D0398874

ALSO BY ZACHARY LEADER

Reading Blake's Songs

Writer's Block

Revision and Romantic Authorship

The Life of Kingsley Amis

The Life of Saul Bellow:
To Fame and Fortune, 1915–1964

EDITED BY ZACHARY LEADER

Romantic Period Writings, 1798–1832:
An Anthology
(with Ian Haywood)

The Letters of Kingsley Amis

On Modern British Fiction

Percy Bysshe Shelley: The Major Works
(with Michael O'Neill)

The Movement Reconsidered:
Essays on Larkin, Amis, Gunn, Davie,
and Their Contemporaries

On Life-Writing

The Life of Saul Bellow

The Life of Saul Bellow

LOVE AND STRIFE
1965–2005

Zachary Leader

ALFRED A. KNOPF New York
2018

THIS IS A BORZOI BOOK
PUBLISHED BY ALFRED A. KNOPF

 Published in the United States by Alfred A. Knopf, a division of Penguin Random House LLC, New York, and distributed in Canada by Random House of Canada, a division of Penguin Random House Canada Limited, Toronto.
www.aaknopf.com

Library of Congress Cataloging-in-Publication Data
Names: Leader, Zachary, author.
Title: The life of Saul Bellow : love and strife, 1965–2005 /
By Zachary Leader.
Description: First edition. | New York : Alfred A. Knopf, [2018] |
Includes bibliographical references and index.
Identifiers: LCCN 2017053381 (print) | LCCN 2017056393 (ebook) |
ISBN 9781101875179 (ebook) | ISBN 9781101875162 (hardcover)
Subjects: LCSH: Bellow, Saul. | Novelists, American—
20th century—Biography.
Classification: LCC PS 3503.E4488 (ebook) | LCC PS3503.E4488 Z7355
2018 (print) | DDC 813/.52 [B]—dc23
LC record available at https://lccn.loc.gov/2017053381

Jacket design by Carol Devine Carson

Manufactured in the United States of America
First Edition

To Alice

Contents

List of Illustrations

The Life of Saul Bellow

I

Fame and Politics in the 1960s

THE LAUNCH PARTY for *Herzog* was held on September 22, 1964, two days after Julian Moynihan pronounced the novel "a masterpiece" on the front page of *The New York Times Book Review* and Philip Rahv called Bellow "the finest stylist at present writing fiction in America" in a review in the *New York Herald Tribune Book Week*.[1] Alfred Kazin was among the guests at the launch, and while waiting for his wife to arrive he amused himself by picking out "the customers for Saul's party from the regulars at 21. It was so easy!" The regulars were better looking, the partygoers, "stamped with the difference of their background and their trade," deeply depressing. In they came, "Arabel Porter and Katy Carver and all the old loves, would-be loves, friends and near friends, the hits and misses—even Vassiliki [Rosenfeld]. All so stale, isn't it? All so bloody familiar?" Only Bellow impressed:

> Saul, our plebeian princeling and imaginative king, standing there, gray, compact, friendly and aloof, receiving his old friends whom he had invited to 21 . . . Saul alone of all the old gang has achieved first-class status. . . . Saul alone has made it, with the furious resistance of personal imagination to the staleness of the round. There's more yet for me, he cries in his heart, more, much more! Nothing is stale, he cries, if only you look at it hard enough, see in it aspects of human fate in general. Put your story on the universal stage of time, and the old Chicago friends will seem as interesting as kings in the old history books.[2]

Two days earlier, when the first reviews of *Herzog* appeared, Kazin had pondered Bellow's public persona. The face he presented to the world, Kazin decided, resembled Charlie Chaplin's "in that first photograph of the tramp—the face absolutely open to life, open, humble, almost childlike, in its concentrated wistfulness and naïve expectancy. Above all a face submissive to the fates." This face, Kazin imagined, was worn by Herzog, and "Saul himself now wears [it] in company. He sits in the waiting room, prepared to be ushered into anything. What will you do with me? he asks, recognising a stronger power than himself." Kazin admired Bellow's air of containment, expectancy, passivity, but also found it irritating. "Saul now wears an aspect mild and submissive," he writes in a journal entry of September 5, before the book was published. "He puts his ear willing to anything you may have to say to him. He is available to you, he is interested in you, and he is most polite. But the minute he has registered what you have to say, he turns it into food for thought—and you find yourself sacrificing 'your' thought for the pleasure of having him develop it." Almost a year later, in a journal entry of August 1, 1965, Kazin complains of "Saul's usual trick of having others make the effort, his immobility in company. . . . Saul is in an interesting state of self-consciousness, of course, because of his present fame and fortune. Having worked so long to make it, he now is suffering even more than usual because he has. He intimated, making almost a physical point of it as usual, that he sought anonymity. . . . He was, as usual, making mental lassos of everyone to himself. And I was tired of adjusting to him."

Within a month of publication, *Herzog* was number one on the best-seller list, supplanting John le Carré's *The Spy Who Came In from the Cold.* Money began rolling in. New American Library purchased the paperback rights to *Dangling Man* and *The Victim* for $77,000 and Fawcett paid $371,350 for the paperback rights to *The Adventures of Augie March* and *Herzog.*[3] "Guys, I'm rich," Mitzi McClosky remembers Bellow declaring. "What can I get for you? Can I buy you something? Do you need any money?" On October 30, Sam Goldberg, his lawyer friend, wrote to Bellow to ask what he should do about the manuscript of *Augie.* "I am sitting with a $25,000 manuscript. I have no safe here which can hold it. . . . Are you going to dispose of the manuscripts this year or are you saving it for 1965"—for tax purposes, that is. On November 18, Bellow received an invitation from Mark Schorer, of the English Department at Berkeley, to teach one course for one semester and deliver two public lectures, for a fee of twelve thousand dollars. He turned it down. In December, he donated the *Augie* and *Henderson* manuscripts to the University of Chicago and turned down a five-thousand-dollar award from *The Kenyon Review*, in both cases because of taxes. He donated Tivoli, the ramshackle house he'd bought in 1956, to nearby Bard College, including the household contents: washing machine, refrigerator, walnut dining table, hi-fi, garden furniture, gas rotary lawn mower, garden tools. Meanwhile, the University of Chicago raised his salary to twenty thousand dollars.[4] Henry Volkening, his agent, negotiated offers for the film rights to *Henderson* (as did Sam Freifeld, to Volkening's consternation[5]). "Don't laugh," wrote Volkening to Bellow on March 24, 1965, "but Peter Sellers is among the other stars with whom it is being discussed." There were also inquiries about *Herzog*. Robert Bolt, Richard Burton, and Fred Zinnemann were interested in filming the novel; Zinnemann suggested that Harold Pinter write the screenplay.[6]

Bellow was kept advised of all these matters in lengthy, at times weekly, letters from Volkening. Throughout the 1960s, he himself was advising foundations and institutes: Yaddo, the Rockefeller, the Guggenheim, the Longview (from Texas, administered by Harold Rosenberg), the Ford, the Salk, the National Institute of Arts and Letters, the Peace Corps, the Princeton University Department of Philosophy. On January 21, 1965, Volkening wrote to Philip Heller of Heller, Strauss and Moses, a Chicago accounting firm, listing payments made to Bellow in 1964 (royalties, serial rights, foreign rights, movie options, etc.). They amounted to $121,682.91 gross and $109,447.22 net. His 1966 tax return reported income of $140,000 (estimated by James Atlas at "about $800,000 in today's terms"[7]), a figure nearly matched in the returns for 1967 and 1968. On February 19, 1965, Bellow wrote to the poet Stanley Burnshaw about his newfound prosperity: "In my simplicity I thought the noise of *Herzog* would presently die down, but it seems only to get louder. I can't pretend it's entirely unpleasant. After all, I wanted *something* to happen, and if I find now that I can't control the volume I can always stuff my ears with money." In March 1965, *Herzog* won the National Book Award, which Bellow had previously won for *The Adventures of Augie March*. Also in March, Volkening and Denver Lindley, of Viking, put Bellow up for membership in the Century Association. As money, honors, and front-page profiles accumulated, even his brother Maury took notice. "The kid finally did it," he declared.[8] On

November 15, 1964, at the end of a typed single-spaced letter devoted to money and business, Henry Volkening apologized and offered advice and reassurance. "Adjustment to success, though less harrowing than adjustment to shall we say figuring out how to 'get along,' does nevertheless pose its problems, does it not? But look, I *know* how these things distract you from things you want to think about. . . . And I'll do my level best to minimize them, *and* have them be a benefit."

Money and its management were distractions for Bellow, but they were also ways of connecting to his brothers and sister. Now Bellow could enter into family business discussions—if not as an equal, at least as a participant. Volkening cautioned Bellow against getting involved in the market ("You have earned all of this big money the hard way," he wrote on May 19, 1965; "it is very much easier to lose money than to increase it"), but when Bellow began to dabble, he put him in touch with his brother, a stockbroker. Now Volkening's letters contained stock tips as well as news of contracts and foreign sales. This was the period when Lesha, Bellow's niece, began to hear him utter the phrase "*Vu bin ikh?*" ("Where am I in this?") when deals and investments were discussed at family gatherings. He hired a Wall Street stockbroker and a prominent Chicago lawyer, Marshall Holleb, who was involved in real estate and property development. Because Bellow never fully engaged with business affairs, he was never very good at them, alternately too trusting or not trusting enough, impatient, shocked at setbacks. After almost fifty years of hard work and money worry, he found it difficult to accept the realities of prosperity. When Robert Hatch, an editor of *The New Republic*, met him in the summer of 1965, all Bellow could talk about was taxes. He had just written a check for forty thousand dollars to the Internal Revenue Service.[9] When David Goldknopf, an old acquaintance, asked Bellow about acquiring an agent, he recommended "a young woman named Candida Donadio" from Volkening's office, later an important agent in her own right; Volkening himself, like Bellow, was "overbusy, all too successful and risen into the nirvana of the harassed."[10] When not harassed about money, Bellow glowed with success. Mitzi McClosky remembers him after *Herzog* as "like a phoenix. The earlier Saul had disappeared. He was on top of the world."[11]

ALMOST A YEAR BEFORE *Herzog* was published, while Bellow was frantically at work on the last stages of the novel, he lost one of his oldest and closest friends. On October 16, 1963, Oscar Tarcov suffered a second heart attack and died at forty-five. The death was especially cruel because Tarcov's fortunes as a writer were at last on the rise. The decision he made in 1958, after his first coronary, to give up work at the Anti-Defamation League in order to write, had been a risk; by 1963, it seemed to be paying off. Tarcov had been writing plays, and they'd been getting some notice. Two of his one-act plays were produced at the Herbert Berghof Studio (Berghof was later to direct a workshop production of *Seize the Day*, with Mike Nichols as Tommy Wilhelm). On March 2, 1963, Bellow wrote to Tarcov, praising his most recent play, "The Interviewer," which he called "thorough, subtle and complete. By far the best thing you've written." He added that he'd "be more than surprised if it's not successfully produced; I'll be shocked." The praise was a great tonic. "I could have kissed you," Tarcov replied.[12] Two months later, on May 11, Tarcov wrote a newsy letter in which he talked about his children and a new play he'd written; he was looking forward to having Bellow and Susan visit soon, but his health was not good: "I'm in a little trouble again." He was experiencing chest pains and other disturbing symptoms and was scheduled to return to hospital for tests. "This will be the eighth hospital visit in less than ten years." In early October, however, there was good news. Kermit Bloomgarden, who had produced *Death of a Salesman*, *The Diary of Anne Frank*, *The Music Man*, and *Look Homeward, Angel*, on Broadway, had taken out an option on "The Interviewer." A summer tour was projected, then a Broadway run. Bellow sent congratulations, in an undated letter written only a week or two before Tarcov died. On October 19, three days after Tarcov's death, a distraught Bellow wrote to John Berryman that he'd "rather die myself than endure these deaths, one after another, of all my dearest friends. . . . Eventually survival feels degrading."

Bellow did not attend Oscar Tarcov's funeral, as he had not attended Isaac Rosenfeld's funeral; he apologized to Tarcov's son, Nathan, in a moving letter of October 22 and visited the family some days later. As Greg Bellow remembers it, his father did not attend the funeral because his wife, Susan, some four months pregnant, "began to have medical problems and he could not leave her."[13] Presumably, the problems cleared up quickly. When Bellow arrived at the Tarcov apartment, he was, according to Ted Hoffman, "distraught," "spooked," "very tender."[14] Edith Tarcov was understanding, or so correspondence suggests, but Greg Bellow, now a sophomore at the University of Chicago, was angry, not so much that Bellow had failed to attend, but that he'd failed to tell him he wasn't going to attend. "We all loved Oscar and I felt it imperative that Saul, Anita [Greg's mother, Bellow's first wife] or I attend the funeral," Greg writes. If Bellow wasn't going to attend, Greg would go in his place, but Bellow "thoughtlessly . . . only told me after the funeral that he had not attended."[15] In the letter to Nathan Tarcov, who was fifteen, Bellow expressed sorrow at Oscar's death and acute sympathy for Nathan. Bellow had been Tarcov's friend for thirty years. That the friendship was unbroken, he wrote to Nathan, in a passage quoted in part in chapter 4 of the first volume of this biography (henceforth referred to by its subtitle, *To Fame and Fortune*), was Oscar's doing, "since I was sometimes hasty and bad-tempered." The friendship began, as did the friendship with Rosenfeld, in the year Bellow's mother died, something Bellow makes much of in the letter.

> I'm sure I brought to these relationships emotions caused by that death. I was seventeen—not much older than you. If I explain this to you, it's not because I want to talk about myself. What I mean to say is that I have a very special feeling about your situation. I experienced something like it. I hope that you will find—perhaps you have found—such friends as I had on Lemoyne St. in 1933. Not in order to "replace" your father, you never will, but to be the sort of human being he was. He invested his life in relationships. In making such a choice a man sooner or later realizes that to love others is his answer to inevitable death. Other answers we often hear are anger, rebellion, bitterness. Your father, by temperament, could make no other choice. Perhaps you wondered why I was so attached to him. He never turned me away when I needed him. I hope I never failed him, either.

In the weeks that followed Tarcov's death, Bellow agreed to help with "The Interviewer," not only by lending his name to the production but by working on revisions. On January 1, 1964, he wrote to Kermit Bloomgarden with a detailed list of "specific proposals" for the play's revision, mostly having to do with a certain vagueness or mystery about the Interviewer's work, but also suggesting ways of speeding up the action and sharpening the dialogue. The letter concludes with a promise to provide Bloomgarden with "a detailed scheme for the revision . . . as soon as there is a practical necessity for it. I expect to have time to work on this play later this winter or early in the summer of 1964. I will do what I can to help the production. My belief in its ultimate success is strong." After what Nathan calls "a certain amount of work," however, Bellow withdrew from the project. Without an author, the producers lost heart and the play was never produced. Edith Tarcov was very upset, and her daughter, Miriam Tarcov, looking back, accuses Bellow of "putting his reputation above his friendship," though she admits that "it was difficult for Saul to lend his name to it or immerse himself in the work when he couldn't quite get it, couldn't find his voice in it." Bellow's claim that her father was a man who "invests his life in relationships" also bothers her. In precarious health, with a wife and two children to support, Tarcov quit a steady job, cashed in an insurance policy of twenty-five thousand dollars, and devoted himself to writing. He, too, she argues, put writing first. "To be a good father, a good husband, that wasn't for him the driving force," Miriam claims.[16]

Tarcov's was not the only death to shake Bellow at this period. A year later, on October 14, 1964, Pat Covici, his editor at Viking, died, also of a heart attack. He was seventy-six, and his death occurred the month after *Herzog* was published and only days before it topped the best-seller list.[17] The novel is dedicated to Covici, "A great editor and, better yet, an affectionate friend." Bellow attended the funeral and contributed to a collection of tributes privately printed a year later by Viking.[18] "I loathe funerals and wasn't planning to attend," he wrote to the novelist Norman Rosten, "but I did love the old man dearly and at the last minute I found I was unable to sit it out in Chicago."[19] Covici and his wife, Dorothy, with the Ludwigs, had been the only out-of-town guests when Bellow and his second wife, Sasha, got married in Reno. In the years leading up to *Herzog*, it was Covici who persuaded Viking to carry Bellow with advances totaling ten thousand dollars, who smoothed over Bellow's tantrums and anxieties, keeping the value of the work squarely in view. "It was years before I understood how necessary his quixotic belief was to me," Bellow wrote in his tribute. "When I sometimes observed that things were not as simple as he thought, he answered that neither were they so very complicated." To Bellow, Covici was "an old prospector" mining for literary treasure, "never doubting he would strike it rich." He'd done it before—others among his authors who wrote tributes were Arthur Miller, Joseph Campbell, John Steinbeck, and Malcolm Cowley—and would do so again. "He would not behave like an elderly man." After his death, Bellow kept in touch with Dorothy Covici and with their son, Pascal, Jr., who was to become chair of the English Department at Southern Methodist University. Shortly after winning the Nobel Prize in Literature, Bellow accepted an invitation from Pascal, Jr., to give a reading at SMU. It was attended by sixteen hundred people. When Bellow finished the reading, he received a standing ovation.

ALTHOUGH BELLOW WAS FAMOUS and successful as a novelist, he received no standing ovations as a playwright. His first play, *The Last Analysis*, opened on Broadway on October 1, 1964, and closed within a month. The most painful review it received was from Walter Kerr, the influential drama critic of the *New York Herald Tribune*, later drama critic of *The New York Times*.[20] Like *Herzog*, the play went through many drafts and versions. The earliest manuscript dates from the beginning of 1958, when Bellow was still writing *Henderson the Rain King*, a work not dissimilar in comic register. In the years leading up to its Broadway production, Bellow worked on the play while working on *Herzog* (having several projects on the boil simultaneously was a common practice with him, one he encouraged other writers to emulate as a way of overcoming creative blockage). On March 6, 1958, Lillian Hellman wrote in praise of the first draft but also with "one small suggestion: remember that on a stage, with people doing the talking, one can cut, hit, sharpen, move on with greater speed, than one can in a novel." Bellow had written the first version "in a week," thinking "like many writers . . . what the hell, anyone can write a play." When Hellman pointed out that his play would take eight hours to perform, he began cutting. Six and a half years later, on the eve of its production, he confessed, "I feel like I've been cutting it ever since."[21] At the end of the summer of 1959, after sending a second version to Hellman, he went to visit her on Martha's Vineyard to hear what she thought. He was not encouraged. "She says I've written a lot of interesting soliloquies, but there's not a play in sight," he reported to his friend Keith Botsford, in an undated letter. A year later, after extensive reworking, Hellman's verdict, in a letter of June 7, 1960, remained unchanged. Though "brilliant in places, very funny, imaginative, the best kind of wonderful wacky . . . I just don't think it's a play. I don't think it's found it's [*sic*] form, it doesn't move far enough from the basic joke."[22]

This joke derives from the play's lead character, Philip Bummidge, a fading television comedian tired of comedy routines and longing for a deeper, more meaningful life. To attain such a life, he sets out to free himself, both from neuroses, variously characterized as "Humanitis" and "Pagliacci Gangrene" ("Caused as all gangrene is by a failure of circulation. Cut off by self-pity. Passivity. Fear. Masochistic rage"),[23] and from his many hangers-on, described by the critic Daniel Fuchs as "a pack of fugitives from *Volpone*."[24] ("I hope you're having a restful vacation," Greg wrote to his father on July 30, 1968, "and that you've escaped all those people who persecute you as a matter of course.") Bummidge has devised a form of therapy called "*Existenz*-Action-Self-analysis" (p. 4), which he intends to demonstrate on himself, broadcasting his treatment on closed-circuit television to an audience of psychiatrists, artists, and comedians gathered at the Waldorf. "It's like a lecture at the New School," his son, Max, explains, "but crazier" (p. 78). The hangers-on, who batten on Bummidge "like green fungus on pumpernickel" (p. 62), are appalled, both at the cost of the scheme and at Bummidge's decision to quit performing as a comic. In the first act, they seek to dissuade him; in the second, they and we watch the broadcast, in which the traumas of Bummidge's life are re-enacted, interspersed with passages from comedy routines. The broadcast ends with Bummidge acting out a rebirth. To the amazement and dismay of the hangers-on, who want him to continue making money in television, the audience of professionals is deeply impressed. The hangers-on are routed, and Bummidge is reborn. Donning a toga, he declares his intention to teach "the poor, the sad, the bored and tedious of the earth." He buys an old theater, the Trilby, to be turned into a center for "*Existenz*-Action-Self-analysis." Graduates of the center will become "missionaries to England, to Germany, to all those bleak and sadistic countries." Bummidge's last words are "I am ready for the sublime." Then he "*raises his arms in a great gesture*" (p. 118), and the curtain falls.

Finding a producer for the play was a protracted business. On April 26, 1962, in a letter to his novelist friend Dick Stern, Bellow reported from Tivoli that Herbert Berghof and Uta Hagen were interested, as was Zero Mostel, the ideal Bummidge. Two weeks later, he reported to Toby Cole, the agent Volkening had enlisted to handle theater and film rights for Bellow (also Zero Mostel's agent), that Gore Vidal had requested a copy of the play. Vidal had had his own play *The Best Man* produced on Broadway in 1960. Now he sent Bellow's play to Roger L. Stevens, who had produced *The Best Man*, and to Joe

Anthony, who had directed it. "I got him his director and I got him his producer," Vidal boasted in an interview (though it took Stevens and Anthony over a year to sign on formally). On August 26, 1962, while Bellow and Susan were on Martha's Vineyard, Herbert Berghof wrote to reiterate his desire to direct the play. He had a producer in mind, and Walter Matthau was interested in playing Bummidge. Other names Berghof mentioned in connection with the part were Jack Warden, Karl Malden, Rod Steiger, Milton Berle, and Martin Balsam. On October 28, Bellow wrote to Cole about Mostel, who was being difficult, both indecisive and moody, "Tell Zero from me that what his mood wants is a swift kick in the rear to hasten its departure," a message Bellow thought better of after a few sentences: "Just give him my regards and say 'Bellow's compliments, and please hurry up a little.'"[25] Five months later, on March 21, 1963, Bellow reported to Cole that Anthony still hoped to direct the play but was at the moment busy with other projects. "Joe is hoping that Zero will accept. He hopes thereby to gain time since Zero is tied up for some months to come." If Mostel didn't accept, Bellow doubted Anthony would. But Anthony remained on board. On July 20, 1963, Bellow told Dave Peltz, the most "street" of his Humboldt Park friends (much discussed in chapter 5 of *To Fame and Fortune*), that he and Anthony had been working on the play for the past five weeks and that, "amazingly, it looks like plays I've read. . . . I don't think I've ever worked harder." His other news was that Mostel would soon return from a holiday in Europe, and that a first production meeting was tentatively scheduled for August. On September 3, 1963, Bellow wrote again to Peltz. He and Susan would arrive in Chicago from Tivoli on September 26 but would return to New York in January, "to spend three months on Broadway. Whether we spend them with Zero is still unknown."

It remained unknown for some time. As Mostel procrastinated, author and director decided "to proceed to cast the play as if he didn't exist" (this to Toby Cole, in an undated note). On November 18, Bellow wrote again to Cole, this time with concerns about Roger Stevens, the producer. "Perhaps we might investigate Lincoln Center further to see whether, if Stevens should poop out in April, we might give the play to [Elia] Kazan etc. Is it unethical? That is still a cut above chaos." On December 3, once more to Cole, Bellow reported that Joe Anthony had begun to waver. "I've taken a very considerable run-around from Zero first (on Joe's say-so) and then from Joe himself, and I'm a bit fed up." At last, Mostel said no, having instead, in Robert Brustein's words, elected "to entertain the Hadassah ladies in *Fiddler on the Roof.*"[26] When Milton Berle also passed on the part, it went to the veteran Broadway actor Sam Levene. That summer, Bellow and Susan spent July and August in a rented house on Martha's Vineyard, part of the time with Bellow's son Adam. Bellow was exhausted, as he explained to his friend and first biographer, Ruth Miller, in a letter of June 13, 1964:

> Since November, things have gone something like this: Finished *Herzog*, rewrote my silly play. Taught school; rewrote *Herzog*, did another version of the play; prepared the novel for the printer, went to NYC to see Adam and cast the play; came home and found galleys, rewrote the book again on the galleys. A batch of fifty of these galleys were taken in a holdup of the Hyde Park post-office. The thieves were caught and the money recovered, but my work was torn to bits (first critical reception?).

The thieves had driven all over the West Side of Chicago in a yellow Cadillac, scattering unwanted mail bags in vacant lots, and it took several days to recover the galleys. In the interim, Bellow received a phone call late at night from a man with a voice like a gangster. He knew where the galleys were and was willing to discuss their return. Bellow was to meet him at midnight beneath the Illinois Central tracks. "Then he let out a loud cackling laugh. It was his brother Maurice."[27] It took the summer for Bellow to recover his energy. In a letter of July 22 to Alfred Kazin, he writes of having "weaned myself from the pills I was taking during the final months of *Herzog*" and of seeing "a bit of Island society." What he says of this society is that "Styron is our leader, here in little Fitzgeraldville. Then there is Lillian Hellman, in whom I produce symptoms of *shyness*" (perhaps because she'd been so tough on the play, or continued to have problems with it). The letter is upbeat: "life is after all simple, decides a complicated mind." Though a momentous autumn loomed, Bellow was gathering strength to meet it. *Herzog* would be published on September 19; *The Last Analysis* would open on Broadway less than two weeks later.

Readying *The Last Analysis* for Broadway was nerve-racking, involving tense meetings with actors and producers and late-night rewrites. Rehearsals took place in the Belasco Theatre, where the play was to open (and where Charlie Citrine's hit, *Von Trenck*, makes his fortune, earning Von Humboldt Fleisher's enduring enmity). Bellow took a room nearby, in the "furnished squalor" of the Hotel Alden on Central Park West. After rehearsals there were interviews, with streams of reporters. Early in the rehearsal period, an interviewer for the *Saturday Review* described Bellow in terms similar to those used by Kazin after the launch of *Herzog*. "At a time when his career seemed to be moving toward a stunning climax, Bellow appears remarkably calm, modest, yet quietly self-assured."[28] Soon after rehearsals began, John Barkham, an interviewer for the Philadelphia *Sunday Bulletin*, described Bellow as "exhilarated by the experience."[29] The interviewer for *The New York Times*, Robert Gutwillig, himself a novelist, had not seen Bellow for four or five years. He described him as "almost alarmingly handsome," with "gray-white" hair and a face that seemed to express "all the life he has seen and understood": "here's a guy who's got more talent than everyone else in the country, and now he's running for Robert Frost, too."[30] With Gutwillig, Bellow was easy, full of jokes; as opening night approached, his mood darkened.

In addition to cutting and rewriting, Bellow faced, in Pete Hamill's words, "the kind of tampering with the original idea that causes a writer either to walk out in a huff, or make the small compromises that make most things possible."[31] Bellow didn't walk out, but in staying, he told Ruth Miller, he was party "to the dismantling of his play."[32] At one point, he and Toby Cole were so alarmed that they tried to get Roger Stevens to shut down the production. That may have been the moment, recounted to Atlas by Joe Anthony, when Bellow was banned from rehearsals. "It was when Saul sensed that we had made wrong judgments that the conflict occurred. There's a bad side to Saul's nature, and once he sensed that the production wasn't going to work, he was quite capable of ruthless indifference to human values—to the point where I had to prevent him from working with us in the theater."[33] According to Bellow's writer friend Edward Hoagland, "an air of despair pervaded the rehearsals"; the playwright's posture, Hoagland recalled, was that of "a man awaiting an announced punishment."[34]

Punishment is what he got. In a brief "Author's Note" to the rewritten version of the play published a year later, Bellow described the Broadway production as "a shipwreck" (p. vii). Several critics laid the blame on the actors and the director. Sam Levene was thought to lack the stature to play Bummidge. Levene had been much praised for his performances in *Guys and Dolls* and *Dinner at Eight*, but the part of

Bummidge, with its long speeches and arcane references, intimidated him, as did Bellow himself, whom he referred to in rehearsals as "the Scholar." Bellow, in turn, described Levene as "a dear man" who "found it hard to speak a sentence with a subordinate clause."[35] Levene's "charming and attractive" girlfriend attended all the rehearsals and took notes for him. "She always had a certain number of questions for me about the words the star couldn't pronounce." "She would ask: 'Is this word pronounced fin-*it*? Fin-*yet*? Fynyte? Or what?' And I would have to tell her. She would then inform the star. Once again the next day he would mispronounce the words."[36] Howard Taubman, reviewing the play in *The New York Times*, praised Levene's performance, but noted that he several times stumbled over lines, which was especially distracting in a role like that of Bummidge, a figure of angst and slapstick, difficult to pin down. "Poor Sam Levene," wrote Robert Brustein, in his review in *The New Republic*, "has been abysmally miscast. At a loss with the part, he has fallen back on the only character he has confidence in, the Jewish garment manufacturer, mugging, grimacing, and ogling until he has flattened the values of the play." For John Simon, writing in *The Hudson Review*, Levene as Bummidge was least convincing when puncturing cultural cliché, "rather as if Milton Berle were reading the lines of, say, Coriolanus." Walter Kerr spread the blame more widely. Are we to take Bummidge seriously or to think of him as a clown? "Bellow sayeth not. Levene sayeth not. Director Joseph Anthony sayeth not."[37]

But Bellow *had* sayeth, in an article of September 27 in *The New York Times Book Review*, published just days before the play's opening. Like the articles Bellow published in the *Book Review* before the publication of *Henderson* and *Herzog*, the purpose of "My Man Bummidge" was to shape the work's reception as well as to explain its character and origins. The aim of the play, Bellow declared, was "to put ideas on the stage in what is possibly their most acceptable form, farce." *The Last Analysis* is only in part a spoof of psychoanalysis; what Bellow "really wanted to reproduce was the common modern mixture of high seriousness and low seriousness" (the mixture of *Henderson*, *Herzog*, Berryman's *Dream Songs*). Bummidge, like Henderson, is in search of his essential self; he's also an autodidact, like Dr. Pep (in "A Sermon by Dr. Pep," a monologue published in May 1949 in *Partisan Review*, discussed in chapter 11 of *To Fame and Fortune*) and Tamkin (in *Seize the Day*). "I am attracted to autodidacts," Bellow explained, "those brave souls who rise to encounter ideas." Bellow claimed to have a specific type of autodidact in mind, though a type that only emerged in the course of revisions.

> I have been especially stirred by jazz musicians, prize fighters and television comics who put on the philosopher's mantle. I find them peculiarly touching. In the tumult of Birdland they are thinking of Kierkegaard. When they turn away from the microphone their painted smiles grow pensive. They are often preoccupied with Freud and Ferenczi, with Rollo May and Erik Erikson, and their private correspondence is very rich in analytic concepts. The self-absorption of people who never tire of exploring their depths is the source of our comedy. Bummidge in "The Last Analysis" is, as another character says, "like a junky on thought."

Getting the balance right between seriousness and comedy was a problem, and as the opening night approached, Levene was not alone in tipping the performance too far toward comedy. Among Bellow's papers in the Regenstein is a set of typed notes, presumably from the producers, titled "Checklist of essential production details which can be achieved readily immediately." The first of these notes concerns Bummidge: "Levene should be given an identifying *signature gesture*, like Jackie Gleason's 'Away we go' movement, which establishes that he is a national comic figure. This could be used by other characters as well, e.g. television technicians could mock him with this instead of words. Every good comic has his signature and Bummidge should have one too."

"Like a junky on thought." Or a junky on speed, jabbering away. In "My Man Bummidge," Bellow recalls the 1962 reading at Aaron and Linda Asher's apartment. He read "as fast as I could. Wildly, excitedly I began to lose my voice before I reached Act II. My own virtuosity exhausted me, and the first victim of my invention was myself." To Pete Hamill, Bellow recalled how one of the theater people present at the reading told him he had "a month's work to do on it," a remark Bellow recounted "with a rueful smile." The play's wordiness was as much a problem for the critics as its mixture of high and low seriousness. Bellow defended himself against the charge of verbosity on generic grounds. "Ask a writer what he thinks of the American theater and he will tell you that it has no language, that it lacks rhetoric or gesture. Ask any professional in the theater what is wrong with plays written by novelists and he will answer that they don't know the difference between the page and the stage." This latter view was Walter Kerr's. Bellow might be a gifted novelist, but he showed "an almost frightening naïveté as a dramatist." To the UPI reviewer, Jack Garver, what the play lacked was "discipline." Bellow called it a farce, Garver speculated, "on the theory that in farce you can get away with any sort of clutter."[38] Several critics complained of the number of minor roles (fretful lawyer, demanding wife, sexy mistress, selfish sister, aggressive son, and so forth). In the published version, several of these hangers-on were dropped, as Bellow "attempted to simplify the cluttered and inconsequential plot, which puzzled the audience (and even the playwright), and tried to eliminate pointless noises and distracting bits of business" (p. vii).

The classicist David Grene, Bellow's colleague at the Committee on Social Thought (an interdisciplinary Ph.D. program at the University of Chicago, also a sort of high-powered academic *salon des refusés*), drew an intriguing parallel between Greek comedy and *The Last Analysis*.[39] In an undated letter to Bellow, Grene sought to clarify comments he'd made at a recent reading of the play for an unspecified student audience. Grene felt the students had missed the play's "explosive" quality, or the nature of its explosive quality. "They wanted to disintegrate the intellectual elements out of which the explosion came," missing what he thought was "most interesting about the work." Though the play mines "a new vein of comedy," it has "something in common with Aristophanes," more so than with "the recent stuff with which people may compare it" (the plays of Ionesco, for example, the current specialty of Rosette Lamont, Bellow's ex-girlfriend). To extrapolate from Grene's suggestion, one might compare Bellow's spoof of psychoanalysis to Aristophanes's spoof of philosophy in *The Clouds*, both plays being simultaneously knockabout and deadly serious. What Aristophanes took aim at in *The Clouds*—the supposed indifference of the sophist philosophers to the truth as opposed to the power of arguments—was a fifth-century B.C. equivalent of mid-twentieth-century nihilism, long Bellow's enemy. Bellow and Grene sometimes taught classes together and had adjoining offices at the Committee. Grene had written a book on Aristophanes and often taught him. That Bummidge dons a toga at the end of the play and sets out to form a center or "school" to be "run like Plato's Academy" (p. 118) partly licenses the comparison. Bummidge, however, is a more serious figure than Strepsiades or any other Aristophanic protagonist. As Daniel Fuchs puts it, he's "ridiculous but in the sympathetic (Don Quixote) rather than the classical (Tartuffe) strain. Like a Don Quixote or a Parson Adams, he is the holy fool mucking through and somehow triumphing in a world of cupidity."[40]

Bellow claimed not to have been put off the theater by his experiences with *The Last Analysis*. During rehearsals, he told John Barkham, the interviewer from the Philadelphia *Sunday Bulletin*, that his next project would be another play. "You derive a certain comfort from not being in your room alone with four walls. In the theater you are in the company of a cast of ten or twelve people. I often envy people who work in offices: they don't have to face the frightful solitude." After the play flopped, he was only briefly daunted, or so he implies in the "Author's Note" to the printed version: "the rehearsals, the previews, the cold and peevish first-night audience, the judgments of the critics, were of the greatest value to me" (p. vii). As he wrote to Stanley Burnshaw on February 19, 1965: "The play was a great disappointment. But instead of making me wretched it only made me obstinate. I've reconstructed (in my field hospital after the massacre) and Viking is printing the text. I'd root out my desire to write plays if I could; I found theater people to be miserable, untrustworthy creatures." Waiting for the reviews in Sardi's, as tradition dictates, was difficult, though in an undated note to Kazin, Bellow describes the opening night party as "very lively." The first reviews were mixed, and the good ones weren't strong enough to save the run. Ten days later, writing to a Viking publicist named Julie, Bellow declined to be interviewed for the *New York Herald Tribune*. "First of all, I don't want to leave Chicago and secondly I don't see why I should come to a *Herald Tribune* affair still wearing the lumps that Walter Kerr gave me." In later years, Bellow joked that the only lesson he'd learned from Broadway was "that prostitution doesn't pay."[41] Yet, within a year, he was at work with Herbert Berghof and Mike Nichols on the stage version of *Seize the Day*, in negotiation with the Guthrie Theater in Minneapolis for a new production of *The Last Analysis*, and consulting with the New York actress and comedienne Nancy Walker, who had come to Chicago in hopes of an Off Broadway staging of "A Wen," a one-act play by Bellow published in *Esquire* in January 1965. Only the Guthrie production failed to materialize.

Nancy Walker, a Broadway veteran, who later earned fame as a television actress, had never directed a play before, but Bellow liked her, and her enthusiasm "stirred my imagination so that on the spot I dreamed up two one-acters."[42] These one-acters were "Orange Soufflé" and "Out from Under." In April 1965, under the auspices of the producer Lyn Austin, an associate producer of *The Last Analysis*, "A Wen" and "Orange Soufflé" were staged by Walker for an invited audience in the Loft on Bleecker Street. Brendan Gill, the *New Yorker* critic whose dismissive review of *Seize the Day* had irked Bellow, was in the audience (presumably, he and Bellow had made up their disagreement). In a note of April 26, Gill praised the plays and the production hyperbolically: "I can't remember *ever* having had such a good time at the theatre" (this from a man who reviewed plays for *The New Yorker* for over twenty years). In the next two years, all three of Bellow's one-acters were staged as a trilogy, in both London and New York, though without Walker as director.[43] A fourth play, "A Work of Art," also written in this period, exists in draft and was never produced. In addition to these theatrical ventures, Bellow lobbied the University of Chicago for a university repertory company, to be housed in two purpose-built theaters, one seating eight hundred persons, the other three hundred. According to a document in the Regenstein headed "Draft/Bellow to the Trustees," he described the function of theater as "bringing the high and the low together in closing the rift between bumps and grinds and the activities of the intelligence. The theater is also—like all the arts—a teacher. It instructs people in conduct. It gives them a style of life. It makes them perhaps more thoughtful." Even so, playwriting remained for Bellow, or so he confessed to Toby Cole, "a holiday from responsibility and earnestness," by which he meant from novel writing. "I enjoy writing these trifles," he told Cole in an undated letter. "Here you are," he wrote on July 12, 1965, "a new trifle, sillier than ever."[44] It is hard not to take Bellow's plays at this estimate, despite moments of cleverness and humor.

DURING THE RUN-UP to the launch of *Herzog* and the opening of *The Last Analysis*, Bellow was accompanied not only by Susan but by the newest member of the family, six-month-old Daniel Oscar Bellow, who was born on March 17, 1964. Susan's parents, Dr. and Mrs. Frank Glassman, were in attendance as well. In late August, Greg Bellow, now twenty and about to enter his junior year at the University of Chicago, arrived. In addition, there were visits from seven-year-old Adam, who was living in Long Island with Sasha. Greg remembers walking down Fifth Avenue one sunny morning with his father, who had been ordered by Susan "to buy me a 'proper' suit" for the launch party and the opening night of the play. "We passed several bookstores, their enormous front windows filled with blue-jacketed copies of *Herzog*."[45] Gregory was as uncomfortable with Bellow's new fame as he was with the wool suit they bought that morning. He was often prickly at this period, prone to anger. In his high-school and college years, he writes, "arguments with both parents were open, direct, fierce, and usually grounded in my highly moralistic sense of right and wrong."[46] It was this sense that had led Greg at sixteen to send Bellow a "scathing letter" early in 1960, upbraiding him for missing his alimony payments to Anita. Bellow wrote back from Puerto Rico in unexpectedly mild terms, explaining his circumstances. He denied being venal or a swindler, told about owing Viking ten thousand dollars, plus other debts and expenses, and asked Greg if he'd ever considered that his mother might be better off financially than his father. Anita had a job and a steady income and was "neither sick nor in dire need." Had Greg forgotten that his father was a writer? "Obviously my unreliable financial situation is related to the fact that I write books. And you might try thinking of this in terms other than the dollar. Those are blood cells in my eccentric veins, not dimes. It's odd that I should have to persuade my son that I'm human." The letter ends: "I'll get by somehow, scrape by, steal by, squeak by. I always have. If I strike it rich, why, I'll buy ice cream and Cadillacs for everybody. And then everyone will say how honest I am and your good opinion of me will return, and your *faith* in me. It's all silly. Your devoted, Papa." In his memoir, Greg is unforgiving: "Fifty years later, what most surprises me . . . is how I took his response in stride. Doubtless I was already subscribing to his self-justification: that his career as an artist entitled him to let people down with impunity."[47]

Greg's relations with his mother in these years were even more strained than those with his father. In June 1962, at the end of his senior year in high school, Anita remarried. Mutual friends had introduced her to a widower, Basil Busacca, who taught comparative literature at Occidental College in Los Angeles. After the marriage, the couple planned to spend the summer in Forest Hills, while Basil taught a course at Queens College. When Greg went off to the University of Chicago in September, Anita would move with her husband to his house in South Pasadena. This plan, as Greg puts it in his memoir, proved "a disaster. Basil tried to impose his will on me, and I fought him at every turn. All that summer Anita was trapped between us as Basil and I battled." Once at university, still smarting from the quarrels of the summer, Greg faced academic difficulties. "For the first time in my life I was trying as hard as I could but getting poor results that made me feel stupid." Bellow and Susan offered advice and sympathy, and Greg often visited their apartment for chats and meals. Susan's cooking was "a decided improvement over dorm food," and there were "many lively conversations."[48] Greg liked Susan, but he also felt that she took advantage of him. "I rarely made a visit there without having to perform a time-consuming physical chore for Susan, which I came to resent." It was, however, Anita with whom he was most at odds. Bellow tried to smooth relations between son and mother; he supported Anita's marriage and, when she was unable to pay her share of Greg's college expenses, took on her half. Greg was furious with his mother: "Anita had reneged on her earlier commitment . . . after she and Basil went through my education fund settling into their new life." The main quarrels Greg had with Bellow during this period, in addition to his anger over his father's having missed Oscar Tarcov's funeral, derived from Bellow's wish "to make up for past absences." Greg needed his space: "At eighteen, the last thing I wanted was to get closer to my father." Only after Ted Hoffman was enlisted by Greg and "got through" to Bellow did he back off.[49] At the end of Greg's freshman year, however, father and son had a "terrible argument" in front of Greg's dorm. Bellow "broke a promise to take my suitcase to New York because Susan had filled the car with her own belongings."[50]

Adam Bellow was more quietly troubling and more troubled, scarred by the wars between his parents. What he remembers of outings with his father in Chicago when he was three is that "I would somehow find myself in the Loop. There'd be a handoff, like a football. He'd take me somewhere. . . . We wouldn't talk very much and he'd ask me questions as though I were a stranger, and then there would always come a point when my mother would come up, as a subject . . . and then he'd become very angry." At this period, "I was not happy—jittery and scared of my father. I would usually wet the bed after I saw him."[51] In 1964, Bellow and Sasha remained locked in bitter disagreements about money. Visits to his father remained "tense," "uncomfortable," partly, he feels, because Bellow sensed his unease, "felt insecure," "felt rejected by me." "Right through the *Herzog* period, he was so enraged with [Sasha]" that "psychologically he really needed [me]," by which Adam means "needed me to take his side": "He expressed it." Another source of tension derived from Bellow's "mystical sense of family resemblance," a sense shared by the protagonists of his fiction (for example, Joseph in *Dangling Man*, Rogin in "A Father-to-Be"). "He was constantly gauging how much Bellow there was." When Adam said he didn't like Aunt Jane's borscht, Bellow's response was "What kind of a Litvak are you?"—the sort of joking remark often made in families, but one Adam thinks may have been more pointed in his case. All Bellow's sons resemble him physically, Adam in particular, but early on, "he may have had some cause to wonder if I was his son." At gatherings in Chicago, "my experience of the Bellow family is that I was like little Pearl in *The Scarlet Letter*."

Adam's memories of summers with his father at Tivoli begin with boredom. "It seemed there was always this cocktail party going on," "a forest of legs." There were no books for children, there was no television, and for the most part there were no other children. His isolation, however, "was as much my fault as anyone's. I came from an isolated background. It was just my mother and I, and we moved around a lot. I became a very introverted child." That the children he met at Tivoli (the Hoffman children, the Botsford children) came from "actual families" "only increased my sense of alienation." He was a "moony, depressive" child, "not good at anything," and his father "didn't like that and just didn't know how to deal with it." Though Bellow was "in many ways a very tender papa, as was his father," with "lots of hugging and kissing," he could also be "the Old Testament God," like Abraham. Also like Abraham was Bellow's belief that it was "up to the son to make himself worthy," a belief Adam feels "explains my whole career." At Tivoli, Adam's mornings were spent alone or with Susan, whose job, Adam felt, was "in large part . . . to protect [Bellow]" from interruption, a job taken on by succeeding "surrogate mothers." In the afternoons, Bellow would make himself available, "be up for things." They'd go for walks or to the river. At Martha's Vineyard or the Hamptons, they'd go to the beach. "He'd explain to me about the various flora, he knew all sorts of stuff, and that was fun." He taught Adam how to make a fire, how to pick a ripe tomato, how to plant corn. As a teacher, he was "laissez-faire—if you did something on your own, he would comment on it, say if you were doing it right." Later in the day, at some adult gathering, "there'd be cocktails on the lawn . . . and he'd be glowing." From time to time, Greg, who was thirteen years older than his half-brother, would come to stay; they'd play catch together, or he'd take Adam to the zoo. "He was very important to me." As for Adam's baby brother, with whom Susan was besotted, "I absolutely refused the existence of Daniel."[52]

SUSAN'S ABSORPTION WITH Daniel "wounded" Adam ("nobody was interested in me"), and her reaction to fame offended Greg. Greg found fame "chafing," like his new wool suit; Susan, in contrast, "was in her element. Outgoing and dressed to kill for every event, she found living in the public eye in New York to be precisely how she envisioned being married to Saul Bellow."[53] When the family returned to Chicago, Susan threw herself into the task of creating a home fit for her famous husband. This home was a co-op apartment at 5490 South Shore Drive, in a handsome high-rise built in 1917 and boasting the largest luxury apartments in Hyde Park. The one she and Bellow chose, purchased by him with the help of a loan from the university, overlooked Jackson Park and the lake, only a block from the modest two-bedroom apartment they had lived in at 1755 East Fifty-Fifth Street. Their fellow co-op owners were psychiatrists, architects, and physicians, not the sort of university types Bellow was used to, and very unlike the writers and intellectuals of the Village or the Upper West Side. Writing to Richard Stern from Menemsha on Martha's Vineyard, at the end of the summer of 1965, Bellow signed off: "Back to the lakefront, the twelve rooms, the psychiatric neighbors and the clap doctor magnates."

The neighbors were not the only aspect of his new home Bellow came to dislike. Susan hired an interior decorator, and the result was for him both too elaborate and too expensive, in a style Adam Bellow calls "conventional Chicago dentist." There was plush green carpet fitted throughout, and the enormous living room faced the lake, as did Bellow's study, with its floor-to-ceiling mirrors, which he hated. Stanley Katz, Susan's cousin, remembers the apartment as "beautiful," "sumptuous"—"everything was always perfect." When Adam came to visit in 1965, he was struck by how much grander it was than the places he and his mother lived in, an impression likely to inflame Sasha, whose fights with Bellow over money were now conducted almost entirely through Marshall Holleb, Bellow's lawyer. Greg "despised" what he calls the apartment's "ostentation," which he saw as Maury-like. When he complained to Bellow about the elaborate furnishings, he was told that they "were of no interest to him, and that wealth did not stop him from writing."[54] But the size of the apartment embarrassed Bellow (Daniel remembers him referring to it in later years as "the Vatican"). It was not where he belonged, for reasons comparable to those offered by Benn Crader in *More Die of Heartbreak*, in explaining his reactions to his in-laws' vast penthouse: "Wandering through endless fields of furniture, strange surroundings, yes, but he was not so impressed as Mrs. Layamon probably felt he should have been. It wasn't the difference in station that got him; not the class idea 'They're bourgeois'; his mind didn't work that way. It wasn't the objects that bothered him but the persistent sense of being in a false position. This was what these articles of furniture symbolized."[55]

The social life Susan arranged for Bellow was as alienating as the apartment's size and decoration. Diane Silverman, who remembers Bellow as "incredibly charming" but also "really self-centered," describes an awkward dinner party at the new apartment, to which Susan had invited the Silvermans and another couple. Diane's husband, "everybody's favorite dinner guest," was tall, smart, political, a property developer with "a fairly large ego." "We had a completely uncomfortable dinner," she recalls. "Saul just wasn't interested in any of the men. . . . These were Susan's friends and he just wasn't interested. He didn't make an effort." Bellow's behavior suggests that relations with Susan were already strained, but even in good times he would have had problems with such guests. He was like Charlie Citrine in *Humboldt's Gift*, who "didn't behave well with the mental beau-monde of Chicago."

> Denise invited superior persons of all kinds to the house in Kenwood to discuss politics and economics, race, psychology, sex, crime. Though I served the drinks and laughed a great deal I was not exactly cheerful and hospitable. I wasn't even friendly. "You despise these people!" Denise said, angry. "Only Durnwald is an exception, that curmudgeon." This accusation was true. I hoped to lay them all low. In fact it was one of my cherished dreams and dearest hopes. They were against the True, the Good, the Beautiful. They denied the light. "You're a snob," she said. This was not accurate. But I wouldn't have a thing to do with these bastards, the lawyers, Congressmen, psychiatrists, sociology professors, clergy, and art-types (they were mostly gallery-owners) she invited [pp. 59–60].

If Bellow had no patience for Susan's friends, she had no patience for David Peltz and other old buddies from Humboldt Park (though she got on well enough with the Tarcovs). Peltz could be coarse. "He was vulgar," Susan's friend Barbara Wiesenfeld remembers, "larger than life, and he was crude." He was also earthy, warm, tactile, whereas Susan "wasn't earthy. . . . She was a very high-standards person . . . but she lacked that earthiness." Wiesenfeld puts the difference in terms of Jewishness. Bellow and Peltz "had a lot of Yiddishkeit; she didn't have enough, though she had a real connection to her Jewishness." Peltz tells of going to visit Bellow and having to meet him in Jackson Park, outside the apartment, because Susan "didn't like his ghetto friends." Bellow would call, and Peltz would drive up from his home in Indiana Dunes, and the two friends would "sit on a bench there and talk and he would unload." On one occasion, Bellow was in an especially bad way, hyperventilating. "I said, 'Saul, you can't breathe, get the fuck out of that relationship. It's smothering you. . . .' He said, 'Come upstairs and maybe Susan will let you have supper with us. She made a pot of chili.' I went up there, and she said, 'No, Saul, we don't have enough.' So I wheeled around and left." Bellow reproduces this scene in *Humboldt's Gift*, describing Denise as "warlike and shrill" as she refuses to have George Swiebel over for supper. Because of her background, Charlie speculates, "she hated George fiercely." "There's not enough. It's just half a pound of hamburger," she cries. "Don't bring him to the house. . . . I can't bear to see his ass on my sofa, his feet on my rug." Denise is impervious to George's vitality, as Susan was impervious to Dave's vitality: "You're like one of those overbred race horses that must have a goat in his stall to calm his nerves," she tells Charlie. "George Swiebel is your billy goat." Later she adds: "Your weakness for your school chums isn't to be believed. You have the *nostalgie de la boue*. Does he take you around to the whores?" (pp. 41–42). George's view of Denise was more circumspect: "that she was a great beauty but not altogether human." This view Charlie comes to share. "Denise's huge radial amethyst eyes in combination with a low-lined forehead and sharp sibylline teeth supported this interpretation. She is exquisite and terribly fierce" (p. 40). Matilda in *More Die of Heartbreak* also has unearthly eyes. Benn describes them as "hyacinth" or "frosted lilac" as well as "amethyst" (p. 116). Like Denise and Susan, she has no time for higher realms or the "strangeness of life" ("Not again with the strangeness!"). For Benn, however, "those huge eyes of hers gave him a frequent thrill of precisely this, of 'unknowable sources'" (p. 119).

"Exquisite and terribly fierce." Barbara Wiesenfeld saw the fierceness in the friend she loved, as well as the beauty. "There was nothing relaxed in her," she recalls. "There was a demanding way about her. . . . It wasn't like she could edit it or stop and think about it." When Susan was hurrying or if she had to rest, she was "peremptory," "imperious." "She didn't understand that she should have tempered that." Barbara thinks Susan's decoration of the new apartment "wasn't all that extravagant," but she blames her for not considering Bellow: "She did not temper it to his taste," "it was thoughtless," "she should have been more sensitive to his life style . . . it didn't fit"; when he objected, "she had a hard time with his criticism." Bellow wanted a wife to take care of him, and Susan thought that's what she was, but "they saw life very differently; she couldn't defer to that." For Susan, Peltz believes, being married to Bellow meant being "an important social person. He didn't want to be used that way." Dr. Layamon tells Benn in *More Die of Heartbreak:* "My daughter will organize a life ideal for your final years. She can be a real bitch, but her bitchiness will be working *for* you" (p. 140). Matilda also wants "a brilliant position for herself," the Doctor elsewhere adds, but that "is no more than a woman like that is entitled to" (p. 161). "I guarantee that your life will be enjoyable," he tells Benn, "if you can learn to like company. You're kind of solitary, but Tilda is very social" (p. 154). When Benn asks Matilda whom they will be entertaining, her answer is "Desirable connections in this town" and "Visitors passing through, people like Dobrynin, Kissinger, Marilyn Horne, ballet dancers, Günter Grass" (p. 144). (Günter Grass was an enemy of Bellow's by the time *More Die of Heartbreak* was published, as we shall see.) In *Humboldt's Gift*, Denise complains to Charlie, "I tried to make a life for you when you insisted on moving back here. I put myself out. You wouldn't have London or Paris or New York. You had to come back to this—this deadly, ugly, vulgar, dangerous place. Because in your heart you're a kid from the slums. Your heart belongs to the old West Side gutters. I wore myself out being a hostess" (p. 43). Denise, like Matilda, has almost none of what Barbara Wiesenfeld calls Susan's "sweetness," or the warmth she showed to Diane Silverman and her three children, "who really loved her." The closest Bellow comes to granting the Susan-characters softer qualities is when Charlie admits that Denise's scolding was "mixed with affection. When I came home in a state over Humboldt, she was ready to comfort me. But she had a sharp tongue, Denise did. (I sometimes called her Rebukah.)" (pp. 115–16).

DANIEL BELLOW THINKS there was a political element in Bellow's objection to Susan's friends, the real-life equivalents of Matilda's "desirable connections in this town." "He didn't want to talk to these people," Daniel says, "because they were all Stevenson people" (by which he means liberals interested in political personalities and electoral politics). He remembers his father saying to him, "Don't disappoint me, don't be one of those people who just line up." As for Adlai Stevenson himself—as opposed to Stevenson people—"my father's view was that he was a putz, he was a dreamer, didn't know his ass from a hole in the ground. He liked looking at all the big Daley Machine people who ate up Stevenson. And my mother was one of the Stevenson people. Classic Jewish liberal." These views were communicated to Daniel in his adolescence, when Bellow's impatience with liberal pieties was greater than it was in 1964, but something of it was alive at the time, prompted by student unrest and by pressure from fellow writers and intellectuals to protest against the Vietnam War. Here he is on the front page of the *Chicago Sun-Times Book Week* in an article of October 3, 1965, entitled "On Chronicles and Partisans": "We now have a large and increasing group of comfortable and privileged citizens who discuss political questions. It is indeed a mark of privilege to sit talking about the highways, De Gaulle, Kashmir. An assured income makes people moderately responsible and even idealistic. Then, too, the pursuit of pure happiness in the personal sphere to which the country was devoted with regressive blindness during the Eisenhower period ended in high frustration. With Kennedy's election came renewed interest in public affairs."

Although suspicious of this interest in public affairs, Bellow was hardly immune to it, nor could he be described as on the right in 1964, in spite of his disapproval of doctrinaire liberals. That was the year in which he seriously considered writing a book about Hubert Humphrey, a man he admired. An editor at Doubleday, Evelyn Metzger, prompted in part by a conversation with Bellow's friend Max Kampelman, now a Washington lawyer, and influenced by the success of a recent Doubleday book entitled *A Day in the Life of a Surgeon*, thought someone should write a comparable book about a day in the life of a United States senator. It was Kampelman who suggested Bellow as author and Humphrey as subject. Metzger jumped at the idea, and Bellow was intrigued, talking of "Liebling's job on Earl Long" as a possible model, though worrying also that Humphrey was too likable for such treatment. "I like the man too well to do him any injury," Bellow wrote in a letter of January 17, 1964, to the Southern journalist Tom Sancton, "but I don't want to paint the conventional oil painting either." In a letter of April 14, 1964, Metzger wrote to Bellow expressing delight "that negotiations on the Humphrey book have reached the stage where you are ready to come to Washington to talk to Humphrey about it." On May 10, after meeting with Humphrey, Bellow agreed to do the book in September, providing LBJ didn't choose Humphrey as his vice-president. When Johnson did just that, the project was dropped. "There was no point in writing about poor Hubert's misery as Vice President," Bellow recalled in a letter of November 23, 1983, to Carl Soberg, quoted in chapter 8 of *To Fame and Fortune*. "He was LBJ's captive." Yet the idea of a political portrait continued to interest Bellow. In the *Chicago Sun-Times Book Week* article of October 3, 1965, for example, he weighs the dangers of writing about politicians one admires, citing his friend Arthur Schlesinger, Jr.'s writings about Kennedy. Bellow describes Schlesinger as "a sophisticated, experienced, cultivated man who writes particularly well when he is angry and mordant, less well when he is generous, and very badly when he is tender."

A year after abandoning the Humphrey book, Bellow accepted an invitation from *Life* magazine to write a profile of Robert Kennedy. This assignment, too, he abandoned, after a frustrating week in June 1966 shadowing Kennedy. Atlas quotes Bellow as explaining how the problem was that "every other sentence was off-the-record. . . . He would say all kinds of things about Johnson, then say 'Don't quote me.'" Bellow also said that Kennedy treated him, in Atlas's phrase, as "an intellectual tutor. 'He had a lot of catching up to do: "Tell me about Veblen, Walter Lippmann, H. L. Mencken."'"[56] In an undated letter, Schlesinger tried to persuade Bellow to do the Kennedy profile, arguing that "circumstances have to some degree cut him [Bobby] off from those who could be his natural allies . . . and I believe that the sooner the liberal-intellectual community begins to perceive Robert Kennedy as he is, and not according to the stereotype, the better it will be both for Bobby and for the liberals." Schlesinger also doubted that Kennedy "held much back from you in your five days of inspection." Bellow was not convinced. Nor was he tempted when Gilbert Harrison, editor of *The New Republic*, asked him to write a profile of Lyndon Johnson. "We would print whatever you write, whatever its length," Harrison wrote in a letter of March 6, 1966; "we would hope to pay whatever you ask." Bellow's scrawled reply (on the letter itself, suggesting that he now had use of a secretary) was a polite refusal. "I've always wanted to write about Washington and politicians and while I was between books I made several attempts to involve myself in politics. I found, however, that one was either inside the [circle] or on the fringes."

Like Bellow, Charlie Citrine is offered the chance of writing a profile of Robert Kennedy for *Life* magazine. "For once my business in the East was legitimate and I was not chasing some broad but preparing a magazine article. And just that morning I had been flying over New York in a procession of Coast Guard helicopters with Senators Javits and Robert Kennedy. Then I had attended a political luncheon in Central Park at the Tavern on the Green, where all the celebrities became ecstatic at the sight of one another." In the helicopter, "whopping over Manhattan," Charlie feels at the top of his game. His physical appearance, like Bellow's, can change radically: "If I don't look well, I look busted" ("Bellow could look eighty one day and much younger the next," according to his friend and ex-lover Bette Howland); while following Kennedy, Charlie "knew that I looked well. Besides, there was money in my pockets and I had been window-shopping on Madison Avenue. If any Cardin or Hermès necktie pleased me I could buy it without asking the price. My belly was flat, I wore boxer shorts of combed Sea Island cotton at eight bucks a pair. I had joined an athletic club in Chicago and with elderly effort kept myself in shape" (p. 11). Charlie likes Bobby Kennedy, who "even seemed to like me. I say 'seemed' because it was his business to leave such an impression with a journalist who proposed to write about him. . . . His desire was to be continually briefed. He asked questions of everyone in the party. From me he wanted historical information—'What should I know about William Jennings Bryan?' or, 'Tell me about H. L. Mencken'—receiving what I said with an inward glitter that did not tell me what he thought or whether he could use such facts" (p. 113). Charlie, who is mourning the death of his old buddy Humboldt, decides to abandon the *Life* magazine assignment and return to Chicago, to the dismay of Denise. Riding in helicopters and hobnobbing with Kennedys is just what Denise wants for him. He returns home on a steamy summer night, the sort when "old smells of the stockyard revive. . . . Old Chicago breathed again through leaves and screens" (p. 114). Denise sits nude on the bed, brushing her hair.

"Her enormous violet and gray eyes were impatient, her tenderness was mixed with glowering. . . . It tired Denise to support me emotionally. She didn't take much stock in these emotions of mine" (p. 115).

Politics and public affairs intruded themselves on Bellow throughout the 1960s. In the summer of 1964, when LBJ picked Humphrey as his running mate, the Republicans chose Barry Goldwater as their presidential candidate. The day of the nomination, July 16, 1964, race riots broke out in Harlem after a policeman shot and killed a fifteen-year-old boy. The riots lasted six days and set off a string of violent disturbances, in Philadelphia, Rochester, Chicago, and several cities in New Jersey. Sometime after the nomination, Bellow wrote to Richard Goodwin, the special assistant to President Johnson credited with inventing the term the "Great Society." The two men had met when Goodwin was working in the White House as a speechwriter to President Kennedy. Bellow's letter expressed disquiet at Goldwater's nomination, and Goodwin, in an undated letter, offered reassurance. "It would be, I believe, a mistake to look at this as a vast groundswell of philosophical reaction to liberalism, etc. If it wasn't for the race issue—which transcends philosophy—Goldwater would be lucky to get 35–40% of the vote. . . . Unfortunately the race issue makes him dangerous. No one can assess the 'backlash.' But all agree it is growing in size and intensity."

Bellow was a supporter of CORE (Congress of Racial Equality) and that year, at its invitation, had written the preface to a book to be entitled "They Shall Overcome," sponsored by CORE's "Scholarship, Education and Defense Fund" (SEDF). The preface, which was clearly written after the riots, is tough-minded and moving. It begins with a simple factual statement: "The lives of Southern Negroes are not protected by law." The truth of this statement, Bellow asserted, was accepted by Republican and Democratic politicians alike, and "until the civil rights movement became effective most Americans accepted it as well." In demanding the vote, the leaders of the civil rights movement, "Negroes and those who joined with them . . . have been persecuted, bullied, terrorized, beaten, abused, jailed, maimed and killed," a situation "documented on every page of this book."[57]

Bellow's introduction devotes several paragraphs to the rural poor, the source, he argues, of most racial violence in the South. He writes with the murders of the Mississippi Freedom Summer volunteers Michael Schwerner, Andrew Goodman, and James Earl Chaney fresh in mind, their bodies having been discovered just outside the small town of Philadelphia, Mississippi, in August 1964, six or so weeks after they had been arrested by the local police.[58] "Everyone knows what a modern metropolis is," Bellow begins, but the myth of Southern agrarian virtue lives on. "Rural America has had a long history of overvaluation," even among "sophisticated social theorists"; the idea that "everyone was better and sounder on the farm, in the woods and hills, less anomic, more self-reliant, fairer, more American. This is simply not so. In provincial America, North no less than South, lives the most unhappy, troubled and alienated portion of the population. . . . In the South the glamor of Confederacy and insurrection, of 'tradition' and 'gentility' has been laid in poster colors over provincial pride, backwardness, xenophobia and rage." The racism of rural Southerners, however, will no longer be tolerated. In the past few years, "a majority of the American people" have signaled that they wish to see an end to "the open and repeated rejection of liberty and equality. . . . Though it may be amorphous and difficult to define, something like a national conscience actually does exist," a conscience activated by volunteers from CORE and other civil rights organizations. In making radical constitutional demands and making them peacefully, they and their followers "have contributed to the moral growth of the American nation. They might have released hatred and destruction, as outcasts often do when their rebellion at last occurs. The peaceful and legal growth of their freedom, for it is bound to increase, will benefit us all."

In addition to supporting the civil rights movement, Bellow took public positions on two other issues of the day: nuclear disarmament and the war in Vietnam. He agreed to act as a sponsor of the National Committee for a Sane Nuclear Policy (SANE), writing to the press to publicize his support, and he made clear his opposition to LBJ's Vietnam policies in letters to *The New York Times* and the *Chicago Sun-Times*. In both cases, however, he was careful to speak out against violent or illegal protest. It was when a SANE rally in Washington turned rowdy that he wrote to *The New York Times* and the *Chicago Sun-Times*, on October 29, 1965, to "make clear that I am wholly opposed to civil disobedience and that I dislike unreasonable rebelliousness and pointless defiance of authority." In the same letter, headed "Author's Testimony on Vietnam" in the *Sun-Times*, he criticized the Johnson administration for its aggressive attitude to political protest: "The government is wrong to attack the political liberties of those who wish to debate its policies and who appeal to it for broader, franker and more responsible explanations. . . . Seldom has any administration dealt so roughly with its foreign policy critics as this one." "That was a wonderful letter of yours in the TIMES," Benjamin Spock wrote to Bellow on November 3, "and it should help the March on Washington."

Although Bellow was outspoken in his opposition to particular government policies, he was unwilling to join protest movements, for reasons he explained in a 1981 interview with Michiko Kakutani of *The New York Times:* "People became organized in camps, and while I was opposed to the war, I just refused to line up with the new groups." Bellow's wariness of groups or camps was particularly intense in New York, where literary alliances were confused with political ones and "you were always being solicited for this cause or that, always being drafted for one thing or another."[59] As he told another interviewer, Susan Crosland, six years later, "Vietnam, civil rights meant writers were 'pressed'—if not quite in the old sense—to line up with the Mailer group, or *Commentary* group, lashed into one ideological column or another. I got tired of having my arm twisted to sign statements insulting Lyndon Johnson and so on."[60] These comments were made in response to a question about why Bellow decided to leave New York, but that decision had been made earlier, before the political pressures he remembered from the 1960s. Nor was life in Chicago free from such pressures. From mid-1965 to the early 1970s, the University of Chicago student newspaper, *The Chicago Maroon*, ran almost daily articles about students protesting the draft and the war in Vietnam; the campus was alive with rallies, teach-ins, demonstrations, occupations. There was similar pressure from Greg, who was in graduate school in social work from 1966 to 1968. He told me that he and his father "were severely at odds over the war, and we were severely at odds over whether I should go to Canada as well. I went to the March on Washington. I went to the civil rights protests. . . . During my senior year, two of my roommates were part of the occupation. There was something about it [the occupation] that put him off . . . too much self-interest."

A very public demonstration of Bellow's reluctance to "line up" was his refusal to join Robert Lowell in rejecting an invitation in the summer of 1965 to a White House Festival of the Arts. Lowell had agreed to attend the Festival, then took back his acceptance, arguing in a letter copied to *The New York Times*, "Every serious artist knows that he cannot enjoy public celebrations without making subtle public commitments." Bellow's position, as reported on June 4 in *The New York Times* and the *Chicago Sun-Times*, was that "the President intends, in his own way, to encourage American artists," an intention Bellow approved. In addition, "I consider this event to be an official function, not a political occasion which demands agreement with Mr. Johnson on all policies of his administration." The administration is "more than the policies of which I disapprove" (these included the "wicked and harmful" intervention in Santo Domingo, as well as the war in Vietnam). The president's record on civil rights was a good one, and the institution of the presidency mattered. He accepted the invitation, he said, "in order to show my respect for his intentions and to honor his high office." In his letter of acceptance, Bellow wrote of his pleasure at being invited but wished "to make it clear that to accept your invitation is not to accept all the policies and actions of your administration."[61] He knew his attendance had "political meaning," but differed with "my friend, Mr. Lowell," in interpreting his responsibility "as citizen and writer." He also differed, he soon discovered, from many other friends, the signatories of a petition supporting Lowell's stand which was circulated by Robert Silvers, co-editor of *The New York Review of Books*, and the poet Stanley Kunitz, and reported on the front page of *The New York Times*. Among those who signed the petition were John Berryman, Robert Penn Warren, Bernard Malamud, Philip Roth, Mary McCarthy, William Styron, Lillian Hellman, Harvey Swados, and Alfred Kazin.[62]

Harvey Swados wrote a harsh letter to Bellow when he heard of his decision to attend the Festival: "Going to the White House on June 1965 is not an innocent amusement [but] an act of solidarity with those who will be bombing and shelling even as you read from your works to the assembled culture bureaucrats." On June 14, the day of the Festival, Bellow responded to Swados's "slap-in-the-face formula and the implied responsibility for death in Vietnam." Swados knew perfectly well that Bellow had publicly opposed what Johnson was doing in Vietnam and Santo Domingo, "but I don't see that holding these positions requires me to treat Johnson as a Hitler. He's not that. He may be a brute in some ways (by no means all) but he is the President, and I haven't yet decided to go in for civil disobedience. Have you? You sound ready to stop paying taxes." Four days later, Swados replied, denying that he had written or implied that Johnson was a Hitler and asking, "Do you really believe it suffices to say, 'but he is the President'? This might do from somebody like say Rex Stout, but not from somebody like Saul Bellow." As for civil disobedience, Swados's answer was "yes, unequivocally," though he would not be withholding his taxes. Instead, he would continue to advise young people "against serving in the armed forces when they are committing criminal acts against other populations," and, more vaguely, to join forces "with 'responsible' others to get it [the army] to stop killing peasants." Swados ended his letter of June 18 by saying he was sorry if his previous letter had wounded Bellow. "I hope you will join us and not be put off by my intemperateness and rudeness." At the Festival itself, Dwight Macdonald, despite signing the Silvers-and-Kunitz petition, was in attendance. Bellow described him as "walking into the Rose Garden in sneakers, the great bohemian himself going around with a resolution endorsing Lowell's boycott."[63] Near the stairs to the East Room, Bellow found himself cornered by Saul Maloff, the editor of the books pages of *Newsweek*. Maloff, described by Atlas as "a noisy ex-radical," was there as a reporter. He berated Bellow for attending and reading from *Herzog*, muttering "ominously: 'We made you, and we can break you.' "[64]

Bellow stuck to his dual view, opposing the Vietnam War and the intervention in Santo Domingo while supporting Johnson's domestic policies. "I had a difficult time knowing where Bellow stood," Mark Harris remembers. Though Bellow clearly opposed the war, "Why then was he embattled with anti-war people when they met?"[65] One answer is that he refused to be a person "who just lined up," the phrase his son Daniel remembers him using (and one found in an article of September 1968 in the *Chicago Sun-Times*, quoted later in the chapter). On July 13, 1966, Bellow and fourteen University of Chicago colleagues had dinner in Chicago with Joseph A. Califano, Jr., special assistant to the president, and two other White House aides, to discuss the Great Society. Califano organized comparable meetings throughout the country, with a total of eighty-one academics and experts from sixteen universities. Bellow was the sole literary academic, the sole writer, consulted. In a letter composed the day after the dinner, Califano asked Bellow and the other academics to produce a memorandum "reflecting your thoughts on the problems that were discussed there and any other problems with which you are concerned. We are particularly interested in these questions: Where should the Great Society go from here? What needs have we left unmet? What new problems do we create as we solve old problems?" Califano also conveyed the president's "personal appreciation for your taking the time to meet with us and pass along your ideas to him through us."[66] When Bellow complained to Philip Rahv about the fallout from his attendance at the White House Festival, Rahv wrote back, on October 15, commiserating with his friend but also reminding him of his new status and visibility. "Success, like failure, has its problems. You were, of course, successful before *Herzog*, though not on the same scale. But on the whole I would say that your position is more secure than that of any novelist in America. But to suffer is our fate."[67]

Political requests and demands arrived almost daily. On November 12, 1965, Nicolas Nabokov asked him to sign a letter to Premier Kosygin of Russia protesting the imprisonment of the dissident writers Andrei Sinyavsky and Yuli Daniel. On December 1, Dwight Macdonald, with Robert Lowell, asked him to sign a similar letter. Bellow signed. The following August, he was asked to contribute to a book entitled "Authors Take Sides on Vietnam."[68] He declined. On October 21, 1967, Norman Mailer wrote asking Bellow to "take a look again" at the "Writers and Editors War Tax Protest," which Mailer himself had agreed to support. Joining the protest, Mailer conceded, would be for Bellow "an unpleasant test of conscience," possibly costing him "a large, even disruptive sum of money" (a possibility that had not deterred Mailer). "So I request you to read this accompanying literature and suffer conceivably the unhappy recognition that one is probably obliged to sign, for until then our protest against the war may be literary yet notably unengaged. Viet Nam, hot damn. Your brother in penmanship, Norman Mailer." Bellow did not sign. On February 17, 1968, he received a telegram from Blair Clark, campaign manager of the anti-Vietnam presidential candidate Eugene McCarthy. Would Bellow serve on a "Committee of Arts and Letters for McCarthy for President"? He would—he scribbled across the telegram, "OK—but have no time for fundraising."

Part of Bellow's reluctance to be pressed by movements and activists derived from firsthand experience. In a letter of August 30, 1969, after agreeing to read a draft of Swados's new novel, he returned to their earlier disagreement over the White House Festival.

> No other two college Trotskyites can have gotten so very far apart. I doubt that I have more use for Nixon and Johnson than you have. My going to the White House was nonsense, probably. It pleased no one, myself least of all. I wouldn't have gone at all if I hadn't been obliged by my own obstinacy to mark my disagreement with all parties. First I made my views on Vietnam and San Domingo as

clear as possible in the *Times*, and then declared that I would go to show my respect for the President's office—the office of Lincoln. I know about Harding, too, and Chester A. Arthur, but I am not at all prepared to secede. I am not a revolutionary. I have little respect for American revolutionaries as I know them, and I have known them quite well. I don't like the Susan Sontag bit about a doomed America. I had my fill of the funnyhouse in Coney Island.

A reliable source tells me that Johnson's view of the White House culture gala was as follows: "They insult me by comin', they insult me by staying away." Could Dwight Macdonald have been more succinct? In fact they have a lot in common.

Bellow's knowledge of what he calls "American revolutionaries" owed as much to his time as a college professor in the 1960s as to his Trotskyist student days in the 1930s. The protesters at the University of Chicago in the 1960s were especially active and prominent, on and off campus. On January 24, 1966, students from the Chicago branch of SDS (Students for a Democratic Society) blocked the entrance to the Illinois Continental National Bank on LaSalle Street, in protest against the bank's part in a forty-million-dollar loan to South Africa. In May 1966, after a week of fruitless negotiations, more than four hundred students occupied the Administration Building for six days. They were protesting against the university's agreement to provide rankings and other academic information to Selective Service draft boards. During the occupation, the students organized a teach-in about the war, in which Dick Gregory, the comedian, made a speech urging them not to give up their fight, and a hundred faculty members signed a petition in their support. Edward Levi, the provost, took the sort of stand Bellow approved: "While the University may work to change the law, it may not disobey it, and in the process endanger its students." Levi also argued that "a student's rank is an individual matter and the University has no right to deny it to him." A year later, a second anti-draft demonstration took place; this time, 120 students took over the Administration Building for a "study-in." Fifty-seven of these students were suspended for Winter Quarter 1967, although many of the suspensions were not carried out.[69] In April 1968, there were riots in Chicago after the assassination of Martin Luther King, Jr., leading to Mayor Daley's notorious "shoot to kill" order. Then came the violence of the police at the Democratic Convention (watched by Bellow on television in East

Hampton, in the company of Gore Vidal and an old Tuley High School friend, Lou Sidran), when seven hundred people were arrested and more than a thousand injured. In October 1968, the *Maroon* reported, fifteen thousand people, many of them students, marched down Michigan Avenue to protest against police brutality. When Edward Levi was appointed university president at the end of the year, SDS members and members of the Hyde Park Area Draft Resisters' Union demonstrated at a dinner held in his honor, in part against the guest speaker at the dinner, McGeorge Bundy, president of the Ford Foundation and former national security adviser to Presidents Kennedy and Johnson.

Several weeks later, on January 30, 1969, four hundred students again occupied the Administration Building, this time in protest against the university's decision not to rehire Marlene Dixon, an assistant professor of sociology, later founder of the Marxist-Leninist Democratic Workers Party, which she led for seven years. The students claimed that Dixon had been treated unfairly because she was a radical, because she put teaching before scholarly publication, and because she was a woman, one of a very small number on the faculty at the time. Edward Levi responded to the occupation by evacuating all staff in the building and placing security guards in the hallways. Unlike other university presidents, he refused to summon the city police to maintain order. The administrators were moved to other campus locations and a faculty committee chaired by Hanna Gray, associate professor of history, later a president of the university, concluded on February 12 that there had been no violation of appointment procedures. Three days later, the students voted to end their sit-in. In the month that followed, forty-one students were expelled from the university, eighty-one students were suspended, and three were placed on probation.

Richard Stern recalled the student radicals as angry and humorless. They formed "improvisatory theater groups, passed out material about such professors as Daniel Boorstin and held rallies. I attended one of these and believe I learned more about revolution there than I'd learned from Carlyle or *Barnaby Rudge*. The radicals were led by the Weatherman, Howie Machtinger. He conducted the meeting masterfully, a young Lenin. . . . My own contribution to the U. of Chicago uprising was a series of satiric poems published in the student newspaper—site of the warring opinions—which earned a denunciation in which Machtinger called me a motherfucker."[70] James Redfield, of the Committee on Social Thought, who describes himself as the most left-leaning member of the Committee, was involved in the negotiations with the students and remembers the 1960s as having "a really shattering effect on people," moving a number of figures on the faculty to the right. He recalls Hannah Arendt, a member of the Committee at the time, arguing with Edward Shils about the protesters. "These children are not criminals," she insisted. According to Atlas, when one of the students at the Committee sought to negotiate with university administrators on behalf of the protesters, Shils, Bellow, and David Grene "threatened to take away his fellowship." Atlas also describes Bellow's outrage when a female student in his Joyce seminar "swept into class in the midst of the national student strike with a list of 'non-negotiable' demands." Bellow's response was to shout: "You women's liberationists! All you're going to have to show for your movement ten years from now are *sagging breasts*!"[71] What Redfield remembers of Bellow at the time of the student power movement was that he was "very quiet" on campus, but "he was heard from in the press." This impression was shared by Jonathan Kleinbard, an assistant to Levi when the sit-ins began. Whereas Shils, in Kleinbard's words, "played a role, I don't think Saul did. I think he was just divorced from it."

What Bellow had to say in the press was tough on the students. On November 30, 1967, he published an article in the *Chicago Sun-Times* entitled "The Young Lack Faith in Leaders." It begins by deploring the Johnson administration's "passion for secrecy," the "harshness and arrogance" of administration spokesmen, the "brutality and abandonment of principle in Vietnam," the president's "refusal to give convincing reasons for his policies," and "his meekness with his generals." Then it turns to the "primitivism" at the heart not only of student protest but of the counterculture in general: "As Marie Antoinette played with sheep, as Gauguin turned to the South Seas, as Rimbaud went primitive, so the kids of Haight Ashbury require from the civilization that produced them the freedom and happiness of primitives." Bellow had little love for "the Washington big business power racket," but the hippie alternative was no answer. "You do not destroy yourself because you think your father a bad man, your mother a fool. Courting dirt because the family was neurotically clean, lying in a trance because Daddy ran to punch the time clock, consenting to a structureless, formless and chaotic inner life, and rejecting all former ideas of order—one cannot make an existence out of such negatives." When Bellow met Mark Harris's daughter, Hester, a high-school senior, who greeted him barefoot, in a long green shawl and a bright-orange leotard, he "appeared not to approve of her, gazing upon her coldly, making her uncomfortable."[72] As for student radicals: "Youth movements are not invariably a good thing. Germany's Hitlerjugend certainly was not. Nor Benito Mussolini's Society of the Wolf. Nor Stalin's Komsomol. Nor do the young Maoist gangs fill one with confidence and hope."

Passages like these alarmed Bellow's acquaintances on the left. A year earlier, on November 12, 1966, Irving Howe had written to thank Bellow for purchasing fifty subscriptions to his quarterly magazine, *Dissent*, presumably to send to friends (that Edith Tarcov was the magazine's managing editor played a part in this purchase). *Dissent* was critical of national liberation theories and the culture of the New Left, but it supported the civil rights movement and organized labor and was sharply critical of Cold War hawks such as Sidney Hook and Irving Kristol. In addition to thanking Bellow, Howe expressed a wish to talk with him when he was next in New York. "I know you're harassed these days. But I've found myself mentally wanting to hold a conversation with you. (We've never really known each other, except through others, like Isaac [Rosenfeld].) There are certain things in what you've recently been writing in articles with which I strongly agree, except that I feel your anger leads you to say things that leave you open to needless demagogic charges. There's a lot of empty verbal radicalism in the air these days: 'peasant revolution' plus tenure."[73]

Howe's letter was sent about a month after Bellow received a letter from his old friend Irving Kristol, at the time executive vice-president of Basic Books and a founding editor, with Daniel Bell, of the quarterly *The Public Interest*. Bellow had raised doubts about Kristol's "editorial integrity" at *Encounter*, the magazine Kristol coedited with Stephen Spender from 1953 to 1958. *Encounter* had been covertly funded in those years by the Congress for Cultural Freedom, at the time a CIA conduit, and though Kristol denied all knowledge of CIA funding and influence, doubts persisted. When Bellow voiced these doubts, Kristol wrote a detailed letter protesting his innocence. "This is one of the few letters I've written defending myself. I've not argued this matter with Jason Epstein, William Phillips, *et al*, because I suspect their motives and am indifferent to their good opinion. But I am not at all indifferent to *your* good opinion, and I do want you to understand that, whatever may have been wrong with *Encounter*'s editorial outlook while I was editor, the wrongness was mine, by God, and no one else's. I may have been, technically, a 'dupe'; but the magazine was not." Like Howe, Kristol hoped he and Bellow could get together "when next you are in New York"; they had known each other for many years, and in 1965 Bellow attempted, unsuccessfully, to bring Kristol and his wife, Gertrude Himmelfarb, to Chicago.[74] The events of the late 1960s drew Bellow closer to the worldview of the Kristols and did little to temper his public pronouncements; they also found their way into a new novel he was writing, about a man named Pawlyk, later named Sammler.

TWO PUBLIC EVENTS of the 1960s were especially influential in Bellow's life: the Arab-Israeli Six-Day War of 1967, and a speech Bellow gave a year later at San Francisco State University, where he was rudely heckled. It was Bellow's idea to go to Israel to cover the war, as does Artur Sammler. In a letter of May 31, 1967, to Ruth Miller, he announced, "On Saturday it struck me that I should go to Israel to report the crisis for *Life*, *Look*, or *The New Yorker*. I have made myself available, there is some interest, and I may be gone in a day or two." Within a week, he was on his way, for *Newsday*, a newspaper rather than a magazine. He wrote four articles for the paper, the first of which appeared on June 9, a day before the war ended, and a day before his fifty-second birthday. It was datelined Tel Aviv and titled "After the Battle: Troops, Sightseers." Like the articles to follow, it stressed the oddity of observing the horrors of war, the bloated corpses of the Sinai, "black and stinking in the desert sun," then returning to a plush hotel in Jerusalem or Tel Aviv. "From the comfortable veranda and the smooth grounds of the King David Hotel in Jerusalem," he reports on June 12, "guests watched the violent fighting last Monday in the Old City. One eyewitness told me that he had just finished his breakfast when he went to look at the battle. He saw an Israeli serviceman hit by a mortar, blown out of his boots; just a moment before, the man had been reading a newspaper."[75] Throughout his dispatches, Bellow stressed the culpability of the great powers in allowing Nasser, Hussein, and the Syrians to arm themselves and threaten "to run the Israelis into the sea, to drown them like rats, to annihilate everyone."[76] In the third dispatch, of June 13, Bellow reports a conversation with a veteran of the 1956 Sinai campaign. The veteran thinks the Egyptian armed forces much improved. "They had prepared their positions skillfully. They had extensive trenches. Their Russian or Nazi teachers—for there are, said my informant, a good many Germans in Egypt who settled down to a useful life after World War II—had some reason to feel encouraged." But the Egyptians had no air cover, and without air cover their army was helpless. The Israelis won the war because they blew up the Arab airfields, even those supposedly out of range, and then shot their aircraft to pieces. "If they had not done this, the war would have been long and bloody."[77]

In the final dispatch, Bellow visits Nablus, in the Jordan Valley, territory taken by the Israelis the previous week. Although unashamedly pro-Israel, he registers the suffering and injustice visited on the Palestinians. "No one can reasonably claim that right is entirely on the Israeli side, and though some Arab leaders exploited the misery of the refugees to intensify hatred of Israel, the Israelis might have done more for the Arabs. It should have been possible, for instance, to set aside money for indemnity and reconstruction. Part of the money paid to Israel by West Germany might have been used for this purpose." If the numbers of rotting slums and demoralized refugees increase, "only Arab extremists can profit from this."[78] The article ends, however, by implying that the misery of the region has its roots not so much in Palestinian displacement as in the Arab mentality, or the current Arab mentality. Bellow and Sydney Gruson, of *The New York Times*, stop in a barbershop in Nablus where an elderly Arab dairy farmer, "very handsome, dark-browed," with "a furious nonsmile," engages them in conversation. He begins by calling Americans spies and complaining about being unable to purchase gas to drive to the relief of his cows (at which point Bellow notes that his farm is only two miles out of town, and that there are plenty of donkeys in the street, as well as many idle men). The farmer talks about "the future, Arab unity, hints of vengeance." Bellow describes him as looking like the actor John Gilbert "playing an Arab role," a description which leads to the article's concluding paragraphs:

> It is instructive to see what Middle Eastern poster artists do with the faces of Hollywood stars, the feelings they impart to them. Robert Mitchum Arabized is strong, honorable, but his features are twisted with foreknowledge of defeat. Fate is dead against him. We know that he is not going to make it. Our gentleman farmer is like that.
>
> Now, having his neck trimmed with a Schick electric razor, he sits with stilted suffering pride. I am unable to give a T. E.

> Lawrence/Freya Stark interpretation to this look. In my cruder Midwestern judgment, it seems all wrong. What good are these traditional dignities? No good at all if they lead to the Sinai roads with their blasted Russian tanks, the black faces of the dead dissolving, and the survivors fighting for a sip of ditch water.[79]

What prompted Bellow to go to Israel as the war approached? He had been there before, several times, though "I have never been a Zionist. I never had strong feelings on the subject. But something about that particular occasion—the fact that for the second time in a quarter of a century the Jews were having a gun pressed to their heads—led me to ask *Newsday*, a Long Island newspaper, to send me as a correspondent."[80] To get to Israel was no easy business. Bellow flew to Rome, where he was told his flight to Tel Aviv would be diverted to Athens. He stayed in the Hotel Grande Bretagne in Athens. After much difficulty, he managed to get a seat on a packed El Al flight (Artur Sammler does this by visiting the Israeli consulate in Athens, then "waiting again at the airport until four a.m. among journalists and hippies" [p. 205]). It was worth it, Bellow wrote in a letter of June 7: "It puts one in touch with reality. Otherwise one's decades begin to feel empty like an old amusement park no longer patronized and oneself the caretaker remembering childhood, boyhood-youth as side shows. . . . This is much better."[81] It is hard to think of the 1960s as empty of stimulus, or insufficiently real, especially for Bellow, but he seems here to have felt that. For Artur Sammler they certainly were, mostly for reasons to do with his experiences as a Holocaust survivor. In explaining why he went to Israel to report on the war, Sammler sounds like Bellow. In the late spring of 1967, Sammler is exhausted by "minor things which people insisted upon enlarging, magnifying, moving into the center: relationships, interior decorations, family wrangles. . . ."

> Civilian matters. Civilian one and all! The high-minded, like Plato (now he was not only lecturing, but even lecturing himself), wished to get rid of such stuff—wrangles, lawsuits, hysterias, all such hole-and-corner pettiness. Other powerful minds denied that this could be done. They held (like Freud) that the mightiest instincts were bound up in just such stuff, each trifle the symptom of a deep disease in a creature whose whole fate was disease. What to do about such things? Absurd in form, but possibly real? But possi-

> bly not real? Relief from this had become imperative. And that was why, during the Aqaba crisis, Mr. Sammler had had to go to the Middle East [p. 204].

The entanglements Sammler wishes to escape are different from Bellow's entanglements, but not all that different. (Bellow's entanglements are more direct or personal, involving his own erotic and marital life rather than those of relatives and friends.) Once in Israel, Sammler, "a man of seventy-plus" (p. 1), heads off to the front "in a white cap and a striped seersucker jacket" (chosen to make him look younger, and worn also by Bellow in Israel). In Gaza, Sammler notices the women in the market: "The black veils were transparent. You saw the heavy-boned mannish faces underneath—large noses, the stern mouths projecting over stonelike teeth" (p. 206). On the battlefield, he, like Bellow, fixes on the strewn corpses: "swollen gigantic arms, legs, roasted in the sun. The dogs ate human roast. In the trenches the bodies leaned on the parapets. The dogs came cringing, flattening up. . . . In the sun the faces softened, blackened, melted, and flowed away. . . . A strange flavor of human grease. Of wet paper pulp" (p. 207). To Sammler, the dead bodies are "the one subject the soul was sure to take seriously" (p. 209). Like Bellow, Sammler sees very few live Egyptians, only a group of captured snipers bound and blindfolded. When he sees them he has to master the trembling of his legs and a wish to cry.

In *To Jerusalem and Back*, published in 1976 and based in part on his *Newsday* articles, Bellow offers a slightly different sense of what was "real" for him about the Six-Day War. It was not merely that it was a war but that it was this particular war. He quotes Professor Jacob Talmon of the Hebrew University of Jerusalem, a figure of "plump professorial propriety . . . finely dressed, tie well chosen . . . not one of your open-at-the-throat, bushy Israeli types,"[82] on the significance of the Israeli victory. In 1967, after the war, Israel could think of itself " 'as one of the few countries in the contemporary jaded world with a sense of purpose,' " an assertion Bellow considers "of first importance."

> The Israelis had war, and not the moral equivalent of war William James was looking for, to give them firmness. They had, in their concern for the decay of civilization and in their pride (pride and concern in equal proportions), something to teach the world. The stunned remnant that had crept from Auschwitz had demonstrated

> that they could farm a barren land, industrialize it, build cities, make a society, do research, philosophize, write books, sustain a great moral tradition, and, finally, create an army of tough fighters [p. 135].

In *To Jerusalem and Back*, Bellow wrestles with the injustices visited upon the Palestinians by the creation of the state of Israel and with the selective nature of the moral outrage these injustices evoke (especially from European radicals, who appear to believe "that the Jews, with their precious and refining record of suffering, have a unique obligation to hold up the moral burdens everyone else has dumped" [p. 136]). He paraphrases another professor, Yehoshafat Harkabi of Stanford: " 'Zionists were not deliberately unjust, the Arabs were not guiltless. To rectify the evil as the Arabs would wish it rectified would mean the destruction of Israel. Arab refugees must be relieved and compensated, but Israel will not commit suicide for their sake' " (p. 158). At the time of the war, these and other demoralizing complications were briefly swept aside by the direct threat Israel faced, a reality which drew Bellow.

The following autumn, at a dinner at Marshall and Doris Holleb's apartment, Bellow met the journalist David Halberstam, who was in Chicago to write a profile of Mayor Daley. According to Doris Holleb, Halberstam told Bellow he loved his novels but that he "shouldn't do reporting, why waste your time on reporting." According to another woman at the dinner, Halberstam also accused Bellow of having "missed the real story" of the war.[83] What Bellow remembers is that Halberstam "made fun of my dispatches, saying that I ran up large Telex bills to describe to Long Island readers the look of a battlefield." Bellow asked Halberstam what he thought "real" journalism was. " 'When an Egyptian general and his entire army were captured,' said Halberstam, 'and a newspaperman asked him why not a shot had been fired, he answered that firing a shot would have given away his position.' And *that*, in Halberstam's view, was one of the most brilliant stories filed in the 1967 war" (*To Jerusalem and Back*, pp. 58–59). Bellow spent the rest of the evening, according to Doris Holleb, silent and angry, though "Halberstam didn't have a clue that he'd insulted him." From Bellow's perspective, Halberstam was superficial, the sort of writer "who was interested in war, but not the things that cause war."[84] Bellow looked for deeper meanings, as he did when considering Vietnam and the controversy it provoked. In Mark Harris's words, as "the debate over Vietnam divided the country, Bellow maintained his view of history as time, breadth, transcendent. In a letter to me he had sarcastically described 'an age' as 'the interval between appearances of the Sunday Times News of the Week in Review.'"[85] As Bellow put it in a 1975 interview in *Newsweek*, "What man with his eyes open at this hour could not be interested in politics? . . . I only wish people talked about it at a deeper level than Chappaquiddick or Scoop Jackson or who's-gonna-get-the-nomination. I don't think we know where we are or where we're going. I see politics—ultimately—as a buzzing preoccupation that swallows up art and the life of the spirit."[86] In Israel, Bellow's family connection, Sabina Mazursky, was struck by the intensity with which he listened: "He listened not only to the story, but beyond that: he listened with all his senses, to body language, to intonation, noticing all details thoroughly and in depth. He was very friendly but needed a lot of space. He was brilliant, sensitive, a unique person."[87]

When Halberstam asked Bellow "why waste your time on reporting," it is likely that he hit a nerve. On September 15, 1968, Bellow published an article in the *Chicago Sun-Times* deploring writers who use up their energy "asserting and publicly establishing the fact that they are indeed writers. They quickly become actors who behave like writers."[88] What matters to these writers is "to be mentioned by the papers or to be seen on television or in the art landscape, to enlist in causes, or to line up with the SDS or the Black Panthers." What also matters is that the public recognize their views as the sort of views writers hold:

> In politics, writers are romantic. They are for dissent, against authority; for the "natural," against the "social"; for sickness and madness, against the square or "normal"; for violence, opposed to bourgeois tameness; for excess and against restraint. This is fairly old stuff, but the public seems to want it, and artists deliver it. People want emancipation. . . . Art itself is secondary now, for the public rejoices in artists rather than in art.

Art itself is seen as secondary, Bellow adds, not only because it is complicated, nuanced, and ambiguous, but because it is often concerned with aesthetic or metaphysical questions, "the life of the spirit." For today's artist, "public and social events dominate all others. News, rumor, scandal, political campaigns, wars, assassinations, youth movements, race riots loom over religion, philosophy, art, private feelings, personal loyalties, love. These are considered the Action, the Center of common experience. . . . The emphasis falls on collective experience and not upon individual vision."[89] In refusing to line up or sign on, in preserving his individuality, in refusing to be "drafted" or "pressed" by politics, Bellow believed he was serving art or literature. When engaged in public debate, he was often irritable or resentful in manner, as if he were wasting his time or angry with himself for wasting his time (having given in to the temptation to play the artist). This was particularly the case when giving talks, undertaken mainly for financial reasons.

BY THE MID-1960S, Bellow was much in demand as a speaker on college campuses, so much so that he hired Bill Cooper Associates (BCA), a New York speakers' agent, to handle requests for talks and readings.[90] In April 1968, BCA organized a five-day tour to five Illinois colleges. Bellow spoke to audiences of 1,000 to 1,800 people, for fees ranging from $1,200 to $1,300. On May 1, he spoke at Wake Forest University in North Carolina, then at William Jewell College in Liberty, Missouri, on May 3, then the University of Washington in Seattle, on May 9, for $1,750 a talk. After speaking in Seattle, he went on to San Francisco State University, where he was to give a talk on May 10. The talk was held in the university's theater-arts auditorium, to an overflowing audience. Bellow had friends at San Francisco State: Wright Morris, whose writing he had praised and published in the magazine *The Noble Savage;* Kay House, Sand House Higson's sister, who was also in the English Department (Sand House Higson was a friend of Bellow's second wife, Sasha); and Phil Siegelman, whom Bellow knew from the University of Minnesota, now teaching political science at San Francisco State. Herb and Mitzi McClosky, close friends also from Minnesota, who now lived in Berkeley, were to put Bellow up a few days after the event. The talk itself, entitled "What Are Writers Doing in the University?" (an alternative to or variant of another talk given on tour, "The Writer and the Public Today"), passed without incident. A friend of Mark Harris's, Hannah Koler, described it as "witty, entertaining & definitely cynical."[91] Matters didn't get out of hand until the question period. After Bellow gave his opinion of LeRoi Jones's distinction between black art and white art ("Why worry about that sort of thing?"), an audience member who had missed all but the final five minutes of the talk stood up in the aisle to ask a question. His name was Floyd Salas, and the year before, he had published a novel entitled *Tattoo the Wicked Cross*, which won several awards and had been optioned by Hollywood (for twenty-five thousand dollars according to a letter of May 22, 1968, Bellow received from Kay House). Salas, who was thirty-seven at the time, had gone to Berkeley on a boxing scholarship, was a prominent radical in the Bay Area ("I was pre–Mario Savio; we set the groundwork"), and claims to have been a fan of Bellow's fiction. "I had read all of his books up to that time, and two of them, *Henderson the Rain King* and *The Adventures of Augie March*, I thought were great. I respected all of his books." Salas had taught writing for several years at San Francisco State but had left in 1967, mostly because "I felt a snobbism and rigidity in the teaching staff that cut itself off from the students."[92]

Bellow's manner during the question period seemed to Salas to show this snobbism and rigidity. "His arrogance was offensive," he told me. "He spoke *down* to the students. He was supercilious, he was vain." According to Kay House, one of his hosts, Bellow "invited this [hostility] by reacting very sharply to questioners."[93] Another woman present at the talk had seen Bellow provoke similar reactions at previous talks.[94] "I don't think I handled myself well," he admitted many years later, "but I don't think that anyone behaved well."[95] The question Salas asked was whether Bellow had said "that the university should be a haven from vulgarity." Bellow's reply, according to Salas, was that he was "sorry that I hadn't been able to get in and knew he looked like a father figure to the students but he wasn't going to answer that question."[96] After this reply, again according to Salas, "the faculty sitting on the stage behind him dutifully clapped at how artfully he had put down this supposedly *hostile* student." In the account given by Atlas, provided in part by House and Leo Litwak, also of the English Department, what Bellow "coldly" replied was "Since you came in late, I have the right to refuse to answer your question," a response he then softened. "I mean, I'm sorry you couldn't get in, but at least other people have notes and you can find out what I said."[97]

According to Atlas's sources, Salas persisted—"I want to challenge you"—and Bellow replied, "But you don't know what you're challenging." "I've read your books," Salas answered. The audience laughed nervously at this exchange. Then a female student asked Bellow how much autobiography there was in his novels, and, according to Salas, "he told her it was none of her business." Another questioner, identified by Salas as a student writer named Frank Olson, stood up and asked Bellow why he didn't call his novel *Bellow* instead of *Herzog*, and why he wrote a novel about a university professor in which not a single student appears, even though "students all over America were demonstrating over the factory machine education they were receiving from faculties that were out of touch with them." Olson, Salas said in an interview, was "brilliant," "a rebel," and striking in appearance, tall, thin, dressed "like a bum . . . like a walking corpse" (Artur Sammler describes a comparably hostile audience at Columbia as "a large, spreading, shaggy, composite human bloom. . . . malodorous, peculiarly rancid, sulphurous" [p. 32]). According to Atlas, Bellow tried to answer the first part of Olson's question seriously: "If you knew more about literature, you'd realize it's very hard to write an autobiography, and once you begin to write, even if it's about yourself, you've invented a fiction and you have to be consistent." Here is Salas's account of what followed:

> The faculty who were sitting behind Bellow on the stage got upset and a low murmur of disapproval rose up from them and spread over the audience at Frank's insolence in bringing up the question of Bellow's autobiographical input in his fiction again when he had already told a student it was none of her business. I then stood up in the aisle where I was sitting and said that they, the faculty, all worshipped this man in his camel hair suit and alligator shoes and got annoyed when he was asked important questions, this effete person who refused to enter into a dialogue with the students (I was implying that this was what was wrong with a university of strictly middle-class white kids and a nearly all white male faculty) when he was the epitome of what was wrong with the university in the first place and probably couldn't even come. (An apt if rather crude comment on the fact that he was obviously separated from the essential, and totally out of touch with the student mood on campuses nationwide, which wanted to bring the common life *into* the university, not protect the university from it.)[98]

The place went wild.

According to Atlas, drawing on Hannah Koler's account, Salas then "went berserk," uttering a string of obscenities. (In *Mr. Sammler's Planet*, the Salas figure addresses the audience directly: "Why do you listen to this effete old shit? What has he got to tell you? His balls are dry. He can't come" [p. 34].) In an interview, Salas denied uttering obscenities, adducing the testimony of several witnesses.[99] He also denies saying, "I want to challenge you." "It's all a lie," he told me, denying also that the following exchange, again reported in Atlas, ever happened: " 'It would have been better if you had heard my speech,' Bellow said patiently. 'I mean, I'm an old soap-box speaker. I used to be a Trotskyite in my youth, and I'm well accustomed to handling this sort of thing, but I don't really like to do it.' 'Because it's *vulgar*?' Salas shot back." To general laughter, Bellow then declared: "I think this meeting is pretty well broken up now. I don't mind answering questions but it's not hospitable to insult your speakers, so let's call it off."

Kay House drove Bellow and Wright Morris to her home in Sausalito, where, "after three drinks in the sun on the deck over there, Saul and Wright started to come out of shock." Bellow was scheduled to spend the night in the St. Francis Hotel in the city but was so shaken that he asked to be taken directly to the McCloskys'. Looking back on the incident, he complained of being "undefended by the bullied elders of the faculty," and found it odd that no one had anticipated trouble. House later said she was "not surprised" at what had happened, having seen, at a talk the historian Richard Hofstadter gave on Black Power, "how much sheer hate and rage could build up in a crowd on our campus."[100] There had been angry student demonstrations on campus before Bellow's talk, and a few weeks later the university's Administration Building was occupied, with protesters demanding ten new minority faculty positions, a "La Raza" Department, a Black Studies Department, the admission of a thousand minority students, and the elimination of ROTC. As Salas puts it, "We, the activists, gave it a good shot and forced the college to set up the Black Studies Department with a Black Panther associate as chair. From that department came the strike that fall." The strike of the autumn and winter of 1968–69 was prolonged and violent, and even Salas thought the strikers went too far, "talking guns, guns, ordering people around, and hostile stuff like that, frightening and alienating lots of faculty and students on the campus . . . making them fear that fascism was going to come from the underclasses instead of the upper classes." In a letter of October 22, 1968, to Mark Harris, who had taught at San Francisco State for thirteen years before moving to Purdue, Bellow described his experiences there as "very bad. . . . Being denounced by Salas as an old shit to an assembly which seemed to find the whole thing deliciously thrilling . . . I left the platform in defeat. . . . It was very poor stuff, I assure you. You don't found universities in order to destroy culture. For that you want a Nazi party." As in his reflections on the Six-Day War, the Holocaust was much in Bellow's mind.

SB and Susan on Martha's Vineyard, mid-1960s (private collection)

2

"All My Ladies Seem Furious"

WHEN FLOYD SALAS JEERED that he bet Saul Bellow "probably couldn't even come," one young woman in the audience felt like standing up and declaring herself a witness in Bellow's defense. The young woman was Maggie Staats, and she had been seeing Bellow for more than two years. They had met in New York in March 1966, at a party given by Harold Taylor, the former president of Sarah Lawrence College. Maggie was twenty-four and worked at *The New Yorker.* She had been brought to the party by Brendan Gill, not Bellow's favorite person, one of two men at the magazine she'd been warned to avoid (the other was the cartoonist Frank Modelli; she later married the magazine's science writer, Paul Brodeur, the first of her five husbands). Maggie had no idea who Saul Bellow was, had never heard of him, despite having done graduate work in English at Yale. "He was good-looking, and he was older, and I had never been with a man who was that old." Bellow was fifty-one. Gill, Maggie's date, was fifty-two, and Joseph Mitchell, another *New Yorker* writer, "one of my closest friends in my whole life," was fifty-eight. "I'd say a lot of Saul's attraction was his age, and he was witty and amusing." They left the party together and set out to find a late-night bookstore where Bellow could buy a copy of *Henderson the Rain King.* Then they went back to his room at the Plaza Hotel, took their clothes off, and got into bed, and Bellow read her the entire novel. It took "two or three days; we were in the Plaza for two or three days." She fell for him completely, as Sasha had done when Bellow read her *The Adventures of Augie March* for a day and a night, "until he was hoarse and, finally, croaked to a halt."[1]

Bellow's affair with Maggie Staats was the longest-lived and most turbulent of his life. Maggie is the model for two female characters in his fiction: Demmie Vonghel in *Humboldt's Gift* (1975) and Clara Velde in *A Theft* (1989). Like them, she is warm, generous, charming, and smart. Physically, she was unlike Bellow's wives or the other women with whom he had significant affairs. Like both Demmie and Clara, she has short blond hair, fashionably cut, blue eyes, slightly protruding teeth, a small upturned nose, and a slim, sturdy figure. Demmie's legs are singled out for praise by Charlie Citrine: "These beautiful legs had an exciting defect—her knees touched and her feet were turned outward so that when she walked fast the taut silk of her stockings made a slight sound like friction"; Clara's eyes, "exceptionally large, grew prominent when she brooded," as attractive a feature to Ithiel ("Teddy") Regler, her much older lover, as to Bellow.[2] Both Demmie and Clara are given minimally disguised versions of Maggie's upbringing. Maggie grew up in Malvern, Pennsylvania, "at the end of the Main Line," almost in the countryside. Her mother was from a prominent Philadelphia family; her father was from a farm in Delaware. In her mother's family, education was important; Maggie's aunts and uncles went to Princeton and Smith. There was money on her mother's side of the family; her father, an only child, went from farming to business and made a fortune in gas and real estate.

Her father was the important influence in Maggie's life. She describes him as "a Bible Belt type," "a ferocious activist and person." She and her older sister and brother were instilled with a deep conviction of hellfire and brimstone. Her father's parenting philosophy was simple and clichéd: "Spare the rod, spoil the child." "It was a terrifying home to grow up in," Maggie recalls. "My father would wake me up and spank me *in case* I did something wrong," which she immediately proceeded to do. "I wanted to get back at him." Although overweight as a child, at twelve she grew five inches, slimmed down (a family doctor gave her thyroid pills and Dexedrine to depress her appetite), and "became a beauty." Her initial education was at a Friends school, where she continued to misbehave. As a teenager, she "hung out with hoody Elvis types," had boyfriends who stole cars. "I was a really bad girl. I had realized how to get to him [her father]." Then she went to the local high school and became "Miss Normal, little Miss High School," though she continued to meet with rough friends away from school.

Like Bellow, Maggie went to Northwestern as an undergraduate.

There she led another kind of double life, joining a sorority yet "secretly" becoming an intellectual. She remembers only two books in her home: "the Bible and Nancy Drew." At university, she studied Greek and German and read many difficult works of literature and philosophy. "If it looked hard I would take the course," she recalled. "It was the Protestant view of the curriculum." She also had an affair with a faculty member, one of the editors of the literary magazine *TriQuarterly*. In 1965, she went on to Yale to do graduate work in English. There she took courses from R. W. B. Lewis, who had taught Sasha at Bennington; Louis Martz, whom she liked; and Harold Bloom, whom she "couldn't stand." She had a "full-time" (i.e., nonsecret) boyfriend at Yale, a law student who was moving to New York. Unhappy in graduate school, she quit and moved to New York herself. Through a relative on her mother's side, she got a job at *The New Yorker*, in the typing pool, but her typing was poor and she was moved to the reviews section, where she worked happily under Gardner Botsford, a senior editor. New York was an eye-opener. "I had never lived in a city. I'd never stayed in an apartment. I'd never been in a subway. I'd never eaten in a coffee shop." She found an apartment at 113 East Ninetieth Street, a building that now houses the Alpine Club, but when her roommate, Margaret McKee, objected that she was dating "too many Jews," she moved out. Bellow then helped Maggie to find an apartment at 230 East Fifteenth Street, not far from Union Square.

Bellow made frequent visits to New York in the spring of 1966, and Maggie went "all over the place with him. There was no question we were a couple." He told her that he was separated from his wife, "but I assumed it wasn't true." "I had no idea what was going on in Chicago," she recalls. "He was much older, he'd been divorced. . . . He just seemed so powerful." In fact, he was still living with Susan, but the marriage had been on the rocks for many months. In the summer of 1965, the second summer he and Susan spent on Martha's Vineyard, they took a house in Chilmark, on Menemsha Pond. Atlas quotes the opinion of Barbara Hanson, the au pair from that summer, who was no fan of Susan's ("She just sort of swanned around; she *loved* being Mrs. Saul Bellow. It was her career") but was sympathetic to Bellow ("constantly reading," affectionate to Adam, whom he hadn't seen since Christmas, "cheerful").[3] In August, the Hollebs accepted an invitation to join the Bellows in Chilmark for a couple of weeks, electing to stay at a nearby inn rather than in the house. When Susan picked them up at the ferry, she was wearing curlers. "Saul was furious," Doris recalls. "It was clear that they were fighting all the time," Marshall adds; "It was not pleasant." That night, at dinner, just the Hollebs and Robert Brustein were present. Bellow and Susan "were testy with each other, snapping at each other," according to Doris. "It was clear they couldn't control themselves." The only social life the Hollebs had during the visit was "daytime social life, not with the Bellows." After ten days, they cut the holiday short and returned to Chicago, certain the Bellow marriage was doomed.

In fact, it dragged on for sixteen more months, for some ten of which Bellow was passionately in love with Maggie. "I didn't believe it possible," begins a letter of April 7, 1966, written after a second meeting (Bellow, Maggie recalls, "was here all the time, every other week").[4] "I thought I had been damaged, or self-damaged, too badly for this. I didn't expect that my whole soul would go out like this to anyone. That I would lie down and wake up by love instead of clocks." He kept himself busy with work and trips "because I need activity and concealment"; though "oppressed and heavy-hearted," he was "grateful": "It's a case of *amo quia absurdum* ["I love because it is absurd," a play on Tertullian's *Credo quia absurdum*, "I believe because it is absurd"]—the absurdity is mine, not yours. My age, my situation! It is absurdity. But what a super-absurdity not to love you." Five days later, Bellow professed himself in love with "everything I can remember of you," declaring, "Although I don't know you I believe that going any distance in every direction with you I can never find anything to disappoint me. I expect to love you whatever happens." This letter was written "instead of prayers. Now I can go about my business." Four days later, in a note written in his office and interrupted by the arrival of his students, he worries about the risks he is running: "In spite of my desire to ease up, I can't let things alone, and I think I'm behaving badly; close to blindness; I sense it. It can't be right to aggravate the disorders at the most disorderly painful stage [of his marriage, presumably]. . . . I think it would be best to force myself to stop, and wait. Only I keep thinking of you." A day later, on April 21, he gives an example of what he means by "the most disorderly painful stage": "One gets home late afternoon and rages inside till midnight, falling into bed and sleeping like a stone in the exhaustion of anger and disappointment. . . . In conversation there have been no holds barred but one. To hear and say such things is degrading. But perhaps everything ought to come out."

Part of the reason Bellow was able to visit New York so frequently was that he had business on Broadway. In April 1965, two of his one-act plays, "A Wen" and "Orange Soufflé," were performed at the Loft on Bleecker Street. In May, they were produced at the Traverse Theatre in Edinburgh, directed by Charles Marowitz. The plays were well enough received at the Traverse to earn a London production, at the Jeanetta Cochrane Theatre in Holborn. Marowitz, best known for his collaborations with Peter Brook, was again the director, and this time a third play, "Out from Under," was added to the evening. *The Bellow Plays*, as they now were titled, got strong reviews. Eric Shorter, in *The Daily Telegraph*, writing on May 27, claimed, "Not since J. P. Donleavy turned his hand to the stage a few years ago has there been such an enjoyable switch by a novelist to the theatre as Saul Bellow's London debut last night." Three months later the plays opened in the West End proper, at the Fortune Theatre. They were now titled *Under the Weather*, since a hurricane figures in "A Wen," a fog in "Orange Soufflé," and a snowstorm in "Out from Under." Once again, the reviews were favorable, giving impetus to talks of a Broadway production. These talks provided a pretext for Bellow's presence in New York, in the period both before and during rehearsals.

Under the Weather opened at the Cort Theater on October 27, 1966, to an audience that included a large party of Bellow's friends and acquaintances, among them two of the plays' backers, Marshall Holleb and David Peltz. Bellow himself put up five thousand dollars to finance the run. This time, neither Susan nor the Glassmans nor any of the Bellow children were present. Just before the curtain rose, Bellow and Maggie slipped into their seats at the back of the stalls, directly behind the investors and critics. At Sardi's afterward, they did not appear until late in the evening. "None of us knew the young lady who worked at *The New Yorker*," commented Doris Holleb, who recalled her as "very attractive." Bellow was "still married to Susan," and the Hollebs thought him "sheepishly protecting himself" by arriving late. When the reviews came in, they were bad. "We all waited around till one or two. It was terrible."

Walter Kerr, now at *The New York Times*, was less caustic about *Under the Weather* than he'd been about *The Last Analysis*, but he was hardly positive, calling the plays "a cerebral construction rather than an easy creative flow"; he thought, rightly, that they lacked "straight-forward comic crackle."[5] Three days later, Richard Cooke in *The Wall Street*

Journal ("Trio by Bellow," October 31, 1966) described the trilogy as confirming an impression created by *The Last Analysis:* "that Mr. Bellow's gifts as a novelist [did not extend] to playwriting." In a review in *The New Yorker* entitled "Look, Ma, I'm Playwriting" (November 5, 1966), John McCarten accused Bellow of writing plays "without submitting to the discipline of the theatre." As with *The Last Analysis,* the plays were accused of being too wordy and of uneasily combining farce and high seriousness. Richard Gilman in *Newsweek* ("Bellow on Broadway," November 7, 1966) was dismayed "to see how manfully short he falls, to see the greater part of his literacy going to waste and his special kind of shrewdness about contemporary manners and mores displaying itself in a thoroughly misconceived framework."

The play that most troubled the reviewers was "A Wen," which Kerr thought "may come to be called 'that second play' as theatergoers get to gossiping about it." Cooke in *The Wall Street Journal* described it as "not only inept but downright unpleasant." Set in Miami in hurricane weather, it revolves around two characters, a man and a woman (only "Out from Under" has a third performer, a cop who appears briefly at the beginning). In this case, the man, Solomon Ithimar, is a Nobel Prize–winning physicist who pays an unexpected visit to a matronly Jewish housewife, Marcella Vankuchen. As adolescents, Solomon and Marcella had played a game called "Show," in which what Solomon saw he never forgot: an apricot-colored birthmark or wen high up on Marcella's inner thigh. In Miami for a conference, he seeks her out, after an interval of thirty years. What he wants is a second view, partly because he remembers their game as the most powerful erotic experience of his life, partly as a release from a life of intellect rather than feeling. After much comic pleading on his part and dithering on hers, the bewildered but flattered housewife accedes to the physicist's request, a scene enacted behind a sofa during a partial blackout caused by the hurricane. Kerr thought this staging a cop-out: "If we're really going to be brave enough to have fun and games crawling beneath a lady's skirts, the sofa is a cheat."

Although "A Wen" and "Orange Soufflé" were published in 1966 by Penguin in a collection titled *Traverse Plays,* they were never republished, and "Out from Under" was never published at all. But they are not without biographical interest. The woman in "A Wen" is a prototype of several characters in Bellow's fiction, all modeled on his high-school love, Eleanor Fox: Naomi Lutz in *Humboldt's Gift,* Amy Wustrin in

The Actual, Stephanie (Louis's girlfriend) in "Something to Remember Me By."[6] The sexual appeal of these characters to the boys who fall for them makes other women mere approximations. That Bellow had Eleanor Fox in mind when writing "A Wen" is suggested by several details in the play: the wife is married to a chiropodist who insists upon being called doctor, as did Eleanor Fox's podiatrist father, and the physicist's "high class discussions" are as baffling to her today as they were thirty years ago, which is what Eleanor Fox felt about Bellow's talk. Eleanor Fox is also evoked in "Out from Under," the play that precedes "A Wen." Harry, a widower, is engaged to Flora, his childhood sweetheart. Like Charlie Citrine in *Humboldt*, Harry Trellman in *The Actual*, Louis in "Something to Remember Me By," and Bellow himself, Harry remembers being "in the park, in winter, under your fur coat—beneath your clothes, it was so warm." "I loved you. First love," Harry recalls (though now he has second thoughts about their being engaged). Flora's first husband was like Eleanor Fox's husband, "nice, but a gambler," in debt to "the syndicate itself." "You'll be driving home one night, but you won't make it. Or you'll turn on the ignition one morning and blow up. They'll find your tongue in a tree."

In all three plays, the women (played by Shelley Winters) are physically stronger than the men (played by Harry Towb), and all the male protagonists fear losing their independence. "Why am I so afraid of slavery?" Harry asks in "Out from Under," contemplating his impending marriage. The best of the plays and the harshest is "Orange Soufflé," about a seventy-eight-year-old industrialist named Pennington and a "Polack whore" named Hilda. For the past ten years, Pennington has visited Hilda once a month, but now Hilda wants something more—she wants a social position, but also for Pennington to know her as a person. "You don't bother yourself about me," she complains. "You never took any personal interest in me." Impersonality, however, is precisely what Pennington wants, as Hilda knows. From his perspective, she explains, the "whole point of a whore" is that "she frees your mind. If you flunk, she doesn't get sore." Flunking in bed is a Pennington worry because he is old; Bellow was only fifty-one in 1966, but his girlfriend was twenty-four. When Pennington learns that Hilda has given up all her other clients, he asks, with naïve vanity, "Am I so special?" "Smiling to herself," Hilda answers, "You don't have to ask." This response, she knows, is what he needs: "Terrific, eh? I hoped it was like that. I had the feeling. Everything about me is wearing out, except." Later, Pennington declares, "I was always virile," which again Hilda plays expertly: "You break all the records." Pennington is a horrible old man, his vanity and egotism like those of Mosby in "Mosby's Memoirs," written at roughly the same time. When Hilda asks, "Why shouldn't we know each other better?" Pennington answers, "I know you plenty." She means know each other as persons, not just sexually. But persons or personal relations don't matter to Pennington:

> What I was as a captain of industry, what I was on the board of directors, what I was on the stock market, that's what I've been here. That's the best of me there is, the truest, anyway. Not what I did with my wife and sons. With them I did what I had to do, not what I wanted.

THE RELATIVE CLAIMS of life and work, the intensity of childhood experience, sexual insecurity—themes familiar from earlier writings—all sound in *Under the Weather*. They also sound in *Humboldt's Gift*, the novel Bellow was groping toward while at work on *Sammler*. Hilda the prostitute lives in Indiana, where Dave Peltz lived. Susan was right to think Peltz had taken Bellow to prostitutes, whose services, Peltz recalled, Bellow was too self-conscious to enjoy. Peltz was much on Bellow's mind in the second half of the 1960s, when they were especially close, and not only away from the desk. In 1967, Bellow began writing, under the titles "Olduvai," "Olduvai George," and "Samson," about George Samson, a prototype of George Swiebel in *Humboldt*, a character very like Dave Peltz. When Denver Lindley of Viking and Henry Volkening, Bellow's agent, saw this material, they were deeply excited, despite knowing that it had meant Bellow put aside the Sammler or "Pawlyk" (sometimes "Pawlyck") manuscript. On August 4, 1967, Lindley begged Bellow to "send along a chunk of OLDUVAI" to brighten his vacation. Four days later, he wrote to say that he'd "read your pages—with great excitement and pleasure and all those little shocks set off by the real thing. It's beautiful, authentic and rich. Samson will be one of your big characters and vivid is a pale word for the supporting cast."[7]

When Bellow told Peltz what he was doing, Peltz objected; he intended to use the same material in an autobiographical novel he was at work on at the time. Bellow was advised to keep writing, but friendship won out, for a while at least. Bellow put the "Olduvai" manuscript aside, a decision that left Volkening "very very sad." On September 14, he wrote communicating this sadness, along with a worry that "just *possibly* [Peltz's book] might not be unpublishable." "At the very least," he continued, "I would like you to make me a gift of my xerox copy." When Peltz failed to secure a publisher, Bellow resumed work on "Olduvai." On November 13, Volkening pronounced his new pages "electrically marvellous stuff"; George Samson was "a hero of shall we say Fielding dimensions and charm—transposed to Chicago." Whether Peltz knew that Bellow had returned to the manuscript is not clear.

A year before Bellow began work on the "Olduvai" or "Samson" manuscripts, which provide versions of the Chicago sections of *Humboldt's Gift* (those dealing with George Swiebel and Rinaldo Cantabile), he started work on what would become the book's New York or East Coast sections, the sections dealing with Humboldt. In late June 1966, while walking in New York with Maggie, Bellow had spotted Delmore Schwartz.[8] Bellow was riding high: in good health, dapper, money in his pocket, with Maggie on his arm. It had been ten years since he'd seen his friend, a period of precipitous decline for Schwartz, who in 1957 had been briefly committed to Bellevue Hospital. Bellow and Katy Carver had organized a fund to pay for his treatment after Bellevue, at the Payne Whitney Clinic, but the delusional Schwartz was convinced that Bellow was conspiring against him. He pocketed the money that had been collected on his behalf, hired a detective to trail Bellow, and began harassing him with phone calls. "He phoned me in the middle of the night," Bellow wrote to James Laughlin on October 27, 1957, "using techniques the GPU might have envied, threatening to sue me for slander and frightening my poor wife." According to Atlas's biography of Schwartz, "No great significance can be attached to Delmore's choice of Bellow as a prominent figure in the conspiracies he perceived, for he had by this time become indiscriminate in his suspicions."[9] In the ten years that followed, Bellow contributed to several efforts to help Schwartz, principally to find him teaching jobs.[10] Schwartz, meanwhile, continued to mock and belittle Bellow's success, as Humboldt mocks and belittles the success of Charlie Citrine.

When Bellow and Maggie saw Schwartz at the end of June 1966 they hid from him. He had only two weeks to live. On July 11, he died of a heart attack, collapsing in the hallway of a derelicts' hotel in the Broadway area. According to an interview with Maggie, after the sighting in June, Bellow sat down and told her what would become "pretty much the whole of the Humboldt parts of *Humboldt's Gift*." When Schwartz died, he began writing down what he'd told her, in the form of a memoir, a partial manuscript of which can be found in the Regenstein. The memoir begins: "My friend the poet D.S. died last week in New York" and goes on to trace Schwartz's life and his relations with Bellow up through the Princeton period, in passages of dialogue as well as description and reflection. When Bellow showed a portion of the memoir to Aaron Asher, now at Viking, and to Henry Volkening, they were more than impressed. In a letter of September 23, 1966, Asher described what he'd read as "astonishing. Within a few paragraphs, the richness of a novel—many novels, following your old dictum urging prodigality. Only you can judge whether to go on with it as fiction. All I can say is that it deserves to be more than a mere epitaph to the poor man." Bellow took Asher's advice. "I sense a lot of momentum in this V. H. Fleisher thing," Asher wrote on December 13, 1967, a year and two months later, "which means that, despite my intention not to be, I'd be surprised if you return to Olduvai."

BELLOW'S PRODUCTIVITY in the second half of the 1960s coincided with an especially difficult period in his personal life. But the actual breakup with Susan was undramatic. Going through their monthly telephone bill, she noticed a large number of long-distance calls to someone named M. Staats. According to Daniel Bellow, recounting what Susan later told him, when she asked Bellow who M. Staats was, "my father said, 'I'm not going to discuss Margaret Staats with you.'" Whether he willfully "failed to cover his tracks or just forgot," Daniel does not know, nor does he know how much time elapsed between Susan's discovery and his father's moving out. Faced directly with evidence of Bellow's womanizing, Susan's response was "If you want to fool around that means I get to fool around, too," which had been Anita's response in Bellow's first marriage (Sasha had just fooled around, a response both more and less direct). Bellow was outraged, Susan later told Daniel, and "almost called me a whore." Two weeks before Christmas 1966, Bellow packed his bags and left. As Susan reported to Mark Harris, he "simply 'moved out,' . . . it was time to go, the end had come, no particular explanations. Although he was a writer he was not on all occasions a man of words."[11] The end of the marriage left her, in Daniel's words, "devastated. It was the great tragedy of her life. She loved him, she couldn't get enough of him."

"I don't think he really liked being married" is how Daniel explains his father's behavior. "He liked being taken care of. . . . He liked beautiful, intelligent, spirited women. He didn't like being bored." According to Atlas, the nominal reasons Bellow gave for moving out were that Susan "nagged him, made unreasonable demands, and was 'cold.'"[12] Susan took the departure stoically, worn down by fights and stony silences, a home atmosphere Greg Bellow remembers as "poisonous."[13] Her friend Diane Silverman believes that, at the last, "she did want the marriage to end when the marriage ended." Atlas quotes a letter Susan wrote to an unnamed friend: "Well, we haven't even received all the furniture we ordered when we moved in here, but it's a lot more pleasant with him gone."[14] Beneath this outward calm, Barbara Wiesenfeld, another of Susan's friends, sensed bewilderment as well as devastation. Susan was unused to being rejected and "unprepared for [Bellow] and his attitudes." What Wiesenfeld remembers of Bellow, whom she felt guilty about liking ("because he wasn't being very nice to my friend"), is that "he was so sort of in charge of himself. It wasn't a fair fight."

Mark Harris was also a witness to the period of breakup, and in his book about Bellow, he gives a vivid picture of Susan, while depicting himself with disarming frankness. Harris first met Bellow in August 1961 in Tivoli, although they had been corresponding since 1959. In addition to writing novels and stories, and teaching writing at San Francisco State, Harris wrote for magazines. In the summer of 1961, after traveling to Vermont to interview Robert Frost for *Life* magazine, he stopped at Tivoli on his way back to New York. Bellow cooked him dinner, read to him from the unpublished *Herzog*, and gave him a bed for the night. Also at Tivoli were Adam and a young woman friend of Bellow's, whose identity Harris does not disclose. Later in the same week, he and Bellow met for dinner in a restaurant in New York, and afterward visited the apartment of a second woman friend. "I hoped it would be the lady I had pondered in the night at Tivoli, but it was not, though it was another as fine." At this second lady's apartment he met seventeen-year-old Greg Bellow.

Bellow liked Harris's profile of Frost, or said he did, and four years later, in 1965, Harris asked if he could write a similar profile of him. This "very good" offer Bellow declined: "The fact of the matter is that I've had about all the public attention I can safely absorb. Anyone who held a geiger counter on me now would hear a terrible rattling. . . . What I want to do now is to lie low and gather a little shadow."[15] Harris's next contact with Bellow came in January 1966, when he visited Chicago to write a profile of the baseball player Ernie Banks (Harris's best known novel is *Bang the Drum Slowly*, about baseball players). Bellow invited Harris to dinner at 5490 South Shore Drive, and there he discovered that Susan "was neither the woman of Tivoli nor the woman of Manhattan but someone other, whose olive beauty made me restless. Her trousers snugly fit her hips."[16] Harris says nothing of marital discord at this time between Susan and Bellow. Later that year, in a letter of July 31, partly at the prompting of Richard Stern, Harris wrote to Bellow broaching the subject of a biography. "Great biography may be creative, too," he wrote. All he asked of Bellow was that "you not say No to me now, nor Yes to someone else, until I have a chance to present my case in person."[17] Bellow did not respond to this letter, nor did he respond to two further letters, one accompanying a copy of Harris's latest novel.

Undeterred, in March 1967, Harris returned to Chicago to plead his case. He telephoned the Bellow apartment and got Susan. Bellow was not there, and Susan had no idea when he would be back. "She was flustered. . . . 'Mark!' she said, deciding not to prolong things (her sharp, crackling firing-off of my name made my heart leap), delivering shocking news with speed, to reduce its impact—'Mark! Saul and I are separated.' " This news, Harris confesses, made him feel "a kind of satisfaction . . . because Bellow had not replied to my letter": "Failure humanized him. . . . We welcome the humility one will acquire from a dose of everyday trouble"[18] (a reaction that recalls Nathan Zuckerman's feelings about Felix Abravanel in *The Ghost Writer*, discussed in chapter 12 of *To Fame and Fortune*). "How had all this happened?" Harris asked Susan. "They had seemed so happy in 1966. No, said Susan, they were not happy even then, their marriage had already begun to crack. It was her first marriage, she said, and she would never marry again." This news makes Harris, though married, eager to meet up with Susan. "Was I interested in seeing Susan or in writing a biography of her husband? Doubtful that I could do both. On the other hand it was a feat worth trying."[19] Harris knows how he sounds here. Throughout the memoir, he presents himself as a comic or semi-comic figure—amorous, emulous, alternately stung, baffled, and amused by his quarry.

At lunch with Susan the next day, Harris wonders how a father can leave a child behind. "After the first one it's easy," Susan replies. When he suggests that Bellow seemed to have worked out his relationship with Greg, Susan replies: "No, Saul hasn't changed. *Gregory* has worked it through." Susan declares Bellow incapable of change, and when Harris disagrees—arguing, "We all make mistakes. We need to be informed by friends and lovers"—she answers, "Friends are harder to find than lovers." She complains of Bellow's neglect of Daniel, his unreliability about visits, a frequent complaint of Sasha's about Bellow's treatment of Adam. Harris mentions Robert Frost, "a man who was also hard upon wife and children, who placed his art before all other obligations," and Susan replies by comparing artists to businessmen. When a businessman places money before other obligations, we "despise" him, "and yet we celebrate the artist for the same offense." "Susan's grief and anger excited me," Harris confesses, fantasizing. "Suppose I were forced to choose between Susan and Bellow, whom would I choose? In that moment, Susan." He quotes Herzog, contemplating Madeleine: "Such beauty makes men breeders, studs and servants."[20] According to Atlas, Harris did more than fantasize, "inviting himself over to her apartment late at night, inviting her over to *his* room, bombarding her with suggestive letters."[21]

As for Bellow at this time, Harris depicts him as prickly and difficult to pin down. "He was witty, charming, and irritable. He scolds. He criticizes freely." Yet he also "raised my consciousness and [gave] me enormously useful advice about writing and living." It is not true, as has been said, "that Bellow is a great artist but a bad friend. Like Frost, he teaches by thorniness."[22] Harris visited Bellow in the small, cramped garden apartment he moved to after leaving 5490 South Shore Drive and staying briefly with Shils. The apartment was a few blocks from Susan and Daniel, in a handsome 1920s building called Windermere House. Here Harris was introduced to what he calls Bellow's "companion, Bonne Amie, a woman who instantly charmed me in a number of ways."[23] The woman was Bette Howland. Stern was there as well, being much in evidence in this period. According to Susan, Bellow phoned the Stern home "four or five times a day," which "must be agony" for Stern's wife, Gay. "'Saul is on the loose,' said Susan, 'dragging Dick through the streets at all hours of the night.'"[24] When Harris, encouraged by Stern, raised the question of a biography, Bellow "was perplexed, or appeared so." Had Bellow not received his letter? "'What letter was that, Mark?'" When Harris explained, Bellow "looked at neither Stern nor me, staring off between our heads, his face whitening as he drew to himself either the idea for the first time, or his renewed resistance to it. Nothing in his face revealed either that he favored my idea or that he opposed it, or even that he heard it. He searched his mind for the letter, not for his response, saying so inaudibly he must have been speaking to himself, 'I didn't receive any letter.'" Harris likens this moment, when Bellow permits the idea of a biography simply to dissolve, to the moment when he moved out of the marital home: "undramatically, no particular explanations, as if now by the invisible power of his impassivity my idea would rise like an odor into the pores of the ceiling, or like a *faux pas* escape notice if we pretended not to have heard it."[25]

Bellow's evasiveness is seen by Harris as characteristic, part of what connects him to the Robert Frost poem "A Drumlin Woodchuck," from which *Saul Bellow, Drumlin Woodchuck*, his book, gets its title (an ill-judged title, like the title of Harris's fifth novel, *The Goy*, which Bellow urged him to change). It was Bellow himself who cited the Frost poem. "Very much liked your Sandburg-Frost article," Bellow wrote to Harris. "How neatly you let Sandburg portray himself. One or two strokes of the dollar sign and the thing was done. Frost is a different kettle of woodchuck altogether. Woodchuck I say because he has more exits to his burrow than any man can count."[26] As Harris sees it, "Bellow knew what Frost was up to with those exits, tunnels, burrows. Escape! Spain, Rome, Yugoslavia, Italy, Dublin, the Dolomites, running off, fleeing, hiding, telephone down, mail mysteriously astray—What letter was that, Mark?"[27]

What Harris does not make enough of is the weight of obligation and expectation Bellow was subjected to post-*Herzog*, "in the nirvana of the harassed," perhaps because he never worked through the bulk of Bellow's correspondence. In addition to demands and requests, there were complaints, not only from wives, children, and friends in need, but from readers and fans: his writing was too popular, his writing was too esoteric, it was not political enough, it was undignified, it was too dignified, it was not Jewish enough. Harris's form as biographer, as in the neat skewering of Sandburg, may also have contributed to Bellow's evasiveness. Harris admired Bellow, but he was needy, by no means free of grievances or immune to slights. He was also, Bellow knew, writing down everything Bellow said. "How did you remember?" Greg asked Harris, when Harris told him they'd first met on August 23, 1961. "'He didn't remember,' said Bellow, 'he looked it up.'"[28] When a prepublication extract from Harris's book was printed in *The Georgia Review* (Winter 1978), Bellow was not happy. Harris asked why:

> "I thought I looked like a turd in it," he impatiently said.
>
> I was astonished. "Really?" It was all I could ask. "Yup," he replied. "Bad-tempered. Nasty, Snappish. I don't see myself that way."
>
> "That's because it's not oneself," I awkwardly said. "It's my version of oneself."[29]

This "version," though, derived from the version Bellow presented him with, in part a product of understandable distrust. That Harris was "astonished" at Bellow's reaction is hard to credit, given the memoir's often acute observations. If he was so surprised, then Harris must have had a poor sense either of himself or of Bellow, or of both—though the same might also be said of Bellow's poor sense either of the impression he was making or of Harris, or of both.

BELLOW'S BAD TEMPER in the late sixties was by no means directed exclusively at would-be biographers, radical students, and aggrieved wives. On July 12, 1966, Tony Godwin, the editorial director of Penguin, his paperback publisher in Britain, invited him to come to London for two weeks in September and October to help to promote the relaunch of five of his novels: *Herzog*, *The Victim*, *Henderson the Rain King*, *The Adventures of Augie March*, and *Seize the Day*. A publicity campaign was planned, with public lectures at PEN, the U.S. Embassy, Edinburgh and Sussex Universities, "as many as possible" engagements on "serious" television programs, and a series of individual interviews "with feature writers and reporters with all the quality papers such as The Times, Telegraph, Guardian, Observer, etc., and with the weeklies. We would also plan a small number of lunch parties in your honour, and a large evening party where critics, booksellers and other influential people would have the opportunity of meeting you." Penguin would make and pay for all travel arrangements, put him up at the Ritz, "and see to it that you are unobtrusively cossetted."

Bellow was appalled. "Is cossetted the word? Two days of your proposed program would put me in the hospital, on tranquilizers for a month," he wrote in an undated reply. "I was willing enough to give a lecture or two, hold one press meeting, tape one BBC program and attend a party. But your lunch parties, trips to Sussex and Edinburgh and 'serious' television programs are out of the question." Although delighted to have Penguin launch his novels "with flame and thunder," he had more than once seen writers "ride bicycles on the highwire, eat fire, gash themselves open to call attention to their books. They end up with little more than a scorched nose, a broken bone." Faced with this reply, Godwin retreated. On August 3, he wrote again with "a reduced, more humane, and civilized programme for your visit," allowing ample opportunity "of mooching around London for a few days on your own." At the bottom of the reply, Bellow scrawled: "I write a silly arrogant letter, and the man capitulates."

There was more trouble in store for Godwin. On September 6, in New York, Bellow was shown the new Penguin covers. According to a letter of September 7 sent by Henry Volkening to Bellow's London agents, Michael Thomas and Cyrus Brooks of A. M. Heath, Bellow "was so outraged and revolted by the vulgarity, bad taste and irrelevance of the Penguin jackets of both AUGIE and HENDERSON that he absolutely refuses to have a damn thing to do with associating himself in any way whatsoever with either of them, or with Tony Godwin either, for that matter (and so of course also with inscribing copies)." The *Augie* cover is a photograph of a Mexican Day of the Dead figure playing a guitar. The *Herzog* cover features an open envelope inside of which the top half of a face, presumably Herzog's, is visible. Candida Donadio of Volkening's office had already phoned Godwin asking that "all public appearances, by TV or otherwise, be cancelled." Godwin, Volkening reported, was "aghast and enraged" and had cabled "justifying the covers, etc., even though they are, we all agree, unjustifiable." Bellow would still come to London, Volkening continued, but only to honor an appearance at a lecture for which tickets had been sold and to have lunch with the American ambassador: "Godwin has been asked at once to cancel all other engagements." As for expenses, "Saul drily says that he'll bear as much of them himself as Penguin might think he should." Godwin's protestations that the covers would sell books "are of no relevance whatsoever."

BELLOW WAS LIONIZED IN LONDON. *Herzog* had received glowing reviews, and even his plays had been well received. Once he arrived, serious profiles appeared in *The Guardian*, *The Observer*, and *The Sun-*

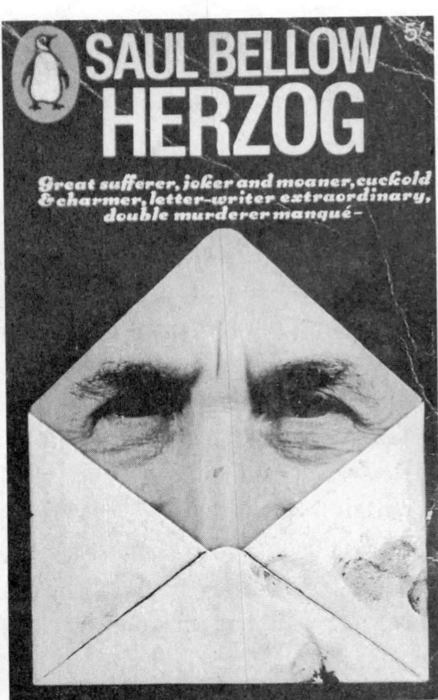

Penguin paperbacks, 1966 (courtesy of Penguin Books, Ltd.)

day Times. "For days he has been pursued for interviews," Terry Coleman wrote in *The Guardian*, "for days he has eluded pursuit; he has been a much wanted man." When Norman Mailer came to London, he and his publishers hired the Mayfair Theatre and filled it, Coleman recalled; Bellow "went one better," having the cultural attaché of the U.S. Embassy send out invitations for his talk, filling the embassy theater with "celebrated people [who] sat in the gangways to hear him, or sat in a little hall at the side, in a little overflow hall, where they could hear but hardly see him." Before reading his talk, Bellow explained that it would be "a rambling discourse. And this, he said, might be all to the good; literature could do with a little more inattention." In the event, the talk was "closely reasoned" rather than rambling. Coleman makes it sound like a version of the talk Bellow would go on to give at San Francisco State. When the talk finished, according to the *Observer* profile, Bellow scurried out "before the audience could leave their seats."[30]

Having dismissed the Penguin people, Bellow turned his anger on Weidenfeld. On September 16, a week before she left Viking to take up a job in London at Chatto & Windus, Katy Carver wrote to Bellow detailing arrangements for the trip, assuring him that Penguin knew neither where he was staying nor for how long, also that the lecture at the Cochrane would be hosted "by the Traverse people, not by anybody you're disagreeing with."[31] She had a warning for him as well: "Word is out in New York that you are moving to Cape, and may be current in London too when you get there, so don't be surprised at anything." London was where the rumors had started, and Bellow did nothing to counter them, pointedly failing to contact Weidenfeld. Only after he had left Britain did Cyrus Brooks raise the possibility of Bellow's changing publishers. In response, on October 18, George Weidenfeld wrote directly to Bellow, pleading his case. He had been Bellow's publisher for fourteen years. They had a personal relationship "which on my part I dared to hope amounted to a friendship." Bellow could have no complaints—had voiced none—about the job Weidenfeld & Nicolson did in launching *Herzog*.[32] As far as Weidenfeld could judge, his central complaint was over the Penguin covers. "I beg you to believe that we are just as upset as you are." Nobody at the firm (or at his British agents, Weidenfeld added) expected Penguin would " 'go it alone' and not let us see the designs in good time. . . . This lapse was very unfortunate but I do beg you not to take too draconian and merciless an attitude." He then reported his distress at discovering that an unnamed British publisher (it was Tom Maschler of Cape) "had not only announced throughout the length and breadth of literary London that he had 'captured' you but that he had also written to another of our most important writers [Margaret Drabble] . . . stating that he had your authority to wean her away from us."

Although Bellow failed to contact Weidenfeld in London, he gave Barley Alison, an editor at Weidenfeld and a friend, a few "brief moments" at Brown's Hotel, where he was staying. To her he indicated that the book he was working on (the "Pawlyk" book) "would not be ready for some time" and that, as Weidenfeld confirmed in his letter of October 18, "your decision about your British publishing plans might be delayed until its completion." Weidenfeld asked that the decision be deferred at least until his annual visit to New York, between Christmas and the New Year. Alison, in a letter of October 22, made a similar request. When Weidenfeld showed up in Chicago on December 19, putting Bellow before other business in New York, he brought with him an offer the author couldn't refuse. The meeting was unexpectedly pleasant, Bellow reported to Alison on January 24, given that he "was vexed with [Weidenfeld] and came prepared to say no." What Weidenfeld offered was a first printing of forty thousand copies for the next book and a uniform edition of all the others. Although Bellow felt obliged to tell Maschler the terms of the deal—the rumors of his moving were true—"it would be insane of me to turn down George's proposal." He was now, he told Alison, waiting to hear from Maschler. He added that he "would not have stayed with W and N had you not been there . . . [and] that the prospect of injuring you by going to Cape did not make me at all happy." He also assured Alison that he had said nothing to Weidenfeld about her own unhappiness at the firm, an unhappiness which led her, in February 1967, to move to Secker & Warburg, with her own imprint, the Alison Press.[33]

BELLOW DID NOT RETURN to the United States immediately after leaving London. He traveled to Holland briefly, and then on to Poland to conduct research for the new novel.[34] The hero of this novel, Meyer Pawlyk, was a Polish émigré living in Queens (in an even earlier manuscript, he lives on the South Side of Chicago). By the time he became Artur Sammler (he'll be Sammler from now on), Bellow had moved him to Manhattan, on the Upper West Side.[35] Sammler is haunted by his experiences during World War II, and Bellow went to Poland to meet survivors of similar experiences and to get a feel for their settings. Among the war veterans he interviewed was Marek Edelman, the last surviving leader of the Warsaw Ghetto Uprising. He met other Polish survivors back in New York, thanks to Edith Tarcov. In reconstructing Sammler's wartime history not only in the camps but "in forests, cellars, passageways, cemeteries" (p. 38), Bellow also drew on printed accounts, in particular David Rousset's *L'Univers concentrationnaire* (1946), discussed in chapter 9 of *To Fame and Fortune*, and Alexander Donat's description of the Polish death camps in *The Holocaust Kingdom* (1965).

Mr. Sammler's Planet was the first Bellow novel to confront the Holocaust directly. In *The Victim*, its presence is implicit, the underlying source of Leventhal's sensitivity to prejudice; it is referred to only once, when Leventhal angrily reminds the anti-Semitic Kirby Allbee that "millions of us have been killed" (pp. 260–61).[36] In *Herzog*, the Holocaust is referred to more frequently, but not centrally. It is one of a host of twentieth-century horrors, "part of the program of destruction into which the human spirit has poured itself with energy, even with joy" (p. 565).[37] The decision finally to confront the fate of the Jews in the Second World War may owe something to Hannah Arendt, Bellow's colleague at the Committee on Social Thought, not only as a result of continuing controversy over *Eichmann in Jerusalem* (1963), but in reaction to her stand in support of student protest. Although she is never named, Arendt's notions of the banality of evil and of Jewish passivity are attacked in all drafts of *Mr. Sammler's Planet*.[38] Sammler himself is hardly passive in resistance, and his views on the banality of evil are clear and forceful: "The idea of making the century's great crime look dull is not banal. Politically, psychologically, the Germans had an idea of genius. The banality was only camouflage. What better way to get the curse out of murder than to make it look ordinary, boring, or trite. . . . Do you think the Nazis didn't know what murder was? Everybody (except certain blue-stockings) knows what murder is" (p. 13). The difference between Bellow's treatment of Arendt's ideas in early versions and in late ones is that in early ones Arendt's views are simply wrong; in late versions, certainly the published version, they are also shameful. According to a letter of March 12, 1982, to Leon Wieseltier, Bellow thought that Arendt lacked "human understanding," her imaginative faculties were "stunted"; in thrall to theory, she was blind to "simple facts," by which Bellow means the facts of Jewish death and suffering.[39] Instead, she uses these facts, in Sammler's words, "to attack modern civilization itself. She is using the Germans to attack the twentieth century—to denounce it in terms invented by Germans. Making use of a tragic history to promote the foolish ideas of Weimar intellectuals" (p. 14), "whose popular American embodiment," according to Daniel Fuchs, "is the Stalinoid Herbert Marcuse."[40] As Ruth Wisse, professor of Yiddish at Harvard, points out, there is a psychological reason for Sammler to be so hard on Arendt: "Had he not undergone the compulsory education that was forced on him by Hitler, he might have sounded just like her. 'Alert to the peril and disgrace of explanations, he was himself no mean explainer.' "[41]

It is shameful to have to explain that life is sacred, a truth understood intuitively, "from the beginning of time." To defy what Sammler calls "that old understanding" is not banality: "Banality is the adopted disguise of a very powerful will to abolish conscience" (p. 14). The phrase "old understanding" calls to mind the title of the Bellow story "The Old System" (1968), composed at roughly the same time not only as *Samm-*

ler, but as the "ur-Humboldt" Schwartz memoir and the "Olduvai" fragments. "The Old System" first appeared in print in January 1968 in *Playboy*, after being rejected by *The New Yorker* on grounds of length. ("*The New Yorker* wanted deletions," Bellow wrote to Meyer Schapiro on March 18, 1968, "so I gave it to *Playboy* in protest—lucrative protest. . . . Hugh Hefner has pleasanter vices than Wm. Phillips.") It was reprinted later in the year in Bellow's first collection of short fiction, *Mosby's Memoirs and Other Stories*, published by Viking. The story sheds interesting light on *Sammler*, and makes clear the complex of ideas and feelings Bellow was wrestling with in the late 1960s, when he was writing at his peak.

The narrator of "The Old System" is Dr. Samuel Braun, a scientist and deep thinker. In the story's opening paragraph, we find Braun in bed at noon on a Saturday, pondering the question of whether human existence is "necessary." Braun distrusts his sense that it is, which might only be "the aggressive, instinctive vitality we share with an ape or a dog."[42] The detachment here is characteristic, crucial to Braun's success as a scientist (his work on the chemistry of heredity has been "written up in *Time*" [p. 91]). Recently, however, "self-observation and objectivity" have begun to strike him as unhealthy: "Existence for the sake of such practices did not seem worthwhile" (p. 90). In lamenting the "great traditions" dislodged by modernity, Braun uses terms that identify the narrative present as contemporary: "Elevation? Beauty? Torn into shreds, into ribbons for girls' costumes, or trailed like the tail of a kite at Happenings. Plato and the Buddha raided by looters. The tombs of the Pharaohs broken into by desert rabble" (p. 91).

In his youth, Braun spent summers with relatives in the Mohawk Valley, in upstate New York. Two of these relatives, Cousin Isaac and Cousin Tina, are recalled in vivid and loving detail.[43] Cousin Isaac embraced the values of the Old System, the intuitive, traditional certainties; Cousin Tina consciously resisted them, though she, too, was "old-fashioned, for all her modern slang" (p. 103). There are parallels here with *Mr. Sammler's Planet*. Like Braun, Artur Sammler is drawn to traditional ways, which he sees as embodied in his nephew, Arnold "Elya" Gruner, a figure not unlike Cousin Isaac. It was Elya, a wealthy gynecologist, who rescued Sammler and his daughter, Shula, from a DP camp in Salzburg in 1947, and it is Elya who has been their protector ever since. Cousin Isaac, fifteen years Dr. Braun's senior, was his protector in childhood, when he showed him great affection and kindness. The differences between Braun and Sammler are of temperament, a product of radically different life experiences. Sammler is only outwardly detached: polite, a considerate father, "muttering appreciation of each piece of rubbish presented to him" (by his daughter, Shula, an urban scavenger); inwardly, he boils with prophetic anger and contempt, and is at times "explosive, under provocation more violent than other people" (p. 20). In the novel's opening paragraph, the practices of detachment and objectivity Braun doubts are called into question by Sammler as well. Ours is an age of explanation, of "fathers to children, wives to husbands, lecturers to listeners, experts to laymen, colleagues to colleagues, doctors to patients, man to his own soul." The effect of these explanations, when not minimal ("for the most part, in one ear and out the other," a conclusion perhaps anticipated by the inversion of "wives to husbands") is pernicious. For Sammler, as for Braun, the knowledge that matters is a product of deep feeling: "The soul wanted what it wanted. It had its own natural knowledge. It sat unhappily on superstructures of explanation, poor bird, not knowing which way to fly" (p. 1).

What leads Braun to recall Cousin Isaac and Cousin Tina is the reputation his detachment has earned him. "It was said of him, occasionally, that he did not love anyone. This was not true. He did not love anyone steadily. But unsteadily he loved, he guessed, at an average rate." For example, "he and Cousin Isaac had loved each other" (p. 91). Isaac is now dead, which leads Braun to wonder, once again characteristically, if he loved him more than his other cousins *because* he was dead. "There one might have something," he thinks. Isaac's soulfulness is suggested in a metaphor that recalls Sammler on the soul. Already in youth, in the 1920s, Isaac "had a mature business face. Born to be a man in the direct Old Testament sense, as that bird in the sycamore was born to fish in water" (p. 92). Isaac is a millionaire property developer, but for all his success as a New World businessman, "his old-country Jewish dignity was very firm and strong. He had the outlook of ancient generations on the New World" (p. 92). Elya Gruner, too, is a millionaire, and no less dignified an Old System figure, "devoted to ideas of conduct which seemed discredited, which few people explicitly defended" (pp. 215–16).

As Cousin Isaac grows rich, he becomes more Orthodox, "an old-fashioned Jewish paterfamilias" (p. 97). He keeps a copy of the Psalms near him at all times, including "in the glove compartment of his Cadillac," "as active, worldly Jews for centuries had done" (p. 98).

What set Isaac on the path to millions was the purchase of a WASP country club.[44] After Isaac demolishes the country club, tearing up its golf course as well, he builds a shopping center in its place. So ugly is this shopping center that Braun thinks it might have been a form of revenge, "an unconscious assertion of triumph" (p. 101) against WASP exclusion—though, as he also points out, "all such places are ugly" (p. 101). Braun wonders if Cousin Isaac felt anything for the lost elms and greenery, "reserved, it was true, for mild idleness, for hitting a ball with a stick" (p. 101) (a remark that recalls Max Zetland in "Zetland: By a Character Witness," on "the laxity and brainlessness of the golf-playing goy"[45]). It seems not. Isaac goes on to fill the Mohawk Valley with housing developments. Although proud of his work, he builds "too densely," is "stingy with land" (p. 101). He is no miser, but he lives modestly, Cadillac notwithstanding. A pillar of the local Jewish community, he is president of its new synagogue, described by Braun as looking like "a World's Fair pavilion." The rabbi of the synagogue, a Madison Avenue type, is "like a Christian minister except for the play of Jewish cleverness in his face." Isaac was elected president, Braun tells us, over "the father of a famous hoodlum, once executioner for the Mob in the Northeast" (p. 101).

To Braun, Isaac is in essential ways untouched by the ugliness and corruption that not only surround him but that he himself contributes to, or is obliged to contribute to. In this, he is like Elya in *Sammler*, whose fortune has come in part from performing abortions for the Mob. Elya's taste is no better than Isaac's, as can be seen from the crowded furnishings of his house, the work of a decorator with "an Oscar Wilde hairdo, suave little belly, and perfumed fingers" (p. 198), or from his dress: the too-narrow trousers (producing a "virile bulge" when he sits), the "matching ties and handkerchiefs from Countess Mara . . . sharp swaggering shoes which connected him less with medicine than with Las Vegas, with racing, broads, and singers in the rackets." Instead of a Cadillac, Elya has a Rolls-Royce and a driver (who once drove for Lucky Luciano). Otherwise, he, too, lives modestly. Aside from the Rolls-Royce, "his one glamorous eccentricity was to fly to Israel on short notice and stroll into the King David Hotel without baggage, his hands in his pockets" (p. 234). Sammler's ability to overlook Elya's aesthetic deficiencies and dubious connections derives in part from an Old World attitude to the law: "The rich men he knew were winners in struggles of criminality, of permissible criminality."

Whenever Sammler tried to imagine a just social order, "he could not do it. A non-corrupt society? He could not do that either" (p. 61). In the Old World, ambitious and able Jews broke or bent the law out of necessity, with no injury to their "Jewish dignity"; to be "a man in the Old Testament sense" meant to provide for one's family, to serve God, and to serve God's chosen people; the needs of the larger community, of the rest of the world, figured only distantly. To be a socialist was likely to put one at odds with Old System values.

Something like this point is made by Braun when he recalls Cousin Isaac's experiences as a member of the governor's commission on pollution. On a boat sent by the Fish and Game Department, Isaac and his fellow commissioners tour the Hudson River from Albany to Germantown. "The towns were dumping raw sewage into the Mohawk and the Hudson. You could watch the flow from giant pipes" (p. 108). Many of the inhabitants of these towns live in dwellings built by Isaac, "squalid settlements of which he was so proud . . . Had been proud" (p. 110). Although he is revolted by the pollution he sees, Isaac's thoughts are elsewhere, with his family. What he thinks should be done about the pollution is hard to discern. The local communities expect the federal government to pay for sewage treatment, which Isaac thinks "only fair, since Internal Revenue took away to Washington billions in taxes and left small change for the locals." When no federal help was forthcoming, the local communities pumped their excrement into the rivers. The next sentence reads: "Isaac, building along the Mohawk, had always taken this for granted" (p. 110) (where "this" means either "this polluting of the waterways" or "this assumption that Washington would help"). At the end of the boat trip, the state game commissioner fishes an eel from the Hudson and drops it on the deck. "It was writhing toward the river in swift, powerful loops, tearing its skin on the planks, its crest of fin standing. *Treph!* [Unclean, not kosher.] And slimy black, the perishing mouth open" (p. 110). Isaac registers the horror of the eel, then turns away, back to family troubles, to Tina in particular. Often during business he thinks not only of family but of God. At building sites he says psalms: "*When I consider the heavens, the work of Thy fingers . . . what is Man that Thou art mindful of him?*" Many doubted Isaac's piety, because he had been "a strong, raunchy young man, and this had never entirely left him (it remained only as witty comment)," also because his mind seemed "a web of computations, of frontages, elevations, drainage, mortgages, turn-around money." "But he evidently meant it all" (p. 105).

Isaac's family troubles derive from the country-club deal, in which his siblings had originally been included. At the last minute they pulled out, leaving him with an hour to come up with seventy-five thousand dollars. At great personal risk, he succeeds in finding the money. Although he loves his brothers and sister, never again will he include them in real-estate deals, a decision that enrages Tina. She accuses him "of shaking off the family when the main chance came," though in fact she and the brothers had deserted him "at the zero hour" (p. 103). Eventually, Isaac and the brothers are reconciled, but Tina remains implacable, refusing to see him, spreading malicious gossip about his business dealings and connections. Every year, on the Day of Atonement, Isaac comes to Tina to make peace, and every year she sends him away. "She said she hated his Orthodox cringe. She could take him straight. In a deal. Or a swindle. But she couldn't bear his sentiment." When Isaac appeals to her "in the eyes of God, and in the name of souls departed," she cries: "Never! You son of a bitch, never!" (p. 106). Only when she is dying of cancer of the liver does Tina agree to see Isaac. But she has one condition: he must pay her twenty thousand dollars.[46]

Braun's opinion of Cousin Tina is that she "had seized upon the form of death to create a situation of opera, which at the same time was a situation of parody" (p. 108) (a form of Herzog's "potato love"). The emotions released at the end of the story are operatic, but they are also powerful. Braun is "bitterly moved" in recalling them—though, being a child of the New World, he also finds them baffling. "What good were they! What were they for! And no one wanted them now. Perhaps the cold eye was better. On life, on death." This view Braun quickly rejects, declaring that at such moments "humankind . . . grasped its own idea, that it was human and human through such passions." The story ends poised between these two views. First the claims of feeling are forwarded:

> Oh, these Jews—these Jews! Their feelings, their hearts! Dr. Braun often wanted nothing more than to stop all this. For what came of it? One after another you gave over your dying. One by one they went. You went. Childhood, family, friendship, love were stifled in the grave. And these tears! When you wept them from the heart,

> you felt you justified something, understood something. But what did you understand? Again, *nothing*! It was only an intimation of understanding. A promise that mankind might—*might*, mind you—eventually, through its gift which might—*might* again!—be a divine gift, comprehend why it lived. Why life, why death.

This qualified affirmation is not given the final word. As Braun lies back in bed, the "intimation of understanding" afforded him by deep emotion vanishes. Braun the scientist is given the final word:

> When Dr. Braun closed his eyes, he saw, red on black, something like molecular processes—the only true heraldry of being. As later, in the close black darkness when the short day ended, he went to the dark kitchen window to have a look at stars. These things cast outward by a great begetting spasm billions of years ago [p. 116].

Mr. Sammler's Planet ends somewhat differently, perhaps because Sammler comes from the Old World. Not only is he less baffled by Old World values than Dr. Braun, he finds the New World repulsive, in part because he was once drawn to it, though mostly because of the horrors he has lived through. He is Old World by default. As Ijah Metzger, the narrator of Bellow's story "Cousins" (1974), puts it, intense family feeling of the sort Sammler now admires is "an archaism of which the Jews, until the present century stopped them, were in the course of divesting themselves. The world as it was dissolving apparently collapsed on top of them, and the divestiture could not continue."[47] The novel ends with Sammler's prayer over Elya's dead body:

> "Remember, God, the soul of Elya Gruner, who, as willingly as possible and as well as he was able, and even to an intolerable point, and even in suffocation and even as death was coming was eager, even childishly perhaps (may I be forgiven for this), even with a certain servility, to do what was required of him. . . . He was aware that he must meet, and he did meet—through all the confusion and degraded clowning of this life through which we are speeding—he did meet the terms of his contract. The terms which, in his inmost heart, each man knows. As I know mine. As all know. For that is the truth of it—that we all know, God, that we know, that we know, we know, we know" [p. 260].

Although the novel's ending is more affirmative than that of "The Old System," it remains only half convinced (as Sammler, who lost an eye in the war, is only half prophet, unlike blind Tiresias or the Oedipus of *Oedipus at Colonus*). Neither Bellow nor Sammler wholly or openly embraces the faith they seek. Early in the novel, Sammler notices some enigmatic graffiti on a vacant building: "On the plate glass of the empty shop were strange figures or nonfigures in thick white. Most scrawls could be ignored. These for some reason caught on with Mr. Sammler as pertinent. Eloquent. Of what? Of future nonbeing. (Elya!) But also of the greatness of eternity which shall lift us from this present shallowness" (p. 72).

What Sammler means by "the contract" is explained in the immediately preceding scenes. As Elya lies on his deathbed, Sammler and Elya's daughter, Angela, wait in the hospital for news of his condition. Sammler wants Angela to make amends to her father: she has been a sorrow to him, spoiled, sexually promiscuous, a child of the sixties. "I should ask him to forgive me? Are you serious?" Sammler is perfectly serious, but Angela cannot bring herself to do as he asks. "It goes against everything. You're talking to the wrong person. Even for my father it would be too hokey." As Sammler persists, bringing up Angela's sex life, she takes offense. What does he know about such matters? Angela is like Cousin Tina in her stubbornness, also in her sexuality (it was Cousin Tina, sullen and stout, who initiated young Braun in the mysteries of sex). Asking for forgiveness "goes against" what Sammler sees as the fashionable freedoms of the day. At Sarah Lawrence College, Angela had "a bad education. In literature, mostly French." This education drew her to outlaw types. She sent money, her father's money, "to defense funds for black murderers and rapists" (p. 7). Angela is "beautiful, free and wealthy" (p. 22), but she is crude, and not only sexually. "I'm sure you love Daddy," she tells Sammler. "Apart from the practical reasons, I mean" (p. 250).

Sammler wants Angela to ask her father for forgiveness because "he's put an immense amount of feeling into you. Probably most of his feeling has gone toward you," but also because "he's been a good man. And he's being swept out" (p. 254). Elya was a better man than Sammler because he treasured "certain old feelings. He's on an old system" (p. 250). Many of the operations he performed as a gynecologist he hated, but "he performed them. He did what he disliked. He had an unsure loyalty to certain pure states. He knew there had been good men before him, that there were good men to come, and he wanted to be one of them." Sammler, in contrast, "was simply an Anglophile intellectual Polish Jew and person of culture—relatively useless. But Elya . . . has accomplished something good. Brought himself through. He loves you" (p. 251).[48] "So he's human," says Angela, "all right, he's human" (p. 251). For Sammler, though, being human is "not a natural gift at all. Only the capacity is natural" (p. 250). Elya's virtues (more spoken of than displayed, a possible fault of the novel) were "feeling, outgoingness, expressiveness, kindness, heart—all these fine human things which by a peculiar turn of opinion strike people now as shady activities. Openness and candor about vices seem far easier. Anyway, there is Elya's assignment. That's what's in his good face. That's why he has such a human look" (p. 251).

SAMMLER'S EMBRACE OF THE OLD SYSTEM goes hand in hand with a ferocious attack on modernity. For Bellow, Sammler was a means of letting rip, something he needed at this period. Creating a protagonist of "seventy-plus" years allowed him, in Ruth Wisse's words, to assume "for the first time the authority of a Jew, and the perspective of a disciplining parent," in defiance not only of the sixties but of traditional patterns of Jewish American fiction: "In a reversal of the immigrant novel that brought Jews to America looking for salvation, *Mr. Sammler's Planet* imports a Jewish refugee from Europe with valuable hard-won wisdom to impart."[49] To begin with, Sammler has no illusions about human depravity. Although not wholly despairing, he is convinced that "liberal beliefs did not seem capable of self-defense, and you could smell decay. You could see the suicidal impulses of civilization pushing strongly" (p. 26).

Although wise, Sammler is powerless, impotent—half blind, with heart trouble that forces him to rest periodically, dependent on the charity of his nephew, too old to live on his own. In the forty-eight hours of the novel's action, his powerlessness is brought home to him in several ways. First and foremost there is his experience with the black pickpocket. The pickpocket works the bus along Riverside Drive. Four times Sammler has seen him in operation, opening handbags, lifting wallets, "without haste, with no criminal tremor" (p. 6). The pickpocket is a big man, about thirty-five, handsome, wearing an expensive camel-hair coat, designer dark glasses, and a single gold earring. Sammler likens his expertise to that of a surgeon, and is appalled and fascinated by the way he "took the slackness, the cowardice of the world for granted" (p. 38). He reports the pickpocket to the police and is greeted over the telephone by a voice "toneless with indifference or fatigue":

> "O.K."
>
> "Are you going to do anything?"
>
> "We're supposed to, aren't we? What's your name?"
>
> "Artur Sammler."
>
> "All right, Art. Where do you live?"
>
> "Dear Sir, I will tell you, but I am asking what you intend to do about this man."
>
> "What do you think we should do?"
>
> "Arrest him."
>
> "We have to catch him first."
>
> "You should put a man on the bus."
>
> "We haven't got a man to put on the bus. There are lots of buses, Art, and not enough men. . . ."
>
> "I understand. You don't have the personnel, and there are priorities, political pressures. But I could point out the man."
>
> "Some other time."
>
> "You don't want him pointed out?"
>
> "Sure, but we have a waiting list."
>
> "I have to get on *your* list?"
>
> "That's right, Abe."
>
> "Artur."
>
> "Arthur" [pp. 9–10].

The effect this exchange has on Sammler, "tensely sitting forward in bright lamplight," is to make him feel "like a motorcyclist who has been struck in the forehead by a pebble from the road, trivially stung." Sammler smiles: "America! (he was speaking to himself). Advertised throughout the universe as *the* most desirable, most exemplary of nations" (p. 10).[50]

DISCUSSING THE PICKPOCKET with Margotte Arkin, the niece with whom he lodges, and with his daughter, Shula, Sammler refers to him as "this African prince or great black beast" (p. 10). He is not without admiration for the pickpocket's manner and appearance. He also discusses him with Lionel Feffer, a graduate student studying diplomatic history at Columbia, one of several students Shula has employed in the past to read to him, to spare his partial eyesight. Feffer is "an ingenious operator, less student than promoter," "a bustling, affectionate, urgent, eruptive, enterprising character" (p. 30). In addition, he's "a busy seducer, especially, it seemed, of young wives." Although his various schemes are moneymaking, he also has time "to hustle on behalf of handicapped children" (p. 31). Sammler finds Feffer charming—like Bellow, he's drawn to "characters"—and he agrees to address a seminar Feffer has arranged as part of "a student project to help backward black pupils with their reading problems" (p. 30). Feffer suggests that Sammler talk about "The British Scene in the Thirties," since for two decades before the war Sammler had been the London correspondent for several Warsaw papers and journals. What such a talk has to do with backward black pupils is unclear, but Sammler, "not always attentive," is often unclear about Feffer's schemes. "Perhaps there was nothing clear to understand; but it seemed that he had promised, although he couldn't remember promising. But Feffer confused him. There were so many projects, such cross references, so many confidences and requests for secrecy, so many scandals, frauds, spiritual communications" (p. 30).

When Sammler arrives at Columbia, Feffer leads him into a large room filled with students, "a mass meeting of some sort." This is the audience he is meant to entertain with anecdotes about R. H. Tawney, Harold Laski, George Orwell, and H. G. Wells. Surprised and frightened, having expected only "a handful of students," Sammler gathers his courage and begins to speak of "the mental atmosphere of England before the Second World War" (p. 32). That the scene is set at Columbia nicely fits Bellow's purposes. Columbia had been much in the news during the writing of *Sammler*. In April 1968, the SDS and SAS (Student Afro Society) led angry protests against the construction of a university gymnasium at Morningside Park, only a few blocks from Columbia but stretching into and through the black neighborhoods of Harlem and Morningside Heights. There were also demonstrations against the university's affiliation with the Institute for Defense Analyses (IDA), a weapons-research think tank connected to the United States Department of Defense. In the course of these protests, several university buildings were occupied, including Hamilton Hall, which housed a number of administrative offices, and Low Library, where the president's office was located. During the occupation, the acting dean was held hostage for a day; a photograph of a student, David Shapiro, sitting in the president's chair, wearing sunglasses, and smoking a cigar, was widely reproduced in newspapers and periodicals; and relations between white and black protesters deteriorated. The black protesters occupying Hamilton Hall insisted that their white counterparts move to other occupied buildings, part of a wider separatist trend among black radicals of the period (as in the purging of white officers from the Congress of Racial Equality, including, presumably, Marvin Rich, editor of the ill-fated volume "They Shall Overcome" [discussed in chapter 1 and its notes], with whom Bellow corresponded over the book's preface). After a week of occupations and fruitless negotiations, Columbia called in the New York City police on April 30, and the protesters were violently ousted; 132 protesters were injured, along with four faculty, and twelve policemen, and there were seven hundred arrests. One policeman was permanently disabled when a student jumped on his back from a second-story window.

Bellow imagines Sammler facing an audience made up of such students. If anything, their behavior is worse than that of the students at San Francisco State. At San Francisco State, Bellow was able to finish his talk; Sammler gets only halfway through his. In the midst of discussing H. G. Wells's "Cosmopolis," his project for a World State, "feeling what a kind-hearted, ingenuous, stupid scheme it had been," Sammler is interrupted by "a man in Levi's, thick-bearded but possibly young . . . shouting at him." The questioner has taken exception to something Sammler said about George Orwell. "That's a lot of shit," he shouts (p. 33).

> "Orwell was a fink. He was a sick counterrevolutionary. It's good he died when he did. And what you are saying is shit." Turning to the audience, extending violent arms and raising his palms like a Greek dancer, he said, "Why do you listen to this effete old shit? What has he got to tell you? His balls are dry. He's dead. He can't come."

Sammler hears several voices raised in protest, but he feels, as Bellow felt at San Francisco State, that "no one really tried to defend him. Most of the young people seemed to be against him" (p. 34). Feffer has left the room, having been called to the telephone. A sympathetic girl bundles Sammler out of the auditorium and down a flight of stairs, "and he was on Broadway at One-hundred-sixteenth Street" (p. 34).

Sammler's treatment differs from Bellow's in that it is unprovoked. Nothing in what he says or the way he says it is aggressive. All that offends about Sammler is his age, his "Polish-Oxonian" accents (p. 32), and his knowledge.[51] Out on the sidewalk, Sammler reflects on the violence of the questioner: "How extraordinary! Youth? Together with the idea of sexual potency? All this confused sex-excrement-militancy, explosiveness, abusiveness, tooth-showing, Barbary ape howling. Or like the spider monkeys in the trees, as Sammler once had read, defecating into their hands, and shrieking, pelting the explorers below. He was not sorry to have met the facts" (p. 34). Sammler can see that his talk might have struck the audience as "downright funny. Inconsequent," and that they might think him an old bore, but "there were appropriate ways of putting down an old bore. . . . The worst of it, from the point of view of the young people themselves, was that they acted without dignity. They had no view of the nobility of being intellectuals and judges of the social order. What a pity! Old Sammler thought" (p. 36). These reflections recall Dr. Braun in "The Old System" on "Plato and the Buddha raided by looters." Sammler is upset by the rudeness of the audience, but also by their contempt for thought itself. He is driven from the stage, as Ruth Wisse puts it, "in the process of trying to fulfill the mandate of the university, there being no one in the university to offer him protection."[52]

Other, more trivial aspects of Sammler's treatment at Columbia have biographical origins. In *Saul Bellow, Drumlin Woodchuck*, Mark Harris recounts his attempts to persuade Bellow to speak at Purdue in 1969. For a second year running, at the behest of colleagues in the English Department, Harris is asked to invite Bellow to Purdue as guest speaker at its annual Literary Awards Banquet. Bellow did not answer his letter of invitation the previous year, so this time Harris phones him, offering a good deal more money: a thousand dollars for a thirty- or forty-minute speech and attendance at the banquet. As instructed, Harris tells Bellow that he is the English Department's unanimous choice, and he mentions previous guest speakers, among them, in a list extending back to 1928, Sherwood Anderson, Theodore Dreiser, William Carlos Williams, and Eudora Welty. Bellow is in a jovial mood when he receives the call. "Why don't you come up to Chicago once in a while," he asks Harris, "and fool around with Dick and me?"[53] When Bellow asks Harris what he'll have to do at Purdue, Harris reads from a memorandum he's been provided with:

> "Topic suggestions," I said, "morning address."
> "Then actually there are *two* talks," Bellow said.
> "I didn't realize that myself until this minute," I said.[54]

Bellow agrees to the morning session as well as to the banquet speech, as long as it's "just a bull session. I don't want to say the same thing over again. Free exchange in the morning session." He has other conditions:

> "No radio stations," said Bellow. "No TV stations."
> "No, no, of course not," I said.
> "No, no, of course not," he replied, "but suddenly there were two speeches instead of one."
> "Nothing between the morning and evening programs," I said.
> "That's *right*," he said.[55]

Bellow tells Harris he is not coming to Purdue for the money: "I need the money like I need a hole in the head. It all goes for taxes." He tells Harris, "I'm doing it for you."[56] In a subsequent phone call, Harris awkwardly informs Bellow that the morning session has changed. Instead of being for twenty or so students, it is now somewhat bigger: "There will actually be six hundred." "I can handle it," Bellow says. Harris tells him he'd be perfectly within his rights to cancel. "I can *handle* it," Bellow replies, "I'm doing it for *you*." In the interval between this exchange and Bellow's arrival, Harris reads an article by Jane Howard in *Life* magazine reporting on a talk Bellow gave at Yale. Howard describes Bellow as relaxed and charming in person, but combative on stage, telling the Yale audience that "campus revolutionaries" were "destroyers . . . just as phony as what they've come to destroy. Maybe civilization *is* dying, but it still exists, and meanwhile we have our choice: we can either rain more blows on it, or try to redeem it."[57] The talk Bellow finally delivers at Purdue is in this vein: tough, provocative, intellectually demanding. Many in the audience have trouble following it and are bored (as the Yale audience had been, according to Howard), but Harris admires Bellow for his single-mindedness: "If he was going to say something he was going to *say* something. That was his radicalism—not to retreat from his aesthetic conviction even to please the crowd."[58] At the morning session the next day, Bellow is told that he will be taped, "yet the promise had been that Bellow was not to be on any tape."[59] At lunch after the session, Bellow is asked by a bearded teaching assistant what the relation is between the author of a novel and its characters or narrator, the very question that led to acrimony at San Francisco State. "I was glancing last night at *Henderson the Rain King*," the questioner says. "You were glancing at it?" Bellow asks. The questioner persists. "What kind of criticism do you prefer?" he asks. "Criticism of a high order," Bellow replies.[60]

THE MOST CONTROVERSIAL of the passages in *Mr. Sammler's Planet* occurs in the scene that immediately follows the talk at Columbia. Sammler again spots the pickpocket on the bus, and the pickpocket sees that he's been spotted. Heart thumping (Bellow began to experience bouts of tachycardia in the late sixties), Sammler quickly exits the bus, crosses Riverside Drive, and enters the first building he comes to, "as if he lived there" (p. 38). After hiding in the stairwell and trying to disguise his appearance, he walks down the street and at last enters the lobby of his own building. The pickpocket has not been fooled. He comes up behind Sammler in the empty lobby and pushes him against a wall. Without uttering a word ("He was never to hear the black man's voice. He no more spoke than a puma would" [p. 39]), he pins Sammler to the wall, first with his body, then with his forearm:

> The pickpocket unbuttoned himself. Sammler heard the zipper descend. Then the smoked glasses were removed from Sammler's face and dropped on the table. He was directed, silently, to look downward. The black man had opened his fly and taken out his penis. It was displayed to Sammler with great oval testicles, a large tan-and-purple uncircumcised thing—a tube, a snake; metallic hairs bristling at the thick base and the tip curled beyond the supporting, demonstrating hand, suggesting the fleshly mobility of an elephant's trunk, though the skin was somewhat iridescent rather than thick or rough. Over the forearm and fist that held him Sammler was required to gaze at this organ. No compulsion would have been necessary. He would in any case have looked.
>
> The interval was long. The man's expression was not directly

> menacing but oddly, serenely masterful. The thing was shown with mystifying certitude. Lordliness. Then it was returned to the trousers. *Quod erat demonstrandum* [pp. 39–40].

What was being demonstrated was not merely the black man's potency, but Sammler's impotence. For Morris Dickstein, a severe critic of the novel, "*Mr. Sammler's Planet* can be read as an inversion of [Norman Mailer's] 'The White Negro,' inspired by the same fantasies and imagery. But Sammler gives Norman Mailer's argument (and William Blake's language) a racist spin: 'The labor of Puritanism now was ending. The dark satanic mills changing into light satanic mills. The reprobates converted into children of joy, the sexual ways of the seraglio and of the Congo bush adopted by the emancipated masses of New York, Amsterdam, London.' "[61]

The "racist spin" Sammler is said by Dickstein to give to outlaw worship, youth worship, and the intellectual primitivism of the sixties is plausible, given his background and history. But it does not originate with him. It originates with views like Mailer's, which helped to create the conditions he deplores. Bellow voiced his opposition to intellectual primitivism as early as 1952, in a review of Ralph Ellison's *Invisible Man* ("Man Underground," *Commentary*, June 1952): "It is thought that Negroes and other minority people, kept under in the great status battle, are in the instinct cellar of dark enjoyment." This view Bellow describes as both untrue—he cites the novel's depiction of Harlem as a place "at once primitive and sophisticated"—and dangerous, in that it "provokes envious rage and murder." But Mailer endorses it in "The White Negro" (*Dissent*, Fall 1957), as Dickstein acknowledges. "By turning the Negro into a psycho-sexual metaphor for the hipster," Dickstein writes, "Mailer ran the risk of distorting the actuality of race in America, which was already fraught with half-acknowledged sexual myths and fantasies."

This distortion is racist. The hipster or White Negro seeks out what Bellow in his *Commentary* essay calls the "instinct cellar" of the black man, and he does so, as Mailer puts it in "The White Negro," "at no matter what price in individual violence." He seeks the removal of "every social restraint," affirms "the barbarian," behaves like a "psychopath," and "psychopathology is most prevalent with the Negro." When Mailer writes of murderous black hoodlums "daring the unknown," he gives them what David Mikics calls "existential panache," precisely the panache Sammler and Bellow anathematize. Bellow's opposition to views like Mailer's was bolstered by his friendship with Ralph Ellison. In 1963, in an essay entitled "The World and the Jug," Ellison took issue with a similar if more muted line adopted by Irving Howe in his essay "Black Boys and Native Sons," published in *Dissent* (Autumn 1963). In Howe's essay, Ellison's comparative moderation in *Invisible Man* is criticized, while the brute fury of Richard Wright's *Native Son* is praised. Ellison's response was to accuse Howe of being "carried away by that intellectual abandon, that lack of restraint, which seizes those who regard blackness as an absolute and see in it a release from the complications of the world." This abandon Sammler and his author abhor, are obsessed with, and, as we shall see, have been infected by.[62]

More puzzling than Sammler's racism is the violence of his references to female sexuality. "In the higher synthesis of *Mr. Sammler's Planet*," writes Dickstein, "sex belongs only to a constellation of moral degeneracy that centers on women, blacks, and young people in general. Sammler constantly thinks of women in terms of their foul odors, their corrupt natures, their unclean organs, 'the female generative slime.' There is no indication of what personal crisis may lie behind this insistence." In the sentence that follows, Dickstein moves from character to author: "No writer since Swift has built his work on such a fascinated repugnance toward female odors and female organs, or expected them to bear the onus of representing a whole culture in decline."[63]

Sammler's misogyny grows out of his traditional notions of women and physicality: "Some parts of nature demanded more control than others. Females were naturally more prone to grossness, had more smells, needed more washing, clipping, binding, pruning, grooming, perfuming and training" (p. 29). Connected to this is a belief in the intellectual inferiority of women. Sammler's daughter, Shula, is one example. The "charming, idiotic, nonsensical girls" taught by Margotte's deceased husband at Hunter College are another. Margotte herself is "a first-class device as long as someone aimed her in the right direction" (p. 12). The bright woman in the novel is the oversexed Angela, and it is Angela who most repels Sammler. "In Angela you confronted sensual womanhood without remission. You smelled it, too" (p. 24). Angela busies herself with "experiments in sensuality, in sexology, smearing all with her female fluids" (p. 230). "We're going to fuck all night!" she cries to her boyfriend, the wonderfully named Wharton Horricker. First, though, she tells Sammler, in whom she often confides, "she had to have a bath. Because she had been longing all evening for him. 'Oh, a woman is a skunk. So many odors, Uncle'" (p. 57). To Elya, her loving father, Angela is "a dirty cunt" (p. 145), "a woman who has done it in too many ways with too many men. . . . Her eyes—she has fucked-out eyes" (p. 146). "I wonder if women really prefer that kind of thing," asks Angela's brother, Wallace, after Sammler describes the black pickpocket's penis. "I assume they have other interests in addition," Sammler replies. "That's what they say," Wallace answers. "But you know you can't trust them. They're animals, aren't they" (p. 245). Angela has already told Sammler what women want: "a Jew brain, a black cock, a Nordic beauty" (p. 54). Sitting next to Sammler in the hospital, waiting for news of her dying father, Angela wears a low-necked satin blouse and "a miniskirt. No, Sammler changed that, it was a microskirt. . . . Sitting near her, Sammler could not smell the usual Arabian musk. Instead her female effluence was very strong, a salt odor, similar to tears or tidewater, something from within the woman. Elya's words had taken effect strongly—his 'Too much sex'" (p. 245).

Sammler's disgust at Angela's physicality and sexual freedom is partly explained by his upbringing. "He had been trained in the ancient mode of politeness. Almost as, once, women had been brought up to chastity" (p. 140). But nothing we are told of Sammler's past, of his marriage or erotic experience, explains the intensity of his disgust. That it is shared by Wallace and Elya lends support to Dickstein's suspicion that it originates in their creator. The evidence that their views are Bellow's, however, except in the sense that they come from characters of his creation, is thin and indirect; there is little of it in Bellow's correspondence. While at work on the novel, Bellow was being harassed by Sasha about money, in divorce negotiations with Susan, and in love with Maggie Staats, whom he frequently visited in New York. In Chicago he was seeing Bette Howland, described by Harris as Bellow's "companion, Bonne Amie," having an affair with his cleaning lady (a black woman, "about twice as tall as he was, and well built, striking," according to Richard Stern), and in pursuit of another woman roughly half his age, Arlette Landes, whom he had met early in 1967, just months after having left Susan. ("It may be a little difficult for you to keep the various wives and girlfriends straight in your mind," wrote Sasha to Bellow in the letter of September 4, 1968, "but do try to remember that I am neither Susan trying to strangle you financially, nor Margy [Maggie] to be read lectures like a misbehaving child, nor Madeleine, believe it or not."[64]) Arlette was twenty-five, the same age as Maggie. She had married at seventeen, while an undergraduate at Hunter College, and had a daughter when she was twenty.[65] Her marriage broke up after four years, when Arlette was twenty-two. When she met Bellow, he had already moved from Windermere House to the Cloisters, an elegant high-rise apartment building at the corner of Dorchester Avenue and Fifty-Eighth Street. Bellow was living in the very apartment, 11E, that Arlette had lived in with her husband and daughter, and they met when her daughter was visiting friends in the building. "You're living in my apartment," she said when she saw Bellow. She knew who he was, had not only read and loved *Herzog* ("I just found it so clever and so terrific, what a book") but had audited one of his classes, though "as a teacher he was a dud, all he did was read from *Mimesis*." Arlette and her daughter lived nearby, having moved to a less grand apartment building on Dorchester. Her daughter, like Daniel Bellow, attended the Laboratory School at the University of Chicago, across the street from the Cloisters.

"I was young and, according to my husband, I was gorgeous," Arlette says of herself in this period, "and, according to his wife, I was very sexy (she said this later, when I must have looked old)." Arlette and Bellow soon began an affair, and Bellow introduced her to a number of his friends at the university, none of whom, she claims, liked her. She did not get on with Shils; Harold Rosenberg "couldn't stand me" (he and his wife were protective of Maggie); Dick Stern described her as "brunette, buxom . . . sluttish," "more overtly sexual than I'm comfortable with, and available" (which didn't prevent him, she recalled, from making a pass at her). Arlette said very little in front of these friends: "I was silent, I was mute." Although at work on a master's degree in teaching at the University of Chicago, she felt "I didn't know enough, I hadn't read enough," and it was not true that she scorned or put Bellow down for his philosophical or spiritual views, like her fictional alter ego, Renata Koffritz, Charlie Citrine's "sex goddess" in *Humboldt's Gift:* "We were kindred spirits in terms of outlook." The only one of Bellow's friends she liked was Dave Peltz: "He was terrific. I loved him." She had very little money when Bellow knew her and very few clothes, though she recalls wearing a flared silver miniskirt and having "big hair." Although she had sympathies with the student protesters, she was neither radical in politics nor countercultural in style; nor was she an advocate of free love. Dick Stern was not the only one of Bellow's friends to make a pass at Arlette. Another friend raped her, she claims.

How serious Bellow was about Arlette is not clear. When he met her mother, "he asked her to keep tabs on me because I was 'vulnerable,'" by which he seems to have meant, according to the mother, vulnerable to the attentions of other men. "I'd like to marry your daughter," he told her, "but I can't unless you see that she behaves," a remark that infuriated the mother. "He's not the person for you," she told Arlette. "He's already thinking of you as giving him trouble." Bellow, in turn, was angry with the mother for not agreeing with him. Nevertheless, Bellow did discuss marriage with Arlette, and for a period she wanted to marry him, "but he never formally asked me." One reason he didn't, she believes, is that "all his friends had got together to see that he didn't marry again." According to another woman Bellow took up with in this period, Frances Gendlin, who will figure in the next chapter, Bellow thought Arlette "a sex goddess." He also admitted that he had treated her badly.

The ending of the relationship with Arlette was neither simple nor clean. In the spring of 1968, Bellow told her that he would be spending the summer in the Hamptons, not with her but with his New York friend, Maggie Staats. "For me that was the emotional end," Arlette believes, though she pleaded with him to change his mind. "I was trying so hard to make him take me." Bellow's excuse was that "the boys are used to [Maggie]." While Bellow was in the Hamptons with Maggie, Arlette spent the summer on Monhegan Island, in Maine, convinced that the affair was over. In the autumn, however, in a grocery store in Hyde Park, Bellow came up behind her, pinched her bottom, "and we started up again." He was no longer with Maggie, he told her. He asked her if she wanted to go to London with him that December, and she said yes, "because he owed me." Although Arlette had begun seeing the man who would become her second husband, "there was a part of me that wanted to be sure." In London, they stayed at the Ritz for a week, then in a small "cottage" belonging to George Weidenfeld, at 42A Hyde Park Gate, near his house in Chester Square, Belgravia. As in Chicago, she was "mostly quiet" in the presence of Bellow's friends: "There wasn't a whole lot I could say to these people." She met the Chancellor of the Exchequer, Roy Jenkins, at a reception he gave for Bellow at 11 Downing Street; Jenkins and Barley Alison had been lovers in the early 1950s and were still close. Arlette could see that Jenkins was wondering, "What are you doing with him?," but all she said was "I met him in Chicago." She claims she had "no designs on [Bellow] at that point, I no longer wanted to marry the man," but she "wanted to see what life with him would be like." "It was no longer the passion," she recalls, "it was not enchanting to me." During the visit, she and Bellow had lunch with Sonia Orwell, who had had several affairs with older literary men. She was not in good shape, and Arlette thought, "Oh my God, I am not going to end up like that."

Arlette felt closest to Bellow after she had spent a weekend alone in Paris. She had gone there in search of her father, as does Renata Koffritz in *Humboldt's Gift*. Arlette's background was as exotic as Renata's. Her mother was born in Amsterdam into a wealthy Sephardic Jewish family. When the war broke out, she was living in France and was imprisoned by the Nazis. She managed to escape and fled the country on a ship bound for Santo Domingo and Cuba. She was forty-one at the time, unmarried, and eight months pregnant with Arlette, her first and only child, the result of an affair with a married Parisian. Arlette spent her infant years in Cuba, where she and her mother were supported by the mother's wealthy brother, who lived in New York. When the brother died, the money ran out, and Arlette's mother moved to New York to look for work, leaving her daughter in the care of a Cuban nurse. The mother, who had never worked a day in her life, took a stenography course and ended up as secretary to the Dutch ambassador. She earned enough money to bring three-year-old Arlette to New York, and after the estate of her brother was finally settled, she received a small inheritance, quit her job, and moved with Arlette to a one-room apartment on Park Avenue. Arlette went to the Jewish Community School at 103rd and Manhattan Avenue, then to a professional children's school, where she studied ballet under George Balanchine, then to the High School of Music & Art on West 135th Street. When she was ten, she and her mother went to Paris to see her father, who refused to see them. When a hip-joint problem ruined Arlette's hopes of becoming a ballerina, she turned to painting.

Bellow paid for Arlette's trip to Paris, as he paid for everything in Europe. She stayed at a hotel on the Rue du Bac; visited Jesse and Laure Reichek, Bellow's friends from his first visit to Paris, in the late 1940s; and set out in search of the shop she knew was owned by her father, a furrier. He was not there when she arrived, though she met his wife of many years. "I left two photos, one of me and one of my daughter, and I never laid eyes on him." On her return to London, Bellow was "nice to me," considerate, sympathetic. When he asked her to join him the following summer at Casa Alison, Barley Alison's house in Carboneras, Andalusia, in southern Spain, she refused. Barley liked Arlette, and Arlette liked Barley, but she would not have been comfortable there, Arlette said. Bellow's world was not for her. When she returned to Chicago alone, to take care of her daughter, she started up again with the man she would marry, a doctor (in *Humboldt's Gift*, the equivalent figure is an undertaker). Bellow was upset when Arlette declined his summer invitation, and he refused to accept that the affair was over.[66] Although they corresponded while he was still in Europe—he did not return until mid-February 1969—on his return she would not go out with him. For a period, "my bell would ring at one a.m., or the phone, and I wouldn't answer it."[67] In explaining her decision to break off with Bellow, Arlette tells a story about shoes. Shortly after her return from London, she was in a shoe shop and couldn't decide between two pairs of shoes, one with high heels, one without. The salesman said, "Buy both," but she couldn't afford both. So she bought the shoes "I could actually wear." In 1970, she married the doctor, to whom she remains married. There was another factor involved in her decision not to stay with Bellow. "He could not satisfy me." The sexual side "meant a lot to me. . . . I couldn't settle. . . . My body was a tyrant," an admission that recalls something Bellow told Dick Stern, that Arlette "wanted to pitch her erotic tent and keep it up all night."[68]

Bellow's difficulties with Arlette were matched by earlier difficulties with Maggie. In his visits to New York, Bellow mostly stayed with Maggie on Fifteenth Street, and they led a busy social life. "It was a day in the sixties in which everybody knew us and we didn't know them; he enjoyed all that." On the whole, they saw Bellow's friends, and Maggie missed seeing her contemporaries. She remembers many outings in which they were joined by Sam Goldberg, the bibliophile lawyer. "I spent my life in the Strand Bookstore." Although she often felt out of touch with her generation ("I sort of heard of it"), she certainly flew its female flag, the miniskirt. When Bellow took her to the Century Association, she wore hot pants: "a very conservative blue suit with pearls, except the bottom was missing." Early in 1967, Bellow pressed Maggie to leave *The New Yorker*, less because his relations with it were uneasy, more because he wanted her free for summers. She left just when the magazine offered her a promotion. In March 1967, she went on holiday with Bellow to Oaxaca, staying in a hotel high above the city. "We had an idyllic time," Maggie remembers. They swam and sunned, and Bellow wrote the whole of the story "Mosby's Memoirs" on the hotel terrace, drawing on visits they'd made to the tombs at Mitla and on their discussions of a Wyndham Lewis book Maggie was reading. Bellow remembered the composition of the story in a letter of April 30, 1969. He wrote the story "on six successive mornings in the Mexican town of Oaxaca without the aid of tequila. I seemed to need no stimulants. I was in a state of all but intolerable excitement, or was, as the young now say, 'turned on.' A young and charming friend typed the manuscript for me. Reading it I found little to change. The words had come readily. I felt as they went into the story that I was striking them with a mallet. I seldom question what I have written in such a state. I simply feel gratitude and let it go at that."[69] The theme of "Mosby's Memoirs," in Maggie's words, is "the humor that can be derived from fucking someone over, and the consequences of doing so."[70] When asked what Bellow's attitude was to such behavior, she replied "mixed."

After his return from reporting the Six-Day War of June 1967, Bellow rented a house at 145 Old Stone Highway, in the artists' colony of Springs, in East Hampton. It was near the bay, and he and Maggie spent July there, the first of two East Hampton summers they spent together. It was "very romantic," she remembers. Bellow "wrote and wrote," and in the evenings "we'd sit at home and cook and read." Alfred Kazin sometimes dropped by, and there were visits with the Rosenbergs, who "looked on me as their daughter," Willem de Kooning, Saul Steinberg and Gigi Spaeth, Benjamin Nelson, Jean Stafford, Penny and Joe Ferrer, and a host of painter friends.[71] Bellow was careful with Steinberg, who could be cruel. "He [Bellow] thought I was young and vulnerable, which I was, and he really thought I needed protection." Maggie remembers reading Betty Friedan's *The Feminine Mystique* that summer and becoming a convert, while acting as Bellow's "handmaiden . . . because that's what you're supposed to do." Ten-year-old Adam came to stay, and she "adored" him; she also made an effort to get to know Sasha, and to smooth relations between her and Bellow. A tricky moment occurred when her parents came east. Although she had secured a job for the autumn, teaching English at St. Hilda's & St. Hugh's, a private Episcopal day school near Columbia, she was still receiving money from her father. Neither parent knew about Bellow, and had they known, "they wouldn't have approved at all." So Maggie moved her things to the Rosenbergs' and pretended she was staying there. She remembers Bellow spying on her parents from a distance.

What Maggie especially valued about her summers with Bellow was the talks they had. She loved the way he thought; she also liked that she could keep up. Bellow was at work on *Sammler*, and they talked a lot about the Second World War and about the Holocaust survivors he had interviewed. The metaphysical questions at play in "The Old System" and *Mr. Sammler's Planet* preoccupied them both, for Maggie shared Bellow's sense that "this can't be the beginning and the end." For Maggie, however, such a sense was a source of dread: "My whole life was wrapped up with the question of whether I was going to go to hell," a question Bellow had "never run into before" but one he took seriously. Bellow respected Maggie's religious feelings, saw her fear of damnation as "a real problem." Like Clara Velde in *A Theft* and Demmie Vonghel in *Humboldt*, Maggie had terrible nightmares. She walked in her sleep and once nearly walked off a roof. Demmie's nightmare voice "was low hoarse and deep almost mannish. She moaned. She spoke broken words. She did this almost every night. The voice expressed her terror. . . . This was the primordial Demmie beneath the farmer's daughter beneath the teacher beneath the elegant Main Line horsewoman, Latinist, accomplished cocktail-sipper in black chiffon, with the upturned nose, the fashionable conversationalist" (pp. 145–46). For Maggie, fear of hell was like "fear of flying, and it was very bad at this date." What joined her to Bellow "wasn't just the sex, it was the death"; "the question of death joined us from day one." Bellow's concern with the soul or spirit, she believes, was his one "true" connection to the world of thought, pursued "without bias for the rest of his life," a view supported in part by *Humboldt's Gift*, *The Dean's December*, and *Ravelstein*.

IN THE AUTUMN OF 1967, during her first year of teaching, Maggie made frequent weekend trips to Chicago, where Bellow introduced her to his friends. She did not like Dave Peltz, finding him sycophantic, but she liked Shils, who "maybe gets a bad rap. . . . I remember him as a very gentle man." Shils was away that autumn, and Maggie stayed in his apartment, presumably to avoid detection by Arlette (Maggie does not remember the reason Bellow gave her for staying at Shils's). One of Bellow's graduate students, a model for Lionel Feffer, recalls several occasions on which Bellow enlisted his help to keep one girlfriend occupied while he was with the other. On January 15, 1968, Bellow came to New York to receive the Croix de Chevalier des Arts et des Lettres at the French consulate. Maggie was at the ceremony, along with Sasha, Sam Goldberg, and Ben Nelson and his wife.[72] Later in the spring, she met up with Bellow in Texas, where he'd gone to visit Keith Botsford, now at the University of Texas at Austin. Maggie liked Botsford, "a character who really *was* a character," "somebody Saul was constantly warned about," "a terrific cook." Before the Texas visit, she and Bellow talked about marriage. "Finally, he said, 'All right, we'll get engaged.'" Maggie even chose a ring, an opal surrounded by thirteen diamonds. They had a small engagement party in Hyde Park. David Grene was there, and other members of the Committee. Maggie had interviews at New Trier High School in Winnetka and at other Chicago-area schools, "because he wanted me to move to Chicago." It was not until Austin, however, that Bellow gave her the ring, "the same ring that figures in *A Theft*." It was also in Austin that Maggie read *Portnoy's Complaint*, "and he made me put a brown paper around it." Later that spring, Maggie accompanied Bellow to California and to the ill-fated talk at San Francisco State.

It was most likely in the spring of 1968, sometime before the trip to California, that Bellow told Arlette that he would be spending a second summer with Maggie. When Arlette discovered that Maggie was in town, she went to Bellow's apartment to see "who was this other woman." There were other people present in the apartment, but when she saw Maggie "padding around . . . I was incensed, enraged." Bellow tried to calm her, whispering in an aside, "This is just a business arrangement" (Maggie had been doing secretarial work for him at this period). "Business is conducted in an office!" Arlette answered. She then asked Bellow directly, in front of Maggie, "Do you want to marry me?" After a long pause, he said, "No." "So I left." What Maggie remembers of this encounter is that when Arlette walked into the room she immediately took her sweater off over her head. Maggie thought, "Wow, this is really out of my league," by which she meant showy, vulgar. She also remembers that, before Arlette was let in, Bellow grabbed his manuscript and hid it in the refrigerator.

RELATIONS BETWEEN Bellow and Maggie were as fraught as relations between Bellow and Arlette, even during their "idyllic" summers and vacation trips. Bellow "lived on turbulence," according to Maggie; "he caused it, and he set scenes." "He would create stories about fidelity," she remembers, "he was jealous of me."[73] She remembers being "afraid of Saul. He could be very harsh in his judgment; in his condemnation about everybody." "Charming and funny," he could also be "condescending and cruel." What was clear to her by the second summer was that "he couldn't stay in a relationship, he couldn't remain faithful." He began visiting nearby Amagansett to receive as well as to send mail—from Arlette, Maggie assumed, or some other woman. Harold Rosenberg, Maggie's protector, "went after him for this. 'You *can't* do this when you have her living with you.'" The memory still rankles: "Why would he fool around? Why would he do that? How stupid! What would make him so destructive, to himself, to me?" During Adam's stay, he and Bellow flew to Martha's Vineyard for a brief visit with Daniel ("I flew from East Hampton in a chartered bumblebee with short wings, through a gale," he wrote in an undated letter to Dick Stern, "we were scared but in heaven. Then we got down on the ground to Daniel's cheers"). At the end of August, while Maggie stayed on in the Hamptons before the school term began, Bellow went off to Italy for a month, to stay at the Villa Serbelloni in Bellagio, on Lake Como, on a fellowship from the Rockefeller Foundation. Here he worked on *Sammler* and had an affair with the poet Louise Glück, who was then twenty-five. As Atlas tells it, quoting another guest at the Villa: "Before post-lunch coffee was served he approached Louise and asked her to show him the grounds. On which walk he kissed her. Fast work. They'd never met." Glück herself recalled Bellow's attentions as "based on the fact that I was nubile rather than intelligent." She was also struck by "something imperial in his manner." His seduction technique, she told Atlas, was "more literary than physical: He read to her from the manuscript of his new novel, and she read him a poem."[74]

Shortly after Bellow left for Italy, Maggie had a checkup and the doctor discovered a lump in her breast. She was taken to the hospital at Southampton by Saul Steinberg's wife, Hedda Sterne, and an operation was scheduled to remove the lump. That Bellow did not return to help her upset Maggie deeply. As she now sees it, "The man was cruel, selfish, and the minute you pressed him he was gone, you make any demands on him, he's off." Their correspondence at the time complicates that picture. On September 4, 1968, Bellow wrote to Maggie praising Bellagio: "It couldn't be better. The very bathroom is situated in a Romanesque tower. Everything is simply beautiful. I am beginning to recover from the flight." That night, he got her phone call telling of the discovery of the lump, and the next day wrote a brief note: "Dearest Maggie—This is very rough, but you can do it. You have the love of many people—it's not just me. You don't need to go through this alone. I know the doctor gave you a bad scare, but it's about two hundred to one that the tumor is benign. If you badly need me, I can fly back, but I will wait for news on Monday." On the telephone, Maggie had stressed to Bellow how alone she felt, and Bellow urged her "not to isolate yourself from friends—don't lose your head, honey. These will be four grim days. They have to be faced. That's not easy. But don't send people away. . . . I wish I were there with you, but since we've got the Atlantic between us I'll wait for the results of the biopsy. It should be just that, only that—a biopsy. Harold [Taylor, her friend, the former president of Sarah Lawrence] will advise you. Take his advice. Bless you, honey. Love, Saul."

On September 11, two days after the biopsy, Bellow had still not heard from Maggie. "Honey, tell me what happened. I was up all night Tue. praying I would not get a call, but this morning I am still in the dark, really. Send me a wire, at least, saying you're okay, if the thing was harmless. But don't lie to me. If it was not harmless I'll want to fly straight back." He wondered if she'd been getting his mail. Was it a good sign that he'd heard nothing? The next day, on September 12, Maggie wrote to say that she was still "a little dopey," still in pain from the operation, but that there was no cancer and she was back in her own bed. She had been terrified before the operation. A woman in the hospital had just had a breast and a leg amputated and "moaned and prayed out loud all night." The nurse who prepared her for the operation "started to shave the wrong breast and then almost cut off the nipple of the right one." Nevertheless, she'd grade her behavior "about 8 on a scale of 10." Although she had no family with her and he was not there, she was not alone the whole time. Friends from the Hamptons visited and brought food and "a beautiful white nightgown." The letter ends by thanking Bellow. He had "really stuck by me," "your name was the first thing I said when I came to in the recovery room." Now that there was no threat of cancer, she hoped he would "be able to concentrate on the novel a little better."

Over the next two days, she fell apart, or so a letter from Bellow of September 14 suggests. He had been short with her on the telephone, for which he apologized. "The reason was we had just had a phone conversation and I wasn't expecting it to be your call. I thought that certainly something had happened to one of the children, for why would anyone else call. And thinking it over, though I don't excuse myself, I think you did not do well to call me. I know your need is great, but this is no way to meet it. . . . You are in pain, yes, but you have just escaped a horrible operation. You don't have cancer. Instead of relief and gratitude you have—this [hysteria, presumably]. It's not good. Not good for you, not good for me. Don't you think, after all this time, that I feel for you, sympathize with you? Waiting here was hellish also. I went to talk to Dr. Bryant, the foundation's doctor here, about your prospects and I sat it out on Tuesday without sleep, or letting up in my panic waiting for an answer to my wire." She obviously needed comforting, but "to give the help you want I would have to come back." And what would that accomplish? "I *have* written, and we have spoken on the phone three times, or is it four, so it's not as if we haven't been in contact. As for your schoolwork, what can I do about it? If you're sick, what can you do? What can anyone do? That's not a thing to phone across the Atlantic about either. Please, Maggie, don't do that anymore, I beg you." He tells her to leave his belongings, including his car, in East Hampton; he'll deal with everything when he gets back. "I've been here now for two weeks and there are only two more, which I don't want to goof up. I want to get something out of them. It's not your fault that the first two haven't been ideal but now, if only for a bit, I want to turn off the heat. I've had a frightful letter from Sondra—just wicked, a horror." (This is the letter that prompted his denunciation of "the abuses I suffered at your hands," discussed in chapter 14 of *To Fame and Fortune*). The letter closes: "You know what our relationship is. It's not what you want, but it is a great deal. It is everything that I can make it. When I put my arms around you it is all there. You know I am YD [Your Darling]. And don't blame the US mails on me. Calm yourself. And honey, lay off the telephone."

In describing his time at Bellagio to Dave Peltz, in a letter of September 20, Bellow is tough and coarse. After the good news about the tumor "came hysterics: all kinds of transatlantic telephone oddities. Time out for sobbing. I thought the whales and the winds were talking to me. The Lord sent relief in the form of a wet dream or two. I've had no other. All my ladies seem furious. Not one of them has written, not even Bette [Howland]."[75] (When Bette did write, on September 24, 1968, she explained that she "didn't know you had gone to Italy alone, and therefore didn't realize that you really wanted mail. . . . I am very tactful with the little girls who call here—those who don't hang up in my face. I tell them that I don't know Mr. Bellow personally, that I am subletting his apartment from the University, and that they should leave their messages with the Committee. They are grateful for this, so grateful that they want to tell me all about you, not realizing of course that even to hear their names would be agony for me.") Around the same time, Arlette wrote (this is several months before the London trip), declaring, "Your being with Maggie was a horror for us. This is a basic fact." The angry letters they had exchanged over the summer and Bellow's refusal "to visit me even once" made her "physically sick": "Somehow I had given you the key to my sense of balance and happiness. I don't think you knew this. Perhaps you did—but it is important that you know it now." It is clear from this letter, dated September 23, 1968, that Arlette had not given up hope of their getting back together, and that Bellow was still involved with her. As for why Bette hadn't written, "she must have done research in my apartment and found sinful evidence. . . . I feel the hook down in my gullet, and I hear that old reel spinning."

In the letter to Peltz, Bellow reports: "Maggie's line with me now is that I must mark time while she tries to develop other interests, especially, she says, since she does this out of rejection and therefore I owe her perfect fidelity. Seeing her twice a month is perfectly adequate. I have no more real needs." On returning from Italy at the beginning of October, he discovered that Maggie did not want to see him at all, or said she didn't, although they continued to communicate in highly charged phone calls and letters. It was at this point that Bellow took up again with Arlette and invited her to come to London with him. Maggie's intensity was wearing him down, he claimed, and on December 9, 1968, he called for "an Armistice, a moratorium, some pause." He loved her and respected her and wished her every good, "but I am trying to save my sanity right now—just probably my very life. I feel it threatened. We must stop. I can't go on without a breather." In *A Theft*, Clara Velde describes a comparable retreat on the part of Teddy Regler: "I turned on so much power in those days, especially after midnight, my favorite time to examine my psyche—what love was; and death; and hell and eternal punishment. . . . All my revivalist emotions came out after one a.m., whole nights of tears, anguish and hysteria. I drove him out of his head" (p. 129).

WHEN ARLETTE DISTANCED HERSELF from Bellow after his return from London in February 1969, Bellow went back to Maggie. He was, she remembers, "desperate" to resume their relationship. He would ring up from the airport and ask to see her. "I can't, I'm seeing someone," she told him, "I need you out of my life." Once, he walked in a blizzard all the way from the Plaza Hotel to Fifteenth Street "to plead his case." The person Maggie was seeing was a young Frenchman, Jacques, "a figure of raw sexuality. . . . He was young and he was great and he was everything that Saul wasn't." One way he differed from Bellow was in personal hygiene ("Flower children are neither as innocent nor as loving as they pretend to be," Bellow told his friend Rosette Lamont, "and they mistake uncleanliness for holiness"[76]). Maggie describes Jacques in a way that recalls Jean-Claude, the young Frenchman Clara takes up with in *A Theft*. Jean-Claude "seldom washed. His dirt was so ingrained that she couldn't get him clean in the shower stall. She had to take a room in the Plaza to force him into the tub" (p. 130). Bellow "was *obsessed* with this guy," Maggie says of her French lover. When Maggie mentioned that Jacques was uncircumcised, Bellow "went nuts," pressing her for details, about size, shape, color, what he was like in bed, what they did there. When she read *Sammler*, Maggie immediately recognized that Bellow had turned her Frenchman into the black pickpocket. "In my mind," Bellow told her, "the pickpocket was this man." Why did he make him black, she asked? "You can use what you want," he answered.

Maggie's testimony suggests that personal history or biography, in the form of sexual jealousy and insecurity, fed into the novel's most controversial episode, charging or intensifying larger and more generalized concerns. Even at moments when Sammler considers the pickpocket's sexual display in its widest context, a note of authorial insecurity can be heard, as at the beginning of the following passage:

> In the past, Sammler had thought that in this same biological respect he was comely enough, in his own Jewish way. It had never greatly mattered and mattered less than ever now, in the seventies. But a sexual madness was overwhelming the Western world. Sammler even now vaguely recalled hearing that a President of the United States was supposed to have shown himself in a similar way to the representatives of the press (asking the ladies to leave), and demanding to know whether a man so well hung could not be trusted to run the country. The story was apocryphal, naturally, but it was not a flat impossibility, given the President, and what counted was that it should spring up and circulate so widely that it reached even the Sammlers in their West Side bedrooms [p. 53].

As Bellow's own sexual history suggests, neither authorial prurience nor repression underlaid Sammler's reaction to the "sexual madness" of the sixties and to female eroticism in particular. Bellow was never more promiscuous than during the sexual revolution the novel deplores. Nor is there anything like Sammler's language in Bellow's letters at this time. None of his letters to Arlette survives, but on the very rare occasions when his love letters to Maggie allude to the body and to sex they do so tenderly. "My pleasure in life," he writes on November 28, 1966, "to think about you. The white valentine. Face when making love. Hair when hands are raised to comb it. Teeth, lips, eyes, all music for my metronome." Maggie and Arlette are thinly and affectionately fictionalized in *Humboldt's Gift*, where their sexuality is a source of pleasure. "I inhaled her delicious damp," Charlie recalls of a morning in bed with Renata (described as "a grand girl," though "I couldn't see her behind my wheelchair" [p. 12]). As Renata secretly pleasures herself in public, when "the company annoyed or bored her," she looks at Charlie with "amusement" and "affection." "How easy and natural she made everything seem—goodness, badness, lustfulness. I envied her this." In describing the moment of climax, there is nothing of distaste. Charlie and Renata are in the Palm Court at the Plaza Hotel, with the oblivious Thaxter, a Botsford character. While Thaxter propounds his latest new scheme ("you'd get fifty thousand bucks on signing"), Renata is at work under the table. Charlie notes "the dilation of her eyes and the biological seriousness in which her fine joke ended. She went from fun to mirth to happiness and finally to a climax, her body straightening in the French provincial Palm Court chair. She nearly passed out with a fine long quiver. This was almost fishlike in its delicacy. Then her eyes shone at me" (p. 351).

Renata is praised by Charlie for her naturalness and vitality. She is very much a person at one with herself. As Charlie puts it, "Some people are so actual that they beat down my critical powers" (p. 347). But she isn't just or wholly a sex goddess, she's no mere idea or symbol. Like Ramona in *Herzog* or Katrina in "What Kind of Day Did You Have?" some part of Renata's sexual allure is worked up, a product of calculation (of what Charlie likes, his antique or French-maid notions of sexiness). "I didn't really believe it was all so natural or easy," Charlie admits. "I suspected—no, I actually *knew* better" (p. 351). In *Humboldt's Gift*, "the modern sexual ideology" is no panacea, "Programs of uninhibited natural joy could never free us from the universal tyranny of selfhood" (p. 39). But there is nothing disgusting about the female body here, none of the repugnance expressed in *Mr. Sammler's Planet*. In early versions, written while Bellow was still at work on *Sammler*, Renata is shown, in Daniel Fuchs's words, "in a light less flattering than that of the novel,"[77] but even in early versions she is associated with vitality, health, strength. In other works, moreover, as we've seen, female fleshiness is anything but disgusting. In "What Kind of Day Did You Have?" Katrina, Victor Wulpy's "manifest Eros," is described as "the full woman, perhaps the fat woman, woman-smelling";[78] Sorella, the heroine of *The Bellarosa Connection*, is courageous, clever, formidable, attractive, and massive: "The more I think of Sorella," the narrator says, "the more charm she has for me."[79] On the evidence of his writing, any feelings of disgust Bellow had about female physicality were more than matched by feelings of attraction. The unqualified repugnance Sammler, Elya, and Wallace express about women's bodies gives a transgressive power to the novel; Bellow means it to shock readers. But it also limits, according to Bellow's own standards. In *Sammler*, a "case" is being made against the culture of the day, and the novel's characters are made to fit the case, particularly the women characters; the fierceness or "fanaticism" of the case is not, in respect to the depiction of women, tamed by truth; there are no complicating, humanizing particulars in the characterization of Angela.[80] Hence Bellow's letter of April 10, 1974, to Daniel Fuchs, in which he claims, "*Sammler* isn't even a novel. It's a dramatic essay of some sort, wrung from me by the crazy Sixties."[81]

A DAY AFTER the coarse letter to Peltz, Bellow wrote warmly to Maggie. Two days later, on September 23, 1968, he asked her how her job was going. She was now teaching at a new school, one closer to where she lived, the Grace Church School in Lower Manhattan. Bellow also recounted the sad news of the death from cancer of his Tuley friend Lou Sidran, who had visited East Hampton that summer with his son, Ezra.[82] "Terrible things keep happening," Bellow writes from Bellagio; "from the peaceful mountains it's all like the plague, down below." After dinner the night before, sitting by the fire, one of the scholars, "John Marshall, Harvard 1921, told me I had meant a great deal to him. My books, and myself. Then he began to weep. He's such a decorous Wasp I hardly knew how to interpret this. He simply said that I was one of the people he loved. And he wept. I wept myself, partly at the oddity of human relations. That there should be so much to jump over—so much apparent difference or distance. And then, in people who are *not* old, whose flesh isn't dead, one could live a life of Harvard or Chicago (dateless horror, Chicago) until love reclaims one for reality."

In *Mr. Sammler's Planet*, it has been suggested, Bellow was unable or unwilling to jump over racial difference or distance, portraying the novel's sole black character as exclusively other, animal.[83] Like Angela, according to this line, the pickpocket is unclaimed for reality. What goes against such a reading is the novel's penultimate scene. In a rush of plot common in Bellow's fictions, Shula's ex-husband, the Israeli sculptor Eisen, attacks the pickpocket by smashing a bag of metal sculptures or medallions into his face. These medallions are made out of iron pyrites from the Dead Sea and depict "Stars of David, branched candelabra, scrolls and rams' horns, or inscriptions flaming away in Hebrew: *Nahamu!* 'Comfort ye!' Or God's command to Joshua: *Hazak!*" (later described as "the order God gave before Jericho, to Joshua: 'Strengthen thyself' ") (pp. 139–40). Sammler is horrified:

> "Don't hit him, Eisen. I never said that. I tell you no!" said Sammler.
>
> But the bag of weights was speeding from the other side, very wide but accurate. It struck more heavily than before and knocked the man down. He did not drop. He lowered himself as though he had decided to lie in the street. The blood ran in points on his cheek. The terrible metal had cut him through the baize [p. 241].

What enters the novel at this moment, as the dazed pickpocket lowers himself to the street, is a long history of African American suffering, a link between the black man and the Jew. What also enters the novel, in the symbolic person of Eisen, is Bellow's warning of the dangers not only of fear and fury but of "realism," the line Eisen takes in his defense: "You can't hit a man like this just once. When you hit him you must really hit him. Otherwise he'll kill you. You know. You fought in the war. You were a Partisan. You had a gun. So don't you know?" This reasoning "sunk Sammler's heart completely" (pp. 241–42). The passage is aimed not only at intransigent Israelis and despairing artists, but at Sammler and at Bellow himself. Sammler because it recalls what is now a moment of shame, when he killed an unarmed German soldier in the Zamosht Forest: "'Don't kill me,'" cried the soldier. "'I have children.' Sammler pulled the trigger" (p. 114). Bellow, provoked and dismayed by increasing tensions in the late sixties between blacks and Jews, especially in Chicago, home of the Black Muslims and other Black Power separatists, by outlaw worship, youth worship, and intellectual primitivism, pulls back from hatred at the end, as does the mature Artur Sammler. Having survived the horror of the Holocaust, the murder of so many Jews, including his wife, at the hands of the Nazis, Sammler

Maggie Staats in New York, late 1960s (courtesy of Maggie Staats Simmons)

takes pleasure in giving in to hatred. When he killed the German soldier, "his heart felt lined with brilliant, rapturous satin." The feeling is addictive: "When he shot again it was less to make sure of the man than to try again for that bliss. To drink more flames. He would have thanked God for this opportunity. If he had had any God. At that time, he did not. For many years, in his own mind, there was no judge but himself" (p. 115). In describing the novel's sole black character as an animal, and disparaging blacks in several passing references, Sammler dehumanizes a race, as the Nazis dehumanized Jews. Sammler's talk of "sexual niggerhood" (p. 133) recalls Nazi talk of "instinctive" Jewish licentiousness, what Adam Kirsch, alluding to Sammler's phrase, calls "sexual Jewhood."[84] Eisen's attack on the pickpocket puts such talk and the hatred that breeds it into focus, partially redeeming both Sammler and his creator.

3

Bad Behavior

EARLY IN 1969, after hearing of Arlette's decision to break with Bellow, Barley Alison sent him a letter of consolation:

> I am really sad about Arlette—I liked her and thought she probably did have a soul tucked away somewhere. . . . But you are not lucky in your choice of women are you? Perhaps you should take up cards? I am not suggesting that it will prove an acceptable substitute, but merely that, with your present record, it should prove immensely financially profitable and enable you to keep more wives in the style to which they hope to become accustomed. No wonder you are upset about Arlette and no wonder that you cannot go straight on with the book you were writing when you were together in London. You did have a premonition that she was not going to prove very durable, however, didn't you? And for all I know, you may have got her back again by now. Or replaced her?[1]

He'd not got her back. He'd got Maggie Staats back. She returned to Bellow sometime that February, having split up with her French lover. But Maggie lived in New York, and in the spring Bellow started an affair with a woman in Chicago, a recently divorced faculty wife, like Arlette. Her name was Frances Gendlin, and she, too, had married young, at seventeen, "just on the cusp of women's liberation." Frances had met her husband, Eugene Gendlin, at the University of Chicago, when she was an undergraduate and he was a graduate student. After they married, he took a job at the University of Wisconsin at Madison, where he taught for five years. In 1963, he was offered a joint appointment in philosophy and psychology at the University of Chicago, and in 1968, the year Frances and Bellow met, she and her family were living in a house at Fifty-eighth and Dorchester, just across the street from the Cloisters. In suburban Madison, Frances had been bored. She took up gourmet cooking, she took flying lessons, like Katrina Goliger in "What Kind of Day Did You Have?" In Hyde Park, she found life more stimulating. She was hired as managing editor of *Psychotherapy: Theory, Research and Practice*, her husband's journal (later, she would edit the *Bulletin of the Atomic Scientists* and *Sierra* magazine). She took courses in Freud and had Italian lessons. "I wasn't a subservient wife anymore."

Frances and Bellow had met at a Christmas party. He was sitting by himself, and the first thing he said to her was "'Tell me what you do to take care of those handsome legs?' So I said, 'Well it's a grave responsibility.' I realized who he was, and we talked the whole evening. We flirted. It was nice. It made me feel different about myself." Bellow asked Frances if she wanted to go to Mexico with him: "It was clearly nonsense." The flirtation, though, was not idle; Frances's marriage was unhappy and would soon be over. At a later party, which she went to alone, "I was walking up the steps and Saul and David [Peltz] were walking down them, and I said, 'Why are you leaving just when I'm coming?' And he laughed, but it was clear that we were both interested in each other." Some months later, before Bellow went off to Italy for a second stay at Bellagio, he pulled his car over to chat. "I said, 'Where are you going, can I come along?' And that's when it started." A few weeks later, Eugene Gendlin moved out: "He had found someone else." When Bellow flew to Austin in late March, to consult with Botsford over their magazine, Frances accompanied him. While he was at Bellagio, she went to Rome for a week's vacation. Although she didn't visit him, they spoke on the telephone. Bellow was working steadily on *Mr. Sammler's Planet*. "Toil until 3 P.M.," he wrote to Maggie, "then tennis, a drink, dinner and a book in bed." On his return to Chicago in September, Bellow called Frances and asked, "'Are you divorced?' and I said, 'Not yet,' and he said, 'Well, I can't go out with a married woman.'" When told that she and Gendlin had separated, however, Bellow was reassured. "Then we had an affair for six years."

AFTER BELLOW'S SECOND STAY at Bellagio, Maggie and Adam joined him in London, where he had rented a house for three weeks from June 22, 1969. Father, son, and girlfriend were together for the first two weeks. In week three, Maggie and Bellow left for Casa Alison, Barley's house in Carboneras in Andalusia, and Adam was joined in London by Sasha. "If you think we can trust Sondra not to break any lousy dishes," Bellow had written to Maggie from Bellagio on June 7, 1969, "she is welcome to finish out week III, while we escape." The house Bellow rented was in Putney, near the Fulham Road. It had three cramped stories and three bedrooms. Adam was "wildly excited" at the prospect of the visit. At twelve, "I already knew more about England than I did about my own country. My Anglophile mother had brought me up on English children's classics. She dressed me up for school in white buttondowns and gray flannel pants, as though I were going to Harrow, not Tarrytown Elementary. . . . She read to me from the Cambridge Shorter History of the Eighth Century and fed me a steady diet of Chaucer, Malory, Scott and historical novels about the Black Prince and the boyhood of Alfred the Great."

These quotations come from a five-page, single-spaced typescript, "A Mug, a Map, and a Brush," written by Adam about a year after Bellow's death.[2] While going through old papers, Adam had come across a diary he'd kept during the London visit. "Written in smudged pencil, the pages covered in a loopy childlike scrawl, it betrayed (among other things) a boyish obsession with minutiae like what time of day we went out, which buses we took, and what everything cost in pounds and shillings." The diary led Adam to reflect on his feelings about his father. At twelve, he writes, he had anticipated the trip as "a sort of Arthurian quest. I had grown up thinking of myself as an exiled prince, stranded in the suburbs of Westchester and Long Island. My father, the famous writer, was the king. Surely one day he would summon me to court, knight me, and acknowledge me as his heir." Arthurian legend deeply stirred Adam. In seventh grade, he recounted in an interview, he'd written his own version of the legend, taking "the point of view of Guinevere—Saul was Arthur, Jack [Ludwig, Sasha's lover] was Lancelot." His propensity to fantasize was fed by how little he knew of his father's life. He had, he writes in the memoir, "no idea" what Bellow was doing in London. "His comings and goings were a mystery to me, and I had never dreamed of asking him about them. Not only was he much older than other boys' fathers, but he was now an international celebrity, and I had gotten used to his jetting off to Europe at the drop of a hat." Bellow and Sasha had separated when Adam was two, after which he saw his father "only intermittently on visits to New York and school vacations." The two-week visit to London "would be our longest to date." Although Bellow was "always affectionate" on these visits, he could also be "remote and intimidating, frequently erupting in anger at my mother." "The lack of familiarity between father and son was unsettling for both of us."

Botsford and his family were in England that summer, and he and Bellow picked Adam up at Heathrow Airport. On the drive to town, Adam sat in the backseat while the two adults conversed, "making no effort to include me." Both men, Adam came later to realize, had a "bohemian" attitude to children: "They were to be liberally begotten, raised by maternal-sexy wives, and treated with benign neglect until their minds had matured enough to be somewhat interesting." The following day, Bellow walked Adam to the Thames. It was at low tide and looked and smelled "like a sewer." Then they went to tea with Bellow's literary agent in Dover Street. After tea, father and son walked to Buckingham Palace, where Adam was disappointed that there was no changing of the guard. Next they went to Westminster Abbey, where Bellow pointed out the memorials of famous men, mostly writers, and they bought postcards. They returned to the house in Putney in time to pick Maggie up for dinner at the Botsfords'. "That, it turned out, was the most active sightseeing day of the week." Much of the rest of the visit was spent "shopping, doing errands, taking his friend Ed Shils to the airport, and browsing in bookstores while my father met with his publisher or talked to someone from the BBC." All the entries in his journal, Adam notes, "begin at 1:00 PM because nothing ever happened before that"; the mornings were reserved for writing. In the afternoons, "I was either brought along or left to my own devices, wandering the streets of a foreign city for hours on end."

After describing himself as wandering the city alone, Adam mentions a tour to the Tower of London, a boat ride to Westminster, a visit to the British Museum to see the manuscripts ("I was fascinated by a scrap of paper with the handwriting of the eight-year-old Princess Victoria"), a day trip to Stonehenge and Salisbury, including a tour of the cathedral, and "a meal of venison at the local inn, stimulating visions of myself at Sherwood Forest," but the impression that predominates is of neglect. The story behind the memoir's title, "A Map, a Mug, and a

Brush," contributes to this impression. Before leaving for London, Sasha gave Adam a list of souvenirs to purchase, including a Kent hairbrush, an antique map of England, and a pewter mug. She also instructed him not to tell his father "that it was *she* who wanted these things, otherwise [he] wouldn't buy them." It was only with great reluctance that Bellow gave in to Adam's nagging about the souvenirs. The pewter mugs Adam dragged him to see were always too expensive. Grudgingly, Bellow agreed to buy a fifteen-dollar Kent brush at Harrods. At the British Museum, "he surprised me by springing for a handsome reproduction of a sixteenth-century map of southern England." This map, Adam now believes, Maggie shamed Bellow into buying. "Over the years I had relied upon an ever-changing cast of wives and girlfriends to act as intermediaries," he writes, "and Maggie in particular had stood, like Hamlet's mother, 'between much heat' and me."[3]

Relations between Bellow and Maggie were not always easy in London. There were fights and *froideurs*. When descending the narrow staircase in Putney, Maggie stepped into an alcove, assumed an Attic pose, and said, "Look, I could actually fit in here." To which Bellow replied, "Why, then you'd be a bitch in a niche," a remark Herschel Shawmut might have uttered in "Him with His Foot in His Mouth." Maggie refused to speak to him for the rest of the day. That whole summer, Bellow was tightly wound, as if affected by the emotions powering *Sammler*. When with his sons, he did not hide his anger or irritation. "It is difficult always to be the jolly, uncritical paternal chum," Bellow wrote to Sasha in a letter of November 2, 1966, when upbraided for telling Adam off. "When I think he is doing wrong, now and then, I feel that I must correct him." Never, he claimed, did he do so "harshly or angrily." Adam was "a gentle, marvelous little boy," his "unusually good manners . . . do you credit." But he "occasionally gives me the Little Prince bit. Generally, I let it pass. This time it was a bit much. It is not for Adam to tell me that he does not wish to continue a discussion."[4]

Adam ends the memoir by listing the most important things he learned from his father. "I now believe I got the best—the very best—of what my father had to offer . . . a habit of mind, a way of looking at the world, a feeling for language, and an irreverent attitude toward reigning intellectual authorities." On this and later visits, he began to learn more about his father's way of life, including his domestic habits and tastes, his sense of himself as a man. Like Abraham, Bellow was handy in the house. He liked to mend things, Adam recalled in an interview;

he liked to wash dishes and clean up. When living as a bachelor, "he was perfectly capable of doing all the housework on his own." He liked to cook and feed people. In addition to spaghetti sauce and carefully prepared but undrinkable coffee, he made good chili, cooked a good steak. He liked bourbon and he liked wine at dinner, though Adam never saw him drunk. He liked certain Jewish foods: black bread, pickled herring, smoked whitefish. He was a careful shopper. A friend recalls his taking forever to choose steaks at the market, closely inspecting each cut, making sure the marbling was just right. He read "a million things at once." He was a good driver, and after the success of *Herzog* he bought expensive cars (Mercedes, Land Rover, BMW). He kept in shape and was physically active. When confronted or challenged, "he would have words with anybody, he would not stifle himself. . . . But he would not look for trouble. He was not a high-testosterone type."

On holiday with Maggie in Carboneras, after a few blissful days in the Netherlands, Bellow was in a bad mood. Barley Alison had found a nearby villa for him to rent, but when he'd done his morning's writing, he and Maggie spent much of the day at Casa Alison. Barley's guests that July were the literary agent Toby Eady; the novelist Margaret Drabble and her husband, Clive Swift, an actor; their three young children; a businessman named David Erskine, an old friend of Barley's; and his younger lover, David Manson. There was much joking about young versus old during the holiday. Bellow, Barley, and David Erskine were twenty or more years older than the other guests, and the joking, according to Maggie, "hurt Saul's vanity."[5] While Barley and the young people stayed up late (Barley was an insomniac, said her friend the agent Gillon Aitken), Bellow retired early, having to write in the morning. If disturbed while writing, he could be "brutal and imperious," once ordering Maggie to tell the maid not to sing while he was working. He was also "incredibly jealous" during the holiday, especially of Toby Eady, with whom he thought Maggie was flirting. One evening, after drinks on the terrace at Casa Alison, as the party headed inside for dinner, Bellow held Maggie back and slapped her so hard in the face "you could see the impact of his hand . . . all through the meal." In recalling the incident over the telephone forty-five years later, Eady could barely contain himself. "I think he's a complete shit," he said. "The only man in my life who I have seen hit a woman . . . Having hit her, he made her sit through dinner."[6] That night, Bellow also made Maggie write a note to Barley, apologizing for flirting. In the morning, Maggie remembers, Barley came down to the villa and "just tore him apart for it, went after him." She told him, "'Maggie has perfect manners. I can't believe you've done this. She is always invited to my house; don't do this again, and don't come to lunch.' And he didn't come to lunch. It was so bad." Maggie tried to leave, threatening at one point to stab Bellow with a scissors if he didn't let her go, but she was persuaded to stay.

Bellow alludes to the Casa Alison stay in a 103-page handwritten novel fragment titled "Rita manuscript" and dated "summer '90."[7] "Rita," the central character, is clearly modeled on Barley Alison, who died in 1989. On the first page of the manuscript, we are told by the narrator, Harold Halsband, that after Rita's death "her family in their unobtrusive insistent London way were after me to write something about her. Not an obit (I am not a journalist) but a memoir or reminiscence to be published privately. They appealed to me as an old friend, which indeed I was." Halsband is a biographer, like many writers in Bellow's fiction, and he shares much of Bellow's history with women. Rita is keen for him to marry "Thalia," a fictionalized portrait of Alexandra Ionescu Tulcea, Bellow's fourth wife, whom he brought to Casa Alison in 1974, in part to be vetted by Barley. "You must do it," Rita insists, which surprises Halsband:

> "Why *must*?"
>
> "She's altogether different from your wives and the girls I've seen you with. What a procession of dogs. The one exception was Maudie, a delightful girl of real character—whom you humiliated."
>
> "I had no idea. You never said so, Rita."
>
> "I didn't wish to interfere, then, but I thought you were unforgivable, Harold. A respectable, handsome and intelligent girl who followed you making no demands for marriage and had the courage to hold her head up under disgraceful circumstances" [pp. 63–64].

Halsband tries to defend himself: "You accept irregularities of all sorts in your circle. . . . Ferocious mad millionaires and young aristocrats running around in silk chemises, copulating in small airplanes with other girls' husbands . . . You accept them as you accept Elliot [a homosexual] and his friends." When Rita expresses relief that Maudie "gave you up," "had enough sense to marry an upright Wall Street man. She has proper treatment at last," Halsband again protests. She then alludes to a summer at her house in southern Spain when "you were composing your Wild Bill book here." (Halsband has written books on Lady Mary Wortley Montagu and the Duc de Vendôme as well as Wild Bill Hickok.) Maudie "would go around the district asking neighbors not to play the radio in the morning because it disturbed your work, and she had no more Spanish than I have." "Maudie did that?" Harold asks. "I was unaware of it" (p. 65).

Relations between Rita and Halsband recall those between Barley Alison and Bellow. "Considering your social origins you've done extremely well, and I expect you to become eventually a very distinguished person," Rita tells Halsband. "You've got excellent instincts, you're good looking, and when you're not boorish you can be most considerate—less with women, I'm afraid, than with personal friends" (p. 67). Barley had similar expectations for Bellow, as suggested in a letter of July 23, 1974:

> I am tetchy and give you a "hard time" (as you describe it) partly because I feel close to you and know you will forgive me, partly because I do love and admire you extravagantly and want you to be *my* idea of perfection (though I allow others to be human and fallible I cannot accept this in a man of your genius. . . . I am afraid I shall always want your character and judgment to be as flawless as your prose). . . . I will continue to criticise you, of course, since I hope that *some* of my bossy, governessy advice is actually useful (being tougher with Susan, letting your family advise on business and legal matters, *not* marrying as soon as you were shed of Susan, marrying Alexandra as soon as possible, etc. . . .) and I hope you know that, underneath the porcupine prickles, I really love you very dearly, and am deeply committed to *your* best interests. (And I *am* ashamed that I criticise you in front of others and determined never to do so again.)

Early in their relationship, Rita, an agent, wants Halsband as a lover or husband as well as an author. Were he to marry her, she would cater to his every need—professional, domestic, erotic. Halsband, however, for unspecified reasons, "could never have made love to Rita. I never did make love to her. I did love her, though. She was dear to me" (p. 6). Rita remains devoted to Harold, despite his rejection of her as a lover. He trusts her advice, even when it takes the form of rebuke. Barley was comparably devoted to Bellow; she "absolutely adored him," according to Rosie Alison, her niece, who added, "She liked difficult, creative men who she could give herself to intensely." In a letter of June 12, 1989, to Michael Alison, Barley's brother, written shortly after her death, Bellow describes her as "a dear and generous friend and one of the most generous persons I ever knew."[8]

AT THE END OF JULY, Maggie and Bellow went their separate ways. Bellow's old girlfriend Rosette Lamont arranged for him to rent an apartment in August on Sunset Hill on Nantucket, not far from her summer cottage. Rosette was now married to Frederick Farmer, her second husband, but she kept a framed photograph of Bellow in the cottage inscribed "*à ma chère cousine*." When five-year-old Daniel came to stay with his father for a summer visit, Bellow spent his time "dealing with little boys, ex-wives, lawyers, fishhooks in the fingers, sunburn, car rentals."[9] To Richard Stern, in a letter of August 1, 1969, he described his time in Europe: "Maggie caused me *grandes dificultades* in England and in the south, but I finished [*Sammler*] just the same. I am obstinate." Three days later, he wrote to Maggie to put off a proposed visit to Nantucket. "It seems too soon. Europe has left me with still raw hurts, not likely to heal in a short time. I don't want them reopened, nor do I want you to be hurt again, and my heart tells me to let things ride, to recover first and not to force anything. For the sake of continuing friendship, we ought to keep away from each other." Maggie came anyway, and described the visit as "a disaster."

They did not see each other again until early December, a separation that was difficult for Maggie. "I had no way to get away from him, I couldn't escape this guy"—they would break up, get back together, break up again. "It kept going like that. There was always somebody else. I'd just get out the door and he'd pull me back." Early in November, Maggie had an operation that kept her in the hospital for nearly two weeks. When Bellow came to New York at the end of the month, partly to look for property to buy in the Hamptons, they saw each other again. He stayed at first at the Hotel Meurice, and Maggie went there to pick up a suitcase for him. In addition to the suitcase, she was passed a phone message that had been left for Bellow. It was from Frances Gendlin. That night, at Maggie's apartment, she and Bellow "had a rip-roaring fight and he stormed out." Maggie, very upset, fell apart completely. In despair, she called Sasha, who in turn called Bellow. Maggie's psychiatrist later ordered Bellow neither to see nor to call her, orders she believes "saved" her. They did not meet again for some nine months. At Barley's invitation, Maggie returned the next summer to Carboneras, this time staying on her own at Casa Alison. In August, after attending Gregory's wedding in San Francisco, Bellow returned to Nantucket, spending part of the month there with Adam ("in the end Adam condescended—he gave his hand like a princess"[10]). When the Nantucket stay was over, he went to New York for a few days, where he saw Maggie, then returned to Chicago. In a letter written on September 27, 1970, almost a month after the meeting, Bellow wrote to say, "I was delighted to see you looking so well and talking so sensibly and the affection we felt for each other was a great improvement over states we've known. Barley wrote a letter of pure praise; she loves you dearly and wants you to come to London." A year and a bit later, in December 1971, Maggie married her first husband, Paul Brodeur, the *New Yorker* science writer. Three years later, the marriage was over and she was married to Nico Rozos, a Greek shipping magnate. Maggie remembers receiving a telephone call from Bellow in 1974, when she and Rozos were in the Hamptons. "I've written this book," he announced, "and you need to know about it." It was *Humboldt's Gift*, with its loving and laudatory portrait of Demmie Vonghel. The fight that led to her breakdown, Maggie believes, had "filled him with guilt, made me an angel."

In *A Theft* (1989), Bellow offers a fictional expansion of these events. Clara Velde, the Maggie figure, begins to assert herself "unreasonably," or so her lover, Ithiel Regler, believes. Ithiel, a Washington foreign-policy adviser, "told himself it would be a bad precedent to let her control him with her fits." It is Clara who is jealous, not Ithiel. "They had bad arguments—'It was a mistake not to let him sleep'—and after a few oppressive months, he made plans to leave the country with yet another of his outlandish lady friends" (p. 132). When Ithiel's ex-wife, Etta, lets Clara know he's in New York, about to fly off with the lady friend, Clara takes a cab to the hotel where she's been told he's staying, identifies herself as his wife, says he sent her, and checks him out, paying his bill and taking his luggage. "She waited until after dark, and he turned up at about seven o'clock. Cool with her, which meant that he was boiling." They fight—"Where do you get off, pulling this on me?"—and Ithiel storms out with his suitcase. "'Don't go now,'" Clara pleads, "'I'm in a bad way. I love you with my soul.' She said it again, when the door swung shut after them" (p. 133). Later that night, in the new hotel he's checked into, Etta, the ex-wife, calls Ithiel to say Clara has attempted suicide. At the hospital, Clara's minister (not her psychiatrist) informs Ithiel that "she had no wish to see him, and had no wish to hear from him, ever." "After a day of self-torment," Ithiel cancels his trip abroad, fends off the sympathy of his ex-wife, "avid to hear about his torments" (p. 135), and returns home. He accepts none of the "handy fixes" about suicide (as "power move," "punitive," "the drama of rescue") offered by friends:

> You could tell yourself such things; they didn't mean a damn. In all the world, now, there wasn't a civilized place left where a woman would say, "I love you with my soul." Only this backcountry girl was that way still. If no more mystical sacredness remained in the world, she hadn't been informed yet. Straight-nosed Ithiel, heading for Washington and the Capitol dome, symbolic of a nation swollen with world significance, set a greater value on Clara than on anything in *this* place, or any place. He thought, This is what I opted for, and this is what I deserve. . . . I got what I had coming [pp. 134, 135].

For all Bellow's "unforgivable" behavior (Rita's word, used of Halsband), Maggie shared with him a sense of soulful connection, the sense Clara feels for Ithiel. "I am *his* truest friend," Clara says of Ithiel, "and he understands that and responds emotionally" (p. 155). "It had become a permanent connection," Maggie says of her relationship with Bellow, one that lasted "till he died."

MAGGIE IS NOT SURE WHY she contacted Sasha after Bellow stormed off. Sasha was "more worldly, a little older, more of the mother role, and clearly I must have identified with her at this point." In an interview, Sasha described Maggie as "a good-hearted person," "very broken-up" after the separation with Bellow. The two women had first met in January 1968, at the French consulate in New York, when Bellow received his Croix de Chevalier des Arts et des Lettres. Sasha's initial impression of Maggie was that she was "very cute, but ditzy, off the wall." Although "never a beauty," she was "so sexy" ("one after another," men fell for her). Later, Sasha realized that Maggie was not only "very, very smart" but "highly organized" (like Frances Gendlin, Maggie would later work at magazines, first as features editor of *Condé Nast Traveler*, then as editor in chief of *Travel Holiday*); she was quite capable of taking charge of Bellow ("That, to him, was love," Sasha claimed). Maggie also deserved credit, Sasha felt, for helping to smooth relations not only between father and son but between father and ex-wife. That Susan was "pinning him to the wall, big time, over money," played its part as well; Susan had taken the baton from Sasha as demon wife.[11]

When Sasha and Adam moved from Great Neck to the Upper West Side, and Adam enrolled in the Dalton School, where Susan had once taught, Bellow willingly paid Dalton's fees (it helped that he'd been unhappy with Adam's schooling in Great Neck). In addition, he paid the costs for Adam's bar mitzvah on March 7, 1970, and for further Hebrew lessons (Adam had been learning Hebrew since he was nine). Sasha "signed Adam up" at the Park Avenue Synagogue and made all the arrangements for the reception, which was held at their apartment on West End Avenue. She ordered smoked fish and other delicacies from Zabar's and cooked "pots and pots" of food. Sam, the younger of Bellow's two brothers, with his wife, Nina, came, but Maury's side of the family was not invited. Anita did not come, nor did Susan—Adam suspects they weren't invited—or Maggie or Greg ("mad at me because Saul had given him his version," presumably of the breakup, and/or fights about money). Nearly the entire congregation of the synagogue turned out for the bar mitzvah, as many as a thousand people, Sasha estimated. Everyone wanted to see the famous author and his son.

THE FAMOUS AUTHOR HAD BEEN much in the news. On February 1, 1970, five weeks before the bar mitzvah, *Mr. Sammler's Planet* appeared in book form, having previously been published in its entirety in two installments of *The Atlantic* (November and December 1969). The novel's critical reception was mixed, but the critics agreed about Bellow's standing in American literature, a consensus summed up by Joseph Epstein in "Saul Bellow of Chicago," a profile in *The New York Times Book Review* (May 9, 1971):

> Saul Bellow is the premier American novelist: the best writer we have in the literary form that has been dominant in the literature of the past hundred years. He has come to his eminence not through

> the mechanics of publicity, self-advertisement or sensationalism, but through slowly building up a body of work, an oeuvre, that with each new novel has displayed greater range, solidity, penetration and brilliance.

The funding foundations, universities, and honorary societies agreed. In May 1969, Bellow was elected a Fellow of the American Academy of Arts and Sciences in Boston. In September, the Rockefeller Foundation gave him money to start a new magazine with Botsford. In October, he was appointed to the Salk Foundation's Council for Biology in Human Affairs (along with James Watson, Jonas Salk, and Jacques Monod, among others). In June 1970, he received an honorary degree from NYU (in a ceremony unflatteringly described in December 1970 in what would prove the sole issue of his and Botsford's new magazine, *Anon*[12]) and was flown to Israel as a guest of the English Department of the Hebrew University of Jerusalem. In Tel Aviv, he was the main speaker at a symposium sponsored by the U.S. Cultural Center, answering questions from a panel of distinguished Israeli writers, including A. B. Yehoshua and Yehuda Amichai. In Jerusalem, he attended a banquet with Golda Meir and Elie Wiesel, commemorating the twenty-fifth anniversary of the liberation of Bergen-Belsen. In March 1971, *Mr. Sammler's Planet* won the National Book Award, Bellow's third. In May, Cornell University gave him an honorary degree. In September, he was elected a member of the American Academy of Arts and Letters.[13] A year later, in June 1972, he received honorary degrees from Yale and Harvard.

There were also personal tributes, including one Bellow received from a woman named Gusta W. Frydman, a New York psychotherapist born in Poland and living on the Upper West Side, "a graduate of Nazism and a Soviet labor camp." Reading *Sammler*, she wrote to Bellow on March 16, 1970, made her "profoundly grateful. . . . You are a testimony to the survival of our sad race." The letter ends with a query: "I noticed that your Sammler occasionally talks seriously to men, but never to women. Why?" Bellow answered on April 1. He "greatly appreciated" Frydman's letter and "was particularly touched by the 'survival of our sad race.'" As for "the unserious conversations Mr. Sammler has with women, I too find them regrettable and I wish I had been able to imagine a woman equal to him in stature. One of these days perhaps I will get lucky." Few if any of Bellow's male characters are "equal" to

Sammler in moral or intellectual stature, though whether his male and female characters are equally unequal, or one accepts his weighting of Sammler in the first place, are different questions.

Gusta W. Frydman was not the only female reader to question Bellow about the depiction of women in *Mr. Sammler's Planet*. Edith Tarcov was especially upset about the character of Margotte Arkin, Sammler's niece. Margotte's intellectual and political views are dismissed by Sammler as "ridiculous" impersonations of the views of her deceased husband, Ussher, Sammler's friend, to whose memory she is devoted. Edith Tarcov was devoted to the memory of her deceased husband, Oscar Tarcov, Bellow's friend, and she had a sister named Margot, whose name she pronounced "Margotte," from the German original. After Oscar's death, Edith took on work as a freelance editor, was, as mentioned earlier, managing editor of Irving Howe's magazine, *Dissent*, and wrote successful children's books, including versions of several Grimm's fairy tales. ("My sister and I still get a few thousand dollars a year through them," Nathan Tarcov told me in 2008.) The character of Margotte is "devoid of wickedness," but she is a high-minded bore, "full of German wrongheadedness," "a bothersome creature, willing, cheerful, purposeful, maladroit" (p. 13), on the "right side, the best side, of every big human question: for creativity, for the young, for the black, for the poor, the oppressed, for victims, for sinners, for the hungry" (p. 15).

Reading about Margotte left Edith Tarcov feeling, in her son's words, "humiliated and exposed." He remembers her saying she felt she "couldn't go outside—people would be laughing at her—and I think she didn't speak to him for a while." When Bellow learned that Edith was upset, he offered "some sort of apology or reconciliation," but this placating was less important than Edith's just "getting over it," accepting that "it wasn't all that terrible." Terrible or not, dismissing the views of women like Margotte wasn't uncommon. As Nathan puts it, "Women of that generation involved in intellectual circles . . . *weren't* taken very seriously by the men." As he also points out, the connections between the fictional Arkins and the real-life Tarcovs were "much more explicitly marked than many of the cases where characters are partly modeled after someone." In later years, however, Bellow arranged for Edith to edit *The Portable Saul Bellow* (1973), and as their correspondence about the volume suggests, he took her opinions seriously.

BELLOW KNEW THAT his reactions were often out of control in the late 1960s and early 1970s. On March 14, 1970, he wrote to William Maxwell, at the time president of the American Academy and National Institute of Arts and Letters, declining an invitation to deliver the organization's annual Blashfield Address. Although "greatly honored" by the invitation, he was in altogether the wrong state to compose such an address: "For the past two weeks I have been writing a polemical essay—*Contra Tutti*. It is intemperate and names names. I've worked myself into a bad mood. . . . If you had asked for fulminations, for wickedness, I'd have been able to accept."[14] The previous spring, according to Atlas, Bellow had sought help for his moods, entering into therapy with Heinz Kohut, an Austrian-born psychoanalyst and past president of the American Psychoanalytic Association. Bellow had known Kohut for some years and may have been treated by him earlier. Among the Bellow Papers in the Regenstein is a postcard from Kohut dated September 3, 1966, written from California, asking Bellow if he would be in Chicago on October 3. There are also bills for "professional services" dated November and December 1966, at the time when Bellow left Susan, and when he was involved with Maggie and others. Whether the services in question were for Bellow or Susan is unclear. In the spring of 1969, when Bellow again turned to Kohut, he was living in an eleventh-floor Cloisters apartment directly opposite Kohut's apartment. To Atlas, Bellow described their sessions as "more literary than professional." Kohut was interested in art and literature and admired Bellow's writing. He had also begun questioning traditional analytic views. In *The Analysis of the Self: A Systematic Approach to the Treatment of Psychoanalytic Narcissistic Personality Disorder* (1971), his best-known book, Kohut deplores the narrow focus of traditional psychoanalysis on drives and internal conflicts, stressing instead the role played in character development by environmental and cultural factors, including relationships. Unlike many orthodox analysts, he was willing not just to acknowledge the role of deliberate or conscious thought and decision in behavior but to take it into account.[15] Bellow would also have approved Kohut's related view of artistic creation: as balance or integration, of inner and outer, perceiving subject and perceived object, rather than as unconscious wish fulfillment.[16]

Bellow's main problems in the late 1960s were not with art but with women, as well as with children, students, editors, and publishers. "I learned to organize my daily life for a single purpose," Bellow wrote to Hyman Slate, looking back on his earlier behavior, in a letter of July 22, 1980. "There *was* one other drive, the sexual one, but even that presently gave way [Bellow writes in the sixth year of his marriage to Alexandra Tulcea, wife number four]. My erotic life was seriously affected, too, in that I diverted myself with a kind of executive indiscriminateness—without a proper interest in women." What caused him to consult Kohut, he told Atlas, was "a period of turmoil," by which he seems to have meant in the nation as well as personally, producing in him extremes of jealousy, paranoia, anger, and aggression. Atlas quotes him as playing down his treatment with Kohut, whom he claims to have seen "only a few times."[17] Kohut left no records of their sessions, but Atlas conjectures that Bellow may have been the model for a patient Kohut describes in one of his books, *How Does Analysis Cure?* (1984). This patient, "Mr. I," is a professor, not a writer, and suffers from "a *Don Juan* syndrome," described as "the attempt to provide an insecurely established self with a continuous flow of self-esteem." Whether Kohut offered such a diagnosis to Bellow, and if so how Bellow responded to it, cannot be known. For Kohut, Mr. I's problem was narcissism, a product of lack of empathy, poor attachment, in particular in relation to the mother. His chasing of women was "motivated not by libidinal but by narcissistic need," the result of poor parenting. He had a "self-absorbed, attention-demanding father [who] had actively belittled and ridiculed him," which could also be said of Bellow; whether Bellow's mother was like Mr. I's mother ("joyless, guilt-producing"), as Atlas suggests, is harder to accept, though the adolescent Bellow could not face the reality of her illness, and as a consequence felt guilty as well as bereft when she died (his reaction is discussed in chapter 4 of *To Fame and Fortune*). Bellow himself says nothing about narcissism in describing his behavior in the late 1960s. His womanizing was a product of the times, of the sexual revolution deplored in *Sammler*. "It was terribly destructive to me; I took it as entitlement, the path to being a free man."[18]

ONE WAY FOR BELLOW to deal with his problems, particularly with women, was to get away from them, a familiar tactic. Shortly after the

February 1970 publication of *Mr. Sammler's Planet*, he set off for Africa with David Peltz, who had been there twice before.[19] The new trip was Bellow's idea, sparked by Peltz's telling him of letters he'd received from a friend he'd made in Nairobi, a guide he'd hired on the second trip, "an ex–Mau Mau terrorist." The guide had written of a beryllium mine in Kenya that Peltz could invest in. Peltz showed the letters to Bellow, who got excited about the prospect not so much of making money as of traveling to Africa. He knew someone at the University of Chicago who could provide him with a letter of introduction to the naturalist George Schaller, who was studying lions and other big cats in Tanzania, in the Serengeti. According to Peltz, both he and Bellow put up fifteen hundred dollars for new equipment for the mine. Bellow told Peltz that if he accompanied him he'd pay his way, a promise Peltz says he failed to honor, perhaps because the investment came to nothing.

The trip began for Bellow with a flight to London, where he stayed "just long enough to get a yellow-fever injection and two visas."[20] Here he also was given the names of some English lawyers in Nairobi. He then flew to Rome, where he met Peltz. The two friends spent several days in Rome, visiting Paolo Milano and Gore Vidal, the latter eager to tell stories of Jacqueline Kennedy. "Gore and I hit it off splendidly," Peltz remembers. "He invited me to Hollywood to meet all the ladies." On the day of their flight to Nairobi, they had a meal with Vidal in his favorite restaurant before taking a cab straight to the airport. Bellow was exhausted on the flight, "knocked out" from the stress of the preceding months. As Peltz recalled, "I said, Put your head down [on his shoulder, he indicated], come and sleep," which Bellow did, soothed as he'd been four years earlier in Jackson Park, when distraught over Susan. Once in Nairobi, Bellow reported in a letter of February 9 to Frances Gendlin, he and Peltz discovered that "the whole mining deal was pure con. Peltz's man w'd not appear. Evidently it was an international swindle. Hugely funny." In a letter to Shils of February 25, after returning to Chicago, Bellow says nothing of being swindled: "In Nairobi, Peltz and I seem to have acquired an interest in a beryllium mine. Of course it is mere playfulness for me. I did it in carnival spirit. Peltz I think is very earnest about it. In any case, it absorbed and amused me for a while and helped to clear my mind of shadows." That the beryllium deal was still on, or back on, is suggested by a note Bellow received on March 13, in which Peltz informed him that he had loaned three thousand dollars to the "Mogul Mining Company Limited," to buy mining rights, equipment, and a Land Rover. Thirty years later, Bellow offered a slightly fuller though no clearer account of the deal. Peltz had been "the intended mark of a gang of con artists who pretended that they had an unlimited supply of semi-precious stones. They had proposed that Peltz should set up a company and that this company should buy them the necessary mining machinery and trucks. Peltz and I had discussed the deal with an English lawyer who advised us to leave town. 'Get away from Nairobi awhile,' he said when he saw copies of the letters Peltz had sent to his associates, 'lest you end up in a courtroom.'"

As Peltz remembers it, he and Bellow did just that. They set out to rent a Land Rover, and, in a crowded street in downtown Nairobi, ran straight into Saul Steinberg, Bellow's neighbor in the Hamptons, who also knew Peltz. Once over the shock, Bellow was struck by the fact that he and Steinberg were decked out in identical tourist gear from Brooks Brothers (including, according to Steinberg's biographer, "a bush jacket of many pockets, shorts, knee socks, sturdy boots, and a pith helmet").[21] Steinberg had been to Africa twice before and was planning a trip to Uganda to visit Murchison Falls and the White Nile, partly to observe crocodiles. Bellow had written a novel about Africa and never actually been there; Steinberg had been drawing crocodiles all his life. He was fascinated by them and found them hateful, "part of the primitive system of nature where certain privileges were given unevenly to different species . . . the son of a bitch is vicious, has terrific teeth, is a great swimmer, and on top of it he's armored." Crocodiles were like dragons, symbolizing any "administration in evil form, political power in general, specifically economic, artistic and cultural. Anything you want—it's a crock."[22]

Having decided to join forces, Peltz, Steinberg, and Bellow flew immediately to Entebbe, where they hired a Volkswagen van and driver. Then they drove to Kampala, from which they traveled to the Paraa Safari Lodge, below Murchison Falls, a well-known tourist destination (it has a swimming pool overlooking the Nile). Bellow described the falls in an address delivered at a 1999 memorial service for Steinberg:

> The huge waters crashed non-stop like a world congress of washing machines and then circled below as if considering what to do next—the hippo mothers and their calves showing nostrils and ears above the surface. The crocodiles, cruising under an agreement millions of years old, gave them a wide pass.[23]

Steinberg had sketched this scene for Bellow, "and there now hangs on the wall behind my desk a Steinberg drawing of a huge hippo looking very much like a New York Department of Sanitation truck. This huge beast came every morning to the Paraa Lodge with her calf and together they overturned the large garbage cans and rummaged in the kitchen waste."[24]

Steinberg was interested in hippos because they were the only creatures crocodiles feared. According to his biographer, Steinberg was especially struck by the way crocodiles could "lie in the mud like a dead log and then suddenly flash into action to devour unwitting prey. Most of all he was mesmerized by the 'toothpick bird' who sat inside the crocodile's open mouth, unconcernedly pecking its food off the gigantic teeth. 'Nobody in the world is as safe as that bird in the crocodile's mouth. They have an understanding, a pact between them, a deep relationship between the two,' "[25] like the "agreement millions of years old" between the hippo and the crocodile.

In the mornings, before the heat built up, the three friends went sightseeing, a rare intrusion on Bellow's writing schedule. One afternoon, they took a motorboat cruise on the Nile. The lodge had arranged the cruise for them and for another of its guests, "a young woman traveling alone—quite a pretty Scandinavian in poplin." Steinberg tried to engage the young woman in conversation, with little success. Bellow describes a moment of drama on the cruise:

> The boat approached a sand bar where crocodiles had laid and buried their eggs and seemed to be dozing in the sunshine and as we drifted by a croc braced herself on her short legs and in a combined swift movement came to her feet and rushed at the boat. The speed of these creatures, because of their Gothic construction and their look of clumsy torpor, takes watchers aback. They pull their prey to the bottom and drown it. The animal tried to board on Steinberg's side of the boat. The young Danish traveler had one elbow on the gunwale, and she went down [inside the boat]. Steinberg also fell into the aisle. I thought: "This is it! Killed in Africa by a crocodile!" The creature had forced its head into the seat. . . . I saw us at the mercy of this overpowering monster. I thought, "Steinberg will be killed. I'll have to write his obituary. But we'll all be killed. There's nothing but an oar to defend yourself with."
>
> But with his oar one of the boatman pushed against the sand-

> bank and the croc slid or fell back into the water, the domain of the hippos and the crocs. All the men laughed at this innocent fun. Steinberg helped the Danish lady to her feet, but there was nothing he could do to please her.[26]

In Atlas's account of this incident, Bellow, too, made a play for the Danish lady, and also got nowhere.[27]

It was in Africa, according to Peltz, that Bellow had his first experience with hashish. On the drive to the falls, Steinberg said to Peltz: "David, we're in Africa, where's the pot? It's time to get a little pot." Peltz asked their guide to procure some and was soon presented with "eighty dynamite joints, rolled like an ice-cream cone, tapered at the end and thick at the top. So I lit up and I called Steinberg and he said I'll be right over, and he got high and we both got high and we were laughing and we met Saul in the lobby." The plan was to go to an Indian restaurant, and Steinberg and Peltz couldn't stop laughing: "Bellow was pissed off, mad we got high." After dinner, Bellow asked to try a joint. "He'd never had one before. He lay down on the bed and I put a lighted one in his mouth and he never inhaled. He was afraid of something unexpected within himself." According to Bellow, he took one puff but the hashish made him sick. It made Peltz and Steinberg, in contrast, "preternaturally cheerful,"[28] a mood maintained all the way back to Entebbe. When it came time to return to the United States, Steinberg and Bellow took a twelve-hour flight to Rome, stopping at Addis Ababa, Asmara, Khartoum, Cairo, and Athens. Peltz took a more direct flight, on which he smuggled all the remaining hashish. When he and Bellow met in Rome, Peltz informed him that he intended to smuggle the hashish into the United States (in the pocket of his raincoat, as he'd done on the flight to Rome). Bellow refused to stand next to him as they went through customs.

The Africa trip was just what Bellow needed. As he wrote to Frances Gendlin from Rome: "This trip I think has met the purpose. I am better, more settled in mind and am willing—no, longing, to come back to 5805 [the address of his Cloisters apartment on Dorchester Avenue]." Back in Chicago, Bellow remained in good spirits. As he wrote to Shils on February 25, partly to explain their missing each other in England: "I didn't want to spend time in Europe: I was eager to get to Africa. It did not disappoint me. Murchison Falls and the White Nile stunned me. . . . I had thought myself ready for nature's grandeur (having seen the movies) but all my preparations were (luckily) driven away by the actual sight of the great river." In addition to settling him, the trip provided material for future stories. In "A Silver Dish"—a loving portrait of Peltz and his father, published in *The New Yorker* on September 25, 1978—Bellow draws on two episodes from the trip: Peltz's hashish smuggling and the motorboat cruise on the Nile. Woody Selbst, a contractor like Peltz, smuggles a bundle of hashish from Kampala to the United States in his trench-coat pocket, "banking perhaps on his broad build, frank face, high color. He didn't look like a wrongdoer, a bad guy; he looked like a good guy. But he liked taking chances. Risk was a wonderful stimulus." Once home, Woody plants the hashish seeds in his backyard. They don't take, "but behind his warehouse, where the Lincoln Continental was parked, he kept a patch of marijuana. There was no harm at all in Woody, but he didn't like being entirely within the law. It was simply a question of self-respect."[29]

The episode from the cruise had been recounted to Bellow by Peltz and Steinberg (Bellow had missed it, Atlas implies, because he was busy chatting up the young Danish woman). A buffalo calf on the shore was suddenly dragged into the water by a crocodile. In "A Silver Dish," Bellow imagines how "under the water the calf still thrashed, fought, churned the mud. Woody, the robust traveler, took this in as he sailed by, and to him it looked as if the parent cattle were asking each other dumbly what had happened. He chose to assume that there was pain in this, he read brute grief into it" (p. 13). Woody makes this assumption because he is incapable of seeing the world as loveless, exclusively red in tooth and claw. His "one idea," from childhood onward, was that love was "the goal, the project, God's purpose . . . that this world should be a love world, that it should eventually recover and be entirely a world of love. He wouldn't have said this to a soul, for he could see how stupid it was—personal and stupid. Nevertheless, there it was at the center of his feelings." At the same time, Woody's aunt wasn't wrong when she said to him, "strictly private, close to his ear even, 'You're a little crook, like your father' " (p. 18).

"A Silver Dish" provides a test of Woody's "one idea," primarily through its account of his father, Morris, whose self-willed energies are presented as admirable but brutish. Just as it is unlikely the water buffalo feels grief, it is unlikely that Morris feels for his son anything like what his son feels for him. When Woody is still a teenager, he takes his father to meet his benefactress, a devout Christian lady, in the hope of securing a loan for the father's laundry-and-cleaning business. When the benefactress leaves the room for a moment, the father steals a silver dish and hides it under his trousers. When Woody insists that he put the dish back before she returns, the father refuses. Woody wrestles him to the floor, there in the Christian lady's parlor; Morris struggles to free himself from his son's grip, punching him several times in the face, kneeing him, butting him with his chin, rattling his teeth. Woody is twenty pounds heavier and eventually subdues him. "Gradually Pop stopped thrashing and struggling. His eyes stuck out and his mouth was open, sullen. Like a stout fish. Woody released him and gave him a hand up. He was then overcome with many bad feelings of a sort he knew the old man never suffered. Never, never. Pop never had these groveling emotions. There was his whole superiority. Pop had no such feelings" (p. 28).

Woody, in middle age, close to the age of Dave Peltz on the Africa trip, is described as "open, lavish, familiar, fleshier and fleshier but still muscular (he jogged, he lifted weights) . . . becoming ruddier every year, an outdoor type with freckles on his back and spots across the flaming forehead and the honest nose. In Addis Ababa he took an Ethiopian beauty to his room from the street and washed her, getting into the shower with her to soap her with his broad, kindly hands. In Kenya he taught certain American obscenities to a black woman so that she could shout them out during the act. On the Nile, below Murchison Falls, those fever trees rose huge from the mud, and hippos on the sandbars belched at the passing launch, hostile. One of them danced on his spit of sand, springing from the ground and coming down heavy, on all fours. There, Woody saw the buffalo calf disappear, snatched by the crocodile" (pp. 32–33). When Woody felt heartache, he would go for a run: "He felt truth coming to him from the sun—a communication that was also light and warmth. . . . And again out of the flaming of the sun would come to him a secret certainty that the goal set for this earth was that it should be filled with good, saturated with it. After everything preposterous, after dog had eaten dog, after the crocodile death had pulled everyone into his mud . . . This was his clumsy intuition. It went no further. Subsequently, he proceeded through life as life seemed to want him to do it" (p. 33). This is how Bellow felt Peltz proceeded through life, a feeling shared by others who knew him.

ONCE BASED BACK IN CHICAGO, Bellow continued his travels: to Washington, D.C., to attend a Jewish Heritage Award Luncheon, to New York for Adam's bar mitzvah, to Texas to consult with Botsford about the new magazine (Bette Howland had been working on the magazine in Chicago while Bellow was in Africa), to Florida to visit Maury and consult with him about business deals. In addition to the deals with Maury, Bellow invested twenty-five thousand dollars in a company drilling for oil and gas in Oklahoma, Texas, New Mexico, and elsewhere, a venture in which Maury's son, Joel, was also involved. A month later, on May 27, Edward Levi, the university president, wrote to Bellow formally appointing him chair of the Committee on Social Thought, "upon the recommendation of the Provost and the Dean of the Division of the Social Sciences." Bellow's appointment was to commence on July 1, 1970, when James Redfield, the current chair, would be on leave in Italy. Redfield expected Bellow's appointment to be for a year only and was upset to learn that it was for three years.

When Bellow agreed to become chair of the Committee, he was probably the most acclaimed novelist in America. He hardly needed the post for his CV, or for his pocket. He was not used to doing things he didn't want to do, and he was not easy to bully or shame. On May 10, writing to Robert M. Adams, the literary scholar and critic, to decline an invitation to deliver the Ewing Lectures at UCLA (two talks for twenty-five hundred dollars), Bellow wondered how being chair would affect him "emotionally" as well as "what freedom it will leave me for junkets." He admitted to being "astonished" at his recent decisions and moods: "I am dégagé where I expected to be anxious, or frantic when I would have predicted nonchalance." One reason why he accepted the post is that he respected the Committee and felt it his duty to take on his share of administrative responsibility. Another is that it provided a distraction from personal difficulties. He owed much to the educational traditions the Committee upheld, which he saw as threatened not only by academic specialization but by recent cultural and political trends. The Chairmanship was meant to rotate among Committee members, and Bellow had been a member for eight years; it was his turn.[30] The influence of Edward Shils may also have figured. Shils was devoted to the Committee. As James Redfield puts it, "Anything that threatened the professional integrity of the Committee was felt by Shils as a personal threat." He was also devoted to Bellow, whom he thought of at this time rather as Barley Alison thought of him. "I . . . want you to be *my* idea of perfection," she had written to him; "I expect you to become eventually a very distinguished person," declares her fictional alter ego, Rita. What Shils wanted for the Committee, he wanted for Bellow: that they meet his ideas of distinction, perfection. While teaching at Cambridge, which he did part of each year, Shils frequently wrote to Bellow about Committee business, offering opinions and advice. He also made clear how much he admired Bellow's writing and valued their friendship.

The vigilance with which Shils looked after what he thought of as the Committee's interests is clear from a letter he wrote to Bellow on December 27, 1962, a few months after Bellow had joined the faculty. After expressing great pleasure in their correspondence ("You have been very sweet to write so frequently") and excitement over *Herzog* (which he was "pining" to read in draft), Shils turns to Committee matters. He has learned that Erich Heller, an influential literary scholar, intellectual historian, and professor of German at Northwestern University, a man Bellow knew and admired, was being considered for the Committee. Shils, too, admired Heller, but with reservations: "I would much prefer to see him in the University rather than at Northwestern. I would much prefer to see him in the German Department in the University with a loose attachment to the Committee on Social Thought rather than solely in the Committee on Social Thought." Heller was lively, and his voice and personality "fill up too much space. They make him too prominent and I would not like him to be the unofficial ambassador of the Committee, which I am sure he would become simply by virtue of the fact that those provincials out there are such suckers for such a 'worldly,' 'sophisticated' person, so flattering and charming, so full of anecdotes about the Common Rooms of the old world and, having no home of his own and no one to cook for him, he would surely be dining out with such frequency and such *éclat* that he would become 'Mr. Committee on Social Thought.'" Shils also voiced "peripheral" objections to Heller's ideas: "He is such a denigrator of the contemporary world. Everything is wrong with us. We are not organic. We have lost our sense for metaphysics. We are just so no good nowadays." Such views, Shils writes, were already over-represented in the Committee and the university. He felt "no bad conscience" about seeking to suppress them, something he might have felt had they been minority views. "Still and all," Shils concludes, "if we are to have him, I will certainly try to make him welcome because, whatever else is wrong with him, he reads widely and is intellectually wide awake." He did not get the job. Months later, on October 14, 1963, Shils offered his views about two potential junior appointments: "I suppose the young'uns must be thrown a bone or a piece of suet occasionally. . . . We cannot have everything that is good. We do have you and Hannah Arendt and we do not have Heller, and all three should be occasion for much gratitude to seen and unseen powers."

Hiring faculty was the most important and difficult part of Bellow's job as chair. The Committee attracted scholars and intellectuals often uncomfortable in traditional disciplines and departments and seen as awkward by colleagues. "Classics wouldn't touch me," admits James Redfield, whose book on the *Iliad* was to employ the methods of social science and ethnography rather than those of traditional Homeric studies. "Philosophy didn't want Hannah Arendt, Art didn't want Harold Rosenberg. They didn't want them around, thought they were destructive personalities." "Every one of them was a prima donna," is how Jonathan Kleinbard, at the time assistant to Edward Levi, later Bellow's close friend and ally ("If he had a problem I was there to help him"), described the Committee faculty. That candidates for the Committee had to be vetted by university departments meant there were bound to be clashes. In 1966, Bellow and Shils were keen to bring Gertrude Himmelfarb to the Committee. When Himmelfarb came to give a talk to the History Department, she was, Bellow and others thought, poorly treated. Shils was in England at the time but was told about her reception by Bellow. On March 3, he wrote to Levi in protest. "She was treated, I am reliably told, with a degree of discourtesy which one would not even expect at a meeting of the *mafia*. If she were an obscure and inconsequential person, such conduct would have been utterly unacceptable in any respectable university. Given the considerable magnitude of her achievements and her own high reputation and dignity of bearing, the conduct of the History Department was all the more unacceptable." In the same letter, Shils protested about the treatment Daniel Moynihan had received at the hands of the Department of Sociology: "It might be that he is good enough to be the Director of the Harvard M.I.T. Joint Center for Urban Studies and not good enough to be appointed to the very remarkable Department of Sociology in the University of Chicago. That is not a view which I myself hold, and I do not think that it could be argued rationally, but even if Moynihan were much less good a man than he is, his own public distinction and the complete propriety of his own bearing merit his being treated in a more gentlemanly fashion than he was treated at the reception which was accorded to him by the sociologists."

Shils's sense of what makes Himmelfarb a person of distinction is not only "the magnitude of her achievement" but her "dignity of bearing." Moynihan's distinction comes partly from the "complete propriety" of his bearing. Although he could be cruelly funny and irreverent, Shils had an old-fashioned sense of dignity; he took himself and his values seriously. Bellow was drawn to and influenced by this seriousness, which shaped or reinforced not only his sense of himself as a writer but what he chose to write about, particularly in his essays. Nor was Shils the only figure at the Committee to take an elevated view of its mission or importance. Redfield opposed Shils and Bellow on a number of issues, was a "young'un," at least in Committee terms, and on the left politically. Here he is in a letter of August 19, 1966, writing to Bellow about the possibility that Irving Kristol, Himmelfarb's husband, might join the Committee.

> In brief, my position is this. Kristol is not an academic, or as you put it, "he's no scholar." There is no doubt that he is a man of considerable quality, but not of that particular quality. Is he then a man for us? The answer to that question depends, I think, on the answer to a prior question: is there a special intellectual tradition, a special form of cultivation, which is kept alive in and transmitted through the universities? I think so. Therefore I think that while it is certainly true that the universities do not contain everything that is valuable, so also not everything that is valuable belongs in the universities. . . . I think the CST has a special obligation, if I may put it this way, of keeping the academic tradition alive; I think that tradition is in danger, and if we don't keep it going, who will?

Bellow himself, of course, was "no scholar," but Redfield pronounces his appointment to the Committee "a complete success." This is because "your work, while not academic, is of quite exceptional substance; at the top all forms of excellence come together." On second thoughts, he decides "your work *is*, in a curious way, academic; I think some of the things you have been saying about the novel fit curiously well with what I just said about the universities." Redfield raises such issues "not because I want to make a fuss about this matter in particular, but because I think the Committee should have a sense of itself, and of its special place." Bellow's sense of himself and his specialness was no doubt fed by this way of thinking and speaking, a way determined in part by the Committee's principled origins, its sense of fostering the highest aims of education.

How Bellow did as chair of the Committee resembled how he did in business—not all that well, judging, at least, by his ability to recruit new appointments. At the end of his tenure, which was extended from three to five years, Bellow wrote despairingly to Shils, in a letter of December 18, 1975: the Committee was "going to disintegrate quite soon, at this rate, divided by disagreements and feuds. I've not been able to do anything to build it up." As in business dealings and investments, he lacked the time, ultimately the inclination, to engage himself fully. "I had books to write and problems to face, many of these arising from my own unsatisfactory character, but I have nevertheless taken my duties seriously. . . . Unless new appointments are made the Committee will cease to exist. In about five years it'll be gone." Redfield thought Bellow lacked political skills, not so much with members of the Committee, with whom he had mostly cordial relations, as with department heads and university administrators. "I think I'm a bit of a joke to the administration," Bellow wrote to Shils on February 27, 1971. "At executive committee meetings the other chairmen seem determined not to let me inhibit their game. I feel like the fifth man in a doubles match and try to stay out of the way. They take a strongly elite view of themselves and behave like crack performers, strong hitters. Some of them seem quite intelligent, but even the intelligent ones betray foolish prejudices." Bellow quotes one of their number: "We don't socialize our Ph.D.s to take ordinary teaching positions in obscure colleges."

This sort of arrogance irritated Bellow. At the beginning of his second year as chair, in a "private communication" to the dean of social sciences, Robert McCormick Adams, an anthropologist and archaeologist, later secretary of the Smithsonian Institution, Bellow made his feelings clear. David Grene was up for reappointment. He was a classical scholar and translator of international reputation, had been teaching at the University of Chicago since the 1930s, and had been a member of the Committee since its inception. Yet Bellow was being asked to furnish detailed documentation in support of Grene's reappointment. "You shall have the David Grene material you requested," he wrote to Adams, but "I think it odd that his case should be studied as if he were an Assistant Professor up for his first renewal. He should be reappointed for the duration, that is, until retirement, and with the usual right to be considered for a final extension." Then Bellow raised "a personal matter."

> I'm sure your duties as Dean are trying and that you are under considerable pressure. But I don't like the bullying tone of the communications you've sent me. I took this job because I wanted to be of service to the Committee and the University. I don't need the glory of a chairmanship. I can easily do without that. If I must take a lot of foolish abuse I will do without it. I think I have done my job properly. If you disagree I will be glad to send in my resignation. I suggest that you find a tone more appropriate to our respective positions in the University.

Bellow could get away with such a letter because the university did not want to lose or upset him. At the end of his time as chair, he sought to secure reappointment for an old friend, Edith Hartnett, whom he'd first known in Paris in the late 1940s, when she was married to the novelist Herb Gold. By 1975, there were powerful forces within the Committee ranged against Hartnett's continuing on the faculty, though, in Redfield's words, she was "not a trivial person" or without credentials. She had a Ph.D. in comparative literature from the University of Michigan and had been an assistant professor at the University of Illinois in Chicago before coming to the Committee in 1973, also as an assistant professor. At the time the decision on reappointment was made, Bellow was away in Israel, and David Grene, his temporary replacement, wrote on November 29, 1975, to say that Hartnett's only hope was that the provost "was sufficiently afraid of you to yield." The strongest case for reappointing Hartnett, the dean of social sciences had told Grene, "was that they wanted you to be happy." In the end, Hartnett was given a two-year reappointment, presumably to placate Bellow and other supporters; there was no question of a permanent appointment.

Within the Committee, Bellow's chief difficulty was managing the tensions between Grene and Shils.[31] In an undated letter of 1976, when Bellow was still on leave in Israel, Grene sought to persuade him to stay on as chair when he returned: "I am afraid that the opposition between Shils and myself has made the job harder to discharge. I hope that it is not true to say that it has been the entire difficulty. It has played a part in your troubles about appointments." Grene then offers to step aside as temporary chair, since, "with me out of any official position in CST, other than teacher, possibly Shils would be easier for you to handle." The tension between Grene and Shils had become obvious almost as soon as Bellow was appointed chair. In addition to the chair and the chair's secretary, the Committee required a third administrator, the executive secretary, a post in the chair's gift (this was the post Edith Hartnett held in the Committee). The job of the executive secretary was to administer the complicated arrangements for predissertation fundamentals exams and to advise students. In 1970, at the beginning of Bellow's tenure as chair, the executive secretary was Herman Sinaiko, who had been a student of Grene's.[32]

Sinaiko was convinced that Shils had opposed his joining the Committee from the start. When Bellow became chair in 1970, according to Sinaiko, Grene and Shils "could hardly be in the same room together," and Sinaiko himself "was always uncomfortable with Shils and Bellow." The case against Sinaiko's reappointment was that he hadn't published enough, but he believed the real problem was that Shils did not rate him as a scholar or a thinker, and that Bellow "depended a lot on Shils." Shils "would make global decisions. This guy is a second-rater." When such decisions were made about students, including those Shils had recommended to the Committee but then found wanting, it was Sinaiko's job to warn them, "You better find somebody else, he's not going to support you."[33] In the end, a deal was struck. Sinaiko was given a year to produce a significant publication. This deal Sinaiko described as "bullshit." The truth, he felt, was that Bellow and Shils wanted him out; he, in turn, "didn't want to be in a place where I'm not accepted."[34]

Was Sinaiko unfairly treated? As he himself admits, he was "not a heavy publisher. I never pretended to be." What he resented was Bellow's manner toward him, which he described as "offensive . . . sly." Bellow should have come to him to tell him what the problem was. But if the problem with Sinaiko was that Bellow didn't rate him, one can understand his reluctance. Sinaiko suspected that there was a political component in Bellow's and Shils's opposition to his reappointment. He was on the left, had taught and sympathized with student protesters. No doubt Bellow and Shils "thought of me as someone who was a bleeding heart for the students." But Redfield was also on the left, sympathized with the protesters, and, unlike Sinaiko, hadn't published a book (his book on the *Iliad* would not be published until 1975). Yet he was not challenged. The difference, Redfield believes, is that Shils and Bellow "were reading my stuff" and recognized its merit. Although Bellow complained about Redfield in correspondence, and often found him exasperating, he had a high opinion of his intellect.[35] He even taught a course on Joyce's *Ulysses* with him. Shils also differed with Redfield on many issues, and there were clashes in temperament. As Redfield puts it, "Shils had an enormous need for deference, which I was ill-suited to supply."[36]

Shils was not alone in being high-handed as well as quick and implacable in judgment. "He really only had two categories of people," Redfield recalls of Grene. "He had people whom he adored and people about whom he'd say, 'Well, you can have my bit of him for Christmas.'" As a teacher, Grene "could be absolutely brutal in seminars and in classes. . . . He talked to the people he wanted to talk to, he had no interest in students per se." Redfield recalls the story of a student who answered a question for the first time in one of Grene's classes. "'Well, you know, I've been teaching a while,' Grene replied. 'I care about it quite a lot. But when you get an answer like that you just want to give the whole thing up.'" Bellow could be tough, but he was more guarded in expressing his opinions than Shils and Grene, especially toward the end of his tenure as chair. He was also more considerate of people's feelings, as in a letter of December 18, 1975, to Shils about the Hartnett case. Shils had opposed Hartnett's retention, again on the grounds that she hadn't published enough (according to Atlas, Shils also complained that Bellow "was filling the department with his 'whores'"[37]). "Hartnett has gotten a two year appointment," Bellow announces in the letter to Shils, "so the matter is settled. I wouldn't have wanted her permanently appointed to the Committee now, nor does she think herself good enough. But I feel that it is no more than fair to give this timid, unassertive woman a chance. She is not frivolous, she knows a lot, and I believe that she will do something with the subject she has chosen. It would have been very damaging to turn her out now." What is striking here is that for Bellow the interests of the Committee—as conceived of by Shils and initially shared by Bellow—take second place to the needs of a friend. Hartnett had published several strong articles, but she was nowhere near as productive or promising a scholar as the Committee usually sought, nowhere near Shils's notions of distinction.

These notions are seen in the list of eminent historians and social and political theorists Shils urged Bellow to pursue during his tenure as chair: Stephen Toulmin, Alasdair MacIntyre, John Pocock, Quentin Skinner, Clifford Geertz, and Arnaldo Momigliano. Shils's notion of a promising junior appointment was the conservative British philosopher Roger Scruton. Eventually, at the end of Bellow's time as chair, Shils managed to bring Momigliano, a historian of Greek, Roman, and Jewish antiquity, to the Committee. In *Portraits: A Gallery of Intellectuals* (1997), Shils has a chapter on Momigliano, who is presented not only as an ideal scholar but as an ideal Committee candidate:

> He was a person of extraordinary range and variety of intellectual and technical competence, and fearless originality. His bibliography lists about 750 papers, books, monographs, and book reviews, excluding innumerable translations into languages other than those in which they were originally written. He also wrote more than 400 articles, some quite long, for encyclopaedias. . . . His name was not bruited about in the newspapers. He did not appear on television. He never became fashionable through the denunciation of bourgeois society and the espousal of Communism; his name did not circulate in the same milieux as those of Chomsky, Habermas, Lévi-Strauss, Sartre, or Foucault. Nevertheless, he was widely known and greatly appreciated by the educated public in Europe and America. . . . His fame rested on the proliferating, tentacular reach of his scholarship.[38]

With the exception of the Sinaiko case, and periods of tension with Redfield, Bellow succeeded in negotiating the internal affairs of the Committee efficiently and with good humor. His manners, according to Redfield, were "formal and generally excellent." At meetings and elsewhere, he was often very funny and "never rude by accident." He was much helped within the Committee by his secretary or administrative assistant, Esther Corbin, who worked for him throughout his tenure as chair. Mrs. Corbin, a kindly person, four years older than Bellow, never had a bad word for anyone. According to her, Bellow was "loved and respected and looked up to" by all his colleagues. "He had such a wonderful relationship with every faculty member." Was he ever prickly? "Oh, no." Was he considerate? "Always . . . he never said a cross word." Did he have enemies? "None I knew of." Was he a good boss? "Good, kind, thoughtful." His relations with Mrs. Corbin were warm but formal. Although he called her Esther, she always called him Mr. Bellow. She soon learned his routine. He was inaccessible until 11:00 a.m., at home writing. Then he would call to find out what was happening and was available to receive calls. He'd come into the office later in the afternoon, to deal with correspondence or to have Mrs. Corbin transcribe something he had written. Only once did Mrs. Corbin undertake research for him. He asked her to find the name of the most expensive woman's watch in the world. The answer she came up with was "an Audemars Piguet with jeweled Peruvian butterfly wings," as worn by sexy Renata in *Humboldt's Gift* (p. 39).

Mrs. Corbin's efficiency meant that Bellow's travels were only slightly curtailed during his tenure as chair. When he was away, she wrote to him daily with Committee business. She also kept him up-to-date with personal and family business. Bellow gave her access to one of his bank accounts, and she paid bills for him. She kept records of all business transactions with his brothers and other relations. Maury, she remembers, was "always calling about investments." She had excellent relations with Sam's secretary and passed on messages from Sam's daughter Lesha, often about business, and from her husband, Sam Greengus ("They were darling"). Joel Bellows, Maury's son, who was Bellow's accountant for a period, was often in touch as well, about tax and other matters. Although Mrs. Corbin had little contact with Adam and Greg, who lived, respectively, on the East and West Coasts, she was very close with Daniel, sometimes picking him up from the Lab School when Susan was busy or unwell. She was on good terms with Susan, who would call her when there were emergencies with Daniel. These were the years of bitter recrimination between Bellow and Susan, and Mrs. Corbin remembers telling Susan early on, "I'll be there for you, but don't say anything to Mr. Bellow." As for Committee faculty, she spoke warmly of David Grene and "loved" Harold Rosenberg and Edward Shils. It was " 'Mr. Shils' and 'Mrs. Corbin,' but he would always stop to see me on his way to the office and we would talk." When she had a serious operation, Shils sent her flowers and "wrote a letter to my husband." After Shils's brother died, Mrs. Corbin knocked on his door and told him she knew how he felt. She, too, had lost brothers. "I put my arms around him and said, I'm so sorry." When her husband had a serious heart attack, both Bellow and Shils were especially good to her. Once, she complained to Bellow that she wished she could lose weight. He told her not to worry: "There's more of you to love." That

Bellow was a considerate boss and admired by his secretary is worth recalling.

ONLY ONCE WAS Mrs. Corbin made uncomfortable by tensions within the Committee, in this case between Shils and Bette Howland, who played an important part in Bellow's life at this time. Bellow had known Howland since 1961, when she was a student in his fiction class at a summer writers' conference at Wagner College in Staten Island (discussed in chapter 10 of *To Fame and Fortune*). He valued her writing and her advice as a reader of his work. At his suggestion, she became a student at the Committee in 1972. Two years later, she passed her fundamentals examination and was ready to begin a dissertation. Shortly before entering the Committee, Howland had published a short story in *Commentary* entitled "Blue in Chicago," the title eventually given to a collection of her stories published in 1978 by Harper & Row. A year or so later, in November 1973, she published a second story in *Commentary*, entitled "To the Country." In 1974, she published a book with Viking entitled *W-3*, about the patients in a psychiatric ward in a large university hospital. The book's unnamed narrator is a patient who has swallowed a lethal dose of sleeping pills. According to the book's dust jacket, "Bette Howland was one of those patients, and her chronicle of that experience is at once her own story and the close-focus, moving depiction of the lives of the community in W-3." The dust jacket describes the book not as a novel but a "journal."[39] It contains a blurb from Bellow praising Howland's writing as "admirably straight and thoughtful, tough-minded but full of powerful feeling."

One striking feature of *W-3* is that it tells us almost nothing about why the narrator—she will be Howland from now on—has tried to kill herself. She had spent a lot of time in hospitals with "various mysterious physical ailments, finally diagnosed as a kidney infection."[40] These ailments "had been going on for years," and eventually she came to see them as symptoms of "what was meant by a breakdown" (p. 125). All she has to say of her mental state in the period just prior to the attempted suicide is the following:

> For a long time it had seemed to me that life was about to begin—real life. But there was always some obstacle in the way. Something to be

> got through first, some unfinished business; time still to be served, a debt to be paid. Then life could begin. At last it dawned on me that these obstacles were my life. I was always rolling these stones from my grave.
>
> These last weeks I had been alone in my apartment, packing up. I had spent the summer months in the hospital, flat on my back; and lost my job, my two sons were staying with relatives. Then a large hand reached out—grabbed me by the scruff of the neck, scooped me up: I was notified of a grant from a foundation to finish a book. We were moving again—we moved very often—this time to a better climate, for our health. Our old flat was bare, dark, curtainless now, the windows gloomy with their long, torn paper shades [pp. 12–13].

Later, Howland describes what it had been like for her as a divorcée with two small children: "A dingy flat, crummy job, constant money worries. Everything you earn goes to doctors and baby-sitters. Then the baby's got a runny nose, the sitter doesn't show, you can't get to work. A life full of reproaches, self-hatred; a woman supporting a manless (unconsoled) existence, beside herself with fear, worry, managing alone." Of another divorcée in W-3, she wonders "where she had managed to find someone who was 'serious' about her and wanted to marry her. That was certainly a preoccupation of mine" (p. 22). She can't stand the impression she gives to men "of being the unattached, *available* woman, walking around like a sort of sexual time bomb" (p. 24).[41]

Howland had great trouble sleeping in the days before her attempted suicide. Once asleep, she dreamed repeatedly of razor blades digging into her wrists. When she got a prescription for sleeping pills, to cure the insomnia, thoughts of suicide became "constant; I dragged them like a weight" (p. 14). When she swallowed all the pills, "I pretty quickly regretted what I had done and called the doctor; he couldn't be reached. I told the voice of the answering service what had happened" (p. 14). Then she undressed and lay down between the sheets "in an orderly fashion" (p. 15). When the doctor got her message, he called the police. She woke up in the university hospital. According to David Peltz, in real life Howland took the overdose of pills in Bellow's apartment. Bellow found her unconscious, she was rushed to Billings Hospital on campus, and later, again according to Peltz, Bellow "had to go to the inner resources of the university to take care of these matters" (which might mean keeping them quiet or keeping himself out of them). Like Clara Velde in *A Theft*, Howland had come close to dying.

Howland's *W-3* is a powerful work and was widely and well reviewed. A year after its appearance, in April 1975, she published a third story in *Commentary*, entitled "Golden Age." Like *W-3* and the other stories in *Blue in Chicago*, it is a hybrid, reportage in fictional form. Its subject is the treatment of old people in Chicago, focused mostly on Howland's aunts and grandmother, but it begins with an account of "Professor Alonzo" and his aged mother, who lives in the apartment above him. Professor Alonzo's apartment is "furnished in books, top to bottom, leather library chairs—billiard table green—curdling cigar smoke, whiskey decanters." Professor Alonzo's mother is proud of her son, showing the narrator clippings about him: " 'He's a famous man you know.' Well he was, he was, much more than she thought. For what could his dry-as-dust essays have meant to her? What could she make of them?"[42] Howland describes Alonzo as "froggy-eyed" and red-faced: "Bluster was Alonzo's trademark, he shouted down everybody. His brilliance bordered on apoplexy. . . . His handful of hairs bristled. You couldn't help being scared of him when he got started" (p. 121). When Mrs. Alonzo becomes unsteady on her feet after a heart attack and begins falling, the professor hears the thud when she lands on the floor. They devise a system for emergencies: "She was supposed to pound on the floor—his ceiling—if she wanted anything." Soon he was listening "to every creaking overhead, and imagined her tripping on her shaggy carpets. She was giving him a hard time" (p. 122). Mrs. Alonzo is then put in a nursing home "in the thick of a desolate black slum" (p. 125) (not far, presumably, from Hyde Park, where she lived in the apartment above her son). The move is inevitable, no sign of coldness or lack of concern on the part of the son. By now she is bedridden, unable to speak.

Edward Shils lived in the apartment below his mother until she had to be put in a nursing home. His apartment, as described by Joseph Epstein in the introduction to *Portraits*, was very similar to Professor Alonzo's apartment. His appearance and personality could also be said to resemble those of Professor Alonzo. The story deeply offended Shils. As Redfield told Atlas, "He felt personally invaded, and thought it was all Bellow's fault."[43] Why he felt it was Bellow's fault is not clear. Perhaps because Bellow introduced Howland to Shils and his mother, or took her with him when he visited the mother during the son's absences in England. Perhaps because, having read the piece, Bellow did not dissuade Howland from publishing it (how could he, given the closeness to life of his own writing?). Shils was a very private person, even with close friends. Joseph Epstein, one of his closest friends, perhaps "the last person to call him by his first name," never knew he'd been married twice, something he only learned "from an enemy of his who told it to me to spite him."[44] As Epstein put it in an interview, Shils steered clear of personal detail and, except when denigrating enemies, he "operated at an . . . elevated sphere of generality." In *Portraits* he says almost nothing of the personal lives of his subjects; one has no idea if they married or had children or what their families were like. Epstein believes an element of malice underlies the opening of "Golden Age," which he attributes to Shils's treatment of Howland. In an interview, he recalled a time in 1973, before "Golden Age" appeared in *Commentary*, in which Bellow brought Howland to Shils's apartment. Epstein was there as well, and remembers that "Edward did not give her a moment's attention. . . . I felt bad about it." Howland didn't fit Shils's notion of the sort of company Bellow should keep. "He wanted Saul to be a great man—Thomas Mann with added jokes." Epstein thinks the Alonzo passages in "Golden Age" were written "in retribution." In an interview, however, Howland told me that though "Shils was a curmudgeon . . . I kind of like curmudgeons." When, in the early 1990s, Bellow put Howland forward for a job at the Committee, Shils objected strenuously. By then he and Bellow had fallen out, but the story also may have put paid to her chances. When Howland gave a job talk in the early 1990s—"a damned good talk," she claimed—Shils's anger was obvious. Mrs. Corbin recalls running into him one afternoon. She was carrying a copy of *Blue in Chicago* and he asked her, "Why would you ever buy such a book?" Thinking quickly she answered, "So no one else will buy it." But she liked Howland, and she liked the book.

HOWLAND'S RELATIONS WITH Bellow at the time of her attempted suicide were complicated. In an interview quoted in the last chapter of *To Fame and Fortune*, she claimed that they had had an affair early on, sometime after they'd met in 1961, but soon became friends rather than lovers. This was not the impression others had, nor is it borne out in correspondence. As late as September 1968, Howland wrote to Bellow, in a letter quoted in the previous chapter, that it was "agony" to be reminded of his affairs with other women. She had spent the summer of 1968, while he was in East Hampton with Maggie, doing secretarial and editorial work for him and looking after the decorating of his apartment in the Cloisters. In the letter, she teases Bellow about how it "amuses" him to think a mutual acquaintance incompetent, "as it amuses you to think of me as a diamond in the rough," adding, "I shouldn't mind if you wanted to hone the edges and polish it yourself." By January 21, 1970, on the eve of Bellow's trip to Africa with Peltz, she is refusing to handle his mail while he's away. The thought of it "makes my heart ache. It reminds me of many sad things in the past. And as a matter of fact, going to your apartment is still a gloomy experience for me. I know it is really a fine and tasteful place, the bachelor's apartment which you really ought to have. . . . To you it is a sanctuary but to me a mausoleum. . . . It would just be unsuitable for me to take on the responsibility of making the circuit between your apartment and office. It would be gloomy."

Frances Gendlin recalls an occasion, sometime in the 1970s, when she and Bellow were in the book section of Marshall Field. Howland walked in, saw them, and turned on her heels and left. According to Bellow's lawyer friend Walter Pozen, Bellow and Howland "had a long romance, and when they broke up she tried to commit suicide." David Peltz, however, believes that if rejection by Bellow played a part in Howland's suicide attempt, it was of her "not so much as a woman but as a friend." The letter of January 21, 1970, lends support to this view. Of the proposed Africa vacation Howland writes:

> It would have been different if you had said, "Look, I need this vacation now by myself; but this is what I am looking forward to doing when we are together." And "this" could have been any number of things—our work on the magazine for instance. What I don't understand is this—you misjudge me if you think it was necessary to tell me that you loved me, because I thought you understood that I belonged to the Truth Party too—I know how to honor it. I know how to respect. I am not only hurt in the way as usual between men and women; but as a colleague, an ally. That is the particular quality of bewilderment and indignation I hope you can distinguish as you file me away. I had hoped to have a real friendship, a life-long friendship.

This friendship Howland and Bellow did have, almost to the end of his life. One sign of the seriousness of Bellow's wish to be a friend to Howland was the help he offered her over a matter raised in the January 21 letter. As an adolescent, Howland had suffered from terrible acne, the facial scars of which were still visible. She now decided "to have that surgical procedure I discussed with you." It would cost $250, and Howland asked Bellow for the money, as payment for her work on the magazine, or for future work on the magazine. This money he gave her. Her expectations for the operation were realistic: "Not that it will create a great change in my life and cause people to admire me and love me; I simply put it in the general category of hiding my light under a bushel basket. Which is sinful. And there is no virtue in 'learning to live with' a condition the solution to which is so trivial."

"Trivial" may not have been the best word to describe the operation, at least according to Bellow's fictional account of a similar operation in *More Die of Heartbreak* (1987). Kenneth Trachtenberg, the novel's narrator, has a less complicated love life than Bellow's, but it is not without complication. Among the women with whom he is involved is Dita Schwartz, an ex-student, a mature-looking woman from a "proletarian" background, the daughter of a Jewish foundry worker. Dita "had an eye on me," a fact Kenneth "couldn't help welcoming . . . for the sake of self-esteem" (p. 174), much needed after rejection by his ex-girlfriend, Treckie, the mother of his daughter. Dita's breath "had a feminine flavor and the look of her dark eyes was a woman's look entirely. You noted this because her skin was not distinctively feminine. It was not a good skin, it was like a mixed weave, a layer of scar tissue from some fiery adolescent disorder." Because of this condition, Dita was always pale of complexion: "Her skin was too dense to show color." Her face gave her "a sore heart." When she sees a photo of Treckie, "the pink face was what Dita concentrated on" (p. 181). As far as Kenneth is concerned, he and Dita are "on friendly terms" (p. 181), "there were no love complications, so we could safely talk about all kinds of things" (p. 183); "she was willing to listen to my troubles, and to put up with my divagations and aberrations, my absurdities, which in fact pleased her" (p. 181). Kenneth admires Dita: "She was a superior woman, and on the basis of cleverness, dignity, feminine warmth, daintiness, princess-style behavior, capacity for attachment, I would disinterestedly have voted for Dita" (p. 196), but he isn't physically attracted to her—rather as Harold Halsband isn't attracted to Rita, the Barley Alison character.

Dita has little money and finds "a downtown fellow who made her a price to remove the top layers of dead skin right in his office, under a local anesthetic. He scrubbed her cheeks, her nose and her chin with a sander, a revolving disk." When the novocaine wears off, the pain is terrible. Kenneth speculates on Dita's motive: "It was her skin, she was convinced, that put me off" (p. 197); more cruelly, "When I saw my friend and pupil with the offputting rind removed, like a kiwi, alligator pear or Ugli fruit, I might fall in love with the angelic face of the real Dita" (pp. 198–99). After the operation, Kenneth drives her back to her apartment: "Dita's bandages were already soaking with blood serum and I was afraid that the gauze would stick to her face and began to think of taking her directly to the nearest hospital. The doctor had given her sample packets of pain pills" (p. 199). She asks Kenneth to sit with her, which he does all day. He is not the best of nurses, but "you didn't open the hand the sufferer reaches for, without touching a new level of familiarity, with warm attachment flowing in very quickly" (p. 200). Warm attachment but not love, or not the love Dita seeks, it is implied. When Kenneth takes off the bandages to change them, Dita looks "as if she had been dragged over the highway on her face." He feels for her, for her bad luck, "because I was the cause of it myself. She wanted to be in a class with Treckie" (p. 200). What Kenneth concludes is that, "however you describe it, I wasn't worth this suffering. Treckie wasn't worth it either, as a rival. In most respects, Dita was effortlessly superior to us both. She had ten times more heart in her, and this produced a kind of beauty we were unfamiliar with" (p. 200).

For the next two weeks, Kenneth nurses and feeds Dita: "I rather enjoyed this domestic stuff, and taking care of a patient." When her scabs finally heal, "Dita didn't have a new face. The extreme pallor went away; the coarse weave, however, remained." The effect of the episode is narrowly or selfishly registered by Kenneth. That her face was not new "mattered less now, for if the experiment didn't succeed, there was a broader relationship between us, we were on a more intimate footing" (p. 202). Bellow, like Kenneth, nursed Howland after her operation, changing her bloody bandages, feeding and taking care of her. If Kenneth's nursing of Dita accurately recalls Bellow's nursing of Howland, the unpleasant details, the blood serum, the scabs, suggest distance as well as intimacy, a novelist's distance, and an increase rather than a diminution of the physically off-putting. "Why does she want me to see her like this?" Bellow asked Frances Gendlin at the time. In the years that followed, Howland's relations with Bellow, according to the cultural anthropologist Constance Perin, a neighbor and friend, became what she claimed to hope they would be: truthful. Perin met Bellow through Howland, and joined them a number of times on social occasions. She and Bellow got on well. Of Howland in the early 1970s she recalled: "I did *not* experience her being in love with Saul, there was no agony between them, they were delightful and total friends, very easy together."

BELLOW'S SUMMERS IN THE EARLY 1970S were spent in the mountains rather than at the sea. On November 27, 1970, he received a letter from the composer Nicolas Nabokov inviting him to spend the following summer in Aspen, Colorado, as writer-in-residence and Guest Fellow at the Aspen Institute for Humanities Studies. Bellow had known Nabokov since the early 1950s, in part through the Congress for Cultural Freedom, whose general secretary Nabokov was from 1951 to 1967. In 1970, Nabokov became composer-in-residence at Aspen, and the deal he offered Bellow was enticing. The institute would pay Bellow's round-trip travel expenses "from wherever you happen to be," give him use of a comfortable independent house, a car, and a monthly honorarium of a thousand dollars. Among the Guest Fellows scheduled for the coming summer were Henri Cartier-Bresson, Senator Jacob Javits, Irving Kristol, the physicist Jeremy Bernstein, and the Oxford historian Alan Bullock. Bellow's duties would be minimal: to give a reading and to lead a discussion. Discussions at the institute were conducted for influential figures in business, government, education, labor, science, and the professions—men and women, mostly men, who had achieved a certain status in life but hadn't had much time to reflect on larger issues, variously identified in publicity material as the nature of man, justice and the individual, the relation of science and technology to humanism, the accelerating rate of social change. These issues were to be discussed largely by relating them to "enduring ideas from the past," as in a Great Books course. Participants were given readings from Plato, Aristotle, Tolstoy, Marx, and so forth, as well as from Eastern thought and culture, and invited to discuss them in groups of fifteen to twenty.[45] The Great Books notion derived from the institute's founder, a Chicago businessman named Walter Paepcke (1896–1960), chairman of the Container Corporation of America. Paepcke first visited Aspen in 1945 and, according to the institute Web site, was inspired by its great natural beauty to transform the town "into a center for dialogue, a place for 'lifting us out of our usual selves.'" He had been a trustee of the University of Chicago and participated in its Great Books seminars. The philosopher Mortimer Adler, whom Bellow had known as an undergraduate at the university and later through his work on the *Syntopicon* (discussed in chapter 7 of *To Fame and Fortune*), was enlisted by Paepcke to design and administer the institute's Executive Seminars and was much in evidence in summer sessions, "scowling at the inability of others to follow the ineluctable logic of his arguments."[46]

Bellow spent parts of each of the next five summers in Aspen, from 1971 through 1975. He went there to write, to hike in the mountains, to get away from Committee meetings and hassles, lecture tours, agents, editors, ex-wives, and ex-girlfriends, and to spend time with Daniel and Adam (Gregory was now married and working in San Francisco), as well as close friends and relatives. In the summer of 1971, his relatives Louis and Helen Gameroff and their daughter Myrna came to visit; two summers later, Joel and Priscilla Bellows visited, as did Walter Pozen and his wife, Joan. Fran Gendlin spent parts of several summers with Bellow in Aspen; she remembers Daniel crawling into bed with her one morning while Bellow worked. Daniel remembers doing so as well. He was eight and missed his mother, "and there was Fran in the bed, and I was, like, Okay, you'll do." "She was awesome," he recalls, "and she had kids my age, too." (When Bellow came into the room, "he was, like, What are you doing in there?" Gendlin said, "leave him alone.") Like all Bellow's girlfriends, Fran was nice to Daniel. "I was a cute kid, and I was his son." She was also fond of Adam, whom she remembers as very smart, with a wonderful sense of humor. When Fran was not with Bellow, he hired babysitters for the mornings; Daniel remembers forcing them to play baseball with him "incessantly." What Fran remembers of afternoons in Aspen, after Bellow's stint at his desk, is that he wasn't as attentive to Daniel or Adam as he ought to have been. "Daniel was always schlepping around after his life. He never took him anywhere where maybe Daniel wanted to go." Nor did Bellow ever just "sit home and play with him." "Saul was too formal. . . . Daniel tagged along, I tagged along, people tagged along." Daniel, however, remembers loving his Aspen visits, "hiking and fishing and jumping from rock to rock" (often across fast-running and dangerous bodies of water, without his father's knowledge). By the second summer, Bellow had found a day camp for Daniel. In a letter of February 5, 1973, to Ferne Hudson, the Aspen Institute program coordinator, he specifies the sort of town house he needs: "A quiet and leafy street is what I would like, away from traffic and hippies. My little boy will be nine in March and if we are within walking distance of Carl's Drug Store where the daycamp bus loads and unloads, I shan't have to chauffeur him back and forth as I do when we're on Red Mountain. . . . I shall be working, working very hard in some cool back room during July and August. Three bedrooms would be best, one to work in, one to sleep in and one for the boy."

Aspen only partly succeeded in calming Bellow. In an unpublished story entitled "Away for the Summer Again," written in 2006, Gendlin fictionalizes an episode recalled from her stay with him in July 1972. To the annoyance of his wife, Julie, a figure who resembles Gendlin, Clay Lewes, a famous poet, invites Marshall and Linda Becker to join them for an afternoon hike in the mountains. The Leweses have already invited Wilson Jones, "a mystery writer who wants to be a poet," to join them. When the story opens, Clay is in good spirits. "I am human with you," he tells Julie. "I've never felt so human before." He dismisses her complaints that the Beckers have been invited, "thinks he will not get riled today. 'He asked if he could come, honey.' His look is helpless as he spreads his hands. 'What could I do?' " (a familiar Bellow gesture). Julie describes herself as "more forceful with people than her husband," suspecting that "he wears out much of his day's power in his early morning writing, while she is still asleep." He often asks her "to handle things" for him, which is "one of the reasons they get along. Clay is not good at taking command."

What Clay and Julie like about Aspen isn't the town, although they attend the music festival "with their summer friends, a few of the other writers and musicians." It is the mountain air, the simple cabins they rent, with views down to the city and the mountains beyond, the grill in the garden, the freshly caught trout. "There are no black moods here," or not many. What annoys Julie about the Beckers is that Marshall doesn't stop talking; she worries about the effect his chattering will have on Clay. To calm her, Clay asks: "Couldn't you hint to Marshall that we like to walk quietly, each with his own thoughts? Please?" Julie also dreads the presence of Linda Becker, with whom she'll have to walk, since the men invariably lead the way. Linda would "stab me if she could, for she thinks 'If only I were married to Clay Lewes, I'd be the one who could finally make him happy.' " "She just thinks your life

SB outside the Belasco Theater, New York, 1964 (courtesy of Howard Gotfryd; photo by Bernard Gotfryd)

Pat Covici and SB, early 1960s (courtesy of the Special Collections Research Center, University of Chicago Library)

Sam Levene on Broadway as Philip Bummidge, the lead in SB's play *The Last Analysis*, Belasco Theater, 1964 (courtesy of Friedman-Abeles/Museum of the City of New York, F2013-41@The New York Public Library)

Hirschfield caricature of Shelley Winters as Hilda "the Polack whore" and Henry Towb as Pennington, a seventy-eight-year-old industrialist, in "Orange Soufflé," one of the three one-act plays in *Under the Weather*, which opened at the Cort Theater in October 1966 (courtesy of Playbill Enterprises, Inc.)

Maggie Staats, SB, and Samuel Goldberg, SB's lawyer-friend, at the French Consulate in New York, where SB was awarded the Croix de Chevalier des Arts et des Lettres, January 15, 1968 (courtesy of the Special Collections Research Center, University of Chicago Library)

Arlette Landes and daughter Bonnie, Chicago, 1967 (courtesy of Arlette Landes)

Bette Howland, 1985 (courtesy of Jacob Howland)

Frances Gendlin, mid-1970s (courtesy of Frances Gendlin)

SB and sons Adam and Daniel on Martha's Vineyard, 1965 (private collection)

"My father, the famous writer, was the king. Surely one day he would summon me to court, knight me, and acknowledge me as his heir." SB and Adam in England, 1969. (private collection)

SB and Daniel on Nantucket, "dealing with little boys, ex-wives, lawyers, fishhooks in the fingers, sunburn, car rentals," August 1969 (private collection)

Greg Bellow, 1969 (courtesy of Greg Bellow)

Saul Steinberg drawing, *Paraa Lodge Murchison Falls Uganda Jan. 1970*, a 1985 present to SB commemorating their 1970 trip to Murchison Falls (courtesy of The Saul Steinberg Foundation/Artists Rights Society, New York)

SB and Dave Peltz, the model for Woody Selbst in "A Silver Dish," with "his broad build, frank face, high color. He didn't look like a wrongdoer, a bad guy; he looked like a good guy. But he liked taking chances. Risk was a wonderful stimulant." (private collection)

David Grene, classicist (courtesy of University of Chicago Photographic Archive, Special Collections Research Center, University of Chicago Library)

Edward Shils lecturing (courtesy of *The Chicago Maroon;* photo by Jackie Hardy)

Floyd Salas in Berkeley in the 1960s; to him SB was "the epitome of what was wrong with the university." (courtesy of Floyd Salas)

Student protester David Shapiro sitting at the desk of Columbia University president Grayson Kirk, whose office protesters had occupied (he is smoking one of Kirk's cigars). A senior, later a poet and critic, he went on to study at Cambridge, returned to Columbia for a Ph.D., and has taught at Columbia and Princeton. (photo by Blake Fleetwood)

SB at the International House in Tokyo, surrounded by its executive director and board members, among them professors of literature and history at Tokyo University and Shigeharu Matsumoto, standing third from right, cofounder of the International House (with J. D. Rockefeller III). The scroll above them translates roughly: "Respect and care, at the end, as in the beginning." (courtesy of the Special Collections Research Center, University of Chicago Library)

Honorary degree recipients, Harvard University, June 1972. Back row, left to right: James Shannon, S.D; SB, Litt.D; Roy Jenkins; LL.D., Paul Samuelson, LL.D.; Northrop Frye, Litt.D. Front row, left to right: Anne Pusey, L.H.D.; Nathan Pusey, LL.D.; Derek Bok (president); Elma Lewis, Art.D. (courtesy of Harvard University News Office)

SB and Herman Wouk hiking in Aspen, 1970s (courtesy of Ferenc Berko Photo Archive)

SB in Aspen, 1974
(courtesy of Ferenc Berko Photo Archive)

James Salter in Aspen, 1970s
(courtesy of Kay Eldredge)

Walter Pozen, SB's lawyer-friend and eventual executor, 1967 (courtesy of University of Chicago Photographic Archive, Special Collections Research Center, University of Chicago Library)

SB, Alexandra, and Florica Bagdasar (Alexandra's mother), sightseeing in Greece; SB doing the "Sirtaki" step, mid-1970s (private collection)

The Bellow party in Stockholm, "Nobel Savages," December 12, 1976. Back row, left to right: Ileana Costea (cousin to Alexandra), Nicholas Costea (her husband, behind her), Alexandra, Greg, SB, Daniel (just peeping out), Adam, Sam Greengus. Front row, left to right: Sam Bellows, Ana Paonescu (Alexandra's aunt), Florica Bagdasar (Alexandra's mother), Nina Bellows (Sam Bellows's wife), Lesha Greengus, Judith, Deana, and Rachel Greengus (daughters of Lesha and Sam), Jane Bellow Kauffman (SB's sister). (private collection)

SB receiving the Nobel Prize from King Carl Gustav XVI of Sweden, Stockholm, December 12, 1976 (courtesy of the Special Collections Research Center, University of Chicago Library)

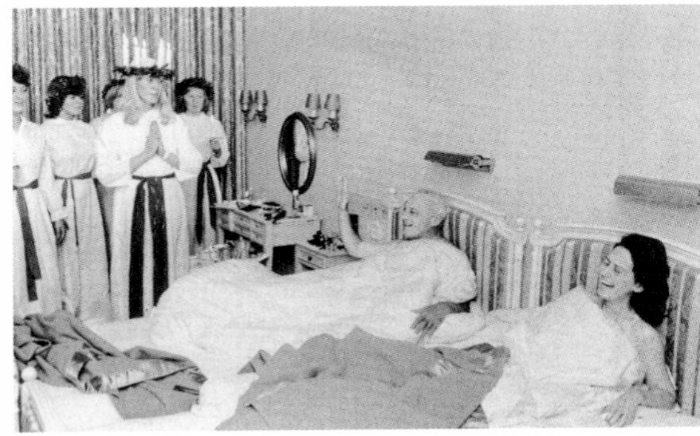

SB and Alexandra surprised in bed by the Saint Lucia ceremony, Stockholm, December 13, 1976 (courtesy of Getty Images, Bettmann)

SB's publishers at the country home of his Swedish publisher Bonnier, December 13, 1976. Front row, left to right: Tom Rosenthal (Secker and Warburg), Thomas Guinzberg (Viking), SB, Barley Alison (Secker and Warburg), Gerald Bonnier, Karl Otto Bonnier. Back row, left to right: George Svensson (also of Bonnier), Jarl Helleman (Finnish publisher), Reinhold Neven du Mont (German publisher) (courtesy of Rosie Alison)

Greg, Daniel, and Adam Bellow, Stockholm, December 1976 (private collection)

Alexandra, SB, Leon Wieseltier, and Daniel, Vermont, 1977 (private collection)

SB's house in Vermont: "He wanted it to be brown and he wanted it to have a slate floor and he went to Europe and it was done." (photo by Alice Leader)

with the famous poet is so glamorous," Clay says. "But would she put up with me the way you do? Not for long." What Julie thinks is: "No, not glamorous . . . Unpredictable is the word that comes to mind. Never anything sure. Rewarding, though."

When the Beckers arrive, Clay's mood momentarily darkens, as does the sky, threatening rain. At the trail, Clay walks ahead, looks back, and calls: " 'We'll meet at the meadow. . . . I'll see you all there.' Then, taking a deep breath and feeling the cool, damp air all around him, he starts. His feeling of peace will return as he walks; this is why he has come." Marshall, however, is hot on Clay's heels as rain begins to fall. Thunder sounds, which makes Clay nervous, and now "he is not liking the walk today at all. He knows his mood is fragile, and he misses Julie's presence." When Marshall catches up to him and misquotes William Blake, Clay asks impatiently: "Please, Marshall . . . can we do without the great thoughts when we walk? Aren't the mountains enough?" The story takes a melodramatic turn at this point, but is of interest for what it suggests of Bellow in dark moods. As the storm increases, Julie tries to persuade Clay to turn back. He won't, because he's in a state, furious that his walk is being spoiled. The reaction of the other characters is interesting as well, for what it says about the power of celebrity:

> "Are we going on?" Wilson's question is the same as Linda's. "I'll defer to you Clay," he says, smiling. "You're the talent and we're the hacks."
>
> "Yeah, you're the expert, Clay," nods Marshall. . . . "What do you say?"
>
> Julie sees a set look come over Clay's face. She tenses. "I am not an expert here," he snaps. He turns to the group. "Can't you understand?" He gets no answer. It is clear they are waiting for him to decide.
>
> "So much for not being riled today," he exclaims to Julie, his voice agitated, and she sees he is upset, more than she had thought. His chest tightens as he turns to the others and speaks. His voice is sharp. "Well, I am going on, rain or no rain." He pauses and stares at them defiantly. "*Talent is going up*," he blurts suddenly, and his voice is cold. "*Hacks can do what they want!*" It is almost a dare.
>
> "Oh no! Lewes!" Julie is frightened. "Don't do this!"
>
> Marshall, his face drawn, looks down on the ground. . . . He nods at Linda. "If Clay thinks it's okay to walk on, I'm game."

> "I did *not* say it was okay," Clay's voice is impatient, scathing. "I *only* said I was going on."

To Julie's disgust, the others choose to follow Clay, with disastrous results. When the full horror of what has happened is revealed (verbose Marshall is hit by a bolt of lightning and killed), Clay returns, sobbing. On the drive back, the rain finally stops, the sky is blue in patches, and with Julie's help Clay calms down. He is like nature itself, the story suggests: grand, terrible, unpredictable. He is also subject to nature, or his nature; neither he nor anyone else can resist his moods, Gendlin suggests, while she also suggests the corrupting as well as inflaming influence of admirers and sycophants.

UNPREDICTABLE BUT REWARDING. In Gendlin's story, the rewarding part of Clay's company is asserted rather than demonstrated. The rewarding part of Bellow's company figures prominently in the recollections of the novelist James Salter, who first met him in Aspen in the summer of 1973. Salter (originally Horowitz) was ten years younger than Bellow to the day, having been born on June 10, 1925. After attending West Point, he spent ten years as a fighter pilot, from 1951 to 1961, flying over a hundred combat missions in Korea. His first novel, *The Hunters*, about his experiences in Korea, appeared in 1957, and was later turned into a movie starring Robert Mitchum. Two years later, Salter was invited to Aspen by a friend and at a party met the then director of the institute's Executive Seminars, Bob Craig, who'd read *The Hunters* and encouraged him to attend one of the seminars. Salter became a regular visitor to Aspen, partly for the ambience of the town and the institute, partly for the skiing. In 1961, he borrowed money to buy a house in town, to be used for winter and summer visits. When he met Bellow in 1973, Lionel and Diana Trilling were also in residence. In an interview, Salter remembered the Trillings as deeply uncomfortable at Aspen (though they would return the next year). "They were not physical people. The altitude bothered them. They were thrown in with a lot of people who had never heard of Lionel Trilling and had never heard of Hawthorne and didn't know about 'authenticity.' . . . I could hardly find anything to talk to them about. They were on an extremely elevated level." The only thing the Trillings seemed to approve of was

Saul Bellow's writing. Lionel Trilling "was tremendously enthused by, supportive of, and in every way a champion of *Augie March*."

Salter met Bellow at a dinner given by the writer and journalist Karyl Roosevelt, "an extremely good-looking woman, very clever." Someone at the dinner showed Bellow a copy of Salter's novel *A Sport and a Pastime* (1967), and Bellow opened it and started reading. The next day, "he came to my house, he came to the door. He had my book in his hand and said, 'Well, I just wanted to talk with you.'" Salter does not remember what they talked about. (He would not say what Bellow thought of his writing, perhaps out of modesty.) What he remembers is being "a bit in awe" of Bellow but liking him. He had not read any of Bellow's fiction and immediately began with one of the early novels, either *Dangling Man* or *The Victim*. He wasn't impressed. Then he read *Henderson the Rain King*. "I just thought, This is simply a gorgeous, a wonderful book. So I esteemed him as a writer—no question about it—both because of his position and because of what he had written." Soon he and Bellow were meeting every afternoon at the local swimming pool. Salter was married at the time, to his first wife, and had four children. "I was not running around." Bellow "began to see Karyl," presumably when Fran Gendlin was not there. "I should marry you," Bellow told her, according to an entry in one of the notebooks Salter kept during the years Bellow visited Aspen. Then Bellow added: "You'd probably only deceive me about ten times in the first year."[47]

Bellow and Salter talked about women, books, and travel, and contemplated a trip to Europe together. Salter's earliest notebook entries about Bellow date from July 1973. On July 5, he writes that Bellow invited him for a drink. When he arrived, Bellow was cooking Daniel dinner, "paper-thin steaks." While Daniel ate, the two novelists drank sour-mash whiskey on ice. They talked of John Berryman's suicide in January 1972. Salter describes Bellow in a notebook entry as having "the face of a not-too-friendly tortoise." He notes "strange silences, almost shyness, his eyes looking to the side as he talks. He's reading Chekhov's letters, *The Kreutzer Sonata*, a book on language and speech. *The Idiot* is open near his bed." Two days later, on an expedition with the journalist Frances Fitzgerald to Roaring Fork River ("She's a good girl, Frankie," Bellow says), they talk of Tolstoy's marriage. "Saul says he has made an exhaustive study of Tolstoy's intellectual positions on marriage," perhaps spurred by thoughts of Susan and divorce, topics he frequently raised in conversation. Salter carries Daniel across the river on his back, "an act he [Daniel] loves." "'My dear Dog,' I say, repeating something Saul had quoted from a Chekhov letter." Then Bellow says: "'No, Chekhov can't have said that. You don't call a woman that. It's badly translated. It might have been Dear Poochie, or something. Too bad Edmund Wilson is gone.'"

In later notebook entries, made in both Aspen and Chicago, Salter characterizes Bellow's talk as "lovely . . . nicely filled with real detail, sexual, sums of money, names of streets, all in the right proportion with an unfailing sense of humor and style." In Chicago, on a visit of October 19–20, 1973, Bellow drives Salter through the city. "Move it, he calls to two black girls sauntering across the path of the car from the trolley platform. Their reply is left behind, fuck something. What'd they say, he asks?" They pass the Shoreland Hotel, once owned by Maury and Marge, then 5490 South Shore Drive, where he and Susan lived. "He'd given it to her as part of the divorce settlement. He'd had a $17,000 equity. She sold it for $40,000." Salter stays in Bellow's apartment in the Cloisters, in the room Daniel sleeps in when he spends the night. He and Bellow lie down in his bedroom to watch the television news: "Israeli generals being interviewed, tough, eloquent men. They speak in the manner of European police commissioners. They were all trained by the English, Saul explains." Then they go for dinner at Gene and Georgetti, a restaurant said to be favored by the Mafia. They serve "the best steak in Chicago," Bellow tells Salter, but they "won't give him a good table." The meal is enjoyable, eaten quickly, without wine, dessert, or coffee. They talk about Karyl Roosevelt, blacks, Israel. The next morning, Salter wakes up to the sound of Bellow typing, the radio blaring classical music.

In an entry from December 1973, Bellow complains of women. He is having problems with Frances Gendlin, "who was nervous, making him nervous. He also has complaints about Karyl Roosevelt and a new girlfriend in Chicago named Gugu, a Romanian mathematician." Salter offers advice about Frances:

> You must calm her, I suggest.
>
> I thought the way to calm them / the way to calm them, I thought, was to go to bed with them.
>
> That does calm them.

Not for long, he says.
It must be repeated.

More generally, Salter's advice is "not to marry unless you are absolutely certain, unless it is impossible not to." In the same entry, he writes of Bellow: "His concerns, his sorrows seem so childish. He will find a woman, I assure him. The world is filled with them."

On another occasion, in Chicago, Bellow takes Salter to the Italian Village, the restaurant where Ijah Brodsky meets his gangster cousin Tanky in "Cousins" (1974). Bellow had eaten there the previous week with the conductor of the Chicago Symphony, Georg Solti. "The head waiter doesn't seem to remember him, but hides it. *Signore*, he calls Saul. *Professore*, Saul corrects." Back in Bellow's apartment, they have a drink "in his large, comfortable, faintly bare living room," then retire to bed. Bellow has given Salter 150 pages of *Humboldt* to read. Salter is struck by the "marvelous names, descriptions. Demmie Vonghel, Uncle Waldemar." He describes Bellow's writing as "compelling, witty, extraordinarily kind. His treatment of his ex-wife, Denise (Susan, in life) is incredibly fair ('just,' he says). The mafia boss whose little dog's paws are infected . . . It is intensely human and at the same time weak." Salter calls it "a book seen naked with its flaws, wanderings, ineptness. An important writer's work in progress." He praises Bellow's "excellent, succinct, *honest* style. Use of homely accurate phrases and words. Also, he often digresses in the midst of things, digresses, not pans away. Very effective." But of the finished book, Salter said in an interview, he was less certain, thought it "flopped around a lot," was "forced."

The friendship between Bellow and Salter at one point included a third party, Bellow's friend Walter Pozen, briefly referred to in earlier chapters. Pozen was younger than the other two men, born in 1933 in East Orange, New Jersey. He went to the University of Chicago, in the same class as Susan Sontag, then to the University of Chicago Law School. He married at twenty-one and in the summer of 1956 got a job in a New York law firm in later years called Fried, Frank. As soon as he arrived, however, he was asked to move to Washington, D.C. Among the firm's Washington clients were several Native American nations: the Sioux and the Laguna Pueblo Indians.

There were three partners in the Washington office, one of whom was Bellow's old lodger from Minneapolis, Max Kampelman. Through his contacts with Hubert Humphrey, Kampelman did all sorts of political work, and Pozen was assigned to take on several jobs for Humphrey. Soon he "got the political bug," took leave from the law firm and went to work for a New Jersey congressman named Harrison Williams, who was running for the Senate. After Williams won, the Kennedys recruited Pozen to work as their campaign advance man in New Jersey. Pozen got to know Congressman Stewart Udall, whom JFK appointed secretary of the interior. Pozen was then asked to be Udall's assistant, because Kenny O'Donnell, the Kennedy aide, knew he'd worked with Indians, and because the Kennedys, who didn't have close ties with Udall, wanted someone in the Department of the Interior whom they knew.[48]

Although Pozen's job was in the Department of the Interior, he frequently did legal and other work for the White House, especially when he and Udall stayed on after Lyndon Johnson became president. Under LBJ, Pozen estimates, he spent almost half his time in the White House. One day, in the autumn of 1965, while at work on a speech for the president, he walked to Lafayette Park for lunch, carrying with him a copy of the *New York Herald Tribune*. The paper contained an article by Bellow on political biography (the article appeared first on October 3, 1965, in the *Chicago Sun-Times Book Week*, under the title "On Chronicles and Partisans," and is quoted from in chapter 1). Pozen was greatly impressed, and when he returned to the White House, instead of resuming work on the speech, wrote a lengthy letter to Bellow, about urban policy and the fate of the inner cities (this was at the time LBJ was thinking of forming the Department of Housing and Urban Development). "I didn't go to the University of Chicago for nothing," Pozen recalled. "I talked about Athens and so forth." Pozen wrote the letter on White House stationery and addressed it to "Professor Saul Bellow, University of Chicago, Chicago." A week later, he received a reply from Bellow, telling him that he'd raised very interesting questions in his letter and that the next time he was in Chicago he should come to see him. "He was most forthcoming, and the long and the short of it was that we more or less kept in touch weekly." Eventually, Pozen went to visit Bellow in Chicago ("my only reason was to go see Saul"), and they struck up a friendship. Now when he received invitations to come to the University of Chicago to talk about government policy he accepted them, and he and Bellow would have lunch at the Eagle or Jimmy's, hangouts Pozen knew from his student days. They talked politics but also money, women, marriage. Bellow was between Sasha and Susan at this period, and Pozen's marriage was in trouble. Like Bellow, Pozen was handsome; both men, in Pozen's phrase, were "chasers."

By the time Pozen came to visit Bellow in Aspen in 1973, he had returned to the law and had a new wife, Joan Kennan, daughter of George Kennan, the Cold War diplomat often called "the father of containment." Bellow gave the Pozens dinner in his "glorious" cabin on Red Mountain—Frances was not there at the time—and read them pages from *Humboldt* (the scene with Cantabile at the Russian Baths).

He also introduced Pozen to James Salter. The three men got along well. This was a time when Bellow, as Pozen puts it, "was always doing these crazy-ass investments," and now he got it in his head to buy a cabin in the Aspen area with Salter, one they would time-share, though Salter, who already had a house in town, would make most use of it. So the three men set out in Salter's rackety VW for Basalt Mountain, which, according to Pozen, had even better skiing than Aspen and was more beautiful. At one point, in their ramble over mountains and through mining towns, in the middle of "absolutely nowhere," the VW broke down. Salter calmly took out a screwdriver, a hammer, and some tape and repaired the thing, while Pozen watched and Bellow sat by the side of the road and read.

In the end, Bellow and Salter failed to find a suitable cabin, but they did find beautiful property—in Missouri Heights, near Carbondale—eighty-one acres, with views of Aspen and the distant mountains. The price was a hundred thousand dollars, and Pozen, too, wanted a piece of the deal. The plan was to divide the property into three ten-acre lots, each with undisturbed vistas, reserving the remaining fifty or so acres for "tasteful development." Each man put up a third of the cost, and Pozen worked out the deal with the realtor, a man straight out of a Bellow novel, totally untrustworthy. Pozen subsequently served as lawyer and banker for the scheme, sorting out water rights and reclamation rights, a more time-consuming business than he'd bargained for. Salter did eventually build a cabin on his acres, but Bellow and Pozen simply retained their plots as an investment, along with the acres held in common by all three. When, eventually, they decided to sell, they had trouble finding a buyer, or a buyer at the right price ("Saul kept thinking it would be worth a fortune," Salter recalls). Finally, over a decade later, in need of money and fed up with handling problems associated with the property ("I was the only one in Aspen"), Salter convinced

Bellow and Pozen to accept an offer of $130,000, described by Pozen as "a loss, considering the costs." As soon as they sold it, Salter recalls, "the land went well up in value."

There were no recriminations. The differences between the friends produced only minor or short-lived tensions. On one of Salter's visits to Chicago in 1973, Pozen came as well, shortly after they'd purchased the land. Over lunch at the Eagle, the three men discussed their joint agreement. For a moment, according to a notebook entry, Salter felt, "I am not really among friends." But he was. There were no double-crossings. Later, Bellow drove him around the city in his new Mercedes, showing him the old neighborhood: Louis Dworkin's bakery, the Russian Baths. During the visit, driving along the Midway, Bellow and Pozen praised its beauty and the many activities that took place there. "Tennis, for instance," said Pozen, "ice-skating." "Rapes," Bellow added. Salter describes Pozen as Bellow's "devoted, admiring friend." Salter, too, was admiring. Although he did not always agree with Bellow about writing, nor did he like all Bellow's books (Salter believed that Pozen admired Bellow's books "beyond all reason"), he thought him "a great figure and a great writer."

Salter did not envy Bellow as a man. "I felt he was harried. He was beset by problems of guilt and behavior." Bellow's breakthrough after *The Victim*, the development of a distinctive voice, set him apart. "I'm never going to be able to do that," Salter admitted, "to bust through to the way I speak and think." This admission was not difficult for Salter. "I'm not like Norman Mailer, I didn't feel that with Saul. It was easy to be friends." When Salter gave Bellow a draft of his novel *Light Years* (1975), Bellow read it carefully, pointing out flaws and weaknesses. In a notebook entry, Salter records his disappointment but also "the accuracy of what he tells me, the knowing, direct appraisal." When the finished novel was published, Bellow read it again, and was full of praise. This time, Salter records Bellow's reaction wryly: "He loved the book. He read the book with delight. The changes I'd made, he said (!) (I'd made very few and those delicate). The deletions! Additions! (I had taken out two meal descriptions). Everything helped tremendously. His main reservation was that there was no objective voice anywhere *pointing out the meaning of the high esteem these people seemed to have for themselves, the real value of privilege*" (a reservation others would share, though what Salter thinks of it, why he underlines it in the notebook, is not clear). With Salter, Bellow was good company, helpful and encouraging, as he was, for the most part, with colleagues on the Committee, with his secretary, who thought him the perfect boss, with other friends. His personal life, however, in particular his relations with lovers and ex-wives, remained turbulent, exacerbated by the gathering pressures of Susan and her lawyers.

SB with English Department students at Sir George Williams University, Montreal, 1968 (courtesy of Alex Dworkin / Canadian Jewish Archives)

4

A Better Man

In Bellow's correspondence from the early 1970s, bad behavior is frequently seen as a product of character as well as a response to external irritants. Faults and vices are acknowledged, at times indulged, as well as excused or denied. In a letter to Edward Shils of February 27, 1972, Bellow enumerates the things that, "as young people say, 'turn me off,'" beginning with James Redfield's "nonsense," continuing with "lawsuits, taxes, business dealings, stock markets, female weakness (in men and women), the gnawing volume of daily mendacity, the obstinate stupidities of the educated in intellectual professions, and my own persistent and wicked habits of soul." "Probably because proximity breeds contempt," he writes on August 3, 1972, to Julian Behrstock, his old friend from college, "I throw away all communication from Northwestern. All the sorority girls who snubbed me—it's them I want to see at class reunions in the full decay of their middle age. I have no other incentive to attend." In June 1971, a revised version of *The Last Analysis* was restaged Off Broadway, at the Circle in the Square, on Bleecker Street, and "handsomely" received by the critics. Clive Barnes in *The New York Times* ("Bellow's Psychology of 'The Last Analysis,'" June 24, 1971) described it as a "peculiar mixture of brilliance and promise, of wild humor and cheerfully careless craftsmanship . . . one of the funniest comedies written during the last few years." In a letter of June 25, 1971, to Constance Perin, Bellow professed himself "delighted" with the reviews, adding, "These are the victories that gratify my litigious character, my vengeful Jewish heart."[1] In a letter of March 5, 1973, to a Tuley High School pal, Louis Lasco, he describes an encounter at the University of Missouri with "Benny Shapiro's brother Manny . . . with his frau and an elegant young son in a Smith Bros. beard. We reminisced about old times on Cortez St. . . . The young man asked what he should do to become a writer. I said 'Shave!' He was much offended, nettled, and turned away from me."

In his denunciation of the editors of *Partisan Review* in "Culture Now: Some Animadversions, Some Laughs" (1971), in the first issue of Philip Rahv's journal *Modern Occasions*, a new violence enters Bellow's polemical prose. In a letter quoted in the previous chapter, Bellow refers to the essay's "fulminations," its "wickedness." Reading William Phillips on Susan Sontag, he says, "is much like going scuba diving at Coney Island in ruinous brine and scraps of old paper, orange rinds, and soaked hot dog buns." Richard Poirier has "made *PR* look like a butcher's showcase, shining with pink, hairless pigginess and adorned with figurines of hand-carved suet which represent the very latest in art, literature, and politics." When Poirier and Phillips were admitted to the Century Association, as mentioned in chapter 14 of *To Fame and Fortune*, Bellow resigned. In the "red letter" or negative appraisal he wrote to the club's Committee on Admissions, he accused the two editors of having "repudiated entirely" the values of Philip Rahv, Phillips's cofounding editor. "Standards have become rather soft, I know, but it's nevertheless difficult for me to understand how anyone who has looked into recent numbers of P.R. could think of its editor as a member of the Century Club."[2] "Red letters" were meant to be destroyed once they'd been read by members of the committee. After Phillips and Poirier were admitted, Bellow reported to F. W. Dupee, "my letter was posted on the bulletin board as evidence of my unbelievable effrontery."[3]

In the publishing world, Bellow's reputation as a difficult author was well established. Like all writers, he wanted his work properly treated. Unlike most writers, he had the power to see that it was. This power he exercised freely, sometimes fiercely, as in his anger with Penguin over the covers of his reissued paperbacks, discussed in chapter 2. Weidenfeld & Nicolson felt his wrath on other grounds as well. On November 30, 1972, he wrote to his British agent, Mark Hamilton of A. M. Heath, with instructions. Although Bellow said he was "very fond" of George Weidenfeld and reluctant to upset him or lose his friendship, "it seems to me as a publisher he leaves almost everything to be desired." Bellow could not find any of his books in the bookstores. His books had not sold well in Britain, though his reputation could not have been higher. "It seems to me that George and Tony [Godwin, of Penguin] have not taken me very seriously. I have repeatedly tried to discuss matters with them but they elude me with a drink or a pleasant chat. In any case, I am tired of this pursuit and of this nagging." Secker & Warburg, where Barley Alison had gone in 1967, would publish his next novel in Britain in 1975. This time there would be no reprieve, as there had been in 1966, when Weidenfeld flew to Chicago to deliver in person a deal Bellow was unable to refuse.

Bellow's power with his American agents was indicated by the nickname they gave him: "God." "God's on the phone at La Guardia Airport. He wants you to meet him in front of the Westbury at six-thirty to pick up the manuscript pages" was a message relayed to Harriet Wasserman in the early 1970s, soon after she began handling Bellow at Russell & Volkening. According to Wasserman's memoir, Henry Volkening would "break out in sweats when Saul came to town." Nor was Volkening alone in this reaction. Bellow "intimidated everyone. Years later, the photographer Tom Victor, who took many wonderful pictures of Saul, said to me, before a photo session . . . 'Saul looks at you like the strictest teacher you ever had in school. The one you were most afraid of.' He has a way of giving a look—sharp and penetrating—that can scare you to death, a no-place-to-hide feeling."[4] Joseph Epstein marveled at Bellow's capacity to instill fear in those who crossed, denied, or let him down. Though physically unintimidating, Bellow somehow managed to convey the impression "that he had strangled a bulldog with his bare hands."[5]

IN 1971, BELLOW AGREED to be a Booker Prize judge, persuaded by the publisher Tom Maschler, a member of the prize's organizing committee. The other judges that autumn were the historian Antonia Fraser, the critic Philip Toynbee, the novelist John Fowles, and John Gross, an English don at King's College, Cambridge. Gross, the chair of the judges, was the author of *The Rise and Fall of the Man of Letters* (1969) and *James Joyce* (1970) and would become editor of the *Times Literary Supplement* in 1974. Gross had met Bellow once before, at an informal dinner at the London home of W. G. ("Garry") Runciman—Viscount Runciman of Doxford, the sociologist—and his wife, Ruth, an adviser to and administrator of charities, quangos, and inquiries. Gross was there with his wife, Miriam, the deputy literary editor of *The*

Observer. Edward Shils had arranged for Bellow to attend the dinner. Like Gross, he was at the time a Fellow of King's College, Cambridge; he had also played a role in recruiting Runciman to the Department of Sociology at Cambridge.[6] What Gross remembered of the dinner was that Bellow spent much of the evening "canoodling" with a young woman he'd brought along (none of the guests can remember her name). When not canoodling, "he would come out with dazzling remarks." Miriam Gross remembers only the canoodling. Gross was also struck by how "neat and dapper" Bellow was, "a very snappy dresser," reminding him of "various uncles on my mother's side, who were always very good dancers."[7]

One of Bellow's conditions on agreeing to be a Booker judge was that he be put up at the Ritz, a condition Gross imagined "must have put a big hole in the Booker budget." When given a room not overlooking Green Park, he complained and was moved. The Booker winner that year was V. S. Naipaul, for *In a Free State*.[8] The main competitor to Naipaul was Elizabeth Taylor, whose novel *Mrs Palfrey at the Claremont* was favored by Gross and Antonia Fraser. Although Gross thought Naipaul a more important writer than Taylor, he greatly admired Taylor's fiction and thought *Mrs Palfrey* "one of her best novels." He also thought Taylor had more to gain from the Booker than Naipaul. Taylor's novels invariably received good reviews and favorable comments from fellow writers, but they never sold—a mystery to Gross, given her accessible style. As he later recalled, it was Bellow who "pretty much blew her out of the water. He said when the first round came . . . 'This is an elegant tinkling teacup novel of the kind that you Brits do very well, but it's not serious stuff.' "[9]

When it came to a vote, Gross remembered, the pro-Taylor judges "weren't so weak that we lay down and died in front of him," but the fact that Bellow "was going to be obviously so against it" played a part in their giving way. During the judges' deliberations, Bellow was "not unamiable." But he seemed to Gross to belong to a different species. "Bellow stood out. He was vivid. He seemed almost a Technicolor personality, where other people were in black-and-white. . . . He had flown in, he was going to fly out." Antonia Fraser recalls sharing a taxi back with Bellow "on a long, long ride from somewhere in the City: he was nattily dressed in a pale green shantung suit, blue shirt, green tie with large blue dots on it; his silver hair and slanting, large dark eyes made him look like a 30s film star playing a refined gangster. Suddenly he leaned forward and asked: 'Has anyone ever told you that you're a very handsome woman?' I pondered on a suitable reply, modest yet encouraging. But having spoken the Great Man closed his eyes and remained apparently asleep for the rest of the journey."[10]

HALF A YEAR LATER, Bellow went to Japan for five weeks, at the invitation of the Japan Society. A letter of March 29, 1972, to Nadine Nimier, a former lover from Paris, explains something of the attractions of travel. Bellow writes from Miami, where he has gone with Adam and Daniel "to cure myself." Although blocked as a correspondent in Chicago, as soon as he lands in Miami: "*Voilà!*—suddenly I am able to reply to your note. Evidently I come back to life when I voyage. Next month I'm off to Japan. I don't know a word of *le Japonais—pas un seul mot*." Nor did he know much of the Japanese, as he explained in a letter of October 20, 1976, to the poet Richard Eberhart. "I was invited by the Rockefeller Foundation to participate in a conference on American-Japanese relations. It has always remained a sevenfold mystery to me why I was asked [his old friend Herbert Passin, an authority on Japanese–United States relations, is the likely answer], why I accepted, and why I observed silence throughout three days. I was mummer than a Trappist, and my silence so deeply impressed the Japanese that I was subsequently invited to Tokyo to determine whether I would ever say anything."

It was not quite true that Bellow knew nothing of American-Japanese relations. As *Herzog* makes clear, he knew a fair bit about Japanese women. Before his marriage to Sasha, and during it, according to Jack Ludwig, Bellow had an affair with a Japanese woman who was the model for Sono Oguki in *Herzog*. Paolo Milano implies as much in a letter of May 29, 1965, confessing, "I am most discreetly interested in the 'Japanese chapter' of your *Herzog*." Moses's evenings with Sono are both sensuous and comic, like evenings with Ramona Donsell. Sono has a wealthy father and has lived in Paris; in New York, she studies design and lives in a brownstone apartment on the Upper West Side, where she pads "back and forth busily on bare feet" (p. 586). She has "a tender heart," and when Moses tells her he is unhappy she cries "instantaneous tears. They had a way of appearing without the usual Western preliminaries." Bathing figures prominently in evenings with Sono. After settling Moses "in the swirling, foaming, perfumed water she let drop her petticoat and got in behind him, singing that vertical music of hers" ("vertical" is perfect, as is a later description of Sono's songs as "sweet and odd, narrow, steep, at times with catlike sounds") (p. 585). After bathing, Sono brings out her erotic scrolls, on which "fat merchants made love to slender girls who looked away comically as they submitted. . . . She pointed to things, winking and exclaiming and pressing her round face to his" (p. 588).

Although Sono has high connections in Japanese diplomatic circles (through whom she has met Nasser, Sukharno, and the secretary of state), all she wants of Moses is to be alone with him in her apartment. " 'T'es philosophe. O mon philosophe, mon professeur d'amour. T'es très important. Je le sais.' She rated him higher than kings and presidents" (p. 589). As Moses puts it, wonderingly: "She did not want me to work for her, to furnish her house, support her children, to be regular at meals or to open charge accounts in luxury shops; she asked only that I should be with her from time to time. But some people are at war with the best things of life. . . . Other men have forsaken the West, looking for just this" (p. 591). When Moses marries Madeleine, Sono returns to Japan. Ever since, as he puts it in an unsent letter, "*When I pass Northwest Orient Airlines. I always mean to price a ticket to Tokyo*" (p. 590). Whether Bellow looked up Sono's real-life model in Japan is not known, but there is evidence he spent much of his trip looking for something like her.[11]

Bellow's responsibilities as Intellectual Exchange Fellow were to offer talks and attend receptions. When not touring the country, he stayed in Tokyo at the International House, in the city's Embassy District. In undated letters to Fran Gendlin, he complains of how hard he is made to work. "I'm told there are castles and blossoms. Haven't seen them myself. I'm kept busy with lectures, seminars and interviews. I get the weekends off for good behavior." In a later letter, he complains of jet lag ("it took more than ten days to recover") and of the drawbacks of celebrity, not just lectures but "interviews, radio programs and Japanese semi-state dinners." To David Grene, in a letter of June 22, he calls Tokyo "a fuming, hissing metropolis," embodying Henry James's coinage " 'numerosity.' There are no small gatherings, only mobs—everywhere mobs of every description." To Gendlin, he complains about Japanese food and dining habits ("sitting on the floor, using chopsticks"), about drinking too much sake, then waking at 4:00 a.m. "utterly wretched most of the time." It was two weeks before the pace slackened and he was allowed out of Tokyo. In Kyoto, "it was relatively tranquil," and he enjoyed the old-style Japanese inn he stayed in, "sleeping on the straw mat and lying on the floors half the day, admiring the little moss garden. Being on the floor was childhood again, and childhood is still the most pleasant part of life."

In the first of the undated letters to Gendlin, Bellow makes an embarrassing confession. "I was disheartened—*appalled* is a probably more accurate word—to find that I had crab-lice. I felt peculiarly shaky and stupid to make that discovery. I'd had nothing at all to do with women here. . . . Cured now, I feel lousy still. Anti-self, anti-others, but above all the old fool." In the later undated letter, he reiterates the point about having nothing to do with women. He has been "perfectly straight, and non-adulterous. There's no inclination, no temptation, and I seem to have lost touch with the seducer's mentality." These assertions are flatly contradicted by Atlas, who describes Bellow as "on the prowl for geishas." He quotes John Nathan, a thirty-two-year-old American scholar of Japanese culture and history, also a filmmaker, later a professor of East Asian studies at the University of California at Santa Barbara, who was asked "to be Bellow's Virgil" in Japan. "The man was obsessed with getting laid," Nathan told Atlas; the claim that he was "straight" or chaste in Japan, he said in an interview, was "patently ridiculous."[12] At one point, it was reported, Bellow got in trouble for trying to smuggle a woman into a Zen monastery.[13] If such reports are to be believed, they help to explain a second confession in the Gendlin letter, of a piece with other admissions of guilt and "wickedness" in this period. "The world seems to expect that I will do all kinds of good things," he tells Gendlin, "and I spite it by doing all kinds of bad things." These bad things, though not "striking sins," produce "unhappiness for myself and others"; "the effect on others is a curse to me night and day." Nathan recalls several such "bad things"—for example, how curt and dismissive Bellow was when interviewed by the Japanese novelist Kenzaburō Ōe, who would himself win the Nobel Prize in 1994. Ōe was a great Bellow fan and excited to meet him. He'd carefully prepared a list of questions about *The Adventures of Augie March* and *Henderson the Rain King*, but when he emerged from the interview he told Nathan, "Bellow had scarcely given him the time of day."[14] On another occasion, Bellow became sullen when he failed to get anywhere with the "dark, literary creature" who had been assigned to look after him before a lecture. He then "ripped through" the lecture (it was about narrative method in Joyce), reading so quickly there was little chance his Japanese audience, packed with admiring English professors, could follow what he was saying. He left without answering questions, a performance Nathan described as "passive/aggressive, hostile."[15]

At other times, Bellow could be cordial. When Nathan took him into a typical Japanese home, he was charming and seemed to enjoy himself. The cutting remarks he made struck Nathan as involuntary, "a kind of Tourette's," recalling Herschel Shawmut in "Him with His Foot in His Mouth." Nathan was well connected in literary and artistic circles in Tokyo. A six-foot-four American with a Japanese wife, he spoke fluent Japanese, had translated Mishima and Ōe, and was at work on a film with Hiroshi Teshigahara, director of *Woman in the Dunes* (1964). He was "thrilled" to meet Bellow and to show him the city. "I was an avid Bellow fan. I wanted to be a novelist. I wanted to be Saul Bellow." Bellow seemed to like Nathan, but at one point he "informed me that I was the best 'squaw man' he had ever met." When Nathan asked what a squaw man was, Bellow explained: it was a white man who married a Native American woman and lived in her tribe. Nathan took the remark as a put-down, as though Bellow were saying, You're a big deal here because you're an oddity, with the implication that you'd be less of a big deal in your own culture.[16] The remark recalls Bellow's hostility toward his Paris-based friend, Harold "Kappy" Kaplan (discussed in chapters 8 and 9 of *To Fame and Fortune*), whom he accused of being more French than the French.

Only at his desk, when such remarks were channeled into art, could one count on Bellow to acknowledge the pain they caused, which is not to say that his awareness would stop him from making them. In "Him with His Foot in His Mouth," Herschel Shawmut acknowledges "the evil I did" (p. 376), inexcusable remarks both "idiotic and wicked" (p. 378), but he sees these remarks as drawn "from the depths of my nature, that hoard of strange formulations" (p. 381). The remarks are made "for art's sake, i.e. without perversity or malice. . . . Yes, there has to be some provocation, but what happens when I am provoked happens because the earth heaves up underfoot, and then from opposite ends of the heavens I get a simultaneous shock to both ears. I am deafened and I have to open my mouth" (p. 390). Elsewhere, Shawmut enumerates the possible sources of these remarks: "seizure, rapture, demonic possession, frenzy, *Fatum* [from Nietzsche, meaning an essential nature "inaccessible to revision," which "can be taught nothing"], divine madness, or even solar storm. The better people are, the less they take offense at this gift, or curse" (p. 412). For Bellow, as for Shawmut, cutting remarks, like other forms of bad behavior, were part of the package, connected in Bellow's case to his power as a writer, his "gift, or curse." When Nathan came to pick him up each day from International House, he would sometimes sit and watch Bellow writing at the little table in his room. "I was delighted to see it . . . the intensity with which he sat there." "I do this to keep sane," Bellow said of his writing routine.[17]

FRAN GENDLIN WAS NOT the only woman to receive a letter from Bellow during his visit to Japan. He also wrote to a young woman with whom he had been having an affair for over a year, to put an end to the relationship. This woman, who wishes not to be identified, recognized herself, or aspects of herself, in Doris Scheldt, with whom Charlie Citrine has an affair in *Humboldt's Gift*. In depicting Doris, she wrote me, Bellow "describes my flat on the near North side of Chicago and my quirky way of dressing at the time. I had a bentwood rocker and though I did needlepoint whilst he read to me, I also knitted matching jumpers for him and Daniel. And yes, I was terrified of getting pregnant. It was before Roe v Wade."[18] The reason Bellow gave for ending the relationship was that he didn't want the woman to end up having to "push him in a bathchair." Bellow was fifty-six when she entered his office on a bet (that she couldn't get into his graduate seminar on *Ulysses*), and she was twenty-one, a fourth-year undergraduate from Columbia, spending her senior year at the University of Chicago.[19] Like Charlie's Doris, she was, still is, petite, attractive, and funny, and after she explained to Bellow why she wished to audit his course, he admitted her. "He didn't know what I could contribute," he said, "but I'd be decorative." At Columbia she had majored in English and urban studies and had ambitions to write. The seminar, to which she occasionally contributed, "was amazing, as you'd imagine." After its penultimate session, she asked Bellow if he'd like a lift home, as it was raining. He declined. After the last session, "he asked if he could have that ride and so I drove him back to the Cloisters. He was obviously attracted to me and as it was the end of the course he asked me out and he made me supper and we went to bed. What can I say? I was terribly flattered."

From then on, they saw each other "about twice a week" for a year. In the summer of 1971, he flew her out to Aspen for a couple of days, shortly after Fran Gendlin's visit. Daniel was there at the time, and he and the young woman were "the kids." In Chicago, the affair was conducted at her apartment, to which Bellow frequently came after playing racquetball at the Riviera Club on East Randolph Street. Mostly they stayed in, though occasionally he'd take her to a restaurant or an event where he was speaking. She met Edward Shils several times and thought he was "a pompous ass," though he treated her courteously. She heard a lot about David Peltz, though she never met him. On one occasion, she and Bellow had supper with her parents, eight years his junior. The family came from a wealthy North Shore township. In *Humboldt's Gift*, Doris's father, Professor Scheldt, is an anthroposophist; the real-life young woman's father was in business. She describes her parents as outwardly establishment but with progressive views. "Their attitude was that I was free, white and twenty-one and if I wanted to get involved with someone thirty-five years older it might as well be a literary eminence. As long as I didn't get hurt." She didn't. As she writes, in an email of June 19, 2015, "I can honestly say that he never hurt me either emotionally or physically in his behavior toward me or when he ended it. It was disappointing but my heart wasn't broken."

She also believes she gained things from the affair. Bellow introduced her to Mozart's operas. She learned how to make a vinaigrette and a martini. Bellow had interesting things to tell about books and writing. The summer after graduation, she got a job in Chicago with the educational publisher Scott Foresman, and sometimes she and Bellow would talk about her work, as when she was asked to prepare biographies of writers or to "expurgate" *The Taming of the Shrew* for students. Mostly, though, Bellow talked about what he was writing, not just *Humboldt's Gift* but "Zetland and Quine," an unfinished novel about Isaac Rosenfeld. When she discovered he had used her as a partial model for Doris Scheldt, "I was flattered. . . . Doris was a pretty fair representation." That Doris is nowhere near as sexy as Renata did not bother her. She'd had little sexual experience when she met Bellow, all of it with equally inexperienced contemporaries, a fact that accounts for her willingness to put up with what she now sees as Bellow's "lousy" lovemaking: "I didn't know any better." Overall, however, she looks back on the affair with warmth and gratitude. "It was a very friendly relationship. I don't think he was ever mad at me. My take on the whole thing is that . . . he was beginning to fear his mortality. His friends were dying. He talked about Isaac Rosenfeld all the time and about Delmore Schwartz and it was during our time that John Berryman died and he was really upset about that." "I made him feel younger. It was a way of avoiding the Angel of Death." Another reason Bellow never expressed anger or irritation toward her, she believes, is that he was "busy venting his feelings on Susan." That he was seeing other women, referred to by her as "your grown-up lady friends," was clear, though she never knew how many there were. She felt no guilt about the affair: since it took place "between Susan and Alexandra . . . the whole thing was kosher." What the affair shows, why it is worth knowing about, is that not all Bellow's relationships with women at this time were fraught and painful, the occasion of inexcusable behavior on his part. That said, exceptions often prove the rule.[20]

SHORTLY AFTER HIS RETURN to Chicago from Japan, Bellow received a letter dated June 2, 1972, from Henry Volkening inviting him to "drunch" at the Century. Two years previously, Volkening's wife, Natalie, had died of lung cancer, and, as Harriet Wasserman puts it in *Handsome Is*, "Henry was lost without Natalie."[21] Volkening himself then developed lung cancer. On January 10, 1971, he had written to Bellow to tell him he was about to be operated on and that the doctors were "as optimistic as they, professionally, can permit themselves to be. 'We caught it early. It's the size of a dime.'" On March 7, Bernard Malamud, also a Russell & Volkening author, wrote to Bellow saying that he had been in New York and "spoke to Henry, in full voice, and apparently coming along well. Speriamo." Weeks later, in an undated letter, Bellow replied less hopefully: "Henry doesn't seem very well. He calls up now and then to say he's better, but he doesn't really sound better. He's putting up a good fight."[22] Both Volkening and his partner, Diarmuid Russell, "smoked like a chimney." According to Wasserman, Natalie Volkening "died of secondhand smoke." A week after Wasserman reported to Russell that Volkening's cancer was inoperable, Russell called her into his office to say that "he'd just got the results of some tests, and his doctors told him he had the exact same kind of lung cancer as Henry."[23] In the summer of 1972, Russell and Volkening sold the agency to Tim Seldes, an editor at Doubleday. The "drunch" Volkening had proposed that June was to introduce Bellow to Seldes. "My sense is that he will be very good and successful," Volkening wrote, "and you of course have long sensed that I won't long be of the health to continue to function efficiently. So this will be a lucky break for me, and for my clients too." Henry Volkening died within the year, on October 18, 1972, followed fourteen months later by Diarmuid Russell.

According to Wasserman, by the time Seldes bought Russell & Volkening, she was "to all intents and purposes" Bellow's agent.[24] She had first met him in January 1969, in her fourth year at the agency, when he came to the office to pick up Volkening for lunch. Bellow stopped in front of her desk when she was on the phone. He "looked me over—up and down. I was skinny then, and I was wearing a great dress. He came behind me, to my free ear: 'You know, you're really very pretty. Do you think you could take care of me? Would you marry me?' " On returning from lunch, Volkening called out in a voice loud enough for the rest of the office to hear: "Saul says Harriet has a pure heart. He says we should pay attention to her—she's got something there. . . . And from then on they paid attention to me."[25] Wasserman became Bellow's agent and remained so until 1996.

Only some of these years were spent at Russell & Volkening. When forced to give up the agency, both its founders wanted Wasserman to purchase it. To do so, however, involved taking out a large bank loan, and "I simply wasn't ready."[26] Seldes became the firm's boss, promising Wasserman a partnership that never materialized. After almost ten years, she began to feel that he was trying to push her out. On September 14, 1981, she left Russell & Volkening to start the Harriet Wasserman Literary Agency, taking Bellow with her. When first she disclosed her plans to leave, "without missing a beat," Bellow told her he'd go with her.[27] This is Wasserman's account. Seldes offers a somewhat different account. He and Wasserman "discussed" a partnership, but he never promised her one. At the beginning, he found her helpful, "very candid and welcoming early on and then sour and disgruntled—for no reason at all." The problem was that "she thought she should have been the boss." There were personality conflicts. She was "a really solitary person," and "eventually she became so difficult that she had to go." With Bellow, in contrast, Seldes's relations were easy. Volkening had told Seldes that Bellow made him so nervous that "he had to go home and have a few drinks before he could talk to Saul." Seldes found Bellow "about as engaging a man as you could want," though also "full of electricity."

Wasserman was devoted to Bellow, her most important author (others included Reynolds Price, Alice McDermott, Ruth Prawer Jhabvala, and Frederick Buechner). Early in their relationship, author and agent spent a single disastrous night as lovers. Bellow came to dinner and made a pass, which unnerved Wasserman ("Is this good for business?"). When he discovered she was wearing a "black Lastex body suit" under her caftan, he told her, "You're not coming to bed in that diving suit!" Once in bed, there were further embarrassments. "I almost laughed," Bellow later confessed, "but I didn't want to hurt your feelings." "I said I almost laughed too. But for me it had been a comic nightmare. . . . That night was never mentioned again. . . . There was no flirting anymore. It was strictly business—and a growing friendship."[28]

Wasserman was tough in defense of her authors' interests, at times abrasive, as agents often are; but she was also insecure, a product in part, her sister Maxine Fields believes, of their father, a dominating, denigrating figure, in part of a childhood illness, scoliosis, which made her self-conscious about her appearance. As a child, Wasserman had a minor protrusion on the right side of her back, which made her think she was deformed, a term her father used about her. In 1954, at fourteen, she had an operation on her back, and had to wear a body cast for a year. After high school, she went to Hunter College, but lived at home, in Riverdale, New York, until she was twenty-five. Although she never married or had a steady boyfriend, she was pretty, smart, and personable. According to her sister, she did well at her first jobs out of college, as secretary to the head of surgery at a New York hospital, then, briefly, in the film business. At Russell & Volkening, both her bosses thought highly of her. With Bellow she was patient and compliant, although she claims always to have given him an "honest response" when asked to read work in progress. Bellow counted on her as "first reader," she says, and when he sent manuscript material, "I'd call at once with a response, no matter what the time of day or night. And I'd tell him I'd get back to him after I read the draft twice more."[29] Early in their relationship, before the embarrassing night as lovers, Wasserman flew to Chicago to discuss a two-book deal Doubleday had offered Bellow. It was for two hundred thousand dollars and the promise of a summer house in Spain. Wasserman "was very cool" (the offer seems to have involved a possible split from Russell & Volkening), advising Bellow to beware, especially if the deal included "a provision that if book number one earns out before you deliver book number two, the contract separates into two individual contracts. Otherwise, the earnings from book number one will pay for the advance of book number two. I think he got it. A gleam came into his eye. 'Oh.'"[30] He continued to be represented by Russell & Volkening.

IN THE SPRING OF 1973, Bellow took an extended break from his duties at the Committee on Social Thought and spent six weeks at Monk's House, in the village of Rodmell in East Sussex, the former home of Virginia and Leonard Woolf. The offer to stay at Monk's House came from the historian Asa Briggs, vice-chancellor of the University of Sussex. The university had received the house from the painter Trekkie Parsons, the wife of Ian Parsons, Leonard Woolf's colleague at Chatto & Windus. In the years between Virginia Woolf's death in 1941 and Leonard Woolf's death in 1969, the Parsonses had been companions to Leonard as well as neighbors. When Briggs came to give a talk at the University of Chicago in 1973, Bellow mentioned that he was having trouble finishing *Humboldt's Gift*. Why not come to Sussex, Briggs suggested, deliver a lecture, and spend a couple of months living in Monk's House? In addition to the attractions of the house itself—oak beams, wood fires, sunny conservatory—there were extensive grounds, including kitchen and flower gardens, rolling lawns, ponds, two tall elms ("Virginia" and "Leonard"), and an orchard filled with plum and apple trees. Rodmell was largely unspoiled, the university was nearby, five or so miles away, as were the South Downs, the River Ouse, and the attractive town of Lewes, home to many Sussex academics.

Bellow's first impressions of Monk's House were communicated in April in an undated letter to Fran Gendlin. "Well, it's beautiful and spooky, the gardens are grand, the house cold, everything creaks but I was not haunted by the ghost of Virginia. I am exhausted, but well. I have no telephone and as yet no car, but I sh'd get the car. The phone is doubtful." In subsequent letters, partly aimed at persuading Gendlin to join him, Bellow complains of loneliness. "I work hard and have made much progress," he writes on May 8, "but the solitude of this existence is trying. I seem to feel quite sorry for myself when I'm alone, and I think Robinson Crusoe had more toys." In other letters, Bellow emphasized the attractions of Monk's House. A charwoman, Mrs. Willard, came daily and did all the washing and cleaning. The garden was "beautiful, and we can sit in the conservatory, which I have brought to life, and smell the jasmine." Gendlin took the bait and has fond memories of their stay: of sunny breakfasts in the conservatory, Bellow tending the kitchen garden in the afternoon, evenings with friends in the cozy upstairs sitting room. To Edward Shils, in a note written on stationery headed "From LEONARD WOOLF," Bellow writes on May 25 of the spring weather and of being happily immersed in his work: "The sun has begun to shine again, and the birds are amorous and the flowers open." The house was not without its inconveniences—Gendlin remembers smacking her forehead on low-hanging door frames and having difficulty getting in and out of the bath without soaking the floor—but it was not true, as has been suggested, that cold and discomfort sent them fleeing.[31]

Nor was it true that Bellow was isolated at Monk's House, as his early letters suggest. The critic and novelist Gabriel Josipovici—thirty-two at the time, a lecturer in English at Sussex—saw a good deal of Bellow that spring. Josipovici was one of only a very few critics whose accounts of his work Bellow approved. Shils had drawn the young academic to Bellow's attention, having been impressed by an essay he published on *Herzog* in 1971 in *Encounter*.[32] On the strength of the essay, Bellow asked Josipovici to write the introduction to the Viking *Portable Saul Bellow*, a task which Marshall Best of Viking thought Alfred Kazin or Lionel Trilling might undertake.[33] Josipovici lived in Lewes, and Bellow invited him over soon after arriving at Monk's House. The two men got on well. Bellow "never looked down his nose at me," Josipovici recalled, and was encouraging about his fiction. What Josipovici remembers of their weekly walks on the South Downs is Bellow's fondness for Chicago stories and locutions.

Josipovici met other guests on his visits to Monk's House, including the South African novelist Dan Jacobson and the Biblical and Jewish-studies scholar Chaim ("Rab") Raphael, a Research Fellow at Sussex. Bellow had known Raphael for many years, having met him in the 1940s, most likely through Alfred Kazin. In addition to writing books on Jewish history and culture, "Rab" (for "Rabinovitch," his original name) wrote crime thrillers under the pseudonym Jocelyn Davey. He had also been a high-ranking Treasury civil servant, and from 1942 to 1957 was posted to the British Information Services in New York, where he and Bellow first met. Josipovici remembers arriving one day at Monk's House to find Bellow entertaining Raphael and Miron Grindea, a Romanian-born journalist, founding editor of the literary journal *ADAM International Review*. Grindea was visibly nervous in the presence of the celebrated novelist, and when Bellow tried to calm him—"Relax, Mr. Grindea, just relax"—he replied: "I am relaxed. I'm just tapping out a little tune." Fran Gendlin also talks of meeting the painter Duncan Grant, who contrasted her favorably with Valerie Eliot. The poet's wife, Grant recalled, "wouldn't deign to see me."

Only occasionally did Bellow play up to his status as literary celebrity. Arriving at the university arts center to give a talk, he refused to begin until a bust of Hemingway was carried from the room. "I'm a writer not a film actor," Josipovici remembers him saying on another public occasion, "though he said it in a film actor's way." Josipovici saw nothing of Bellow's unpleasant side. When asked to address one of Josipovici's classes, Bellow offered a reading instead. "He read the opening of *Henderson* wonderfully and then came back to tea." At tea, Bellow met Josipovici's formidable mother, Sacha Rabinovich, a poet and translator. "She said, 'He's my sort of person,' and she had no time for posturing." When one of Josipovici's research students showed up at Monk's House with his small son, Bellow took the little boy on a tour. "This house belonged to a *very strange woman*," he told the boy when they reached the bathroom. "This is where she had her bath and in the end it was water which did her in."

That Bellow spent only six weeks rather than the full two months at Monk's House was partly the fault of Virginia Woolf, or the cult of Virginia Woolf, partly that of the University of Sussex. "He was very ambivalent about the fact this was Virginia Woolf's house," Josipovici remembers. "He wouldn't sleep with me in the big room," Gendlin recalled, because Leonard Woolf had slept there. "He slept in Tom Eliot's room." "It was the literary tourists who drove him out," she believes. "One sunny morning, when Saul was sitting out in the garden writing, some strangers just wandered in through the gate, saw him, and asked whether he was getting his inspiration from Virginia Woolf. Well, we left two days after that." Bellow may also have wanted to leave because the University of Sussex presented him with a bill for his stay. "He was furious that the university was making him pay," Josipovici remembers. "Asa said, 'Come, be my guest.' Is this the way they treat you?" The day before the decision to leave Monk's House, Bellow would not speak a word to Gendlin. He was in a state like the one fictionalized in her Aspen story. At dinner, she finally said, "Tomorrow you *have* to talk to me. I don't care what you say, but you have to talk to me," at which point he declared, "'Oh, Frances, I can't stand it here anymore.' So we wound up spending a week in Barley Alison's in London" (Barley was out of town at the time). In Gendlin's view, "Virginia Woolf was oppressing him and Virginia Woolf just did him in."

The affair between Bellow and Gendlin had been going on for four years at this point and would last another year. "We had a good relationship," she recalled. "It was domestic. We traveled or we didn't. I had my life and my work, he liked that, though every once in a while it would make him crazy." Their sex life was "extremely passionate." "It was the first time I'd had a longtime sexual passion. Whether or not he was the best lover in the world had nothing to do with it. . . . It was really something that meant a lot to me." Socially and intellectually, life with Bellow was exciting; he was "showing me a new life. He was so funny, so smart." They traveled to Italy together, meeting writers and celebrities. In Milan, Inge Feltrinelli, Bellow's publisher, threw a party for him. Gendlin had no fancy outfits, and "there were all these elegant Italian ladies." So Bellow took her shopping. After trying on a number of dresses, she came out with one they both liked. "This dress made me look long and willowy. 'Oh, Frances,' he said, 'you look like the queen of a small country.' Isn't that wonderful?" The trip to Jerusalem was more somber, to attend the commemoration of the twenty-fifth anniversary of the liberation of Bergen-Belsen. Gendlin remembers Golda Meir's speech at the commemoration, which consisted of a single sentence in Yiddish: "No matter what they do to us, we will beat them." Meir, the prime minister, looked to Gendlin "just like Lyndon Johnson." It was Meir's office that supplied Bellow with a car and driver, while Teddy Kollek, the mayor of Jerusalem, acted as their guide. Alfred Kazin was also present at the commemoration (along with Elie Wiesel), and when Bellow whispered to Frances during the speeches, Kazin thought he was translating for her. In fact, she told Atlas, "he was whispering, 'Has Kazin made a pass at you?' "[34]

While he was with Gendlin, Bellow became interested in the ideas of the anthroposophist Rudolf Steiner. They frequently tried out exercises Steiner had developed to train what he called "spiritual perception." "One of them was to walk down to the end of the block and say what we had seen. And it was totally different. It was great. And we'd do this exercise of trying to remember the day" (that is, from the present back to the moment of waking). During their time together, Bellow was at work on "Charm and Death," one of the unfinished Zetland novels, and on *Humboldt's Gift*, which in early versions contained Zetland-like

Greenwich Village episodes. Partly to recapture the Village milieu, Bellow had David Peltz build an orgone box in the hall closet of his Cloisters apartment. Gendlin remembers taking turns with Bellow to sit naked inside the box. "He did it," she recalls, "but he had humor about it. I thought it was a hoot."

In addition to including Gendlin in his spiritualist and other investigations, Bellow also, she claims, taught her how to write. She would come home from editing the *Bulletin of Atomic Scientists*, and he would read to her what he'd written that day. "I'd say, This is fabulous, and the next day he would change it, and it was better. The first day I wouldn't understand why it was better, but the second day I knew it." The process was not without its pains. Bellow could be undiplomatic in his reactions, crude as well. After reading a review Gendlin wrote of a biography of Einstein, "he put his hands on my breasts and said, 'Oh, Frances, isn't it lucky you have other things you do so very well.'" Yet she continued to show him her writing, which eventually improved. "The last thing I wrote was an article on climate change, and he read it and looked up and said, 'Frances, there's nothing wrong with this.' I grabbed the paper and was running around saying, 'There's nothing wrong with this, there's nothing wrong with this.'" Gendlin's attempts to educate herself sometimes involved embarrassment. In her desire to keep up with Bellow's range of reference, she was like Katrina in "What Kind of Day Did You Have?" ("There was a lot in that story which was about our relationship"). The first year they were together, "I kept reading in the encyclopedia about all these people I thought I should know. I read about Baudelaire and Stendhal one day and got them totally mixed up. He kept telling me I wasn't good enough, and so I wanted to be good enough." Eventually, she felt she was. "There was nothing to put down anymore."

From the beginning, Bellow was open with Gendlin about his feelings, calling her his "best friend" but admitting he "could only love her so far," that she "didn't touch his soul." At Monk's House, as with Maggie in the Hamptons, "he was doing something strange with the mail. Hiding some letters." It was no secret to Gendlin that Bellow was "juggling all sorts of relationships" (causing her, in turn, to go off at times with other men). He could, she admits, treat her "like crap." Once, in Chicago, when Peltz and his wife, Doris, were over, Frances said, "You know, sometime I'd like to live in Rome." Bellow said, "'Well, why don't you go now? Why don't you leave?' I said, 'You want me to leave now?' He said yes. It was so awkward. I should have left." But she didn't. "He was in a mood" is how she explains not leaving, the sort of state in which he made caustic and cutting remarks "about everyone." David Peltz's view was that Gendlin "was too nice, that I lacked an element of bitchiness Saul needed . . . There should have been more push and pull." Gendlin recognized the masochistic element in her relationship with Bellow. " 'I want you, I don't need you,' " Bellow warned her, " 'don't get addicted to me,' and I *was* on some level addicted to him." "It was my responsibility. If I didn't like it, I could leave." But when she said she was leaving, "that's when he'd come closer." Once, her therapist asked her what name she thought would have best suited her, and she went off and asked Bellow the same question. "He answered right away. It should have been a Russian name: 'Nearbyfaroff,' " by which he meant, as Gendlin puts it, "come closer, come closer, oops, you're too close."

In the summer of 1970, Greg Bellow got married in California, and Bellow asked Gendlin to accompany him, though she hadn't been invited to the wedding. While Bellow was at the ceremony, she went to the movies, and when he came back to the hotel, she had not yet returned. The wedding upset Bellow, not because he disapproved of Greg's marrying, or of Greg's bride, JoAnn, but because, as Greg explains in his memoir, it was small and "self-financed" and he had invited "all of the doting Goshkins and Saul, but none of the other Bellows—all of whom had ignored me during my childhood. . . . Saul was sore as a boil and complained bitterly at having his family snubbed, being outnumbered by Goshkins, and seeing Anita happily settled in Los Angeles with Basil, while he was between marriages."[35] The movie Frances had gone to see was *M*A*S*H*, and when she finally appeared, Bellow "was furious." He insisted that she see it again with him, and afterward said he "hated it." In "What Kind of Day Did You Have?" Bellow fictionalizes this episode. As Katrina recalls it, "she got into trouble in San Francisco when she insisted that he see *M*A*S*H*. 'I've been to it, Vic. You mustn't miss this picture.' Afterwards he could hardly bear to talk to her, an unforgettable disgrace. Eventually she made it up with him, after long days of coolness." What Wulpy hated about *M*A*S*H* is not specified, but the anecdote is prefaced by Katrina's saying that "he was unnervingly fastidious about language. As others were turned off about grossness, he was sensitive to bad style" (p. 292).

Bellow's friend and first biographer, Ruth Miller, recalls a conversation she had with him in 1979 about the real-life version of Katrina's *M*A*S*H* "disgrace." Gendlin, identified by Miller as "a woman he had once admired," had "gone on and on explaining to him what the movie was all about. As he had sat there in the theater, he had said to himself, My God! What am I doing here?" Shaking his head, Bellow told Miller, "The most important thing in his life were his books and no one seemed to care at all about them."[36] Katrina's praise of *M*A*S*H* in "What Kind of Day Did You Have?" identifies her with a level of culture which Victor Wulpy, like Bellow, not only despised but saw as a threat. In the story, movies in general get it in the neck. At the airport, Victor and Katrina run into an old acquaintance and admirer of Victor's from Greenwich Village days, Larry Wrangel, now a big success in Hollywood. Victor remembers Wrangel as an ex–philosophy student from NYU, "a character who longed to be taken seriously. The type who bores you when he's most earnest" (p. 308). He treats him with "angry restraint and thinly dissimulated impatience" (p. 315), qualities Susan Bellow's friends noted in Bellow's treatment of the talk of their husbands, wealthy real-estate agents, architects, and physicians. Bellow's books were serious, and they grew, he felt, out of a more exacting or demanding culture than that of the movies, even movies at their best (he also hated *Psycho* and *The Godfather*). By eroding the standards of a wide literate audience, *M*A*S*H* was debasing as well as debased. The "unforgettable disgrace" Wulpy feels when watching the film ("What am I doing here?") derives from his attraction to a woman whose erotic appeal, in addition to her niceness, causes him to lose sight of what is "most important." "Her idiocies irritated me to the point of heartbreak," Victor says of Katrina, a sentence Gendlin calls "beautiful," but one that "made me feel sad."[37]

BELLOW'S QUICKNESS TO DEFEND not only his books, "the most important thing in his life," but literature in general, and to see both as everywhere threatened, led in this period to an embarrassing contretemps with Lionel Trilling. On November 14, 1972, Bellow delivered a lecture at the Smithsonian Institution in Washington, D.C., entitled "Literature in the Age of Technology."[38] The lecture was the first of five Frank Nelson Doubleday Lectures commemorating the seventy-fifth anniversary of the founding of the Doubleday publishing firm (the other lecturers were Daniel Bell, Peter Medawar, Arthur C. Clarke, and

Edmundo O'Gorman). The Doubleday Lectures were black-tie events, accompanied by lavish dinner parties. Bellow's fee was five thousand dollars plus expenses. In a letter of November 9, Ruth Boorstin, the wife of Daniel Boorstin, the Smithsonian director, wrote to report that Betty Beale had mentioned Bellow in her gossip column in *The Washington Star*, along with items about Jackie Onassis and Margaret Truman. Almost two years later, in the August 1974 issue of *Harper's* magazine, Bellow republished the essay under the title "Machines and Storybooks: Literature in the Age of Technology." Before it appeared, however, his attention was drawn to a damaging misreading it contained of an essay Trilling had published in *Commentary* entitled "Authenticity and the Modern Unconscious." Trilling's essay was drawn from the final chapter of his most recent book, *Sincerity and Authenticity* (1971), a book Bellow had not read. Although Bellow was unable to alter or remove the offending passages in the *Harper's* version of the lecture, he wrote to Trilling in advance of its publication to express "regretful second thoughts" and "remorse" about what he had written.

The starting point of Bellow's lecture is that literary culture is under threat on a number of fronts. Among the figures he quotes as colluding in this threat, or complacent in reporting it, are novelists and poets as well as critics, including Arthur C. Clarke (his fellow lecturer), Theodore Roszak, André Malraux, Paul Valéry, his friend Harold Rosenberg (for whom, as Bellow puts it in the lecture, "most modernist masterpieces are critical masterpieces . . . Joyce's writing is a criticism of literature, Pound's poetry a criticism of poetry, Picasso's painting a criticism of painting"), and Lionel Trilling. The high esteem accorded movies is symptomatic. Early on in the lecture, Bellow abruptly asks of the Stanley Kubrick film *2001*, "Will this sort of drama replace *Othello*?" Everywhere he goes, he hears of the triumph of science and technology: "Now, as power-minded theoreticians see it, the struggle between old art and new technology has ended in the triumph of technology." In defiance of these theoreticians, Bellow declares that "man is an artist and that art is a name for something always done by human beings. The technological present may be inhospitable to this sort of doing, but art can no more be taken from humankind than faces and hands." Even those who deplore the present situation do so in ways that "narrow the scope of the novel . . . make the novelist doubt his own powers and the right of his imagination to range over the entire world. The authority of the imagination has declined." The effect of such jeremiads is either to silence the imagination or to drive it into overassertiveness: "Writers have capitulated to fact, to events and reportage, to politics and demagogy."

Trilling is the last of the lecture's enemies of literature, but chief among those "who preside over literary problems." Bellow cites "Authenticity and the Modern Unconscious," beginning with the following quotation: "It is an exceptional novelist today who would say of himself, as Henry James did, 'that he loved the story as story,' by which James meant the story apart from any overt ideational intention it might have, simply as, like any primitive tale, it brings into play what he called 'the blessed faculty of wonder.' Already by James's day, narration as a means by which a reader was held spellbound, as the old phrase put it, had come under suspicion. And the dubiety grew to the point where Walter Benjamin could say some three decades ago that the art of story-telling was moribund."

Bellow was not impressed. "Here one cries out, 'Wait! Who is this Benjamin? Why does it matter what *he* said?' But intellectuals do refer to one another to strengthen their arguments." To Benjamin, as quoted by Trilling, stories have an "old-fashioned ring"; to Trilling, as quoted by Bellow, they are "inauthentic for our present time—there is something inauthentic in our time in being held spellbound, momentarily forgetful of oneself, concerned with the fate of a person who is not oneself." This quotation leads Bellow to conclude that for Trilling "literature itself is now inauthentic." After Bellow alerted Trilling to the *Harper's* essay, and Trilling read it, he was not inclined to accept Bellow's apology or to think of him, as Bellow imagined he would, as merely "silly." "The adverse words which occur to me," Trilling wrote to Bellow on July 25, 1974, "are, I am sorry to have to say, rather graver than that." Nor would it do for Bellow to attribute his misreading of the article to a failure to read the book from which it was excerpted: "Reading the whole book would have done nothing to preserve you from the extravagant error of your treatment of it [the article]." What Bellow has done, Trilling claims, is to misinterpret his intention "to the point of exactly inverting it."

> Let me put it this way: if someone were to say that in Mr. Sammler you had portrayed a voluptuary nihilist who despised England and nursed a secret admiration of Nazism, was gratified by all the manifestations of contemporary culture which deny the traditional

> pieties, and was incapable of love or solicitude for any fellow-being, your purpose would not have been more distorted than are my views in your representation of them.

That Trilling's article reports on the devaluation of storytelling "with regret" was something he claims "any passably intelligent reader will recognize." "No part" of the description of Benjamin's position, as derived by Bellow from Trilling, is true: "All the characteristics of the art of storytelling which you say explain Benjamin's fancied objection to it are in point of fact the reasons for the love and admiration he gives it and for his thinking that something peculiarly human is lost when the telling of stories is no longer cherished." How, then, to account for Bellow's misreading? "On the one hand, that you should simply have failed to comprehend what I say and what Benjamin says in my paraphrase of him I can scarcely credit, given your known competence in the reading of texts far more difficult than mine. On the other hand, it is scarcely to be conceived, let alone believed, that you would consciously and deliberately pervert the meaning of what I had written." He goes on to question why, in the months since the Smithsonian lecture, Bellow never asked himself if he'd dealt "fairly and accurately" with Trilling's views. "To the best of your knowledge of me," Trilling asks, "have you ever heard me say, either in my life or in my work, that I hoped 'for the end of art as the surest indication that man had achieved maturity and ultra-intelligence'?" Bellow's decision to publish his Smithsonian lecture in *Harper's* was "tantamount to a conscious and deliberate intention *not* to comprehend or present truthfully what I have said."[39]

In late June, before Bellow received Trilling's letter, Edith Tarcov, who was helping him not only with *The Portable Saul Bellow* but with other publishing tasks, forwarded to him an earlier letter, either written or forwarded to her, in which Trilling made his discontent clear.[40] On June 28, after receiving the forwarded letter, Bellow wrote to Tarcov admitting that he'd "put my emphasis in the wrong place, like an idiot," and suggesting that they insert the following footnote in reprinted versions: "Rereading Mr. Trilling's essay with a calmer mind, I see that I misrepresented his position. I repent of my hasty error in attributing views to him which he does not hold. Those views are, however, held by others and although I may have been unjust to Prof. Trilling I have not entirely wasted the reader's time." Bellow then instructs Tarcov to "make what changes you like to save face for me, but I have a shamed face as big as the new harvest moon." He also admits he'll have to apologize directly to Trilling. The letter to Tarcov offers an explanation for the misreading: "I think I dislike T's way of reading so much that it inflames my brain." The upshot of Trilling's angry letter of July 25, 1974, was a period of estrangement, made particularly difficult by the fact that the two men were to appear together later in the summer at an Aspen Institute conference entitled "The Educated Person in the Contemporary World." The relationship never recovered. Trilling died on November 5, 1975. In an undated letter to Karyl Roosevelt written that autumn, Bellow confessed to being "upset abt Lionel. With all his faults I like him" ("like" versus "liked" suggests that the letter was written before Trilling's death). It was in Jerusalem that he learned of the death and wrote a belated note of condolence, to which Diana Trilling responded in a letter of January 15, 1976. In her letter, Trilling reiterated her husband's "astonishment" not only that Bellow should have so misread him but that he persisted in his misreading. Then she softened somewhat, admitting: "Both of us were aware in Aspen that you wished that none of it had happened. At least, when I undertook to bridge the gap you plainly knew that was my intention and responded with a warmth and simplicity that I much appreciated as Lionel did too."

IN THE LATE SPRING OF 1974, shortly after another trip to San Francisco with Gendlin, Bellow made a brief visit to London, before spending the early months of the summer in a villa near Casa Alison in Carboneras. The trip to California had involved a visit to his first grandchild, Juliet Bellow, daughter of Greg and JoAnn. In a letter of January 2, 1974, to Philip Siegelman, Bellow was undoting, or posed as undoting (later, he would become especially fond of Juliet, who is now a professor of art history). "Juliet was born about five weeks ago. I have a picture of her and she doesn't yet look worth flying to California to see. But I don't think I have the guts to break with conventions, so I suppose I'll be coming out soon." It was after the trip to California that Bellow and Gendlin broke up. Atlas says it was Bellow who ended the affair, after the trip to London. Gendlin says she ended it, deciding to move to New York to break her "addiction" to him. "I feel like I'm possessed by demons," she told Karyl Roosevelt in the summer of 1973. "I had a lousy time while he was here [in Aspen, where she'd stayed on] and I'm glad he's gone. . . . I can understand why he loses a woman with every book—he's certainly lost me with this one [*Humboldt*]. 'Talk to me,' I said to him, and he thought awhile and said, 'Well, I think at this point, Charlie—.' 'Shut up,' I told him, 'I only want to hear things about me.' Silence . . . He just couldn't understand that I wanted to see if the relationship was going to lead to something."[41] Less than a year later, in an undated letter to Mitzi McClosky, Gendlin attempted to explain her decision to call it quits. In the past, "when there were lies and deceits I stepped back, when I could see them, and stayed away 'til they were over. But now I am in confusion and I can't deal with that. . . . I no longer understand the situation, so I have to leave, because it's muddy and dirty. . . . I feel so sad at losing such a dear dear person." The withdrawal pains were severe: "I was devastated for a year. . . . I missed our relationship." Eventually, though, she recovered. "I remember him with love and gratitude and with appreciation," she told me in an interview, "and with great relief that I escaped when I did. . . . Our relationship had terrific ups and terrible downs."

AFTER THE SPLIT with Gendlin, Bellow spent June and the early part of July in southern Spain, working toward the completion of *Humboldt's Gift*. He was not alone there. When he learned that Harriet Wasserman was coming to Spain to conduct some business in Barcelona, he invited her to stay with him at his villa. There was difficulty coordinating dates, but finally Bellow cabled that he was "happy to put you up. Driver will meet you at airport and bring you to me. Saul."[42] When Wasserman arrived, the driver was waiting with a message: "Dear Harriet. Your driver Juan who speaks no English will take you to the home of Barley Alison where you'll be her guest. My maid is too messy. I'll meet you at Barley's house at one o'clock and then we can go for a swim. Saul." Wasserman had never met Barley Alison, who quickly brushed aside her apologies for intruding. After a shower and a rest, she went down from her room to pre-lunch drinks on the veranda. There Bellow sat, "flanked by Barley and her other houseguests," none of whom Wasserman had met before.

> Saul hadn't risen to greet me. I noticed he was deeply tanned. "What's new in New York?" was the first question he put to me. Before I could answer, Barley piped up. "Well, we're all going to convince Harriet to stay, even though Saul is leaving tomorrow."

> Everyone looked embarrassed, obviously they already knew the big news.
>
> I turned to Saul, who was gazing at the tile floor, and asked, "Is that true?"
>
> Without looking at me he nodded his head.[43]

Later, driving to his villa, Bellow asked: "Are you sore at me? This is good for you. You're not social enough." At lunch, they talked mostly about Bette Howland, whom Bellow had recommended to Wasserman as a client, and who was distressed when Viking complained upon discovering that *W-3* was not a work of fiction. Wasserman attributes this misunderstanding to Bellow, who had described *W-3* as fiction both to her and to the editor at Viking, though "for self-protection" she couldn't say so to either author or editor. ("To have confessed to him would have made his situation no better, only mine worse.") Bellow asked, "Why did they take it if they thought it was a novel?" and Wasserman replied: "You have tremendous power over Viking. If you suggest it, they'll take it. They can't say no to you."[44] Bellow's ignorance about business matters is a theme in Wasserman's memoir. The next day, before his departure, he asked Wasserman if he could borrow some money, suggesting that when she arrived in Barcelona she could ask his publishers, Plaza y Janes, to "advance you against my next earnings." But Plaza y Janes had not been Bellow's publisher for several years: "He didn't know that. He doesn't follow business. With a few important exceptions, he doesn't know who his European publishers are, let alone the local subagents."[45]

In Wasserman's memoir, Bellow's business ignorance combines with a penchant for Machiavellian plotting. After he left Almeria, Wasserman stayed on for several days, enjoying Barley's company. "Barley was a truly generous hostess. . . . Often she kept me by her side, wanting to talk." When she returned to New York, however, she was greeted with a furious letter from George Weidenfeld: "Barley had written to him that I had come to Almeria to discuss moving Saul from Weidenfeld! The trip to Almeria had been a setup. But I took the hint. Saul's way of making his will known is reflected in one of his favorite jokes: 'Let's you and him fight.' Now I knew what he wanted. I was the one who strong-armed him to leave Weidenfeld and move to Secker." A second motive for luring Wasserman to Almeria, she thought, was that "Saul wanted Barley to check me out as an agent."[46]

Here, as elsewhere in Wasserman's memoir, doubts arise. Why

would Bellow need Barley to check her out? Wasserman had been acting as Bellow's agent for several years at this point, and as her memoir makes clear, she was devoted to him. It is true that Bellow valued Barley Alison's advice, on everything from linens and handmade shoes to foreign publishers. It is true also that he had her check out new girlfriends. But Wasserman was not a new girlfriend. If he wanted to shift the blame onto Wasserman for leaving Weidenfeld & Nicolson, he hardly needed the plot she describes to do so. Nor does it sound like Barley Alison to lie about Wasserman's role in Bellow's move to Secker. "Barley had recently changed firms, to Secker and Warburg," Wasserman writes, before declaring that the stay at Casa Alison had been a "setup." But Barley had left Weidenfeld & Nicolson in 1967, seven years earlier.

An alternative account of the episode is possible. For reasons he did not wish to disclose to Wasserman, Bellow had suddenly to leave for Madrid. In trying to soften her upset at his departure, he called upon Barley for help. Would she put Wasserman up for a few days? It would be a good thing for agent and publisher to get to know each other; they could talk about his move to Secker & Warburg. Wasserman says nothing of the reason Bellow gave for having to leave so suddenly. If she asked for one, did he evade answering, gazing at the floor as at Casa Alison (or at the ceiling, as when pressed by Mark Harris about writing his biography[47])? Perhaps "for her protection," Wasserman did not press Bellow about his reasons for leaving. She presents Bellow as unaware of his power, but the guilt-inducing high-handedness of his behavior in this period can in part be seen as testing this power. In the memoir, there is little evidence of Wasserman's criticizing Bellow's behavior, whereas Barley Alison told him what she thought of it directly. Though no less devoted to Bellow than Wasserman, Barley could tease and cajole him, as in an undated thank-you letter of 1972, written after a visit to Chicago. The letter begins by praising the decoration of Bellow's apartment in the Cloisters, "the rugs particularly, but I also liked the mixture of modern chairs, old chests and tables and antique sculpture with gay modern prints." It then moves to Bellow's personal life. "I still worry, of course, about the monstrous regiment of women who surround you but I cannot see what you could really do about it. If you were fat, ugly and dull your reputation would still attract them. . . . If you got rid of the present collection there would be another lot forming up behind them immediately I fear. But just don't marry them at the moment or let them move in on you even if it means constant trips to Japan, London, Yugoslavia or Israel to keep you one jump ahead."

A similar letter, written shortly after Wasserman's stay at Casa Alison, holds a key both to Bellow's sudden departure and to his reluctance, spoken or signaled, to explain its cause. On July 23, 1974, Barley wrote to Bellow, "We all got *very* fond of Harriet W. And I think that towards the middle of her stay she got over her shyness and enjoyed herself." The letter ends: "I do hope Madrid was a success, I *do* hope Alexandra agreed on a definite date, I *do* hope Chicago was not harrowing, and I hope, above anything else, that Aspen is as good to work in as the [Casa] Pillet tower proved to be."[48] "Alexandra" here is Alexandra Bagdasar Ionescu Tulcea, Bellow's houseguest before Wasserman's arrival, the woman who would become his fourth wife. He had gone to Madrid to be with her. "I do hope Madrid was a success, I *do* hope Alexandra agreed on a definite date." Bellow had at last produced a girlfriend Barley Alison approved of as a possible wife. Alexandra recalls Barley as "a woman of sterling character. She was completely devoted to Saul, a trusted friend. Later she became my friend too. Saul undoubtedly wanted Barley to check me out. The line in Barley's letter very likely refers to a wedding date." As for Bellow's attitude to Harriet Wasserman, "it became clear to me that Saul did not want us to meet, whence the complicated arrangements. After this somewhat awkward episode, if my memory serves me right, Saul and I met again in Madrid for a few days."[49]

ALEXANDRA IONESCU TULCEA WAS in some ways an unlikely choice for Bellow. She was not literary, she was not Jewish, and she was not American, having been born and educated in Bucharest, the daughter of prominent Romanian physicians. She was very intelligent, however, a professor of mathematics at Northwestern (she'd come to Carboneras from MIT, where she'd been teaching for six months). She was also attractive, elegant, refined in manner and appearance, and recently divorced. They had met in 1969, when Alexandra was thirty-four, some nineteen years younger than Bellow. Her ex-husband, Cassius Ionescu Tulcea, had been her mathematics professor at the University of Bucharest, and when, in 1957, he was invited to participate in a special two-year mathematical program at Yale, she enrolled to study for a mathematics Ph.D. at the university. They had left Romania, she told Greg Bellow, "determined not to return."[50] Two years later, Alexandra received her doctorate in mathematics, under the direction of Shizuo Kakutani, "famous already for his fixed-point theorems" (famous also, in later years, as the father of Michiko Kakutani, the *New York Times* book critic). After Yale, the Tulceas went on to teach at the Universities of Pennsylvania and Illinois and then, in 1967, became members of the mathematics faculty at Northwestern. According to Arthur Copeland, Alexandra's friend and colleague from Northwestern, her husband received the senior appointment because he was older and better known, "but she was the better mathematician."

Alexandra's interest in mathematics was partly inherited. Her father, Dumitru Bagdasar, a brain surgeon trained in the United States, founded the first neurosurgery clinic in Romania, and became minister of health in the first communist government. "When he wanted to relax, he would either work out an integral, read poetry, or work on his embroidery—to keep his fingers nimble for surgery."[51] He died of cancer in 1946, when Alexandra was eleven. Her mother, Florica, a child psychiatrist, "was keenly interested in child education, particularly the teaching of arithmetic." She was a great admirer of Hypatia, the female mathematician of antiquity who taught at the Academy in Alexandria. Florica's maternal grandfather, an engineer, had taught mathematics in high school. Her younger sister, Minna, studied mathematics at university and "according to family legend . . . she would first put on a string of pearls and then sit down at her desk to study. She was a woman and she was a mathematician: the two were not incompatible." When Alexandra was little, her mother teased her "that the love of mathematics was in our genes."[52]

When Alexandra's father died, shortly after his appointment as the first Romanian ambassador to the United States, a post he was never able to take up, her mother was appointed in his place as minister of health. Two years later, she "fell in disgrace," the victim of a campaign that would reach its climax in the early 1950s, "the peak of the Stalinist terror in Romania." There was a real threat that she would be arrested or even executed. Her crime was having "dared" to accept help from the West after the war, shipments of medicine and food.[53] "My mother and I had become pariahs, Untouchables." Their Bucharest friends dropped them. At school, Alexandra's teachers "were afraid to be seen talking to me." She became extremely guarded, rarely speaking or voicing her opinions. Alexandra's sense of danger from the state fed her commitment to mathematics. "I came to realize that of all the disciplines, Mathematics is perhaps the most immune to political pressures and it made Mathematics tremendously attractive, even more attractive than before." As a student at university, she had taken courses in astronomy, mechanics, and thermodynamics. For a while, she was attracted to astronomy, "but I soon realized that none of these other disciplines could compete with Mathematics in clarity, precision, elegance."[54] Nor would they be as free from government surveillance and interference.

BELLOW AND ALEXANDRA MET at a party in Hyde Park given by Mircea Eliade, a professor of comparative religion at Chicago and a member of the Committee on Social Thought. Eliade and his wife were Romanians, but Alexandra had only recently gotten to know them, and this was the first time she'd been to one of their parties. She knew none of the other guests at the party, nor did she have "the faintest idea of who Saul Bellow was. People were fawning all over him." When introduced, she told him that she'd never read any of his books. He told her he'd never read any of hers. Then he asked her to marry him. "I was speechless. Of course I was very flattered but I was also taken aback. Later I learned that it was one of his favorite opening lines with the ladies, a sure ice-breaker." Bellow told Alexandra about meeting Bertrand Russell, who complained about the women in his life. "Saul said, You know why he had so much trouble with women? Because they didn't know any mathematics."

It was some time before Bellow and Alexandra met again. "I should tell you, I was charmed by him. I was also frightened." They didn't start "seriously dating" until 1973, before Alexandra went off to teach at MIT. Gathering her courage, she called to tell Bellow her news, "and that piqued his interest." In the short period before she left Chicago, as Alexandra puts it, "we became close." Once she was at MIT, "he came and visited me; there were telephone calls and visits" (though no letters—she was not comfortable writing letters to Bellow). "We were attracted to each other. I remember thinking, This is the world outside of mathematics, which I know very little about, and he was indeed very charming, very funny, very witty, and he knew an enormous amount of things and he had a fabulous memory. He had read everything, and he offered such a contrast to the mathematicians I had known and to the life I had led before, and it really made an enormous impact." Like those of many mathematicians, Alexandra's cultural interests were musical rather than literary. Also like many mathematicians, she had "a very strong sense of the aesthetic, because really good mathematics is elegant, perhaps even austere." Elegance for Alexandra "means streamlined simplicity. . . . An ideal proof is a string of words in which every word counts and is irreplaceable." Shortly after they married, she gave Bellow G. H. Hardy's *A Mathematician's Apology* (1940), which stresses the aesthetic appeal of mathematics, "and he was absolutely fascinated by it." What especially struck Alexandra about life with Bellow was how exciting it was: "One of the most striking statements that he made to me is that life isn't really black-and-white, life is essentially gray most of the time, but there are these surges of color that make life worthwhile. That stayed with me. That was an eye-opener."

Adam Bellow was seventeen when he first heard of Alexandra. He was in Aspen with his father in the late summer of 1974 and knew that, after he was due to leave, a woman he hadn't met was coming for a visit. About this woman Bellow "was very reticent." All he told Adam was that she was "closer to his [Bellow's] age, she was a foreigner, quite an accomplished person in her own right, and she was different." Later, having met Alexandra, and seen her with his father, Adam sensed "that he respected her and that he wanted to be the man that she saw in him. He wanted to be that guy" (roughly, a distinguished figure, which is what Barley Alison and Edward Shils also wanted him to be). "He sort of did the Dido and Aeneas routine. He came to her like a refugee from a burning city. He told her the story of his trials and sufferings. She was very receptive and provided a high-octane sympathy." Alexandra, in turn, saw Bellow "as a truly serious man. Someone she could look up to like her father," the father she lost at the age of eleven. The desire to be seen in this way had a powerful appeal to Bellow, Adam believes. "If you've been through three failed marriages and a bunch of long relationships . . . and knowing that you haven't been at your best, I can really understand Alexandra's appeal. . . . She brought out a side of him—courtly, indulgent, fond, paternal—I hadn't seen."

"Courtly" is the word Joseph Epstein uses in recalling Bellow's demeanor with Alexandra. Despite her distinction as a mathematician, there was something childlike and vulnerable about her. Epstein thought Bellow treated her at times "like a daughter who didn't pick up on things." Partly this was because Alexandra came from a very different world (one Richard Stern said "amused Bellow and then alienated him"), partly because of the abstract nature of her concerns, partly because she was a non-native English speaker. Her speech was slow and precise ("actually" is pronounced as four distinct syllables), with odd emphases (Epstein, a friend, recalls her telephoning "to touch *base*"). The Copelands, also with affection, describe her as "notoriously absentminded." When Bellow first visited Alexandra in her apartment, she asked him if he'd like a drink. As Lynda Copeland remembers the story: "So he went to the refrigerator, and not only was it empty, but there were no ice cubes." Yet, as Adam Bellow puts it, "she had, still has, an unspoiled sweetness . . . a wonderful capacity to be just thunderstruck by a sunset." To teenage Adam her formality was a virtue: "She set a tone of civility and aesthetic values"; she was considerate, wrote thank-you notes, made sure Bellow remembered his sons' birthdays. All the Bellow family, with whom she remains close, took to Alexandra, and she took to them. "It was a wonderful feeling to know that I belonged to a new family, having left everyone behind. They were wonderful to me."

Adam first got to know Alexandra in Carboneras in the summer of 1975. "They were staying in this house [Casa Pillet, near Casa Alison], and she was independent," he recalled. "She'd go into her study, doing her mathematics. . . . You respected her." Alexandra remembers the summer as "very relaxing, very easygoing." There was household help, and after the morning's work at their desks, there were visits to the beach, then a late lunch, a siesta, a late dinner: "We had a wonderful time." Bellow's description of the summer comes in a letter of July 2, 1975, to David Peltz: "Adam smiles at his peevish pa and goes on reading science fiction and thrillers"; "the queen" (Alexandra) is "in her parlor eating mathematical bread and honey." "For a long time it worked," Adam says of the relationship: "the match was a good one, and Saul did live up to her expectations" (which partly means he didn't stray). As Adam sees it, "He was delighted to have an opportunity to redeem himself. I was seventeen. He told me all about this. He got some strength and a sense of personal redemption out of this." Alexandra had "existential depth," a product of "having lived her early life under communism." Bellow had read all he could about the Gulag and the camps, and "it gave him a salve to his wounds to meet the standards and the expectations of a woman like Alexandra, who had lived through that."

Bellow and Alexandra were married in November 1974, after signing a prenuptial agreement on October 22. The ceremony was low-key. "Saul didn't want any publicity. One day he took me to Marshall Field and bought me a beautiful Victorian ring, which was very unusual, and told me this is what ladies used to wear in Victorian times as a wedding band. It was not your standard wedding. . . . He had been married three times before, and his name had been in the papers a great deal." They were married by a Circuit Court judge in front of what Alexandra describes as "Joel Bellows and someone else." "I did not tell my mother we were getting married till not long before. . . . I knew she would be worried sick, and she was worried until she actually saw us together." Alexandra owned, still owns, an apartment on Sheridan Road, on the North Side of the city, not far from Evanston; Bellow's apartment was on the South Side. "For a while we lived in both places, but for me it was increasingly difficult." Alexandra had numerous obligations at Northwestern: many Ph.D. students, a heavier teaching load than Bellow, committee meetings. Bellow's apartment in the Cloisters was "beautiful," and he "took great pride in having done it himself without the help of an interior decorator or any adviser of any kind," but it was very much his apartment. "I felt like a permanent visitor in this place."

Proud of his new wife's distinction as a mathematician, Bellow made efforts to understand her work. "We would go out, and he'd often say, We have to go home because my wife has to prepare her class on stochastic integrals for tomorrow. Or I don't know much about Martingale theory, but she has to give a talk on it, so we cannot stay very long." Alexandra tried to explain her work "*grosso modo*," and when Bellow asked her to give him a simple mathematical proof involving numbers, she gave him a proof "that the square root of 2 is an irrational number. This is a consequence of the Pythagorean theorem, and he was extremely taken with that, and he tried to understand it and then he memorized the steps and he reviewed it a number of times, and eventually he got sick and tired of it. He really never developed that kind of interest. I think he was smart enough to understand mathematics if he applied himself to it, but he was so completely involved in literature and writing and everything else that there was no room left for it." Alexandra was comparably involved in mathematics, and though she had more access to Bellow's work than he did to hers, she, too, lacked the interest or time fully to understand or appreciate it.[55]

Alexandra likens mathematicians to gold miners. "You have to be prepared to work hard, to sweat, to overcome long periods of frustration for the sake of getting those few gold nuggets that illuminate your whole existence." The most important of the nuggets to come her way before she met Bellow involved "Martingale theory." In "A Mathematical Life," Alexandra offers the following *grosso modo* explanation of Martingale theory, in a single sentence: "The notion of Martingale in Probability Theory is a model for a fair game of chance."[56] To nonmathematicians, this sentence is of little help. An equally unenlightening footnote (again, to nonmathematicians) is provided in Atlas's biography, where Alexandra is described as "an authority on Banach spaces, named after the Polish mathematician Stefan Banach, a pioneer in the field of topological vector spaces."[57] Alexandra's working methods were as incomprehensible to Bellow as the substance of her work, but, then, his working methods were incomprehensible to her. The concentration demanded of the mathematical prospector meant physical and mental removal for long periods. "When I worked hard on a Math problem," she writes, "I went into seclusion for hours."[58] Bellow worked with comparable intensity, but for shorter periods and with music blaring. Alexandra marveled at the "ironclad discipline" of Bellow's morning work routine, from nine till about twelve or one, but also at his ability to handle distractions: "He very often answered the phone and engaged in these very lively conversations, and then he'd go back to work with just as much energy and zest as before." With her own work, "I need complete silence, no distractions. I even close the curtain. It is to shut out the lake, the magnificent view of the lake [from her Sheridan Road apartment]. Saul, on the other hand, opened the curtains wide, listened to *Don Giovanni* full blast." Bellow's apartment, fortunately, was big enough for them to work without disturbing each other. "We worked in different quarters," Alexandra recalls. "He did not interrupt me."

Alexandra is the model for several characters in Bellow's fiction, most obviously Minna in *The Dean's December* and Vela in *Ravelstein*. There are also traces of her in Benn Crader, the genius botanist in *More Die of Heartbreak*, described by his nephew Kenneth as "humanly more confused than many persons of normal gifts." (Benn resembles Bellow in that his confusions concern Matilda Layamon, a woman modeled largely on Susan.) In *The Dean's December*, the preoccupations of Minna, the scientist wife of Albert Corde, the dean, are "astrophysical, mathematical." The closest Corde comes to describing them is through metaphor: "bringing together a needle from one end of the universe with a thread from the opposite end. Once this was accomplished, Corde couldn't say what there was to be sewn. . . . Face it, the cosmos was beyond him" (p. 14). On the flight to Bucharest, where her mother is dying (as Alexandra's mother was dying in 1978, when she and Bellow flew to Bucharest), Minna's valise is packed with astronomical papers, "giving them priority over dresses. On the trip she couldn't be separated from these books and reprints. They weren't checked through but had to be carried as cabin luggage" (p. 18). Minna is "superconscientious" about her work:

> Nothing was allowed to interfere with duties. Mostly it amused [Corde] that this beautiful and elegant woman should behave like a schoolgirl, with satchel and pencil box. When she was getting ready to set out for the day, he sometimes joked with her. "Got your compass and your protractor? Your apple for teacher?" Together with her big fragrant purse, a bag of scientific books and papers was slung over her shoulder—ten times more stuff than she needed. But occasionally the gold-star pupil stuff did get him down, and she was cross with him, interpreting his irritation as disrespect for her profession. It had nothing to do with that. She put in a ten-hour day, never missed a visiting lecturer, a departmental seminar. Her tutorials, rehearsed far into the night, must have been like concerts. What he minded was her fanatical absorption. He often had dinner waiting for her, and toward seven o'clock began to listen for the sound of the key in the lock. . . . She gave him (it was absurd!) wifely anxieties [pp. 253–54].[59]

Minna's mother, like Alexandra's mother, was a forceful woman who had fought hard to secure her daughter's well-being. "For safety" she had assigned Minna "to the physical universe—not exactly the *mysterium tremendum;* that was religion. But science! Science would save her from evil." As a consequence, Minna is "an innocent person. . . . She did stars; human matters were her husband's field" (p. 256); Corde's responsibility is "keeping his wife posted on sublunary matters" (p. 261). Her innocence of human matters, though, is deceptive. "She was as intelligent—phenomenally intelligent—as she was childlike. The boundaries between intellect and the rest meandered so intricately that you could never guess when you were about to trespass, when words addressed to the child might be interpreted by a mind more powerful than yours" (p. 257). When "brought back to earth," Corde tells us, Minna is not only superintelligent but "a tigress" (p. 24), like her mother. Unlike her mother, though, "she had no practical abilities, she had never needed them. Valeria had done all that" (pp. 170–71). Nor has she much knowledge of the issues that matter most to Corde. "My wife is a simple person," he declares. "No politics. Her mother wanted her out of it, brought her up that way. No politics, no history" (p. 63). Valeria sends her "directly into cosmic space. Nothing but particle physics, galaxies, equations. Minna had never read the *Communist Manifesto*, had never heard of Stalin's Great Terror" (p. 65). As he gets to know her, Corde is amused to discover that Minna, "who had grown up in a Communist country, should have to be told by her American husband who Dzerzhinsky was, or Zinoviev" (p. 261). Nor has Minna any interest in contemporary issues, particularly those of the city she lives in. After Bucharest, she can't stand to hear of them. "Her mother's death had taught her death. Triviality was insupportable to her. Her judgment was rigorous, angry. She wanted no part of his journalism, articles, squalor. Suburban pimps or smart-ass lawyers beneath contempt and the great hordes, even of the doomed, of no concern to her, nor the city of destruction, nor its assaults, arsons, prisons and deaths" (p. 288).

With her mother's death, Minna is engulfed by "mortal weakness, perplexity, grief—the whole human claim. Minna hadn't made the moves frequently made by scientists to disown this claim: 'Don't bother me with this ephemeral stuff—wives, kids, diapers, death'" (p. 256). Alexandra speaks of herself as having been comparably engulfed at the time of her mother's death. "That trip to Romania was so traumatic and so somber and so macabre that, to tell you the truth, many of the details have faded for me, perhaps out of an instinct of self-defense. It was so dramatic that Saul didn't have to invent much or to change much. It was probably quite close to the real story." To Corde, the trip to Romania, in which the authorities are punitively obstructive, immovable, makes clear that Minna is "rich . . . in human qualities" (p. 57) as well as "unskilled in human dealings" (p. 308), a mixture Adam Bellow sees in Alexandra, who is warm and full of feeling while also "treating emotional life as if it were mathematics." Hence, in part, Alexandra's adherence to etiquette and decorum. Minna "disliked noise, disorder, notoriety, any publicity" (p. 261), as does Alexandra (she can be reticent and uncomfortable in interviews, for example, while clearly wishing to help). Minna is no more comfortable speculating about social or philosophical matters. At her mother's death, she is appalled at how angry she feels. Her emotions, she says, are "horrible. Not like a grown woman. I feel vicious" (p. 258). Corde tries to explain her fury in wider terms, talking of "how schizoid the modern personality is," invoking Jung on "the civilized psyche" as "tapeworm." "Why do you think you should tell me this now?" Minna asks. "It might be useful to take an overall view," Corde replies. "Then you mightn't blame yourself too much for not feeling as you should about Valeria."

> "What comfort is it to hear that everybody is some kind of schizophrenic tapeworm? Why bring me out in the cold to tell me this. For my own good, I suppose."
>
> "This might not have been the moment," he said.
>
> "I tell you how horrible my mother's death is, and the way you comfort me is to say everything is monstrous. You make me a speech. And it's a speech I've heard more than once" [p. 263].

The events that were fictionalized in *The Dean's December* took place in the winter of 1978. In addition to stressing the accuracy of the novel's account of these events, Alexandra describes Bellow's fictional portrait of her in the novel as "loving and respectful." In Romania, his behavior was exemplary, both in relation to her and her family and to the hostile officials with whom he had to deal. "That was probably his finest hour in our marriage." The novel depicts Corde's attraction to Minna in terms that recall Adam Bellow on his father's attraction to Alexandra. In chapter 16, toward the novel's close, Corde describes himself as having behaved badly in the past, though this behavior is nowhere dramatized in the novel.[60] At times, Corde is insensitive and self-absorbed (as in his speech to Minna about the civilized psyche), or cruel and cutting, but never do we see him lash out because he is in a mood, or insult admirers, or slap a woman. There is little evidence of underlying bad character, the sort Bellow began to suspect in himself after leaving Susan. Hence the puzzling nature of his account of the risks Minna takes in marrying him, an account which encourages biographical readings.

> She loved him but he was suspect. And so he should be. We were a bad lot. For a complex monster like her husband, goodness might be just a mood, and love simply an investment that looked good

> for the moment. Today you bought Xerox. Next month, if it didn't work out, you sold it. It was an uncomfortable sort of judgment, but Corde was beginning to realize that this was how he wanted to be judged. Minna gave him a true reflection of his entire self. The intention was to recognize yourself for what you (pitiably, preposterously) were. Then whatever good you found, if any, would also be yours. Corde bought that. He wasn't looking for accommodation, comfort [p. 289].

IN THE EARLY 1970S, what Bellow was looking for was to be a man or a mensch, not a jerk. He sought to become a man in several ways: in his conduct as chair of the Committee on Social Thought; in his relations with family, both immediate and extended; and in wider social and political engagement. On October 3, 1975, on the eve of stepping down as chair of the Committee, Bellow hosted a dinner in celebration of its thirty-fifth anniversary and in honor of its founder, Professor Emeritus John U. Nef. The dinner was held in the university's Swift Hall, and Bellow paid for the banquet. Two years earlier, in the manner of Elya Gruner in *Mr. Sammler's Planet*, he had mounted a campaign to get his maternal cousin Mischa Ulman, an electronics engineer and "refusenik," out of Latvia.[61] With the help of Walter Pozen in Washington, Bellow made appeals on Mischa's behalf to Hubert Humphrey, Henry Kissinger, Senator Charles Percy, Soviet Ambassador Anatoly Dobrynin, Senator Jacob Javits, and President Richard Nixon (though Bellow had voted against Nixon and had openly supported George McGovern, both as Democratic nominee and as presidential candidate[62]). He also wrote telegrams to the Soviet minister of culture and the chair of the Soviet Writers Union. Mischa Ulman's mother, Bella, had been allowed to immigrate to Israel. Mischa was her only child, and the plan was for him to join her. After he lost his job in Latvia, however, she did not hear from him for several months, and feared that he might be in prison, as a "parasite" as well as a refusenik. In the spring of 1973, she flew to New York, where she telephoned her Chicago Bellow relatives. Soon after the call, Bellow came to New York, met Bella, and began a campaign to persuade the Soviet authorities to allow Mischa to emigrate. (Sam and Nina Bellows also campaigned on Mischa's behalf, as did several Jewish organizations.) On May 1, 1973, Bellow wrote to "Dear Cousin Mischa" to inform him that he had "made formal application to bring you to the United States. My desire is that you should live in Chicago where I will make myself responsible for you, seeing to all your needs until you are able to make your own way. . . . I speak for the entire family when I say that we shall be very happy to have you here." By December, the campaign had succeeded. Mischa was allowed to leave Latvia for Israel, from where he would eventually move to the United States; he later returned to Israel to make his home.

A year after Mischa's arrival in Israel, Bellow and Alexandra flew to Jerusalem. Bellow had agreed to address the thirty-ninth annual PEN International Congress, a visit agreed to the previous June. Here he met Mischa for the first time, at family gatherings of the Gordins, Mazurskys, and Ulmans, maternal relatives. Bella, "a medical worker of some sort" in Riga, was now a department-store cashier; Mischa, however, had found work with Sony as an electronics engineer.[63] In his PEN address, among his papers in the Regenstein, Bellow quoted a recent statement by Soviet President Nikolai Podgorny warning Russian writers against deviating from the principles of Soviet realism, and stressing the need for Soviet art "to constantly raise its ideological arsenal, its irreconcilability to manifestations of alien views, to combine the assertion of the Soviet way of life with the deflation of apolitical consumerism." He then contrasted these quotations from Podgorny with one from Goethe: "I have never bothered or asked in what way I was useful to society as a whole. I contented myself with what I recognized was good or true." A similar stress on the artist's obligation to the good and the true is sounded in a letter Bellow wrote on January 7, 1974, to *The New York Times* in defense of Alexander Solzhenitsyn, "a man of perfect intellectual honor." To Solzhenitsyn, as to all "the best Russian writers of this hellish century it has been perfectly clear that only the power of the truth is equal to the power of the state." In a period of détente, it was unlikely that American diplomats or the heads of great corporations would protest against the Soviet treatment of Solzhenitsyn, "but physicists and mathematicians, biologists, engineers, artists and intellectuals should make clear that they stand by [him]. . . . Americans have a special responsibility in this matter. What Solzhenitsyn has done in revealing the unchecked brutality of Stalinism, he has done also for us. He has reminded every one of us what we owe to truth."

An earlier letter of protest, from October 15, 1973, written nine days after the outbreak of the Yom Kippur War, never appeared in print, though Bellow alludes to it at the beginning of *To Jerusalem and Back* (p. 6). Addressed to the editors of *Le Monde*, it opened as follows: "It was France at the end of the eighteenth century that began the political liberation of the European Jews. In our own times, however, the French attitude toward the Jews has been painfully variable. The century began with the Dreyfus Case. In the Forties there was Vichy. Now there is the Pompidou government which, with a small show of neutrality and objectivity, has taken the Arab side in the present war. It associates itself politically with all of Israel's enemies, even the most bizarre of African and Asian demagogues [Idi Amin, most recently]." Bellow then asks what France would do if Israel lost the war "to the attacking coalition of Egypt, Syria, the oil billionaires and the Russians. . . . For everyone understands that there are two questions here. One is the question of justice to the Arabs, the other is that of the destruction of the Jews. There are also two traditions involved in this matter, those of Revolutionary France on the one hand and those of French anti-Semitism on the other." The letter ends:

> Why should France not take into account the fact that Israel is democratic, while the Arab nations are oppressive, xenophobic, feudal? Does a French government owe no loyalties whatever to liberty and equality, to what is best in French civilization? Or shall we on the outside begin to think of that civilization as nothing but another export commodity like wine and cheese and perfumes and armaments?

To make sure that the letter reached *Le Monde*, Bellow gave one copy to the playwright Eugene Ionesco and a second to the novelist Manès Sperber, both to be delivered directly to the paper's editor. "The letter was never acknowledged."[64]

BELLOW'S CONNECTIONS TO HIS SIBLINGS and their families were especially close in this period. In November 1973, he traveled to Montreal to receive an honorary degree from McGill University and to give a lecture on James Joyce. Accompanying him were his sister, Jane Bellow Kauffman, his brother Sam, and Sam's daughter, Lesha. Together they visited Gameroff relatives in Lachine and Montreal. Maury was by now living in Florida, but Bellow remained in contact through joint business ventures.[65] In December 1971, Maury began construction of a sixty-unit apartment building in North Miami, a deal for which his son Joel did all the tax work. Bellow initially invested forty-four thousand dollars in the deal. Pleased with Joel's work, in August 1973 Bellow made him his tax accountant.[66] A year later, Bellow invested in a second deal with Maury, for the development of a warehouse and shopping center, again in Dade County (Bellow had 25 percent interest in the scheme, Joel 10 percent , Maury 48.75 percent, and a fourth partner 16.25 percent). Other deals would follow, and although Bellow made money from them, in the end they generated bad feeling. The money mattered to Bellow in this deal-making, but so did the closeness to Maury. "I admired my brother, not because he was a 'creative businessman,' as they said in the family," admits Herschel Shawmut in "Him with His Foot in His Mouth," "that meant little to me—but because . . . Well, there is no 'because,' there's only the *given*, a lifelong feeling, a mystery" (p. 395). In *Humboldt's Gift*, Charlie Citrine describes a comparable admiration for his brother Julius, known also as Ulick. "Are you fluid?" Ulick asks. "Have you got about fifty thousand? I may be able to put you into something."

> From time to time Ulick telephoned me from Texas and said, "Send me a check for thirty, no, make it forty-five." I simply wrote the check and mailed it. There were no receipts. Occasionally a contract arrived six months later. Invariably my money was doubled. It pleased him to do this for me, although it also irritated him that I failed to understand the details of these deals and that I didn't appreciate the business subtlety. As for my profits, they had been entrusted to Zitterbloom [accountant], they paid Denise, they subsidized Thaxter, they were taken by the IRS, they kept Renata in the Lake Point Towers, they went to Tomchek and Srole [lawyers] [p. 372].

Other investment opportunities and stock tips came from Sam. Though Jane initiated no deals, she was a keen investor, and often badgered Bellow and Sam to press Maury about dividends and returns. Joel Bellows describes her as "*really* single-minded about money," "mean as a snake" (according to Lesha and her daughters, Jane was in part a model for Isaac Braun's sister Tina in "The Old System"). Bellow may have been, as Joel says, "an amateur when it came to thinking about money," but part of his sense of what it was to be a man was to be involved with money.

It also mattered to be an involved parent. Bellow's efforts to be a good father were mixed in this period. Greg, the most prickly of his sons, was now himself a father. In addition to living farthest away from Bellow, he was wary of Bellow's efforts to keep in touch. "Maintaining a geographic distance from Saul was the first in what became a series of insulating layers that afforded me some distance from his demands for attention and control." Complaints about lack of attention from his father now alternated with complaints about threats to his independence. Shortly after Bellow and Alexandra married, they began spending summers in Vermont. For the first few years, Greg and his wife, JoAnn, and daughter, Juliet, joined them for family vacations. "But sitting around all morning and keeping a lively child quiet while my father wrote and Alexandra did academic work reminded me of my childhood boredom. Eventually I balked at such family vacations and stopped making the effort, placing yet another barrier between us."[67] In Greg's view, Bellow was too critical, too controlling. "By my late twenties I had tired of judging myself by his standards."[68]

Relations were better with Adam, now a teenager and relatively happy at the Dalton School, after a rocky first year.[69] What Adam describes as "the experience of feeling like nobody" had begun to fade. He became involved in drama at Dalton, developed a circle of friends, had a growth spurt, and slimmed down. Increased confidence fed a lively wit and turn of phrase, judging at least from letters kept by Bellow. "Dear Papa," begins a letter of October 27, 1970, written when Adam was thirteen:

> How are things at your end of the line? Everything here is pretty much fastened to the deck. How's your book, your apartment, your family, your peace of mind, and your squash? I just finished reading "Ethan Frome" for English. You have heard tell of this strange, dull book, mayhap? It matters but little. All I can say is, if they want us to write essays, can't they make the subjects a bit more interesting? Anyway, if this sneak preview of life at Dalton (such as it is) alarms you, don't let it! Nohow and contrariwise, I consider figuring out how the Greeks lived from painted vases quite interesting.

Sasha attributes Adam's newly confident manner with his father in part to her being out of the picture. Adam and Bellow could now arrange visits and meetings directly; she was no longer "the referee."[70] These were the years in which her own relations with Bellow began to improve, as noted previously. On February 8, 1973, she received a letter from Stewart Richardson, an editor at Doubleday. "Saul Bellow suggested that I contact you," the letter begins, "I am writing in the hopes that we can get together to discuss editing and job opportunities in the field." Nothing came of the contact, but it is evidence that Bellow had softened toward Sasha.

Daniel was the son Bellow saw most of in the 1970s, and Daniel was having a rough time. He was six at the beginning of the decade, seriously asthmatic and emotionally fragile. Bellow saw him every Sunday and during the holidays. Daniel knew from an early age that his father was a celebrity. Everywhere he and Bellow went in Hyde Park, "people wanted to shake his hand. High-school students on the bus would say, 'Tell me about your father.' I'm, like, 'I'm only seven.'" The Sunday routine was for Daniel as it had been for Adam when he and Sasha lived in Skokie. "We'd go to the museum, we'd take a walk in the park, we'd go to Daphne's [a greasy spoon at Fifty-Seventh and Dorchester]." Or they'd visit relatives or friends of Bellow's. After moving from 5490 South Shore Drive back to an apartment at 1755 East Fifty-Fifth Street, both within minutes of the Lab School, the Cloisters, and Bellow's office, Susan decided to move with Daniel to the North Side. Bellow was furious. "My father said, I wasn't consulted about this. My mother said, Fuck you, I'm not married to you, I can do what I want." When asked if Bellow could control himself in talks with Daniel about Susan, Daniel answered, "No, nor she about him. They would yell at each other—'you're poisoning the child against me.'" Bellow and Susan reached an initial divorce settlement in 1968, when Daniel was four, but continued to argue about money and child care and were soon back in court.

For more than a decade, while producing novels, essays, a book about Israel, lecturing all over the world, chairing the Committee on Social Thought, advising foundations and grant committees, visiting the White House, winning a Nobel Prize, a Pulitzer Prize, a third National Book Award, Bellow was up to his ears in lawyers. They bogged him down and bled him dry, in one of the longest, most expensive and acrimonious divorce settlements in Illinois history. Neither he nor Susan would give in. Struggles over the divorce wore at Bellow's nerves and his patience, hampering his efforts to be the man he wished to be. At his desk, however, these struggles proved a source of rich material, much of it, as we shall see, very funny.

SB and Alexandra on train platform in London, mid-1970s (private collection)

5

Distraction/Divorce/Anthropoposophy

IN JANUARY 1975, Bellow was invited to address the University of Chicago Board of Trustees' Annual Faculty Dinner. His subject, "distraction," was introduced by a quotation from Wordsworth, who "in 1807 warned that the world was too much with us, that getting and spending we lay waste our powers, that we were giving our hearts away and that we saw less and less in the external world, in nature, that we could respond to." As Bellow saw it, the situation was worse today: "We are in a state of radical distraction, we are often in a frenzy," he declared, a state produced by "the history of the twentieth century," "an unbroken series of crises." "Social and economic problems" wholly preoccupy us: "taxation and terrorism . . . street crime, racial tension, corruption in government, inflation, depression, Arab oil, détente, the technological future, arms talks." Culture—high culture, that is—barely figures, even in the thoughts of what he calls "serious people," "American intellectuals," the assembled faculty he is addressing. Such people "cannot be said to take literature very seriously. It is simply not that important to them. It is not a power in life. Power is in science, in technology, in business, in institutions, in government and politics, in the mass media, in the life of nations. It is not in novels and poems."[1]

At the end of the month, on January 30, a third visit to the White House offered corroborating evidence of the lack of attention to literature and culture, at a banquet given in honor of Harold Wilson, the British prime minister, described by Bellow as "fatty, stooped, and short, without the slightest interest in the people being introduced to him."[2] In the East Room, Bellow and Alexandra joined the other guests: Cary Grant, Danny Kaye, Henry Kissinger. The only person there Bellow could actually claim to be acquainted with was Hubert Humphrey, who was "in one of his public states. The fit was on him. He couldn't bear to be confined to the two of us. He was looking for someone more suitable, for the most suitable encounter, the one it could be death to miss."[3] Nelson Rockefeller, the vice-president, walked over to Bellow to shake his hand. "He had taken me for someone else and recognized his error in mid-course when it was too late to turn aside. He did the handshake bit, I murmured my meaningless name, and the Vice President went on to seek a more significant encounter."[4] After the banquet, there were difficulties finding a cab to the hotel. Back in the room, Bellow lay in bed and "understood a little the phenomenon described by neurologists as an insult to the brain. As I closed my eyes, the night opened mercifully before me and my spirit gracefully left this world."[5]

The theme of distraction—the seedbed of such insults to the brain—was not new to Bellow, but it became especially prominent in his writing from 1975 onward, for personal or biographical as well as historical reasons.[6] It is at the center of *Humboldt's Gift*, in which the lesson Charlie Citrine learns from Humboldt is that "you don't make yourself interesting through madness, eccentricity or anything of the sort, but because you have the power to cancel the world's distraction, activity, noise, and become fit to hear the essence of things" (p. 305). In his Nobel Prize lecture in December 1976, Bellow says the novelist's job is "to cut through the whirling mind of a modern reader . . . to reach the quiet zone."[7] In "An Interview with Myself," conducted in the *Ontario Review* (founding editor Joyce Carol Oates), Bellow begins with how difficult it is "to possess your soul in peace for a few minutes":

> It is easy to observe in bars, at dinner tables, everywhere, that from the flophouse to the White House, Americans are preoccupied by the same questions. Our own American life is our passion, the problems of our social and national life with the whole world as background, an immense spectacle presented daily by the papers and the television networks—our cities, our crime, our housing, our automobiles, our sports, our weather, our technology, our politics, our problems of sex and race and of international relations.

> These realities are real enough. But what of the formulae, the jargon, adopted by the mass media—the exciting fictions, the heightened and dramatized shadow events presented to the great public and believed by almost everyone to be real. Is reading possible for a people with its mind in this state?[8]

This question persisted for Bellow, in essays such as "The Distracted Public" (1990) and "There Is Simply Too Much to Think About" (1992), and in correspondence as well, often in the form of excuses. He has had no time to write letters, he complains; he is hounded by worthy causes, political, literary, and educational. "I am writing a short book about life in Jerusalem," he reports to Karyl Roosevelt, in a letter of November 7, 1975, "while with the left hand I try to keep my novella going and, in spare time, study a bit of Hebrew and with my fanny direct operations at the U of C and follow up half a dozen other serious interests. Women used to take up so much of my time that I thought marriage w'd free my mind. Not a bit!" A year later, back in Chicago after three months in Jerusalem, he writes to Teddy Kollek on November 19, 1976: "People of America have begun to talk of the protection of natural resources. I have decided that I am such a national, and even international, resource and am issuing an appeal for protection. Here and now I have a choice to make between becoming a Jewish diva [Kollek wanted him to attend fund-raising events for Jewish and Israeli organizations] or remaining a writer. Your situation is different: you have a political vocation and you have to deal with all of these outfits. My duty—to myself, I mean—is to say no to all of them." "I have too many things going all at once," he complains in an undated letter to Mel Tumin, "and all keep me in that essential state of turmoil which, Pascal says, prevents people (*saves* them) from thinking about salvation. I hump along among unfinished works, promises unkept, things undone, lawsuits without end and the rest of the weak comic furniture of *Life*." "Stone walls may not a prison make," he writes to Barnett Singer, a Canadian academic and fan soon to figure more prominently in his life, "but I have enough manuscripts here for a lockup. Today I was presented with three, yours and two others of the same dimensions, all required reading *sous peine d'amende*. When am I supposed to cook curry, wash the dog or examine my toes?"[9]

The demands on Bellow multiplied in 1975, with the publication of *Humboldt's Gift* in August, the award of the Pulitzer Prize the following May, and the publication of *To Jerusalem and Back* in October 1976, accompanied by a front-page rave review from Irving Howe in *The New York Times Book Review* (it began, "The best living American novelist is also a man of brains").[10] Five days after Howe's review, Bellow was named winner of the 1976 Nobel Prize in Literature, the eighth American writer to be so honored. This was followed by a rush of congratulations, further honors, and invitations, most notably to deliver the Jefferson Lectures for the National Endowment for the Humanities, to receive the American Academy of Arts and Letters Gold Medal for the Novel, the National Arts Club Medal of Honor for Literature, and the Emerson-Thoreau Medal. He was also asked to be a judge at the 1976 Miss USA Contest. On March 23, in a letter of invitation from Cindy Adams, a contest official, Bellow learned, "A poll of contestants of the Miss USA Pageant reveals that you are their number one author. Thus, they would like me to invite you to join the celebrated panel of Judges at the 1976 Miss USA Beauty Pageant which comes out of Niagara Falls. Last year we had Leon Uris, the year before Robin Moore, the year before that Jacqueline Susann and Irving Wallace."[11]

"I suppose I could have said 'No' to all the publicity like Beckett did and seen nobody," Bellow told a reporter from *The Guardian*, "but I thought I would go along for a bit and see what it was like and then draw the curtains again."[12] The day before the Nobel announcement on October 21, he received a call from the Swedish Embassy asking whether he'd accept the Prize if offered it. That night, he and Alexandra went to dinner with a reporter from *Newsweek*, who had arrived in anticipation of such a call. Alexandra had scheduled movers to arrive the next day, to transport Bellow's things to her apartment at 5901 North Sheridan Road. When a reporter from the *Chicago Tribune* arrived at Bellow's apartment that morning, he found the new Nobel laureate on the sidewalk, surrounded by armchairs, padded tables, sofas, chiffoniers. As the president of the university, John T. Wilson, waited impatiently to drive Bellow to the campus for a formal press conference, Bellow instructed the movers about which pieces of furniture were to go to Sheridan Road and which into storage. He was stylishly dressed in a matching green turtleneck shirt and suit and a black leather jacket—a dude. *Newsweek* described him as "silver-haired and trim at 61."[13] When asked by the *Tribune* reporter whether the award meant he was now going to be more engaged politically, Bellow answered: "It'd be a good idea if more people were out of politics." When asked what the award meant to him, he answered, "It means I can stop thinking about recognition. Now I can think about more serious matters."[14]

At the press conference, Bellow claimed to have no plans for the $160,000 prize. "At this rate," he quipped, "my heirs will get the money in a day or so." What was he feeling? "I'm glad to get it. I could live without it."[15] The phone hadn't stopped ringing, he said, with calls from family and friends, also "old professors who are pleased with my progress."[16] His sister, Jane, called and wept to remember their father's contempt for Bellow's literary ambitions. Maury called from Georgia (where he'd bought a property big enough for his wife, Joyce, to keep horses). Greg called from California, and Bellow joked, "Now you know why I was after you to be quiet thirty years ago."[17] In a sidebar to its report on the prize, the *Chicago Daily News* unearthed the authors of the two undergraduate stories that had been judged better than Bellow's "The Hell It Can't!" at Northwestern in 1936 (in a competition discussed in chapter 5 of *To Fame and Fortune*). Neither author went on to write fiction; both warmly welcomed Bellow's success.[18] Also pleased was Sydney J. Harris, in a *Chicago Daily News* column of November 15, 1976 ("One of Us Won the Nobel Prize . . ."), recalling how forty years ago he and Bellow "sat around our dining room table and planned the books we were going to write." Harris felt "reflected pleasure," not "reflected glory," "that these two steeds did actually come out of the same stable, even though one of them is Pegasus and the other Dobbin."

A more troubling reaction came from Ted Hoffman, Bellow's old friend from the Salzburg Seminars and Bard College, who wrote to Bellow in a letter of November 8, 1976. Hoffman was now at NYU, and he and Bellow had been out of touch. His letter is rambling, ill-judged, and long, six single-spaced typed pages. It begins by briefly acknowledging the award, which "surprised me, given literary politics on a grand scale; I'd have expected there would have to be two Arabs, a Bulgarian, and an Asian South African to be taken care of first." Perhaps there was some truth in "the contemptible suggestion made in some indefensible quarters that quality of some sort was involved in the deliberations, but we're above that sort of nonsense, aren't we?" Then Hoffman turned to his many trials and tribulations. Four pages later, when Bellow is next mentioned, it is to contrast his good fortune, personal as well as professional, with Hoffman's current state. How, Hoffman asks, has Bellow, "the old Tripartite loser of love," managed to find a "paragon" (Alexandra) or at least "a plausible solution, since one of the givens of the humanistic tradition is that a Bellow could never find the right woman"? Might Alexandra "possibly know someone for me, someone outside the conditions in which I exist, an Albanian physicist, a Macedonian horticulturalist, a Bosnian biologist?" If Bellow's "extraordinary career in Saint Sebastianism" can end in "serendipity," maybe there's a chance for Hoffman. "I don't want an astrological projection. Or a Poor Saul's Almanac. I just want some household hints."

At the letter's close, Hoffman moves from heavy irony to "truth-telling," the sort Bellow associated with the therapy culture of Greenwich Village.

> I wish I still knew you. I wish you were concerned with me. I don't like, at heart, your literary exploration of geriatric experiencers of a world going down the drain, of loves and energies dissipated in an enervating society. I read Herzog as a fool. I think Sammler had a bad education. Humboldt's gift was a treachery. I never identified with Tommy. Augie March always extracted more out of me than he gave.

"What the hell am I doing here?" Hoffman then asks, breaking off the beginning of his answer with an ellipsis: "Oh yes, of course . . ." The ellipsis turn out to be a setup.

> Oh yes, of course . . . I trust you have not lost that minor curse of finishing the ridiculous sentences of others, of extending and completing inane rhetoric, of topping some egregious narrative with the ultimate punch line, which ends with the summary Bellow characterology of combined visceral defiance and abysmal sinking into the floor. (Can I ever forget Ada Green: "Oh, Mr. Bellow, in that cap you look just like an archaeologist." Bellow: "And you look like something I just dug up." Yes you actually said that, I testify. Five Andrew Jacksons, in a plain brown wrapper, and I'll promise never to retail it at a cocktail party at which Jason Epstein or Norman Podhoretz are present. . . . So I guess I will be discreet about your infamous relationship with Ada Green, of whom I have not heard since that puissant afternoon in 1953.)

The letter ends "on a querulously affectionate note." Although Hoffman assumes that Bellow is "still preternaturally vulnerable," he trusts that his Nobel address "will subsume this formidable element of your essential mettle. Love, as ever. Ted."

IT IS POSSIBLE THAT Hoffman had been drinking when he wrote this letter. Six years after receiving it, Bellow published "Him with His Foot in His Mouth," which takes the passage about Ada Green as its starting point. As so often in Bellow's life, a wounding experience—not just Hoffman's aggression but the bad behavior he makes Bellow recall—is put to artistic use. On the heels of a great popular success, the musicologist Herschel Shawmut receives a letter from his old friend Eddie Walish. Walish recalls a moment in the 1940s when he and Shawmut were teaching at Ribier College, a thinly disguised Bard. Shawmut, new to the faculty, owes his job partly to Walish, as Bellow owed his job at Bard partly to Hoffman. Shawmut describes himself as "keen to learn" from Walish, "because I have never seen a progressive college, never lived in the East, never come in contact with the Eastern Establishment, of which I have heard so much" (p. 377). All of which was true of Bellow in the 1940s. Like Hoffman, Walish has a Harvard background and a limp, and is prone to "clever intricate analysis," the sort popular in Greenwich Village in the 1940s. Walish, Shawmut admits, "gives me the business in his letter":

> Why was it, he asks, that when people groped in conversations I supplied the missing phrases and finished their sentences with greedy pedantry? Walish alleges that I was showing off, shuffling out of my vulgar origins, making up to the genteel and qualifying as the kind of Jew acceptable (just barely) to the Christian society of T. S. Eliot's dreams. Walish pictures me as an upwardly mobile pariah seeking bondage as one would seek salvation. In reaction, he says, I had rebellious fits and became wildly insulting. Walish notes all this well, but he did not come up with it during the years when we were close. He saved it all up. At Ribier College we liked each other. We were friends, somehow. But at the end, somehow, he intended to be a mortal enemy. All the while he was making the gestures of a close friend he was fattening my soul in a coop till it

> was ready for killing. My success . . . may have been too much for him [p. 379].

Bellow's treatment of Hoffman in "Him with His Foot in His Mouth" is typical. He exaggerates the aggression in Hoffman's letter partly in revenge, partly as a way of making a larger observation, throwing into relief the complex feelings aroused by literary success. Bellow was rarely disposed to let slights and insults pass, including half-conscious ones such as those in Hoffman's letter. A comparable vigilance, again involving the Nobel, can be seen in his response to a letter of February 27, 1979, from Isaac Bashevis Singer. When Singer won the Nobel Prize in 1978, Bellow sent him a note of good wishes: "My wife and I happily congratulate you" (October 5, 1978). But relations between the two writers were never easy. Singer resented Bellow's part in the success of "Gimpel the Fool," his first story to be published in English, the story that, in Bellow's words, "got him started." The story appeared in *Partisan Review* in May 1953, the year *The Adventures of Augie March* was published, having been brought to Philip Rahv's attention ("Hey, where'd you find him?") by Bellow (in fact, it was Irving Howe who found him, enlisting Bellow as translator). That Singer neither thanked Bellow for his translation of the story (discussed in detail in chapter 11 of *To Fame and Fortune*) nor ever asked him to translate anything else of his was nettling and ungracious. "I think he cherished his eccentricities a little bit too consciously," Bellow told Norman Manea. "I was not one of those people who found them charming. I thought he was a conniving old Ganev [thief]." Bellow told Manea an anecdote about Singer he had heard from Philip Siegelman. When Siegelman was a graduate student at the University of Minnesota, Singer came to give a talk, and it was Siegelman's job to look after him during his visit. On the way to the talk, Singer asked Siegelman a favor. Would he, during the question period, ask him a question, one Singer particularly wanted asked? Siegelman said he would, and duly asked the question. Singer began his reply with the words "That's the stupidest question I have ever been asked in public."[19]

The letter Bellow received from Singer in 1979 was relayed through his secretary. It began: "Mr. Singer has been meaning to write to you for some time now. It was told to him that you felt uneasy about his comments in Stokholm [*sic*] concerning your speech [the newspapers reported that Singer had found Bellow's speech boring]. He never meant to comment on the text of the speech, but rather and this is what he said, that the speech was read very quickly and it was difficult to understand. Mr. Singer is sending his very best personal regards and hopes that this misunderstanding has been cleared." A week or so later, on March 8, Bellow replied:

> Dear Miss Menashe,
>
> I don't believe everything I see in the papers, I know what troublemakers journalists are. On the other hand, I did not read the speech quickly. I read it slowly and carefully and distinctly, and none of the papers I read reported faulty delivery. Besides, Mr. Singer was not in the audience. This is, however, a trivial misunderstanding and I propose to say no more about it. I avoid making disobliging comments about my colleagues in public.
>
> May I call your attention to the fact that you have misspelled Stockholm.
>
> Sincerely yours,
> Saul Bellow

ALTHOUGH ISAAC BASHEVIS SINGER was not at the Nobel ceremony in Stockholm to hear Bellow's speech, many of Bellow's family were. In addition to Alexandra, all three of Bellow's sons accompanied him, dressed for the ceremony in white tie and tails. Alexandra's mother came from Bucharest, along with Alexandra's aunt, and the aunt's daughter and son-in-law. Sam and Nina Bellows came, as did their daughter, Lesha, and son-in-law Sam Greengus, plus the three Greengus daughters: Dina, Rachel, and Judith, ages eighteen, sixteen, and fifteen, respectively. Maury's family stayed at home, but Bellow's sister, Jane, came. For Bellow's speech, Jane insisted on a seat in the first row, just in front of the podium. She soon fell asleep and had to be prodded awake several times, thus exemplifying its warnings about distraction, the difficulty of reaching an audience "agitated in private life and tormented by public questions" (Jane's agitation was mostly a product of having had to fly from Florida to Chicago to get her mink coat out of storage). All together, sixteen family members came to the event, "an unprecedented number that made front-page news in the Stockholm papers."[20] Adam had T-shirts printed up for the Bellow party with the words "Nobel Savages." What Bellow described to a Nobel official as "this huge contingent of Bellows" pretty much took over the Grand Hôtel, located on Stockholm's waterfront.[21] "There wasn't anybody there who wasn't called Bellow. It became a kind of joke."[22] Bellow and Alexandra had a suite, with two bedrooms separated by a sitting room. Greg, now thirty-two, slept in the second bedroom. The two younger boys, Adam, nineteen, and Dan, twelve, shared a room. As Greg recalls, Adam and Harriet Wasserman "were chiefly responsible for keeping Dan under control, but he still managed to order a great deal of food from room service, which infuriated Saul when the bill arrived."[23]

The presentation of the prize took place in the late afternoon on Saturday, December 12, 1976, which meant that Sam and Nina, Orthodox Jews, and other members of their family had to walk from the hotel to the concert hall at Hötorget, where the ceremony was held. The walk was not long, perhaps fifteen minutes, but it was snowy and cold. Earlier, the family had taken a trial walk, also attending a Sabbath Morning Service at the Great Synagogue of Stockholm and a Kiddush Service in the community hall "in honor of all the Jewish Nobel Prize Laureates." The economist Milton Friedman, Bellow's fellow University of Chicago laureate, and Baruch S. Blumberg, co-winner of the Nobel Prize in Medicine, were present; Bellow was not, nor had he responded to a personal invitation from Rabbi Morton Narrowe of the Great Synagogue, sent on behalf of the city's Jewish community. Rabbi Narrowe complains in his memoirs about Bellow's rudeness, "but it is of course the Nobel Prize for Literature and not for manners that he is about to receive. His brother, on the other hand, lets us know that several other family members will be glad to come."[24]

Bellow's polite, civic-minded brother, Sam, was in serious trouble at this time. In November, after a lengthy trial, he was convicted of defrauding patients in his nursing homes by selling them drugs from companies offering kickbacks. "I can't go into the details of this," Bellow told Norman Manea in their interview, "but it really wasn't his fault; it was somebody else in the family for whom he was covering."[25] Sam's sentence was sixty days in the Metropolitan Correctional Center and a fine of two hundred thousand dollars. Before he served his sentence, however, the judge allowed him to fly to Europe to watch his brother be awarded the Nobel Prize, also to visit with Lesha and her family, who were living in London at the time (Sam Greengus, a Biblical scholar at Hebrew Union College in Cincinnati, was on a research grant). That all the Greenguses were in London made it possible for them to join Sam and Nina in Stockholm. According to Lesha, in an undated letter written before sentencing, "This ordeal has certainly aged my poor father." To Bellow, Sam's presence in Stockholm was a "last opportunity to make public his attachment to a famous brother, to lessen the sting of the fact that he was going to prison."[26]

For Alexandra, the week in Stockholm "was like a fairy tale": the ceremony itself was "absolutely gorgeous," the Swedish king and queen "this most handsome young couple," the banquet and ball a flurry of "beautiful gowns, beautiful music, everybody had a wonderful time." "I was so proud of Saul and so proud to be at his side." Greg, too, was proud of his father, telling him so "just before we left for the ceremony."[27] The next morning, December 13, was St. Lucy's Day. Bellow and Alexandra were woken up by the St. Lucia ceremony, a Swedish tradition in which white-clad maidens carrying candles, coffee, and saffron buns serenade sleepers with songs in honor of St. Lucy. The hotel manager had let them into Bellow's suite, along with a troupe of photographers. "We thought it was a joke," Alexandra recalls, "someone was putting something over on us. Pulling our legs. It was quite a shock." Bellow barely composed himself. As he recalled to Atlas, "They came bearing a tray of bad coffee and some buns which they set down on my bathrobe so that I couldn't reach it. And behind them was the press, in force. I scowled, and then my face formed the smile which is obligatory on such occasions."[28] There would be other such smiles during the week. "I found I was carrying my entire family on my back," Bellow recalls. "I had to take everyone else into consideration." It was "a kind of family circus." "The prize officials were very amused by this circus. They knew all about it and were signaling each other behind my back. That's all right. They have to get something out of it, too."[29] In addition to the Bellow circus, there were tensions with Alexandra's mother, who "didn't approve of me." "She had this competitive streak in her," Bellow recalled. "If they gave the Nobel Prize to mathematicians," she told him, "my daughter would surely get one." "Well of course she would," Bellow replied.[30]

Bellow's publishers were also at the ceremony, in boisterous good humor—Tom Rosenthal and Barley Alison representing Secker & Warburg, Thomas Guinzburg representing Viking. Atlas quotes Guinzburg: "It was only light for about an hour and a half a day. Everyone was drunk all the time, knocking back little glasses of schnapps. Bellow looked great. It was the one time I saw him really happy."[31] But looks can deceive, as with Bellow's smile on the morning of the St. Lucia ceremony. The day after Bellow gave his speech, his Swedish publisher, Gerald Bonnier, gave a luncheon in Bellow's honor at his country home, Manila, attended by the whole Bellow family plus a host of American, British, German, and other European publishers. Harriet Wasserman describes the scene:

> The house had lofty rafters throughout and, in the dining room, oil portraits of the numerous Nobel Prize winners Bonnier published. The portraits hung all around the room—even on the beams. There were four round tables, with ten guests at each. I was sitting with Alexandra, who was quite happy, composed, and elegant. One of Saul's sons sat at each of the remaining three tables.
>
> At the end of the luncheon, Bonnier gave a short speech, offered a toast, and sat down. Daniel clinked his glass with his fork. When he had gotten everyone's attention, he said: "I'd just like to say my father has been so busy, but he still had time for me. Thanks, Pop."
>
> Up stood Greg, who was at his father's table. "My young brother has given me the courage to say something I've always wanted to say."
>
> Greg's voice was cracking. Alexandra put her elbows on the table and her face in her hands. Adam was at the table across from Saul's. He didn't blink. He didn't move. I looked at both of them, Adam and Saul, they were absolutely fixed and still.
>
> Greg was standing there, his walrus mustache trembling slightly. "I never thought you loved me, and I never understood what the creative process was. You were behind a closed door all the time, writing, listening to Mozart." He was looking straight at his father. "I was young. I didn't know what you were doing behind the closed door. I didn't understand the creative process."
>
> All the European publishers, all of them men, were sitting very stiff and upright. . . . Looks of total shock—horror almost—on their faces. They'd never seen a father and son like this before, and you could sense them experiencing a vicarious pain and embarrassment at this public display.
>
> "And then . . ." Greg was barely controlling himself. "And then

I had my own child. I witnessed the birth of my own child and I understood what the creative process was, and I understood then that you really did love me."

No one moved. All eyes turned away. Greg sat down and after a stunned silence people began to leave their tables. Saul was one of the first. He stood up quickly and went straight over to his middle child, put out his hand, and shook Adam's. "Thanks, kid, for not saying anything."

And off he went, in a stretch limo, entourage at his side.[32]

"Do you have emotions? Strangle them," says Joseph, the hero of Bellow's first novel, *Dangling Man*, published the year Greg was born. "To a degree everyone obeys this code," except Joseph: "To hell with that! I intend to talk about mine." According to Greg, "My father told me the only thing he enjoyed about the week in Stockholm was a quick visit to August Strindberg's study on his way out of town."[33] To Manea, Bellow claimed that the Nobel Prize "had absolutely no effect on me. Especially when I saw how my family misbehaved . . . My mother would have liked it very much. She was the one person who I would've been interested in telling it to. Or my father—he would've liked it."[34]

Bellow liked at least one other thing aside from the visit to Strindberg's house. Amidst ceremonial and familial distractions, he and Wasserman worked feverishly on his speech, which was far from ready when he arrived. He had three days to finish it, each fully scheduled. Ingemar Lindahl, who had been assigned to look after Bellow by the Swedish Foreign Office, made arrangements to allow him at least a couple of hours each day to work on it. On the second morning, he found an exhausted-looking Bellow staring at heaps of scribbled paper spread out on his desk. He was drinking a glass of greenish liquor and offered Lindahl some. "This is a kind of moonshine Romanian plum vodka," Bellow explained. "It's called Zuica. My mother-in-law has brought it. Romania produces two good things: that drink and beautiful women" (a remark partly addressed to Alexandra).[35] Bellow's difficulties with the speech may have come from worry about losing his powers, an effect winning the prize was said to have had on previous winners, John Steinbeck most recently. This worry Bellow voiced shortly after the award was announced, both privately and publicly. He confided it to Sasha in a tearful phone call on the day of the announcement, to her astonishment. He also admitted it to *The New York Times*, in an article of October 22, 1976. When Bellow's old Reichian therapist, Dr. Chester Raphael, read the article, he immediately wrote encouragingly: "Your writings already give assurance that the trauma of the 'ultimate' recognition you have just received will not inhibit you but will spur you on to ever greater literary achievements."

At the grand ball held the night before Bellow was to deliver his speech, he watched with alarm as twelve-year-old Daniel joined in all the toasts, "beginning to glow with the excitement and the wine."[36] Before leaving, "under great pressure," he asked Harriet Wasserman to come to his suite at nine-thirty the next morning to type out his speech, which was to be picked up by the press at noon. When Wasserman arrived in the morning, she discovered there was no script. Pale from worry and the night's festivities, Bellow began dictating from notes, "revising as he went along." "When he finished, he looked at me and asked what I thought. 'Good,' I replied." Then they went off for lunch at the hotel's Wintergarden restaurant, where the orchestra immediately started playing "Chicago, Chicago, that toddlin' town." Bellow waved in acknowledgment and told Wasserman, "Now this part I really like."[37]

THE DISTRACTIONS OF the Nobel Prize followed what was meant to have been a year of recuperation. It had begun in June 1975, when Bellow delivered the proofs of *Humboldt's Gift* to Viking. He had been at work on the novel for almost a decade and was glad finally to have it off his hands. This time, as he explained in a letter of April 15, 1975, to Joyce Carol Oates, there would be no "essay to go with it, hitting everyone on the head. I did that when *Henderson the Rain King* appeared [also with *The Adventures of Augie March*] and a very bad idea it was too—guaranteed misinterpretation. . . . You shouldn't give readers two misinterpretable texts at the same time." While at work on the proofs, Bellow had turned sixty. He and Alexandra were scheduled to be in New York for the week of his birthday, to attend Adam's graduation from the Dalton School, and Harriet Wasserman had planned an elaborate surprise birthday party. On June 9, the day before the birthday, thirty-five of Bellow's and Alexandra's friends were invited to a cocktail party at Wasserman's apartment. Twenty of these friends were also given secret instructions to go on from the party to a "birthday banquet" at a nearby Chinese restaurant. It was Herb Passin's job to get

Bellow to the restaurant after the party, which was not easy. In addition to being tired and not particularly hungry, Bellow was upset at having to cut short a conversation he had been having with John Cheever, a particular favorite. When, reluctantly, he entered the restaurant and was greeted with cries of "Surprise!" and a chorus of "Happy Birthday" from a crowd including Philip Roth, Saul Steinberg, Aaron Asher, and Cheever himself, "Saul took a look at John, and threw his head back and laughed."[38]

Soon after the birthday party and the final submission of galley proofs, the Bellows headed off to Europe, to a mathematics conference in the Black Forest in Germany, where Alexandra had a paper to deliver. From there they traveled to London, where Bellow met Alexandra's mother for the first time. "He deliberately set out to win her over," Alexandra recalled, "and when we met abroad he really spent lots of time talking to her and endeared himself to her . . . and she was not easily swayed." Bellow was helped in his campaign by Barley Alison and her younger brother, Michael, a Conservative MP, who later became Margaret Thatcher's parliamentary private secretary. Barley entertained the Bellows and Alexandra's mother in the evening and Michael took them to lunch at the House of Commons and gave them a tour of the Parliament buildings. There was another important first meeting on this London visit, with Owen Barfield (1898–1997), the English writer and barrister. Barfield was an authority on anthroposophy, a "spiritual philosophy" developed by Rudolf Steiner (1861–1925) at the end of the nineteenth and beginning of the twentieth century. Bellow had written to Barfield, having read several of his books, and thought of him, with Steiner, as allied against the forces of distraction, and also as capable of helping him "to become fit to hear the essence of things," as Charlie Citrine puts it in *Humboldt's Gift* (p. 305).

From London, the Bellows, accompanied by Adam, flew to southern Spain, to recuperate in Carboneras, as described in the previous chapter. "I arrived in an exhausted state and have been sleeping, eating, swimming, reading and little else," Bellow wrote to David Peltz in the letter of July 2, 1975 (this is the letter in which Alexandra is described as eating mathematical bread and honey). "Life lays a heavy *material* weight on us in the States—things, cares, money. But I think that the reason why I feel it so much is that I let myself go, here, and let myself feel six decades of trying hard, and of fatigue. My character is like a taste in my mouth. I've tasted better tastes." A day earlier, he had written to Harriet Wasserman to apologize for taking so long to thank her "for the magnificent party and the dinner." He was "oddly tired. This is Sixties fatigue, and I'm not talking about the last decade. It's only now, after a week in Carboneras, that I'm able to face a piece of paper." On August 8, in a letter to Philip Roth, Bellow described the birthday party in New York as "the one and only party in memory that felt to me like a real party. I didn't know what I was saying or doing. It was bliss. I do remember trying to talk to you about The Jewish Writer but I was quite drunk and you were wasting your time. So let's try again."

By the time Bellow returned to Chicago for the launch of *Humboldt's Gift*, he had recovered sufficiently to impress interviewers with his appearance and good humor. The reporter from the *Chicago Sun-Times* was struck by his clothes: "A subtle, rich-looking green-and-blue tie, the shirt turquoise, the suit olive, single-breasted with a quarter belt in back, the shoes two-tone dark chocolate brown and black. Completing the look are a neat, pinched black Savile Row fedora, a tightly rolled umbrella."[39] To Martha Fay, in an interview for the Book of the Month Club, "Bellow, face to face, is a natural charmer, a laugher, amused and playful, no matter how ascetic, how mournful he sometimes appears."[40] John Aldridge, not a Bellow favorite, began an admiring review of *Humboldt's Gift* in the *Saturday Review* by noting Bellow's age. At sixty, "most American novelists have ceased to live in expectation of doing important new work and many have given themselves up to producing menopausal recapitulations of their important old work. Bellow on turning sixty has done neither. He has marked the occasion by publishing a novel, his eighth, that contains abundant evidence of the continued expansion and deepening of his creative powers."[41] Alfred Kazin, too, was impressed. "How marvelous. How grateful I am," he records in his journal, on July 23, 1975. "Here I have been mooching along, more than half wishing for easeful death, waiting for the fire to blot me out completely . . . and Saul is insisting that he must continue! continue!"[42]

ONCE PUBLICITY DUTIES for *Humboldt's Gift* were out of the way, Bellow took a three-month sabbatical. Alexandra had been invited to Israel in the autumn of 1975 to give a series of lectures on probability theory at the Hebrew University of Jerusalem. As early as the PEN Congress of the previous December, Bellow had expressed an interest in an extended visit to Jerusalem, and on learning of this interest, the mayor, Teddy Kollek, wrote on December 29, 1974, to say how delighted he was at the prospect, asking "if there are any special arrangements you would like me to make." On April 14, 1975, as soon as Alexandra had received her invitation, Bellow wrote to John T. Wilson, at the time only acting president of the University of Chicago, to tell him he planned to accompany her. Though he could simply have taken the autumn off, confining his teaching at the Committee on Social Thought to the winter and spring quarters, he decided "to make a gift of my salary for the Fall quarter." The British philosopher Stephen Toulmin had agreed to stay on through the autumn, "so that we won't be short-handed." In addition to taking it easy, Bellow thought he might use the visit to write what he described to Kollek, in a letter of September 26, 1975, as "a short personal book about Israel." "It would be best for me to avoid VIP treatment . . . (interviews, lectures, television programs, etc.). If I'm to write a book, I should avoid all such entanglements." To Owen Barfield, in a letter of February 25, 1976, he said that, though his intention had been "to wander about the Old City and sit contemplatively in gardens and churches," once he arrived, he realized what he must already have known: that "it is impossible in Jerusalem to detach oneself from the frightful political problems of Israel. I found myself 'doing something.' I read a great many books, talked with scores of people, and before the first month was out I was writing a small book about the endless crisis and immersed in politics. It excites me, it distresses me to be so immersed."

The excitement, the distraction, the immersion began as Bellow and Alexandra waited to board the flight from London to Tel Aviv. As he reports at the opening of *To Jerusalem and Back*, in the departure lounge they found themselves surrounded by Hasidim ("the corridors are jumping with them") on their way to Israel to attend the circumcision of the firstborn son of their spiritual leader, the Belzer Rebbe. "Far too restless to wait in line [they] rush in and out, gesticulating, exclaiming," behavior that anticipates Israeli driving: "cars as a matter of course rushing into the reserved bus lanes, screwing everything up and honking madly" (p. 24). As the Bellows entered the plane, they were "enfiladed by eyes that lie dark in hairy ambush" (p. 1). The young Hasid seated next to Alexandra leaned across to ask Bellow if he spoke Yiddish. "I cannot be next to your wife," he says. "Please sit between us. Be so good." Pimply, unprepossessing, not permitted even to look at women unrelated to him, let alone to sit next to them, "he seems a good-hearted young man and he is visibly enjoying himself." Bellow was amused—as he had been fifteen years earlier, on a comparably noisy flight from New York to Puerto Rico (described in chapter 14 of *To Fame and Fortune*). His neighbor then, a cigar-smoking priest, carried a dozen cigars in his upper coat pocket, which he described to Bellow as "just about enough for the trip." The Hasidim, like the earlier Puerto Ricans, are described as "vividly enjoying themselves, dodging through the aisles, visiting chatting standing impatiently in the long lavatory lines, amiable, busy as geese. They pay no attention to signs" (p. 2).

When the young Hasid discovers Bellow has not ordered a kosher meal, he sets out to convert him.

> "I must talk to you. You won't be offended?"
>
> "No. I don't think so."
>
> "You may want to give me a slap in the face."
>
> "Why should I?"
>
> "You *are* a Jew. You must be a Jew, we are speaking Yiddish. How can you eat—*that*!"
>
> "It looks awful, doesn't it?"
>
> "You mustn't touch it. My womenfolk packed kosher-beef sandwiches for me. Is your wife Jewish?"
>
> Here I'm obliged to lie. Alexandra is Rumanian. But I can't give him too many shocks at once, and I say, "She has not had a Jewish upbringing."
>
> "She doesn't speak Yiddish?"
>
> "Not a word. But excuse me, I want my lunch."
>
> "Will you eat some of my kosher food instead, as a favor?"
>
> "With pleasure."
>
> "Then I will give you a sandwich, but only on one condition. You must never—never—eat *trephena* [unkosher] food again."

Clearly enjoying himself, Bellow cannot make such a promise. So the youth offers him a deal. If Bellow will from now on eat nothing but kosher food, "for the rest of your life I will send you fifteen dollars a week" (p. 3). When Bellow demurs, the Hasid offers him twenty-five dollars a week, to which Bellow answers, "I can't accept such a sacrifice from you," turning to his British Airways chicken "with the chill of death upon it" (p. 2), his appetite spoiled.

Though keen not to receive VIP treatment, Bellow was happy to be put up by Mayor Kollek in the guest house of Mishkenot Sha'ananim, southeast of the Old City, not far from the King David Hotel. Mishkenot serves as a cultural center for Jerusalem, hosting visiting celebrities, conferences, recitals, exhibitions, and readings. Its name means "peaceful habitation" (from Isaiah 32:18: "My people shall dwell in a peaceful habitation, and in sure dwellings, and in quiet resting places"). Surrounded by a park and gardens, it directly overlooks the Old City, in a district of small stone causeways and elegant white stone dwellings. The Victorian banker and philanthropist Sir Moses Montefiore was its founder, acting on behalf of a wealthy Jewish merchant from New Orleans. When it was created, in 1860, Mishkenot was intended as an almshouse, but since 1973 it has served its current function. Several days after his arrival, Bellow wrote to eleven-year-old Daniel to tell him about his new surroundings. At "this very moment," he was looking across at Mount Zion. Like Daniel, he was studying Hebrew, "to write something about the city. It's a funny experience, at the age of 60, to do the things you did as a small boy." In *To Jerusalem and Back*, Bellow describes the white stone of Jerusalem, the stone of Mishkenot, as "hoarier than anything I ever saw." Its "brilliant" light, like the "broadcast" light he found in Mexico in 1940, makes "the American commonplace 'out of this world' true enough to give your soul a start" (p. 10). Later in the book, Bellow describes the light as having "purifying powers," likening it to "the outer garment of God" (p. 93), a comparison that recalls the "angelic" hoops of light reflected off the water glasses in *Seize the Day*. Yet "even on a sunny morning the stone buildings of Jerusalem chill your hands and feet. Stepping out, I feel a bit numb, like a wasp in autumn" (p. 22).

IN THE COURSE OF immersing himself in Israeli culture and politics, Bellow interviews government leaders and public figures, journalists, professors (of history, sociology, international relations, philosophy, mathematics, English), novelists and poets, relatives, the barber at the King David Hotel, a masseur who comes to Mishkenot to unknot his back. Accounts of these meetings, in the form of sketches or vignettes, are interwoven in the book with snippets and summaries of his reading, from Elie Kedourie, Malcolm Kerr, Bernard Lewis, Theodore Draper, Walter Laqueur, Yehoshafat Harkabi. Pro-Palestinian and

Israeli positions are presented as intractable, even when outlined by moderates. Mahmud Abu Zuluf, the editor of *El Kuds*, the largest Arab newspaper in Jerusalem, sets out the Palestinian case in a tone "somewhere between boredom and passion." The Jews "must divide authority with the Arabs. They are too reluctant to accept realities, too slow. The longer they wait the worse things will be." Bellow describes Abu Zuluf as "hated by the leftists. His life and the lives of his children have been threatened. His automobile was once blown up, but he continues to follow the line of conciliation and peace." As Abu Zuluf talks, he grows more agitated, smacking the top of his desk with the flat of his hand. The only solution is for Israel to "come forward quickly with peace plans and initiate negotiations, show a willingness to negotiate." Later that day, Bellow takes tea with David Shahar, an Israeli novelist ("a good one"). "The Jews have not been inflexible and negative," begins Shahar. "Concessions are continually offered. They are rejected. The original U.N. partition plan of 1947 was turned down because the Arabs could not tolerate any Jewish state, not even a minuscule one. If a state was what they wanted, they might have had it years ago. They rejected it. And they invaded the country from all sides, hoping to drive the Jews out and take the wealth they had created" (pp. 36–37). Soon Shahar is shouting and banging on the table, like Abu Zuluf at his desk. Six generations of Shahar's family have lived in Jerusalem. "You don't know them," he says of the Arabs, "the West doesn't know them. They will not let us live." Bellow had come to have tea with Shahar, but "there are no peaceful moments in Jerusalem, not for those who are making inquiries. Immediately you are involved in a tormenting discussion" (p. 36).

Part of what inflames Shahar is what Bellow calls "my American evenhandedness, my objectivity at his expense. It is so easy for outsiders to say that there are two sides to the question" (pp. 37–38). In Chicago, when the brutality and injustice reported in the newspapers oppresses Bellow, he refuses to open his newspaper. "In Israel, one has no such choice. There the violent total is added up every day. And nothing can be omitted. . . . Unremitting thought about the world situation parallels the defense effort. These people are actively, individually involved in universal history. I don't see how they can bear it" (p. 46). In Israel, when you put down the newspaper, immediately you are met with "a gale of conversation—exposition, argument, harangue, analysis, theory, expostulation, threat, and prophecy. . . . I listen carefully, closely, more closely than I've ever listened in my life, utterly attentive, but I often feel that I have dropped into a shoreless sea" (p. 25). The only relief Bellow finds outside his rooms in Mishkenot, at least the only relief he records, is with the poets Harold Schimmel and Dennis Silk, who take him sightseeing. They want to know what Theodore Roethke was like. Silk has written an article about John Berryman and asks Bellow to recite some of Berryman's poems "in Berryman's own manner" (p. 78). Returning to Mishkenot, Silk offers details about Moses Montefiore, about whom he has written "a curious, half-imaginary account." Bellow thinks Montefiore sounds "as indefatigable as Kollek himself" (for Kollek, Montefiore's founding of Mishkenot, the first settlement outside the Old City, matters for political reasons, as a way to buttress "the legitimacy of Jewish claims in Jerusalem") (p. 79). At the end of his outing with the poets, Bellow tells them: "When I came to Jerusalem, I thought to take it easy here. This is the first easy day I've enjoyed in a month" (p. 79).

Bellow's impressions of the Israelis he meets, also of the Americans he interviews before and after his Jerusalem stay, are characteristically vivid. Extended sketches are offered of Mayor Kollek, the writer John Auerbach, Foreign Minister Abba Eban, Minister of Defense Shimon Peres, and the philanthropist Meyer Weisgal, founder of the Weizmann Institute. Deft touches appear throughout. The curmudgeonly columnist Joseph Alsop "argues by linking a long series of aggressive questions, punctuated by 'Hey?' 'Eh?' 'Isn't that so—ekh?' " (p. 178). At lunch, Abba Eban, "a type with which I am completely familiar," orders chicken. "It is Jewish chicken, boiled in its skin, sitting on waves of mashed potatoes and surrounded by shores of rice and brown gravy. . . . Hungry Mr. Eban is full under the chin. His voice is Oxonian, his views are highly organized. He is not a listener" (p. 40). Harold Fisch, an Orthodox professor of English, tells Bellow that " 'the liberated territories' must be colonized and reclaimed by the Jews. The West Bank is Promised Land." Fisch is English by birth and declares "fiercely in his Oxbridge voice that we American Jews are not Jews at all. It is a strange experience to hear such a judgment in such an accent" (p. 70). At dinner, the children of friends of Alexandra's from the Hebrew University, a boy and a girl, "come up to the table and examine us boldly, pacing around the room like small lions. They look into our plates to see how foreigners eat cutlets." Everyone laughs. Then, "as usual" (p. 116), the conversation becomes serious.

That Bellow was exotic was a feeling shared by adult Israelis. Amos Oz saw him twice during his stay in Jerusalem, both times at Mishkenot. In the first visit, in the early hours of the afternoon, the two novelists spoke for ninety minutes, mostly about the revival of Hebrew. Oz remembers "a certain undertone of disbelief that Hebrew could be used as a living language after being virtually dead for seventeen centuries." "He asked me about writing modern literature in Hebrew. How is it possible?" Oz found Bellow "very formal and schoolteacherly. He asked polite questions and kept his distance, curious, eager to know, almost impersonal, though in the course of conversation he warmed up." The second meeting took place five or six weeks later, and this time they talked about politics, American as well as Israeli, and about the translation of Bellow's novels into Hebrew. Oz was struck by the fierceness of Bellow's anti-communism, in particular his resentment of Soviet policies toward the Middle East.[43] What he remembered "most vividly," however, was "a brief exchange about death. I don't know how we came to speak about death, I don't remember the context," but Bellow "made a stunning remark. I said I was hoping to die in my sleep, and Saul responded by saying that, on the contrary, he would like to die wide awake and fully conscious, because death is such a crucial experience he wouldn't want to miss it."

ALTHOUGH *To Jerusalem and Back* does not ignore the injustices visited on the Palestinians, the bulk of Bellow's indignation is reserved for the hypocrisy of their supporters, the French in particular, an emphasis or tactic urged on him by Edward Shils. In a letter of February 12, 1976, Shils confessed that he had "been thinking a lot about your book on Israel. I attach great importance to it. There is no one who has written or who is likely to write on this subject whose eminence in the world of letters is such as to guarantee him a considerable audience. This audience will be European as well as American; the book is likely to be translated into the major European languages." If Bellow keeps in mind "the dominant prejudices against Israel in the Western European societies, you will be directing yourself toward them, and that will make your book more effective." Bellow was unlikely to have needed this advice, though it may have buoyed him. Soon after describing the airplane flight to Israel and settling into Mishkenot, he rehearses the story of *Le Monde*'s refusal to print his 1973 letter, criticizing Sartre for his selective outrage (and for the naïve belief "that more popular or leftist Arab regimes would find Israel's existence easier to accept" [p. 123]). But it is not just Europeans he criticizes. "Between 1950 and June 1975 the United States contributed more than $600 million to the United Nations Relief and Works Agency fund for the relief of Palestinian refugees. Israel gave more than $6 million. The Soviet Union contributed nothing, the Chinese nothing, the Algerian government, so concerned about the Palestinians, nothing" (p. 127). Bellow openly admits "that Israel might have done more for the refugees, over the years. The efforts made to indemnify those who had lost their lands were far from adequate." He cites Hannah Arendt, approvingly for a change, for her suggestion "that a part of the German reparations should have been set aside by Israel for the relief of the Palestinians." The responsibility of other interested parties, however, must not be forgotten. "Many Palestinians have suffered greatly, but it was not because of their suffering that Nasser went to war in 1967. Nasser didn't want them resettled; he kept them rotting in refugee camps and used them against Israel. The British did not create the Arab-Jewish conflict, though they may have aggravated it. If the Arab states did not deliberately exploit the Palestinians for political purposes, then the kindest interpretation of their conduct is that they were utterly incompetent" (pp. 121–22).[44] More broadly: "In India, in Africa, in Europe, millions of human beings have been put to flight, transported, enslaved, stampeded over the borders, left to starve, but only the case of the Palestinians is held permanently open. Where Israel is concerned, the world swells with moral consciousness. Moral judgment, a wraith in Europe, becomes a full-blooded giant when Israel and the Palestinians are mentioned" (p. 135).

Bellow describes a single visit to the West Bank, with Alexandra, Sam and Nina Bellows, a friend of theirs named Shimshon (described as "religious, philanthropic" [p. 13]), and Cousin Nota, "two years out of the Soviet Union" (p. 19), a tough reality-instructor. "You are no match for them," Nota tells Bellow, speaking of the Russians. "You do not understand with whom you are dealing" (p. 19). Nota Gordin was a captain in the Russian army and fought the Germans until 1945: "He has the family look—the brown eyes, arched brows, dark coloring, and white hair." Nota's view of Bellow is his view of Americans in general: "amiable, good-natured, attractive perhaps, but undeveloped, helpless" (p. 19). Shimshon, it turns out, is a supporter of the settlements, a benefactor of those "determined for religious reasons to colonize the West Bank." Bellow disapproves, though his disapproval is implicit, partly, one suspects, to maintain a pose of reportorial neutrality; the settlements are "held by some to imply a rejection of Zionism, for the Zionist pioneers were satisfied with a sanctuary and did not try to recover the Promised Land" (pp. 131–32). Shimshon, "very observant and busy in Jewish affairs," takes the party to Gush Etzion, where a Jewish colony had been wiped out by the Arabs before the war. A benefactor of the settlers there, he "proudly shows us the yeshiva, a newly built fortress of Orthodoxy" (p. 132). Bellow notes the rugged appearance of the settlers: "The young men wear skullcaps but their frames are big and their forearms thick with muscle. Their beards are far from tame and rabbinical; they bristle" (p. 132).

The evenhandedness of *To Jerusalem and Back* infuriated hard-liners from both camps. For Isabella Fey in *The Jerusalem Post*, the book was a "weary little collection of hedgings and evasions. . . . It is the careful *neutrality* of the current book which grates on the truth-nerve of the reader." She accuses Bellow of withdrawing from "the real issues of Israel," which mostly means from Arab intractability, though intractability—the fact that "the Arabs would not agree to the existence of Israel"—is what the book sees as "the root of the problem" (p. 179).[45] On its final page, Bellow praises the May 1976 Israeli peace proposals, recently reported in the wire services of the *Chicago Tribune*. "They indicate that Israel has not become immobile, inflexible, paralyzed by stubbornness of political rivals, or lacking in leadership" (p. 182). Fey was not impressed: "This reproach is the very heart of Arab and left-wing propaganda against the State of Israel. Did Bellow ever believe it, that he seems so relieved to find some big American paper denying it?" The response from the left was even more scornful. For Noam Chomsky, Bellow's book might have been written by the Israeli Information Ministry. He takes issue with almost every political assertion made in the book, quoting myriad sources and filling his review with phrases such as "of this we hear nothing," "he fails to mention," "had he bothered to look," "hardly the most objective source." Bellow's attacks on *Le Monde* and Sartre are treated with particular contempt, as gross distortions. The review ends: "Bellow has an engaging ability to skim the surface of ideas. He also has a craftsman's talent for capturing a chance encounter or an odd circumstance. Beyond that, his account of what he has seen and heard is a disaster. The critical acclaim it has received is revealing, with regard to the state of American intellectual life."[46]

The final view of the Arab-Israeli conflict offered in *To Jerusalem and Back* is the one Bellow openly declared two years after its publication as a supporter of Peace Now. He was a signatory, along with Irving Howe, Daniel Bell, and Lucy Dawidowicz, of the "Letter of 37" published in *Moment Magazine* in 1978, a declaration organized by Leonard Fein, the magazine's cofounding editor (the other cofounding editor was Elie Wiesel). The aim of the "Letter of 37" was to express solidarity with the Israeli Peace Now movement, spearheaded by Amos Oz and others, which urged Prime Minister Begin not to let talks with President Sadat of Egypt collapse, and advocated both a two-state solution and a negotiated settlement to the Israeli-Palestinian problem. That these were Bellow's implicit positions in *To Jerusalem and Back* is suggested by the prominence he gives toward the end of the book to the views of Yehoshafat Harkabi in Israel, whose objectivity is scoffed at by Chomsky, and of the sociologist Morris Janowitz back in Chicago. In a passage partially quoted in chapter 1, the once hard-line Harkabi—chief of Israeli Intelligence from 1955 to 1959, now, at the time of writing, professor of international relations at the Hebrew University—is initially unencouraging, at least as paraphrased by Bellow:

> He concedes that the Arabs have been wronged, but he insists upon the moral meaning of Israel's existence. Israel stands for something in Western history. The questions are not as simple as ideological partisans try to make them. The Zionists were not deliberately unjust, the Arabs were not guiltless. To rectify the evil as the Arabs would wish it rectified would mean the destruction of Israel. Arab refugees must be relieved and compensated, but Israel will not commit suicide for their sake. By now the Arabs see themselves as returning in blood and fire, and Israel will not agree to bleed and burn [p. 158].

These views Bellow characterizes as "rather better balanced than [those of] most of the people with whom I have discussed Arab-Israeli problems" (p. 158). They are also properly attentive to moral questions. They would lead Harkabi to support the movement for a two-state solution and to advocate negotiations with the PLO. A similar position is voiced by Janowitz, an old friend and colleague of Bellow's at the University of Chicago. Soon after his return to Chicago, Bellow tells us, he invited Janowitz, described as "torrentially sensible" and coming from "a family deeply involved in the issues of Zionism . . . a supporter of Israel" (p. 164), to meet him in Hyde Park, at the Eagle, to discuss the Middle East. It is Janowitz's belief "that the West Bank territory, with mutual adjustments, would serve as the basis of a Palestine state" (p. 167); "that while 'military force created Israel and keeps it alive, only a political settlement will insure its survival—physically and morally' "; that "Israel's leaders must oppose the further expansion of . . . settlements"; and that there must be "guarantees of military security and the prevention of terrorism" (p. 167).

THROUGHOUT THE 1970S and beyond, Bellow was bedeviled by legal problems. These began on February 14, 1968, when, after seven years of marriage, Susan divorced him on the grounds of desertion and mental cruelty. The terms of the divorce, as laid out in a written order from the Circuit Court of Cook County, were that Susan was to get $150,000 in alimony and $250 a month in child support. The child-support figure was pegged at 10 percent of $30,000, Bellow's estimate of his annual projected income, an estimate that would get him into serious trouble. He arrived at it by adding $10,000 for speaking fees, royalties, and investments to his University of Chicago salary of $20,000, describing the resulting figure as "an attempt to average out into the future as I had averaged back into the past." In court, when questioned about the estimate, he admitted that his lawyer "seemed to feel that the lower the figure the better."[47]

According to court records, in 1964 Bellow earned $89,670; in 1965, he earned $79,157; in 1966, he earned $90,085; in 1967, he earned $128,104; in 1968, the year of the estimate, he earned $149,631. As for later years, in 1969 he earned $163,622, and in 1970 he earned $169,165, figures that were dwarfed by his earnings in the mid-1970s, particularly after 1976, when he won the Nobel Prize and when the royalties from *Humboldt's Gift*, which won a Pulitzer Prize, started to come in.[48] In 1977, Susan calculated that Bellow earned $461,303, a figure derived largely from *Humboldt's Gift*, which spent nine months on the best-seller list, and for which Avon paid $175,000 for paperback rights. In addition, he received $160,000 for winning the Nobel Prize. Despite these figures, Bellow argued that he had been fair in his estimates. In a letter of July 26, 1976, to his lawyer friend Sam Goldberg, he complained, "Judges and lawyers simply don't understand how a writer makes his way through life. . . . I didn't misrepresent. I simply had no idea what my future income would be. It's true that I took an advance of fifty thousand [for *Mosby's Memoirs and Other Stories*, several of which, Susan argued, were written "in the marital residence" and "discussed with me"[49]], but suppose I had been unable to complete the book?" In addition to underestimating his projected earnings, Bellow was accused of a second misrepresentation, involving the co-op apartment at 5940 South Shore Drive. Although Bellow claimed to be sole owner of the apartment ("I paid for it and assumed that it was mine"), in fact it was held in joint tenancy. When Susan realized the importance of this finding, she filed a petition on June 30, 1969, to vacate the original settlement. To his lawyer, Bellow countered that Susan had signed the settlement "in full knowledge of everything. She knew of my income from the prosperous years ('64 through '67). She knew also of the lean years and understood beyond any doubt that the figure of $30,000 was an estimate based on my lean year income. She knew of the title of the co-op apartment because she signed the joint tenancy document. She lived in the apartment and she had every opportunity to check ownership. She knew all the facts relating to our joint bank account. . . . She need not have accepted the figures I named."[50] It would take five years of legal wrangling for the courts to rule on Susan's June 1969 petition.

Bellow's lawyer in the original settlement was Stanton Ehrlich, of Ehrlich, Bundesen and Cohn, an expensive firm on LaSalle Street, Chicago's Wall Street. Ehrlich was recommended to Bellow by Marshall Holleb, who did not do divorce work. Joel Bellows, himself now a LaSalle Street lawyer (he would later act on Bellow's behalf), thinks the failure to report co-tenancy of the apartment was an oversight on Ehrlich's part rather than a deliberate act of deception. In his ruling on Susan's petition on July 25, 1974, Judge David Linn declared that Bellow had procured the original agreement "by fraud and misrepresentation" and ordered him to pay Susan $2,500 a month in alimony, backdated to 1968, plus $600 a month child support, plus lawyers' fees. As Joel remembers it, Linn didn't like Bellow at all. "Susan was a good witness. Bellow wasn't a good witness, and he was successful and he was an intellectual." In *Humboldt's Gift*, Charlie Citrine provokes similar hostility from Judge Urbanovich, who sides with Denise in divorce proceedings. Denise claims Charlie will earn at least $100,000 a year for the next fourteen years, until he's seventy. "I can't help being a little amused by this, your honor," Charlie responds. "Ha ha! I don't think my brain is strong enough, it's my only real asset. Other people have land, rent, inventories, management, capital gains, price supports, depletion allowances, federal subsidies. I have no such advantages." Judge Urbanovich is genial but having none of this. "You're a clever person, Mr. Citrine. Even in Chicago that's obvious. . . . In the property division under the decree Mrs. Citrine got less than half and she alleges that records were falsified. You are a bit dreamy, and probably were not aware of this. Perhaps the records were falsified by others. Nevertheless you are responsible under the law." After raising the possibility that Charlie's recent lowered productivity might be a deliberate attempt "to balk the plaintiff," the judge begins "diverting himself" with Charlie.

> "I am sympathetic to the problems of intellectuals and I know you may get into special preoccupations that aren't lucrative. But I understand that this Maharishi fellow by teaching people to turn their tongues backward toward the palate so that they can get the tip of their tongue into their own sinuses has become a multimillionaire. Many ideas are marketable and perhaps your special preoccupations are more lucrative than you realize," he said [p. 226].

By October 1971, Bellow had dismissed Stanton Ehrlich and his associate, Chuck Sproger, who in Bellow's fictional account become Charlie Citrine's lawyers, Forrest Tomchek and Billy Srole, "two honest-looking deceitful men" (p. 214). In real life, Bellow's new lawyer was Barry Freeman, who took over his appeal against Susan's petition. Susan, meanwhile, had replaced her original lawyer, from the firm of Lipnick, Barsy and Joseph, with Jerome Berkson, who would later become partner in the LaSalle Street firm of Beermann, Swerdlove, Woloshin, Barezky, and Berkson. In *Humboldt's Gift,* Denise is represented by Maxie "Cannibal" Pinsker, "that man-eating kike," a "brutally hairy" man who enters court in a bright-yellow double-knit suit and "a large yellow cravat that lay on his shirt like a cheese omelette" (p. 224). On the side, Denise also receives legal advice from "Gumballs" Schwirner, with whom Srole thinks she is carrying on. " 'That son of a bitch,' said Tomchek, violent. 'If I could prove that he was banging the plaintiff and interfering in my case I'd fix his clock for him. I'd have him before the Ethics Committee'" (p. 215).

Bellow's lawyer-friend Sam Freifeld advised him against employing Stanton Ehrlich, as he was later, in a letter of December 19, 1966, to warn him against underestimating his projected income. Perhaps as a consequence, the two friends had a serious falling-out, and their relationship never recovered. Freifeld may have wanted to represent Bellow himself. Bellow may have been angry with Freifeld for interfering (at one point, Freifeld wrote to Ehrlich to caution him against overcharging). In *Humboldt's Gift*, the Freifeld character is Alec Szathmar, who thinks Tomchek is too important for Charlie. "He wouldn't put you in his fish-tank for an ornament." "He's a crook all the same," Charlie replies. "Denise is a thousand times smarter. She studied the documents and caught him in a minute. He didn't even make a routine check of titles to see who legally owned what" (p. 204). Like Denise, Susan spotted who owned what, being obsessed with the case as well as intelligent. Early in 2015, Daniel Bellow boxed up his mother's papers relating to the divorce and shipped them to me to look through and then deposit "in the midden heap of the Regenstein to gross out future historians." The papers are covered with Susan's shrewd, bitter, furious instructions, queries, and outraged interjections, often directed at her own lawyers. "Dear Miles," begins a handwritten note dated March 16, 1982. "It's nice to know you are still practicing law, but I must confess I gained no particular information from your note. . . . Equal Justice Under Law says the pediment on the Supreme Court Building. Under Law is a pretty dark and heavy place to be." Atlas quotes Herb and Mitzi McClosky. "It was her profession," they claimed, speaking of Susan's involvement in legal proceedings. "She wanted to divorce Saul and punish him and still stay married to him."[51] "*Of course* Berkson's documents are tendentious," writes one of Bellow's lawyers in 1982, fourteen years into the case. "If they weren't, Berkson wouldn't be Berkson (besides he has *Susan* to try to control)."[52] This is not to say that Susan's vigilance was misplaced.

As soon as Judge Linn ruled in Susan's favor, Bellow appealed, arguing that what remained of the $150,000 granted in the original settlement (some $130,000) had first to be returned. This appeal was denied and on July 1, 1977, Judge Mary Ann McMorrow entered an order for Bellow to pay temporary alimony and child support pending final disposition of the case. Susan was to receive alimony of $2,500 a month if unemployed, $1,500 a month if employed, plus $650 a month child support. In addition, Bellow would pay all Daniel's medical bills and private-school fees. Joel Bellows, now acting for his uncle, urged Bellow to accept the judgment, which he thought a good one. Instead, Bellow fired Joel and appealed the ruling, refusing to pay the interim alimony. On October 18, 1978, some $11,500 in arrears in alimony payments, Bellow was ordered by Judge McMorrow either to pay up or to post bail of $50,000. If he failed to post bail, he faced a ten-day jail sentence for contempt of court. The next day, Bellow's new lawyer, George Feiwell of Feiwell, Galper and Lasky, 23 North LaSalle Street, declared that Bellow would pay up only if Susan agreed to return the $130,000 left over from the original settlement. Then Bellow posted bail. On October 20, articles about the threatened jail sentence appeared in the *Chicago Tribune* and the *Sun-Times*. Eleven days later, *Newsweek* reported that, "for now, Bellow is spared the slammer."[53] It was not until May 17, 1979, that the Illinois Appellate Court upheld Judge McMorrow's July 1, 1977, ruling, and Bellow was forced to pay Susan the sum of $45,634.66.

By this date, such a sum must have seemed to Bellow a drop in the ocean. Half a year earlier, in September 1978, a "final" judgment had at last been rendered on his appeal against Judge Linn's 1974 ruling. This judgment, handed down by Judge James Bales of the Circuit Court, a downstate appointment from Dixon, Illinois, awarded Susan alimony of $650,000, minus the original $150,000. Like Judge Linn, Judge Bales did not care for Bellow. Atlas reports that he told one of Bellow's lawyers, "I don't like that son of a bitch, he writes pornography."[54] According to Daniel Bellow, it was "true that the judge hated him." Bellow's view was that "the judge was an anti-Semite. . . . He thought [Bellow] was a Jew who wrote dirty books." The amount awarded Susan included all her legal expenses, amounting to $200,000 (having to pay them, the judge said of Susan, "would exhaust her meagre savings and undermine her economic stability"). In addition, Bellow was ordered to pay $800 a month child support, an increase of $150 a month, plus medical and educational expenses. Against the advice of his lawyers, Bellow appealed Bales's judgment and received an order to stay payment, excepting child support. "If the brutal order holds in the Appeals Court," Bellow wrote to Edward Shils on September, 3, 1978, "I shall have to borrow to pay my persecutors, and I have no reason to be confident in the judgment of the Court of Appeals. . . . The whole thing is monstrous—simply monstrous. It has taught me a great deal, though. I don't say this menacingly, or with excessive bitterness. I plan no vengeance. I mean only to say that it has expanded my understanding of human beings very considerably." To Julian Behrstock, his friend from Northwestern, in a letter of October 9, 1978, Bellow described the sum he had to pay as "stupendous, and the legal fees, two hundred thousand, also stupendous. If these judgments hold I will be where I was in 1937 on the campus, living on an allowance of three bucks a week. I may ask the President to revive the WPA for my sake."

Two years later, the Appellate Court modified Judge Bales's order. In addition to lawyers' fees, Bellow had now to pay Susan a lump sum of $102,000, plus child support and monthly alimony installments of $2,000 until Daniel's eighteenth birthday (some 121 months, totalling $242,000). In 1981, Bellow wrote to his Tuley High School friend Hyman Slate "of news of a new lawsuit by Susan. The wicked never let up. The lawyers learn no kindness. My own are as bad as hers."[55] A year later, Bellow fired George Feiwell, in a letter of August 16, 1982, complaining, "I haven't heard from you in some time. My questions are not answered, my calls are not returned, you have offered no suggestions. . . . Since I have no notion what actions the other side may be preparing, and since there is not the slightest sign of interest or concern from you I have no choice but to find another lawyer." In the letter to Behrstock, Bellow likened Susan's lawyers to the Philistines hounding Samson—though, "come—oddly—to think about it, most of the fellows who have ganged up on me are fully and legitimately circumcised." Eventually, the lump sum was reduced, the $102,000 figure whittled down to $59,209. In 1984, Susan's lawyers were still busy, begging her to sign papers allowing them to sue Bellow for failure to pay certain legal fees. By then, after sixteen years, Susan had had enough. Two years earlier, she had declared herself "the doubly defrauded party and the big loser in this nightmare of legal entanglement. It is a bit hard to end up on the losing end with my lawyers as well. . . . The costs of 'justice' or 'equity under the law' or whatever I thought I was after have been terrible for Daniel and me."[56] For over a dozen years, both parties had been unyielding. Atlas quotes one of Susan's lawyers on Bellow: "He didn't want to resolve it, he wanted to go on fighting." He also quotes Bellow's lawyer George Feiwell: "They wanted to hurt each other. It was a matter of who was going to hurt who the worst."[57]

It was Daniel who was hurt the worst. From when he was four to the age of sixteen, his parents were at war, with only rare truces. "I am coming to Daniel's bar mitzvah," Bellow wrote to Richard Stern on October 1, 1977, "but I may be arrested in front of KAM [a synagogue in Hyde Park] next Saturday despite my truce agreement (for the weekend) with Susan. The court held me in contempt because—I will tell it in legal language—pursuant to advice of counsel I refused to comply with the alimony assessment of the court but appealed the decision. Until the appeal is formally filed, I am in contempt." The bar mitzvah boy's parents were civil to each other at the bar mitzvah, even danced together at the party after the ceremony. Two days later, they were back in court. The adult Daniel is clear on their behavior: "It's like a textbook approach about how not to get divorced. I mean, if I ever get divorced I hope I'll act with a lot more class than either of them. I see people get divorced all the time, but they behave with some dignity and some restraint and with some compassion for their children. None of that happened." When Susan decided to leave Hyde Park for the North Side, removing Daniel from the Lab School and sending him to a school associated with "this big *macher* [big-shot] synagogue on the North Side," Bellow objected. "My father said, 'I wasn't consulted about this.' My mother said, 'Fuck you, I'm not married to you, I can do what I want.'" Exchanges like these helped to turn Daniel into "a willful, headstrong, angry child." "Like all bright children, I learned to do what my parents do," he recalls. "I don't want to discuss my mother with you," twelve-year-old Daniel had announced to his father (both parents ran each other down to Daniel), in a tone that caused Bellow to slap him, something he did "maybe three or four times." Bellow had been slapped by his father, but there was a difference: "Saul felt bad when he hit me, and his father didn't feel bad when he hit him." Daniel knew his father loved him, as Bellow knew his father loved him, but Bellow "could make you feel so bad, so small, so disgusting. He didn't need to hit you, he could just look at you."

The worst moment for Daniel came when his father sued for custody and Daniel was called to testify. Throughout what came to be known among Bellow's friends as "The Long Divorce," Daniel's welfare was a key battleground. In an undated document from the early 1970s, Susan sought child support "at a level that will protect me from Bellow's view of Daniel's interests and his conviction that money for Daniel means money for me. I do not want to be hassling with Bellow year in year out about whether Daniel needs psychiatric care (it took from the time

Daniel was 4 until he was 9 to convince him of that) or whether 8 weeks in camp will do him good." These complaints about Bellow and child care were not unique to Susan, as she well knew. Bellow also "suffered over writing child support checks to his two older sons."[58] In addition, as a way of getting back at her, Bellow suggested she was a negligent parent, a charge she often leveled against him. On February 14, 1972, Barry Freeman, Bellow's lawyer, wrote to Jerome Berkson, Susan's lawyer, to convey a complaint. When seven-year-old Daniel returned from school, he sometimes found no one at home. "In these situations he is instructed to walk three blocks to a drug store, crossing Hyde Park Boulevard in the process, and to read in a phone booth until his mother comes for him. The perils of this practice should be obvious."

On March 31, 1977, Susan wrote a ferocious letter to Bellow, accusing him of neglecting Daniel and caring only for himself. "You're the father, not the child. You still grieve over how your father treated you. Do you have a tear or two left for Daniel. . . . Doesn't your prized human understanding perceive even a fraction of all this. You're a fraud." The letter is three pages long, single-spaced, every sentence a damning accusation. In a letter of May 7, 1979, she tried to persuade a therapist of Daniel's to be deposed by her lawyer, as part of a campaign to get Bellow to pay Daniel's "extraordinary medical expenses," which the court had ordered him to pay. Susan's lawyers were eager to rebut Bellow's "usual charge that treatment for Daniel is a whim of mine."[59] Four months later, on July 12, 1977, Bellow wrote to Shils that "the disgraceful, disheartening legal battle continues. . . . Wicked wastefulness, gratuitous destructiveness. I was summoned to appear although Susan knew that I had just brought Daniel to the summer place, and although no judge had been assigned to the case. . . . Harassment was the only object, and my lawyers, not always effective, got me out of that at least." On February 22, 1979, Bellow wrote to Jack Goldstein, dean of the Graduate School at Brandeis University, "Litigants and lawyers still keep me nailed down in Chicago, and there is simply no escape possible until the court has ruled on my appeal. There are subtle and delicate threads that hold me down like Gulliver. I am bristling with Lilliputian arrows, they itch horribly. I am putting myself under the care of a dermatologist—that is literally true." Bellow's enemies were not only Lilliputians, they were midges, blackflies, spiders.

Daniel was not consulted about Bellow's plans to gain custody. "It was very unpleasant," he recalls. "He didn't say, 'Dan, would you like to come live with me?' He's like, 'I'm suing for your custody because I don't think it's right for you to be living with [your] mother.' And I said, 'But I want to live with my mother.'" This was in 1978. "I was fourteen years old and I didn't want to leave my mother. What was my mother going to do without me? It was just so implausible. It was ridiculous. He said, 'We'll fix up the room for you. . . . You could go to the Lab School with all your friends.'" Instead, Daniel went to New York with his mother.[60] Joel Bellows thinks Bellow may have been "helplessly" (the quotation marks were conveyed vocally by Joel, signaling irony) swept along "by a lawyer who said, 'Have Daniel testify and suggest he stay with you.'" I had no choice, Bellow might have said, or so Joel conjectures, which was partly how Bellow justified his decision to dismiss Joel as counsel, on the grounds that Edward Levi advised him to hire a lawyer from the firm used by the University of Chicago. As Joel reconstructs his uncle's thinking, "What's a man to do?"

Much of the wrangling over Daniel concerned therapy and schooling. Bellow had little faith in psychiatry, and he thought Daniel's problems in school were largely of his own making.[61] On April 3, 1979, he wrote to Susan objecting to Daniel's changing schools, the third change since the seventh grade. It wasn't the school's fault that Daniel was unhappy and doing poorly; "I see no reason why he should not turn in his homework." Daniel's problem, Bellow claimed, was Susan. "I can't see him making any progress solving his problems as long as he is with you." At the time of this letter, Daniel had only just turned fifteen and was unhappy at his school on the Upper West Side, near where he and Susan had moved from Chicago. A handsome boy, he was charming, mischievous, and hard to control, as at the Nobel ceremony. While still in Chicago, he recalled in an interview, "At thirteen I walked into court one day and I said to the judge, Let me take you to lunch and we'll figure out how to sort this out. My father never forgave me for that, never. I just wanted my parents to stop fighting." Daniel often cut classes, to hang out in the park or at CBGB, the New York punk-rock club. Susan was working, entirely taken up with the divorce, and "I don't think she noticed. They didn't tell her, but I wasn't showing up in school. . . . I was cutting school because I was miserable and the teachers were clueless and the kids were really mean." Although the second school Daniel went to in New York was better than the first, it wasn't until Susan took Bellow's advice and sent him to board at Northfield Mount Herman in Massachusetts that his life improved. "It was the best thing that ever happened to me. I had a great time," Daniel remembers. "I made a great group of friends. I didn't have to live at home anymore, that was what was needed, and I did okay in school, so everybody left me alone."

THE DIVORCE GROUND ON into the early 1980s, draining money, souring Bellow's mood, helping to account for his bad behavior. It may also have played a part in his increasing attraction to Steinerian ideas. In *Humboldt's Gift*, Charlie Citrine is enmeshed in the material realm of money, power, sex, crime, "the human world and all its wonderful works" (p. 305). Lately, though, he has begun to think "the painted veil isn't what it used to be. The damned thing is wearing out. Like a roller towel in a Mexican men's room" (p. 20). Worldly preoccupations have a similarly soiling effect on Charlie's character, for which "I'll never get any medals" (p. 13), especially after he becomes a celebrity. Being known—a "notable," in Chicago parlance—makes Charlie "ambitious cunning complex stupid vengeful" (p. 209). Vain, too, as well as undignified, as when he finds himself considering plastic surgery to remove the bags under his eyes (p. 190). "Once you had picked up the high-voltage wire and were *someone*, a known name, you couldn't release yourself from the electrical current" (p. 305). You also required increasingly powerful jolts. Forced by the small-time gangster Cantabile's threats onto the "fiftieth or sixtieth floor" of a half-finished skyscraper, "a headless trunk swooping up, swarming with lights," Charlie finds himself in open space. With "the wind ringing in the empty squares of wound-colored rust and beating against the hanging canvases," he clings to a pillar, fearful of falling to his death. Yet "my sensation-loving soul was also gratified. I knew that it took too much to gratify me. The gratification-threshold of my soul had risen too high" (p. 102).[62]

What Charlie wants is escape, most immediately from the ruinous divorce proceedings. So he flees to Europe, pursued by dunning letters from Chicago: "I knew that Tomchek and Srole would send in a staggering bill for losing my case and that Judge Urbanovitch would let Cannibal Pinsker help himself from the impounded funds" (p. 425). "Long ago I read a book called *Ils ne M'Auront Pas* (*They Aren't Going to Get Me*)," he says earlier in the novel, "and at certain moments I whisper, 'Ils ne m'auront pas'" (p. 141). He several times invokes Harry Houdini, "with whom I think I have some affinities" (p. 66). "The great Jewish escape artist," from Appleton, Wisconsin, Charlie's hometown, "defied all forms of restraint and confinement, including the grave. He broke out of everything. They buried him and he escaped. They sank him in boxes and he escaped. They put him in a strait jacket and manacles and hung him upside-down by one ankle from the flagpole of the Flatiron Building in New York" and he escaped. Charlie has written an article on Houdini, about his escapes but also about the intensity of his love for his mother, his years spent debunking spiritualists ("he exposed all the tricks of the medium-racket"), and his death, when he was "punched experimentally in the belly by a medical student and died of peritonitis. So you see nobody can overcome the final fact of the material world" (p. 424). "As a boy I was not a remarkable runner," Charlie tells us at the beginning of the novel. "How was it that in my middle fifties I became inspired with flight?" (p. 12).

Charlie means figurative flight, but he might also mean literal flight. Here he is on an airplane, with luscious Renata at his side:

> My head lay on the bib and bosom of the seat and when the Jack Daniel's came I strained it through my irregular multicolored teeth, curling my forefinger over the top of the glass to hold back the big, perforated ice cubes—they always put in too many. The thread of whisky burned pleasantly in the gullet and then my stomach, like the sun outside, began to glow, and the delight of freedom also began to expand within me. Renata was right, I was away. Once in a while I get shocked into upper wakefulness, I turn a corner, see the ocean, and my heart tips over with happiness—it feels so free!

Charlie explains this feeling of freedom in terms that recall the Romantic poets and their followers, in particular spiritualists like Rudolf Steiner and Owen Barfield. As he looks out the window of the plane, "I have the idea that, as well as beholding, I can also be beheld from yonder and am not a discrete object but incorporated with the rest. . . . For what is this sea, this atmosphere, doing within the eight-inch diameter of your skull?" (p. 306). In such seeing, "the earth is literally a mirror of thoughts. Objects themselves are embodied thoughts" (p. 256), perceiver and perceived unite. The glow Charlie feels links him to the glowing sun, recalling a similar glow in childhood, a time of "*personal* connection with the external world" (p. 199). "In the first decade of life" he recalls, "I knew this light and even knew how to breathe it in."

Hemmed in by shades of the prison house, Charlie loses touch with the light, or dismisses it, "for the sake of maturity or realism (practicality, self-preservation, the fight for survival)." Now, however, he finds it "edging back" (p. 175), as at moments like the one on the airplane with Renata. Such moments, though, are only in part spiritual or elevated. They also have lower or worldly origins. "Sipping whisky, feeling the radiant heat that rose inside, I experienced a bliss that I knew perfectly well was not mad. They hadn't done me in back there, Tomchek, Pinsker, Denise, Urbanovich. I had gotten away from them. . . . I could find no shadow of wistful yearning, no remorse, no anxiety. I was with a beautiful bim" (p. 306).

Charlie's mystical tendencies are undermined not only by the fact of women like Renata and Denise but by their cutting impatience with higher aspirations. "What you really want is to get rid of everybody," he reports Denise telling him, "to turn out to be a law unto yourself. Just you and your misunderstood heart" (p. 45), a judgment Charlie "would not argue with" (p. 45). Reading Barfield or Rudolf Steiner may help him to feel "the one life within us and abroad" (a phrase from Coleridge, the subject of a book by Barfield), but it may also be a way of blotting out the needs of others.[63] When he reads Steiner, Charlie often feels "unusually light and swift-paced, as if I were on a weightless bicycle and skipping through the star world. Occasionally I saw myself with exhilarating objectivity, literally as an object among objects—the physical universe. One day that object world would cease to move and when the body collapsed the soul would simply remove itself" (p. 216). The image of a "weightless bicycle" floating away like a balloon suggests the child's world, as does "skipping," just as the spiritual insights Charlie finds in Steiner corroborate emotional certainties from earliest infancy, the sort challenged or disputed by reason. "Matters of the spirit are widely and instantly grasped," Charlie asserts. "Except of course by people who are in heavily fortified positions, mental opponents trained to resist what everyone is born knowing" (p. 91). As Charlie puts it at the end of the novel, speaking of death and the afterlife, "the prevailing beliefs seldom satisfy my need for truth. . . . I never believed that oblivion *was* the case" (p. 348).

What Charlie looks for in Steiner and other mystical writers is corroborating evidence, support for what he *knows* is true. His faith, the faith he's tempted by, is in instinct, "an illusion, perhaps a marvellous illusion, or perhaps only a lazy one, that by a kind of inspired levitation

I could rise and dart straight to the truth" (p. 156). That this faith is "religious" he is prepared to admit, if by religious one means believing "there's something in human beings beyond the body and brain and that we have ways of knowing that go beyond the organism and its senses. I've always believed that. My misery comes, maybe, from ignoring my metaphysical hunches" (p. 131). For too long, Charlie has allowed himself to be governed by received opinion, "the going mental rules of a civilization that proved its right to impose [its] rules by the many practical miracles it performed" (p. 50). To fight against its hold, he practices Steinerian meditative exercises, aimed at strengthening spiritual perception, as in "my exercise in contemplation of Spirit-recollection (the purpose of which was to penetrate into the depths of the soul and to recognize the connection between the self and the divine powers)" (p. 141). Charlie gets these exercises from Steiner's *Knowledge of the Higher Worlds and Its Attainment* (1947) and finds them difficult to perform, because "characteristically I had been trying too hard" (p. 110). Bellow, too, performed Steiner's exercises, in particular the "I Am, It Thinks" meditation, to which he was "particularly faithful," crediting it with giving him "a certain daily stability."[64]

Yet Charlie, like Bellow, never fully commits to his metaphysical hunches or to Steiner. "It was now apparent to me that I was neither of Chicago nor sufficiently beyond it, and that Chicago's material and daily interests and phenomena were neither actual and vivid enough nor symbolically clear enough to me, so that I had neither vivid actuality nor symbolic clarity and for the time being I was utterly nowhere." Charlie's unclarity drives him to "long esoteric conversations" (p. 254) with an anthroposophist named Professor Scheldt, father of the nubile Doris. What he hopes to gain from these conversations, as from his reading of Steiner and Barfield, is "once and for all . . . to find out whether there was anything behind the incessant hints of immortality that kept dropping on me" (p. 347). These hints are supported by a sense that "each thing in nature was an emblem for something in my own soul" (p. 348), a sense which promises, in ways not explained, reunion with his "significant dead, remembered every day" (p. 110). So intense is Charlie's longing for this reunion that he is willing to put up with Professor Scheldt's esoteric idiom, with its talk of "Moon Evolution, the fire spirits, the Sons of Life, with Atlantis, with the lotus-flower organs of spiritual perception or the strange mingling of Abraham with Zarathustra, or the coming together of Jesus and the Buddha" (p. 257).

These are the equivalents of Steiner's talk of Angels and Spirits, as in the "bewitching pamphlet" in which he identifies "our duty . . . to collaborate with the Angels. They appear within us (as the Spirit called the *Maggid* manifested itself to the great Rabbi Joseph Karo). Guided by the Spirits of Form, Angels sow seeds of the future in us. . . . Among other things they wish to make us see the concealed divinity of other human beings. They show man how he can cross by means of thought the abyss that separates him from Spirit" (p. 287). How literally Charlie takes this sort of thing is not clear, to himself or to the reader. "There were passages in Steiner that set my teeth on edge. I said to myself, this is lunacy. Then I said, this is poetry, a great vision" (p. 427), a doubleness that recalls Bellow on Reich, or Henderson on King Dahfu, who has life wisdom but whose "enthusiasms and visions swept him far out" (p. 221). "The strange things he said," Charlie recalls of Professor Scheldt, "were at least deep things" (p. 255).

BELLOW'S INTEREST IN STEINER was supported by his reading of Barfield's *Saving the Appearances* (1957) and *Unancestral Voice* (1965).[65] Barfield, whose background was literary, was the most influential of Steiner's English-speaking disciples. At Oxford, where he read English, he became a founding member of the Inklings, along with C. S. Lewis, J. R. R. Tolkien, and Charles Williams (none of whom shared his anthroposophical beliefs). When Lewis left Oxford at the end of 1954 to take up a chair at Cambridge, he lobbied for Barfield to replace him as lecturer in English at Magdalen College, but the appointment fell through. Barfield's first work of nonfiction was *Poetic Diction: A Study in Meaning* (1928), a revised version of his Oxford B.Litt. thesis. It was published five years after he joined the Anthroposophical Society of Great Britain and is "anthroposophical" in aiming to show not only how words change their meanings over time but how consciousness changes as well, in the process unfixing supposedly objective "representations," what in *Saving the Appearances* Barfield calls "collective representations" or "idols." For Barfield, as for Steiner, perception is "participatory"; "the actual evolution of the earth we know must have been at the same time an evolution of consciousness. For consciousness is correlative to phenomenon."[66]

This is Romanticism, derived ultimately from Goethe, Steiner's great mentor ("Barfield is to Steiner," G. B. Tennyson has written, "as Steiner was to Goethe"[67]). For Steiner, it is Goethe the scientist who matters, author of *The Metamorphosis of Plants* (1790) and *The Theory of Colors* (1810), works that challenge, respectively, Linnaean taxonomy and Newton's theory of optics. Goethe's science is "Romantic" not only in these challenges, but in its belief in a supersensible reality wholly different from that of mainstream science. To the physicist, the underlying or supersensible reality, Goethe's *Ur-Phänomen*, is the subatomic particle, inaccessible to human perception; for Goethe, as for the English Romantic poets, the *Ur-Phänomen* is accessible through "creative" perception, an active, which is to say imaginative, attention to surface reality.[68] "He who wishes to see a Vision; a perfect Whole," Blake writes, "Must see it in its Minute Particulars."[69] In Goethe's science, the outer form or *natura naturata* discloses an inner form or *natura naturans* that shapes the outer appearance. From infancy, Bellow believed something similar. "If a man or woman looked a certain way it meant something to me, about their characters." In such cases, what is seen is in part the creation of the perceiver, as in Blake's famous answer when questioned about the rising sun: "Do you not see a round disc of fire somewhat like a guinea? Oh! No, no! I see an innumerable company of the heavenly host crying 'Holy, holy holy is the Lord God Almighty!' I question not my corporeal or vegetative eye any more than I would question a window concerning a sight. I look through it and not with it."[70]

IT WAS BARFIELD who put Bellow in touch with the Chicago branch of the Anthroposophical Society in America. There Bellow joined a study group organized by one of its senior members, Peter Demay, a seventy-five-year-old retired mechanical engineer. Demay was in several ways unlike Professor Scheldt in *Humboldt's Gift*, being a bachelor (no nubile daughter), well under six feet, and born and educated in France.[71] He became a member of the Chicago branch of the Anthroposophical Society in 1931, and in 1942 was elected its president. Demay took on the task of guiding members in discussion of Steiner's books and lectures. He also conducted discussions for the general public. The study group Bellow joined met weekly at 7:00 p.m. in Demay's apartment, overlooking Lincoln Park, on the North Side of the city. The group consisted of seven or eight men, of whom Bellow was the oldest.

Each week they were assigned readings, usually one of Steiner's lectures. Sessions lasted two hours. Bellow joined the group in 1975 and attended sessions regularly for a little over a year.[72]

Only one other member of the group was literary: William Hunt, a poet, urban reformer, and school administrator.[73] Hunt, a light-skinned African American, born in 1937, had studied at the University of Chicago. After university, he worked for the community organizer Saul Alinsky, with whom Barack Obama later worked, and then, less happily, at the Department of Labor. In 1975, he was employed as an administrator at the Esperanza School, for children with developmental difficulties, mental health problems, or other special needs. The teachers at Esperanza mostly came from Steiner-based Waldorf schools and the Camphill Movement, which also ran Steiner-inspired schools for children with learning difficulties. Although Hunt met Bellow for the first time in Peter Demay's study group, he had known Susan Bellow since 1970, through Richard Hunt, an African American sculptor (no relation) whom she dated after the break with Bellow. At the time of their meeting, William Hunt was looking for a Waldorf kindergarten for his son, and Susan was considering a Waldorf school for Daniel (who did attend such a school in New York). Either through Susan or through one of the teachers at Esperanza, Hunt came across a pamphlet by Steiner entitled *The Work of the Angels in Man's Astral Body* (1918), which led to his joining Demay's study group.[74] He and Bellow became friends and soon began meeting for dinner before the sessions.

Hunt was struck by Bellow's contained manner in the study group. He remembered him as "snooty and on edge" in literary discussion, as in question periods after talks and readings.[75] With Demay he was "deferential," also "professorial, letting others talk." Demay could be hard to follow, carrying his thoughts into what Hunt calls "the imaginal." Bellow was "very circumspect and kind and sort of amazed at some of the things Peter would go off on—he couldn't follow him, I couldn't follow him." After Bellow won the Nobel Prize, he was often away from Chicago, especially burdened by requests and invitations, and he attended the group infrequently. When Demay had a serious heart attack, the group disbanded.[76] Bellow and Hunt, however, continued to meet, at first at Bellow and Alexandra's apartment at 5901 North Sheridan Road—though, as Hunt recalls, Alexandra "didn't stay in the room much after the topic of Rudolf Steiner came up"—then at several bookstores in Evanston, one an Evanston landmark called

Great Expectations, the other, nearby, devoted to historical books, particularly having to do with Chicago. Although Hunt made a point of arriving at these meetings on time, Bellow was always there ahead of him. Bellow's attention "was very intense," and Hunt felt he "needed to be a bit more alert" at their meetings. After meeting, they'd adjourn to The Spot, a neighboring coffee shop, to talk not only about anthroposophy but about Chicago politics, social issues, race relations, prison violence. The meetings, often weekly, continued from 1976 to 1982, when Hunt moved to Great Barrington, Massachusetts. Hunt, who had been raised on the South Side of Chicago, knew the problems of the inner city firsthand, though in the years he and Bellow were closest and would meet in Evanston, he lived in Wilmette, immediately to its north. After the move to Massachusetts, the two men would visit each other every summer.

WHEN BELLOW INTRODUCED HIMSELF to Barfield in a letter of June 3, 1975, he was almost sixty. He would be in London, he wrote, from June 10, the birthday itself, to June 15, after which he and Alexandra would travel to Dornach, Switzerland, to visit the Steiner Center, and then go on to Spain for the holiday with Adam described earlier. Would Barfield come up to London from Kent to talk with him about spiritual matters? He would, and the two men met in London on the fifteenth. Bellow's manner with Barfield was deferential, disciplelike, as it had been in his initial letter. A month later, on July 15, he wrote a belated letter of thanks. "That you should come down to London to answer the ignorant questions of a stranger greatly impressed me. I daresay I found the occasion far more interesting than you could." In the initial letter of June 3, Bellow played down any doubts and uncertainties: "There are things that seem to me self-evident, so markedly self-evident and felt that the problem of proving or disproving their reality becomes academic." Yet he also confessed to finding aspects of *Unancestral Voice* puzzling. In the book, a fictional English lawyer named Burgeon (Barfield was a lawyer) reads of Rabbi Joseph Karo and the Maggid, and begins to hear a voice of his own, speaking in English not Hebrew. This voice, the titular "unancestral voice," comes "from the depths within himself."[77] Burgeon calls it the "Meggid," after Rabbi Karo's voice, and quizzes it about pressing social issues. The answers he receives derive, the Meggid tells him, from the archangels Gabriel and

Michael, who initiate and preside over stages in the evolution of consciousness. The archangel Gabriel is responsible for the period between the scientific revolution and the end of the nineteenth century, a period when matter was most fully the vehicle of spirit; Michael, in contrast, "does not work indirectly through the flesh or through the senses. His field is the thinking that has been set free from the flesh" (p. 44). The two great antagonists of Gabriel and Michael are Lucifer and Ahriman, enemies of cultural development. Lucifer's aim is "to conserve the past too long; to maintain, in the present, conditions that rightly obtain in the past, but should now be superseded." Ahriman, in contrast, would destroy the past completely in the name of the future, in the process creating what "can only appear in the present as a wicked caricature. . . . Ahriman is both the peculiar opponent and the peculiar underling of Michael. He is in truth the dragon underneath the Archangel's feet" (pp. 58, 59). These are the "powers of darkness" whom Bellow professed not to understand in his June 3 letter to Barfield. In the letter of July 15, he continues to find *Unancestral Voice* "hard going" while retaining "a strong hunch that you are giving a true account of things." The illumination Bellow seeks still eludes him, though "lately I have become aware, not of illumination itself, but of a kind of illuminated fringe—a peripheral glimpse of a different state of things."

Nine days later, on July 24, 1975, on the eve of his return to Chicago from Spain, Bellow writes to Barfield that he continues "to pore over *Unancestral Voice*." He wants another meeting: "It is most important that you should be willing to discuss it with me." The origin of his pursuit of the truths of spirit is deep disillusion, a feeling "that the interest of much of life as represented in the books I read (and perhaps some that I wrote) had been exhausted." The source of this feeling Bellow explains in terms familiar from his writing on distraction. "I concluded that the ideas and modes by which it [the interest of life] was represented were exhausted, that individuality had been overwhelmed by power or 'sociality,' by technology and politics." That Barfield and Steiner make similar points accounts in part for Bellow's attraction to them. The letter ends with a deferential bow. "You speak of yourself as the servant of your readers, but this reader, though eager to talk with you, hesitates to impose himself."

Edward Mendelson connects Bellow's deference here to a passage in a later letter to Barfield, of February 25, 1976, in which Bellow recounts what he thought was a joke on Barfield's part:

> You asked me, very properly, how I thought a writer of novels might be affected by esoteric studies. I answered that I was ready for the consequences. That was a nice thing to say, but it wasn't terribly intelligent. It must have struck you as very adolescent. You asked me how old I was. "Sixty," I said. Then you smiled and said, "Sixteen?" It was the one joke you allowed yourself at my expense, and it was entirely justified. It's a very American thing to believe that it's never too late to make a new start in life. Always decades to burn.

Barfield replied on March 17 that Bellow had "read into that 'sixty' and 'sixteen' exchange a whole lot of meaning that simply wasn't there. All that actually happened was that I did for an instant actually *hear* 'sixteen' and thought the error ludicrous enough to be worth sharing."[78]

After the letter of March 17, Bellow begins to temper his earlier manner toward Barfield—partly, one suspects, because of this exchange, partly because Barfield admits to having trouble reading Bellow's novels. "I did get hold of Humboldt's Gift," Barfield tells Bellow, "and may as well confess that I couldn't get up enough interest in enough of what was going on to be held by it. If it's any comfort to you—and the possibility that you don't particularly need comforting ought not to be altogether ruled out—I had very much the same experience with the Lord of the Rings." Not only did *Humboldt's Gift* fail to interest Barfield, but he found its passages about anthroposophy confused. These passages had been copied out by a friend and sent to Barfield, who "read them through and then sat back and then asked myself what exactly you had got from Anthroposophy; and I found I couldn't answer. Your literary mind is so active—or perhaps agile is the word I really want—that it was like trying to catch a flea!" Though Bellow is unlikely to have appreciated the flea comparison, he was relatively restrained in response. "Perhaps it was wrong of me to put this longing for spiritual fruit in a comic setting," he wrote to Barfield some months later, on August 13, 1976. "I knew that you could never approve and would think it idiotic and perhaps even perverse. But I followed my hunch as a writer, trusting that this eccentric construction would somehow stand steady."

Barfield was precisely the sort of reader for whom Bellow's construction was unlikely to appeal or "stand steady." A believer, he had little patience with Charlie Citrine's persistent doubts and equivocations. Nor, as he later revealed, was he much inclined to distinguish between author and character, especially in cases like *Humboldt's Gift*, where the two share similar traits. One aspect of Barfield's Englishness was the "robust" nature of his observations, at times indistinguishable from tactlessness. Yet he was not without sensitivity or self-knowledge. He knew full well the sort of figure Bellow wanted him to be, and firmly but not unkindly declined to meet expectations. In the letter of March 17, Barfield begins by apologizing for addressing Bellow as "Bellow." "I feel uneasy with 'Mr.' but have never got comfortably acclimatized to the contemporary practice of jumping straight from there to first names." He then turns to Bellow's projected sense of him. "I daresay you noticed, during our two conversations, that, whatever I may have somehow managed to write in some book or other, I am not personally much at home in a 'wise old Dr. Barfield' role."

This admission may have helped to put the relationship on a truer level. In subsequent letters, Bellow feels freer to confess to his difficulties in reading Steiner. On February 5, 1977, he writes: "I am drawn to him because he confirms that a perspective, the rudiments of which I always had, contained the truth. . . . I keep my doubts and questions behind a turnstile and admit them one at a time, but the queue is long." Nor would it be right, he tells Barfield, to omit these doubts and questions in his fiction: "I can't put into what I write the faint outlines I am only beginning to see. That would muddle everything, and it would be dishonest, too, in a novice." He remained eager, however, to stay in touch with Barfield and sought to arrange a third meeting in April 1977, when next he would be in London. This eagerness is especially remarkable given the letter to which Bellow is responding, one written by Barfield almost five months earlier, on September 18, 1976. In this letter Barfield fails to acknowledge or comment on *To Jerusalem and Back*, a copy of which Bellow had sent him "in lieu of a letter." Instead, Barfield draws Bellow's attention to a hostile review of *Humboldt's Gift* by Seymour Epstein in the Winter 1976 issue of the *University of Denver Quarterly*. The review, "Bellow's Gift," complains of the novel's "self-indulgent clownishness and cultural detritus," its repetitiveness, its inability or refusal to offer any solution to "the failure of Western Civilization to sustain the individual," identified as "Bellow's theme." "Bellow—or any novelist—owes us no answers," Epstein's review concludes, "but the novelist who has raised important questions owes us the integrity not to trivialize those questions by repetitive improvisations on a theme, no matter how adroit." Unsurprisingly, Bellow "disliked" Epstein's review, as he confessed to Barfield in the February 5 letter. He also "felt sure you would ask me about it." He identifies the review with "the work of Ahriman, his chilling of everything in human thinking which depends on a certain warmth," an accusation that might in part have been leveled at Barfield himself, formal or "English" in manner, a thinker with little gift for humor, ambivalence, or fictional indirectness.

Yet Bellow continued to be interested in Barfield's writings. A little over a year later, in the spring of 1978, one of the participants in the Demay reading group, an enterprising University of Chicago undergraduate, persuaded Bellow to organize a Barfield reading group, to discuss *Saving the Appearances* and *Worlds Apart: A Dialogue of the 1960s* (1963).[79] The other participants in the group were Wayne Booth of the English Department, a Kantian philosopher named Warren Wick, also from the University of Chicago, and a young mathematical colleague of Alexandra's at Northwestern named Sandy Zabell, "who had seen a copy of *Saving the Appearances* on my table," Bellow recalled to Barfield in a letter of September 19, 1978, "and was keen to discuss it with me." As Bellow reported to Barfield, "Booth was extremely sympathetic, keenly interested, Wick was laconic and pulled at his pipe and told us that we didn't really know Kant; we would be hopelessly muddled until we had put in a year or two at the critiques of This or That. But even he found you an attractive writer." Booth later commended the balance the group struck "between having a seminar of inquiry and a seminar that is merely an excuse for spiritual meditation."[80] Yet the group did not last long: it disbanded in May 1978, after only four sessions.

A year or so later, in a friendly letter of August 15, 1979, Bellow apologized to Barfield for being a poor correspondent, insisting that he was neither "fickle" nor had "dropped away."

> No, it is not at all like that. I am however bound to tell you that I am troubled by your judgment of the books I have written. I don't ask you to like what you obviously can't help disliking, but I can't easily accept your dismissal of so much investment of soul . . . and although I can tolerate rejection I am uneasy with what I sometimes suspect to be prejudice. . . . You don't like novels?—very well. But novels have been for forty years my trade; and if I do acquire some wisdom it will inevitably, so I suppose, take some "novelistic" expression. Why not? . . . I find some support in Steiner ". . . if a man has no ordinary sense of realities, no interest in ordinary realities, no interest in the details of another's likes, if he is so

> 'superior' that he sails through life without troubling about its details, he shows he is not a genuine seer." (*Anthroposophy: An Introduction*, p. 202).

The letter ends with Bellow declaring that "my affection for you is very great, and I am sure you know how much I respect you. For my part I feel safe with you—i.e. I know you will forgive my idiocies." In reply, in a letter of August 23, 1979, Barfield gives evidence of having "an ordinary sense of realities." He admits to having been troubled by the effect his comments about *Humboldt* have had on Bellow. "You speak of my judging. . . . I thought I had made it clear that I did not feel confident enough to do anything of the sort. . . . Seriously, I imagined you regarding it as something of a joke that in spite of all we have philosophically and spiritually in common my personal limitations (you know I was born in the reign of Queen Victoria) prevented me from seeing in *Humboldt's Gift* what nearly everyone else sees plainly enough." Bellow did not realize, Barfield adds, "what a Nobel prizewinner feels like from outside. I wrote as breezily as I did because I supposed that any lack of appreciation from this quarter could do about as much damage as a peashooter will do to an armoured car." Then, in a moment of self-doubt, Barfield wonders if the continued affection in Bellow's letter, which makes him feel "unpleasantly guilty," might have "misled me into a sort of cantankerous exaggeration of the remoteness and imperviousness of an armoured car. Whatever the cause I am seriously distressed by the thought of having wounded you, however slightly."

Bellow replied to Barfield on November 11, 1979, by saying that his letter "moved me by its warmth, kindness and candor." He apologized for having put Barfield in the position of judge, though the position not only "carries no duties, you owe me nothing," but was earned. "I see you—it came through in your letter—as a man who has learned what to do with the consciousness-soul, has managed to regenerate severed connections and found passages that lead from thought to feeling." For Bellow, though, what is sought is a move from feeling to thought, which, for all his reading of Steiner, he has not yet found. Bellow knows that his praise embarrasses Barfield ("you may think it bad form"), but he means it. He thinks of himself as a lesser person than Barfield: "So it amused me to be described as a tank surrounded by pea-shooters." After "four or five years of reading Steiner," he has been altered "considerably." He believes that he is undergoing "some sort of metamorphosis." But when he sits down to write to Barfield, he finds himself "at a loss for words."

It would be another three years before the two men again exchanged letters. On July 23, 1982, Barfield wrote to Bellow about *The Dean's December*, which he had recently reviewed for the anthroposophical journal *Towards*. Barfield reports having suggested to the journal's editor that Bellow be sent a copy of the review, which was not due to appear until the issue of Spring 1983. Perhaps Bellow would like to write a reply.[81] Bellow declined, but a month later, on August 21, 1982, he wrote directly to Barfield. The letter is polite, but makes clear that he was hurt by the review. Chief among Barfield's objections to the novel was that it focuses on social and political issues.[82] Barfield also complains, in the manner of Seymour Epstein, of the Dean's limitations, which he sees as Bellow's and the twentieth century's limitations, the cause of what he describes as the book's formlessness:

> Extremity of self-consciousness, together with unwillingness to essay the leap beyond it, is the general problem of the age in which we live. Its inherent antagonism to any sort of form or structure is the particular problem of literature and the arts; and there are those who believe that the correct solution is to abandon structure altogether. The author of *The Dean's December* drops an occasional hint that he is well aware of the problem. . . . He has confirmed as much, too, in interviews given since the Nobel Prize, and he had already disclosed in the novel that came before it, *Humboldt's Gift*, that he is no stranger to the writings of Rudolf Steiner. In *The Dean's December* he has chosen to remain, with most of his contemporaries, perched on the apex of excruciating self-consciousness at which the Western mind has arrived, ignoring any prospect of taking flight above it.

Bellow's reply to this criticism makes clear what he must long have known: Barfield would never approve his fiction. "I felt as I read your review, that you found me very strange indeed. I was aware from our first meeting that I was far more alien to you than you were to me. American, Jew, novelist, modernist—well of course I am all of those things. And I wouldn't have the shadow of a claim on anybody's attention if I weren't the last, for a novelist who is not contemporary can be nothing at all." Barfield, in contrast, has qualities Bellow knows:

"English, of an earlier generation, educated in classics, saturated in English literature. Your history is clearer to me than mine can ever be to you. . . . Few Europeans really know anything about America. . . . And I hope you won't take offense at this, but in my opinion you failed to find the American key, the musical signature without which books like mine can't be read. You won't find anything like it in any of the old manuals. There is nothing arbitrary in this newness." Barfield thinks Bellow's fiction formless, Bellow claims, because form grows out of "one's experience of the total human situation," in his case the total American situation. That the reflections of the Dean are "crowded" into small corners of sentences (Barfield had complained that the Dean "was, more or less in secret, serious about matters he couldn't discuss . . . for instance, the union of spirit and nature") is what that situation demands, fits "the American key, the musical signature." "Without the signature the Dean is impossible to play. Reading becomes a labor, and then of course one needs frequent rest, and the book has to be put down. And what is this mysterious signature? It is Corde's passion. If the reader misses that he has missed everything."

Bellow also takes issue with complaints about Corde's "extreme interior self-awareness" and "abnormally vivid external" awareness, qualities that Barfield thinks obscure spiritual knowledge. It is not true, as Barfeld implies, that *The Dean's December* is "Henry James in shorthand. Not at all. Nothing like it. The Dean is a hard, militant and angry book and Corde, far from being a brooding introvert, attacks Chicago (American society) with a boldness that puts him in considerable danger." As for the most important of Barfield's objections to the novel—its failure to "leap beyond" self-consciousness, "the general problem of the age in which we live"—this objection Bellow deals with in a postscript. It is the last thing he would write to Barfield.

> About the "leap beyond": certain knowledge isn't it either, but it would have to be a leap into a world of which one has some experience. I have had foreshadowing very moving adumbrations, but the whole vision of reality must change in every particular and the idols dismissed. Then one can take flight. It can't be done by fiat, however much one may long for it.

The leap of faith was no more possible for Bellow in 1982 than it had been seven years earlier, when he first contacted Barfield. "From

Barfield's perspective," writes Simon Blaxland-de-Lange, his biographer, "there could be no reconciliation with such a standpoint."[83] Even toward the end of his life, as his hold on the world weakened, Bellow continued to equivocate. In the interview with Norman Manea, conducted when Bellow was eighty-five, he had "no trouble at all" admitting that he didn't think "the world developed or evolved at random, hit-or-miss. It seems to me inconceivable that all this development should have been random and not directed by some sublime intelligence." He then adds, "I don't say that the conclusions I reached are the correct conclusions. All I say is that it's time I stopped pretending I don't believe in them."[84] As for the existence of God, "it's not a real question. The real question is how have I really felt all these years, and all these years I have believed in God; so there it is,"[85] an answer that is also an evasion. Bellow's belief in the afterlife is similarly powered by intense feeling rather than thought. "I say to myself, very often, when you die you will see them again, and it's a kind of perennial attachment, and so you wish you will see those people you loved again. My mother,

"I'm glad I got it. I could live without it." SB at a press conference announcing the award of the Nobel Prize, University of Chicago, October 22, 1976 (courtesy of the Special Collections Research Center, University of Chicago Library)

first and foremost. We probably all have such feelings, that we'll be reunited with those people whom we loved." A wish is not a leap. In a letter of October 17, 1997, to Cynthia Ozick, Bellow writes of reunion with the dead with irony. "As might be expected at my age, I think a lot about the life to come, but for me it always begins with a reunion. I see my parents again and my dead brothers and cousins and friends. Since my life has not been as virtuous as I would have liked it to be, I expect to be reproached by those I have injured and punished. But afterwards, eternity will have to be filled up, and it's eternity that stops me in my tracks. Will God give us work of eternal significance to do in the billions of worlds he's developing?" In the end, Bellow never fully commits to the ideas of Steiner and Barfield, as he never fully committed to the ideas of Reich. Yet these ideas were important for the man and the writer—as a way of combatting the dominance of science and technology, as an encouragement in the search for higher truths, as a form of escape.[86]

6

The "Chicago Book" and *The Dean's December*

On March 30, 1977, in Washington, D.C., Bellow delivered the first of his two Jefferson Lectures. The lectures were sponsored by the National Endowment for the Humanities under the title of "The Writer and His Country Look Each Other Over." Both lectures contain moving evocations of the Chicago of Bellow's youth. The first opens with a contrast between the Gold Coast houses of the ultra-rich, who lived within sight of Lake Michigan, and those of the landlocked slum dwellers who passed them in summer on their way to the shore. "This was how the children of immigrant laborers first came to know the smell of money and the look of luxury."[1] Bellow writes about the disparity between rich and poor without rancor, partly because, as we learn in the lecture's second paragraph, he now lives, as do many of the friends he grew up with in landlocked Humboldt Park, in one of the tall apartment buildings "that have risen along the shore on the north side of the city" (p. 117).

It isn't just that Bellow and his fellow immigrant children feel they have made it. Life in the working-class neighborhoods of their youth wasn't that bad: "No one had money, but you needed very little" (p. 119). Bellow's memories of Chicago during the Depression, of Tuley High School, of the University of Chicago, of his early years as an impecunious "*romancier*," are affectionate. It was a professor, Nathan Leites, a political scientist, who called Bellow a *romancier*, a mocking term that

Bellow hated but admits he deserved, having accepted "the prevailing assumption—and the Romantic presumption still prevailed—that man could find the true meaning of life and of his own unique being by separating himself from society and its activities and collective illusions" (p. 125). Undiscouraged—charged, in fact—by this assumption, Bellow set out, "for the sake of us all (I was very young then), narrow and poor as I was, [to] try myself to leap towards the marvelous," a phrase borrowed from Harold Rosenberg's 1940 essay "On the Fall of Paris."[2]

Two days after delivering the first Jefferson lecture, Bellow delivered the second, a darker talk, in the Gold Coast Room of the Drake Hotel, a venerable Chicago landmark. The Drake overlooks Oak Street Beach, the destination of the slum dwellers he described in lecture one as heading to the lakeshore. As in Washington, the Chicago audience was glittering, on this occasion made up of officials and guests of Chicago's cultural establishment, including members of the Chicago Historical Society, the Field Museum, the Illinois Humanities Council, the Newberry Library, Northwestern University, and the University of Chicago. In Washington, the ball-gowned and dinner-jacketed audience included very few Chicagoans. In Chicago, friends, colleagues, and cultural notables were joined by local big-money benefactors, the sort who funded rather than ran museums, opera companies, orchestras, and arts clubs. Bellow distrusted such types, seeing their motives as boosterish, materialistic.[3] But he looked just like them: prosperous, silver-haired, expensively dressed.

At the conclusion of the second Jefferson lecture, according to an article by Paul Carroll, who attended as the cofounder of the Chicago Poetry Center, Bellow received only muted applause.[4] The lecture opened with several paragraphs about American success, then turned on its audience, who embodied it, attributing to them an unspoken or repressed "feeling that this miraculously successful country has done evil, spoiled and contaminated nature, waged cruel wars, failed in its obligations to its weaker citizens, the blacks, the children, the women, the aged, the poor of the entire world" (p. 138). That women and blacks were listed as among the country's "weaker citizens" may have unsettled some listeners. Other unsettling passages were to follow. Bellow returned to Chicago in the 1920s and 1930s, to the neighborhoods populated by immigrants from Poland, Italy, Ireland, and Eastern Europe. These neighborhoods he described as places of relative harmony and industry. Today, thanks to the 1924 Immigration Act, everything had changed.

> No more carpenters, printers, mechanics, pastry cooks, cobblers, sign painters, street musicians, and small entrepreneurs entered the country from Greece, Serbia, Pomerania, Sicily. Such trades were infra dig for the children of immigrants. They improved themselves and moved upward. The neighborhoods they left were repopulated by an internal immigration from the South and from Puerto Rico. The country people, black or white, from Kentucky or Alabama, brought with them no such urban skills and customs as the immigrants had. Assembly-line industries had no need for skilled labor.
>
> What we have taken now to calling "ethnic neighborhoods" fell into decay long ago. The slums, as a friend of mine [Harold Rosenberg] once observed, were ruined. He was not joking. The slums as we knew them in the twenties were, when they were still maintained by European immigrants, excellent places, attractive to artists and bohemians as well as to WASPs who longed for a touch of Europe. The major consequences of the devastation of these neighborhoods, invariably discussed on these occasions—the increase in crime, the narcotics addiction, the welfare problem, the whole inventory of urban anarchy—I will spare you. I will appease the analytical furies by mentioning only three side effects of the change: the disappearance of genial street life from American cities; the dank and depressing odors of cultural mildew rising from the giant suburbs, which continue to grow; the shift of bohemia from the slums to the universities [p. 145].

What came next in the lecture seemed at first a digression: a detailed description of the domestic architecture of working-class Chicago, in particular its bungalows and six-flats (residential buildings containing six apartments one on top of another, with separate entrances), mass-produced but nevertheless bearing "trimmings, nifty touches, notes of elegance and aspiration" (p. 147), saving graces like those of the city's "loutish-looking" cottonwood trees, which nevertheless produce a day or two of fragrant spring catkins and summery white fluff (p. 147). The faculty of the University of Chicago live peacefully in the six-flats of Hyde Park. Only a few blocks away, in the black slums, "a different sort of life, in Woodlawn and Oakwood, tears apart the six-flats and leaves them looking bombed out. They are stripped of saleable metals, innards torn out, copper cable chopped to pieces and sold for scrap, windows all smashed, and finally fire and emptiness. Sometimes there is no one at all in these devastated streets—a dog, a rat or two." The wooden fences meant to enclose the front lawns of slum six-flats have been "torn up . . . stolen, burned. The grass plots themselves have been stamped into hollow clay" (p. 148).

In an attempt to discover why, Bellow had talked to police and firemen, welfare and community workers. He had visited inner-city schools, hospitals, courts, clinics, the county jail, read learned articles about race and crime, interviewed their authors. "The first fact that strikes you," Bellow declared of his visits to criminal court, "is that so large a part of Chicago's black population is armed—men, women, children even" (p. 148). The slum schools are "now almost entirely black and Puerto Rican" (p. 149); they could not be more different from the schools of Bellow's youth. Their teachers "have the highest salary scale in the country," but what they teach "is hard to determine, and *whom* they teach is even more mysterious. I have entered classrooms in which pupils wandered about knocking out rhythms on the walls absorbed in their transistors. No one seemed to grasp that the room had a center. No one heeded the teacher when she spoke" (pp. 149–50). "Some of the kids are like little Kaspar Hausers—blank, unformed, they live convulsively, in turbulence and darkness of mind. They do not know the meaning of words like 'above,' 'below,' 'beyond.' But they are *un*like poor innocent Kaspar in that they have a demonic knowledge of sexual acts, guns, drugs, and of vices, which are not vices here" (p. 150). Similarly, in the courts, the young black men or women on trial strike Bellow as "unreachable, incomprehensible. It is impossible to know what they are thinking or feeling." In a rare qualification, he adds: "I am speaking, please notice, of what sociologists call the underclass, not of black Chicago as a whole, the orderly, churchgoing black working people or members of the growing middle class. These struggle to maintain themselves in a seemingly disintegrating city and to protect their children from beatings in school corridors and assaults in hallways and toilets, from shootings in the playgrounds. No one goes out carefree for a breath of air at night" (p. 150). After this nightmare vision, Bellow ends the lecture with a moment of self-correction, like the moment of sympathy and fellowship extended to the black pickpocket at the end of

Mr. Sammler's Planet, when Eisen, the Israeli sculptor, batters the pickpocket to the ground. Here are the lecture's final sentences:

> When he visited the Lower East Side, [Henry] James was alarmed by the Jewish immigrants he saw, appalled by their alien, ill-omened presence, their antics and their gabble.
>
> There is no end to the curious ironies all this offers to an active imagination—and, in particular, to a descendant of East European Jews like myself [p. 152].

The muted applause that greeted these words was followed by a reception. As Carroll reports, "Much of the audience is missing; few who do come to sip champagne bother to shake the hand of the Nobel laureate or to congratulate him on his success." Carroll suggests that the audience was put off by Bellow's crack about the "stench of cultural mildew from the suburbs." They may also have been irked that Bellow "failed to tell his audience—the Cultural Establishment—how important they were and how grateful he was for their support." Perhaps the prominent blacks who were present (Carroll could see no prominent Puerto Ricans or Appalachians) "and hard-line liberals from the universities and Highland Park took umbrage at that 'lack of culture' business."

Reaction from the university community was swift. Citing a description of the lecture in the *Chicago Sun-Times*, the University of Chicago newspaper, *The Chicago Maroon*, published a two-column letter of protest to the editor on April 14. It was titled "Bellow: False and Racist?" and signed by "The University of Chicago Committee Against Racism, accompanied by 14 signatures by members of the University community."[5] The authors of the letter described the remarks quoted from the lecture in the *Sun-Times* as "outrageous," hoping they were inaccurately reported. They then "strongly" urged Bellow to "1) Issue a statement clarifying his position. 2) Issue an apology for what, regardless of his intentions, can only be regarded as racist statements. 3) Take steps to insure that the racist statements are eliminated before the lectures appear in published form." Bellow did not reply, but at least one of the quotations excerpted in the *Sun-Times* was cut in the published version of his lectures. The *Sun-Times* quoted Bellow as having said, "In the slums today comes a savage fury directed at the middle class." When the lectures were published in *It All Adds Up: From the Dim Past to the Uncertain Future* (1994), this sentence did not appear, perhaps because the preponderance of black crime in the slums is lower-class black-on-black crime. The signatories also complained of Bellow's failure to mention the causes of disintegration in the black slums, in particular "the discriminatory policies of real estate companies and banks," the redlining that consigned blacks and Latinos to old or shabby housing by refusing them home-improvement loans or insurance (on the grounds that they lived in areas deemed a poor financial risk). Far from holding the city together, as the signatories to the letter claim Bellow implied, the banks and universities "are among the principal beneficiaries of racism, and in fact . . . have promoted the disintegration of the city. . . . The University of Chicago is directly responsible for the devastation of Woodlawn."[6]

What upset Carroll about the lecture was Bellow's claim that the black, Appalachian, and Latin slums were without culture. They might be without high culture, but what of popular or street culture, the black or Latino equivalents of the culture celebrated in *The Adventures of Augie March*, "largely unwritten, oral, and often ungrammatical, lacking the paintings and the great royal and private collections of Europe, and involving worship in such 'low' churches as the Baptist and the Methodist. About this, Bellow left his audience in the dark, and uncomfortable stirrings and quick, uneasy whispers were heard." Bellow, of course, knew a great deal about the popular culture of black immigrants from the South, not only from the classes he took with Melville Herskovits at Northwestern, but from his time as an undergraduate at the University of Chicago, renowned for its research into "Negro-White relations." Bellow's friend Herb Passin was also a source of such knowledge. When he and Bellow were closest, in the early 1940s, Passin was a student of the anthropologist and ethnographer Robert Redfield, director of the American Council on Race Relations from 1947 to 1950. This was also the time when Bellow's fiction was centrally concerned with racial discrimination. The earliest of his manuscripts, the unpublished novel fragment "Acatla" (1940), contains scenes in which an interracial couple are victims of prejudice; his first completed novel, "The Very Dark Trees" (1942), concerns a white man who wakes to find he's turned black.[7] In the first Jefferson Lecture, however, racial prejudice, like black street culture, is barely mentioned. Bellow's concern in the lecture is with the consequences, not the causes of discrimination, their destructive effect on African Americans, the anger, fear, and incomprehension they breed in whites, emotions dramatized in the story "Looking for Mr. Green" (1951) and in *Mr. Sammler's Planet*. The refusal to focus on causes in the lecture is a matter of calculation rather than ignorance, a strategy, like the refusal to qualify or hedge. The lecture means to wound, to force his listeners and readers to face what they have chosen not to face. Like Socrates, the stinging fly, Bellow sees or treats the elite of his city as complacent, a handsome horse in need of a good shock, what in *The Apology* Socrates calls "stimulation."

Though he did not reply to the letter in the *Maroon*, Bellow was himself stung by the reaction to the lecture, or so a letter of May 19, 1977, from the University of Chicago sociologist Morris Janowitz suggests. In addition to talking to Janowitz about Arab-Israeli relations, Bellow consulted him on race (Janowitz had served as consultant to the 1947 Commission on Civil Rights established by President Truman and had co-authored a book about racial prejudice with Bruno Bettelheim[8]). "Please do not feel sensitive about those handful of students—if they can be called students—who talk about racism," Janowitz reassured Bellow. "There is no doubt that there is no racism in your lecture—and no one on campus believes that there is any. A small group of students—and the striking aspect is that they are so personally unhappy—on all campuses are searching for a new issue. Nuclear power plants, university investments in South African companies, tuition rises—and very little seems to come of all of this, it looks like."

There were many demonstrations at the University of Chicago in the 1970s, as at other universities, the biggest being against the Vietnam War, which Bellow also opposed. In May 1970, an estimated 75 percent of students stayed away from classes in protest against the war. In November 1974, two hundred students protested against the visit of Henry Kissinger to the university. In addition, as Janowitz suggests, there were calls for the university to stop investing in South Africa, a move Bellow, too, approved, arguing that the trustees should consider human-rights decisions in all investments. " 'We have relations with all kinds of governments that seem pretty wicked,' he told reporters from the *Maroon*. 'If you want to divest from all of them I'm with you.' "[9] The undergraduate Philip Grew remembers being told that Bellow had watched him as, with a bullhorn, he addressed a campus demonstration against investment in South Africa in 1977. For Grew and others, the university was as culpable in its investment policies in Hyde Park and surrounding black neighborhoods as it was in South Africa.[10] In

January 1970, thirteen students, all from SDS (Students for a Democratic Society), were briefly suspended for demonstrating against the university's "racist policies." In April 1972, Dwight Ingle, professor of physiology at the university, was shouted down in a debate about black IQ scores. A year later, the political scientist Edward Banfield was prevented from speaking, also accused of racist beliefs.[11] In these cases, the number of student protesters involved, as Janowitz suggests, was small. How he knew they were "personally unhappy" is unclear.

BELLOW WROTE ABOUT Chicago throughout his life, but the city only became an object of direct or systematic investigation for him in the late 1970s, sometime after he returned from Jerusalem. The Jefferson Lectures were the first fruit of this investigation, but they were merely an offshoot of a larger project, commonly referred to by researchers as the "Chicago Book," a work that was never published and exists only in parts. Other offshoots of the "Chicago Book" include the two Tanner Lectures, delivered at Brasenose College, Oxford, on May 18 and 25, 1981, the television program *Saul Bellow's Chicago*, aired locally on March 27, 1981, and the Chicago sections of *The Dean's December* (1982), a novel that seems to have begun life as a long short story or novella set in Romania.[12] In the course of fictionalizing the trip he and Alexandra made to Bucharest in December 1978, a trip discussed in chapter 4, Bellow began adding to the backstory of the Alexandra figure's husband, Albert Corde, a Bellow-like dean of students at an unnamed Chicago university. Soon the story had grown into a novel, a tale of two cities, Chicago and Bucharest, each depressing in its own way. "I wrote it in a year and a half," Bellow told an interviewer, "and had no idea it was coming."[13] Many passages in the novel are taken from the "Chicago Book," sometimes word for word.

What survives of the "Chicago Book" is an eighty-four-page autobiographical manuscript and shorter notelike sections with such titles as "American Materialism," "A Visit to County Jail," "Newspapers." (The book's title is taken from the heading of a section dated April 5, 1979.) In addition, Bellow compiled sixteen research files or folders for the book, containing clippings, notes, ephemeral publications, and correspondence on a range of Chicago topics and personalities. There are folders on Jake "The Barber" Factor, the gangster pardoned by President Kennedy; on Mayor Daley; on the 1979 mayoral race between

Jane Byrne and the incumbent Michael Bilandic, Daley's successor.[14] The book was to resemble *To Jerusalem and Back* (1976), mixing reportage and reminiscence in a way that appears influenced by the "New Journalism" of Tom Wolfe, Truman Capote, Gay Talese, and Norman Mailer. In 1974, Wolfe edited an influential anthology of such journalism, claiming in its introduction that the novel was dead and New Journalism was its rightful successor, and issuing a direct Kipling-inspired challenge to Bellow: "The Huns are at the Gate, Saul!" Two years earlier, in *New York* magazine, Wolfe's challenge was "Damn it all, Saul, the Huns have arrived!"[15]

William Hunt, Bellow's friend from the Steiner reading group, was a sounding board for his thoughts about the city. By the late 1970s, their discussions in The Spot in Evanston were as likely to be about race and city politics as about anthroposophy. Hunt was born and raised in Woodlawn, just to the south of Hyde Park, a no-go area for many whites by the late 1970s. Before working at the Esperanza School, he was employed by several social-service organizations in the area. As the projects he worked on were for the most part federally funded, they were less corrupt than city projects, so his knowledge of city corruption was "like what a child would imbibe while overhearing his elders arguing behind closed doors." He had one city job, as the director of a public-information division of Chicago's anti-poverty agency. Here he learned how employees were hired. There was "a two-tiered structure. One tier involved professionals hired to maintain the requirements of services; the professionals included attorneys, medical personnel, social workers, city planners, and the like. The other tier was composed of the personnel recommended for jobs by the city's ward committeemen; their work credentials were validated by the expectation that they would do the bidding of the ward committeemen during the weeks leading up to elections, especially local elections."

Over the course of their meetings, Hunt found Bellow's views on the city "increasingly dystopian." In addition to political and judicial corruption, and the lawlessness and nihilism of the black slums, Bellow was much preoccupied with the influence of drugs on college youth culture, by the willful blindness of liberals, and by the irrelevance and frivolity of the press. Bellow was as hard on newspapers in the "Chicago Book" as he is in *The Dean's December*. When Clayton Kirkpatrick, editor of the *Chicago Tribune*, tried to defend his paper's reporting, sending reprints of articles he thought supported his defense, Bellow was unmoved. In the "Newspapers" section of the "Chicago Book," he complains that as much as 80 percent of the *Tribune*, as of other Chicago papers, is made up of advertising. "It would be impossible if one read only the Chicago papers to know what was happening in the world" (p. 1). But readers want the ads, Kirkpatrick answered, and they read them "with passionate attention. To the majority of Chicagoans they are really the most valuable part of the paper." This claim Bellow thought "we have no way to ascertain," though admitting, "It is impossible to estimate [i.e., overestimate] the place of commodities in the life of the city" (p. 7). Albert Corde, in *The Dean's December*, a journalist before becoming a dean, is a figure of notoriety in Chicago, having written two articles for *Harper's* magazine detailing the horrors of the city, articles that reproduce material from the "Chicago Book." The hostility these articles provoke is Bellow's imagining of the hostility he himself would have faced had the "Chicago Book" been published (a taste of which he received after the second Jefferson Lecture). "Where the press is concerned," Corde is told, "you caused great resentment by your articles, implying they were lazy and cynical, and now you are their target of opportunity" (p. 150). Dewey Spangler, an old friend of Corde's from high school, now a globe-trotting columnist in the mode of Joseph Alsop, congratulates him privately on the articles ("You were eloquent, you were superexpressive" [p. 113]), then accuses him in print of having been "carried away by an earnestness too great for his capacities." Spangler also quotes private remarks bound to upset Corde's bosses at the university, notably a crack about how "a tenured professor and a welfare mother with eight kids have much in common" (p. 303).

A GOOD DEAL OF THE MATERIAL Bellow gathered for the "Chicago Book" is lurid—newspaper articles and interview accounts of grisly murders and sexual crimes—and a number of these accounts find their way into the Dean's articles for *Harper's*. They are part of what makes the experience of reading *The Dean's December*, as Bellow himself put it, "hard": "The language knocks you hard. . . . It demands your attention, the way a man does when he grabs you by the lapels."[16] One case concerns a retired air force pilot, Lieutenant Colonel Duane Swimley, who had to go to court a number of times, at great expense, to divorce his wife, an attractive brunette in her thirties who had been convicted of hiring a hit man to kill him. The wife appealed her conviction, posted bond, and resisted Swimley's attempts to obtain a divorce. Bellow saved clippings about the case, went to interview Swimley, as the Dean does his fictional equivalent, and wrote up his notes from the interview.[17] According to the *Chicago Tribune*, when the divorce finally came through, Swimley was "obliged under the property settlement to pay [his wife] $147,000 as her share of the home in which they had lived."[18] The newspaper reported Swimley asking, "Why should a guy whose wife tried to kill him get horsed around by these judges?"

Bellow's sympathies in this case may account for an uncharacteristic mistake. Swimley, in his mid-forties, is described in the notes as "in his early sixties," Bellow's age at the time. In the notes, Swimley describes the several attempts his wife made to murder him. First she put ant poison in his food; then she paid a neighbor's son twenty-five hundred dollars to shoot him. On a hunting trip with the neighbor's son, when Swimley realized what was going on, he stopped his truck, held a pistol to the boy's head, and said, "If you don't tell me what the hell you're doing you'll never leave this truck alive." Later, Mrs. Swimley tried to get her son from her first marriage to murder Swimley. She also retained two Mafia hit men from California, who were picked up by the police and gave testimony against her, after which she "tried to beat his brains out with a telephone while he slept" (p. 1). In addition to the cartoon comedy aspects of the case, Bellow highlights the behavior of the judiciary, which he, like Swimley, sees as corrupt and incompetent, a judgment based as much on "research" as on personal experience. While working on the "Chicago Book," according to William Hunt, Bellow regularly attended early-morning sessions at the State Street courthouse. In addition to courtroom proceedings, "he was also able to sit in on backroom negotiations in chambers, where the litigants were represented by their attorneys."[19] Bellow's old Tuley pal, Julius "Lucky" Echeles, a criminal lawyer known for defending mobsters, accused murderers, and loan sharks, was one of several attorneys who helped him obtain access. Here is Bellow's description of the treatment Swimley received from the courts:

> She [the wife] was convicted and appealed the case, posting a bond. She and the children occupied the family house. The Circuit Court made him pay $1,000 a month in alimony and support. He could not obtain a divorce. The house was owned in joint tenancy and it was impossible to agree on the division of property. Besides, he

> wanted a divorce on the grounds that she had tried to kill him and the court would not allow this. Judge Feltman insisted that the grounds be mental cruelty. . . . The matter dragged on. For nearly four years he paid her $1,000 a month in maintenance and there were other expenses and fees. At one time the Colonel was held in contempt and sentenced to fifty days in County Jail. He detested the four judges before whom he appeared [p. 3].

Bellow's notes on the case end with the news of Mrs. Swimley's conviction and sentence: six years in prison (her son got four). "I hate what to think they're up to," Swimley tells Bellow, "and she'll be out in about three years." "What then?" Bellow asks. "She'll probably try again," Swimley replies. "What, with her record, and people watching her?" Swimley gives Bellow a cool look. "What people?" "Good question" (p. 4).

Much darker and more demonic is the case of Linda Goldstone, a young Evanston housewife, a mother and natural-childbirth instructor, who was raped and murdered in 1978 by Hernando Williams, an African American from the South Side. Williams, who was twenty-three and the son of a preacher, kidnapped Mrs. Goldstone while out on bail for a previous kidnapping and rape. Clippings about the case are in one of the "Chicago Book" folders, and Bellow lightly fictionalizes it as the "Spofford Mitchell" case in *The Dean's December.* Corde goes to interview the public defender assigned to Spofford Mitchell, and his account of the interview and of the case itself proves "by far the most controversial part of his article" (that is, of the *Harper's* article) (p. 193). The terrible details of the real-life case, which are almost identical to those of the fictional case, show the depravity both Corde and his creator are obsessed with and try to force readers to face. Corde's account stresses not only the horrors of the crime but the varied forms of civic evasion that accompanied it, the refusal to intervene, the looking the other way.

> The victim was a young suburban housewife, the mother of two small children. She had just parked in a lot near the Loop when Mitchell approached and forced her at gunpoint into his own car. The time was about 2 p.m. Spofford Mitchell's Pontiac had been bought from a Clark Street dealer just after his recent release from prison. Corde didn't know how the purchase was financed. (The dealer wouldn't say.) In the front seat, Mitchell forced Mrs. Sath-

> ers to remove her slacks, to prevent escape. He drove to a remote alley and assaulted her sexually. Then he locked her into the trunk of his Pontiac. He took her out later in the day and then raped her again. By his own testimony this happened several times. At night he registered in a hotel in the far South Side. He managed to get her from the trunk into the room without her being seen. Possibly he was seen; it didn't seem to matter to those who saw. In the morning he led her out and locked her in the trunk again. At ten o'clock he was obliged to appear at a court hearing to answer an earlier rape charge. He parked the Pontiac, with Mrs. Sathers still in the trunk, in the official lot adjoining the court building. The rape hearing was inconclusive. When it ended he drove at random about the city. On the West Side that afternoon passersby heard cries from the trunk of a parked car. No one thought to take down the license number; besides, the car pulled away quickly. Towards daybreak of the second day, for reasons not explained in the record, Spofford Mitchell let Mrs. Sather go, warning her not to call the police. He watched from his car as she went down the street. This was a white working-class neighborhood. She rang several doorbells, but no one would let her in. An incomprehensibly frantic woman at five in the morning—people wanted no part of her. They were afraid. As she turned away from the third or fourth closed door, Mitchell pulled up and reclaimed her. He drove to an empty lot, where he shot her in the head. He covered her body with trash [p. 194].

"The dealer wouldn't say." "Possibly he was seen; it didn't seem to matter to those who saw." "The rape hearing was inconclusive." "Passersby heard cries from the trunk. . . . No one thought to take down the license number." "No one would let her in." In the real-life case, one of the passersby *did* take down the car's license plate and gave it to the police. They did not act on the tip. Another difference is that when Mrs. Goldstone rang doorbells one person answered, a Chicago fireman, who said he'd call the police, which he did; but he did not let Mrs. Goldstone into the house, and Williams, who had been following her, led her away to a back alley, where he shot and killed her.

The young public defender assigned to Mitchell in *The Dean's December*, Sam Varennes, answers Corde's questions about the case coolly, collectedly. Corde knows that to be appointed public defender in Chicago "you generally needed some sort of backup or sponsorship"

(p. 195), to be connected in some way. Varennes, however, strikes Corde as conscientious, well qualified, and liberal. In the course of their conversation, Varennes pays close attention to the way Corde phrases his questions, looking for signs of bigotry. What Varennes reveals about his planned defense is that it will make much of the victim's opportunities to flee and of her failure to do so. Corde's view is that she may have been "dazed" by what happened to her ("As dazed as all that?" Varennes asks). In addition, Corde suggests that she may have "felt that she was already destroyed" (p. 196). From here, with the recklessness that marks his *Harper's* articles, Corde weaves a theory about the human "sex nerves" and how, "if people think they're going to get murdered anyway when it's over, they may desperately let go." "That's quite a theory," says Varennes. Heedlessly, Corde begins a riff about "the peculiar curse of sexuality or carnality we're under—we've placed it right in the center of life and connect it with savagery and criminality" (p. 196). For Corde, as for Artur Sammler, "our conception of physical life and of pleasure is completely death-saturated. . . . Spofford Mitchell was on the fast track for death—fast, clutching, dreamlike, orgastic. Grab it, do it, die" (pp. 196–97). Varennes comments: "My team and I are on these homicides year in year out. We can't get up the same fervor as an outsider" (p. 197).

The effect of these words is to return Corde to his "interviewer's detachment or professional cool." He looks again at Varennes, whose "serious eyes and strong bald head" he admires; he thinks Varennes "a nice man" (p. 197), even as he knows he's being checked out by him, to see "whether I could be trusted, what my angle was, why I wasn't somehow one hundred percent contemporary in my opinions" (p. 198), which means not only "did I play by Chicago rules" (p. 198), acknowledging traditional powers and practices, but were "my liberal sympathies . . . in order." "Chicago rules" are anathematized throughout both the "Chicago Book" and *The Dean's December*. As for "liberal sympathies," here is Corde's scornful summary, versions of which Bellow used to tease liberal friends:[20]

> We are for everything nice and against cruelty, wickedness, craftiness, monstrousness. Worshippers of progress, its dependents, we are unwilling to reckon with villainy and misanthropy, we reject the *horrible*. . . . Our outlook requires that each of us is naturally decent and wills the good. The English-speaking world is tempera-

> mentally like this. You see it in the novels of Dickens, clearly. In his world, there is suffering, there is evil, betrayal, corruption, savagery, sadism, but the ordeals end and decent people arrange a comfortable existence for themselves, make themselves cozy [p. 199].

Bellow had his Dickensian side, as well as his Dickensian brilliance, but in the late 1970s the more likely influence, given the bleakness and intensity of his focus on the ruinous consequences of materialism, is Dostoevsky. In the second Tanner Lecture, Bellow declares: "The overwhelming power in Chicago remains the power of money and goods. People of course wanted fun, they seemed to want religion too—they joined hands, they prayed, they joined the Moral Majority and responded to appeals for contributions. But as you watched the programs and turned the pages of the *Sun-Times* and the *Tribune*, you were aware that the economy was a sort of divinity. You said, with some reluctance, a bit dazed, somewhat disheartened—but this was confirmation, not a fresh discovery—'These be your gods!'"[21] (p. 188). For Corde, America's children are as unreachable as the black underclass: "It was impossible to educate either, or to bind either to life. It [America] was not itself securely attached to life just now. Sensing this, the children attached themselves to the black underclass, achieving a kind of coalescence with the demand-mass," characterized by Bellow in a 1980 interview as a "malignant Mammonism . . . very different from what I knew as a kid."[22] As Bellow explains in the second Tanner Lecture, "It was not so much the inner city slum that threatened us as the slum of innermost being, of which the inner city was perhaps a material representation" (p. 201). He quotes Morris Janowitz on "the shift in popular culture from 'idols of production' to 'idols of consumption.' He bases his observations on a study by Leo Lowenthal which shows that before 1924 the idols of the mass media, such as they were then, were the Fords and the Edisons, empire builders, makers of goods and machinery. By the end of the twenties, idols of consumption were, however, at the center of the pantheon. The gods were fat, eating and drinking and driving about in luxurious machines" (p. 196).[23] In *The Dean's December*, Corde describes the effective black "image" today as that of the "outlaw chieftains" who run gangs like the Rangers and the El Rukins—"black princes in their beautiful and elegant furs, boots, foreign cars" (p. 149), a passage that recalls the black pickpocket in *Mr. Sammler's Planet*, also princely, also expensively dressed.

Liberals, Corde would claim, rarely talk of the city's real or deep problems. Corde tells Varennes of a recent magazine article in which prominent Chicagoans were interviewed about how to make the city "more exciting and dynamic." These were the Chicagoans Susan Glassman wanted Bellow to entertain: gallery owners, architects, business executives, lawyers, advertising men, journalists, TV commentators, artistic directors, publishers, city planners. From Corde's and Bellow's perspective, their suggestions are criminally myopic: "Some said we needed outdoor cafés like Paris or Venice, and others that we should have developments like Ghirardelli Square in San Francisco or Faneuil Hall in Boston. One wanted a gambling casino atop the Hancock Building; another that the banks of the Chicago River should be handsomely laid out." All the suggestions are of this sort. "But no one mentioned the terror. About the terrible wildness and dread in this huge place—nothing. About drugs, about guns . . ." When Varennes objects that the magazine article is "hardly a serious matter, the opinions of those people, what the interior decorators are saying, what the features editors print," Corde agrees: "Quite right, but it made me think it was high time to write a piece, since I grew up here" (p. 202). When he does write his piece or pieces, "most of the poison-pen notes" he receives are from "the suburbs, where the diehard Chicago boosters all lived" (also the "hard-line liberals" from Highland Park). "Commuters who escaped from race problems and crime were indignant because he had told it as it was" (pp. 144–45).

That Bellow thought something similar when he began work on the "Chicago Book" accounts for folders with titles like "Blacks—Criminal Activity" and "Black Welfare," or his lengthy detailing of living conditions in Cook County Jail and the Robert Taylor Homes. Hence also his detailed portrait of Winston Moore, the first black man to serve as County Jail's warden and to try seriously to reform it, wresting control from the barn bosses, convicts with whom previous wardens felt forced to cooperate. In County Jail, we learn from the portrait, "money has always been in circulation, guards have always been on the take. Dope and weapons have always been obtainable, sodomizing rapists have always had their way unchecked. . . . In winter, prisoners have been known to make their own weapons by soaking rolls of newspaper in the toilet and hanging them out of the window to freeze. A blow from these ice-clubs can maim or kill" (p. 15). During Moore's tenure there were no killings, fewer suicides, and, "yearly, [he] returned more than a million unspent dollars to the County treasury" (p. 16). Despite these successes, Moore was relieved of his post. He was accused of beating prisoners and condoning their beating, trumped-up charges ultimately dropped. Like Rufus Ridpath in *The Dean's December*, Moore was ousted for ignoring "Chicago rules." Ridpath's lawyer explains: "County Jail has a big budget. Suppliers and contractors came to the office (you understand who was sending 'em) and he wouldn't do business. He said, 'If I don't buy your meat boned I can save sixty cents a pound. I'm having it boned right here.' Too many savings. He saved a million dollars out of his budget and refunded it to the county.... Rufus got a bad name with the top guys. They thought he might become dangerous politically, too" (p. 154). Albert Corde interviews the head of the meatpackers' union to ask about these matters, encountering the closed-mouthed G. O. O'Meara, "about ninety years old... packed with guile, terribly pleased with himself!" O'Meara "still cut a figure among the big shots of Chicago." He answers none of Corde's questions, and when Corde gets up to leave says, "You wanted me to talk, but I didn't tell you a thing, did I?" (pp. 155–56). Whether Bellow actually went to Meat Cutters' Hall to check out the real-life version of O'Meara is unclear, though among the "Chicago Book" materials is a copy of the meatpacking union's magazine, *The Butcher Workman.* The visit Bellow made to County Jail, in contrast, is recorded. By May 17, 1979, the date of the visit, Moore had been relieved of his post. No one Bellow met mentioned Moore's name, though the improvements he had brought to the jail were visible. "The new modern prison technology exhibits itself in all its pride. Medical and dental facilities, gymnasiums and recreation halls, computerized supervision, modern highly sanitized guard posts, the remote control of locks." Only the rodent population remains unalterable: "The rats come at night and eat the crumbs or lick what gravy or icing have fallen to the lower gratings."[24]

The shameful treatment Moore received from the Chicago newspapers was proof for Bellow of their collusion with the city's ruling powers or "big shots." In headlines and photographs, Moore was depicted as "a dangerous gorilla... more violent than the wild men of County Jail... a crude giant, swollen with self-importance." In fact, as Bellow discovered when he met him, Moore was mild in manner, "firm" in build but not big, with "a certain reserve, an air of watchfulness" (p. 17). (That Corde accuses the Chicago newspapers of depicting Rufus Ridpath in just this way is partly what earns him the enmity of Dewey

Spangler and his fellow journalists.[25]) Though defamed in the press, Moore was exonerated in court. After a lengthy Federal Grand Jury financial audit ("eight or nine months of combing through his checkbooks and savings accounts"), no evidence was found of corruption. Another lengthy examination followed, in which Moore was acquitted of all charges of prisoner abuse (though, as Bellow says of Ridpath, "people remembered the charges and forgot the acquittal—the usual pattern" [p. 149]). On the day of the acquittal, Moore was sacked by the county sheriff, Richard Elrod, a Democratic Party loyalist, the son of a West Side committeeman. In 1969, Elrod had been paralyzed when trying to restrain a demonstrator during the "Days of Rage" protests staged by the Weathermen faction of SDS. A hero to the police and the Democratic machine, Elrod got his way over Moore, despite Daley's having initially hired Moore and approved his work. In the end, Moore lost his job because "he was determined to keep County Jail out of politics." How he lost it "is not difficult for seasoned Chicagoans to conceive": "Someone sets the fix apparatus going and arranges with more or less finesse to destroy a man's career and his reputation. The intention is not necessarily malicious. You may rig a jury or spray your man with sewage but you don't necessarily bear him ill will. As for the man, it is not a good idea for him to accuse his enemies, they sit safely in their offices and by reaching for the telephone can easily make him unhappy" (p. 18). Having allowed Elrod his way, Daley found Moore another job, as director of security for the Chicago Housing Authority, heading up the police in public housing.

In discussing black crime and black communities, Bellow concludes that no one knows what to do—neither the press nor the city government nor the courts nor liberals, nor the federal government, nor its advisers, including sociologists, economists, criminologists, professors of urban studies. "None of the poverty programs ever had a sense of what to do," Bellow told the novelist William Kennedy, in their interview in *Esquire*. "We're now in the fourth or fifth welfare generation, people who've never worked, people sealed out, set aside, and they look to me like a doomed population. And from the social organizations, educators, psychologists, bureaucrats—nothing. Just zilch. They've racked up a most extensive failure which has cost billions of dollars and employed millions of people and achieved nothing. The cities continue on this giant slide." Later in the interview, Bellow complains, "You read Encounter, Commentary, Foreign Affairs, books by psychologists, sociologists, and you can't find out what's happening—at least what's happening humanly."[26] "Excuse me if I offend," Rufus Ridpath's lawyer tells Corde in *The Dean's December*, talking of conditions in County Jail, "but professor-criminologists *were* brought in, but they were afraid to go into the tiers and put down the barn bosses, or even look at them. You can't blame them for it, but they sat in the office and wrote reports, or articles for criminology journals, while the suicide figures went up and up, the murders higher and higher. They didn't dare go into the jails and they couldn't take charge" (p. 153).

It was in his new capacity as director of security that Moore showed Bellow around the Robert Taylor Homes, offering the novelist a first-hand view of life "in the great public highrises on the South Side where thousands of welfare families live" (p. 19). Bellow knew something of the black areas of the city in the 1930s, but almost nothing of them in the late 1970s. "For many years I lived in Hyde Park," he writes in the "Chicago Book," "on the thirteenth floor of an apartment house and I could see the city for many miles around, the Gothic university buildings in the foreground, and beyond them endless miles of slum. On summer evenings, there were often spectacular fires to watch, and every night the dazzling blocks of the projects along South Street. They stood in the midst of vast clearings" (p. 19). The first thing Bellow noticed when he visited the projects was just this sense of separation and ruin, how they were "isolated from the rest of the city by acres, miles of devastation" (p. 20)—as they still are. Most of the inhabitants Bellow saw on his tour were children, "thousands of black kids and their mothers. There are few fathers. . . . Most of the mothers are young women on welfare. Busy with their infants, busy with men, it is inevitable that they should neglect the older children" (p. 20). The Robert Taylor Homes house "twenty-eight thousand people, six thousand of whom are adult"; 80 percent of families in the Homes are fatherless (pp. 20, 22).[27]

The state of the high-rises that make up the Homes appalled Bellow, in particular the galleries and common areas.

> These galleries are fenced to the ceiling with strong wire grills to prevent falling or being pushed or thrown over the railings and also to protect people on the ground from being pelted with garbage or bricks or pieces of iron. Every fixture is sure to be tested. Detached, it can be thrown, used as a weapon. Everything will be pried, wrenched, burned, scrawled over, pounded, sprayed with

> urine. There is an ammoniac stench on the open staircases and in the elevators. The paint has been knocked from the metal elevator walls. Built to last thirty or forty years, an elevator in one of these buildings has a life of about six months. Young men lying in wait for the guards to take their guns have been known to ride atop the elevator cabs and to open the escape hatch and threaten to douse the trapped guard with gasoline and set him afire. At the Robert Taylor project, I was told, one guard was burned this way. Garbage collects in the galleries near the incinerator drop on every floor, for the tenants bring it in bags too large for the opening and the spillage kicked aside is not often swept up [p. 20].

The tenants of such projects are mugged for their welfare checks and food stamps, sexually assaulted in elevators and janitors' closets, especially on the higher floors.

> In these housing developments there is a direct statistical correlation between the number of stories and the figures for robbery, rape and killing. The taller the building, the higher the crime rate. These highrises making "economical" use of the land for which there was no special demand, gave the politicians, the managers, the sellers of services every advantage. You could crowd two precincts into one housing project, and on election day the voters did not have to leave the premises but could be herded down to the polls by the captains. In these buildings it was intended that a potentially threatening population should be cut off and controlled and that there should be, of course, the usual boodling opportunities for suppliers, contractors, labor unions and patronage bosses [pp. 21–22].

Corde's descriptions in *Harper's* of the real-life horrors in such places are at times surreal. In the Cabrini-Green projects, "some man had butchered a hog in his apartment and had thrown the guts on the staircase, where a woman, slipping on them, had broken her arm, and screamed curses in the ambulance. She was smeared with pig's blood and shriller than the siren" (p. 131).

On the day Bellow visited the Robert Taylor Homes, a five-year-old child had been killed in a fall from an eighth-floor window. She had been left alone in the apartment with the television set on. Moore introduced Bellow to the maintenance engineer at the Homes, who explained to him that vandalism in the projects cost the city a million dollars a year in repairs and replacements, a third of his budget. As an example, he told Bellow of ninety new "commodes" designated for the apartments. Within two months of their arrival, only three were unbroken. The tenants "flush the garbage down them because they are afraid at night to go to the incinerator drop. Then the bones stick in the pipes and they try to snake them out. There goes your commode—cracked" (p. 22). The destruction of property, Bellow adds, is as widespread among the white uptown slums of the Appalachians ("the more respectful word for hillbillies" [p. 23]) as among black and Latino slum dwellers. Why this urge to destroy property, he asks, to destroy one's own habitat? Liberals see it as "a revolutionary protest against deprivation and oppression"; conservatives believe that "where you have loyalties—even loyalties to property—you have persons; not perhaps of the most desirable sort, but persons nevertheless who are aware of being such," an answer Bellow sees as "equally lacking in imagination" (p. 24). But, then, it isn't an answer at all, not to the question of *why* slum dwellers act as they do, how they came to be "unpersoned."

IN THE "CHICAGO BOOK," as in *The Dean's December*, a reforming impulse wars with despair, the roots of which lie for Bellow not only in material culture, the culture of commodities, but in matter itself, in particular the human body. The refusal to see—and the punitive element in forcing truth on the reader (to William Kennedy, in a letter of August 22, 1980, Bellow described the "Chicago Book" as "something of a cherry bomb or small grenade")—is ultimately a refusal to face death, about which Bellow, having entered his sixties, was increasingly preoccupied. Although he had many years to live, the anger in the "Chicago Book" and *The Dean's December* is the sort one sometimes sees in the eyes of the dying. At the funeral of the Dean's mother-in-law, Corde imagines her cremation:

> At this very instant Valeria might be going into the fire, the roaring furnace which took off her hair, the silk scarf, grabbed away the green suit, melted the chased silver buttons, consumed the skin, flashed away the fat, blew up the organs, reached the bones, bore down on the skull—that refining fire, a ball of raging gold, a tiny sun, a star [p. 220].

First the carefully assembled burial outfit, then the body itself, devoured by a "refining" fire. The passage, like the novel as a whole, undermines material claims; they are easily engulfed, liquidated. A similar motive underlies a scene at County Hospital, also recounted in the "Chicago Book." In *The Dean's December*, a Chinese medical technician tending an aged patient blunders:

> A valve has been left open on the tray, and immediately everything is covered with blood. The suddenness of this silent appearance and the volume of blood with which the tray fills makes my heart go faint. I am almost overcome by a thick and sweet nausea, as if my organs were melting like chocolate in hot weather [p. 167].

There are other such passages in *The Dean's December*. Corde recalls to Varennes "an eyewitness account of rats eating their way into corpses, entering at the liver and gnawing their way upwards, getting so fat they had trouble squeezing out again at the mouth" (p. 200). Dewey Spangler is especially struck by a long passage in the *Harper's* article about a mammoth sewer project costing the city "more than the Alaska pipeline."

> Capacity forty billion gallons, as wide as three locomotives side by side, running for a hundred miles deep under the city, maybe weakening the foundations of the skyscrapers. And all those tons of excrement, stunning to the imagination. It won't be the face of Helen that topples those great towers, it'll be you-know-what, and that's the difference between Chicago and Ilium.

Recounting this passage, Spangler asks Corde: "Now tell me, whom were you writing for? You pushed the poetry too hard" (p. 238). In passages like these, Corde is writing for everyone. In Troy, the facts of death, dissolution, bodily mess are both openly admitted and heroically defied. In Chicago, they are buried deep underground or in the unconscious.

BELLOW'S ANGER AT the material values that dominated the city, shaming and inflaming the poor, particularly the black poor, was accompanied by fear. The dangers of living in Hyde Park in the late

1970s were real and well publicized—too well publicized, according to some. In the July 1975 issue of *Chicago* magazine, an article entitled "How Hyde Park Made Me a Racist" caused widespread comment. Its author, Terry Curtis Fox, a recent alumnus of the university, moved to New York the week after the article was published, for reasons the article makes clear. A second article in the same issue, entitled "Magnums on the Midway," by C. D. Jaco, another university alumnus, concerned faculty members who carried guns. On July 11, in response to the two articles, the *Maroon*, which had been planning its own series on crime in Hyde Park, published a lengthy survey of reactions. "Absolute nonsense!" was the first quoted response. What followed were qualified and embarrassed assents. "It's hard to answer the Terry Curtis Fox article," a Hyde Park mother is quoted as admitting, "because it's reality here. . . . We live around the fear. You tell your kid not to argue if someone wants your bike. Don't argue. It's hard to get used to it." Another parent, once active in community affairs, moved his family to Winnetka because of fear of crime. "With his four daughters growing up, he and his wife felt that they were being overprotective of them in response to the threat of crime in Hyde Park. 'We restricted their lives in a way that wasn't fair. . . . We were developing a fortress mentality.' " As an inducement to live locally, the university offered faculty special mortgage benefits. It also sought, with only minor success, to overcome the reluctance of stores and restaurants to locate in the neighborhood.[28]

During the years Bellow worked on the "Chicago Book," the *Maroon* amply documented crime and violence in Hyde Park. On April 13, 1976, it reported, a university student was shot at and wounded in an attempted robbery just outside a university building on Fifty-Ninth Street, on the north side of the Midway. In an article of October 13, 1978, entitled "Crimes Mark Year's Start: Area Crime Rate Goes Down," it was reported that, in the first three weeks of the autumn quarter, more than twenty university students had been assaulted within a few blocks of campus, and that one week before classes a student and a female research technician were raped. Three other rapes occurred in Hyde Park between September 15 and 24. The technician was raped on a weekday morning while jogging on the lakefront, moving the assistant dean of students to advise women never to jog alone. The article was prefaced by a claim from the dean that the crime rate had gone down in Hyde Park; it was accompanied by a photograph of one of the university's one hundred security men. In the winter quarter, in an article of January 19, 1979, it was reported that the sixty-six-year-old university track-and-field coach was robbed and shot in the leg in front of his house. Three months later, in an article of April 24, 1979, the *Maroon* reported the sudden appearance of bright-red graffiti all over the campus and surrounding streets. The words "Woman Raped Here" or "Women Against Rape" were sprayed over fifty separate Hyde Park locations. According to the *Maroon*, the spray painters, twenty-five of them, were "drawn from the community, the University, and the student body." Their aim was not only to warn women to be on guard and to avoid certain areas, but "to prompt University officials to release crime statistics for Hyde Park." A report on these statistics had been commissioned and completed and was supposed to have been made available at a long-planned meeting between university officials and the Women's Union. When the meeting was canceled, Hanna Gray, the university president, was questioned about the report, which she claimed not to have read. Meanwhile, the university was seeking to discover the identity of the spray painters in order to bring them before a disciplinary committee.

As Bellow turned from the "Chicago Book" to *The Dean's December*, crime and violence continued to figure in Hyde Park. According to an article in the *Maroon* on July 27, 1979, a twenty-four-year-old university hospital worker was shot and killed as he tried to flee a holdup attempt on Harper Street, one block west of Dorchester, the street Bellow had lived on for many years. A year later, the *Maroon* reported the shooting of an off-duty police officer on East Fifty-Fifth Street, and the robbery at gunpoint of a student in her apartment. The robbery of the student took place in the afternoon. "She escaped a rape-attempt by leaping from her second-floor window," breaking her hip.[29] The next year, in an article of April 3, 1981, the *Maroon* reported the abduction late in the winter quarter of two male University of Chicago students, who were forced into a car at knifepoint and driven to Cabrini-Green, a notorious black housing project. The students were taken in an elevator to the eighth floor of one of its high-rises and robbed; they eventually escaped, when their abductors began fighting over whether to "get rid of them." In the fall of the same year, on October 7, at 10:00 p.m., a foreign student at the university was beaten outside the university's Rockefeller Chapel by three teenage boys, two from Woodlawn and one from Hyde Park.[30]

In a welcoming article at the beginning of the autumn quarter of

1981, the *Maroon* devoted a page to "Fear, Crime and Urban Living." After acknowledging that "one of the first things a new student will hear in Hyde Park is a scary crime story," it sought to reassure. "By being conscious of the problems, using common sense and the security facilities available to students, your time at UC can be a safe one." Students who were nervous about walking in Hyde Park alone could get an escort from campus security; student government organized a bus service to the Loop on Friday and Saturday nights, for those "who wish to avoid the more dangerous public transportation"; white emergency telephones on and around campus connected callers directly to the university police. Students were advised "at all times" to carry a whistle, "to alert others and the police if a crime is occurring." Of the three means of rail transportation between Hyde Park and downtown, the safest was the Illinois Central, which has two Hyde Park stations, one for Fifty-Fifth, Fifty-Sixth, and Fifty-Seventh Streets, and one for Fifty-Ninth Street. Although the wait for trains was shorter at Fifty-Ninth Street, "that station was the site of a series of rapes not long ago, and the shooting of an IC security officer earlier this month. It would be best to get a schedule and not arrive at the station much before the train."[31] In a separate article on the same page by Susan Aaron entitled "Starting a Personal Security System," female students were given advice about how to walk in Hyde Park: "briskly, with a sense of purpose, towards your destination. Have your keys (preferably with a whistle attached) in your hand when you walk. Carrying them can make you appear and feel more alert. Wear shoes and clothing you can run in. Carry your books and possessions so that you always have a free hand." If you are attacked, "your chances are best if you resist immediately," though resisting "doesn't insure that you won't be hurt further in addition to being raped."

The North Side neighborhood Bellow moved to in October 1976 was not much safer, or so he suggests in the second Tanner Lecture, in which he describes local condominium residents as "afraid to go out at night. They triple-lock their doors and set the alarm system. . . . They fear, with good reason, that in the garages below their cars are being ripped off. There are gangs of thieves who prop the axles up on bricks. Cars themselves are driven away to the chop shops and taken apart, engines and transmissions sold in other cities, even in Central America" (p. 211). Alexandra's apartment, on the twelfth floor of a luxury building, was in fact two adjacent apartments, both of which she owned.

Dave Peltz had knocked a wall through to connect them. They looked out onto the lake. At their back, just across Sheridan Avenue, the neighborhood was dangerous, and beyond that, only a few miles farther west, lay Cabrini-Green. In an interview in *U.S. News & World Report*, Bellow recalls an encounter with a woman in the neighborhood. "We bought this condominium," she told Bellow, "and now look what's happening right across the way. I can't even go across the street to shop. My neighbor's arm was broken by a purse snatcher because she had the strap wound around her arm. I can't have my grown daughters come here from the suburbs to see us, because I am afraid for them. We thought we were providing for our old age, and we are trapped here now."[32] In a letter of October 21, 1982, to his son Adam, who was traveling at the time in Africa, Bellow writes of arriving home from the airport by cab. The cab pulled up in front of Alexandra's building, and while Bellow was paying the driver,

> a black woman who pretended to be studying the names of the tenants on the board panhandled me for a dollar, which in my distraction I handed over with uncustomary softness to the touch, but then the cabdriver, a young Iranian, also surrendered a dollar when she said she was hungry. My impression was that she was hungry for human flesh. She was a strong and very tough woman who towered over us both. The driver had taken out a roll of bills, and when she saw how much money he was carrying, she asked him for a ride to Broadway, where she could buy a sandwich. Alexandra said I should have warned him, but I was tired and without my normal presence of mind.

That night, too distressed to eat supper, Bellow was unable to sleep. The next morning, he "combed" the *Tribune* for items about cabdrivers. In this state, he wrote the letter to Adam, the main purpose of which was to convey upsetting news about a planned meeting he and Adam were to have in Jerusalem, to interview Menachem Begin together. Begin's schedule had changed, the interview was off, and Bellow would not be traveling to Israel. The letter opens, though, with the tough woman panhandler. It begins: "By now you must be off in the bush running over lions or being raided at night by baboons, and I can't feel terribly sorry for you when I look out the window at the baboons on the sidewalk." This remark comes in a private letter. In *The Dean's December*, as was mentioned, Corde deplores the depiction of Rufus Ridpath as a gorilla, as, in the "Chicago Book," Bellow deplores the depiction of Ridpath's real-life model, Winston Moore, as a gorilla. In the William Kennedy interview in *Esquire*, Bellow described the Chicago sections of *The Dean's December* as a protest against "the dehumanization of the blacks in big cities. I'm speaking up for the black underclass and telling the whites they're not approaching the problem correctly." As he also points out, "the people (in the book) who stand out in moral stature, who each in his own way tries to do something, are blacks." In private, however, when upset or distracted or angry, he was capable of remarks like the one in the letter to Adam, comparing black women to baboons, especially when such remarks accompanied or facilitated wordplay or verbal flourishes or jokes, even feeble ones, as here.

IN PUBLIC CONTEXTS, both in his writing and in his actions, Bellow's concern for black people, together with his insistence on facing hard truths, was obvious, which is not to say that what he thought of as "truths" were unchallengeable. For Bellow, the first truth to face about "the hard core of the welfare society" is that it is "doomed." He elaborates in the *U.S. News & World Report* interview:

> There are no prospects for these people. Nobody ever took the trouble to teach them anything. They live in a kind of perpetual chaos, in a great noise. And, you know, they really are startled souls. They cannot be reasoned with or talked to about anything.
>
> Isn't it time for us to admit this? For a long time the subject lay under a taboo. Nobody was going to talk about it. Now people are beginning to do so. Though I consider myself a kind of liberal, I have to admit that the taboos were partly of liberal origin. It was supposed to be wrong to speak with candor. But lying in a good cause only aggravates disorder. . . .
>
> Writers are part of this whole dismal picture that is dominated by an evasion and unwillingness to come to grips with the profoundest human facts. . . . I include myself in this. I seem to have been overtaken by a kind of fit in my old age [he is 67] in which I want to say things definitely and firmly—and hit hard.

The Chicago sections of *The Dean's December* set out to do just this, picking up the baton, wrenching it, from the "Chicago Book." In the interview with William Kennedy, Bellow described the decision to expand Corde's backstory, importing material from the "Chicago Book," as inadvertent, "one of these things that came over me." In the same interview, he also connected the decision with an encounter in 1965, at the ceremony at which he was presented with the National Book Award for *Herzog*. That year, the journalist and biographer Louis Fischer was also presented with a National Book Award, for *The Life of Lenin*. After the ceremony, Fischer and Bellow exchanged inscribed copies of their books. Fischer's inscription read "To Saul Bellow, for deeper thought," which Bellow took to mean "his book had bigger status than mine, that he was writing about great disasters of the 20th century and that they should be described properly, but I was only writing about private life. . . . Let's think big. Let's not think about these schnook professors (like Moses Herzog) with their cuckoldries and broken hearts." The Fischer anecdote was recalled by Bellow in the Kennedy interview in the midst of a defense of fiction over journalism, "new" as well as old. Although Bellow had done a fair bit of journalism in his life, covering Khrushchev's visit to the United Nations, the Six-Day War, contemporary Israel (in *To Jerusalem and Back*), to Kennedy he announced, "I'll never have any more to do with it." "The very language you have to use as a journalist works against the true material." To say what needs saying about Chicago, to communicate "what's happening humanly," one needs fiction or poetry. "We live in this age of communication, drowned with communication which comes in the form of distracting substitutes for reality. But the reality of our day comes in art."

THE MARK GROMER MURDER CASE, as fictionalized in *The Dean's December*, provides a way of testing Bellow's faith in art over journalism, in fiction as a path to reality. Although by no means the most gruesome of the real-life Chicago stories the novel draws on, it is especially tightly and centrally woven into the narrative. The Gromer case began in the early hours of July 6, 1977, when Mark Gromer, a twenty-five-year-old graduate student in English at the University of Chicago, fell to his death through the window of his third-floor apartment in Hyde Park, at 5344 South Woodlawn Avenue, three blocks west of Dorchester. The cause of the fall was disputed, as was almost every aspect of the case. According to an article in the *Chicago Tribune* published in a late edition on July 6, the police were seeking two black youths who had attempted to rob the apartment. The youths had threatened Gromer with a knife, stuffed a rag in his mouth to stop him from crying out, and tied a cloth strip around his head in an attempt to blindfold him. They then filled a suitcase with items, apparently including a small television and a stereo. Gromer's wife was asleep at the time, but, when wakened by voices, wandered into the hallway leading from the bedroom to the living room. One of the youths grabbed her from behind, pushed her into the kitchen, and ordered her at knifepoint to kneel on the floor. She heard the sounds of a struggle in the living room, of breaking glass, and of the attackers fleeing. When she ran to the living-room window and looked down, she saw her husband lying motionless on the sidewalk. Although still alive when the ambulance arrived, he died two hours after being admitted to hospital.[33]

The next day, more details were revealed in the newspapers. The police said the youths entered the apartment around 4:30 a.m. through a back door that had been left open because of the heat—it was a typically steamy July night in Chicago. According to his wife, Gromer had been up late, studying in the living room (the dean of humanities at the university described him as "an excellent student and well thought of").[34] It was also reported that the South East Chicago Commission—formed in 1952, partly to plan and implement the urban renewal of Hyde Park, partly to monitor crime in the Hyde Park–Woodlawn area—had offered a five-thousand-dollar reward for information leading to the arrest and conviction of Gromer's attackers, urging anyone with information to contact the police, and promising anonymity.[35] The executive director of the commission and one of its founders was Julian Levi, professor of urban studies at the University of Chicago Law School, who was the older brother of Edward Levi, president of the university from 1968 to 1975. It took a day for the offer of the reward to bear fruit. On July 8, the papers reported that Deola (Dee Dee) Johnson, thirty-four, a prostitute and heroin addict, had been linked with a piece of jewelry stolen from the Gromer apartment. It was Gromer's wedding ring, which Johnson had left with a friend to hide. It was also reported that Johnson had been seen the night of Gromer's death dressed boyishly, and that she had a boyish Afro hairdo. This information was passed to the police by Johnson's friend Joseph Booth, an ex-convict and reputed South Side drug dealer, in search of the reward.[36]

Then a new witness, Levar Lewis, came forward, claiming that on July 6 an acquaintance of his named Ellis McInnis, with whom he worked at a deli-restaurant in Hyde Park called Unique, had told him in confidence that he and Johnson had been in a nearby bar, the Tiki Lounge, on the night of Gromer's death, and that there they met a white guy, Gromer, who invited them to his apartment for a "party."[37] McInnis and Johnson quickly hatched a plan to "rip him off." McInnis claimed that neither he nor Johnson pushed Gromer out the window, but that he fell in the course of a struggle. The next day, Lewis saw McInnis at work. He showed McInnis a newspaper article about the death. McInnis said he was worried that Gromer might have talked before he died. He asked Lewis to find out if Johnson had been arrested. Later that day, Lewis learned of the reward and went to the police to report what McInnis had told him. Four months earlier, Lewis had pleaded guilty to a charge of attempted burglary and received sixty days work release and three years on probation. At the time he came forward as a witness, he had a violation of parole pending.[38]

After Lewis spoke to the police, and McInnis and Johnson were arrested, Lewis was again in the Tiki, where he ran into a young white undergraduate, Philip Grew, the bullhorn-wielding demonstrator, who also worked part-time at Unique. Grew had just finished his second year at the University of Chicago. He was nineteen, a prominent protester on campus, active in student government, and a photographer for the *Maroon*. Lewis claimed that Grew threatened him for talking to the police, warning him not to testify against McInnis. He said Grew told him, "You better watch your back," and that the next night, walking home from work at Unique, he'd been shot at by an unknown person standing in a gangway. In late August, it was incorrectly reported in the press that the assistant state's attorney, T. J. McCarthy, had issued an arrest warrant for Grew, whom he described as having "fled" Hyde Park for Ann Arbor, Michigan, where his parents lived. Grew denied that he had threatened or shot at anyone, and that he had fled. Four months later, in December 1977, after Grew's parents were forced to remortgage their house and his mother to postpone retirement in order to meet legal expenses, a criminal-court judge dismissed the indictment, citing "prosecutorial abuse" of a county grand jury.[39] The assistant state's attorney, the judge ruled, had acted improperly in not waiting for a preliminary hearing before testifying to the grand jury (in *The Dean's December*, Corde is advised, of the McCarthy character, "The court will give your friend Grady hell for rushing to the grand jury" [p. 88]). In effect, Grew was let off on a technicality. On October 9, 1980, after lengthy appeals, Ellis McInnis, having been found guilty of murder and armed robbery, began serving a term of twenty-five to forty years in prison. Because Deola Johnson had pleaded guilty to the same charges, her sentence was only fourteen years. After sentencing, Johnson told lawyers for McInnis that she was now willing to testify on his behalf and that her testimony would corroborate his. "She said her previous refusal to testify was based on the mistaken belief that the defendant's counsel was responsible for her having to plead guilty."[40] A motion to reopen the trial to allow Johnson to change her testimony was denied.

In *The Dean's December*, the Gromer case becomes the Rickie Lester case. As Albert Corde sits shivering in Bucharest, failing to comfort his distraught wife, Minna, ineffectually wrestling with the petty tyrannies of party functionaries, chief among the problems he ponders is the fallout from his decision as dean of students to offer a five-thousand-dollar reward for information leading to the perpetrators of Rickie Lester's defenestration. It is Corde's only nephew, Mason Zaehner, Jr., a character very loosely based on Philip Grew, who gives him the most grief. Mason's deceased father was "a high-powered Loop lawyer . . . tough, arrogant, a bulldozing type" (p. 32) (an American equivalent of the hospital director in Bucharest). Mason, Jr., shares both his father's "bullying lusterless put-down stare" (p. 37) and his contempt for "the dud dean" (p. 42). He orchestrates campus protests against the university's role in prosecuting the two suspects in Rickie Lester's death. These suspects are Riggie Hines, a boyish-looking prostitute, and Lucas Ebry, a black dishwasher at the restaurant where Mason works part-time. In Corde's summary, "The radical student line was that the college waged a secret war against blacks and that the Dean was scheming with the prosecution, using the college's clout to nail the black man. . . . Mason argued that there had been no murder. Rickie Lester hadn't been pushed from the window, he had stumbled, he fell. Anyway, it was all his [Lester's] fault, he went out that night looking for trouble, had been asking for it" (p. 30). The university's behavior in the case was of a piece with its attempt to restrict black housing in the neighborhood, its refusal to divest itself of South African investments, its slowness on affirmative action. Mason identifies with blacks like Embry and Hines: "Those are my people and you made them all seem subhuman . . . wild-ass savages from the Third World. And now I see that you are writing something about County Jail" (p. 47).

Corde admits that Mason "had a cause," but sees his animus as personal. "Mostly he was eager to needle his uncle and he hoped—craved, longed—to drive his needle deep" (p. 35). An Oedipal element is at work in the nephew's hostility. Mason resents Corde's closeness to his mother and her idealizing of him. "I'm the one who makes her unhappy," Mason, Jr., tells Corde. "You're the one that protects her" (p. 49). Brother and sister "have something palpable between us. Mason, somewhere, is aware of this and he doesn't like it" (p. 90). "I was always having you rubbed into me," Mason says. "Uncle Albert this and Uncle Albert that. A big man, and smart, and a notable" (p. 49). By the end of the novel, Mason flees to Mexico, having been indicted by the assistant state's attorney for threatening witnesses. His mother asks Corde if he believes Mason capable of shooting at anyone. "Not necessarily," Corde answers. "But I don't necessarily disbelieve it. He's in real earnest about his pal Ebry. By working in the restaurant kitchen he got to be an honorary black. He cornered those witnesses." The prosecutor indicted Mason "because he raised hell with the witnesses. You can't expect a prosecutor to let the kid ruin his case. . . . He threatened those street characters. He said he'd get 'em." "Without them," Corde adds, the prosecutor "had no case" (p. 86).

PHILIP GREW DESCRIBES his politics in 1977 as to the left of those of his parents, ardent Stevenson supporters, but as neither extremist nor radical, a position not dissimilar, he claimed in an interview, to that of the young Saul Bellow, a Trotskyist unwilling to toe the party line (though Bellow joined the Trotskyists, whereas Grew belonged to no political parties or formal groupings).[41] Mason, Jr., was also a nonjoiner, perhaps calculatedly. "A definite ideology would have made him easier to deal with," Corde thinks, "and Mason didn't intend to make anything easy. No, Corde couldn't identify the young man's position, if he had a position. Maybe there wasn't really any" (p. 31). In 1977, Grew certainly looked like a radical, with curly hair down to his shoulders, so long that, when it was washed and slicked down, he could, if he leaned back, sit on it. He also talked like a radical, with "black" or hipster inflections and in a manner not unlike Mason, Jr.'s, judging by his reconstructions during our interview. Corde describes Mason, Jr., as affecting a "bright bitterness barrels-of-fun line" (p. 34); "His ultra-bright hey-presto look was insolent" (p. 35). Although Grew was deeply serious in the interview, at one moment moved to tears, there were also times when he recounted the ironies and injustices of the Gromer case with just such a "bright bitterness."

Grew's father was a professor at the University of Michigan, a fact, he believes, that contributed to the passion he brought to the Gromer case. The issue that galvanized him was racial injustice. He had gone to school with black children and "really believed from a very early age in Martin Luther King." "I grew up believing literally in King's dream. I was living it." "In junior high school and high school I had loved Malcolm X, Richard Wright, Eldridge Cleaver. This kind of African American awareness had been very much around me, was part of my upbringing." Arriving in Hyde Park, "I was just *shocked* by race relations. . . . I had completely failed to realize what the black-white situation was going to be like in Chicago." What also shocked Grew was the discovery that white liberals, university people, often "held feelings about race which were in some sense the most pernicious."[42] In his first year in Chicago, he lived in a dormitory on the north side of the Midway, below which lay Woodlawn. Bellow referred to the Midway as the "Maginot Line" or "Passchendaele"; Grew referred to it as "the DMZ, the Demilitarized Zone."

Unique, where Grew, McInnis, and Levar Lewis worked, was on Fifty-third Street, on the northern edge of Hyde Park. Although a predominantly white neighborhood, it was one in which blacks were a presence, particularly at night in bars and restaurants. Tiki was one of those bars, an "unsavory" place to some (T. J. McCarthy, for instance). It stayed open after 2:00 a.m., and drugs could be found there as well as drink. Grew remembers that drugs were also passed in the alley behind Unique, where the dishwashers played craps. Mason accuses the Dean of despising such types: "Those people of the *underclass*, dopers or muggers or whores: what were they, mice? To the 'thinking population,' to establishment intellectuals, they were nothing but mice! Thus Corde spelled out, parsed his nephew's message. He even agreed, in part" (p. 36). Like Mason, Grew is proud that he knew something of the black underclass, a term he hates (as does Mason, who tells Corde, "That's what your sociologists around here call them. They're hoping that drugs and killings and prison will eliminate that lousy, trouble-making underclass" [p. 35]).[43] In knowing and working with the African American kitchen staff and dishwashers at Unique, Grew felt he was keeping faith with Martin Luther King's dream. At the same time, he was clearheaded about his fellow workers. Ellis McInnis he describes as an alcoholic, a pathetic figure who looked in his thirties, not his twenties, "one of those black kids gone wrong but from a good mom, a good family." Although he was pretty much "unhirable," the owner of Unique, a woman named Pat Bradley, "scooped [McInnis] up out of the gutter. . . . He was her pet project, at least at the beginning."

Because Grew found it hard to believe that McInnis "could have been involved in this," also because McInnis "seemed to be heading in the right direction," Grew "couldn't stand by and do nothing." He began investigating the charges, partly for the university newspaper, partly to aid McInnis's attorney. He was soon convinced, is still convinced, that McInnis and Johnson were "railroaded": "there was absolutely no pretense that this was a fair trial." To begin with, there was "too much circumstantial evidence that things were being fabricated, things were being made up, there was all this interference." The testimony of the witnesses kept changing. There were questions about the testimony of Gromer's wife, who seemed to Grew and others to be holding something back. The word on the street (and later witness testimony in court) was that Gromer was high that night on drugs as well as drink, and in search of sex. In addition to the reward money, Levar Lewis and Joseph Booth, key prosecution witnesses, hoped for leniency in their own cases. In pleading guilty and accepting the prosecution's account of what happened in the apartment, Deola Johnson was seeking a reduced sentence. Despite these complications, Grew recalls, "in the white environment I lived in there was a unanimous leap to say this was a murder. We were brought up, we were trained, by the university to expect to be the victims of black-on-white crime. In actual reality, this black-on-white crime didn't take place so much."

Like Mason, Jr., Grew cannot say for certain what went on in the apartment the night Gromer died.[44] What he is certain of is that McInnis and Johnson were denied due process and that the guilty verdict was by no means beyond reasonable doubt. Especially upsetting to him was the role the university played in the case. From the start, the assistant state's attorney was in close contact with university officials and the South East Chicago Commission (the university's "Special Ops" division, Grew calls it).[45] In Bucharest, Corde learns that he's been subpoenaed by Mason, Jr.'s lawyer (another hostile relative, Corde's cousin, Maxie Detillion), "to establish the heavy involvement of the college in this case" (p. 177). According to T. J. McCarthy, during the Gromer case Jonathan Kleinbard, a university vice-president and Bellow's friend, was often in touch on the telephone, as was Michael J. Murphy, executive director of the South East Chicago Commission. Kleinbard first contacted McCarthy while he was "doing a work-up" on the case. He was "gracious but insistent. He wanted to be kept informed of what was going on." Soon "Jonathan and I struck up a very good rapport." When, however, McCarthy told Kleinbard that he planned to leave the State's Attorney's Office before the case went to trial, to go into private practice, Kleinbard was distressed. "He said, 'Well, why? You know these two police officers, you've worked with them before, you've developed this rapport.'" Kleinbard then asked McCarthy, who was only three years out of law school, the name of the firm he was going to, which happened to be headed by two generous donors to the University of Chicago. After joining the firm, McCarthy learned that a deal had been struck between the State's Attorney's Office and his new employers, presumably suggested or orchestrated by figures from the university. McCarthy was to be seconded to the State's Attorney's Office and sworn in for the duration of the trial as a special prosecutor ("this was unheard of"). At the trial's conclusion, he would return to his position in private practice. Kleinbard's mission, in McCarthy's words, was "to make sure that the people of the Hyde Park–University of Chicago community were aware that the State's Attorney's Office was doing everything possible to bring the case to a proper conclusion," by which was meant not only a speedy and successful prosecution but a tightly focused one: "Jonathan had the parameters very clearly marked in his mind." Sexual speculation, the sort that might upset the grieving Gromer family as well as reflect badly on the university community (depicting Hyde Park as a place where students mixed with drug dealers and prostitutes), was to be avoided. Such matters, in McCarthy's words, "had no bearing on the actual underpinnings of the case"; they were "proprietary, confidential," so "we didn't really go into all of that, nor did we allow it." According to Grew, the university also sought to shape coverage of the case in the *Maroon*. Soon after Gromer's death, the editor of the paper was discouraged by unnamed university officials from interviewing potential witnesses or airing doubts about the police account of what had happened that night. McCarthy also felt pressure from the university to come down hard on Philip Grew, leader of what Kleinbard called "this scurrilous campaign by student groups," and he had no problem accommodating Kleinbard, not only because he thought Grew a "smart-ass," but because "I think he crossed the line with our witnesses. I still think that to this day." Indicting Grew was the right thing to do, he believed, though it "kind of fanned the flames."[46]

What Grew saw as the university's interference in the case outraged him, in part because of his background. "I was a faculty brat and thought universities should be held to a higher standard." Grew also admits to an Oedipal element behind his outrage, like that of Mason, Jr. That Bellow gives Mason, Jr., such a motive is striking, part of what he means about art's capacity to attend to "what's happening humanly." Also striking is Corde's refusal to dismiss Mason, Jr.'s doubts about Rickie Lester's death, about how the alleged perpetrators ended up in the apartment, about the reliability of "bought" witnesses, or the more lurid alternatives he offers about how Lester met his death. "Though it went against the grain," Corde admits, "he suspected that his nephew might have been right, that on the night he was killed Rick Lester had been out for dirty sex, and it was this dirty sex momentum that carried him through the window" (p. 130). Mason is obnoxious, but none of his arguments, which were and remain Grew's arguments, is refuted. In the novel, as opposed to the newspapers, justice is done not only to "what humanly matters," but to the complications and uncertainties of the case.

However, the Dean's doubts about the case do not extend to the verdict. Lucas Ebry, he believes, was rightly convicted of murder. He believes this because he also believes that Rick Lester's death occurred in the course of an armed robbery and therefore counted as "felony murder," regardless of whether he was pushed or fell, was drunk and/or stoned, or lost his balance in a struggle. Corde has no sense of connection with people like Ebry and Hines; nonetheless, he thinks Mason's attitude toward them is both naïve and typical. "In Mason you saw an attempted reversal, a connection to be made on black terms. What terms were those? Lucas Ebry's terms? They didn't exist. Unreal! Young Mason's idea of boldness put him in the servile position" (p. 149). When pressed by Mason's mother, Corde admits that his nephew was unlikely to have shot at anyone. "*If* shots were fired—

a doubtful proposition—somebody else might have fired them" (p. 187). He is convinced, though, as McCarthy is of Grew, that "Mason did threaten the witnesses, gang style, that does seem to be a fact" (p. 87). There is also no question in the novel that Mason goes into hiding. "He must be thrilled to pieces to be a fugitive. It's a terrific luxury for a kid like Mason. You corner two street people. You deliver a death threat. They take you *seriously*—that's a real thrill. It means you're pretty close to being black yourself. You don't have to be ashamed of your white skin" (p. 87). At this point, Mason, Jr.'s story and Philip Grew's story diverge dramatically. Grew went home to visit his family in Ann Arbor before he knew anything of the indictment. As soon as he received word of it, he returned to Chicago with his father and presented himself to the State's Attorney's Office. In the novel, Bellow sacrifices the reality of Grew's response to the indictment, which he must have known, to "art," to the serving of deeper truths. Corde accepts that Rick Lester, in one sense, brought his fate upon himself: "It was the evil that had overtaken the boy that did it" (p. 28). "Did it" means "got him killed," and "the evil that had overtaken the boy" refers to an internal as well as an external evil. Rick Lester turned up at two in the morning at a bar like the Tiki. According to the bartender, " 'He made a pest of himself, acted up, just about the only white person in the place, making sex signals.' . . . Maybe this boy had hot pants, or drank more than he could hold, or was freaked out on Quaaludes" (p. 29), allegations that were made against Mark Gromer, in court as well as in the news.

Philip Grew has an interesting story to tell about the claim that he intimidated witnesses. The only prosecution witness he talked to was Levar Lewis. "I talked to Levar a number of times. Levar and I worked together. Who is Levar? Levar is an opportunist. . . . He was gonna make it, he was gonna get rich . . . the kind of upcoming black guy who could appeal to white people." Grew had met Lewis many times at the Tiki and elsewhere, and Lewis had told him that he was going to be given witness protection and "live in the lap of luxury." His story was that, the day after Gromer's death, he and McInnis "were just shooting the breeze" and McInnis, "his good friend," told him the story of what had happened when he suddenly committed murder. At a later meeting, the crucial meeting, Grew now realizes, Grew was again in the Tiki, and "Levar was there and I went over to him and I knew that Levar was getting paid to testify against Ellis. This was a tense situation. Levar was with some girl . . . lighter skin than him. So I went over to Levar's table and tried to have a frank conversation about this. 'Levar, you got to do what's right. I know you want the money. I know you want to cooperate with the South East Chicago Commission, but you can't tell things you don't know.'" The conversation got heated—they'd had several beers each—"it was certainly tense. I put it right before him, very frankly, that I thought what he was doing was morally wrong, and legally pretty risky, because you could get into a lot of trouble lying to the man. Also, there was a lack of solidarity to the black community. None of that shit fazed him." So Grew took a different tack. "Levar had a proselytizing sister, so I made the Biblical argument. I said, 'Thou shalt not bear false witness.'" This infuriated Lewis. "He got up and he stomped out of Tiki."

Had Grew threatened Lewis? Did he say to him, "You better watch your back"? By now, after lengthy interviews, my impression of Grew was that he could not have shot at Lewis. He would not have owned a gun. He was not a person to use a gun. Lewis may have heard gunshots after his encounter with Grew, but if he did, there is no proof that they were directed at him. It was not until 1983, Grew claims, six years after his indictment, that he realized what really happened that night at the Tiki. The realization, an "epiphany," came to him while recounting to a friend the events of the summer of 1977. When Levar stomped out,

> I realized he'd left behind a pack of Kool Lights, Newports, something on the table, a soft pack. It was sopped with beer, mentholated cigarettes. I smoked Gauloises, so I had no interest in them. But almost a full pack of cigarettes. I wasn't going to hold his cigarettes for him—what if he had hidden something else in the pack? I went as far as the door of the Tiki, and as he was leaving, I yelled, "Levar, Levar, want your pack?"
>
> I was interrogated by my lawyer, by my lawyer's lawyer, by my father . . . for years and years, by everybody in the world for hours and hours and hours, and nobody could even get close enough to me to loosen me up to the point where I could recount in such detail that particular conversation with Levar, that little detail I'd completely forgotten about. When Levar said I had said, "Watch your back," he really believed it, he thought that's what I said.

I believe this story. I certainly believe that Grew believes it. He had always wondered why Levar had not retrieved his cigarettes ("I could never figure it out"). What Bellow would have done with the story, had he known it, is hard to say. When Bellow interviewed McCarthy, McCarthy recalled, "he was completely prepped, he had his questions in mind, he had his notes." McCarthy was uncomfortable in the interview, because Bellow persistently asked him about a possible sexual dimension to the case. His questions, McCarthy thought, were not only irrelevant but prurient; the information he sought was "confidential, privileged." Bellow, like Corde, seems to have thought not only that sex played a part in what happened to Gromer, but that it did so in a way important to an understanding of American culture generally, particularly of American youth culture. For Corde, the material, the sexual, and the mortal go together: "Our conception of physical life and pleasure is completely death-saturated." For African Americans reduced to "savagery and criminality," as for the youth who glamorize them, "the full physical emphasis is fatal" (p. 196). *The Dean's December* pays no more attention to the prejudice and discrimination that have produced black "savagery and criminality" than Bellow does in the second Jefferson Lecture. Bellow's focus here, as in the lecture, is on the behavior bred by prejudice and discrimination. He is comparably "hard" in his attitude to those who endanger the existence of the university, while openly admitting the injustices visited on them by the university's protectors. In the words of Julian Levi, "The University had taken the initiative in the organization of the South East Chicago Commission to combat the forces of uncertainty and deterioration at work in the neighborhood." The aim of the commission was to create "a community in which our faculty and students will be secure."[47] Bellow allows Mason, Jr., to list, unchallenged, the unfair practices the creation of this community involved, the collateral damage suffered by those who lost their properties and businesses, however "blighted" or "slum," to the forces of renewal.[48]

In *The Dean's December*, as in *Mr. Sammler's Planet*, no member of the black underclass is given a voice. For Corde, as for Bellow in the second Jefferson Lecture, types like Ellis McInnis and Deola Johnson are "unreachable, incomprehensible. You will never know what they are thinking or feeling," at least not directly. The closest Bellow gets to depicting such types "humanly" in *The Dean's December* is through the characters who deal with them daily: Rufus Ridpath, modeled, as we've seen, on Winston Moore, and Toby Winthrop, also an African American, modeled on Matt Wright, who was described in the "Chicago Book" as having been "a criminal, a Mafioso dope addict in and out of prison, tried more than once on a charge of murder."[49] Bellow went to interview Wright at the detoxification center he ran, as Corde interviews Winthrop at "Operation Contact," his detoxification center. Both real-life and fictional African Americans are described as tough-minded, willing to face illiberal-sounding realities (about welfare, the black family). "There are two black men in the book," Bellow told Eugene Kennedy in the interview in the *Chicago Tribune:* "I looked far and wide for men of moral imagination. And I found only these two. One was an ex–hit-man. . . . The other the former director of Cook County Jail . . . They had grasped the real problem, which has had every unavailing solution thrown at it. Programs, plans, money. Theirs was an elementary application of the imagination," which is to say, one involving courage, firsthand knowledge or experience, intense caring, and passionate judging.[50] To some, the complications and contradictions I've been tracing in Bellow's attitudes to race will be seen as evasions. "As he grew older," James Atlas declares of Bellow, "the bones of a deeply conservative, xenophobic vision of life emerged more clearly. Like his ill-concealed racism, which made exceptions for blacks who were his friends (Ralph Ellison, William Hunt, Stanley Crouch), Bellow's misogyny was a cultural anachronism for which he almost gleefully refused to apologize."[51] Atlas is comparably certain about both the "murder" of Mark Gromer, "who was pushed to his death," and the subsequent trial, "in the midst of which potential witnesses were shot at by a student radical sympathetic to the defendants."[52]

DURING THE YEARS Bellow worked on the "Chicago Book" and *The Dean's December*, he and Alexandra spent their summers in Vermont, initially at her suggestion. Alexandra knew the area through friends from Northwestern, Lynda and Arthur Copeland, who had a house in West Halifax, just over the Massachusetts border. "I knew he liked New England," Alexandra recalled, and that "he missed the house in Tivoli in New York." Bellow himself had friends locally: "He was particularly fond of Robert Penn Warren, Bernard Malamud, and Meyer Schapiro, whom he adored . . . so I thought it made perfectly good sense." The Copelands scouted out summer rentals for the Bellows for the first few years, and in 1981 helped them to find land on which to build a house of their own, on property in West Halifax known as the Old Larrabee

Farm. Arthur Copeland, a colleague of Alexandra's in the Department of Mathematics at Northwestern, was one of several mathematicians who summered in the area, among them Shizuo Kakutani, who had taught Alexandra at Yale, and Marshall Stone, retired chair of the University of Chicago Mathematics Department, and a former colleague of Bellow's at the Committee on Social Thought. To William Kennedy, Bellow described his Vermont social life as "at the heart of an extended group of mathematicians from Yale, Amherst, Boston, Dartmouth." At least once or twice a week, the Bellows joined members of this extended group at dinner parties or concerts at the nearby Marlboro Music Festival. Lynda Copeland remembers Bellow in Vermont summers with amused affection. "Saul was King of the Earth wherever he was." At social gatherings, "he was a quiet, a very quiet presence, but let me tell you, you knew he was there." Mostly Bellow's talk took the form of "interjections, one-liners, often barbed . . . never a wasted word." "You always knew that he was a powerful intellect, someone to reckon with, he did not suffer fools gladly, and was probably half the time in social occasions bored to death, but he did not indicate it." Although Bellow liked to tease the Copelands about their liberal politics, "we never saw Saul behave in a rude manner. I'm sure he did, but never with us."

In the unedited typescript of his *Esquire* interview with Bellow, conducted in Vermont in the summer of 1981, William Kennedy describes Bellow and Alexandra's daily routine. "Rise about seven or eight, long leisurely breakfast, workdays in separate studios in the old house, a long afternoon walk together. They have been summering here five years, renting, mostly in willful isolation from the assault on their time that goes with life back home in Chicago. Sometimes, Alexandra said, the phone doesn't ring once all day long." Bellow did his writing in a sparsely furnished second-floor room with a double skylight and a balcony looking out onto the Vermont landscape, composing in longhand on a lapboard. Among the many books scattered in the living room, Kennedy noted "Zamyatin's essays, *The Teachings of Gurdjieff, Chaucer's Bawdy* by Thomas Ross, and four novels: *Joseph Andrews*, Feyodor Sologub's *The Pretty Demon*, Djuna Barnes' *Nightwood*, and Rousseau's *La Nouvelle Héloïse*." To break the daily routine, there were afternoon excursions to Brattleboro, where old friends often turned up. In a letter of August 22, 1980, to Edward Shils, Bellow describes his part of Vermont as "thickly populated with writers and savants. I don't see them often but I never know when I may run into them. Last week in Brattleboro (Kipling's old haunt) I bumped into Sidney Hook on Main Street. He was spry but shaky, assisted in mid-street by his wife and calling out to numerous grandchildren who ran in and out of ice-cream parlors and Dunkin' Donuts. And a few days later Meyer Schapiro telephoned, keenly alert but his voice quite weak. He told me how hard he was working, and he was vigorous and amusing—and doddering a little, and also a shade melancholy. I suppose that description covers all of us."

To help meet divorce costs and lawyers' fees, Bellow took on more than his usual number of guest lectureships, talks, and readings. Shortly after the visit from William Kennedy, Bellow and Alexandra traveled to Syracuse University, where for three weeks Bellow would be the Jeannette K. Watson Distinguished Visiting Professor in the Humanities, an appointment for which he was paid fifteen thousand dollars plus hotel and transport costs. His duties were minimal: to deliver one public lecture, one reading, and four seminars. Almost four years earlier, in the fall of 1977, Bellow and Alexandra had accepted jobs for the fall quarter at Brandeis University in Waltham, Massachusetts, Bellow as Frances and Jacob Hiatt Visiting Professor of English. Bellow taught a weekly seminar on Conrad at Brandeis, but was otherwise rarely seen on campus. At a Halloween costume party in an undergraduate dormitory, the first prize went to a young man who put a sheet over his head and wore a sign saying simply "Saul Bellow." The Bellows were more visible in Cambridge, where they took an apartment in a high-rise on the Charles River, at 1010 Memorial Drive, and led a busy social life. "I am much in his doghouse because of a social error," Bellow wrote on November 7, 1977, to Bernard Malamud, who had asked after a mutual friend, "a confusion among Wednesdays. We missed a cocktail party and have not yet been forgiven."

In Cambridge, as in Vermont, Bellow and Alexandra saw "quite a number of mathematicians." Alexandra had friends in Harvard's Department of Mathematics and served on its "ad hoc" committee, to evaluate job candidates. Graeme Segal, a young visiting professor from Oxford, remembers meeting the Bellows at a lunch on Christmas Day given by the chair of the department, Shlomo Sternberg, and his wife, Aviva Green, a painter. At sixty-two, Bellow was much the oldest of the guests (Alexandra and the Sternbergs were in their early forties, Segal and a friend he'd brought in their early thirties). Segal was struck by how well dressed Bellow was, and how he was "very much like the guest of honor." The Sternbergs are Orthodox Jews. Segal, though Jewish, describes himself as "aggressively secular," from a family of outspoken anti-Zionists. When the subject of Israel came up, Segal recalled, Bellow "played a very straight bat"[53] (Segal had not read *To Jerusalem and Back*, published the previous year). There was also "some sort of Jewish grace" before the meal, and Bellow asked Sternberg if he wanted him to wear a yarmulke. After the lunch, the Bellows drove the young English guests back to Harvard and got stuck in Cambridge's one-way traffic system. When Segal and his friend volunteered to walk the short distance to Currier House, Bellow insisted on driving them to their door, "with only a slight hint of testiness." Segal remembers no literary conversation, no friction, no putting on of airs, nothing but good humor on Bellow's part. Of Alexandra, whose reputation as a mathematician he knew, all he remembers is how beautiful she was. What Aviva Green wished to emphasize about Bellow at this time (they'd met previously in Jerusalem, where the Sternbergs have a house) is how supportive he was to her as an artist. In addition to buying one of her paintings, he gave her two pieces of invaluable advice: first, to go to her studio every day, since "nothing can happen in the studio unless you *are* in the studio"; second, to put aside "the business of art . . . just don't think about it. He recognized I was very ambitious and was saying, Don't let the business of art intrude."

Although Bellow had several old friends living in the Cambridge-Boston area (Monroe and Brenda Engel, whom he'd known since the 1940s; Eugene Goodheart, whom he'd known from Tivoli days), he made new friends as well. In the case of Alan Lelchuk, a novelist who taught creative writing at Brandeis, he firmed up a friendship. Lelchuk had met Bellow in May 1966, when he was twenty-eight and in his last year as a graduate student in English at Stanford. That spring, Bellow had been invited to Stanford by the Creative Writing Center to give a public lecture and teach a few classes. When Lelchuk gave him a tour of the Stanford campus, they got on well, and the next afternoon Bellow invited him to lunch. Later, he asked to see some of Lelchuk's writing, and recommended his stories to Gordon Lish at *Esquire*. In the intervening years, he had written several Guggenheim letters for Lelchuk. When Lelchuk finished at Stanford, he got a job at Brandeis. There he befriended Philip Rahv, Bellow's old editor from *Partisan Review*. In addition to teaching in the English Department, Rahv edited a short-lived periodical while at Brandeis, *Modern Occasions*, on which Lelchuk worked as associate editor. Bellow published "Culture

Now: Some Animadversions, Some Laughs" (1971) and "Zetland: By a Character Witness" (1974) in *Modern Occasions* (the latter appearing in the year after Rahv's death), which helped to keep him in contact with Lelchuk. Before he came to Cambridge, he wrote to Lelchuk asking about Brandeis, and about where in the Boston-Cambridge area he and Alexandra should live.[54] Lelchuk thought Bellow would like Brandeis. He would be a "big figure" at the university (along with Abraham Maslow, the psychologist, and Herbert Marcuse, the radical Frankfurt School critical theorist, no Bellow favorite).[55] Lelchuk's wife, Betty, who was writing her Ph.D. dissertation on Bellow, audited his Conrad seminar. She thought the seminar brilliant, though others in the class complained both about Bellow's views and about the certainty with which he expressed them. Like the Sternbergs, the Lelchuks have only positive memories of Bellow that autumn. They named their son after him.[56]

The most important of the new friends Bellow made in the autumn of 1977 in Cambridge was Leon Wieseltier, recently arrived at Harvard from Oxford to do a Ph.D. in Jewish studies. Like Lelchuk, Wieseltier had grown up in Brooklyn. Shortly after arriving at Harvard, he was given Bellow's number and told to call him (by whom, Wieseltier can't remember). He and Bellow quickly struck up a friendship. "We just were crazy about each other. We used to see each other a lot," often for walks along the Charles or for lunch. "I took a shine to Wieseltier immediately," Bellow recalled in a letter of January 31, 1977, to the Israeli novelist John Auerbach. "I should be happy to feel he returned my warm feelings." Wieseltier, facetiously, describes himself in 1977 as having "this reputation that preceded me as the hottest thing in Jewish Studies since white bread." Like Bellow, he had—still has—a sharp tongue, and a taste for intellectual gossip. He also shared Bellow's love of English Romantic poetry (Wordsworth, Blake, Shelley's *Epipsychidion*). Metaphysics, however, was the real key to their friendship: "We bonded over Steiner and Barfield." Wieseltier remembers Bellow as "very respectful of Steiner, very interested in Steiner, in, what shall we call it, nonmaterialistic understanding. He was prepared to give the benefit of the doubt." Though Wieseltier himself had "a high tolerance" for such figures, he remembers asking Bellow, "What's a rough stringent Jew like [you] doing corresponding with Owen Barfield?" Bellow's answer, which made clear that *Saving the Appearances* "meant a lot to him," contained a remark that especially struck Wieseltier: "The truth, whatever it is, is strange." To Wieseltier, this remark, at once "anti-rational, but sort of reasonable to understand," became "a sort of principle about how he operated." Later in the same interview, Wieseltier described Bellow as "the most brilliant dupe I ever knew," drawn to "outlandish totalistic explanations . . . one doctrine after another, as long as it explained everything." Yet "the fiction *doesn't* fall for these types," never "makes the leap." Bellow may have "deeply resented rationalism," sought to "*épater* the rationalists," but he was too smart to oppose reason itself.

Wieseltier thinks his friendship with Bellow was helped by the fact that "I didn't want anything from him." At Columbia, he had been taught and befriended by Lionel Trilling and Meyer Schapiro. At Oxford, Isaiah Berlin "more or less adopted me" (he also studied with A. J. Ayer and Peter Strawson). "I was the luckiest student who ever lived."[57] At Harvard, though, Wieseltier was determined that there would be no more "sitting at the feet of great men." "Enough fathers. I was done with discipleship." Instead, he and Bellow "were true, raucous, spiritually bonded friends." The raucousness owed something to Yiddish. On his first visit to 1010 Memorial Drive, Wieseltier and Bellow watched the televised arrival of Pope Paul VI in Boston. As the Pope got off the plane, he bent down to kiss the tarmac. "*Habemas Pacem*" ("We have [come in] peace"), he declared. To which Bellow muttered, "*Habemas behaymes*," from the Yiddish *behayme*, meaning "dolt" (or, literally, "beast"). The only politics Wieseltier recalls discussing with Bellow concerned Israel (Wieseltier, "a mere graduate student," organized a letter of protest that Bellow and others signed against settlement activity on the West Bank). Like the Sternbergs and the Lelchuks, he remembers no talk of race or inner-city crime and corruption, issues Bellow would immediately return to in Chicago. Nor did Bellow talk much of legal problems, though that September he was threatened with jail over the failure to post bond. Only after the Bellows left Cambridge in the new year did Wieseltier get a full sense of Bellow's difficulties at home. In a letter of January 18, 1978, Bellow apologized for not responding earlier: "I thought I knew corrupt Chicago, the money world, the legal and accounting professions and all their psychological types and all the political parallels—I did, of course, but it was an intelligent person's closet knowledge and fate decided that I should get a finishing course, that I should feel all the fingers on my skin and have my internal organs well squeezed."[58]

SOMETIME TOWARD THE END of 1979, Bellow put aside the "Chicago Book" and "Far Out," the novel about 1950s Greenwich Village he was working on simultaneously (it is discussed in chapter 6 of *To Fame and Fortune*), to begin work on what would become *The Dean's December*. "I brought with me to California a bundle of work in progress," Bellow wrote to Bette Howland on January 31. "Instead of progressing I laid it aside, quickly sketched out the plan of a short book, altogether new, and proceeded quickly to write it. I've done more than half of it since Christmas and am subject to nightly vibrations that prevent me from sleeping. The usual flood of the nerves, breathless excitement and insomniac happiness." Three weeks later, in a letter of February 25 to Hyman Slate, he was complaining that he had "overworked myself, and consequently I don't sleep well. I go around like a Zombie." Bellow was writing from Pasadena, at Caltech, where Alexandra had been invited as a Sherman Fairchild Fellow in Mathematics. In January, the historian Daniel Kevles, executive officer for the humanities at Caltech, was asked to arrange something for Bellow to do. The chair of the Mathematics Department had been told that Alexandra's husband was "well-known in his field." Kevles arranged for Bellow to offer a series of seminars, after agreeing to certain Bellow provisos—namely, "no assignments, no agenda, just literary discussions for the Caltech community."[59] The seminars were held in the new Beckman Laboratories, right across from Baxter Hall, home of the Division of Humanities and Social Sciences at Caltech, where Bellow had an end office with a view of the San Gabriel Mountains. "The term 'seminar' suggests an intimate and informal discussion," Kevles's wife, Bettyann, writes in a recollection of Bellow's time at Caltech, "but these meetings were neither. Saul Bellow's fame then [the chair of the Mathematics Department notwithstanding] was akin to Richard Feynman's after the *Challenger* hearings, so it was not surprising that the auditorium was filled from the first meeting to the last." Bellow's subject was the early-twentieth-century novel, and at the end of each session he took questions. "The students who signed up for it," Bellow remembered, "were as mystified by Joseph Conrad as I was by jet propulsion."

> When we discussed *Typhoon* one of them said that he was bothered by the disorderly thinking of Captain MacWhirr. He began his analysis by assigning the Captain and his first mate to subset-a, the

crew to subset-b, and the Chinese passengers to subset-c. Then he went to the blackboard and began to write out an equation.

"I'm afraid you've lost me," I said.

Then all the boys and I stared at each other in shocked silence.[60]

Bettyann Kevles remembers a question period in which Bellow was asked, "Just how do you start writing every day?" He answered, "By explaining that first he checked his typewriter to see that all the letters of the alphabet were still there."[61]

Not all Bellow's interactions with the Caltech audience were like this. One listener in particular caught his attention, "a white haired, close-cropped man of about my own age" whose attendance record he recalled as "flatteringly perfect." Bellow thought the man might be a faculty member and wondered if he "might possibly explain how these clever boys, elite engineers and technocrats in training, viewed the paleo-technic freighter Nan Shan [from *Typhoon*], its old fashioned, literal-minded Captain, its engineer and all the Coolie passengers in the hold." The man's name was Clair Patterson, and he was, indeed, a faculty member, as Bellow had guessed, a professor of geology. In addition, Bellow learned, he was a graduate of the University of Chicago. As Bellow wrote many years later, in his foreword to *Clear Hands, Dirty Hands* (1999), a Festschrift for Patterson, "In the early thirties, the worst years of the great Depression, both of us had been Chicago undergraduates, on opposite sides of the quadrangle—the sciences and the humanities separated by lawns, trees and tennis courts." Over lunch at the Faculty Club, Bellow asked Patterson his question about what the Caltech students were likely to make of *Typhoon*. "Patterson's answer was that these brainy students had been brought up on Mickey Mouse and Superman and their picture of human life was inevitably a caricature." At later lunches and on walks, Bellow learned just why Patterson lamented this ignorance. He also learned a great deal about lead.

As Bellow writes in the foreword, Patterson struck him as being like William Jennings Bryan, "speaking for the Free Silver Democrats almost exactly a century ago." Whereas Bryan "cried out against the Cross of Gold. Pat Patterson's cross was made of lead." It was made of lead because Pattterson was convinced that lead was contaminating the whole planet:

> He told me that for several millennia now the lead levels of sea water and of the air had risen steeply. Patterson had measured lead residues in human and animal bones, in arctic ice strata and was able to prove, I was persuaded, that the brains of civilized man had suffered lead damage as well. Moving to conquer nature as the Enlightenment had told us we must, man had fatally damaged the earth, had poisoned its air and its waters. Already our brains were affected by the lead wastes we had ingested, our descendants would be even more seriously and progressively brain-damaged.

Patterson's theories and dire predictions recall Wieseltier's sense of Bellow as drawn to "outlandish totalizing explanations." For Bellow, what Patterson had to say resembled "prophetic revelation"; "as such, I could appreciate it for its comprehensiveness and its somehow poetic splendor."

Patterson was hardly alone as prophet of doom. As Bellow puts it, "Many great thinkers have held that we are sick creatures." He cites two examples: "Baudelaire wrote that modern man was like a hospital patient who believed that he would recover if only he were moved to another bed. Freud was convinced that the repression of our instinctual desires was the cause of our lifelong illnesses." For much of his life, Bellow opposed views like these, which he accused of creating the sickness they diagnosed, a sickness he thought of as spiritual. Patterson's diagnosis attracted him in part because it was neither Freudian nor modernist (that is, void-mongering, *Waste Land*–like), in part because it attributed sickness to science. The science Patterson attributed it to, though, was of a particular kind: not pure or classical science but the science of engineering technology. Pure scientists like himself, according to Bellow, writing to the Norsk Nobel-Komité, strive "for non-utilitarian knowledge, appreciate the value of human life and hold the worth of humanity in high regard."[62] Hence the crusade against lead, one aspect of which, affecting the inner city, was bound to attract Bellow, leading him to create the character of Sam Beech in *The Dean's December*. That Beech is meant to be recognized as Patterson is clear. His fame as a scientist, like Patterson's, derives initially from his use of radioactivity "to measure the age of the planet"; his campaign against lead promises to bring about the sort of crucial reform Patterson's campaign brought about in 1970, the year Congress passed the Clean Air Act, which not only called for the removal of lead from gasoline in the United States but encouraged comparable acts on an international scale. The Clean Air Act was largely Patterson's achievement, the product of a decade of lonely proselytizing. In a letter recommending Patterson to the Nobel Prize Committee, on January 20, 1981, Bellow praised him for his refusal "to accommodate or placate special interests, either within the scientific community or outside." In *The Dean's December*, when Corde contemplates taking on Beech's cause, he realizes it will mean challenging powerful industrial interests, the sort that "bring the university much financial support" (p. 221).

Given the issues that obsessed Bellow in the late 1970s, he was bound to be drawn to Patterson's claim that the poisonous effects of lead contamination were especially dangerous to children in urban settings. As Beech puts it, "Millions of tons of intractable lead residues [are] poisoning the children of the poor. . . . It's the growing children who assimilate the lead fastest. The calcium takes it up" (p. 137). Sam Beech has read Corde's *Harper's* articles about blacks "in public housing and the jails. . . . And when I read your description of the inner city, I said, 'Here's a man who will want the real explanation of what goes on in those slums. . . . The concentration is immeasurably heaviest in those old slum neighborhoods, piled up there for decades" (p. 137). Using almost exactly the words Bellow uses in his foreword to the Patterson Festschrift, Beech explains: "If you watch the behavior of those kids with a clinical eye, you see the classic symptoms of chronic lead poisoning. . . . It comes down to the nerves, to brain poisoning" (p. 137). The symptoms of such poisoning are "irritability, emotional instability, general restlessness, reduced acuity of the reasoning powers, the difficulty of focusing, et cetera" (p. 139).

In Bucharest, Corde wonders if, when he returns to Chicago, he should publicize Beech's views. Did he, to begin with, believe them? Beech might be a "crank," but he was "an eminent man of science. That was unanimous. He had authoritatively dated the age of the earth, had analyzed the rocks brought back from the moon" (p. 138). Patterson's standing at Caltech was similarly elevated. What first impressed Jane Dietrich, editor of the Caltech magazine, about Bellow was that he took up so quickly with Patterson, by no means the most famous but arguably the most interesting scientist at Caltech. In *The Dean's December*, Minna is keen for Corde to take up Beech's cause, "thinks it would *upgrade* me to associate with a man of science" (p. 223). But Corde has other worries aside from whether Beech is a crank. Of course the anti-lead campaign is worthy—Corde, too, wants "bad things to stop and good things to go forward"—but "I don't want to become an environmentalist. For me it would be a waste of time, and I haven't the time to waste" (p. 219). The prospect of having to read Beech's "stuff" makes Corde gag. "I'd rather eat a pound of dry starch with a demitasse spoon than read this. Truth should have some style" (p. 226). That Patterson sensed comparable reservations on Bellow's part is suggested in a letter of March 12, 1981. "What seems easy to you is difficult to me," Patterson wrote, of his efforts to publicize his findings. "I work to gain knowledge and, through a chain of circumstances involuntary but unfortunate for me, have learned vast and terrible things. This in itself is laborious, but it is even more difficult for me to turn to the role of an educator and explain what I have learned because there are no existing terms and concepts to use—they have to be forged." As for "what is, in turn, difficult for you"—Patterson means both the science of the cause and understanding the sort of person he is, for fictional purposes—"I *can help* you . . . without too much effort on my part."

As he describes himself, Patterson is like Beech, who "wants his case stated not only to the general public but also to the Humanists" (p. 136). Patterson knows Bellow "is writing some fiction about scientists, which includes my work." In the March 12 letter, he promises to send Bellow a tape "concerning emotional insights in to my past life that are of no value to me but perhaps may be useful to you." Corde listens to a comparable tape sent him by Beech. The incidents both men recount, to quote again from the March 12 letter, will "help to define for you the scientist personality," and thus to create the scientist Beech. Though he is pressed with deadlines for scientific papers and grant proposals, Patterson assures Bellow, "you loom large in my world." In the future, Patterson is certain, scientists will need to turn their attention from "discovering knowledge of the world we live in to discovering new knowledge concerning our place as humans in that world. . . . Our contact may prove either unproductive or ineffectual, nevertheless it is actually a part of the leading edge of an activity which will in time constitute a new era in the relationship among science, the humanities, and society." A striking feature of Patterson's letter, written more than thirty years ago, is the other great danger he singles out, one only now, in the second decade of the twenty-first century, coming into prominence. "I assure you with absolute certainty," the letter concludes, "that my scientist followers will, in the future, inexorably disclose which of *your* followers are hollow men—defeated by the android world of misguided engineering technology, and which are true artists—fighting for humans with every new advantage they can seize—always—even if we humans are eventually destroyed by the androids."

For all Patterson's scientific eminence, it was hard for Bellow to accept lead poisoning as the *fons et origo* of urban violence, squalor, and despair. As with Charlie Citrine's attraction to the theories of Steiner and Barfield, so with Albert Corde's attraction to Beech's theories. He can't bring himself to make the leap.

> "There would be no difficulty in agreeing that inner city black kids should be saved from poisoning by lead or heroin or synthetic narcotics like the Tees and Blues. The doubtful part of his [Beech's] proposition is that human wickedness is absolutely a public health problem, and nothing but. No tragic density, no thickening of the substance of the soul, only chemistry or physiology. I can't bring myself to go with this medical point of view, whether it applies to murderers or to geniuses. At one end of the scale is Spofford Mitchell. Did he rape and murder a woman because he put flakes of lead paint in his mouth when he was an infant? At the other end, are Beethoven and Nietzsche great because they had syphilis?"
>
> . . .
>
> "Where Beech sees poison lead I see poison thought or poison theory. The view we hold of the material world may put us into a case as heavy as lead. . . . The end of philosophy and of art will do to 'advanced' thought what flakes of lead paint or leaded exhaust fumes do to infants" [p. 227].

Bellow's time at Caltech introduced one other element into *The Dean's December*. Shortly before he and Alexandra were to leave Pasadena, Dan and Bettyann Kevles decided to give a dinner party for them. Bettyann Kevles in particular was grateful to Bellow, for reasons similar to those of Aviva Green at Cambridge. Bellow had offered her advice about a historical novel she was writing and had encouraged her. She was also keen to meet Alexandra. The other guests at the dinner were carefully picked. They were an astronomer named Marshall Cohen, and his wife, Shirley, who taught mathematics at a local public high school, and a philosophy professor named Will Jones, whose wife was a child psychologist at Pomona College. The evening was a great success, no one wanted to leave, and Cohen suggested that they all get together the following week for a visit to the Palomar Observatory. Cohen would make arrangements, ensuring access to the telescope and arranging a Caltech limo for the drive. The plan was to have a picnic supper on the way and arrive at Palomar just at dark. Unfortunately, the day was drizzly and overcast ("California is drowned sodden, tormented by mudslides," Bellow wrote on February 20 to his new colleague at the Committee on Social Thought, Allan Bloom; "the land of beautiful living, of exquisite lawn-cultivation and of saran-wrapped lotus flowers is suffering, quivering under the vertical indignities of nature. I rather like the place, though"). When the party arrived at Palomar, they were told that the dome would not be opened unless it stopped raining. So they sat down in an office in the observatory and ate their picnic, then explored the enormous space of the closed dome. Suddenly, as Bettyann Kevles describes it, "I heard a grinding noise and looked up to see the dome parting. As I stared, it opened with deliberate speed and the stars—seemingly closer than they would have appeared were I standing outside in the woods—glowed in the clear sky. We were all excited by our change of fortune and sought each other to share the moment." All, that is, except Bellow, who as soon as the dome began to open had gone directly to the gondola and was rising slowly above the rest of the party in the direction of the prime-focus cage at the top.

What Bettyann Kevles remembers of the ride back to Pasadena is that Bellow was silent, "struck mute by the experience, perhaps, or fixing the impression in his mind." At the end of *The Dean's December*, Corde and Minna journey to California, where Minna has booked time on the twenty-four-inch telescope at Palomar. Corde thinks Minna too frail to go up in the cage, after all she's been through in Romania and then in the hospital. But Minna insists. What strikes Corde about the observatory is how cold it is: "If you came to look at astral space it was appropriate that you should have a taste of the cold *out there*, its power to cancel everything merely human" (p. 310). The cold makes him recall how freezing the crematorium was at his mother-in-law's cremation, "the killing cold when you returned and thought your head was being split by an ax" (p. 311). Invited to go up in the cage with Minna, Corde sees a sky "tense with stars." This is not "the real heavens." Rather, it is "as much as could be taken in through the distortions of the atmosphere." What he thinks is that, in seeing, "you were drawn to feel and to penetrate further, as if you were being informed that what was spread over you had to do with your existence, down to the very blood and the crystal forms inside your bones. Rocks, trees, animals, men and women, these also drew you to penetrate further, under the distortions (comparable to the atmospheric ones, shadows within shadows), to find their real being with their own." Here, on the novel's penultimate page, Corde offers a poetical condensation of Barfield's *Saving the Appearances.* It is not enough. *The Dean's December* ends with a fragment of dialogue between Corde and the largely unintelligible young astronomer, a junior colleague of Minna's, with whom he has toured the dome.

> The young man pressed the switch for the descent. "Never saw the sky like this, did you?"
>
> "No. I was told how cold it would be. It *is* damn cold."
>
> "Does that really get you, do you really mind it all that much?"
>
> They were traveling slowly in the hooked path of their beam towards the big circle on the floor.
>
> "The cold? Yes. But I almost think I mind coming down more" [p. 312].

Because the worlds below are so terrible. In this ambivalence, Bellow resembles Keats in the sonnet "Bright Star," where the desire to be "stedfast as thou art," addressed to the star, is immediately qualified:

SB about to deliver the second Jefferson Lecture to an audience of cultural "notables" in the Gold Coast Room of the Drake Hotel in Chicago, April 1, 1977 (courtesy of The Chicago Maroon; *photo by Dan Wise)*

"Not in lone splendour hung aloft the night," but "Pillow'd upon my fair love's ripening breast, / To feel for ever its soft fall and swell." The immortality Keats seeks is human (living, breathing, warm), an impossibility given the dependence of human beauty and pleasure on time and mortality (the true love's breast is "ripening," as in the "Ode on Melancholy," where melancholy "dwells with Beauty—Beauty that must die," or with "Joy, whose hand is ever at his lips / Bidding adieu"). Wordsworth, too, registers this impossibility. In the "Lucy" poem "A Slumber Did My Spirit Seal," the beloved is imagined "Rolled round in earth's diurnal course, / With rocks, and stones, and trees" (echoed in Corde's "rocks, trees, animals, men and women"). Like Keats and Wordsworth, Bellow will not pretend. To embrace the cold of the stars, to seek oneness with "rocks, and stones, and trees," is impossible, for all the horrors of the human realm, including those of the inner city.

7

Nadir

ESCAPE WAS ON Bellow's mind when he finished *The Dean's December*. Exhausted and apprehensive about the novel's reception, he accepted an invitation from the English Department at the University of Victoria in British Columbia to spend the winter term as a visiting professor, from January to March 1982. The invitation was issued by the chair of the English Department at the time, Michael Best, a Shakespearean, but the impetus for it came from two other figures in the department: Lionel Adey, an authority on C. S. Lewis, who was to write a monograph on what he called the "Great War" between Lewis and Owen Barfield, and Patrick Grant, a specialist, like Adey, on the relations between religion and literature.[1] Both Adey and Grant had corresponded with Barfield and knew of Bellow's interest in his writings and in anthroposophy more generally. This interest was still very much alive in 1982. In Victoria, Bellow agreed to write, and may well have written, a foreword to a new translation of eight lectures Rudolf Steiner gave in 1920 entitled *The Boundaries of Natural Science* (1983). After describing the lectures, he ends the foreword by quoting Barfield approvingly, calling him "one of the best interpreters of Steiner."[2] Winter term in Canada promised not only a vacation from the horrors of Chicago and American materialism, but spiritual allies.

The city of Victoria is small and attractive. Although it is the capital of British Columbia, its population in 1982 was less than seventy thousand. In "Him with His Foot in His Mouth," the story Bellow wrote, or began writing, in Victoria, the narrator, Herschel Shawmut, flees the United States for Canada (the city of Vancouver, to be precise, seventy-one miles from Victoria). Shawmut has money and legal problems (Bellow had similar difficulties, in addition to his divorce from Susan, and at one point was advised by his lawyer, as was Shawmut, to flee the United States for Canada[3]). As he lies in bed, Herschel realizes "there isn't a soul in British Columbia I can discuss this with. My only acquaintance is Mrs. Gracewell . . . who studies occult literature, and I can't bother her with so different a branch of experience. Our conversations are entirely theoretical" (p. 382).

What Bellow wanted in Victoria, for a while at least, was to disappear. On September 26, 1981, some months before publication of *The Dean's December*, he wrote to his friend Julian Behrstock to say that he and Alexandra would be in Canada "hiding from the anticipated publication storm." On November 18, 1981, he described his reasons for going to Victoria to Bette Howland as "partly to get out of Chicago, partly to escape the *Sturm und Drang* of publication. . . . Once I reach Victoria I'm not likely to communicate with anybody." Philip Roth understood this decision. On December 5, after reading *The Dean's December*, he wrote to Bellow describing the novel as "terrific" but also issuing a warning: "You look the worst right in the face and will take much shit as a result."[4] Some weeks later, in a reply to Roth written on the last day of the year, Bellow described himself as "clearing out for the winter to British Columbia which I look forward to as a sanitarium."

> I've warned them in the English Department there that if they run me too hard I may have a breakdown. I'm not pretending, I'm ready for a padded cell. *The Dean* took it out of me. I can't even describe it.
>
> I discovered some time ago that there was nothing to stop me from saying exactly what I thought. I expected flak, and unpleasant results are beginning to come in but I'm getting support too, which I hadn't looked for.

The English Department took Bellow at his word. As Lansdowne Visiting Professor, he had only a couple of public lectures and readings to deliver, in addition to meeting informally with students and faculty.[5] With no scheduled classes, he held office hours on Tuesday afternoons (in an office bare of books, he noted indignantly, apart from a short row of first-year textbooks on English composition).[6] At Caltech, Alexandra had been the celebrity, with Bellow's light duties arranged at the behest of the Math Department; at UVic (as it is known locally), the

English Department arranged with the Math Department for Alexandra to have a visiting professorship as well. The house the English Department rented for the Bellows in Victoria was at the edge of town, near a nature preserve and a small lake (Swan Lake). Bellow thought the house "dinky," like Herschel Shawmut's "little box of a house, which is scarcely insulated" (p. 381). He also found the house "full of kitsch."[7] British Columbia was mild in January. "Because of the Japanese current," Shawmut's lawyer tells him about Vancouver, "flowers grow in midwinter, and the air is purer." Shawmut observes that "there are indeed primroses out in the snow" (pp. 378–79). "It is very beautiful here," he later adds, "with snow mountains and still harbors." Watching the freighters at anchor "is pleasant. They suggest the 'Invitation au Voyage,' and also 'Anywhere, anywhere, Out of the world!' [poems of escape by Baudelaire]. But what a clean and civilized city this is, with its clear northern waters and, beyond, the sense of an unlimited wilderness beginning where the forests bristle, spreading northwards for millions of square miles and ending in ice whorls around the Pole" (p. 384). On February 4, 1982, in a letter to William Kennedy, Bellow described his first reactions to British Columbia in similar terms. " 'The Dean' " was written over "eighteen months of high excitement, a long spree for a codger." By fleeing to Victoria, not only had he and Alexandra escaped "the ensuing noise of battle . . . We got away from a disastrous winter, too. Here it rains and rains, but the green moss is delicious to see and there are snowdrops out already. The nervous system was not attuned to this sanctuary. For the first month I suffered acutely from what I called boredom: it *was* boredom but with a wash of deep fatigue, black-and-blue spread over the gray." When asked what he wished to do in Victoria, Bellow answered, "Take silent nature walks" (this to the loquacious Barnett "Barney" Singer, his fan, a historian at UVic); the stay in Victoria, he told Singer, was "my *kuhr ort*" (rest cure).[8]

It was a rest cure with outings and parties. The Bellows were much entertained in Victoria, as always on academic visits. The Adeys invited them to tea and dinner; Lionel Adey took them on "long, picturesque nature walks."[9] The poet Charles ("Mike") Doyle remembers inviting Bellow to accompany him and his eldest son "on a hike or walk, ninety minutes or so through light woods around a lagoon." Doyle "felt responsible for the conversation," which he did not find easy. When at one point he mentioned that the English Department's next Lansdowne Professor would be Hugh Kenner, "this was met with silence.

Some time later, however, Bellow stopped us on the woodland pathway, and confronted me. . . . 'Did you do that on purpose?' he asked, looking indignant. 'What?' I said, perplexed. 'Mention Kenner,' he said. 'No. He just happens to be our next visitor,' or some such. 'Have you read Harper's?' " Doyle had not read the issue of *Harper's* to which Bellow referred, missing Kenner's harsh review of *The Dean's December*. "Bellow needed convincing that my Kenner reference was by chance. We completed the walk affably enough."[10]

Doyle had been recommended to Bellow by the poet and artist P. K. Page, "a charming sociable person, who welcomed all visiting writers/artists."[11] On at least one occasion, however, Page and Bellow, according to one witness, "nearly came to blows" ("she took issue with me" is how Bellow put it). The argument was over Canadian culture, which Bellow claimed was borrowed from the United States. It was popular or low culture he had in mind. As Singer puts it, "The way Canucks believe they are cleaner than Americans, more upright, less sullied—the way they *condescend* to watch American films, switch on American TV, eat American foods, etc. 'They don't like hearing these things,' Bellow continued."[12]

In Herschel Shawmut's case, what the Canadians don't like hearing about is politics. "When I arrived, I was invited to a party by local musicians [Shawmut is a musicologist], and I failed to please. They gave me their Canadian test for U.S. visitors: Was I a Reaganite? I couldn't be that, but the key question was whether El Salvador might not be another Vietnam, and I lost half the company at once by my reply: 'Nothing of the kind. The North Vietnamese are seasoned soldiers with a military tradition of many centuries—*really* tough people. Salvadorans are Indian peasants.' . . . Two or three sympathetic guests remained, and these I drove away as follows: A professor from UBC observed that he agreed with Alexander Pope about the ultimate unreality of evil. Seen from the highest point of metaphysics. To a rational mind, nothing really bad ever happens. He was talking high-minded balls. Twaddle! I thought. I said, 'Oh? Do you mean that every gas chamber has a silver lining?' " (p. 384). This is the exact line Bellow uttered at a dinner in Victoria, after Singer had told him of an old friend who often said, "Nothing bad ever happens." "He went right home that night or the next morning and put it into the short story he produced from his Victoria stay, attributing the line 'nothing bad ever happens' to a fictional Vancouver professor."[13] Alexandra also remembers an awkward moment at a dinner party given by Connie and Leon Rooke, "a glamorous literary couple in the English Department" (both writers—he a novelist, she the author of short stories and also fiction editor of *The Malahat Review*). Over dinner, Bellow raised the question of Poland and Solidarity; Łech Wałęsa and Marek Edelman had disappeared without trace. After "lashing out" against Pierre Trudeau, who had recently criticized Solidarity in the newspapers, he was greeted by an awkward silence. According to Alexandra, the source of the anecdote, "This was a Trudeau stronghold and we had not realized it."[14]

For the most part, however, Bellow was in good humor, nonconfrontational, during his stay in Victoria, uncomplainingly attending dinners and parties given by Alexandra's Math Department colleagues, including one who lectured him at length on "the subtleties of the English language." The chair of the department cheerfully announced on another occasion that he'd not read a single one of Bellow's novels and that he never read fiction. He was, however, a good cook, and served Oysters Toscanini. "Naturally," as Alexandra puts it, Bellow found a pearl in his oyster.[15]

During the visit, Bellow's irony, as recalled by Barnett Singer and others, was mostly benign. When cautioned to watch out for the traffic in town ("They whiz along at fifty. You can get killed"), he smilingly replied, "I better *not* get killed. I only came for a rest." At the end of the stay, when asked by a professor in the UVic English Department how he could go back to Chicago after having enjoyed the beauty of Vancouver Island, he "replied quietly that he wasn't yet ready for utopia." To Singer, the most ardent of his admirers, Bellow seemed nearest "not to Henderson, as some critics maintain, or to Herzog (except perhaps when he's around women), or to natty Citrine, but to old Mr. Sammler, 'distant from life.' I realize that his performances [the stories and novels] bring out the blood and the guts, maybe the truest spirit; but this daily Bellow beside me is a bit thin-blooded. Academe and the monasticism of the writer's life, a certain New England model, must have taken away some of the original bite." Elsewhere, Singer describes Bellow's face "in its usual neutral. He has the artist's essential aloofness at almost all moments of outward life. Inwardly it's another story—oh, another. With him what you get is emphatically what you *don't* get." When Singer apologized "for not knowing exactly how to be around him," Bellow, who had been critical of Singer's self-deprecation, "apologized for having reproved me too much."[16] "Him with His Foot in His

Mouth" ends with Mrs. Gracewell, who talks to Shawmut of the withdrawal of the Divine Spirit from the visible world. Shawmut listens to this talk with "no mischievous impulses." After what he calls "much monkey business," he is ready "to listen to words of ultimate seriousness" (p. 413). In Victoria, Bellow seems to have been comparably unmischievous—under the influence, perhaps, of Shawmut's example.

In the end, Victoria provided the Bellows with the escape they sought. Alexandra regretted they hadn't done more sightseeing and told Singer she hoped "to return some spring" for a proper visit. In addition to wanting, as Bellow put it, to "lay low," they'd had visitors.[17] Alexandra's seventy-six-year-old aunt, Ana Paunescu, the model for Aunt Gigi in *The Dean's December*, came for a week in January. Bellow had been instrumental in getting Ana a passport to leave Romania and reunite with her daughter in Los Angeles.[18] In Victoria, Ana had many stories to tell of her last months in Bucharest. According to Alexandra, Bellow "was quite fond of her, endearingly calling her *jeune fille roumaine* and encouraging her on the verge of her new chapter in life, the American chapter." In February, there was a second visit, from Bellow's son Greg and his family, again for a week. Greg, his wife, JoAnn, with their eight-year-old daughter, Juliet, and the infant Andy, stayed in the house while Bellow and Alexandra moved into a hotel nearby, "a decision that everybody was happy with." Alexandra remembers the week as a success, with "plenty of fun family activities, very little work." She recalls only a single unsunny moment. After Greg and Bellow managed to find time to be alone, "both looked preoccupied" when they returned. Alexandra never found out why. What she mostly remembers is "love, genuine love, between Saul and Greg."[19]

BARNETT SINGER, whose memoir, "Looking for Mr. Bellow," is the source of many of these anecdotes about the Victoria stay, is among the most perceptive of Bellow obsessives (or ex-obsessives, he would now claim), a type that often interested Bellow. In 1970, when Singer was twenty-four, *Seize the Day* set his obsession in motion, revealing "emotions that were in me and that had never been properly articulated." Singer grew up "in Toronto (the Good) . . . in the cocoon of a bourgeois family." The appeal of Bellow's writing partly derived from "my condition as a Canadian, trying to become more flamboyantly American and elude the decorousness of my home." It was *Herzog*, however, that hooked Singer. "I devoured my new find—reading *Herzog* once, twice, four times, ten times. . . . *Herzog* entirely took me over." The novel altered many aspects of Singer's life, including his attitude to his career. "I was seduced by the way Bellow dropped his feet into the intellectual pool but refused to take the full bath—refused to become *only* abstract and give in to shorthand views of life. . . . After getting a Ph.D., I myself would be both intellectual and wary of being intellectual. I henceforth played a tightrope game in academe."[20] Refusing to confine himself solely to scholarship (studies of French colonial proconsuls and military figures), Singer wrote a well-regarded biography of Brigitte Bardot and dozens of local newspaper columns, and appeared frequently on local radio.

He also began writing unsent letters to Bellow, in the manner of Moses Herzog. It was not until the autumn of 1972 that he finally mailed one of these letters, "noting my admiration for Bellow's work and how it followed similar passions I'd had for the historian D. W. Brogan, the sportswriter Arthur Daley, the philosopher Pascal."[21] Three weeks later, Bellow replied, briefly, in what Singer aptly describes as "unornate deft handwriting." After apologizing for his delay in responding, Bellow revealed that "he only acknowledged good letters, and that mine was very good."[22] Though the letter closed "with a formula that invited no further intimacy," its effect on Singer was "magical":

> For I now began a totally one-sided correspondence with the master, at first mailing one out of every ten or twenty letters I wrote. The ones I did send were sometimes prefaced with an apology—"Excuse previous crappy letter, sir"—and in most of the letters I put myself down plenty. What counted was that the epistolary mode allowed me to say what I wanted in the way I wanted, and to someone I felt sure would understand. . . . It began to consume my existence. . . . At first I was super-imitative of Bellow himself; only gradually did I rely more on my own idiom. Eventually I became wilder, bolder, I started mailing most of what I wrote. I used swear words, I used weird paragraphing techniques, I went farther and farther with free associations, and yet I also made the letters compact, gave myself limits.[23]

Every six months or so, Bellow would reply, usually on a card or in a short note, though each reply contained "a bit of verbal gold."

Singer describes himself smiling "compulsively" as he read Bellow's letters, "my lips softened, and my heart opened, and I went back to the masterpieces—to the Herzog, to the Sammler." Bellow became for him, as he became for other young male admirers, "a kind of invisible father-figure; but I was also having plain fun."[24] The charged nature of Bellow's prose, Singer believes, attracts "an awful lot of nuts, a lot of quivering schmucks. . . . But I think I took the cake." "With me the Bellow thing was an absurd passion, a compulsion to connect and to repeat. Eventually I must have read *Herzog* a thousand times [by 1982 "maybe closer to 2,000"], to the point where I could recite great chunks with pretty accurate fidelity. . . . At least I wasn't picking through garbage." There was also, he admits, "an element of self-hate" in the compulsion.[25]

In the spring of 1975, before stopping in Chicago on his way to a meeting of historians, Singer gathered the courage to ask Bellow if they could meet. At this date, Singer estimates, he had sent Bellow something like three hundred letters. The reply he received from Bellow's secretary, as he remembers it, was that "Mr. Bellow would be 'delighted' to meet one of his 'principal correspondents.'" In "Looking for Mr. Bellow," Singer conflates the 1975 visit with two subsequent ones. Like Mark Harris, another obsessive, in *Saul Bellow: Drumlin Woodchuck*, Singer is open about his flaws and weaknesses, at one point paraphrasing a letter Bellow had written to him from Spain: "No wonder you like Herzog—you resemble him, being always *after* yourself, a kind of self-persecution. Objectively that's funny. Sub., not." It is also irritating, judging by the acid nature of some of the responses Singer recalls provoking, and by the lack of response (Harris, too, records Bellow's discomfiting silences). Before the first meeting, Singer describes himself as "brimming with fears." Sitting in Bellow's office, awaiting his arrival, he could barely credit the mundanity of the scene, but, then, "I refused to believe that he ate or smelled or paid his parking tickets or opened his bank account." When invited to Bellow's apartment on a later visit, Singer was bowled over: "*This* is an author's apartment floor; this is his Windex, these are his *Atlantics* and *Commentarys*, his pre-Columbian artefacts, his bar selection, his book shelves, his view of Chicago, his alarm system. My overvaluing intensity bordered on insanity."[26]

Singer is good on Bellow's appearance and manner. Not just the neat suit and silk vest, but the "wide smile" he gives his secretary. Bellow speaks "without pedantry," "frugally," "normally and humbly," with "the slight lisp of a fine-grained intellectual."[27] "I was flabbergasted by how natural he was; there was not a hint of inflation in what he said," a trait Alfred Kazin noted when meeting Bellow for the first time, when both were in their twenties. Singer asks if he's boring Bellow and Bellow replies no, "with a charming hint of irony in his large eyes. Think of the look in Tony Randall's eyes and you will have it." This look leads Singer to describe Bellow (a description anyone who knows Bellow's papers will confirm) "as having eternally to say 'no' to people; a man of real social instincts and sympathy forcing himself because of his art to keep aloof." When Bellow finds Singer irritating, he says so without embarrassment. Singer complains of the conventions of scholarship, and Bellow replies, "almost negligibly," that "stock brokers must remember their hog belly prices." Was there much crime by the lake? Singer asks. "Enough to keep me away," Bellow answers. When Singer refers to the "big-wigs" of the English Department, Bellow registers "a definite message of irony; I knew exactly what he thought of mediocre professors. Worse than mediocre ball players or plumbers, or even racketeers." At one point during Bellow's stay in Victoria, Singer complained of feeling "restricted" by how much time he had to spend with his girlfriend. Bellow claimed to have been faithful to Alexandra during their marriage. "Why does it restrict you?" he asked. "Well she's jealous." "What do you want to do," Bellow snapped, "fuck every woman in Victoria?"[28]

Bellow's refusal to let Singer know that he was coming to Canada or to get in touch may have derived from an increasing unease with Singer's letters, the source also, perhaps, of the vehemence of his response to Singer's complaints about his girlfriend. Singer himself describes his letters of this period as "entirely out of control—too personal, too sexual."[29] On February 12, 1979, in a letter quoted in part in chapter 5, Bellow sent him what he took as a "warning."

> Dear Barney,
>
> Stone walls may not a prison make but I have enough manuscripts here for a lockup. Today I was presented with three, yours and two other of the same dimensions. All required reading *sous peine d'amende* [under threat of punishment]. When am I supposed to cook curry, wash the dog or examine my toes? I do expect to be in Chicago on the 25th of March and if I have not

> disappeared under hundreds of reams of paper I'll be glad to talk. In moderation. I don't grudge you the time but I don't want to be discomfited by your hurricane breeziness. You probably don't know what I'm talking about but I will give you a clue: my father, an old European, was incensed when one of my brothers complained to him (my father was then in his seventies) that he had never been a pal to his sons. My father justifiably exploded. "Pal! Had he gone mad? Has he no respect for his father?" I was taught to be deferential to seniors. If historians can't understand that, who can?
>
> Yours in candor,

"Finally he'd blown the whistle," Singer comments, "as I guess I'd always wanted him to do."[30] Yet his unwelcome breeziness persisted, as in a letter of April 5, 1980, which begins with "advice" to Bellow (to put in more "very open" passages in his writing, like those found in *Sammler*), then reports on his sex life ("all of a sudden, broad-wise, it doesn't rain but it pours"). The "warning" letter of February 5, 1979, was, unsurprisingly, the last Singer heard from Bellow before the Victoria visit.

AT THE END OF Bellow's first week in Victoria, Singer decided to seek him out. He found him in the UVic Library, where he had been spotted by Singer's girlfriend, who worked there. "Surprised, he looked up quizzically from beneath his glasses, as placid as Lawrence's snake at the trough. 'Hello, Barney.' " With his finger still on the open page, Bellow apologized for not getting in touch. "Said he'd been tired and he'd been laying low." When introduced to Singer's girlfriend, Bellow gave her "a soft glowing courteous smile. Though he was always tamping it down, his excessive humanity could easily flare up, especially around females." Singer was struck again by "how very anchored and committed" Bellow was, "something I'd known from the books, but around him you really feel it. It's the same impulse that in one story makes him celebrate the first moment of opening a container of coffee—'only a moment, but not to be missed.' I mean he's right *here*. Everything counts and can end up potentially processed as art."[31]

Observations like these help to explain why Bellow never fully broke with Singer, also why he encouraged him to write.[32] In Victoria, however, his reservations were clear. "His cool glance seemed to say: I went through that Herzog stage once. Now I want peace. I don't need to be around messy characters anymore." Singer, though, couldn't stop confessing his problems and obsessions, "the very worst thing I could bring him, the absolute evidence of being a child in search of a better parent."[33] "I enjoyed your shy yet not so shy visit," Bellow wrote to Singer in a letter of June 6, 1978, after their second meeting in Chicago. The letter ends: "No I don't need the thirty bucks, but you need to send it to me. You put me *in loco parentis.* I've already got my Oedipal work cut out for me with my own children and am not in a position to offer you the same relationship." Singer's "breeziness," what he himself calls his "passive-aggressive manner," also figured in Bellow's wariness.[34] In "Looking for Mr. Bellow," Singer recalls driving Bellow to the center of town. Bellow has difficulty digging out his seat belt. "Wouldn't want the great author flying through the windshield," Singer writes.[35]

As Singer himself realizes, he is a type. "I knew that Bellow had attracted, by his seeming stability and understanding, by his softness and talent, a slew of terminal literary neurotics, headed, I suppose, by the poets Delmore Schwartz, John Berryman, and Anne Sexton." In addition, Bellow has had "half a lifetime of dealing with amateurs and sycophants and self-servers, trying to get close. As soon as these artist-nudgers came too near he'd obviously arch the old pincers, mostly in a civilized way, to be sure; but mostly he wanted to protect himself."[36] Singer likens his relation to Bellow to Richard Aldington's relation to D. H. Lawrence. In Aldington's words, Lawrence "needed cool handling and not too close an intimacy. Unluckily it was nearly always over-sensitive and emotional persons like himself who were most drawn to him, whom he was as bound to hurt as they hurt him." That Bellow "has hurt me or I him" Singer denies, even as he evokes "all those needy hearts in Chicago [who] must sometimes feel his cool wrath at being invaded." But Singer suffers humiliations in the great man's presence, as when, after dinner, "clumsily, I took Alexandra's small hand and kissed it; she did not seem pleased by the gesture," or when he describes himself, after Bellow complains that he's "always switching," as being "either too uptight or too saucy" when with him, failing to "be myself."[37] At the end of the visit, at a pleasant farewell dinner with the Bellows, Singer continued to feel ill-at-ease. The dinner was held at a restaurant owned by Singer's friend Howie Siegel, a local celebrity. Bellow found Siegel amusing and was in good spirits at the dinner.

Why, then, couldn't Singer show "what I really feel about this delicious couple. . . . I mean they are so goddamn *nice*—so informed, so polite, so witty, so receptive, so handsome! Suddenly I realize how lonely I'll be when they're gone."[38] When "Looking for Mr. Bellow" was published, Singer wrote to Bellow to apologize. Bellow replied on January 17, 1983: "Dear Barney, Why should I be mad at you? I've got my hands full with the major lunatics."

HE WAS NOT EXAGGERATING. For all his neuroses, Singer belongs on the saner end of a line of unstable correspondents whose letters Bellow felt worth reading and keeping (in files labeled "Abuse," "Problem Mail," "Nuts"). At this time, Bellow grouped Singer with clever, vituperative Dean Borok, Maury's illegitimate son. "Send this back, please, in silence," Bellow instructs his secretary, after receiving a hostile letter from a poet whose poems he was late in returning. "Signs of hysteria here, and I already have Singer and Borok."[39] Borok was in high spirits at the time *The Dean's December* was published, declaring in a letter of January 1, 1982: "The world is gonna have to brace itself for a new generation of Bellows. When it sinks in that you named your new book after me, nobody's ever going to oppress me again, which is what I wanted all along. THE DEAN'S DECEMBER. That's outasite. . . . Now I can build myself a pedestal and climb up on it, and everybody will have to accept it because I am the artist nephew of a Nobel Prize–winning author who named his latest hit after me. I feel better already. I'll never write you another rude letter (you shouldn't hold those letters against me. I mean, really, who else was I going to complain to? I take it all back). . . . Nobody's going to doubt that you are my uncle, and that you care about me. That's all I wanted. Love, Dean." The rude letters soon resumed.

Borok was unbalanced and Singer was obsessive. Others of Bellow's obsessive correspondents were certifiable. One young man warns him of the dangers of computers, which give you headaches and make you vomit blood. He asks Bellow to introduce him to Norman Mailer, whose diet he wishes to study. Another writes that he has been "robotized by brain radio manipulators . . . causing me to urinate and defecate in my clothing and to suffer a robotized flow of sperm while I was sleeping." In 1976, a delusional twenty-six-year-old student contacted Bellow about applying to the Committee on Social Thought. He continued to write to Bellow for a decade, voluminously, in French and Italian as well as English. He also sent Bellow manuscripts of novels and stories, among them "A Jewboy Answers" and "Loving Your Country, a Novel in Five Segments, Less Two Unknown," a work of some 344 single-spaced pages. In one letter, the student expresses a willingness to be circumcised in order to marry Bellow's daughter Junie (the name of Moses Herzog's daughter). In another, he confesses: "Oh Mr. Bellow I'm so confused. I thought I was dead last night, and most of the day yesterday." When Bellow's secretary tells him that Bellow is finding it impossible to keep up with his correspondence, the student writes that he understands, because he, too, has been under great stress. Another secretary writes to Bellow to inform him that the student has phoned and left a message: "Some of his letters to Mr. Bellow are not to his own satisfaction, and he apologizes for any inconvenience caused to you Lillian or to Mr. Bellow or to his daughters. He hopes that Mr. Bellow is receiving the mail that he is sending because he is making commitments that rely on his requests to Mr. Bellow. If [the student] has not heard to the contrary within two weeks, he will take that to mean that Mr. Bellow has agreed to assume the requested obligation." At one point, a few months after this message, the university legal counsel, Raymond Kuby, wrote to the student to warn him not to use Bellow's name on his letterhead. The student's letters to Bellow sometimes end with the salutation "Votre fils à l'esprit."[40]

One of the earliest and most promising of Bellow's obsessive correspondents, eccentric rather than unstable or deranged, closer to Barnett Singer than to the "major lunatics," was Louis Gallo, a proofreader who lived with his mother in Queens, and who submitted a story which Bellow and Botsford published in the fourth issue of *The Noble Savage*. The story was titled "Oedipus-Schmoedipus" and was about a proofreader who lived in Queens with his mother. Gallo could hardly believe it when he received a letter of January 15, 1961, which began, "Dear Louis Gallo—You have a friend and admirer—Saul Bellow. 'Oedipus Schmoedipus' will appear in *The Noble Savage* #4, unless I perish in the plane [to Puerto Rico]." Gallo replied on January 30, and again on February 12, before receiving a second letter from Bellow, written on February 15: "Your letter was a little sassy but it was amusing, too, and on the whole I thought you meant well but were being awkward, and what's the good of being a writer if you must cry every time someone makes a face." Gallo's "sassiness" included criticisms of *The Adventures of Augie*

March, the only Bellow novel he had so far read ("your hero wasn't someone I could take seriously"), criticisms Bellow described as "pretty sound," admitting that in writing *Augie* "I became so wildly excited I couldn't control the book and my hero became too disingenuous."

The "sassiness" Bellow identifies in Gallo's letter is like Barnett Singer's "breeziness." Bellow's initial letter was followed by eleven long letters from Gallo, from the end of January 1961 to the end of June. In these he presents himself as alienated and unhappy, much preoccupied with the way writing cuts the writer off from life. Of his time as a student at Columbia, he writes on February 17: "It never really 'took.' The education didn't; the City didn't." He has had four pieces published in magazines and is at work on "something that may not (probably won't) be published until after we're both dead (a journal)." He has an older brother who sounds like Bellow's brother Maury, "a powerhouse of a personality." The letters refer often to friends, several of whom read his work and to whom he has read Bellow's letters. These friends aren't writers and are sometimes rude not only about his writing but about Bellow's letters. Bellow chides Gallo for his *Waste Land* views: "I—we—can't believe, ugly as things have become, and complicated, that human life is nothing but the misery we are continually shown." But Gallo is unconvinced, describing himself in a letter of February 15 as "not just miserable, I'm living in torture. . . . I've gone further, I think, than you. . . . I stopped affirming altogether: myself, life, the universe, everything," a comment he asks Bellow to take "in the correct spirit of comedy." This spirit Bellow acknowledges in a letter of April 4, praising Gallo's "knotty and bitter sense of comedy," which, "far more than *position* [about life's "meaninglessness," for example], is what gets me."

Like Singer, Gallo skates close to the edge. He begins reading other Bellow novels, partly at Bellow's suggestion, and tells him what's wrong with them. In the first half of *Seize the Day*, "I was against you . . . and I had reasons, I could enumerate them, good reasons, concerning method, how you were going about doing your job, how you could do it better."[41] Only the first hundred pages of *Henderson the Rain King* work. "The primary disappointment for me is that my attention is on you, on the writer, sitting at his desk." Although drawn to writing, Gallo sees writing as psychosis. In a letter of April 7, he claims "our particular psychoses attract each other." Writers hide their real selves. How can Bellow claim to be Gallo's "friend," as he does in the original acceptance letter, on the basis of a single story? Gallo approves of the way his nonwriting friends put down his writing "without a second thought," interacting with him as persons, "who *they* are separated from their social roles (*their* psychoses)." When Bellow, in a letter of April 4, claims he shares Gallo's feelings, in that "I've never known what it was to live an accepted life," Gallo and his friends find his claim ludicrous. "There you are," Gallo explains, "a professor, a magazine editor, twice married, a father, published in *The New Yorker*, *Partisan Review*, and *Esquire*—who are *you* kidding."[42] When the friends advise Gallo not to write this to Bellow, he does so anyway, then the next day regrets having done so. "They were right. That letter (also this) is madness." Bellow takes no offense, but begins to withdraw. "I have a taste for bluntness, just like yourself," he admits in a letter of May 9, "but I don't want to write you the story of my life. I haven't the time even if I had the inclination. I'm writing a book [*Herzog*]." The letter closes with reiterated praise of "Oedipus-Schmoedipus," which he calls "the stripped model, every superfluity carefully removed and nothing but the essences allowed to stay." At the end of the last letter he writes to Gallo in 1961, Bellow repeats this praise, after commenting briefly on Gallo's reflections on "the hatred of art among great writers" (Tolstoy, Rimbaud), a topic that "interests me enormously." "Now and then," he says, your writing "hits the mark with a real clang. You're erratic but you have a true aim."[43]

The correspondence stops at the end of June 1961. What seems to have halted it was Gallo's habit of showing Bellow's letters to friends and relaying their comments. One of these friends, "Fred," made a remark that was anti-Semitic, or so Gallo suggests in a letter he wrote to Bellow early in 1966, after he sought to revive the correspondence. "I've assiduously so far avoided discussing the main issue, Fred. He's the villain. Because of him you told me—four and a half years ago—to drop dead."[44] Gallo deplores Fred's remark while admitting that he and Fred have been friends for many years ("it's complex . . . he demands love"). Gallo's reason for getting back in touch with Bellow now is that he has decided to publish their 1961 correspondence, together with "Oedipus-Schmoedipus," under the title *The Bellow-Gallo Letters.* A printer has been engaged, and the book is in production. On January 24, 1966, in a letter now lost but quoted by Gallo in a letter of February 9, Bellow accused him of behaving dishonestly by not telling him of his plans or gaining his permission to publish in an earlier letter. Gallo had admitted he'd been dishonest, but called his dishonesty "an incidental element, unintentional, deeply regretted. . . . I won't plead innocent, but I do feel the crime I've committed is capable of an interpretation that would show it to be less wicked than at first view it may have seemed."[45] If Bellow insists, and gets back to him in time, he will remove his side of the correspondence. Bellow never replied, nor did he answer two subsequent letters from Gallo, full of apology and self-recrimination. In the end, Gallo published only his side of the correspondence, which appeared in 1966 under the title *Like You're Nobody: The Letters of Louis Gallo to Saul Bellow, 1961–1962, plus "Oedipus-Schmoedipus," the Story That Started It All.*[46] Like Singer's letters, Gallo's letters combine insecurity with aggression. Only in the clear bold hand of the originals, littered with spidery arrows, interjected phrases, circled words, blocks of text wholly inked out (visual equivalents of habitual self-checking), is their author's true eccentricity revealed.

IN THE EARLY 1980S, Bellow's relations with his real sons, as opposed to sons "à l'esprit," were also tricky. Daniel was then at Wesleyan University, in Connecticut, and smoking a lot of pot and taking LSD. He'd been reading Allen Ginsberg (praised by Herschel Shawmut in "Him with His Foot in His Mouth"[47]) and Jack Kerouac and believed that LSD "brought me face to face with the facts of my existence." As for pot, "I *loved* smoking pot." Daniel credits his father with trying to give him space: "He really did his best to conceal his expectations and his hopes for me, because he didn't want to influence me unduly. He wanted to be fair, and it was confusing." It was confusing not just because Daniel could see through these efforts but because he knew of his father's own early years. "My old man was like the ultimate rebel. Wrote his own ticket through life. Never gave a *shit* what anybody thought and was so monumentally focused on his project." How was Daniel to rebel, "to defy *my* parent"? "How do you rebel against somebody who is in a way the symbol of personal freedom? What was going to impress him?" All Daniel could come up with was "nihilism, drug use, refusal, a refusal to get my act together until well into my twenties." Shortly after arriving in Pasadena in January 1980, Bellow wrote to Daniel, who was almost sixteen, and had been out of touch. "I wish that I could see you more, I often miss you and I think somehow that you have arranged matters so in your own mind that the absence is mine from you and not yours from me. But the move East was after all by your choice. No reproach,

I just think you should bear it in mind along with other facts, realities, truths."[48]

Adam's solution to the problem of impressing his father was partly intellectual. At Princeton, he had majored in Renaissance studies and done a fair bit of acting. After graduating in 1979, he took a year off to learn Italian "and read Dante in the original. I thought I'd either be a professor or writer." After an internship at the New York *Daily News* he thought he'd be a journalist-writer, "like John McPhee or Paul Theroux." He also began writing stories. He got a little apartment in Manhattan and "set up shop as a writer." He'd always believed he'd be a writer. In high school, "I wrote very easily." Bellow's attitude to Adam's literary ambitions was, "quite naturally," mixed. Part of him was pleased. It was flattering that Adam wanted to be a writer: "It was a way of reassuring my father that I really loved him and really identified with him as a son. You could say it represented a symbolic victory over my mother. On the other hand, he knew that I was setting myself up for a difficult road. . . . He also knew that I would suffer from comparison with him." In addition, Adam suspects, there was the matter of privacy. "This is a guy who really did write from inside his life. He rewrote his story to get control—the Prospero story is very important to him, in that Prospero was also wounded and angry; he had a lot of material to work out." For Adam to become a writer raised worrying questions. "Who's writing the story? For someone within the family to do what he did, to tell the story, that's threatening. I might expose certain things. I might contest his version of things."

When Adam showed Bellow his writing, he received qualified praise. "He said, You do some things very well and other things not so well." Bellow was much more enthusiastic about the literature essays Adam sent him while at Princeton (on *Ulysses* and *Madame Bovary*). During visits, talk about books formed "the heart of our relationship"; they gave Adam, or so he felt, "access to my father." "It was a relief to both of us not to be talking about family issues and the deficiencies in our relationship." When Adam planned a visit to Kenya late in 1981, Bellow offered advice in a letter of November 17: "I don't know whether you want a purely parental comment on your project. Chances are you don't but it would give me too much trouble to repress it, so here goes." Adam needed something to do when in Africa: "Without some sort of purpose the trip is just another trip. . . . You don't need anything elaborate in the way of a purpose. You might write pieces for a magazine but you must have *something.* You shouldn't travel such a distance without a *theme* of some sort." It was after this trip that Adam was to meet Bellow in Jerusalem, for their joint interview with Menachem Begin.[49] "I was going to be John Quincy and he was going to be Adams. It was going to be the making of me." After the interview was canceled, Bellow's praise of Adam's account of the Kenya trip ("this is very good, this is real writing") was some compensation. Still determined to be a writer, Adam decided that what he needed was a greater sense of how the world worked, to learn something of "history, economics, some political theory. . . . I needed a way of looking at the world." He asked his father about applying to study at the Committee on Social Thought. Bellow "was flattered," and Allan Bloom said, "Come to Chicago, we'll fix all that." At the Committee, Adam studied political science with Nathan Tarcov, dropped out of a class with Edward Shils after two sessions, and lasted only a year, returning to New York in 1983. He left partly to be with Rachel Newton, whom he'd met in New York the previous summer, and who would eventually become his wife. Although the Committee wasn't quite right for Adam, the year in Chicago brought him closer to his father. Bellow "liked very much our relationship, which became more and more intellectual. He would have liked me to stay."[50] Adam attributes what he calls a "noticeable softening" in Bellow to Alexandra, "the only childless wife." "All the sons felt that. She made sure that he remembered your birthday. You got a phone call, you got a check. It was a good period in all our lives. You felt it was a family."

This is not what Greg felt, though he, too, praises Alexandra. Greg was in his late thirties in the early 1980s, married, with two children. He had been living in California since 1970, first in San Francisco, then in Redwood City, just outside Palo Alto. The move to California, he writes, was "the first in what became a series of insulating layers that afforded me some protection from his [Bellow's] demands for attention and control."[51] Both Greg and his wife, JoAnn, were psychotherapists, Greg specializing in the treatment of children, and Bellow's distrust of therapy and psychoanalysis had hardened over the years.[52] Greg was hurt by what he describes as his father's "discomfort and notable lack of interest in the priorities I gave to my family and my career as a psychotherapist. . . . Saul maintained, with considerable pride, that he had decided to ignore his psychological problems. Long ago he had put his faith in willpower." Looking back, Bellow described his experiences in therapy as largely unhelpful—harmful, even—and, as Greg puts it,

"No doubt, he found Freud's boiling down creativity to the sublimation of libido an offensive notion." Greg, in contrast, describes his experiences in therapy as positive. Thinking about psychological problems, he believes, is "a valuable form of facing emotional truth, for my patients and for myself."[53] These disagreements were exacerbated by Bellow's interest in Rudolf Steiner and spiritualism. Whereas Greg talked of "an 'inner self' . . . limited to the secular realm,'" Bellow talked of "a 'human soul,' which included a spiritual dimension."[54]

Politics also played a part in the tensions between Greg and Bellow, in particular what Greg describes as "Saul's refusal to consider the merits of disenfranchised groups." This refusal he describes as "a reversal that was out of character." Bellow's political views "diverged from our family ethos of fairness, respect, and concern." That Greg argued back "brought out the worst in my father. Arguing with him only increased his ferocity. . . . I was appalled at what he said."[55] Bellow's "repellent" views were voiced "with venom, ridicule, and contempt designed to obliterate opposing views."[56] Greg's own quickness to anger and obvious upset were part of the problem, as was Bellow's sense of how a son should speak to a father. "When he got older," according to his niece Lesha Greengus, Bellow "didn't like to be argued with. He was not happy when I disagreed." Although Greg recalls Bellow as "plagued by self-criticisms," racked with "regret and shame" over past mistakes, he also describes him as incapable of "admitting that he was wrong or even had once been so." He needed "to alter, repudiate, and occasionally deny that past." For Greg, these "revisions of his personal history compounded the reversals of his socio-cultural beliefs and became new hot spots in a long cold war that further eroded our already tenuous common ground." When Bellow "went too far," misrepresenting "people toward whom I felt loyal," "I disinterred what he was trying to bury, which infuriated him because he knew I had a historical point."[57]

Greg's daughter, Juliet, is interesting about Bellow and her father. That the two men loved each other was clear; it was part of what made the relation so fraught. Juliet's earliest memories of Bellow are from when she was six or seven (she was born in 1973). She describes him then as "very warm, very sweet," also as "difficult," "changeable." At one moment, "he'd call me kitty-cat and I'd sit on his lap"; then "he'd be very distant, he'd be disapproving"; "you didn't know what to expect." When Bellow was cold or critical, Juliet suspects, "he was trying to fight with my father through me, as a conduit." She remembers Bellow's complaining to her about her father's move out west. "He took it personally" (not without reason, according to Greg's memoir). When Bellow was proud of Juliet, "he would always say, 'You look like my mother,' which I think wasn't true but which he decided was true. . . . In a letter he'd say, 'It's great to have such a beautiful and clever granddaughter.' " "He was in many ways a very thoughtful and kind person, but I think his need to be the top dog, the best, was very deep." He could be "incredibly acute about people's characters," while at the same time ignorant of "the complexities of his own motivations." When Bellow described the faults of a relative or friend, "you had consciously to guard yourself. 'I know these people, there's more to it than this.' " Juliet remembers Bellow expounding the virtues of monogamy, which "took my breath away." He also once said, "I don't think my children ever suffered very much from my divorce." Juliet was a teenager, or late teenager, when he said this. "I was shocked."

Bellow disliked visiting California, and mostly saw Greg and his family when they came to Chicago, which they did once or twice a year, for a week or so at a time. That they always stayed with JoAnn's family irritated Bellow, as did Greg's reluctance to have much to do with his paternal aunts and uncles. Greg resented the way the Bellows had treated him and his mother after his parents divorced. As Juliet puts it, "The Bellows wanted nothing to do with these people [the Goshkins], and my grandmother's family took him in and took care of him" (as in later life Greg took care of them). According to Juliet, her father felt the Bellows had "written him off, and he didn't really care." Hence, as we've seen, Greg's decision not to invite the wider Bellow family to his and JoAnn's wedding in 1970, which made his father "sore as a boil." Bellow's bitter complaints further embittered Greg, who was "never completely free from being hurt by his displeasure, whether it was expressed, implied, or conveyed by others."[58] That Juliet "tried so hard" to have a good relationship with Bellow "was really about my father, trying to heal this wounded guy, and I realized that that's never going to happen." She cites a letter Bellow wrote to her in her last year of high school. "Your father says that when university decision time comes my opinion might be solicited. I am always very free with my opinions. They are to be had for the asking. I am sure that as I never forget the essentials you'll not forget to ask my advice." To Juliet, "the entirety" of what Bellow could be when interacting with her was suggested in such letters, which were "warm and funny and silly and difficult and demanding and sometimes mean."[59]

THE LEAST TRICKY FILIAL RELATION, or would-be filial relation, Bellow had in the early 1980s was with Martin Amis, who came to Chicago to interview him for *The Observer* in the last week of October 1983. The idea for the interview had been Amis's. In 1974, in Spain, he'd read his first Bellow novel, *The Victim*, and immediately felt, "Here's a writer who is addressing me personally, doesn't care what anyone else thinks. And I'm going to have to read everything," which he then did.[60] In Chicago, Bellow met Amis for lunch, informing him that he would be identifiable "by certain signs of decay." In fact, what identified Bellow, according to the *Observer* profile, was "his dapper, compact figure" and "his expression—one of courteous vigilance."[61] At sixty-eight, Bellow's hair was white, his "generous yet combative" eyes "the color of expensive snuff." "It is clear from his books, his history, his face, that Bellow has weathered considerable turbulence." In repose, Amis thought, Bellow looked "like an omniscient tortoise." The profile begins with Bellow's claims as a writer, which Amis thinks indisputable, unlike the claims of his contemporaries. "Saul Bellow really is a great American writer. I think that in that sense he is the writer that the twentieth century has been waiting for."[62] Amis believes this because "the present phase of Western literature is inescapably one of 'higher autobiography,' intensely self-inspecting," and Bellow has not only made his own experience "resonate more memorably than any living writer," but is "the first to come out the other side of this process, hugely strengthened to contemplate the given world." So highly does Amis rate Bellow that he is willing to set aside the newspaper journalist's traditional hope that his or her subject will manifest "lunacy, spite, deplorable indiscretions, a full-scale nervous breakdown."[63]

The talk at lunch began with Reagan's recent intervention in Grenada, which Bellow declared "an opportunist PR exercise" meant to distract from the Beirut suicide bombing of the previous Sunday (in which at least 230 American marines were killed). PR, Bellow tells Amis, is now mostly in the hands of television, which is "ugly, ignorant, self-righteous and terrifyingly influential." Ronald Reagan may be in "a long gallery of dumb-bells," but he's been "TV-tested." Bellow's own celebrity since winning the Nobel Prize has given him a taste of that sort of testing. The "micro-inspection" is appalling; "one is asked to bare one's scars to the crowd, like Coriolanus." There's also "the ingratiation, the danger of becoming a cultural functionary, the extra mail ('suddenly even more people think that what I want to do is read their manuscripts')." Staying in Chicago, which is "huge, filthy, brilliant and mean," affords at least some insulation ("The main thing about Chicago is that it's not New York").[64] Chicago's other advantage is that it offers an unimpeded view of "money-mania, corruption, urban vileness," the chief evils of American society. "You can say this for Chicago—there's no hypocrisy problem here. There's no *need* for hypocrisy. Everyone's *proud* of being a bastard."[65] Proud also of their low literary tastes, in which novels, as Amis paraphrases Bellow, are treated "as how-to books about life, or about life-style. The writer is no curer of souls; he is on the level of the etiquette page and advice to the lovelorn."[66]

Amis's Bellow profile was a big hit with *The Observer*, which ran it as a "Review" front. Its subject was pleased with it as well, at least according to Harriet Wasserman, who told Amis that she'd read it to him over the phone. "The whole thing?" Amis asked (the piece was "like 4,000 or 3,000 words"). "Yes," Wasserman answered, "and when I finished he said: 'Read it again.'" "That impressed upon me that with all his prizes and distinctions, the right kind of praise is tremendously important. Because he'd been duffed up a bit, too. And it's terribly nice for a novelist to have a young [novelist] admirer, it's a sort of guarantee of limited immortality."

THE MOST RECENT DUFFING had come from John Updike, reviewing *The Dean's December* in *The New Yorker*.[67] Updike had been critical of Bellow before. His review of *Humboldt's Gift*, also in *The New Yorker*, complained that the novel had too many characters, all of whom sounded alike, that its incidents were "abstract and hurried," that the writing was "not always grammatical, feels fallen away from a former angelic height." On the morning the *Humboldt* review appeared, Bellow's lawyer friend Sam Goldberg called him to ask "whether I had read the review in the *New Yorker* by that anti-Semitic pornographer." Bellow had, and it had hurt. As he told Maggie Staats (not yet Maggie Simmons), in a letter of September 15, 1975, "No one has ever accused me of writing bad English—I'm sure I slipped up here and there, in a book of five hundred pages that would be inevitable. This morning I'm actually frozen, covered with a thick ice of Jewish inhibitions. Shall I write my next book in Yiddish? But perhaps the grammatical lapses were all Charlie's. Besides, did H. W. Fowler ever write an American novel?"

Updike's criticisms, characteristically, were balanced by praise. "Of course there are passages that no one but Bellow could have perpetrated—scenes that are, in the flow of their wit and felt detail, simply delicious." "Bellow is not only the best portraitist writing American fiction, he is one of our better nature poets." The review of *The Dean's December* has a similar mixture, but is tougher. "Literature can do with any amount of egoism, but the merest pinch of narcissism spoils the flavor. And [here] there is more than a pinch." "We are told much and shown little in the course of the narrative, and if Bellow's eye is still magical his ear seems dulled, allowing the voice of exposition to overwhelm the voices of character." "The switching back and forth between the two cities, both demoralized but in such different ways, is as wearying as the effort of holding in the mind's eye an image of Albert Corde different from the one on the back of the jacket." Most tellingly, given Bellow's several references to Henry James's *The American Scene*, with its offensive remarks on the Jews of the Lower East Side: "One wonders if to, say, Henry James the ethnic neighborhoods of Chicago so engagingly particularized in 'Augie March' might not have seemed as much a hopeless wasteland as black Chicago appears to Albert Corde."[68]

Bellow rarely mentions Updike in letters or essays, invariably a sign, according to Adam Bellow, that a writer mattered or was a potential rival. There are only two references to Updike in Benjamin Taylor's edition of Bellow's correspondence.[69] In addition to the letter to Maggie Staats, Bellow writes on May 18, 1988, to Cynthia Ozick, explaining why he won't be attending an American Academy meeting: "New York is a ten-hour round trip from Vermont and I can't face that. Not for the privilege of sitting next to John Updike." Only once does he discuss Updike's fiction in print, in a published version of a lecture of January 21, 1963, at the Library of Congress. This lecture, entitled "Recent American Fiction," was subsequently reprinted as a pamphlet by the library, but also, slightly altered, in *Encounter*, as "Some Notes on Recent American Fiction." About the title story in Updike's collection of stories *Pigeon Feathers* (1962), Bellow voiced reservations, while praising its "virtuosity":

> There is nothing to see here but the writer's reliance on beautiful work, on an aesthetic discipline and order. And sensibility, in such forms, incurs the dislike of many because it is perceptive inwardly, and otherwise blind. We suspect it of a stony heart because it functions so smoothly in its isolation. The writer of sensibility assumes that only private explorations and inner development are possible and accepts the opposition of public and private as fixed and indissoluble.[70]

Whether Updike saw this judgment is unknown. Nor is what he said of Bellow outside of reviews recorded, at least not by his most recent biographer, Adam Begley, who also has nothing to say of the reviews.[71] Updike's sunny public persona masked as competitive a streak as Bellow's. For John Cheever, writing in a letter of June 1, 1965, to the novelist Frederick Exley, Updike was "a brilliant man," but after traveling with him in Russia in the autumn of 1964, Cheever decided that in the future he "would go to considerable expense and inconvenience to avoid his company. I think his magnanimity specious and his work seems motivated by covetousness, exhibitionism and a stony heart."[72] Before the trip, Cheever was an active Updike supporter, not only nominating him to the National Institute of Arts and Letters, but championing Updike's novel *The Centaur* over Thomas Pynchon's *V* for the 1964 National Book Award for Fiction. If Cheever really had turned against him—for more than the moment of the 1965 letter to Exley, that is—Updike had no idea that he had. Cheever saw a good deal more of Updike than he did of Bellow, and relations between the two men were always cordial.[73] When, in 1988, a posthumous collection of Cheever's letters was published, Updike reviewed them in *The New Yorker*. The collection contained the Exley letter, which "chastened" Updike, but which he claims to have found "edifying," attributing its malice to an all-but-universal competitiveness among writers. "The literary scene is a kind of *Medusa*'s raft, small and sinking, and one's instincts when a newcomer tries to clamber aboard [Cheever was born in 1912, Updike in 1932] is to stamp on his fingers."[74]

On the Russia trip, Cheever and Updike "joked about being the last non-Jewish writers in America."[75] They also joked about the Soviet literary figures and functionaries they'd encountered. Cheever made up little stories about them, turning them into what Updike remembered as "a bright scuttle of somehow suburban characters"—or "Cheever characters," as Begley puts it.[76] What Updike came away with from the trip was a story titled "The Bulgarian Princess," about a "fortyish young man, Henry Bech, with his thinning curly hair and his melancholy Jewish nose." Bech, Updike's composite version of a New York Jewish novelist, is described by Begley as "less wholesome" than Harry Angstrom of the *Rabbit* novels. In later stories, Bech's experiences recall those of Bellow, though also of Malamud, the Roths (Philip, Henry), Mailer, Singer, Salinger. In Cheever's June 1, 1965, letter to Exley, Bellow figures as a foil of sorts to Updike: "My admiration for Bellow's works is genuine; but Updike . . ." The malice that follows leads Cheever back to Bellow, whose "mind is, of course, erudite, bellicose and agile and as a companion I find him one of the most difficult men to part with." After a month in daily contact with Cheever in Russia, in the year *Herzog* topped the best-seller list, it is likely that Updike heard at least something of Cheever's admiration for its author.

When the Bech stories were gathered into *Bech: A Book* (1967), Updike introduced them, in the manner of Nabokov, with a "foreword" by Bech himself, who suavely congratulates his creator while noting "something Waspish, theological, scared, and insulatingly ironical" in the collected stories. He doubts that "your publishing this little *jeu* of a book will do either of us drastic harm." Not all Jewish readers—certainly not Samuel Goldberg—will have liked the "*jeu*" joke here, cleverly insulated by being "Bech's." That Bech and Updike in some respects resembled each other, says Begley, as Harry Angstrom and Updike did, "dawned on Updike only gradually."[77] A similarly gradual recognition dawned on Philip Larkin, admired by both Bellow and Updike, in respect to Jake Balokowsky, the Jewish American biographer Larkin imagines for himself in the poem "Posterity." Jake is fed up with working on Larkin and wants to go to Tel Aviv to study "Protest Theater," but " 'Myra's folks'—he makes the money sign— / 'Insisted I got tenure.' "[78] There is affection and good fun in Updike's creation of Bech (more than in Larkin's creation of Jake), but it is not hard to imagine Goldberg's crack about "that anti-Semitic pornographer" striking a chord with Bellow, both the "anti-Semitic" bit and the "pornographer" bit, given the relative absence of explicit sex in Bellow's writing.[79]

JOHN CHEEVER WAS as much a WASP as Updike, but he and Bellow loved each other and never fought or fell out. Cheever had admired

Bellow's writing from the start, years before they met, praising him as "the first American novelist of parts who writes neither in sympathy with nor in opposition to the Puritan tradition. He writes as if it didn't exist."[80] Of *Dangling Man* Cheever declared: "Here is the blend of French and Russian that I like." It wasn't until *The Adventures of Augie March*, however, that Cheever was offered "the experience, that I think of as great art, of having a profound chamber of memory revealed to me that I had always possessed but had never comprehended." For all their superficial or social differences, Cheever sensed similarities. "His optimism I share, having reached it by my own, crooked, lengthy, leaf-buried path. We cannot spend our lives in apprehension."[81] When finally they met, in September 1956 at Yaddo, Cheever's excitement was registered in his journal. "I am conscious of being in the same room with Saul," he writes, describing Bellow as "about my size," with "that sometime tragic fineness of his skin, that tragic vitality. His nose is a little long, his eyes have (I think) the cheerful glint of lewdness, and I notice his hands and that his voice is light. It has no deep notes."[82] On a long walk after dinner, the two men forged what Cheever thought a "mystical" bond. "I cast around for some precedent of two writers with similar aims who are strongly drawn to one another. . . . I do not have it in me to wish him bad luck: I do not have it in me to be his acolyte." The rapport Cheever felt with Bellow was on several levels. "We joke, fool, as I like to," he reports. Both were drawn to eccentrics, particularly as fans: "Why, I wonder," asks Cheever, "should my admirers always be mad." Their attraction to the luminous, Cheever called "very near botanical": "It seems to me that one's total experience is the drive toward light—spiritual light," a drive increasingly prominent in Bellow's writing.[83]

The two men saw each other infrequently. In October 1971, during a time of marital discord and creative blockage, Cheever flew to Chicago to participate in *Playboy* magazine's International Writers' Convocation. During his stay, he and Bellow met at the Riviera Health Club, where Bellow played racquetball. Cheever arrived while Bellow was still on court and agreed to meet him for a steam after his match. Six years later in New York, on February 23, 1978, while presenting Bellow with the Gold Medal of Honor at the National Arts Club, he recalled the meeting. "Saul appeared from the clouds, stark naked and wearing a copious wreath of steam. I stood in my own cloud. As we shook hands I said, as I am pleased to say tonight, that our friendship is obviously not of this world."[84] The two writers met again at Bellow's sixtieth birthday (described in chapter 5), then, in January 1976, when both were visiting Stanford, Cheever with his son Federico, who was thinking of applying there as an undergraduate, Bellow with Alexandra, who was considering an appointment in the Math Department. During their visits, the novelists gave readings. Bellow was testy at the time and, when asked by Dana Gioia, a graduate student looking after Cheever (later a poet and chair of the National Endowment for the Arts), which contemporary novelists he most admired, snapped: "Literature is not a competitive sport." He then listed "Wright Morris, J. F. Powers, and a man standing in this room . . . *John Cheever*." To Gioia, Bellow was "intimidatingly confident," projecting "unapproachable dignity and reserve." "At sixty he was still trim and handsome. . . . A king's haberdashery would not have surpassed his wardrobe." Cheever, in contrast, struck Gioia as modest and self-effacing, easy with undergraduates, none of whom seemed to have heard of him.[85] As his biographer Blake Bailey puts it, Cheever behaved, "in the best possible sense, like a man who realized his books were out of print."[86]

Cheever had only six years to live, but in these years his reputation rose dramatically. He had stopped drinking in 1975, a year before the Stanford visit. In 1977, he published *Falconer*, which Bellow read and praised in galleys, and which reached number one on the best-seller list. Cheever's face appeared on the cover of the March 14 issue of *Newsweek*, the first writer's face to appear on the front cover since September 1, 1975, when the face in question was Bellow's. In 1979, Cheever was awarded an honorary doctorate from Harvard, along with Alexander Solzhenitsyn, who used the occasion to denounce the degenerate West. Two years later, in the summer of 1981, he was diagnosed with cancer, only a few months before *The Stories of John Cheever* were published to universal acclaim (they would go on to sell 125,000 copies in hardback). In March 1982, *Oh What a Paradise It Seems*, a novella, was published. Bellow wrote to call the novella charming. The next month, on April 27, 1982, Cheever was awarded the National Medal for Literature at the American Book Awards ceremony at Carnegie Hall, where his shrunken appearance shocked the audience. Two days before, he had written to Bellow about the ceremony. Whenever he received a prize, it was his habit to dig out "a yellowed newspaper copy of your beautiful Nobel Prize speech and crib from this." As the copy was very fragile, he'd neatly packed it between boards. Now he couldn't find it. "I can't very well say that I'm unable to thank them because I lost Saul Bellow's Nobel Prize speech. I have another day."[87] The speech Cheever came up with, at moments, resembles Bellow's Nobel speech, as when he declares that "a page of good prose seems to me the most serious dialogue that well-informed and intelligent men and women can carry on today."

Cheever died on June 18, 1982. Six months earlier, Bellow had learned of his friend's cancer and wrote movingly of their closeness, in a letter of December 9, 1981:

> What I would like to tell you is this. We didn't spend much time together but there is a significant attachment between us. I suppose it's in part because we practiced the same self-taught trade. Let me try to say it better—we put our souls to the same kind of schooling, and it's this esoteric training which we had the gall, under the hostile stare of exoteric America to persist in, that brings us together. . . . Neither of us had much use for the superficial "given" of social origins. In your origins there were certain advantages; you were too decent to exploit them. Mine, I suppose, were only to be "overcome" and I hadn't the slightest desire to molest myself that way. I was, however, in a position to observe the advantages of the advantaged (the moronic pride of Wasps, Southern traditionalists, etc.). There wasn't a trace of it in you. You were engaged, as a writer should be, in transforming yourself. When I read your collected stories I was moved to see the transformation taking place on the printed page. There's nothing that counts really except this transforming action of the soul, I loved you for this. I loved you anyway, but for this especially.

The letter ends with an offer to fly to New York "whenever it's convenient for you."

The themes from this moving letter were sounded in Bellow's eulogy for Cheever, delivered at a service in Ossining, New York, on June 23, 1982. Bellow agreed instantly to the Cheever family's request that he come and speak at the funeral (something he had been unable or unwilling to do at the deaths of Isaac Rosenfeld and Oscar Tarcov). Picking up on Cheever's image of the "nearly botanical" attraction the two writers had to light, and on a later comment of Cheever's, in a letter of April 3, that the chief authority on his sort of cancer lived in Bucharest (Cheever imagines him there "watering his cyclamens," plants that feature in *The Dean's December*), Bellow describes their friendship as "a sort of hydroponic plant [which] flourished in the air . . . healthy, fed by good elements . . . a true friendship."[88] On both sides, "there was instant candor," also understanding, since "each of us knew what the other was up to. We worked at the same trade." Cheever is praised for being "not in the least grudging or rivalrous."[89] Their differences helped rather than hindered the friendship, more, even, than their similarities:

> He was a Yankee; I, from Chicago, was the son of Jewish immigrants. His voice, his style, his humor, were different from mine. His manner was reticent, mine was . . . something else. It fell to John to resolve these differences. He did this without the slightest difficulty, simply by putting human essences in first place: first the persons—himself, myself—and after that the other stuff—class origins, social history. A fairly experienced observer, I have never seen the thing done as he did it—done, I mean, as if it were not done at all. It flowed directly from his nature.[90]

A LITTLE MORE THAN A YEAR after Cheever's death, on November 13, 1983, Bellow's lawyer friend Sam Goldberg died of cardiac arrest, after a long period in and out of emergency wards and hospitals. Bellow had known Goldberg since the early 1950s (he is partly the model for Mintouchian, the divorce lawyer who appears at the end of *The Adventures of Augie March*). In addition to practicing law, Goldberg, a bibliophile, once thought seriously of going into business as a book dealer. Bellow described him as "an eccentric rich Manhattan lawyer . . . whose hobby it was to buy rare books for nickels and dimes from Fourth Avenue dealers who didn't know what they were selling."[91] Goldberg bought many books for Bellow—not rare books, but new ones, mostly of social and political theory and history and philosophy. He was also a serious art-collector (not just of the paintings of his friend Nahum Tschacbasov, Sasha Bellow's father). It was Goldberg who arranged the sale of the manuscript of *Mr. Sammler's Planet* to the New York Public Library, persuading Frances Steloff, founder of the Gotham Book Mart, a client of his for over forty years, to donate twenty-five thousand dollars anonymously to the library's Berg Collection. Without this donation, the library could not have met the sixty-thousand-dollar asking price for the manuscript. The Gotham Book Mart was a New York institution and a Bellow haunt. Goldberg also helped to set up the Steloff Lectures at the Hebrew University of Jerusalem, and Steloff was "particularly proud" when Bellow agreed to deliver the first such lecture.[92]

IN LATE FEBRUARY 1984, Bellow and Alexandra traveled to Paris, where, on March 1, he was made Commander of the Legion of Honor by François Mitterrand. As Mitterrand tied the decoration around his neck, Bellow told an interviewer, "I said to him in French, 'Better to be decorated than hanged!' I hope he didn't hear me. . . . At a solemn moment, you know, when a man puts his arms around you and he's fastening a knot around your neck . . ."[93] Later in the spring, Bellow received a second honor, one that moved him to tears. A letter arrived from the mayor of Lachine, Quebec, Guy Descary, announcing that the town library was going to be renamed the Saul Bellow Municipal Library, and inviting him to attend a naming ceremony on June 10, his sixty-ninth birthday. "He seemed genuinely moved by the gesture," the mayor recalled. "He said he had nothing named for him anywhere."

Bellow returned to Lachine with Alexandra, his niece Lesha Greengus, his sister, Jane, and Harriet Wasserman, his agent, who had also arranged for *People* magazine to cover the event. On the way to the ceremony, they stopped in Stowe, Vermont, to visit Marvin Gameroff, son of Shmuel David Gameroff, in part the model for Isaac Braun in "The Old System." They arrived in Montreal several days before Bellow's birthday, to stay at the Ritz-Carlton Hotel, on Sherbrooke Street, a far cry from St-Dominique Street, in the Jewish district of the city, where the Bellows moved after Lachine. That night, there was a big family dinner, attended by a number of relatives, including Marvin Gameroff, who drove up separately from Stowe (with his newly adopted son, Lamont, a ten-year-old African American boy). In the morning, Bellow and his party, including a photographer from *People*, drove to Lachine, where they visited his birthplace, the modest two-flat house at 130 Eighth Avenue. A French Canadian woman in her thirties came to the door and graciously showed them round the apartment.[94]

The ceremony at the library, at 3100 St-Antoine Street, began around noon. It was a hot and muggy Sunday, but when Bellow and his party alighted from Mayor Descary's limousine, they were greeted by what Wasserman describes as "the whole town," plus an orchestra, L'Harmonie de Lachine, playing "Chicago," "When the Saints Go Marching In," and "Happy Birthday."[95] The street in front of the library was closed to traffic, and a tent was set up on the library lawn. The mayor gave a brief speech of welcome, calling Bellow *"le plus grand écrivain de notre époque."* A plaque was unveiled at the library entrance, and Bellow, tearful again, gave a speech, in French and English. This speech, much drawn on in chapter 2 of *To Fame and Fortune*, recalled Bellow's happy childhood in Lachine. After the ceremony, there was an "exclusive" hundred-dollar-a-plate brunch for 250 people at the Maison de Brasseur, a converted brewery bordering the St. Lawrence, the proceeds of which were to go to the Lachine Hospital. Among the invited guests were Mordecai Richler and Leonard Cohen. A second brunch was held the next day, for what the *Montreal Gazette* called "the less-famous." It was free. There was singing and dancing on the library grounds, and nothing like the number of speeches from the day before. Among the sixteen speakers at the first brunch was Ruth Wisse, who taught Yiddish literature at McGill (she would not become professor of Yiddish at Harvard until 1993).[96] The next night, Bellow had dinner with Wisse and her husband and another of the speakers, Louis Dudek, also a professor at McGill. Wisse, a hard-line conservative, took Bellow to task over politics, accusing him, among other misdemeanors, of "temporizing" in his support of Israel. Bellow took no offense.[97] In fact, she recalls, "he loved how passionate we were about Israel." At another party during the visit, Wisse and Bellow sat next to each other and conversed in Yiddish. When Wisse got up to bring sweets and fruit to the table, Bellow, playing on her name, said, "*Zi heist rut nor zi rut nisht,*" which Wisse translates as "Her name is Ruth but she does not rest."[98]

More awards and recognition brought 1984 to an end. In September, Andrei Sinyavsky (Abram Tertz) and his wife, Masha, visited the Bellows in Vermont, and Bellow traveled to Capri to receive the Malaparte Prize. In October, he was interviewed by Diane Sawyer, "that blonde beauty," on *60 Minutes* and gave readings in San Francisco and New York. Though *The Dean's December* had received very mixed reviews, *Him with His Foot in His Mouth and Other Stories*, published in May 1984, was much praised.[99] In addition to the title story, the collection included "What Kind of Day Did You Have?," "A Silver Dish," "Cousins," and "Zetland: By a Character Witness." Typically, only Anatole Broyard of *The New York Times* failed to see merit in these stories.[100]

A YEAR AND A HALF AFTER Sam Goldberg's death, Bellow's first wife, Anita, died, in March 1985, four months after her second husband, Basil Busacca, to whom she had been married for twenty-five years. Anita had worked all her life. At the time of her death, she was running the Hollywood office of the Department of Social Medicine at Kaiser Permanente, a large health-care company in California.[101] When Bellow heard of Busacca's death, he asked Greg whether he should call Anita to offer his condolences. Sensing that this was "something he really did not want to do, I left it up to him. He never called, though he should have." When Anita died, however, Bellow "was at his absolute best. . . . Saul's tenderness was palpable as he said, 'Come to Chicago. Your loving father will be waiting.' " For all the tensions in the relationship between Bellow and his oldest son, "seeing me suffer always cut through to our fundamental emotional connection."[102]

Within two months of Anita's death, Bellow's seventy-seven-year-old brother, Maury, died from colon cancer.[103] Maury had been unwell for some time, with prostate cancer and heart trouble. He died in Thomasville, Georgia, where he had moved from Miami in 1976 with his second wife, Joyce, and their two children. They lived on a fifteen-acre plantation named White Haven, where Joyce raised Paso Fino horses, prized for their smooth gait; at one point, she owned twenty-two of them. Maury was then in the antiques business, buying up fine furniture on twice-yearly visits to England and storing his purchases in large warehouses in Thomasville. Shortly after his death, Ruth Miller paid a condolence call on Bellow, at the apartment on Sheridan Road. Bellow told her that, on his last visit to Thomasville, in April, he'd bought three pieces of furniture from Maury: "a revolving bookcase, a fine old bureau, and a small desk. He didn't need them, but he bought them and they were beautiful."[104]

Maury knew he was dying at the time of Bellow's visit but talked only of how lucky he was. "He told Bellow," Miller reports, "how all his life was good, was right, how fine a woman his second wife was, and his children, and his home, and all his fine furniture, and Bellow sat there listening, grieving."[105] The brothers knew they were unlikely to see each other again, but Bellow said he would return if Maury needed him, he would fly right down. Maury did, in fact, call, according to Miller, advising Bellow that, "if he meant it, if he wanted to come, now was the time. He had better come now." Before Bellow left for the airport, he received a second call, from Joyce: Maury had died.[106] As Bellow recounted the story of his brother's death, he sipped aquavit; he was okay, he said, not panicky. Miller was struck by the suit he was wearing, "a beige silk and wool suit, a very dashing well-cut suit with a vest." It had belonged to Maury, who had bought it after losing a great deal of weight. Fat again, and dying, Maury pressed the suit on Bellow, who did not want it but took it anyway. As Miller puts it, "Maury was always giving Bellow a suit, and so, at the last, they reenacted the ritual between them."[107]

In "Him with His Foot in His Mouth," Herschel Shawmut flies to Texas to visit his older brother Philip on his estate near Houston. "Here he lived in grandeur, and when he showed me around the place he said to me 'Every morning when I open my eyes I say, "Philip, you're living right in the middle of a park. You own a whole park."' " Shawmut senses something false in his brother's praise of the estate, as if "he was stuck with it. He had bought it for various symbolic reasons, and under pressure from his wife" (p. 395). This wife, Tracy, raises pit bulls, not horses, terrifying animals "bred for cruelty" (p. 398). "She was difficult to know but she was a true woman," Philip said of her, "her fanatical fidelity to him was fundamental." "Tracy is a wonder, isn't she? There's terrific money in these animals. Trust her to pick up a new trend. Guys are pouring in from all over the country to buy pups from her" (p. 397). Philip is fat, unwell, seeing a doctor, and on a physical-fitness program designed by Tracy. Herschel is made to watch him work out, "to witness that under the fat there was a block of primal powers, a strong heart in his torso, big veins in his neck, and bands of muscle across his back" (p. 398).

The visit to Texas partly involves business. Some time ago, Philip cut Herschel in on a deal. By investing six hundred thousand dollars in an auto-wreckage business, "a foolproof investment" (p. 394), the brothers became partners. With money to invest, Herschel at last gained Philip's attention. "For once he spoke seriously to me, and this turned my head" (p. 395). The problem now was that he was yet to receive anything back. "We waited and waited, and there was not a single distribution from the partnership. 'We're doing great,' Philip reassured him. 'By next year I'll be able to remortgage, and then you and I will have more than a million to cut up between us. Until then you'll have to be satisfied with the tax write-offs' " (p. 399). What Herschel discovers is that, "on the credit established by my money," Philip and Tracy had been acquiring and reselling land, much of which "lacked clear title, there were liens against it. Defrauded purchasers brought suit." Philip is convicted of fraud, jumps bail, escapes to Mexico, is caught and extradited, and dies "while doing push-ups in a San Antonio prison" (p. 402). Herschel then discovers that Philip "had made all his wealth over to his wife and children." As the sole general partner in the business, "I was sued by the creditors." In court, Herschel is represented by "energetic but unbalanced" Hansl Genauer, his wife's brother (Hansl is the lawyer whose eyes are "like the eyes you glimpse in the heated purple corners of the small-mammal house" [pp. 409, 412]). It is Hansl who advises Herschel to hide his assets and flee to Canada.

The real-life business dealings between Bellow and Maury were in several respects similar to those between Herschel and Philip. When Bellow came into money, after the success of *Herzog*, Maury involved him in several business ventures (mentioned in chapters 4 and 5). By 1972, according to Maury's son, Joel, Bellow had invested "maybe $100,000" ($130,000 in fact) in the purchase of a large four-story apartment building well located in North Miami. Joel was Bellow's accountant at the time, while also keeping books for Maury. He, too, was involved in the deal, as was his aunt, Jane Kauffman, Bellow and Maury's sister. Like the fictional deal, the real-life one failed to produce returns. Bellow began to complain, unconvinced by Maury's excuses. As Joel recalled in an interview, "Saul didn't want to hear about drawdown, real-estate taxes." Joel knew about such matters, but he, too, questioned the inexplicably high expenses and vacancy rates his father cited by way of explaining the absence of returns. The most aggrieved investor was Jane, who, according to Joel, "really loved money" and "could push Saul Bellow's buttons; Jane was working over Saul, who was working over me."

In the summer of 1976, Joel and Bellow flew down to Florida to confront Maury about the lack of returns. "I became Jane and Saul's link to Maury," Joel remembers, "a lever with which to pry money."[108] Hoping to be a peacemaker between his father and his uncle, he had little sympathy "for either of them and certainly none for Jane." On the flight from Chicago to Miami, Bellow talked to Joel "about what was really important in life." This talk Joel describes as "the highpoint of my relationship with my uncle." From it, he absorbed a conviction that "knowing," "the process by which one knows," was "paramount," a lesson that changed his life, but one that, in hindsight, he saw as ironic,

The Cloisters, 5805 Dorchester Avenue, Hyde Park (photo by John Hellmuth)

The Cloisters, ground floor corridor, Hyde Park (photo by John Hellmuth)

5490 South Shore Drive, "The Vatican," Hyde Park (photo by John Hellmuth)

5825 Dorchester Avenue, Hyde Park (photo by John Hellmuth)

Rudolf Steiner, father of anthroposophy, to whom SB was drawn "because he confirms that a perspective, the rudiments of which I always had, contained the truth" (Wikipedia)

Owen Barfield, at Orchard View, South Darent, Kent, c. 1975 (courtesy of the Marion E. Wade Center, Wheaton College, Wheaton, Illinois)

Peter Demay, convener of SB's Steiner reading group and a leading figure in the Chicago branch of the Anthroposophical Society (courtesy of William Hunt)

William Hunt, poet and Steinerian, early 1970s (courtesy of William Hunt)

SB and Joseph Epstein, 1970s
(courtesy of Joseph Epstein)

John Cheever, John Updike, and their wives at the National Book Award ceremony, 1964
(courtesy of Getty Images; photo by David Gahr)

SB and Edward H. Levi at the second Jefferson Lecture, Chicago, April 1977. From 1968 to 1975 Levi was president of the University of Chicago; from 1975 to 1977 he was U.S. Attorney General under President Ford.
(courtesy of the Special Collections Research Center, University of Chicago Library)

SB and President Jimmy Carter, March 1979, at the White House to celebrate the Egypt-Israel Peace Treaty (courtesy of the Special Collections Research Center, University of Chicago Library)

A broken elevator forces children to play in the hallways of an upper floor at the Robert Taylor Homes on Chicago's South Side, 1971. (courtesy of Getty Images; photo by Robert Adam Senstacke)

Clair Patterson, the model for Sam Beech in *The Dean's December*, photographed at Caltech's 1993 commencement ceremony (courtesy of *Engineering and Science;* photo by Yigal Erel)

Winston Moore, Warden of Cook County Jail, the model for Rufus Ridpath in *The Dean's December*, playing horseshoe with prisoners, 1971 (courtesy of *Ebony* magazine; photographer unknown)

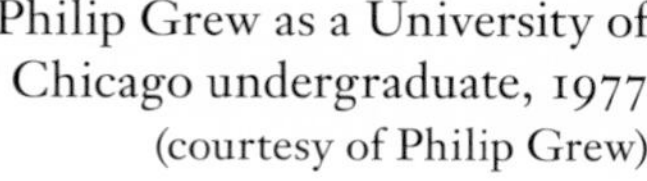

Philip Grew as a University of Chicago undergraduate, 1977 (courtesy of Philip Grew)

Where Mark Gromer fell to his death in July 1977 (courtesy of John Hellmuth)

Jonathan Kleinbard, University of Chicago vice president for University News and Community Affairs, and SB's friend, 1983 (courtesy of *The Chicago Maroon;* photo by Arthur U. Ellis)

Philip Grew, age fifty-eight, Umbria, 2016 (courtesy of Alice Leader)

T. J. McCarthy, assistant state's attorney in the Mark Gromer case, early 1980s (courtesy of T. J. McCarthy)

Marion Siegel, Barney Singer, SB, Alexandra, and Howie Siegel in front of Siegel's restaurant in Victoria, British Columbia, 1983 (courtesy of Howie Siegel)

Lesha Greengus, Jane Bellow Kauffman, and SB in Montreal, on the occasion of the naming ceremony of the Saul Bellow Municipal Library in Lachine, June 1984 (private collection)

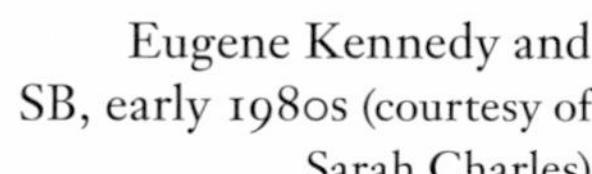

Eugene Kennedy and SB, early 1980s (courtesy of Sarah Charles)

SB and Allan Bloom on the porch of the Vermont house (courtesy of Janis Bellow)

Harriet Wasserman, SB's longtime agent (courtesy of Special Collections, Duke University Library)

Andrew Wylie, SB's agent, replacing Harriet Wasserman in 1996 (courtesy of the Wylie Agency)

Barley Alison, SB's British editor and friend (courtesy of Rosie Alison)

Joel Bellows, SB's nephew and sometime attorney and accountant, with wife Laurel (courtesy of Joel Bellows)

Adam Bellow and Rachel Newton at the time of their marriage, 1986 (courtesy of Daniel Bellow)

Daniel and Susan Bellow, his mother, who died in late 1996, when Daniel was thirty-two, undated (courtesy of Daniel Bellow)

At the wedding of Daniel Bellow and Heather Hershman, with Susan Bellow on the left and SB at the right, Miami, January 1996 (courtesy of Daniel Bellow)

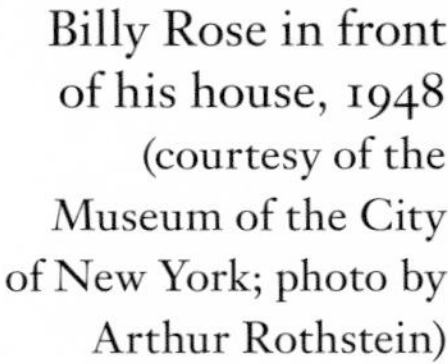

Billy Rose in front of his house, 1948 (courtesy of the Museum of the City of New York; photo by Arthur Rothstein)

since at the time Bellow "was going for the money that it was obvious he wasn't gonna get." The meeting with Maury took place at a steakhouse on Biscayne Boulevard in downtown Miami. "We sat down without pleasantries. Then Saul turned to me and said words to the effect of 'Tell him why you wanted me to come'" (which "wasn't the only time that he ducked responsibility").[109] Feeling "like a patsy," though still affected by their talk on the plane, Joel complied:

> I told my dear father that he had become unilateral in his dealings with his investors. Fortunately, Maury did not prolong the discussion. He said to us, "You will piss blood before you see a penny from me." We stood up and left before our drink order was served. We got on a plane and went home without exchanging another word until we landed at O'Hare.[110]

Whether Maury had been cheating Bellow is not clear. "In a way" he was, Joel believes. "There were too many excuses. We should have got *something* from the investment. I didn't think the situation could be so difficult that there couldn't have been something." Maury was "taking liberties," using money invested by Bellow, Jane, and Joel to support other ventures. "For guys like Maury," Joel explains, "there's little they won't do or say to justify their actions to themselves." His attitude was "Who the fuck are you to question my word?" When consulted about the deal, Sam, who hadn't gone in on it, said only, "Well, you know Maury."

In a letter of August 27, 1976, after the meeting, Maury dispensed with Joel's services as accountant and attacked him as unfeeling: "It seems at this time that your heart has shrunk to a walnut." On November 18, 1976, "after serious consultation with Saul and prolonged soul searching," Joel wrote to his father to protest his having "liquidated our interests at an amount which you claimed to be the fair market value of the property," but which "less than six months later, you sold . . . for a $400,000 profit. In the latter transaction you appropriated all the cash at the closing; certainly, we were entitled to a portion of those funds." After further complaints, Joel declared, "Saul and I are weary of what we can no longer consider to be a modest fucking and request that you desist from unilateral and arbitrary decisions regarding our interests."

In a letter of reply of December 1, Maury invites Joel to examine the books for the period in question, one in which Joel not only acted as an accountant for Maury and his companies, but was well aware, Maury claims, of the reasons for his decisions. Maury finds "offensive" Joel's and Bellow's "insinuations of dishonesty" and will not change his way of doing business. The letter ends defiantly: "You are welcome to pursue your options." According to Joel, "Eventually, the property was sold and Saul and I received no part of the proceeds. Shit happens. But, I finally realized that familial feelings notwithstanding, I had better things to do than be used by my father in games with his brother, or by my uncle in much more subtle games with my father. That said, this round definitely went to Maury."

Several years later, on his birthday, Joel received a phone call from Maury. It was the first conversation they had had since the confrontation in Miami. After brief small talk, Joel, "meaning no disrespect," asked about Maury's health, assuming that something must have been wrong with it for him to call. Maury admitted that he'd just undergone cobalt treatment for prostate cancer. From then on, until Maury's death, father and son exchanged phone calls on each other's birthdays. Bellow's relations with Maury took longer to repair, judging at least from the letter he wrote to Maury's illegitimate son, Dean Borok, on June 17, 1980, quoted in chapter 3 of *To Fame and Fortune.* "He sees none of us," Bellow reported, "brothers, sister, or his two children by his first marriage, nor their children—neither does he telephone or write."

After the news of Maury's death, Bellow and Sam's daughter Lesha flew to Georgia. Joel was already there, along with his son, Kyle, who had arrived from Florida, where he was at university. Joel got to Thomasville in time to say goodbye. "I kissed him and told him, 'I love you Dad.' He said, 'I love you too David' [Maury's son from the second marriage]. As I say, one has to have a sense of humor."[111] When Bellow and Lesha arrived, after an arduous journey (a flight from Chicago to Tallahassee, then a four-hour drive to Thomasville), Bellow immediately asked Joel to drive them to the undertakers. "And I said: 'He's here.' So Uncle's taken aback. I said, 'In the other room.' . . . We start walking to the front of the house and they're looking around in the parlor for where the casket is and I say 'Right there.' And it's one of those black canisters. . . . I think it's the first time that either of them had ever seen or heard of cremation for a Jew. The two of them in unison just sat down." Joel thinks Maury wanted to be cremated because he "just did not want anyone pissing on his grave, and that was that. . . .

And undoubtedly Joyce had influence." A small service in the backyard, overlooking the pasture and stables, was conducted by a friend of Maury's, a local minister. A rabbi did the blessing, but the minister gave the eulogy, which Kyle remembers as "about what a kind soul Maury was and how he had this wonderful warmth and community sense and love of the land and the people. And we're sitting there like, who the hell is he talking about?"

At the end of *More Die of Heartbreak*, published two years after Maury's death, aspects of his final years, including his relations with Joel and Bellow, are woven into the narrative. Benn Crader, the novel's central character, flies to Miami a day after the death of his uncle, Harold Vilitzer. "The last time we saw him he was in a bad way," Benn tells his nephew Kenneth, "but he was still a man, a person. Now he's a packet of ashes, inside a black box" (p. 312). On his arrival, Benn immediately asks to see the body: "I had been preparing to have my last look at him on this earth" (p. 315). There is no body, but "just inside the wide plantation-style door . . . on a red marble or porphyry shelf there was a box." The box is "no bigger than my binocular case." Benn's surprise at seeing his uncle reduced to ashes "came up from the ground, as it were, and caught [him] around the knees, so that he had to sit down" (p. 315). Kenneth wonders why Benn is so moved, since Vilitzer had cheated him in a development deal. "He didn't really care for you, and I don't see why you're broken up over that old crook" (p. 312). Kenneth also wonders why Vilitzer wasn't buried. "Harold arranged all that himself," Benn explains. "His order was immediate cremation, Fishl [Vilitzer's son] told me. The minute the death certificate was signed. Before sunset it was done, and he was brought back and set on the shelf. It turns out that he couldn't bear the very idea of a burial. Couldn't stand to be underground. He was revolted by it" (p. 315). As Kenneth comments, "There are some who can't wait to get rid of themselves. Whereas others can't bear to let anybody go." "It's true," Benn replies, "I couldn't bear to surrender Uncle Harold. It's also the way with my memory. Once my memory has fastened on to some phenomenon it grips it tight" (p. 316). Fishl is like Joel in that he has been estranged from his father ("He's no son of mine," Vilitzer once told the press [p. 165]). When he learns his father is dying, Fishl flies down to Florida immediately, "determined to make up [with him]. Wishing the impossible as so many of us do" (p. 313).

Joel's sister, Lynn, refused to go to Thomasville. In 1961, Maury had reneged on a business promise to her husband, Leonard Rotblatt, who oversaw the finances of several of Maury's businesses. Leonard had married the boss's daughter, and after the birth of their first child, Mark, the boss offered him a deal. Maury had recently acquired a failing chemical company. If Leonard turned the company around within six months, he would give him half-ownership. This Leonard did, but Maury had second thoughts. He had been funneling profits from the company to Joyce. Now he decided she should take full ownership, at which point all relations between Maury and his daughter and her family were severed.[112] It was not until Leonard's death—fourteen years later, at the age of forty-five—that father and daughter saw each other again. At Joel's urging, Maury attended Leonard's funeral in May 1975, where he met Mark and Maureen, his grandchildren, for the first time. For the next three years, according to Mark, "my mother and Maury tried to have the semblance of a relationship." Lynn, though, made the mistake of asking Maury's advice about Leonard's business, and, as Mark puts it, "Of course he came in and said, This is wrong and this is wrong, and made all these changes . . . and basically he took control." Lynn finally accepted that it was impossible to maintain a relationship with her father, and in 1978 they broke apart and never saw each other again. "Do you not feel bad that your father died?" Mark asked his mother in 1985. "I feel bad that I don't feel bad," she answered. "My father died many years ago."

SAM BELLOWS DIED ON June 1, 1985, within weeks of Maury's death. He had been ill with colon cancer since the previous November, as well as having prostate cancer. On December 1, 1984, the colon cancer was operated on at Memorial Sloan Kettering Hospital in New York. Sam was in the hospital for a month. The cancer was stage D, incurable, but back in Chicago, Sam bowed to pressure from Nina, his wife, and agreed to undergo chemotherapy. According to Rachel Schultz, his granddaughter, a medical student at the time, the chemotherapy was unlikely to prolong his life and was "just awful—against everything he stood for." Rachel and Bellow tried to persuade Nina to discontinue treatment, as Sam himself wished. So enervating and humiliating were the side effects of the chemotherapy that Sam stopped eating and on several occasions tried to pull out his feeding tube. Bellow was at Sam's bedside much of the time. He had been in New York for the operation, staying in the same hotel as the family. In Chicago, "he made a concerted effort to be there all the time." He also made an effort to get on with Nina, whom he did not like. Unlike his brothers, Sam steered clear of conflict, hated it, believing in the religious ideal of *shalom bayit* (Yiddish for "domestic harmony"). On Bellow's visits, Rachel remembers, before Sam was bedridden, the two brothers would sit in the den, a "dark, soothing room," just talking. When Bellow and Lesha flew to Georgia, Nina tried to hide the news of Maury's death from Sam, but, as Greg puts it in his memoir, Sam was "no fool, had gotten the picture." Ruth Miller asked Bellow how he and Sam got on: "Sam, he said, always tried but he never knew what to say to his brother Saul." The two men had lived very different lives. Sam was *frum*, observant, correct, dutiful, deeply embedded in the Jewish community of North Chicago. He remained married to the same woman, stayed at home, looked after his father and sister, always made money, eventually a great deal of money. Although he may not have known what to say to Bellow, he loved him. Bellow, he told Rachel, was "the only sibling I have who doesn't give me a hard time." In his last days, Sam was surrounded by friends, including what Rachel calls a "Disney parade" of rabbis, some of whom, Bellow told Miller, were "trying to get him to leave a large sum of money to the synagogue, the yeshiva, an old people's home, to this, to that, and he greeted them all."[113] The funeral service was held at the Hebrew Theological College in Skokie. Bellow sat shiva with the family. The obituary in the *Chicago Tribune* described Sam as "a leader in Jewish education and causes for Israel," the recipient of "many honors and awards," and the brother of Saul Bellow. No mention was made of his problems with the law, or of stories in the press about his nursing homes.

"As we began so are we ending," Sam told Bellow on his deathbed. "You were there at the beginning. You're here now. It's all on you now."[114] Bellow took the injunction seriously, making time for nephews and nieces and their children, offering advice but not pushing, writing references, making calls when needed. Lesha and Lynn, in particular, adored him, as did their children. "He was wonderful," Mark Rotblatt remembers. "It's far less complicated to be the uncle. I really loved Uncle Saul, because I was so grateful that he gave my mother what she needed. She needed approval. . . . And Uncle told her she was smart, she was attractive." Mark remembers trips to Vermont with his sister and mother. Before leaving Chicago, they would go to a

North Side delicatessen, "and my mother would get, like, five pounds of corned beef and the rugula, the big rugula. We'd carry it on the plane and get off in Gentile Brattleboro, and we'd lay it all out in the kitchen, and Uncle Saul was, like, in heaven. And it was nice, because he was appreciative. It was also love, what my mother was so appreciative to do. One of the things that he loved about my mother was that my mother really looked to him for emotional approval. So many people who cozied up to him were looking for something else." Bellow was also close to Lesha Greengus, offering advice and encouragement in correspondence, inviting her to accompany him on trips. Before going to medical school, Rachel Greengus majored in English at Cornell. She remembers that Bellow sent her lists of books to read, and contacted M. H. Abrams, the Cornell Romantics scholar, to make sure she was well looked after. The great-nephews and great-nieces, like the cousins (the Dworkins, Missners, Gameroffs, Gordins, Ullmans, Baronovs), mostly remember Bellow as "generous," "warm," "full of family feeling," "funny," "appreciative," "with a lot of joy in life." Keeping in touch with family was more than an obligation or a source of material for Bellow, it was also centering, as it is for Ijah Brodsky in Bellow's story "Cousins" (1974). "I had remembered, observed, and studied the cousins," Ijah declares, "and these studies seemed to fix my own essence and to keep me as I had been" (p. 239). With his immediate family, his sons and wives, matters were different.[115]

NINE DAYS AFTER SAM'S DEATH, Bellow turned seventy, a fact that "obsessed" him, according to Aaron Asher, now at Harper & Row. In a memo to colleagues who were already worried about Bellow's unhappiness with the marketing of *Him with His Foot in His Mouth and Other Stories*, Asher warned against saying anything about the birthday, much less making a fuss over it. Bellow wanted "no congratulations or any other acknowledgment of this event."[116] On May 28, just days before Sam died, Bellow had business in New York, where Gerald Freund, unaware of his feelings, unaware also of the current state of his friendship with Alfred Kazin, held a joint birthday dinner for the two men, born five days apart (Kazin on June 5, Bellow on June 10). Freund had been the first director of the MacArthur Foundation Prize Fellows Program, for which Bellow served as an "evaluator."[117] When Bellow's term as an evaluator expired, he became an evaluator for the Whiting Writers' Awards program, which Freund headed.

The small dinner party Freund and his wife, Peregrine, arranged for Bellow and Kazin was held at their apartment on the East Side. The only guests were Bellow and Alexandra, Kazin and his third wife, Judith Dunford, and Adam Bellow and his girlfriend, Rachel Newton, soon to be his wife. Newton, the main reason Adam left Chicago for New York, had been Gerald Freund's assistant at the MacArthur Program, her first job after Harvard. Bellow and Kazin had known each other for over forty years. But they did not always get on. Bellow never fully forgave Kazin for his hostile review of *Mr. Sammler's Planet* in *The New York Review of Books*, and Kazin found it difficult to stomach Bellow's increasingly right-wing politics.[118] The most recent of their infrequent meetings, however, had been civil. On May 8, 1979, when Kazin was in Chicago, Bellow took him to lunch at the Arts Club. They had not seen each other since 1970, the year of the *Sammler* review. In a journal entry for that day, Kazin described Bellow at the lunch as "quiet, very cordial, elegant and precise in his speech and manner . . . Sad in a reserved kind of way . . . The waiters all bowing to him."[119]

At the Freund dinner, according to Dunford, everything "started off reasonably well," with a "feeling of nostalgia" between the two men: "All these years, we have all these years together." Then politics entered the conversation. Unlike many of his contemporaries, Kazin remained steadfastly on the left ("militantly" on the left, according to his biographer, Richard M. Cook). Israel was discussed, and Kazin made clear his hatred of Prime Minister Menachem Begin and the Likud Party.[120] There was also talk of Leon Wieseltier's criticisms of Hannah Arendt in *The New Republic*.[121] Bellow was no fan of Arendt's writing; Kazin deeply admired her. When Spain was discussed, according to Cook, Bellow mentioned that Franco had at least saved the Jews, which "outraged" Kazin. "But Bellow stood his ground. 'I was a Trotskyite and you were writing for Luce!' he retorted."[122] In Adam Bellow's words, the atmosphere was "awkward," "embarrassing." Kazin mentioned that *The New York Times* was becoming increasingly conservative, to which Bellow replied, "How can you call a paper conservative that publishes Anthony Lewis?" Looking back on this moment, Dunford says of Bellow: "I don't think he meant to create a bad mood. I don't agree with his politics at all, but I think he was saying something which was a reasonable thing to say . . . when you have Anthony Lewis [an unwavering liberal] writing two or three times a week." In Cook's account, Bellow "blew up" when he made the Lewis point. Adam Bellow describes his father as "loaded for bear when we arrived." But Dunford remembers Kazin as the one who lost control: "It was waiting to come out. That was often the case with Alfred. . . . Alfred was furious and hurt; it was very hard with Alfred to tell the difference between furious and hurt."

The next morning, in his journal, Kazin was bitter about Bellow, "congested in his usual cold conceit . . . the little pasha . . . He did not even try last night to offer much conversation, and I, determined not to taunt the little 'conservative,' went on talking just to avoid a case of the blahs." On June 1, 1985, the day of Sam's death, Kazin was still angry: "God how I hate these princelings baked in their own conceit. The Big Ego always throws me into a rage—no doubt of envy as well as principled antagonism to dictators, despots, spiritual bullies and the like."[123] Dunford, too, recalled Bellow's "sense of his own importance," while also being struck again by his intellect, "a sort of electric halo of intelligence that some people have, as though you're near a live wire." In Kazin's journal, it is Bellow's manner, as much as his politics, that infuriates. Unlike Bellow, in Dunford's view, "Alfred felt that he could scramble for something, not that he was destined for something." When Bellow left the party—after a birthday cake had been brought out, with one candle for Bellow and one for Kazin—he did not say goodbye, or so Kazin claimed. Adam remembers the birthday cake, "a nice touch," but not that his father left without saying goodbye. It is hard to imagine Alexandra leaving without saying goodbye; Adam and Rachel "certainly did." That Bellow avoided saying goodbye to Kazin is not hard to imagine.[124]

ADAM BELIEVES THE DEATH of Maury and the impending death of Sam partly accounted for his father's combativeness at the Freund dinner. "I know he took the deaths of both his brothers very hard. He also had a terrible time with turning seventy." Only days after Sam's death, Bellow left Chicago with Alexandra to spend the summer in Vermont, their third summer in the West Halifax house built for them on the land Bellow had purchased in 1982. She describes herself as "ecstatic" over this house, for which she organized a housewarming in June 1983.

In 1985, her mood was quite different. She and Bellow celebrated his seventieth birthday "quietly," and two months later celebrated her fiftieth birthday "contentiously." The marriage was by now in its end stage. In 2010, in notes for the draft "Chronology" Benjamin Taylor was to include in his forthcoming edition of Bellow's *Letters*, Alexandra offered additions to the entry for 1984. She suggested he add the following sentences: "In March Bellow and Alexandra travel to Paris, where Bellow is awarded the order of Officer of the Legion of Honor. The marriage begins to disintegrate." The trip to Paris had been "dismal," she recalled in an interview. To a sentence about Bellow's traveling to Capri in September for the Malaparte Prize, she suggested Taylor add: "Alexandra does not accompany him." At the end of the 1984 entry, she suggested he add the following sentences: "The marriage continues to unravel. Hopes that the new house will stabilize the marriage, begin to fade, as the tempestuous year 1984 ends." She then offered additions to the beginning and end of the 1985 entry: "The downward spiral of the marriage continues, at an accelerated pace, as the calamitous year 1985 unfolds"; "In December Alexandra asks for divorce."[125]

In my interviews with Alexandra, she was reluctant to elaborate on the causes of the split. In "A Mathematical Life (*Una Vida Matematica*)," her brief memoir of 2001, all she says of the split is that "balancing a career in Mathematics and marriage to a writer was an arduous, demanding task. . . . By and large life together was high-voltage and a study in contrasts. In the end the needs of a writer and the needs of a mathematician were so divergent, that the marriage dissolved in 1985, after 11 years." The paragraph that follows bears indirectly on the breakup: "I had gone from East to West, from the Old World to the New World, I had crossed the bridge between the Humanities and the Sciences and I had paid my dues. If there was one constant in my life, it was Mathematics."[126] Alexandra's reticence, her habitual reserve, was reinforced by emotional pain. When her mother was dying, as we've seen, she found everything "so traumatic and so somber and so macabre" that "many of the details have faded from me, perhaps out of an instinct of self-defense." So, too, with details of the Freunds' disastrous birthday dinner, which "is all a big blur in my mind, too much upheaval, too much confusion, too much heartache at that time." Subjected to nasty gossip after the breakup, she maintained a dignified silence: "I'm not going to disparage or demonize Saul or our marriage, out of respect for the eleven years we spent together and ultimately out of respect for myself. I should also add that I learned very much from Saul and he opened many vistas for me, he enriched my life tremendously."

Family and friends have been less reticent about the causes of the breakup. Adam Bellow offers several explanations, beginning with Bellow's mood that summer, a product of "his ensuing depression over the deaths of both his brothers and his own hastening decline. He was always moody, but these events really put him in a dark place that must have made him hard to live with." The "childlike" quality Bellow and others noted in Alexandra (discussed in chapter 4) he now found irritating rather than endearing. For her part, according to Adam, Alexandra "felt she had been misled." Bellow "told her a version of his life story in which he was always innocent. . . . The only thing that could be said against him was that for some reason he had attracted these people like Gersbach and Madeleine [from *Herzog*] and Cantabile." Initially, Adam believes, the marriage was "a reform project" for Bellow. "He was delighted to have an opportunity to redeem himself," not only by having a successful marriage, but by marrying a woman of distinction. It was not true, Bellow hoped to show, that he was incapable of sustaining a marriage. One thinks of Herschel Shawmut's motives for marrying his late wife, Gerda, in "Him with His Foot in His Mouth": "Which was the real Shawmut, the man who made insulting jokes or the other one, who had married a wife who couldn't bear that anyone should be insulted by his jokes?" (p. 390).

Bellow and Alexandra had what Adam calls "a good long run," including "at least four or five largely happy years." By the early 1980s, however, their differences began to tell. Alexandra's intelligence was unquestioned, as were her independence and seriousness, but her knowledge of Bellow's world, of literature, culture, politics, was "limited." She didn't get his references or his jokes; it made no sense for him to read her what he was writing. Like all three of Bellow's sons, Adam is fond of Alexandra and grateful to her for her kindness and for the influence she had on Bellow as a father. That "she was not comfortable outside mathematics," he believes, was a problem for the marriage, as was Bellow's sense that she treated emotional life "like mathematics." Bellow may also have sensed, Adam came later to believe, that as he aged, Alexandra "was not going to take care of him," that "on a deep level the attachment was not strong enough for him to rely on."

"How's the marriage going?" Adam remembers asking his father.

"There are days when I feel like throwing myself off the balcony," he replied. In the terrible summer of 1985, Adam and Rachel visited Bellow and Alexandra in Vermont. At dinner at Le Petit Chef, a favorite local restaurant, Alexandra asked the waiter if the veal was good. Bellow turned to the table and said, "This is her feeble-minded idea of asking the help what he thinks of the food." Alexandra remembers "walking about in a daze" that summer, "totally bewildered by the anger, the hostility that my mere presence provoked."[127]

As Bellow lost patience with Alexandra, she lost faith in him as a man. "It was a moral question for her," Adam believes. "He was a man who used other people." Three years into the marriage, Alexandra had sided with Bellow when Dave Peltz, whom she was especially fond of, was upset over the story "A Silver Dish," which fictionalizes episodes from his life. As with material Bellow drew on in *Humboldt's Gift*, Peltz asked him not to use these episodes, which he intended to write about himself. Alexandra, with Bellow's agreement, asked Adam to read the story and give his opinion about whether "Saul has the right to do this and Dave has the right to be upset." Adam read the story ("one of the greatest things I'd ever read") and answered "Yes" to both questions, which relieved Alexandra. What especially struck Adam about Bellow at this moment, when the marriage was strong, was how "vulnerable" he seemed "in this 'seminar' over which Alexandra presided." "He was really hanging on my judgment, and I felt that I had to be careful." In later years, Alexandra changed her views about an author's right to draw on real-life characters and episodes. Adam remembers her complaining about the use Bellow made of her family in *The Dean's December*. It had been "wrong" to depict her mother in the novel, "however admiringly." Her privacy and that of her mother and aunt had been violated. As Daniel puts it, Alexandra is "very old-school, very old-fashioned, very private."

Greg Bellow remembers other complaints in the last years of the marriage. Alexandra did not take sufficient interest in the building of the Vermont house, leaving Bellow to make all the decisions. Bellow was furious, Greg remembers, at finding himself "being forced to choose from a catalog filled with bathroom fixtures." Although he was impressed by Alexandra's achievements as a mathematician, her devotion to her career, Bellow told Greg, "wore on him"[128] (one recalls Henderson's first wife, Frances, in *Henderson the Rain King:* "When Berthe [the children's governess] had her appendix out there was nobody but myself to visit her in the hospital. My wife was too busy at the Collège de France" [p. 212]). Bellow complained that the marriage "lacked warmth"; he was only sticking with it "as he did not want to go through another divorce." At the end, the bad feeling between Bellow and Alexandra was unignorable. Lesha, who also spent summers in Vermont, described "the same cold war of interminable silences that [Greg] had witnessed between Susan and Saul twenty years earlier."[129] To Alexandra's friends the Copelands, the strains first came to the surface "as the house was being built. We went over for dinner one evening . . . and the bleakness was just stultifying, stifling. . . . That house never had any warmth in it from the time it was built."

This is not the way Alexandra remembers matters. One of the reasons she was "ecstatic" about the house was that "I really loved Vermont." It was to be "a dream house for our retirement." She has warm memories of entertaining and overnight guests (Harriet Wasserman, Barley Alison, John Auerbach, Allan Bloom, various family members). She "loved my little office on the second floor with its wrought iron balcony and the view of the forest." "I had hoped that the beautiful new house in Vermont would strengthen the marriage. Instead the marriage deteriorated to the point of no return. The summer of 1985 was nightmarish."[130]

Bellow's complaints about making all the decisions concerning the house are only partly corroborated by Frank Maltese, who built it. Maltese, a local handyman, had been helping the Bellows in Vermont since 1977. A straight talker, Maltese "bonded very quickly" with Bellow. What he especially liked about him as an employer was that "you didn't have to explain things twice. . . . He didn't pull punches, he said what he meant. We got along real good, there was no dancing around." Maltese had never built a whole house before, but Bellow gave him free rein. "He wanted it to be brown and he wanted it to have a slate floor and he went to Europe and it was done." As for billing, "He told me what he would like to spend and the price was agreed" (partly because, as Maltese puts it, "he wasn't going to be around"). When bills came in, Bellow "always complained about the price," but, then, "everybody likes a deal, and Saul liked a deal." In previous Vermont summers, it was Alexandra who found places to stay, paying for them herself. With the new house, Maltese dealt exclusively with Bellow. This arrangement he approved, since "men want the job done . . . and women want to control how the job is done." He knew Bellow well enough to know what he wanted. He wanted "quietude," so Maltese made sure all the rooms were properly insulated for sound. He also wanted escape, so Maltese thought carefully about ingress and egress. "In Saul's house every room has two doors," he explains, "because he didn't ever want to be cornered in any place." What Maltese remember of Alexandra is that she "wasn't comfortable" in the country, "didn't like the isolation." But what she was uncomfortable with was the marriage, and being isolated in the country with Bellow.

Harriet Wasserman visited Bellow and Alexandra in Vermont late in the summer of 1985. Bellow was at work on *More Die of Heartbreak*, and when Harriet arrived "the atmosphere was extremely tense." Alexandra had been "going into rages," Bellow complained. To Wasserman, Alexandra was "very polite," but she and Bellow "barely spoke to each other." When a close friend of Alexandra's invited them over for a visit, there was a tug of war between Bellow and Alexandra over whether to accept. Bellow wouldn't go, but Wasserman felt she had to, though she feared "Saul's wrath" for "siding" with Alexandra. In past years, Wasserman recalled, Bellow had found Alexandra's "somewhat halting" English and odd inflections attractive. Now "he had taken to teasing her with jokes and statements she couldn't quite follow." At one point, over drinks at the house, the teasing was so mean that Wasserman felt she had to intervene. On the drive to Le Petit Chef, no one spoke. After dinner, the plan was to watch a video of *The Godfather Part II*. Bellow started the video while Alexandra was upstairs fetching a sweater. When Wasserman protested that Bellow should wait, he "sat back in his seat, all excited with the satisfaction of one-upmanship."[131] Wasserman's memoir is bitterly anti-Bellow, but the tension and hostility she describes were noted by others.

Ruth Miller heard complaints about Alexandra's lack of warmth as well as her absorption in her work. Bellow had at least tried to understand her world. In contrast, he claimed, she took "no interest at all in what he was doing." He also began questioning the value of her research. "The power of even the ablest mathematicians begins to decline in the third decade," he wrote to Barley Alison. "Alexandra is now in her fifties [so the letter, which is undated, was written sometime after August 30, 1985, when Alexandra turned fifty]. She may enjoy trotting around to congresses where she is sure of a warm welcome because she is pretty and, thanks to me, well-heeled, also. She can stand the young prodigies to lunch, but she has little to contribute to the proceedings. She told me with heavy emphasis not many months ago that for a long time she had not been able to obtain significant results in her researches, and that it was ALL MY FAULT."[132]

Back in Chicago in September, tensions increased, partly because of the proximity of Bellow's colleague Allan Bloom, whose friendship with Bellow will be discussed in the next chapter, along with the relationship of his politics to Bellow's. On October 6, Bellow began a letter to the Chicago novelist Harry Petrakis by apologizing for having been out of touch. "The communication system is the first to go when I'm having personal difficulties. I had rather a bad summer." He and Alexandra had been traveling a lot since leaving Vermont, and "the traveling hasn't quite stopped—Alexandra has to go to Vancouver, and I have to go abroad briefly." The trip abroad was to Dublin, where Bellow spoke at Trinity College, on October 12, after which he spent several days in London.[133] He returned to Chicago for a week, then flew to New York to address the Whiting Foundation Writers' Program Ceremony on October 31.[134] In New York, he caught flu; as he wrote to William Kennedy on November 21, "It was all I could do to get through the ceremony much less greet my friends." The flu would not go away, he reported to John Auerbach from Chicago, in a letter of November 18, which meant he could not return to New York on November 25, "to be one of twenty speakers at a banquet in honor of [Teddy] Kollek." In a letter of December 6 to Kollek, Bellow describes the flu as "real and earnest . . . involving the head and the gastric regions and exorbitant thermometer readings." They would see each other soon, though, as he and Alexandra had been "pressed into attending" the World Jewish Congress in Jerusalem, where they would be in residence at the Hilton from December 24 to 30.[135]

Then the marriage finally came apart. Sometime before the end of December, Alexandra asked Bellow for a divorce, just over half a year after his seventieth birthday and the deaths of his brothers.[136] It was a decision he claimed took him by surprise. That he'd been difficult to live with he knew; it was "unnatural to grieve so much," he admitted to Barley Alison in a letter of September 6. But Alexandra's kicking him out and demanding a divorce left him, as William Hunt recalls, "pretty broken up." The decision to end the marriage was hers. "I wasn't the architect."[137] Her reasons for doing so, he decided, had less to do with how difficult he had been than how difficult he would become. As his son Greg puts it, in words that recall Adam's conjecture about Bellow's fears of not being taken care of, "he had convinced himself that Alexandra lacked the emotional strength to see him through his final passage."[138] Alexandra herself described the breakup as inevitable. "It had to happen sometime," she told Barley Alison.[139] Thirty years later, in 2016, she elaborated, attributing the fault to Bellow, as he had attributed the fault to her: "He needed to renew himself. . . . He needed new sources of inspiration. Toward the end of our marriage he would say, 'Look, she locks herself up in her study, I don't hear from her all morning, she doesn't care about me'—but that's the way things were from the very beginning, when he took great pride in me. He needed change, the old muse had to be deposed, and the new muse was waiting in the wings to be installed and anointed. So that was the natural process of things, I think now, in retrospect, but at the time I was very bewildered."[140]

SB's brothers, Maury and Sam Bellows (courtesy of Joel Bellows; courtesy of Lesha and Sam Greengus)

8

Janis Freedman/ Allan Bloom/Politics

THE NEW "MUSE" DID NOT THINK of herself as such. Her name was Janis Freedman, she was a graduate student at the Committee on Social Thought, and she had been Bellow's secretary since June 1982, working twelve hours a week, mainly handling correspondence. Janis took the job, as had her predecessor, Lillian Doherty, after finishing her fundamentals examination, a requirement for all Committee students. Her duties, Bellow explained to a university official, would "be mainly of a literary nature, and these should assist and enhance her studies. As Miss Doherty will be glad to testify, her duties have in no way interfered with her preparation for the Ph.D." Janis herself could determine her working hours. There would be "no interference with classwork, and the tasks are such as to leave ample study time. Miss Doherty has signified her willingness to train Miss Freedman in the organization of my papers and in the handling of correspondence."[1]

Janis Freedman's training was mostly a matter of learning "who was important and who wasn't," as the scale of the correspondence was impossible to deal with without form letters. Bellow "wasn't around very much." When he did come to the office, it was to receive mail or dictate letters. His relations with his new secretary, a slim, dark-haired young woman with a warm, intelligent voice, were friendly but professional. He was "Professor Bellow" to her, as he was in the courses she took from him. In her first year at the Committee, in the fall quarter of 1980, she took a seminar co-taught by Bellow and Allan Bloom on Machiavelli's *Mandragola* and several plays by Aristophanes. The following year, she took a second Bellow-and-Bloom seminar, on Rousseau's *Nouvelle Héloïse*, and arranged a reading course with Bellow on Balzac's *Lost Illusions*. She was, she recalls, "fascinated by him from the first time I set foot in class. He was extraordinary. I thought he was, hands down, the most intelligent person I'd ever met. But did I have a crush on him, the way I had a crush on teachers in high school or university? No." For his part, Bellow thought highly of Janis as a student, judging at least by the reference he wrote for her when, being a Canadian, she applied for a fellowship to the Social Sciences and Humanities Research Council of Canada:

> This quiet and polite young woman turns out to be a person of considerable intellectual force and independence. She doesn't so much attend seminars as ingest them. In class she is superattentive, most intense, I have seldom been made to feel even by the most alert students that I am being not only anticipated but perhaps exceeded. Her comments show this to be a distinct possibility. She seems to be traversing the subject, going back and forth on an invisible high wire. As you can see I hold a very high opinion of Miss Freedman. I expect her to accomplish great things.[2]

Janis enjoyed her work as Bellow's secretary, especially when he dictated letters to her, "because I learned so much." In addition to admiring Bellow, "I grew to like him a lot. He was a good boss," "very grateful for help" (the mass of correspondence, he told her, "weighed on him and made him sick"). Although happy to please him, Janis claims not to have had romantic illusions about their relationship. "He was so distant from my student life. He lived in another world. He lived in the North End. He had a very glamorous wife. He was a Nobel Prize winner. He was also very much older than me." Forty-three years older. Janis had met Alexandra, and they had got on well. She'd had Bellow and Alexandra to dinner, and in the summer of 1984 she was invited to Vermont for a few days to go through "a whole stack of letters." Alexandra was "very pleasant" during the visit; there wasn't "a single bad vibe." In the mornings, while Bellow wrote and Alexandra did her math, Janis did her own work; then she and Bellow had sessions with the correspondence. Janis met Alexandra's friends the Copelands, and went riding or took walks with them. "I had a great time." Unlike other visitors that summer, she was struck by "how nicely" Bellow and Alexandra greeted each other, how physically affectionate Bellow was with her.

Eighteen months later, after Alexandra broke with Bellow, Janis and others of Bellow's students helped to move his things from the Sheridan Road apartment back to 5825 Dorchester, where Jonathan Kleinbard had found him an apartment two floors below the apartment he'd lived in with Alexandra before their move to Sheridan Road. He was not at that time the building's only Nobel Prize winner. Milton Friedman lived there, as did George Stigler, also an economist, and S. Chandrasekhar, the physicist. According to Janis, Bellow had "some sort of hideous flu" at the time of the move, which "looked like pneumonia." Lesha came to Chicago to look after him and to cook him chicken soup. Alexandra herself was alarmed, inviting Janis to lunch and telling her Bellow "was in bad shape" and needed extra help. In *Ravelstein*, Vela, the Alexandra figure, harbors suspicions about Rosamund, the Janis figure. "Your little Rosamund is dying to take care of you," she tells Chick. After visits to their lakeside apartment to help Chick with his calls and correspondence, Rosamund likes to go for a swim. Vela thinks she does so, she tells Chick, "because you can see her beautiful figure" (p. 119). Janis thinks this exchange is completely fictional: Alexandra "thought of me as beneath her notice"; besides, "she looked better in a bathing suit than I did." Janis felt affection and sympathy for Bellow, but that, she claims, was all. "Still there was nothing. This was an old sick person who had been beat up."

JANIS FREEDMAN WAS BORN on September 3, 1958, the second of Harvey and Sonya Freedman's three children. Harvey, a psychiatrist, came from Romanian and Polish Jewish stock. He was the first member of his family to go to university, receiving his medical degree from the University of Toronto, where he later taught in the Faculty of Medicine. In addition to teaching, Harvey had a busy private practice. He also helped to found the Gestalt Institute of Toronto, having studied in New York with Fritz Perls, the founder of Gestalt therapy. Sonya Freedman (née Rosen), a second-generation Canadian, came from Russian Jewish stock. At the University of Western Ontario, she studied music, then trained as a concert pianist and taught the piano for many years. By the mid-1980s, she was also writing short stories. The Freedman children were high achievers. Janis's younger brother, Robert, an architect, was for ten years director of urban planning for the city of Toronto; her older sister, Wendy, an eminent astronomer, now at the University of Chicago, was previously director of the Carnegie Observatories, in Pasadena and Chile, codirector of the team that discovered the Hubble Constant, and a co-winner of the Gruber Cosmology Prize, astronomy's equivalent of the Nobel Prize. All three children went to local public schools and the University of Toronto. Janis describes herself as literary from an early age, "through the influence of my mother." Bright and serious, a straight-A student, she "worked like a maniac" at university; when she enrolled at the Committee on Social Thought in 1980, she had narrowly missed out on a Rhodes Scholarship.

The Freedmans were "a tight pack," and they still are. They have no tales of sibling rivalry or adolescent rebellion. Right through college, the children liked to retreat from the city with their parents, spending weekends and holidays on a small family farm forty miles from Toronto. The farm was purchased in 1971, when Janis was thirteen, and it came with horses, to which were added cows, rabbits, a dog, and many cats, at one point twenty-one of them. Here the Freedman children and their friends skated on the pond, went cross-country skiing, and rode horses; Janis describes her adolescent self as having "a thing about horses." The Freedmans were well off but not rich; there were family holidays to Europe, Israel, and the Caribbean, but they did not have enough money to educate the children privately (had they wanted to, which they didn't). Although raised in Orthodox Jewish families, Harvey and Sonya did not belong to a synagogue (except, presumably, when Robert had his bar mitzvah); Wendy and Janis did not have bat mitzvahs. As Wendy puts it, though they were not religious Jews, "culturally we identified with where we came from." The family hosted seders and on Friday nights lit candles and ate challah bread, but they did not say prayers. Nor was the family political. When asked to sum up his politics, Harvey answered, "A plague on both your houses." "We raised a family that was apolitical. We see the folly on the left and the folly on the right and consider ourselves smug, snobbish, and superior." When asked about voting, his answer was "Every four years, vote for the other guy."

It was at the University of Toronto that Janis discovered philosophy, taking courses in Kant and Aristotle, along with courses on Shakespeare and the Romantics. She had "a hard time with anything having to do with math," and panicked when she took a logic course, until Harvey, the scientific parent, stepped in. "My father was always astonishingly calm about everything, and he said, You know what you have to do here? Everything one step at a time, and you can do this, calmly, easily, and well. . . . I needed a lot of that coaching through college, both from Wendy and from my dad." Janis ended up with the top mark in her logic class. The class that mattered most to her, however, was on Plato's *Republic*, a large lecture class taught by Allan Bloom. Janis describes Bloom's lectures as "absolutely astonishing." What distinguished him from other professors was "the seriousness with which he took what he was teaching" and his intellectual "adventurousness." Bloom made his students feel that there was more to education "than just going into a profession." His popularity with students, Janis believes, contributed to the hostility with which he was viewed by some of his colleagues at Toronto. She remembers her ethics professor announcing, "Anyone who uses Allan Bloom's translation of the *Republic* gets a fail." At the end of Janis's sophomore year, Bloom left Toronto for a position at the Committee on Social Thought, and Janis went on to take courses from his ex-students Clifford Orwin and Thomas Pangle, by then colleagues at Toronto. After her Rhodes disappointment (she "blew" the interview), she was admitted to study for a Ph.D. at the Committee. It was the only graduate program she had applied to, partly because it would allow her to combine philosophy and literature, partly because of Allan Bloom (whom she had never met, despite taking his Plato course), and partly because she wanted to read Homer in Greek with David Grene. When she set off for Chicago in the autumn of 1980, she was the first member of her family to move away from home.

IT WAS EDWARD SHILS who had masterminded Allan Bloom's appointment to the Committee on Social Thought. On February 17, 1976, Shils wrote to Bellow listing several possible job candidates, including Bloom, whom he described as "really quite outstanding." That Bloom had himself been a graduate of the Committee was an advantage. He was also, Shils thought, "probably the best of Leo Strauss's pupils." Shils's only worry was that Bloom could be "a bit of a fanatic on all the important questions discussed by Strauss," though "I have become informed that he has become a bit more polished in his manners and a bit easier to get on with." David Grene, no ally of Shils, also welcomed the appointment. He knew Bloom well, had supervised his thesis, and could be counted on to welcome the appointment. Opposition came, however, from the Departments of Philosophy and Political Science. On June 8, 1978, Bellow wrote to John Wilson, president of the university, protesting, not for the first time, the requirement that outside departments approve Committee appointments, what he called "this insulting fashion of dealing with our nominations." A year later, Bloom's appointment was approved.

Bloom remembered meeting Bellow in the 1950s, while Bloom was a graduate student at the Committee. They had been introduced at a party in Hyde Park, where Bellow and Jack Ludwig were among the guests. Bloom told Nathan Tarcov that he was so disgusted with Ludwig's fawning over Bellow that he steered clear of them both. Bellow had no recollection of this meeting, but when Bloom came from Toronto to be interviewed, Bellow was charmed by him. Tarcov remembers that Bellow told him Bloom resembled Tarcov's father, Oscar, "which was to me strange but interesting, since one was my father and the other was a very influential teacher of mine. The resemblance had never occurred to me." The summer before Bloom took up his appointment, which began in 1975, Bellow wrote to him about arrangements for a seminar they had agreed to teach in the spring:

> We'll run a tutorial on any afternoon convenient to you. I refrain from coming to the campus in the morning. My habit is to work until noon at whatever I happen to have to hand and then seek refreshment in Hyde Park. We should have a splendid time with Stendhal and Flaubert, against a background of Jean-Jacques. There must be a few students at the Committee who read French. . . . Whenever I taught with David [Grene], there was always a preliminary session for the two of us—at Jimmy's naturally. You and I can find another suitably grimy spot, if Jimmy's is too much for you. Some people can't take it.
>
> With great expectation,
> Ever yours,
> Saul

ALLAN BLOOM WAS BORN in Indianapolis in 1930, the child of Jewish social workers. Two years after the family moved to Chicago, he entered the University of Chicago. He was fifteen. Three years later, he graduated with a bachelor's degree in liberal arts. As an undergraduate, Bloom fell under the influence of Leo Strauss, a professor in Chicago's Department of Political Science. Strauss, a German Jewish émigré, moved to the United States in 1937, after brief research stints in Paris and England. He was a research fellow at Columbia, taught for ten years at the New School, and in 1949 took up his post at Chicago, where he taught for two decades. In later life, he taught for a year and a half at Claremont Men's College (not yet Claremont McKenna College) in California, and then went to St. John's College, Annapolis, in 1970, where he stayed until his death in 1973.

Through Strauss, Bloom became a devotee of Plato and the classical tradition. In *The Closing of the American Mind: How Higher Education Has Failed Democracy and Impoverished the Souls of Today's Students* (1987), Bloom writes, "When I was fifteen years old I saw the University of Chicago for the first time and somehow sensed that I had discovered my life."[3] He received his Ph.D. from the Committee on Social Thought in 1955, for a dissertation on the Greek rhetorician Isocrates. What David Grene remembered of Bloom as a graduate student is that he was "frightfully enthusiastic and very dogmatic, very funny."[4] From 1955 to 1960, Bloom taught courses in Chicago's Basic Program for Liberal Education for Adults. During these years, he also studied for periods in Heidelberg and Paris. In 1960, he moved first to Yale, where he taught until 1963, then to Cornell, where he taught until 1970, and where student militancy had a profound effect on him, as it had on Bellow. So appalled was Bloom by the violence of the militants at Cornell and what he saw as the cowardice of the administration that he left the university in disgust.

In the chapter of *The Closing of the American Mind* entitled "The Sixties," the events at Cornell are given pride of place. At their heart lay problems of race. In 1963, when Bloom arrived at Cornell, there were only twenty-five African American students out of an undergraduate population of eleven thousand. The newly appointed president of the university, James A. Perkins, previously chairman of the board of the United Negro College Fund, set out to increase the number, and by 1969 it had grown to 250 out of fourteen thousand. Despite their increased numbers, many African American undergraduates felt alienated from the university. Influenced both by the Black Power movement and by a series of real and perceived slights and threats to their safety, they sought measures to separate themselves from the main student body. The newly created Afro-American Society (AAS) lobbied for curriculum reform and segregated programs and facilities. When the university dragged its feet over the society's demands, frustrated protesters disrupted classes and damaged property, insisting upon the right of black students to devise and administer their own courses and to restrict admission to some classes on the basis of color.

By 1969, these and other separatist demands were accompanied by threats of violence and disruption. In one instance, during a symposium to discuss the university's investments in South Africa, an AAS student rushed onstage and grabbed President Perkins by the collar while he was speaking. When the university's supervisor of public safety moved to defend Perkins, another AAS student climbed onstage and threatened him with a wooden plank. The story made the front page of *The New York Times*, and the AAS immediately expelled the two protesters. The administration, however, was reluctant to punish African American students, or to punish them severely, and some administrators and faculty expressed admiration for the moral convictions of the protesters.

Then things got worse. On the night of April 17, 1969, a burning cross appeared on the lawn of Wari House, a cooperative residence for black women. The next morning, the AAS occupied Cornell's student-activity center, Willard Straight Hall, evacuating students, their visiting parents, and all university employees, and chaining shut the doors.[5] In solidarity, 150 white students from SDS formed a barricade around the building, condemning the "racist and capitalist policies" both of Cornell and of America at large. When twenty-five white fraternity students tried to invade the building to end the takeover, leaving after a brief scuffle, rifles were smuggled in to the occupiers. The administration ordered the campus police not to intervene. Over a megaphone, an armed AAS leader shouted, "If any more white students come in, you're gonna die here." Later in the day, an agreement was reached between the AAS and the administration. In exchange for the occupiers' vacating the building, the administration agreed to recommend that they not be punished, that punishments for previous disturbances be nullified, that the university would help the protesters with legal counseling and pay for any damages to Willard Straight Hall, and that Wari House would be given round-the-clock protection. As the last AAS occupiers left the building, they did so carrying rifles and making Black Power salutes. An Associated Press photograph of the moment appeared on the cover of *Newsweek* and won a Pulitzer Prize.

To many students and faculty, peace at Cornell had been bought at the price of a shameful capitulation on the part of the administration. Bloom was outspoken in his opposition to the administration, directing students, some carrying signs reading "Berlin '32, Ithaca '69," to hand out extracts from Plato's *Republic*.[6] When the faculty met to discuss the administration's recommendations, they accepted some measures, but by a wide margin rejected the amnesty granted to earlier demonstrators. The presence of guns on the campus made it "impossible for the Faculty to agree at this meeting to dismiss the penalties imposed." In reaction, an AAS leader denounced the withdrawing of the amnesty on campus radio, calling its supporters racists and threatening four administrators and three named professors, one of them Allan Bloom. He gave out their home addresses and warned that if the faculty did not reverse its vote by 9:00 p.m. "they would be dealt with." He ended his speech by announcing, "Cornell has three hours to live." Bloom and the other threatened faculty and administrators checked themselves and their families into motels under assumed names. Bloom also helped to protect a black student who had opposed the takeover, putting him on a late-night bus to Montreal and arranging for him to finish his studies at Harvard.

When the Cornell faculty reconvened, under threat of violence not only from AAS militants and their SDS supporters, but from the intervention of armed state authorities, they overturned their previous vote, repealing all penalties. During the debate, forty-nine faculty members sympathetic to the AAS students threatened to go on strike, and twenty-six faculty members declared their readiness to participate in further occupations. The reversal of the earlier decision was covered in *The New York Times*, as was the resignation of President Perkins in June, and the furious departure of a number of well-known faculty, including not just Bloom but Walter Berns, a past chair of the Department of Government; Allan Sindler, the current chair; Donald Kagan, the historian and classicist; and Thomas Sowell, a black assistant professor of economics who was later to describe the AAS occupiers as "hoodlums" with "serious academic problems."[7]

In *The Closing of the American Mind*, Bloom attributes the uprising at Cornell to affirmative action. In the drive to recruit black students, he claims, the university sought them out in inner cities as well as among the privileged. "And, of course, in order to get so many, particularly poor blacks, standards of admission had silently and drastically been altered. Nothing had been done to prepare these students for the great intellectual and social challenges awaiting them in the university. Cornell now had a large number of students who were manifestly unqualified and unprepared, and therefore it faced an inevitable choice: fail most of them or pass them without their having learned." For these students, integration was seen as "an ideology for whites and Uncle Toms." Hence the demand for black-studies courses, "decidedly attractive to the kids who were the victims of the university's manipulations" (p. 94). Hence also the appearance of separate tables in the dining halls, "which reproduce the separate facilities of the Jim Crow South" (p. 95). As Bloom saw it, "The worst part of all this is that the black students, most of whom avidly support this system, hate its consequences," principally the sense "that whites are in the position to do them favors" and "that everyone doubts their merit, their capacity for equal achievement." Bloom's conclusion is that "democratic society cannot accept any principle of achievement other than merit" (p. 96). Of the need for a level playing field in determining merit, Bloom says little. This is similar to Bellow's failure in the Jefferson Lectures to acknowledge, or adequately acknowledge, the role of discriminatory practices in the disintegration of the black slums.

NATHAN TARCOV, as a student at Cornell in the late 1960s, knew and admired Bloom, and took his courses in the Department of Government. In 1968, he wrote an article in the fall issue of *The Public Interest*, edited by Daniel Bell and Irving Kristol, deploring Cornell's failure to stand up for what he called "the fundamental characteristics of education in the arts college."[8] Tarcov had come to Cornell in 1964 a moderate leftist. In his freshman year, he joined SDS, not yet a radical organization, and served as its treasurer. He soon drifted toward the center, steering clear of mass rallies both for and against the Vietnam War. Instead, he and five fellow students, one of them Paul Wolfowitz, formed what they called the "Committee for Critical Support of the United States in Vietnam." Wolfowitz, later deputy secretary of defense and president of the World Bank, had been a student of Bloom's, as had the political scientist Francis Fukuyama. Other students of Bloom's included Edith Jones, who would become chief judge of the United States Court of Appeals for the Fifth Circuit; William Galston, later an adviser to President Clinton and a senior fellow at the Brookings Institution; and Alan Keyes, former presidential candidate and assistant secretary of state. Keyes was the black student Bloom sent to Montreal and then to Harvard. According to Tarcov, neither Bloom nor the majority of his students could rightly be called conservatives at this time, certainly in terms of electoral politics. Bloom voted for Johnson in 1964, for Humphrey in 1968, for Carter in 1976, and had he lived to see the 1992 election would have voted for Clinton.[9] In "Western Civ," the opening essay in *Giants and Dwarfs: Essays 1960–1990* (1990), Bloom himself declares: "I am not a conservative—neo- or paleo-. I say this not to curry favor in a setting where conservatism is out of favor [the essay is a reprint of an address delivered at Harvard University on December 7, 1988]. Conservatism is a respectable outlook, and its adherents usually have to have some firmness of character to stick by what is so unpopular in universities. I just do not happen to be that animal. Any superficial reading of my book will show that I differ from both theoretical and practical conservative positions."[10]

Like Janis, Tarcov and his fellow students at Cornell were drawn to Bloom by his power as a teacher. Tarcov has several objections to Bellow's portrait of Bloom in *Ravelstein*, but what he mentions first is its failure to portray Bloom as a teacher. According to Clifford Orwin, an exact contemporary of Tarcov's at Cornell, and Bloom's colleague later at Toronto, "In one year at Yale, teaching in Directed Studies where the best undergraduates were to be found, [Bloom] inspired two of them to transfer to Cornell immediately, and another four to resolve to attend graduate school there. These decisions to transfer were made within weeks of the students' first meetings with Allan."[11] As undergraduates at Cornell, both Orwin and Tarcov won room-and-board scholarships to Telluride House, a residence hall described by Tarcov as "a designated hatchery for intellectuals." Everyone there, Orwin remembers, was obsessed with Bloom, who had been a faculty resident the previous year. They either "loved or hated him. The two parties therefore fell to warring for the souls of us freshmen. The Bloom question raged unabated, inside the residence and on the campus generally, for my entire four years at Cornell." For Orwin and his friends, "Allan was the foremost issue of the Sixties, with which all the others were hopelessly entangled." When Orwin went to Harvard to do a Ph.D., he again found that "a great many people were obsessed with Allan. He remained throughout his life the consuming topic of discussion whenever his acquaintance gathered."[12]

Orwin, like Tarcov and Janis, stresses Bloom's appeal as a teacher. "His presence . . . was astonishing"; "If nervous energy was radioactive his casualties would have dwarfed Chernobyl." (In non-teaching contexts, Bellow captures this intensity in *Ravelstein*, along with many physical and other eccentricities, as all who knew Bloom, including friends who deplore the novel, agree.) Bloom made his students feel, in Orwin's words, "that study was something exalted, one of the rarest human privileges. . . . Through knowing him it suddenly became credible that a life devoted to a couple of dozen mostly old books was one of surpassing nobility and joyfulness." Like his mentor, Leo Strauss, Bloom often structured his courses around single texts (the *Republic*, *The Prince*, *Gulliver's Travels*, *Madame Bovary*), each read in its entirety. Mixing explication with jokes and provocative questions, he sought to show how current social, cultural, and political problems "upon examination always proved variants of age-old human problems." For Bloom, Plato was not only, as Orwin puts it, "speaking to *us*," but "had thought more deeply about the problems that most gripped us than we had ever been going to think about them ourselves."

Although Bloom is thought of as anti-liberal, when discussing politics, according to Orwin, he "was every bit as hard on 'conservatism' as on 'liberalism.'" Orwin believes his reputation as anti-liberal owes something to the fact that "all of his best students began on the Left, even if few remained there." The related view that Bloom was "elitist" applies in some respects but not others. Although no social snob ("he was committed to liberal education for everybody," according to Nathan Tarcov), Bloom believed that some people were smarter than others, just as some books were more intelligent or valuable than others. In defending the Great Books tradition in his Harvard speech, he was, he teased, challenging "elite education," which champions "a new 'nonelitist,' 'nonexclusionary' curriculum in the humanities and in parts of the social sciences. . . . I have always been a supporter and a beneficiary of the movements toward practical equality." These words come from the beginning of the speech, which opened with the words "Fellow elitists," an acknowledged allusion to FDR's salutation in an address to the Daughters of the American Revolution: "Fellow Immigrants." Bloom goes on to declare, "*Elite* is not a word I care for very much—imprecise and smacking of sociological abstraction—but if any

American institution of any kind merits it, it is Harvard, and it lends that tincture to everyone associated with it."[13]

The charge of elitism derives in part from Bloom's association with Strauss's method of reading and writing, an inheritance from those he wrote about, including Maimonides, Al-Farabi, and Socrates. According to Strauss, the teachings of these figures can be read in two ways: to most readers, what Strauss calls "*exoteric*" readers, they can be seen as suggesting the compatibility of religion and philosophy; to "*esoteric*" readers, more attentive readers, a different and truer meaning, dangerous and therefore disguised, suggests the incompatibility not only of philosophy and religion but, in religious societies, of philosophy and the state. This theory of esoteric and exoteric writing is most directly described by Strauss in *Persecution and the Art of Writing* (1952): "Persecution, then, gives rise to a peculiar technique of writing, and therewith to a peculiar type of literature, in which the truth about all crucial things is presented exclusively between the lines. That literature is addressed, not to all readers, but to trustworthy and intelligent readers only."[14] Strauss's view has been controversial and widely challenged, by classicists, medievalists, and historians of modern thought. Among journalists and political commentators in the period leading up to the Iraq War, it spawned what the political theorist Mark Lilla calls "absurd" rumor and speculation about Straussian "duplicity," and the influence it had on United States policy. In Lilla's words, it was claimed that Strauss "never wrote what he thought, that his secret antidemocratic doctrines were passed on to adepts [like Bloom and his students] who subsequently infiltrated government. At its ideological fringes the term 'cabal' was occasionally employed, in ignorance (one hopes) of its anti-Semitic connotations."[15]

Like many Straussians, Bloom did not write much, partly because of his devotion to teaching. Much of what he did write grew out of this teaching and was intended to serve it, as in his translations of the *Republic* and Rousseau's *Émile*, with their detailed introductions. The advice he gave to Ph.D. students was to find one great writer and stick to him; over his lifetime, he stuck to four great writers: Plato, Shakespeare, Rousseau, and Nietzsche. Bloom differed from Strauss not only in how little he wrote but in the audience he addressed: Strauss wrote for scholars, Bloom for students, albeit advanced students, and the general public. Like Bellow, but unlike Strauss, Bloom had ambivalent feelings about popular or material culture, about which he knew more than one might suppose from his writings. Nathan Tarcov thinks Bellow and Bloom only selectively acknowledged these feelings. "My view is that both of them sort of took an official policy of contempt for American vulgarity and materialism, and *loved* American vulgarity and materialism, in different ways." In *The Closing of the American Mind*, Bloom writes dismissively of rock music, but at Telluride House, which had only a single hi-fi in the early 1960s, Tarcov remembers being told that "he actually sided with those who liked rock over classical music."[16] Tarcov also remembers "the strong sympathy Bloom had for African Americans, which somehow doesn't come out in much of the official statements. He really liked the vitality of democratic American life, and so does Saul. . . . They both subscribe to an official position that is more elitist and more anti-American than their real feeling."

Not everyone found Bloom compelling. Maggie Staats Simmons thought that he fawned over Bellow, and when, for a moment, it seemed possible that she and Bellow might get together again, in the period between their respective fourth and fifth marriages, she was put off partly by the realization that life with Bellow would mean lots of time with Bloom. To Joseph Epstein, a Shils partisan, Bloom was "pushy," "forward," "clownish" ("He looked like Jackie Mason's agent"). Harriet Wasserman thought he looked "like Milton Berle before a nose job."[17] As Clifford Orwin admits, Bloom "had vices," and "because his personality was so forceful, these were obtrusive. His nervousness and intensity put people off. He could be abrasive and overbearing, and sometimes argued unfairly. He loved attention, and he insisted on it. He dominated social situations so thoroughly as to drive hostesses to despair." Epstein recalls Shils saying to Bloom, "Allan, it is true you haven't read many books, but you have read twenty-five or thirty books intensely, and they should tell you that it doesn't matter a shit that Reagan fell a point and a half in the opinion polls." Shils and Epstein had personal rather than political objections to Bloom; James Redfield, who had little time for Bloom politically, got on well with him personally, liking the very qualities that put others off, "his good energy," "wild energy."

JANIS, WHO ATTENDED ALL THE SEMINARS taught jointly by Bloom and Bellow, was struck by the easy familiarity between the two men and their shared sense of humor. In addition, they seemed to her to be "learning from each other." Bloom kept drawing Bellow out about the literary aspects of the works discussed, while Bellow sought from Bloom their philosophical implications or underpinnings. When Nathan Tarcov attended a seminar the two men taught on *The Red and the Black*, he had a similar impression, though in terms that may help to explain Maggie Staats Simmons's sense of Bloom as fawning. "One of Allan's personas was as a kind of talk show host or MC, which was quite different from his charismatic, theatrical persona. . . . My sense is that much but not all of the time he would play that role in the classes with Saul. He would try to get Saul to say things. Saul being Saul, it would sometimes be hard to get Saul to come out and pronounce on things. And there was this weird dynamism, that very often it seemed that Allan wanted to talk about literature, to get Saul to talk about literary questions, and Saul would want to talk about philosophy, to get Allan to talk about philosophical issues." Bloom once asked Harriet Wasserman if she knew a place where he could stay on Martha's Vineyard before a summer visit with Bellow in Vermont. "I need to be in shape to spend some time in the Green Mountains with Saul. I want to go and relax, and he wants to talk about Nietzsche, Rousseau, etc. I've got to be on my toes the whole time."[18]

Like Shils, whose position as friend and intellectual crony he supplanted, Bloom offered Bellow a theoretical frame for his intuitions, which is not to say he offered him a system. As Leon Kass, a colleague at the Committee, puts it, Bloom "had at his fingertips most of the important human philosophical questions, questions of personal psychology, questions of politics, and he knew what the great arguments were about these things." Bloom's sense of these arguments owed much to Strauss. That he was a "Straussian" all agree, though what this means is as much a matter of dispute as the charge of "elitism." In America, a number of Bloom's students became involved in Republican and neoconservative politics. For Mark Blitz, one such student, who served as director of the United States Information Agency under Ronald Reagan and is now a professor of political science at Claremont McKenna, "The elements in Strauss that prepared and allowed an affinity with conservatives" were "anti-communism (and not amelioration), the virtue of individual responsibility (and not excessive social welfare), individual rights (and not affirmative action or feminism), market competition (and not excessive regulation or quasi-oligarchy), and educational and artistic excellence (and not 'politicization' or self-indulgence)." Strauss was certainly anti-communist and pro-virtue (as well as pro-excellence in education), but as Mark Lilla points out, "There is not a word in his works about such topics as welfare, affirmative action, feminism and the like."[19]

One point of connection between Strauss and his American followers, Bloom included, was historical or experiential rather than theoretical. Strauss had been a student of Heidegger. When, in his Rector's Address at the University of Freiburg in 1933, Heidegger hailed Hitler and the rise of Nazism, Strauss felt betrayed not only by his mentor but by the German liberals who had capitulated to Nazi threats and intimidation. To Bloom and others, Bellow included, the disturbances at Cornell and other American universities recalled Weimar Germany, with liberal faculty and administrators repeating the mistakes of German liberals. As Bloom puts it: "The American university in the sixties was experiencing the same dismantling of the structure of rational inquiry as had the German university in the thirties" (p. 313). James Redfield remembers both Shils and Bellow making similar comparisons at the time of the student uprisings in Chicago.

Strauss's most influential book, *Natural Right and History* (1953), argues against a view of truth as historical or evolutionary, positing instead a tradition of "classical natural right" in which, for example, Socrates and Thomas Aquinas shared not only a sense of the difference between nature and convention but also a conviction that justice is what accords with nature. This conviction is expressed in terms such as "We hold these truths to be self-evident" from the Declaration of Independence (one of two epigraphs to *Natural Right and History*, the other being from 2 Samuel 12, a parable of "self-evident" injustice). It was Machiavelli who inaugurated the most influential attack on these views, according to Strauss, leading, in Lilla's summary, "after intermediate stops at Locke's liberalism and Rousseau's Romanticism . . . [to] historicism and nihilism."[20] Lilla quotes from the introduction to *Natural Right and History*, where, with Heidegger in mind, but also Max Weber, Strauss declares, "The contemporary rejection of natural right leads to nihilism, nay, it is identical with nihilism."[21] Within a university context, by which is meant an undergraduate context, it is the Great Books, repositories of natural or universal truths, that are rejected or at least marginalized. Students are drawn away from the actual words of the Great Books to the contexts out of which they grew, as elaborated by historicist and other critics, or the Great Books themselves are replaced by Not-So-Great Books, the sort assigned, according to their

Straussian detractors (if not Strauss himself), in black or feminist or other "identity" programs of study.

"I DON'T THINK I READ a single work of criticism the whole time I was there," recalls Janis of her years at the Committee. She read Plato with Nathan Tarcov, Maimonides and Spinoza with Ralph Lerner, Homer with David Grene, and, in the joint seminars of Bloom and Bellow, she read Balzac, Dickens, Flaubert, Proust, Stendhal, Rousseau, and Joyce. To these were added language courses: French, Greek ("the hardest thing I ever studied"), Russian ("easy compared to the Greek"). Presumably, there were secondary or critical reading lists for these courses (Tarcov's list of secondary reading for a course on Leo Strauss runs to several pages), but Janis prospered at the Committee without them, gaining a distinction on her fundamentals examination. The texts she chose to be examined on were *War and Peace*, the *Republic*, *Émile* and *La Nouvelle Héloïse*, *King Lear*, *Antony and Cleopatra*, *The Tempest*, *Ulysses*, *Antigone*, and Thucydides's *History of the Peloponnesian War*.

To be a favored student of Bloom's at the Committee could bring financial as well as intellectual benefits. Nathan Tarcov explains the source of these benefits. In 1983, Bloom found himself seated on an airplane next to Michael S. Joyce, executive vice-president of the Olin Foundation, a conservative philanthropic organization that had been established in 1953 by John M. Olin, president of Olin Industries, a chemical-and-munitions manufacturing business.[22] The Olin Foundation had remained largely inactive until 1969, when Olin, at the age of eighty, reacted with outrage to the disturbances at Cornell, his alma mater. Through grants to conservative think tanks, media outlets, law schools, and graduate programs at influential universities, including Harvard, Yale, Stanford, Duke, Pennsylvania, and the University of Chicago, Olin set out to counter radicalism in all its forms. To prevent any softening of will over time, he directed that the entirety of the foundation's assets be spent within a generation of his death. Between 1969 and 2005, when the foundation was disbanded (twenty-three years after Olin's death in 1982), $370 million of its assets had been distributed to conservative projects and venues.

Michael S. Joyce was impressed with Bloom during their conversation on the airplane, and before parting suggested that he come up with a program that the foundation might fund. Bloom immediately set out to devise such a program, conferring with Nathan Tarcov, now teaching in the University of Chicago's Department of Political Science (he did not join the Committee until 1990). Tarcov remembers sitting with Bloom on a bench in the Midway and devising what came to be called the John M. Olin Center for Inquiry into the Theory and Practice of Democracy. The aims of the center, which opened in 1984, are set out on its Web site: "to provide a forum for the reconsideration and analysis of the fundamental principles and current practices of American politics and society, along with a thoughtful examination of classic philosophical, theological, and literary texts."[23] These aims were to be realized in several ways: by developing "scholars and practical men and women who will make a lasting contribution to the future of our society"; by running conferences and lecture series for advanced students and scholars; and by financing publications, some growing out of the center's conferences, others the work of center faculty, or their allies and influences (among them, Leo Strauss, transcripts of whose classes were word-processed and published by the University of Chicago Press). The Olin Junior Fellows scheme, largely controlled by Bloom and Tarcov, awarded full-tuition grants to graduate students drawn mainly from the Committee on Social Thought and the Department of Political Science. Janis Freedman was one of ten Committee students in her year to become Olin Junior Fellows.

Bellow was listed among the center's Senior Fellows and often attended its lectures, frequently dining afterward with visiting speakers. "Bloom provided a very rich social life," Janis recalls, "much good talk and laughter." A lot of this talk and laughter came from the political right. Among the visiting speakers Bloom invited Bellow to dine with were Antonin Scalia, Jeane Kirkpatrick, Vladimir Bukovsky, Robert Conquest, Irving Kristol, and Bernard Lewis. He may also have dined with more left-leaning visitors, including Christopher Lasch, Michael Walzer, Conor Cruise O'Brien, and Bill Bradley. Bellow also attended and spoke at the center's first conference, held in the summer of 1984, in Marlboro, Vermont, a short drive from his house. The title of this five-day conference was "The Writer in the Contemporary World," and contributors included Czesław Miłosz, A. B. Yehoshua, Leszek Kołakowski, Andrei Sinyavsky, Ruth Prawer Jhabvala, Allan Bloom, Werner J. Dannhauser (who was, like his friend Bloom, a student of Strauss's), and Bellow himself. There were also fourteen student fellows, including Janis (who joined the conference after her stay at Bellow's house to help him sort out his mail) and her boyfriend, Peter Ahrensdorf, who would later go on to teach political science and classics at Davidson College. During the conference, the student fellows were put up in a modest hotel, while, as Janis puts it, "the big shots stayed at the White House," a historic inn in Wilmington, Vermont, near Bellow's home. The Israeli novelist A. B. Yehoshua remembers being met at the airport in New York by Janis and another student, and being driven, together with his wife, to the conference. The other things he remembers about the conference were how lavish it was (he and his wife were given a car to use during their stay, and there were lots of grand meals at restaurants) and "the way that Allan Bloom was all the time surrounded by students, like Socrates surrounded by students. This impressed me very much."

BELLOW'S INTEREST IN the philosophical underpinnings of Bloom's politics, in particular its Straussian stress on natural right, derived in part from his attraction to the sorts of extra-rational "truths" required of, say, a follower of Rudolf Steiner. As ever, what he sought was intellectual support for his intuitions, principally about the soul and the afterlife, his conviction (in *The Closing of the American Mind*, Bloom calls it an "awareness" or "divination") "that there is a human nature, and that assisting its fulfillment is his task" (p. 20).[24] In *More Die of Heartbreak*, Bellow identifies this need for intellectual ballast as characteristically American. "If you venture to think in America," declares the novel's narrator, Kenneth Trachtenberg, in some respects a Bellow stand-in, "you also feel an obligation to provide a historical sketch to go with it, to authenticate or legitimize your thoughts. So it's one moment of flashing insight and then a quarter of an hour of pedantry and tiresome elaboration—academic gabble. Locke to Freud with stops at local stations like Bentham and Kierkegaard. One has to feel sorry for people in such an explanatory bind. Or else (a better alternative) one can develop an eye for the comical side of this" (p. 183).

BELLOW'S INTEREST IN domestic politics and foreign affairs, as opposed to cultural politics, remained peripheral. He was wary of joining political movements and organizations. Although happy to listen to and help to entertain the Olin Center's parade of mostly right-wing speakers, he was quick to withdraw his support from other groups. In late 1976, he agreed to lend his name to the Board of Directors of the recently formed Committee on the Present Danger, which sought to alert the country to what it saw as the weakness of America's foreign and defense policies. In *To Jerusalem and Back*, Bellow himself had expressed dismay at America's ignorance of "the real dangers of Russian ambitions," particularly but not exclusively in the Middle East.[25] Bellow had little problem at first with the committee, none at all with its initial statements of intent, released at an inaugural press conference on November 11, 1976.[26] These statements listed the committee's chief tenets: that détente was "illusory" and ought to be abandoned; that defense spending, which "is lower than at any time in twenty-five years," ought to be increased; and that "there is a crucial moral difference between the two super powers in their character and objectives. The United States—imperfect as it is—is essential to the hopes of those countries which desire to develop their societies in their own ways, free of coercion." The committee claimed to have "no political axe to grind," welcoming the support of all political parties. It also claimed to have "no organizational affiliates. All members serve in their individual capacities." Its concern would be "with broad principles and policy objectives," as opposed to "short-range tactics or maneuvers." It would "not urge the election or defeat of individual candidates for office." Instead, it would "encourage, conduct, and participate in conferences and seminars across the nation, involving as many sectors of society as our resources permit."

Among the names listed on the committee's stationery were Eugene V. Rostow, executive director; Paul Nitze, chairman, Policy Studies; Max Kampelman (Bellow's old lodger), general counsel; and Donald Rumsfeld, Richard Perle, Richard E. Pipes, Dean Rusk, Norman Podhoretz, Lane Kirkland of the AFL-CIO, Jeane Kirkpatrick, and Clare Boothe Luce. Just one month after its inaugurating press conference, the committee published a letter in *The New York Times* that took what Bellow judged to be precisely the sort of specific position it had said it would avoid. On January 13, 1977, Bellow wrote to Rostow, withdrawing from the committee and requesting that it make no further use of his name. As he explained:

> I joined the Committee on the Present Danger because I agreed in principle with your views on the growth of Russian military

> power—I do still. But it was my impression that yours was a group formed for the purpose of discussion and for public information and enlightenment. . . . What I did not know was that the Committee was prepared to take specific political actions. Now, I don't know enough about military matters to back legislation, to recommend appropriations, etc. That is not my dish. As a writer I have no business to assume such a role. It is necessary for me to do things in my own way and to impose my own limits on positions publicly taken. I certainly cannot allow others to write my own letters for me. . . . I shall continue to support you in my own fashion on specific occasions, but I am obliged to withdraw from the Committee and request that you make no further use of my name. I have gotten out of my depth. With good wishes.
>
> Sincerely yours,
> Saul Bellow

In 1984, Bellow resigned from a similar group, the Committee for the Free World. Bellow's reasons for joining this committee were partly personal. It was founded in February 1981 with the help of the Olin Foundation and other conservative philanthropies. Its director was Midge Decter, Norman Podhoretz's wife. Bellow liked Decter, he told Kazin in a letter of January 24, 1983, and agreed to join the board of her committee "for old times' sake," but he disliked the other board members, many of whom had been members of the Committee on the Present Danger. "I belong because the other side smells so bad. Unbearable!" At the time of the committee's launch, in a letter of February 4, Bellow provided Decter with a statement: "Sensible people charged with anxiety over the state of the world and bitterly frustrated every day by the lack of sense, principle and coherency they feel when they read the newspapers welcome the founding of the Committee for the Free World. Someone to monitor the long long slide of the Gadarene swine is just what I need. And when my tongue is in traction the Committee can speak for me." What Bellow expected it to speak about, however, was foreign and defense policy.

In the 1983 letter to Kazin, Bellow confessed to being a lax member of the committee board. "I never attend the meetings, because it interferes with the writing of stories." The following year, he resigned over an issue of the committee's newsletter, *Contentions* (known to its detractors as *Conniptions*, misnamed by Bellow as *Confrontations*). In 1983,

Decter had been a Pulitzer Prize juror for fiction, which she described to Bellow in a letter of January 24, 1984, as "one of the most appalling experiences of my life." "With perfect accuracy," she predicted that Alice Walker's *The Color Purple* would win, "an outcome entirely unaffected by the fact that I may have been the only juror who actually read, carefully and conscientiously, every one of the books submitted." At Decter's suggestion, *Contentions*, edited by her daughter, Naomi Podhoretz Munson, whose husband, Steven Munson, was deputy director, devoted an entire issue (October 1983) to reviews of the books chosen as winners that year by Pulitzer, National Book Critics Circle, and American Book Award jurors. In an editor's note on the first page, readers were advised that, though the jurors' choices "may tell us little about the nature of genuine literary achievement, they nevertheless speak volumes about the current condition of our cultural life and the values that govern it."

The *Contentions* reviewers were unimpressed, in almost every case deploring the authors' political opinions and ways of life, with much briefer discussion, if any, of literary or stylistic features. The reviewers, identified only by initials, were Decter herself, her daughter Naomi, her son John, her son-in-law Steven, and Neal Kozodoy, the committee secretary, later editor of *Commentary*. Among the authors pilloried or patronized, in addition to Alice Walker, were Gore Vidal (for a collection of essays), Robert A. Caro (for the first volume of his LBJ biography), and Stanley Elkin (for the novel *George Mills*). Tom Gidwitz, a writer and editor who did not know Bellow, wrote to him on December 23, 1983, after having read the October issue of *Contentions*, a publication he had never seen until he was loaned this particular issue by a friend, and about whose politics he knew nothing. Having noticed Bellow's name listed among board members, he wrote to ask if he endorsed the contents of the issue. "These books may not deserve awards," Gidwitz wrote, "but if they don't, the critics have not shown why. The articles struck me as being malicious and smug and highlighted these critics' intolerance of lifestyles and philosophies, rather than their perceptions. Your association with the Committee for the Free World is understandable, however your connection to this issue of *Contentions* is not. Perhaps I've misinterpreted the articles or your own position."

Bellow replied a month later, on January 23, 1984: "I have read the pages you sent, and I agree in part with your objections. I have resigned from the Committee (I had been contemplating resignation anyway)."

The resignation had been submitted five days earlier, on January 18, in a letter to Midge Decter.

> Inquiries and complaints—mainly complaints—having been made about my participation in or sponsorship of your Special Issue of *Confrontations* ("Winners"), I read the offending number, which I had missed, and although the prize books you attacked seemed squalid enough your own reviews were in such bad taste that it depressed me to be associated with them. . . . About Nicaragua we can agree well enough but as soon as you begin to speak of culture you give me the willies. . . . I can't allow the editors of *Contentions* to speak in my name. When there are enemies to be made I prefer to make them myself, on my own grounds and in my own language. . . .
>
> I am resigning from the board and request that you remove my name from your announcements. Sorry.
>
> Yours sincerely,
> Saul Bellow

Bellow's letter to Decter offers another reason for his unhappiness with the Committee for the Free World. On February 12–13, 1983, the committee held a conference at the Plaza Hotel in New York entitled "Our Country and Our Culture" (a title taken from the 1952 *Partisan Review* symposium discussed in chapter 10 of *To Fame and Fortune*). According to Joseph Epstein, who spoke at the conference, Ruth Miller told Bellow that Epstein had attacked him in his speech. In his resignation letter to Decter, Bellow accused Epstein of "ascribing to me views I do not hold and pushing me in a direction I wouldn't dream of taking. . . . It was uncomfortable to be misunderstood and misused in a meeting of which I was one of the sponsors and even more uncomfortable to see his speech reprinted in *Commentary*."

Epstein had been a fan and friend of Bellow's since the early 1970s. In 1973, as we've seen, in a lengthy profile in *The New York Times Book Review*, he called Bellow "the premier American novelist: the best writer we have in the literary form that has been dominant in the literature of the past hundred years." Although ten years later Epstein's feelings about Bellow as friend and writer had changed somewhat, he did not, he insists, attack him in his conference speech. What he said, to quote from the expanded version of the speech published in *Com-*

mentary ("Anti-Americanism and Other Clichés," April 1, 1983), is that American literature had begun to seem "rather backwater, a bit beside the point, somehow or other less than first-rate."

In support of this judgment, Epstein invoked Bellow, whose views, voiced "not long ago" in an unidentified interview, he paraphrased. In the interview, Epstein says, Bellow complained that American writers "no longer had the great subject."

> The great subject of our day, he said, belonged to those writers who had survived totalitarian regimes and lived to write about them: Pasternak, Solzhenitsyn, Sinyavsky, Kundera. . . . What Bellow seemed to be saying was that these writers, often wretched in the conditions of their lives, were nonetheless privileged as writers in their experience, for their experience had brought them face to face with terror and evil, goodness and heroism—in short, with the largest human feelings and with destiny played out on the grand scale.

Bellow, according to Epstein, thought contemporary American writers faced a more complicated task:

> They had to come at things less directly, more obliquely, with comedy and irony being perhaps their chief literary weapons. That is, of course, a description of the way Saul Bellow himself proceeds. But at an even slightly lower level than Bellow is able to work it, this vein of writing, relying so heavily on irony and comedy, quickly becomes desiccated and dreary in the extreme.

This is hardly an attack on Bellow. Epstein today has very little to say in Bellow's favor, but in this case, "I thought—and still think—this a legitimate and honorable thing to say." He goes on to add: "None of this would have occurred if he had called me and asked if Ruth Miller was correct about my defaming him. But, as you know, he was a man with a short fuse, especially when it came to the defense of his own reputation." When Miller wrote to *Commentary* to support Bellow's complaint that Epstein had ascribed to him views that he did not hold, Epstein answered in the same issue by referring readers to an interview printed in the *Chicago Tribune Magazine* on September 16, 1979. He quotes the following passage from the interview: "We American writers can hardly expect to compete with those who have known the worst of war in their own cities, or who have been condemned to slave-labor camps. . . . But perhaps we can do in the realm of comedy what we are unable to do in the realm of horror."

In the *Commentary* version of Epstein's speech, which Bellow claims to have read, Epstein disparages not only ironists but also those authors who "feel that they *are* writing with the wind of history at their back." These are the writers who "think the worst" of America. "The contemporary literary scene is rife with writers whose chief stock in the trade of ideas is a crude anti-Americanism." Among their number he includes Robert Coover, Robert Stone, Joseph Heller, E. L. Doctorow, Ann Beattie, and John Updike. Someone listening to rather than reading these sentences (Ruth Miller, for example) might well have received the impression that for Bellow American literature was bound to be second-rate, a view he fiercely rejected throughout his life, though this is not what a careful reading of the printed version of the speech suggests.

JOSEPH EPSTEIN'S DETERIORATING RELATIONS with Bellow involved Bellow's relations with Edward Shils and Allan Bloom. Epstein, born in Chicago in 1937, was closer in age to Bloom than to Bellow or Shils. He was educated at the University of Illinois at Urbana-Champaign and at the University of Chicago, and taught for thirty years at Northwestern, from 1972 to 2002. From 1974 to 1997, he edited *The American Scholar*. A very funny man, Epstein can also be cutting, making him, in this respect at least, a worthy companion of either Shils or Bellow. During the period of his friendship with Bellow, which began soon after the interview in *The New York Times Book Review*, they met "perhaps every other week." There were racquetball games at the Riviera Club in Chicago, where Bellow met the dapper gangster Gus Alex, the model for Vito Langobardi in *Humboldt's Gift;* they dined frequently at the Whitehall Club in the Whitehall Hotel, just west of Michigan Avenue on Delaware Place; they browsed bookstores after lunch, and occasionally "went out together with lady friends." "We got on very well," Epstein told me in an interview, "but it was never a relationship of equals. I never pressed him, never said, 'Oh, Saul, that's bullshit.'" "We were fairly close friends for nearly a decade," Epstein explains, "close but not intimate, if such a distinction is permissible." Bellow read portions of *Humboldt's Gift* to Epstein, who would offer occasional corrections (for example, "the weight of a linebacker—he didn't really know"). "I felt honored to be read to by this fellow I thought was a great man."

Relations between the two friends began to cool for several reasons. Epstein thought Bellow had defamed his friend Hilton Kramer, the art critic and editor of *The New Criterion*, gratuitously portraying him in *Humboldt's Gift* as cowardly and a careerist ("he threw it in at no extra charge," writes Epstein of the novel's Kramer-like character). When Kramer rang Bellow to complain, according to Epstein, Bellow blew him off. "Call the police," Bellow told him. It was Bellow who ended the friendship, according to Epstein. "I didn't pull away, I was pulled away from." This was in part because of Epstein's growing closeness to Shils, to whom Bellow had introduced him. Shils and Bellow had themselves drifted apart by 1983, for several reasons. Shils had blocked Bellow's attempts to get jobs for Edith Hartnett and Bette Howland at the Committee on Social Thought, telling Epstein, "I refuse to let him use the Committee as a rest home for his old *nafkas*" (Yiddish for "whores").[27] Epstein does not believe, as do others, that Shils became jealous of Bellow after the Nobel Prize; Shils had "a sure sense of his merit." Nor does he believe that politics broke them up. "The split was not political but 'characterological.' "

The critic David Mikics believes the roots of the breakup between Bellow and Shils can be detected in *Mr. Sammler's Planet*. After publication of the novel, which Shils read and commented on in draft, the two friends began to quarrel. Mikics thinks that this is because Shils saw Sammler, correctly, as a version of himself, "mandarin, detached, and professorial," and that the novel was Bellow's way of "working through his relationship with Shils." By the end of the novel, in this view, Sammler has changed, learning to appreciate the value of human particulars, of individual personality or character. "Sammler gets shaken out of his theorizing, his arm's-length way of fending off the chaos that surrounds him. By the book's conclusion he no longer looks down on people—he looks at them. . . . Sammler passes the test; Shils, to Bellow's mind, failed it. This is Bellow's trick on the intellectual type: trap him in life and see what happens. Shils remained aloof, refusing to be captivated by Bellow's key value, personality."[28]

Jonathan Kleinbard, a friend of both Shils and Bellow, lends support to the first part of Mikics's account of the estrangement. Shils "deeply resented *Sammler*, as he thought the character was based on him." Although there is little direct evidence to suggest that Shils himself saw the novel as an implicit attack on theory or sociology, his annotations of the *Sammler* manuscript lend indirect support to Mikics's view. Nowhere are these annotations more agitated and emphatic than in the scene at the end of the novel in which the nameless black pickpocket is beaten by Eisen, Sammler's former son-in-law. What Shils objects to about this episode is its praise for the pickpocket. Here is the offending passage, from the manuscript version:

> Sammler was in a rage with Eisen. He had given those atrocious blows to a better man than himself. It wasn't hard to be better than Eisen. And you had to reckon in Eisen's madness, he counted as a War-victim, even though he might have been mad. But he belonged in the mental-hospital. Homicidal maniac: Artist-type. Maybe this is why his life-studies had a mortuary look. But why was the Black man better? The impression was based on a certain princeliness—the clothing, the Dior shades, the sumptuous matching colors. And his manner, barbarous-majestical. Cornering a poor old White man, but not violent, making a superior noble gesture. He showed his patent of nobility and let the obvious conclusion be made.

"I don't understand at all," Shils writes in the margin of this passage. "Why did or would S. think the pickpocket better than Eisen? This is too far-fetched either as an argument in itself or as reasoning in character for S." On the back of the page, Shils reiterates his objection: "I think that the whole episode . . . deforms the character of the old man as you have presented it so far." In a marginal comment on the page that follows, he adds that Sammler's disapproval of Eisen's "ecstasy of murder" might be "OK, but not the imputation of majesty to the megalomaniac negro. It is just this that S. opposes throughout the book and having him turn around 180 degrees . . . is not well prepared and undoes all the moral good sense of the book so far. I am very perplexed."[29]

Bellow responded to Shils's objections by altering the passages slightly. He removed the sentence "He had given these atrocious blows to a better man than himself." He also rewrote the passage imputing nobility to the pickpocket.

> The black man? The black man was a megalomaniac. But there was a certain—a certain princeliness. The clothing, the shades, the sumptuous colors, the barbarous-majestical manner. He was prob-

> ably a mad spirit. But mad with the idea of *noblesse*. And how much Sammler sympathized with him—how much he would have done to prevent such atrocious blows [p. 293].

The references to the pickpocket's "superior noble gesture" and "patent of nobility" (his exposed phallus) are cut, and in their place comes Sammler's admiration for his "idea of *noblesse*." What Bellow refuses to give up is the complexity of Sammler's reaction to the pickpocket, which is in part ironic, in part an acknowledgment of the princeliness with which he manifests his "idea," that of the supremacy of the body, both in itself and as metonym for the material realm. As Mikics puts it, "By dunking Sammler so thoroughly in the mad social reality of his time, Bellow argues that a novelist can do something that a sociologist simply can't. The novelist gravitates toward the chaos that sociology tries to tame and categorize. Novels give disorder a voice [not the best phrase, given that the pickpocket never speaks], letting us see our own strange or hidden thoughts."[30] Shils was perfectly capable of acknowledging anomalies or inconsistencies of thought, the awkward particulars of personality, but his need to judge or place or "tame" them, on moral grounds or in the service of coherent character-drawing, seems to have taken precedence in this instance over the novelist's desire to depict human complexity. The differences Mikics points to between novelist and sociologist are not so much "characterological," in Epstein's phrase, as discipline-based or vocational.

But character *is* involved. Joan Kleinbard, Jonathan's wife, attributes the deterioration of the relations between Bellow and Shils to Shils's annotations: "At one point, Saul just got tired of Shils trying to change it [the *Sammler* manuscript]." Janis takes a similar line: "He tried to form and shape and direct people, and Saul wasn't having any of that. . . . There are six or seven people who had had a close relation to Shils. . . . There was the embrace and then after that complete rupture." Epstein thinks Shils did not give Bellow "enough deference," a view exactly opposite that of Richard Stern, who attributed the break between the two men to Bellow's no longer deferring to Shils. According to Daniel Bell, "The big problem was the implication that Shils was giving Saul the ideas in the novel"; the person who spread this idea, Bell claimed, was "Joe Epstein, who adored Shils." By the time Janis arrived on the scene, though Bellow and Shils saw each other in Committee corridors or at meetings or university functions, they had ceased dining together or seeing each other alone. Masters of invective, each would entertain Epstein with insults about the other, until Bellow broke with Epstein. "Have you noticed that our friend Saul is the kind of Jew who wears a hat in the house?" Shils once asked Epstein. Bellow, learning that Epstein had dined the previous night at Shils's apartment, asked, "Still got the leather palate, Joe?" Bellow once described Shils as looking like "an unlanced boil";[31] Shils took to referring to Bellow as "the Old Gentleman" (though Shils was five years older than Bellow). "If the old Gentleman were allowed to sit for two hours on the lap of the Queen of England," Shils told Epstein, "our good friend Saul Bellow would say two things about the Queen: she understands nothing of the condition of the modern artist and she's an anti-Semite."

Shils was marginally less insulting about Bloom, whom he described to Epstein as "a gifted teacher but a fool." Epstein suspects Bloom chose Bellow over Shils partly because Bellow was easier to get on with, partly because, "although Shils was much the greater man than Bellow, Bellow, for Allan, had more social cachet." According to Bloom's partner, Michael Z. Wu, Bloom was "very grateful" to Shils for having brought him to the Committee, and early on the two men often dined together. But Shils "could be unpleasant." As Leon Kass, also a member of the Committee, later chair of President Reagan's Council of Bioethics, puts it, Shils "had the nastiest wit of any person I'd ever met." In Committee meetings, however, again in Kass's words, "a very nice courtesy" prevailed. Animosity rarely colored discussion of student admissions or the marking of fundamentals examinations. "It wasn't Harlan County," another Committee member, Ralph Lerner, a political theorist and philosopher, told me. Social occasions, however, could be awkward. Janis remembers going to a party with Bellow at the home of Jack Cella, manager of the Seminary Bookstore, a Hyde Park institution. When Shils and Epstein entered the elevator to Cella's apartment and discovered it occupied by Bellow and Janis, they turned their backs on the couple without acknowledgment. All four occupants traveled up to the party in silence, as Janis recalls.[32]

The strained relations between Shils and Bellow are clear from a letter Shils wrote to Bellow on April 29, 1988:

Dear Saul:

I was not indifferent to your having turned and come back to speak with me yesterday afternoon. I was also a little surprised. In the gloom of the late afternoon and the surprise of your approach, as well as the fact that I had been thinking about something quite remote, it was not possible to engage in a conversation. Perhaps that's what you desired but I might be quite wrong about that. But if you do desire a conversation I would not be averse.

I still have the same telephone number. I do not have yours. You may call me if you wish or you may come to see me.

Please do not misunderstand this note. It intends no more than it says.

Yours sincerely,
Edward

JANIS DESCRIBES HERSELF in her first year at the Committee as intimidated by Bellow and Bloom. In the initial seminar she took with them, "I didn't talk at all." Like other first-year students, she angled to sit as far away from the two men as possible: "I didn't want to be called on." Seminar discussions were lively but scary. Bloom and Bellow would "mostly come in laughing," often about aspects of the text they'd been discussing over lunch. With the students there was "lots of laughing and also sassy talk, a lot of quick, American-style banter, back-and-forth, put-downs." "You'd say something and you'd be chopped down and then you'd come back. Bloom loved that, loved if his students were witty." "I didn't have any of that." The only banter Janis remembers directed toward her was when Bloom asked, "Don't you ever do anything but read?" There were other reasons Janis was quiet in seminar. She was busy "writing it all down, every word." She also felt in a minority among the students, most of whom "were tilted toward political philosophy," whereas she was "tilted toward literature." "I had high-minded ideas about how I was going to write about Shakespeare. I also loved the Romantics." She considered writing about Wordsworth's *Prelude* as well.

At first Janis lived in the International House on the corner of Fifty-Ninth Street and Dorchester, the next building along from Bellow's apartment. Everything seemed new to her. "The things I was used to, like living in the countryside and privacy, I lost, but it was very exciting." All the students read a newspaper, something she hadn't done in Toronto ("That's how I blew the Rhodes"). The university was also, she felt, "the first really Jewish place I'd ever been" (ever lived in, she means: she'd visited Israel with her family). She had little time to examine Chicago beyond Hyde Park, because the courses she took—not just the Bloom-and-Bellow seminars and the language courses, but Ralph Lerner on Maimonides and Spinoza, Nathan Tarcov on Plato's *Laws*—were demanding as well as absorbing. Also absorbing was her relationship with Peter Ahrensdorf. They began seeing each other in October 1980, a month after she arrived in Chicago, traveled together in the States, often with another couple from the Committee—Richard Ruderman, Peter's best friend, and Anne Crippen, both of whom would go on to teach political philosophy in Texas. On a trip to Paris in September 1984, Ahrensdorf proposed to Janis, "but she wanted me to convert to Judaism before she accepted my proposal." This he never did. When he finished his dissertation in 1985, he was offered a job at Kenyon College in Gambier, Ohio. He and Janis were still together, and he asked her to come with him, but she was at work on her own dissertation and reluctant to leave Chicago. After much soul-searching, she decided to stay. "I thought if I go to Kenyon College, I'm never going to finish, and that was probably true." They ended their relationship in May 1986, according to Ahrensdorf, by what he calls "mutual agreement." "It ended well," Janis believes. "We had already decided we were not getting married, and neither of us felt bitter about parting." "I think we both knew it made sense not to carry on."[33]

Janis had great difficulty finishing her dissertation, for several reasons. Although she began it under the supervision of Bloom and David Grene, she had been thinking about its themes since her undergraduate days at Toronto. The title of the dissertation was "Passionate Longing: Women in the Novel from Rousseau to Flaubert," though originally Janis had intended to include later examples. The kernel of the dissertation derived from Bloom's lectures on *Madame Bovary* in Politics 101, a popular undergraduate course at Toronto. It also owed something to Bloom and Bellow's seminars on Rousseau's *La Nouvelle Héloïse* at the Committee, and to Bloom's reading of Rousseau's *Émile*, as elaborated in essays and the introduction to his translation of the work.

The dissertation seeks to describe what "passionate longing" is for women, to identify its sources, and to trace its consequences, in fiction and in life. For Janis, as for Bloom, Rousseau begins the discussion by dividing woman's nature in two. In Janis's paraphrase: "On the one hand she is drawn towards her children and has social needs which can be satisfied only in the family. Women, he asserts, are bound by a strong instinctive sense of duty and loyalty. On the other hand, they are also in the grip of passionate (and frequently lawless) desires and are by nature less tractable than males. Their drives are more urgent and their love-longings more extreme."[34] It is these wild urges, particularly as depicted in Flaubert's writing, both early and late, that the dissertation examines, beginning with Rousseau's account of them in *La Nouvelle Héloïse* and *Émile* and ending with their depiction in *Madame Bovary*.[35]

In the chapters on *Madame Bovary*, Emma is seen as both Baudelaire and Allan Bloom see her, as a passionate extremist. In Baudelaire's words, *"elle poursuit l'idéal"*; in Bloom's words, she is the novel's "true high stakes player" (p. 173). The cruelty of Flaubert's treatment of Emma derives from what he saw as the inadequacy of the object of her longing: "The rewards of flesh and blood are simply insufficient. . . . Far from leading to 'tous les mystères' love only stands in the way of higher aspirations"; "Flaubert fiercely resists the idea that love between a man and a woman could bring us to the blue [a reference to Emma's search for a "realm of purity," "the azure realm"] or be at the center of existence" (p. 168); for Flaubert, "to the blue spaces [Emma] brings nothing but love-clichés" (p. 175).

In her conclusion, Janis describes passionate female longing as "mysterious": "Far from being the *donnée*, or given, of every woman, it apparently is found only in the most powerful, excitable, responsive natures" (p. 182). In the works Janis discusses, "these women lacked the gifts, the imagination, the scope for independent striving; they had neither the ability to ask the right questions nor the guides to whom they might have put their questions" (p. 180). Rousseau had no hope for such women; Flaubert's account of them was "bleak and nihilist" as well as hostile. "To the question what are women to do with their highest longings, [Flaubert's] answer is: Nothing."

In the next sentence, Janis asks: "Is there no other reply possible?" (p. 183). Her answer comes in an afterword to the dissertation, where she cites contemporary novels and memoirs in which female longing is less hostilely treated. She also discusses the fate of such longing in an age in which "women have fully realized freedoms previously reserved for males" (p. 185). Do the types of women she has been examining belong only "to the literature of days gone by" (p. 185)? Not by the evidence of the afterword's "small foray" (p. 188) into contemporary fiction.[36] "Although we may have expected the sexual revolution to have snapped this thematic thread, no break in feminine feeling appears to have occurred. . . . Many remote descendants of the Julies and the Emmas are springing up in every corner." Women still seek through love for "azure-tinted tranquillity," though "the complete and perfect satisfaction of persistent longings is as elusive as ever" (p. 192). The question of whether these longings are a product of "the *nature* of women" or "an ideological product springing from ideas about happiness" (p. 190) is left open, here and throughout the dissertation.

These themes were at the heart of Janis's thinking when she began work as Bellow's secretary, became his lover, and then his wife. Shortly after she and Peter Ahrensdorf broke off their engagement, in the spring of 1986, she met Bellow as she was coming out of the Regenstein Library. It was late in the afternoon, perhaps four or five, and Janis had had enough of studying and was going home. Bellow told her she looked tired, and she admitted as much. In fact, she had been unhappy for a while and had become "a little bit of a recluse," "dragging through my dissertation." Since the break with Ahrensdorf, "people would try to fix me up, and I was a little disgusted by all this." Bellow said to her, "why don't you come over to my house for dinner, and I said sure. I didn't think anything of that, and when I arrived he was wearing an apron and holding a spatula, which was very funny. . . . I'd never seen him wearing an apron." "It was a fish dinner and we had a very lovely conversation and I ended up staying there and after that we never had a night apart." By this date, Janis was living in an apartment on Blackstone, one street east of Dorchester: "I never spent another night in that apartment."

FOR A LONG PERIOD, the couple was "not out of the closet, as it were." Steering clear of Hyde Park, they drove into Chicago "in a regular sort of way. He'd take me to the Loop and we'd go to Marshall Field and we'd do little errands here and there." "There was a place he went for fruit in the old neighborhood, and a place he went to for a special type of bread. Then he'd take me to the zoo. We spent a lot of our courtship looking at animals in the zoo." As Janis remembers it, "He seemed much of that time like a seventeen-year-old. . . . He really did think of himself as a kid. He had a lot of energy. He was always singing. He'd be teaching me songs from vaudeville Chicago. He had endless opera." Bellow read her poetry or recited poetry he knew: "It was very moving. I think he felt he was being resurrected, and so some of the poems were about that. He had kind of been a flop at the end, after Alexandra, and he didn't really feel like there was going to be a reawakening or another chance or the possibility that somebody would ever love him. And it was astonishing to him, that we immediately and deeply fell in love with each other."

The final break with Alexandra, who had wanted a divorce for a while but insisted on it sometime in December 1985, had occurred in the new year, in humiliating circumstances for Bellow. On returning to the Sheridan Road apartment after a visit to Greg and his family in California, he opened the door to discover that every item in the apartment had been marked with either a blue dot or a red dot—blue for her, red for him. There was a note as well. Bellow was to vacate the apartment as soon as possible and should take all his possessions with him. The night was bitterly cold, according to Bellow's friend Eugene Kennedy, and when Bellow called to tell him, "Alexandra has left me," Kennedy agreed to come over the next morning. What he saw shocked him: "You knew this was very strange behavior." Bellow seemed "dazed" by what Alexandra had done. "He looked around the apartment and he looked at me and he said, 'I guess she just went dotty.' "[37]

When Bellow recovered from the initial shock, and the severe flu that accompanied it, he became angry. Alexandra, he wrote to Barley Alison, had "done one of her most exquisite snowjobs [on Alison, he means]. . . . You are one of a regiment of friends whom she has entirely convinced that I wanted to divorce her. . . . It all makes exquisite sense: two brothers die, I turn seventy, and then I put myself out on the street. Do you know this anecdote about the Duke of Wellington? He is approached on the street by a gentleman who asks, 'Sir, are you Mr. Jones?' Wellington answers, 'Sir, if you can believe *that*, you can believe anything.' " Bellow's view of the breakup was no easier to believe. "Suddenly there was an outbreak of bitterness about Alexandra," Richard Stern recalls. It made Stern "uncomfortable," as when Bellow told him that *The Dean's December* didn't work "because I let her off too easily."[38] "She's got parts missing," Bellow told the attorney Walter Pozen, "her heart, for example."

Some friends took Bellow's side unquestioningly. Eugene Kennedy thought Alexandra "paranoid" and believed Bellow's claims that she took less care of him than he did of her and offered little in the way of companionship. Not only did Kennedy think Alexandra was suspicious of a homosexual element in the relationship between Bellow and Bloom, but he thought she entertained similar suspicions about his own friendship with Bellow.[39] In the spring of 1986, Bellow wrote again to Barley Alison, saying that he would give his account of Alexandra and the breakup when he came to London. "Like one of the more forbidding tales in Herodotus, that will be, the one in which the severed head of a defeated prince is plunged into a tub of blood by the barbarian who has killed him. A little of that will go a long way."[40]

For Adam and Daniel, Bellow's anger at Alexandra was difficult to handle. Greg, who knew Alexandra least well, simply "accepted Saul's rationale" about her leaving because she lacked the emotional strength to see him through old age. "Out of what I considered loyalty to him," Greg admits, he "kept my distance from Alexandra for a number of years."[41] For Daniel, now twenty-one, the divorce "was so upsetting. It was like my own parents. . . . It was worse." When Bellow said "mean things" about Alexandra, Daniel thought, "This is all bullshit, it just doesn't square with what I know about her. . . . She was a good wife to him. She took care of him. She put up with his shit." Adam felt that a key factor in the breakup with Alexandra was her resentment of Bloom. "He was being put in the position of having to choose" (the position Maggie Staats Simmons felt she'd be likely to put Bellow in if she took up with him again). Adam does not believe Bellow's attraction to Bloom was homosexual ("Saul would have been repelled by that"), but he does believe that it was intense. For Adam, the precipitating moment in the breakup, the moment that caused Alexandra finally to put a stop to the marriage, was when Bloom barged into the room where she was dressing, a scene fictionalized in *Ravelstein* (and discussed in chapter 12). As if in reaction to Alexandra's suspicions, Bellow spread rumors about her. She was seeing someone else, he had been told, the mathematician Alberto P. Calderon—whom she would marry three years later. "This was his line—he wanted it to be that *she* was unfaithful," Adam recalls. "When Saul would enter the endgame of a marriage, he would start building a case that the wife was crazy [Adam is obviously thinking of his own mother], and he had an enormous theoretical construct around it, having to do with modernity . . . and television."

ANGRY, FEARFUL FOR HIS FUTURE, depressed: this was Bellow's state in early January 1986, when he boarded a plane for New York to attend the forty-eighth International PEN Congress, a weeklong gathering of seven hundred delegates, including four dozen all-expenses-paid "guests of honor," plus assorted journalists, commentators, and celebrities. The congress did not improve his mood. Like fellow members and guests, he was put up at the St. Moritz Hotel, in one of two hundred rooms donated by the young real-estate tycoon Donald J. Trump. There were glitzy parties at Gracie Mansion, the Metropolitan Museum of Art, the Arts Club, the New York Public Library, and the "quintaplex" penthouse (floors fifteen to nineteen) of Saul P. Steinberg, described by Richard Stern as "the virtuoso of leverage, arbitrage, and golden parachutes."[42] Steinberg and his wife, Gayfryd, served dinner to two hundred members and guests. According to Rhoda Koenig, who was covering the congress for *New York* magazine, the foreign writers who attended the party "had been deeply alienated, indeed stupefied, by the superabundance of brocade, marble, old masters, and Louis this and that."[43]

The congress was organized by Norman Mailer, president of American PEN, together with his vice presidents, Kurt Vonnegut and Donald Barthelme.[44] Bellow had been persuaded to attend by generous letters of invitation from Mailer and Vonnegut. The theme of the congress was "The Writer's Imagination and the Imagination of the State," a title dreamed up by Barthelme, and in addition to attending parties, dinners, press conferences, and speeches, Bellow agreed to address a panel on the topic "The State and the Alienation of the Writer." David Lehman, reporting on the conference for *Partisan Review*, described the panel as bound to appeal, since most writers were "presumed 'alienated' unless proven otherwise" (at *Partisan Review* in the 1940s, according to an old joke, the office typewriters were said to have "a special key that typed out 'alienation' on command").[45] The panel was held at the Essex House Hotel on January 13, and its other members were the South African writers Nadine Gordimer and Breyten Breytenbach, the Spanish novelist Juan Benet, the exiled Soviet novelist Vassily Aksyonov, and the Harvard philosopher Robert Nozick. Among the writers in the audience were Günter Grass, Salman Rushdie, and the Canadian novelist Robertson Davies.

Bellow spoke from notes rather than a finished text. He began by agreeing with Aksyonov, the previous speaker, that exile was not necessarily equated with alienation. He then offered five meanings or "resonances" of the term: "Rousseau's *amour propre* . . . the vanity which is the fast route to hypocrisy and self-distortion"; "Stendhal's Julien Sorel as an example of *amour propre* transcending itself to *amour passion*";

"Marxist alienation, in which history is a nightmare from which only the proletariat can awaken us"; "spiritual alienation," in which "the soul does not seem to count for much . . . Life has lost its sacredness"; and the naïve belief, especially relevant in the context of this congress, in "a simple natural goodness that is vitiated by our government" (or, as Amos Oz put it in a later session, the "Rousseauian assumption that governments and establishments are wicked—all of them—whereas 'common people' are born pure and sweet in heart").[46] In America, Bellow argued, our present "spiritual alienation" derived from the strengths of democratic capitalism. "We didn't start very high, and we didn't rise very high either. . . . We have shelter, health, protection, and a certain amount of security against injustice. . . . American democracy recognized no gods, no demons, and no philosophical idealisms; Romanticism was routinized and demystified. . . . Consequently, we do not believe in the existence of powers not guaranteed by the senses."[47] That these views owed something to Bellow's conversations with Bloom, to their joint seminars, and to his reading of *The Closing of the American Mind*, which he encouraged Bloom to write, discussed with him, helped to get published, and commented on in draft, is suggested by his account of the congress in "Writers, Intellectuals, Politics: Mainly Reminiscence" (1993), in which he paraphrases his address and then offers "a brief quotation from an exceptionally clear-minded political theorist, Allan Bloom." This quotation, Bellow adds, "will show better than I can the direction I meant to take in my speech. . . . 'Civil societies dedicated to the end of self-preservation cannot be expected to provide fertile soil for the heroic or the inspired. They do not require or encourage the noble. . . . One who holds the "economic" view of man cannot consistently believe in the dignity of man or in the special status of art and science.' "[48]

As Bellow also recalls in the 1993 essay, when he finished his speech, Günter Grass rose to attack him. This Grass did by completely ignoring the main thrust of the speech, its stress on "spiritual" alienation. "He said he had just visited the South Bronx and the poor blacks who lived in those monstrous streets could not agree that they were free and equal" (p. 111).[49] In effect, Grass "lighted the ideological fuse and out came a tremendous boom, a blast of anger from delegates and visitors. Replying as well as I could in the uproar, I said that of course American cities were going to hell in a hurry; they had become monstrous. I tried also to indicate that corrective actions could be taken only by a rich society, and this seemed to prove that the material objectives of the Founders [the objectives that marginalize American writers, along with notions of spirit or soul] had indeed been met" (p. 111). As Rhoda Koenig reported, after admitting that "no writer is devoid of political feelings," Bellow went on to say that, "on the other hand, one must not get megalomaniac notions of the powers of writers."[50] "In this connection," Bellow recalls in the essay, "I mentioned Brecht and Feuchtwanger in Germany. Grass protested that he was always being put down as a Communist" (pp. 110–11).

"You have to hand it to the social visionaries and liberators," Bellow continued in the essay: "They know how to get the high ground and keep it. They are masters also of the equivalence game: you have spoken well of the American system [though hardly unreservedly in Bellow's speech] because you are an apologist for it and a stooge; you are not concerned about the poor, and you are a racist to boot. . . . Grass seemed to believe I was justifying the establishment—that moth-eaten shroud. No, I was simply describing what there is to see" (p. 111). *Time* magazine reported the exact words that Bellow here paraphrases. After saying that it was admirable of Grass to think of the South Bronx, and that he, too, thought of it, Bellow answered: "I was simply saying the philosophers of freedom of the seventeenth and eighteenth centuries provided a structure which created society by and large free, by and large an example of prosperity. I did not say there are no pockets of poverty." The *Time* reporter, R. Z. Sheppard, described the tone of this reply as one of "patient grace."[51] Not all observers agreed. "The man looks as if he was born sneering," Robertston Davies said to Rhoda Koenig. Koenig herself described Bellow's speech as "maddening for its frigid superiority." When Grass said he often thought of the dictatorships propped up by the United States, Bellow replied "acidulously": "That's *very* commendable. I think of them, too."[52]

Salman Rushdie also rose to challenge Bellow, asking him what he thought the writer's "task" was in the context of America's international power. Irritated by now, Bellow replied, "We don't have any tasks, we just have inspirations," a view seconded at another congress session by Nadine Gordimer, for whom the imagination of the writer "must be private not collective." In Gordimer's view, the state thinks of the imagination of the writer as merely "something that can be put into service."[53] The tensions debated at the congress between the writer's responsibility to his craft and to the state, between art and politics, were ones Bellow had negotiated throughout his life, with leftist groups in the 1930s and 1940s, with liberals and conservatives alike in the 1950s and 1960s, and then with the various groupings, mostly on the right, discussed in this chapter. While refusing to be cowed by what he saw as liberal prejudice, he was equally vigilant, in public settings at least, in resisting identification with conservative and neoconservative doctrine, especially in relation to cultural issues.

To David Lehman, the confrontation between Bellow and Grass "was, perhaps, the week's pivotal moment, the one that most observers remembered most vividly after the shouting had died down."[54] Lehman was also struck by an exchange between Aksyonov and Allen Ginsberg during the discussion period. Ginsberg, addressing his fellow delegates as "members of the so-called free world," accused them of failing to recognize, or to acknowledge, that their freedom was dependent on "the exploitation of others." Aksyonov then called on delegates, especially Grass and his fellow German delegates (among them, Hans Magnus Enzensberger and Peter Schneider), "to think twice before making parallels between the U.S. and the U.S.S.R. [which had boycotted the congress]." The next day, in a panel on "The Utopian Imagination," Grass showed no second thoughts, "wondering out loud whether capitalism is any better than gulag communism. Grass later denied saying this, but dozens of reporters, several of them armed with microcassette recorders, heard him answer his own rhetorical question by saying: 'I don't think so.'" The bellicose attitude taken by German delegates toward the depredations of American capitalism was much discussed at the congress. Lehman quotes an unnamed writer speculating that "the burden of guilt for the Nazi past supplied a secret subtext to Grass's South Bronx–equals–gulag gambit. If the South Bronx is no better than the gulag, and the gulag is not much better than the death camps, doesn't that somehow let the Germans off the hook?"[55] Bellow was more generous in his attitude toward the Germans. In the press conference after the panel, he claimed to understand why Grass, described by Stern as "the Chief Confronter,"[56] took the positions he did. He felt "sympathetic" to German writers, caught as they were between East and West, in the middle of "a life and death struggle" between the two superpowers. At the same time, in a complaint made equally of pressure groups on the right, he resented not only the "stampeding of writers into political boxes," but the language used by both those who do the stampeding and those who are stampeded: "You immediately hear anchormen jargon and the jargon of militant radicals going back to the thirties. The language we use is heavily polluted by politics. And we're forced to speak about life-and-death matters on these unfavorable terms."[57]

At a party at the Metropolitan Museum of Art the night after Bellow's panel, the critic Daniel Fuchs, author of one of the few studies of his writing that Bellow approved, confronted Grass. Had he read *The Dean's December* or Bellow's story "Looking for Mr. Green," works that clearly show Bellow had thought about places like the South Bronx? Had he read *Mr. Sammler's Planet,* for that matter, or *Seize the Day,* which show that Bellow was "hardly oblivious to the negative effect of capitalism. Grass seemed to agree but repeated that he objected to Bellow's saying that people in America were not alienated. (Is that what Bellow said?)"[58] Bellow himself confronted Grass the next morning, at breakfast at the St. Moritz. Adam Bellow, who was with his father at the time, describes the confrontation.

> We entered the room and everyone was looking at him. He went directly up to Günter Grass, who had attacked him the day before. He was sitting at a table with Bill and Rose Styron. Saul went straight up to Grass and shook his finger in his face and said, "That was very bad what you did yesterday." You could see that he was hurt by what had happened.

Adam's view of his father's speech at the panel, or his manner in delivering it, was that "he'd asked for it, hadn't he?" Presumably by identifying writerly hostility to the state, to all states, as naïve or "Rousseauistic."[59]

ON MARCH 18, 1986, two months after Bellow's return to Chicago, Bernard Malamud dropped dead of a heart attack. He was only a year older than Bellow. At the PEN Congress, Malamud had not looked well. Richard Stern, who hadn't seen him in years, "felt queasy at how age and illness had worked him over."[60] The day after Malamud's death, Bellow flew to London to give another PEN talk, this one entitled "American Writers and Their Public—The American Public and Its Writers." English PEN paid for his flight and put him up at the Capital Hotel in Knightsbridge, which he didn't like, though London itself he had grown to like. He was close to Barley Alison, his London publisher, and on previous visits had befriended her brother, Michael, Mrs. Thatcher's parliamentary private secretary since 1983. Michael and his wife, Sylvia, dined with Bellow several times at the House of Commons, and Bellow became a friend of their family as well.

Bellow's agreeing to give the English PEN address may have been influenced by the success of a visit to London five months earlier. On that visit, he was filmed in conversation with Martin Amis, for the first of four television programs on Channel 4 in a series entitled *Modernity and Its Discontents*. The first program's title was "The Moronic Inferno" and it was moderated by Michael Ignatieff, the Canadian author and public intellectual, later leader of the Liberal Party of Canada. According to Amis's account of the visit, which features as an episode in a draft of his forthcoming autobiographical novel, *Inside Story*, Bellow judged the filming to have gone "very smoothly." Bellow was staying at Durrants Hotel, not far from Oxford Street, and he and Amis had tea there the day after filming. Amis describes the hotel as "all lace and chintz" and Bellow as "very sure of himself in London," "very Asser and Kisser" [from Turnbull & Asser, the Jermyn Street shop where Bellow bought his shirts]. At one point in the novel, Bellow "delighted" Amis when he said, "*They treat me very well here*—he meant his publishers and facilitators—*because they think me a toff*" (that is, upper-class, from "tuft," which, according to Amis, was "used to denote the gold tassel worn on the cap by Oxbridge undergraduates"). "London was a town where Saul Bellow could legitimately feel like a toff," the fictional Amis recalls, an impression confirmed by the real-life Amis, in an interview. "*The universal eligibility to be noble:* this was one of Saul Bellow's core principles."[61] Four or so months had elapsed by the date of this visit since the deaths of Bellow's brothers, and although relations with Alexandra were poor, she had not yet kicked him out. He was no longer stricken. Amis likens his voice—in the novel, that is—to Ijah Brodsky's voice in the short story "Cousins" (1974), "dreamy, prosperous," having deepened over the years into a *basso profundo*. "When I offer a chair to a lady at a dinner party," says Ijah, "she is enveloped in a deep syllable."[62]

In *Inside Story*, Amis invites Bellow to dinner after the filming, as he did in real life. The novel's version of the dinner corresponds to Amis's account of it in an interview, but it also draws on details from an earlier Bellow visit and dinner in 1983. (In the novel, to complicate matters further, the dinner is set in 1984, for what Amis calls "reasons of my own.") "I happen to know you like a nice piece of fish," Amis tells Bellow, when issuing the invitation. Bellow replies, "It would be futile to deny it." Amis tells Bellow he will be bringing along what he calls his "serious girlfriend," a philosophy lecturer, soon to be his wife (it was at the 1983 dinner, not the 1985 one, that the philosophy lecturer Antonia Phillips, soon to be Amis's wife, met Bellow for the first time). "Do you mean that she's serious or you're serious?" Bellow asks. Amis means both. Would Bellow be bringing anyone? "My dear wife is in Chicago, so, no, I'll be alone." The dinner is at Odins, a fashionable restaurant in Marylebone; it is paid for by *The Observer*, as was the real-life 1983 dinner. Bellow arrives elaborately turned out in "fedora, checked suit with a crimson lining (not loud exactly, but *a bit sudden*, as the English say)." He is sixty-nine, making Amis "exactly half" his age. Physically, Bellow is described in the novel as "just below average height," but with "that ever-surprising solidity of chest and shoulder, like a stevedore." At the dinner in the *Inside Story* draft, Amis's philosopher girlfriend is reserved at first (as Antonia Phillips was in 1983, though less so in 1985), and she has mixed feelings about Bellow's fiction. She had liked *Henderson the Rain King*, but when Amis presses *The Adventures of Augie March* on her, her response after twenty-five pages is "Does anything actually happen?" She also has reservations about *To Jerusalem and Back*, on political grounds. Bellow soon wins her over, using a recent scandal involving a West Virginia pastor to explain the difference between ethics and morals in American public life. Ethics involves money, morals involves sex, so that "relieving old believers of their disability cheques—that's ethics. Pairing hookers in a hot-sheets motel—that's morals." Like Antonia Phillips in real life, at this the fictional girlfriend lets out a laugh Amis "never dreamt she had in her. . . . Then they ordered their nice pieces of fish and their expensive white wine, and the evening began."[63]

BEFORE BELLOW'S VISIT to London in March 1986, he had a business errand to attend to, a toff's business errand. On February 4, he wrote to Mr. J. Carnera, High Class Boot and Shoemaker, at New & Lingwood, a Jermyn Street shop across from Asser and Kisser:

> Dear Mr. Carnera,
>
> The last pair of shoes you made for me are cruel to my feet. I have patiently tried to break them in and have not been able to soften them at all. They cut into my foot below the ankle bone

and I doubt that you can do anything with them. I shall appear in London the week of March 22 to return them. As you can see, the Atlantic is not broad enough to obstruct my claim for justice. Yours in much disappointment,

Saul Bellow

The writer Bellow saw most of on this March 1986 visit to London was Philip Roth, who had been living there with the English actress Claire Bloom since 1976. "He was very lonely," Roth recalled. "He was seventy; he had to start all over again."[64] It was on this visit that Roth's wariness of Bellow began to soften. "He was so needy, one's instinct was to help him out." The first of Bellow's needs was to change his hotel. "I phoned him and he said this hotel is terrible or they didn't have a room or something." So Roth got him a room at the Royal Automobile Club in Pall Mall, where he was a member (Roth liked to swim, and the RAC has a large swimming pool). "I went over in a taxi to his hotel, and there he was, sitting in the lobby, looking utterly defeated, sitting in a chair." Roth and Bloom had tickets that Sunday for the Borodin Quartet playing the last three Shostakovich string quartets, and were able to get a ticket for Bellow. In the taxi to the concert, thinking of Malamud, Bellow stared out the window and said, "Well, Schaffner is gone," an allusion to his joke about how Bellow, Malamud, and Roth were the Hart, Schaffner & Marx of the Jewish American novel (Hart, Schaffner & Marx are upscale men's clothiers). In his present mood, Roth realized, Bellow "needed the last quartets by the Borodin Quartet like a hole in the head." After the concert, which Roth remembered as "astonishingly beautiful," Bellow "was very silent."[65]

Later in the visit, at a dinner given by Roth and Bloom, Bellow perked up slightly, after an awkward beginning. The Irish novelist Edna O'Brien was there, along with the writer-journalist Timothy Garton Ash and his Polish wife, Danuta. Garton Ash had just read *The Dean's December* and started asking Bellow about "his very interesting Romanian wife," not knowing of the recent breakup. It was Edna O'Brien who lifted the mood, being, "of course, anything but Romanian, and refusing to be brought down by any of this gloom, East European or otherwise. I'm not sure how much of it was her influence, but I remember it in the end as a good evening, with the two American novelists matching each other with acid doses of wit."[66] Bellow also attended a dinner given by George Weidenfeld, his old publisher, who found him "sweet and touchingly vulnerable in his self-pity." Weidenfeld listened patiently as Bellow "kvetched about this one and that one." He also recalled that Bellow asked him, before the dinner, to "screen the female guest list for availability."[67]

By Easter weekend, Bellow was back in Chicago, and sometime in the next month or so, he and Janis began living together. In June, Bellow traveled to New York, where on the fifteenth Adam and Rachel were married in an outdoor ceremony in Riverdale, at the home of old friends of Rachel's family. Alexandra was not there, despite Adam's affection for her. Nor was Janis. Harriet Wasserman had been invited; she remembers the newlyweds standing "together between two 'majestic' trees," with Bellow standing against the tree on the right, in a "white suit and panama hat," and Sasha standing against the tree on the left, "the two parents framing the young couple, and glaring at each other."[68]

It was at the wedding that Bellow told Adam about Janis. Adam was shocked. He knew Janis well, not only from his year as a fellow student at the Committee, but from her role as Bellow's secretary, "the go-to person for me." Adam liked Janis and speculates that "if Janis and I had dated I would have stayed in Chicago." But Janis was with Peter Ahrensdorf, "and we were very good buddies." As news of Bellow's relationship with Janis spread, Adam says, "everyone was horrified by Saul." The split with Alexandra had left him "clearly very frightened and worried about his situation." Adam told Janis that he understood why she would be attracted to Saul, but he was concerned for her: "Life with him would not be a picnic." He thought of Roth's novel *The Ghost Writer*, with Bellow as Lonoff, not Abravanel, and Janis as both Amy Bellette and Lonoff's wife, Hope (with the prospect of a life like Hope's). "I knew what Saul expected of his wife: secretarial services, household major domo, surrogate parent." What Adam didn't know, what he underestimated, "was their potential to make it work. They *did* make it work." He also underestimated "the amount of steel in Janis."

IN MARCH 1986, while Bellow was in London, Allan Bloom was putting the final touches on *The Closing of the American Mind*, which was published a year later by Simon & Schuster with a foreword by Bellow. The book grew in part out of an essay Bloom had published in the *National Review* on December 10, 1982, entitled "Our Listless

Universities," the themes of which he had been airing and expanding to Bellow and others in Hyde Park.[69] Harriet Wasserman was pressed by Bellow into representing the book and finding Bloom a good deal with a trade publisher (not an easy task for a book with chapter titles like "From Socrates' *Apology* to Heidegger's *Rektoratsrede*"). The initial print run was ten thousand, but by the end of the year, to the surprise of all concerned, Bloom in particular, five hundred thousand copies had been sold. It was Christopher Lehmann-Haupt in *The New York Times* who set the ball rolling. Within two weeks of his rave review of March 23, 1987 ("remarkable . . . hits with the approximate force and effect of what electric shock-therapy must be like"), the book was number eleven on the paper's best-seller list, at a date, in Wasserman's words, "too soon after publication to even think of the best-seller list."[70] "All the reviews came at once, so no matter where people looked—TV, radio, newspapers—within a two-week period they were somewhere made aware of the book. . . . William Buckley called, MacNeil/Lehrer called. *Newsweek* did a spread, *Time* did a spread, the *Washington Post* did a spread in the Style section."[71] There were cartoons about the book in *The New Yorker* and *The Washington Post;* Bloom appeared "on almost all the shows—Evans and Novak, *Open Mind*, ABC, NBC, CBS, PBS, CNN—but he longed for only one: 'I want Oprah. I want Oprah.'" Harriet Wasserman is good on Bloom's appearance on *The Oprah Winfrey Show:*

> The theme of the program was General Knowledge, and it opened with a quiz of the audience. One of the questions: "What is the Magna Carta?" Oprah pointed the microphone at some guy, who answered "It's a bottle of champagne!" Then she asked, "Does the earth move around the sun, or does the sun move around the earth?" Oprah pointed her microphone, and this woman answered, "I think the sun moves around the earth, because we don't feel it!" Then a schoolteacher was asked, "Who was the second president of the United States?" She didn't know! There was one more question. It was a very good one: "What is Gdansk?" And somebody answered, "A polka."
>
> Then Oprah brought out Allan Bloom. He loved being on her show. He said she was just wonderful. He loved her. She felt the material of his suit and complimented him.[72]

Sales of *The Closing of the American Mind* were remarkable from the start, well before Oprah. A week after publication, Bloom got his friend Leonard Garment, Richard Nixon's lawyer, to call the head of Simon & Schuster, who approved a twenty-five-thousand-a-week reprint. Within weeks of publication, the book went from number eleven on the *New York Times* Best Seller list to number five, then to number four. Then it reached number one, where it stayed for ten weeks; both hardcover and paperback editions were on the list for a year. When Bellow's novel *More Die of Heartbreak* came out in June 1987, it stayed at number four for two weeks, then dropped to nine or ten, then, after fifteen weeks, disappeared completely, while *The Closing of the American Mind* remained at one or two. In addition to its year on the *New York Times* list and the sale of over a million copies in the United States, it was a worldwide best-seller. Bloom was a millionaire, and famous. Wasserman negotiated a large contract for his next book, *Giants and Dwarfs* (1990), a collection of essays, and signed him up for lucrative lectures.[73] When Simon & Schuster sent Bloom his first royalty check, "a nice round number,"[74] he paid off all his debts and then went out and bought new Persian rugs, a Lalique chandelier, giant stereo speakers, medieval tapestries, Renaissance paintings, and a twenty-three-hundred-year-old Greek torso on a pedestal.

Bellow was delighted with Bloom's success. Delighted also to see his friend's ideas so widely and sympathetically received. In his foreword, he confesses to being especially moved by the book's concluding pages, in which "what is essential" about the Platonic dialogues is said to be "reproducible in almost all times and places," a statement Bellow sees as containing "the seed from which my life grew."[75] In supporting this statement, and confronting the forces or trends ranged against it in the modern university, Bloom provides the sort of exegesis Bellow especially sought from him: "He explains with an admirable command of political theory how all this came to be, how modern democracy originated, what Machiavelli, Hobbes, Locke, Rousseau and the other philosophers of enlightenment intended, and how their intentions succeeded or failed" (p. 18). Bloom also deliberately sets out to cause controversy, accusing American universities of claiming to support "openness" (principally by removing core requirements) while in fact stifling it. Among the many causes of this stifling or "closing" are radical feminism (which he accuses of defying "nature"), the decline of parental authority, divorce, drugs, rock music, the New Left, Black Power, historicism, cultural relativism, and political correctness (a term not yet in wide use). Higher education, according to the book's subtitle, has *Impoverished the Souls of Today's Students.* The remedy, Bloom believes, is to return to a core curriculum composed of the Great Books.

The Closing of the American Mind was widely attacked as well as praised, its author denounced as racist, sexist, reactionary, and elitist. To his friend Werner J. Dannhauser, a fellow student of Strauss's and professor of government at Cornell, these attacks were inevitable; Bloom "was hitting the left where it lived, the universities, the stronghold it has always taken for granted, and with good reason."[76] Bloom was accused of lacking "a sense of compassion" as opposed to a sense of justice.[77] He was also accused of being a Straussian—which he was, though Strauss's name appears only once in the book—and of therefore indulging in what Strauss calls esoteric writing. "When Bloom writes about democracy," goes the charge, as paraphrased by Dannhauser, "he does not mean what he says or say what he means."[78] Martha Nussbaum, a philosopher at Brown University, later at the University of Chicago, attacked Bloom's scholarship in *The New York Review of Books,* pointing out his failure to give "any indication that these texts [of Plato, Aristotle, Cicero, and Plutarch] are difficult to interpret, that scholars disagree about their meaning." Bloom, she also claims, is "silent" about evidence that goes against his views, "evidence that is not obscure, but is well-known and essential." She argues that a distinction needs to be drawn "between Bloom's official allegiance to Socrates [the self-described "idiot questioner"] and the more dogmatic and religious conception of philosophy to which he is deeply drawn."[79]

ON JANUARY 3, 1988, *The New York Times Magazine* published a profile of Bloom by James Atlas, a staffer on the magazine. The article was entitled "Chicago's Grumpy Guru: Best-Selling Professor Allan Bloom and the Chicago Intellectuals." A month before the article's appearance, Atlas had flown to Chicago from New York to conduct interviews. He interviewed Bellow on December 2, 1987. At some point before this, Philip Roth, among others, had suggested to Atlas that he write a biography of Bellow, who had admired Atlas's life of Delmore Schwartz. Atlas had signed a contract to write a biography of Edmund Wilson, but after five years he had not written a word, principally because "I felt no emotional connection with my subject, no 'elective affinity,' to borrow Goethe's phrase. As a figure with whom I could identify—or at the very least through whom I could tease out, however subliminally, the hidden themes of my own life—Wilson left me cold."[80] Bellow, by contrast, was a "natural choice for me." Atlas's parents came from the same Chicago milieu as Bellow. Atlas was Jewish, also a writer, the author of a recent novel he describes as having "annoyed the critics." "To write a biography of Saul Bellow would be, in a sense, to write my own autobiography, a generation removed."[81] He had sent a letter to Bellow in the summer of 1987 about the possibility of writing such a biography, "broaching the matter in a gingerly fashion," and after a few weeks telephoned to ask him if he had given the matter any thought. Bellow "professed to be flattered that I thought him worthy of a biography, and he had kind words for my biography of Delmore Schwartz. But he was intending to write a memoir of his own and didn't think he could both reminisce to me and write. Maybe later on . . . And there we left it."[82]

A few days after his return to New York, Atlas received a call from Adam Bellow, reporting that Bellow was "very sore at me. According to Adam, his father thinks that I'm trying to make a career out of him."[83] But when the Bloom article came out, Adam called again to say that his father had liked it, also that he "appreciated the unctuous letter I sent him stressing that my article really was about Bloom while acknowledging that I hoped to write about B later. All is forgiven; I am back in B's 'good graces.' So far so good."[84] Atlas then told Adam that he intended to go ahead with the book, and he wrote to Bellow for permission to examine his papers. He received no reply. In the spring of 1989, however, "on an impulse," Atlas flew to Chicago and called Bellow, who suggested that he come to his apartment. Atlas found Bellow "formal," "wary." He told Atlas he felt "burned" by Ruth Miller's book, about to be published, adding: "I'm not ready to be memorialized. I don't have all the answers. I'm still trying to figure things out." (Ruth Miller's book will be discussed in chapter 10.) He agreed to see Atlas "from time to time . . . but doesn't want to become too involved." As for his papers, Atlas could see manuscripts but not correspondence. "Maybe I'll simmer down," he added. For the next ten years, Atlas was a presence in Bellow's life, "The Shadow in the Garden," the title Atlas gave to a memoir which appeared in *The New Yorker* on June 26 and July 3, 1995 (and from which I have been quoting). The memoir worried and upset Bellow and increased his wariness. The title came from Bellow himself, misremembered from notes Atlas had taken from an interview with Eugene Kennedy. What Bellow actually told Kennedy, according to Atlas's checking of his notes, was that biographers were "the shadow of the tombstone falling across the garden."[85] The story of the biography and of Bellow's shifting feelings about it is taken up in subsequent chapters.

MORE DIE OF HEARTBREAK was published in June 1987.[86] The book had taken Bellow only six months to write; it was begun in the summer of 1986, six months after Alexandra insisted that he vacate the Sheridan Road apartment.[87] Its botanist hero, Benn Crader, is another "outstanding 'noticer'" (p. 184), though what he notices is plants, in particular arctic lichens. Benn's noticing, like Bellow's, moves through surface detail to inner meaning. He "saw into or looked through plants" (p. 19), "sure that nature has an *inside*" (p. 128); "there was something *visionary* about the distinctness with which 'plants came before him'" (p. 97). Benn's appearance suggests both perceptual power and otherworldliness. His eyes are "cobalt blue" (p. 157), "marine-blue, ultramarine" (p. 6), his face "like the moon before we landed on it" (p. 114). Benn's thirty-five-year-old nephew, Kenneth Trachtenberg, the novel's narrator, is an assistant professor of Russian literature who teaches at the same unnamed Midwestern university as Benn. Kenneth calls Benn "a contemplative, concentrating without effort" (p. 245), a description that recalls the infant Bentchka, a fictional representation of the infant Bellow, in "Memoirs of a Bootlegger's Son," "dreaming at" phenomena.[88] Benn's problems occur when he looks or dreams at human beings rather than at plants, at women in particular: "He couldn't make the psychic transfer to human relations" (p. 98).

The reason for Benn's failure with women is that, for all his otherworldliness, he, too, has been infected by modernity, in particular by modernity's debasement of love into sex. After fifteen years as a widower, "dredged in floury relationships by ladies who could fry him like a fish if they had a mind to" (p. 22), he is still in thrall to "*love* longings" (p. 270).[89] To Kenneth, watching "Uncle" seek for love is like watching "a bad driver fail to back into a parking space" (p. 5). The love Benn longs for is love "in a classic form" (p. 15), Plato's form, the form of Diotima in the *Symposium*. This was also the ideal of love Allan Bloom espoused, in his teaching and his writing, and which devoted students, including Janis, embraced. Benn is like Abe Ravelstein: "not one of those people for whom love has been debunked and punctured—for whom it is historical, Romantic myth long in dying but today finally dead. He thought—no, he *saw*—that every soul was looking for its peculiar other, longing for its complement. . . . Love is the highest function of our species—its vocation. . . . He never forgot this conviction. It figures in all his judgments" (*Ravelstein*, pp. 139–40).[90] In his mid-fifties, Benn falls disastrously in love with a "perfect" beauty, a woman twenty years his junior. He marries this woman, Matilda Layamon, despite misgivings from the *daimon*-like clairvoyant power that allows him to see into plants, a power he wrongly distrusts when focused on humans. As he tells Kenneth: "I was warned . . . not to marry. It was a sin to disobey the warning. But a man like me, trained in science, can't go by revelation. You can't be rational and also hold with sin" (p. 290).

In marrying Matilda, Benn enters what the critic Ellen Pifer calls "the maelstrom of American greed, ambition, desire."[91] The Layamons are a family straight out of Balzac, scheming about power and money. Some part of Benn, Kenneth conjectures, "had *wanted* to come down . . . had a special wish to enter into prevailing states of mind and even, perhaps, into the peculiar sexuality associated with such states" (p. 158). What draws Benn into the Layamon world is "admiration of beauty; desire to be bound to a woman in love and kindness; and finally, sexual needs, which, let us speak frankly, are seldom if ever free from crotchets, if not downright perversities" (p. 186).

It is not only his *daimon* that warns Benn. Matilda's appalling father, Dr. William Layamon, describes her, in a passage quoted earlier, as "a real bitch," though one whose bitchiness "will be working *for* you. . . . [She's] great with brilliant people and she can invite them because of you, a big name in your field" (pp. 154–55). (Benn's supposed status as a "world-famous botanist" [p. 147] recalls the improbable Bellow-like status of Chick in *Ravelstein*, or Albert Corde in *The Dean's December*.) To be married to Matilda, her father warns Benn, he'll need to make a good deal more than the sixty thousand he earns as an academic. "If you're going to share the bed of this delicious girl of high breeding and wallow in it, you'll have to find the money it takes" (p. 163).[92] Will Matilda take care of Benn? Fortunately, this is not what Benn needs, since with her "classic face" and "hyacinth hair" (terms from Edgar Allan Poe) Matilda "wasn't going to do the dishes" (p. 45). Benn can do the dishes, in fact "rather liked" housework, a trait he shares with his creator, who was as happy to parade the names of cleaning products as of philosophers. "He poured blue Vanish into his toilet," Kenneth tells us. "He preferred 409 to all other kitchen cleaners. He did his socks with Woolite. Jobs that drove other men wild, like peeling spuds, cleaning out the cheese grater, scrubbing scorched saucepans, doing the floors on his knees, didn't bother him at all" (p. 44).[93] How to get the money to keep Matilda has already been worked out by the Layamons. Benn must win back the inheritance he has been cheated of by his eighty-year-old uncle, Harold Vilitzer, an "old-time pol and ward boss, a machine alderman . . . as crooked as they came" (p. 32). If he succeeds, Dr. Layamon adds, speaking colloquially of money alone, "we think you can be made whole" (p. 163).

The corruption of Benn's longing for love is partly explained by Bellow in an interview of May 31, 1987, with Eugene Kennedy in the *Chicago Tribune*.[94] The interview appeared only days before the novel's publication. "In sexual relationships people have become extremely literal," Bellow told Kennedy. "They don't view each other as persons but only as bearers of erogenous zones." The result is disastrous, since "you cannot excise human nature and not expect people to die of heartbreak."[95] Hence the new novel. "In *More Die of Heartbreak*, I am trying to deal with the fact that the more we become objects to one another, the less well we get along together. . . . People act like trunk murderers in their relationships, dismembering everybody they meet, taking the part they want and discarding the rest."[96] This view of modern sexuality goes some way toward explaining one of the strangest features of the novel. Bored during a visit to the Berkshires, Matilda badgers Benn into taking her to see Alfred Hitchcock's *Psycho*. Benn hates the movie and becomes obsessed with the resemblance between Anthony Perkins's shoulders and those of Matilda, also by how far apart her breasts are ("She isn't wide only across the shoulders but also in front. . . . The distance between them has an effect on me" [pp. 254–55]). Kenneth's explanation is that "these defects jump out at you because love punishes you for drafting it against its will; it's one of those powers of the soul that won't be conscripted. It makes beauty, it makes strength. . . . Without it, critical consciousness simply reduces all comers to their separate parts, it disintegrates them" (p. 257).

One consequence of Benn's insistence that what he feels for Matilda is love is that he loses something of his clairvoyant power with plants.

Decked out in custom-made tweeds from his father-in-law's tailor, his hair done over by Matilda's "stylist" (p. 156), Benn wanders through the alien glamour of his in-laws' enormous apartment, his only comfort a beautiful azalea glimpsed through the open door of Matilda's mother's private study. When at last he sees the flower up close, he is shocked to discover that it is a fake, a silk replica. This shock he registers in an idiom hard to square with his supposed otherworldliness:

> A stooge azalea—a stand-in, a ringer, an impostor, a dummy, a shill! I was drawing support for weeks and weeks from this manufactured product. Every time I needed a fix, a contact, a flow, I turned to it. Me, Kenneth! After all these years of unbroken rapport, to be taken in [p. 292].

IT IS NOT HARD TO SEE why Bellow should create a character like Benn Crader, with his history of failed love relationships. Nor is it a mystery that he should imagine his falling for a perfect beauty like Matilda, a version, in part, of Susan Glassman. Most of the novel's real-life correspondences are, however, partial, fragmentary, multiple. Benn's unearthliness is as much Alexandra's as Bellow's; Matilda's sexual allure is partly Alexandra's as well as Susan's. For Roger Kaplan, Harold Kaplan's son, in part the model for Kenneth, Bellow "to some extent sees himself as Benn, meant to represent (not just 'represent,' I mean just be a story about) vulnerability despite superior brainpower. At the same time, Kenneth also has much of Saul in him [as in Kenneth's relationship with Dita Schwartz, discussed in chapter 3, modeled in part on Bette Howland]. First of all, Kenneth is, like Benn, vulnerable despite his intellectual power. Second, Kenneth is to some extent Saul looking upon Saul and trying to give Saul advice."[97]

The novel's plot—nothing much happens till halfway through—owes something to real-life experiences and people, in particular to the business conflicts between Bellow and Maury. Benn loves his swindling uncle Harold, despite Uncle Harold's having robbed him of his inheritance (by undervaluing the land on which their family house stood and buying it from Benn and his sister for a fraction of its eventual worth). When Benn and Kenneth visit Uncle Harold to confront him over his swindling, he reacts angrily, as Maury did when confronted in Miami by Bellow and Joel. Like Maury's, Uncle Harold's "main objective was to pile up a huge personal fortune and the hell with everything else" (p. 189). Also like Maury, he had started out "on the street, right here in town," in his case "taking bets, paying off the police. As a bookie, he was such a success out in the fresh air that when he had a big loss the cops collected 50,000 bucks among themselves to keep him in business. It was worth it to them. Next thing we knew, he was in politics" (p. 35). When Benn and Kenneth's mother take Uncle Harold to court, they are bound to lose, since "there's no saying how many judges he owned" (p. 36).[98]

Uncle Harold's son Fishl, as was mentioned in chapter 7, loves his father, though, like Joel, he has been cut off from him for years, in Fishl's case fifteen years. When Benn and Kenneth urge Fishl to intervene with his father, as Bellow urged Joel to intervene with Maury, Fishl refuses indignantly, "in an overflow of feeling" that reveals an "inner" self or "soul" (p. 182). Fishl is not Joel, but Joel's relations with his father and uncle provided Bellow with a starting point from which to imagine Fishl's relations with his father. So, too, I suggest, did Bellow's sons, Gregory in particular, judging by the speech Bellow gives Fishl explaining why all his life he felt that his cousin Benn "was better than me."

> He didn't invest his whole life in a struggle with his parents. I meet people of eighty who still are furious over their toilet training, or because their dad wouldn't take them to the ball game. Imagine such an infantile life! Such bondage to papa and mama. A whole life of caca-pipi! No self-respecting person would submit. Part peacefully from your parents if you can, and if you can't, tell them to fuck off. You have to go your own way at twenty, at least. I'm typical, still pursuing my father at the age of fifty, hating and loving and begging him to let the prodigal come back [pp. 171–72].

Fishl sees himself as Edgar in *King Lear*, cursed by old Gloucester. "That's why I'm in this shit-house office while my brothers are up in pig heaven. Bind fast his corky arms! Put out his eyes and spurn them with your foot! My dad has never been exactly a good guy, but I'm his son and long to save him. . . . I want to prove that there's only me, the rejected son, defending that rugged ogre, that I'm the devoted one" (pp. 173, 174).

Ugly Harold Vilitzer, "deeply tanned," with "clever" lumps in his face and white hair "combed straight forward to the edge of his forehead," is as much in thrall to the material world as beautiful Matilda (p. 34). And just as Matilda's love of sleep and hatred of waking allies her to death, so Vilitzer is allied to death. In extreme old age, his body a mere husk ("only the pacemaker under his shirt had any weight" [p. 280]), he is immovable, unrepentant. "Where money is concerned," he declares, "the operational word is *merciless*" (p. 274). As Kenneth sees it, trying to make sense of Vilitzer, "Death is merciless, and therefore the ground rules of conduct have to include an equal and opposite hardness. From this it follows that kinship is bullshit. . . . Fishl's emotions towards his father were further evidence [to Vilitzer] of his unfitness, his ignorance of the conditions of existence" (p. 274). Vilitzer is like Dr. Adler in *Seize the Day*, as Fishl is like Tommy Wilhelm, a resemblance seen also in Fishl's history of failed and dubious business ventures, "the credit card scam, the yoga, the acupuncture" (p. 167).

The horrors of modernity are seen also in Kenneth's love life, which is almost as disastrous as Benn's. Kenneth is more worldly than Benn, with his Parisian, UNESCO, Euroculture background (though, as Martin Amis puts it, "*everyone* is more worldly than Benn"[99]). He is estranged from his girlfriend, Treckie, who lives in Seattle with their young daughter, and with a ski-instructor lover. That Kenneth still adores Treckie, he realizes, opens him to the charge of falling from "*l'amour propre* to *l'amour passion*" (p. 57). (Kenneth may have taken a course from Allan Bloom.) What draws him to her is another "sexual peculiarity," her childlike body. He is "turned on by a . . . child-woman" (p. 303). Like Bellow, especially in the period after the breakup with Alexandra, Kenneth is pursued by women.[100] These include Treckie's mother ("The pleasant nights we'd spend together would give us strength for anything. Would you like to try one to see what it might be like?" [p. 209]), and, as we've seen, Dita Schwartz, an ex-student of Kenneth's who "had taken my Russian Seminar 451 on The Meaning of Love" (p. 247). After telling the story of Dita's horrific operation, and his nursing of her, Kenneth flies to Seattle in a doomed attempt to revive the relationship with Treckie. Treckie, a masochist, "didn't want any part of me. I failed to turn *her* on" (p. 304). What turns Treckie on is rough sex. She's also into "California-type stuff," "applied Zen," "group psychotherapy" (p. 306), embodying many of the modern traits and symptoms deplored in *The Closing of the American Mind*. Ellen Pifer is good on Kenneth's confrontation with Treckie: "As their daughter watches television cartoons in the next room, [Treckie] tells Ken, 'We're a pluralistic society after all. Multiple acculturation is what it's all about' [p. 308]. To Ken, in search of 'a desperately needed human turning point' [p. 307], Treckie's relativistic chatter is virtually indistinguishable from the 'cartoon sound effects' coming from the television set: 'the bangs, whistles, buzzings, blams and tooting' [p. 308]."[101]

The reviews of *More Die of Heartbreak* were mixed, and the sales moderate.[102] On May 24, 1987, in a review entitled "An Instinct for the Dangerous Wife," William Gaddis praised the novel on the cover of *The New York Times Book Review*. He called it the product of "a mind not only at constant work but standing outside itself, mercilessly examining the workings, tracking the leading issues of our time." On May 31, in a review in the *Chicago Sun-Times* entitled "Saul Bellow's Magic," the novelist Anne Tyler called Benn "Bellow's most vibrant character since Henderson the Rain King . . . one of the most richly textured and endearing characters in recent fiction." On June 15, in a review entitled "Victims of Contemporary Life," Paul Gray in *Time* described the novel as "crackling with intelligence and wit," "consistently funny," "proof that Bellow, 72, can live up to his own standards."

Other prominent reviewers, however, saw the novel as a falling off. Alfred Kazin, in "Trachtenberg the Rain King," a review of June 26 in *The New York Review of Books*, complained about Kenneth's "exultantly sour views of modernity, sexuality, women, the local and international scene." Kazin claimed his objections were not so much to Kenneth's opinions (though the review ends, "This is a book fired by misogyny") as to "the fact that he is always sticking them in your eye. The problem is familiar: Bellow does not always know what to do with his own overwhelming authorial presence." Terrence Rafferty, in "Hearts and Minds," a *New Yorker* review of July 20, also had trouble with Kenneth's "punishing gusts of theory, history (global and personal), and physical detail," especially in the first third of the novel, which he calls "phenomenally boring," "like an impossibly long letter from a relative to whom not very much has happened in the years since we last heard from him." Craig Raine, in the *London Review of Books* ("Soul Bellow," November 12), begins his review by citing dozens of brilliant moments in Bellow's earlier novels, "little miracles of particularity." In *More Die of Heartbreak*, in contrast, far too many similarly striking perceptions turn out to have been recycled from earlier work. The novel "is ruined by repetitions and echoes." There are other important flaws: the novel has "no form to speak of"; "the characters are mere tokens"; the main theme, about the centrality of heartbreak in Western as opposed to other cultures, is "nutty in its presentation" (since "suffering is manifold and it is very stupid to make meaningless comparisons"); the talk of "soul" and "*daimons*" is "hollow," "irritating." Raine is among the most ardent of Bellow's British defenders, but *More Die of Heartbreak* is, he concludes, "a dismally thin performance." Finally, in "Soul and Form," a review of August 31 in *The New Republic*, Leon Wieseltier described the novel as "a sorry tale of male self-pity," a description which soured relations between Bellow and Wieseltier for some time. "I missed him," Wieseltier said of their estrangement, "because he was one of the most charismatic persons I've ever met. . . . He was a magical Jew, a magical man."[103]

On March 8, 1987, an article by Bellow appeared in *The New York Times* seeking to shape the reception both of *More Die of Heartbreak* and of *The Closing of the American Mind.* The article, entitled "The Civilized Barbarian Reader," was adapted from Bellow's foreword to *The Closing of the American Mind.* In it, Bellow is much concerned with his depiction of know-it-all intellectuals, Kenneth Trachtenberg's predecessors. What the critics missed in these depictions was the humor extracted from them, the fact that "many of my books, in retrospect, are comedies of wide reading." What makes characters like Moses Herzog and Charlie Citrine comic is partly America's indifference to their concerns, partly the fact that the books they read "led to deserts of abstraction. After many years of attentive and diligent study, we are left with little more than systems of opinions and formulas that hide reality from us. Personal judgment is disabled, crippled by theoretic borrowing. . . . I was making fun of pedantry! . . . I meant to show how little strength 'higher education' had to offer a troubled man." What the critics also missed was the moments of insight his disillusioned characters were offered. In terms that pave the way for *More Die of Heartbreak* as much as *The Closing of the American Mind*, Bellow recalls Moses Herzog's return to balance at the end of *Herzog:*

> In the greatest confusion there is still an open channel to the soul. It may be difficult to find because by midlife it is overgrown, and some of the wildest thickets that surround it grow out of what we describe as our education. But the channel is always there, and it is our business to keep it open, to have access to the deepest part of

ourselves—to that part of us which is conscious of a higher consciousness, by means of which we make final judgments and put everything together.

The independence of this stricter consciousness, which has the strength to be immune to the noise of history and the distractions of our immediate surroundings, is what the life struggle is all about. The soul has to hold and find its ground against hostile forces, sometimes embodied in ideas that frequently deny its very existence, and indeed often seem to be trying to annul it altogether.[104]

MORE DIE OF HEARTBREAK ends with Benn fleeing Matilda, tricking her in the process, a sign that something of her family's ethos has rubbed off on him.[105] Benn lights out for the frozen North: "I signed on three days ago, to check out lichens from both poles, a comparative study, and work out certain morphological puzzles. . . . Nothing but night and ice will help me now. Night so that I can't see myself. Ice as a corrective. Ice for the rigor" (p. 326). As in *The Dean's December*, the purer realm looked for is an inhuman one, the cold of the frozen North like that of the starry heavens viewed from the Palomar Observatory. If

Black students at Cornell leaving Willard Straight Hall, Ithaca, New York, April 1969 (courtesy of Steve Starr/AP/Rex/Shutterstock)

not a defeat, the ending is for Benn a tactical withdrawal, the sort Bellow might well have imagined for himself after the failure of his marriage to Alexandra. Benn is left with his work and with Kenneth. While producing the novel, Bellow may have thought of himself as left with his writing and teaching—or co-teaching—with Allan Bloom. Kenneth, with his nonstop loquacity, his theorizing and philosophizing, can be seen as a figure of Allan Bloom as well as Roger Kaplan. Though the novel at times sees Kenneth as comical, in the line of Moses Herzog, Benn takes his advice seriously, as he does Kenneth's habit of viewing personal problems from the most elevated perspective ("As is evident by now," Kenneth admits, "I have a weakness for the big issues" [p. 284]). The bond between the two men owes something to the bond between Bellow and Bloom. If Bellow was tempted, like Benn, to give up on "love longings," settling for work and friendship, the temptation was short-lived. By the time *More Die of Heartbreak* was published, he and Janis were inseparable. When I asked Janis why she thought Bellow had married so many times, she answered, "He was looking for me."

9

To Seventy-Five

IN APRIL 1987, ten months after the wedding of Adam and Rachel, Bellow and Janis set off for Europe and then Haifa, where an international conference had been organized to discuss Bellow's writing. The trip was their debut as a couple. The intervening months had been spent by Janis learning how to live what Bellow called "a literary life." At last, he told her, he was "with somebody who understands me. We can talk about everything." (After Philip Roth read Janis's admiring reviews of his work, he said much the same thing: "At last Bellow married a woman who understands me."[1]) To Bette Howland, Janis was not only in love with Bellow, she "idolized him." Janis also says she was unperturbed to discover how powerful his will was, "not just in terms of his ideas and writing but everything. And I was receptive to that. I didn't buck it. . . . That didn't matter to me. I enjoyed it." Bellow had "very definite habits, and everything about him had his stamp." In the morning, he got up early, and it was important that the coffee was right, "so he wouldn't be juddering and he wouldn't be sluggish, so he could wake the right way." She learned to make coffee "the Ralph Ellison way, the right amount, in a particular cup." He was also particular about breakfast. With cereal, he liked bananas, but "only seven slices." Getting the morning right "was directed toward an end . . . the sanctity of the writing time." In the morning, often in the afternoon as well, "he was essentially solitary, and we fit together very well that way."

Bellow usually spent four hours a day at his desk, with distractions. After a bad phone call with an accountant or a family member, he'd go right back to work. "Use your anger," he told Janis; "your anger is burnable fuel." When not writing, he read, "always reading, reading aloud. We read in bed. I read to him while he was driving sometimes." In Chicago, he wrote until one, then took his bath. When not teaching or attending meetings, "he liked to kick off in the afternoon." They visited old neighborhoods, shopped in the Loop. In Vermont, there was the garden to tend to, long walks along tree-canopied dirt roads, swimming in the spring-fed pond behind the house. For both of them, Vermont was "The Good Place," the name Bellow gave to a 1990 article for *Travel Holiday* magazine, an article rich with loving details. In Vermont, on warm rainy days, "you are kept almost dry by the packed leaves, and you hear the drops falling from level to level." In the morning, "the dew takes up every particle of light. . . . Grass snakes come out of their sheltering rocks to get some sun. The poplar leaves, when you narrow your eyes, are like a shower of small change. And when you walk down to the pond, you may feel what the psalmist felt about still waters and green pastures."[2] On their walks, Janis recalls, "he'd spin out all kinds of ideas," or he'd ask her about the philosophy she'd studied, seeking "a survey of Kant or Strauss." It mattered that Janis knew Bellow's tradition. It mattered also that she was a good cook, since "every food item had interest for him" and he had strong preferences. "He loved persimmons, but they had to look a certain way, have a certain ripeness." The spices he favored were lemon, ginger, dill. Earlier in his life, he drank Jack Daniel's. In his last twenty years, he drank only wine, two glasses at dinner, or they'd split a bottle of beer. On expeditions to town—Brattleboro in Vermont, the Loop in Chicago—or on a trip, he'd buy Janis presents, "when he happened upon them." He was not one for flowers or valentines—"he hated that." As Janis sees it, speaking more widely, "I felt like he was giving me stuff all the time . . . a feeling of such luck . . . and delicious intimacy."

When Janis read *More Die of Heartbreak*, she recognized "a lot of Saul" in Benn. He, too, like Benn, suffered from "the many mistakes he'd made. He beat himself up over these things. He didn't shy away from examining all of his mistakes, big mistakes, tragic, ugly, wrong-headed moves, that whole Reichian period when he was perfectly crazy." Bellow could be frightening to new acquaintances—mostly, Janis believes, because "his powers were exponentially greater than those of other people." When displeased, he didn't mince words. "He wasn't diplomatic about what he didn't like" is how Janis puts it. "He wasn't going to pretend or mollify," and she came to respect this. "Certain people hold you up to high standards. It's very exacting and can seem—is—harsh. But with this person you're going to see something and achieve something." The example Janis gives concerns cooking. "There was no one on earth more appreciative of food, but if he didn't like it, you knew that, too. And the first few times it happened it's like a knife wound: 'You know what? Flush this down the toilet.'"

A story about Bellow, purportedly told by Bellow himself, sheds light on this side of his character. The story exists in several versions, including a version fictionalized by Joseph Epstein in a story entitled "Another Rare Visit with Noah Danzig" (1990). It turns on a harsh remark Bellow made at a dinner, in one version to a visitor to the Committee on Social Thought, in another to a pompous German Jewish psychoanalyst. In the latter version, the psychoanalyst is a guest of Bellow's sister, Jane, who, having just moved into a new apartment, invites her neighbors to dinner. Her famous brother is invited as well, to impress them. At some point during the meal, the talk turns to literature, and the German Jewish psychoanalyst pronounces Shakespeare much better in Schiller's translation than in English. Bellow looks up and says: "You know, I don't need to listen to any more of this German-Jewish bullshit." He then picks up his knife and fork and resumes eating. In Epstein's fictional version, the dinner takes place at the Whitehall Club and involves "Noah Danzig," obviously based on Bellow, and his host, a man he had met at a party who speaks four or five languages. The host's daughter, a senior at Radcliffe, is also present. Danzig makes the same remark about "German-Jewish bullshit" that Bellow is said to have made to the psychoanalyst but prefaces it by saying, "I'm sorry to have to say this with your daughter at the table." "What did you do then," asks the narrator, "walk out?" "'No,' said Noah. 'Why should I? He invites me to dinner, why should I leave just because he proves a bore? But I have to admit that what I said did put a chill on the wine.'"[3] Bellow, when in good humor, could be considerate and charming, but when in a mood or faced with nonsense, he could be consciously offensive. He could also offend unintentionally. In social situations, according to Bette Howland, "he could only handle one person at a time. If he's talking to X and you're standing next to him, then he's not going to introduce Y." There was also the matter of his being unable to stop himself from making hurtful remarks, wisecracks, jokes—like Herschel Shawmut in "Him with His Foot in His Mouth." Most of Shawmut's wounding remarks Bellow himself had made.[4]

Offense and consideration figure in an evening that has been written about by Martin Amis and Christopher Hitchens as well as by Bellow himself. The evening took place on a visit Amis and Hitchens paid to Bellow and Janis in Vermont in the summer of 1989. This was Amis's third Vermont visit; Hitchens, who had never met Bellow, "knew I was being greatly honored by the invitation" (elicited by Amis). On the way to Vermont from Cape Cod, where Amis was staying that summer, Hitchens was warned not to say anything political, "let alone left-wing, let alone anything to do with Israel. ('No sinister balls,' which was our colloquialism for a certain kind of too-easy leftism)."[5] Over drinks and most of dinner, which Hitchens describes in his memoir, the conversation was "by turns genial and sparkling." Then Bellow made a remark about anti-Zionism, reaching for a periodical Hitchens had noticed lying nearby on a small wicker table. The headline for its bannered cover story read: "Edward Said: Professor of Terror." Bellow read several passages from the article, which Hitchens, a friend of Said, described as "a very coarse attack."[6]

As he listened to Bellow's "disgusted summary" of the anti-Zionism detailed in the article, Hitchens decided he would have to say something. Amis describes what happened next:

> Very soon Janis and I were reduced to the occasional phoneme of remonstration. And Saul, packed down over the table, shoulders forward, legs tensed beneath his chair, became more laconic in his contributions, steadily submitting to a cataract of pure reason, matter-of-fact chapter and verse, with its interjected historical precedents, its high-decibel statistics, its fortissimo fine distinctions—Christopher's cerebral stampede.[7]

After the stampede, no one said a word. As Amis recalls, "A consensus was forming in the room, silently: that the evening could not be salvaged. . . . But for the time being we sat there rigid, as the silence raged on. Christopher was still softly compacting his little gold box of Benson & Hedges. He seemed to be giving this job his full attention." He also seemed to Amis uncharacteristically abashed.

> During the argument the opinions of Professor Edward Said had been weighed, and this is what Christopher, in closing, wished to emphasise. The silence still felt like a gnat in my ear.

—Well, he said. I'm sorry if I went on a bit. But Edward is a friend of mine. And if I hadn't defended him . . . I would have felt bad.

—How d'you feel *now*? said Saul.

In addition to being funny, Bellow's rejoinder is simultaneously cutting and considerate—cutting to Hitchens, considerate to Amis, whose distress at the turn the evening had taken was visible. The next day, after he and Hitchens returned to the Cape, Amis was still, in his wife, Antonia Phillips's words, "very upset . . . regretful." He called Bellow to apologize, feeling "shocked, indignant and guilty."

—And tell Janis I'm sorry.

—Please don't worry about it.

—You deserved a night off, I thought.

Saul was emphatic:

—Martin, you're *not* to be hard on yourself about it.

—Thank you. But when you bring—

—Listen, I'm used to it. I get that kind of thing all the time.

—That's what the *Hitch* said!

We couldn't avoid laughing at that; and accordingly the case began to close.[8]

Bellow's account of the evening, in a letter of August 29, 1989, to the novelist Cynthia Ozick, a passionate supporter of Israel, differs in several respects from the account Hitchens and Amis give. As Bellow remembers it in the letter, the offending article was by Said, not about him. The article Hitchens remembers appeared in *Commentary*, in the issue of August 1, 1989, and was written by Edward Alexander, a professor of English at the University of Washington and a friend of Ozick's. Bellow says nothing of this article, instead mentioning something Said had written in the latest issue of *Critical Inquiry*, a left-leaning University of Chicago periodical.[9]

My young friend Martin Amis, whom I love and admire, came to see me last week. He was brought here from Cape Cod by a chum [in fact, it was Amis who did the bringing] whom I had never met, not even heard of. They stayed overnight. When we sat down to dinner the friend identified himself as a journalist and a regular contributor to the *Nation*. I last looked into the *Nation* when Gore

> Vidal wrote his piece about the disloyalty of Jews to the USA and their blood-preference for Israel. . . . His [the chum's] name is Christopher Hitchens. During dinner he mentioned that he was a great friend of Edward Said. Leon Wieseltier and Noam Chomsky were also great buddies of his. At the mention of Said's name, Janis grumbled. I doubt that this was unexpected, for Hitchens almost certainly thinks of me as a terrible reactionary—the Jewish Right. Brought up to respect and to reject politeness at the same time, the guest wrestled briefly and silently with the *louche* journalist and finally spoke up. He said that Said was a great friend and that he must apologize to Janis but loyalty to a friend demanded that he set the record straight. Everybody remained polite. For Amis's sake I didn't want a scene. Fortunately (or not) I had within reach several excerpts from Said's *Critical Inquiry* piece, which I offered in evidence. Jews were (more or less) Nazis. But of course, said Hitchens, it was well known that [Yitzhak] Shamir had approached Hitler during the war to make deals. I objected that Shamir was Shamir, he wasn't the Jews. Besides I didn't trust the evidence.[10]

In this letter to Ozick, Bellow, who had restrained himself over dinner, lets rip. Hitchens represents "the political press in its silliest disheveled left-wing form." "These Hitchenses . . . drink, drug, lie, cheat, chase, seduce, gossip, libel, borrow money, never pay child support, etc. They're the bohemians who made Marx foam with rage in *The Eighteenth Brumaire*." Amis's attraction to Hitchens Bellow forgives. "This is a temptation I understand. But the sort of people you like to write about aren't always fit company, especially at the dinner table." Looking back on the visit, after some twenty years, Hitchens believed Amis "suffered more agony than he needed to, because Bellow as an old former Trotskyist and Chicago streetfighter was used to much warmer work and hardly took offence at all." He reported that Bellow later wrote him "a warm letter about my introduction to a new edition of *Augie March*."[11] The edition did not appear until 2003, however, when Bellow's memory had largely disappeared.

BEFORE THE 1987 CONFERENCE in Haifa, which took place on April 27–29, Bellow and Janis went on a holiday to Europe. They flew from Chicago to Zürich to Lugano, where Bellow was to film an interview, a nine-hour journey; after visiting Milan on a side trip, they flew to Nice, where Bellow rented a car and drove through pouring rain to Aix-en-Provence. They stayed there from April 11 to 14, giving Bellow a chance to collapse and collect himself. From Aix they drove to Avignon and spent the night there. The next morning, they walked the ramparts in bright sunshine, lugging their bags, which were full of books and lecture manuscripts. They had to run to catch their train to Lyon, an episode remembered by Janis as a "terrible ordeal." In Lyon they stayed two nights on the forty-eighth floor of a hot, airless, modern hotel. "The trip had not given Bellow his much-needed rest," Janis recalled. "Packing, moving, worrying. We were tremendously dispirited." One morning in Aix they sat in a café, planning what to do with the rest of their holiday. "We'd pretty much decided that a trip to Torino would suit us best. And just as we were about to leave the café and head to the agency to book the tickets B spotted the headline in the paper: Primo Levi dies. . . . B was crushed. We were going to Turin so that B could meet with Levi again (they had met only once in NY). We staggered away from the café and I could feel how shaken B was by the arm I'd taken to guide him through the crowd."[12] From April 15 to 23, they finally got some rest, staying just outside Avignon at the Auberge de Cassagne in Le Pontet, in a quiet, dark room, with walks along an avenue of sycamores. On April 24, they took a 6:00 a.m. flight from Lyon to Zürich to Haifa. Though close and loving throughout the trip, Janis and Bellow were often exhausted, and Bellow was sometimes depressed. "It was the difference in years, his pattern of unsuitable mates, and of course always death and what approaches a need sometimes, to give yourself to it." Against such darkness, there was for Bellow "this aching need for life. There's this spring all around us in Le Pontet." In such a state, the couple arrived in Haifa.

The conference, the first to be devoted exclusively to his work, was not easy for Bellow, and at times he was unwilling or unable or barely able to disguise his feelings of discomfort, disapproval, boredom. The idea for the conference came from its organizer, Ada Aharoni, a lecturer in the Department of English at the University of Haifa. Aharoni had completed her Ph.D., on Bellow, in 1975, and claims to have been the only Israeli academic working on him that year. She also met him in 1975, during his stay in Jerusalem with Alexandra. At a conference in the autumn of that year, she asked him, "When will you come to Haifa?" He answered: "If you invite me, I'll come." Eleven years later, having got approval for the conference from the rector of the University of Haifa, Aharoni enlisted the help of the novelist A. B. ("Bully") Yehoshua, who also taught at the university. In addition, she contacted the American founders of the Saul Bellow Society, Leila Goldman and Gloria L. Cronin, academics "who were very helpful in organizing people from Japan and all over."

The conference was large and ambitious. There were six sessions spread over three days, plus social events on either side, stretching the proceedings to five days. Among the speakers were three of Israel's most prominent novelists: Yehoshua, Aharon Appelfeld, and Amos Oz. Martin Amis was invited by Yehoshua and gave a talk on *More Die of Heartbreak*, due out in June. The novelist Alan Lelchuk, a friend of Bellow's, talked about the story "What Kind of Day Did You Have?" Lelchuk and Amis appeared together in a session chaired by Allan Bloom, who was in ebullient form after the initial rave reviews of *The Closing of the American Mind*, published the month before. That night, the second night of the conference, Bellow gave an address entitled "The Silent Assumptions of the Novelist." It was introduced by Shimon Peres, at the time leader of the Israeli Labor Party and foreign secretary of Israel, formerly prime minister. The academics were impressed by how well Peres knew Bellow's works and how intelligently he talked about them. Bellow, too, was impressed, commenting that not since Woodrow Wilson had an American president shown a comparable interest in literature. Among the academics who gave papers were Daniel Fuchs, whose work Bellow approved, Ellen Pifer, and Jonathan Wilson. Like most of the other speakers, they had all published articles in the *Saul Bellow Journal*, founded in 1982 and edited by Cronin and Goldman. The conference was attended by more than a hundred scholars and writers from Israel, the United States, Canada, Britain, Italy, Germany, Japan, and India. Bellow's talk was attended by an audience of a thousand.

According to Ada Aharoni, Bellow "sat through all the sessions." But he was not always happy with what he heard. Bellow was wary of academics who presumed to explain his works, particularly English-literature academics. "I love coming to Israel," he told Aharoni and Goldman in an interview conducted during the conference and published a year later. "I am grateful for the opportunity of being in Haifa again. However, the experience of being dissected and laid on the table for three days reminds me of the anecdote about the three Jewish mothers who boasted about how much their sons loved them. The first one said:

'My son loves me so much he bought me a mink coat.' The second one said: 'My son loves me more; he bought me a brand new Cadillac.' The third one said: 'My son loves me the most; he goes to the psychoanalyst every week, pays $100 for each visit and talks, talks, talks, all about me!' That's how I feel about it. I am grateful to the Saul Bellow Society and to Haifa University for inviting me and for organizing this conference, but sometimes people think a celebrity has all the answers. To myself I'm not a celebrity, and I don't have all the answers."[13] Bellow bridled at being pinned down or pigeonholed; he thought of scholars and critics of his work as denying him the freedom to grow or change. Reading the *Saul Bellow Journal*, Atlas quotes him as saying, gave him an "in-memoriam" chill: "I'm not about to order my cenotaph."[14]

On the eve of the conference, Aharoni gave a party for the speakers and conference organizers and baked a big cake with Bellow's name on it. An American academic came up to Bellow and told him he thought parts of *Dangling Man* were taken from Jean-Paul Sartre. As Aharoni remembers it, Bellow "became very defensive about that, and the man tried to explain: 'It's all right, I loved it.' It sort of got Bellow in a bad mood, and he went off to talk with Allan Bloom." Andrew Gordon, a scholar from the University of Florida, the author of several essays published in the *Saul Bellow Journal*, introduced himself to Bellow. They talked of the Robin Williams film of *Seize the Day*, released the year before, which Bellow did not like: "They got it wrong; it's supposed to be a funny story. There were no humorous lines." Bellow admitted he didn't care much for American movies. He told how Jack Nicholson had bought the rights to *Henderson the Rain King* in 1979 but said he had heard nothing since. This was fine with Bellow, who had been paid his option money. "I got the best of it—the movie without the movie being made." Then Gordon asked Bellow if he'd been involved in training and hunting eagles in Mexico, as had Augie in *Augie March*. "He said nothing and glared at me." This glare Gordon describes as "withering." Yet, minutes later, Gordon and Bellow were telling jokes and laughing. An Indian scholar joined them and said to Bellow, "I've spent ten years studying your work." Bellow's reply, described as "mordant" by Gordon, was "I hope your time wasn't wasted." A young assistant professor told Bellow he'd just written a book about him, a revised version of his dissertation. " 'I see,' said Bellow. 'I was your ticket. Well, I won't read it.' And he turned away." When Gordon's wife met Bellow, she said he reminded her "of some senior professor who's had tenure so long that all he does is sneer down his nose at everyone."[15] Ann Weinstein, the most ardent of fans, recalls getting into an elevator with Bellow and finding Leila Goldman there. Weinstein introduced Goldman to Bellow as the editor of the *Saul Bellow Journal*, president of the Saul Bellow Society, and "the woman who made the conference possible." "Much to my disappointment as to Leila's, all Bellow did was nod, acknowledge her presence, without so much as expressing one word of thanks for her grandiose [*sic*] efforts to promote his work. . . . My heart ached for her."[16] Bellow may have been embarrassed or preoccupied when confronted with Goldman, but he may also consciously have slighted her; he had no high opinion of the Saul Bellow Society or of its members, most of whom he thought second-rate, and made little effort to hide his feelings.

Politics played a part in Bellow's uneasiness during the conference, mostly concerning questions of national identity and gender. In the unedited transcript of his interview with Goldman and Aharoni, among his papers in the Regenstein, he is asked to "say something about the women in your novels," a topic raised by several speakers at the conference. "That has the air of an FBI question," he replies. The interviewers press him: "The issue is very important." He answers "that we belong to the same spirit and are mutually dependent upon one another and that after all we are all possessors of a soul. . . . I think we should be very careful about these things and not go crazy in the field of ideology because it has gotten us into so much trouble in this century." He is asked if there will be a heroine in his next book, since "your central character is always a hero." He replies, "Well I know more about people who wear trousers, but now the women are wearing them too, perhaps I can be more at home with them." "You're not helping very much," the interviewers tell him. "Of course I'm not helping very much," he replies. Later in the interview, when talking of the dual loyalties and responsibilities of American Jews, Bellow argues that it would be wrong to abandon the American project, the democratic project, "which you Israelis [only Aharoni was Israeli] also have an interest in." Israelis often argue that only in Israel is a Jew safe and wholly or truly a Jew, a view Bellow rejects. "I think it would be both inconsistent and even cowardly, I won't say unmanly for fear of being stoned, but how can one turn his back on his own life?"

Martin Amis's recollections of Bellow at the conference differ from those of Aharoni. Amis remembers Bellow as "not often to be found at the Saul Bellow Conference Centre." After sitting through a talk that Amis characterizes as "hopelessly academic and abstract," Bellow "was heard to say that if he had to listen to much more of this he would die, not of heartbreak but of inanition" (the title of the talk, Amis believes, was something like "The Caged Cash Register: Tensions Between Existentialism and Materialism in *Dangling Man*"). Bellow's unhappiness at the conference, Amis thinks, may have been a product not only of boredom and embarrassment but of a principled opposition to the way literature was taught in American universities. He quotes Bellow's essay "A Matter of the Soul" (1975), in which American English departments are said to teach students to discuss "what Ahab's harpoon symbolizes or what Christian symbols there are in *Light in August*," but fail to instill "passion for novels and poems."[17]

In addition to Bellow's disapproval of literary academics, there were awkwardnesses over Janis, the sort they would encounter elsewhere. The conference paid for flights and accommodation for Bloom, Janis, and Bellow, putting them up in the city's most expensive hotel. Aharoni's secretary was instructed to ring Bellow in Chicago to ask if she should book him a double room or a single room. He said a single room. Then he rang back and said a double room. The organizers knew he was divorcing Alexandra but weren't sure about Janis's status. When she arrived, according to Aharoni, "everyone was saying, Is she your daughter?" Ellen Pifer remembers that Janis was at Bellow's side throughout the conference. At a reception hosted by the rector of the university, Janis and Pifer chatted for a few minutes. When Pifer asked her if she was Bellow's secretary, "with great timing, poise, and a subtle sense of irony, she answered deftly: 'Sometimes.'"[18] Yehoshua and his wife had met and liked Janis during the 1984 Olin Center conference, but they were disturbed to find that Bellow was now in a relationship with her, in part because she was his student and forty-three years his junior, in part because they had also met and liked Alexandra. "The difference of ages," Yehoshua admits, "we didn't like it. I'm very much a conservative in my marriage, in my relationship with my wife." Bellow enjoyed Yehoshua's company, admired his writing, and expected that they would spend time together in Haifa. They barely exchanged a word, and in a letter of July 10, 1987, he hinted at his disappointment. The reasons for this disappointment come in a letter of August 5. It was at Yehoshua's urging, Bellow reminds him, that he had accepted the invitation to come to Haifa, and "all my arrangements were made solely with you." Once he arrived, though, "I fell into the hands of the ladies who had organized the conference." These ladies he calls "career parasites," just the types he had "done everything possible to avoid. . . . I found myself surrounded and utterly cut off. . . . Nor was there a single private conversation in which I might have explained all this to you. I thought that I should have had at least fifteen minutes of your private time and I don't think you can blame me for wondering why you and I were unable to manage even a brief conversation."

Yehoshua admits he could have behaved better: "I was faulty for not inviting him to the house." On July 27, in reply to Bellow's letter of July 10, he wrote that he understood why Bellow was "slightly annoyed with me," but reiterated his belief that "from a completely objective point of view the conference was a great success." There were several "outstanding" lectures; Bellow's "left a lasting and deep impression"; the conference was "widely reported" in the Israeli press; "good and friendly relations" were established among conference participants; and "people who had not met with you before were impressed by your easy-going personality and humanism." From the evidence of Gordon and others, this last assertion is hard to credit. Bellow's behavior with the academics was sometimes ill-mannered.

BELLOW'S WILLINGNESS TO OFFEND, particularly when it came to questions of literary value or standing, extended to close friends. At around this time, Edith Tarcov sought to publish a collection of the writings of her deceased husband, Oscar. She went to see Morris Philipson, director of the University of Chicago Press, to see what he thought of the idea. Philipson was interested, but would only publish if Bellow agreed to write an introduction to the volume. When Edith sent Bellow a letter about her meeting with Philipson, she heard nothing back. After weeks of silence, Nathan Tarcov went to Bellow's office to ask him if he'd received his mother's letter, "because I knew she was suffering from not having heard back from him."

> It took him a while to answer at all, and finally he said something like "Oscar was a better husband and father but he wasn't that good a writer and I don't really see any point in your doing this." I was quite shocked. . . . I think he was trying to say this in a calm and respectful way, but to me it just seemed some kind of reappearance

> of this long-ago teenage rivalry which he should have gotten over already. He had a Nobel Prize and was the most famous American novelist, and my father was dead and no competition and all Edith was asking was that he write an introduction to this volume, and he could do that even if he didn't think these were the greatest writings ever. So I was pretty shocked and horrified. . . . Maybe he was just very busy and always being bombarded with requests. . . . But, then, he could have said that.

AFTER THE HAIFA CONFERENCE, Bellow, Janis, Bloom, Martin Amis, and Antonia Phillips, Amis's wife, traveled to Jerusalem, where they were put up at Mishkenot Sha'ananim, the guesthouse for writers and artists. "We'll have a ball yet," Bellow told Amis, and they did. "We were very privileged," Amis remembers, "it was a fantastic week," the highlight being a dinner they all had with Mayor Teddy Kollek to celebrate Jacob Rothschild's birthday. The Amises had met Rothschild, a friend of Antonia's, on the plane to Israel. Also at the dinner were Jacob's younger half-brother, Amschel Rothschild, and his wife, Anita, whom the Amises knew from London. Kollek was much as Bellow depicts him in *To Jerusalem and Back*, a bustling figure who disappeared between courses and then, in Amis's words, "potently rematerialized, his city so much the calmer or the more solvent after some appearance he had put in or phone call he had made." Jacob and Amschel were visiting Jerusalem in their capacity as trustees of Yad Hanadiv, the Rothschild family foundation which gave the Knesset and the Supreme Court buildings to Israel. They operated in what Amis calls "that (to me) mysterious arena of power and public relations, of endowments, of pro-bono unveilings. 'I'm the Princess Di of Israel,' said Anita (née Guinness), semi-seriously: 'I *am*.' "

During the dinner in Jerusalem, Amis watched Bloom closely, attracted both by his demeanor "of constant expectation of amusement" and by "the physical greed with which he went through his Marlboros." Noting "the pleasure Saul took in him" did not prevent Amis from engaging Bloom in "a loud, long, and in the end unrancorous argument about nuclear weapons" (Bloom was for them, as deterrent, Amis against them, having written a long prefatory essay about their use in *Einstein's Monsters*, a collection of stories published that year). As the argument heated up, Amis backed off, as Bellow was to do two years later when arguing with Hitchens about Edward Said. Both Amis and Bloom resisted what Amis calls "the deep attractions of escalation." "There are times," he continues in *Experience*, "when manners are more important than the end of the world." During their stay at Mishkenot, Amis asked Janis if she thought Bellow would like the idea of meeting with him for a little chat, the sort Yehoshua had ducked in Haifa. She advised him to drop Bellow a note. Over tea on the terrace at Mishkenot the next day, Amis felt they were moving beyond friendly acquaintance to genuine friendship.[19] Antonia Phillips remembers that Bellow was "quite protective in a funny way with Martin." There was "a tenderness between the two of them," perfectly understandable on Martin's side "from his relations with Kingsley; after all, Saul actually read things that Martin wrote." The next summer, Martin and Antonia were invited to Vermont with their young sons, Jacob and Louis. In an undated thank-you note, Amis remembers Bellow "robustly carrying Jacob down the lane (I think that was more or less the only time he was unconscious for the whole of our stay). You were marvellously hospitable and beautifully patient. We must come again—and quickly, in the brief interlude before the boys start smashing cars and taking crack and knocking up their girlfriends."

BY JUNE 1987, following not only their travels but the publication of *More Die of Heartbreak*, Bellow and Janis were back in Vermont and exhausted, Bellow in particular. The summer, however, was restorative, despite many visitors and a short trip to New York.[20] Among the visitors were members of Janis's family, several of whom Bellow had got to know on trips to Canada. Early in their courtship, before any question of marriage, Janis brought Bellow to the family farm outside Toronto, where he met her father for the first time. Her mother he had already met. When Sonya Freedman first came to Chicago to visit Janis, "before there was any romance," she sat in on a Bloom-and-Bellow seminar and was introduced to both men. By the second visit, Janis had told her mother of the relationship with Bellow, and when they met up again, her mother says, "Bellow seemed nervous." At a meal that night, though, "the conversation was fine, and afterwards I said to him: 'Well, that wasn't so difficult, was it?' and he just burst out laughing, and that was sort of the end of the strangeness between us. And he came to the farm, many times, before they were married."

When the Freedmans first learned of a romantic relationship between Janis and Bellow, they were naturally concerned. For two reasons, according to Harvey Freedman: "He was a famous man, and there's always some discomfort in a first encounter with a famous man, and he was sleeping with our daughter." Although the Freedmans assumed the relationship would not last, after the first visit "it became obvious that this was more than a fling." Janis's sister, Wendy, also thought that the relationship would not last, that Janis was rebounding from Peter Ahrensdorf and Bellow from Alexandra. But, like her parents, she soon saw that Janis "was happy, very, very happy. . . . I was convinced by Janis. I could see what she had." The only member of the family to take serious objection to the relationship was Janis's maternal grandmother, the family matriarch, "who was really upset . . . but not for long." She was brought round by Bellow himself, as well as by Janis. According to Janis, Bellow made a concerted effort to win the old woman over. He traveled with Janis and her family to Hamilton, Ontario, where she lived, and, according to Sonya Freedman, "got all dressed up . . . and came to tea and charmed her. She was giggling."[21]

Harvey Freedman's acceptance of Bellow was also quickly won, in his case on Bellow's first visit to the farm. "We picked him up at the airport," he remembers. "He came to the car, he sat down, and we had rather a large golden retriever, and it kept licking him." Bellow did not complain; in fact, "he seemed rather at home." That night, Sonya Freedman was nervous about dinner: "I was cooking, and I was a bit cowed, because this man had eaten at some of the best restaurants in the world. And he sat down at the counter in the kitchen and there was some kosher salami and some pickles and he just loved them. . . . He was our kind of person." "There were no airs about him," Harvey recalls; "he spoke honestly, you were not getting a phony person. . . . That was apparent from the first meal we had, that he was the straight goods, which we valued, and we were relieved. The other reassuring thing was that Janis is a pretty good judge of character . . . and if she was going to be involved with Saul Bellow it wasn't just because he was Daddy Warbucks or a famous man, but that there was a human being of substance." Freedman was also impressed by Bellow's "capacity for clarity," describing him as "the Michael Jordan of clarity."

The next morning, Bellow chopped wood with Freedman. "There he was [at seventy-one, fourteen years older than his future father-in-law], chopping up half a cord of wood. He was quite powerful. . . . I couldn't keep up." Later that day, Sonya Freedman was struck by the appearance of Bellow and Janis together: "It was strange, as though we had two kids here. Janis wanted to show him all her favorite places on the farm. I remember watching them holding hands walking down the path, like two young lovers." Later, the Freedmans felt, as Harvey Freedman puts it, that "there was a—I use the word metaphorically—spiritual union here. They were soulmates, they understood each other poetically and emotionally, sort of kindred souls." The parents took the relationship on Janis's terms, trusting in her happiness and certainty. They also recognized the benefits for Bellow. As Wendy puts it, "For Saul, here's a young woman who is very bright, very knowledgeable about literature, very interested in ideas. From his perspective, he found somebody with whom he could share a lot of things . . . and Janis is a very loving person, an extremely warm and loving individual. And she really fell in love with the man. And they went for it." This sense of Janis's having committed herself wholly to Bellow was shared by her friend Alane Rollings, a poet, and also a friend of Alexandra's. Rollings herself was involved with a much older man, Bellow's friend Richard Stern, whom she later married. She stresses Janis's seriousness about her relationship with Bellow, and her comparable seriousness about literature. Rollings believes Janis made "a conscious decision . . . to give up my life to this man." Being with Bellow was exciting; providing and being what he needed was fulfilling, but it was also, Rollings imagines Janis thinking, "the thing I could do with my life, the most important thing I can do for society." To Adam Bellow, Janis "couldn't possibly have known what she was getting into, but she didn't care. . . . She went for the idealization of the couple. . . . She had made a big statement."

DURING THEIR FIRST YEARS TOGETHER, Bellow published two novellas, *A Theft* and *The Bellarosa Connection*, both in 1989. A year later, he published what many consider his finest short story, "Something to Remember Me By." In these years, he was also at work on two novels, "A Case of Love" and "All Marbles Still Accounted For," neither of which he completed. The longest and most finished of the manuscripts for "A Case of Love" is 207 typed pages. The comparable manuscript for "All Marbles Still Accounted For" is 279 typed pages. Both manuscripts were finished enough to be shown to publishers, as examples of work in progress. "A Case of Love" (henceforth "Case") has a female protagonist and a female narrator. Its central concern, as Janis puts it, is "the idea of whether or not a woman's love was at the center of life for her." Another concern of the novel is what to do "if the guy turns out to be a total jerk." "All Marbles Still Accounted For" ("Marbles") has a ninety-three-year-old protagonist, Hilbert Faucil, who ends up in New Guinea, a wealthy proprietor of a national tabloid, a cross, somehow, between the *National Enquirer* and a highbrow publication (said to offer "the soul's real response to the crisis of modernity").[22] Both novels have wildly improbable plots, closer to *Henderson* than to any of Bellow's other works.

The record of Bellow's struggles with these novels is drawn from excerpts from Janis's journals. From 1987 to 2002, Janis wrote down notes about her life with Bellow.[23] The notes provide information not only about "Case" and "Marbles," but about several other unfinished works: a novella about Barley Alison; a novel about Allan Bloom, parts of which would find their way into *Ravelstein;* and a short story called "Imenitov." Bellow himself used Janis's notes as an *aide-mémoire*. At a dinner party in Paris in 1992, attended, among others, by the historian François Furet and the British politician George Walden, Walden was especially struck by Bellow's "novelist's instincts." "When for some reason we got on to rabies, and someone mentioned that the only person in recent history who had died of the disease in France was said to have been a mayor in a small town who was inspecting his loft when a bat pissed in his eye, Bellow asked Janis to make a note."[24]

Here are entries about "Marbles," the first from May 21, 1989. "I" in what follows is Bellow, who is also "B," or sometimes "he."

> I've been trying to find a person who will have the kind of wide-ranging consciousness, the diverse range of awareness that my ninety-year-old man has. . . . I came up with Nathan Tarcov . . . someone who is also eccentric, quirky, whose life is complicated, full of irregularities, brilliant flashes, and who has the breadth of intelligence to see the whole picture. . . . That isn't to say that the ninety-year-old man has to be anything like Tarcov in what he has done with his life; he wouldn't have taken a degree in political science. I'm talking about the core of the man. It helps to have a real person in mind, to zero in on the core of this person's consciousness, to see what's essential. It doesn't have to be Tarcov, I was just running through in my mind types I had known with great intel-

lectual powers. . . . When I was writing *Henderson* I had someone clearly in mind. It wasn't that this man was Henderson. He'd never done the things Henderson did. It was that this man could have, would have been capable of imagining these sorts of things.

Now what I have in mind is that the ninety-year-old man used to tell stories to his granddaughter, stories dug up from his early incomplete anthropological training. She grows up and takes the whole business seriously in a way granddad never did. It's her idea to send him off to New Guinea. He doesn't particularly want to go on such a trip but he has other reasons for wanting to leave [these reasons concern his accountant, who has cheated him "of six or seven million bucks—as much as ten percent of my fortune," a figure six or seven times greater than the one Bellow claimed he had lost, according to Janis, because of his accountant].[25]

Yesterday after B read to me from "Marbles" again . . . he feels it isn't right yet, it doesn't check out. It's very painful for him to write about Bobby, that's the man sick with brain fever. . . . Here's all this human tragedy working its way into what's supposed to be a Hendersonian novel about a man who goes off to New Guinea and discovers his reincarnated professor [Bellow's old anthropology professor from Northwestern, Melville Herskovits, or a character based on him, was going to be reincarnated as a native]. The whole thing has to be done quickly, with a light touch. . . . Meanwhile it continues to expand in these strange directions, the stuff about old age is quite grim, bitter.

Today June 11 was another story altogether. . . . He woke feeling well, went to the studio. . . . He was redoing "Marbles" from page 1. The tone has shifted. It feels right. It had almost imperceptibly slid into place. I was trying to make it Hendersonian but that didn't work. Henderson is a clown . . . and preposterous, actively preposterous, and that's not at all to my present purpose. . . . B's old man is thoughtful. . . . B hasn't cut the fun from the story . . . but the tone will be all his own not Henderson's.

Janis's notes give a flavor of her life with Bellow, as well as of his methods of composition. In an entry of August 19, 1988, Bellow discusses "Marbles" but also Billy Rose, from *The Bellarosa Connection*, which he is at work on at the same time. In addition, he has new thoughts about the heroine of "Case," whose name is Ursula, and about the "total jerk" she falls for, named Milo. When Bellow thinks of Milo, he sees Jack Nicholson. On February 12, 1989, Bellow walks into Janis's study and reads her the last three pages of the short story "Something to Remember Me By," at the time titled "Louie—Words from an Ancestor," with its thinly fictionalized account of his mother's last days in wintry Chicago in February 1933. "His voice trembled. We both started to cry. Then he took a Kleenex from my pocket, and blew his nose, and put it back. And I started to laugh and cry and I embraced him and kissed his head. 'It's so simple,' he said to me. 'But it has everything in it.'" Weather had sparked the story. They had come to Vermont from Chicago for a little vacation, and all they found was snow.

What entries like these make clear is that, while Bellow engaged in public controversy, gave talks, taught, wrote and published *A Theft*, *The Bellarosa Connection*, and "Something to Remember Me By," worried about his family, mourned the deaths of friends and loved ones, and began a new life with Janis, he was thinking about the plots, themes, characters, registers, and settings of as many as half a dozen unpublished narratives. In a note of February 21, 1990, he explains to Janis that he thinks about these narratives simultaneously, "in a day-to-day way. None of them have actually been shelved, or put on a back burner. He described it to me this way: 'I go around with all my pans in front of me, and every day something falls into each of them.'" That day, what fell into the "Case" pan concerned Ursula's jerk lover. Bellow thought he should be a TV anchorman, not an actor. He and Ursula would meet years later at a White House reception. Her rich husband would leave the reception before her; then she and Milo would try to flag a cab in the pouring rain. "Can you imagine how she feels watching the face of the man she loved night after night on television—seeing the transformation of the features?"

Several weeks later, in March 1990, Bellow's thoughts were of "Kamo," the manuscript about Barley Alison, later to be titled "Rita." After a "brainstorming session" with Janis on the night of June 13, he returned to "Marbles." Two days later, he was back with "Kamo," which he mostly worked on through mid-July, "then more MARBLES." At the end of June, Bellow told Janis he was ready to sign a contract. "I laughed: For which one?!" "'Well I've got two sure things,' he replied," by which he meant "Case" and "Marbles." "Now he's on his way back from the studio. I can hear him singing below my study window. . . . Yesterday he replied to my q. about how the morning had been with distinct enthusiasm: it went VERY well. . . . But what is he working on? MARBLES OR A CASE?" Through August, he worked on "Kamo/Rita" and "Marbles" simultaneously. On August 24, 1990, however, he began a new version of "Case."

> He has a new slant, and a new start. Ursula will relate her tale from a detached perspective. . . . He has worked out the whole episode in the White House in which Ursula runs into Milo and has a quickie with him in one of the State Rooms. Ursula has been through the love disease; the determination to live for love has gone sour on her.

In addition to switching from one work to another, Bellow kept restarting works from the beginning. On December 17, 1990, it was "Marbles" he decided to rewrite: "Typing a fresh start has given him fresh energy," Janis's note reads. "He had been exhausted, dispirited, feeling old. CASE wasn't drawing him sufficiently." In January 1991, Bellow signed a contract for "Case," to deliver a ninety-thousand-word manuscript by April, which in a later note Janis calls "a very bad idea": as soon as he signed, he found himself writing a new short story, "Imenitov." This story he worked on "right through February 1991," "all the while he's worrying about CASE." The story was never finished. The nature of Bellow's worries is suggested in an entry of January 7, 1991: "He feels he doesn't have time to get himself mired in a long story or book. It's a gamble to be immersed in a work that may not pull together in the end. 'I've always written that way,' he explained. 'I let what's inside me unfold without too much external planning.'" A bewildered entry for February 12, 1991, reads: "A new start [for "Case"]. Really. All over again, from page one, in a hand-written version—hard cover—navy notebook. He's tired." In March, Bellow decides that "Case" should not be narrated by Ursula, the heroine, but by her friend Amanda, based on Lillian Blumberg McCall, a figure he knew from the Village and whose memoir he and Janis had been reading (McCall figures in chapters 10 and 11 of *To Fame and Fortune*). The book will now include episodes from Amanda's backstory, including one in which she is asked to write the entry on "Love" for the *Encyclopaedia Britannica* (the *Syntopicon* volume, presumably), and is blocked by Hannah Arendt. "That'll account for why a lot of her theories find their way into her 'novel' about Ursula instead. And this was something that happened to B. Edward Shils had put him forward as the best person to do the entry on love. And he didn't want to, hadn't the time for the research or the writing, but he never even had the chance to decline. Yammering Hannah stepped forward to nip the idea in the bud: How could B. be the one entrusted with such a subject?!"

A second addition to this newest version of "Case" widened the story to include current affairs. As Janis records on March 11, 1991: "Milo goes off on some Middle East journalist romp and is kidnapped. Ursula goes to Syria to intercede with Hafez al-Assad. . . . We had fun with this. I thought Carstens [the millionaire husband Ursula marries after splitting with Milo] might have a U.S. company that could provide something Assad needed for weapons manufacture, and that Carstens might agree to some awful, illegal deal in the negotiations to free Milo." On April 3, 1991, Janis records that, "when we got to p. 24 of the computer version of CASE, B. decided that he was going to start typing a new draft from page one. And so it is this new typed version that I have been putting into the computer at night. Now Amanda is fully incorporated into the story, and B. was typing along with great enthusiasm until the past couple of days. He has been wildly excited, hasn't been sleeping well. But it hasn't been Ursula who has been keeping him awake, he just told me, and he feels that this is a 'betrayal.' This book [not "Case"] is still a sideline for him, and he must push on with it ["Case"] because he signed a contract. But what is at the center for him now is the Bloom book."

THE THEME OF LOVE IS DISCUSSED with Janis in several notes. On July 9, 1991, she records Bellow's conclusion, contra Rousseau, that "there IS such a thing as love. It isn't a manipulative product of the imagination. It's a real power. Not a winning one, no one ever said that, but real nonetheless. We're always talking about the EMILE and B has been dipping into Bloom's essay on Rousseau in GIANTS AND DWARFS. He succeeds in offering a counter-example to the modern type in Ursula." At the end of the entry, in which possible plot schemes for "Case" are discussed, Janis concludes: "OK. So there's much going on. And B., for all his troubles has produced 152 manuscript pages (I have barely put 100 into the computer, and have barely touched my own work)." Less than a week later, on July 14, 1991, Bellow announces another breakthrough:

When he came in (for his salade nicoise) at 1:00 yesterday, and read me the morning's work, he was triumphant. He called time-out and made room for a very serious core statement by Amanda. About what love is. A spiritual power. First you know nothing but your own reality, the fact of your own being. When you fall in love for the first time you know about the existence of another: in the fullest sense, you discover being. (Take that Heidegger.) Amanda delivers her soliloquy on love so simply. Just stating the facts . . . Here is B. speaking to people who, through their yearning, have earned the right to hear such things. I think readers will respond to this revolutionary statement with the same kind of longing that they poured into Henderson's "I want I want."

B. was very emotional as he read those pages to me. This is straight from the heart stuff. Later in the afternoon, as we were driving back from our town-run he voiced doubts about how such a message would be received. "Critics will attack me for delivering a highfalutin' sermon, as though I was looking down on them about the most important things." He reminded me that there were all sorts of creeps out there waiting to take pot-shots at him. I told him that anyone hearing Amanda's statement who has any drop of soul left in him will immediately understand what's being said.

. . .

Over lunch he wasn't having any of these doubts—he was just on fire with what he'd written in his blue notebook. He told me that he's waited all his life to understand these things, and that part of his understanding came from me. . . . He said it was the reciprocal love that was so new, so important. I laughed and told him I was glad to be able to teach him about something.

Later in the entry, Janis talks of reading bits of her dissertation to Bellow, "from my pages on Emma riding in the woods with Rodolphe. He was pleased by my tone—more authoritative. . . . It was a high pressure day yesterday. Clear crystal blue sky without a trace of cloud. Perfect conditions said B., for his best work. We biked and swam. He was so much himself. . . . B. asked me to try to remember some of what we'd talked about at breakfast, and to take some notes."

Janis's notes make clear not only how involved she and Bellow were in each other's work but how they shared a sense that they were living out the themes of their writing. Bellow had always worked on several things at once, but had mostly done so alone. He had regular readers—Bette Howland in particular, also Harriet Wasserman—but neither had anything like the daily contact Janis had, or the daily access to his thoughts. In their early years together, Susan Glassman had been intimately involved in Bellow's writing, but Janis was better informed about Bellow's tradition than Susan, in addition to being wholly sympathetic, untricky, and, in Martin Amis's words from an interview, "barbarically loyal." As Howland puts it, "Janis really could combine all these things. She could tie his shoes and she knows Greek and she's from Canada and she was Jewish and she was trained in the Committee. . . . They really were a couple, and she *did* laugh at all his jokes."

BELLOW'S PROBLEMS WITH "Case" and "Marbles" led him to fears about his powers as a novelist, worries about what he could or should write. Such worries, he told Janis, were "a torment once you hit fifty." His propensity to start over rather than to rework was especially hard on Janis: "Every time he'd start again, I'd go down with him." Bellow confided his fears to close friends as well as to Janis. After telling Amis that he'd completed *The Bellarosa Connection*, in a letter of November 14, 1988, he announced that he was " 'kissing off' the lengthy novel ('kissing off' being an older form of 'spinning off,' both expressions refer to the stifling of a relationship, or the slow and gentle suffocation of the beloved). 'Too little time' is, I suppose, what people of my age keenly feel, and if you add to that Sydney Smith's plea, 'Short views, for God's sake!' you can see where I'm at." Complaining to John Auerbach, in a letter of October 23, 1989, he provides a striking image to illustrate the drawbacks of "free-style" composing: "Lack of time comes in the nick of time for I haven't got anything to work on. I wrote one hundred pages of a very funny narrative ["Marbles"] during the summer, but it was like a skyscraper in the desert. I had overlooked the water problem." In another letter to Auerbach, of July 7, 1991, he describes similar problems with "Case":

> I have X-plus pages to write and I do it under the shadowy threat of "too late." So . . . I am trying to meet a deadline imposed by a contract I signed in order to spur myself to work more quickly. But I haven't got the energy I once had. Well into my late sixties I could

> work all day long. Now I fold at one o'clock. Most days I can't work without a siesta. I get out of bed and try to wake up. I ride the bike or swim in the pond. After such activities I have to rest again. It's evening, it's dinnertime. Nine-tenths of what I should have done it now seems too late to do. . . . I water the garden and promise myself to do better tomorrow.

INTENSE PERIODS OF WORK and Vermont quiet were broken for Bellow and Janis by glamorous outings and occasions. On December 8, 1987, they attended a state dinner at the White House to celebrate the signing that afternoon of the INF Treaty, in which the United States and the Soviet Union agreed to ban the use of intermediate-range nuclear weapons. According to *The New York Times*, this dinner was "the most coveted invitation in the capital in many a year," attended by "126 stars of business, science, sports, politics and the arts." Bellow sat next to Jimmy Stewart's wife and enjoyed meeting Joe DiMaggio; Janis tried out her Russian. After toasts by Presidents Reagan and Gorbachev and a lavish meal, they decided to skip the entertainment (Van Cliburn playing Shostakovich) and hailed a cab back to their hotel, as Ursula and Milo do in "Case." Bellow enjoyed himself at the dinner, but Janis sensed that he wasn't all that interested in the occasion and had accepted the invitation "for me." The treaty itself was controversial, criticized by former president Richard M. Nixon, Henry Kissinger, and William F. Buckley, Jr., as well as by prominent members of the Committee on the Present Danger and the Committee for the Free World.

Bellow's attitude to the politicians and political types he met in Washington is captured in an article he wrote for *Newsday* about the March 1979 signing of the Egypt-Israel Peace Treaty, a companion piece to "White House and Artists" (1962), which describes the state dinner President Kennedy gave for André Malraux (discussed in chapter 14 of *To Fame and Fortune*).[26] Here, too, as with the Malraux dinner and the INF Treaty dinner, Bellow notes the pleasure the assembled "eminences" take in recognizing and greeting each other, "embracing enthusiastically, grappling affectionately, kissing." The treaty itself is greeted realistically, as the INF Treaty was to be. "Most of those present were moved. Some said they were moved against their better judgment." In his capacity as reporter, Bellow visits Egyptian Foreign Minister Boutros Boutros-Ghali, "a diplomat whose smooth

Egyptian-French surfaces easily deflected unwelcome questions. There were no unmannerly rejections, only an easy, practiced turning aside of things he didn't care to discuss. For these things he substituted certain rhetorical practices of his own. I have done much the same on some occasions, with less style."

The *Newsday* article ends with a description of Bellow's brief encounters with major political figures: Fritz Mondale, Henry Kissinger, Daniel Moynihan, and James Schlesinger, "a person of monumental presence, a great pillar smoking his pipe . . . Senator Moynihan told me how greatly the afternoon ceremony had moved him. Mr. Kissinger told me nothing, but coldly endured my handshake. He was very like Queen Victoria, it struck me. Some of my mischievous remarks in print apparently had displeased him. 'We are not amused.'" That Bellow says so little about James Schlesinger, Carter's secretary of energy, previously secretary of defense under Nixon and Ford, is odd. Among the Saul Bellow Papers at the Regenstein is the draft of a letter dated October 23, 1998. Whether the letter was sent is not clear.

> Attention: James Schlesinger
>
> A Piece of unfinished business
>
> You and I met at Carter's dinner celebrating the Camp David Agreement. When we were introduced you tilted your wine glass, picked up my necktie and poured a large amount of wine over it. I was about to punch you in the nose but friends—probably friends of yours—said that a fist fight would be out of place and I was pulled from the scene. I've had this on my mind for many years now [almost twenty], and when I saw your name in the Wall Street Journal recently I decided to send you a note.
>
> I don't know if you were malicious or merely drunk. In some places you may be an eminent statesman but in my book you are a shit.
>
> Saul Bellow

Bellow was not alone in his view of Schlesinger. President Ford fired him in 1975, and President Carter fired him in 1979. According to the journalist and Clinton speechwriter Paul Glastris, writing in the *Washington Monthly*, Carter fired Schlesinger "in part for the same reason Gerald Ford had—he was unbearably arrogant and impatient with lesser minds who disagreed with him, and hence inept at dealing with Congress."[27] Janis several times heard Bellow tell the story of his encounter with Schlesinger; each time "he threw back his head and laughed. . . . This was the kind of episode he adored." There is also a fictionalized version of the encounter in "All Marbles Still Accounted For," in which Secretary of Defense Schlesinger becomes Secretary of Defense Brushmore.[28]

After the INF Treaty dinner, there was one other visit to the White House. In July 1988, President Reagan awarded Bellow the National Medal of Arts, along with eleven other recipients, among them Helen Hayes, I. M. Pei, Rudolf Serkin, Jerome Robbins, and Brooke Astor. When asked about Reagan by Norman Manea, Bellow said of him: "I never saw anybody in public life who was so at ease and who played his role so well, with the vitality of an artist. I think that this was his great moment as an actor, when he was President."[29] Whether Bellow had voted for Reagan is not clear. Adam Bellow thinks he probably did not, which is what Janis thinks. "I think Saul's view of Reagan evolved as mine did," Adam told Gloria L. Cronin in an interview. "He probably considered Reagan to be a sort of third-rate actor, though he may have been more aware of Reagan's record as governor than I was. Ultimately, it was Reagan's anticommunism that drew his approval. . . . Although for my father and I as Jews it was still very difficult to identify as Republicans, socially and culturally."[30] Daniel Bellow believes: "When Ronald Reagan got elected he [Bellow] was happy because he thought Reagan was a man of character and an anticommunist. I would say 'He deregulated the banks and let the thieves loose in the treasury,' but Pop had lived through the Harding administration so he wasn't impressed. He thought Adlai Stevenson was a fool, easy pickings for Mayor Daley. Pop respected strength and savvy in a politician, and when a politician did not display those qualities, Pop considered that he was not fit for office."[31]

Daniel's view is given support by Bellow's encounter with another head of state. In a trip to Britain in 1990, George Walden arranged for him to meet the prime minister, Margaret Thatcher. Walden was at the time minister of higher education and knew Bellow through Allan Bloom. Having been greatly impressed by *The Closing of the American Mind*, Walden and his wife, Sarah, called on Bloom in Chicago on a trip to the United States in the spring of 1988. The two men liked each other, and Bloom invited Walden to return that autumn to give a lecture at the Olin Center. At the lecture, Bellow sat in the front row, "an unnerving experience" for Walden, and joined the Waldens and Bloom for dinner afterward at the Italian Village. For Walden, the dinner was "the funniest, most free-spirited evening I could remember," "a perpetual double act" in which Bloom and Bellow "kicked around the gravest of ideas in a series of running gags."[32]

In February 1989, Bloom came to London to appear on television, and Walden arranged for him to be introduced to Mrs. Thatcher.[33] His motive for arranging the meeting was to counter the view, fashionable in government circles and shared by Mrs. Thatcher, that university courses of no direct importance to the economy were an indulgence. To Walden's surprise, Mrs. Thatcher invited Bloom to Sunday lunch at Chequers, the country-house retreat of the prime minister. To his greater surprise, she stayed up the night before until 2:30 a.m. reading Bloom's book. "It had never occurred to me that she would open it, let alone read it." Over lunch she was at her best: "Instead of telling Bloom the book he ought to have written, as she might easily have done, she not only asked detailed questions: she listened to the answers."[34]

In May 1990, Bellow and Janis came to England, where Bellow was to deliver the Romanes Lecture at Oxford, the Annual Public Lecture of the University. His subject was "The Distracted Public." When Walden learned of the visit, he "made the mistake of trying to repeat the success of the Bloom-Thatcher encounter." This time the meeting was at Downing Street, for tea. When the prime minister's office rang Walden to ask what would be discussed, he suggested "the black problem in America," which he knew was much on Bellow's mind at the time. In St. James's Park, on the way to Number 10, Bellow asked Walden the same question, and got the same answer. This time, Mrs. Thatcher was not at her best. She arrived for tea "between meetings, pretending not to be exhausted, and on a talking high." "She was all keyed up and tired," Walden recalls, "and, of course, she hadn't read any of Bellow's novels."

> "You're from Chicago. Now that's most interesting. They tell me Chicago has a bad racial problem. I would much like to hear your views."
>
> "Well . . ." Bellow made to put down his tea.
>
> "My own feeling is . . ."
>
> Bellow stuck with his tea, listening with every appearance of

> interest while Thatcher told him all there was to know about the problem of blacks in America. When she seemed on the verge of talking herself out her guest was finally invited to give his view.
>
> "If you'd really like to know my opinion . . ." Bellow began with a lightning smile.
>
> "Absolutely!" said Thatcher.
>
> And off she went again.

In the final minutes of the meeting, Bellow was able to say what he thought, "which was mild and unprovocative." When he finished speaking, "the Prime Minister said how much she had enjoyed the conversation, thanked me for bringing the most interesting people to meet her, and away she swept. Subsequently Bellow remarked, with amusement: 'I didn't get a word in. Not even edgeways.' "[35]

Janis records in her journal how she was greeted by Mrs. Thatcher. "Her glance went by me without a second's pause and it felt as though a searchlight had swept by." She was "much more attractive than she appears in photos," "impeccably groomed, skin glowing, radiant, smooth." Her first words to Bellow were "They can't have given you the Nobel Prize for nothing—you must have something to tell me." Later, after speaking briefly of Allan Bloom, she declared: "The problem with intellectuals is that they are unwilling to speak out, and if they do speak out they are unwilling to act. There is no force behind their pronouncements." The meeting lasted thirty minutes, "but it all seemed to happen in the blink of a steel blue eye." To Martin Amis, in a letter of June 3, 1990, Bellow offered a metaphorical account of the meeting: "Well, you're cruising on an interstate highway and a few hundred feet ahead you see a perfectly ordinary automobile like any other GM, Chrysler or Japanese product, and then suddenly it turns on its dangerous blue police lights and you realize that what you took for a perfectly ordinary vehicle is packed with power. It's that unearthly blue flash that makes the difference." "Packed with power" recalls Daniel Bellow's view of his father's respect for strength. Though the visit was not a success, Walden did not regret introducing Bellow to Thatcher: "I thought she really ought to know that this man exists, because he was generally recognized as the greatest novelist of the day."

To decompress from the rigors of Oxford and Mrs. Thatcher, Bellow and Janis boarded a train to Sidmouth, a resort on the South Devon coast. There they stayed in an "ancient" hotel, were relieved not to be talked to by any of the other guests, ate gigantic cooked breakfasts, and went for long walks in the countryside and along the Esplanade, not returning to the hotel until dinner. On country walks, they came across little tearooms "out of nowhere." Janis was reading Hardy, in whose Wessex novels Sidmouth is "Idmouth" (in Thackeray it is "Baymouth"). The local railway stopped at the village of Ottery St. Mary, Coleridge's birthplace. The break was idyllic; in Janis's summary, "We loved it."

THAT "THE BLACK PROBLEM IN AMERICA" was much on Bellow's mind in 1990 was a product of recent developments in Chicago. In 1988, there was an outbreak of anti-Semitism among African Americans. Steve Cokely, an aide to Eugene Sawyer, the city's black mayor, claimed that Jews were involved in an international conspiracy to control the world and that "the AIDS epidemic is a result of doctors, especially Jewish ones, who inject AIDS into blacks." It took Mayor Sawyer a week to fire Cokely, an act only three of Chicago's eighteen city councilmen approved. In addition to his remarks about Jewish doctors, Cokely attacked Sawyer's predecessor, Mayor Harold Washington, the city's first black mayor, for having Jewish advisers. The previous November, on the forty-ninth anniversary of Kristallnacht, Cokely accused North Side Jewish merchants of breaking their own windows in an effort to gain sympathy. When Cokely was invited to explain his views to the City Council's health committee, its chairman, Alderman Allan Streeter, also an African American, criticized the "continued Jewish dominance of the news media" and accused the Anti-Defamation League of having a "hit-list" of black leaders.

There were other well-publicized instances of black anti-Semitism in Chicago. In May 1988, a student exhibition at the Art Institute was criticized for including a painting of Mayor Washington dressed in women's underwear. Streeter and two other black aldermen arrived with police officers and confiscated the painting, triggering a First Amendment crisis and a civil lawsuit. Streeter claimed, incorrectly, that "the fellow who drew that picture is Jewish." The influential black activist Lutrelle ("Lu") Palmer, in a column in the *Metro News*, defended Cokely and Streeter, defying "anyone to deny that Jews as a group are greatly disliked by our community. Cokely said it publicly. Most blacks say it privately." The head of the city's Commission on Human Relations, the Reverend B. Herbert Martin, also defended Cokely. The black community, he claimed, heard "a ring of truth" in Cokely's remarks about an international Jewish conspiracy: "There is a growing opinion among younger blacks, grassroots black people, that Jews are running things, that Jews are unfair, unloving." When Jewish leaders objected to Martin's remarks, State Representative William Shaw, an African American, threatened to organize a boycott "on everything dealing with the Jewish community." He also claimed that black leaders were being "picked off one by one" by Jews.

These details come from articles in *The New York Times*, in particular an article of July 26, 1988, written by Bellow's friend Eugene Kennedy.[36] The title of the article, "Anti-Semitism in Chicago: A Stunning Silence," derived from Kennedy's claim that aside from the deceased Mayor Richard J. Daley's son Richard M. Daley, the Cook County state's attorney and soon to be Chicago's mayor, "hardly any Chicagoan of major influence in government, religion, education and business has spoken out strongly, unambiguously and consistently against the anti-Semitism that has infected the city's life." As Kennedy put it in an interview, "The Jewish people, of course, had been in the vanguard of fighting for the rights of African Americans, but there was a hysterical paranoid fervor in this city, and there were guys getting on television programs and talking about this. It was really bizarre." Kennedy's article upset many Chicagoans, and the *Chicago Tribune* ran an editorial denouncing him for writing about Chicago's problems in *The New York Times*. When Bellow read the editorial, he called Kennedy and told him, "I'll never forget you for doing this" (Allan Bloom, Kennedy remembers, was also "very grateful"). As Kennedy saw it, "The Jewish people needed someone who wasn't Jewish to raise the issue and to raise it as strongly as possible."

On August 14, 1988, some weeks after its editorial, the *Tribune* published an article by Bellow defending Kennedy. The article began by accusing the paper of sweeping the issues raised by Kennedy's piece under the rug (there to form "gruesome lumps"), shifting attention "from Cokely's illiterate mob incitement to Kennedy himself, as if Kennedy were the guilty party." The *Tribune* complained in its editorial that Kennedy was wrong to take Cokely seriously, describing the mayoral aide as "barely able to keep a grip on himself, let alone Chicago's black community," and citing a June poll it had commissioned in which only 8 percent of blacks opposed Cokely's firing.[37] Of the support Cokely received from the leaders of black Chicago, detailed by Kennedy and repeated by Bellow, the *Tribune* said nothing, though the paper's star columnist, Mike Royko, had earlier warned of a dangerous rise in "inflammatory, irresponsible racial rhetoric," virtually all of it "coming from blacks." Royko's column, "Put Up or Shut Up Time in Chicago," appeared on May 18, 1988, and in a personal letter of May 26 Bellow praised him as "the brainiest and the bravest of newspapermen. It takes guts to do what you are doing." The articles by Royko, Kennedy, and Bellow eventually bore fruit when Cokely was condemned by the city's most widely read African American columnists, Clarence Page in the *Tribune* and Vernon Jarrett in the *Sun-Times*. What most upset Bellow about the whole episode, he wrote in his *Tribune* piece, was the "curious inability" of Chicago journalists and politicians "to respond to what is monstrous in a monstrous situation. Does no one remember Stalin and his 'Jewish doctors' plot'? Has everyone forgotten Hitler?"

That Richard M. Daley was one of the few Chicago politicians to take an early stand against Cokely and his defenders earned him Bellow's support. When Daley ran for mayor the following year, Bellow and Kennedy agreed to campaign for him in Jewish neighborhoods. After he was elected, Daley gave them a tour of the mayor's office, the whole time holding an unlit cigar in his hand, the very image of a big-time Chicago pol. "We had a hilarious time," Kennedy remembers. "Saul just loved that sort of stuff." Daley asked Bellow to speak at his inauguration in April 1989, and Bellow agreed, movingly describing his love for the city. He also spoke of how pleased he was that Daley had chosen a writer to speak. "This is a first for Chicago," he told the assembled notables. "Our mayor-elect might have asked Mike Ditka [the football player] to say a few words, but Chicago is already sufficiently identified with Bears, Bulls, with Wrigley Field and Comiskey Park. And I take it as a good sign for the city that he put a writer on the program. . . . [Chicago] has a place in American literature and world literature which it owes to the writers I represent here today." About Daley himself, Bellow was cautiously optimistic. "I take seriously his efforts to bring together a divided city and his determination to remind the people that a city of this size and complexity cannot afford wild dissent, dramatics and demagoguery."[38]

IN THE SUMMER OF 1989, in Vermont, after living together for three years, Bellow and Janis married. Bellow wanted no fuss over the wedding. Janis invited her parents to Vermont, but said nothing about her getting married. There was some question whether the parents would be able to come, and when they called back to say the trip was on, she told them the news. The wedding took place on August 25, 1989. The Freedmans arrived from Toronto with champagne and flowers. They and Walter Pozen, who also spent summers in Vermont, were the only witnesses (Allan Bloom was in Paris and could not attend, but he knew of the planned wedding and approved). Janis wore a dress Bellow had bought for her in Paris, and Bellow wore one of Maury's suits. They were married in the town hall in Wilmington, Vermont, and then drove with Pozen and Janis's parents to the home of their friends and neighbors, Herb and Libby Hillman, where everyone drank the champagne and ate challah and honey. It was the wedding Bellow and Janis wanted. There was "absolutely no valentine stuff," as there'd been no valentine stuff when Bellow proposed, which was fine with Janis. Both partners felt they were taking "a gamble" in getting married. Bellow "must have had terrible fears," Janis believes, physical equivalents of his fears about writing. As it turned out, they were "very lucky, hugely happy." "We had more than most married couples in terms of married happiness and passion." At seventy-four, Bellow was to Janis "still physically beautiful. He didn't have the skin and the body of an old man. . . . He had this incredible strength."

SHORTLY AFTER THE WEDDING, the Bellows left Vermont for Boston, where Bellow had been invited to teach for a term at Boston University. This was a golden period for Janis. "I was somebody nobody knew," she remembers, no longer Bellow's "student or secretary or wife number 657 or whatever, as in Chicago." The invitation came from John Silber, president of the university, previously a friend and colleague of Keith Botsford's at the University of Texas. Silber, a Texan, trained as a philosopher at Yale and chaired the Philosophy Department at Texas from 1962 to 1967. In 1967, he became dean of the College of Arts and Sciences, a post he held until 1970, when he was fired by the chair of the regents of the university. For much of his life, Silber was a figure of controversy. On social issues, he was a liberal, supporting racial integration and Head Start programs for preschool pupils and opposing capital punishment. As a university administrator, he was a radical. In his three years as dean at Texas, in an attempt to clear out what he called "dead wood," he replaced twenty-two heads of department. According to a lengthy obituary in *The New York Times*, both his politics and his "executive aspirations" led to his firing.

That same year, 1970, Silber was appointed president of Boston University, a job he held from 1971 to 1996, ruling with what the *Times* called "tigerish ferocity." When he arrived at BU, he faced falling enrollment and budget deficits. He froze salaries, cut budgets, refused to negotiate with staff, and came down hard on student protest, actions reported in the national news media. In the course of many battles, he built Boston University into one of the country's largest private universities, raising endowments from $18 million to $422 million and research grants from $15 million to $180 million. Although tuition fees rose to Ivy League levels, enrollment increased, from twenty to thirty thousand. The university's property portfolio was tripled, and $700 million was raised for new construction. For these and other initiatives, Silber paid himself the highest salary of any college president in the United States, twice that of the president of Harvard. When he resigned in 2005, he received a record severance package of $6.1 million.[39]

Silber had been in pursuit of Bellow for some time, first as dean at Texas then as president of BU. While a graduate student at Yale, listening to a books program on the car radio, he heard Bellow discuss *The Adventures of Augie March.* It was winter, and snowing in New Haven, and "I thought, This guy is fascinating, this guy is wonderful, and I got to thinking about him and ran into a truck in front of me. Saul is embedded in my mind in connection with this little accident." Silber then read *The Adventures of Augie March*, and he thought, "This is a figure to contend with." He first met Bellow in the late 1960s in Texas, at Keith Botsford's house. Botsford had moved around a good deal since Bellow lodged with him in Puerto Rico in 1961, living in locations in Europe and South America. In 1965, he was appointed director of the Ford Foundation's National Translation Center, which was to be based at Texas. At the same time, he was made a professor of English at Texas.[40]

Bellow several times flew to Austin in the late 1960s to consult with Botsford about a successor publication to *The Noble Savage.* At a dinner party Botsford gave for him on one of these visits, the guests included Silber and a philosopher named Oets Bouwsma (an American, born of Dutch American parents), an authority on Wittgenstein and Kierkegaard. Silber was Bouwsma's head of department at the time and admired his work. During dinner, Bellow made a point that interested Bouwsma, who began peppering him with questions. Although Silber could not remember what this point was, he remembered that Bellow stopped Bouwsma in his tracks. "I don't play these games," he told him calmly. Some guests thought this reply rude. Others suspected that Bellow refused to answer "because he wasn't smart enough." This is not what Silber thought. "I thought he was just as smart as a rat in a barn. I really liked the idea that this wasn't his area, something he cared about, so why the hell should he get in the ring with a guy who boxes by rules he didn't even know. I thought he'd done enough in his life and he didn't need that, so why should he subject himself to it." After he became dean, Silber tried unsuccessfully to lure Bellow to Texas.

When Silber became president of BU, he poached a number of faculty from Texas, including William Arrowsmith, whom Bellow had known and admired at Princeton in the 1950s; Donald Carne-Ross, another eminent classicist; "and a lot of other bright people," among them Botsford. It was Botsford who suggested to Silber that Bellow's love of Vermont might be a way of getting him to BU. As Silber recalled: "I said, You know, it's a shame to be about eight or nine hundred miles from your house in Vermont when you could be just a couple of hours or three hours' driving from Boston. Why don't we just move you to Boston? We'd make it as convenient for you as possible, see to housing, which is always a problem." Again Bellow declined. In 1988, Silber tried a third time, laying out terms in a letter of March 6. If Bellow came to BU, he would receive "a University Professorship and a Professorship in English with a salary of $80,000." University Professors, Silber explained in an interview, were appointed not just because they were well known but "because the caliber of their work went beyond a single discipline. You take a person like Saul, who is working in the fields of sociology, philosophy, psychology, history, as well as literature. There's no way that he could have done his work just sticking to literary matters. . . . Look at the range of that man. . . . And every University Professor was like that." Bellow's teaching responsibilities, Silber assured him, would be light. He would be expected to teach "one course and give one public lecture and a public reading."

Bellow offered a counterproposal. He and Janis would come to Boston for a term, in the autumn of 1989 (when Bloom would still be in Paris). They would only come, however, if certain conditions were met. In a letter of March 11, Bellow spelled out these conditions:

> I would have to have suitable living quarters (with an unlisted telephone number) because I work at home; I should not be able to pay two rents—I can't sublet my Chicago apartment, and it costs me $1,200 a month to maintain. An appropriate salary would be more like fifty than $40,000. That would be no more than fair since I am paid somewhere between five and $10,000 for each lecture or reading. In Chicago I teach one course per term, a seminar for fifteen to twenty students, meeting once a week, and here I do not have the headaches and disorder of new surroundings. What I had envisioned for B.U. was a course in selected literary classics of the Twentieth Century, Italian, French, German, English and American—perhaps a Russian or two for good measure. I function best when my mornings and early afternoons are given over to the intensest kind of work. It seems to me that if I am to sing a divinely beautiful swan song it is better not to have to cope with geese. Decades in Chicago have taught me how to protect my privacy. . . . No luncheons, no cocktail parties, few dinners and no banquet speeches. . . . I am mindful of the tasks I want to finish and I believe that I can count on your understanding and perhaps even your sympathy.

He could count on both. In September, Bellow and Janis moved into an apartment Janis describes as "like a palazzo" at 69 Bay State Road, overlooking the Charles River. They were very well treated by everyone, especially Silber, who "bent over backwards," and Botsford, who was "incredibly good to us." "I know a lot of people say negative things about him," Janis says of Silber, "but he was *so* good to Saul. There was nothing he wouldn't do to court him or to woo him. There were dinner parties with Christopher Ricks [lured to BU from Cambridge University]. He [Ricks] was so funny. The atmosphere there seemed so lively. . . . Saul needed that. I think Bloom was the only person who brought that out in him, that kind of back-and-forth wit." Although he'd sworn off banquet speeches, Bellow gave several talks and readings that autumn term, always to packed audiences. Charles U. Daly, the head of the John F. Kennedy Presidential Library and Museum, previously an administrator at the University of Chicago and at Harvard, arranged for him to speak at the Harvard Kennedy School. On November 9, he gave an early version of the Romanes Lecture (it was titled "A Writer Looks at Twentieth-Century History"). He also gave a reading of "A Silver Dish" at the Tremont Temple Baptist Church in Boston, where Charles Dickens and Abraham Lincoln had once spoken.[41] The church was packed, though the night was cold and rain-swept, almost as inclement as the night Woody and Morris Selbst trudged through in "A Silver Dish." Weekends were spent in Vermont, in a glorious New England autumn. On December 6, Bellow wrote to Catherine Lindsay (now Catherine Choate), the "big beauty" John Berryman had once pursued, to congratulate her on a new job and to tell her his news. He had "taken some time off from Chicago to spend a few months in Boston, not far from my place in Vermont." Boston he "rather liked"; it was a respite from Chicago, which "has been taken over by racial politics—blacks and whites in a contest for control. I find it very disagreeable. On the 15th the Boston holiday ends and we go back."

A THEFT WAS THE FIRST of the two novellas Bellow published in 1989. It appeared in March in an unexpected format, as a paperback original rather than a hardback, published by Viking at $6.95. Harriet Wasserman had offered the novella to *Esquire* and *Atlantic Monthly*, also, according to Atlas and others, to *The New Yorker* and *Vanity Fair*. All turned it down, ostensibly on the grounds of length (it is approximately twenty thousand words long, around a hundred pages in book form). When Bellow was asked to trim, he refused. As Wasserman puts it, its "length fit the story perfectly; it could not be cut."[42] The decision to publish as a paperback original was daring. *The New York Times* speculated that only "Mr. Bellow, a Nobel laureate in literature, and a very few other novelists," could publish their books first in paperback without putting their reputations "at risk."[43] Bellow himself had concerns about his reputation, worrying to Wasserman whether the reason given for the magazine rejections was "just the reason they gave you." Wasserman writes that she offered the novella to Viking in part because it had been Bellow's original company, in part because it was headed by Peter Mayer, who had bought the paperback rights to *Humboldt's Gift* for Avon and made a huge profit out of the deal.[44] To *The New York Times*, Bellow speculated that by publishing first in paperback he would reach well beyond his normal readership, estimated as between 100,000 and 250,000, though in the event sales remained at around 100,000.

On March 13, 1989, Viking launched *A Theft* at Hubert's Restaurant on Park Avenue, in the Beekman apartment building. Review coverage was disappointing. *The New York Times Book Review* failed to give it the usual front-page coverage, though Joyce Carol Oates reviewed it at length on page 3. *The New Yorker* and *The New York Review of Books* grouped it with books by other writers, which Atlas describes as "unheard-of for a work by Bellow."[45] The book's shortness may explain this treatment, along with related grumbles about thinness: "skimpy" was the adjective used by both John Updike in *The New Yorker* and Robert Towers in *The New York Review of Books*. Joyce Carol Oates, like Updike, began by praising Bellow (for Updike, "our preeminent fiction writer"; for Oates, "consistently brilliant and defiantly risky . . . our genius of portraiture"), but found *A Theft* "strangely lacking in the richly textured and sharply observed ground bass of reality that has always been his strength." Oates also voiced reservations about the novella's depiction of women, as when the heroine prepares an elaborate meal for her lover in the nude, something she thought would cause women readers to "smile, or wince."

A Theft is not among Bellow's stronger works, but it is interesting biographically. It is also unusual. To begin with, it has a female protagonist. According to Updike, "Until *A Theft* [Bellow] had not presented a woman as an autonomous seeker rather than a paradise sought" (presumably Updike is excluding older women such as Grandma Lausch in *The Adventures of Augie March* or Hattie in "Leaving the Yellow House," or the various fictional incarnations of Rosa Gameroff, in *Herzog*, "The Old System," and "By the St. Lawrence"). The setting of the novella is the Upper East Side in New York, more Edith Wharton or Henry James than Saul Bellow (it was James who called the novella "the beautiful and blessed *nouvelle*"[46]). The main characters are moneyed and powerful, inhabitants of the Washington and Manhattan circles Bellow had been moving in for some years. The story is more tightly plotted than most Bellow narratives, with carefully laid surprises. The writing is less street than in other Bellow works, and larger social and political concerns are mostly pushed to the margins. There is relatively little theorizing or esoteric/mystical speculation (though the male protagonist "more than half expects" to see his loved ones "in the land of the dead . . . because we loved each other and wished for it"[47]). As in a James novel or *nouvelle*, the story turns on a small but symbolically important item, an emerald ring, like the golden bowl or the spoils of Poynton. As the critic and novelist John Banville puts it, the ring "increases steadily in significance, turning from a trinket into a talisman," the source, the narrator tells us, of the heroine's "very stability" (p. 155).[48]

The autobiographical impulse behind *A Theft* is celebratory rather than score-settling. The story was written between the breakup of Bellow's marriage to Alexandra and the early years of his relationship with Janis, during or shortly after the period when Maggie Simmons briefly considered getting back together with him. Clara Velde (a Jamesian name) is given versions of Maggie's appearance, upbringing, marital history, education, and professional career. The novella's plot is based on a real-life theft or loss, also of a ring, an engagement ring Bellow gave to Maggie in the spring of 1968, on one of his visits to Austin. Clara Velde's au pair, Gina, is, like Maggie's au pair, a wellborn young woman from Austria. In *A Theft*, the au pair's lover is Frederic, a good-looking young Haitian. Like Maggie's lover from an earlier period, the young Frenchman named Jacques, and Clara's early lover, Jean-Claude, Frederic is a figure notable for sexual stamina and poor hygiene. In a letter of April 9, 1989, written shortly after the novella's publication, Maggie reported to Bellow that her au pair "called me yesterday. She's living in Boston, and was listening to a radio show about the book and recognized the story. She was stunned, to say the least."

Clara Velde, like Maggie, is a "rawboned American woman," "ruggedly handsome" (p. 117), also smart, stylish, and sexy (she's the one who does the nude cooking). Clara is on her fourth husband, a version of Maggie's third husband, described as "big, and handsome, indolent." All Clara's husbands are "gesture-husbands" (p. 118) or "utility husbands" (p. 136) or "dummy husbands, humanly unserious" (p. 143). Only number three, an Italian oil tycoon (Maggie also had such a husband), excited her much. At first she had "real feeling" for this husband, thought that "once he got to know my quality I'd mean more to him. . . . I don't say I'm better than other women. I'm not superior. I'm nutty, also. But I am in touch with the *me* in myself" (p. 136). The real love of Clara's life, the figure with whom she has a "permanent connection," she never marries. This real love is Ithiel "Teddy" Regler, a fictional version of Bellow. Ithiel, too, believes that "his attachment, his feeling for [Clara] was—to his own surprise—permanent. His continually increasing respect for her came over the horizon like a moon taking decades to rise" (p. 138). Given the resemblances between Clara and Maggie, it is hard not to see these sentences as an expression of

Bellow's own feelings, despite his inability to live with or stay faithful to Maggie, like Ithiel's inability to live with or stay faithful to Clara. As Clara sees it, she and Ithiel "have this total, delicious connection, which is also a disaster" (p. 121). "We'll never be man and wife," she tells him. "You love me, but the rest is counterindicated" (p. 157). In fact, "you continued to love me *because* we didn't marry" (p. 158). As Maggie sees it, the novella was "an act of expiation." Bellow "considered our connection permanent and it was. He sent me an advance copy in June of '89 with his inscription: 'To Maggie—So need I say more? Love, Saul.' That's how he viewed it."

The reasons Teddy is given for his unwillingness to marry Clara are those Bellow gave when distancing himself from Maggie. In youth, Clara's emotions were "so devouring, fervid, that they may have been suprapersonal" (p. 127). These emotions, "whole nights of tears, anguish and hysteria," finally drove Teddy "out of his head" (p. 129). Although he gave her the emerald engagement ring, which "appeased her for a while," he "was not inclined to move forward, and Clara became more difficult" (p. 129), "asserted herself unreasonably" (p. 132). The other element Clara sees as contributing to the dissolution of their relationship was "the insignificance of the personal factor" in Teddy's life (p. 132), his preoccupation with "issues" and work, "his grotesque game theories, ideology, treaties, and the rest of it" (p. 132), the powerbroker's equivalent of Bellow's life at his desk. Bellow knew that Maggie would be upset by parts of the novella, for all its praise and affection for her. But "the personal factor," her worries about "how my family was portrayed—and me," if not a matter of "insignificance," took second place to "work" or "the work." Maggie acknowledges that she had been idealized ("his treatment of me was the opposite of his treatment of Susan"), but nonetheless "was very happy to see the book go out of print."[49]

Clara's emerald engagement ring was bought for her by Teddy twenty years before the story begins. Twenty years before publication of *A Theft*, Bellow had bought Maggie her engagement ring, an opal surrounded by thirteen diamonds. Clara held on to her ring "through four marriages." Maggie has held on to her ring through five marriages. In the novella, Frederic steals the ring. In real life, according to Maggie, her au pair "discovered what we used to call free love in my apartment while I was at work," and her lover took the ring.[50] "The circumstances

Saul describes," Maggie writes, "are almost identical except it was a girlfriend not a boyfriend that [the au pair] had become attached to and she stole the ring. According to Josie [Maggie's housekeeper], [the au pair] realized there would be trouble because I had hired a detective to investigate and she saw him in the apartment and later got the ring back from the other girl."[51] In both the novella and real life, the rings are lost and recovered twice. "As I remember," Maggie writes, "I lost the ring, got the insurance money, used it to go to Europe and then found it under my bed when I came home! This would be sometime after Saul. I actually called the insurance agent and they said they'd never had such a call and to keep the money!" In the novella, the insurance company isn't notified: "Clara was not prepared to return the money" (p. 139).

Although Clara is furious with Gina for allowing her boyfriend into the house, she also admires her. She, like Gina, had come to New York, "Gogmagogsville," "to learn about such guys as Frederic" (p. 14); "Clifford, a convict in Attica, still sent Clara a Christmas card without fail" (p. 148). That Bellow chose to make Gina's lover a young Haitian male rather than a white female is a provocation, like describing Michael Jackson as a "little glamour monkey" at the beginning of *Ravelstein* (p. 4). As with the pickpocket in *Mr. Sammler's Planet,* other motives for making him black are in play: sexual insecurity, doom-laden theorizing about materialism and the body. Hence the uncharacteristic violence of the language Bellow gives Clara when she realizes the ring has been stolen:

> This love-toy emerald, personal sentimentality, makes me turn like a maniac on this Austrian kid. She may think I grudge her the excitement of her romance with that disgusting girl-fucker who used her as his cover to get into the house and now sticks her with this theft.
>
> Nevertheless Clara had fixed convictions about domestic and maternal responsibilities. She had already gone too far in letting Gina bring Frederic into the apartment and infect the whole place, spraying it with sexual excitement.
>
> . . . These people came up from the tropical slums to outsmart New York, and with all the rules crumbling here as elsewhere, so that nobody could any longer be clear in his mind about anything, they could do it [pp. 153–54].

At the end of the novella, after the ring is recovered, Clara attempts to bring Gina into a relationship with Ithiel. This part of the story can be thought of as Jamesian, with Clara as a sort of Fanny Assingham. It also has a biographical dimension, since, after breaking with Bellow, Maggie remembers many intense discussions with him about Janis. "I think it's right that I encouraged Saul's feelings for Janis, but that was made easier because I had just come off of Saul's and my attempt to get back together and he was entirely under Bloom's spell and I knew I could never put up with that—or his political views. In other words, I'd lost any romantic interest. Over the years we talked a lot about our spouses in the way true friends do."[52] "You want us to meet," says Ithiel of Gina, "and she'll come under my influence. She'll fall in love with me. . . . And she and I will cherish each other, and you will have the comfort of seeing me in safe hands, and this will be your blessing poured over the two of us." "Teddy, you're making fun of me," says Clara, "but she knew perfectly well that he wasn't making fun, that wasn't where the accent fell, and his interpretation was more or less correct, as far as it went" (p. 165). Maggie's feelings for Janis were not Clara's feelings for Gina, as Gina was not Janis, but Clara's impulse to see Ithiel properly settled was in part Maggie's impulse: "She wanted to find a suitable woman for Ithiel. It was a scandal, the wives he chose" (p. 169).

Although Ithiel Regler resembles Bellow in several respects, notably in his messy sexual and marital history, he is also a figure of fantasy.[53] He is what Bellow imagines he might have been had he gone into politics—powerful, influential, like Henry Kissinger only better-looking. Ithiel advises governments and large corporations, when he is in the mood. "He took on such assignments as pleased the operator in him, the behind-the-scenes Teddy Regler: in the Persian Gulf, with a Japanese whiskey firm looking for a South American market, with the Italian police tracking terrorists. None of these activities compromised his Washington reputation for dependability. He testified before congressional investigative committees as an expert witness" (p. 126). "He might have gone all the way to the top, to the negotiating table in Geneva, facing the Russians [like Max Kampelman, Bellow's friend and lodger from Minnesota], if he had been less quirky" (p. 125). As his friend Steinsalz explains (Steinsalz is a portrait of Bellow's lawyer friend Samuel Goldberg, according to Maggie), Ithiel "values his freedom, so that when he wanted to visit Mr. Leakey in the Olduvai Gorge, he just picked up and went" (pp. 130–31). Ithiel is closed-mouthed about his activities, which is part of his appeal. "Power, danger, secrecy made him even sexier. No loose talk. A woman could feel safe with a man like Ithiel" (p. 126). "I've always discouraged small talk about my psyche" (p. 144), Ithiel says, a description Maggie calls "disingenuous," although she voices no complaint about Clara's description of Teddy as "more plainspoken about his own faults than anybody who felt it necessary to show him up" (p. 124).

In addition to being politically influential, Ithiel, according to Clara, "might possibly be a dark horse in the history of the American mind" (p. 169), knows "the big, *big* picture" (p. 173), "could be the Gibbon or the Tacitus of the American Empire" (p. 145). These claims the novella does little to support, except insofar as it tempts the reader to identify Ithiel with his creator. Ithiel's sexual appeal is also exceptional. "When Ithiel comes to town and I see him at lunch," Clara confides, "I start to flow for him. He used to make me come by stroking my cheek" (p. 121). Clearly, Clara, too, is exceptional, as she is in other ways, something she acknowledges. "I never feel so bad as when I feel the life I lead stops being characteristic—when it could be anybody else's life" (p. 159). The people she values are exceptional, too. Gina is "a special young woman" (p. 164), no "sample from the population" (p. 165). What is uncharacteristic—for Bellow, that is—about these exceptional characters is how privileged they are, a product in part of the novella's Upper East Side milieu. Gina's specialness derives in part from her being "a young upper-class Vienna girl" (her fiancé, we learn at the end of the story, is a "man from Daddy's bank" [p. 169]). The emerald ring itself is exceptional, "conspicuously clear, color perfect, top of its class" (p. 125). When it is recovered, the detective Clara hired to find it worries that she might wear it on public transportation. "She looked disdainful. . . . He didn't seem to realize how high her executive bracket was" (p. 161).

The element of privilege in the novella is distracting, given the claims made for the depth and seriousness of the connection between Clara and Teddy. The "big, *big* picture" Teddy knows, in the passage quoted above, which accounts for his capacity to identify exceptional people like Clara, is meant to have nothing to do with money or status. Immediately after using the phrase, she adds: "he doesn't flatter, he's realistic and he's truthful. I do seem to have an idea who it is that's at the middle of me. There may not be more than one in a zillion, more's the pity, that do have" (p. 173). Clara's privileged claims are distracting in another way, because not wholly convincing. Clara is believably exceptional in her powers of perception—about people, herself included—but her business acumen, like Ithiel's world-historical intellect, is gestured at rather than dramatized. Although she devises the novella's concluding twists and turns, and runs everything in her life "single-handed: mortgage, maintenance, housemaids, au pair girls" (p. 119), she never sounds like a business type. What she sounds like is Ithiel, an incongruity she acknowledges (as if Bellow were anticipating criticism). Here is Clara's analysis of Gina's affair with Frederic, which she calls "just another case of being at sea among collapsing cultures—I sound like Ithiel now, and I don't actually take much stock in the collapsing-culture bit: I'm beginning to see it instead as the conduct of life without input from your soul" (p. 162).[54] Clara's openness, as in her belief in "soul," is also incongruous in "a good corporate person" (p. 118), even one who works in fashion or publishing, as the narrator also acknowledges. It was "odd," we are told, that Clara should become "an executive, highly paid and influential," since, for all her sophistication, "at any moment she could set aside the 'czarina' and become the hayseed, the dupe of traveling salesmen or grifters who wanted to lure her up to the hayloft" (p. 137). Maggie Simmons might possess both business acumen and soulful self-awareness. In *A Theft*, it is hard to see this combination in Clara Velde, or to believe in it. What is missing is what Joyce Carol Oates calls "the ground bass of reality." Hence the impression of skimpiness, a product neither of length nor of failing powers, but of the story's imperfectly realized setting or world. *A Theft* lacks the vivifying particulars characteristic of Bellow, the product of affection as well as familiarity, as much for what is deplored as for what is valued.

IN CHICAGO IN THE SPRING of 1988, while wrestling with "A Case of Love" and the final revisions to *A Theft*, Bellow spent much time thinking about Jewishness and the history of the Jews in the twentieth century. He had agreed to deliver a talk in Philadelphia entitled "A Jewish Writer in America" on May 1, before traveling to New Hampshire as a Montgomery Fellow at Dartmouth, a four-day visiting lectureship for which he was paid seventy-five hundred dollars plus travel and expenses. The venue for the Philadelphia talk was the Jewish Publication Society, the oldest publisher of Jewish books in the United States, with roots predating the Civil War. This was the hundredth anniversary of the society, and Bellow, Cynthia Ozick, and the ninety-three-year-old historian Salo Baron were being awarded Centennial Medals. Like many of Bellow's talks, the JPS talk took the form of a "personal history." It begins, though, at a stage before personal history, what Bellow thinks of as a less "mental" or "educated" stage, that of "my first consciousness."[55] In this consciousness, "I was among other things a Jew. We were all Jews. We spoke Yiddish, we spoke English, we observed Jewish customs, accepted Jewish superstitions, we prayed and blessed in Hebrew, our parents spoke in Russian. . . . My first consciousness was that of a cosmos, and in that cosmos I was a Jew" (p. 1). When Bellow outgrew this consciousness, the thought of turning away from or rejecting his Jewishness "always seemed to me an utter impossibility. It would be a treason to my first consciousness, my core consciousness, to unJew myself . . . to go beyond the given and re-enter life at a more advantageous point" (pp. 1–2).

Bellow illustrates the disadvantages of Jewish identity, as they pertain to a young American Jew who wishes to be a writer, with examples drawn from his own experience. In high school, he read Spengler's *Decline of the West* (1918–22), in which he learned that Jews were Magians in a Faustian age, representatives "of an earlier type totally incapable of comprehending the Faustian spirit . . . fossils, spiritually archaic" (p. 2). In college, he encountered the anti-Jewish slights and suspicions of "the Protestant Majority" (p. 3), in academic as well as literary circles, including those of such literary idols as Henry Adams, Henry James, Ezra Pound, and T. S. Eliot, whose traditionalism Bellow describes as "profoundly racist" (p. 15). Whereas fellow aspiring writers who were Jewish worried "what T. S. Eliot or Edmund Wilson would be thinking of them," or flirted with Anglicanism, or "came up with different evasions, dodges, ruses and disguises," Bellow was unmoved. "If the Wasp aristocrats wanted to look upon me as a poacher on their precious cultural estates then let them. It was in this defiant spirit that I wrote *The Adventures of Augie March* and *Henderson the Rain King*" (p. 4).

Slights and suspicions notwithstanding, Bellow knew early on that he was better off in America than in Europe. The hostility faced by the Jewish writer in America was of a different order from that faced by the Jewish writer in Europe, where, inevitably, "Wagnerism in one form or another would reject them" (p. 8). Although the Jewish writer in America "could not afford to be unaware of his detractors," his identity as an American was not denied. When Bellow's friend Paolo Milano died in April, exactly a month before the JPS lecture, "his obituaries mentioned that this brilliant man was of Hebrew birth. So he was. No mention was made of the fact that his Jewish ancestors had lived in Italy for two millennia" (p. 25). Although less discriminated against than his European counterparts, Bellow felt, like other American Jewish writers of his generation, that "without coarsening himself, he had to thicken his armor" (p. 10), adopting "the Nietzschean *Spernere se sperni*, to despise being despised" (p. 11). "Irreverent, prickly, rude," these were the qualities many American Jewish writers, particularly those from New York, cultivated; their arrogance "was partly defensive. . . . You had to train yourself in infighting and counterpunching" (p. 14). Bellow quotes Irving Howe: "When up against the walls of gentile politeness we would aggressively proclaim our 'difference,' as if to raise Jewishness to a higher cosmopolitan power" (p. 12). In his early seventies, Bellow believed he had passed "this phase of meeting arrogance with arrogance, I appear to have grown calmer. More philosophical," a condition belied by the vehemence with which he explains it:

> "Philosophical," in common usage, often translates as passive. I don't think I grew passive. I was less easily nettled, harder to offend, increasingly indifferent to criticism and to the cultural claims of self-appointed Wasp spokesmen. In the end their Ivy League fortresses capitulated in the Sixties to protesters and strikers and after Kingman Brewster had declared that no black could expect a fair trial in a Federal Court, the Establishment could no longer be taken seriously. There was no point in fighting a gutless antagonist [p. 15].

This moment of political aggression presages—derives from?—reflections on the Holocaust and Israel, which begin with a quotation from Lionel Abel's memoir *The Intellectual Follies* (1984). During the war, Abel heard vague reports of extermination camps in Eastern Europe:

> But I had no real revelation of what had occurred until sometime in 1946, more than a year after the German surrender, when I took my mother to a motion picture and we saw in a newsreel some details of the entrance of the American army into the concentration camp at Buchenwald. We witnessed the discovery of mounds of dead bodies, the emaciated, wasted but still living prisoners who were being

> liberated, and of various means of extermination in the camp, the various gallows and also the buildings where gas was employed to kill the Nazis' victims en masse. It was an unforgettable sight on the screen, but as remarkable is what my mother said to me when we left the theatre: She said, I don't think the Jews can ever get over the disgrace of this. She said nothing about the moral disgrace to the German nation, only . . . about a more than moral disgrace, and one incurred by the Jews. How would they ever get over it? *By succeeding in emigrating to Palestine and setting up the state of Israel* [p. 17].

Bellow describes his own reaction to such newsreels as "identical to that of Mrs. Abel" (p. 17). He also shares a belief that "the founders of Israel restored the lost respect of the Jews by their manliness. They removed the curse of the Holocaust, of the abasement of victimization from them, and for this the Jews of the diaspora were grateful, and repaid Israel with their loyal support" (p. 16). Yet he recognizes the still-living dangers of the "curse" and "abasement," both for individual Jews, himself included, and for the Jewish nation. "I sometimes glimpse in myself, an elderly Jew, a certain craziness of extremism, the crumbling of my mental boundaries. I sometimes think I see evidences in Israeli politics of rationality damaged by memories coming from the Jewish experiences of this century" (p. 19). The violence of Eisen, the Israeli sculptor, at the end of *Mr. Sammler's Planet*, provides a fictional example of such damage.

In one respect, Bellow sees the Holocaust as lending force to Jewish values, principally to an aversion to "the modern world of nihilistic abysses and voids" (p. 18). "Through the horror of their sufferings and their responses to suffering [Jews] stand apart from the prevailing nihilism of the West" (p. 19). When true to their culture and their vocation, American Jewish writers "remind the convulsive modern psyche of ancient visions of order or moral law, of something opposed to the prevailing polarity: at one end a hideously vivid consciousness stirred by terror and slaughter, and at the other pole unconsciousness, the light of the critical mind put out" (p. 21). As Bellow says later in the talk, American Jewish writers must give voice to a "Jewish preoccupation with the redemption of mankind from its sins and injustices. . . . Somebody should be representing the decencies. . . . Somebody should remember the eternal background of our ephemeral doings" (p. 29). In such representing and remembering, certainly in Bellow's case, "contemporary wisdom," the wisdom of "historians, psychologists, and behavioral scientists," proves of little assistance. Bellow turns instead "to philosophy, to Kabbala and to Christian hermeticism. And there I find, curiously enough, the help I have not found among exoteric intellectuals" (p. 23). The esoteric as opposed to exoteric authority Bellow cites in the lecture is Valentin Tomberg (1900–1973), an Estonian Russian mystic. What interests Bellow about Tomberg is his theory of the *egregore*, " 'an artificial being who owes his existence to collective generation *from below*' . . . To the Hermetics *egregores* are phantoms of humanity. That is to say, they are nourished by men collectively. In thinking of a catastrophe like the Holocaust one cannot overlook the possibility that such an evil had its origin in a powerful collective fantasy, a ghostly double or *egregore* of the German people" (pp. 23–24).[56]

Tomberg was a Christian mystic, but Bellow describes the willingness to take concepts like the *egregore* seriously as Jewish. "Since the Old Testament assumes the intercourse of man and spiritual beings, since God, in our Jewish tradition, reveals himself to Man face to face, a respect for revelation has been bred into the Jewish mind. So that when secular education fails us we are tempted by religious thought. Secular accounts of evil—political, anthropological, psychological—do not go deep enough to meet our extraordinary needs. . . . If to a Marxist Nazism is explainable by the failures of capitalism I far prefer the Hermetic serpent or Antichrist and that collective phenomenon, the *egregore*" (p. 24). In the end, Bellow urges the American Jewish writer to combine the role of "participant-observer in the life of his country" with a more traditional Jewish role, that of tracking "the history of the Jews in our time" (pp. 21–22). These have been his own roles, he implies on the lecture's last page. "A writer who is an American and a Jew," he declares, "has been able to explore and develop his own consciousness freely, and in this consciousness, a Jewish preoccupation with the redemption of mankind from its sins and injustices. To hold to this in barbarous times without pretensions is the decent thing to attempt" (pp. 29–30).[57]

AFTER THE JPS LECTURE, banquet, and attendant speeches of commemoration ("These got worse and worse with the rank and wealth of the speakers"[58]), Bellow and Janis traveled to Vermont, and to Bellow's visiting lectureship at Dartmouth. There and in Vermont, they waited to hear the fate of *A Theft*, already rejected by *Esquire* and *Atlantic Monthly*, soon to be rejected by *The New Yorker*. In Vermont, Bellow also came up with the idea for *The Bellarosa Connection*, the second of his novellas to be published in 1989. The idea came to him toward the end of May, partly as an outgrowth of the JPS lecture, partly inspired by a story he had been told at a dinner party in Vermont. In her preface to Bellow's *Collected Stories* (2001), Janis Bellow gives a vivid account of this dinner party and of its effect on Bellow.[59] The dinner took place at the home of Herb and Libby Hillman and was arranged partly to cheer everybody up after weeks of black flies and bad weather. In the course of the dinner, Bellow raised the question he had been brooding over since the Philadelphia lecture: "Should the Jews feel shame over the Holocaust? Is there a particular disgrace in being victimized?" Janis describes herself as "ferociously opposed to this argument," which soon gave way to "gags, jokes, old chestnuts" and dessert. As Janis and Bellow were getting ready to leave, Herb Hillman, a retired chemist, recounted the story of a colleague of his who had been a European refugee in the 1940s. Hillman's story provided Bellow with the starting point for *The Bellarosa Connection*. On May 24, "the first fine day of the season," Bellow returned from the studio Frank Maltese had built for him behind his Vermont house; he had an announcement to make: "I'm on to something new. I don't want to talk about it just yet." The next day, on the drive to Brattleboro for weekly supplies, he revealed what it was he was on to, as recounted by Janis in her preface:

> "I haven't found a shape for the new story yet, but it's based on what Herb told us over dinner. . . . A refugee is imprisoned by the Italian fascists, but prior to his imprisonment, having become aware that his arrest is imminent, he has written overseas to the Broadway impresario Billy Rose on the advice of a friend. (In the story as Saul eventually wrote it, the hero makes no such appeal to Billy Rose and in fact has never even heard of him.) A mysterious plan is concocted while he waits in his prison cell. . . . All happens as planned, and with the aid of . . . emissaries he escapes to the States. There, he is denied entry because of the quotas, but makes it to Cuba. Years later when he is back in the United States he tries to contact Billy Rose and to thank him in person. But it seems Rose, who has helped a lot of people, will have nothing to do with the refugees he has saved, perhaps fearing that they will lean on him or mooch from him

> indefinitely. The rescued man is quite shaken by the cold shoulder he gets from Broadway Billy" [p. vii].

At this point, only a day after the Hillman dinner, "the story was no longer about Herb's friend, but already about a character—Harry Fonstein—'Surviving Harry,' as Saul would later call him, borrowing from John Berryman's 'Dreamsong' (dedicated to Saul) about 'Surviving Henry'" (p. vii). Several things drew Bellow to the story Herb Hillman told him. In the 1950s, when Bellow was often in Greenwich Village, he knew a man who worked as a ghostwriter for Billy Rose: Bernie Wolfe. Bellow described Wolfe to Janis as "a very bright, very savvy and strange man who took an unusual interest in New York people and their motivations." If he was to do something with Herb Hillman's story, Wolfe could act as the point of contact between Rose and the Fonstein character—an idea he later dropped, though Wolfe is mentioned in the story. That Bellow had once seen Billy Rose in Jerusalem and was struck by his appearance was another draw. Janis asked what Rose looked like: "Well, he was small, Jewish; he might have been handsome but for the tense lines in his face. He looked strained, greedy, dissatisfied with himself" (p. vii).[60]

On May 29, Bellow had pages to read to Janis, including those that recount Fonstein's escape from prison. He had by now also decided to contrast Fonstein, a European Jew, with the narrator, an American Jew. "He wanted his reader to feel the difference in tone between the two men's lives. He could mine his own experience and call upon his memories of Wolfe for the American" (p. viii). Bellow had already made use of such a contrast in his story "The Old System" (1968), in which Samuel Braun, the narrator, is a New World, American figure, with much of Bellow's childhood experience and relatives modeled on Bellow's Canadian relatives, the Gameroffs, and Isaac Braun, his much older cousin, the story's central character, is a fictional version of Shmuel Gameroff. Though not a European, Isaac has "the outlook of ancient generations on the New World" (p. 92). A successful businessman from upstate New York, a millionaire like Fonstein, he leads "an ample old-fashioned respectable domestic life on an Eastern European model completely destroyed in 1939 by Hitler and Stalin" (p. 104). In Janis Bellow's recollection, Bellow had not yet, by May 29, given Fonstein a comparably respectable domestic life. Nor had he dreamed up Fonstein's wife, Sorella. On June 2, however, he told Janis he'd found a possible model for Fonstein. This was the nephew of his stepmother, Fannie Gebler Bellow, a "chess-playing sober young refugee" (p. viii) of whom Bellow was especially fond. "This late immigrant arrival with his singsong Polish accent, his gift for languages, and his business smarts . . . would give flavor to his European character, Harry Fonstein" (p. ix).

The memory of the young refugee provided another key ingredient in the novella. Despite Bellow's fondness for him, they had been out of touch for three decades. Over the winter, Bellow learned that the nephew had been dead for some years. He brooded over the fact that he hadn't known of the man's death. In Janis's summary, what struck Bellow about having lost touch with the nephew was the importance of memory in his life: "Someone occupies a place in your life, takes on some special significance—what it is you can't really say. But you have made a real connection—this person has come to stand for something in your life. Time goes by, he may even be dead for all you know, and yet you hang on to the idea of the unique importance of that individual. What a shock to discover that memories have become a stand-in for that warehoused person" (pp.viii–ix) ("warehoused" comes from an earlier phrase in the novella, "the warehouse of intentions" [p. 70]). As the narrator of *The Bellarosa Connection* broods over the meaning and significance of Fonstein, "who had survived the greatest ordeal in Jewish history" (p. 38), and of his having lost touch with Fonstein, he sets about recollecting and reconstructing Fonstein's life, to write a memoir about him.

The importance of memory to Bellow, as to the novella's narrator, is hard to overstate: memory provided him with material for his fiction, and hence with a livelihood; it was a way of keeping the past alive, also a way of keeping alive the people he valued or loved; the vividness and intensity of Bellow's memories of departed loved ones offered the hope of reunion in an afterlife. Less happily, memory served as reprimand, for misdeeds as well as inattention, for inattention to misdeeds, or to something much worse, as in his failure or unwillingness for many years to face or remember the Holocaust. In a letter to Cynthia Ozick, written on July 17, 1987, Bellow openly admits his culpability in the 1940s and 1950s. He had averted his gaze from the destruction of European Jewry, the central event of modern Jewish history:

> I was too busy becoming a novelist to take much note of what was happening in the Forties. I was involved with "literature" and given

> over to preoccupations with art, with language, with my struggle on the American scene, with claims for recognition of my talent or, like my pals of the *Partisan Review*, with modernism, Marxism, New Criticism, with Eliot, Yeats, Proust, etc.—with anything except the terrible events in Poland. Growing slowly aware of this unspeakable evasion I didn't even know how to begin to admit it into my inner life.

As Bellow put it in the JPS lecture, the American writer who is Jewish has a responsibility to track "the history of the Jews in our time" (p. 22). By combining the European refugee Fonstein's story with the American narrator's unwillingness to face it, as well as with his overcoming his unwillingness, Bellow hoped to fulfill his responsibility as a Jewish writer in America.

On June 12, 1988, two days after his seventy-third birthday, Bellow announced to Janis that he'd started the Hillman story over again from scratch. Among other things, he'd crammed too much into the beginning: "All this stuff about the American versus the European Jew. This must unfold gradually." Behind the contrast between European and American Jews lay a larger Jewish theme. As he told Janis, "What the story is really about is memory and faith." For the Jew, "there is no religion without remembering. As Jews we remember what was told to us at Sinai; at the Seder we remember the Exodus; Yiskor is about remembering a father, a mother. We are told not to forget the Patriarchs; we admonish ourselves, 'If I forget thee, O Jerusalem . . .' And we are constantly reminding God not to forget his Covenant with us. This is what the 'chosenness' of the Chosen People is all about. We are chosen to be God's privileged mind readers. All of it, what binds us together, is our history, and we are a people because we remember" (p. xi).

At some point in the summer of 1988, Bellow decided that the American Jew in the Fonstein story, its unnamed narrator, would be "founder of the Mnemosyne Institute in Philadelphia," the business of which was to train "executives, politicians, and members of the defense establishment." Now retired and in his "twilight years," the narrator would like "to *forget* about remembering," in part because of fears he was losing his own memory.[61] This fear began one day as he was walking down the street humming "Way down upon the . . ." and failed to remember the name of the Swanee River, "a song I'd sung from childhood, upwards of seventy years, part of the foundation of one's mind. A classic song, known to all Americans" (p. 72): it is also a song about remembering. According to Janis, "This actually did happen to Saul during the winter in Chicago, while strolling around downtown on his way back from the dentist." Like Fonstein, "until Suwannee came to him he was beside himself" (pp. xi–xii). Although the narrator laments having lost touch with Fonstein, he remembers details from their times together, a number drawn from Bellow's own life. In their youth, Fonstein was an object of admiration to the narrator's father, having survived real suffering and danger—unlike his son, the narrator—a judgment Abraham Bellow had leveled at his sons. Fonstein's aunt, the narrator's stepmother, like Bellow's stepmother, "parted her hair in the middle and baked delicious strudel" (p. ix); Fonstein's aversion to a particular shade of blue-gray, the color of the shroud in which his mother was buried, was Bellow's aversion, that being the color of the shroud in which *his* mother had been buried.

Although the narrator's memory has earned him "an income of X millions soundly invested" and "an antebellum house in Philadelphia" (p. 35), it hasn't made him wise. The data that fill his memory not only lack significance but distract from significance. Bellow writes of distraction and information overload as dangers of the modern age in "The Distracted Public," his Romanes Lecture, and again in "There Is Simply Too Much to Think About" (1992), and, as we've seen, they were themes of his fiction as well.[62] Augie March complains, "There's too much history and culture to keep track of, too many details, too much news, too much example, too much influence, too many guys who tell you to be as they are, and all this hugeness, abundance, turbulence, Niagara Falls torrent. Which who is supposed to interpret? Me?" (pp. 902–3). Charlie Citrine in *Humboldt's Gift* is not so much overwhelmed as knocked out by information, or so he claims, having "an exceptional gift for passing out." In snapshots of himself from the 1930s and 1940s, when, he adds, millions were being killed, he is pictured in "an ill-fitting double-breasted suit . . . smoking a pipe, standing under a tree, holding hands with a plump and pretty bimbo—and I am asleep on my feet, out cold. I have snoozed through many a crisis" (p. 108). Like Charlie, the narrator of *The Bellarosa Connection* has missed the crisis at the heart of Fonstein's story, partly because he's been distracted, partly because he couldn't face it. "I wouldn't do it," he recalls of his "snoozing through" the Holocaust. "First those people murdered you, then they forced you to brood on their crimes. It suffocated me to do this. Hunting for causes was a horrible imposition added to the original 'selection,' gassing, cremation. I didn't want to think of the history and psychology of these abominations, death chambers and furnaces. . . . Such things are utterly beyond me, a pointless exercise." Hence his advice to Fonstein, brooding on Billy Rose's refusal to meet him: "My advice to Fonstein—given mentally—was: Forget it. Go American" (p. 49).

Why the narrator finally decides to face Fonstein's story is explained partly by his understanding of Billy Rose, who wants nothing to do with memory, whose Americanness is connected with letting memory go. Billy Rose ("Bellarosa" to Fonstein, before he learns who he is) shares qualities with Bellow's brother Maury. He has gangland connections, is "the business partner of Prohibition hoodlums, the sidekick of Arnold Rothstein" (p. 40). He is a voracious consumer, of paintings, fancy clothes ("the tailored wardrobe was indispensable—like having an executive lavatory of your own" [p. 58]), of "bimbos." A syndicated newspaper columnist, he deals in Broadway gossip and scandal and has "a buglike tropism for celebrity" (p. 41). He is hard, hot-tempered, when pushed will retaliate, believing, like the narrator, that "if you can retaliate you've got your self-respect" (p. 57). Although unsentimental, he has "spots of deep feeling." The narrator describes him as "spattered," like a Jackson Pollock painting: "and among the main trickles was his Jewishness, with other streaks flowing toward secrecy" (p. 41). Like Maury, he wants nothing to do with the old times and old ways, and this is partly why "he refused to be thanked by the Jews his Broadway underground had rescued" (p. 41). He has no interest in his own old times. "I don't care for stories," he says. "I don't care for my own story. If I had to listen to it, I'd break out in a cold sweat" (p. 65). The narrator speculates about Billy's motives for never looking back: "Afraid of the emotions? Too Jewish a moment for him? Drags him down from his standing as a full-fledged American?" (p. 46). (This is what Fonstein thinks: "It's some kind of change in the descendants of immigrants in this country" [p. 46].) Money and material goods mark Billy's sense of having made it as an American, as they did for Maury. In addition, though, for Billy, celebrity matters, however vulgar or tawdry. As the narrator describes him:

> Billy Rose wasn't big; he was about the size of Peter Lorre. But oh! He was American. There was a penny-arcade jingle about Billy, the popping of shooting galleries, the rattling of pinballs, the weak

> human cry of the Times Square geckos, the lizard gaze of side-show freaks. To see him as he was, you have to place him against the whitewash glare of Broadway in the wee hours. But even such places have their grandees—people whose defects can be converted to seed money for enterprises. There's nothing in this country that you can't sell, nothing too weird to bring to market and found a fortune on. And once you got as much major real estate as Billy had, then it didn't matter that you were one of the human deer that came uptown from the Lower East Side to graze on greasy sandwich papers [p. 47].

Although Fonstein takes offense at Rose's refusal to meet with him, it is his wife, Sorella, who "made up my mind that Billy was going to do right by him" (p. 65). Sorella's determination recalls Bellow's Philadelphia lecture. She sees facing Billy Rose as a way of concluding a chapter in her husband's life, one that "should be concluded. . . . It was a part of the destruction of the Jews. On our side of the Atlantic, where we weren't threatened, we have a special duty to come to terms with it" (p. 66). In what will be her final meeting with the narrator, she expresses an anxiety shared both by him and by Bellow: "If you want my basic view, here it is: The Jews could survive everything that Europe threw at them. I mean the lucky remnant. But now comes the next test—America. Can they hold their ground, or will the U.S.A. be too much for them?" (p. 69). The narrator has an additional anxiety, a larger one: "If you go back to the assertion that memory is life and forgetting death . . . I have established at the very least that I am still able to keep up my struggle for existence" (p. 73). Facing the Holocaust means facing the impossibility of forgetting death. For all his mnemonic powers, the narrator will never defeat death, as he will never fathom the Holocaust, a truth the American in him could not face—and so chose not to face. "I had discovered how long I had shielded myself from unbearable imaginations—no, not imaginations, but recognitions—of murder, of relish of torture, of the ground bass of brutality, without which no human music is ever performed" (p. 82), a companion image to one in *Humboldt's Gift*, of death as "the dark backing a mirror needs if we are to see anything" (p. 256).

At the end of the novella, in a telephone conversation, the narrator learns of the recent deaths of the Fonsteins and of the fate of their only son, Gilbert, a mathematical prodigy and compulsive professional gambler. Gilbert's system when playing cards is to memorize the deck. "That's up your alley," says the young man who answers the Fonsteins' telephone. Gilbert, he tells the narrator, is now living in Las Vegas with his girlfriend. "Does she enjoy Las Vegas?" the narrator asks. "How could she not?" the young man replies, cynically. "It's the biggest showplace in the world—the heart of the American entertainment industry. Which city today is closest to a holy city—like Lhasa or Calcutta or Chartres or Jerusalem? Here it could be New York for money, Washington for power, or Las Vegas attracting people by the millions. Nothing to compare with it in the history of the whole world" (p. 88). In the course of the phone call, the young man mocks the narrator, who is concerned about the fate of the Fonsteins and Gilbert. "He was taunting me—for my Jewish sentiment" (p. 88). The episode seems to confirm Sorella's fears about the fate of the Jews, or of Jewish values, in America, what in his Philadelphia lecture Bellow calls "the old decencies," "the eternal background." After hanging up on the young man, the narrator considers phoning him back to "call him on his low-grade cheap-shot nihilism," to talk to him "about the roots of memory in feeling . . . what retention of the past really means. Things like: 'If sleep is forgetting, forgetting is also sleep, and sleep is to consciousness what death is to life. So that the Jews ask even God to remember, "*Yiskor Elohim*."' God doesn't forget, but your prayer requests him particularly to remember your dead. But how was I to make an impression on a kid like that? I chose instead to record everything I could remember about the Bellarosa Connection, and to set it all down with a Mnemosyne flourish" (p. 89).

SORELLA FONSTEIN, the novella's heroine, is both autonomous seeker and paradise sought, to adapt Updike's formulation. A French teacher before her marriage, knowledgeable as well as intelligent, she is the only American character in the story to understand from the start the value of facing the Holocaust—something she forces the narrator to understand as well.

> I wasn't inclined to discuss Jewish history with her—it put my teeth on edge at first—but she overcame my resistance. She was well up on the subject, and besides, damn it, you couldn't say no to Jewish history after what had happened in Nazi Germany. You had to

> listen. It turned out that as the wife of a refugee she had set herself to master the subject, and I heard a great deal from her about the technics of annihilation, the large-scale-industry aspect of it. What she occasionally talked about . . . was the black humor, the slapstick side of certain camp operations. Being a French teacher, she was familiar with Jarry and *Ubu Roi*, Pataphysics, Absurdism, Dada, Surrealism. . . . I didn't want to hear this [p. 49].

Sorella's problems in finding a husband are attributed by the narrator to her stupendous girth ("She made you look twice at a doorway. When she came to it, she filled the space like a freighter in a canal lock" [p. 60]). She meets Fonstein through her uncle, his employer in Cuba. Like many "worthy girls to whom men never proposed," Sorella had to find a husband "in Mexico, Honduras, [or] Cuba" (p. 44), among European refugees anxious to gain entry to the United States. Initially, the narrator thinks of the marriage as one of convenience, unable "to imagine what Fonstein and Sorella saw in each other when they were introduced. . . . My tastes would have been more like Billy Rose" (p. 44). It takes a while for him to recognize Sorella's intelligence and charm, in part because, as his father puts it, he's a "spoiled American." "Eastern European men had more sober standards," the narrator admits, adding, "Your stoical forebears took their lumps in bed" (p. 44), a remark Billy Rose might have made. Soon, however, he recognizes that, though "technically she was a housewife," none of the "things, or powers, or forces [of housewives] (for I see them as powers, or even spirits), could keep a woman like Sorella in subjection" (p. 56). "She was an ingenious and powerful woman who devised intricate, glittering, bristling, needling schemes" (p. 61). These schemes, like her strengths, are fully dramatized, unlike those of Clara Velde. Nor, as he gets to know her, is Sorella without physical attraction to the narrator. As was pointed out in chapter 2 of *To Fame and Fortune*, the narrator admires her neat ankles, small feet, and pleasant feminine voice. "She set her lady self before him, massively," the narrator says. "The more I think of Sorella," he later admits, "the more charm she has for me" (p. 68).[63]

Bellow's capacity to imagine a woman like Sorella may have been influenced by several real-life models, none like Sorella in appearance. In the late 1980s, directly after they were together at the centennial celebrations of the JPS in Philadelphia, he and Cynthia Ozick conducted a serious correspondence about the Holocaust, Israel, and the Jewish writer's responsibilities. Ozick is among Bellow's greatest admirers, describing her feelings for him as "something more than admiration, something closer to adoration." They first corresponded when a poem of hers, "The Street Criers," was published in *Noble Savage*, volume 2 (1960). Over the years, they met only very occasionally. "When I looked around you were gone, and I was greatly disappointed," wrote Bellow after the JPS ceremony. "Our contacts make me think of a billiard game—one light touch and then we're again at the opposite ends of the table. . . . It always does me good to see you, and I think it's time we met face to face for a conversation. Perhaps you and your husband would like to take in a Marlboro concert. If so, we could give you dinner and a night's lodging." Ozick was too shy to take up the offer (from the letter of May 18, 1988). "I never had the nerve to be a friend," Ozick confessed in an interview. "There were invitations that might have led to [friendship] but I never felt equal to those invitations. . . . I'm told that in writing I'm ferocious, but in life not."

In the early spring of 1988, as Bellow was revolving the themes of "A Jewish Writer in America," Ozick wrote him a response to a letter of July 17, 1987, one she described as "the most elating I have ever had in my life." This was the letter in which Bellow confessed his guilt at having been "too busy becoming a novelist to take note of what was happening in the Forties." That the letter also praised and criticized Ozick's writing (for its "virtuosity") accounted in part for Ozick's eight-month delay in replying, though ill-health played a part as well. In her reply, on March 22, 1988, Ozick mentions her reaction to Bellow's foreword to *The Closing of the American Mind*. In that foreword, Bellow writes of his determination "to decide for myself to what extent my Jewish origins, my surroundings (the accidental circumstances of Chicago), my schooling, were to be allowed to determine the course of my life." For Ozick, in contrast, as she writes in the March 22 letter, "it's otherwise. . . . I keep wanting to become my mother and father—day and night I long for my parents' drugstore (may it be reconstituted in Eden!), and as I get older, I'm surprised now and again by the discovery of the music of their brains in my brain. I'm not any sort of runaway." Elsewhere in the letter, Ozick fiercely defends Israel against its critics, "those who put the onus for progress entirely on Israel, as if the Arabs were some sort of impersonal force of nature from whom it would be foolish to expect fundamental human responsibility or accountability," or for whom "the establishment of Israel was a 'historic injustice.'" Ozick's obvious intelligence and learning are as clear in her letters to Bellow as in her published writing. Together with the embrace of her Jewish heritage, and her willingness to take on Israel's critics, she anticipates Sorella, just as Bellow's acknowledged unwillingness to be determined by his Jewish heritage or to confront the Holocaust underlies his creation of the narrator in *The Bellarosa Connection*.

Bellow sent Ozick galleys of *The Bellarosa Connection* with an inscription that scared her, since it said she would "instantly see" what he was up to ("Suppose I didn't, couldn't, wasn't smart enough? But I saw, I saw"). Of Sorella ("I decided to pronounce her name not SorELLa, but as the Yiddish diminutive, SORella"), she wrote: "Oh, tremendous. One mourns her when her death is unveiled. She knows it all, and asks the question YOU are the only American novelist with the guts to ask." This is the question about whether the Jews can "hold their ground" in America, or whether "the U.S.A. will be too much for them." Of this question Ozick writes: "Answer: Broadway Billy Rose, in all his manifestations (including the universities)." As for the narrator, he is "ten times more ingenious" (as a fictional creation, she means): "The Memory Master, the *baal-zikaron* has attenuated all the old connections and in certain ways now begins to stand for America. 'Half-Jewish, half-Wasp,' in a mansion next door to the Biddles. A big American money-maker. But on memory! Memory isn't an American commodity. In an ironic flash you put the Mnemosyne Institute practically on top of Independence Hall. (The closest thing America has got to a Mnemosyne Institute.)" The letter ends as unsentimentally as the novella, lamenting others who "made the Billy Rose connection. In one form or another. But without Billy Rose's 'spurt of feeling' for his fellow Jews," an absence that "scandalizes" Ozick. Bellow's answer to this letter, on August 29, 1989, is the one where he tells of the Vermont visit of Hitchens and Amis and lets rip over Hitchens and other "Fourth Estate playboys." In the same spirit, he writes that "the movement to assimilate [on the part of European Jews] coincided with the arrival of nihilism. The nihilism reached its climax with Hitler. The Jewish answer to the Holocaust was the creation of a state." Enemies of this state are everywhere, but, then, "it's so easy to make trouble for the Jews. Nothing easier. The networks love it, the big papers let it be made, there's a receptive university population for which Arafat is Good and Israel is Bad, even genocidal." These, of course, were and are Ozick's views, as they are the views of Ruth Wisse and Janis, who are also like Sorella—in their Jewishness, their intelligence, and their fierce loyalties. "It's like your family," Wisse says of Israel. "You protect it instinctively and you don't put it at risk. . . . Janis and I share views very, very much. I don't know the subjects we'd ever differed about."

AS BELLOW'S SEVENTY-FIFTH BIRTHDAY approached, he often wrote of feeling his age. The years 1985 to 1990 had seen the deaths of close friends and relations, beginning in 1985 with his brothers Maury and Sam and his first wife, Anita. Bernard Malamud and his childhood friend Sydney J. Harris died in 1986. Paolo Milano died in 1988. In June 1989, Barley Alison died, the editor to whom he was closest, "a dear and devoted friend and one of the most generous persons I ever knew";[64] in September, Robert Penn Warren died, "a great-souled man."[65] At the beginning of 1990, on January 16, Edith Tarcov died, at seventy. Two months later, on March 13, Sam Freifeld died, at seventy-three. "For a man approaching the seventy-fifth year of his age I am not doing badly," Bellow wrote to John Auerbach on February 5. But they were chopping in his part of the woods. "As more news of deaths arrives," Bellow wrote, "(the latest death was that of Edith Tarcov, a dear woman whom I think you knew) the less I feel the victory of my survival. There is a strange scratchiness in the viscera when I think matters over." There may also have been remorse. Both Edith and Sam Freifeld thought Bellow had treated them badly. Shortly after Freifeld's death, Bellow encountered his ex-wife, Marilyn Mann, at a theater in Skokie. "He was visibly shaken," she recalled to Atlas. "'They're really going,' he told her."[66] Bellow attended Edith Tarcov's funeral in New York, but according to her son, Nathan, the two old friends had been estranged for some time. "There are no letters from Edith's later years," Nathan recalls, the years following Bellow's hurtful refusal to write an introduction to a volume of Oscar Tarcov's shorter fiction.

WITH THE LOSS OF HIS BROTHERS, of Sam in particular, Bellow took on something of the role of family protector, especially for his sister, Jane, but also at times for his nieces and nephews and their children. About his brothers and sister he remained clear-sighted. On March 11, 1988, in a letter to Lesha's daughter, Rachel Schultz, he wrote frankly not only about her grandfather Samuel Bellows but about Maury and Jane as well.

> I loved him without any expectation of a return [which is not to say he received no return]. He forgave me even my numerous and preposterous marriages, by which he must have, in some way, felt threatened. But I didn't ask him for anything and I knew that he would never understand what I was up to. I learned to love both my brothers and my sister to the extent that they were lovable and even a bit beyond and it made not the slightest difference to me that I couldn't even begin to talk to them. I had to forgo all communication except what long-standing family love going back to childhood made possible. But that was a great deal. Some four-thousand years of Jewish history went into it—I don't mean Talmudic history or anything of that sort, I mean the history of Jewish feeling.

Two months later, on May 25, Bellow wrote to Rachel's uncle, Shael Bellows, Sam's son, on behalf of his widowed aunt Jane. Jane was an investor in the rest-home business Shael had taken over from his father, and her dividends as a limited partner had recently been much reduced. According to Shael, this was in part because revenues "simply aren't what they used to be" (Bellow's paraphrase or quote from the letter of May 25), in part because Shael felt that his father "made overlarge distributions to his limited partners . . . he 'spoiled' them." Although Jane often complained about money, in this case she was in genuine difficulties. She had already lost one son, Larry (whose suicide was described in chapter 13 of *To Fame and Fortune*), and her other child, Robert, was gravely ill in Florida with AIDS. Since Robert was too weak to work, Jane was obliged to pay his bills, "about fifty thousand dollars since the beginning of the year." Bellow wrote to Shael in his capacity "as your Aunt Jane's only surviving brother." He reminded Shael that his father "left Jane (and other members of the family) in your care, and he would most certainly have expected you to look after them, especially in their declining years. Jane is part of your legacy. . . . You can't blame her for being shaken, nor can you blame me for asking you to behave less like a general partner and more like your father's son." On July 19, Bellow wrote again, agreeing with Shael that Jane should sell her holdings, and raising another family matter. Lisa Westreich, a cousin, and her daughter, Sabina Mazursky, had written to Bellow asking if he would intercede with Shael to find out what had happened to the money they had sent to him for investment and about which they had heard nothing. Bellow wrote Shael: "The amounts are trifling to us but these are the slowly accumulated savings of Lisa and her daughter and I feel that it would not be out of place to give an explanation of what you are doing. You need not send your explanation to them, send it to me and I will transmit the information." Bellow signed the letter "Your affectionate Uncle, Saul."

A WEEK AFTER THE LETTER to Shael, Bellow wrote to Sanford Pinsker, an English professor at Franklin and Marshall College in Pennsylvania, a specialist in Jewish literature and culture, in response to an invitation. "Because I don't travel as easily as I once did," Bellow explained, "I have been obliged to set a minimum fee to discourage invitations. Although I would dearly love to see you at Franklin and Marshall I have set a fee of $10,000 per engagement. Even at that price I am obliged to refuse invitations. . . . You will understand this if you will remember that I am somewhere between my seventy-third and seventy-fourth birthdays. . . . I simply have to limit my air miles and conserve my strength."[67] These complaints about reduced powers often occurred when Bellow was turning down invitations, and must be measured against evidence to the contrary: a travel schedule as crowded as ever; the production of his best short fiction; Janis's sense of his strength and vigor. Nor were there signs of mellowing. On June 5, 1990, five days before he turned seventy-five, Bellow wrote to the scholar and critic Roger Shattuck apologizing for a recent bout of ill-temper. Shattuck had teased him about some aspect of the language of his novels, at a dinner party at the poet Rosanna Warren's house in Vermont, and the next day Bellow "burst into" Shattuck's office at BU with a list of references in support of his usage. This behavior he calls "unforgivable," but "when I am criticized in a matter of usage I can be a bit crazy." "If we knew each other better, I'm sure I'd come to accept this teasing, even to enjoy it, and you might make friendly allowance for an occasional eruption." The letter closes with a reference to the possibility of a permanent move to Boston University. "The daring of a major move at my time of life," he writes, "sets my teeth on edge but nothing is impossible to unrealistically (perversely?) youthful types like me."

BY THE DATE OF THIS LETTER—by the date also of the 1988 Pinsker letter, with its talk of conserving energy—Bellow had taken steps to maintain his youthfulness. He had become a patient or customer of Dr. Harry B. Demopoulos, whose "pure" vitamins and amino acids, if consumed in large enough doses, promised "to slow or even *reverse* the aging process." According to an article of November 8, 1989, in *The Wall Street Journal*, in consuming Dr. D's costly "Fountain of Youth" pills, Bellow joined such celebrities as Doris Duke, William S. Paley, Sylvester Stallone, and Clint Eastwood. So convinced did he seem to be of the efficacy of the pills that he agreed to appear in advertisements for a book Dr. Demopoulos co-wrote to promote them, *Formula for Life* (1989). In advertisements for the book, Bellow praised its "detailed and reliable information" about preventing "the premature slipping away of vital mental powers." It was Jonas Salk (a fellow evaluator for the MacArthur Foundation) who first told Bellow about Dr. Demopoulos—a reason, perhaps, for Bellow's faith in him. "I've been on the regime for four years," Bellow told the *Journal*. "My energy level has been high, there has been no decline in my mental abilities. I can work for long stretches of time."[68]

In "All Marbles Still Accounted For," a figure not unlike Dr. Demopoulos appears. Hilbert Faucil, at ninety-three, is in "excellent" condition, partly attributable to medical assistance he describes as "a dense, complex and partly uncomfortable side of my existence." At a spa called the Doral Saturnia, a "super-elegant health-resort," Faucil meets Dr. Clavel, who takes an interest in his remarkable strength and liveliness. Faucil goes to the Saturnia for "the inimitable pleasure of sitting under a warm waterfall, or maybe a cascade. I do it by the hour while I test my memory of poems that have been very important to me" (p. 47). Although he thinks of the fitness craze in America as "one of the more demeaning aspects of modern life" (p. 49), when he is introduced to Dr. Clavel, a "world famous" endocrinologist now into geriatric medicine, he is impressed by the strong color in his face, his "black hair growing straight up," his "peremptory eyes," his "man-of-the-world style" (p. 51). Dr. Clavel no longer practices, but he advises "a few people in Hollywood as well as prominent TV personalities and sports figures" (p. 54). "He gave me a narrow look, the narrowest yet. . . . He was offering me access to scientific knowledge such as only he in all the world had at his specialized fingertips" (p. 56).

"For your stage of life, I know exactly what to recommend," says Clavel. "People who take it actually grow younger from it" (p. 59). "It" here is human growth hormone, which "restores your muscle mass. . . . You get your legs back. To an extent you eliminate signs of age from your skin. It tends to turn crepey on the inner arms, the inner thighs and the neck. There's also a rise in the energy level. Think what life could be if you were back at normal energy for, say, age fifty" (p. 59). After Clavel talks to Faucil "about free radicals, anti-oxidants, and dietary methods of fortifying the body against cancer," he offers to take him on as a patient and to provide him with the requisite medication.

> "I do have an inside line. After decades of research. I think I could promise you a twelve-month supply." He asked me to guess what the price would be.
>
> "Good I was warned. I'll brace myself. . . . Ten thousand?"
>
> "What would you say to forty-grand?"
>
> "I'd say it was a deal. . . ."
>
> His look expressed considerable respect. "Well, you are a plunger. I don't even hear you asking about possible risks in this therapy. It's taken intramuscularly by injection."
>
> He was amused by my way of doing things. . . . On the physical side I always was a headlong type [pp. 61–62].

These scenes recall Bellow's fictionalizing of his Reichian therapy in the "Zetland" manuscripts, in which admiration for the therapist, Dr. Sapir, combines with clear-eyed skepticism. It also recalls his inability, in life as in his novels, wholly to commit to the theories of Rudolf Steiner, even as he continued to pore over and recommend his writings.[69]

IN MAY 1990, while Bellow and Janis were in Britain, over a hundred of his friends and relatives received invitations to a surprise birthday party for him on Saturday, June 9, the day before his actual birthday. The party was organized by Janis and held at Le Petit Chef in Wilmington, Vermont, where Betty Hillman, Libby and Herb's daughter, was chef, and where the Bellows often dined. Guests came from all over. There was a Chicago contingent, including Zita Cogan, Al Glotzer, the Kleinbards, Bette Howland, the Missners, and Wolf Baronov, Bellow's cousin from Riga, who gave a toast in Yiddish (Allan Bloom and Michael Z. Wu were in Paris; Yetta Barshevsky Schachtman, Bellow's friend from Tuley High School, was unable to travel; Richard Stern and Alane Rollings were absent because of Richard's recent surgery; all sent long letters explaining why they couldn't come). Eleanor Clark was there—a year after the death of Robert Penn Warren—as was their daughter Rosanna Warren, who brought John Auerbach, to whom *The Bellarosa Connection* was dedicated, and his wife, Nola Chilton, who had come from Israel. Other Russian cousins came, only recently arrived from the Soviet Union. Philip Roth and Claire Bloom were there, as were William Kennedy and his wife, and William Arrowsmith and his wife. Janis's parents couldn't come—Harvey, her father, was ill—but Sonya's brother came, accompanying their mother, Janis's grandmother, who had initially opposed Bellow's marrying Janis. Among the New York guests were Maggie Simmons, Harriet Wasserman, Vicki (Lidov) Fischman (a friend from the 1940s), Walter Pozen, and Saul Steinberg, who arrived by helicopter. Vermont neighbors and friends came: the Hillmans, of course, and the Copelands, Ann Malamud, Frank Maltese (who built Bellow's house), even the owner of the Marlboro inn that Janis had completely filled with party guests (finding hotels for guests, she remembers, "was the hard part"). Lesha and Sam Greengus came, as did their daughter Rachel Schultz and her husband and two-year-old son. Adam Bellow and family were there (Cynthia Ozick was offered a ride with Adam, but was too shy to accept). Daniel and his family came, and though Greg was absent, having just returned to California after touring colleges on the East Coast with Juliet, his daughter, Greg's son, Andrew, came with his mother, to represent the family.

Bellow had no idea about the party. The RSVPs had been sent to Janis's parents in Toronto, no one let the secret out, and Bellow and Janis were abroad most of May. Janis invited everyone she could think of, including ex-girlfriends and would-be girlfriends ("I didn't realize . . . how many women were still in love with him"). When Bellow and Janis arrived at Le Petit Chef, he looked at all the cars in the parking lot and said: "Oh shit, it looks like somebody's having a party tonight." As they entered the restaurant, "there was grandson Andrew and John Auerbach from Israel, and the Russian cousin Baronov." Atlas quotes an unnamed guest on the moment of arrival: "Whammo! great screams and cheers!"[70] As Bellow later told Janis, "He had the sensation that it was as though there was some meeting after you die where all the people come together." To Philip Roth, the party "was Chekhovian . . . with people popping up suddenly to make speeches, to break into tears, to tell you how much they loved you. Chekhov and no one else would have thrust forward the Russian cousin to announce, 'I chav a song!' The little Jewish chef of Vermont, her proud mama, your very different sons, the exquisite tiny Lily [Adam's daughter], the speech by your niece ('even though he is seventy-five . . .'), Maggie's kisses and tears . . . enough to keep the Moscow Art Theater busy for many, many seasons."[71] In addition to speeches and songs and tears, there was champagne, a lavish meal of smoked salmon, boeuf Wellington, and chocolate cake. Bellow, according to Janis, "loved it, he just loved it. Totally surprised him. It was a triumph." Julian Behrstock, his old friend from Northwestern days, couldn't come from Paris, but sent a birthday message. On June 26, Bellow wrote to thank him and to offer a brief description of what he'd missed: "You would have enjoyed the occasion. It was attended by seventy people, two of them greenhorn cousins of my own age just out of the Soviet Union. And children, of course, and grandchildren and old pals, the durable kind like yourself." Bellow described Janis as "an incredibly gifted organizer" ("he was so

SB and Janis on their wedding day, Vermont, August 25, 1989 (courtesy of Janis Bellow)

proud of me," she recalled). The next day, on Bellow's actual birthday, everyone came over to the house. Betty Hillman did all the cooking. Guests wandered in and out, under the maple tree, down the stone steps, by the pond. On July 10, Bellow reported to Saul Steinberg that, "after the birthday shouting, the silence of Vermont came back. Real life is represented by the cat, who appeared just now to show us the bird he had killed, and to fill Janis's mind with thoughts of vegetarianism."

10

Papuans and Zulus

AT THE END OF SEPTEMBER 1990, Janis and Bellow returned to Chicago and a second seventy-fifth birthday party: this one a grand celebration organized by Mayor Richard M. Daley, on October 6. "The scene was unprecedented in Chicago," the reporter from the *Tribune* wrote. "Chicago politicians chatting up literary savants over sautéed medallions of veal." Richard Stern, who had recently recovered from surgery, was amazed, calling the event "downright un-American." The dinner was held at the Art Institute, where the mayor praised Bellow in a speech Stern described as "very awkward and touching." Not only had Bellow brought "vitality" to the city through his works, he had inspired the mayor personally, helping him to become "a more compassionate man." In addition to the dinner and the speeches, performers from the Lyric Opera sang songs and snatches from Bellow's favorite arias. Allan Bloom flew in from Paris to toast his friend. In his speech, Bloom declared: "Bellow is to Chicago what Balzac was to Paris. He has always understood that even if you are on your way from Becoming to Being, you still have to catch the train at Randolph Street." The mayor's wife, Maggie, presented Bellow with a handcrafted volume containing a selection of his writings about the city, illustrated by original woodcut drawings; Janis received a bouquet of roses. The mayor announced that a sculpture of Bellow would be commissioned and displayed in the new Chicago Public Library. On October 30, Bellow praised the party in a thank-you letter. "It was not a ceremonial occasion but a *real party* not something 'laid on.' Everyone (almost without exception) was simple and natural. You and Maggie were the source of this easiness. You said exactly what you felt and thus liberated us from stiffness and artificiality." At the dinner itself, Bellow's parting words to the mayor were "You're a class act."[1]

BLOOM'S HAPPY RETURN to Chicago for the belated birthday party was soon followed by debilitating illness. He was diagnosed with Guillain-Barré syndrome, a rare neurological disease that causes paralysis and atrophy. The initial onset of the disease almost killed him, wrecking his body, leaving his limbs stick-thin. He was bedridden for months, had to relearn to walk, and never regained full use of his hands. On December 3, 1990, Bellow wrote to John Auerbach about Bloom's condition and its effect on those close to him. "Since he has no wife, no children, no one to take care of him but his friends, Janis and I would run back to Chicago from San Antonio, Montreal, Miami, etcetera as often as possible. For a while he was in mortal danger. He's better now. His chances for recovery are good. He may be able to walk again." By December 30, writing to Martin Amis, Bellow was less sanguine. He and Janis had planned to spend the winter quarter, from February to May, in Paris, where Bellow would be loosely connected to the Centre des Recherches Politiques Raymond Aron, a research branch of the École des Hautes Études en Sciences Sociales. He had been invited by the historian François Furet, the center's founder, who spent every autumn at the University of Chicago and had recently joined the Committee on Social Thought from the Department of History.[2] The trip to Paris was canceled. "Our friend Bloom has for some months been down with the paralyzing Guillain-Barré syndrome, and we can make no travel plans until we know whether the paralysis is temporary. Or not. He's making progress but there won't be any holidays until we've seen him through." A month later, on January 29, 1991, Bellow wrote to his old friend Julian Behrstock with no better news: "We couldn't possibly take a holiday in Paris under the circumstances."

Although Bloom never fully recovered his health, for a few months he was able to return to his normal routine, or much of it. He taught seminars, held reading groups, and kept up with politics and debates over higher education. Clifford Orwin, his student at Cornell and his colleague at Toronto, who was in Chicago for most of 1992, was impressed with the way Bloom fought to keep up appearances. "As he had always done, he welcomed countless visitors and spent hours on the telephone with friends, many of them his former students." He also worked steadily to complete a book he had contracted with Simon & Schuster, for which Harriet Wasserman had secured a large advance. The book was *Love & Friendship* (1993), described by Orwin as "the work for which he wanted most to be remembered."[3] All the novels and plays discussed in the book were ones Bloom had taught with Bellow over the preceding twelve years. On its posthumous acknowledgments pages, his executors, Nathan Tarcov and Hillel G. Fradkin, report that Bloom "often remarked upon how much he learned about them from this experience."

Love & Friendship was dictated in its entirety to Tim Spiekerman, a student at the Committee and an Olin Fellow. Spiekerman wrote his dissertation under Bloom and Bellow and took on part-time jobs for both men. For much of Bloom's last year, he spent mornings with him on the book, staying on for lunch. "Every afternoon," Spiekerman recalls, Bellow would come over to visit. The work Spiekerman did for Bellow was office correspondence. So voluminous was this correspondence that "I found myself becoming rather protective. There were lots of requests to sign petitions, which I rarely passed on." Spiekerman had first encountered Bellow as a teacher in a joint Bellow-Bloom seminar on Flaubert's *Sentimental Education*. Bloom was "more dynamic," "the superior teacher," but he treated Bellow respectfully, as "the one in the room who had actually made great literature." Spiekerman was surprised to find Bellow "rather shy," both in and out of class; what did not surprise him was his "quick and astute" judgment of people.[4]

On several occasions when Bellow and Janis were away, Spiekerman looked after the apartment at 5825 Dorchester. In the bedroom, he noticed a full bookshelf devoted to the works of Rudolf Steiner and his followers. This interest of Bellow's "infuriated" Bloom. "If he has to dabble in mysticism," Spiekerman remembers Bloom complaining, "why not Jewish mysticism?"[5] Bloom, though, "adored" Bellow, and Bellow "went out of his way on a couple of occasions to tell me how smart and thoughtful Allan was." To Spiekerman, the relationship between the two men fed Bloom's intellectual interest in friendship. Bellow appears twice in *Love & Friendship*, both times briefly. In a chapter on *Madame Bovary*, Bloom recalls: "Once in class I said, with a rhetorical flourish, that all nineteenth-century novels were about adultery. A student objected that she knew some which were not. My co-teacher, Saul Bellow, interjected, 'Well, of course, you can have a circus without elephants.'" In a chapter on *Romeo and Juliet*, Bloom claims that, with the possible exception of Tybalt, everybody in the play "is nice, and there are no villains. Good intentions are to be found everywhere and one cannot help remembering Saul Bellow's firm, 'The Good Intentions Paving Company.'"[6]

Bloom's relative recovery lasted until December 1991, when, according to Orwin, he suffered "a sudden and nearly fatal onset of acute diabetes." From this setback he again recovered, and again sought to resume normal activities.[7] He then suffered a perforated ulcer and liver failure, and rallied only briefly. He died on October 7, 1992, almost two years from the initial diagnosis of Guillain-Barré syndrome. Throughout his ordeal, Bloom was nursed by his partner, Michael Z. Wu, and attended by a host of friends and students. Bellow, in particular, "was my salvation."[8] In *Ravelstein*, Bloom's end is controversially fictionalized (it will be discussed in chapter 12). What Wu remembers of Bloom's death was how "impressive" it was: "He was not frightened at all. . . . He was very, very clear-minded. He really didn't care, in a way. He was not trying to prove anything. He was trying to finish his book; he was just too weak. He did what he had to do till the end. A serious person." What Orwin remembers of Bloom's final months is somewhat different. "The last thing he would have wanted was for me to depict him as J.-L. David painted Socrates, all noble gesture and moral uplift. He feared death as much as (and loved life more than) the next man, but he faced it squarely. He wanted his friends around him, and he wanted to prepare them for the worst, but he also wanted to make this as easy for them as possible. For a man who had so many books in his head and who had taught them so eloquently, a signal achievement of his last months was that he never struck an edifying note."[9]

BELLOW WAS "HAMMERED FLAT" by Bloom's death.[10] He was also softened by it, though there had been signs of softening earlier. In February 1992, during a period of remission for Bloom, he and Janis flew to the University of Florida, where he had agreed to participate in its annual Writers Festival. On the evening of February 21, Bellow gave a half-hour reading from *Humboldt's Gift* (Citrine's visit to Humboldt's "rural slum") to an audience of nine hundred. He left directly after the reading, without answering questions or signing autographs, though that evening he briefly attended a reception in his honor at a local writers' hangout. The next morning, he spent an hour answering questions from a smaller gathering of students, and returned to Chicago later in the day. He was paid sixty-five hundred dollars for the two-day visit. The invitation had been issued by the novelist Padgett Powell, whose work Bellow admired. Powell, the director of the creative writing program at Florida, hosted a dinner for the Bellows the night before the reading in a downtown Gainesville restaurant. Among those at the dinner was Andrew Gordon, who had last seen the Bellows at the Haifa conference five years earlier, when Bellow had struck him as uncomfortable and standoffish.

At the dinner in Gainesville, Bellow's behavior was quite different. "He was hospitable and gracious," Gordon writes, "showing a side of him I had not seen at the conference." At the question-and-answer session the next morning, Bellow patiently answered queries from graduate students and faculty in the Department of English. Gordon describes him as "in fine form, relaxed but sharp and witty."[11] Many of his comments concerned aging, a sense that "life is running a lot thinner now." He also stressed the prominence of early memories in his work, nowhere more so than in "Something to Remember Me By" and *The Bellarosa Connection*, his most recent writings (reprinted the previous autumn, along with *A Theft*, in a single volume entitled *Something to Remember Me By: Three Tales*). Early memories mattered to Bellow for the reasons they mattered to Wordsworth: because they come from the period when one is most alive or awake, and because they concern individuals (recent Jewish immigrants in Montreal and Chicago) who, like the rural inhabitants of Wordsworth's poems, "had not yet been pressed into shape by the forces of modern life."[12] There was a new openness in Bellow's answers. In talking about *The Bellarosa Connection*, he gave the impression, to Gordon at least, "that he felt he had done the same thing to some people in his life that the elderly narrator had done. . . . Like the narrator, Bellow judges himself harshly because he has a tendency to put people in storage, to place them in a 'mental warehouse' and assume he is intimate with them but not have to deal with them further. 'If he loved them, then how could he find it in his heart to check them in his locker and lose the key? When he tries to find these people he loves so much, they've all been filed away. If you live long enough, you'll do this to people. You say "Yes, I've got them inside me."'"

Bellow increasingly sought to counter his tendency to lose touch with people, both those he loved and those he liked or admired. After he left Chicago for Boston, he received a note from Tim Spiekerman asking for a reference. Bellow readily agreed and produced a glowing letter. He also wrote Spiekerman a personal letter, the quiet tone of which may owe something to their shared connection with Bloom. The letter is dated July 26, 1993.

> Dear Tim,
>
> There are not many Chicago people whom I miss, but somewhat to my surprise you are one of that small number. I say to my surprise because our relations were never intimate. If anything they were on the cool side, but as I am increasingly aware they were not as cool as they seemed. Behind the formal style adopted by both of us I sensed a good deal of thoroughly concealed warmth in you as well as a considerable gift for clear thought and expression. If you can be lured away from your defenses and give out a bit I am convinced that a significant number of people will sit up and take notice. For one reason or another I didn't reply as I should have done to the letter you wrote two or three years ago, but it's not too late now I feel for us to begin to level with each other.
>
> As a for a letter of recommendation, I am only too glad to write one and to work in what to my certain knowledge Bloom would have said in his letter of recommendation about you.
>
> All best,
> Saul

A similar example of softening or mellowing can be seen in Bellow's relations with his colleagues at the Committee on Social Thought. By the end of the 1980s, the Committee was in a bad way. Its members had been unable to agree on new faculty for almost a decade. Bloom and Leszek Kołakowski, the philosopher and historian of Marxism, were its most recent members, Bloom in 1979 and Kołakowski in 1981. So exercised was the dean of social sciences about the Committee's failure to hire anyone that he raised the possibility of shutting it down if it failed to agree to recruit four or five new members from within the university and two from without. It was then agreed that François Furet would join the Committee from the Department of History and be appointed chair, even though he would continue to spend only the autumn quarter in Chicago, ten weeks a year. The other internal appointments agreed on were the anthropologist and linguist Paul Friedrich, the historian Mark Kishlansky (who was poached by Harvard almost as soon as he joined), the theologian David Tracy, and Nathan Tarcov. The external appointments were two philosophers, Robert Pippin and Jonathan Lear. Ralph Lerner was appointed co-chair, to conduct meetings and arrange Committee business during the quarters when Furet was in Paris; in 1991, Lerner was succeeded as co-chair by Tarcov.

Tarcov attributes the Committee's failure to hire anyone in the 1980s in part to Edward Shils. Although Shils was "always very nice to me, very encouraging," to others he could be "ferocious and rude." "Unlike most of us, if he didn't think well of people he didn't feel obligated to treat them with courtesy or respect, or just to ignore them. It was unusual enough for me to note it." Tarcov remembers one occasion on which a job candidate, a sociologist, was brought to Chicago at Shils's suggestion to give a talk to the Committee. She was regarded as Shils's candidate. "When she spoke, he tore her apart, in a humiliating way, and opposed her appointment. No wonder we weren't making appointments." By 1990, Tarcov believes, Shils "had no allies, though some people, including Wheatley [Paul Wheatley, the chair before Furet], were clearly afraid of him," which made them equivalent to allies, "as we know from great power politics."

Shils's waning influence, and Furet's abilities as chair, meant that Committee business became less contentious. Tarcov remembers the first meetings he attended in 1990 as "rather congenial." Bellow, an obvious power because of his eminence, was "charming and witty," with "an ironic gleam," "a certain remove." His association with Bloom could not have been closer, and Bloom not only had great influence, because of the Olin money, but also managed to get on with everyone, including left-leaning members of the Committee (James Redfield, Wendy Doniger), as well as Shils. As Tarcov puts it, Bellow was surrounded by "many friends, Allan, François, Ralph Lerner, myself. I didn't see the Iron Age. What I saw was a period when he was rather comfortable." This was an impression shared by Robert Pippin, who would eventually take over from Furet as chair. He remembers Bellow as quiet during the several job talks he gave before joining the Committee but easy and welcoming at subsequent dinners. The Committee had been looking for years for someone who wrote on and could teach Hegel and Nietzsche and Heidegger. After coming close to hiring the

Canadian philosopher Charles Taylor, who accepted the post but then withdrew, the Committee turned to Pippin, a much younger man. Pippin accepted on condition that the appointment be approved by the Department of Philosophy, with which he wished also to be affiliated. He had come from the University of California at San Diego, where he was chair of the Department of Philosophy, and it was assumed that at some point he would become chair of the Committee.

Pippin and Tarcov were both born in 1948, and this constituted something of a generational change for the Committee. "They hadn't hired anyone our age virtually ever," Pippin believes. At a time of great interest in French and German theory in American universities, Pippin was much in demand, for he knew the primary texts that influenced Derrida and Foucault (texts by Husserl, Heidegger, Nietzsche) "better than anyone in the Committee or the English Department." His courses were very popular (they are still), and his approach to the philosophers he writes and lectures about is acceptable to those who are wary of Continental philosophy and the use to which it is put by "theorists." Bellow's *de haut en bas* attitude to theory is seen in a letter of October 27, 1994, to Huston Smith, a professor of religious studies at Berkeley (a former colleague of Timothy Leary and Richard Alpert): "My own view of the questions raised by Derrida and company is that they don't really need to be raised and that the incredulity of sophisticated theorists does not concern me very much." Yet Bellow approved Pippin. As did Edward Shils. In the winter quarter of his first year at the Committee, Pippin taught a course on Hegel's *Philosophy of Right*. "Shils came to every class, staring at me for fifty minutes, never said a word." When the course was over, Shils told Pippin, "The approach you used was the right one."

Bellow's relations with Pippin were not without tension. From the start, Pippin made it clear that he thought that students at the Committee should be accredited by traditional departments as well as by the Committee; that their Ph.D.s should be issued jointly. As a consequence, most doctoral candidates would need to satisfy coursework requirements from outside the Committee. In the case of the Department of Philosophy, "the most conservative of the departments we deal with," Committee students were required to take its courses for two years. Pippin concedes that this was a high price to pay, and that some Committee students might end up taking very few Committee courses. He thought that joint degrees would help Committee students find better jobs, and in doing so they would help the Committee to recruit better students. "Our students weren't getting good jobs," he recalls, and if the trend continued, enrollment would suffer. Few top universities and colleges hired applicants from interdepartmental programs, and it would be "professional suicide" to allow Committee graduates to be disadvantaged in this way.

Bellow did not agree, nor did Bloom, though it was Bellow who made the case against joint degrees to Pippin. This was because, a week after Pippin moved to Chicago to take up his post, in August 1992, "Bloom went into a tailspin, went into the hospital, and never came out." Pippin had long admired Bellow, who was "an important writer to me since high school. I was pretty much in awe of him and he was very nice to me . . . never indicating anything other than enthusiastic support." When Pippin's advocacy of joint degrees became known, however, Bellow intervened: "One day Saul came to my office." Although it might be true, Bellow admitted, that Committee students weren't getting the jobs they merited, "we ought to respect the choice they made when they came to the Committee." Pippin stuck to his guns, "but I could tell that he was very disappointed." Soon he began hearing that Bellow had voiced his disappointment to others. When told this was happening, Pippin recalls, "I'd always say how sad I was." Shortly before Bellow left Chicago for Boston University, however, in the spring of 1993, he wrote Pippin "a little note." This note Pippin has lost, but he remembers its gist: "I understand you think I'm disappointed with your hire. Nothing could be further from the truth. I'm very glad we hired you. I'm very glad you're here."

AT THE BEGINNING OF DECEMBER 1991, shortly before acute diabetes almost killed Bloom, Bellow and Janis traveled to Italy, where Bellow had agreed to give a talk to mark Mozart's bicentennial. The invitation came from Bruno Bartoletti, artistic director and principal conductor of the Chicago Lyric Opera, to which Bellow and Janis subscribed. In addition to his jobs in Chicago, Bartoletti was director of the Maggio Musicale Fiorentino, a music festival in Florence, and it was at his house in Fiesole that the Bellows had dinner the night after the talk. The night before, they and the Bartolettis dined with the mayor of Florence and his wife, and Bellow began to worry about his speech. "As often happens," he recalled to Ruth Wisse, in a letter of February 20, 1992, "I was obliged to rewrite my talk in the hotel room." He was pleased with the result, and two years later chose the talk, retitled "Mozart: An Overture," to open the prose collection *It All Adds Up: From the Dim Past to the Uncertain Future* (1994).

"Mozart: An Overture" begins, as do a number of pieces in the collection, autobiographically, with recollections of his sister, Jane, at the piano, early violin lessons, student years as an unpaid usher at the Auditorium Theatre. Then it turns to the question of Mozart's genius, in particular to its seeming independence from "environmental or historical theories." Einstein is invoked, calling Mozart "only a visitor upon this earth." Mozart's genius "forces" one "to speculate about transcendence," but such speculation makes Bellow uncomfortable, since it is often associated "with crankiness or faddism—even downright instability and mental feebleness."[13] Bellow persists, convinced that "there is a dimension of music that prohibits final comprehension and parries or fends off the cognitive habits we respect and revere" (p. 5). About this dimension, Mozart himself was in the dark. He was, says Bellow, "a 'stranger' who never understood the nature of his strangeness" (p. 11).

There are implicit, perhaps unconscious, connections in the talk between Bellow and his subject. Mozart's powers as a letter writer are likened to those of a novelist. He has the novelist's "gift of characterizing by minute particulars. . . . His manner of seeing comes directly from his nature, perhaps from a source close to the source of his music. The two styles, the verbal and the musical, have something in common" (p. 7). Mozart was only peripherally interested in politics, and his management of his own affairs, his biographers agree, was "disastrous" (p. 9). His music was "fertile, novel, ingenious, inexhaustible"; it came to him "readily, easily, gratuitously" (p. 11). At the same time, as in Bellow's writing, "we recognize also the signature of Enlightenment, of reason and understanding" (p. 11). How, Bellow wonders, does one reconcile this "signature" with Mozart's "clownishly demonic" behavior, his "liking for low company," his "tricks," "gags," "insults," "lewdness" (p. 10)? This recalls Herschel Shawmut, who senses a connection between his propensity to put his foot in his mouth and creative power. Shawmut describes a put-down he receives from his mentor, Kippenberg, "prince of musicologists," as "genius . . . it was a privilege to have provoked it" (p. 384). "I never intentionally insulted anyone," Shawmut claims in a passage quoted in part in chapter 4; his insults were involuntary, a product of "seizure, rapture, demonic possession, frenzy, *Fatum*, divine madness. . . . The better people are, the less they take offense at this gift, or curse" (p. 412).

Mozart's "gift, or curse," a much greater thing than Shawmut's, is illustrated for Bellow by a story involving "a certain Frau Pichler." As she sat at the piano playing "Non più andrai" from *Figaro*, Mozart came up behind her, pulled up a chair, and, while she played, "began to improvise variations so beautifully that everyone held his breath, listening to the music of the German Orpheus. But all at once he had had enough; he jumped up and, as he often did in his foolish moods, began to leap over table and chairs, miaowing like a cat and turning somersaults like an unruly boy." Bellow quotes Wolfgang Hildesheimer, Mozart's biographer, who calls outbursts like these "physical necessities, automatic compensation for a transcendent mind" (p. 10). Here and throughout his essay, Bellow pays wondering tribute to Mozart's genius and to his irreducible individuality. The writing has a relaxed, meandering quality and ends: "How deeply (beyond words) he speaks to us about the mysteries of our common human nature. And how unstrained and *easy* his greatness is" (p. 14).

INSTEAD OF RETURNING DIRECTLY to Chicago after the Mozart speech, the Bellows traveled by train to Siena, then drove into the countryside near Montalcino, where they stayed for a week. Bellow wrote a travel piece about this stay, "Winter in Tuscany" (1992), also reprinted in *It All Adds Up*. Like the Mozart talk, the piece has a relaxed, informal feel. It begins with a description of the view from their hotel in the Tuscan countryside, all the way to Siena, a distance of some forty kilometers. The ancient landscape "carries the centuries lightly," as do the region's ancient ruins and buildings. "Romanesque interiors in fact are a good cure for heaviness." December in Tuscany is cold. On the day of their arrival, "the *tramontana* was battering the town. . . . It forced open windows in the night and scoured our faces by day" (p. 252). Coming in winter, however, has its advantages. Everyone is welcoming. "They take your off-season visit as a mark of admiration for the long and splendid history of their duchy" (p. 253).

At the cellars of the Fattoria dei Barbi, a tourist highpoint, the vats of wine "resemble the engines of 747 jets in size." The guide, Angela, "a young woman whose pretty face rivals the wine display in interest," has an assistant, "a cat with a banner tail." The cat leads the group "up and down, in and out, from cellar to cellar. We take to this tomcat, who has all the charm of a veteran of the sex wars." At the tour's end, "the cat leaves the building between our legs" (p. 254). Later, at the Taverna dei Barbi, Bellow samples the Brunello wine. "Your susceptibility returns at the same rate as the glass fills. Once again it makes sense to be a multimillionaire. The Brunello fragrance is an immediate QED of the advantages of the pursuit of riches" (p. 254). Less expensive pleasures follow. On the way to the Palazzo Piccolomini in Pienza, "a fine group of old gents standing outside the open door of a café acknowledge us with dignity as we move down the all-stone pavement" (p. 254). Once inside the palazzo, Bellow discovers "that fifteenth-century popes were reading Thucydides and even Aristophanes, and as we enter the papal bedroom I think how difficult it would have been to handle these folios in bed." The palazzo is freezing, and though the fireplace in the bedroom is wide enough to accommodate eight-foot logs, "you'd have to stoke it for a week to drive out such an accumulation of cold" (p. 255). Outdoors, there is a café. They order cappuccinos, which "lose heat so quickly that you'd better down them before ice forms" (p. 256).

The article ends with two very different outings. The first is to an herbal specialist in Montalcino, where Bellow goes to treat a sprained shoulder. Known in the village as "Il Barba," the herbalist is an immensely tall old man with a stubbly beard. In his long, narrow kitchen, Bellow is seated on a stool and asked solicitously about the cause of his sprain. "I took a header over the handlebars of a bike last summer in Vermont," he tells the herbalist, an answer that, given Bellow's age, "doesn't make much sense to him." As Bellow strips to the waist, the herbalist pours a mixture into a small saucepan and heats it over the stove. Olive oil is added to the mixture, which is then rubbed into Bellow's shoulder. Il Barba uses his hand "like a housepainter's brush." His diminutive wife, in close attendance throughout, produces a salve to follow the oily mixture, also applied by hand. Bellow enjoys the treatment, even thinks it might cure him, "because I have a weakness anyway for secret herbal remedies, and the treatment in the kitchen has its occult side" (p. 256). As he and Janis leave, Il Barba holds the door open for them: "He is so tall that we don't have to duck under his arm. We go down the stairs into the night very happy" (p. 257).

The second outing describes a pleasant but unprofitable truffle hunt in the woods near San Giovanni d'Asso, led by a guide and hunters who seem impervious to the cold. A black thread has come loose from the guide's cap and hangs over his face unnoticed, so intent is he on his explanatory lecture. "With his large objectives," Bellow explains, "he didn't notice trifles" (p. 257). Here, too, there are noteworthy animals: three dogs, Lola, Fiamma, and Iori. Although the ground is frozen, the dogs "will sniff out a truffle under a foot and a half of earth. . . . Hurrying after them, you find yourself breathing deeper, drawing in the pungent winter smells of vegetation and turned-up soil." The hunt yields a mere three truffles. Before getting into the car, Bellow and Janis shake hands with the guide and the other hunters. Their ungloved hands "are warmer than ours. For all our leather and wool and Thinsulate." On the drive back to Montalcino, "we consider the mystery of the truffle. Why is it so highly prized? We try to put a name to the musk that fills the car. It is digestive, it is sexual, it is a mortality odor." Bellow is no fan. "Having tasted it, I am willing to leave it to the connoisseurs. I shall go on sprinkling grated cheese on my pasta" (pp. 259–60). So the piece ends.

For all its pleasures, the Italian jaunt was fatiguing. But instead of flying home, Bellow and Janis flew to Israel, for two or so weeks in Jerusalem, from December 16 to January 3, 1992. Here they saw old friends (David and Shula Shahar, Judith Herzberg, Dennis Silk), relatives (Nota Gordin, Lisa Westreich and her daughter, Sabina Mazursky), and assorted notables (Nathan Sharansky, the mayor of Bethlehem, and the director of the Jerusalem Museum, who took them on a private tour). Bellow gave a reading of "Something to Remember Me By" to a large audience at Mishkenot, where, apart from a visit to the Auerbachs at their kibbutz, Sdot Yam, they stayed throughout. Teddy Kollek, ever "the schemer, the finagler, the arranger," once again treated them royally, while pressing Bellow to write a book "using the concept of the ties of Jews of the Diaspora to Jerusalem . . . a fascinating subject. It would be good if it could appear by the end of 1995."[14] In a letter to John Auerbach on March 2, 1992, Bellow described the return to Chicago:

> I took to my bed for some weeks—most of January—with accumulated fatigue. Then there were more weeks of testing—medical knocking and rapping, blood tests and tubes in the esophagus, prostate examinations. From all this I came out relatively clean. An increase in quinine doses and a new prescription for reading glasses. They (the doctors) say, "You're in good condition," and they add "for a man of your age."

A YEAR LATER, five months after the death of Allan Bloom, Bellow and Janis took up François Furet's invitation to come to Paris for a quarter, from March to May 17, 1993. A comfortable apartment was found for them on the Left Bank, at 141 Rue Raymond Losserand, in the Fourteenth Arrondissement. It belonged to the American poet William Jay Smith, and, though hardly luxurious, it was good for writing. As usual, Bellow worked at home every morning, while Janis exercised, shopped, prepared meals, walked through every quartier in the city, often retracing her steps with Bellow in the afternoon. She also wrote a review in *Bostonia* magazine of Philip Roth's *Operation Shylock*, which she and Bellow thought had been "unfairly manhandled by the press."[15] After lunch, when not retracing Janis's morning walks, they strolled through the Luxembourg Gardens to the École des Hautes Études, where Bellow's teaching duties are recalled by her as "not taxing" ("several lectures at the Raymond Aron Institute," is how he described them to Teddy Kollek, in a letter of February 26, 1993), or visited places they especially enjoyed: the Picasso Museum, the Marais, St-Germain. At night, there were dinners with Harold "Kappy" Kaplan, his old Northwestern friend Julian Behrstock, Furet, and other Paris acquaintances and friends. But there were also quiet evenings at home or at a favorite local brasserie, L'Univers, in the Rue d'Alésia.

Twice in April the Bellows left Paris for brief excursions. The rector of the Collegium Budapest invited Bellow to give a talk entitled "Intellectuals in the Period of the Cold War." They were put up for three nights, April 2–4, in the Hotel Gellért, overlooking the Danube, and taken to a late night performance of Handel's *Solomon*, described by Janis as "the most stirring and beautiful concert we had ever attended." (Rosamund sings a chorus from *Solomon*, having heard it "in Budapest a few months earlier," as she sweeps Chick through the water in *Ravelstein* [p. 186].) Later in the month, Bellow was invited to give a talk in Lisbon by the Fundaçao Luso-Americana, established in 1985 to further relations between Portugal and the United States. Again they were put up in splendor and entertained lavishly. At one dinner, Janis found herself seated next to Manuel Soares, the president of Portugal. A car and driver were made available to them during their stay, and they spent several nights in the nearby resort town of Sintra, where Bellow wrote outdoors and "many happy hours" were passed wandering the cliffs overlooking the sea.

The person the Bellows probably saw most of in Paris, aside from Furet, was Roger Kaplan, Kappy's son, in part the model for Kenneth Trachtenberg in *More Die of Heartbreak*. With Kappy himself, there was an element of rivalry, over women, over writing, over Kappy's Francophilia. According to Roger, "Saul felt my Dad did not work enough in developing his talent. . . . I think he felt that a life in the foreign service and the careers that followed, however much work that all represented, was a way to avoid the hard work Saul thought Dad should have done in writing."[16] With Roger, himself a writer, relations were easier, helped by the fact that he lived near the Bellows' apartment. After the death of Roger's mother, Celia, with whom Bellow was especially close, Kappy married a Frenchwoman and moved from a small rented place on the Boulevard St-Michel, which he retained, to her large apartment in a house in the Parc Monceau, on the Right Bank. Roger describes that apartment as "the most beautiful place you ever saw," and his stepmother as "behaving like a *grande dame*." Another reason for the closeness between Roger and the Bellows was that he was nearer Janis's age than most of the other people they saw in Paris.

Bellow had long encouraged Roger in his writing; after asking to see an early unpublished novel, he not only wrote him "a fabulously nice letter," but passed the novel to an editor at St. Martin's Press, a former student, though nothing came of it. In Paris that spring, Roger was working as a journalist for the *Reader's Digest*. Bellow urged him "not to let that 'lost' novel discourage me from starting another one."[17] As has been mentioned, Roger had no objection to the Kenneth Trachtenberg character in *More Die of Heartbreak*. On the contrary, "I was quite taken with the way Saul used me and my own problems. I think over the years he saw in me and my awful and comic (viewed objectively) relations with women some of his own experiences. . . . He realized very well that the stories he drew from his own experiences were universal. . . . It was scarcely me, but all kinds of men of his and my and the next and the next and the previous and the previous generations who would have these experiences."

In 1989, Roger wrote an article for the *Reader's Digest* about François Furet, to coincide with the bicentennial of the French Revolution. In addition to being a historian, Furet was a well-known public intellectual in France. For many years, he had written about contemporary politics in *L'Observateur* (later *Le Nouvel Observateur*), which he had helped found, and he had served for eight years as president of the École des Hautes Études en Sciences Sociales (1977–85). Furet was the foremost French theorist of the Revolution (as Roger saw it, "number two isn't even running on the same track"), but it took some persuading to get the *Digest* to agree to Roger's writing the article. What helped was Furet's famous formula of "*dérapage*" (from the verb *déraper*, meaning to skid out of control), used to describe the effect the Jacobins had on the Revolution once they seized control of the Assembly. Roger remembers talking about this formula with Bellow, who characterized Furet's opponents as *bien pensants*, sophists who "found all kinds of clever reasons to say it was all worth the horror, because they really wanted to hit somebody else, somebody today, you know, in their own time." He and Bellow often talked more generally about France, since, "like Saul, I have a tic about the French and how they think."[18] Bellow thought Roger should write a book about France.

> "Just write a first paragraph and get it going," he said. " 'France is a country in Western Europe whose capital is Paris. When I arrived here a few years ago, the Socialists were in power, and they were interested in staying in power more than in applying socialist policies.' That's it. There's your lead. The reader knows right off you are writing on France and more specifically you are writing about the end of the doctrinaire left. . . . It isn't easy. You just have to have confidence you will get it done. Look, it is not the most interesting theme in the world, let's face it, but I have always liked what you have written and I see no reason why you shouldn't make something with all this data you have collected."

Roger had been an undergraduate at the University of Chicago and did graduate work in the Department of Theology. But he knew and was taught by a number of people in the Committee on Social Thought, and he and Bellow sometimes discussed them. What he remembered of Shils is that he was "fantastically brilliant and often very funny in a deadpan way." He knew nothing of the chill between Shils and Bellow until Bellow told him of it. He admired Mircea Eliade, and in discussion with Bellow was upset to learn of Eliade's support for the fascist Iron Guard in the 1930s and 1940s. There were lots of stories about Bloom. When Bloom came to Paris, flush from the success of *The Clos-*

ing of the American Mind, he and Roger saw a fair bit of each other. He was "like Groucho Marx," Roger remembers, living in a palatial duplex apartment near the U.S. Embassy, excitedly showing off "the kinds of beds you see in French castles and Hollywood movies," "the most ornate bathroom I had ever seen," "the rustic kitchen with the latest equipment." Roger noticed a copy of Plato's *Republic* on a small table next to the bathtub. "You know, I always wanted to study business," Bloom declared, "but there's so much more money teaching philosophy. I couldn't afford to pass it up." When Roger was asked to host a *Reader's Digest* dinner for Bloom, he and the guest of honor spent the evening cracking "outrageous jokes." "Allan and I had an uproarious time," Roger remembers, "but it was a disaster." People thought they were making inside jokes. Bloom kept "talking with food in his mouth and spilling wine all over the place," to the horror of the wife of Roger's boss, a prim matron from a conservative Catholic family. "It was the beginning of my falling out of favor," Roger believes. When he asked Bellow what Bloom thought of him, Bellow answered, "He was quite fond of you, about as fond as he could be of a young man who did not know Greek and did not study philosophy."

Bellow's manner with Roger was avuncular, like Benn's with Kenneth in *More Die of Heartbreak*. After Roger told him of a second awkward moment with the boss's wife, Bellow urged caution. He also spoke respectfully of the *Reader's Digest*, which surprised Roger. "You can't be juvenile in an important job like this," he recalls that Bellow warned him. "These people take their jobs seriously. They should, too. Don't underestimate them or what they do." Roger was struck again on this visit by how carefully Bellow chose his words, especially about Bloom, how level his tone was, how clearly expressed his opinions were. Janis also had advice for Roger—it was "not nice" to let colleagues think you were mocking them—advice Roger took seriously. "Janis is extremely sensitive about that. She had antennae that could detect the line between meanness and humor. She was really good at that." Much of the advice Bellow gave Roger, or the support he offered him, concerned his problems with women. At the time of the Bellows' stay in Paris, Roger owned an apartment on the Boulevard St-Michel. He also kept a small studio off the Rue de l'Ouest, a few blocks from the apartment Bellow and Janis had rented. He was now sleeping on a pull-out couch in the studio, having been kicked out of the other apartment by his second wife, Nancy, the mother of their son, Josh. During the Bellows' stay, Nancy asked Roger to give them her phone number: "I thought about it for a while and gave it to Saul without comment. He did not comment either and did not call her."

On their first night in Paris, Roger took Bellow and Janis to dinner at a local Vietnamese restaurant, "for months the only place I ate at." "I wouldn't eat anywhere else, either," said Bellow after their meal. The restaurant was a favorite of Roger's current girlfriend, Rabia, who also lived in the neighborhood, and whom the Bellows, Janis in particular, would see much of in the coming months. Rabia, an Arab woman from Algeria, was a professor of sociology. The Bellows pumped Roger about her, "smiling as I hemmed and ah'ed." He described her as "very cute . . . but ferocious when roused." "I have no confidence in sociology Ph.D.s in general," he added, "but she's an exception." He told them of her "crazy ideas about Zionism and international Jews. 'La Juiverie internationale,' she would say. But she said it with such heavy sarcasm that you knew it was complete and utter nonsense, she had just not figured out what else it was. . . . She knew it was a lie but she did not know what the truth was."

Politics notwithstanding, Rabia and Janis became friends. The day after they met, Rabia walked over to Rue Raymond Losserand in the morning, and while Bellow read the *International Herald Tribune*, she told Janis which butchers to use in the neighborhood, where the better *boulangerie* was, which were the best wine stores and markets. Later, she took her to the *marché découvert* and pointed out the best stands. To illustrate what he liked about Rabia, Roger tells a story about his deafness, a characteristic shared by Kenneth in *More Die of Heartbreak*. "I always hated talking about myself," he writes, "but I often met girls who wanted to know about me. . . . Girls are nosy creatures, like spies and tabloid reporters." Instead of describing himself, "both the public me or the private me," or explaining his hearing problems, Roger sometimes told them to read Bellow's novel, where "you'll learn more about me than you ever could by listening to my evasions." If a woman had no idea who Bellow was, or no interest in reading him, "I knew in advance our fling wasn't going anywhere." Rabia was no such woman. As for the deafness, "one of the things I liked about Rabia was that (in this she foreshadowed the African girls I successively fell in love with), she did not seem to give a hoot."

Roger was aware that the Bellows had a wider social life, "were taken to fancy places by Furet and whoever Furet delegated," or by people Bellow knew "from way back and all over," but his impression was that they preferred staying close to home, eating at L'Univers, or climbing the stairs to Rabia's tiny apartment, where she served "something simple and delicious." At 141 Rue Raymond Losserand, Bellow worked on the lectures he owed Furet and "the important work he was starting on Allan." In the late afternoon, he and Roger sometimes met at a local café, while Janis and Rabia were "out carousing or shopping or having fun." Roger suspects that Bellow had begun writing his book about Bloom, "but he had not figured it out yet. It seemed to me he was thinking about a memoir or a biography, or both together. But the event was close and I did not think he was ready to decide for sure what form this book would take." (He heard nothing of Bellow's two unfinished novels, "Case" and "Marbles.") Janis's memories of the Paris stay confirm Roger's impression that simple pleasures were those that mattered: strolling, arm in arm, through the city, walking home at night after dinner without fear, an impossibility in Hyde Park. The Paris spring, with its little embedded holidays, was for Janis "the most free and enjoyable time of our lives."

THE DANGERS OF HYDE PARK influenced the decision Bellow and Janis made to leave Chicago, a decision they arrived at in the months after Bloom's death. In Paris, that spring, Bellow wrote to friends to say that he had finally agreed to take up John Silber's offer to become a University Professor at Boston University.[19] He and Janis would be returning to Chicago on May 17 to pack their belongings and move them to Vermont and Boston. John Silber had waited only a matter of weeks after Bloom's death in October to approach Bellow with a new offer. Bellow took a while to reply, but on December 27, 1992, he wrote encouragingly. The offer was "splendid" and "generous," the effect it had on him was to make "my whole life flash before me like the experience of the drowning." There were, however, matters to consider:

> Problems of moving and resettlement arise. And then as I grow older I think of reducing the time spent in teaching.
>
> Since Boston and BU have a great many attractions, would it be possible to teach half-time? I could make the public appearances—I don't mind those too much, and it would be agreeable to live in Brookline or the Back Bay. Would it be possible to find a teaching

> position for Janis? She has just gotten her Ph.D. while studying in the Committee on Social Thought. She taught college courses in political theory and also in literature, and she would be ideally suited for your undergraduate Humanities program.

Silber quickly dealt with these problems, offering Janis a job and Bellow a salary of $155,000 to teach two courses a year, both in the period from January to June, spring being mud season in Vermont.

When the University of Chicago learned of Silber's offer, it made efforts to match it. Robert Pippin's understanding of these efforts, drawn "from those on the inside," is that Hanna Gray, the president of the university, offered pretty much the same salary and teaching load, and that the only differences between the offers concerned secretarial help and the nature of the teaching position Janis would be given. On paper, the position offered her at BU looked better, though in the end, Pippin believes, it may not have been. Some observers thought that Hanna Gray could have been more accommodating, though her letters to Bellow, at least those I have seen, are warm and friendly. Bellow's decision to accept Silber's offer was communicated to Gray in a letter of April 25, 1993, from Paris. Although some friends suggested that he felt he had been neglected by the university, this is not what the letter suggests.[20]

> Dear Hanna,
>
> As of June 30th I am resigning from the University. This, after thirty years or more, makes my heart very heavy. I have always been happy in my situation and will always think of the Committee on Social Thought as my intellectual home. I shall miss my colleagues—David Grene, Nathan Tarcov, François Furet—and friends like the Kleinbards. My resignation is not due to any dissatisfaction with the University, which has shown me nothing but generosity.
>
> I feel that I must leave the city. It has become unendurably difficult. I am less and less able, at my age, to cope with the streets. So I have decided to end my life where it began, on the Eastern seaboard. I can get away from Boston to Vermont as often as I need to. After dinner I can walk without fear on the country roads. I hope to find as much intelligent conversation as I may require in my declining years.

With thanks for your many kindnesses and best wishes for the future.

Yours sincerely,
Saul Bellow

The same day, Bellow sent Jonathan Kleinbard a copy of the letter, along with a personal note describing it as "largely true. I can't cope with Chicago. A month in Paris had brought back to me the life I knew in the past—free movement, peaceable crowds in parks. . . . I don't feel like breathing my last in the Maginot Line (5825, Apt 11E)." The note hints at other reasons for the decision. "Allan said to me, 'You're planning the moves you'll make when I die.' That was a bad moment for me, but he was right of course, and I was silent. But after a time I said, 'Yes, but I'll be catching up with you soon enough.' He agreed with that and we went back to discussing the Bulls' chances against the Knicks." On May 24, after failing to persuade Bellow to stay, Hanna Gray wrote to say that she was "very sad that you are leaving." Although "no one could understand better than I the attraction of being so close to Vermont . . . it is a great loss for your colleagues and for the University, and a real personal loss as well." On May 12, David Grene wrote to express "great sorrow that you had at last decided on Boston," and to assure Bellow that their friendship of over thirty years "won't dissolve." Nevertheless, "the joy in it gets diminished by not having the fruits of it, in the every-now-and-then lunches and the times at meetings of CST, and otherwise, when I could find you on my side. Not at all least when we taught together both in the old days, quite long ago, and in the last three or four years with Allan . . . Please give Janis my dear love and tell her that I will miss her bitterly also."

By May 24, the news of Bellow's decision had reached the newspapers. Eugene Kennedy wrote an article about it in the *Chicago Tribune* headlined "Say It Isn't So: Another Legend Leaves Chicago." Two days later, in *The Chicago Maroon*, Richard Stern was quoted offering reasons for Bellow's decision: the closeness of Boston to Vermont, a lighter teaching load, the effect of his recent stay in Paris. "These things are not defined," he added. "You decide at a certain time of your life to move on. He's a marvelous, unique man and we've been lucky to have him here, but maybe Boston should have a shot at him."[21] Before the decision, in a letter of April 24, Bette Howland emphasized the part Janis's needs played in Bellow's decision. "I've thought all along you

Nathan Tarcov at thirty-five, professor at the Committee on Social Thought, the Department of Political Science, the Committee on Social Relations, and the College at the University of Chicago, 1983 (courtesy of *The Chicago Maroon;* photo by Patricia Evans)

Allan Bloom in Chicago, 1987 (courtesy of Paul Merideth)

Leo Strauss, professor in the Department of Political Science, University of Chicago, undated (courtesy of the Special Collections Research Center, University of Chicago Library)

A partial gathering of faculty of the Committee on Social Thought, 1987. Back row: Edward H. Levi (law), Karl J. Weintraub (history). Next row down: Ralph Lerner (political philosophy), Anthony Yu (literature and religion), Leon Kass (science, medicine, education), Paul Wheatley (geography). Next row down: A. K. Ramanujan (poet, scholar of literature and religion), James Redfield (classicist). Next row down: David Grene (classicist), Allan Bloom (political philosophy). Next row down: SB and Wendy Doniger (Indian religion and mythology). (courtesy of Paul Merideth)

SB and Ada Aharoni, poet and literary scholar, organizer of the 1987 conference on Bellow at the University of Haifa, April 1987 (courtesy of Ada Aharoni)

SB, Shimon Peres, and a University of Haifa official, April 1987 (courtesy of Ada Aharoni)

SB and Teddy Kollek, Jerusalem, April 1987 (courtesy of the Max Jacoby Estate; photo by Max Jacoby)

SB receiving the National Medal of Arts from President Reagan, August 9, 1998 (courtesy of the University of Chicago News Office; photo by Mary-Anne Fackleman-Miner/The White House)

Mark Harris, 1984, author of *Saul Bellow, Drumlin Woodchuck* (1980), an attempted biography (courtesy of Neil Boenzi/New York Times/Redux/eyevine)

Ruth Miller, Boston, 1987, before falling out with SB over *Saul Bellow: A Biography of the Imagination* (1991) (courtesy of the Geddes Language Center, Boston University)

James Atlas, 2016, author of *Bellow: A Biography* (2000) (courtesy of Pantheon Books; photo by Michael Lionstar)

Brent Staples, author and editorial writer for *The New York Times*, New York, 2005 (courtesy of Fred Conrad/New York Times/Redux/eyevine)

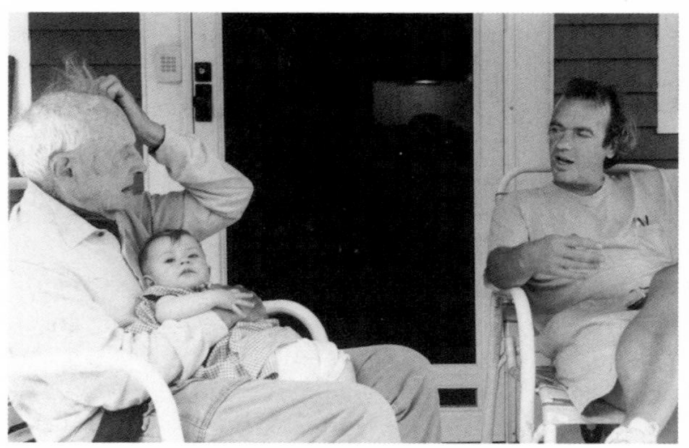

SB, Rosie, and Martin Amis, Vermont, summer 2000
(courtesy of Isabel Fonseca)

Cynthia Ozick, who described her feelings for Bellow as "something more than admiration, something closer to adoration" (courtesy of Nancy Crampton)

James Wood and SB, c. 2000
(courtesy of James Wood)

Ruth Wisse and SB, 2001, Brookline
(courtesy of Ruth Wisse; photo by Janis Bellow)

SB and Chris Walsh in front of the Crowninshield Road house, Brookline, mid-1990s (courtesy of Chris Walsh; photo by Janis Bellow)

SB and Keith Botsford, Boston University, early 2000s (courtesy of Keith Botsford)

Crowninshield Road house, Brookline, 2017 (courtesy of Asaf Galay; photo by Asaf Galay)

John Silber in his office at Boston University (courtesy of Getty Images, Rick Friedman)

Guests assembled outside the Vermont house the day after SB's surprise seventy-fifth birthday party (courtesy of Janis Bellow)

SB, Richard Stern, and Alane Rollings (courtesy of Alane Rollings; photo by Janis Bellow)

SB and Philip Roth on the Connecticut River, Brattleboro, Vermont, 1998 (courtesy of Cella Manea and the Wylie Agency)

Dave Peltz at ninety-four, still driving, Chicago, 2009 (courtesy of Alice Leader)

Stephanie Nelson and Janis Bellow as they were awarded Ph.D.s, with David Grene and SB, University of Chicago, 1993 (courtesy of Janis Bellow)

Roger Kaplan and daughter Chloe, Paris, early 1990s (courtesy of Roger Kaplan)

SB and Janis, with Janis's parents, Sonia and Harvey Freedman, in the background and Rosie, barely visible, between them, undated (courtesy of Janis Bellow)

François Furet of the Committee on Social Thought and the École des Hautes Études en Sciences Sociales, Paris, undated (courtesy of Sygma via Getty Images; photo by David Niviere/Kipa)

Greg Bellow in 2005, the year of SB's death (courtesy of Greg Bellow)

Juliet Bellow, late 1990s (courtesy of Daniel Bellow)

Janis and SB, Brookline, 1996 (courtesy of Thomas Barnard)

SB's grave, Morningside Cemetery, Brattleboro, Vermont, 2008 (courtesy of Alice Leader)

should go to Boston, because, though your choices weren't so clear, it seemed clearly better for Janis. That was good and sufficient reason, but there is more to it. The central question is making a life, now, for the two of you. I've seen your life in Chicago, and I've seen your life in Vermont, and Vermont is better," a comparison, she admits, that's not "entirely fair." In Vermont, "Alexandra isn't in the picture; there is something very satisfactory about the way things play out.—You built the house to appease a woman who couldn't be appeased; now you have it to make another woman happy. . . . Anyway, you will be doing this, whatever you do, because you want to make Janis happy; and the experience will be blessed."

In 1999, looking back on the decision at the age of eighty-four, Bellow offered Norman Manea other reasons for the move.

> When people asked me why are you leaving Chicago, I said because I can't walk down the street any more without thinking of my Dead, and it was time. I had a girlfriend here or went to a party there or attended a meeting there and so forth. Most of the people whom I had known so well and loved so well were gone, and I didn't want to be occupying a cemetery. Because that was how it was beginning to feel. There was also another angle. That is to say, I had become a cultural big shot in the town. I didn't really like to play that role. I thought there was something very bad about it. I didn't want to be idolized by people for whom I had no respect. . . . Just didn't want to play their game, to any degree. Because I knew them too well. So I thought, let's have a new cast of characters.[22]

By the time of this interview, David Peltz, Bellow's oldest friend, had fallen out with him, for reasons that will be discussed in chapter 13. When asked by Atlas to explain Bellow's move to Boston, Peltz offered exactly the opposite reason from the one Bellow gave to Manea: "fresh adoration." Atlas also quotes the reaction of Bellow's bookseller friend, Stuart Brent: "Who will you have to talk Yiddish with? Not those *farshtinkener* Goyim."[23] To which Bellow might have answered, Ruth Wisse, professor of Yiddish at Harvard, among others.

AT THE END OF MAY, over the Memorial Day weekend, Bellow attended the sixtieth reunion of the Tuley High School Class of 1933.

After lunch, he gave a brief speech to 124 of his fellow graduates. The speech was in praise of their teachers. Bellow looked terrible, worn out from recent travels and the emotional and other difficulties associated with relocation. "It was Janis who actually moved us," he wrote to John and Chantel Hunt on August 5, 1993, from Vermont. "I was spared the worst. My end of the deal was to keep anarchy from overwhelming us. I didn't do at all well at my detail." To Julian Behrstock, on August 18, Bellow confessed that he hadn't fully appreciated his stay in Paris "until we arrived in Chicago on a particularly *morne* [dismal] afternoon, got into a taxi cab stinking like a latrine and plunged through the bungalow belt. . . . I turned to Janis and said, 'This ain't Paris!'" In his short stay in Chicago, "I visited a few doctors." He and Janis flew to Boston directly after the Tuley reunion, then drove to Vermont. Two weeks later, Janis returned to Chicago to complete the move. Then they set about finding a place to live near BU, a process that Bellow says took "a few months." "Under such circumstances one doesn't get much work done." In addition to news, the letter to Behrstock conveys warm feelings. Behrstock was one more person Bellow was determined to keep from "the warehouse of intentions." "Although I have always enjoyed your company," he wrote, "our recent encounters moved me very much. I thought that I already knew how gently, quietly intelligent you were. Well, you were even more so this time. Or maybe we feel these things more as we grow older."

Shortly after Bellow's arrival in Vermont, he received a letter of June 4 from Nathan Tarcov, in his capacity as chair of the Committee on Social Thought, formally extending "the invitation I made to you last week." He asked Bellow to return to Chicago for a week next autumn, perhaps in November, to give an informal two or three seminars to Committee students on "some short text you would like to talk about with us. It would surely be the highpoint of the Committee's year, give your many friends in the Committee a chance to see you, and help us all to take your departure as less of a rupture." Bellow accepted the invitation, and returned to Chicago early in November, when he also unveiled the bust of himself that Mayor Daley had promised to commission and install in the recently opened Harold Washington Library Center, the main Chicago public library. Two hundred people attended the unveiling ceremony, over which the mayor presided. Bellow approved the bust, but joked that he was "sorry Picasso wasn't around to do one of me with two noses. For one nose, it's fine."[24] He then flew on to the University of Iowa, where he lectured to Frank Conroy's writing group, and to Toronto, where he and Janis visited her parents, and he delivered the convocation address at the University of Toronto.

THE BOSTON RESIDENCE the university made available to the Bellows was an apartment at 73 Bay State Road, a few doors down from the palatial apartment they'd lived in during the autumn of 1989. The new apartment was also palatial; Silber would eventually take it over himself. The *Chicago Tribune* described it as "baronial," with a grand staircase, high ceilings, polished wooden floors, plush rugs. Bellow told the *Tribune* it was "almost too grand." His office, in contrast, on the sixth floor of a nondescript building housing the Department of Theology, was described in the *Tribune* as "grimy," with "cardboard boxes on the worn purple carpet. It felt like the office of a cheap detective."[25] On September 21, Bellow made one of the public appearances he had told Silber he "didn't mind . . . too much," addressing the Inaugural Convocation of the Boston University Academy, the university's equivalent of the Lab School at Chicago, on the topic of education. Once again, Bellow began autobiographically, with his years at Tuley High School, but he soon went on to lament current trends: the marginal role of literature in modern culture, the malign influence of historicism and cultural relativism in universities.

In January 1994, when spring term began, Bellow taught an undergraduate lecture course entitled "An Idiosyncratic Survey of Modern Literature." "I've never taught this sort of class before," Bellow admitted. "I got tired of having people say to me, 'You old-timers never pay attention to the younger contemporary writers.'" The course met on Wednesday afternoons for two hours and was devoted to novels by "living writers I find especially interesting." Among the novels assigned were Denis Johnson's *Resuscitation of a Hanged Man* (1991), Cormac McCarthy's *The Orchard Keeper* (1965), Martin Amis's *Money* (1984), and Philip Roth's *Operation Shylock* (1993). As with his courses at the University of Chicago, students wishing to attend had first to be interviewed by him. There were some twenty-five students in the course, undergraduates and graduate students, plus a few auditors, Janis among them, and although Bellow mostly lectured, he also answered questions. One student, Josh London, a senior English major, described Bellow as "very relaxed, very accessible. . . . Everyone's given ample time for their opinions, whether they agree with him or not."[26]

Another student, Chris Walsh, in the second year of a Ph.D. program in American studies, became an important figure in Bellow's life. After graduating from the University of Rochester, Walsh spent two years in the Peace Corps in Africa. While in Africa, he read all of Bellow's novels he could lay his hands on, starting, naturally enough, with *Henderson the Rain King*. In 1992, he came to BU, and in the next academic year signed up for Bellow's first course: "Rarely has a student been so well prepared to write a paper for Saul Bellow." The preparation paid off; Bellow was impressed with Walsh's work, and in the spring, at the end of the course, invited him up to Brattleboro "for a beer." They talked about politics, Walsh remembers, and when he asked Bellow why he bothered keeping up with them, he was struck by the answer: "Well, as a novelist you have to." In the summer, Walsh was invited up to Vermont a second time, and brought his girlfriend. The visit was relaxed and friendly. Next academic year, in the spring of 1995, Walsh audited a Bellow course on Conrad, and at some point that semester Bellow asked him if he could recommend anyone to replace his secretary, who was leaving in the summer to join a jazz group in New York. As Walsh remembers it, "I wound up appointing myself." His job title was as "personal assistant" or "executive secretary"; Bellow assured him he'd be able to write his dissertation, adding that he expected him to go on "to great things." His duties were to deal with correspondence, type manuscripts (including the whole of *Ravelstein*), keep the checkbook, drive Bellow to social and other appointments, and let him know who had called or come to the office.

Walsh was struck by how robust Bellow was for a man of seventy-eight, his age in 1994, when they first met. When crossing the street, Bellow "wasn't one to heed traffic; he sort of barreled along." He was also "very down-to-earth," "a small-'d' democrat with other people—the electrician, for example." Bellow was drawn to Walsh, he told him, because he wasn't "cultic," by which he meant "professionalized," the kind of graduate student who used expressions like "resonant paradigms." Like all the students and secretaries who worked for Bellow, Walsh thought him a good boss, considerate, never rude or angry to underlings or employees. He remembers no illiberal remarks, and the only comment about race he recalls was when Bellow expressed "great disappointment" at learning of a racist remark made by one of the

Southern Agrarian writers (which one Walsh cannot remember). As they got to know each other better, Walsh came to recognize a wary or embattled side to Bellow's character, his sense that forces were ranged against him. He would joke about this, but he was also serious. "There's a big black line running down the middle of my life," he told Walsh, "and you're either on one side or another." Janis shared this them-or-us sense.

The Bellows saw a number of old friends in Boston: Monroe and Brenda Engel, Eugene Goodheart, Ruth Wisse. They also saw a good deal of Keith and Nathalie Botsford. Nathalie, Keith's second wife, was French, but she grew up in New Jersey and lived for long periods in London and Paris. She met Botsford in Paris in 1984, while working as a translator at *Grand Prix* magazine. Botsford had moved to London in 1971, to become a full-time journalist (when Silber brought him to BU, it was as a professor of journalism). He was a sports reporter for the *Sunday Times*—hence the visit to *Grand Prix*—a food columnist for the *Independent*, and a features writer and U.S. correspondent for *La Stampa*. As Nathalie remembered it, a taxi was booked to pick him up and take him to the airport after his visit to *Grand Prix*. He was off to Goa, he told her, "to marry a child bride, because he was fed up with uppity Western women." The taxi never arrived, he missed his flight, and he and Nathalie went to a nearby café for a drink. After what she remembered as "a couple of bottles of wine," Nathalie volunteered that she "didn't think his child bride would like life in London with Keith and his seven kids [five from his first wife, who described marriage to him as "like taking a course in comparative gynaecology"] and that he should marry me instead, and he agreed." They were married a week later, eventually moved into an old stone house in Italy, a disused mill, cold and drafty, where "we were broke all the time." Silber rescued them in 1988 when he hired Botsford to teach at BU. That autumn, they moved to Boston with their son, Thomas, Botsford's eighth child.

Nathalie was interesting on the relations between Bellow and Botsford. "I'm a snob and Saul was a snob," Botsford declared in an interview. "If someone said they'd been to the symphony," Nathalie recalled, "Keith would say, 'I can't possibly go to the symphony in this country.'" Or he'd say, "I never go to the theater in this country, not after the theater in London in the 1940s." "It was always better somewhere you couldn't possibly get to yourself" (Walsh remembers Botsford telling him, "You wouldn't have stood out at Chicago"). Bellow's snobbery, Nathalie thinks, was different. "He could veer between being very approachable and very haughty and arrogant, and I believe Keith brought out the haughty, arrogant side of Saul—there was a little bit of a sense of always having to put Keith in his place." Once, at a dinner party, Nathalie accused Botsford of having a streak of anti-Semitism. "Keith looked horrified and said, 'I can't believe you said that,' and Saul said, 'Well, I understand why she said it. It's true.'"[27] Once, she heard Bellow call Botsford "his sidekick, and Keith was very offended," having "always struggled to accept that he'd never made it as Bellow had." "Keith revered him," Christopher Ricks recalls, "but you don't have to be Harold Bloom to think that there is a parricidal side to these things."

There was genuine affection between the two men, as there was affection in Nathalie's and Walsh's memories of Botsford. "It was fascinating being married to Keith," Nathalie said, "and had there not been a child involved I probably could have continued to be married to him."[28] Bellow was drawn to Botsford not only because they went back so far but because of his great stories, a number of which are true or partly true. Bellow admired Botsford's nerve and originality, his flouting of rules, his erudition and talents. Botsford really does, as he claims, speak many languages (he reads eleven, he told *The New York Times*), know the literatures of most European countries, write concertos and choral works as well as novels. He really did work in the theater with John Houseman and train as a lawyer in London. Janis remembers how he would recommend writers one had never heard of, and how they invariably turned out to be worth reading. In literary conversations with Bellow, Nathalie believed, "Keith brought an international dimension." This dimension is seen in his lineage as well as in his exotic life. On his mother's side, one quickly learns, he is a direct descendant of Machiavelli; his father, Willard Hudson Botsford, was a tennis-playing American expatriate who lived in Brussels (where Keith was born) and London. According to Botsford, "He kept his own plane at Croydon and flew to his matches. He won the Coupe Lambert (Belgian Rothschilds) against Gottfried von Cramm . . . played doubles with [Bill] Tilden, and slaughtered [Jean] Borotra." The Botsford family immigrated to America in 1639 and "founded Connecticut."[29]

Bellow has great fun with Botsford in *Humboldt's Gift*, where he becomes Charlie Citrine's pal Pierre Thaxter. When Thaxter fails to pay his share of a defaulted loan, Charlie forgives him, explaining, "I love Thaxter, whatever he does."

> Broke but grandiose [Thaxter] had ordered a check from his Italian bank for me, the Banco Ambrosiano of Milan. Why the Banco? Why Milan? But all of Thaxter's arrangements were out of the ordinary. He had had a transatlantic upbringing and was equally at home in France and California. You couldn't mention a region so remote that Thaxter didn't have an uncle there, or an interest in a mine, or an old château or villa. . . . Thaxter wanted people to believe that he was once a CIA agent. It was a wonderful rumor and he did everything to encourage it. It greatly added to his mysteriousness, and mystery was one of his little rackets. This was harmless and in fact endearing. It was even philanthropic, as charm always is—up to a point. Charm is always a bit of a racket [pp. 75–76].

When Charlie receives a letter from Thaxter, whose letters, like Botsford's, are often very long, he imagines it being written "in his orange grove near Palo Alto where he sat thinking in a canvas officer's chair. He wore a black carabiniere cloak, his feet were bare, he drank Pepsi-Cola, he had eight or ten children, he owed money to everyone, and he was a cultural statesman. Adoring women treated him like a man of genius, believed all that he told them, typed his manuscripts, gave birth to his kids, brought him Pepsi-Cola to drink" (p. 195).

Although unreliable, Thaxter is trusted with Charlie's confidences. "Whenever Thaxter and I met we had at least one intimate conversation. I spoke freely to him and let myself go. In spite of his eccentric nonsense, and my own, there was a bond between us. I was able to talk to Thaxter. At times I told myself that talking to him was as good for me as psychoanalysis. Over the years, the cost had been about the same" (p. 270). Botsford was untroubled by his depiction as Pierre Thaxter: "A tiny part of me had been transformed magically, into a character in a novel, enlarged upon, recreated."[30] During Bellow's Boston years, they taught together and even started a successor to the earlier periodicals, *The Noble Savage* and *Anon*. They would publish *News from the Republic of Letters* "as long as we have good enough material to fill it." A statement on the contents page of their new collaboration reads: "If you would like to acquire your citizenship, Saul Bellow and Keith Botsford welcome your adherence."[31]

The Botsfords entertained frequently at their home in Dorchester, a suburb of Boston described by Nathalie as "*un quartier mal formé.*" Before their first dinner party for Bellow and Janis, the guest of honor telephoned to ask where Keith was, expecting him to guide them personally to the house. Nathalie answered that she thought he "had given you directions and that you'd find your way," to which Bellow replied, " 'Oh, in that case let's just forget it.' That's the arrogant side of Saul." At dinner, Nathalie said she was serving rabbit. Bellow told her he didn't eat rabbit. Fortunately, she had leftovers from a veal stew, a blanquette de veau, which she heated up for him. He was "very impressed." Among the guests the Bellows saw at the Botsfords' were Christopher Ricks and his wife, the photographer Judith Aronson; John and Kathryn Silber; the novelist Claire Messud and the critic James Wood; and Roger Shattuck and his wife, Nora, an ex–ballet dancer. The Bellows "tended to arrive quite early and to leave early." Nathalie was pleased when she heard Bellow say of her, "She doesn't talk much but she says a lot." That he liked Nathalie "leavened some of Saul's irritation with Keith." At parties, she was struck by the way Bellow "had no need to make himself the center of attraction." This quality Christopher Ricks also noted and approved, along with Bellow's "desire not to talk about his work. He wanted to talk about other great writers." "Remarkably," Ricks adds, he and Bellow never had a disagreement in these talks; Bellow never took him to task, even over his defense of T. S. Eliot against the charge of anti-Semitism.[32] "Bellow was a great anecdotalist," Ricks believes, as opposed to someone who liked literary argument. He enjoyed Ricks's company and was interested in him, Janis believes, because Ricks is clever and funny. It helped also that they were both, as Ricks puts it, "*persona non grata* with members of the English Department"—for what he calls "complicated reasons, some having to do with their deeply disliking Silber, or, rather, shallowly disliking him."

ON DECEMBER 1, 1993, Bellow wrote a letter to the MacArthur Foundation supporting Alfred Kazin's nomination for a fellowship. Kazin's curriculum vitae, which Bellow said he had never seen before, "was impressive," and though he didn't always agree with his views, "I read him with respect. . . . His work is first rate." The unnamed person who nominated Kazin compared him to Edmund Wilson, but Wilson, Bellow wrote, "did not always read contemporary literature; he frequently declared that he had no patience with most of it. Kazin has always been much more open and hospitable to innovation. I urge the Selection Committee to be generous with him." Given their recent disagreements, Bellow's letter was itself generous. Six weeks later, on January 14, 1994, a letter arrived from a fact checker at *The New Yorker* asking Bellow a series of questions in connection with an article by Kazin that was soon to appear in the magazine. Some of the questions were easy to answer. "Do you like teaching?" "Yes, of course." "Do you consider yourself an ex-Trotskyist?" "Yes, I am an ex-Trotskyist. I became ex in about 1937." Other questions irked him. "Do you like Reagan?" "I don't ["know him" should appear here] well enough to like or dislike. I don't froth at the mouth when his name is mentioned. I think he played a significant role in bringing the cold war to an end." In a later response about Reagan: "How I vote is none of your business." "Do you consider *The New York Times*, which publishes Anthony Lewis, is not a conservative newspaper?" "Only a nut would call the NYT a conservative paper. It's our fountainhead of liberal clichés." Bellow was not asked: "What did you mean when you said, 'Where is the Tolstoy of the Zulus? The Proust of the Papuans? I'd be glad to read him.'"

When Kazin first read these words, he tells us in "Jews," a memoir published in *The New Yorker* on March 7, 1994, "my heart sank." The words Kazin had read were in a 1988 profile of Allan Bloom in *The New York Times Magazine*. Bellow had not written them; he had spoken them, in the course of an interview with the profile's author, James Atlas, who quotes them parenthetically in a paragraph about Bloom and multiculturalism:

> Gleefully he [Bloom] shows me a clipping from *The San Francisco Examiner* that recounts the efforts of radicals at Stanford to do away with the Western civilization class on the grounds that it's racist. ("Who is the Tolstoy of the Zulus? The Proust of the Papuans?" says Bellow. "I'd be glad to read them").[33]

Few words by Bellow have done more to alienate liberal and academic opinion than these, or to banish his fiction from college syllabuses. Robert Pippin remembers being "stunned that even at the University of Chicago so many people expressed contempt for Bellow, hated him, for that remark." The impact of the remark was increased by another contemporary publication. On February 6, 1994, a month before Kazin's article appeared, *The New York Times Magazine* published an extract from a forthcoming memoir by Brent Staples entitled *Parallel Time: Growing Up in Black and White*.[34] Again, Atlas was involved, having picked out and edited the extract. Staples, an African American, also a member of the *Times*'s editorial board, had grown up in poverty, the son of an alcoholic truck driver. In the extract printed in the *Times Magazine*, he describes his years as a graduate student at the University of Chicago in the 1970s and his conflicted feelings about Bellow, whose works he revered but also recoiled from, because of their depictions of black men, particularly in *Mr. Sammler's Planet.* Staples was not literary. The dissertation he was at work on at Chicago was in psychology, on "the mathematics of decision making. The cool indifference of numbers appealed to me." In 1975, Bellow was approaching his zenith. *Humboldt's Gift*, which would win the Pulitzer Prize the next year, the year Bellow was given the Nobel Prize, had just been published, "and copies were placed in every one of the university bookstore's several windows." The novel generated "endless gossip" among Staples's circle of graduate students, especially about the supposed real-life models of its characters. Unlike other novels Staples had read, which he calls "merely" fictional, *Humboldt* was "local geography, people included." It was also, he admits, "one of the first novels I'd read of my own free will. Most of the others had been assigned in college and I'd ransacked them for facts to be used in term papers and essays."

In the extract, Staples sketches the plot of *Humboldt's Gift* and describes it as "cast as a farce." Then he says, "The novel ceases to be a farce when a black man steps out of the shadows and with no motive slits a white woman's throat. Black people in the novel were sinister characters. Rinaldo [Cantabile, "a would-be mafiosi"] refers to them as 'crazy buffaloes' and 'pork chops.' Crazy buffaloes populate the slums around Hyde Park. A pork chop chases Charlie down the middle of his street, presumably at night. These passages made me angry. It was the same anger I felt when white people cowered as I passed them in the street." As Staples knows, and documents in the extract, and as early chapters of this book have made clear, Hyde Park in the 1970s was a dangerous place, with many instances of assault, theft, and murder, crimes mostly perpetrated by young African Americans from the surrounding neighborhoods. As for "crazy buffaloes" and "pork chops," a character like Rinaldo Cantabile would hardly refer to the perpetrators of these crimes as "African Americans" or "Negroes" or even "blacks" (certainly without an accompanying profanity); "crazy buffaloes" and "pork chops" are uncomplimentary, but they are already concessions to liberal opinion. It is hardly unfair or inaccurate or racist of Bellow to have imagined as black the perpetrators of seemingly motiveless assaults and street crimes in Hyde Park. Nevertheless, Staples's anger is understandable. There are no counterbalancing black characters in the novel (though neither are there any admirable Italian Americans to counterbalance Cantabile), and little is said of the discriminatory practices that help to create these crimes, practices outlined in earlier passages from the Staples extract.

Matters are more complicated in the case of *Mr. Sammler's Planet*, where questions of race figure centrally. For Staples, as for many readers, the novel's "most vivid description," that of the black pickpocket's penis (discussed in chapter 2 of this book), returns "again and again as a symbol of spiritual decay, of the 'sexual niggerhood' that 'millions of civilized people' had deluded themselves into wanting." Given the anger and hurt the description produced in Staples, it is striking that he not only went on to read a third Bellow novel, but that he found in it something like a portrait of his world. The novel was *Dangling Man*, which "captured it all: the chrysalis character of graduate school. The idleness and sterility of Hyde Park. The vast emptiness of the wintertime streets. The ice clinging to the gutters in spring, and the desperate longing for warmth. This novel was the ground beneath my feet."

The conflicted nature of Staples's feelings about Bellow is nowhere more obvious than in the extract's most controversial passages. "I felt for Bellow what the young Charlie Citrine had felt for Von Humboldt Fleisher. I envied his luck, his talent and his fame. I wanted to be near him—but not too near. His sentiments about black people made me wary. So did the way he dissected you with his eyes." That young Charlie Citrine envied Humboldt "his luck, his talent, and his fame" we learn midway through the novel's first paragraph; by the end of the paragraph, envy and wariness fall away. "Humboldt was very kind. He introduced me to people in the Village and got me books to review. I always loved him." Young Staples wants to get close to Bellow, as Citrine wants to get close to Humboldt, but he also wants to punish Bellow. When Staples learns that Bellow's apartment at 5825 Dorchester overlooks his running route, "I envisioned him looking down at the lone runner trudging along. I raised my arm and waved."

The wave is not altogether friendly. On evening walks, Staples makes it a point to pass Bellow's building. The nearby intersection at

Fifty-Ninth and Dorchester "was the dark stretch of sidewalk where I had played the cruelest innings of Scatter the Pigeons." This game was invented as a form of revenge. Staples explains:

> I liked walking at night. I found the quadrangles tranquil and beautiful after dark, the turrets and towers lit by the autumn moon. At night, the quiet beauty was mine alone. If I had attended the official tours and lectures of orientation week, perhaps I'd have found out why. People were frightened of crime, and with good reason.

Initially, when encountering others at night, Staples would smile reassuringly. Then he realized, "I'd been grinning good evening at people who were frightened to death of me. I did violence to them by just being. . . . I kept walking at night, but from then on I paid attention. I became expert in the language of fear. . . . It occurred to me for the first time that I was big. I was 6 feet 1½ inches tall and my long hair made me look bigger."[35] In addition to smiling reassuringly, Staples took to whistling Beatles tunes or Vivaldi, which had a similarly calming effect. Then one night, for reasons he didn't understand, he stopped smiling and whistling. A couple was walking toward him, laughing and talking. As he approached them, they grew silent. Instead of giving way, he headed straight at them, forcing them to separate to avoid walking into him. "A few steps beyond them I stopped and howled with laughter. I came to call this game 'Scatter the Pigeons.'"

A security gate and steps separate visitors from 5825 Dorchester. When Staples fantasized about confronting Bellow, he wished he could do so at the base of the building, "because there were shadows there to linger in." What exactly he'd do in such a confrontation he was not sure. "Perhaps I'd lift him bodily and pin him against a wall. Perhaps I'd corner him on the stairs and take up questions about 'pork chops' and 'crazy buffaloes' and barbarous black pickpockets. I wanted to trophy his fear." After several months of what he calls "stalking," Staples finally spotted Bellow twenty yards ahead of him at Fifty-Eighth and Dorchester, "a little man in an overcoat, hurrying along the sidewalk." He could have caught up with Bellow if he'd run, but "the game was to wait for a chance to place me squarely between the tower [what he calls Bellow's building] and him. That way, he'd have to face me in the dark. This was not to be the night. He threw back a glance, wisps of white hair flying, then picked up his pace. He showed surprising bounce getting up the stairs. When I reached the tower, I saw only his shoe disappearing through the gate."[36]

Bellow was outraged when he read this description of his scurrying to safety, and he even had Walter Pozen call the *Times* to threaten suit. The effects of the extract, when combined a month later with Kazin's article, were rapid. On March 13, Bellow delivered the opening remarks at the annual Literary Lights Award fund-raising dinner for the Boston Public Library, the oldest free municipal library in the United States. He himself had received one of its awards. As Harriet Wasserman recalls in her memoir, "Preceding the ceremony by days was a column in the *Boston Globe* that began by stating that the chairman of the Literary Lights Committee had been asked to uninvite Saul as honored guest." According to the column, this request had been "prompted" by the Staples and Kazin articles.[37] After other such incidents were brought to Bellow's attention, he decided to respond. On March 10, three days after the Kazin article, he published an op-ed piece in the *Times* defending himself against accusations of racism. The title the *Times* gave the piece was "Papuans and Zulus." Bellow's decision to write the piece is explained in a letter of May 31 to Milton Hindus of Brandeis:

> My "awful" remarks about the Zulus had gone out on the networks, nationwide. MacNeil and Lehrer had asked Camille Paglia whether I wasn't a racist. All garbage, of course . . . And yet one should step up to the plate every now and then and try for a homer. So my black friend Stanley Crouch opined (do you know his essays?) and so when Brent Staples went after me in the Times a few months ago, Crouch advised me to pick up my bat and step forward.

The key point Bellow makes in his defense in the op-ed piece is that the quotation about Papuans and Zulus was taken out of context. It was made, he claims, in the course of a telephone interview with a journalist ("I can't remember who the interviewer was") and in reference to "the distinction between literate and preliterate societies." Kazin's heart sank when he read the remark in Atlas's profile of Bloom, Bellow implies, because there it looks like "an insult to Papuans and Zulus, and . . . a proof that I was at best insensitive and at worst an elitist, a reactionary and a racist—in a word, a monster." In Kazin's article, the remark is recalled in a similarly damaging context, that of Bellow's "moving right . . . like many Jewish intellectuals from the immigrant working class." No mention is made in either Kazin's article or Atlas's of the distinction between literate and preliterate cultures. Atlas remembers no such distinction being made by Bellow during their interview; the "Zulu" remark, he felt, was an allusion to the growing "culture war" debate.[38] In his op-ed piece, Bellow says nothing of Atlas's profile of Bloom, though it is hard to believe that he hadn't remembered it. As was reported in chapter 8, he told Atlas he had read and liked it; he said the same to his son Adam. It is possible that, when writing the op-ed piece, he had some other interview in mind—a telephone interview—in which he made the remark while distinguishing between literate and preliterate societies. I have found no such interview.[39] In the op-ed piece, Bellow explains why it would have been natural for him to have made such a distinction: "I was once an anthropology student . . . a pupil of the famous Africanist M. J. Herskovits, who also devoted many decades to the study of the American Negro." In fact, "immediately after the telephone interview I remembered that there was a Zulu novel after all: 'Chaka' by Thomas Mofolo, published in the early 30's. In my Herskovits days, I had read it in translation. It was a profoundly, unbearably tragic book about a tribal Achilles."

Bellow's critics had a field day with his remark, taking it, as he says in the op-ed piece, as signifying "contempt for multiculturalism and defamation of the third world. I am an elderly white male—a Jew, to boot. Ideal for their purposes." He reminds readers, "Nowhere in print, under my name, is there a single reference to Papuans or Zulus." He insists that the remark, in what he claims was its original context—a claim Atlas disputes—was neither contemptuous nor defamatory in intent: "It is no slander to describe a people as preliterate." Although he implies he was not alluding to the culture wars when making the remark, in defending it he implicitly supports Bloom's position. "Preliterate societies have their own kinds of wisdom, no doubt, and primitive Papuans probably have a better grasp of their myths than most educated Americans have of their own literature. But without years of study we can't begin to understand a culture very different from our own." Nor can it simply be assumed that we understand our own culture. "The literacy of which we are so proud often amounts to very little. You may take the word of a practicing novelist for it that not all novel readers are good readers. . . . Besides, as we all know, certain forms of literacy are decidedly repulsive."

Bellow does not name his critics. He does, however, venture the opinion that "many . . . could not locate Papua New Guinea on a map." He might also have pointed out that he had been a student of preliterate cultures throughout his life, not just at university. At the time he was writing "All Marbles Still Accounted For," a work begun before December 16, 1987, the date Atlas says he heard him make the remark about Papuans and Zulus. "Marbles" was to be partly set in New Guinea, about which, as we shall see, Bellow had been reading widely, particularly among anthropological studies. In addition to naming no critics, Bellow makes no explicit reference to accusations of racism in his fiction. What he does say, perhaps with Staples in mind, is that "the ground rules of the art of fiction are not widely understood. No writer can take for granted that the views of characters will not be attributed to him personally." He ends the op-ed piece by likening his unnamed critics to "thought-police" and "Stalinists." Nothing controversial or jokey is permitted today, all is "righteousness and rage." "As a onetime anthropologist, I know a taboo when I see one. Open discussion of many major public questions has for some time now been taboo. We can't open our mouths without being denounced as racists, misogynists, supremacists, imperialists or fascists."

In the week in which Bellow's op-ed piece appeared, Sarah Lyall referred to it in a "Book Notes" column in *The New York Times Book Review*.[40] Bellow "seemed to feel quite put upon," she notes. Staples, her colleague, "finds himself under attack, too, both for his account of following Mr. Bellow and for his views, which he says are misunderstood. (The New Republic called him a 'political corrector.')"[41] Staples points out that his memoir contains "page after page of laudatory examinations of the guy's work. Nowhere did I mean to imply that his work was any less brilliant for the flaws I found in it." When Staples accuses Bellow of "being a bit sensitive," he does so, Lyall points out, "oddly enough, in the same way Mr. Bellow himself condemned in his recent Op-Ed piece." Staples concedes that there's "room for discussion" over the extent to which "an author is responsible for the opinions of his characters," but he also says, somewhat incoherently, that it "just shows how far gone we are that every discussion of race quickly generates [degenerates?] into a discussion of character."

Three days after Lyall's piece appeared, on March 19, Bellow wrote to his friend George Walden, who had sent him the draft of an article provisionally titled "A Non-Interview with Saul Bellow." In the article, Walden discusses the Papuans-and-Zulus quote, which he calls "rash":

> Was he sorry he said it? No, because it's true. Not that he despises primitive cultures: he read anthropology at University (later even a Zulu novel, *Achaka*) and shares the universal attraction to simple truths. But he has an uncomplicated truth of his own: that the greatest cultures accrete over millennia—the writing, the music, the cities. This, he implies (he dislikes cultural big talk) is the soil we should be tilling and planting now.

Bellow's response to this passage was to correct the name of the Zulu novel; to amend the third sentence by adding, after "primitive cultures," "of course primitive societies have their arts and their wisdom"; and to add a concluding sentence: "And in the West the books are under attack" (he might also have cut the parenthesis about disliking cultural big talk). Perhaps the most welcome letter he received about the controversy was written by Melville Herskovits's daughter, Jean, a professor of African history and politics, who had recently visited the State Department to discuss African affairs. The "Papuans and Zulus" article had just appeared, and "all through that day and the next . . . at the State Department, on the Hill, even at the Pentagon, and meals with friends, including some who work at AID [Agency for International Development] on matters nearly Papuan and others who are journalists, your piece was resonating and they were cheering." Once she was back in New York, a Nigerian friend, an ex-soldier and minister, asked her to "convey his applause."

The op-ed piece did Bellow little good, even among the minority who read it carefully. For Hilton Kramer, on the right, Bellow's claim that the "Papuans and Zulus" remark was made in reference to the distinction between literate and preliterate cultures "is such a transparent copout—such an egregious attempt to by-pass the explosive subject of multiculturalism—that one feels embarrassed on his behalf."[42] In answering his attackers, Bellow "never really engages the central charge that Brent Staples and Alfred Kazin have brought against him, which has little, if anything, to do with distinctions between literate and preliterate cultures." This is not fair, or not quite fair, given what Bellow implies when he speaks of the difficulty of understanding preliterate cultures or the ignorance of supposedly literate Westerners. Still, Kramer has a point. It takes some unpacking to get to Bellow's position on multiculturalism in the op-ed piece, which suggests to Kramer that he, too, was "fearful of the cultural ostracism that awaits the writer today, no matter how famous, who goes into battle against the radicalization of our culture."[43] Fearfulness or uneasiness may also underlie Bellow's description of himself as attacked for "a remark I was alleged to have made." But he did make the remark. "Alleged" is bound to raise doubts, the sort raised by his claim not to remember to whom the remark was made or to mention its appearance in Atlas's profile of Bloom.

It is hard to believe that when Bellow made the Papuans-and-Zulus remark—and when he read it in Atlas's article—he was unaware of what it sounded like. It was meant to be funny, but it was also meant to provoke. Herschel Shawmut might have said something like this, or Albert Corde in *The Dean's December*. Twelve years before the op-ed piece, Bellow has Corde make a similar remark, with disastrous consequences. In conversation with his journalist friend Dewey Spangler, Corde says: "Some professors work hard. . . . Most of them do. But a professor when he gets tenure doesn't *have* to do anything. A tenured professor and a welfare mother with eight kids have much in common." In the next sentence we read, "The damage that these sentences would do was as clear as the print itself" (p. 303); Dewey Spangler prints the sentences, and Corde is forced by his provost to resign. "Read charitably," Robert Pippin claims, Bellow's Papuans-and-Zulus remark "didn't say anything all that controversial. It was more the way he said it." The way he said it derived from contempt not for preliterate societies or third-world countries but for thought-police, verbal hygienists.

It may also owe something to anger at the black anti-Semitism discussed in the previous chapter. In his biography of Bellow, in the course of discussing the Papuans-and-Zulus remark, Atlas quotes Richard Stern on Bellow's "obsession with black-Jewish relations. . . . He couldn't leave it alone." Bellow deeply resented the anti-Jewish remarks made by African American politicians and commentators in Chicago in the late 1980s. To others of his friends, according to Atlas, Bellow complained that the city of Chicago gave black workers preferential treatment. Again, these complaints were spoken, not written, a distinction Bellow invokes in his defense. But the Papuans-and-Zulus remark was made to a journalist who was embarked on his biography.

Early in May, Bellow and Janis traveled to New York, where he was to participate in a panel discussion at the 92nd Street Y on anti-Semitism. The other participants were Cynthia Ozick, John Gross, and William Phillips of *Partisan Review*, then located in Boston. The proceedings were taped, and *Partisan Review* was keen to publish Bellow's talk, an abbreviated version of "A Jewish Writer in America," his 1988 speech in Philadelphia. At its end, Bellow briefly discusses Black-Jewish relations:

> I do give a lot of thought to the special and in some ways occult place assigned to Jews. To me, this is of course more than a theoretical curiosity. My interpretation of the recent increase of hostility among American blacks toward Jews is that the blacks have a clear reason for dissociating themselves from these eternal expendables, for they see that in making common cause with the Jews they would risk exchanging transitory disadvantages for permanent ones. Jew-hatred, moreover, is never wholly unpopular, and this is as clear to black demagogues as it was to Germans, Russians, Frenchman, Rumanians, and others in the past. I have a very particular sympathy for what I see as the distortions in black life, a sympathy rooted in my lifelong familiarity with deformities in Jews produced by their experiences in the pale. I think often of an essay by Rebecca West in which she discusses the Jewishness of Kafka: "Russia," she observes in an aside, "has succeeded in oppressing its Jews until they have become nightmare figures which the Western Jew did not like to recognize as brethren. . . ." But what she sees as a Russian deformation has existed in other forms for centuries.

At the end of *Mr. Sammler's Planet*, as the black pickpocket is beaten to the ground, Bellow reminds his readers of the shared suffering of blacks and Jews, and of the damaging effects of prejudice and discrimination, both psychological and material. This, say his defenders, is the real Saul Bellow, not the "off the cuff" Bellow grousing to friends about the preferential treatment of black workers. "In daily life," Bellow told Norman Manea, in a quotation cited in *To Fame and Fortune*, "I don't ask myself what is honorable and what is dishonorable but I do when I'm writing." The novelist, he says elsewhere, with Dostoevsky in mind, "cannot permit himself to yield to cruel, intemperate, and arbitrary personal judgments," the sort made in an interview or to friends. "The writer's convictions, perhaps fanatically held, must be tamed by truth. The degree to which you challenge your own beliefs and expose them to destruction is a test of your worth as a novelist."[44]

On the morning of the 92nd Street Y panel, the young journalist David Remnick came to the Lotos Club on the Upper East Side to interview Bellow for the "Talk of the Town" section of *The New Yorker.*

Bellow "looked fit (he is seventy-eight), and was outfitted like a moderate dandy. But he was glum." He missed Chicago: "Janis does, too." New York depressed him, particularly the Upper West Side. Walking down Broadway "doesn't necessarily scare me, but it's disgusting. . . . There's an obvious drug scene now, the hustle of the homeless. . . . You try to take an over-all view of the thing that is more elevated, benevolent. But the fact is you resent it and you think it's degrading." Despite Bellow's growing reputation as a conservative, he thinks of himself as "some sort of liberal, but I don't like where liberalism has gone in this country in the last twenty years . . . these terrible outbursts from people whose principles are affronted when you disagree with them." When Remnick asked Bellow "about today's racial politics, he had winced, saying he hoped we could find 'an undangerous way' to talk about it all." He was preoccupied with Louis Farrakhan, of the Nation of Islam, a figure he had been watching "for many years." Black anti-Semitism in Chicago might not be deep, "but it is certainly conspicuous. There is this sort of attitude among the blacks; whatever else we may be, whatever handicaps we may labor under, we are, nevertheless, not Jews." Saying such things, Bellow realized, could get one into trouble. "There seems to be such a taboo on open discussion that no habits of discussion have developed, no vocabulary for discussion, no allowance made for intellectual differences, because you are immediately labelled a racist." He lists Ralph Ellison, the sociologist William Julius Wilson of the University of Chicago, and Stanley Crouch as exceptions, "blacks with whom you can talk openly. And they do the same. . . . But there are very few people in general who don't respond to the taboo." Remnick asks Bellow if this new atmosphere "affected his writing? Would he hesitate for fear of attack?" He would not. "I write as I write. If I'm going to take heat from it—well, that's the name of the game." Away from his desk, he was also fearless, and, in the case of the Papuans-and-Zulus remark, heedless, to the cost of his reputation and the fortunes of his fiction.

ON JUNE 1, 1994, in a letter to the Marxist historian Eugene Genovese, Bellow was still smarting. "The *Times* is a terrible topic. When I say that I hate it, it sounds to me as though I were saying that I can't stand Nero or Caligula. It's *their* empire. It's also our 'paper of record.' In the Book Review Becky Sinkler is our muse and in the Sunday Magazine we have James Atlas and on the Editorial page that unsigned hero

Brent Staples. I read *The Wall Street Journal* as an antidote to the *Times* and as a supreme antidote when the going is really rough I read a book of the Testaments. Old or New."

Bellow's attitude to James Atlas, as was suggested in chapter 8, was fickle, changeable, hard for Atlas to read, sometimes warm and friendly, particularly early on, at other times prickly and grudging. Early letters begin with the salutation "Dear Mr. Atlas"; later ones begin "Dear James"; still later ones begin "Dear Mr. Atlas." Atlas tracks Bellow's mood shifts in his 1995 *New Yorker* memoir, "The Shadow in the Garden," the title he later used in his book-length memoir. The *New Yorker* memoir takes the form of transcribed or reconstructed journal entries.[45] At first, Bellow gave permission for Atlas to read manuscript material in the Regenstein but not letters. On a visit Atlas made to Chicago in February 1991, Bellow called him "Jim." When, however, Atlas asked him "a bunch of factual questions," Bellow wondered "Why do you want to know all this. . . . B takes me in with that keen, appraising look of his, the wide saucerlike eyes suspicious: *Who is this guy?* It's beginning to dawn on him: I'm really going to exhume his past, unearth and reconstruct it in every detail. I'm going to write his biography." In October 1991, Atlas called Bellow and noted in his journal that "he seems pleased to hear from me." At this point, Atlas had been at work on the biography for three years and asked Bellow again if he could see the letters. " 'I don't want my last tatters exposed . . . my poor porous fig leaf,' [Bellow] replies. He sits, silent, in the gathering dusk, then says, with feeling, 'I don't give a damn. It's really for Janis's sake. It hurts her to read about all this. She doesn't think I should do it." At the end of the interviewing session and a tour of the old neighborhood, Bellow told Atlas he "really enjoyed" the day, and tried to reassure him: "You'll probably learn as much from me as from the letters. I don't mind at all talking to you. I don't want to get involved, but from time to time."

The next entry in Atlas's *New Yorker* memoir is dated August 30, 1992. Bellow has invited him to dinner in Vermont. Janis is away. Bellow takes him to Le Petit Chef. It seems to Atlas that Bellow enjoys talking to him. When Atlas tells him over dinner that he thinks his life "interesting," Bellow answers, " 'All you have to do to live an interesting life is be a damn fool.' I babble something about how it's a wonderful project for me. B, deadpan: 'I'm glad I haven't lived in vain.' " At the end of the evening, Bellow says "in a heartfelt way that he's had a good time; asks what to call me, Jim or James. 'There's always business to conduct,' I say, and hand him a letter I've drawn up, giving me permission to consult the files of Marshall Holleb, one of Bellow's lawyers in Chicago. He hands the letter back: 'It's just legal stuff.'" As Atlas drives back home—he, too, has a house in Vermont, forty-five minutes away—he is exhilarated: "I'm shouting in the car, 'It's fun! Fun!' I don't feel rejected by his refusal to let me see these papers. It *is*, after all, just legal stuff. . . . I also realize that I don't need his permission—the creative part, the original part, is my interpretation." He then records his "greatest fear": "that we'll have a falling-out someday. The person with whom I used to experience a huge paternal transference doesn't exist as powerfully for me anymore; I feel independent of him, but also sad. There is no Dad. Certainly not this difficult, prickly character." Still, the next time they meet, Atlas records: "Bellow is wearing—guess what?—a railroad cap *identical* to mine."

In October 1993, Atlas visits Zita Cogan, Bellow's old friend since Tuley High School. She has all sorts of materials to show him, but the only letter "is one in which I'm referred to disparagingly, and in which B makes clear his position about the book." Atlas does not quote the letter, but it is written in reply to one Cogan wrote to Bellow on July 1, 1990, in which she alerts him that Atlas is coming to Chicago and will be staying with her ("because I remembered his two grandmothers"). She reassures him: "As usual, you can rely on me—as far as you're concerned, I'm mum. Any suggestions?" Bellow's reply, in a letter of July 18, is "You're kind to Mr. Atlas. I am no more keen about a biography than I am about reserving a plot for myself at 26th and Harlem Avenue. I keep putting it off. I say this in order to make clear that I am not supporting Atlas, nor am I asking my friends to oblige him with recollections of my misconduct." That night, after reading these words, Atlas had dinner with Edward Shils. "On impulse," he asked Shils to read his manuscript, by now some seven hundred pages long. Shils agreed.[46]

The next entry in Atlas's *New Yorker* memoir is dated August 3, 1994, the summer after the Staples and Kazin articles and Bellow's op-ed piece. The Bellows are in Vermont, and Atlas comes to visit. The entry has a title: "The Fight." Although Janis is warm and welcoming, Bellow is described as "looking crabby." He brings up the Brent Staples article, asking, "Why didn't Brent come see him . . . instead of lurking in the dark?" He is "appalled" at having been stalked and calls Staples "barbaric." The discussion takes place in Bellow's study, and "he sharply rebukes me for putting my iced coffee on a book, then shows me again his mother's old passport. . . . He wants to make a point: 'Why did you say that my name is Bellows?' Suddenly I remember—the article I wrote in the *Times Magazine* last winter defending biography. I had referred to his change of name from Solomon to Saul, even though I knew he was incredibly sensitive about it. Why did I do that?"[47] Then Atlas voices a grievance of his own. Why did Bellow deny that he made his controversial Papuans-and-Zulus remark "about the multicultural debate . . . and [say] that what he had said had been 'misconstrued' by 'the interviewer' "? Bellow "doesn't reply. Instead, he goes on about how he's had a 'brutal' year: Brent's book, an attack on him by Hilton Kramer in *Commentary*. (B is surprised there weren't many letters to the editor: 'They must be killing them in the office.') He's also annoyed about a piece by David Remnick that made him out to be a curmudgeon." There then follows "a long wrangle over the papers. He won't give me permission for this latest batch of excerpts unless I explain how the passages are being used. Finally, he relents a bit. 'I'll give you all the stuff that makes me look good,' he says with a laugh. But he's still mad. He looks at his watch, uncharacteristically; it's something he's never done before. He wants me to leave. They're going out to supper. Janis is in the garden. I say, 'We had a fight.' 'Bring your swimsuit next time.' She's cheerful. 'It will be more fun.' "

In *The Shadow in the Garden: A Biographer's Tale* (2017), Atlas's book-length memoir and meditation on biography, he incorporates and expands upon these journal entries, adding several striking details. At the August 3, 1994, "Fight" meeting, in addition to challenging Bellow about the context of the Papuans-and-Zulus remark and about his claim not to have remembered the identity of the "interviewer," Atlas revealed the source of the Staples piece:

> As it happened, I had edited Brent's piece in the *Times Magazine*. . . . No, not as it happened. I had plucked the excerpt from the galley myself. It was beautifully written; it was about Bellow; it was news. A black journalist stalking a white Nobel Prize–winning novelist known for his controversial views on race through the streets of Chicago . . . what a story! But there must have been other factors involved in creating the awkward situation in which I now found myself. Could I have been making Brent's aggression a stand-in for my own? Then there was the most obvious motive of all: it would be good for *my* book.

> I confessed to Bellow my role in the publication of Brent's piece. There may have been a tangled web, but at least there was no deceit, just the usual murk of mixed motives—unconscious acting out, ambivalence, good intentions, bad faith, enthusiasm, opportunism, and a thousand other impulses, all of them imperfectly understood.[48]

"I had never seen him so angry before," Atlas writes in the book-length memoir, on the occasion of "The Fight." Bellow spoke of being persecuted by *The New York Times*, citing, most recently, a slight from Rebecca Sinkler, the editor of the *Book Review*, and a lukewarm review of *It All Adds Up*, his nonfiction collection, by Peter S. Prescott. "They were out to get me," Bellow claimed of people at the *Times*.[49]

The final journal entry in Atlas's *New Yorker* piece is dated August 26, 1994, three weeks after "The Fight." It also has a title: "The Reconciliation." Atlas had provided Bellow with thirteen pages of "content," to show how he would be using the passages he wished to quote. Over the telephone, Bellow was "very conciliatory; the letters seem harmless. We agree to meet." When Atlas arrives at the meeting, Bellow "tells me, giving me a direct and forthright look, that he never meant to interfere in my project; that I misunderstood; that he just wanted to know what I was quoting. B is concerned about what certain people are saying about him. How will I know to be fair? I answer that it's my job, that I'm a writer, too; I know how to judge character. He says, 'But you're not the catcher in the rye.' I reply, 'It's true, I can't save you every time.' We both laugh." After two hours going over quotations and signing permissions, Bellow is tired. "He doesn't want me to stay afterward; he gets up from the kitchen table." Atlas, too, is tired, "drained." In *The Shadow in the Garden: A Biographer's Tale*, he describes returning home and looking up the passage in *The Catcher in the Rye* in which Holden Caulfield imagines himself standing by a cliff and saving children from going over it. "I sat on the couch and wept," Atlas writes. "I was Holden. But I was also the cliff."[50]

ONE FEELS SYMPATHY FOR both biographer and subject. Bellow never really wanted a biography, not while he was alive, but, having allowed Atlas to spend seven years on the book, he can't stop him. But he doesn't trust him. "It's true," Atlas tells Bellow, "I can't save you every time." But that's what Bellow wants. Why should he want instances of misconduct recollected, or cooperate in their recollection? "He thinks I won't be embarrassed about these things," Chris Walsh remembers Bellow saying about Atlas. Whether Bellow considered or cared how his distrust and distance would affect Atlas is unclear, though his conciliatory tone after their fight suggests that he did. Atlas's decision to publish journal entries showing Bellow as difficult, prickly, and inconsiderate he looks back on in the book-length memoir. "How could I resist? Or rather, how could *I* resist? A more prudent biographer would have considered the possible consequences and demurred. But I had become accustomed to thinking of Bellow not only as a father figure, but as a father, whose unconditional love—or at least forgiveness—I could count on no matter what I did."[51]

On May 24, 1995, a month or so before the journal entries appeared in *The New Yorker*, Atlas wrote to Bellow to tell him of their impending publication, reminding him that at one time ("on January 3rd, 1993, to be precise") he (Bellow) had encouraged him to write a book about his experiences as a biographer. Bill Buford of *The New Yorker* had learned of the existence of the journals and asked Atlas if he could see them, "so I showed them to him." In the letter of May 24, Atlas recalls thinking, perhaps wishfully, that Bellow wouldn't object to their publication, would at least tolerate them, and in places might even enjoy them. An extract from the biography had recently been published in *Granta*, which Bellow "seemed to have liked."[52] Atlas was on Bellow's side, he assured him; he would be objective but sympathetic; he also had a deep appreciation of his writing. That his presence was "in many ways unwished-for (and perhaps resented)," he realized, but the resulting biography would serve "a positive function"; Bellow would not regret having allowed it to go ahead. In the book-length memoir, Atlas looks back on the 1995 decision to publish excerpts from his journal in *The New Yorker*. What he now feels, he sums up in a Yiddish phrase: "*Gottenyu*. Dear God." Earlier, in a reference to the biographer as "gravedigger," he describes himself in 1995 as seeming "in an awful hurry to bury the person I was raising up."[53]

It took some weeks for Atlas to gather the courage to call Bellow after the *New Yorker* piece appeared. Their conversation, reconstructed in *The Shadow in the Garden: A Biographer's Tale*, is frosty. Here is how it ends: "'I wish you well,' I said, hoping to convey an apology without apologizing. *Accept the consequences of your acts.* I hung up, shaken. I had really done it this time."[54] Although they were to meet again, from this point onward, Bellow consistently disparaged Atlas in correspondence and discouraged his friends from cooperating with him.[55]

BELLOW'S DIFFICULTIES WITH earlier biographers, or would-be biographers, ought to have prepared Atlas for this treatment. He had read and reviewed Mark Harris's *Saul Bellow, Drumlin Woodchuck* (1980), a book, as we've seen, about Harris's failed attempts to write Bellow's life. "Mr. Harris received no decisive rebuff, and implies that Bellow even gave tacit encouragement," Atlas wrote in the review. "When the biographer, after a decade's elusive pursuit, demanded to know whether Bellow wished him to discontinue his project, Bellow replied with an amiable postcard that made no reference whatever to the question."[56] As Atlas recounts in his biography, Richard Stern had warned Harris that Bellow would say neither yes nor no—just as he was to say neither yes nor no to Atlas. When an extract from the book came out in *The Georgia Review*, Bellow told Harris that he hated the way it made him look ("I don't see myself that way"). When the book itself was published, he didn't read it, or so he told William Kennedy, in a letter of January 7, 1991, "and I rather enjoy the pummeling he's getting in the press."[57]

Atlas also knew what had happened to Ruth Miller, Bellow's lifelong friend and ex-pupil, when she sent him a draft of *Saul Bellow: A Biography of the Imagination* (1991). At the last minute, after the manuscript had been typeset, Bellow refused Miller permission to quote from unpublished letters and manuscripts, threatening her publishers with legal action unless "a satisfactory resolution" of his many objections to the book's claims and assertions was found. These objections were set out on four typed pages, single-spaced; enough of them were met to avoid legal action.[58] In addition, the following sentences were added to the end of the book's introduction:

> To thank Saul Bellow for the many hours of conversation we have shared over a long span of years may suggest he is in part responsible for what I have written. He is not. Indeed, I understand that Bellow disagrees with much of what I say in this book and, I am told,

> now denies having said many of the things I quite clearly recall him saying, things I often recorded in my journal at the time. Of course, I must stand by my memory and my notes. I express my gratitude to him for allowing me to read his letters and papers deposited in the archives of the Regenstein Library at the University of Chicago, although he ultimately decided not to let me quote from them.[59]

Bellow felt "burned" by Miller's book. He wrote to the publisher Herb Yellin on July 9, 1991, describing its "attacks" on him as "horrifying." "I abominate Ruth," he told Yellin. "She is a stinker, vulgar and vile." At the same time, he admitted to having been "largely to blame" for the book. "I should have known better, even half a century ago—not extended my patronage to her or let her think I had admitted her to intimacy." This was the mistake he made with Mark Harris and then with James Atlas, or so he would come to feel. Adam Bellow describes the mistake as habitual, by no means confined to biographers or would-be biographers. All sorts of people, his children included, wanted things from Bellow, wanted time with him. "He had this tremendous appeal, and people wanted more and more of it . . . the whole invasive thing, the constant promising things." When faced with requests, Bellow's responses, Adam believes, were often ways "of keeping people at bay. . . . He couldn't just say no, that was the thing. He couldn't say yes and he couldn't say no." If people later assumed that they knew what he thought or that they had his approval, "he'd act very surprised . . . even indignant."

Bellow's complaints when the Miller book came out were less about content than style. "In truth," Atlas writes in his biography, "Miller did have a tin ear. She made Bellow sound earnest and solemn. . . . 'Between the time she'd left my apartment and the time she got home, she forgot what I'd said, so she made it up herself,' he complained" (presumably in an untaped interview with Atlas, which he, too, went home and reconstructed in his journal). In the letter to Yellin, Bellow describes his friends as unaware of "how thick my protective armor is. The fact is I have not suffered horribly from her attacks." But this is not the impression conveyed in the letter itself, or in other correspondence. What makes Bellow's behavior difficult to understand in this instance, if what Miller told Atlas is to be trusted, is that when she showed him the final draft, in Vermont during the summer of 1990, he embraced her and said it was " 'the best book, bar none, written about him.' "[60] In Atlas's May 24, 1995, letter to Bellow, he had assured him that he was "not Mark Harris or Ruth Miller." This is not how Bellow saw him, or came to see him.

ON MARCH 13, 1994, three days after the appearance of Bellow's Papuans-and-Zulus op-ed piece, the London *Sunday Times* asked leading authors and critics in Britain to name the greatest of living writers in English. Bellow came first. Later that spring, Viking published *It All Adds Up*, to mostly admiring reviews (even Prescott in *The New York Times* admitted, "Mr. Bellow couldn't write a dull page if he tried"). The collection had been Harriet Wasserman's idea.[61] Bellow had published no book-length fiction in five years. His most recent short story, "Something to Remember Me By," had been published in 1990. "Case" was nowhere near finished (three years had passed since its April 1991 delivery date), and neither was "Marbles," the work that now, according to Wasserman, "wanted his full attention."[62] "Why not such a collection in the year or two before the new novel would be finished and brought out?" Bellow was resistant at first, worrying that the book would be seen as "a kind of filler." Only after he was assured that he would be able to select, organize, introduce, and where necessary revise the pieces himself, as well as give the volume its title, did he approve the project.[63] Meanwhile, he plowed on with "Marbles. "The rumors of a novel are true," he wrote to Andrew Noble, a lecturer in English at the University of Strathclyde in Glasgow, on June 12, 1994. "I've been trying for a couple of years now to bring it to completion. This summer one of us must crack." In August, he turned down an invitation from Rebecca Sinkler of the *Book Review* to write an essay on James Hogg's *Private Memoirs and Confessions of a Justified Sinner*, a neglected classic and a book Bellow greatly admired. "I am finishing a book which was several years in the writing," he told her, in a letter of August 9, "and I can't possibly do an essay on the *Justified Sinner*, or any other sort of sinner until I have rid myself of my burden."

By the end of the summer, "Marbles" was still not finished. The final section was to be set in New Guinea, and Bellow's plan was to complete it in November, in a tropical setting like the one he would be writing about. Jonathan and Joan Kleinbard had suggested Grand Case, a small fishing village on the French half of the Caribbean island of St. Martin. There the Bellows stayed in a beach-front apartment in a complex called Flamboyant Beach Villas. "The blue of the Caribbean I see from this open door," Bellow wrote on November 10 to Gene Kennedy. "We have no phone in our small flat . . . and no newspapers are available. NO mail is being forwarded. My one daily lapse or cop-out—cheating on the cure—is literary. I work each morning on my *Marbles* book. I may actually get that monkey off my back before X-mas." The "cure" in question was from "too much *festination* [pathological shortening of the stride and quickening of the gait; more loosely, frenetic activity], as Dr. Oliver Sacks would put it. . . . His account of festination and catatonia went straight to that waiting throbbing target, my heart." The blue of the Caribbean, Bellow writes, "is my form of El Dopa." Twice a day, he and Janis bathed in the sea. The "daily lapse or cop-out" he explained to Wasserman in a telephone conversation: " 'After I write, we sit on the beach and read Shakespeare. *The Tempest*, *A Midsummer Night's Dream*. Can you send me some Shakespeare? And if you want, you can send me a little treat.' The treat he meant was chocolate and caramels, his favorites." She sent the books and some chocolate turkeys and caramels by Federal Express, so that they would arrive in time for Thanksgiving.[64]

Janis remembers the apartment on Grand Case as "unpleasant from the beginning. There were trails of little insects that appeared near the tables in the kitchen where Saul wrote. We kept the doors and windows open for the breeze, but it seemed stifling inside. I remember the terrible pink artificial smell of the Jergens lotion that we would rub on our hands and feet at night."[65] The bed in the apartment was small; the bedroom was narrow and airless. The only relief came from a little terrace at the front, with beautiful hovering butterflies and a lime tree for shade. During the mornings, Bellow worked surrounded by the anthropological studies they'd lugged from Boston, gruesome texts about cannibalism. In the afternoons, when they swam, "we did carry each other in the water and sing Handel duets from Solomon." At dusk on the terrace, they drank wine and ate olives and watched the calm sea before walking out along the beach in search of supper, "carrying our sandals, and talking about the day's work." One evening, some days before Thanksgiving, they found a restaurant in town. Bellow ordered red snapper, served cold with mayonnaise. In *Ravelstein*, Chick, on holiday on St. Martin, orders just such a fish at just such a place and time.

"The snapper at room temperature was clammy," he recalls. "The mayonnaise was like zinc ointment." Rosamund, the Janis figure, tastes it and agrees: "It wasn't cooked through. It was raw at the center" (p. 188). Bellow, like Chick, couldn't finish his meal. Within a week, he was in the hospital, in a coma, close to death.

Janis, SB, and Allan Bloom, at the belated birthday party given for SB by Mayor Richard M. Daley, Chicago, October 6, 1990 (courtesy of Janis Bellow)

II

Intensive Care

THE RED SNAPPER was contaminated with a toxin called ciguatera. Just to the north of Grand Case, the fishing village where the Bellows were staying, is a coral reef, an island tourist attraction. Ciguatera toxin is found in over four hundred species of coral-reef fish, of which red snapper is one. The toxin is tasteless and odorless and cannot be removed by ordinary cooking. Its initial effects on Bellow were general malaise, loss of appetite, aversion to food. Janis took him to a local doctor, who diagnosed dengue, a mosquito-borne fever, the first symptoms of which are similar to those of ciguatera. Dengue can be treated and usually passes within a week; there is no effective treatment or antidote for ciguatera poisoning, though in some cases recovery can be aided by vitamin supplements and steroids. Ciguatera poisoning can last for weeks or years; in extreme cases, it results in long-term disability and death.

The local doctor did not help. Soon Bellow developed other symptoms: headaches, muscle aches, numbness, vertigo, hallucinations. He collapsed on the bathroom floor, and Janis refused to take him to the local hospital (in *Ravelstein*, which offers a fictional version of the trip to St. Martin, an ambulance is summoned, and Chick, the Bellow character, refuses to get in). After consulting with her father, Janis insisted that they return to Boston immediately. John Silber arranged for Bellow to be admitted to the Boston University Hospital on Thanksgiving Day, by which time he was suffering from double pneumonia, the principal concern of the doctors who received him in intensive care; other problems, either caused or exacerbated by the toxin, including threatened heart failure, had also to be treated. Dr. John Barnardo, a pulmonary specialist, saw Bellow the day he arrived: "He was quite ill . . . and he got sicker and sicker and developed respiratory failure and had to be put on a ventilator. I thought if he were not treated with the ventilator he wouldn't have made it." Bellow hated the ventilator, tried to pull it out, and tried also to pull out the IV tubes to which he was attached. When he was particularly agitated at one point, Janis climbed into bed and held him to keep him still, as Woody Selbst climbs into bed to still his struggling father, Morris, in "A Silver Dish." The doctors in ICU then put Bellow into a medically induced coma.

Dr. Barnardo was not sure that Bellow would make it, and said so to Janis. "The thing that worried me," he remembers, "was not only whether he would come out of this, but how he'd come out of it." Janis remembers the following possibilities: "(A) he's going to die, (B) if he doesn't die he's going to be hooked up to machines for the rest of his life, (C) if he ever should come out of this . . . he'll be in a chronic care facility."[1] When word of Bellow's condition reached his niece Lesha Greengus, she informed her daughter, Rachel Schultz, an anesthesiologist at the University of Texas Health Science Center in Houston. As Rachel remembers it: "Uncle Saul was already on a ventilator and when I first talked to Greg and Janis about the specifics (the vent settings and such), it didn't look good. We all thought this might be the end, and my initial concern was that he be made comfortable. I know how miserable it can be on a ventilator." When Bellow's ventilator settings began to stabilize, and it looked as though he might pull through, Rachel began to worry that the doctors in Boston wouldn't be able to get him off the ventilator, because of the drugs they were using to sedate him. "So I spoke with the doctor in the ICU . . . about using a different more short-acting sedative." According to Janis, the doctors knew full well the effects of the sedatives they were administering. The drug Bellow was switched to was Versed, which cost more: "To me it was a no-brainer," Rachel recalls, "and I insisted that they make the switch. Not everyone was happy about the extra expense, but I really pushed for this. And about a week later, Saul was extubated!"[2]

Rachel was not the only person with views about Bellow's treatment. The day after Thanksgiving, Adam Bellow left a message on Harriet Wasserman's answering machine saying that his father had been flown from St. Martin to Boston and was in intensive care. Wasserman then received a call from Harvey Freedman, Janis's father: "Janis asked me to call," he told her. "Saul is a very, very sick man. We have to pray for him, he's in a very bad way." Adam also called her to say that one of Bellow's lungs had ceased functioning and that the other "was having difficulties." In addition, there were problems regulating his heartbeat. Wasserman asked Adam "for permission to get hold of the infectious-diseases specialist who had prescribed exactly the antibiotic that saved my life when I got [a] staph infection." Adam said okay, but then Greg Bellow called her from California "and bawled me out. 'You're not to call that specialist. We are only going to have one line here. I'm the oldest and I'm in charge. I'm in touch with the infectious diseases doctor and Saul's primary doctor. You are not to interfere.'" Wasserman asked if she could come up to Boston for the weekend. "'No. You are not to come this weekend.'" Later, she was called by Walter Pozen, who had been called by Harvey Freedman, who had been called by Janis. Could she advance money to cover bills at the beginning of the month? "If you can't do it," Pozen said, "I'll do it." Wasserman told Pozen there was plenty of money; she had recently deposited two large checks into Bellow's account. Just in case, Pozen wrote Janis a check for ten thousand dollars. More phone calls followed, "including one asking who had power of attorney." Then Greg called to apologize "for having raised his voice. I told him I understood."[3]

By the time of Greg's apology, he and his brothers had joined Janis in Boston. As he saw it, "Our tiny world was like a series of concentric circles that surrounded and protected him. In the innermost ring was Saul, protected by Janis. She was in a complete state of exhaustion after staying up for days, and her health worried the nurses and the three of us. But Janis refused to go home, claiming she needed nothing but a toothbrush and a few clean T-shirts. The next ring held Dan, Adam, and me; we agreed our primary job was to protect Janis and Saul. Once the news of his illness got out, that job expanded to keeping people who were worried about him informed but at bay. Lesha wanted to come to Boston but agreed to settle for phone calls several times a day. She, in turn, kept the rest of the family up-to-date. The ring beyond his immediate family included his agent, Harriet Wasserman, his lawyer, his friends, and his colleagues." According to Greg, when Wasserman pressed to come to Boston, he and Adam did put her off, knowing that "her meddling would upset Janis. We tried to keep her occupied with a chore: securing some ready cash for Janis, who, it turned out, did not have access to Saul's bank accounts." When Wasserman persisted and would not agree to stay in New York, "I lost my temper and she relented."[4]

Everyone was overwrought. When Janis brought a recording of Handel's *Water Music* to the hospital, to play to Bellow as he lay unconscious in bed, Greg thought of his mother, who would have been eighty that day, as well as of "the good times during my childhood. I burst into tears and ran out of the room as the impact of losing one parent and the possibility that I'd lose the other hit me. When I returned I explained my tears to a sympathetic Janis." While in Boston, Greg learned of the death of Isaac Rosenfeld's son, George Sarant, to whom he had become close. "With my emotions already worn thin, I could not remain sitting in a hospital room. I needed a break and went to New York." He extended his stay to attend Sarant's funeral: "After Saul's failure to attend Isaac's or Oscar Tarcov's funeral, I was determined to ensure a Bellow was present at the time."[5]

Janis was quickly bolstered by her family. Sonya Freedman came immediately, for the first of three visits during Bellow's hospitalization (Harvey Freedman was unwell at the time). Janis's sister, Wendy, also arrived to help, relaying news to the rest of the Freedman family and taking care of domestic chores. Janis remembers a rare night at home, after days and nights of sleeplessness at the hospital. "Blessedly back in my own bed . . . I was unable to calm myself." Wendy was there, and "she spent most of the night reading Auden poems to me." At dawn, Janis headed back to the hospital.[6]

Janis's state worried everyone, not just the Bellow sons and the ICU doctors and nurses. When Sonya arrived in Boston, she found her daughter "sleeping on a chair. She was a wreck." "I was very concerned," she recalls. "She just neglected her health. She didn't leave him for a moment. She was beside him, talking to him, reading poetry to him, singing to him, and a lot of people said, What are you doing? This is ridiculous. But it turned out that when he regained consciousness, he was aware." "No one should take anything away from Janis's dedication to him," Adam believes. Nor was this dedication without benefit to Bellow's recovery. Although overwrought, Janis took meticulous notes about symptoms and medicines; she was also clear and controlled when consulting with doctors. As Adam puts it: "There's a part of Janis that's very capable, but she was not looking after herself. . . . There was a real question of whether she was capable. . . . She was not willing to look after herself. . . . She has to be willing to listen to help." One bit of help she listened to was forced upon her. "In and around this time," she recalls, "I had two day surgeries—removal of what turned out to be non-malignant tumors."[7]

Dr. Barnardo was especially concerned about Janis when Bellow was first intubated, but "she held up pretty well." He describes her as "a very strong factor in him getting out of the hospital as quickly as he did." Bellow "didn't have a voice. . . . We had him very heavily sedated." Janis was his voice. "Because he was so overwhelmed," Dr. Barnardo remembers, "I wasn't sure he was interested in all the torture we were going to put him through, if he'd known about the tube [the ventilator] and so forth." In addition to intubation, the torture included lumbar spinal taps, endoscopies, cystoscopies, MRIs, CAT scans, catheterizations, and "interminable medications," to deal not only with blacked-out lungs but bladder infections and heart failure. Only after Bellow was extubated could the doctors "tell he was pushing himself to get back. I remember vividly he was sitting there with a pile of books at his bedstand doing research. I said, 'What are you doing?' He said: 'I'm writing.' "

Bellow's memories of his time in intensive care were sparse and confused, a product in part of delusions or hallucinations, in part of retrograde amnesia, both caused by heavy sedation. In a speech of April 13, 1997, in Chicago, at a medical conference ("Contemporary Health Care and the Ethic of Medicine: What Is a Physician to Do?"), as well as in a memoirlike story of the same year, "View from Intensive Care," he remembered being certain of only three things: "someone pounding me on the back and ordering me to breathe"; being turned over "many times"; and Janis's presence. "While I struggled to breathe, she would lift the oxygen mask and swab the inside of my mouth. . . . My divided consciousness recognized at all times that she was present and that she was determined that I should live."[8] He had no idea where he was. Often, in his delusions, it seemed to him that he was underneath Kenmore Square in Boston. In "View from Intensive Care," he recalls thinking he was in a vast cellar with soiled brick walls "as white as cottage cheese" (p. 74). One especially vivid delusion, recounted in the medical-convention address, caused real-life physical pain:

> Before my release from ICU I climbed out of bed, thinking that I was at home in wintry Vermont, and that one of my granddaughters was skiing around the house. I was annoyed with her parents for not having brought her in to see her afflicted grandpa. . . . It was a win-

> ter morning, so I thought. Actually it must have been the middle of the night. I climbed over the bed rail without noticing that I was attached by needles and tubes to hanging flasks and intravenous needles. I saw, as if they were someone else's, my bare feet on the sunny floor. They seemed unwilling to bear my weight but I forced them to obey my will. Then I fell, landing on my back. At first I felt no pain. All I was aware of was my helplessness. An orderly ran up and said, "I *heard* you were a troublemaker. . . ." I had been out for many weeks [pp. 1–2].

Bellow was on heavy doses of heparin, a blood thinner, at the time of the fall. He began bleeding internally, and his "hugely inflamed" back looked, he was told, "like a forest fire." The nurses decided to put him into a restraining vest, so "I asked my grown sons to call a cab; I'd be better off at home, soaking in the bath" (p. 2).

A version of this delusion appears in "View from Intensive Care," as does the unfriendly orderly, whom the narrator says he'd "taken notice of" earlier (noticing being "part of my job description"). As the orderly hangs Christmas tinsel and mistletoe from the wall fixtures, the narrator notes "his sloping shoulders and wide backside" (p. 75). Later in the delusion, the orderly kicks him out of the hospital, saying, "We need the space" (p. 76). The narrator identifies himself as "a tabloid publisher" (but if so why is "noticing" part of his job description?). For those with knowledge of "All Marbles Still Accounted For," the novel Bellow was at work on in St. Martin, it is tempting to see the narrator as a depiction of Bellow himself under a toxin-induced or sedation-induced delusion: that he was Hilbert Faucil, the novel's hero, a tabloid publisher.

In another delusion recounted in "View from Intensive Care," the narrator's ex-wife appears. Her name is Vela, which is the name of Chick's ex-wife in *Ravelstein*, a character modeled on Alexandra. In the delusion, Vela is described as having left the narrator on his seventy-fifth birthday, after ten years of marriage. She "declared and also silently asserted that she was a real beauty. And something else, which may be rendered, translated or explicated as: 'Judge for yourself what sort of match I made in marrying this deficient person—nothing but a tabloid publisher' " (p. 77). A companion joins her: "a Spanish-looking and very elegant male person in his mid-to-late twenties" (a cross between Maggie Simmons's young French lover, Jacques, and the elderly Argentinian mathematician Alberto Calderon, whom Alexandra married after

Bellow, and whom Bellow suspected she'd been seeing during their marriage). Vela explains to the narrator: "Until now I never had any experience of glamorous sex and I figured, in what you always call the sexual revolution, I should have a sample of it—to find out once and for all what I was deprived of with you" (p. 78). Later, Vela and the narrator are in a bank and she suggests to him that he freeze himself for a hundred years, through cryonics, while she "did lewd things with the Spanish boyfriend." At the end of "View from Intensive Care," the delusions seem to give way, though the narrator's wife is not so sure. " 'That meeting in the bank you believe in,' my wife, the real wife, later said, after I described this moment to her. 'Why should it be always the *worst* things that appear to you so real? I'll never be able to talk you out of being sadistic to yourself.' " In the story's last sentence, the narrator identifies this real wife as "Trudi" (p. 81).

IT TOOK A MONTH, Bellow recalls in the medical conference address, for the pneumonia to be defeated, the sedation to be reduced, the delusions and hallucinations to recede, and for him to be transferred from ICU to a regular room, " 'on the floor,' in hospital lingo" (p. 2). Dr. Barnardo and another doctor from ICU came to visit, bearing gifts. The other doctor brought "soup from her own kitchen"; Dr. Barnardo "made some lasagne and meatballs and brought it in and [Bellow] actually ate them."[9] At this point, with his lungs cleared, everything else that was wrong with Bellow needed addressing. "My body was wasted—unrecognizable. My sphincters were haywire. I could not walk. I had lost the use of my hands. The extent of recovery possible could not be estimated; I would soon be eighty years of age." Among smaller problems, "my upper lip was (to put it in my own way) lame. Even when I spoke or laughed it was strangely immobile or partially paralyzed" (p. 3). When given paper and pen and asked to draw something, he couldn't. He couldn't sign his name or eat his soup.

In the intensive-care unit, Bellow had been dimly aware of resisting death. Now he had to decide "whether I should or should not make efforts to recover" (p. 4), a decision that required he be "as clear as possible, or as frank as I had the strength to be," about what he could expect. For example, "I could not expect to recover the powers of a sixty or seventy year old" (p. 5). Janis's determination to keep Bellow alive figured heavily in his calculations, "so that in addition to what 19th century old timers called *aviditas vitae*, I had to keep going in order to deserve a wife who put up such a fight for my not-so-precious-life" (p. 4). The doctor in charge of Bellow's recovery was the senior neurologist at the hospital, Daniel S. Sax, who "overwhelmed" Janis with questions but refused to speculate on Bellow's long-term prospects. When Dr. Sax learned that Bellow played the recorder, he encouraged Janis to bring it in for Bellow to play: for the good it would do his fingers and paralyzed facial muscles as much as his spirits. Sometimes Bellow asked Dr. Sax larger questions, about tenacity and the kind of life worth living: "He steered me towards other subjects—books, music, anything except my dilapidated biological foundations. But he came several times a day to see me, at odd hours. . . . He asked me a great deal about a course I was giving in the next term. He wanted to hear all about the reading list. Before I knew it he had me outlining lectures. . . . He brought me back to the subject again and again with great cunning" (p. 6). Bellow "longed" to be told he would regain his strength (p. 5). Only in retrospect, when writing up notes for the medical-conference speech, did he come to appreciate "how much tact there was in the doctor's conduct and to see that he knew perfectly well how much I needed him to see me through" (p. 6).

It was Dr. Sax who made the diagnosis of ciguatera, almost a month after Bellow had been admitted to the hospital. That his colleagues at the hospital doubted and disputed this diagnosis, Bellow suspected, may have had something to do with the frequency of his visits (it may also have mattered that his patient was famous, though Bellow says nothing of this). "I was able up to a point to separate [Sax's] professional motives from his other interests. The fact is that he knew I needed his 'personal' visits, his daily presence—that I depended on it" (p. 7). When asked about Dr. Sax, Dr. Barnardo described him as "a classic neurologist who was trained in the old school: clinical history and physical examination told you everything; *then* you get the CAT scan, then you go to the technology. He was a neurologist who got his information from his patients and developed everything around what he heard and what he sensed from his patients first." Under Dr. Sax's care, Bellow gradually recovered the use of his hands and fingers; he was able to pick up a ballpoint pen, though "the best I could write was a cramped small circle." Sax set him long-division and multiplication tasks, the sort that reminded Bellow of the challenges thrown to David Copperfield by his stepfather: "Nine dozen cheeses @ 2 pounds, eight shillings, four pence. It shouldn't take you more than three minutes." Soon Bellow was adept enough with the pen to sign checks "and began to pay hundreds of bills." In his early days "on the floor," when he failed to name the day of the week, Dr. Sax was tough with him: "Now don't tell me you live on a superior plane and don't have to know exact dates. . . . From now on you'll know the date, like any normal person. You'll check it out every morning and you'll be sure from now on to know the day of the week and the exact calendar date." Soon after, Sax came in "and pinned a calendar on the wall for me. The doctor had observed that my days were a morass of negligence and I was demoralized and drifting and losing heart in slackness and disorder" (pp. 5, 8).

In the medical-convention speech, Bellow refers to Dr. Sax as Dr. X, because, he explains to Sax in a letter of January 5, 1998, three years after the event, "I was unwilling to use your good name without permission. . . . In any case you are the Doctor X who brilliantly diagnosed my disorder—a case of cigua-toxin; from which, with your help, I am still slowly recovering." In the speech itself, he praises Sax more fully, while also considering the differences between medical virtues and those of his own profession:

> I am deeply grateful to the doctors and nurses who saved me within intensive care. But I wonder if I would have been able to come back without Dr. X. And I have given Dr. X a lot of thought. And what I see for him goes something like this. The doctor's outlook, if you prefer, his ideology, is humane. But his training is in science. And science does not see nature as having a soul. But the neurologist, Dr. X, whether he was aware of it or not, did have a soul. He was capable of compassion. So he came early in the morning or late at night, and on the weekends. Nothing is more disheartening or killing than a sickness late in life, when your capacity for recovery is low. I often think that Dr. X understood my condition in the widest sense—beyond blood pressure, beyond the loss of muscle mass (one of his terms), beyond the nerve damage. I can't say [what] he understood of his understanding and that he was "conscious" of it. But that is the difference between his kind of work and my kind of work [p. 11].

ON JANUARY 5, 1995, after over a month in intensive care and almost two weeks on the floor, Bellow returned to the apartment at 73 Bay State Road. The class that Dr. Sax had taken such an interest in would start two weeks later. It was on Joseph Conrad and, understandably, had been canceled when Bellow was in ICU. After rescheduling, it was held in the apartment, and Bellow taught it alone. The class was small. Chris Walsh, who was auditing, remembers Bellow as "hollowed out by his illness. Mentally altogether there, physically drained but trying to husband his energies, and slowly rebounding." The day after the first session, on January 19, Bellow wrote to John Silber to thank him for "saving my life": "The doctors agree that if I had not been rushed to the hospital on Thanksgiving Day, I would not have lived through the weekend." Silber wrote back, on January 22, to say that all he'd done was to contact the dean of the School of Medicine, who ensured that Bellow was immediately put into intensive care, "where you belonged": "The person who really saved your life was Janis."

HALF A YEAR LATER, on June 18, 1995, a week after his eightieth birthday, Bellow wrote to his friend John Hunt to tell him of his illness. While in the hospital, "I wasn't certifiably unconscious but neither was I in any ordinary sense conscious. . . . 'Recovery' was a euphemism for infantile weakness. I had to learn to walk again, to go to the toilet like an adult, to tell time, etcetera." He was now better, but still not "normal." "I take huge doses of blood-thinners, and I am warned that to swallow two aspirins may be fatal. I *do* now and then write something, and I can read again. . . . All the granite I depended on has turned to loose sand and gravel. This is the *dérèglement de tous les sens* [disordering of all the senses] Rimbaud was sold on." A week later, Bellow received a letter from Alexandra—Vela in his delusions, also in his fiction. She had heard of both his illness and his recovery: "Now I hope you will go on to enjoy the years ahead and to prove that there is life after eighty, just as you proved that there was life after the Nobel Prize. As always, ergodically yours, Alexandra." On July 28, Bellow reported to Saul Steinberg that he "was again caught in an undertow—one of the drugs I was taking had swollen my tongue and my palate to such an extent that I was unable to swallow.—I was, in short, choking to death. And once more, rallying, I pulled through." On September 30, he apologized to Martin Amis for not having written. "For the better part of a year," he had been convalescing, "unable to pull myself together." Often he felt "that I never shall recover—I'm too old to do it." Despite medication and a pacemaker, the persistent fluttering of his heart produced "unbearable sluggishness. . . . I have just enough stamina to write for an hour or two, and then I go back to bed for a siesta! I take a good many drugs—'beta-blockers'—and these affect the brain weirdly. I am easily depressed. The days fly away, the weeks are uncontrollable, the months and the seasons are like the merry-go-round." "Derangement and drift," he tells Amis, mark his days, relieved only by the pleasure of "being in Janis's company, and in the weather, the summer blues and greens." Only toward the end of the letter does Bellow rally slightly, with something of his old bite. Debility is not all loss. "I haven't been well enough to see the shoulderless Atlas—*that's* an unmixed benefit—a very considerable plus."

JAMES ATLAS WAS NOT the only person to rouse ill-feeling in Bellow after his release from the hospital. Rachel Schultz was rebuked for urging the doctors to prescribe Versed: "Uncle Saul hated the way it made him feel. He said he was a person who really worked hard to remember things and he was angry that he was given a drug that was meant to make him forget. He said he struggled to remember while they were giving the drug to him and that it was quite a battle. He was angry at me when I told him it was my idea to switch him from the Valium (which also does the same thing as the Versed). . . . He gave me a real earful!" But Rachel stuck to her guns, explaining to Bellow her fears about weaning him off the ventilator had he not switched sedatives. He forgave her "grudgingly," recognizing that Versed "was the lesser of two evils."[10]

There were problems with Greg as well. As Greg writes in his memoir, shortly after Bellow "was wakened from his induced coma, Janis made it clear that she was in charge and, despite appearances, had the strength for the job." After two weeks "hanging on every medical detail . . . I had no reason not to trust Janis. I told her I had no wish to be burdened with his physical care or to make decisions." Greg gives no indication of why Janis may have thought otherwise, adding, "Silently

I thought that a man who had left three sons in the custody of their mothers could not expect them to care for his day-to-day welfare."[11] Some months after Bellow left the hospital, Lesha visited him in Vermont, a visit Greg describes in his memoir:

> With Janis sitting quietly by, Saul, in a rage at his sons, told her that while he was in a coma, Adam, Dan, and I expressed a desire for our father to die so that we could inherit his estate. Lesha shot back, "That's ridiculous, the boys came to Boston to help." Further angered, Saul challenged Lesha to check it out for herself if she didn't believe him. Shocked and frightened by the damage that could result, Lesha called me. Angry about a report I knew to be false, I grudgingly repeated the entire chronology that I had relayed to her over the phone from Boston while Saul was in a coma.[12]

Daniel, too, faced accusations. In a letter of January 16, 1995, less than two weeks after Bellow's release from the hospital, Daniel wrote to him both to explain why he had been unable to come to Boston "when you called to say there was a crisis" and to regret Bellow's anger in reply. "I'm sorry you took it so badly and said the things you did. I'm quite aware of the fact that you nearly died, because I watched the whole thing from the side of your hospital bed and it scared me worse than anything I've ever seen. I've been sure only since Christmas, as your voice sounded stronger with every phone call, that you were going to make it." Bellow's outburst had occurred "just as things were getting so much better between us. I was so happy to be able to see you so often and have the kinds of conversations we've been having. I take what you say very seriously, so you should be careful what you say to me. It pains me that you seem to believe things about me that just aren't true, and that you don't seem to know other things that are true." The letter ends with a desire to come to Boston to "clear the air," perhaps that weekend: "Just call me. I hope Janis is feeling better. Heather and I send our love."

A second and much more painful confrontation occurred three or so months later, in Vermont. Bellow had invited Daniel up "for our favorite lunch of salami and rye bread and pickles, and I was happy to see he was doing better after the nightmare winter he had had. He told me about the dream he'd had in the hospital . . . about Alexandra, which was just as disquieting as it later looked in print [in *Ravelstein*]. Everything was going OK until he said 'I hear my sons were discussing my inheritance in my hospital room while I was there unconscious.'" It took Daniel a minute to compose himself. Then he asked Bellow: "Who told you that?" At this point Janis entered the room: "Oh, here she is!" Daniel said. He was furious and deeply hurt. "That's the most despicable lie that I ever heard told about me." He remembers feeling "hot all over"; tears came to his eyes. "I nearly lost my job because of all the time I spent down in Boston by your bed. I don't get to go on vacation this year because you were sick. I was afraid you would die!" As he said this, Janis was "white in the face" while Bellow "was watching us both." Daniel felt his father "was forcing me to enact the first scene of King Lear. And my stepmother was telling lies to set him against me. . . . I'd read enough Russian novels to know things were to go very badly for me and my brothers." As the silence continued, Daniel finally said, "Do you believe it?" "No," Bellow answered. "No I don't." The tension in the room eased, but Daniel was still furious. "I've been a better son to you than you deserve," he told Bellow. "'I have to go back to work now.' I left them both there and slammed the door on my way out." Later, Daniel wondered if Bellow was testing Janis as much as himself. Although he speaks of his father with love and affection, he describes Bellow's behavior at this moment as "disloyal, and in a way I never forgave him for it, never trusted him again."[13]

GREG, LIKE DANIEL, believes that Janis may have been the source of Bellow's accusations. This she denies. She claims to have said nothing to Bellow about the behavior of his sons or of Lesha. "There were plenty of other people who talked to him about this, people who were there." In his memoir and in interviews and emails with me, Greg speaks only of the worry and concern he and his brothers felt on their father's behalf.[14] What Adam recalls is that Janis "took very ill the well-meaning but also dismissive interference of people who felt they had to step in." He also speaks of a "general coldness of the family towards her—especially on the part of the old inner circle . . . Lesha, Gregory, Harriet." Daniel speaks of "a lot of conflict between Janis and Greg in the ICU," with Greg "acting like he should be in charge. And if Janis felt stiffed by that, she was. But everybody was under such tremendous strain." Greg compares Janis's actions in the months that followed Bellow's release from hospital to "a coup d'état,"[15] presumably because they overthrew the influence of this circle. Adam remembers that Lesha, who had been

Bellow's executor and often advised him about financial matters, felt "driven out" by Janis, which, in a sense, "she was," though relations were hardly severed.[16]

Daniel doubts Janis acted alone, as Gregory suggests, because "she never did anything that he [Bellow] didn't want her to do." This view irritates Janis. "I stood up to him plenty. . . . When he said 'poor me,' played the Herzog role, I teased him mercilessly. I never let him talk in a way that was ridiculous. 'Poor you. Of course Alexandra should have come home from a day of mathematics and gone straight to the kitchen to cook you brisket.' He *wanted* to be checked; he loved me to disagree with him. I let him have it often." Chris Walsh remembers a drive to the airport. He and Bellow were sitting in the front, Janis in the back. Bellow said something about delays and women with their cosmetics. "WHAT?" came a cry from the backseat. "What did you say, Saul?" It was mock outrage, but it was also calling Bellow out. Chris could mock as well, as when Bellow complained about Janis's frequent calls to her mother and sister. "Why not lock her up? Then she'll have no chance to talk to them." Only once—when Bellow could no longer be allowed to drive—did Janis's defiance lead to a serious fight. "He loved to drive, he loved his cars," Janis recalls. "When he finished *Ravelstein* he bought himself a little black BMW as a treat." The fight happened sometime after Bellow had agreed not to drive, which on this occasion he either forgot or chose to forget. Janis hated driving, had only become confident behind the wheel when Bellow was in the hospital. When Bellow refused to move, she threatened to walk home. Furious, he finally gave in. In this sense at least, out of necessity, Janis was in the driver's seat.

Greg emphasizes the role money played in the distancing and disaffection between father and sons. As he puts it in the memoir, both he and Lesha knew that "touching on filial greed and patricidal wishes elicited the most powerful forces in the Bellow family—the spectre of Abraham's chronic threats to disinherit his children, along with images of King Lear and the hated father Karamazov."[17] Early in his stay in intensive care, when it looked as though Bellow would not survive, Janis was focusing exclusively on his immediate comfort and treatment, but there were talks among his sons and others about what needed to be done if he died. The Bellows are emotional people and feelings were especially high during this period. In such circumstances—when discussing power of attorney, costs, conflicting advice from lawyers and doctors—heated or tactless remarks, hurt feelings, fears, and suspicions are common, even in the most harmonious or unemotional families. In Greg's words, not always borne out in his memoir: "I've learned never to draw any permanent connotation from how people act when under duress."[18]

Janis will say nothing of the behavior of the sons during Bellow's time in the hospital. She has "no wish to say negative things about the boys," and repudiates the suggestion that she was responsible for distancing them from their father. Of Greg she will only say, "I'm not going to go anywhere near Greg and his behavior in intensive care." When she and Bellow married, "I wanted the sons to be made happy," describing attempts to bring the family together as "reparations." "I had this Pollyannaish idea—I come from this [close] family—we can all be a family. I would do anything to make this happen." Bellow was not optimistic: "'No, this is going to be difficult.' And I would say, 'Come on, we can do it, let's have a family dinner.' I didn't understand how complicated and how difficult this was, but I tried very hard, very, very hard, and also to help him after these little gatherings. For all his faults, he loved his kids. He was not some ogre, some beast." Janis readily acknowledges that the sons returned Bellow's love; she has sympathy for them, even for their attitude to her. "These poor kids. I mean, what can you expect: And here's *another* woman. What am I going to be? The step-step-stepmother? They'd already each had a stepmother. What a bizarre thing to have to accept. No, they couldn't accept me. But at the minimum what you would want would be some kind of respect, decency, getting along, but it wasn't to be. . . . You know why I stood it? I stood it because I loved their father. I would have done anything to make things better, and I swallowed quite a lot. That's not really my nature, but I did it."

Greg, too, remembers swallowing a lot, especially "being demonized when my brothers and I tried to protect Janis and our father while both were so vulnerable." He was "incensed" at Bellow's "accusation of malice and greed," which "followed on the heels of what appeared to be Janis's friendliness and cooperation," and what he calls his "accession" to her status as Saul's caretaker ("accession" is a strange word to use in this context, given that Bellow had been living with Janis for nine years and married to her for five). A year and a half later, "when Bellow had recovered most of his strength," Greg returned to Boston "to clear the air." Bellow, he writes, apologized for not having remembered that Greg had been there when he was in a coma, and said he no longer believed that his son had been "sitting around in the hospital waiting for him to die so that I could get my hands on some dough." He also acknowledged Greg's "thirty years of financial independence."[19] On June 10, 1995, long before this apology, Bellow turned eighty. Atlas says Janis threw a party for him in the house in Vermont, "with all three sons and their children,"[20] but Janis has no recollection of this party (or any record of it in her journal), nor have Gregory, Adam, or Daniel, though Daniel thinks it possible "that Heather and I, and maybe Adam and Rachel, went out [to Vermont] to dinner." If there was a party, Daniel believes, "I can't imagine it was much fun." A week after the birthday, on June 16, Daniel sent Bellow a Father's Day card with a poem: "Roses are reddish / Violets are bluet / You're my ol' man / And that's all there is to it."

ON JANUARY 23, 1995, within a month of Bellow's release from the hospital, Edward Shils died. As Bellow knew through the Kleinbards, Shils had been terminally ill with cancer for some time. Before the trip to St. Martin, Kleinbard encouraged Bellow to attempt a reconciliation. When Shils learned of this, he rejected the idea. "I'm not going to do that," he told Kleinbard. "It's over. He behaved badly." To Joseph Epstein, Shils said much the same thing: "I'm not making it easy for that son of a bitch. I don't want him over. . . . I'm not going for this sentimentality at the end." Shils's intense animus toward Bellow had long been clear but is given its fullest expression in his annotations to the draft of Atlas's biography. These annotations are contained in two letters, dated March 17 and April 13, 1994, amounting to some thirty-two single-spaced pages. Shils begins by describing the draft as "compellingly readable," "vivid," and "very well written." As with his annotations to *Mr. Sammler's Planet*, a novel he greatly admired, Shils corrects what he sees as mistakes of fact and emphasis, the sort any author would be grateful to receive. These corrections also consistently malign Bellow's character and work. "Consecration to his art" is the only virtue Shils allows his former friend: "With all his troubles mostly of his own making he has never lost that sense."

According to Shils, Bellow's failings as man and artist are various. He advises Atlas to say more of "the wider setting of European romanticism which had seeped into the United States. I refer specifically to the image of the artist as a spurned and misunderstood genius whose sensitivity separates him from and elevates him above the rest of philistine humanity." This image, Shils claims, helps to account for Bellow's "hostile and resentful attitude to American society and particularly to *Goyim*," a quality "he shared but with additional vehemence with the other young Jewish intellectuals of his generation." Bellow has "no sense of obligation to any other human being or to any institution. They were there for him to enjoy, benefit by and discard, as the spirit moved him." More generally, "A great novelist has to have some moral sense. That has been Bellow's blind spot in most of his writings." Bellow's heroes "are self-indulgent persons—'slobs'—yielding to every impulse. Bellow has always written about them with obvious sympathy." His supposed love of Chicago Shils characterizes as *nostalgie de la boue*. "In many respects [the city] represents to him the dregs of all human existence. It must be recognized that Bellow has a powerful attraction to dregs. . . . He is fascinated by corruption, obscenity, sheer dishonesty, cruelty. He has a nose for bad odors to the point where he seldom smells anything else." Shils claims that Atlas is wrong to suggest that Bellow has any sense of citizenship. "I had countless conversations with him. He never spoke of any sense of responsibility for any events occurring in the public sphere in the United States or any other country. There was never anything about which he thought he ought to do something."

When Atlas quotes Bellow on the need "to work out one's destiny freely," Shils scoffs. "This is characteristic of Bellow's nonsense. . . . I do not think there was ever a world in which individuals are free to work out their destiny freely. So, he is even more ignorant than I thought he was." Elsewhere, Shils condemns Bellow's refusal to "take sides. . . . That is, in fact, one of his greatest deficiencies as a writer. . . . If Bellow really took the moral life seriously, he would have taken it seriously. There is no evidence that he did as he floated from one woman to the other. The one thing he took seriously was his literary art and that is something very different from moral seriousness." In daily life, Shils writes, Bellow was ungenerous. He "practically never" invited anyone to dinner, and when he himself was invited "he tried to monopolize the conversation, took affront easily and acted as if he were the most important [person invited] to the dinner and that everyone else had been invited to have the distinction of having his company." Bellow's attempts to persuade the Committee on Social Thought to hire Edith Hartnett and Bette Howland, neither of whom was "remotely qualified," need "more refined analysis." Only his "subterfuge" and threats "to leave the University" explain their having been considered. He put them forward for personal reasons, "at the expense of the University of Chicago. . . . In the case of Mrs. [Howland] I know very well that he was very connected with her sexually. This kind of 'generosity' seemed to be more characteristic of him than in many more of the ordinary kinds." On March 24, 1994, Atlas wrote back to thank Shils for his "percipient and just" comments (the sort of thing anyone might say in a letter of thanks). Then he went on: "I think what you have to say about Bellow as a Romantic, and about his attitude toward America, is very provocative. It's obvious to me that, despite whatever personal differences you and he may have had over the years, you see this man with remarkable clarity."[21]

SHORTLY AFTER BELLOW got out of the hospital, he began work on a new story, "By the St. Lawrence," a work "planned and matured . . . under the respirator and with only intervals of clear consciousness."[22] The story would be a test, Bellow told Richard Stern, "to see whether there was a charge still in the batteries. And of course repetitions—deploying old troops—wouldn't do."[23] The story was published in the July 1995 issue of *Esquire*, for reasons Bellow explains to Julian Behrstock in a letter of September 13: "The New Yorker was willing to print me, but I was told that the word rate was lower for fiction than for non-fiction—i.e. libelous 'exposés' and the trashing of quite inoffensive people. So I accepted Esquire's higher offer. Their fiction editor, Rust Hills, has a soft spot for me." "By the St. Lawrence" is the last story Bellow published. Six years after it appeared in *Esquire*, he chose it to open his *Collected Stories*. Whether it is free of "old troops" is open to question, as it draws on thinly fictionalized characters and situations from Bellow's childhood, some of whom, and some of which, appear in earlier works ("The Old System," *Herzog*, "Memoirs of a Bootlegger's Son"). The narrator, Rob Rexler, only just recovered from "a near-fatal illness,"[24] feels a need to return to the place of his birth, Lachine, Quebec (as Bellow, just out of the hospital, returns to Lachine in writing the story). Rexler recalls how "more than seventy years ago" his mother, "mute with love, had bundled him with woolens and set him down in the snow with a small shovel" (p. 2), a real-life incident recounted by

Bellow on several occasions. Rexler's aunt Rozzy is the last of several fictional versions of Bellow's aunt Rosa Gameroff; her sons, Rexler's cousins, are modeled on Bellow's Gameroff cousins.[25]

What is new is the story's fascination with viscera and body parts. Rexler's body is contorted by polio, contracted in his twenties. The disease turns him into "a crustacean" (p. 3), humping his back and curving the bracket of his left shoulder into "a contorted coop or bony armor" (p. 11). He walks through Lachine "with a virile descending limp, his weight coming down on the advancing left foot" (pp. 3–4). It is autumn in the narrative present, but in Rexler's mind it is a day in June, when he was seven or eight. On that day, his much older cousin, Albert, an *homme à femmes*, takes him along on what he says is an errand. They pull up in front of a large bungalow with a spacious porch. Albert tells Rexler to stay in the car, that he is likely to be some time. From the car window, Rexler watches as young women "came and went on the broad porch. They walked arm in arm or sat together on the swing or in white Adirondeck chairs." Albert's "errand" takes "as much as an hour" (p. 5), and the adult Rexler wonders if his child self had any idea what Albert was up to in the house. "He might have had," he decides, given "all those young women passing through the screen door, promenading, swinging between the creaking chains" (p. 5). He certainly knew not to "say anything to Aunt Rozzy about the house with all the girls" (p. 7).

The key moment in the story occurs on the drive back home. Rexler and Albert are stopped at a level crossing: there has been an accident, a man has been hit and killed by a train, the scene has not yet been cleaned up, and when Rexler stands on the running board of the car, he sees "not the corpse, but his organs on the roadbed—first the man's liver, shining on the white, egg-shaped stones, and a little beyond it his lungs. More than anything it was the lungs—Rexler couldn't get over the twin lungs crushed out of the man by the train when it tore his body open. The color was pink and they looked inflated still" (p. 6). That night, at dinner, Aunt Rozzy notices Rexler isn't eating. "I think it was the accident that took away his appetite," says Cousin Albert, who recounts how the man's body had "burst open. . . . We came to a stop and there were his insides—heart, liver." Young Rexler stares at his bowl of chicken soup and at the gizzard Aunt Rozzy has served him as a special treat: "It had been opened by her knife so that it showed two dense wings ridged with lines of muscle, brown and gray at the bottom of the dish." The gizzard reminds Rexler the child not only of what he had seen that afternoon, but of the trussed chickens he had watched being slaughtered in St-Dominique Street, in the Montreal slum where his family once lived, as had Bellow's family: "first fluttering, then more gently quivering as they bled to death. The legs too went into the soup" (p. 7).

These memories conjure a much later memory, when Rexler was summoned to Lachine to say goodbye to Cousin Albert, now the last of his Lachine relatives. Albert is eighty and dying of skin cancer, "his legs forked under the covers like winter branches" (p. 11). He recalls nothing of the accident or the strewn body parts, and Rexler doesn't press him. In Albert's "still-shrewd eyes," Rexler reads an awareness that the cancer "had metastasized and he hadn't far to go" (p. 10). If Albert remembered anything from that day, Rexler thinks, it would have been what happened in the bungalow rather than at the level crossing: lying with a girl "chest to chest, his heart and lungs pressing upon hers" (pp. 10–11). Looking at the drip to which Albert is attached, Rexler notices "in the upside-down intravenous flask a pellucid drop was about to pass into his spoiled blood" (p. 11).

The two memories—of dying Albert and the accident at the level crossing—come to Rexler as he walks "lopsided" through Monkey Park, along the Lachine Canal and the St. Lawrence. "He turned his mind again to the lungs in the roadbed as pink as a rubber eraser and the other organs, the baldness of them, the foolish oddity of the shapes, almost clownish, almost a denial or refutation of the high-ranking desires and subtleties. How finite they looked" (p. 10). The qualifications here—"almost clownish," "almost a denial," "how finite they looked" (as opposed to "were")—suggest incredulity rather than equivocation. "In part the story had to do with anatomy," Bellow told Werner Dannhauser in a letter of August 25, 1995, "the vital organs scattered on the tracks—all the absurd-looking parts on which the spiritual life rests."

In the narrative present of the story, Cousin Albert has been dead for years, buried with the rest of his family, among what Cousin Ezra, Albert's older brother, called "my dead" (p. 11), an expression Bellow used of his own deceased relatives. Toward the end of the story, Rexler imagines that his crippled body "must have been formed by his will on the hint given that afternoon at the scene of the accident. Don't tell me, Rexler thought, that everything depends on these random-looking parts—and that to preserve them I was turned into some kind of a human bivalve?" (p. 11). The question is rhetorical: "everything," ultimately, depends on the body (even if Rexler is right about the role of his will in deforming his body). This is a truth the story faces squarely, as it is faced in *The Dean's December*, most memorably at Minna's mother's funeral, when the roaring furnace of the crematorium "flashed away" her fat, "blew up" her organs. On the last page of "By the St. Lawrence," Rexler turns his thoughts to death, only recently escaped. He likens it to "a magnetic field that every living thing must enter" (p. 11). This thought comes to Rexler beside the "platinum rush" of the St. Lawrence, a rush to the North Atlantic, into which it dissolves. The river is drawn to the sea like metal to a magnet, like Rexler and Bellow to Lachine. For both narrator and author, the St. Lawrence is sublime in its power, but unfeeling, inhuman, like Shelley's Mont Blanc, or the night sky at the end of *The Dean's December*. Lachine is the place from which they come, but there is little of Wordsworth's sense in "Ode: Intimations of Immortality" of the ocean as the place "which brought us hither," an "immortal" place, which, consolingly, "Our Souls have sight of" in privileged moments. If the story is new, what makes it so is its unwavering focus on the vulnerability and dissolution of the body.

IN LATE MAY 1995, shortly before Memorial Day weekend, Harriet Wasserman picked up a message on her answering machine from the agent Andrew Wylie. He was calling about Saul Bellow and asked Wasserman to get back to him. Wasserman thought the call was about Saul Steinberg, a Wylie client, one of whose drawings (given to Bellow after their adventures in Kenya) was being considered as a cover for the Penguin Classics edition of *Henderson the Rain King*. When she returned it, Wylie immediately announced, as she reconstructs it in her memoir, "I've spoken with Saul Bellow, and I want to buy the backlist from Russell and Volkening and handle his foreign rights." Wylie then went on to say that Bellow had described his relationship with Wasserman as "sacrosanct," both as an agent and as a friend. Wylie could only handle the backlist and foreign rights "if it's all right with you." Wylie then asked if he could come to Wasserman's office "to talk to you for about an hour." The rest of the phone conversation was unpleasant. Wasserman had heard that Wylie had spat on a copy of *More Die of Heartbreak* and stubbed his cigarette out on it. This Wylie denied. She reminded Wylie that she had been Bellow's agent "for twenty-five years," to which Wylie answered: "I can do a better job than you can." When Wasserman accused Wylie of wanting not only Bellow's backlist and foreign rights but "all of him," Wylie said he would provide her with a signed letter saying that this was not so, adding that he had taken on lots of estates recently and was good at revitalizing backlists. Wasserman returned to Wylie's treatment of *More Die of Heartbreak* and asked him why he wanted to represent Bellow. He answered, "He's the greatest writer we have."[26]

Wasserman was keen to know if Wylie had contacted Bellow or Bellow had contacted Wylie. "I called him," Wylie answered. To Bellow, later, she was adamant that the proposed arrangement would never work. "You don't divide up lists," she said. "You can only have one agent." He had to choose. Some months passed after this initial exchange with Bellow. "By the St. Lawrence" was sold to *Esquire* by Wasserman, and business continued "as usual." In mid-September, however, Bellow called and asked her to reconsider Wylie's scheme "about the foreign rights and the backlist." Wasserman reiterated that there could be no division of the job. Bellow said he'd think things over. In a subsequent telephone call, before a reading Bellow was to give at the 92nd Street Y at the beginning of October, Wasserman pressed Bellow. He had still not made up his mind. She insisted, "I have to know where I stand!" and Bellow answered by telling her not to raise her voice. Then she hung up. Bellow called the Wasserman agency lawyer, Edward Klagsbrun, who also did work for him in connection with nonagency matters, and the lawyer advised Wasserman: "The poor guy, he hasn't made up his mind. Call him up. He thinks you're firing him. He thinks you're resigning." After the reading at the Y, Wasserman contacted Bellow. He had still not made up his mind. In the following days, she got several telephone calls from her lawyer saying that Bellow kept calling him to ask if Wasserman was still his agent: "Is she resigning? Is she firing me?"

Despite these queries, Wasserman was convinced that Bellow had made up his mind to go with Wylie. On October 23, she sent him a fax saying: "It is my understanding that you have dismissed me as your agent. It doesn't all add up that you keep asking if I'm resigning, if I'm firing you." Bellow did not answer until November, when a note from him informed her, she writes, "that a new lawyer would be requesting that I gather all his material, contracts, etc. The lawyer asked for a meeting. I came to his office. He told me that Saul hadn't made up his mind yet, that he himself was a neutral third party, engaged to look over all my work and Wylie's proposition and advise Saul." In early December, Wasserman finally heard from Bellow, who told her he had to go into hospital again, for a gallbladder operation.[27] As Wasserman remembers it, nothing was said about her fax or about Wylie. Bellow's manner was friendly. After the operation, he telephoned to ask Wasserman to negotiate a contract with Viking Penguin for his collected short stories. A week later, the new lawyer told Wasserman that "Saul would like Andrew Wylie to handle his backlist and his foreign rights and for you to be his primary agent under Wylie's supervision." Would Wasserman be willing to meet with Wylie? She wouldn't. On February 8, 1996, the lawyer tried again: "Saul has made up his mind. I hate to do this, it's the kind of call I hate to make, but he's going with Andrew Wylie." The next week, on Valentine's Day, an item appeared in the *New York Times* "Book Notes" column announcing that Bellow was about to join the Wylie Agency, among whose clients were Norman Mailer, Philip Roth, Martin Amis, Salman Rushdie, Pat Barker, and Susan Sontag. The next day, Bellow rang to say it wasn't true. According to Wasserman's own account, she again hung up on him.

> "Saul, are you writing?
>
> "Yes."
>
> "Write good, bye-bye."

A half hour later, the new lawyer called to say, "You know that article's absolutely not true. . . . I officially terminated you for the backlist and the foreign rights. You would still be Saul's primary agent, under the supervision of Andrew Wylie." The lawyer's tone was now friendly. He had heard "many good things about you from a number of people." Bellow asked the *Times* to print a correction, but nothing came of it, for reasons not altogether clear from Wasserman's account. Wasserman then heard that Bellow was complaining that she no longer communicated with him, so she formalized the break. "I knew he wished me to infer and carry out a final duty on his behalf. In true Bellovian fashion, I was to fire myself."

Wasserman felt betrayed by Bellow, but her memoir suggests that she played her hand poorly, flying off the handle out of injured pride. "Her reaction to the call I made," Wylie remembers, "was sort of crazy, because Saul could not have been clearer with me: If she's not happy, it's not going to happen. So he was *completely* honorable in regards to her interests, completely, and he was very distressed when she, as he put it, cast him into outer darkness." She might have fought off Wylie, or addressed the issues Wylie raised when wooing Bellow. But at this stage she was unable to do so. Janis is hard on Wasserman. What she remembers of the split is that "she was both not effective and difficult to deal with." She had "troubles"; "there was nobody who could really talk to her or get along with her." The process of separating "was long overdue and painful. . . . He did not want to do her in and hurt her." Wylie has no memory of meeting Wasserman either before or after the split with Bellow, and claims to have no animus against her. "I don't think she was a bad person. I think she was just scatterbrained and she had her passions." Wasserman has stout defenders among her authors; she also had authors who have sued her.

Wylie's initial decision to contact Bellow came after browsing in a bookstore, something he often did, looking for the books of authors he admired. The way their books were displayed, what their covers looked like, often told a story. Bellow's books were published by different houses and he could see little coherence in their presentation. "A lightbulb went on in my head, and I thought the reason why Saul's books were not presented in a uniform format and with coherence is that Wasserman used to work as a receptionist for Seldes [Tim Seldes, who took over Russell & Volkening in 1972, by which time, Wasserman claims, she was already, in effect, acting as Bellow's agent, hardly a receptionist] . . . and when she left [in 1981] Saul went with her." Wylie knew Seldes, and called him up to say, "Tim, I'd like to buy the representation of those books of Saul's you represent" (that is, all the books published while Bellow was with Russell & Volkening, the last of which was *The Dean's December*). In the course of the call, Seldes made clear that "there was no love lost between himself and Harriet." He asked Wylie what he would "like to pay" for the right to receive commission on the books. Wylie answered, "Whatever you'd like." Seldes said that he'd think about it but that any deal would have to be approved by Bellow.

So Wylie called Bellow in Boston—he got the telephone number from James Atlas—and asked if he could come to see him. He had never met Bellow, who asked what he wanted to see him about. As Wylie recalled in an interview: "I said, Well, I want to buy the representation of your backlist. He said, What does that mean? and I said, That's what

I'd like to come to talk to you about." Wylie then called Martin Amis and Philip Roth (or perhaps he called them after seeing Bellow; he's not sure) and asked them "to put in a good word." In Boston, he told Bellow: "The reason your books aren't presented coherently in the marketplace, not just here but abroad, is that you've got two people working on the case and the two don't get along, so there's no coordination. . . . This is very damaging. So what I'd like to do is buy the representation to the early [books], because I don't have a problem with Harriet—which was true" (recalling this moment, Wylie began to laugh). When Bellow asked Wylie why he wanted to buy out Seldes's rights, Wylie answered, "Because I love your work and I want to make money. [Bellow] said, You think you'll make money this way? I said, I know I'll make money this way. He said, Well, why do you suppose Tim Seldes doesn't want to keep hold of them [the rights]? And I said I guess he feels there's a price at which it would make sense to unload [them], because he doesn't have a connection with you . . . if the price is right."

When Bellow asked Wylie what the price was, Wylie said, "He hasn't told me yet, but I've assured him that I'll pay whatever he asks. And Saul said, Why would you do that? And I said, Well, Tim's a gentleman, and he'll ask less than it's worth. So Saul said, very distinctly, The only way I would be okay with this is if you report to Harriet. So, if you can work out a deal with Harriet to represent the foreign rights for her books as well as Tim's, if you acquire Tim's, fine, but in any case you've got to report to Harriet." Wylie began to push: "I said, Okay, I think I know more than she does. . . ." Bellow cut him off: "You have to report to Harriet." Wylie said okay, and Bellow said: "So you go back to New York, you call Harriet, and if she's okay with it, we're on." Back in New York, Wylie came to an arrangement with Seldes ("He mentioned a price; I said fine") and contacted Wasserman. Wylie's account of this call is somewhat different from Wasserman's. "I explained to her what I had in mind, and she said, Have you spoken to Saul about it? I said, Yes, I went to Boston and I explained to him. He said it was okay with him if it was okay with you."

Wylie claims he tried not to antagonize Wasserman, saying: "The problem, Harriet, was not with you, it was the fight you had with Tim. . . . There's this division in the work and division in the representation. You've got one person selling some books and another selling the others, and the two of you don't talk to each other, so how the hell can you coordinate anything? The result is that Saul's work is out of print all over the place, and nobody cares about it, because, with the more recent work coming along as it has, there's no reference made to the earlier titles that Tim was representing. Because not only do you not represent them [this wasn't quite true, as we shall see] but you don't want them to do particularly well. . . . It's a broken system, and the unwitting victim in this is Saul." In Wylie's reconstruction, this is how the call ended: "She said, I know who you are. I said, What do you mean? She said, You're Mike Ovitz [the Hollywood agent]. I said, No, I'm not, I'm Andrew Wylie. And she said, Yeah, okay, I'll get back to you, and hung up." A series of emotional calls followed. "I understand why they were emotional," Wylie says, "but the exchanges are a matter of record. I think Harriet's account is not very accurate. . . . And eventually she resigned, just resigned, said, That's it." When Wylie took over all Bellow's representation, "I continued to send her every cent she was due . . . including half the foreign revenue [for post-1982 titles]. She never cashed any of my checks." After three years of uncashed checks and unanswered letters and emails, Wylie stopped sending her checks, having first warned her that he would do so unless she got back to him within three months. As he puts it, "We wanted a record in case she went legal."

Wylie's view is that Wasserman's position was impossible: "She could never do what needed doing, because Seldes would never sell her the backlist. If you represent Saul Bellow and the receptionist leaves with Saul Bellow, you want to kill the receptionist, by means of severe torture if possible. That's how I'd feel. . . . Neither Tim nor Harriet wanted Saul to suffer, but no one had tried to solve the problem, and the problem was visible in the bookstore." In a footnote in her memoir, Wasserman offers a different but comparably discrediting account of her position vis-à-vis the backlist, for which she claimed sole responsibility, a service she agreed to perform gratis, as a courtesy. If the footnote is correct, she alone was responsible for the incoherence Wylie drew to Bellow's attention. That Seldes got the commission and Wasserman acted for free, may account for her lack of attention to old titles, though at the time of the split, she claims, a uniform reissue of all Bellow's novels was in the pipeline, in the Penguin Twentieth-Century American Classics series. What Wylie remembers is that when he took over as Bellow's agent, in February 1996, he discovered that there were two separate networks of foreign subagents for Bellow's work, one for the Seldes titles, one for Wasserman's. "In some cases, licenses had expired and not been renewed; there was no attempt to use new work to reinvigorate the presentation of older work . . . so the new work declined in value and the old work went out of print." Wylie went to Paris to talk with Gallimard, Bellow's French publisher, who agreed to retranslate his books and to put the new translations in the paperback La Pléiade series. "Basically, we just got things into print," he recalls, "and used new works to make sure the old ones were still in print."

Relations between author and agent also improved, without any of the difficulties there had been with Wasserman, including those experienced by Janis, whom she treated, according to Adam, "like a servant."[28] The only tricky moment between Wylie and Bellow occurred when Wylie acquired James Atlas as a client. "I had not negotiated Jim's relationship with Saul, and I had not negotiated his contract for the book. . . . Later, when the Bellows became disenchanted with Jim's biography, obviously, the issue was raised: How could you represent him? And I said, How could I not? I'm his agent. . . . So I had conversations with Saul and Janis, advising them. I had conversations with Jim, advising him. . . . It was difficult for Saul. I know he got paranoid at one point, and I tried to calm him down."[29]

ON DECEMBER 5, 1995, two weeks before gallbladder surgery in Boston, Bellow returned to the University of Chicago to deliver a talk to an audience of a thousand in Mandel Hall. The title of the talk, cosponsored by the Committee on Social Thought, was "Literature in a Democracy: From Tocqueville to the Present." It began with memories of Bellow's undergraduate days at the University of Chicago—of Mandel Hall in particular, where he claimed to have spent more hours playing pool than he could afford, "trying to master reverse-English while my conscience grew more and more swollen."[30] As in "By the St. Lawrence," the talk draws heavily on "old troops," and not only in the opening pages of reminiscence. The claims of the novel are once more forwarded, even though the present is an age in which "we, the likes of us, are its material" (no Julius Caesars, etc.). So, too, the claims of the imagination (as opposed to "ideas," "cognitions," "ideologies") (p. 4). The dangers of distraction are again emphasized ("around us ideas proliferate madly") (p. 8). Tocqueville does not figure until the second half of the talk, when he is quoted as saying that in democratic America "each man instantly sees all his fellows when he surveys himself" and that "in the end democracy diverts the imagination from all that is external [social rank, wealth] and fixes it on man alone. . . . Here, and here alone, the rude sources of poetry among such nations are to be found" (p. 10).

For Bellow, Tocqueville is thus "a younger contemporary of Wordsworth, and like Tocqueville Wordsworth in his lyrical ballads wrote of simple people. . . . In low, rustic life Wordsworth looked for 'the essential passions of the heart' . . . aiming at a poetry purged of civilized prejudices" (p. 11). Toward the end of the talk, Bellow deplores "contemporary writers functioning as mere illustrators for leading thinkers. With a little practice you can see easily where these writers are coming from philosophically" (p. 17). Where they should be coming from is the human heart, "the inner life." In an expanded version of the talk, published in a 1999 Festschrift for David Grene, Bellow describes the inner life as opposed not only to the exposition or illustration of "leading thinkers" but to "the paltriness of our daily doings, the events we read in the papers and watch on television" (an allusion to Tocqueville's complaint about the "paltry interests" that crowd the lives of most Americans). The inner life may be "intimidated and frightened," but it "nevertheless persists," in the work of true novelists and poets, the source of "a multitude of mysterious qualities and powers."[31]

Richard Stern, who was at the lecture, pronounced his old friend "about 75% of what he was a dozen years ago, maybe a bit less." When they were alone, "he was much the old Saul, inquisitive, full of memories."[32] In the run-up to the talk, Bellow was characteristically finicky, revising it at least five times "and still fiddling with it just before he eased on stage." The talk was difficult in places (the printed version is also difficult), and "not everyone absorbed every word," according to the reporter from the *Chicago Tribune*. "To some it was enough to be in Bellow's presence, to welcome him back to the place where his career took off." As Stern told the reporter, laying it on thick: "If Shakespeare were going to make his last appearance somewhere, wouldn't you want to see him?"[33] In the course of making a case for instinct or the heart over intellect or ideas, Bellow refers to dozens of works and writers, including philosophers and social theorists as well as novelists and poets. He points to *Crime and Punishment* as illustrating the dangers of intellectual hubris, as when Raskolnikov compares himself "not only to Napoleon but to Mohammed and other founders." For Bellow, "Raskolnikov is fighting the impotency of thought. As he lies in his attic revolving entire universes in his mind, he is incapable of freeing his sister from her humiliations or of obtaining a few rubles for his rent. His crime is committed, and he swings his murderous axe, in order to save his intellectual honor" (p. 7).

BELLOW HAD RECENTLY REREAD *Crime and Punishment*, for the first time in forty years. He did so because it figured in a course he was to teach in January 1996 at BU, "The Ambitious Young Man" (other texts for the course were Bellow staples: *Père Goriot*, *The Red and the Black*, *Great Expectations*, *Sister Carrie*, and *The Great Gatsby*). Chris Walsh was by this time Bellow's assistant, but he took no part in conducting the class. He did, however, devise instructions for student papers, under Bellow's supervision. The instructions give a sense of the mood Bellow sought to establish in class and of his manner with students. On the question of due dates, the instructions were firm. "As a favor to you, *no late papers will be accepted*." In choosing a topic for final papers, students were advised to "consult with Professor Bellow." The topic they chose to write on had to be "substantial enough to justify your essay's length" (eight to twelve pages). One topic was banned: "No papers on Color in *The Great Gatsby*, please." As for titles, they should be "brief but informative," or, better still, "brief but provocatively informative, without being contrivedly cute." The main stylistic advice was "write concisely." More specifically, verbs should be "strong, expressive, active," and special care should be taken with words "that seem ready at hand," including "parameters transcend irony ironic dichotomy mindset thus therefore furthermore relationship showcase paradox internal parallel closure utilize it would seem one might argue." In addition, students were encouraged to "take special care with every other word you use." The instructions end with the heading "Ignore": "Ignore the above, and try to write in your own voice. Read your paper aloud, to a friend if possible. Then read the above. Revise. Don't lose your own voice. Revising helps singing."[34]

In addition to teaching, Bellow was a responsible colleague, assessing job candidates, fellowship applicants, marking comprehensive examinations (the equivalent of "fundamentals" exams at the Committee on Social Thought). He also involved himself in the politics of the University Professors program. The director of the program, Claudio Véliz, a Chilean economic historian, had been appointed by Silber in 1990.

Rosanna Warren—poet, daughter of Robert Penn Warren and Eleanor Clark, and one of the younger University Professors—remembers a banquet at which Véliz rose to offer a toast to Pinochet, at the time under house arrest in Britain. Véliz ran the University Professors program as his personal fiefdom, "wanted to control everything. No faculty meetings, everything private." The arts-and-literature group among the University Professors (Warren, Bellow, Roger Shattuck, William Arrowsmith, Geoffrey Hill, Donald Carne-Ross, Mary Ann McGrail) were soon openly hostile to him. There were disputes over fellowships for arts-and-literature students; hiring preferences; bias in favor of social-science faculty; the intellectual standing of new hires; extravagant banquets and glitzy "*conversaciones*" ("flummery," in Christopher Ricks's phrase). At one point, relations reached the boiling point, and Silber called an emergency meeting. In the course of the meeting, which was held in the wood-paneled splendor of the president's office, Véliz insulted Roger Shattuck, who told him, "In another era, Claudio, I would challenge you to a duel." Shattuck was serious. During these crises and confrontations, according to Warren, Bellow "was very generous as a colleague. . . . He got involved. He wasted a lot of his precious energy and time fighting shoulder to shoulder with us. . . . He cared about the quality of the program he was teaching in." Warren credits Bellow with giving the arts-and-literature group "a sense of solidarity with each other."

A YEAR AFTER BELLOW'S RECOVERY from the poisoned-fish episode, he and Janis flew to Florida to attend the wedding of his youngest son, Daniel, and Heather Hershman, who had recently completed an M.A. in criminal justice at American University in Washington, D.C. The family all liked Heather. To Janis she was "always a love to Saul and to me. Quiet, kind, sensitive, generous." The wedding was held on Sunday, January 14, 1996, at the Biltmore Hotel in Coral Gables, the Art Deco palace where Al Capone stayed before his arrest for income-tax evasion in 1931. Heather's father, a Miami physician, spared no expense. The three hundred guests dined from lavish buffet tables organized by region (Middle Eastern, Chinese, Southwestern), drinking champagne and twenty-year-old Scotch.[35] Janis remembers getting "all gussied up. . . . It was a very swank occasion." Adam described it as a wedding "out of *Goodbye, Columbus*, which amused everybody." Bellow hadn't seen Susan since Daniel's bar mitzvah, and Adam was relieved to find that at the wedding he was "gracious to her, he was on good behavior." Daniel, however, remembers his father's refusal to go to the rehearsal dinner hosted by Susan, dining instead at a "fancy restaurant." (Daniel later learned from Lesha that Bellow had "tried to talk the rest of the family into boycotting it as well, and Lesha gave him hell for it.") Only at the last minute did Daniel ask Bellow to escort Susan down the aisle during the ceremony. "I didn't ask you before," Daniel admitted, "because I didn't want to give you a chance to back out on standing up with me." As he put it in an interview, "He had to take his medicine like a big boy." When Daniel stomped on the glass, "everyone said *mazel tov*, and then there was dancing with chairs up in the air, and it was a tremendous party."

Bellow had been determined to attend the wedding and to behave well at it, despite having a note from his doctor saying that he was too weak to expose himself to fatigue. As he wrote to Sophie Wilkins on January 19, 1996, "I didn't want the kid accusing me of disappearing on *all* important occasions. So I did it all, including a second trip to the altar with my ex-wife, Daniel's mother. There wouldn't have been a Stoic in all of Rome who wouldn't have congratulated me on my philosophic poise." Father, son, and stepmother had recovered from the painful confrontation in Vermont. Or, rather, they had got over it enough to be civil, even cordial, at the wedding. Nor were there difficulties with Bellow's other sons, with his two wives, with Lesha and her family, or with Maggie Simmons. "Who was that attractive woman you were talking to?" Susan's friend Margo Howard asked her. "One of Saul's old mistresses," Susan said. "During whose marriage?" the friend asked. "Mine," she answered.

SOME MONTHS AFTER THE WEDDING, in the spring of 1996, relations between Daniel and Bellow were tested again, by an autobiographical story Daniel wrote and sent to Andrew Wylie for comment. Before doing so, he showed Bellow what seems to have been a proposal for the story "where I name names and refer to actual events" (presumably to be altered in the story itself). Bellow objected to parts of the proposal, and in an undated letter Daniel responded to his objections. "After careful consideration," he writes, he has decided to rework "the discussion of my parents. I believe I make it clear I am not talking about the way things are now, but about the way they were then." The parents, he reminds Bellow, won't be the main focus of the story, but they need to be characterized "in order to show how the narrator leaves home and begins his journey of self-discovery." The memories Daniel will recount are as painful to him as to Bellow, but, then, "describing our own experiences in literature can be hurtful to those around us, as you know." His justification sounds familiar: "My career and my desire to be a writer must be weighed against my immortal soul and the effect of my actions on those I love. In 100 years, we'll all be dead." The letter ends with controlled feeling: "I was glad this morning that you were still speaking to me. I hope your visit to the doctor was not serious. I doubt you would tell me anyway. I look forward to seeing you this weekend."

After hearing from Wylie that he liked the story, Daniel sent him a rewritten version, on June 27, 1996. His parents appear now, he writes in a cover letter, only briefly, in two "tantalizing glimpses." Daniel then describes his father to Wylie in a way that captures not only the complexity of his feelings about him but the state of their current relationship:

> My father, whom you know, is a brilliantly talented writer and thinker who should never have been allowed around small children. His reaction when he read the story: "You little bastard! I knew you were up to no good, and this just filled me in on the details."
>
> My attitude towards him has mellowed in recent years as I realized that while he never took me sledding, he made sure I had read Dickens, Twain, Conrad, London and Kipling before I was 12. What I took for neglect and cruelty I now recognize as the standard Russian Jewish child rearing method, seldom seen in this country anymore.[36]

A similar mixture of feelings underlie several stories Daniel tells about his father's political attitudes. In the years since his graduation from Wesleyan University in 1987, Daniel had worked as a reporter in New England. At the time of his wedding, he was covering politics and government as a city-hall reporter on *The Berkshire Eagle*, a seven-day morning newspaper in Pittsfield, Massachusetts. Daniel's politics lay somewhere between Adam's on the right and Greg's on the left, but at times he could say things that set his father's teeth on edge. "He hated to hear me repeat propaganda. Almost to the point of physical violence he hated it. He would say, 'No son of mine is going to be ignorant about this. Read this book and don't talk to me until you're finished.' "[37] What Bellow especially liked was when Daniel's articles attacked government, either civic or national. "Pop loved all this. He thought my ideals were a bunch of misty bullshit, but he liked to watch me make trouble. When I worked for the [*Brattleboro*] *Reformer*, he read my stories every day. If a couple of days went by and I didn't have a by-line in the paper, he'd call me up and say, 'Are you alright, is everything okay, you sick?' Once he said to me, 'I've been watching you and you're very interesting. You don't join the organizations. You are not a joiner. You're a cat who walks by himself. . . . So I'm very proud of you."[38]

Daniel describes Bellow as "a great chain-yanker" in argument. "He liked to dig a pit and cover it with branches so you'd come walking along, whistling away, and fall right in it. Then he would stand at the edge and watch you as you sort of thrashed around. He liked that."[39] But he could, of course, also lose control. Daniel recounts a conversation about Bernie Sanders, at the time the mayor of Burlington, Vermont. Daniel followed Sanders for the *Reformer* and "knew how Bernie would say one thing in Brattleboro and another in White River Junction." When Bellow launched into a "tirade," denouncing Sanders and the political left for its nihilism, insincerity, and hypocrisy, Daniel thought the tirade directed at him, despite his having voiced doubts about the mayor. "Did Abbie Hoffman just walk into the room behind me?" he asked Bellow. "I mean, who are you talking to? Don't you know me any better than that?" Bellow stopped fulminating, "and on the way to the car, he apologized. Pop was the best. I'm so proud to be his son."[40]

A YEAR AFTER THE JULY 1995 publication of "By the St. Lawrence," Bellow was back at work on "Marbles." He had never abandoned it, even in hospital, when weak and despairing. "On the first night when he almost died," Janis recalled, in a journal entry of June 1, 1995, "he was talking to me about the book. Before and after, and the next day in MICU [Medical Intensive Care Unit] too." At one point while in the hospital, according to Janis, Bellow announced he "would *never* go back to it," a view connected to the darkness of the New Guinea scenes he had been working on in St. Martin, involving cannibalism, the disease called kuru, and the findings of the American physician and medical researcher Daniel Carleton Gajdusek, whose journals he'd brought with him from Boston. Gajdusek had also won a Nobel Prize in 1976, in Physiology or Medicine (shared with Baruch S. Blumberg), and he and Bellow had kept in touch. His best-known work was on kuru, a degenerative disorder of the nervous system that turned the brain to sponge. In New Guinea, where Gajdusek conducted his research, the spread of kuru, known as "the laughing death" (for the smilelike rictus it produced), was connected to the practice of funerary cannibalism, the ritualistic consumption of the brains of deceased relatives. This connection Gajdusek proved by infecting primates with liquefied brain samples from New Guinea natives. Gajdusek's Nobel citation described his discoveries as representing an "extraordinarily fundamental advance in human neurology and in mammalian biology and microbiology," an advance crucial to the investigation of other forms of spongiform diseases of the brain, including bovine and human forms of "mad cow disease."

In addition to the gruesomeness of the disease itself and of Gajdusek's experiments, the journals contain disturbing accounts of sexual practices in New Guinea, particularly concerning children. In the journals, he discusses the Anga tribe in New Guinea, whose young boys come to manhood by having sex with older village men. Gajdusek records having been offered children as sexual playmates, or having boys themselves openly approach him for sex, and describes sleeping in the same bed with boys. In the mid-1960s, he began bringing boys from New Guinea back to the United States to live with him. When he won the Nobel Prize, several of them accompanied him on the stage to receive the award. In later years, seven of the boys Gajdusek had adopted testified that they had had sex with him, and Gajdusek admitted having masturbated boys and approving of incest. In April 1996, he was charged with child molestation, and spent a year in prison. From the time of Bellow's first denguelike symptoms on St. Martin, he was, according to Janis, "tortured" by details from Gajdusek's journals, the source material for the New Guinea scenes of "Marbles." But he did not give up the novel. After leaving hospital and finishing "By the St. Lawrence," he returned to "Marbles" once more. On June 1, 1995, according to Janis's journal, he began yet another new version, "handwriting again from PAGE ONE." In this version, the model for Hilbert Faucil was no longer Nathan Tarcov. Now it was Philip Roth, "a P.R. who late in life decides he might still love" (an idea sparked by a conversation

Bellow and Roth had during a visit Roth paid to 73 Bay State Road, after Bellow's return from the hospital). Another factor drawing Bellow back to "Marbles," according to the June 1 journal entry, was his eagerness "to incorporate his new sense of what it means to be old, and 'to have two wheels over the median line.'"

For a while, Bellow went at the novel with renewed confidence, even sending a twenty-eight-page extract to Bill Buford at *The New Yorker*. "I must finally be feeling strong about this book," he told Janis, "otherwise I would never have consented to publish part of it." It was the first time in five years that he had "felt up to letting any part of it go." But again, as the same June 1 entry records, confidence waned, partly because he lacked stamina. In Vermont, in the summer of 1995, Bellow found he could no longer follow his usual routine. "I know he's in trouble when he suggests, as he did a couple of days ago, that we do the grocery shopping in the morning. This morning over breakfast he told me that he's tired of the book again." Roth hadn't worked out as a starting point for Hilbert; now he was considering Arthur Lidov, the starting point for Basteshaw in *The Adventures of Augie March*.[41] In the June 1 entry, Janis admits: "I've given up trying to guess whether Hilbert will make it or not. I asked B why this book had gotten hold of him and tied him up for 5 years, and he said, 'Well, love in old age is a subject that interests me.'" Four months later, in an entry of October 15, Janis records that the model for Hilbert has become Lou Sidran, Bellow's friend from high school. She also records Bellow's complaint that he "doesn't know anymore" where he is in the novel, in the current draft of the novel, so many drafts have there been. The strand of the novel he's at work on now is "confused with other strands from other drafts."

There was also a problem of tone or register. On the one hand, "there's this absorption with death (at least every third thought). And there's this central q[uestion] he brought back from his own crisis, which is, What did I fight for? B didn't come back for the sake of a *Brillig's* [Hilbert's tabloid], or a Magnusson [Hilbert's old friend, part Peltz, part "Kappy" Kaplan], or even a Chickie [Hilbert's girlfriend, some forty-plus years younger]." On the other hand, "this is a comic novel." Although it is perfectly possible to mix the silly with the serious, Bellow couldn't find the right key. As Janis puts it in the journal: "What B has experienced in coming back from death is far more serious than anything he is allowing Hilbert. What he has seen or felt on the comic side he has rendered brilliantly in *Herzog*, but his own history is not the history of a schlemiel." This problem Bellow and Janis discuss throughout the morning, invoking Heidegger and Nietzsche and Flaubert and *Lear* and *Measure for Measure*. At the end of the journal entry, Janis asks: "Have I succeeded in transmitting any of this morning's talk? We were both very excited. . . . We went into a lot more detail about Flaubert than I have indicated here."

THREE MONTHS LATER, on January 26, 1996, Bellow began writing a completely different fiction, *The Actual*, a novella published in April 1997 as a Viking Penguin paperback (like *A Theft* and *The Bellarosa Connection*). Its original title was "Changing Places"; its theme, Bellow told Janis, was "how out of place love is in the modern world," though it soon became apparent that "love in old age" would also be a theme. The idea for the novella came from an episode in "Marbles." Hilbert Faucil, at ninety-three, encounters the spitting image of his high-school love, Nellie Bassix, whose face "I had carried in recollection upwards of seventy years and saw more regularly than the orbits of the moon."[42] In *The Actual*, the lovers in question, aging if not old, are Harry Trellman, a businessman returned to Chicago after years in the Far East, and Amy Wustrin, a divorcée, twice married, who decorates the apartments of North Shore notables. Harry has loved Amy, whom he dated briefly in high school, for more than forty years. That they never became lovers or married is his fault, and he bitterly regrets never declaring himself, never competing for or pursuing her. The figure who brings them together resembles the wealthy benefactors of Victorian fiction: Sigmund Adletsky, a "trillionaire" businessman aged ninety-two. Adletsky is small and shrewd; his wife, Dame Siggy, also shrewd, is even smaller. Seated in their warm limo, Dame Siggy looks "something like a satin-wrapped pupa. . . . Her bird legs, aslant, were laid together or set aside until they should be called upon to move."[43]

The real-life starting points for these characters were fixed early. According to Janis's journal entry of May 6, 1997, Bellow identified Herb Passin, a friend since high school, later a professor of East Asian studies at Columbia, as the model for Harry Trellman; Marilyn Mann, the second wife of Sam Freifeld, also a friend from high school, as the model for Amy Wustrin (Marilyn Mann, too, was an interior decorator); and Freifeld himself as the model for Amy's second husband, Jay Wustrin, about whom we hear many unflattering things. Other characters have comparably recognizable points of origin. Adletsky resembles Abe Pritzker, founding father of the Pritzker business empire (Hyatt hotels and the Royal Caribbean cruise line, among other enterprises) and many Chicago philanthropies (the Pritzker School of Medicine at the University of Chicago, the Pritzker School of Law at Northwestern University, Frank Gehry's Pritzker Music Pavilion in Millennium Park). Like Adletsky, Pritzker lived to a ripe old age. He died aged ninety, having turned the family businesses over to his sons and grandchildren (Adletsky's sons and grandchildren now run his businesses, though they "still report to him" [p. 5]). According to Marilyn Mann, Pritzker several times consulted her over questions of interior design and decoration.

Although no trillionaire, Harry Trellman is rich, having "a gift for putting together business deals" (p. 3). One such deal, buying damaged Burmese antiquities, shipping them to Guatemala City to be restored cheaply, then selling them in North America, has earned him "a lifetime income" (p. 9).[44] Harry's habitual reserve, useful in business, is inherited from his mother, who "kept her own counsel." He has a vaguely Asiatic look, enabling him "to drown my emotions in my face, Chinese style" (p. 67). Like Herb Passin's mother, Harry's mother had a disability ("She limped"), which she used as an excuse to place her son in a Jewish orphanage; then she traveled "from sanitarium to sanitarium, mainly abroad" (p. 2), trips paid for by her brothers, rich sausage-makers. Harry's father, a carpenter, seems not to have objected. Perhaps because Harry is so reserved, people confide in him, "though I didn't ever encourage confidence." He's Bellow's cat who walks alone, deriving "an almost incomprehensible satisfaction to deny almost everyone access to my thoughts and opinions" (pp. 62–63). Among the many things most people didn't know about Harry are "what I did in Indochina or Burma. Whether there were women in my life. Or children" (p. 69). What the reader knows is that he had a wife, who strayed, but no children, and that there were other women. Hence, in part, Amy's assumption "that I could never be domesticated" (p. 84).

When Adletsky meets Harry at a dinner party, he finds him astute and intriguing. "In my active years," he tells Harry after summoning him to his office, "I did very little socializing. I have to do it now. And there must be a way to make it pleasanter" (p. 16). Harry, another "first-class noticer" (p. 15), is enlisted by Adletsky to be such a way. He will explain the forces at work on such occasions as the recent dinner—the motives, the interests, the powers. Harry will also be called upon to advise Adletsky "on matters of taste" (p. 16), an additional topic not much attended to by the businessman. Adletsky, Harry thinks, is like Napoleon on St. Helena, bored in exile: "Old age was Adletsky's exile" (p. 75). When Adletsky asks Harry why he's returned to Chicago, Harry answers with characteristic reserve: "I have a connection here" (he means Amy). He might also have said: "I was fond of winter, of the snow on the ground and the old-fashioned raccoon coats high-school girls used to wear—coats with big braided-leather buttons. . . . I valued highly the smell of animal musk released from the fur by the warmth of Amy's body when she unfastened those buttons" (p. 76), a passage that recalls Bellow's memories of petting with Eleanor Fox, his high school love, in wintry Humboldt Park, versions of which appear in "Something to Remember Me By" and *Humboldt's Gift*.[45] "By and by I came to see what kind of hold she had on me," Harry says of Amy: "Other women were apparitions. She, and she only, was no apparition" (p. 84). When asked why, he answers: "After forty years of thinking it over, the best description I could come up with was 'an actual affinity' " (p. 100). "What made it actual?" Amy asks. "Other women might remind me of you, but there was only one actual Amy" (p. 101). Although Adletsky hears none of this, he, too, it turns out, is a first-class noticer. At the end of the novel, he brings the two lovers together at the graveside of Amy's second husband. As Harry puts it, "At ninety-two, Adletsky was pioneering in compassion, a new field for him" (p. 81).

Amy is Harry's erotic ideal, in part because he encountered her in adolescence, the time when "this tremendous feeling came . . . this love, direct from nature, came over me" (p. 70). For forty years, "I kept her preserved as she had been at fifteen years of age" (p. 19). Encountered in later life, the real Amy is at first unrecognizable. Ten years ago, Harry ran into her in the Loop and didn't know her, "the woman with whom I was virtually in daily mental contact" (p. 19). Over the years, "with their crises and wars and presidential campaigns, all the transformations of the present," the Amy of memory is unchanged. "There's the power of Eros for you" (p. 21). That Harry failed to recognize her in the Loop, looking "as gray-faced as a maid-of-all-work—an overworked mother," was because she "was in the real world. I was not in it" (p. 19). Like many Bellow characters, Harry lives much of his life, his most vivid life, in memory. Amy is indignant, furious not to have been recognized, and as he collects himself, he sees her as she is: "More mature. Or subdued. I'm looking for a tactful way to say it" (p. 19). Then he considers the circumstances. "Under the el tracks when the weather is overcast, everything turns gray. . . . The thick, dried urban gumbo of Lake Street made everything look bad." In addition, "her difficulties with her husband, Jay, were acute just then, and she feared she wasn't fit to be seen" (p. 19).

In the narrative present, ten years later, Harry encounters Amy at the Adletskys', where she has come to advise them on furnishings. She is dressed in a blue knitted suit, wearing a good deal of makeup, "especially around the eyes, where it was most needed. Her round face was calm, though her inner reckoning machines ran at high speed" (p. 35). The Loop meeting is forgotten: "Age sometimes brings slovenliness to a woman of a full build. But it was plain that she was still in control of her appearance; her traits and faculties were rounded up—they were on view in the corral. She was a beauty, her skin still smooth; she even breathed like a beauty" (p. 35). As ever, Harry's way of talking makes Amy uneasy (as Bellow's way of talking made Eleanor Fox uneasy). But Amy knows full well the place she holds for him (as Eleanor Fox knew full well the place she held for Bellow). As they talk, Harry pictures Amy, the Amy in front of him, in the shower: "The double cheeks of her backside are still well modeled, and she washes with the experienced hands of the mother who has bathed small children. A whole lifetime of self-care is apparent in the soaping of her breasts" (p. 21). The process of blending the ideal Amy and the flesh-and-blood Amy has begun.

Amy's sexual allure is not wholly a creation of memory or adolescence. A real thing, it has survived both time and the sullying of the world, of Jay Wustrin in particular. In high school, Jay, "an attractive man with a deliberate erotic emphasis in his looks" (p. 22), took Amy from Harry. He and Amy then split up and found others to marry. After those marriages fell apart, they got together again. Before they married, Jay, a swinger, invited Harry to join them after lunch in a threesome in the Palmer House, a postprandial shower (the reason Harry pictures the current Amy in the shower). Jay's aim, Harry believes, was "to cure me of my sentiments . . . his version of cure or correction in accordance with realistic principles" (p. 64). Amy agreed to the shower, Jay tells Harry, with a shrug. "Why not?" (p. 24). (On another occasion, Harry observes, "When she shrugged, the soft breasts in her sweater added weight to her shrug" [p. 83].) After twenty minutes, Jay, a lawyer, is called away to appear in court. "It was then that I kissed her under the breast and on the inner thigh" (p. 24). At some point, Harry recalls, "Amy opened her mouth toward me, yearningly. But she didn't speak. Nor did I" (p. 25). And that was it. "At the Palmer House, when you had the opportunity, you didn't take it," Amy recalls. Harry has thought long and hard about this moment and has his answer to hand. "Just because you were available to me. As you had been available to Jay," an explanation Amy understands: "The generic product, as druggists say, not the name brand. Not you and me, but any male with any female. Looking back, I might have felt like a sex tramp" (p. 20).[46] After Jay and Amy married, Harry recalls, "I was a frequent dinner guest. Friend of the family" (p. 25).

Jay Wustrin was piggish about sex, always on the make, kinky, gross. Five years before his death, he sued Amy for divorce, having secretly taped her sex talk with a lover from New York. These tapes he played to the judge in chambers (and to Harry). Amy was left penniless, an object of salacious gossip. Harry is unfazed: "I wasn't jealous of Jay Wustrin gripping Amy before the wall mirror or of the New York man. . . . I couldn't have expected Amy to mark time while I was inching toward her" (p. 21). It is important that Amy's erotic appeal is set in the context of such doings, also that Harry knows of them. When Amy asks Harry if Jay recounted his sexual antics, Harry tells her, "I didn't care to hear the blow-by-blow." To the reader, Harry is more forthcoming: "I looked down on his activities, but I never tired of hearing (translating them into my own terms) about these seductions. Of the girls by him. Of him by them. More than forty years of it, starting with his father's laundry . . . On bags of soiled towels and bedding, after five p.m., when his Pa put him in charge of locking up for the night" (p. 65).

The erotic ideal Amy embodies for Harry is realizable in the flesh, and always has been. In addition to the warm musk of the raccoon coat as she opens it to him, Harry was drawn to the adolescent Amy by other particulars:

> The imperfect application of her lipstick was another point of identity. That was the whole power of it—the beauty of this flesh-and-blood mortality. Just as mortal was the shape of her bottom as she walked, a mature woman swinging a schoolbag. She didn't walk like a student. There was also the faulty management

> of her pumps. They dropped on the minor beat. This syncopation was the most telling idiosyncrasy of all. It bound the other traits together. What you were aware of was the ungainly sexuality of her movements and her posture [p. 20].[47]

The novel ends with Harry's proposal, and a final scrutiny. "I stood back from myself and looked into Amy's face. No one else on all this earth had such features. This *was* the most amazing thing in the life of the world" (p. 104). "I stood back from myself" suggests that what Harry sees is not solely the Amy of memory. "This is the time to do what I'm doing now," he tells her in the novel's last sentence, "and I hope you'll have me." Not all love in the modern world need be profane; love in age is a reality.

Harry conquers his habitual reserve, but Amy's feelings remain unclear, her pain in particular. This is a point Philip Roth raises with Bellow, in a letter of April 22, 1997. He has now read the novella several times, calling it "a delight in its masterful ease of movement and its sharp momentary effects—the quick portraits of people, *weather*, the surprises . . . yet it seemed to me that undetonated impulses of either thought or sentiment kept reining it in. . . . There isn't much that is recognized or depicted as pain. The pain is treated as far, far away . . . and the invention and the recording of the pain may be what I felt missing." To this letter Bellow replied on May 7. Given the " 'humorously' cynical" nature of the characters (Harry is cynical about everyone except Amy), "I concluded that the pain had to be taken for granted": "Probably they feel they can wear their pain out, or attenuate it, or outlive it." As for Amy, Bellow admits that Harry "gave her no inducement to think of *him*. Still, he does see that he has come somehow to belong to Amy. Because she is his actual." Not everyone will think this much of an answer. The emphasis remains on Harry and his feelings.

The novella has its imperfections. There are improbabilities of plot, as in Adletsky's initial contacting Harry for advice, or the "joke" that Jay contrives, occasioning his reburial (having himself buried next to Amy's mother, who hated him). Also improbable, or uncharacteristic, is Harry's sudden denunciation of the debased modernity of "commonplace people . . . lacking in higher motives" (p. 43). This is the bit of the novella Roth liked best: "where the narrator comes out of hiding and lets the judgment rip." James Wood, writing in *The New Republic*, called it "a marvelous Bellovian tumble of accusations."

> They were run-of-the-mill products of our mass democracy, with no distinctive contribution to make to the history of the species, satisfied to pile up money or seduce women, to copulate, thrive in the sack as the degenerate children of Eros, male but not manly, and living, the men and women alike, on threadbare ideas, without beauty, without virtue, without the slightest independence of spirit—privileged in the way of money and goods, the beneficiaries of man's conquest of nature as the Enlightenment foresaw it and of the high-tech achievements that have transformed the material world. Individually and personally, we are unequal to these collective achievements [pp. 42–43].[48]

Harry is thinking these accusations, not speaking them—to speak them would be wholly out of character—but it is hard to imagine him even thinking them, or thinking them in these terms. Although he is said to "look down on" everyone, Amy excepted, there is little evidence elsewhere in the novella to suggest that he sees the world from this elevated perspective, so transparently Bellow's perspective, the perspective of the Mandel Hall lecture. Like Bellow, Harry is devoted to higher motives, but these motives are particularized, not built into a

The view from the Flamboyant Beach Villas, Grand Case, St. Martin (courtesy of Flamboyant Beach Villas; photo by Ralf Hildebrandt)

theory. It is Amy he seeks. More believably Bellow-like is his chancing his hand in love, at last declaring himself.

At the time *The Actual* was written, Bellow himself was chancing his hand. Janis's devotion to him in his weeks of illness and recovery had kept him alive. They had been together for more than a decade. He loved her and needed her. Now, on the eve of her forties, she desperately wanted a child. He was in his early eighties; his record as a father had not been good; he had more work to do, and less energy. These were his realities. He told several friends he did not want another child. Janis's realities were also to be considered. He was unlikely to have many years left; the clock was ticking; with a child, he would live on for her, their life together would live on, and not only in memory. One way of looking at the decision Bellow made was that he needed Janis and he owed her; another way was that he knew how much Janis wanted a child and that he did it for her. In other words, he did it for love.

12

Ravelstein

In the "marbles" typescript, dated June–October 1994, Hilbert Faucil, aged ninety-three, also chances his hand.[1] Chickie MacNellis, the daughter of Hilbert's housekeeper (in New Hampshire, where he summers), has been his girlfriend for many years. Every other week, Hilbert flies to her from his home in Florida. They have traveled together to Paris and Budapest. Chickie is a contemporary of Hilbert's granddaughter Immy, who now sees her as a threat to her inheritance. By the age of eighteen, Chickie was Hilbert's lover, but when she pressed him to marry her, he demurred. "You're never going to do it," she says. "You'd be embarrassed to marry a teenage girl. Besides you're one of those widowers that play the field" (p. 69). So Chickie marries MacNellis, a veteran of the Korean War, who has been in and out of prisons and VA hospitals. Now, in her early forties and divorced from MacNellis, she and Hilbert are together again, and she wants his baby.

Chickie has made a name for herself as a brewer or fermenter of miso, "familiar to all who shop in healthfood markets . . . as common here as baseball and topless bars are in Japan" (p. 69). In addition to taking Dr. Clavel's human growth hormone, Hilbert has been adding her miso to his soups and fishes, as well as taking it "neat by the spoonful like cod liver oil." Chickie knows nothing of Dr. Clavel's magic pills and credits Hilbert's "all around physical soundness" (p. 70) to her miso. She loves Hilbert and explains to him her reasons for wanting a child at forty. "I don't care how you argue it, while you're not exactly out of commission it's not a one hundred percent pleasure to look into the future. So why not have a child? What woman wouldn't be delighted to have one by a prodigy like you" (p. 232)? Chickie has no illusions about Hilbert, despite her sense of him as prodigy. "It wasn't as though she didn't know my failings and shortcomings. She saw important human qualities—the abiding ones in me. I must add that she did not think those qualities were well-represented in my descendants" (p. 72). It is these descendants who figure in Chickie's current feelings about marriage. "I regularly offered to take her to the altar," Hilbert says. "No, she said, she wasn't going to be denounced as a gold-digger. But she was still capable of conceiving and would remain so for a few years yet, and if she conceived and delivered she would accept my marriage offer. It would have to be an absolutely foolproof case of paternity. With the now dependable genetic tests nobody could accuse her of putting it over on a doddering sugar-daddy. Anybody could see that I was of sound mind, 'If Immy takes us to court'" (p. 72).

Although vain about his health and appearance, Hilbert has a clear sense of what it is like to make love to a nonagenarian and what his chances are of getting Chickie pregnant. As he admits, "there *is* something messy—simian—about people in old age, grotesquely disfigured, deeply wrinkled, but still performing the act of love" (p. 58). Performance is no problem: "Whenever I felt inclined to do it, it has always been doable. Imagination is at the bottom of it if you ask me. . . . I'm sure it's the affection of the woman and the expectation she has of you. So it is the appeal to your imagination" (p. 57). It helps that Chickie is the sort of woman for whom "the act of love is as natural as breathing" (p. 72). Her attitude to parenting is similarly easy. She advises Hilbert "to consider how you'd really feel about becoming a daddy and having to bring up a child," but she assures him, "Naturally I promise to spare you the night feedings, diaper changing, crying and fussing. All you'd have to do is dandle the kid when you felt like it" (p. 222). When Hilbert warns that "there couldn't be the usual baseball or football or any of that all-American stuff," Chickie suggests, "You could recite *The Owl and the Pussycat* or *Mother Goose*." In wishing to have a child with Hilbert, Chickie claims to have the greater good in mind, as well as her own needs: "In human terms it would be a great loss to life in general if your type wasn't preserved" (p. 222)—though what of granddaughter Immy? one wonders.

Hilbert is a celebrity, and his reputation is that of an eccentric. Fathering a child at his age will be "a fabulous send-up, setting a record for screwball ingenuity." Dr. Clavel takes a similar view, dreaming of money and fame. When he is told what Hilbert intends: "Bang! His color changed. . . . The blood that came into his face and even under his chin-beard was a cranberry flood." "If at my time of life I could be somehow engineered into fatherhood," Hilbert says of Clavel's reaction, he "would join the band of Twentieth Century immortals headed by Einstein and the double-helix twins Watson and Crick. . . . The covers of *Time* and *Newsweek* were a sure thing" (pp. 83–84). Yet there's Chickie to consider. "I would never involve Chickie in anything macabre or suspect—nothing that would subject her to cynical comment or be a source of vulgar amusement. I dearly love Chickie MacNellis. By which I mean to say our souls are connected. . . . I had to wait sixty years or so for a female profile to fit my own" (p. 78). Hilbert's fears for Chickie are sparked in part by past history. In "primitive" rural New Hampshire, when she was a teenager and he a long-haired city slicker at least three times her age, "there was a small satellite of suspicion circling us. . . . Go tell such people that the broadening of Chickie's mind was based on love and that true educational impulses have an erotic base." It was Chickie who made the first move. "She simply stated one day that the time had come. It's common knowledge that there are girls who find old men sexier than young ones. To her my baldness and my wrinkles seemed to have been signs of character" (p. 79).

When Chickie sings Hilbert's praises—"a person of a rare type . . . rare types owed it to society to reproduce themselves"—he immodestly agrees. Yet he is not without modesty. "It was painfully blissful to hear such things. She had a way of spreading them on my responsive quaking heart like honey butter. Though you know yourself too well to believe such stuff. It still sends tremors through the system. It may be that the good in you, even if you have offended or betrayed it hundreds of times, has refused to give up" (pp. 79–80). Hilbert thinks of the Bible story of Sarah and Abraham: "how she had laughed to think of conceiving at her age, and asked whether she would be pleasured after the manner of women. But her pregnancy is an event of vast historical significance." Immediately Hilbert regrets his presumption, declaring, "The only resemblance is that of great age and the improbability of conception" (p. 81).

Although kindly, Hilbert's impulses are also violent. The desire to be strong, he admits, is only partly a product of motives connected with Chickie. "I could never get rid of fantasies of retribution for offenses going back seventy years. It comes over me that I should still be ready to punch so-and-so in the mouth. And if so-and-so has gone to his reward, as is usually the case, I have to get what emotional satisfaction I can from his death." These feelings Hilbert sees as "pathetic and almost painful—an old man who is still a street kid and won't back away from a fight" (p. 111). "If you ask me whether it isn't unseemly to fancy at ninety that you can drive your fist into a hated face my answer is, 'Sure thing, certainly. I will never stop trying to shake it off' " (p. 112). Here, as elsewhere in "Marbles," one thinks of Bellow, an identification not always fictionally plausible. For example, Hilbert attributes his feistiness to his experiences as an artist—experiences little in evidence in "Marbles." "Some of this I conclude reflects the struggle of an artist, having to stand up to the dazzling cultural changes experienced during and after the pop-Sixties. One had to fight. Willy-nilly we slipped into something like the state of nature and the war of all against all. In such a war you get no protection from the former reverence for the aged and the sage" (p. 111). At this point, Hilbert recalls the story of former Secretary of Defense Brushmore pouring wine over his tie, a fictionalized version of the incident in which former Secretary of Defense Schlesinger poured wine over Bellow's tie.

The "practical difficulties" connected with Hilbert's decision to father a child with Chickie much preoccupy him. "First off," he is sent by Dr. Clavel to "a private, discreet lab" for a sperm test. He is also prescribed Pergonal, a hormone specifically aimed at increasing fertility. At the lab, he faces "the humiliation of having to produce samples, the astonishment and disbelief of biotechnicians in their white jackets who evidently thought I was funny as hell and coming to them with senile delusions, and their hair-raising experience of finding viable sperm. It was also the burden of justification, not least to myself" (p. 131). When the baby comes, Hilbert's response is:

> The baby!
> At my age!
> What have I done!

Then, to himself: "Don't give me that. You've done just what you wanted. . . . Glad to have the capacity still, nearing the century mark" (p. 245). When, later, he questions the morality of "begetting an orphan. How else was I to think of it with a life expectancy like mine," his next thought is that "it was heroic to become a dad at ninety-five" (p. 263). The final word on Hilbert's fathering a child at his age is Chickie's. "I think you kept alive because of me. Also you go to the trouble of dreaming up new projects because you won't die as long as you have unfinished business. Behind it all maybe is the fact that you had to wait so long to find the woman in your life and you're not ready to part with me. I believe also I got into miso to lengthen your life and then it occurred to me also that we could have a kid together" (p. 268).

BELLOW AND JANIS THOUGHT of having a child "long before we were married." "From day one" they never took precautions. Before marriage, they also began consulting fertility charts "and schlepped them with us everywhere we traveled"; "Those were in the days when you took your temperature and then made sure to have a lot of fun at those peak times. He didn't have to be coerced—it was something he very much wanted. As long as I was prepared to change all the diapers, he was in!"[2] The difficulties they faced were of several sorts. In addition to worries about the viability and motility of Bellow's sperm, Janis had fertility problems. Despite the absence of symptoms, she turned out to have severe endometriosis and was operated on. When she recovered, she got pregnant, around the time of Bellow's seventy-fifth birthday. A "terrible" miscarriage followed, but they did not give up. As she later told an interviewer, speaking of this painful period, "I wasn't the kind of person who was interested [in babies], only then it grabbed me with a ferocity."[3] They turned to IVF ("an extremely expensive process," Bellow told Walter Pozen), which can not only overcome female infertility but also aid male fertility. Four failed attempts at IVF followed, one of which led to pregnancy and a second miscarriage. A fifth attempt remained, but Janis "had given up." It was Bellow who encouraged her to try one final time. "Everyone else said enough, enough for God's sake. He was the only one who said you'll never forgive yourself." On the fifth and last attempt, Janis conceived, the pregnancy was carried to term, and on December 23, 1999, Naomi Rose Bellow was born.

Janis's parents were among those who had given up. "I had reconciled myself that she would be childless," Harvey Freedman recalled in an interview. "I don't know how many miscarriages she had," Sonya Freedman added, "at least three." Harvey remembers twice talking to Bellow about becoming a father again, including once after Janis was pregnant with Rosie. "On both occasions he started, 'Am I nuts? Am I nuts?' and I said that's got nothing to do with it. It's a *fait accompli*, and I said it's going to turn out either beautifully or it's going to be a disaster and it's not up to you, it's up to this unborn child. If it's a winning child with a decent temperament it could be the best thing that ever happened to you, if it's the opposite it could be terrible." "He knew how much Janis wanted it" is Sonya's view. "He did it for her." Most of their friends were delighted at the news. Bette Howland, however, to whom Bellow had confessed reservations, thought that Janis's family had "worked on" him, "indoctrinated" him, and that he "just folded." Howland became angry, and "by the time Rosie was born," she recalled, "I couldn't take any more." "Everybody was totally surprised," Jonathan Kleinbard recalls. "When Janis had the baby, Bette totally broke off."

BELLOW WAS EIGHTY-FOUR when Rosie was born. Four months later, on April 24, 2000, his last novel, *Ravelstein*, was published, to acclaim and controversy. Once again Bellow was in the news, partly for admitting that Bloom was the model for Ravelstein, partly for "outing" him as a homosexual and suggesting that he died of AIDS, and partly because he'd produced a work of such quality at eighty-four (as *Newsweek* put it, "What else would you expect from an 84-year-old man who fathered his fourth child last December?"[4]). The idea for writing the book, a fictional memoir, came, Bellow claimed, from Bloom himself. That Bloom expected Bellow to write about him was clear to his companion, Michael Z. Wu. That he would have wanted a book as revealing as *Ravelstein* Wu denies. Several of Bloom's closest friends, friends also of Bellow, dispute the suggestion that the novel was solicited by Bloom, as Ravelstein solicits Chick to "do me as you did Keynes, but on a bigger scale. And also you were too kind to him. I don't want that. Be as hard on me as you like. You aren't the darling doll you seem to be."[5] For Wu, who is depicted in the novel as Ravelstein's partner, Nikki, this speech is pure fiction: "I just don't believe it's true that Bloom said write about me and be honest."

Whatever the book's origins, Bellow was thinking about it as early as the spring of 1990, well before Bloom's death in October 1992. In an April 1991 journal entry largely devoted to Bellow's problems with "A Case of Love," an entry noted earlier, Janis records, "At the center for him now is the Bloom book." In Paris, in the spring of 1993, the

"Bloom book" was again Bellow's prime concern, according to Roger Kaplan. It seemed to Kaplan that Bellow was trying to decide whether it should be a novel or a memoir or a mixture of the two. The solution to this dilemma—if solution it was—did not occur to Bellow for more than three years. On July 17, 1996, four months after reading to Janis the final pages of "Changing Places," soon to become *The Actual*, her journal records: "HE HAS STARTED THE BLOOM BOOK!"

RAVELSTEIN SPARKED A COMPLEX CONTROVERSY, one that needs recounting before the novel itself is discussed. Bloom's homosexuality was no secret to his friends and to those who followed his career, but he rarely discussed it with them and said nothing of it in print. "Allan was a very private person," Jonathan Kleinbard declares. "We never talked about Allan's homosexuality . . . until he was dying." Wu speaks of valuing "discretion, manners, it's just private things; what is your life is your life." In addition, "there are people who accept you but do not want to know details. . . . You don't say anything and they don't ask." ("It was sort of, don't ask, don't tell," Bloom's student Paul Wolfowitz, Philip Gorman in the novel, told an interviewer from *The New York Times*.) The prudence of this view, especially in influential conservative circles, is suggested in a *Wall Street Journal* article of February 2, 2000. The article was written by Sam Tanenhaus, a friend of James Atlas, and titled "Bellow, Bloom, and Betrayal." It was accompanied by a drawing of a man being stabbed in the back. Tanenhaus, who had not yet read the novel, implies that Bloom's reputation could be undermined by its revelations. "This is important because Bloom has lost the iconic status he once enjoyed among conservatives, who initially hailed his work but have been more subdued in recent years, owing mainly to uneasiness about his homosexuality."[6]

A week before the Tanenhaus article, *The New York Times* published an interview in which Bellow admitted to mixed feelings about the revelations in *Ravelstein*. On the one hand, he told the interviewer, Dinitia Smith, he confessed to "a feeling he [Bloom] would mind" the exposure of his homosexuality. On the other hand, Bloom had "asked him to write a memoir of him that was, in the words of the novel, 'without softeners or sweeteners,'" and, despite his public silence about his sexuality, "he didn't have anything to hide."[7] The Smith interview was not the fullest and most influential of prepublication "outings" of Bellow's novel. On April 16, *The New York Times Magazine* published an article entitled "With Friends Like Saul Bellow," accompanied by a photographic montage: the left half of Bloom's face, the right half of Bellow's face, and between them a typewriter with a sheet of paper bearing a drawing of a dagger.

The author of the article, D. T. Max, later the biographer of David Foster Wallace, sketches Bloom's history, the story of the Bloom-Bellow friendship, and the genesis of the controversy surrounding *The Closing of the American Mind.* The disclosures in *Ravelstein*, Max claims, have "created a furor," in particular over the suggestion that Bloom's death, "ascribed in his obituaries to internal bleeding and liver failure," was attributable to AIDS. Is *Ravelstein*, Max asks, "an act of friendship or of betrayal?" To answer this question, Max interviewed a number of Bloom's close friends and ex-pupils, including Bellow, Nathan Tarcov, and Werner Dannhauser, a student of Bloom's and a fellow Straussian and political philosopher. Bellow had sent Dannhauser a partial draft of the novel, and Dannhauser (the model in part for Ravelstein's friend Morris Herbst) had objected to its inclusion of "too many details about Bloom's private life: 'Did my objections register?' Dannhauser remembered with an unhappy laugh. 'Yes, but he decided to do it anyway.'" Dannhauser told Max that Bloom had been "wary of being written about" but that "over time, [he] gave up his secrets. 'When Allan liked someone, he wasn't very calculating.'" Among the secrets Bloom gave up to Bellow, the novel suggests, was that, like Abe Ravelstein, he "relished *louche* encounters, the fishy and the equivocal" (p. 31), also thought "a lot about those pretty boys in Paris" (p. 138).

Nathan Tarcov told Max, as he told me, that he "doesn't believe Bloom died of AIDS. Nathan was Bloom's medical executor and present during his final days. 'The word AIDS was never mentioned when Alan died. . . . I think I would have known.'" Max also spoke to Bloom's doctor, Nicholas Davidson, who signed Bloom's death certificate, which makes no mention of AIDS or HIV. When asked about the cause of death by Max, Dr. Davidson answered that it was "pretty much irrelevant"; Bloom was a man who "was in heart failure, kidney failure. . . . The body was winding down."[8] All Michael Wu said to Max of Ravelstein's death was "It's fiction, not a biography." In Nathan Tarcov's interview with me in 2008, he called the suggestion that Bloom died of AIDS "a factual error," but he admitted that Bloom had been HIV-positive. He "does not know" whether there was any connection between Bloom's HIV and his liver failure. He also offered a "correction" to his statements at the time of Bloom's death. "I will admit now, sixteen years later, that my publicly contradicting that [the suggestion that Bloom was HIV-positive] . . . was in a way my substitution for expressing my disgust at the portrayal of Nikki, which I did not want to talk publicly about. . . . There was at least one article in *The New York Times* [Max's article] that said it was obviously based on Michael Wu."[9]

The question of whether Bloom died of AIDS, which is of importance to accounts of Bellow's life if not to *Ravelstein* the novel, is further complicated by the correspondence between Bellow and Dannhauser, correspondence not available to Max. According to a letter Bellow wrote to Dannhauser on October 6, 1999, after Dannhauser had read a *Ravelstein* draft and registered his objections, Bellow "promised to eliminate what you thought to be objectionable material and I wrote a revised version." The fate of this version he goes on to describe:

> It took quite a lot of doing and the doing went against the grain. When I was done the results were highly unsatisfactory; what was lacking was the elasticity provided by sin. In the midst of this lengthy, time-consuming and ultimately sterile procedure I remembered how displeased Bloom had been with *The Dean's December*. He objected to the false characterization of Alexandra and he didn't spare me one bit. But now the shoe is on the other foot and I saw no reason why I should do in *Ravelstein* what Allan had so strongly objected to in the earlier novel. After all, I was trying to satisfy Allan's wishes, and I couldn't have it both ways—I couldn't be both truthful and camouflaged. So I did as I think he would have wished me to do. And I know I am going to alienate a lot of my Straussian friends. Some of these old friends I can well afford to lose, but you are not in that number. . . . Believe me, none of this is literary frivolity. I have taken the whole matter with great—the greatest—seriousness.[10]

Bellow's letter to Dannhauser began: "It's about time I heard from you." In his undated reply, Dannhauser, too, laments the silence between them. His problem had not been with the revelation of Bloom's homosexuality, but with the suggestion that Bloom died of AIDS. Given "how hard he [Bloom] tried to keep the AIDS details secret," Dannhauser writes, it is difficult to credit Bellow's claim that revealing them in

Ravelstein is "what he would have wanted me to do." The letter ends with the hope that they can soon meet up, perhaps when Dannhauser comes to Boston College to lecture on Strauss and Bloom.[11]

Several questions are raised by Dannhauser's letter. It is possible that "the AIDS details" were kept from Nathan Tarcov, his medical executor, not only by Bloom but by the physicians, acting on Bloom's orders. Another possibility is that Tarcov was himself honoring Bloom's wishes by denying the story about AIDS. If Dannhauser is correct about Bellow's knowing "how hard [Bloom] tried to keep the AIDS details secret," then Bellow, for all the love and admiration he felt for Bloom, could be accused of "betraying" him. In his interview with Max, Bellow admitted, as Max puts it, that "Bloom had been oblique about his illness, as he was oblique about many things. He had never spoken to Bellow about his having H.I.V. or AIDS. 'I don't know if he died of AIDS, really,' Bellow admitted. 'It was just my impression that he may have.'"[12] This was also the impression of other close friends. According to Jonathan Kleinbard, "Near the end he [Bloom] would kiss Joan [Kleinbard's wife] on the lips." Kleinbard asked the doctor if this was okay, and the doctor told him not to worry—an answer open to interpretation. That fear of AIDS lay behind the question is clear.

It was this fear that Bellow had underestimated, along with religious and other objections to homosexuality. "Where he had erred," he told Max, "was in misjudging people's sensitivities about homosexuality and AIDS. 'You know, I've discovered that this is a very itchy subject, and the people carry over attitudes more appropriate to the Middle Ages.'" Among those who carried over such attitudes were influential Straussians, the most controversial of whom was Harry V. Jaffa, a professor of government at Claremont McKenna College, where Strauss taught briefly after leaving the University of Chicago. Jaffa and Bloom had co-authored a book, *Shakespeare's Politics* (1964), dedicated "to Leo Strauss our teacher," but they grew apart in the 1970s. Jaffa was a prolific scholar, best known for an acclaimed account of the Lincoln-Douglas debates, the author also of studies of natural law, Aristotle and Aquinas, the American Revolution, and the Declaration of Independence. He had been a speechwriter for Barry Goldwater and was the author of the slogan: "Extremism in the defense of liberty is no vice! And . . . moderation in the pursuit of justice is no virtue." A friend of William F. Buckley, Jr., and a frequent contributor to Buckley's magazine, the *National Review*, he was a key figure in forging links between secular intellectual conservatives and Christian evangelicals and fundamentalists.

One such link concerned attitudes to homosexuality, consistently referred to by Jaffa as "sodomy." In the fall of 1988, Jaffa published a lengthy review of *The Closing of the American Mind* in *Interpretation: A Journal of Political Philosophy*, a Straussian journal numbering among its general and consulting editors, including deceased editors, Strauss himself, the English philosopher Michael Oakeshott, Arnaldo Momigliano, and Harvey C. Mansfield, Jr., of Harvard, a friend of the Bellows in Boston. After applauding Bloom for his stance on the evils of relativism, feminism, and sexual promiscuity, Jaffa laments the absence of any mention of "the so-called 'gay rights' movement," which he calls "the most radical and sinister challenge, not merely to sexual morality, but to all morality."[13] For Jaffa, "Nature is the ground of all morality, but maleness and femaleness is the ground of nature. . . . The so-called 'gay rights' movement is then the ultimate repudiation of nature, and therewith the ground of morality. . . . This has constituted the great moral crisis of the eighties on American campuses, and Bloom is almost entirely silent about it." Jaffa then turns to AIDS, which he sees as a boon to opponents of sodomy:

> The chronology of the AIDS epidemic corresponds precisely with this public movement to establish sodomy and lesbianism as a recommended lifestyle. In nothing has the power of relativism—and the disgrace of American higher education—manifested itself more than in its endorsement of homosexuality. But whatever the attitude of the educational authorities, God and nature have exacted terrible retribution. This lifestyle has proved to be a deathstyle. . . . Thanks to AIDS then, we have a little breathing time to assert the true arguments—the "enriching certitudes" (as in the *Nicomachean Ethics*), not merely Bloom's "humanizing doubts." Morality must be seen, as Aristotle sees it, as a means to implement the desire for happiness, and not merely as a restraint upon the desire for pleasure. The arguments must be made not only as to how one may avoid a bad death, but how one can pursue a good life. But one will not find those arguments in *The Closing of the American Mind*.[14]

Jaffa was the most combative Straussian to hold these views, but he was not alone in doing so (for Harvey Mansfield, testifying in 1993 against gay-rights statutes in Colorado, homosexual sex is "shameful," and homosexuality, if unchecked, is likely to "undermine human civilization"[15]). For whatever reason, Bloom was not prepared to defend his sexual proclivities against the views of men like Jaffa and Mansfield.[16] He showed little public interest in forming, or opposing, political alliances with the Christian right, preferring to influence politics by placing his students in government (which is true also of Ravelstein, who loved "to have the men he had trained appointed to important positions" [pp. 57–58]). When Bellow expressed regret at having "exposed" Bloom in *Ravelstein* and admitted to feeling a "sense of neglected responsibility and even recklessness on my part," he was admitting that he had underestimated the homophobia not merely of a general or exoteric audience but of a Straussian or esoteric one. "I didn't mean any harm to Allan," he told Max. "He was so open about himself that you never thought of it as being harmful."

JANIS BELLOW SIDED WITH Dannhauser and Tarcov about disclosing details of Bloom's sexuality. In abandoning his revised version, Bellow was overriding her reservations as well as theirs. In retrospect, in "Rosamund and *Ravelstein:* The Discandying of a Creator's Confection," an essay of 2015, what bothers Janis more than the use of "details about Bloom's private life" is Bellow's openness with Max about their truth to life. "Rather than wait for critics to out the writer who had scandalously outed a dear friend, Saul agreed to speak to a reporter." She quotes the passage in Max's article in which Bellow calls Bloom "in some sense a great man" and admits that he "wanted to get him down on paper."

> A handful of words, and instead of protecting himself, his friend, and his book, the author demolished the wall separating novel from memoir. Saul threw his own dynamite stick at the *roman à clef.* How delicious: these weren't characters, they were people, and more to the point, famous people with dirty secrets and compromising illnesses. No one felt obliged to wear kid gloves when mining the wreckage for juicy bits.[17]

Bellow himself came to accept this view of where he had been mistaken, expressing regret for the *New York Times* interview in a letter to Martin

Amis of February 7, 2000. In *Ravelstein*, he admits, "the mixture of fact and fiction has gotten out of hand."

> There are other elements besides, because the facts are so impure. There's fact and then there is journalistic fact with its usual accents. You can even see the journalists transforming fact into scandal and, towards the top, scandal lapsing over into myth, moving into the medieval territory reserved for plague. I was not prepared to hear a leper's bell ring at the crossroads of affection and eccentric charm.
>
> It seems that many people knew the truth about Allan. If not the pure truth then the bendable, versatile kind that academic politics is familiar with. So I found myself challenged by fanatical people. I discovered very soon that Allan had enemies who were preparing to reveal that he had died of AIDS. At this point I lost my head: when the *New York Times* telephoned to have it out with me I fell apart—I was unable to outsmart the journalists. So here I am, the author of a tribute which has been transformed into one of those civilized disasters no one can be prepared for.

Bellow did make some slight changes in deference to Dannhauser's and Janis's reservations. These were listed by Max in his article: "Ravelstein and Nikki's sexual connection was now just implied. The phrase 'He was H.I.V.-positive, he was dying from it' had been changed to 'He was H.I.V.-positive, he was dying of complications from it.' The words 'from H.I.V.' had been excised from the sentence 'And not only his death from H.I.V., but a good many other deaths as well.' The phrase 'Abe was taking the common drug prescribed for AIDS' had become 'Abe was taking the common drug prescribed for his condition.' " None of these changes obscures the fact that Ravelstein dies of AIDS.[18]

By the time of the book's publication on April 24, 2000, Bellow was only marginally more consistent in explaining its character than he had been to D. T. Max, or so an interview of April 24 in *Time* magazine suggests. Back in place, at least at the start, was the wall between novel and memoir. The interviewer, Paul Gray, asks Bellow about the notion "that his new novel is principally an outing or an exposé":

> This is a problem that writers of fiction always have to face in this country. People are literal minded, and they say, "Is this true? If it is true, is it factually accurate? If it isn't factually accurate, why isn't it

> factually accurate?" Then you tie yourself into knots, because writing a novel in some ways resembles writing a biography, but it really isn't. It is full of invention. If there were no invention, it wouldn't be readable. Invention, freedom. If you need circumstances, you create them in your own mind. But it is obviously not a project for literal-minded people. Habitual readers of fiction have an inkling of that, but so many people do not. I get impatient.

This impatience surfaces in the interview. Gray raises the subject of Bloom and AIDS: "I'm sorry to see you getting me on this particular track because I don't want to be on it." All Bellow offers by way of an answer is that Bloom said: "I trust you to write this. I know it's going to be fiction. . . . I'd like you to do this."

IN THE LATER STAGES of writing *Ravelstein*, Bellow worked closely with his editor from Viking, Beena Kamlani. Kamlani had been at Harper & Row when Bellow was there, but only got to know him after he moved to Viking from William Morrow in the spring of 1988. Kamlani was friends with Bellow's regular copyeditor, Marjorie Horvitz, whom he insisted on retaining at Viking. On *A Theft*, though Horvitz did the copyediting, Kamlani "did the editing, such as it was, very cautiously." Kamlani and Horvitz had worked together in the same way on *The Bellarosa Connection*. Kamlani remembers querying sentences "which might have been deliberately repeated—and Marje would ask and come back and tell me that Bellow very much appreciated this." It wasn't until *It All Adds Up* that Kamlani met Bellow. She and Horvitz drove up to Vermont, where they stayed in a bed and breakfast, "and after that our relationship [Kamlani's and Bellow's] developed." After Horvitz's death in 1988, Kamlani took on both roles, editor and copyeditor.

With *Ravelstein*, Kamlani received sections of manuscript, suggested revisions, then received radically revised versions of the same sections. Sometimes she received radically revised versions *before* she could suggest revisions. The book "kept changing," and the whole thing "didn't really come together until that very last manuscript," itself revised in production. "He rewrote proofs, he rewrote galleys, he even rewrote blues [the printer's photocopy, costly to emend], for God's sake." A pattern was established early on, one that would last until Bellow's death.

Kamlani would travel from New York to Boston or Vermont to discuss the latest manuscript material. She would sit down across a table from Bellow and "query something but in a very mild way, and he'd come around and say, 'You don't like this, huh?' Then he'd come across something and he'd stumble over it and he'd say, 'So this is what is bothering you. I see what's bothering you.' And he'd sit back and rewrite the whole page, perhaps another page and a half. . . . Then he'd cut out this yellow sheet and throw it in the bin and start again. . . . If I said 'hmmm' he'd ask, 'You like that, kiddo?' or 'You like that, kid?'" Kamlani calls the experience of working with Bellow "truly astounding. . . . He was so engaged in the process, so alive when working it out. . . . The veils of aging were pushed to one side and he came through almost like the sun. He was there. If I sensed that, I would mine that for everything. . . . I would bring up all [my concerns]. I'd say, 'I think you can do better than that,' and he'd say, 'You're right, I can do much better than that,' and he'd be writing, and then he'd finally nail it. And then he was so pleased. You'd just see his face light up." Even when Bellow was not on form, it was useful for Kamlani to hear him read out versions, "because it gave me the opportunity to intuit where he was with something. So he'd read it out and, depending on how he read it out, I could tell [how engaged or committed he was]." What Kamlani especially remembers is that "he was razor-sharp when he was fully on. There was nothing in the world that could compete with him. No. It's there in the book. The images, the sharpness with which he saw things. It was incredible."

Kamlani's visits during the composition of *Ravelstein* were frequent. "Every two weeks I was on a train," usually for a stay of four days, though one Vermont visit lasted eight weeks. Janis was never present during work sessions. In Boston, before Rosie was born, she was often out of the house, "at a whole lot of different things." Kamlani would arrive at nine or nine-thirty, and she and Bellow would work until lunchtime. Sometimes work sessions would continue into the afternoon, even into the evening. After they'd worked out a passage or problem to Bellow's satisfaction, Janis would read it. "We were incredibly knit, and there were times when, over dinner, I would say to Janis, I'm a little concerned about this, and she'd say, Well, why don't you try this way or see if that will work. And so we'd go back to it the next day and look at it fairly differently." At several dinners, the question of Ravelstein's sexuality came up. "I don't think it came up at a legal level," Kamlani remembers. "I think he was caught between a need to describe this person truthfully, to describe him as he saw him, and I think there was something horrible to Saul about losing this man to such a horrible disease, and I don't know how one can make AIDS into smallpox or measles." The question was "to what extent should this be changed . . . and I know he considered it very, very carefully. . . . It kept him up at night. I know he thought long and hard. I know this."

The problems Kamlani remembers most vividly from their sessions on *Ravelstein* were formal or structural, a matter of plot strands rather than character drawing. The novel has an unconventional, nonlinear narrative: its story of a life and a friendship is told through what Helen Small calls "meaningful repetitions, variations on themes, deepening meditations on certain problems,"[19] an approach recommended by Ravelstein himself: "Do it in your after-supper-reminiscence manner, when you've had a few glasses of wine and you're laid back and you're making remarks. I love listening when you are freewheeling" (p. 129). As Kamlani saw it, the novel's freewheeling contents needed to "mesh," in particular the scenes involving Rosamund, based on Janis, on the one hand, and the main portrait of Ravelstein and his friendship with Chick, on the other. "At first the Janis bit was there but much smaller," Kamlani recalls, then "he expanded it a lot" (she recalls a similar expansion of minor plot strands in *A Theft* and *The Bellarosa Connection*). How "the Janis bit" (i.e., the Rosamund bit) fit the Ravelstein bit bothered Janis as well. For Janis, the novel was "about the friendship between two men. A once-in-a-lifetime friendship. Two men who laugh, and argue, and disagree about almost everything" (p. 112). In early drafts, when Rosamund was still a minor character, Janis asked Bellow to remove her: "Pull one thread and be rid of the prissy girl. Nothing would unravel. No scar would be visible in the fabric. What could so slight a character add to a story already teeming with vibrant human types?" Janis claims "largely" to have kept her feelings about Rosamund to herself, even though the experience of "being seen or not seen" through the character was "excruciating." "Don't do this to me," she remembers thinking. "I'm not that woman: servile, prim, obedient. Is that the way you see me? Wounded vanity might be endured. But to be invisible to the person you love" (p. 114).[20]

Bellow refused to budge. When she complained, "the rejoinder was brief: Rosamund is a character. A minor character. The book is about the friendship between two men" (p. 114). Then he expanded Rosamund's role, so that in the final draft she could hardly be called minor. On St. Martin, when Chick collapses, "obedient" Rosamund shows "an underlying hardness" (p. 199). In the ICU, "I was tempted to drop out," Chick admits, "but she had concentrated her soul wholly on my survival" (p. 227). Janis quotes Chick: "Rosamund was determined that I should go on living. It was she, of course, who had saved me—flew me back from the Caribbean just in time, saw me through intensive care, sleeping in a chair beside my bed" (p. 225).[21] Although tenderhearted (as when lifting to safety the salamanders she and Chick come across in the road, out of a surfeit of "humane impulses" [p. 184]), Rosamund is hardly weak. Nor is she always prim or proper. Chick recalls her surreptitiously scooping after-dinner truffles into her purse at Lucas-Carton, the fanciest of French restaurants. "Don't give me that well-bred-young-lady, lace-paper-doily routine," Ravelstein says, "I saw you swiping those chocolates." Ravelstein is teasing here, for "he liked minor crimes and misdemeanors," disapproved of "uniform good conduct." He also liked that Rosamund had fallen for Chick. " 'There's a class of women who naturally go for old men,' he said. . . . He was drawn to irregular behavior. Especially where love was the motive" (pp. 23–24).

It is love—"the highest function of our species—its vocation"—that connects the Rosamund sections of the novel to the Ravelstein sections. The topic of love "simply can't be set aside in considering Ravelstein. He never forgot this conviction. It figures in all his judgments" (p. 140). In addition to being the central subject of his teaching and writing, it determines his friendships. The Floods, for example, "to whom Ravelstein and Nikki were greatly attached" (who are thinly fictionalized versions of the Kleinbards), "very simply loved each other. More than any other human connection this naïve (but indispensable) one was valued by Ravelstein" (p. 158). It is what he approves also in the Battles, an elderly couple who come to him for advice about suicide: he told them "they had a great love affair." "Among millions or hundreds of millions of people they alone lucked out. They had a great love affair and decades of effortless happiness. Each amused the other with his or her eccentricities. How could they bear to cheapen it with a suicide" (p. 155). Rosamund had been Ravelstein's student for five years, studying "Rousseauian romantic love and the Platonic Eros" (p. 231)—just as Janis studied love for five years with Bloom. In her essay on *Ravelstein*, Janis quotes Chick on Rosamund, who "knew far more about [love] than either her teacher or her husband" (p. 121; *Ravelstein*, p. 231). After the quote, in a passage hard not to read as autobiographical, Janis disagrees: "Rosamund did not know more about love than her husband or her teacher. It wasn't about knowing. She was in love, and had limitless expectations about its endlessness—more oceanic, certainly, than her fine education ought to have allowed" (p. 122).

Kamlani points to paired moments of tenderness in the Ravelstein and Rosamund plot strands. When Chick visits Ravelstein in the hospital, "now and then I put my hand to my friend's bald head. I could see that he wanted to be touched. I was surprised to find that there was an invisible stubble on his scalp. He seemed to have decided that total baldness suited him better than thinning hair, and shaved his head as well as his cheeks. Anyway, this head was rolling toward the grave" (p. 177). The poignancy of Ravelstein's wanting to be touched and of the invisible stubble on his head have their equivalents a few pages later in the scene in St. Martin when Rosamund (referred to as "Janis" by Kamlani) "towed or carried me in water just shoulder-high. She put her arms under me and walked back and forth. . . . The music she sang as she sailed my body through the water was from Handel's *Solomon*. We had heard it in Budapest a few months earlier. 'Live forever,' she sang, 'Happy-happy Solomon'" (pp. 185–86). Chick, in his seventies, is Ravelstein's senior "by a good many years" (p. 15); the scene takes place after Ravelstein's death. As Chick lies in Rosamund's arms, he thinks of the form his book should take. Then he and Rosamund change places, and he carries her through the water. As he does so, he feels "the sand underfoot ridged as the surface of the sea was rippled, and inside the mouth the hard palate had its ridges too" (p. 186). It is love, as well as Chick's habitual alertness to surface particulars, his "childish" (p. 97) way of seeing (with the wonder of "first epistemological impressions" [p. 96]), which allows him a glimpse of the "one Life within us and abroad."[22]

A much darker point of connection between the two plot strands offers a way of understanding Bellow's decision to use AIDS as the cause of Ravelstein's death. On St. Martin, as the ciguatoxin works its way through his body, ordinary cooking smells repulse Chick, as do the "strange stinks of jungle plant-life and rotting animal matter" (p. 195). As he and Rosamund pass the market stalls on the main street, grinning touts hold up live lobsters, "swinging them by the antennae or the tail. If some part of the creature fetched loose and fell to the ground, that was part of the fun" (p. 184). Elsewhere, "through the smoke and fire of curbside grills . . . the skinny local hens seemed to be growing hair, not feathers" (p. 194). Chick's revulsion at such sights and at the island's stinks is intensified by his reading: the Gajdusek journals he has brought from Boston, with their accounts of cannibalism, the savory smell of roasted human thigh, the ground "rich in red blood," "black headless bodies in a jungle where crimson orchids stream downward for hundreds of feet" (p. 193).[23] Gajdusek defends native practices by invoking the Siege of Leningrad, and Japanese soldiers, cut off in the Philippine jungles, who ate their dead. (He also, as we've seen, defends native sexual practices, including sex between adult males and young boys, though these practices are unmentioned in the novel.) On the plane to Boston, Chick recalls a young friend of Radu Grielescu (a character based on Mircea Eliade, Bellow's Romanian colleague at the Committee on Social Thought), "who was murdered in a stall of the men's room. . . . He died in the middle of the act—easing himself. They shot him at close range" (p. 202).[24] Once back in Boston, beached in intensive care, Chick suffers bodily indignities—the catheter, the ventilator, the drip. In recovery, he is "held upright in the shower and felt humiliated as I was soaped and rinsed by kindly nurses who had seen everything and were not shocked by my body" (p. 227). That Ravelstein dies from AIDS connects to the horrors of St. Martin and the ICU in a way smallpox or measles or TB could not. In the popular imagination of the day, AIDS, too, involved taboos, forbidden practices, infection, impurity. In the Tuileries, a setting as beautiful in its way as a tropical or jungle paradise, Ravelstein meets the pretty boys of Paris. In his letter of October 6, 1999, to Werner Dannhauser, Bellow dismisses alternative causes of Ravelstein's death as "lacking the elasticity provided by sin." By "elasticity" I take him to mean associative power, what T. S. Eliot calls "tentacular roots reaching down to the deepest terrors and desires."[25]

A final parallel between the Ravelstein and Rosamund sections concerns Chick's intellectual needs. Rosamund is smart as well as loving and "unlike most other observant persons . . . also thought clearly" (p. 41). One of the things she thought clearly about was Chick, so that, like Ravelstein, she is able to tell Chick things about himself that make him think. When he claims he has learned how foolish he was in his early years never to admit he was wrong, Rosamund's reply, more applicable to Bellow than to Chick (about whose early years we know very little), is "You needed to be right and you couldn't get by and be right, also" (p. 166). As Ravelstein's devoted pupil, Rosamund shares his intellectual interests, so that, as Chick puts it, "if I needed to know what Machiavelli owed to Livy I had only to ask." More important, "there was nothing I could say to this woman that she wouldn't understand" (p. 151). Often what Chick has to say to Rosamund concerns the Holocaust, as much his obsession as Bellow's. "In my original take on the Rosamund character," Janis admits, "I missed the role she played as sparring partner to Chick when he turns his face towards what he elsewhere calls the central event of our time: the destruction of European Jewry" (p. 117). In the *Ravelstein* essay, Janis recalls that, "in the twenty years I lived with him, only once did the books on the Holocaust disappear from the bedside. I remember this time because I enforced the ban. I told him that we would not have Hitler in bed with us while I was pregnant. That did not stop us from talking in the middle of the night, or over breakfast, or after a morning's work. That ban would have been too large to enforce" (p. 119).

For some, the problem with the Rosamund sections of the novel is not their failure to connect with the Ravelstein sections, it is Rosamund herself. Although Rosamund is heroic, she lacks complexity as a character, being perfect. She also lacks size, certainly in comparison with "great-souled" Ravelstein (though Ravelstein dwarfs all characters in the novel). Bellow's love for Janis, Leah Garrett conjectures, "overtakes his capacity to render her character, Rosamund, in anything less than an idealized light"[26] (as does Chick's love for Rosamund, one might add). In a fax of May 4, 1999, Bette Howland urged Bellow to "take the Rosamund character out. Let it go. You don't really need a woman until the ending—the last things—Chick's harrowing of hell," by which she means the fish poisoning and the weeks in ICU. She suggests that Chick should travel to St. Martin alone, where he runs into "an elderly Jewish widow (of course—probably more than once); around 70 I'd say. . . . Still, she's fishing; she's hoping; she's not giving up. . . . Chick sees what's up, it doesn't take binoculars, and besides it happens all the time. It's too late in the day for subtlety. But not only is he not interested—he's sick. He's been poisoned. . . . He develops an actual aversion to the poor woman—that is, to life, to the sensuous facts. The smell of her perfume or powder or hair spray, or more personal scents; the oiliness of her lipstick; her accent, her voice. Her urgency, her hanging on . . . But it is this woman who sees he's in danger; it's this woman, in his crisis, who does what needs to be done. She gets him out." One thinks of Dita Schwartz, the Bette Howland figure in *More Die of Heartbreak*.

Daniel Bellow also disapproved of the Rosamund character. "I thought the portrait of Janis was the most idealized bullshit." In addition, he was shocked to see Bellow distressed by criticism from "all those neocons [who] took us into Iraq." "I'd never seen him do that before," he says of Bellow's equivocations and expressions of regret. Bloom was half in the closet, a "fifties-style" homosexual; like Ravelstein, he "couldn't bear the fluttering of effeminate men" (p. 99); but he was also, as Daniel puts it, "gay as a party hat."[27] In Daniel's eyes, those who criticized *Ravelstein* for "outing" Bloom were weak or hypocritical. "Inability to hear the truth is a sign of weakness," he declares, a lesson he learned from his father, along with the importance of being true to one's nature. "I was faithful to what I was," Bellow declared; "I lived that way and I tried to write that way."[28] As criticism of the "outing" of Bloom grew, Daniel "was filled with rage that they were doing this to Pop." When Bellow told Daniel, "Nathan Tarcov's really angry with me," Daniel replied: "Pop, get a hold of yourself. This is what you told me, write what you see. . . . This is their problem. . . . They're frightened that they're going to be thrown out of the Republican Party."

Bellow's idealizing of Rosamund is paired with his demonizing of Vela, Chick's ex-wife, a character clearly based on Alexandra. "Why would he do that?" Alexandra asked Joseph Epstein after she had read the novel. "It was a shock for me, a shock for my friends," she remembers. "I reeled in terror at the picture of this wife." Some reassurance was offered by the reaction of her "younger feminist friends" who "thought it was downright hilarious that I should be described as a *femme fatale*, that in the space of a few years this wife, or ex-wife, should go from translucent Minna gazing at the stars, to ferocious, chaos-dispensing Vela. . . . They thought it was absolutely hilarious." For Philip Roth, the character of Vela is "a mistake," a view shared by Bette Howland. "He went overboard with Vela," she said in an interview, "and the result was somehow that she didn't come alive" (unlike, presumably, the comparably overboard fictionalizing of Sasha in *Herzog* or Susan in *Humboldt's Gift*). Both Adam and Daniel were shocked by the violence of the portrait, which Daniel calls "very unfair, really unfair." Beena Kamlani, acknowledging the unfairness, admits that the same "point" could have been made "without necessarily being so violent." In partial mitigation, she cites narrative context: "What is being described in Vela is a certain anger in [Chick], which then manifests itself in his conversations with Ravelstein. Now, how are we to appreciate the level at which these two men are talking about a marriage which is crumbling without seeing first his anger? One can't just separate things and say, Be kind to this person, without there being a consideration of the larger work."

Vela is criticized by Ravelstein as well as Chick, in ways not always flattering to Chick. At first, for the sake of his friendship with Chick, Ravelstein is "extremely careful not to offend Vela," is "warm, markedly attentive when she spoke," "deferred to her," suspending "deeper judgment" (p. 111). After Vela turns on him—"she began to say that you and I were carrying on together" (p. 112), Chick tells him—Ravelstein becomes openly hostile. "Vela will soon be through with you," he predicts, citing her frequent absences from home, "off to conferences all over the world" (p. 84). For Chick, Vela is "a beauty impossible to rival" (p. 123); for Ravelstein, "she's got the makings of a beauty but she's not a beauty" (p. 84). Chick ungallantly describes Vela's morning makeup preparations as "at a West Point or Hapsburg hussar level" (p. 107), picking up on Ravelstein's reference to her having "some sort of European military correctness about her. And when she inspects you, you just don't make the grade with her" (p. 84). When Chick complains about Vela's domestic failings—"What we had was a loose arrangement—a household, not the locus of married love or even affection" (p. 85)—Ravelstein takes him to task just as Janis says she took Bellow to task over Alexandra: "She's a high-grade scientist, they tell me, and she may not feel like cooking your dinner—clocking in at five o'clock to peel the potatoes. . . . The idea of leading a warm family life is her number one antipremise" (pp. 87–88).

What also counts against Vela, Ravelstein claims, is her association with Radu and Nanette Grielescu, thinly disguised portraits of Eliade and his wife, Christinel. Grielescu, in Vela's eyes, "sets the standards for male conduct," what Ravelstein calls "the courtly gentleman bullshit" (p. 106). "Yes, that's more or less it," says Chick. "The considerate man, the only right kind, remembers birthdays, honeymoons, and other tender anniversaries. You have to kiss the ladies' hands, send them roses; you cringe, move back the chairs, you rush to open doors and make arrangements with the maître d' " (p. 106). Grielescu, like Eliade, is "a famous scholar, not exactly a follower of Jung—but not exactly *not* a Jungian." Glamorous Nanette had once been "one of those *jeunes filles en fleur* you read about long ago" (p. 105). That Grielescu had also been a strong supporter, if not a member, of the Romanian Iron Guard, a prewar fascist movement (referred to by Chick as "the meat-hook people" [p. 202]), again like Eliade, Vela overlooks.[29] Ravelstein chides Chick for socializing with the Grielescus; he is as keen to free him from Vela and her circle as Vela is to free Chick from Ravelstein (putting Grielescu in his place, Ravelstein suspects). "They use you as their cover," Ravelstein tells Chick. "You wouldn't have become chummy with those Jew-haters. But these were Vela's friends, and you put yourself out for them, and you gave Grielescu exactly what he was looking for. As a Romanian nationalist back in the thirties he was violent toward the Jews" (p. 125). In real life, it was Philip Roth, through his friend Norman Manea, who warned Bellow off the Eliades.

In Chick's eyes, Vela's chief failing is her incapacity to love. Hence her attitude to sex, which she treats as performance or weapon. As Chick puts it, "There's a hint of artificiality about it. Like a stratagem. Like a lack of affect" (p. 121). "She had a sex-hex on you," Ravelstein tells Chick (p. 128). "Lucky for you . . . you have a vocation. So this is just a side thing. It's not a genuine case of sex-slavery or psychopathology" (p. 112). Still, the "sex-hex" has its effect: witness Chick's hallucinations in ICU (taken directly from Bellow's "View from Intensive Care," quoted in the previous chapter), which combine suspicions about Vela's infidelities with performance anxiety (her complaining of all the "glamorous sex . . . I was deprived of with you" [p. 214], her bragging about the "lewd things" she does with her Spanish boyfriend [p. 218]). Earlier, in a vivid scene, Chick describes Vela wandering into his bedroom in the nude. As he lies reading, she "came to my bedside and rubbed her pubic hair on my cheekbone. When I responded as she must have known that I would, she turned and left me with an air of having made her point. She had won hands down without having to speak a word. Her body spoke for her, and very effectively too, saying that the end was near" (p. 86).

This end, Vela's kicking Chick out of the apartment and filing for divorce, occurs at what Ravelstein calls "the worst moment possible" (p. 128), within a week of his burying his brothers. Vela engineers the breakup just as Alexandra engineered the breakup with Bellow, according to the account Bellow gave to Eugene Kennedy (Sam Pargiter in the novel). "I found the house filled with large, colored stickum circles—the green identified my possessions, the salmon-colored were glued to hers. . . . They produced a snowstorm effect—'a meum-tuem blizzard,' as I said to Ravelstein" (p. 122). Here truth to life is sacrificed to anger or hurt—Bellow's, that is. Six months separated the deaths of Bellow's brothers and Alexandra's kicking him out and filing for divorce. In the novel, the interval is less than a week, which makes Vela's actions especially heartless. The heartlessness is accentuated by having the "meum-tuem" scene recounted immediately after a scene in which Chick visits his dying brother, Shimon, Bellow's last fictional depiction of his brother Maury. Shimon is dying of cancer, and Chick comes to Tallahassee to say goodbye to him (as Bellow went to Georgia to say goodbye to Maury, and Charlie Citrine goes to Florida to say goodbye to Julius in *Humboldt's Gift*, and Herschel Shawmut goes to Texas to say goodbye to Philip in "Him with His Foot in His Mouth"). Shimon, with death in his face, compliments Chick on his shirt: "That's got class, the red-and-gray stripe." Then he warns Chick against buying a diesel Mercedes: "It'll be nothing but trouble" (p. 121). "After a long exchange of silent looks," Shimon is exhausted and tells Chick he wants to climb back into bed.

> He was too far gone to do this. He had been a ball player once with strong legs, but the muscle now was all gone. . . . And then his head twisted toward me and his eyeballs turned up—nothing but blind whites. The nurse cried out, "He's leaving us."
>
> Shimon raised his voice and said, "Don't get excited."
>
> This was what he said often to his wife and to his children when they differed or began to quarrel. . . . He was unaware that his eyeballs had rolled back into his head. But I had seen this in the dying and knew that he was leaving us—the nurse was right [pp. 121–22].

No such moment occurs in Bellow's accounts of Maury's death or in the fictional deaths of Julius Citrine or Philip Shawmut. But the feel of the moment, its mix of pathos and comedy (the inability to climb into bed, "Don't get excited"), matches the feel of earlier accounts and is comparably affecting.

Vela is not the only character in *Ravelstein* born of anger or strife. Edward Shils, who is fictionalized as Rakhmiel Kogon, is also given a kicking. Just as suffering Minna gives way to heartless Vela, so Richard Durnwald, the Shils character in *Humboldt's Gift*, whom Charlie Citrine "admired and even adored," gives way to "wicked" Rakhmiel Kogon in *Ravelstein*. Both Durnwald and Kogon share Shils's appearance, professorial expertise, and personal history. Durnwald is "reddish, elderly but powerful, thickset and bald, a bachelor of cranky habits but a kind man";[30] Kogon is "a non-benevolent Santa Claus, a dangerous person, ruddy, with a red-eyed scowl and a face in which the anger muscles were highly developed" (p. 36) (elsewhere Chick calls him "a tyrant, with the tyranny baked into his face" [p. 133]). Chick tells us about Kogon, who is recently deceased, in order to avoid thinking about Ravelstein's death: "I would much rather think of Rakhmiel's death" (p. 131). Although Kogon's ideas of decency "went back to the novels of Dickens," "not even a genius like Rakhmiel was able to conceal the storminess or, if you prefer, the wickedness of his nature" (p. 132). In his letter to Atlas, Shils granted Bellow a single virtue, "consecration to his art." In *Ravelstein*, Bellow grants Kogon two virtues, though only one unequivocally. "My belief is that on the side he grew a little herb garden of good, generous feelings. He hoped, especially when he was wooing a new friend, that he could pass for a very decent man. He was also very learned" (p. 133). When Ravelstein heard this description, he "shouted with laughter," telling Chick, "That's how I want to be treated, too. That's it. I want you to show me as you see me, without softeners or sweeteners" (p. 133). All that Chick has missed in his account of Kogon, Ravelstein tells him, is "his sex life—a major omission, he believed. He told me authoritatively, 'You've missed it—Kogon is attracted to men'" (p. 134).

THE NOVEL'S *DRAMATIS PERSONAE* can be divided into camps. On the one hand, Ravelstein, Rosamund, and the lovebird Floods and Battles, characters born of love; on the other hand, Vela, Kogon, Grielescu, and graceless M. Bédier, the proprietor of Le Forgeron, the restaurant on St. Martin where Chick is poisoned. These are the characters created out of a desire to wound or punish. Chick describes M. Bédier as "a pig who was taught manners, but they didn't take" (p. 191). If the love camp prevails, it does so through the portrait of Ravelstein, the last of Bellow's larger-than-life protagonists. We meet him first in Paris, ensconced in a penthouse suite in the Hotel Crillon. A year earlier, he had been a hundred thousand dollars in debt. Then "the vast hydraulic forces of the country" (p. 15) picked him up, catapulting him to worldwide fame and fortune ("his Japanese royalties alone were, he said with wild pleasure and no modesty, 'ferocious'" [p. 61]). Thanks to the most improbable of best-sellers, described by Chick as "a spirited, intelligent, warlike book" (p. 4),[31] he could at last finance his need for luxury goods: "for Armani suits or Vuitton luggage, for Cuban cigars, unobtainable in the U.S., for the Dunhill accessories, for solid-gold Montblanc pens or Baccarat or Lalique crystal to serve wine in—or to have it served" (p. 3). Other luxury cravings scattered through the narrative include high-end audio systems, custom-made Sulka shirts, expensive sofas, a full-length fur-lined leather coat, a giant wall-screened television, a new eighty-thousand-dollar BMW (for Nikki), Jensen teapots, Quimper antique plates, Pratisi linens, fancy formal wear ("cummerbund, diamond studs, patent leather shoes" [p. 15]), neckties flown air-express from Chicago to Paris, to be dry-cleaned. After dinner at Lucas-Carton, Ravelstein signs the enormous bill "in an ecstasy" (p. 23).

Ravelstein invites Chick and Rosamund to breakfast in his suite. "He had every right to look as he looked now, while the waiter set up our breakfast. His intellect had made a millionaire of him. It's no small matter to become rich and famous by saying exactly what you think—to say it in your own words without compromise" (p. 4). In addition to present success, a five-million-dollar book offer is on the table. "And he was a learned man after all. Nobody disputed that. You have to be learned to capture modernity in its full complexity and assess its human cost" (p. 14). You also have to be "as familiar with entertainers like Mel Brooks as with the classics" (p. 11), to value the artistry of Michael Jordan, to know who Michael Jackson is and appreciate the weight of his celebrity. Jackson and his entourage are also staying at the Crillon, occupying a whole floor of the hotel. "Terrific, isn't it," asks Ravelstein, "having this pop circus?" (p. 2).

Ravelstein's appearance, like that of all Bellow characters, provides clues to his personality. The blue-and-white kimono he wears at breakfast—presented to him in Japan, where he lectured the previous year—is "loosely belted and more than half open," showing his underpants, which "were not securely pulled up" (p. 4). Beneath the kimono, his legs are "paler than milk. He had the calves of a sedentary man—the shinbone long and the calf muscle abrupt, without roundness" (p. 10). Indifferent to fitness ("to prolong his life was not one of Ravelstein's aims" [p. 54]), "he treated his body like a vehicle—a motorbike that he raced at top speed along the rim of the Grand Canyon" (p. 10), an image that parallels his attitude to money, "something you threw from the rear platform of speeding trains" (p. 15). He was "one of those large men—large, not stout—whose hands shake when there are small chores to perform. The cause was not weakness but a tremendous eager energy that shook him when it was discharged" (p. 3). This energy—"the excitement, the wringing, the tension of his pleasures, of his mental life" (p. 18)—was a key to Ravelstein's success as a teacher: "a vital force was transmitted. Whatever the oddities were, they fed his energy, and this energy was spread, disseminated, bestowed" (p. 53). It was also what kept him awake at night, led to disorder in his personal life and his physical awkwardness. Hence his barging in on Vela, the occasion of their first falling-out: "Impatient, in high spirits, keen to see me, Ravelstein called out from the anteroom and without waiting for an answer he rushed in. He intended to hug me—or Vela, if she should happen to be first. But she was in her slip and she wheeled round and ran, slamming the bathroom door" (p. 104). A memorable scene involves Ravelstein's purchase of a forty-five-hundred-dollar Lanvin jacket, "golden, with rich lights among the folds" (p. 34). As soon as he puts it on, he spills coffee ("his third *espresso serré*" [p. 41]) on its lapels, an episode that reminds Chick of Ravelstein's Hermès and Ermenegildo Zegna neckties, "dotted with cigarette burns" (p. 41). While lecturing, "he coughed, stammered, he smoked, bawled, laughed, he brought his students to their feet and debated, provoked them to single combat, examined, hammered them" (p. 19). Lighting up "with his Dunhill flame" in front of "a large *No Smoking* sign," Ravelstein tells his audience: "If you leave because you hate tobacco more than you love ideas, you won't be missed" (p. 156).

Paris matters to Ravelstein not only for its "sexy mischief" but for all the "arts of intimacy": "In every *quartier*, the fresh-produce markets, the goods bakeries, the *charcuterie* with its cold cuts. Also the great displays of intimate garments. The shameless love of fine bedding. '*Viens, viens dans mes bras, je te donne du chocolat*'" (p. 31). All this in addition to architecture, history, French literature. "For a civilized man there was no background, no atmosphere like the Parisian" (p. 45). Chick's feelings about Paris are more mixed. He "looked down on Paris, rather," citing the Jewish freethinker's saying "*wie Gott in Frankreich*. Meaning that even God took his holidays in France. Why? Because the French are atheists [like Ravelstein] and among them God himself could be carefree, a *flâneur*, like any tourist" (p. 171). Paris is the perfect place to meditate modernity and the nihilism that shapes it, source ultimately of "a general willingness to live with the destruction of millions. It was like the mood of the century to accept it" (p. 169). In prewar years, "to many in France, it was Jewry that was the enemy, not Germany" (p. 203). Much of the serious talk between Ravelstein and Chick concerns Jews and Jewishness, with Chick pressing the point of French anti-Semitism. Not that Ravelstein needed to be told of the prejudices of the French. When illness prevents him from returning to Paris, he fears losing a ten-thousand-dollar *dépôt de garanti* on his apartment, "because the tenant is a Jew, and there's a Gobineau in the landlord's family tree. These Gobineaus were famous Jew-haters. And I'm no mere Jew but, even worse, an American one" (p. 70).[32]

Chick is as open with Ravelstein as Ravelstein is with him, "free to confess what I couldn't tell anyone else, to describe my weaknesses, my corrupt shameful secrets, and the cover-ups that drain your strength. As often as not he thought my confessions were wildly funny. Funniest of all were the thought-murders" (p. 95), the sort that produce characters like Vela and Kogon. Chick also feels bound to communicate what he calls his "incommunicables" or "private metaphysics" (p. 95), including his belief in an afterlife, which Ravelstein mocks.[33] In the end, Chick is forced "to surrender my wish to make myself fully known to him by describing my intimate metaphysics," Ravelstein being "too close to death to be spoken to in such terms" (p. 97). This is not to say that Ravelstein himself has no metaphysics. His metaphysics comes directly from Plato's dialogues. As Chick soon realizes, "there wasn't the slightest hope of following Ravelstein's thoughts if you were ignorant of them entirely. . . . By now I am as much at home with Plato as with Elmore Leonard" (p. 117).

Although a follower of Plato, Ravelstein recognizes the value as well as the sensuous appeal of appearances. He "had come to agree that it was important to note how people looked. Their ideas are not enough—their theoretical convictions and political views. If you don't take into account their haircuts, the hang of their pants, their taste in skirts and blouses, their style of driving a car or eating a dinner, your knowledge is incomplete" (p. 136). Chick, however, carries noticing too far, according to Ravelstein. He is too fixated on "ordinary daily particulars . . . not the noumena, or 'things in themselves'" (p. 193), convinced that they lead to deeper truths. In the process, knowing for Chick replaces action.

> Either you continue to live in epiphanies or you shake them off and take up trades and tasks, you adopt rational principles and concern yourself with society, or politics. Then the sense of having come from "elsewhere" vanishes. In Platonic theory all you know is recollected from an earlier existence elsewhere. In my case, Ravelstein's opinion was that distinctiveness of observation had gone much further than it should and was being cultivated for its own strange sake. Mankind had first claim on our attention and I indulged my "personal metaphysics" too much, he thought. His severity did me good. I didn't have it in me at my time of life to change, but it was an excellent thing, I thought, to have my faults and failings pointed out by someone who cared about me. I had no intention, however, of removing, by critical surgery, the metaphysical lenses I was born with [pp. 97–98].

Ravelstein points to Chick's indulgence of Grielescu as an example of observational irresponsibility. "The fact was that I enjoyed watching Grielescu" (p. 125), Chick admits, as opposed to avoiding or attacking him, or doing what Ravelstein calls "the unpleasant work of thinking it all through" (p. 167). In company, Grielescu was a performer, "off inwardly on some topic from myth or history about which you had nothing to tell him." This monopolizing, Ravelstein claims, was "how he steered the conversation away from his fascist record" (p. 126).[34] Although Chick accepts Ravelstein's criticism, he later defends himself by recalling an argument with Grielescu, who was proposing myth as a complement to "ideas" or "culture." For Chick, all three are of less value than "a gift for reading reality—the impulse to put your loving face to it and press your hands against it" (p. 203).

As Ravelstein nears death, his intellectual allegiances shift perceptibly. "If he had to choose between Athens and Jerusalem, among us the two main sources of higher life," Chick declares of Ravelstein, "he chose Athens, while full of respect for Jerusalem. But in his last days it was the Jews he wanted to talk about, not the Greeks" (p. 173). As he saw it, the Jews "had been used to give the entire species a measure of [that is, a way of measuring] human viciousness" (p. 174). On his deathbed, "I could see that he was following a trail of Jewish ideas or Jewish essences. . . . He was full of Scripture now. . . . Sometimes he was coherent. Most of the time he lost me" (p. 178). Ravelstein urges Chick to take Rosamund to synagogue on the approaching high holidays. He disparages myth, Grielescu's great subject, not as a Platonist but as a Jew. "The Jews had better understand their status with respect to myth," he reminds Chick. "Why should they have any truck with myth? It was myth that demonized them" (p. 127). What matters to a Jew is history: "A Jew should take a deep interest in the history of the Jews—in their principles of justice, for instance" (p. 179).

AFTER THE ST. MARTIN EPISODE, the novel ends by returning to Ravelstein. That it does not end with Ravelstein's death is one of the reasons we don't see the cutting short of his life as tragic, for all his great-souled virtues and attractions. As Helen Small puts it, in *Ravelstein* "we are invited to see the quality and the intensity of the engagement with life, not the duration of the life, as paramount."

> Relatedly, we are continually aware of Chick's age, but he is (until the very end of the novel) fit, still working, still held in high public esteem, still enjoying life. This is not quite the Epicurean disconnection of the good life from temporality, but it shares something of the Epicurean disregard for longevity, and much of the hedonism. What matters is immersion in the present and, to a degree, comic insouciance about the inevitable end point.
>
> . . .
>
> [Chick's] resistance to the forward drive of the life-story is, finally, a refusal to accept that proximity to the end must structure how one lives in old age. It would be impossible to live happily on those terms, Bellow suggests. This rejection of chronological progress takes additional support from his refusal to see his own (or Ravelstein's) life as an isolated unit, closed in on its own narrative form.[35]

Hence the novel's last pages. Chick recalls that Ravelstein "ordered me to write this memoir, yes, but he didn't think it was necessary for me to grind away at the classics of Western thought," an order Chick approves, declaring, "I would rather see Ravelstein again than to explain matters it doesn't help to explain" (p. 231). The novel ends, therefore, with a picture of Ravelstein. I quote the description in full, as it is among Bellow's richest endings, a marvel for an author at any age, let alone one in his eighties. The setting is Hyde Park. Ravelstein is dressing to go out and talking to Chick at the same time, walking from room to room.

> The music is pouring from his hi-fi—the many planes of his bare, bald head go before me in the corridor between his living room and his monumental master bedroom. He stops before his pier-glass—no wall mirrors here—and puts in the heavy gold cufflinks, buttons up the Jermyn Street Kisser & Asser striped shirt—American Trustworthy laundry-and-cleaners deliver his shirts puffed out with tissue paper. He winds up his tie lifting the collar that crackles with starch. He makes a luxurious knot. The unsteady fingers, long, ill-coordinated, nervous to the point of decadence, make a double lap. Ravelstein likes a big tie-knot—after all, he is a large man. Then he sits down on the beautifully cured fleeces of his bed and puts on the Poulsen and Skone tan Wellington boots. His left foot is several sizes smaller than the right but there is no limp. He smokes, of course, he is always smoking, and tilts the head away from the smoke while he knots and pulls the knot into place. The cast and orchestra are pouring out the *Italian Maiden in Algiers*. This is dressing music, accessory or mood music, but Ravelstein takes a Nietzschean view, favorable to comedy and bandstands. Better Bizet and *Carmen* than Wagner and the *Ring*. He likes the volume of his powerful set turned up to the maximum. The ringing phone is left to the answering machine. He puts on his $5,000 suit, an Italian wool mixed with silk. He pulls down the coat cuff with his fingertips and polishes the top of his head. And perhaps he relishes having so many instruments serenading him, so many musicians in attendance. He corresponds with compact disc companies behind the Iron Curtain. He has helpers going to the post office to pay customs duties for him.
>
> "What do you think of this recording, Chick?" he says. "They're playing original ancient seventeenth-century instruments."
>
> He loses himself in sublime music, a music in which ideas are dissolved, reflecting these ideas in the form of feeling. He carries them down into the street with him. There's an early snow on the tall shrubs, the same shrubs filled with a huge flock of parrots—the ones that escaped from cages and now build their long nest sacks in the back alleys. They are feeding on the red berries. Ravelstein

looks at me, laughing with pleasure and astonishment, gesturing because he can't be heard in all this bird-noise.

You don't easily give up a creature like Ravelstein to death [pp. 231–33].

The wonderful parrots, "noisy green birds from the tropics," have appeared before. "Doesn't the snow get them down?" Ravelstein asks on a first sighting. Chick is struck by how long the birds hold Ravelstein's attention, as Ravelstein "had little interest in natural life." Perhaps they do so, he conjectures, "because they were not merely feeding, but gorging, and he was a voracious eater himself" (pp. 141–42). Perhaps, also, because he was noisy, colorful, no less incongruous and amusing a presence in gray Chicago. In a later sighting, Ravelstein grins and tells Chick: "They even have a Jew look to them," and Chick compares their sacklike nests to "Eastside tenements" (p. 170).[36]

Janis, Marje Horvitz, SB, and Beena Kamlani, Vermont, 2000 (courtesy of Janis Bellow)

13

Love and Strife

RAVELSTEIN APPEARED SIX MONTHS before the publication of James Atlas's biography of Bellow, just in time for Atlas to discuss it. He calls it "the most compelling book Bellow had written in years" and "Bellow's greatest act of literary portraiture," adding a characteristic qualification: "He could finally share the stage with someone else."[1] Other deflating or negative remarks appear in the biography. In *The Shadow in the Garden: A Biographer's Tale*, Atlas admits to a dozen, a number later whittled down to six.[2] Bellow always feared Atlas would recount instances of bad behavior, but that these would be accompanied by moments of authorial animus he seems not to have anticipated, at least not until April 22, 2000, the week *Ravelstein* was published. That morning, in *The New York Times*, Brent Staples, Bellow's stalker, published an op-ed article entitled "Mr. Bellow Writes On, Wrestling with the Ghost of Edward Shils." The article begins by recounting Shils's career, his friendship with Bellow, the possible causes of their falling-out, and his depiction in *Ravelstein* as Rakhmiel Kogon. The possible causes of the falling-out, according to people "who knew both men" (Atlas? Joseph Epstein?), are "that Shils had tired of being caricatured in the novels, that Bellow was angered that the man he 'admired and adored' did not take him seriously as an intellectual—and even that the two of them had argued over a woman [Bette Howland?]." Shils died in 1995, so it seemed that, in their mutual hostilities, Bellow would have the last word. This, Staples now announced, might not be the case:

> When Mr. Bellow's biographer, James Atlas, publishes the writer's biography next fall, the book will have been shaped to some degree by none other than Edward Shils, who read a draft—annotating it in that famous green ink—and disgorged on his death bed a 16,000-word edited memorandum. In revising the book, Mr. Atlas told me recently, "I sat at the keyboard with this memo, communing with a dead man."
>
> We may have known for half a century what Mr. Bellow thinks of Mr. Shils. Come the biography, perhaps we can glimpse, at least after a fashion, what Mr. Shils thinks of him.

Two days after these words appeared in the *Times*, Atlas wrote to Bellow to apologize, prompted by a call from Andrew Wylie, his and Bellow's agent. As Atlas recounts the call in his memoir, Wylie told him that the Staples piece was "the last straw" for Bellow: "He'd had enough of this biographer; he would rescind permission to quote from his papers. I immediately sat down and wrote him an apologetic letter."[3] Atlas begins this letter—actually a fax, dated April 26—by saying that he had no intention of causing Bellow pain and that his aim in asking Shils to read the manuscript (as he'd asked others "of that generation" to do) was "to give me an accurate sense of the period, its issues and social history, its *feel*." He describes himself as no friend of Shils, who didn't like him; he claims he chose Shils as a reader because he knew he'd be tough (as he chose Dwight Macdonald to read the manuscript of his Delmore Schwartz biography, "and you know what he was like"). Atlas then offers Bellow a "general sense" of what Shils had to say about the manuscript: he criticized its length and the inadequate attention it gave to anti-Jewish prejudice at that time; he offered factual corrections; and he congratulated Atlas "on having got so far." What Atlas does not mention, understandably, are the many disparaging remarks Shils makes about Bellow in his memo. The fax ends: "Will you like everything about this portrait? Will I have gotten everything right? I doubt it. But I'm doing the best I can; my book is fair and—I like to think—generous."

This is not quite what Atlas says of the biography in *The Shadow in the Garden: A Biographer's Tale*. Prompted by what he calls the "splenetic reviews" his biography received ("There were also many positive ones," he adds in a footnote), he reread it in search of the bias identified by his critics: "Had I disparaged Bellow's intellectual pretensions? Was

I as hostile to my subject as my critics claimed? Had I gone on too much about the women?" The dozen places "where I felt I had gotten it wrong—not in fact but in tone," he identifies, variously, as "ungenerous," "judgmental," "neurotic," "small-minded."[4] Their presence in the book he attributes in part to the cumulative effect of the interviews he conducted, many of which were with witnesses whose "testimony was harsh, and they didn't seem to care if it was on the record." He also considers the possibility that his personal contacts with Bellow may have had a deforming effect—understandably, given how difficult and changeable Bellow was with him, alternately wary, welcoming, snappish, warm, evasive. "Somehow knowing him was proving a hindrance to understanding him."[5] Then there was the "servile role" Atlas found himself adopting in Bellow's presence. This role he claims not to have minded at the time, though "normally" he was "a proud and stubborn person, bristling, easily wounded, short-tempered when 'dissed.'" In Bellow's presence, he reverted "to a second-grade self, afraid of girls, sports, Skate Nights." "Could it be that I feared my own aggression? That the chauffeur might inadvertently slam his passenger's fingers in the door?"[6] What is striking about this image is how close it is to one used by Barnett Singer in his memoir, recounted in chapter 7. Singer is chauffeuring Bellow around Victoria, British Columbia, and as Bellow digs about for his seat belt, Singer thinks: "Wouldn't want the great author flying through the windshield." There is an element of aggression in the feelings of both men: admiration, even reverence, mixes with hostility. Earlier in *Shadow in the Garden*, Atlas quotes Richard Holmes, the British biographer and theorist of biography, who writes "of the biographer extending 'a handshake' toward his subject." "At some point," Atlas admits, "without realizing it, I had withdrawn my hand."[7]

BELLOW DREADED THE APPEARANCE of the biography. On October 6, 1999, in the letter in which he explained to Werner Dannhauser why he had stuck with AIDS as the cause of Ravelstein's death, he claimed to be "taking heat on three fronts: i) Paternity—a fresh start at the age of 84, ii) The messy explosive mixture that James Atlas is preparing for me in the form of a biography, iii) The hue and cry about my book against which I must brace myself. Janis occasionally says to me that maybe we should move to Uruguay." Ten months later, on August 12, 2000, Bellow wrote to Richard Stern, declaring, "I don't intend to read Atlas. There is a parallel between his book and the towel with which the bartender cleans the bar. What strikes me uncomfortably about Atlas is that he has a great appeal for my detractors. He was born to please them." When Stern read the biography, which he admired in part, he wrote to Bellow, in a letter of July 28, 2000: "I don't think you and Janis need to read it. Would Hector and Andromache read their story if Thersites had written it?" This crack he repeated in a review, though, as a friend of Atlas as well as of Bellow, he also called the biography "fascinating, sometimes brilliant."[8] "When is this book of yours coming out," Bellow wrote to Atlas a few weeks before publication. "I feel I should go off to Yemen."[9] According to Ruth Wisse, before the book was published, "he [Bellow] and Janis talked about moving to France. I don't think they were serious. But he was terrified. . . . They were sure they were going to be pulverized." Wisse was distressed at Bellow's distress.

Philip Roth, who had originally suggested to Atlas that he write Bellow's biography, was also worried, and had been for several years. In the summer of 1998, while visiting the Bellows in Vermont, he proposed to Bellow "that he and I do an extensive written interview about his life's work." He would reread Bellow's books and "then send him my thoughts on each, structured as questions, for him to respond to at length however he liked." In the end, the project was not completed, "despite Saul's willingness and my prodding." What answers Bellow did provide—about the novels up to and including *Humboldt's Gift*—were full of interest, which partly explains Roth's reluctance to "let [Bellow] be."[10] But he was also reluctant for the reason that had prompted him to suggest the project in the first place. As he explained to Bellow in a letter of July 28, 1998, "I would like this interview to do everything that Atlas isn't going to do," by which he means as an interpreter of Bellow's works. In an undated letter of September 1998, Roth praises Bellow's full comments on *Augie March*, "because you more than likely never told this to Atlas. Let's just load this thing up with stuff that [he] doesn't know." A year later, in a letter of September 27, 1999, having not heard from Bellow, Roth is disappointed: "I remind you that it's now over a year since we launched this project. And I continue to think, as I did at the outset, that it is terribly important—when Atlas's book appears, and there is a long overdue public discussion of your work as a result—that our interview be a central part of that discussion. . . . David Remnick at the New Yorker is eager to publish the interview when it is completed.

I think it would be a good idea for it to appear there in the spring of 2000, when Atlas's book is scheduled to be published." In the end, an edited version of what they had completed of the interview was published in *The New Yorker* on April 25, 2005, three weeks after Bellow's death, in similar hopes of being at the center of a discussion of Bellow's writing. When Atlas's book was published in October 2000, it appeared a week after Roth published an article in the October 9 issue of *The New Yorker* entitled "Re-Reading Saul Bellow," a discussion of the novels from *The Adventures of Augie March* to *Humboldt's Gift*.

ROTH'S FRIENDSHIP WITH Bellow blossomed in the early 1990s, though, as we have seen, he had admired him from his earliest days as a writer. In 1975, he dedicated a collection of essays and interviews, *Reading Myself and Others*, to Bellow, described as "the 'other' I have read from the beginning with the deepest pleasure and admiration." In the 1980s, the two men saw each other only occasionally, in part because Roth was living half the year in London with Claire Bloom, whom he married in 1990. After he and Bloom moved back to the United States, he would see Bellow when he came to Chicago to visit his older brother, Sandy. Roth believes it was Janis's enthusiasm for his fiction that led Bellow at last "to read me seriously." He also believes that she urged Bellow to be more openly friendly toward him. "What's the matter?" he imagines Janis saying. "This guy really likes you, he really admires you, he wants to be your friend." When *Operation Shylock* (1993) was published, Bellow phoned Roth, "saying, basically, 'Kid, that was terrific.'" He was similarly enthusiastic about *American Pastoral* (1997). In the late 1990s, Roth paid several summer visits to the Bellows in Vermont, sometimes with friends (Norman Manea or Ross Miller, an English professor at Columbia, the nephew of Arthur Miller). For Janis, Roth and Martin Amis were "twin pillars" in Bellow's last years. She also believes her role in bringing them together has been exaggerated. "It's not like I was kicking him under the table"; he was "hungering for a connection to Philip."

In the course of this new closeness, the novelists made a pact of "mutual candor" when discussing each other's work.[11] This pact Bellow tested when writing to Roth about his novel *I Married a Communist* (1998). Although it was always "a treat" to read a Roth manuscript, Bellow wrote on January 1, 1998, in this case "the overall effect was not satisfactory." The problem with the novel, Bellow believed, was one of "distance. . . . There should be a certain detachment from the writer's own passions." The irony of such a complaint coming from the author of *Herzog*, he fully recognized, but Herzog was "a chump—a failed intellectual and at bottom a sentimentalist," an altogether different character from "the man who gives us Eve and Sylphid," characters in *I Married a Communist* thought by many readers, certainly by Bellow, to be thinly fictionalized versions of Claire Bloom and her daughter, Anna Steiger. Bloom had written harshly about Roth in her memoir *Leaving a Doll's House* (1996), and Bellow's letter implies a revenge motive in Roth's depiction of the characters of Eve and her daughter, Sylphid. Moreover, the communist of the title, Ira Ringold, is "probably the least attractive of all your characters. I assume that you can no more bear Ira than the reader can. But you stand loyally by this cast-iron klutz—a big strong stupid man who attracts you for reasons invisible to me." Anticipating Roth's response, Bellow continues: "You will say that all of that is acknowledged in *IMAC*. Yes, and no . . . One of your persistent themes is the purgation one can only obtain through rage. The forces of aggression are liberating, etc. And I can see that as a legitimate point of view. But Eve is simply a pitiful woman and Sylphid is a pampered, wicked fat girl with a bison hump. These are not titans."

On January 10, Roth wrote back, beginning with Bellow's point about "distance." He and Bellow must be "broadcasting on different frequencies." Two-thirds of the novel is narrated by "the *brother* of a Communist, the *brother* of a killer, who is himself opposed to his brother's politics and spends a lifetime trying to educate and subdue his brother's violent impulses. I believe Murray [the brother] is strongly there (as is his wife and his daughter) and that it's impossible to understand this story separate from his/their presence. The remaining third of the story is narrated by the former protégé of the Communist and the killer [Nathan Zuckerman], who is neither of those things himself, and who explains what Ira's appeal was to a certain kind of morally precocious boy in the 1940s. . . . For some reason, in IMAC, you won't see narrators anywhere, though mine don't shut up from beginning to end, endlessly reflecting on the story." When Bellow describes one of Roth's "persistent themes" as "the purgation one obtains only through rage," Roth replies that this is precisely the opposite of the theme of *I Married a Communist*, as it is the opposite of the theme of *American Pastoral*. Throughout the book, Ira "is trying to be liberated *from* violent rage.

He fails, but the story is about the effort." Roth also disputes Bellow's account of *Herzog:* "You're forgetting the intellectual ferocity, the sheer *human* ferocity, of that book. . . . You were writing about betrayal and so you wrote about betrayers and the betrayed. You faced things. *Everything.* If Herzog was a sentimentalist none of us who think of that novel as a masterpiece would have bothered to read it. Herzog is a moralist, and, like any moralist with a brain, brokenhearted."

At the end of his letter, Bellow anticipates and seeks to soothe Roth's feelings. "There aren't many people to whom I can be so open," he declares. "You'll be sore at me, but I believe that you won't cast me off forever." Roth's letter ends with a comparable softening: "Cast you out forever? You've been in my bloodstream since I read *Augie March.* It's going to take more than candor for me to cast you out for half an hour, let alone 'forever.' " The great respect, the reverence, Roth feels for Bellow underlay his response to *Ravelstein* as well, occasioning what Claudia Roth Pierpont calls a slight "bending" of their pact of mutual candor. Roth thought *Ravelstein* "deeply flawed," despite "some wonderful scenes and portraits." "I knew what was wrong with it," he said in an interview, "and I knew it was not right to tell him, because he didn't have the strength." He thought it was a mistake to make Ravelstein "wonderful from the first line of the story, so there's nowhere to go." He felt the same way about "the evil of the Eliade character." Had Bellow been younger and stronger, he would have advised him to "mix them up." "It's hard to write a book at eighty-four," he told Pierpont. "It's hard to remember day to day what you've done" (something he himself would experience, retiring from writing fiction at seventy-seven). What he said to Bellow, he told Pierpont, was that "he couldn't properly evaluate 'Ravelstein' because he was 'out of sympathy' with the character of Abe Ravelstein," by which he also meant out of sympathy with Allan Bloom. Within the Bellow circle, some attributed Roth's lack of enthusiasm for *Ravelstein* (wrongly, Roth insists) to his response to Bellow's remarks about *I Married a Communist.*

Roth was not alone among Bellow's friends to face candid criticism of their work. At Bellow's request, Richard Stern submitted a story to *News from the Republic of Letters,* the literary journal Bellow and Botsford had founded in 1997. In a letter of June 18, 1998, Bellow rejected the story. "I'd be all for it if it had been written in a different way," he explained. "It has too much extraneous data for a short story, too many lists of names. . . . So much lavish documentation makes the reader (this reader, anyhow) impatient. But Botsford and I have set ourselves up to be the saviors of high culture—saving it from itself—so we've put extraordinary demands on ourselves and everybody else. I seriously doubt whether he and I could meet our own standards." Stern, like Roth, was forgiving. A more pained response, one seriously damaging to their friendship, came from Bellow's rejection of a story by David Peltz. The story, entitled "Side Effect," was never published (Peltz gave me a copy). It is narrated by a man much like Peltz himself, a builder and ex–aluminum-siding salesman. Like Peltz, the narrator decides to produce his own version of a Jackson Pollock painting, which he hangs in a prominent place in his living room. The materials he uses for the painting come from his twin brother, with whom he's always been competitive (unlike the narrator, Peltz had sisters but no brothers). This brother "was organized. He was focused. Without a misstep he went on to become highly achieved as an oncologist. The unexpressed comparison between us followed me like an albatross. I was the undeveloped one. The inferior half." So good a painter was the oncologist brother that he put the narrator off painting for many years.

Bellow's rejection of Peltz's story came in a letter of July 10, 1997:

> I'm sorry to say that Botsford and I can't persuade each other to print your piece. The idea behind it is good but your handling of it is faulty. You make too much of your rivalry with the brother you never had. To have a rivalry with one's brother is one thing, but to have it in for a brother who never existed is ill-natured. It's like washing dirty linen in public; and furthermore washing sheets you never slept on. So your story toils on and you deal with problems nobody wants to hear about. After all, it's a jolly inspiration to do a Jackson Pollock of one's own to put it over on one's wife as a work of genius. But you reveal throughout, one way or another, that at this light-hearted moment you have also brought a large burden of unsettled scores to church, and you drag every last one of them into the confession box with you.

Peltz's story is not very good, certainly not good enough to go into a magazine aiming to save high culture from itself. But Bellow's rejection is harshly personal. The passages about the narrator's brother are, indeed, extraneous, but that the brother had no real-life model is irrelevant. Bellow, reading biographically, sees the brother as a figure for himself, and has taken offense: "To have a rivalry with one's brother is one thing. To have it in for a brother who never existed is ill-natured. It's like washing dirty linen in public; and furthermore washing sheets you never slept on."

Peltz was wounded. Nor was he softened by the rejection letter's concluding sentences: "Don't hate me too hard or too long. Just ask yourself how many other contributors get a letter as long as this." As Peltz interpreted the letter, "He is not my brother, is what he's saying: Get off it! Are you pretending to be my level? I have a reputation, and I don't want to taint it by publishing a work that's not up to my level." Peltz admitted that "the story was a metaphor of our relationship," but it was in no way critical of Bellow; the story's narrator is not critical of his brother, only envious of him. Peltz was upset not so much by the rejection, or the harshness of the criticism, as by the absence of any word of encouragement: " 'David, this is not good but stay with it. I want the best for you, but I cannot publish it.' That's all." "I'm not anti-Bellow," Peltz insisted in an interview. "I'm anti his not acknowledging me in terms of our relationship." Bellow's letter was "unforgivable" in its failure to acknowledge their friendship and history. "Outrageous. How petty . . . How I hungered for this, I hungered for him to say, Dave, show me what you're doing, we'll go over it together. He did it with students and strangers; why didn't he do it with me?"

These are later reflections. At the time, Peltz was more conciliatory, though openly pained. "Since your letter," he wrote to Bellow on August 12, 1997, a month after Bellow's letter, "more than once I have pulled off to the side of the road to find that what I am really searching for is not the right house but the right response to the cruelty of having learned that I never had a brother and I shouldn't be wasting literary efforts laundering feelings in a public way for a brother I never had. . . . But I did have fun doing it. And I did try to make it readable and hoped it would earn a word of praise." His letter ends: "Saul, it is built into my well-being not to hate at all. Pissed off, yes. But not for long. Happily, I am off the floor, upright again, and working on another story." This was not quite true. Ten years later, he was still angry with Bellow in interviews with me, as he no doubt was when interviewed by James Atlas, and the harshness of Bellow's letter figured prominently in his complaints.

Bellow had form in cases like this, where the claims of friendship seemed to him to impinge upon what he saw as the claims of literary merit, including the costs involved in creating works of literature and finding an audience for them. One thinks of his refusal to write an introduction to a collection of Oscar Tarcov's stories. In the Tarcov case, discussed in chapter 9, Bellow's refusal was more tactfully phrased than the Peltz rejection letter, but for Nathan Tarcov it was no less wounding and incomprehensible. In explaining his decision to Nathan, Bellow gestured toward the sacrifices required of a literary vocation. Oscar Tarcov was a better father and husband than he was, he told Nathan, but "he wasn't that good a writer and I don't really see any point in your doing this." Nathan sees this answer as "petty" (a word Peltz also used), a resurfacing "of a long-ago teenage rivalry." But it could also be a sign of the sole virtue Edward Shils allowed Bellow: "consecration to his art." Another answer, a related answer, is that in life, including in correspondence, Bellow was not always as careful, sensitive, or thoughtful as he was in his fiction. When people are wounded by his fiction, on the whole they're meant to be wounded. Neither Roth nor Stern nor Nathan and Miriam Tarcov were meant to be wounded. Peltz is another matter.

Bellow's regrets figure prominently in the correspondence from his early eighties, often occasioned by the deaths of old friends and acquaintances. On March 20, 1997, he wrote to his old friend Al Glotzer (he figures in chapters 5 and 6 of *To Fame and Fortune*) with news of Bellow's third wife, Susan's, death. Susan died on September 17, 1996, at sixty-two, two days after collapsing from an aneurysm, the same sort that her father, Frank Glassman, had died of at fifty-eight.[12] Daniel, who was thirty-two, was devastated. When he called his father, Bellow burst into tears, his first confused words being "Tell your mother I'm sorry." What Daniel remembers of him at this time is that "he was never more kind to me." Bellow offered to attend the funeral in Chicago, but he was frail, still not wholly recovered from the fish poisoning, and Daniel told him not to make the trip. As he explained to Atlas, "I didn't want to lose both my parents in the same weekend."[13] Daniel remembers telling Bellow, "Pop, you're a great guy. I really admire you," and Bellow answering, "I'd like it if you were a better man than me." In the same letter to Glotzer, Bellow comments on the death of Irving Howe. "We got off on the wrong foot," he admits. "David Bazelon introduced us (in the Village days) and I was—well . . . [his ellipses] ungracious. For which I was never forgiven."

Susan's death in 1996 had been preceded in the same year by the deaths of two other people who had been important to him. Eleanor Clark, Robert Penn Warren's widow, the mother of Rosanna Warren, died in February. In March, Meyer Schapiro died. Both were old friends and part of Bellow's life in Vermont. The next year, in July, François Furet died suddenly, on the tennis court. On September 1, 1997, Bellow wrote to Werner Dannhauser, suffering from "pangs of conscience."

> I haven't written to my correspondents because . . . because, because, because. I haven't added up the deaths of friends during the past six months. Furet you knew and perhaps you remember Zita Cogan who died a few weeks ago. The others were long-time buddies: a college classmate, in Paris [Julian Behrstock]. In New York, Yetta [Barshevsky] Shachtman, the widow of the Trotskyite leader. She and I would walk back from school in Humboldt Park (Chicago) discussing Trotsky's latest pamphlet on the German question. . . . She was an earnest girl—the dear kind—Comrade Yetta. Her pa was a carpenter, and his old Nash was filled with tools, shavings and sawdust. And now she has gone—human sawdust and shavings. There was also a clever, clumsy man named [Hyman] Slate who believed (when we were young) that a sense of humor should be part of every argument about the existence of God. Laughing was proof that there was a God. But God in the end laid two kinds of cancer on him and took him away very quickly. . . . Next came the news that David Shahar had died. So many women in his life. When I met him with yet another one on some Jerusalem street he would lay a finger to his lips as he passed. . . . I did like him but my deeper sympathies went to Shula [his wife].

A month after this letter, in November 1997, Catharine "Katy" Carver died, at seventy-six. She and Bellow had fallen out over John Berryman. They were discussing him in a bar on Dover Street in London, and Carver angrily told Bellow, "This is no place to be talking about John," to which Bellow replied: "'On the contrary, John would have thought it appropriate to be mourned in a bar-room.' After that she refused to meet me or return my telephone calls. . . . I think she felt my introduction to Berryman's posthumous novel was disrespectful." Bellow remembered Carver in her youth as "a very pretty and lively young woman . . . kind and attractive."[14] A month later, to round off the year, Owen Barfield died, perhaps the most important of Bellow's spiritual guides. He was ninety-nine. In the letter to Dannhauser, Bellow, at eighty-two, described himself as "dying piecemeal. My legs aren't functioning as they ought. Day and night they ache. And I am this, that and the other in many respects, physically. It seems that my tear ducts have dried up, and the eyeballs feel gummy. The details are not worth going into. It's possible that I may never recover from the damage done by cigua toxin." The next summer, in June 1998, Alfred Kazin died. Born five days before Bellow, he died at eighty-three. The next year, in May 1999, Saul Steinberg died.

As old friends fell away, new ones entered the picture. Chief among these was the young British critic James Wood. When he first met Bellow, in 1990, Wood was twenty-five and a freelance book critic for *The Guardian*. In a letter to Harriet Wasserman, he described himself as a great fan of Bellow's and asked if he could interview him for a *Guardian* profile. The interview, he assured Wasserman, would be literary, nonjournalistic, nonsensational. "And Wasserman said it was fine, just call him, and I did." When he met Bellow in Chicago, he found him not at all the formidable figure he'd expected. "He was very warm, he laid the table for tea, Russian tea, and we had a free-ranging conversation for a couple of hours. At a mere twenty-six, or whatever I was [he was twenty-five], I felt I should be very serious, and in addition to discussing his fiction I thought we should talk seriously about the state of America, modernity, post-modernity, and so on. And I remember Bellow, charmingly at the end, saying this conversation has been a bit serious, and he wanted a bit more levity." Then, "very thrillingly," Bellow suggested that they walk together to a local bookshop, "and people were spotting Bellow on the street and whispering—I enjoyed that." Bellow recommended Czesław Miłosz's poetry and the Frances Steegmuller book *Flaubert in Egypt*, "which he said was a riot, a real laugh." Then they got into Bellow's Range Rover, and he drove Wood back to his hotel in the Loop. "So he could not have been nicer. I was absolutely nobody. I was just a young admirer. So as you can imagine it left a very nice impression."

The resulting profile by Wood began as it meant to go on. "Why poke around by torchlight if there are stars to see by? It seems strange at times that anyone bothers with ordinary writers after reading Saul Bellow." What followed was a Bellow-like description of Bellow's face, which looks "as it should. . . . Deeply grooved with creases of laughter, it is heroically formed. The brow is large, domed; it blazes, as do the eyes which are heavy-lidded and comically recessed—they suggest reserves of brilliant slyness. His nose is noble, elevated, slightly veined with age now; his mouth is voluptuous and resembles Mr. Sammler's in *Mr. Sammler's Planet:* 'a heavy, all savouring, all-rejecting lip.'" The profile, "Einstein of the Common Life," was published on April 21, 1990, and Wood sent a copy to Bellow. On August 15, 1990, Bellow wrote back saying he'd read and been impressed by Wood's reviews in *The Guardian* and that he was "delighted with your visit and also of course by [the profile]. . . . You gave me first-class treatment and I am not one of those monsters who are senselessly provoked by good deeds."

IN 1996 THE BELLOWS MOVED from Bay State Road to a house in Brookline, on Crowninshield Road, a quiet residential street off Commonwealth Avenue. The house had four bedrooms, four bathrooms, separate studies for Bellow and Janis, a dining room, a living room, a front porch, a television room, and a kitchen with a central station. The Bellows fell in love with it as soon as they saw the light-filled kitchen and the yard beyond, with its handsome chestnut tree. The property was rented from the university, a five-minute subway ride away (on the Green Line). Sometimes Bellow and Janis walked to BU along the back roads that run parallel to Commonwealth Avenue, past grand Victorian mansions, a bird-and-wildlife sanctuary, a large pond. The urban attractions of Brookline were first outlined to Bellow by the novelist Alan Lelchuk, who stressed its Jewish character. In a letter of March 27, 1976, in anticipation of Bellow and Alexandra teaching for a semester at Brandeis, Lelchuk praised Brookline's "solid bourgeois Jewish familiarity and warmth. . . . I think this is a better town than Newton because it's not really a suburb, but a town in itself with a center or two, and it's right down the street from Boston, across a little bridge from Cambridge." While at Brandeis, the Bellows lived in Cambridge but had been attracted to Brookline. In a letter to Lelchuk of March 22, 1976, Bellow said that Brookline reminded him of "the Montreal I knew when I was a kid." Twenty years later, a Brookline resident, he ate nearby at Rubin's Kosher Deli on Harvard Street, described by Ruth Wisse as "the best we can do in Boston," bought his fish at Wulf's Fish Market, and shopped and browsed at other stores at Coolidge Corner, a neighborhood much frequented by Russian Jewish immigrants, including several Gordin cousins. As Janis puts it, Coolidge Corner "replicated all the little shops and things of Chicago," and "you could hear Yiddish spoken there."

In May 1999, Chris Walsh, Bellow's assistant, finished his Ph.D.[15] As his thesis adviser, as opposed to his boss, Bellow had been "pretty disengaged, but that was what I wanted." As his boss, in addition to being considerate, he'd been fun, full of silly stories and cracks: about the BU philosophy professor described as "always dropping his own name" (followed by "That was pretty good, wasn't it?"); about addictions ("mine's to ill-nature"); about feeling low ("Whenever you are feeling down, Chris, remember it's a blessing that you were not born with Russian cousins"); about a poor student ("Always a disappointment when you find a Jewish kid who's not smart. I think his father's Irish," a crack aimed at Walsh); about a sentence in a Russian novel: "He had one rather clean shirt" ("a very Russian sentence"). After finishing his dissertation, Walsh was keen to return to Africa, where he'd been with the Peace Corps before coming to BU. In May 2000, having been awarded a Fulbright Fellowship, he accepted a two-year teaching post in Burkina Faso and was replaced as Bellow's assistant by an ex–BU student who would remain on the job for five years, until the end of Bellow's life.

The student's name was Will Lautzenheiser. An English major, he had graduated Phi Beta Kappa and summa cum laude in 1996. For the next four years, he worked first at the James Joyce Research Center at BU, under the eccentric Joyce scholar John Kidd, and then for the provost of the university. When he heard that Bellow was looking for a new secretary, he immediately emailed Walsh, who told him to come by the house. Will had never met Bellow, or taken any courses with him, though as a senior he'd attended a reading Bellow gave of "Leaving the Yellow House." The only Bellow novels he'd read were *Herzog* and *Henderson the Rain King*. The interview took place in the living room at Crowninshield Road. Janis was nursing six-month-old Rosie. Moose, the cat, introduced as "an important member of the family," was present throughout. Bellow was relaxed and easy. "I see this as a very simple thing," he told Will. "I want you as my secretary." "It was very intuitive," Will recalls, it "wasn't even an interview." Will's father was also born in 1915, he told Bellow; "Well, that should inspire filial piety," Bellow answered. "And he was right about that; the bond that was established happened very quickly."

The first job Will was given was to help move the family to Vermont at the end of the month. Once the Bellows were settled, Will returned to Boston to collect mail from the Crowninshield Road house and Bellow's office at BU. Every two weeks, he returned to Vermont "for a few days or even a week," armed with Bellow's correspondence. Sitting together on the front porch of the Vermont house, they would go through the hundreds of requests Bellow received. At first, Will recalls, "I ran most everything past him," but he soon learned "what he wouldn't do." Later, Will was set the task of organizing Bellow's books in Vermont, which were grouped by country. Frank Maltese was called in to build more bookshelves. The first literary conversation Will had with Bellow concerned Melville, how funny he was (in the sense of amusing). That summer, there were lots of visitors and nights out, concerts at Marlboro, family outings for ice cream. There was a morning routine. Bellow would come downstairs at nine or nine-thirty, have his coffee. The papers came a day late, through the mail, and most mornings Bellow would read a little of *The New York Times* or *The Wall Street Journal.* Then he'd go to his office in the house, on the ground floor, not to the outside studio, "and he'd do some reading, and he would write, and he'd sometimes do some letters." His manner with Janis was "loving"; the first summer with infant Rosie was "beautiful, magical."

Bellow was now eighty-five, and the writing he returned to was "Marbles." He could write paragraphs, Will remembers, "but that was all." After *Ravelstein,* he also turned his attention to the ordering of his *Collected Stories,* helped by Janis as well as Beena Kamlani. James Wood wrote an introduction to the volume, Janis a memoirlike preface, and Bellow a brief afterword, in which he confessed to "emphatically agreeing" with Chekhov's "mania for shortness," a necessity in modern America, with its "plethora of attractions and excitements—world crises, hot and cold wars, threats to survival, famines, unspeakable crimes" (p. 440). He makes no mention of age as a factor in writing short. Kamlani continued to visit Bellow after *Ravelstein.* "My prime function," she recalls, "was to get him started." "For a while, something would capture his imagination, and he'd say, Okay, let's give it a shot. And we'd spend four mornings working on it, and then it would peter out. . . . But of course he was old by then, and his attention span was not quite what it was."

In addition to visitors—the boys and their families, Janis's family, Lesha and family, Joel Bellows, friends from Chicago and Boston—there were Vermont friends—the Copelands, Walter Pozen, the cellist

David Soyer of the Guarneri Quartet and his wife, Janet Putnam, a harpist, and Laura and Franklin Reeve, she a novelist, he a poet and Russianist, as handsome as his son Christopher. Especially welcome were visits from Rosanna Warren and her husband, Stephen Scully, a classicist, often accompanied by their teenage daughters. Rosanna had inherited her parents' Vermont house, along with a family tradition of reading Shakespeare plays out loud. On several occasions, the Bellows joined in. They read *The Tempest*, with Bellow as Prospero and Janis as Miranda. When they read *King Lear*, Bellow was Lear and Janis was Cordelia. Bellow was Falstaff in the *Henry IV* readings. "If you wanted to, you could prepare," Warren remembers, "but we'd all been living with these plays all the time." The readings began at 6:00 p.m., and the first three acts were read before supper; the last two acts were read after dessert. The children were given minor parts, and other parts were switched around, but with Lear and Prospero "there was no question of his being someone else." As an actor, Bellow "was extremely expressive . . . completely magical and with such authority. Everybody was intensely gripping our texts. . . . The room was no longer Vermont. In a weird way it was no longer Saul. We were all alive to the complex registers of Saul having such roles." On these evenings, Warren was struck by how generous Bellow was with her children, "really attentive, very sweet to them. . . . The children loved it."

Bellow's difficulties with his writing, his inability to concentrate, his lapses of memory, were apparent when he and Will went through office work, including finances and correspondence. "We would sit down with the checkbook," Will remembers, and Bellow would ask, "What is this?" or "What is this Verizon all the time?" "He'd make a joke out of it, but it was real." In the following spring, when Bellow taught a course on Conrad, there were one or two complaints from students about being asked to look at passages they'd looked at just previously. Will attended all the classes. "There was some impairment, but we got through it." As James Wood understands it, that spring someone had gone to the dean to complain. Silber was informed, but his view was "When you get a really great eagle, you don't clip his feathers." Bellow had no desire to give up teaching—quite the contrary. He enjoyed the contact with young people. One solution was for him to co-teach, as he'd done in Chicago (with Bloom and David Grene and others). Fortunately, just the right co-teacher was at hand. In autumn 2001, James Wood's wife, the American novelist Claire Messud, had taken a job as writer-in-residence at Amherst College. In 1995, after five years as lead fiction reviewer at *The Guardian*, Wood had become a senior editor at *The New Republic*. When he visited Boston, Martin Peretz, the owner of *The New Republic*, held a dinner for him. Peretz invited Janis and Bellow, who was just out of the hospital after the poisoned-fish disaster. Wood was struck by how much older and weaker Bellow looked, how "his hand trembled as he passed the salad bowl. But we talked happily. We talked about Dreiser and how much he liked Dreiser." By 2001, Wood was living in Northampton, within driving distance of Boston, and he and Messud were frequent visitors to the Bellows. Sometime that autumn, Janis asked Wood if he'd help out with Bellow's spring-semester course. A meeting was arranged with the dean at BU, who eagerly approved the arrangement, and almost immediately Wood and Bellow devised a syllabus: "Just a few things Saul liked and a few things I liked. It was a fairly light course in terms of reading. . . . " 'The Dead,' *The Secret Agent*, *The Death of Ivan Ilyich*, some Chekhov stories, *Notes from Underground*, *Hunger* [Knut Hamsun], *Sea and Sardinia* [Lawrence]."

By the spring of 2001, Bellow's memory problems had been drawn to the attention of his doctor, Thomas Barber, an internist who had been the family physician since Bellow's release from the ICU in January 1995. In mid-April, Bellow contracted pneumonia and was admitted to hospital for four or five days. After his release, "something was acutely worse," according to Barber. Tests were conducted, and on May 9, 2001, Barber recorded a "probable diagnosis of dementia," a scan having shown a "suggestion of early Alzheimer's." Martin Amis was visiting Boston at this date, and, over a meal at a restaurant near the Crowninshield Road house, was told of the diagnosis the day it was delivered. "He was very resilient about it," Amis remembers, "more so than Janis, refusing to be daunted."[16] Bellow's physical health was pretty much normal for an eighty-five-year-old middle-class male: "moderately high cholesterol, moderately high blood pressure, slightly overweight, living a North American lifestyle." His pacemaker, installed in August 1998, had kept atrial fibrillation in check; he could again drink coffee and wine. As for the memory loss, among patients in their eighties, "it's the minority who have all their mental faculties." According to Janis, even as Bellow suffered increased confusion, "anecdotes, limericks, songs [were] bubbling up all the time, a huge poetic energy." Barber, too, remarked on Bellow's energy: the moments of not being himself, of slowed mental capacities, were moments, at least up until a year or so before his death. "He never had full-blown Alzheimer's." At times, especially when physically unwell or under stress, "he'd be distant and an old man and sometimes he'd be on the phone and wholly there." "Even on bad days," Will Lautzenheiser recalls, "he could seem well. . . . His sense of humor, his wit, never diminished."

That August, a distressing incident highlighted Bellow's increasing confusions. Janis had been invited to attend a conference in Toronto on Conrad's *Under Western Eyes*. Toronto was where her family lived, and help would be available, so Rosie and Bellow accompanied her. Will drove the family to the airport the day before the conference, and "everything was going to go wonderfully." The next night, Will went to the movies, a six-hour showing of the whole of Lars von Trier's *The Kingdom*. When he returned to his apartment at 1:00 a.m., there was a message on his answering machine, recorded a half-hour earlier. It was from Bellow: "I am coming in from the airport and should be home in forty minutes." Will immediately called Crowninshield Road and got no answer. When he finally made contact (he can't remember if he called again or received a call), Bellow "seemed anxious and exhausted": "He was home and said I'm just in. I said I'd be right over. It's a mile away and I ran. I'd never run so fast in my life, through the dark [the streetlights weren't working; there'd been a power outage in Brookline]."[17] Will asked Bellow why he'd come home alone, and Bellow answered that "he felt like Janis was leaving him." "No, no, Janis loves you," Will told him. "Well, that's what I've always thought. But I'm not sure. I'm not sure today." Will told him it would "all be sorted out," and Bellow "seemed skeptical but hopeful, too." How had Bellow got to Boston? "I bought a plane ticket." When Will called Toronto, "everyone was terrified, there was a police search."

Will later learned that, when Janis went off to the conference in the afternoon, the plan was for Bellow to wait in the hotel room until he was picked up to be taken to dinner with friends, Clifford Orwin and his wife, Donna. He thinks Bellow "was in the hotel and he felt like he was being neglected." He may also have felt anxious when left alone. Harvey Freedman, Janis's father, thinks "he wasn't used to the fact that this was her thing." Janis thinks he acted on "a flash of pique [which] he apologized for and regretted."[18] There was also, according to Will, "some tension between the in-laws and Saul. . . . Maybe that's what he meant when he said I'm just not sure that Janis loves me." This tension or irritation he communicated to others—to Walter Pozen, Philip

Roth, Maggie Simmons. He was spending too much time with Janis's family, he complained; he was being treated "like a piece of excess baggage." It was the Orwins who discovered he'd gone. At the hotel, they were told that Bellow had checked out. How Bellow managed to get himself to Boston baffled everyone. As Will puts it, "We were all kind of laughing at it—because he had actually done it. We were all elated to some extent." At the airport, Bellow had bought a ticket not to Boston but to New York; he thought he was living in New York. "Then somehow he was redirected. Someone at the airport—some good Samaritan working for the airline—redirected it. . . . He had to swap tickets and they got him on the right plane." Will has no idea how Bellow found his phone number and was able to call from the airport; "he certainly hadn't memorized it." At Crowninshield Road, "he was totally calm. He was sad if anything, because he felt like the relationship was in trouble. He was defeated. We might as well have been talking at one in the afternoon instead of in the [morning]. Then I put Walter on the phone with him and Walter was very reassuring and then Saul calmed down. And I got him upstairs and into bed. And that was it, and I stayed there." Janis was "beside herself."

IN THE SPRING OF 2002, James Wood thought Bellow had "the ability to concentrate long enough to read a hundred pages or so. . . . But in class, he was quite capable of forgetting what had been said fifteen minutes before." Yet "you could still touch the brain for the deep meaning. That was part of my job. One part of my job was to do some formal close reading . . . take the students through passages; the other part was just to say to Saul: 'Tolstoy, Dostoevsky, there used to be an either/or battle when you were growing up, and you had to choose one or the other,' and he'd be off, telling what it was like being a young man reading Tolstoy in Chicago. . . . And there were wonderful formulations, too. He was sometimes absent or a bit supine or a little bit sleepy, and other times he proved that he was absolutely still there." Wood remembers Bellow's describing hate in Dostoevsky (a desire for revenge, rage, resentment) as "really a love." Another time, he spoke of "the secret resources of the weak."[19]

Wood was struck by the pleasure Bellow took in teasing the students. He also recalls his "losing a sense of chronology." In one class, he described Dostoevsky's antiheroes as wandering the streets of St.

Petersburg, fulminating with rage against its peaceable citizens. They reminded Bellow of a character in the funny papers in Chicago when he was growing up. The character's name was Desperate Ambrose. Then he looked around and asked, "Any of you remember Desperate Ambrose?" Since the faces of the students were blank, he described how "Desperate Ambrose would go sloping around the streets of Chicago muttering to himself—'Too tame! Too tame!'" The memory delighted Bellow, and he "put his head back and laughed, and if anyone joined in laughing it was only because they were enjoying his self-pleasure. They weren't getting it at all." On this occasion, Wood was not sure if Bellow was teasing when he asked his students whether they remembered Desperate Ambrose. There were other such moments in the course, but overall Wood thought it "wonderful." There were "a lot of mature students, quite a number of auditors, it was always full (easily over thirty), with people standing. Sometimes Keith Botsford would turn up, and Beena—let's say eight to nine auditors, grad students. There was just a good feeling. It was an exciting class." Before class, Wood and Bellow would have lunch together at Crowninshield Road and talk about the day's reading, then they'd drive or take the subway to campus. After class, "a group of us" would go back to Crowninshield Road. "We'd have tea or sometimes dinner, and then I'd drive back to Northampton late at night. I never wanted that to end. On the other hand, I felt that that should have been Saul's last year, and it wasn't."

MARTIN AMIS THINKS Bellow never took in September 11, 2001, but Beena Kamlani, who was in Boston at the time, is pretty sure that he understood, at least for a moment. At Crowninshield Road, "we were glued to the television," but "at that point he wasn't always separating reality [from delusion]." The next morning, scanning the newspapers, "he asked me what is all this excitement about, and I explained, and he shook his head with such horror that I think he did get it, but he was trying to connect the dots." Several weeks later, she recalls, "in one of those full-on moments, he understood exactly what had happened." (A year and a half later, on March 19, 2003, just before the invasion of Iraq, Eugene Goodheart told Bellow, "It looks like we're going to war." "With whom?" Bellow replied.) In a letter of condolence of April 16, 2002, to his Vermont friend Herb Hillman, after the death of

Herb's wife, Libby, Bellow's difficulty separating reality from delusion is explicitly acknowledged.

> Dear Herb,
>
> Just as I was sitting down to write this note I discovered that my elder brother, Sam, had died. He died not this year, or the year before, but in 1990 [in fact, he died in 1985]. Until half an hour ago I had assumed he was alive and well. Eighty years ago, I could have told you what sort of dinner he had eaten last night.
>
> This is what life prepares for us in our closing years. In his closing years, no man can assume that his mind is as it once was—intact.
>
> I should have written weeks ago to tell you how marvelous a woman your wife was.
>
> You could, if you were familiar with my handwriting see for yourself that I am, as the kids like to say, "all shook up" and not to be held strictly accountable.
>
> Janis and I—and Rosie as well—hope to see you in June.
>
> As you know well, we have no choice but to soldier on—Rosie, sporting a new barrette or pony-tail holder, has come to claim my attention. Janis is at the University today.
>
> Yours affectionately,
> Saul
>
> My original intention was to try to comfort you for your great loss but my mind is not following orders today. My heart appears to be in the right place but my mind is only lightly attached.

Around the time of this letter, Andrew Wylie traveled to Boston to spend a day with Bellow, "and when I came back I reported to Philip [Roth] that I thought Saul was depressed, and Philip's response was like a Zen master's. It was said with a hardness. 'You'd be depressed too if that universe was shutting down on you.' " Adam Bellow tells of the first time he began seriously to worry about his father. It was sometime in 2002. Janis had gone to Toronto to visit her parents, "and I was filling in." He and Bellow decided to go out to lunch at a local pizza place. Bellow was wearing the long down coat he liked, but on this occasion, it seemed to Adam, the coat made him look like a homeless person.

After they ordered a couple of slices of pizza, Adam watched as "the guy gives him some change. Saul doesn't say anything. He just stands there, looking kind of off, mouth slightly open, expression glazed, maybe he's having an episode." Finally, the pizza man gave Bellow another bill, and Bellow returned to Adam. "That guy was trying to cheat me. So I just stood there, and finally he gave me the ten." What struck Adam about the episode was that he couldn't be sure whether what Bellow said was true "or some sort of delusion." The look on Bellow's face was so odd and vacant that Adam seriously considered that the pizza man might have thought him a homeless person and given him the money "to get rid of him. And that's when I thought he wasn't going to get better."

ONE INCIDENT IN PARTICULAR in Bellow's last years was especially distressing to his family. On September 26, 2002, Greg Bellow's daughter, Juliet, married Charlie Schulman, a close friend of Daniel's. The wedding was to be held in Prospect Park in Brooklyn, and Juliet was keen for Bellow and Janis to attend. According to Janis, "We fully intended to go, we were longing to go. . . . He loved Juliet, and he would never have denied her in a million years. I had bought the tickets to go, and Saul got sick, and Dr. Barber advised against him going. And it's a hassle to cancel Amtrak tickets." "He could not go," Janis reiterates; "the doctor said he could not go." Juliet and her father do not believe this account. "I was very upset," Juliet remembers. "He kept saying he was going to come, and then he didn't. . . . I was so angry. We were willing to do anything to get him to come." She remembers Bellow telling her, " 'You'll have to forgive me' . . . It wasn't like 'please forgive me.' " "My father called [him] and said: 'This is it, if you do this to me.' " Juliet admits that "it is possible" that Bellow was, indeed, too sick or weak to come.[20] "But my ninety-year-old grandmother, who was deathly afraid of flying, got on a plane to come from Chicago. If you want to be somewhere, you'll do it. But it is possible. It's not my understanding that he was [bedridden], but I was not there." "I only saw him once after that."

Adam remembers attempting to intervene. "I took on a role that I don't usually take. I tried to persuade him." Bellow told him: "My doctor's advice is that I shouldn't go, and so I can't." Adam suspects that Bellow "didn't want to go," though "part of it is that he *was* elderly and unwell." "The wedding was held outdoors in Prospect Park. . . . There was no place he could have gone to rest and recuperate. . . . [though]

he didn't know that. But it was just as well he didn't come. He would have been miserable." Adam also suspects that Bellow's not coming "must have had something to do with Gregory, the unresolved conflict between them." Greg offers a detailed account of this episode in his memoir. When the wedding was announced, Bellow called promising to move "heaven and earth" to be there. But "a few weeks before the wedding," he called again. "Offering no explanation, he said, 'You must forgive me, but I cannot come to your wedding.'" There was then a "heart-wrenching" conversation between Greg and Juliet "about how Saul could inflict so much pain by making commitments and failing to fulfill them." Bellow's reversal, Greg believes, was the moment Juliet realized why "I had erected the self-protective barriers between my father and myself." At Adam's prompting, Bellow called Greg again, but "simply announced he would not be at the wedding, again offering no explanation." In a third call, "a few days later," Bellow at last offered an explanation. He "laid the responsibility on his doctor, who forbade travel. But in his belated medical excuse, I recognized a familiar pattern of hiding behind someone else when he had done something hurtful."[21]

It is hard to believe that Bellow would have lied about his doctor's advice, or that Janis would join him in doing so, though this is what Greg and Juliet believe. Easier to believe is that, out of pride or something in Greg's manner that irked him, Bellow replied defensively, stubbornly refusing to offer reasons for his decision. Dr. Barber could not remember the specifics of the episode, but among his records is a note about seeing Bellow on September 4, 2002.[22] Adam telephoned Will, asking, as Greg puts it, "if there was any constructive way for him to intervene. Will said no," an answer that Greg took as "confirming my impression that Saul had dug his heels in and would not budge."[23]

This is not how Will remembers Bellow's reasons for staying in Boston during the wedding. In an interview, he said nothing of Bellow's digging in his heels. "Saul was not able to go, physically not able [to go] from Boston to New York." Of Greg, he says: "I spoke with him. Janis might have tried to avoid speaking with him. I didn't have a break with them [the sons]. I would think that what I was saying would seem to be somewhat objective. I'm not lying to them." When he received the invitation, "Saul was beginning to be on a roller coaster of pneumonia and not pneumonia. . . . Now he's better, now he's worse. He had basically been in bed for two weeks, three weeks, and beginning to lose mobility and barely coming downstairs. He couldn't have made a trip. It would have been terrible. And Gregory wouldn't accept that. What couldn't you accept? He couldn't make the trip." When reminded that, three weeks after the wedding, Bellow was well enough to fly to Cincinnati to see Jane, again accompanied by Daniel, Will said simply, "His condition had improved." Asked about this recovery, Dr. Barber replied, "I can imagine easily . . . that he was in an unsteady state . . . and that it may have felt impossible to make the trip to Juliet's wedding, and then he was more stable a short time later."[24] Greg's conclusion, given the trip to Cincinnati and a later trip with Janis and Rosie to Toronto at Christmas, was that "clearly he was able to travel. . . . He did not attend because, surrounded by those who knew him well, he could not hide memory losses and did not want to be embarrassed in public."[25] This is Daniel's view as well:

> I knew how bad Greg wanted Pop to come, and I knew how bad it would be if he didn't. So, when Janis said he couldn't make it, I offered to come and get him in Boston and drive him to Brooklyn and take care of him the whole time. My offer was rebuffed, even though I accurately predicted to Janis how bad it would be if she didn't let me do it. My theory, developed through close observation of him the next month, was that he was just compos-mentis enough to know he was not capable of playing the role of Saul Bellow in public, where everyone wanted to meet him and say something clever and have him acknowledge it. He was very dependent on Janis and really didn't like to go anywhere without her. And she didn't want to go, because she hates Greg.

On the day of the wedding, Bellow wrote a letter to Juliet enclosing a check. The letter is typed and may have been dictated:

> Dear Juliet,
>
> Your grandfather sends you his best wishes for a long and lasting marriage together with the enclosed check to give the situation more reality than such wishes generally are joined to. If you should decide to spend it on a bash, you have my approval in advance. This, I realize, is an old-fashioned gesture, but I am bound to these fashions by my age and other limitations. My whole life testifies to my belief in the institution of marriage. I need only point out that I am, at my great age, still married. I would not

allow myself even to dream of dying single. While I have not had a history of durable unions, I do believe in them, and I hope yours will be—all kidding aside—endlessly durable. I wish you endless happiness.

With grandfatherly assurances,
Saul Bellow.

Three weeks later, on the trip to Cincinnati, there were times when Bellow didn't know where he was. Daniel also remembers that Bellow was stopped at airport security for carrying toenail clippers in a wash bag. He was threatened with a strip search. Jane Kauffman, Bellow's sister, was ninety-five in 2002, both her sons and her husband were dead, and she was living in what Bellow called a "luxury funny farm."[26] Lesha Greengus and her husband, Sam, lived in Cincinnati, and she was the relative responsible for Jane's care. Lesha had summoned Bellow to Cincinnati to get his opinion about whether Jane should be transferred to what Daniel calls "a really horrible part of the old folks' home." Jane was as feisty as ever. "Which one are you?" she asked Daniel. "Who was your mother?" "The pretty one," Daniel answered. "Oh, yes, the pretty one. She thought she was better than us, she went around with her nose in the air." Daniel replied: "That's what she said about you." "Pop laughed at that." When it came time to look at the wing of the old folks' home to which Jane might be transferred, Bellow refused to go. "Dan, you go look and bring me a full report" (Dan remembers often being asked to bring back full reports). "It's just awful," Dan said after seeing the wing. "It looked pretty depressing up there, and you wouldn't want to be there." Dan thinks that, at some point after this exchange, Bellow may have thought "we were going to ditch him there." He remembers telling Lesha: "Don't you see? We're the grown-ups now."

After his last telephone conversation with Bellow, Greg did not speak to him again until early spring of 2004, eighteen months later. "I did not wish to see him, talk to him, or hear about him." He did, however, write Bellow two letters, neither of which Bellow answered. The letters, quoted in full in Greg's memoir, are moving and characteristically conflicted. In January 2003 (no day of the month is given for the letters), Greg began by accusing Bellow of being incapable of putting anything "beyond your own needs" and as a consequence rending "the fragile fabric that holds this family together." He claimed no longer to be concerned about Bellow's welfare, having "no desire for contact—to visit, to speak to you, or to hear family reports." If Bellow wished to re-establish contact, "the initiative rests with you." If Greg didn't hear from Bellow (personally, not through surrogates), he would take it to mean "either you did not receive this letter, you are incapable of remedying the situation, or the absence of a relationship going into the future is your desire." How, exactly, Bellow was to be faulted if the first of these possibilities was the cause of his silence seems not to have been considered. Nor is anything said about the possibility that illness or debility, as opposed to pride or pique, might be the cause of Bellow's silence (perhaps because other family members had kept Greg apprised of Bellow's health). The letter ends, "In any case I remain your son—even in absentia."

Although this letter received no reply, Greg wrote again in May 2003 (he did not call, "as I did not want a repeat of our last phone conversation"). Nothing in the May letter is said about either Bellow's nonattendance at the wedding or the January letter's insistence that contact would only be re-established if Bellow took the initiative. The impediments to the relationship were now said to be disagreements "about politics, money, educational philosophy, or the nature of family obligations." Greg wishes these disagreements weren't so strong, but "as we both get older changes have occurred. You, on the one hand, have become less tolerant of differences between yourself and others. I have come to have faith in myself and the correctness of my own ideas." Although Greg sees little hope of improved relations, "as a child you are my pop and I love you. This will never change. As a man I will not abandon myself and you should not ask me to do so. I never mean to hurt you, but when it comes to a choice between my values and hurting someone—even you—my values will prevail. This is the man my parents brought me up to be and this is the man I am. G."[27]

Bellow was almost eighty-eight and suffering from dementia when he received this letter. If he took it in, it is unlikely to have pleased him, given his notions of the respect due to a father. What Greg wanted was for his father "to apologize to me or to his granddaughter." Some months after sending his May 2003 letter, Greg received an email from Monroe Engel, "gently trying to encourage me to visit my ailing father" (that Engel showed "no interest in my side of the story" leads Greg to describe him as "just another messenger on an errand from Saul"). Greg then called Will to discuss a possible visit. When Will "insisted on putting him [Bellow] on the phone"—something Greg hoped to avoid, given their last calls—Greg said he'd be coming to Boston soon and would like to see him. It was now the autumn of 2004, and Bellow "was bedridden, and was not expected to survive." When Greg arrived at Crowninshield Road, Janis and Rosie were out. He was led up to Bellow's room by Maria, the housekeeper. Bellow was in bed, drifting in and out of sleep. When awake, he "spoke coherently though softly." "I needed to clear the air as we always had," Greg writes, "particularly if this was to be our last conversation." So he told Bellow of the pain he felt at his not attending Juliet's wedding. Bellow answered, "I did not mean to hurt you, but the disease takes over." In his memoir, Greg describes what followed:

> "But you did hurt me and my child!" I exclaimed. Just then his attendant came in, ostensibly to check on him, though she immediately insisted that Saul was a very sick man who could not tolerate any emotional upset. Alone again, I asked if there was anything more he wanted to say. He said no. I ended with "We always had an honest relationship and I don't see any reason to change it now." He nodded in agreement. As I left to have lunch, the attendant was giving Janis, who had returned, a report. I concluded that she had been instructed to listen at the door and interrupt if I brought up the problems between us.

In looking back on this moment, Greg begins by saying, "Saul's statement that he wished me no harm went a long way toward healing my wound." Although he was often angry about Bellow's behavior, Greg writes that he had mostly been spared "the kind of pain Saul could cause when he let people down." As a child, he was protected by fatherly love; as an adult, by his own efforts, principally "physical distance and layers of emotional insulation." In the case of Juliet's wedding, however, "I had let my guard down out of love for Juliet, and I had paid the price. . . . The disappointment I had experienced was just a full dose of the selfishness everyone else had been enduring for years."[28]

Will Lautzenheiser offers a different account of Greg's visit, which he describes as having ended with a "meltdown." "Greg threw a tantrum. Saul was in the hospital bed, and Greg screamed at him [presumably the moment in the memoir in which Greg says he "exclaimed," "But you did hurt me and my child!"]. He was upstairs talking, and he started accusing his father of indifference and not going to the wedding and all this kind of thing. Saul was helpless. He was physically frail, he was mentally frail at that time. It was horrible, and Greg had no excuse [what he told Sasha, Adam's mother, was "I felt I had to tell him off"]. He left: 'I'm going to get a pizza.' Janis wasn't there. She'd make sure she was away. She'd orchestrate being away." Will himself was in the house but in another room. "The person who was actually there, who said, basically, You have to go, was Maria, the housekeeper; Maria was bringing something up or whatever. . . . It was supposed to be a reconciliation or something. I do know that, but it's not the way it went." As Will saw it, "Saul was very impaired and Greg let his anger run away. . . . Saul didn't know what was happening, didn't understand Greg's anger, had no way of responding." Maria told Janis that she was so alarmed by Greg's behavior that she considered calling the police.

According to Greg, an hour after leaving the house he returned, fearing that this would be the last time he'd see his father alive. "I tried to find a way to say goodbye without using the word *death*. I was standing by his bedside and Saul put his hand on my heart. I told him that I loved him as I always had. I kissed him and walked out of his room. Saying 'Goodbye, Pop' under my breath, I wished him a peaceful end." As so often in his final years, Bellow rallied from what seemed like the end. There were other visits and phone calls from Greg, calmer ones. On one visit, Greg reports, Maria, "the kind woman now charged with his physical care, reported that Saul called me his 'little boy' and spoke of me often."[29] At what turned out to be Greg's last visit, in the winter of 2004, Bellow called him "Sonny Boy," mimicking Al Jolson, as he'd done when Greg was a child ("Climb upon my knee, Sonny Boy"). In their last phone conversation, "I remember shouting into the phone, 'I love you sweetheart,' the last thing I ever said to my father."[30]

IN THE SPRING OF 2003, Bellow taught his last course. He had been teaching literature in universities for over sixty years. His original plan was for James Wood to co-teach with him again. But Wood procrastinated, couldn't bring himself to say yes or no (or to explain that he thought 2002 should have been Bellow's last year of teaching). Then Claire Messud got a position teaching creative writing at Kenyon College, in Gambier, Ohio, which made commuting weekly out of the question. On October 2, 2002, Bellow wrote to John Silber with a plan for having weekly visiting lecturers teach with him. The names he gave

Silber were Martin Amis, the only lecturer to come from outside the United States; Jonathan Wilson, who taught at Tufts; and Ruth Wisse, Keith Botsford, Stanley Crouch, Roger Kaplan, Cynthia Ozick, and Philip Roth. In a follow-up letter of October 21, Bellow estimated that the travel and accommodation costs for these lecturers would be nine thousand dollars. Silber agreed, and in the end all but Roth taught on the course. In addition, Keith Botsford volunteered to lead the seminars each week, an arrangement with which, as Will puts it, "Saul more or less agreed." Will himself attended all the seminars, and helped with course administration. According to several attendees and lecturers, Botsford not only led the seminars but took them over, intruding not only on Bellow but on the visiting lecturers, some of whom complained of condescension and impertinence in his attitude to Bellow. "He would call Saul 'Ducky,'" Will remembers. "Saul would turn to a page and he'd say, 'No, Ducky, the other page.' It was very belittling. . . . I thought he was cruel, maybe unintentionally." Bellow was "not particularly aware of it. . . . He had a serenity. I think he did notice but he couldn't do anything about it. . . . He was tired. It was bad."[31] Like Bellow, Botsford was touchy and had a high opinion of himself. He must often have suffered as well as benefited from being in Bellow's shadow.

What Ruth Wisse and others noticed about Bellow in the last two years of his life was that "he began to tune out. He couldn't hear very well and didn't want to, I felt. . . . I realized one day that he didn't need to hear any more, preferred to sit at the table having things go on around him." Increasingly, "he wasn't interested anymore in making the effort, and he would smile."[32] Wisse describes Bellow's smiling silence as "noble. . . . He never complained, never, never alluded to anything that was missing." Maggie Simmons, whom Bellow often called, felt "he did mellow out and he did become humble. . . . He certainly did become gentler." She was also impressed that as he approached death he was "not at all afraid." Martin Amis remembers that in the last year or so, he saw Maria, the housekeeper, carry Bellow up the stairs. "She'd put her arms around his chest, lean backwards, and carry him." Bellow's expression was "resigned." "It was very sweetly done, cheerfully done." Was there a mellowing? Had he become nicer? "Nicer!" said Daniel. "He was never 'nice.' It's too weak a term in relation to him." Yet, at the end, Daniel remembers, "he just loved me. . . . It was just sweet at the end." Adam has similar memories. "He became sweet and childlike. He calmed down. . . . I like to think he became more plantlike, more like a flower, which he was always fascinated by, the life of plants and trees." Some thought Bellow had softened because he had no choice, being so reduced and dependent upon others, but not all elderly people soften when reduced. James Wood emphasizes that "he was surrounded by people who were acolytes and vastly his junior, people like Martin and me and Will; it wasn't the old tussling thing like with Kazin. The most Kazin-like relationship was with Botsford—and it was quite fraught. . . . If you played along he was serene." In Wood's case, the playing along was sometimes literal, as when Bellow played the recorder and Wood the piano, or when Wood accompanied him on the piano when he sang from a book of French folksongs, the words of which he knew by heart. A number of friends said how much he liked to sing in his last years.

Bellow's silences provoked questions. Many times a day, people would ask him what he was thinking or how he was feeling, which he found tiring. "I'm making a list," he once told Will, "of the things I've done and the things I haven't done." On another occasion, he said, "I feel that I lost my way some days ago and I'm not sure that I can find my way back." Will reassured him: "There's still time. Don't worry." To which Bellow answered, "Yes, but I have to devote all my energy to the project." "There's a person inside of these symptoms," Oliver Sacks told Will, during a visit to the Bellows in Vermont. Wood recalls telling Bellow about Henry Green's novel *Loving*. At one point, the serving maid goes into her mistress's room and finds her in bed with a man. In her shock, the mistress sits up and her breasts are exposed. Later, the servant tells the butler of this incident, describing how the mistress sat up "with her fronts bobbin' at him like a pair of geese." "Bellow stopped and said to me: 'Fronts?' 'Yes, fronts,' and then he sat back with his slow quiet laugh: 'Ah, ah, ah, ah.' " Later, "quite near the end," Wood remembers, at dinner, "we were talking about George Herbert, and Janis said Saul loves that poem 'The Flower,' and she said, 'Saul, why don't you read it?' Saul said, 'I don't want to,' and Janis said, 'Well, I'll read it.' And Janis started reading it, and there's a moment about having been in a long winter and then the artist, like the spring, awakening ('once more . . . I relish versing') and clearly it had been a great text for Janis and Saul about recovering after the fish incident. And Janis got to that bit, and there was a catch in her voice, and she was clearly overcome, and Saul said, '*I'll* read it,' and then Saul read the whole poem out. That was an extraordinary moment. He read it to the table." Here, as at other moments, as Will puts it, "Saul was still Saul." In June 2004, he received an honorary degree from BU and climbed up to the stage unassisted. The last time Martin Amis saw Bellow, "he could still give you a very good idea of that Norwegian fascist, Knut Hamsun." Amis remembers reading him a passage from an article in the *Atlantic* in which Bellow was called the greatest American novelist. "I said the only American novelist who gives you any trouble was Henry James, and there was a cry from the bed: 'Jesus Christ!' It was very funny." Amis then amused Bellow by "slagging off Henry James a little bit. James has a terrible stylistic flaw, which is elegant variation. 'He crossed the Ponte Vecchio and looked back at that noble structure.' Instead of 'it.' Pretending you give a bit of extra information. I think Saul *is* a greater writer than Henry James."

The most painful consequences of memory loss for Bellow involved deceased friends and relations. Greg Bellow remembers him trying to call Sam Freifeld and breaking into tears when told he was dead. Janis remembers the same reaction when she had to tell him, in the spring of 2004, that David Grene had died two years earlier. Several times, Bellow asked about his sister, Jane, who died in 2003, and each time he was devastated to learn she had died. Wood remembers "a time (and I think Martin had this, too) when each time I met him he would say 'Hello, James.' So he got the name right, but then there was an abyss. You felt he didn't have any available data except you were a face and a name." One way to get Bellow to talk, Wood remembers, was to prod him with a name. "You'd say, 'Like John Berryman, Saul,' except that would backfire when he would say, 'Is he still alive?' and Janis would say, 'No, he's dead, Saul,' and that was awful." In addition to memory loss, there were terrible delusions and anxieties, often about travel: He thought he'd lost his wallet. He didn't have a passport. Will would say, "You have it here, you're all set." He thought he was in a hotel when he was at home. "I want to check out," he told Will. "Give me ten dollars, get me out of here." When put right, Bellow would say, "I'm all mixed up today." "During the day you didn't see the dementia as much," Janis recalls, but "during the night he would put his fists up and think there was someone in the room. And I would have to get out of bed." He also had terrible delusions about Janis's betraying or leaving him. Nathalie Botsford used to visit on Sunday afternoons, when Maria was off, so that Janis and Rosie "could go off and do things." Before the very end, she and Bellow would do the *New York Times* crossword together, but later she'd just sit by his bedside. "One day I was sitting next to the bed, and he knew I was there, but when he said what he said I realized he didn't know who I was. I thought he was sound asleep, and all of a sudden, in a very loud clear voice, he said, 'Did you sleep with that guy last night?' And I thought, he's talking in his sleep, and I didn't say anything. I'm not going to answer. And thirty seconds later he said, 'I'm still waiting for an answer.'"

ROSIE WAS A GREAT SOLACE to Bellow. She was a beautiful child; she didn't ask him what he was thinking; there was no question of forgetting who she was; she was a daughter, not a son (to Harvey Freedman, "The blessing of a granddaughter far surpasses that of a grandson . . . being cherished by a granddaughter"). She also reminded him of his own childhood memories, which never left him. Will once said of Rosie, "Looking at her just exhausts me," and Bellow said, "No, she enacts my feelings." Will has film of Bellow patiently dandling Rosie on his knees in the summer of 2001, on the porch in Vermont. At two and a half, Rosie's behavior became worrying, to Janis and others if not to Bellow. She was willful, wouldn't follow, wouldn't be led or listen to instructions, wouldn't eat with a spoon. She was prone to tantrums, in Will's words, "beyond what you'd think as normal." As Nathalie Botsford recalled, it became more and more difficult to have a conversation at dinner if Rosie was present. "Why are you always holding her wrists?" Janis remembers being asked. "To prevent her from suddenly running out into the street." At this time, Rosie was diagnosed with ASD (autism spectrum disorder), a term encompassing a range of symptoms and conditions that impede social interaction and communication. The symptoms were acute for Rosie in her early years but have, now that she's in high school, tapered off. She is a gifted musician, a violinist (her father's first instrument was the violin), and is now a member of the New England Conservatory Youth Symphony.

For the most part, Rosie's condition passed Bellow by, as his problems were unrecognized by her. For Janis, in the last two years of Bellow's life, caring for them both was exhausting, mentally as well as physically. Neither could be left alone. Maria helped out, and Will, and Rosie's therapists. "We had a little family: it was all the caregivers . . . and the occasional visitor" (Stephanie Nelson, who was a young Classics professor at BU, previously a student and then companion of David

Grene's at the University of Chicago, Nathalie Botsford, Ruth and Len Wisse, Brenda and Monroe Engel, Chris Walsh, Gene Goodheart, and from farther afield, Walter Pozen, Joan and Jonathan Kleinbard, Martin Amis, Philip Roth, Janis's family). Nathalie Botsford jokingly took to calling herself "Janis's catastrophe friend," because "if she ever called me it was often when Saul was in the hospital—which was University Hospital, nearby to where I lived—so I could help Janis by going over there when she really did need to be at home with Rosie, or I could bring him some hot food, which was better than hospital food. What was amazing about Janis was that she was doing all this and trying to preserve the air of some sort of normalcy. . . . It was almost as though she could will it to be something that was okay and manageable, even though that wasn't necessarily the case"—"I don't know how she did it." One of the worst memories for Janis was of the time Bellow fell and she had to call 911 because she couldn't get him up. Another was Christmas Eve, 2004, when all the caregivers were away and she was alone in the house with Bellow and Rosie. "What am I supposed to do? I've got Saul in the hospital bed, and Rosie, and I could *not* take care of the both of them at the same time, because if I got up to take care of her he's going to get up out of bed and fall. . . . I could hear him when he tried to get out of bed." On Christmas Day, "he thought I was on a train somewhere and there was all this jealous stuff." Rosie's teacher came over that morning and took her out for the day.

Rosie has memories of her father. Of going to the zoo, being pushed by him in a stroller, seeing the lions ("He was crazy about the lions"), being waved to as she rode the carousel. She has no memory of Bellow's ever being angry with her. She remembers sitting by his bed and watching him sleep. He sang songs to her in French, picked blueberries in Vermont and fed them to her. And they would read together.[33] In March 2002, Bellow wrote a fan letter to the children's author Arnold Lobel (who had been dead for about a decade and a half). "As an octogenarian who continues to father children," it begins, "I think it only right that I should tell you how grateful I am to you for your delightful children's stories. Every time I read *Uncle Elephant* to my two-year-old daughter Naomi Rose, I think how I used to labor through Dr. Seuss and other boring texts. . . . Any line that I miss my little daughter knows by heart, so I can admire both her powers of memory and your gift for writing kid's books. Respectfully yours, Saul Bellow."

A letter of February 19, 2004, to Eugene Kennedy, perhaps the last he wrote, gives a sense of how stimulating Rosie was for Bellow, for his memory as well as his spirits. He was eighty-eight at the time.

> I don't do much of anything these days and I spend much of my time indoors. By far my pleasantest diversion is to play with Rosie, now four years old. It now seems to me that my parents wanted me to grow up in a hurry and that I resisted, dragging my feet. They (my parents, not my feet) needed all the help they could get. They were forever asking. "What does the man say?" and I would translate for them into heavy-footed English. That didn't help much either. The old people were as ignorant of English as they were of Canadian French. We often stopped before a display of children's shoes. My mother coveted for me a pair of patent-leather sandals with an elegantissimo strap. I finally got them—I rubbed them with butter to preserve the leather. That is when I was six or seven years old, a little older than Rosie is now. It is amazing how it all boils down to a pair of patent-leather shoes.

DR. BARBER BELIEVES THAT in his last days Bellow had a series of minor strokes and that that's how he died, of slow vascular insufficiency. There was no evidence of a main-vessel stroke. The idea of putting him in the hospital at the very end was considered but rejected; the prognosis was not good, but he didn't need to be in the hospital. Bellow died on April 5, 2005, at 5:15 p.m. In the last months before his death, according to Will, there were repeated ups and downs: "He would be terrible, and then he'd be okay, and we were thinking he'd be able to get out somewhere." Adam saw him for the last time three months before he died. "I went to the house, and Janis had got him up and dressed him, and he was waiting for me at the entry hall. He looked puffed up, like the Michelin Man, wrapped up in layers. . . . He knew me, but when he sat down with me on the sofa in the living room, he asked me a couple of questions; I asked him a couple of questions. He tired very quickly, but I still felt a spiritual connection, a deep connection." Later, over the telephone, Bellow told Adam: "'I want you to know you've been a good son and I'm proud of you.' And I felt he was telling me something he wanted me to know. So I took that and put it in the bank." Daniel remembers a lunch in the winter of 2004–5 at a Thai restaurant on

Commonwealth Avenue, a short walk from Crowninshield Road. He and Heather and their two children, Stella and Ben, were visiting, and Bellow was well enough to leave the house and join them, along with Rosie and Janis. "All the kids were a handful, especially Rosie, and so all the adults were in a man-to-man defense and Pop was kind of dreaming away with nobody paying him much attention. After we had eaten all the yummy ducks and squids and other Thai delights, they brought in the dessert tray and Pop looked at me clear as day and he said 'Daniel, you'd better not eat any of that, it's full of nuts' " (Daniel has been allergic to nuts since infancy). "I said, 'Pop, I'm forty years old, I'm a big boy, I can take care of myself.' He drew himself up proudly and said 'I'm your father!' "[34]

In his last months, Bellow's nature, according to Will, "was usually very gentle and thankful, grateful and sweet. . . . 'Thanks, Will, I don't know what I'd do without you.' " In his last weeks, he was having trouble breathing and swallowing. And he mostly slept. It was at this time, slipping in and out of consciousness, that he asked Eugene Goodheart the question quoted on the opening page of *To Fame and Fortune*: "Was I a man or was I a jerk?" Will thought the end was very close, but "people were saying, 'Oh no, no, no, he'll pull through it,' and other people said 'No, he won't pull through.' So I called around the family, saying, 'Look, this is not good.' I called all the sons, and the friends, Walter or Philip, saying, 'Look, I'm really not sure.' " The day before he died, Greg asked, "Should I come out?" Adam: "Should I come out?" "They were asking *me*, and I'm like, 'I can't make this decision. . . . You're a mature adult; if you want to come out, come out.' And Greg was saying, 'Well, I don't want to get there and he's unconscious,' or 'I don't want to get there and he's dead already.' " Will said: " 'This is pretty dire. We're not sure'—and we weren't sure." In the end, given the uncertainty, none of the boys came.

On the morning of the day Bellow died, both Chris Walsh and Will were in the house, Will in Bellow's room. As Will recalls, "Saul was very confused about where we were, thought we were on a boat, a transatlantic boat, didn't really know who I was. That was the worst time for me." Then Bellow lapsed into sleep. By that time, his food was almost all liquid, with a thickener, but he wasn't eating or drinking. "Basically, we sat with him all day, and it was pretty clear that he wasn't going to pull through, so I left the room and Maria left the room." Over these months, Janis had been getting no sleep. While looking after Rosie and Bellow, she was also keeping up with her teaching job.[35] "She was always on call," Will remembers. "It was just incredible that she kept it all together." Rosie's teachers knew Bellow was dying and came and took her out for the day, and Janis "spent an hour or two with Saul." Then Will and Maria came back into his room. "Maria sat on one side of the bed and I sat on another, and Janis was at the head of the bed, leaning over Saul and stroking his head, and his breathing was very labored and sounded awful. So you knew he was dying, and it was very hard to be there. His breathing was slowing . . . and so Janis kind of started talking to him. 'It's okay, my baby, it's okay,' and she said something his mother would say to him, a Russian phrase . . . and he kept on breathing, and he opened his eyes and he looked at her, and she looked at him, and he was in awe, he was, like, okay. It was really beautiful, a transcendent moment. He looked at her with such love, and she at him, and then he died. It was incredible. He had been going in and out of a coma for weeks. He was totally unconscious for a day or two. That he gave that look was like a gift, and it was right at Janis, a focused, direct look, and then he died. It was beautiful. We were all weeping and sat there for a long time."[36]

WHEN THEY GOT UP, the world flooded in, with its animosities, anxieties, importunities. Will called the sons, then called Walter Pozen and Stephanie Nelson, "and pretty soon there were phone calls all night."[37] Within an hour and a half, two hours at most, news of the death was on television and radio. Greg maintains he was not called. Will says, "I certainly tried, but obviously didn't reach Gregory. . . . I certainly wasn't going to leave a message like 'Saul died' on an answering machine. . . . I was floored/shocked/appalled when the phone rang—maybe Mark Rotblatt [Bellow's great-nephew]?—and we learned that Saul's death was on the news—because I knew we hadn't gotten through to all the sons. The timing was very, very fast—I'm talking fifteen or twenty minutes after I tried making calls. . . . The fact that the story got out to the press so quickly was a distressing element in a very distressing day. I did my best to inform people, but it got away from me." Greg had "spent the day on tenterhooks, anticipating the call from Boston that never came";[38] he learned of Bellow's death on his car radio. His daughter, Juliet, also heard of the death through the media.[39] Both blamed Walter Pozen. "I will never forgive him for that," Juliet said in an interview.

"It's the most degrading, humiliating thing to have happened to a person, and I'll never forgive him for that." Juliet doesn't blame Janis but is convinced that "somebody called *The New York Times* and told them before they told the family members." "My dad wouldn't deal with any of these people," Juliet says, referring to what Greg calls the surrogates. "His line was 'I'll only deal with Saul.' He didn't pay fealty to any of them. . . . That didn't win him any friends with those guys.' "

As Walter Pozen remembered it, "Will called me to say that Saul had died, minutes before. And I said, 'How's Janis?,' and he said, 'Well, Walter, as you can imagine.' And I said, 'You better call Andrew [Wylie].' He called Andrew, and Andrew called me right back. This all happened within minutes." Wylie then called the Associated Press and told them what had happened and gave out Pozen's number, as Pozen was Bellow's lawyer and the executor of the Bellow estate. "And before I could even collect my thoughts, the phone rang. It was *The New York Times*." The calls never stopped; he was on the phone for two hours straight. "I was just wiped out." When told that Greg never received a call and learned of his father's death on the car radio, his reply was "I don't know who should have done what. . . . I didn't even think of that." Pozen, it is true, was no admirer of Greg, but he seems to have assumed that someone at Crowninshield Road would have informed family members. The next day, he traveled to Boston with Philip Roth. Martin Amis was already there.

The funeral, attended by a hundred or so family and friends, was held in the Jewish section of the Morningside Cemetery in Brattleboro, Vermont. The Jewish section of the cemetery is green and peaceful, but it is reached through a litter-strewn gully, or at least it was in 2005.[40] Not all the family, certainly not Greg or Lesha, approved. Lesha had found a gravesite in Chicago, adjacent to that of Bellow's parents and of his sister, Jane, and her family. It was for sale and, as Greg puts it in his memoir, "sufficient to hold Saul, Lesha, and her husband." He says nothing in the memoir about whether it would have held Janis. As Greg saw it, "Burial next to his parents would confirm the sentimental connection between Saul and his family of origin in perpetuity. But when Lesha pressed Saul for a decision, she was met with obfuscation and delay. Finally, with my father present but silent, it was Janis who told Lesha that the two of them would be buried together in Vermont."[41]

There was crying at the funeral, but also much worldly agitation. What Nathalie Botsford dreaded about the ceremony was the possibility that Keith might not be included among the pallbearers. Keith thought Martin Amis and Andrew Wylie were talking business at the gravesite. Adam's wife, Rachel, wore fishnet stockings and a short skirt, which Nathalie Botsford saw somehow as aimed at Janis. Rachel asked Will what he was planning to do now that Bellow had died, describing the funeral as a good place to network. Adam could not stop crying. When he saw his father's coffin, it made him think of the loss not only of his father but of his writing self. When Adam gave up writing in order to become an editor and to support his family, "I think it disappointed him and may have made it harder to see himself in me. . . . From that point on he began to feel ambivalence toward me, which he would express to others (Roth, my brothers, everyone)." Sasha, Adam's mother, came to the funeral, which raised eyebrows ("I was certainly invited, personally invited by Saul's family"). She was affected not only by Adam's sobbing and Greg's "stony" expression, but by how "decrepit" Monroe and Brenda Engel looked (the Engels had not been nice to her many decades ago, in Princeton). Sasha spoke at the little gathering after the burial and then returned to New York. Greg presided over the speeches and spoke in praise of Janis. Ruth Wisse spoke of Bellow's Jewishness, Martin Amis of his achievements as a writer.[42] Rabbi William Hamilton, of Congregation Kehillath Israel in Brookline, closed the gathering with a speech about the love between Janis and Saul, which for Greg "solidified my view of how she romanticized their relationship."[43]

Bellow wanted a plain, traditional Jewish burial. The rabbi explained the parts of the funeral and how, in Jewish tradition, as Ruth Wisse puts it, "friends have to bury the deceased themselves without leaving it to strangers."[44] In his memoir, Greg describes the scene at the gravesite:

> Pins with black ribbon were affixed to the mourners and were roughly torn to represent our loss and grief. Saul's thin wooden casket was so light that I had to remind myself that I was carrying my father, who had often seemed larger-than-life. At the gravesite, the black cloth with a white Star of David was removed from the casket, and Saul was lowered into the ground. Next to the rectangular hole stood a pile of sand with a shovel placed back side up to represent the unusual task to which it was about to be put. Janis carefully balanced a bit of sand on the shovel's back and threw it into the casket, where it landed with a hollow sound. Next came my turn. I picked up a handful of sand, kissed it, said "Rest easy, Pop," and threw it

into the hole. Adam and Dan followed with their shovels of sand before the other mourners took their turns at the required task of filling the grave level to the earth.[45]

It was a warm April day, overcast, and Nathalie Botsford was worried when she saw some of the old men among the mourners shoveling dirt on the coffin: "I thought we might be burying more than one man here." James Wood remembers the three middle-aged Bellow boys "hugging each other by the side of the grave." During the burial, Philip Roth told Wylie, "I wonder if the earth knows what it has just received." Frank Maltese, who had built Bellow's house, took on the lion's share of burying, along with younger mourners such as Chris Walsh. When Leon Wieseltier stepped forward to do his bit, he staggered and was steadied from behind by Roth. In an interview, he urged me to include this detail as "the only known act of kindness in Roth's life" (a crack easily countered, not least by Roth's kindness to Bellow). When Lesha's brother, Shael, took his turn, Greg shouted for him to "put one in for Grandpa." Then Shael also put one in for his father, Sam, for Jane, and two for Maury, "whom we all agreed required an extra because he took a double share of everything." Harvey Freedman, Janis's father, thought Greg's behavior "flippant," "disrespectful." After the funeral, Greg's family and Lesha's family gathered at Dan and Heather's house, "where we shared family stories over dinner."[46] Neither Lesha nor Bellow's three sons came to the shiva at Crowninshield Road, which was attended by Bellow's Boston friends and neighbors, Janis's family, and Martin Amis, who came every day for the whole week. "He was like a son," said Harvey Freedman of Amis, one of several spiritual sons at the funeral. At the shiva, Ruth Wisse was struck by how bereft Amis looked, "as though he were experiencing the death of his own father again." Roger Kaplan remembers being told by Dan's wife, Heather, "You're the fourth Bellow boy."[47] At the shiva, in addition to stories about Bellow, people sat in the kitchen and recited passages from his books—in Wood's and Amis's case, often from memory.

To Ruth Wisse, it was Philip Roth who seemed, among all the mourners at the funeral, "the most bereft." She was not the only mourner to remark on Roth's appearance. To Harvey Freedman he seemed "more in grief than anyone there." To James Wood and Claire Messud, he looked "old and hollowed out . . . dazed. He seemed to wander around all day with his mouth open, looking lost."[48] Roth's grief was obvious, but he was also, in the spirit of the man he mourned, at work. Within a year, he published a short and harrowing novel, *Everyman* (2006), which begins with the protagonist's funeral. Among the mourners at this funeral "were his two sons, Randy and Lonny, middle-aged men from his turbulent first marriage, very much their mother's children, who as a consequence knew little of him that was praiseworthy and much that was beastly and who were present out of duty and nothing more." The detailed description of the sons at the beginning of the novel was seen by a number of mourners, including Adam and Daniel, as taken from Bellow's funeral:

> Then came the sons, men in their late forties and looking, with their glossy black hair and their eloquent dark eyes and the sensual fullness of their wide, identical mouths, just like their father (and like their uncle) at their age. Handsome men beginning to grow beefy and seemingly as closely linked with each other as they'd been irreconcilably alienated from the dead father. The younger, Lonny, stepped up to the grave first. But once he'd taken a clod of dirt in his hand, his entire body began to tremble and quake, and it looked as though he were on the edge of violently regurgitating. He was overcome with a feeling for his father that wasn't antagonism but that his antagonism denied him the means to release. When he opened his mouth, nothing emerged except a series of grotesque gasps, making it appear likely that whatever had him in its grip would never be finished with him. He was in so desperate a state that Randy, the older, more decisive son, the scolding son, came instantly to his rescue. He took the clod of dirt from the hand of the younger one and tossed it onto the casket for both of them. And he readily met with success when he went to speak. "Sleep easy, Pop," Randy said, but any note of tenderness, grief, love, or loss was terrifyingly absent from his voice.[49]

The protagonist of *Everyman* is not Saul Bellow, and his sons are not Bellow's sons, but there are resemblances between the real-life people and the fictional characters. In a later passage, the sons are described by their father as "the source of his deepest guilt," but the impatience with which this admission is made is Bellow-like. The protagonist has given up trying to explain his behavior to his sons.

> He had tried often enough when they were young men—but then they were too young and angry to understand, now they were too old and angry to understand. And what was there to understand? It was inexplicable to him—the excitement they could seriously persist in deriving from his denunciation. He had done what he did the way that he did it as they did what they did the way they did it. Was their steadfast posture of unforgivingness any more forgivable? Or any less harmful in its effect? He was one of the millions of American men who were party to a divorce that broke up a family. . . . What could have been avoided? What could he have done differently that would have made him more acceptable to them other than what he could not do, which was to remain married and live with their mother? Either they understood that or they didn't—and sadly for him (and for them), they didn't.[50]

There are two burials in *Everyman*, one of the protagonist, the other of his father. The father, like Bellow, was buried according to Jewish tradition. The protagonist stands at the edge of his grave and watches as the dirt reaches the coffin lid with its carving of the Star of David: "His father was going to lie not only in the coffin but under the weight of that dirt, and all at once he saw his father's mouth as if there was no coffin, as if the dirt they were throwing into the grave was being deposited straight down on him, filling up his mouth, blinding his eyes, clogging his nostrils, and closing off his ears." "I've never seen anything so chilling in my life," the protagonist's daughter says. " 'Nor have I,' he told her."[51] Roth's stricken expression at the Bellow funeral might have owed something to his picturing just this "chilling" image. It might also have owed something to literature, to the moment when Woody Selbst climbs into his father's hospital bed in "A Silver Dish." Woody's dying father, referred to as "Pop," is writhing about in bed, "the dirt already cast into his face."[52]

THE DEATH OF SAUL BELLOW was front-page news around the world. The next day, April 6, *The New York Times* published a long obituary, written by Mel Gussow and Charles McGrath. On April 7, it published an "Appreciation" of Bellow on its editorial page. The author of this appreciation, entitled "Mr. Bellow's Planet," was Brent Staples, who recounted his first sighting of Bellow in Hyde Park and claimed to have learned from him "how books were put together." Nothing was said in the appreciation about Staples's subsequent stalking of Bellow, or about his objections to the racist attitudes of Bellow's characters. That same day, Staples's colleague James Atlas sent a fax to Janis. *The New York Times Book Review* had asked him to compose a page drawn from Bellow's earliest writings, including unpublished letters and pieces of college journalism. Atlas needed Janis's signed approval "by the end of today or tomorrow," which he would then forward to the Regenstein. He admitted that his biography of Bellow had not turned out as Janis, or he himself, would have liked, but "suffice it to say that I loved him very much. . . . I would like to do this for Mr. Bellow and his readers." He offered to have his name removed from the page. Across the top of the fax, now among Bellow's papers in the Regenstein, Janis has written: "*IGNORE*" and "Absolutely *NOT*."

THESE, THEN, WERE BELLOW'S WORLDS— a love world, or spiritual world, figured in the final intense look at Janis; and a world of strife and jostling, figured in the animosities and anxieties exhibited at the funeral and in the hours after his death. In this world, among other things, romantic love is doubted or mocked or cheapened. Both worlds live in Bellow's fiction. The possibility of love is rendered movingly, with delicacy and tact, as is the possibility of the soul or the existence of God. The world of flux and worldly ambition is rendered with comic gusto as well as fierce criticism; the energies, pleasures, and temptations of American materialism, seen from the inside, are crucial to Bellow's style and are as much the object of his intense noticing as any spiritual intimation. The fullness of the fiction mirrors the fullness of the life. In the end, as Bellow himself acknowledged, it is the fiction, not the life, that is most admirable, honorable, and truthful, for all his desire to love, to be worthy of love, to be a man, not a jerk; for all his feeling for family and for right conduct; for all his regret and remorse. The fiction is his great gift—the great gift of his life.

SB and Will Lautzenheiser, Vermont, August 12, 2003
(courtesy of the Avedon Foundation)

Acknowledgments

My first debt is to Andrew Wylie, whose idea it was for me to write Bellow's biography. I am indebted also to the executors of the Saul Bellow Literary Estate, the late Walter Pozen and Janis Freedman Bellow. Bellow's sons, Greg, Adam, and Daniel, have been generous with their knowledge and time, granting lengthy interviews and enduring numerous queries. Bellow had five wives. His first and third wives, Anita Goshkin Bellow and Susan Glassman Bellow, died before I began work on the biography. His second wife, Sasha Tschacbasov Bellow, his fourth wife, Alexandra Ionescu Tulcea Bellow, and his fifth wife, Janis Freedman Bellow, generously granted me interviews, as well as helping in innumerable small ways, with queries and introductions. Bellow took a keen and loving interest in his larger family and I have been much helped by a number of his relatives, in particular by his nephew, Joel Bellows, and his niece, Lesha Bellows Greengus, together with her husband, Sam Greengus, who was especially generous in helping me to find family photographs. The children of Bellow's nephews and nieces also granted interviews and answered queries. Other Bellow relatives were generous with their time as well. Soon after I began work on the biography I was put in touch with Benjamin Taylor, editor of *Saul Bellow: Letters* (2010) and *There Is Simply Too Much to Think About: Collected Nonfiction* (2016). Ben has been a friend since my biography's inception. A full list of those who agreed to formal interviews, subsequently helping with inquiries, is provided in the Note on Sources.

For advice and assistance I am grateful to the administration and staff of the Special Collections Research Center at the Joseph Regenstein Library at the University of Chicago, in particular to Dan Meyer, Alice Schreyer, Eileen Eilmini, Ashley Locke Gosselar, David Pavlich, Barbara Gilbert, and Julia Gardner. I also owe thanks to Raymond Gadtke of the Regenstein. In Winter Quarter 2008 I was a Visiting Professor at the Committee on Social Thought at the University of Chicago, where Bellow taught for more than thirty years. There I conducted a seminar on his novels and stories and learned a great deal from the responses of my students, both those from the Committee and those from other departments. I am especially grateful to Robert Pippin, Chair of the Committee, for arranging my visit; to Anne M. Gamboa, the Committee's Administrative Assistant, for smoothing my way once I'd arrived; and to those Committee members who knew and worked with Bellow, offering me interviews, advice, and assistance, among them Nathan Tarcov, Paul Friedrich, Wendy Doniger, Ralph Lerner, James Redfield, and Leon Kass. David Nirenberg arrived at the Committee after Bellow but was a friendly and informative colleague throughout my stay. The late Richard Stern, Bellow's great friend from the English Department, also welcomed me, as did W. J. T. Mitchell, another English Department member. Finally, I am grateful to Donna Sinopoli of the University of Chicago's Housing Services, who found my wife and me an apartment on the twelfth floor of the Cloisters, the splendid 1920s apartment building where Saul Bellow lived for over a dozen years. Although I have doubts about a "footsteps" approach to biography, it was good to live in a building Bellow lived in, to share much the same view he had, and to walk each morning to an office at the Committee on Social Thought along the routes he would have taken.

I am grateful to the Guggenheim Foundation for a fellowship in 2009 to free me from teaching. I am also grateful to the Department of English and Creative Writing at the University of Roehampton for Research Leave in 2014. The first chapter of *To Fame and Fortune* was written outside Genoa at the Liguria Study Center for the Arts and Humanities, on a monthlong fellowship from the Bogliasco Foundation. A similar monthlong fellowship in the summer of 2015 from the Civitella Ranieri Foundation in Umbria, as the Kirby Family Foundation Fellow in Writing, enabled me to write chapter 6 of this second volume. In 2018 I was awarded an Author's Foundation grant from the Society of Authors. At the University of Roehampton I am grateful for the support of my colleagues, in particular Laura Peters, Jenny Watt, Patricia

Tomlinson, and Sara Wake of the Department of English and Creative Writing. I also want to thank Lynn Dobbs, Deputy Vice-Chancellor, for her support. At the Wylie Agency I owe thanks to Jeffrey Posternak in New York and James Pullen in London. At Jonathan Cape I am indebted to the continued support of Dan Franklin and at Knopf to the continued support of Erroll McDonald, both of whom published my biography of Kingsley Amis. Nicholas Thomson of Knopf was especially helpful and efficient in the preparation of the manuscript and in helping with illustrations and permissions. At Jonathan Cape, I am grateful to Michal Shavit and Clare Bullock for help with permissions fees. For advice about permissions I owe special thanks to Karen Mayer, also to Michele Park, both of Knopf. Douglas Matthews prepared the index for this volume as he did for volume 1.

For careful reading of the entire manuscript I am again grateful to Lindsay Duguid, who improved the book at every stage of its composition. Andrew Gordon, Chris Walsh, and David Mikics also read and improved the whole manuscript. For comments on portions of the manuscript I am grateful to Nathan Tarcov, Miriam Tarcov, and Janis Freedman Bellow. Jonathan Roy Turner, a resourceful and efficient research student at Roehampton, helped in checking quotations.

For help in archives, libraries, foundations, and institutions I am grateful to the following: Cheryl Schnirring, Abraham Lincoln Presidential Library, Springfield, Illinois; Helene Tieger, Bard College Library; Anne Garner and Isaac Gewirtz, Berg Collection, New York Public Library; Robert Rothstein, Mark Lewis, and Francis Antonelli, Geddes Language Center, Boston University; Ellen Keith, Matt Krc, and Debbie Vaughan, Chicago History Museum; Susan Art, Sharon Hudak, Jeanine I. Alonso, Heatherlyn Mayer, Rita Vazquez, Office of the Registrar, University of Chicago; Rare Book and Manuscript Library, Butler Library, Columbia University; Laurie Rizzo, Special Collections, University of Delaware Library; Andre Bernard and Edward Hirsch, Guggenheim Foundation; William Furry, Illinois State Historical Society; Shannon Hodge and Eva Raby, Jewish Public Library Archives, Montreal; Barbara Cline and Tina Houston, Lyndon Baines Johnson Library; Graham Ball, Harvard University Public Affairs and Communications; Erin George and Elizabeth Kaplan, University of Minnesota Archives, Elmer L. Anderson Library; Frank Blalark, Office of the Registrar, University of Minnesota; Liat Cohen, Elie Derman, Ofira Ratsab, Mishkenot Sha'ananim, The Jerusalem

Foundation; Maria Molestina, The Morgan Library and Museum; Patrick Quinn and Janet C. Olson, Northwestern University Archives; Tamara Thatcher, Council of the Humanities, Princeton University; Kristen Turner, Mudd Manuscript Library, Princeton University; Rare Books and Special Collections, Firestone Library, Princeton University; Cheryl Van Emburg, Salzburg Seminars; Georgette Ballweg, Office of the Registrar, University of Wisconsin; Lori B. Bessler and Lee Grady, Wisconsin Historical Society; Leslie L. Leduc, Corporation of Yaddo.

I am grateful to the following individuals for answering queries, advice, and hospitality: Victoria Aarons, Martin Amis, Janet Ariad, James Atlas, David Bell, Moshe Bellows, Julie Ann Benson, Judith and Lawrence Besserman, Dina Binstock, Alan Brownjohn, Emily Budick, Shirley Cohen, Jay Corcoran, Gloria L. Cronin, H. M. Daleski, Philip Davis, Carol Denbo, Morris Dickstein, Jane Dietrich, Richard and Christianne Dimitri, Peggy Eisenstein, Paul Ekman, Esther Elster, Anne Feibleman, Maxine Fields, Catherine J. Fitzpatrick, Judith Flanders, June Fox, Liz Frank, Rani Friedlander, Abraham Fuks, Asaf Galay, David Gooblar, Grey Gowrie, Selina Hastings, the Hellmuths (Mary, John, Alison, Spencer, and Molly), Christopher Hitchens, Lewis Hyde, Nicole Jackson, Eric Jacobson, Scott and Fredda Johnson, Leslie Kaplan, Shirley Kaufman, Edmund Keeley, Rhoda Koenig, Mark Lambert, Scott Latham, Will Lautzenheiser, Zoe Leader, Victoria Lidov, John Lloyd, Peter Manning, Bobby Markels, Anita Maximilian, Carolyn McGrath, Josine Meijer, Edward Mendelson, Michael Mewshaw, Elena Mortara, Janet Nippel, Richard O'Brien, Doris Palca, Thomas Passin, Matt Phillips, Arnold Rampersad, Michael Roberts, Mary Rynerson, Rosemarie Sanchez-Fraser, Dr. Rachel Schultz, Sasha Schwartz, Tim Seldes, Adam Shils, Elaine and English Showalter, Margalit Steinberg, Erik Tarloff, Patricia Vidgerman, Chris Walsh, Annie Dubouillon Walter, Jacob Weisberg, Catherine Wells-Cole, Rose Wild, Hana Wirth-Nesher, Nancy Bass Wyden, and Steven J. Zipperstein.

Finally, I thank my wife, Alice Leader, the dedicatee of both volumes of this biography; our sons, Nick and Max Leader; and our daughter-in-law, Nicole Jackson. Like my friends and colleagues, they have heard a great deal about Saul Bellow this past decade.

A Note on Sources

Unless specified, all unpublished or manuscript material by Saul Bellow, including letters, is to be found among the Saul Bellow Papers in the Special Collections Research Center of the Joseph Regenstein Library at the University of Chicago, cited within the text and notes as Regenstein. I have been given unrestricted access to the Bellow Papers and have looked through every item in every folder in every box.

Before 2017 and the complete recataloguing of the Saul Bellow Papers, scholars and researchers faced numerous problems negotiating and referencing the collection. From 1960 onward, in a series of gifts and deposits, Bellow sent his papers (including notebooks, galley proofs, unpublished speeches and essays, hand-corrected manuscripts, typewritten drafts, letters, and miscellaneous items pertaining to his life and work, including interviews, profiles, photographs, tax returns, legal and financial documents, and reviews of his novels, stories, essays, and plays) to the Regenstein. Before 1968, writers were eligible to receive a tax deduction for such gifts; when the law involving cultural property changed, in reaction to enormous deductions obtained by visual artists, Bellow's gifts became deposits, held but not owned by the library, an arrangement agreed in the hope that the new law would be reversed and deposits could then become donations. After Bellow's death in 2005, at the age of eighty-nine, the executors of his literary estate decided that his papers should be kept together at the Regenstein. As a result of this decision, roughly 150 boxes of materials joined the two hundred boxes already housed in Special Collections.

These boxes were organized by deposit or gift. In the case of correspondence, letters from longtime friends and associates were scattered in dozens of locations with separate inventories. In the case of manuscript material, there were related problems. Bellow was a demon reviser, he rarely dated manuscripts, and the old inventories made only a few shrewd attempts at ordering drafts. Daniel Fuchs, the author of *Saul Bellow: Vision and Revision* (1984), still the best study of Bellow's composing process, gives reference names and numbers to the manuscripts he discusses but does so from what were already outdated inventories. Fuchs's study is an invaluable resource for students of Bellow's writing, but it was—still is—very difficult, at times impossible, to identify the draft versions he cites, not only for researchers but for the collection's efficient and professional archivists.

Given the partial nature of the inventories prior to the complete cataloguing and the high likelihood of the collection's being rationalized and properly processed in the near future, in *To Fame and Fortune* I decided against providing folder, box, and deposit numbers and names for unpublished correspondence or draft material. The decision not to specify folder and box in the current volume partly derives from the fact that it was largely written and researched before the newly catalogued collection was made available to Bellow scholars. In both volumes I do, however, provide names, dates, and estimated dates for individual items, and readers who wish to consult originals will have very little difficulty locating them, thanks to the excellent new online "Guide to the Saul Bellow Papers 1926–2015," the work of Ashley Locke Gosselar, lead archivist of the newly catalogued collection. It took Gosselar more than a year to catalogue the Saul Bellow Papers and to produce its "Guide," a project largely financed by Robert and Carolyn Nelson, generous University of Chicago alumni.

A selection of Bellow's correspondence, *Saul Bellow: Letters* (New York: Viking and Penguin, 2010), ed. Benjamin Taylor, "includes about two-fifths of Saul Bellow's known output of letters" (p. 533). On occasion, passages omitted by Taylor are restored from the original letter. Taylor lists the locations for all published Bellow letters not located in the Regenstein (pp. 553–56). The fullest annotated bibliography of works by and about Bellow remains Gloria L. Cronin and Blaine H. Hall, *Saul Bellow: An Annotated Bibliography*, 2nd ed. (New York: Garland Publishing, 1987), available electronically on http://www.saulbellow.org/bibliography. The *Saul Bellow Journal*, edited by Gloria L. Cronin and Victoria Aarons, has been in publication since 1981 and currently appears twice annually. It publishes updated "Selected Annotated Bibliographies," edited by Gloria L. Cronin and Robert Means, and is available electronically on EBSCO. Published Bellow texts cited in the notes refer to the editions used by the author. Full publication details for these editions, along with details of original publication, can be found in the notes. After an initial note, quotations from Bellow's fiction are cited in the text by page numbers.

All unattributed quotations in the biography come from the following interviews with Zachary Leader:

Ada Aharoni, 23 May 2010 (Nesher, Israel); Gillon Aitken, 10 July 2014 (London); Rosie Alison, 1 December 2007 (London); Martin Amis, 5 December 2014 (Brooklyn, N.Y.); Aharon Appelfeld, 21 May 2010 (Jerusalem); Linda Asher, 9 January 2009 (New York); Thomas Barber, 18 March 2017 (telephone); John Barnardo, 2 August 2010 (Boston); Wolf Baronov, 23 July 2008 (Chicago); Daniel Bell, 11 May 2008 (Cambridge, Mass.); Adam Bellow, 23, 27 March, 20 May 2008 (New York); Alexandra Bellow, 5 February, 1, 3 April 2008 (Chicago); Daniel Bellow, 11, 15 May 2008, 31 May 2017 (Great Barrington, Mass., telephone); Gregory Bellow, 20 August, 30 December 2008 (Redwood City and San Francisco, Calif.); Juliet Bellow, 20 December 2008 (San Francisco); Lily Bellow, 27 March 2008 (New York); Rachel Bellow, 7 August 2010 (Cambridge, Mass.); Sasha (Sondra) Bellow, 30 July 2007, 22, 23 March 2008 (New York); Janis Freedman Bellow, 5, 6, 7 August 2010 (Brattleboro, Vt.), 25 February 2017 (Boston); Bambi Bellows, 19 January 2008 (Chicago); Joel Bellows, 19 April, 28 June 2008, 26 August 2015 (Chicago); Kyle Bellows, 24 April 2008 (Chicago); Keith Botsford, 13, 14, 15 March 2008 (Cahuita, Costa Rica); Nathalie Botsford, 12 May 2008 (Boston); Polly Botsford, 5 November 2009 (London); Leon Botstein, 26 July 2007 (Annandale-on-Hudson, N.Y.); Jack Cella, 8 April 2008 (Chicago); Arthur and Lynda Copeland, 6 August 2007 (Brattleboro, Vt.); Esther Corbin, 10 July 2007 (Homewood, Ill.); Paul Dolan, 18 May 2008 (New York); Wendy Doniger, 1 February 2008 (Chicago); Margaret Drabble, 1 July 2014 (London); Judith Dunford, 10 January 2009 (New York); Toby Eady, 7 July 2014 (telephone); Brenda and Monroe Engel, 3 August 2007 (Cambridge, Mass.); Joseph Epstein, 18 April 2008 (Chicago); Maxine Fields, 12 June 2015 (telephone); Eileen Finletter, 18 May 2008

(New York); Isabel Fonseca, 5 December 2014 (Brooklyn, N.Y.); Joseph and Marguerite Frank, 19 August 2008 (Stanford); Harvey and Sonya Freedman, 6 August 2010 (Vermont); Wendy Freedman, 7 August 2008 (Pasadena, Calif.); Judy Freifeld, 13 August 2007, 19 February 2008 (Chicago); Paul Friedrich, 11 February 2008; David and Simon Gameroff, Leonard and Shelley Lewkowict, 18 September 2009 (Montreal); Frances Gendlin, 17 May 2008 (New York); Herbert Gold, 18 August 2008 (San Francisco); Sydney Goldstein, 29 December 2008 (San Francisco); Eugene Goodheart, 2 August 2007 (Cambridge and Watertown, Mass.); Mikhail Gordin, 30 May 2010 (Holon, Israel); Naum and Jana Gordin, 4 August 2010 (Brookline, Mass.); Jana Gordin, 30 May 2008 (telephone); Aviva Green, 12 October 2015 (telephone); Lesha and Sam Greengus, 28 August 2010 (Cincinnati, Ohio); Ethel Grene, 4 September 2010 (Wilmette, Ill.); Philip Grew, 23–24 July 2015 (Civitella Ranieri, Italy); John Gross, 26 October 2007 (London); Miriam Gross, 18 June 2015 (London); Christopher Hitchens, 19 February 2008 (Washington, D.C.); Doris and Marshall Holleb, 3 March 2008 (Chicago), Bette Howland, 2 July 2008 (Logansport, Ind.); Chantal and John Hunt, 18 September 2008 (Lyons, France); William Hunt, 3 August 2010 (Westport, Mass.); Gabriel Josipovici, 15 June 2014 (London); Beena Kamlani, 6 January 2009 (New York); Max Kampelman, 23 May 2008 (Washington, D.C.); Harold Kaplan, 6 May 2008, 28 March 2009 (Paris); Roger Kaplan, 23 May 2008 (Washington, D.C.); Leon Kass, 25 April 2008 (Chicago); Stanley Katz, 26 March 2008 (Princeton, N.J.); Eugene Kennedy, 16 April 2008 (Chicago); Jascha Kessler, 20 July 2007 (Los Angeles); Bettyann and Dan Kevles, 4 August 2010 (Centerville, Cape Cod, Mass.); Joan and Jonathan Kleinbard, 20 February 2008 (Philadelphia, Pa.); George Kliger, 26 June 2008 (Minneapolis, Minn.); Amos Kollek, 29 May 2010 (Jerusalem); Irving Kristol, Gertrude Himmelfarb, 19 February 2008 (Washington, D.C.); Arlette Landes, 22 May 2008 (Bethesda, Md.); Will Lautzenheiser, 12 May 2008, 25 February 2017 (Brookline, Mass.); Alan Lelchuk, 8 October 2015 (telephone); Ralph Lerner, 25 February 2008 (Chicago); Paul Levy, 30 April 2010 (Oxford); Frank Maltese, 7 August 2007 (Brattleboro, Vt.); Norman Manea, 9 January 2009 (New York); Sabina Mazursky, 25 May 2010 (Tel Aviv); T. J. McCarthy, 26 August 2015 (Chicago); Mitzi McClosky, 17 August 2008 (Berkeley, Calif.); Susan Missner,

29 July 2009 (Chicago); Vivien Missner, 11 July 2009 (Skokie, Ill.); John Nathan, 16 September 2014 (telephone); Evelyn Nef, 5 August 2007 (Great Barrington, Mass.); Amos Oz, 27 May 2010 (Tel Aviv); Cynthia Ozick, 6 December 2014 (New Rochelle, N.Y.); Jean Passin and Miriam Tarcov, 8 December 2009 (Phoenix, Ariz.); Sid Passin, 25 March 2008 (New York); David Peltz, 9, 15 February 2008 (Chicago); Antonia Phillips, 7 May 2016 (London); Robert Pippin, 31 January 2008 (Chicago); Norman Podhoretz, 23 March 2008 (New York); Walter Pozen, 22 January 2008, 25, 30 January and 12 May 2014 (Brattleboro, Vt., New York, and telephone); Antoinette Ralian, 29 October 2012 (telephone); Piers Paul Read, 19 June 2014 (telephone); James Redfield, 14, 21 January 2008 (Chicago); Laure Reichek, 15 August 2008 (Petaluma, Calif.); Christopher Ricks, 11 July 2010 (London); Tom Rosenthal, 3 November 2009 (London); Mark Rotblatt, 14 February 2008 (Chicago); Philip Roth, 20 March 2008 (New York); Floyd Salas, 28 November 2008 (Berkeley, Calif.); James Salter, 10 August 2010 (Bridgehampton, N.Y.); "Doris Scheldt," 12 June 2015 (London) [this is my anonymous interviewee]; Rachel Greengus Schultz, 1 April 2016 (telephone); Joan Schwartz, 25 March 2008 (New York); Graeme Segal, 20 September 2015 (London); Tim Seldes, 24 July 2010 (telephone); Ellen and Philip Siegelman, 16 August 2008 (Berkeley, Calif.); John Silber, 13 May 2008 (Boston); Diane Silverman, 29 January 2008 (Chicago); Eleanor Fox Simmons, 9 July 2007; Maggie Staats Simmons, 20, 21 May 2008, 31 March 2014 (New York and telephone); Herbert Sinaiko, 6 February 2008 (Chicago); Barbara Probst Solomon, 30 July 2007 (New York); Carol and Jay Stern, 8 September 2010 (Wilmette, Ill.); Richard Stern, 8 January, 29 May 2008 (Chicago); Shlomo Sternberg, 12 October 2015 (telephone); Miriam Tarcov, 7, 8 December 2009 (Tucson, Ariz.); Nathan Tarcov, 24, 31 January, 28 February 2008 (Chicago); Sylvia Tumin, 25 July 2007 (Princeton, N.J.); Bella and Mischa Ullman, 30 May 2010 (Hod Hasharon, Israel); Patty Unterman, 18 August 2008 (Berkeley, Calif.); George and Sarah Walden, 21 November 2009 (London); Chris Walsh, 12 May 2008, 24 February 2017 (Boston); Rosanna Warren, 14 September 2010 (New York) and 4 January 2017 (telephone); Lord Weidenfeld, 14 December 2007 (London); Renee Weiss, 25 July 2007 (Stonebridge, N.J.); Leon Wieseltier, 19 February 2008 (Washington, D.C.); Barbara Wiesenfeld, 7 August

2008 (Santa Monica, Calif.); George Wislocki, 10 June 2008 (telephone); Ruth Wisse, 1 August 2007 (Cambridge, Mass.); James Wood, 13 May 2008 (Cambridge, Mass.); Michael Wu, 5 June 2008 (Chicago); Andrew Wylie, 15 September 2010 (New York); A. B. Yehoshua, 24 May 2010 (Haifa, Israel).

Notes

EDITIONS OF SAUL BELLOW'S WORKS CITED (INCLUDING FIRST PUBLICATION DETAILS)

Novels

Dangling Man (New York: Vanguard, 1944); Library of America, 2003 (in *Saul Bellow: Novels 1944–1953*).
The Victim (New York: Vanguard, 1947); Library of America, 2003 (in *Saul Bellow: Novels 1944–1953*).
The Adventures of Augie March (New York: Viking, 1953); Library of America, 2003 (in *Saul Bellow: Novels 1944–1953*).
Seize the Day (New York: Viking, 1956); Library of America, 2007 (in *Saul Bellow: Novels 1956–1964*).
Henderson the Rain King (New York: Viking, 1959); Library of America, 2007 (in *Saul Bellow: Novels 1956–1964*).
Herzog (New York: Viking, 1964); Library of America, 2007 (in *Saul Bellow: Novels 1956–1964*).
Mr. Sammler's Planet (New York: Viking, 1970); Penguin, 1972.
Humboldt's Gift (New York: Viking, 1975); Penguin, 1977.
The Dean's December (New York: Harper, 1982); Penguin, 1998.
More Die of Heartbreak (New York: Morrow, 1987); Penguin, 2004.
The Bellarosa Connection (New York: Viking Penguin, 1989); Penguin, 2002 (in Saul Bellow, *Collected Stories*).
A Theft (New York: Viking Penguin, 1989); Penguin, 2002 (in Saul Bellow, *Collected Stories*).
The Actual (New York: Viking Penguin, 1997); Penguin, 1998.
Ravelstein (New York: Viking, 2000).

Collected Stories

Mosby's Memoirs and Other Stories (New York: Viking, 1968); Penguin 1996 (excluding stories reprinted in *Collected Stories*, Penguin, 2002).
Him with His Foot in His Mouth and Other Stories (New York: HarperCollins, 1984); Penguin, 2002 (in *Collected Stories*, which contains all the stories in this volume).

Something to Remember Me By: Three Tales (New York: Penguin, 1990); Penguin, 2002 (in *Collected Stories*, which contains all three stories in this volume).
Collected Stories (New York: Viking, 2001); Penguin, 2002.

Nonfiction

To Jerusalem and Back (New York: Viking, 1976); Penguin, 1998.
It All Adds Up: From the Dim Past to the Uncertain Future—A Nonfiction Collection (New York: Viking, 1994); Penguin, 1995.
Saul Bellow: Letters, ed. Benjamin Taylor (New York: Viking Penguin, 2010).
There Is Simply Too Much to Think About: Collected Nonfiction, ed. Benjamin Taylor (New York: Viking Penguin, 2015).

Plays

The Wrecker, in *New World Writing*, no. 6 (New York: New American Library, 1954); reprinted in *Seize the Day* (New York: Viking, 1956).
The Last Analysis (New York: Viking, 1965); Viking Compass, 1969.
Orange Soufflé, in *Traverse Plays*, ed. Jim Haynes (Harmondsworth, U.K.: Penguin, 1966). One of three one-act plays performed on Broadway and in London in 1966 as *Under the Weather*.
A Wen, in *Traverse Plays*, ed. Jim Haynes (Harmondsworth, U.K.: Penguin, 1966). One of three one-act plays performed on Broadway and in London in 1966 as *Under the Weather*.
Out from Under (unpublished in English). Italian translation, *C'è speranza nel sesso* (Milan: Feltrinelli, 1967); English version cited in manuscript, in Saul Bellow Papers, Special Collections Research Center, Joseph Regenstein Library, University of Chicago.

ABBREVIATIONS USED IN THE NOTES

Atlas, *Biography* James Atlas, *Bellow: A Biography* (New York: Random House, 2000).
Cronin and Siegel, eds., *Conversations with SB* Gloria L. Cronin and Ben Siegel, eds., *Conversations with Saul Bellow* (Jackson: University of Mississippi Press, 1994).
"I Got a Scheme!" "'I Got a Scheme!': The Words of Saul Bellow," *The New Yorker* (25 April 2005), an edited and rewritten interview between Saul Bellow and Philip Roth.
Koch interview An eight-hour interview Saul Bellow gave in 1987 to Sigmund Koch, a "University Professor" (as Bellow would himself become) at Boston University, one of seventeen such interviews with writers Koch conducted between 1983 and 1988 as part of the Boston University Aesthetics Research Project. The interviews were videotaped and are held at the Geddes Language Center at Boston University.
Manea, "Conversation" Norman Manea, "Saul Bellow in Conversation with Norman Manea," *Salmagundi* 2007, 155/156 (page numbers from the Literature Online version, http://lion.chadwyck.com).
Regenstein The Special Collections Research Center at the Joseph Regenstein Library, University of Chicago.
SB Saul Bellow.
SB, *CS* Saul Bellow, *Collected Stories* (New York: Viking Press, 2001).
SB, *IAAU* Saul Bellow, *It All Adds Up: From the Dim Past to the Distant Future—A Nonfiction Collection* (1994; Harmondsworth, U.K.: Penguin, 1995).

SB, "Memoirs" Saul Bellow, "Memoirs of a Bootlegger's Son," an unfinished manuscript among the SB Papers in the Regenstein.

Taylor, ed., *Letters* Benjamin Taylor, ed., *Saul Bellow: Letters* (New York: Viking, 2010).

1. FAME AND POLITICS IN THE 1960s

1. See Julian Moynihan, "The Way Up from Rock Bottom," *New York Times Book Review*, 20 September 1964; and Philip Rahv, "Bellow the Brain King," *New York Herald Tribune Book Week*, 20 September 1964.

2. Kazin's Journals are located in the Berg Collection of the New York Public Library. Unpublished entries involving SB were kindly provided to me by Richard M. Cook, ed., *Alfred Kazin's Journals* (New Haven and London: Yale University Press, 2011), and are reprinted here by permission of the Berg Collection. The entry for 22 September 1964 is printed on pp. 335–36 of Cook's edition; subsequent entries are unpublished.

3. These figures come from James Atlas, *Bellow: A Biography* (New York: Random House, 2000), p. 339 (henceforth cited as Atlas, *Biography*).

4. These and other financial details come from Atlas, *Biography*, pp. 339, 368–69. But see also chap. 5, n. 47.

5. After Volkening had complained of Freifeld's interference, SB wrote on 25 February: "When I do the mental balance of what people playfully call my 'career,' I find that my love for H. Volkening is among the biggest of the credits. You can never get into the Freifeld class. He's a sort of brother I must always make allowances for, dependably incompetent Sam. He'll *never* understand."

6. According to Robert Goldfarb of CMA (Creative Management Associates), in a letter of April 1965 to Henry Volkening, forwarded to SB in a letter of 19 October 1965. "On the subject of movies agents . . . the three of us have chosen Mr. Goldfarb and CMA to work with us after long and careful thought."

7. Atlas, *Biography*, p. 368.

8. Quoted in ibid., p. 339.

9. Letter of Robert Hatch to Dwight Macdonald, 14 July 1965, quoted in ibid., p. 347.

10. SB to David Goldknopf, n.d. Goldknopf, a writer, had known SB for over a decade. He was the author of *Hills on the Highway* (1948), a novel, and of a critical study, *The Life of the Novel* (1972).

11. In an interview, Mitzi McClosky recalled the following exchange. "How has success affected you?" she asked SB. "I used to get letters: 'You should have done this, you should have done that in your book.' . . . I'd believe them but I'd feel terrible about it when I didn't do anything about it. Now when I get these letters I say: 'So! Write your own *Herzog*!'"

12. Tarcov's letter has a penciled date of 1 March [1963]; it is, however, a reply to a letter from SB dated 2 March, though this date is not in SB's hand.

13. Greg Bellow, *Saul Bellow's Heart: A Son's Memoir* (London and New York: Bloomsbury, 2013), p. 114.

14. Quoted in Atlas, *Biography*, p. 327.

15. Greg Bellow, *Saul Bellow's Heart*, p. 114.

16. As it happened, Tarcov found lucrative part-time work as a freelance acquisitions editor at Collier Books, and eventually made more money than he'd earned at the Anti-Defamation League.

17. There is some confusion about Covici's date of birth. He was born in 1888, though Wikipedia gives his date of birth as 1885 and Atlas, *Biography*, p. 339, says he was sixty-three when he died.

18. A copy of the privately printed tributes is among the SB Papers in the Regenstein.

19. Quoted in Atlas, *Biography*, pp. 339–40.

20. Kerr may have known Bellow from Northwestern, or at least known of him. Both wrote for *The Daily Northwestern* under the editorship of Bellow's friend Julian Behrstock, and both graduated in 1937. Kerr was the paper's drama-and-arts editor and an Evanston native. Perhaps (this is pure speculation) he harbored a grudge over Bellow's mockery of Evanston types in his "Pets of the North Shore," a humorous piece published in *The Daily Northwestern* on April Fools' Day, 1936. Perhaps he also knew of and took offense at Bellow's pseudonymous attacks on Northwestern in the December 1936 issue of *Soapbox* (Bellow's student journalism is discussed in chapter 5 of *To Fame and Fortune*). Or he may simply have thought the play no good, or thought the play no good *and* harbored a grudge.

21. Quoted in Pete Hamill, "A Look at Saul Bellow, Writer at the Top," *New York Herald Tribune*, 27 September 1964.

22. On 18 March 1962, Robert Lowell wrote to SB apologizing for not being able to attend a reading of *The Last Analysis:* he and Elizabeth Hardwick would be in Puerto Rico at the time. He was especially sorry to miss the reading since he had finally redone one of his own plays "to fit Lillian Hellman's strictures. . . . The process is back-breaking."

23. SB, *The Last Analysis* (New York: Viking Press, 1965), pp. 77–78. Further quotations from the play and SB's "Author's Note" are cited within the text by page numbers.

24. Daniel Fuchs, *Saul Bellow: Vision and Revision* (Durham, N.C.: Duke University Press, 1984), p. 182.

25. The letter also expresses pleasure at the news that the play had been optioned by Giorgio Strehler, the theater director and cofounder of the Piccolo Teatro di Milano.

26. Quoted in Atlas, *Biography*, p. 331.

27. Quoted in ibid., p. 328.

28. David Boroff, "Saul Bellow," *Saturday Review*, 19 September 1964.

29. John Barkham, "A Writer's Diary," *Philadelphia Sunday Bulletin*, 4 October 1964.

30. Robert Gutwillig, "Talk with Saul Bellow," *New York Times Book Review*, 20 September 1964, reprinted in *Conversations with Saul Bellow*, ed. Gloria L. Cronin and Ben Siegel (Jackson: University of Mississippi Press, 1994), p. 24 (henceforth cited as *Conversations with SB*).

31. Pete Hamill, "A Look at Saul Bellow, Writer at the Top."

32. Ruth Miller, *Saul Bellow: A Biography of the Imagination* (New York: St. Martin's Press, 1991), p. 163.

33. See Atlas, *Biography*, p. 332.

34. Edward Hoagland, "The Job Is to Pour Out Your Heart," *New York Times Book Review*, 4 October 1981, quoted in ibid., p. 332.

35. Atlas, *Biography*, p. 331.

36. In SB, "Draft/Bellow to the Trustees," 10 December 1965, in SB Papers, an appeal to the trustees of the University of Chicago for the creation of a university repertory company and two new theaters. Sam Levene shows up again disguised as Murphy Verviger in *Humboldt's Gift*, where his girlfriend bothers Citrine just as Levene's girlfriend bothered SB: "The Belasco was like a gilded cake-platter with grimed frosting. Verviger, his face deeply grooved at the mouth, was big and muscular. He resembled a skiing instructor. Some concept of intense refinement was eating at him. His head was shaped like a busby, a high solid arrogant rock covered with thick moss." Verviger's girlfriend, Denise, eventually Citrine's wife, takes

down rehearsal notes "with terrible concentration, as if she were the smartest pupil in the class and the rest of the fifth grade were in pursuit. When she came to ask a question she held the script to her chest and spoke to me in a condition of operatic crisis. Her voice seemed to make her own hair bristle and to dilate her astonishing eyes. She said 'Verviger wants to know how you'd like him to pronounce this word'—she printed it out for me, FINITE. 'He can do it *fin*-it, or *fine-ite.* He doesn't take my word for it—fine-ite!' " (SB, *Humboldt's Gift* [Harmondsworth, U.K.: Penguin, 1977], p. 58) (henceforth cited within the text by page numbers).

37. Howard Taubman, " 'Last Analysis' of Saul Bellow Arrives," *New York Times,* 3 October 1964; Robert Brustein, "Saul Bellow on the Drag Strip," *New Republic,* 24 October 1964; John Simon, "Theater Chronicle," *Hudson Review,* vol. 17 (1964–65), p. 557; Walter Kerr, "Bellow's 'Last Analysis,' " *New York Herald Tribune,* 3 October 1964.

38. Jack Gaver, quoted in "Saul Bellow's First Play Draws Mixed Reviews," *Chicago Sun-Times,* 3 October 1964.

39. For the Committee on Social Thought, see chapter 14 of *To Fame and Fortune.* SB was on the faculty of the Committee for thirty years, from 1963 to 1993. Other notable Committee faculty include Hannah Arendt, Mircea Eliade, Leszek Kołakowski, Friedrich Hayek, T. S. Eliot, J. M. Coetzee, Jacques Maritain, Paul Ricoeur, Adam Zagajewski, and Wendy Doniger.

40. Fuchs, *Saul Bellow: Vision and Revision,* p. 181. SB himself came to share Grene's view of *The Last Analysis,* as in a letter of 26 June 1971 to Edward Shils, written after the play's 1971 revival by Circle in the Square: "I refused to go to New York for the revival of my revised farce. It seems to be having a *succès fou.* You don't approve of it, I know, but it has a few Aristophanic moments."

41. Fuchs, *Saul Bellow: Vision and Revision,* p. 178. Three months after the play closed, SB complained to Tom McMahon, a friend from the English Department at the University of Puerto Rico, that "the profession of the theatre was anything but a profession" (quoted in Miller, *Saul Bellow: A Biography of the Imagination,* p. 165).

42. Nancy Walker originated the role of Hildy Eszterhazy in *On the Town* and won Tony nominations for several Broadway hits, including *Do Re Mi* (1960) with Phil Silvers, a potential Bummidge. She was Ida Morgenstern on the *Mary Tyler Moore* show and its spinoff, *Rhoda,* directing episodes for both series. SB's comment about having his imagination stirred comes in a letter to Toby Cole, quoted in Atlas, *Biography,* p. 351, without a date. In another letter to Cole, written on 23 January, before Walker's visit, SB announces "that a lady named Nancy Walker has been reading my dramatic works, and wants to direct 'The Wen' on Bleecker Street, in a loft. And that is probably where it belongs." In the July 1965 interview with Gloria Steinem in *Glamour,* reprinted in *Conversations,* ed. Cronin and Siegel, p. 56, SB says he's finishing off "the last of three one-act plays and looking forward to seeing them produced Off-Broadway. . . . Nancy Walker . . . is doing a great job with them. She's wonderful. Brains in the theatre are very rare."

43. By 12 July 1965, SB was less sure about Walker, as he expressed in a letter to Toby Cole. He had written a new play: "I don't know how Nancy and them others will like it. If they don't, we might (Ted Hoffman suggests) turn the three plays over to Oliver Rea for off-Broadway. Though I love her dearly, I think the inadequacies come from her, not from the play."

44. The two quotations preceding the 12 July quotation come from undated letters to Toby Cole. Atlas, *Biography,* p. 351, quotes the second, along with the subtitle to the unpublished and unproduced one-acter, "A Work of Art": "Silliness in one act."

45. Greg Bellow, *Saul Bellow's Heart,* p. 116.

46. Ibid., p. 105.
47. Ibid., p. 106.
48. Ibid., pp. 108, 114, 113.
49. See ibid., p. 114, for Greg's difficulties with Susan, Anita, and SB (over his failure to attend Oscar Tarcov's funeral). On 12 January 1964, Ted Hoffman wrote to SB from Stanford, where Greg had been visiting. He and Greg "had a couple of man-to-man talks." It was "the same old story—you've been rational when he wanted love, showered love when he wanted explanation, and manage to accept everything about him except what he wants you to accept. Same thing with Anita . . . What's funny is how little he knows about you, how differently he interprets the past, how absent so many facts are—not radically different, just different. I kept wanting to say NO, look, here's the life you lived; here's what happened then; here's what he believed, felt, tried to do, etc., but what's the point? The boy doesn't attack you or Anita. He accepts you. He appreciates your concern. But he's making his own life, as we all do, and I guess we can only make our own life by assuming that its materials are beyond the comprehension of our parents."
50. Greg Bellow, *Saul Bellow's Heart*, p. 114.
51. Adam's sense of being handed off owed something to the frequency with which he and Sasha moved in his early years. "My experience of the world was just of being yanked around."
52. In a letter of 24 October 1966, Sasha wrote to SB to complain about his bad-mouthing her in front of nine-year-old Adam: "Adam expresses the problem this way, and I quote directly: 'Papa wants me to love him more than I love you, but he doesn't understand that I want him to love me more than he does Daniel.' "
53. Greg Bellow, *Saul Bellow's Heart*, p. 116.
54. Ibid., p. 117.
55. SB, *More Die of Heartbreak* (1987; New York and London: Penguin, 2004), p. 125 (henceforth cited in the text with page numbers).
56. Atlas, *Biography*, p. 359.
57. The book seems never to have been published. CORE's papers are held at the Wisconsin Historical Society, and its files on "They Shall Overcome" contain correspondence, several copies of Bellow's introduction, and what appears to be a rough draft of the book itself. According to the letters on file, the book was to be published by Norton in the autumn of 1965, but correspondence stops abruptly with discussion of Bellow's introduction. SB's contribution was not the problem. "Thanks so much for your introduction to the CORE book," wrote Marvin Rich on 9 September 1965. "It was really very much to the point." The reason the book was never published is suggested by two letters from George Brockway, president of W. W. Norton and Co., one to SB, the other to Henry Volkening. To SB, Brockway wrote on 12 October 1965: "In my opinion, THEY SHALL OVERCOME, the CORE book to which you have contributed an introduction, will sell about 6,500 copies. On this sale, CORE will realize about $7,000. As you know, the bookstores have been flooded with books on the race problem. If it were not for your introduction, we doubt very much whether this book would sell even as well as STEP BY STEP, a volume we published last year for a Cornell committee, which has earned them less than $1,000. We should, therefore, value your contribution at about $6,000." On 27 April 1966, Brockway wrote to Volkening: "Dear Henry: Here's the Bellow introduction. Sorry. Yours, George."
58. In email to the author, 15 January 2014, Lee Grady, reference librarian at the Wisconsin Historical Society, writes of "They Shall Overcome" that it is "described as a 'documentary' of 'the movement' with an emphasis on the three civil rights workers who were murdered in Mississippi (Goodman, et al)."
59. Michiko Kakutani, "A Talk with Saul Bellow: On His Work and Himself,"

New York Times Book Review, 13 December 1981, reprinted in *Conversations with SB*, ed. Cronin and Siegel, p. 187.

60. Susan Crosland, "Bellow's Real Gift," *Sunday Times*, 18 October 1987, reprinted in *Conversations with SB*, ed. Cronin and Siegel, pp. 233–34.

61. Undated draft of the letter, in the Regenstein.

62. When Lowell heard of Bellow's plan to attend the festival and to publish his opposition to the Vietnam War in the papers, he several times telephoned "to concert a strategy for the afternoon. I gathered that he and his group were giving me a clearance to participate—somebody like me *should* be inside." (Quoted in SB, "Writers, Intellectuals, Politics: Mainly Reminiscence," *National Interest*, Spring 1993, reprinted in SB, *It All Adds Up: From the Dim Past to the Uncertain Future—A Nonfiction Collection* [1994; Harmondsworth, U.K.: Penguin, 1995], p. 110 [henceforth abbreviated as *IAAU*]).

63. Ibid., p. 110.

64. Atlas, *Biography*, p. 346.

65. Mark Harris, *Saul Bellow, Drumlin Woodchuck* (Athens: University of Georgia Press, 1980), p. 59.

66. Details of Califano's meetings with the academics are found in a memo to President Johnson dated 9 August 1966. Attached to the memo are "a few of the better letters" Califano received. The memo and a list of the academics consulted can be found in the LBJ Library in Austin, Texas. If Bellow answered Califano's three questions, the answers are not among LBJ's papers in Austin, according to the library's archivist, Barbara Cline.

67. Among the SB Papers in the Regenstein is a letter of 12 November 1969 from Frederick M. Kravitz on stationery of the University of Chicago Festival of the Arts Committee. Two days earlier, SB had declined to participate in the festival. Kravitz's letter reads in part: "I am sorry to note your gastro-intestinal disorder, which if memory serves, did not stop you from feasting at Lyndon Johnson's table while the abomination of the war in Vietnam was being executed." SB forwarded Kravitz's letter to "Tom" (there is no last name) with a note at the bottom reading: "This has to do with our last talk. What I said in the first place was that I w'd not participate in a festival with the above-named artists ["artists" is ironic; the speakers named in Kravitz's letter were Paul Goodman, Jimmy Breslin, Dwight Macdonald, and Studs Terkel]. What a provocation, eh? Please return this. SB."

68. See Cecil Woolf to SB, 17 August 1966. Among the book's dozens of contributors were Kingsley Amis, W. H. Auden, Isaiah Berlin, Graham Greene, Arthur Miller, Harold Pinter, Iris Murdoch, Anthony Powell, Bertrand Russell, Stephen Spender, and Leonard Woolf.

69. For the student occupations and sit-ins of 1966 and 1967, see especially issues of the University of Chicago student newspaper, *The Chicago Maroon*, for 13 and 27 May 1966, 24 and 28 January 1967; and the University of Chicago Library Special Collections Web site entry for "University of Chicago—Student Activism," http://www.lib.uchicago/e/scrc/collections/subject/activism.html. The quotation from Edward Levi was reported in Jeffrey Blum, "The Sit-In: Three Days That Made UC History," *Chicago Maroon*, 30 September 1966.

70. Email to the author, 5 October 2008.

71. Quoted in Atlas, *Biography*, pp. 386–87.

72. Harris, *Drumlin Woodchuck*, p. 82.

73. For Irving Howe's views on the New Left, see his *Margin of Hope: An Intellectual Autobiography* (New York: Harcourt Brace Jovanovich, 1982), p. 309: "Each day the New Left kept moving away from its earlier spirit of fraternity toward a hard-voiced dogmatism, from the ethic of nonviolence toward a romantic-nihilist fascination with a 'politics of the deed.' . . . To see the Leninist-Stalinist contempt

for liberal values elevated to Herbert Marcuse's haughty formulas about 'repressive tolerance'—formulas used to rationalize the break-up of opponents' meetings by some new Left groups—made one despair of any authentic Left in America."

74. "How is the Kristol movement coming?" wrote Shils to SB on 20 September 1965. "I am very eager that it should be successful." That SB was spearheading this effort is suggested by a letter of 19 July from James Redfield detailing objections to Kristol. The attempt to bring Himmelfarb to Chicago was foiled by objections from the History Department, though there were also objections from some members of the Committee on Social Thought. See Edward Shils to SB, 3 March 1966: "I do not think anything about the University of Chicago and my association with it has ever depressed me as much as the performance of the History Department in the Kristol case. Of course I do not gainsay the right of any scholars to pass judgment on the work of other scholars, but they have a powerful obligation to behave like gentlemen in doing so, whether they do in writing or orally. . . . I doubt whether the Kristols would now consider coming to the University of Chicago." This letter was accompanied by the letter to Levi, of the same date, in which Shils complained in particular of "the case of Mrs. Kristol . . . [who] was treated, I am reliably told, with a degree of discourtesy which one would not even expect at a meeting of the *mafia*." Shils also complained of the treatment of Daniel Moynihan, turned down for an appointment in the Department of Sociology. Moynihan, he concedes, might, indeed, be "good enough to be the Director of the Harvard–M.I.T Joint Center for Irving Studies and not good enough to be appointed to the very remarkable Department of Sociology at the University of Chicago," but it was not the failure to appoint that he objected to (wrong as he thought it, as he thought the failure to appoint the Kristols wrong), but "the crudity of manners" of the departments in question.

75. SB's four *Newsday* dispatches were dated 9, 12, 13, and 16 June. The last three are reprinted in *IAAU*, under the general title "Israel: The Six-Day War." This quotation is from the 13 June dispatch, p. 208.

76. Ibid., pp. 206–27.

77. Ibid., p. 209.

78. Ibid., pp. 214–15.

79. Ibid., p. 216.

80. Quoted in Atlas, *Biography*, pp. 369–70.

81. SB to Maggie Staats, 7 June 1967. Maggie Staats will figure prominently in the next chapter.

82. SB, *To Jerusalem and Back* (Harmondsworth, U.K.: Penguin, 1976), p. 133 (henceforth cited within the text by page numbers).

83. This woman was Arlette Landes, who will also figure prominently in the next chapter.

84. SB, interview, *San Francisco Chronicle*, quoted in Harris, *Drumlin Woodchuck*, p. 24.

85. Ibid., p. 25.

86. Quoted in Walter Clemons and Jack Kroll, "America's Master Novelist: An Interview with Saul Bellow," *Newsweek*, 1 September 1975, reprinted in Cronin and Siegel, eds., *Conversations*, p. 129.

87. Sabina Mazursky email to the author, 3 May 2010.

88. "Are Many Modern Writers Merely Becoming Actors Who Behave Like Artists?," reprinted in *Observer*, 7 December 1968, under the title "Perils of Pleasing the Public." See also SB, "Skepticism and the Depth of Life," in *The Arts and the Public*, ed. James E. Miller, Jr., and Paul Herring (Chicago: University of Chicago Press, 1967), reprinted in SB, *There Is Simply Too Much to Think About: Reflections from Seven Decades*, ed. Benjamin Taylor (New York: Viking Press, 2015):

"Writers of talent do occasionally manage to make a beginning in New York, but their tendency is to compensate themselves too handsomely and too fully for the hardships they endured on the way up. They are often transformed into Major Literary Figures and for the rest of their lives do little more than give solemn interviews to prestigious journals or serve on White House committees or fly to the Bermudas to participate in international panel discussions on the crisis in the arts. Often the writer is absorbed by the literary figure. In such cases it is the social struggle that has been most important, not the art" (p. 227).

89. See also SB to Gloria Steinem, in the 1965 profile in *Glamour* magazine, reprinted in *Conversations with SB*, ed. Cronin and Siegel, pp. 51–52: "It is difficult," Bellow went on, "for writers to escape the temptation to be exemplary. The public wants them to be heroes, philosophers, to point the way. . . . The hard thing to do—the thing few Americans think is necessary—is to make the choice, close the door, and say 'this is it, this is all I can do.' "

90. See Bill Cooper to SB, 9 December 1966, in a letter containing a list of ten talks for the spring of 1967: "We will set up the entire itinerary, hotels, flights, etc., and, as I told you, you can get out on 30 days notice on any of these dates."

91. Harris, *Drumlin Woodchuck*, p. 119.

92. These comments come from an interview with Salas.

93. Quoted in Atlas, *Biography*, p. 376.

94. The other woman was Maggie Staats. Carol Stern—the girlfriend, now wife, of SB's friend and pupil Jay Stern (the model for Feffer in *Mr. Sammler's Planet*)—recalls a similar encounter a year later, on 2 May 1969, when SB gave a talk at Roosevelt University in the Loop, where she taught. The talk was entitled "The Artist and the University," and SB "was given the Sammler treatment."

95. SB, quoted by Leah Garchik, *San Francisco Chronicle Book Review*, 2 January 1983; Atlas, *Biography*, p. 376n., quotes an account of the San Francisco State episode published the following day in the *San Francisco Chronicle*. In the account, SB is described as "prematurely old and cranky," "an alienated super-intellectual afflicted with defensiveness and hostility."

96. This quotation and the account that follows come from an eleven-page typed transcript of an unpublished talk by Salas entitled "The Sit-in at State—68." The transcript is dated 30 October 1999.

97. For Atlas's account, quoted from in the following paragraphs as well, see *Biography*, pp. 374–77.

98. When asked why he made the comment about Bellow's not being able to come, Salas answered: "This was the beginning of the summer of love, . . . Fuck don't fight—that's probably where the come thing came from." In "*Mr. Sammler's Planet:* Saul Bellow's 1968 Speech at San Francisco State University," in *A Political Companion to Saul Bellow*, ed. Gloria L. Cronin and Lee Trepanier (Lexington: University Press of Kentucky, 2013), p. 157, Andrew Gordon provides useful background to the incident: "Then called San Francisco State College, now San Francisco State University, it was a commuter school, largely working class, multi-ethnic, including some black, Chicano, and Filipino students who banded together under the label of the 'Third World Liberation Front' (echoing the North Vietnamese Liberation front or NLF) and called for Black Studies and Ethnic Studies programs." To Gordon, Salas was "a working-class Chicano writer in the vanguard of a movement of students and teachers who were trying to transform the university and the society to make it more culturally inclusive" (p. 160).

99. Salas provided me with a copy of an email of 11 June 2001 from Richard Hanlin, to be used in possible legal action against Atlas and Random House: "All I can tell you about Floyd's confrontation with Bellow is this: Floyd was standing in the aisle less than six feet from where I was sitting. The whole thing lasted less

than forty seconds. He did not swear. I recall what he said and there was no profanity unless one considers the word 'come' as a swear word. Other witnesses: my guest Lee Combs who is now close to eighty years old . . . Maureen Putnam, the wife of Floyd's teacher and colleague, was there and doesn't recall Floyd or anyone swearing." Hanlin had been in correspondence with Random House about the incident: "In my last phone call to them they told me they'd talked to Atlas and he stood by his account and for them the issue was over" (they would not, therefore, be supplying the "transcript" of the confrontation Atlas refers to in an endnote on p. 642).

100. Atlas, *Biography*, p. 376.

2. "ALL MY LADIES SEEM FURIOUS"

1. This quotation comes from p. 72 of Sasha's unpublished memoir, "What's in a Name?" (henceforth cited within the text by page numbers). The memoir consists of two parts, 121 typed pages written sometime in 2006, and a postscript entitled "The Years Between" written in 2008. This postscript, which deals with Sasha's life from age twelve to twenty, goes on to p. 130, and is followed by a letter to her son, Adam, dated May 2008, in which she explains how difficult it was "to dredge up memories" of what she calls the "dark ages" of her life. The memoir, she tells Adam, "is not an autobiography. In fact, it is fairly fragmented, surprisingly incomplete in many respects and, significantly, does not even touch on the last thirty plus years (my best) at all." The letter is numbered as though part of the memoir (pp. 131–32). My dating of the first two parts of the manuscript is conjectural, based on the May 2008 letter to Adam and the first sentence of the postscript: "I spent nearly two years trying to tackle the years 12–20 that are missing in the memoir." Sasha gave me a copy of the memoir in 2010, the year before she died. The memoir records the difficulties she encountered over her various names when at Bennington. In her second year, she needed a birth certificate to travel to Mexico with a roommate: "Because I had no other recent, official record of my legal existence, I had to get signed and notarized affidavits from my mother and my aunt, attesting that Saundra and Sandra Richter, Sondra and Alexandra Tschacbasov were all the same person" (p. 2).

2. SB, *Humboldt's Gift* (Harmondsworth, U.K.: Penguin, 1965), p. 19 (henceforth cited in the text with page numbers); SB, *A Theft* (1989), published as a paperback original by Penguin; reprinted in SB, *Collected Stories* (New York: Viking, 2001), p. 117 (henceforth cited in the text by page numbers).

3. Atlas, *Biography*, p. 347. See also, on p. 348, this quotation from Hanson's diaries: "Mr. Bellow is one who loves his family, and as far as I can see it, his family now consists of himself and his sons. . . . He is the only connecting link between his three sons, and his family life will always be a bit incomplete."

4. SB's letters to Maggie are in her possession.

5. Walter Kerr, "Saul Bellow's 'Under the Weather,'" *New York Times*, 28 October 1966.

6. Eleanor Fox is discussed in chapter 4 of *To Fame and Fortune*.

7. The "Olduvai" manuscripts and SB's decision to give them up are discussed in the introduction to *To Fame and Fortune*.

8. This episode is also mentioned in the introduction to *To Fame and Fortune*.

9. James Atlas, *Delmore Schwartz: The Life of an American Poet* (1977; New York: Avon Books, 1978), p. 315.

10. See, for example, SB to Meyer Schapiro: "It's possible that Edward Honig at Brown may know of a job. I heard of one there, but I was told that John Berryman would probably be taking it. Perhaps it's still open. But I'd guess that Syracuse was

Delmore's best bet. I hope he's well enough to function. Teaching makes him more stable, but Syracuse is a small town where he would be continually observed by people who had heard of his troubles etc. . . . But then I haven't seen Delmore since '57 or '58, the year of the crisis, and I've no idea what he's like. But I wish him well."

11. Mark Harris, *Saul Bellow, Drumlin Woodchuck* (Athens: University of Georgia Press, 1980), p. 21.

12. Atlas, *Biography*, p. 360.

13. Greg Bellow, *Saul Bellow's Heart: A Son's Memoir* (London and New York: Bloomsbury, 2013), p. 119.

14. Atlas, *Biography*, p. 360.

15. Quoted in Harris, *Drumlin Woodchuck*, p. 15, where no date is given.

16. Ibid.

17. This portion of the letter is quoted in ibid., p. 18.

18. Ibid., p. 20.

19. Ibid., p. 21.

20. Ibid., pp. 23, 29, 30.

21. Atlas, *Biography*, p. 365.

22. Harris, *Drumlin Woodchuck*, pp. 35, 36.

23. Ibid., p. 41.

24. Ibid., p. 40.

25. Ibid., p. 42.

26. Quoted in ibid., p. 14 (see also p. 157 for SB's disapproval of *The Goy* as a title). On pp. 55–56, Harris lists several woodchuck references in Bellow's writing. Grandma Taube in *Herzog* has "teeth like a woodchuck." "Thoreau saw a woodchuck at Walden," we learn in *Humboldt's Gift*, "its eyes more fully awake than the eyes of any farmer." Woodchucks are smart as well as alert, and sensibly hibernate "when Humboldt comes 'skedaddling dangerously' in his Buick." In *Seize the Day*, Tommy worries "that all my life I had the wrong ideas about myself and wasn't what I thought I was. And wasn't even careful to take a few precautions, as most people do—like a woodchuck has a few exits to his tunnel."

27. Ibid., p. 56.

28. Ibid., p. 23.

29. Ibid., p. 182.

30. See Henry Brandon, "Writer Versus Readers," *Sunday Times*, 18 September 1966; Terry Coleman, "Saul Bellow Talks," *Guardian*, 23 September 1966; for the anonymous *Observer* profile, 25 September 1966, see Atlas, *Biography*, p. 359.

31. SB was introduced by Malcolm Bradbury at the Cochrane Theatre on Sunday, 25 September, according to Carver's note of 16 September. Carver's note also mentions various people eager to meet him or have him to dinner, including Peter Brook, Lawrence Gowing (of the Tate Gallery, also a painter and an art historian), and Julia Strachey, Gowing's former wife (a writer and member of the Bloomsbury circle).

32. Among the services Weidenfeld performed for SB was lobbying and jockeying on his behalf for the ten-thousand-dollar Formentor Prix International de Littérature. As Barley Alison predicted in a letter of 28 October 1963: "I must tell you that the Prix Formentor will be a good deal less Moravia dominated when George [Weidenfeld] is the President than in the past. . . . Also the Americans bring Herbert Gold who is an old friend. . . . I long for you to win it, partly because I think you deserve it, partly because . . . you would then have to go to the meeting in 1965 in order to make a gracious, modest little speech." SB's friend Mary McCarthy was chairman of the judges for the 1965 competition (though she spoke in favor of Ivy Compton-Burnett's *A God and His Gifts*). SB narrowly beat Witold Gombrowicz when the French jury changed its vote from Yukio Mishima to SB.

The competition was held at Valescure, on the French Riviera, and publishers from thirteen different countries (Weidenfeld was the English publisher) provided teams of judges (among Weidenfeld's judges were John Gross and Francis Wyndham). Despite Alison's hopes that SB would come to Europe to collect the prize, in fact he did not receive it until 1966, at a ceremony in the offices of the Grove Press in New York (Barney Rosset of Grove Press had headed the American delegation). Herb Gold, who presented SB with the award, remembers Rosette Lamont arguing with him, "The really great writer, the one who should have been given the prize . . . is Ionesco. He's international." (Herbert Gold, *Still Alive: A Temporary Condition: A Memoir* [New York: Arcade, 2008], p. 15.) In "Bellow Observed: A Serial Portrait," *Mosaic*, vol. 8, no. 1 (Fall 1974), pp. 256–57, Lamont recalls an episode on the morning before the ceremony. SB went out to buy a new pair of shoes for the occasion, accompanied by Paolo Milano and Lamont, but was reluctant to carry the old pair to the Grove offices. The old pair was still in good condition, and, finding himself in front of the New York Public Library, SB decided to place it on the front steps. Then he and his friends stood aside, waiting to see if anyone would pick the shoes up. No one did. "As we boarded the number 4 on the way downtown," writes Lamont, "Paolo Milano reflected: 'I guess there isn't anyone ready to step into Saul Bellow's shoes.'"

33. Weidenfeld had made a similar offer, Alison wrote to SB on 5 February 1967, but his terms were "a non-starter and likely to bankrupt me sooner rather than later." After the move to Secker, she thanked Bellow in a letter of 4 March. His praise and support had led to all sorts of offers, the best of which was Secker's.

34. He was back in time to deliver the keynote address at a University of Chicago conference on "The Arts and the Public" (16–21 October) as part of the celebration of its seventy-fifth anniversary. In his talk, SB argued that New York was not the literary capital of America, though it was the capital of literary business in America. Granville Hicks's report on the conference in the *Saturday Review* ("Mass Media's Gifts to the Muse," 19 November 1966) quotes the address: "'The literary life of the country is concentrated mostly in university communities. The university has come to be in the Sixties what Paris was to Fitzgerald and Hemingway in the Twenties.'" Whether SB attended subsequent sessions is unclear. He is unlikely to have listened to Anthony West, Leon Edel, or Studs Terkel, though he might have stayed for William Arrowsmith, Wright Morris, and Harold Rosenberg.

35. Perhaps the earliest of the *Sammler*-related manuscripts is an undated and unpublished story among the SB Papers in the Regenstein entitled "Out of Bounds," about a magazine writer and failed playwright named Alex Goodkin (author of a play entitled *Trenck*, later used as the title for Charlie Citrine's hit in *Humboldt's Gift*). Like Oscar Tarcov, Alex has a heart condition, has had a coronary, and has witnessed a black pickpocket on the Riverside Drive bus (it was Tarcov who first told SB about having seen such a pickpocket). Alex tells his wife, Erna, what he's seen, and after a second sighting is confronted by the pickpocket, who deals with him "as a tomcat might deal with a fish head." His feelings about the pickpocket are contrasted with those of his truculent, hip daughter, Patsy. "He had been greatly frightened by that Negro," who to Patsy was "someone who was *with it*, on top of things. In short, a master spirit. Which her daddy was not. In some respects he thought her right. He had the Thirties' playwrights' outlook, and old-fashioned compassion. To her, though not in those words, the Humanistic crap." Another possible early version, the earliest discussed in Fuchs, *Saul Bellow: Vision and Revision* (Durham, N.C.: Duke University Press, 1984), pp. 209ff., takes the form of manuscript material related to a story entitled "The Future of the Moon," in which Pawlyk is attacked by "two slim negroes" and there is "no pick-

pocket, no Columbia scene, no Feffer, no Wallace." This material was deposited in the Regenstein in a gift of 1967, which leads Fuchs to conclude that "it was not until the late sixties that the novel's subject matter really presented itself" (p. 209).

36. As Atlas, *Biography*, p. 126, suggests, the Holocaust is alluded to twice more: in Leventhal's nightmare dream of a crowded railway station with blaring loudspeakers and guards pushing people onto trains, and in Allbee's turning on the gas stove in Leventhal's kitchen.

37. Earlier in the same passage, one of the effects of the Holocaust on Jews of the New World, including those who suffered before emigrating, is said to have been to silence any claims to exceptional suffering, the sort Father Herzog used to make: "We are on a more brutal standard now, a new terminal standard, indifferent to persons" (p. 565). "It took a long time for me to get a grip on it," Bellow admitted to Norman Manea, when asked about the Holocaust. "I ask myself often nowadays: why were you so slow in picking this up? I don't know why" ("Conversation," p. 15).

38. Fuchs, *Saul Bellow: Vision and Revision*, p. 226.

39. SB offers examples of these facts in the letter to Wieseltier, by way of the testimony of a survivor: "I once asked Alexander Donat, author of *The Holocaust Kingdom*, how it was that the Jews went down so quickly in Poland. He said something like this: 'After three days in the ghetto, unable to wash and shave, without clean clothing, deprived of food, all utilities and municipal services cut off, your toilet habits humiliatingly disrupted, you are demoralized, confused, subject to panic. A life of austere discipline would have made it possible for me to keep my head, but how many civilized people lead such a life?' Simple facts—had Hannah had the imagination to see them—would have lowered the intellectual fever that vitiates her theories." Donat's views find their way into the novel as Sammler reflects on his shooting of an unarmed German soldier: "The thing no doubt would have happened differently to another man, a man who had been eating, drinking, smoking, and whose blood was brimming with fat, nicotine, alcohol, sexual secretions. None of these in Sammler's blood. He was not then entirely human. . . . Not much there for human appeal" (p. 114).

40. Fuchs, *Saul Bellow: Vision and Revision*, p. 19.

41. Ruth R. Wisse, *The Modern Jewish Canon: A Journey Through Language and Culture* (New York: Free Press, 2000), p. 303.

42. "The Old System" is reprinted in SB, *CS*, p. 90. Further references to the story itself are cited within the text by page number.

43. They are both discussed in chapter 2 of *To Fame and Fortune*, in connection with Bellow's Canadian cousins the Gameroffs.

44. The deal is described in detail in chapter 2 of *To Fame and Fortune*.

45. SB, "Zetland: By a Character Witness" (1974), reprinted in SB, *CS*, p. 243.

46. The choice of this figure was coolly calculated, and no less coolly analyzed both by Braun in retrospect and by Isaac: "He must have known all along that he would have to pay the money. . . . Tina from the deathbed had made too strong a move. If he refused to come across, no one could blame him. But he would feel greatly damaged. How would he live with himself? Because he made these sums easily now. Buying and selling a few city lots. Had the price been fifty thousand dollars, Tina would have been saying that he would never see her again. But twenty thousand—the figure was a shrewd choice" (pp. 113–14).

47. SB, "Cousins" (1974), reprinted in *CS*, p. 206.

48. For a related sense of the Old System contract and of the importance of family, see Irving Howe, *A Margin of Hope: An Intellectual Autobiography* (New York: Harcourt Brace Jovanovich, 1982), p. 269: "Again and again I would 'fail' my father through what he took to be my disordered life—a broken marriage, a sud-

den unexplained stay in California. But his solidarity never wavered, and I came to feel that it was a solidarity more than familial, deriving from some unexpressed sense of what a Jew owed his son."

49. Wisse, *Modern Jewish Canon*, p. 298.

50. A likely source for the episode with the black pickpocket, also for the phone conversation with the police officer, is "The Pickpockets" (1961), a story by Oscar Tarcov. The narrator of the story, Mr. Karpen, lives on the Upper West Side (like Tarcov himself, who lived at 37 Riverside Drive at the time he wrote the story) and takes the "Riverside–Fifth Avenue bus" to and from work. Karpen's neighbor also takes this bus and recounts having seen two black pickpockets, a tall one and a short one, plying their trade on the bus (Tarcov himself had witnessed something like this). The outraged neighbor is no liberal, and Karpen thinks to himself: "In this day and age, goddammit, can't Gabler view a couple of thieves simply as men—lousy men, O.K.—and not as two niggers?" Some days later, Karpen himself spots the pickpockets, watching them "intently." The two thieves go about their work coolly. When one of them only just misses snatching a wallet, quickly exiting the bus, Karpen lets the other one know he's been spotted. "When the small man started to move to get off the bus, Mr. Karpen said to him, 'Tell your friend that he's too obvious.' The small man smiled and said, 'I don't know that man but I sure wished I did.'" Then he gets off the bus. When Karpen's wife asks why he didn't do something about the pickpockets, he replies: "'I'll make a fuss in the bus and nothing will happen. I can't arrest them and search them.'" After several more such sightings, Karpen sees them attempting to rob "an elegantly dressed, very old man who had palsy. They made no effort to use their skills. The tall man shamelessly jostled the old man to the point of utter bewilderment while the small man openly went through the helpless old man's pockets until he found his wallet. The two pickpockets calmly got off the bus, for the first time together." Karpen thinks back on this moment, "smoldering." Previously, he'd been impressed by the smooth professionalism, the "craftsmanship" and imperturbability of the pickpockets. Now he thinks: "The dirty bastards—they threw their skills, their finesse, out the window and shamelessly and ruthlessly frisked the old man—they didn't care if he knew what was happening because he was too helpless to stop them."

Karpen feels shame not only at having been too cowardly to intervene but at having admired the pickpockets. He calls the police to complain, and "after several transfers" finally gets through to a lieutenant, who politely tells him "they were short of staff in his detail but after the summer they would put someone on this. . . . Was there anything else he had to say that would be helpful?"

> "They were Negro," Mr. Karpen said.
>
> "Oh, nigger pickpockets," the lieutenant said.
>
> "Negroes," Mr. Karpen said strongly. "Negroes."
>
> And as he said this, hating the lieutenant, he imagined himself on a bus pointing to the two pickpockets and yelling thieves! And he saw the passengers' faces looking at the small man and the tall man and saw their lips spitting out the words, dirty niggers.

The connections between SB's novel and Tarcov's story are obvious, particularly in relation to feelings of shame, guilt, fear, prejudice, and the inadequacies or weaknesses of liberal sentiment.

51. A personal memory: In graduate school, I attended a series of lectures by Northrop Frye on the Bible as literature. At one point, Frye digressed to tell us about an argument he'd had with a radical student at Berkeley in the late 1960s. Frye did not specify the topic of the argument, or if he did, I do not recall it. What

I recall is the quiet contempt with which he described the student's refusal to continue arguing: on the grounds that Frye had more knowledge than he did and thus put him at an unfair disadvantage. A different view, more in connection with the students, is offered in an entry of 15 April 1967 from Alfred Kazin's Journals: "Youth and age . . . Saul and his hatred of the young. I was thinking, too, going up to Stony Brook Thursday morning, about the pompous oily look of success worn these days by Professor Leon Edel, Professor Oscar Handlin, Professor Richard Hofstadter, Professor Saul Bellow, goodness what successes we all have become, and how successful and happy and pompous some of us look."

52. Wisse, *Modern Jewish Canon*, p. 302.

53. Harris, *Drumlin Woodchuck*, p. 136.

54. Ibid., pp. 136–37.

55. Ibid., p. 137.

56. Ibid., p. 138.

57. Ibid., p. 139. See Jane Howard, "Mr. Bellow Considers His Planet," *Life*, 3 April 1970, reprinted in Cronin and Siegel, eds., *Conversations with SB*, p. 78, when Howard adds: "Bellow the public figure can be acerb, aloof and elusive. But in private he is different."

58. Harris, *Drumlin Woodchuck*, p. 146.

59. Ibid., p. 156.

60. Ibid., p. 159.

61. Morris Dickstein, *Leopards in the Temple: The Transformation of American Fiction 1945–1970* (Cambridge, Mass.: Harvard University Press, 2002), p. 175; the quotation from *Mr. Sammler's Planet* is from p. 25. For an intelligent comparison of *Mr. Sammler's Planet* and Mailer's *An American Dream* (1965), also a novel in which a Jewish intellectual is threatened by a sexually powerful black man, see Susan Glickman, "The World as Will and Idea: A Comparative Study of *An American Dream* and *Mr. Sammler's Planet*," in *Saul Bellow in the 1980s: A Collection of Critical Essays*, ed. Gloria L. Cronin and L. H. Goldman (East Lansing: Michigan State University Press, 1989), pp. 209–23. Bernard Malamud has an interesting relation to SB and Mailer over these issues. According to a friend of Malamud's, Claude Fredericks, quoted by Philip Davis in *Bernard Malamud: A Writer's Life* (Oxford, U.K.: Oxford University Press, 2007), p. 267, "Bernard increasingly questions in himself the validity of the kind of order his own writings, he thought, demanded: the sacrifice of a life—like Flaubert. And the animal energy of the black is the image of that very life he hungers for now too late." A year after *Mr. Sammler's Planet*, Malamud published *The Tenants*, a novel about two writers, a Jew named Harry Lesser and a black named Willie Spearmint. The two writers, tenants in the same decaying building, argue about art. Lesser accuses Spearmint's writing of lacking form, Spearmint hits back, in Davis's words, that his individualism "was the art; form and genre were Jewish coercion. In the battle between content and form, ideology and art, this is an extreme and transmuted version of the muddled controversy between Ralph Ellison, the author of *The Invisible Man*, and the Jewish critic Irving Howe that simmered on throughout the 1960s."

62. My comparison of SB and Mailer draws on David Mikics, *Bellow's People: How Saul Bellow Made Life into Art* (New York: W. W. Norton, 2016), pp. 78, 160–62. In addition to discussing the Ellison and Howe essays, Mikics quotes Edward Shils's attacks on the Mailer line: "Blacks, according to this view, were entitled to exemption from the obligations of law-abidingness and of assimilation of the higher culture of American and Western society. They gained merit from the fact that they lived in slums, in wretched dwelling" ("Learning and Liberalism," in *The Selected Papers of Edward Shils*, vol. 3 [Chicago: University of Chicago Press,

1980]). Ellison's essay, "The World and the Jug," appeared in *The New Leader*, 9 December 1963.

63. Dickstein, *Leopards in the Temple*, p. 175.

64. SB's womanizing was common knowledge. See Norman Rosten, 11 September 1967: "Did your nice friend from the New Yorker come out? Saul, I think of you juggling all those oranges—girls, wives, children—and I think, Is God nice to him or just fattening him up for some fearful retribution?" Or Paolo Milano, 18 September 1968: "My 'lovely acquaintances,' who are also 'impressionable' as you prefer them, are already impressed by the sheer possibility of meeting *il cantor di Ramona*."

65. Arlette's husband was four years older than she was and had been a graduate student in economics at Columbia. After a spell at Stanford on a Ford Foundation grant, he got a post at the University of Chicago, teaching law and economics.

66. Barley Alison sought to comfort SB about Arlette in a letter of 26 February 1969, quoted at the beginning of chapter 3.

67. Arlette's letters from late January 1969 report on the controversy at the University of Chicago over Marlene Dixon. On 30 January, she wrote: "The university is being attacked again by those great democratic forces the mob and equality. A sociology instructress, Marlene Dixon, has been dismissed because she was not doing what instructors must do to stay on: publish. Instead, she taught and was politically vocal. As I see it, these kinds of teachers are still half-way between student and teacher. Endearing to the student and hateful to the teacher." The next day, she wrote that Bruno Bettelheim, the child psychologist, a University of Chicago professor, had called a news conference "in which he said the student upheaval paralleled German pre-Nazi student behavior." Bettelheim had spent eleven months in Dachau and Buchenwald. Arlette also had a theory about black militants and Jews. She thought "the real hatred and resentment" came from the pressure to act and achieve: "Fighting the Jew with whom he has always dealt is fighting the representative of social participation."

68. My interview with Arlette took place in the garden of her home in Bethesda, Maryland. She is a serious painter, smart, funny, down-to-earth. A handsome woman off to work, she wore jeans, running shoes, and a fleece, not exactly the dress of a sex goddess.

69. This letter was written to Whit Burnett, editor of *Story* magazine.

70. For a discussion of "Mosby's Memoirs," see chapter 6 of *To Fame and Fortune*.

71. Maggie still has her engagement diary from the second (1968) summer at East Hampton, and among painter friends lists Ben and Jean Gollay, Herman Cherry, Warren Brandt and his wife, Grace, and Syd and Annie Solomon, presumably friends also from the previous summer.

72. Ben Nelson, an acquaintance of SB's from Hyde Park days, was a historian and a social theorist. He and SB became good friends at the University of Minnesota, where Nelson was a colleague. An authority on medieval usury and immensely learned, Nelson was the model for the scholar-theorist Egbert Shapiro in *Herzog*.

73. See, for example, SB to Margaret Staats, 18 June 1966: "For the first time, I feel out to a dangerous depth with you. Friday P.M. gave me a bad shock. You didn't tell me you were going out with anyone. . . . The Friday man did not seem to me a casual date, but, judging from your changed tone towards me, one that means something to you. You didn't want to express feeling towards me in his presence. I thought, in fact, that you wanted to get rid of me. I've never before felt that you were anything but straight with me; but these last twenty-four hours I've felt it, terribly, wondering whether my being in love with you isn't my ticket

to destruction. . . . When I guessed what the doorbell meant, you sounded guilty. You sounded ashamed. Maggie—what are you up to?"

74. See Atlas, *Biography*, pp. 380–81.

75. They had been furious for some time. As SB wrote to Richard Stern on 16 July 1968: "*Toujours poursuivi des femmes, pourtant tracassé. Des circonstances assez marrant. Elles sont* toutes *fâchées—au nord, ouest, et ici même. Mais je continue tout de même de faire mes devoirs.*" In Benjamin Taylor's translation: "Still pursued by women: worried nonetheless. An amusing situation. They're *all* furious—north, west, and even here, but I continue to do my duty" (*Letters*, p. 274n).

76. Lamont, "Bellow Observed," p. 254.

77. Fuchs, *Saul Bellow: Vision and Revision*, p. 250.

78. SB, "What Kind of Day Did You Have?" (1984), reprinted in SB, *CS*, pp. 312, 335.

79. SB, *The Bellarosa Connection* (1989), reprinted in SB, *CS*, p. 68.

80. Another way to look at characters like Angela (or Wallace or Eisen), and hence at the novel itself, is to see them as different in phenomenological type from Sammler or Elya. To Mark Shechner, in *After the Revolution: Studies in the Contemporary Jewish American Imagination* (Bloomington: Indiana University Press, 1987), pp. 146–47, "these caricatures are 'humors' characters, flat figures with one or two exaggerated tendencies, as in the plays of Ben Jonson."

81. In "*Mr. Sammler's Planet:* Saul Bellow's 1968 Speech at San Francisco State University," in *A Political Companion to Saul Bellow*, ed. Gloria L. Cronin and Lee Trepanier (Lexington: University Press of Kentucky, 2013), p. 154, Andrew Gordon makes the fair point that the novel "never mentions Vietnam." He goes on to argue, "The absence of any mention of the Vietnam War, the motor for much of the widespread political protest and questioning of authority during the late 1960s, turns the young radicals in the novel into lunatics, running amok and tearing down the universities for no apparent reason." Adam Kirsch makes a related observation in "Flower Children," an essay on *Mr. Sammler's Planet* in the Jewish online magazine *Tablet* (14 March 2012): "For a man who survived the Holocaust, Sammler seems very little interested in social and political questions. The disaster he sees unfolding around him is, instead, spiritual, moral, and above all sexual." Kirsch objects to this emphasis on novelistic rather than moral grounds: "What Bellow is criticizing in the 1960s—the topsy-turvy elevation of youth over age, energy over wisdom—really has nothing to do with what Sammler experienced in the 1940s. As an American Jewish novelist, Bellow tries hard to seek a point of imaginative contact with the Holocaust, but the concerns of the present overshadow the realities of the past. Indeed, one feels that a man with Sammler's experiences would not condemn the American present in quite such absolutist terms. At the intersection of Broadway and 96th Street, for instance, Sammler feels that the dismal scene seems to say 'that the final truth about mankind was overwhelming and crushing': But surely a man who was buried alive under the corpse of his wife would not need Broadway and 96th Street to enforce such a feeling."

82. See SB to Margaret Staats, 27 September 1968: "Shirley [Sidran] kept saying that he was so happy to have come to East Hampton before, and talked of nothing else. He had come to say goodbye to me, and knew it. He got my card from Bellagio and hoped I'd get back before too long." Lou Sidran worked in advertising but had previously been an associate editor at *Esquire*, for which he wrote. He also wrote for *Reader's Digest* and *Coronet* magazines and had literary interests (according to Atlas, *Biography*, p. 378, his library "boasted complete sets of *transition* and *Scrutiny*"). That summer, SB, Maggie, Sidran and his son, and Gore Vidal watched the Democratic Convention together, appalled by the violence in the streets.

83. See, for example, Ethan Goffman, "Between Guilt and Affluence: The Jew-

ish Gaze and the Black Thief in *Mr. Sammler's Planet*," *Contemporary Literature*, vol. 38, no. 4 (1997), pp. 705–25.

84. Kirsch, "Flower Children."

3. BAD BEHAVIOR

1. Barley Alison to SB, 26 February 1969.

2. A copy was given to me by Adam Bellow. An edited version of the essay was published in the London *Sunday Times*, 5 June 2005, under the title "Lost and Found, My Nobel Father."

3. Shortly before SB's death in April 2005, Adam took his wife and two daughters to visit London, his first trip there in thirty years. In the memoir, he contrasts his father's irritation and impatience about the souvenirs with his own generosity toward his girls, who "thought nothing of asking me to stop for a rest or a snack, to see (or not to see) a given monument, to buy them souvenirs and other things their hearts desired. And it was my pleasure to do so."

4. In an email to the author, 24 January 2018, Adam Bellow writes: "It . . . seems worthwhile to note the letter [SB] wrote to Sasha describing my 'little prince' routine and making me out to be spoiled and arrogant pertained to a conversation we had had at a restaurant in Great Neck in which he had started to get wound up about my mother and I told him, following her own well-meaning advice, that I would rather not discuss my mother with him. He exploded in a rage and hurled the Ten Commandments at me as a result of which I knocked my ice cream sundae to the floor where it smashed with a loud bang. I was seven or eight at the time."

5. Email to the author, 2 June 2014.

6. Telephone interview with Toby Eady, 7 July 2014.

7. The manuscript is in the SB Papers in the Regenstein. Its dating is in Janis Bellow's hand: "Unfinished Rita manuscript summer '90."

8. That SB himself was a good friend to Barley Alison is suggested not merely by her loyalty to him and by the warm memories her family—including her brother, his wife, and their daughter Rosie—have of him, but also by a long letter of 4 November 1974, in which she tells him about her problems concerning her mother, who had been diagnosed with cancer. The letter was clearly written to someone she felt she could count on for sympathy, comfort, and understanding.

9. Quoted in Atlas, *Biography*, p. 392, presumably from a letter but not identified.

10. SB to Margaret Staats, 27 September 1970. See also SB to Benjamin Nelson, 11 September 1970: "*Le Destin* has been against me, using its familiar agents—children, hostages to fortune. I longed to go to Montauk, but Gregory announced that he would be married in August, in San Francisco. He chose the middle of the month, just to make things interesting—a little test of his value to his dear Pa, with a slender golden edge of the will to Power. To pass this new test I had to spend a large part of August in San Francisco. Next it was the turn of Adam, who is thirteen, to do his stuff. His choice fell on Nantucket. No, it hasn't been one of my better summers."

11. Sasha Bellow, "What's in a Name?," p. 116.

12. SB, "Mr. Wollix Gets an Honorary Degree," *Anon*, December 1970, reprinted in SB and Keith Botsford, *Editors: The Best from Five Decades* (London and Connecticut: Toby Press, 2001). See also Rosette Lamont, "Bellow Observed: A Serial Portrait," *Mosaic*, vol. 8, no. 1 (Fall 1974), p. 253: "Early in the summer of 1970, Bellow was awarded an honorary doctorate by New York University. He flew in from Chicago to receive it. Mrs. Vincent Astor was appointed his sponsor, and arrived in her chauffeured car to call on the writer at his hotel, the Plaza.

Together, they went on to the ceremony. There, reports Bellow, the main speaker began to mouth the kind of elegant liberal clichés he thought he was expected to produce. The parents of the graduating students, all hard-working, middle of the road members of the *bourgeoisie,* soon broke into hisses and boos. Mrs. Astor who was sitting next to the writer seemed highly amused: 'Are we going to have a bit of a scuffle?' she inquired, a gleam in her eyes. Saul Bellow appreciated the great lady's defiant wit. He himself could not feel as objective, faced as he was with the misanthropy he deplores on the day of being signally honored."

13. SB had been a member of the National Institute of Arts and Letters since 1958, a separate body from the American Academy of Arts and Letters, founded by National Institute members in 1908. In 1976 the American Academy and the National Institute merged; SB was by then a member of both. The American Academy Web site lists him as having been a member since 1958.

14. The essay was "Culture Now: Some Animadversions, Some Laughs," delivered at Purdue University on 30 April 1970, reprinted in *Modern Occasions,* vol. 1 (1971). Among those attacked in the essay are William Phillips and Richard Poirier, editors of *Partisan Review,* from whom Philip Rahv, editor of *Modern Occasions,* had parted acrimoniously.

15. In a review of Eduard Hitschmann's *Great Men: Psychoanalytic Studies* (1956) in *The Psychoanalytic Quarterly,* vol. 26 (1957), reprinted in *The Search for the Self: Selected Writings of Heinz Kohut, 1950–1978,* 2 vols., ed. Paul Ornstein (New York: International Universities Press, 1980), vol. 1, p. 89, Kohut takes issue with Hitschmann's view of Albert Schweitzer. For Hitschmann, Schweitzer's moral scrupulousness derives from "an unconscious guilt feeling which originated in early years and was renewed by regression." For Kohut, Schweitzer's "keen awareness of the misery existing in the world and the determination to live a life devoted to the suffering are the autonomous attitudes of a mature ego." Schweitzer's work in Africa as a medical missionary was for Kohut a product of control and compassion rather than conflict and unconscious psychic compromise. This attitude was bound to appeal to Bellow, a fierce opponent of the view, as Herzog puts it, that "what a man thinks he is doing counts for nothing. All his work in the world is done by impulses he will never understand" (p. 28).

16. For Kohut's views on artistic creation, see his essays on Thomas Mann, Beethoven, and creativity and childhood, also in volume 1 of *The Search for the Self,* ed. Ornstein.

17. Quoted in Atlas, *Biography,* p. 384.

18. Both Kohut and SB quotations are from ibid., p. 385.

19. Peltz's first trip to Africa was to visit a relative, a State Department official working in Dar es Salaam; his second was to see Lake Victoria, the largest lake in Africa.

20. SB to Edward Shils, n.d.

21. Deirdre Bair, *Saul Steinberg: A Biography* (New York: Nan A. Talese/Doubleday, 2012), p. 421.

22. Ibid., p. 422. Bair's quotations come from a marked transcript of an interview Steinberg had with Grace Glueck, "The Artist Speaks: Saul Steinberg," *Art in America* (November–December 1970), pp. 110–70. There is a good deal more about the symbolic properties of crocodiles in the published interview. There are also slight differences in quotation.

23. This address, among the SB Papers in the Regenstein, is where he reports having been advised by lawyers in Nairobi to get out of town. A version of it was published in *Republic of Letters,* vol. 7 (November 1999), reprinted in SB and Botsford, eds., *Editors,* p. 422. For Steinberg's account of the visit to Murchison Falls

with SB and Peltz, see "Saul Bellow in Uganda," *Saul Bellow Journal*, vol. 4, no. 2 (1985).

24. SB, "Saul Steinberg," in SB and Botsford, eds., *Editors*, p. 448.

25. Bair, *Saul Steinberg: A Biography*, p. 422.

26. SB, "Saul Steinberg," in SB and Botsford, eds., *Editors*, p. 449.

27. Atlas, *Biography*, p. 396.

28. SB, "Saul Steinberg," in SB and Botsford, *Editors*, p. 449.

29. SB, "A Silver Dish," reprinted in SB, *CS*, p. 13 (henceforth cited within the text by page numbers).

30. According to Atlas, *Biography*, p. 405.

31. The nature of these tensions seems to have been personal; on Shils's part, it did not preclude recognition of Grene's intellect or of his importance to the university and the Committee on Social Thought. On 8 January 1987, Paul Wheatley, at the time chair of the Committee, wrote to Shils to thank him "for raising the question of the University's lack of recognition of David Grene. Of course, I am entirely in agreement with you that the University should formally honor a lifetime of devoted and inspiring teaching, and I shall make representations to the Provost in the manner you suggest." But see Shils to SB on 4 June 1975: "I am pleased that you are going ahead with a dinner in honor of John Nef. I myself find him utterly repulsive, but he was a very outstanding scholar, and in his unpleasant way he was a most valuable member of the University." In an undated letter from the summer of 1974, SB writes to his secretary: "Dear Esther: Take out of Mr. Shils's memorandum the clause 'ass though he is.' Let that sentence read 'It would please Nef and he does deserve some recognition from the University and the Committee.' For God's sake, don't fail to suppress the ass."

32. Before joining the Committee, Sinaiko had held teaching posts in the Department of Oriental Languages at the university and at the college. He had studied Chinese for ten years and taught it for seven, originally intending to write a Ph.D. dissertation on Plato and Confucius. While still teaching in the Department of Oriental Languages, he decided, at David Grene's urging, to drop the Confucius part of the dissertation, writing on Plato alone. The resulting work was good enough to be published by the University of Chicago Press but counted for little when Sinaiko came up for tenure in the Department of Oriental Languages. He was then hired to teach in the college, which awarded him tenure. In 1964, Marshall Hodgson, a Sinologist, was chair of the Committee. With the support of Redfield and Grene, he obtained a junior appointment for Sinaiko. When Redfield became chair, after Hodgson, he made Sinaiko executive secretary.

33. When the Committee was canvassed about Sinaiko, it was split: Grene and Redfield in support, Bellow and Shils opposed, with a middle group made up mostly of part-time faculty (Harold Rosenberg, Victor Turner, Hans Jonas, Hannah Arendt), who tended to defer to the majority.

34. Sinaiko could have fought the decision, since he had been awarded tenure in 1964, while still teaching in the college, but decided it wasn't worth it. He returned to the college, where he had a long and successful career teaching undergraduates.

35. At one point, in a letter to Shils of 27 February 1972, SB says he can "no longer bear James Redfield," who has written "a long emotional letter . . . to Adams [the dean of social sciences] complaining of my high-handedness in the Committee. I would say pure nonsense if that weren't a tautology—nonsense is pure by nature."

36. That Shils never went after Redfield may, in part, be because he knew and admired Redfield's father and grandfather, great figures in their fields and in the university. It may also have helped that Redfield was not as closely associated with Grene as Sinaiko, though he declared himself "devoted" to him.

37. Atlas, *Biography*, p. 406. Joseph Epstein remembers Shils saying something like "Saul thinks he's going to use the Committee on Social Thought as the farm team for his *nafkas*."

38. Edward Shils, *Portraits: A Gallery of Intellectuals* (Chicago: University of Chicago Press, 1997), pp. 220, 231.

39. In *Handsome Is: Adventures with Saul Bellow* (New York: Fromm International, 1997), pp. 33–34, Harriet Wasserman, SB's agent after Henry Volkening, describes a conversation they had over a writer SB had "encouraged me to take on as a client. Her contract had been negotiated at Viking earlier in the year. The author was particularly high-strung and difficult. Unfortunately there had been a misunderstanding as to whether the manuscript was fiction or nonfiction. The editor had understood Saul to describe the work as a novel. . . . I too understood it to be a novel. . . . The author complained bitterly to Saul and then phoned me in a rage." When SB wondered why Viking had accepted the manuscript if it proved not to be a novel, presumably forgetting that he'd been the one who'd described it as such, Wasserman answered: "You have tremendous power over Viking. If you suggest it, they'll take it. They can't say no to you." This exchange took place early in the summer of 1974, the year in which *W-3* was published. As Wasserman points out, "Viking had been Saul's publisher since 1948, more than twenty-five years."

40. Bette Howland, *W-3* (New York: Viking, 1974), p. 9 (henceforth cited within the text by page numbers). In real life, SB's inability to reciprocate Bette's feelings—or to reciprocate them as she'd wish—was a motive for her attempted suicide. In an email of 18 December 2017, Joseph Epstein claims SB once told him that Bette "expected me to marry her. I would never marry a woman who attempted suicide."

41. One other circumstance tormented Howland: the fact of having to pretend all the time:

> I couldn't take it any more, no longer could bear this burden of concealment. Things seemed bad enough without adding extra weight. I wanted to be rid of it all, all of it. I wanted to abandon all this personal history—its darkness and secrecy, its private grievances, its well-licked sorrows and prides—to thrust it from me like a manhole cover. That's what I had wanted all along . . . what I hoped to obliterate. That was my real need [p. 25].

42. Bette Howland, *Blue in Chicago* (New York: Harper & Row, 1978), p. 120 (henceforth cited within the text by page numbers).

43. Atlas, *Biography*, p. 477.

44. Joseph Epstein, introduction, in Shils, *Portraits*, pp. 27–28.

45. Among the SB Papers in the Regenstein is "A Brief Overview" of the Aspen Institute for Humanistic Studies, from which my account is partly drawn. It was sent to SB together with a "Lecture and Film Series" schedule and a list of "Brief Biographical Sketches" of the 1971 "Scholars and Artists in Residence." See also the current Aspen Institute Web site: http://www.aspeninstitute.org/about.

46. Robert Reingold, "Scholars Assay Meaning of 'the Educated Person,'" *The New York Times*, 10 August 1974.

47. There are five of these notebooks, Salter told me. The photocopied pages he gave me from them he gave "in the interests of Saul Bellow's life being well written." The joke-sarcasm of SB's remark to Karyl Roosevelt is taken from the notebooks.

48. Udall had been appointed secretary of the interior for delivering Arizona for Kennedy, as opposed to Johnson.

4. A BETTER MAN

1. The production was directed by Theodore Mann, opened on 23 June 1971, and closed on 1 August, after forty-six performances. For some reason, Walter Kerr also reviewed it in *The New York Times* ("Basic Freud, Bad Bellow," 4 July 1971), after SB's "delighted" letter to Perin. Kerr was as dismissive in 1971 as he'd been in 1964, calling the play "excruciating," the work of an author with "no feel for the way the stage functions." He was no kinder to Joseph Wiseman, who played Bummidge, than he'd been to Sam Levene. Wiseman went on to play Dr. Adler in the 1987 television film of *Seize the Day*, with Robin Williams as Tommy Wilhelm and Jerry Stiller as Tamkin. Wiseman's best-known role was as "Dr. No" in the James Bond film of 1962.

2. The letter to the Committee was written on 29 September 1972. In it, SB describes the *Partisan Review* under Phillips as "trivial, fashionable, mean and harmful. Its trendiness is of the pernicious sort. It despises and, as much as it can, damages, literature. . . . I think it has become the breeding place of a sort of fashionable extremism, of the hysterical, shallow and ignorant academic 'counter-culture.'"

3. Quoted in Atlas, *Biography*, p. 497n. See also SB to Fred Kaplan, 10 February 1978: "I resigned from the Century Club because Poirier and Wm. Phillips were admitted to membership. I *am*, after all, some sort of snob myself. . . . I said in resigning that there were people I simply didn't care to meet in the club rooms. My letter was posted on the bulletin board as evidence of my unbelievable effrontery. All this gave me the greatest pleasure. . . . I am not one of your *resigned* types. One fights on."

4. Harriet Wasserman, *Handsome Is: Adventures with Saul Bellow* (New York: Fromm International, 1997), pp. 7, 9–10.

5. See also Wayne Booth to SB, 21 September 1975: "My trouble with you is that though I am the ideal reader of your books . . . I am personally intimidated by you and therefore never speak out."

6. According to Gross, Shils had been brought to Cambridge not only to give academic credibility to sociology, a new department in the university, but to lure figures like Runciman to the faculty.

7. Rosette Lamont is good on Bellow and clothes and furnishings, in "Bellow Observed: A Serial Portrait," *Mosaic*, vol. 8, no. 1 (Fall 1974): "Now that he can afford it, Bellow enjoys a certain amount of luxury. . . . He goes to London to pick up shirts he has ordered, and he may add to that a beautiful Rembrandt print for his otherwise pristine apartment. His Chicago tailor may line his jackets with Indian foulard, the same as that which he uses for his ties. But except for a glorious pale green Chinese rug on the living room floor, a beautiful Dutch tile in the center of his circular dining-room table, and rare editions of books, mostly in French or English, the place where Bellow lives is designed for the comfort of work. He has, of course, his small foibles, and is the first to laugh at them: he collects boots and borsolinos." In Nairobi, Saul Steinberg turned to SB and inquired: "'What, you don't wear cashmere socks? A man in your position?' So they bought cashmere socks."

8. There was much controversy later over Naipaul's *In a Free State*, though it did not involve Bellow. Fowles publicly complained that it was a collection of stories rather than a novel, an issue Gross thought had been resolved in preliminary meetings. In the end, the panel stuck by its decision that the book's three stories were closely enough linked to qualify as a novel.

9. Aside from the Naipaul, the other novel Gross remembers Bellow praising was *Goshawk Squadron* by Derek Robinson, which Gross also "rather liked." Bellow

described it as "red-blooded unlike Elizabeth Taylor," a judgment Gross called "a defect of taste. I don't think he got that right." His suspicion was that Bellow was irritated "by the Englishness" of Taylor's novel. Mrs. Palfrey is an elderly woman living in a shabby-genteel residential hotel off the Cromwell Road. To Gross, the novel "is about old age, very, very touching; I think he didn't get it." But Bellow himself had written touchingly about old age and shabby gentility, in "Leaving the Yellow House," also in "Dora" and "The Gonzaga Manuscripts." Gross thinks it possible that with the Taylor novel Bellow may have "lost patience after twenty pages," though in discussing the other short-listed novels Bellow seemed to have neither skimmed nor skipped.

10. Review section, *Guardian*, 6 September 2008.

11. The Sono scenes in *Herzog* are recollected, and the novel's present is c. 1960. In that present, we are told that Sono "had gone back to Japan long ago. When was it? He turned his eyes upward as he tried to calculate the length of time" (pp. 584–85). If SB's Japanese lover was the model for Sono, she may have returned to Tokyo sometime in the mid-1950s.

12. Atlas, *Biography*, pp. 416, 417.

13. Nathan thinks the episode referred to was at International House, which had, still has, very strict rules and cell-like rooms for guests. In an interview, he conjectured that if SB was chaste while in Japan it was only because he mostly frightened or intimidated the young girls with whom he flirted. He wasn't all that well known in Japan, Nathan explains, and "he was old and they were young." In a letter of 5 September 1973 to Professor Yuzaburo Shibuya of Meiji University in Tokyo, SB recalls the visit as five weeks in which "I was guilty of no crimes. A charming young lady from International House, Miss Shizuko Asahi (against whom I committed no offense), sent me cards and presents for a time but I haven't heard from her in many months now and am worried about the poor girl who disappeared so suddenly."

14. Although SB seems not to have known or admired Kenzaburō Ōe's fiction, he admired the novels of Junichiro Tanizaki (1886–1965), praising *Diary of a Mad Old Man* (1961) and *A Blind Man's Tale* (1931) in *To Jerusalem and Back*, p. 137.

15. Atlas, *Biography*, p. 417.

16. Nathan found the remark especially wounding. As he explains in *Living Carelessly in Tokyo and Elsewhere: A Memoir* (New York: Free Press, 2008), pp. 150–51, "His appraisal felled me like a crowbar. Seven years later, his words were still ringing in my ears when I resolved to distinguish myself with accomplishments that had nothing to do with exoticism and tried to put Japan behind me." Later, he considers "the possibility that I possessed the wherewithal to distinguish myself only as an exotic foreigner in an insular island country. I was determined to prove myself on home ground" (p. 198). For "squaw man" as disparaging, see SB, *Herzog*, p. 519: "Sono wanted me to move in with her. But I thought that would make me a squaw man."

17. Atlas, *Biography*, p. 417. Before agreeing to visit Japan, SB sought assurances that he would be able to keep up his writing routine. "I said I had some work in progress," he wrote to Yoichi Maeda, chairman of the Japan-U.S. Intellectual Interchange, reporting in a letter of 31 January 1972 an exchange with Professor Charles Frankel of Columbia about the visit, "and that I would not find it agreeable to suspend it for five weeks. He [Frankel] thought there would be no great objection to my continuing to work for two or three hours each morning. After that I would be entirely at your disposal."

18. From an interview with the author. For a description of Doris Scheldt, see SB, *Humboldt's Gift*, p. 111; also pp. 254–55.

19. Returning home to Chicago in the summer of 1970 after her junior year at

Columbia, she got "a really interesting job" for the summer at the periodical *Urban Crisis Monitor* (the offices were located in the basement of the Shoreland Hotel, once owned by Maury and Marge). She transferred to the University of Chicago for her senior year partly to continue working at the *Monitor.*

20. A second exception is suggested by James Atlas in *The Shadow in the Garden: A Biographer's Tale* (New York: Pantheon, 2017), pp. 335–40. It concerns Roberta ("Bobby") Markels (1926–2014), a voluminous correspondent of SB's for nearly fifty years, though one who seems never to have figured in his letters to other correspondents or in interviews, either with him or his friends. She is mentioned once in *To Fame and Fortune* (p. 578) and Benjamin Taylor prints two letters to her in *Letters*, pp. 373, 434. Markels contacted SB in 1956 when she lived in Evanston and was working on a novel. They had a brief affair in the early 1960s and kept in touch after she moved to California later in the decade. In California, Markels wrote a column in the local paper titled "Babbling with Bubbela," a title no less apt for her letters to SB. Many of these letters are in the Regenstein. They are very long and almost wholly self-involved. SB, however, was encouraging about Markels's writing. In 2014, the year she died, Atlas obtained a manuscript of hers which he describes as "a kind of epistolary memoir—letters back and forth interspersed with commentary." This manuscript, he claims, offers "a more vivid portrait of Bellow than any I had ever read" and describes a warm and lasting friendship. SB is remembered by Markels as "patient, generous, and kind."

21. Wasserman, *Handsome Is*, p. 23. See Volkening to SB, 17 June 1969: "It's a slow and painful process, this trying to become used to being alone, after forty-three years of not being. . . . Thanks for your having been so very thoughtful of me during all of the four terrible months since Natalie first went to the hospital."

22. Malamud's letter was accompanied by a newspaper clipping headlined "Saul Bellow Wins Book Award," below which Malamud's photo appears with the caption "SAUL BELLOW." After praising *Sammler* in the letter, Malamud adds: "My only regret—from what I see in the newspapers—is that you're losing your looks."

23. Wasserman, *Handsome Is*, p. 23.

24. Ibid., p. 6.

25. Ibid., pp. 4, 6.

26. Ibid., pp. 15, 16.

27. Ibid., p. 85.

28. Ibid., pp. 13, 14.

29. Ibid., pp. 10–11.

30. Ibid., pp. 25–26.

31. That cold and discomfort drove SB from the house, a view taken from the letters, is repeated in Victoria Glendinning, *Leonard Woolf: A Biography* (New York: Simon & Schuster, 2001), p. 437; and Joseph Epstein in "The Long, Unhappy Life of Saul Bellow," a review of Taylor, ed., *Letters*, in *New Criterion*, December 2010.

32. Gabriel Josipivici, "Bellow and Herzog," *Encounter*, vol. 37, no. 5 (1971), later a chapter in Josipovici's first critical work, *The World and the Book: A Study of Modern Fiction* (London: Macmillan, 1971).

33. On 9 December 1970, Best wrote to SB that he "supposed" Kazin would make a good editor, though "I don't like the grudging note in his admiration. . . . On the other hand, at lunch with Trilling the other day, I learned of his extreme enthusiasm, especially for MR. SAMMLER. . . . It was touching to hear him say that he had abandoned, at least for now, a novel he had been talking about for years, because you had done so perfectly what he had wanted to do."

34. Atlas, *Biography*, p. 402.

35. Greg Bellow, *Saul Bellow's Heart: A Son's Memoir* (London and New York: Bloomsbury, 2013), p. 135.

36. Ruth Miller, *Saul Bellow: A Biography of the Imagination* (New York: St. Martin's Press, 1991), pp. 197–98.

37. Gendlin thinks Ruth Miller's account of the *M*A*S*H* episode "unfair," but it is possible to see the two versions as compatible. SB returns to the hotel in a foul mood, compounded by Gendlin's not being there. She returns full of praise for the movie and insists he must see it, an insistence that further infuriates him. He, in turn, insists that she see it again, with him. In no mood to approve what he sees, he finds the film debased and debasing.

38. Reprinted in SB, *There Is Simply Too Much to Think About: Collected Nonfiction*, ed. Benjamin Taylor (New York and London: Viking Penguin, 2016).

39. In David Mikics, email to the author, 6 July 2017, commenting on this exchange: "But there is a real argument here between SB and Trilling—not that it justifies SB's misprision, but it's there. Trilling and Benjamin think in terms of eras: modernity has put the kibosh on storytelling power. SB will have nothing of this waste-land theory (as he sees it). Technology is not the culprit, for SB; his reason for disliking movies was probably the insistence that movies are the twentieth-century art form, and that novels are passé."

40. Bellow's lecture was to be reprinted in a volume of Doubleday Lectures entitled *The Frontiers of Knowledge* (1975), and Edith Tarcov may have forwarded the earlier Trilling letter because of her involvement with the printing of the lecture in book form.

41. This exchange was related immediately after it happened in an undated letter from Karyl Roosevelt to James Salter. For Atlas on the end of SB's affair with Fran Gendlin, see *Biography*, p. 422.

42. Wasserman, *Handsome Is*, pp. 30, 32.

43. Ibid.

44. Ibid., p. 34.

45. Ibid., p. 36.

46. Ibid., pp. 38, 39.

47. See chapter 2 for an account of this episode, drawn from Mark Harris, *Saul Bellow, Drumlin Woodchuck* (Athens: University of Georgia Press, 1980), p. 42.

48. Edgard Pillet (1912–1996), a French artist, designed Casa Alison, as well as several neighboring houses. The "Pillet tower," where SB and Alexandra stayed, was one of those houses.

49. Email to the author, 23 September 2014.

50. Greg Bellow, *Saul Bellow's Heart*, p. 134.

51. From p. 3 of an English translation given to me by Alexandra Bellow of "Una vida matemática" ("A Mathematical Life"), originally published in *La Gaceta de la Real Sociedad Matemática Española*, vol. 5, no.1 (January–April 2002), pp. 62–71, from a talk given at the Royal Academy of Sciences, Madrid, Spain, in September 2001, at the festive inauguration of the project "Estimulo del Talento Matemático" for the year 2001–2.

52. Ibid., p. 2.

53. Ibid., p. 3. See also Alexandra Bellow, "Asclepius Versus Hades in Romania: Some Facts About My Father," pp. 15–19, for the details of her mother's "disgrace" (for arranging aid from the United States) and subsequent removal from her post as minister of health in 1948. These page numbers are from an English translation given to me by Alexandra Bellow of her article, which appeared in Romanian, in two separate installments of *Revista*, vol. 22, no. 755 (24–30 August 2004) and vol. 22, no. 756 (31 August–6 September 2004): "I can still recall the disbelief on my mother's face when, in a special New Year issue of *Scanteia*, the official party newspaper, she read a fulminating article against the 'warmongering imperialist circles and their lackeys' who were trying to enslave people economically and

politically through their infamous 'Marshall Plan'" (p. 18). Shortly after reading the article, Alexandra's mother was removed from her post and "marginalized" by "an official campaign." Later on, in her work as a child psychiatrist, she was hounded by the authorities. In 1953, "my mother was accused of: 'cosmopolitanism,' of 'stooping obsequiously before the decadent imperialist ideology and pseudo-science' (such accusations in those days were tantamount to treason), of introducing and promoting in child psychiatry 'obscurantist tendencies, such as of Freudian type, which degrade man and at the same time serve . . . as a diversion . . . to distract the attention of the masses from the class struggle'" (p. 19). Alexandra's mother lost her job and her husband's pension, and she and Alexandra were obliged to share their apartment with another couple. At the time, Alexandra was in her last year of high school.

54. Alexandra Bellow, "A Mathematical Life," p. 4.

55. According to SB's friend Walter Pozen, Alexandra "just didn't understand" SB's writing: "'Why is he so good?'" To her mother, she "was clearly an equal [to SB], if not more so"; the mother thought of him as "a trophy husband."

56. Alexandra Bellow, "A Mathematical Life," p. 7.

57. Atlas, *Biography*, p. 423.

58. Alexandra Bellow, "A Mathematical Life," p. 8.

59. And later in *The Dean's December:* "He had got into the habit of attempting whatever Minna needed. He no longer asked whether this suited him, whether he was risking his dignity by pushing a cart in the supermarket, reading recipes, peeling potatoes" (p. 258).

60. Corde's bad behavior, principally with women, is alluded to by others in *The Dean's December*. According to Corde, "It was because people said such things about the wicked Dean that [Minna] was attracted to him. She wanted to marry a wickedly experienced but faithful man, a reformed SOB, a chastened chaser, now a gentle husband; and she got what she wanted" (p. 260).

61. A "refusenik" was a person, usually a Jew, who was denied permission to emigrate by the Soviet authorities.

62. See SB to George McGovern, 20 January 1971: "Dear Senator McGovern, I heartily endorse your candidacy for the office of President and shall do everything possible to help. We badly need you. I am convinced of that and trust that the voters will agree." McGovern replied on 19 April, saying he was "honored that you will be with me in the challenging months ahead."

63. SB, *To Jerusalem and Back*, p. 129. The acronym "PEN" stands for "Poets, Playwrights, Essayists, Novelists."

64. Ibid., p. 9. In addition to alluding to his letter of 15 October 1973 to *Le Monde*, SB devotes several pages at the beginning of *To Jerusalem and Back* to *Le Monde*'s pro-Arab bias: "It supports terrorists. It is friendlier to Amin than to Rabin. A recent review of the autobiography of a fedayeen speaks of the Israelis as colonialists. On July 3, 1976, before Israel had freed the hostages at Entebbe, the paper observed with some satisfaction that Amin, 'the disquieting Marshal,' maligned by everyone, had now become the support and the hope of his foolish detractors. *Le Monde* gloated over this reversal" (p. 9).

65. SB frequently took advantage of opportunities to visit Florida, as in November 1974, when he accepted an invitation from Mel Tumin to attend the Palm Court Symposium, sponsored by ITT. SB was on a panel entitled "Human Nature and the Control of Human Destiny," with the scientist James Watson, codiscoverer of the structure of DNA, and the sociologist Gunnar Myrdal. "Just tell them about Kierkegaard and Spinoza, à la Sammler," Tumin wrote to SB on 31 May: "we should have a lovely time." For his contribution, SB was paid twenty-five hundred dollars plus travel expenses and was free to leave the symposium immediately after

the panel. In January 1976, he flew to Miami to accept the S. Y. Agnon Gold Medal for Literary Achievement from the American Friends of the Hebrew University, and spent several days with Maury. In November, he agreed to give a public reading at Southern Methodist University in Dallas at the invitation of Pat Covici's son, Pascal Covici, Jr., chair of the English Department, visiting Miami first to discuss property deals with Maury.

66. "My relations with you," SB writes on 27 June 1973 to Charles Strauss, of the accountants Laventhol, Krekstein Horwath and Horwath, "have always been cordial and I regret bringing them to an end. But business, as people always tell me, is business."

67. Greg Bellow, *Saul Bellow's Heart*, p. 135.

68. Ibid., p. 136.

69. In his first year at Dalton, according to Sasha, Adam was so unhappy he suggested that he needed a psychiatrist. Sasha, too, went to see this psychiatrist, and SB "came in when requested . . . He really resisted this and did not like the psychiatrist at all. But it was clearly proving enormously helpful to Adam" (Sondra "Sasha" Bellow, "What's in a Name?," p. 118).

70. Ibid., p. 120.

5. DISTRACTION/DIVORCE/ANTHROPOSOPHY

1. From SB, "Remarks," 55th Annual Board of Trustees' Dinner for the Faculty, 8 January 1975, reprinted as "A World Too Much with Us," *Critical Inquiry*, vol. 2, no. 1 (Autumn 1975). See Regenstein for both the original typsescript and printed galleys of the "Remarks."

2. SB, *To Jerusalem and Back*, p. 31; in addition, see "An Interview with Myself," *New Review*, vol. 2, no. 18 (1975), printed also in *Ontario Review*, vol. 4 (1975), and in *IAAU*, pp. 80–87.

3. SB, *To Jerusalem and Back*, p. 31.

4. Ibid., p. 32.

5. Ibid., p. 33.

6. For an early airing of this theme, see SB, "Distractions of a Fiction Writer," opening essay in *The Living Novel: A Symposium*, ed. Granville Hicks (New York: Macmillan, 1957), discussed in chapter 12 of *To Fame and Fortune*, pp. 531–32.

7. SB, "Nobel Lecture," *IAAU*, pp. 92–93.

8. SB, "An Interview with Myself," in *IAAU*, p. 82.

9. "I have become a sort of public man," SB later complained to Nathan Gould, in a letter of 4 August 1982: "I thought, in my adolescent way, that I would write good books (as writing and books were understood in the Thirties) and would have been happy in the middle ranks of my trade. It would have made me wretched to be overlooked, but I wasn't at all prepared for so much notice, and I haven't been good at managing 'celebrity.' . . . I can't do the many things I'm asked to do, answer the huge volume of mail, keep up with books and manuscripts and at the same time write such books as I want and need to write."

10. Irving Howe, "People on the Edge of History—Saul Bellow's Vivid Report on Israel," *New York Times Book Review*, 16 October 1976. An abbreviated version of the book had appeared on 12 and 19 July in *The New Yorker*.

11. He did not accept. SB had been seriously considered for the Nobel Prize in 1975. On 25 October 1975, Harriet Wasserman wrote to his secretary, Esther Corbin, to express her disappointment: "I had a call from Sweden saying that the panel could not decide between Bellow and Graham Greene and so put off the English-language for another year." SB was invited to give the Jefferson Lectures in the Humanities on 30 May 1977 (in Washington, D.C.) and on 1 April (in Chi-

cago, in the Gold Coast Room at the Drake Hotel). The lectures were sponsored by the National Endowment for the Humanities and brought a ten-thousand-dollar honorarium. These lectures had been given since 1972 (for a list of previous speakers, see *To Fame and Fortune*, p. 685n5). SB requested that the following guests be invited to the lecture in Washington and the dinner afterward: Mr. and Mrs. Morris Janowitz, Mr. and Mrs. Wayne Booth, Richard Stern, Harriet Wasserman, Edward Shils, Mr. and Mrs. Victor Turner, Mr. and Mrs. John U. Nef, Dr. Sanda Loga (a Romanian refugee, and friend of Alexandra's), Adam Bellow, Katharine Graham, and Joseph Alsop. As for other honors and awards: The American Academy of the Arts Gold Medal for the Novel, awarded once every six years, was bestowed in March 1977; the National Arts Club Medal of Honor for Literature was awarded in February 1978 (introduced by speeches from Bernard Malamud and John Cheever); and the Emerson-Thoreau Medal was also awarded in 1977, by the American Academy of Arts and Sciences (the prize was established in 1958, and the previous recipient was Robert Penn Warren). In addition to these major awards: in January 1976, SB was awarded the S. Y. Agnon Gold Medal for Literary Achievement, by the American Friends of the Hebrew University of Jerusalem; in March 1976, he received the Merit Award from the Decalogue Society of Lawyers; in April 1976, he was appointed to the Advisory Council of the Department of Comparative Literature at Princeton (the lengthy correspondence with its chair, the classicist Robert Fagles, suggests SB was almost never free to do any advising); in May 1976, he was awarded a doctorate of letters from the University of Dublin (using the occasion to visit David Grene on his farm in County Cavan); in October 1976, he was presented with the Distinguished Service Award for *Humboldt's Gift* from the Society of Midlands Authors; in November 1976, he received the America's Democratic Legacy Award from the Anti-Defamation League, the league's highest honor; in January 1977, he was made an honorary member of the Covenant Club (his brother Maury's club) and was named Chicagoan of the Year by the Chicago Press Association; and in February 1977, he was made an honorary doctor of letters by the University of Illinois at Chicago Circle. According to Atlas, *Biography*, p. 476, "Now that he was a Nobel Prize winner, the English Department [at the University of Chicago] had grudgingly invited him to become a member, though he never attended a department meeting."

12. W. J. Weatherby profile, "Saul Bellow," *Guardian*, 10 November 1976.

13. Walter Clemons, with Chris Harper in Chicago, "Bellow the Word King," *Newsweek*, 1 November 1976.

14. Timothy McNulty, "Saul Bellow: 'Child in Me Is Delighted,'" *Chicago Tribune*, 22 October 1976.

15. "A Laureate for Saul Bellow," *Time*, 1 November 1976.

16. McNulty, "'Child in Me Is Delighted.'"

17. Quoted in Atlas, *Biography*, p. 457; Richard Stern also heard SB say to Greg, "You're a good son, I love you."

18. "Bellow's 'Betters' Are Glad He Won," *Chicago Daily News*, 22 October 1976. Constance Davis, later women's news editor of the Elyria *Chronicle-Telegram*, won first prize in the 1936 contest; Mary Zimmer, who went on to work in advertising, won second prize.

19. Manea, "Conversation," p. 39.

20. Harriet Wasserman, *Handsome Is: Adventures with Saul Bellow* (New York: Fromm International, 1997), p. 54.

21. SB to Baron Stig Ramel, 26 November 1976.

22. Manea, "Conversation," p. 36.

23. Greg Bellow, *Saul Bellow's Heart: A Son's Memoir* (London and New York: Bloomsbury, 2013), p. 137. At the banquet following the ceremony, Daniel joined

in the toasts and got tipsy. In the lobby of the hotel, he played "fall down" with the children of Baruch S. Blumberg, co-winner of the prize for medicine, and was reprimanded by hotel staff (Wasserman, *Handsome Is*, p. 64).

24. Morton Narrowe, *En tretvinnad trad: Amerikan Jude Svensk* (Stockholm: Albert Bonniers Forlag, 2005), p. 215, trans. for this book by Marion Helfer Wajngot.

25. According to SB, in Manea, "Conversation," p. 36, Sam "just accepted the charge. It was embarrassing." As Joel Bellows puts it, "The story in the family is that Sam took the fall." "They're all holier than [thou]," he explains, but the general feeling was "It's a victimless crime. If God didn't want them shorn [the patients in the nursing home] he wouldn't have made them sheep." Joel believes Sam was hurt badly, "but he did the right thing." Did he know what was going on? "Yeah." Neither he nor Maury was a crook, but "did they pay every last penny? No."

26. SB, quoted in Manea, "Conversation," p. 36.

27. Greg was less impressed than Alexandra with the Swedish royals. "The recently crowned queen of Sweden, a former German beauty queen, far outshone the king, who for a moment stood alone during the reception. I felt a rough pull, was dragged over to His Highness, and was told to make conversation. Later, Count Something-or-other, the man who had grabbed me, apologized and explained that it was not seemly for the king to have no one with whom to speak" (*Saul Bellow's Heart*, p. 139).

28. Atlas, *Biography*, pp. 461–62.

29. Manea, "Conversation," p. 36.

30. Ibid., p. 37.

31. Atlas, *Biography*, p. 460.

32. Wasserman, *Handsome Is*, pp. 67–68.

33. Greg Bellow, *Saul Bellow's Heart*, p. 138. In James Atlas, *The Shadow in the Garden: A Biographer's Tale* (New York: Pantheon, 2017), p. 332, Greg recalls how uncomfortable he was during the Nobel festivities: "I had a bad time in Stockholm, when Bellow won the Nobel. My feeling was, 'Fuck that. I'm not going to put up with that shit.'"

34. Manea, "Conversation," pp. 36–37.

35. These quotations come from Ingemar Lindahl, "A Day with the Nobellows," his translation of an article he published in what he described, in an email of 27 March 2015 to the author, as "A now defunct [Swedish] magazine, *ARK*, no. 2, March 1977."

36. Wasserman, *Handsome Is*, p. 61.

37. Ibid., pp. 65, 66–67.

38. Ibid., p. 45.

39. Timothy McNulty, "Saul Bellow: 'Child in Me Is Delighted.'"

40. Martha Fay, "A Talk with Saul Bellow," *Book-of-the-Month Club News*, August 1975.

41. John Aldridge, "Saul Bellow at Sixty: A Turn to the Mystical," *Saturday Review*, 6 September 1975.

42. Alfred Kazin entry of 23 July 1975, in *Alfred Kazin's Journals*, ed. Richard M. Cook (New Haven: Yale University Press, 2012), p. 435.

43. In the Spring 1978 issue of *Dissent*, the Israeli historian Shlomo Avineri published an article entitled "A Meeting with Saul Bellow" in which he took strenuous objection to SB's account in *To Jerusalem and Back* of a meeting they had at the Hebrew University of Jerusalem on November 10, 1975. In that meeting, according to Avineri, SB pressed him on "the aggressive designs of the Soviet Union against Israel." Avineri's position was that Soviet aggression "reinforces

Arab hostility" but "is not the source of the conflict." The source of the conflict is "the stubborn position of the Arab countries, which refused to recognize the right of Israel to exist as a sovereign Jewish state." In *To Jerusalem and Back*, p. 43, SB presents Avineri as complacent about Soviet influence, not only in the Middle East but in Eastern Europe, where "life has immensely improved." In SB's opinion, this misguided optimism is characteristic: "Israel's utter dependency upon the United States leads Israeli intellectuals to hunt for signs of hope in the Communist world." Avineri complained that this account of his views was completely distorted, "misconstrues the whole tenor of our meeting," being the work of a novelist rather than a researcher. For the novelist, "reality is like clay in the hands of the potter; he can expand or contract it as he sees fit."

44. See Shils to SB, 12 February 1976: "While it must be admitted that Israel did less than it should have done to indemnify and help settle those who elected to leave their homes and property and to flee from what became Israel, the Arab states deliberately—and where not deliberately, through incompetence—made the Gaza strip into a running sore."

45. Isabella Fey, "Strategic Withdrawal," *Jerusalem Post*, 16 November 1976.

46. Noam Chomsky, "Bellow's Israel," *New York Arts Journal*, Spring 1977, reprinted as "Bellow, *To Jerusalem and Back*," in Chomsky, *Towards a New Cold War: Essays on the Current Crisis and How We Got There* (New York: Pantheon, 1982), pp. 299–307.

47. Quoted in Atlas, *Biography*, p. 369.

48. These figures come from court records, *Bellow v. Bellow*, no. 61454. On 14 July 1974, Susan successfully petitioned that the original 1968 divorce settlement be set aside; on 25 July 1974, SB appealed. Two years later, on 14 July 1976, SB's appeal of this judgment was rejected. The figures I have cited come from p. 3 of *Bellow v. Bellow*, no. 61454, the 14 July 1976 rejection, delivered by Mr. Justice Dieringer. There are differences between the figures listed here and the figures listed in chapter 1, which come from Atlas, *Biography*, pp. 368–69, and derive from tax records and court records, as well as from the files of Marshall Holleb and Miles Beermann. I have let the discrepancy stand because, throughout the divorce papers, reported income is calculated differently. The figures quoted here are also reported in Edward I. Stein, "Today's Institute Report on Family Law: Divorce/ Sec. 72 of the Civil Practice Act," *Daily Law Bulletin*, 16 August 1976.

49. The quotation from Susan Bellow is from an undated typescript entitled "Mosby's Memoirs and the Manuscript," presumably intended for her lawyers. It is among divorce papers given me by Daniel Bellow to be deposited in the Regenstein among the SB Papers.

50. SB to Barry Freeman, one of his lawyers, 14 September 1973.

51. Atlas, *Biography*, p. 381.

52. Henry L. Mason, III, to SB, 9 November 1982.

53. Michael Zielenzigar, "Saul Bellow Sentenced to Jail in Alimony Hassle," *Chicago Sun-Times*, 20 October 1977; Charles Mount, "Bellow Appeals Jail Term, Posts Bond in Alimony Fight," *Chicago Tribune*, 20 October 1977.

54. Atlas, *Biography*, p. 367.

55. Ibid., p. 494.

56. Susan Bellow to Miles Beerman, 29 June 1982. In a letter of 31 January 1983 to her accountant, Susan was certain "there is an old-fashioned Chicago answer to your puzzlement as to how my lawyers received $125,000 in fees, $33,999+ in interest and that I got a 'settlement' of $8,000 taxable to me."

57. Atlas, *Biography*, p. 381.

58. The undated document from Susan is among the divorce papers given to me by Daniel Bellow, to be deposited among the Saul Bellow Papers at the Regen-

stein. Susan, too, could be late with or reluctant to write checks, as correspondence with her lawyers indicates. She, however, had nothing like Bellow's resources. See Burton Joseph, of Lipnick, Barsy and Joseph, to Susan Bellow, 28 January 1972.

59. Susan Bellow to Dr. Sandor Abend, 7 May 1979.

60. In a letter of 27 June 1996 to Andrew Wylie, Daniel explained his having to testify and what happened after he did:

> My father had sued for my custody, on the grounds that my mother was allowing me to wander the streets at all hours. This was not strictly true. On the stand, under cross examination by my father's lawyer, I said I would rather move to New York with my mom, and so we did, the evidence against her being weak and the judge being unwilling to rule against me.
>
> In New York, on the old upper West Side of kosher butchers and bodegas and movie six-plexes, I realized that my mother, upon whom I had always relied, had no better grip on things than I did. As she struggled in a dead-end city job, I had trouble in school. . . . I skipped a lot of class, wandering the streets and watching people, scared to death half the time.

61. SB was convinced Daniel did not need further psychiatric care. In a letter of February 9, 1979, to Dr. Sandor Abend, the psychiatrist who was to testify as to whether Daniel needed more therapy, Bellow insisted, "I have never refused Daniel anything that might help him. The prospect of more psychiatry, however, does not cheer me. Daniel has seen some eight or ten psychiatrists over the years, and I am not at all sure that they were able to do much for him. . . . When Daniel's last therapist died, Susan consulted five child psychiatrists in Chicago. Each of them opined that Daniel was not ready to resume treatment."

62. Charlie's condition recalls Wordsworth in the preface to *Lyrical Ballads*, on the age's "craving for extraordinary incident . . . this degrading thirst after outrageous stimulation."

63. The Coleridge quotation is from "The Eolian Harp" (1795): "Oh! The one life within us and abroad, / Which meets all motion and becomes its soul, / A light in sound, a sound-like power in light, / Rhythm in all thought, and joyance everywhere." Barfield's book is *What Coleridge Thought* (1971).

64. SB to Owen Barfield, 25 February 1976. Steiner identified six essential exercises, one for the cultivation of objectivity; one for the cultivation of will; one for the control of feeling, in which one practiced expressing a quiet or contained emotion; one for the cultivation of positivity; one for the cultivation of open-mindedness (the how in this case is not specified); and one for harmony, which involves practicing the other five exercises in various combinations to find a balance between them. Other Steinerian exercises involve drawing the same landscape or plant over a year, and reviewing the day's events in one's mind, at night going backward in sequence, an exercise Bellow especially valued and taught to his sons and to various wives and girlfriends. As mentioned in the previous chapter, Fran Gendlin remembers performing Steinerian memory exercises with SB in the early 1970s. For more on the exercises see http://steinerbooks.org/research/archive/outline_of_esoteric_science/outline_of_esoteric_science.pdf.

65. In a letter of 2 July 1976 to Howard Nemerov, SB suggests that it was Barfield who brought him to Steiner: "I admire Barfield and I owe him a great deal. . . . Yes, he did get me to read Steiner. I'm still at it."

66. Owen Barfield, *Saving the Appearances* (London: Faber and Faber, 1957), p. 65.

67. The G. B. Tennyson quotation comes from *Owen Barfield: Man and Meaning*, a documentary he and David Lavey co-wrote and produced in 1996. It was

directed and edited by David Levin and is available via the Owen Barfield Web site at http://davidlavery.net/barfield/.

68. Accessible but ineffable, gestured at in vague strivings, as in Wordsworth's "a presence," "a motion and a spirit," "a sense sublime," from "Lines Composed a Few Miles Above Tintern Abbey" (1798).

69. William Blake, *Jerusalem: The Emanation of the Giant Albion* (1804–20), plate 30, ll. 20–21.

70. These are the concluding words of William Blake, *A Vision of the Last Judgement* (1810), a prose description of an 1808 painting of the same name exhibited by Blake in 1810. SB's quote about the relation of looks to character come from an interview he gave in 1987 to Sigmund Koch, a University Professor (as SB would become) at Boston University. See "Abbreviations Used in the Notes" for further details of the interview.

71. Like Peter Demay, however, Professor Scheldt worked in science and technology, having been "a physicist at the old Armour Institute, an executive of IBM, a NASA consultant who improved the metal used in space ships" (p. 255).

72. These details about Peter Demay (not Lemay, as in earlier biographies) come from interviews with William Hunt as well as Hunt's emails to the author, 12, 14 July, 3, 11 August, and 16 September 2010. I have also benefited from a typescript Hunt sent me of a talk he gave on 18 September 2009 ("Talk Given at Rudolf Steiner Library") about Bellow and anthroposophy. The library in question was the Rudolf Steiner Library in Ghent, New York.

73. Hunt's poems have been published in *Poetry*, *The New Yorker*, *Partisan Review*, *New American Writing*, and *The Nation*. In 1974, he received the Langston Hughes Memorial Award from *Poetry* magazine; in 1967, he received a fellowship from the National Endowment for the Humanities. Among the places he has taught creative writing are Loyola University in Chicago, Northwestern University, and the University of Illinois.

74. Hunt says he was drawn to Steiner and anthroposophy for the same reasons Bellow was. Both were distressed "by the direction the country seemed hell-bent on pursuing," a direction depicted in Bellow's novels *Mr. Sammler's Planet* and *The Dean's December*. As Hunt puts it in his "Talk Given at Rudolf Steiner Library," on reflection not altogether tactfully, "his [SB's] interest and mine in Steiner and Anthroposophy was like the behavior of shipwreck victims bobbing in the water and reaching out for any bits of floating debris to hold them afloat" (p. 3).

75. Also in private conversations. As Hunt recalled, in an email to the author, 12 July 2015: "He went nearly over the edge with anger the few times I said anything about his writing. So we mostly talked about Steiner, about Chicago politics, and about other matters." See also SB to Herman Kogan, 22 August 1976: "You know how it is—it gives me the willies to face cultural gatherings in Chicago."

76. According to Hunt in an interview: "Peter said that while he was unconscious from the heart attack he experienced a specific joy: 'I felt that I was about to learn all that I ever wanted to know.' But then someone began pounding on his chest to get the heart started up again. Peter said, 'So then I regained consciousness—I was never so disappointed in all my life.'"

77. Owen Barfield, *Unancestral Voice* (London: Faber and Faber, 1965), p. 163. Henceforth cited within the text by page numbers.

78. See Edward Mendelson, "The Obedient Bellow," *New York Review of Books*, 28 April 2011 (a review of Benjamin Taylor, ed., *Saul Bellow: Letters*). The entirety of the SB-Barfield correspondence is reprinted and discussed in Simon Blaxland-de-Lange, *Romanticism Come of Age: A Biography of Owen Barfield* (Forest Row: Temple Lodge, 2006), pp. 49–66.

79. Like some of Barfield's other books, including *Saving the Appearances*, *Worlds Apart* takes the form of a fictional dialogue, in this case between a physicist, a biologist, a psychiatrist, a lawyer-philologist, a linguistic analyst, a theologian, a retired Waldolf schoolteacher, and a young man employed at a rocket-research station. During a period of three days, the characters discuss and debate spiritual issues.

80. Wayne Booth, *The Vocation of a Teacher: Rhetorical Occasions, 1967–1988* (Chicago: University of Chicago Press, 1988), p. 256.

81. The title of the review was "East, West, and Saul Bellow." *Towards* magazine was published periodically from 1977 to 1989 by Clifford Monks, an English-born Waldorf educator living in California. Its aim was "to explore and make better known the work of Owen Barfield, Samuel Taylor Coleridge, Wolfgang Von Goethe, Rudolf Steiner and related authors" (see http://davidlavery.net/barfield/Barfield_Resources/Towards/Towards.html).

82. See Blaxland-de-Lange, *Romanticism Come of Age*, p. 62, which paraphrases this objection. As Barfield saw it, SB preferred "to regard the modern disintegration of the individual human spirit as an incentive to study the disintegration of society," as opposed to the other way around, "which would by implication be Barfield's way."

83. Ibid., p. 65.

84. Manea, "Conversation," p. 43. See also SB to M. Thomas (unidentified), 6 March 1985: "I have never been able to accept the idea of random collisions and am revolted by the thought that our existence is accounted for by probability theory. It makes creation feel so boring. But natural scientists are in love with this hypothesis. Their preference may have some connection with the vulgar origins of most of them. My origins are probably as vulgar as theirs, but my aspirations are as lofty as can be."

85. Manea, "Conversation," p. 18.

86. There are other instances of Bellow's caution or reservation. In 1983, at the age of sixty-eight, Bellow was invited to address a seminar on Steiner at the Goethe Institute in Chicago. The seminar was also to be addressed by Hagen Biesantz, a member of the Vorstand at the Goetheanum in Dornach (Bellow had met Biesantz on a second visit to Dornach, in April 1977). One of the organizers of the seminar was Traute Lafrenz Page, head of the Esperanza School and a prominent Chicago anthroposophist (also, in the late 1930s, a member of the White Rose, twice imprisoned by the Gestapo for anti-Hitler activities). In declining the invitation to speak, Bellow confessed to Page, who was only four years his junior, "that he was too old to get his head around the subject of Steiner sufficiently to speak about him in public." Hunt, the source of this anecdote, partly connects Bellow's withdrawal from Steiner and anthroposophy to an increasing interest in Judaism and in Jewish mysticism, with a concomitant distrust, perhaps unconscious, of the Christian element in Steiner's and Barfield's thinking, their belief in Christ's incarnation as a key moment in human evolution, not only redeeming the Fall but unifying and inspiring all religions. Support for Hunt's view comes from SB's letter of 23 July 1990 to the anthroposophist Rudi Lissau: "One remark in your letter is certainly straight to target. I have always had peculiarly Jewish difficulties with Christianity in all its forms. . . . I have read much and thought much about the Jewish side of life during two Christian millennia, about being one of those on whom so much evil has been cast and I can't help but trace some of this evil back to the Gospels themselves. On this question none of the Steiner literature has satisfied me."

Another anecdote from Hunt comes from near the end of SB's life. Hunt had told him of a meeting he had had with James Atlas in which Atlas referred to SB's "anthroposophic episode." "Bellow laughed heartily at that. He repeated the word 'episode' and laughed more." Yet, in one sense, Atlas was right. "Are you an anthroposophist?" Hunt heard an interviewer ask Bellow in the early 1980s. "The tone of the question sounded a bit like the McCarthy era question 'Are you or have you ever been a Communist?'" Bellow's answer was "I'm trying to become one" (from Hunt's "Talk Given at Rudolf Steiner Library," p. 2). In 1985, Ruth Miller asked Bellow if Steiner and Barfield "had been of much use to him during those years of turmoil [from 1976 to 1982, between *Humboldt's Gift* and *The Dean's December*]. Bellow replied no. He was less involved in anthroposophy since the friend with whom he had long discussions died"—Peter Demay, who died in 1983 (*Saul Bellow: A Biography of the Imagination*, p. 231).

6. THE "CHICAGO BOOK" AND *THE DEAN'S DECEMBER*

1. SB, *It All Adds Up: From the Dim Past to the Uncertain Future: A Nonfiction Collection* (New York: Viking Penguin, 1994), p. 117 (henceforth cited as SB, *IAAU*).

2. Rosenberg's essay and SB's reaction to it are discussed in chapter 7 of *To Fame and Fortune*, pp. 273–74.

3. In the first of SB's two Tanner Lectures, delivered in Oxford in May 1981, at Brasenose College, he quotes Wyndham Lewis in *America and Cosmic Man* (1949). The cultural monuments of big American cities, Lewis writes, include "big universities, theaters, art schools, and a Symphony Orchestra—the latter *de rigueur*. There are large libraries, usually very good museums. . . . But all this immense apparatus of culture, of learning and taste, is a discreet screen to cover the void. . . . And, of course, such things are there to advertise the city, not to promote letters, fine arts and science" (*The Tanner Lectures on Human Values*, ed. Sterling M. McMurrin [Salt Lake City: University of Utah Press, 1982], pp. 178–79).

4. See Paul Carroll, "Bellow's Culture Shock," *Chicago*, September 1977, the source of all subsequent quotes from Carroll.

5. The names of the signatories are not given in the *Maroon*, nor has the paper any record of them.

6. I could find no such claim in the published version of the lecture in *IAAU*.

7. For discussion of "Acatla," see chapter 6 of *To Fame and Fortune*, pp. 231–32; for discussion of "The Very Dark Trees," see the same chapter, pp. 222–23, 238–42.

8. Bruno Bettelheim and Morris Janowitz, *Social Change and Prejudice* (New York: Free Press of Glencoe, 1964), an updating of their 1950 collaboration, *The Dynamics of Prejudice*.

9. Richard Biernacki, "Faculty S. Africa Reaction Mixed: Bellow Takes Human Rights Stand," *Chicago Maroon*, 4 April 1978.

10. For a detailed account of the university's policies concerning Woodlawn, which between 1950 and 1960 changed from 86 percent white to 86 percent black, see John Hall Fish, *Black Power/White Control: The Struggle of the Woodlawn Organization in Chicago* (Princeton, NJ: Princeton University Press, 1973), p. 15: "The University, in danger of being engulfed by a blighted and black neighborhood, spearheaded a major renewal and rehabilitation effort as the only alternative to moving from the area. The goal of the renewal program was to stop the cycle of deterioration and to develop a stable, integrated, middle- and upper-income neighborhood which would be compatible with the style and goals of an academic institution." In 1960, as part of this effort, the university proposed to expand its campus to the south, clearing a one-block-deep and one-mile-wide section of Woodlawn. The university already owned 60 percent of the land it hoped to develop, and most of the buildings to be cleared, it argued, could be termed "blighted" or "slum" properties.

11. In January 1972, perhaps to counter such accusations, the university gave three hundred thousand dollars to the Black Culture Center "to improve black social life," prompting the *Maroon* to ask "why blacks should have a social life when no one else does" (according to the timeline accompanying Mark Wallach, "The University: Notes on the 70s," *Chicago Maroon*, 22 January 1980).

12. SB often worked on several manuscripts at once. In the period 1977–82, in addition to the "Chicago Book" and its offshoots, he was also at work on "Far Out," an unpublished novel that survives in a typescript of a hundred pages. These pages were sent by Harriet Wasserman to Harvey Ginsburg of Harper & Row, the novel's contracted publisher. "Far Out" is set in the 1950s and is discussed most fully in *To Fame and Fortune*, chapter 6, pp. 215–16, and chapter 10, pp. 395–97.

13. Interview with William Kennedy, "If Saul Bellow Doesn't Have a True Word to Say, He Keeps His Mouth Shut," *Esquire*, February 1982. A fuller typescript of this interview can be found among the SB Papers in the Regenstein. The interview was conducted in the summer of 1981 but not printed until February 1982, the month when *The Dean's December* was published.

14. Each of these topics offers examples of corruption, incompetence, or malfeasance. Michael Bilandic lost the mayorship in part because of the disastrous job the city did in cleaning up two terrible snowstorms before the election. SB saved a Mike Royko column from the *Chicago Daily News* that discussed, with knowing Chicago irony, what went wrong. Peter Schivarelli, who was in charge of the city's Snow Command, had been passed over by Bilandic, in favor of a comparably "connected" figure from Buffalo. "If I were one of Schivarelli's many Chicago mob friends," Royko wrote, "I would be hurt that he didn't think of me first." In a section of "the Chicago Book" entitled "Notes on Meeting with Sen. Neistein—April 30, 1979," Neistein gives SB a different reason for Bilandic's loss. "Bilandic just didn't belong to the Irish City Hall gang. Those are the boys who understand the art of politics. They know what to do for everybody. Change Crawford to Pulaski Road for the Poles, parade for the Puerto Ricans, a couple of judgeships for the Jews—you've got to give them that—and keep all the main things for themselves. You've got to hand it to them, they're born with the knack" (p. 3).

15. See Tom Wolfe and E. W. Johnson, eds., *The New Journalism* (New York: Harper & Row, 1973), and "The Birth of 'The New Journalism,'" *New York*, 14 February 1972 (reprinted as the first of the four Wolfe essays that make up the first section of the 1973 book, entitled "Manifesto"). In an interview in the May 1997 issue of *Playboy*, SB was asked about Tom Wolfe's jokey call to arms. He was not in good humor at the time: "Yes, and the Huns were taught to read English and then they bought *The Bonfire of the Vanities*, which was a whole series of the most stunning billboards along the highway I ever saw. Let me tell you something: I'm a Jew, and when Jews hear the language of the Holocaust, because that's what it is—the world will be *Novelrein*, just as Hitler wanted to make Germany *Judenrein*, OK?—I say to myself it's all meshuga. I am used to hearing this eliminationist talk."

16. Quoted in Eugene Kennedy, "Bellow Awaits Heat from a Novel of Hard Knocks," *Chicago Tribune*, 10 January 1982.

17. See "Notes on Meeting with Lt. Col. Duane Swimley, 21 April 1979," in the "Chicago Book" papers in the Regenstein (henceforth cited within the text by page numbers).

18. William Juneau, "Marlene Swimley to Begin Sentence," *Chicago Tribune*, 4 November 1978.

19. See William Hunt, "Talk Given at Rudolf Steiner Library," 18 September 2009, pp. 2–3 (in the possession of the author).

20. According, at least, to Lynda and Arthur Copeland in an interview.

21. "Variations on a Theme from Division Street," the second of SB's two Tanner Lectures, was delivered on 25 May 1981 at Brasenose College, Oxford, under the general title "A Writer from Chicago," and printed in *The Tanner Lectures on Human Values,* ed. Sterling M. McMurrin (Salt Lake City: University of Utah Press, 1982), p. 188 (henceforth cited within the text by page numbers).

22. D. J. R. Bruckner, "Interview with Saul Bellow on 13 June 1980," a typescript of which begins by discussing SB's hopes for *Saul Bellow's Chicago,* the television documentary broadcast on Channel 5 in Chicago on 27 March 1981.

23. Morris Janowitz's theories, as cited by SB in the second Tanner Lecture, come from *The Last Half Century: Societal Change and Politics in America* (Chicago: University of Chicago Press, 1978).

24. Quotation from SB, "Notes on Visit to County Jail," 17 May 1979, p. 2.

25. See *The Dean's December,* p. 59, for the newspaper depiction of Ridpath; the Winston Moore quotes that follow come from p. 16 of the main biographical section of the "Chicago Book."

26. See also Eugene Kennedy, "Bellow Awaits Heat," in which SB says of "the black condition" that it "had every unavailing solution thrown at it. Programs, plans, money."

27. According to Dominic A. Pacyga, *Chicago: The Biography* (Chicago: University of Chicago Press, 2009), p. 332, the Robert Taylor Homes were built in the early 1960s to replace the demolished Federal Street slum, "which some called the longest slum in the world." The Homes consisted of twenty-eight identical sixteen-story buildings containing 4,415 apartments. Within these apartments lived twenty-one thousand children and seven thousand adults, almost exclusively black. Although the Homes were situated on ninety-five acres, only 7 percent of this land was occupied by the buildings themselves.

28. Hyde Park today, to the pride of its more high-minded residents, continues to offer a comparatively narrow range of shops and places to eat. It must be the only setting of a major American university without a Gap, a Banana Republic, a Foot Locker. What it has instead are excellent used-book shops, as well as the finest academic bookstore in America, the Seminary Co-op, which numbers Barack Obama among its members.

29. Jeff David and David Glockner, "Two Injured in Attacks," *Chicago Maroon,* 25 July 1980.

30. Robin Kirk, "UC Security Let Mugger's Father Convince Victim," *Chicago Maroon,* 23 October 1981.

31. Robin Kirk, "Fear, Crime and Urban Living," *Chicago Maroon,* 25 September 1981.

32. Alvin P. Sanoff, "A Conversation with Saul Bellow," *U.S. News & World Report,* 28 June 1982.

33. Joseph Sjostrom and Jerry Thornton, "Student Killed in Robbery," *Chicago Tribune,* 6 July 1977.

34. The dean was Catherine Ham, as quoted in Edward J. Rooney, "Two Terrorize Wife Before Fatal Struggle," *Chicago Daily News,* 7 July 1977. See also William Sluis and Joseph Sjostrom, "Man Dies Fighting Invaders," *Chicago Tribune,* 7 July 1977; Leon Pitt and Hugh Hough, "Grapples with Robber, Dies in Three-Floor Plunge," *Chicago Sun-Times,* 7 July 1977.

35. Nathaniel Clay, "Offer $5,000 Reward in Slaying," *Chicago Defender,* 7 July 1977.

36. Edmund J. Rooney, "Stolen Jewelry Found, Woman Linked to Student Death," *Chicago Daily News,* 8 July 1977. See also Tom Page Seibel, "Woman Fugitive Seized in UC Student Murder," *Chicago Daily News,* 19 July 1977.

37. This account was corroborated by other witnesses. The movements of Gromer and his wife on the night of 5–6 July were very different from those first reported. Apparently, they had decided to go out that night to escape the heat of the apartment. They arrived at a Hyde Park bar called Jimmy's at midnight and stayed for about forty-five minutes. There, according to his wife, Gromer had a couple of bourbons. Then they returned home and, again according to the wife, she went to bed while Gromer stayed in the living room. But not for long, she was to learn. According to witnesses, at 1:30 a.m. on 6 July, Gromer was seen wandering around barefoot, smoking marijuana outside the Tiki, then bothering people inside the bar. The bartender asked him to leave. At 2:00 a.m. he was seen in his car with Deola Johnson. These and other details come from *People v. McInnis* no. 79–27, reporting the 9 October 1980 decision of Justice Mel Jiganti, of the Appellate Court of Illinois—First District (Fourth Division), not to rehear the appeal of Ellis McInnis (see http://www.leagle.com/decision/198064388IllApp3d555_1561/PEOPLE%20v.%20McINNI).

38. In *People v. McInnis* no. 79–27, McInnis's lawyers are said to have contended that Lewis "was promised by the State that it would talk to the judge in the case [that is, in Lewis's violation-of-probation case], in an effort to get his probation extended if he cooperated; that Lewis was housed in witness quarters while the case was pending; that he had sought and received help from the State in relocating from his former neighborhood; that the State was paying his rent in his new building; and that he hoped to collect a $5,000 reward."

39. Philip Grew's "indictment" and "flight" were reported in several papers: see Jay Branegan, "Witness Threat Cited, Hunt Student in Gromer Death Case," *Chicago Tribune*, 31 August 1977; Thomas J. Dolan, "'Call Off Your Dogs,' Judge Warns Defendants' Pals," *Chicago Sun-Times*. (The only pal mentioned in the story, which gets the identity of the threatened witness wrong, is Philip Grew, whose neighbors are reported to have said he'd "fled" to Ann Arbor.) The dropping of the supposed indictment was reported in Charles Mount, "Gromer Case Figure Indictment Dropped," *Chicago Tribune*, 8 December 1977.

40. As reported in *People v. McInnis* no. 79–27.

41. In my interview with Grew (July 2015) he described himself as "a Michael Harrington Democrat," though never a member of the Democratic Socialists of America, which Harrington helped to found in 1982. In his first year at the University of Chicago, Grew volunteered to write press releases for the Student Council president, Alex Spinrad, a close ally of another campus politician, David Axelrod (later to mastermind Barack Obama's presidential campaign). Both Spinrad and Axelrod were members of the Democratic Organizing Committee or DSOC, the Harrington wing of the Democratic Party.

42. Grew recalls the lyrics of a song sung by undergraduates about their University of Chicago professors: "They're scared to leave the campus for the streets at night / 'Cuz the targets of their theories put 'em too uptight."

43. "I felt a little bit alone," Grew told me, "in terms of feeling so comfortable with African Americans. . . . As a group we could go to Teresa's . . . owned by Buddy Guy and Junior Wells. They [white friends] would go as a *group*, but couldn't individually—or wouldn't individually—do so." If you had what Grew and his friends referred to as a "WCB" or "Working Class Background" ("Saul Bellow had this"), it was "a card you could play to get to know blacks comfortably." Grew remembers a talk given to residents of his dorm on his first day at the university, about "how we had to be aware of where we were, and how dangerous it was and we were living in the middle of a ghetto and you couldn't walk to the Museum of Science and Industry."

44. After our interview, Grew sent me an email, 25 July 2015, detailing his understanding of the Gromer case. Here are portions of the email: "I witnessed the construction of a court case designed to rewrite the record so the graduate student, Marc Gromer, would go down in history—and later in fiction—as the victim of black-on-white crime. The entire case rested on hearsay. Administrators, staff, and consiglieri from the University of Chicago, largely through the South East Chicago Commission, in close cooperation with police and prosecutors, in a climate of support from the student and faculty communities, were able first to choreograph a plausible scenario for the events of 5–6 July and then to script a series of statements that were staged during a sham trial to convict a local black man, Ellis McInnis. Had crime been involved, it would have consisted of an attempted armed robbery whose side effects caused the death, i.e., felony murder. This implies several material elements, including a dead person, a cause of death attributable to the felony of armed robbery, a weapon, and an item to be robbed. Of these four elements, only the first existed when I returned to Hyde Park from a Fourth-of-July visit to Ann Arbor. That is, Marc [*sic*] Gromer was dead." Over the course of the next five weeks, "the three missing elements—crime, weapon, and loot—got added to the narrative." Of the witnesses who helped to add these elements, "I cannot recall a single one whose primary motivation appeared to be civic duty. In many cases there were obvious stimuli in the form of positive or negative sanctions. Often, an incentive consisted quite simply of the hope of a share in the reward money. The other main positive sanction was a reduced sentence or other lighter treatment at the hands of the 'legal' system. The negative sanctions whose avoidance motivated people to recount their stories ran across a broader range, a continuum that stretched from mild hassles with authorities through a variety of threats to fear of outright torture. . . . These negative sanctions were in no way unique to the Gromer case. They were business as usual, part of the climate. If the prosecutor told the press that someone was a fugitive from justice, for example, the person in essence became an outlaw, even when no arrest warrant existed. That was what happened to me. . . . In late July and early August, the missing three elements—connection to a crime, desired loot, and a weapon—were added into the plot through bought and coerced testimony. A late night hitting the books turned into a late night hitting the bars. The bedsheet hung as an improvised curtain over the window became a gag in the mouth of the white guy. Various items such as suitcases and stereos failed to materialize as the potential loot. At the final curtain, the only booty was a ring from Gromer. . . . The ring was a rather weak tie, since it might have been transferred from Gromer earlier that night or after his fall, thus failing to place even Deola, let alone Ellis McInnis, in the apartment. The weapon, however, was real physical evidence. Although the final account apparently placed the knife in Gromer's kitchen in the hand of an investigating policeman who had approached a paramedic kneeling alongside the fallen student, during dress rehearsal the knife had also put in an appearance upstairs with the watermelon, or was it cantaloupe." (It was cantaloupe, according to *People v. McInnis* no. 79–27; according to McInnis's testimony, "They started to smoke some reefer in the living room. Johnson asked for something to eat and the victim brought out a cantaloupe and three plates. The victim kept telling Johnson he wanted to go to bed with her so the defendant told them he was going to leave and he did so. He got home about 2:30 or 3:00.")

45. Here is how the *Chicago Tribune* describes the South East Chicago Commission's aims and activities, in an obituary of Julian Levi on 18 October 1987: "The issue for the city, community and the university was stability, as neighboring areas such as Kenwood and Woodlawn saw whites flee as the first African-Americans

moved in. Edgy university administrators were considering plans to move the campus to Lake Geneva, Wis. Led by Chancellor Lawrence Kimpton, the university committed itself instead to stay. It offered to contribute $14 million to the city, to be matched by $42 million from Washington, to buy slum property around the university and improve it to encourage stability and integration. This required new legislation, and Mr. Levi helped lead lobbying efforts for an amendment to the Housing Act of 1949 that became the key to rebuilding Hyde Park and, later, other communities through urban renewal. It was a controversial process that angered many who saw it as a land grab by the university." Philip Grew was certainly angered, accusing the commission of "actively paying to burn down buildings so that the territory that belonged to the university could expand southwards towards South Shore." In the Gromer case, "There was no doubt about them paying for a conviction. . . . I can't believe this is a university doing this stuff. This is not what academics [such as Julian Levi] do. That's not what universities are for." The university set up the commission, he believes, to deal with "anything that would be embarrassing to espouse a public position on."

46. Both Kleinbard and McCarthy were moved by the suffering of the Gromer family. For the duration of the trial, McCarthy remembers—some three weeks—the university put the Gromer family and Gromer's wife up at the Drake Hotel, at considerable expense. After the trial, the wife, in a fragile state, lived with Kleinbard and his wife, Joan, for several months.

47. Julian Levi, "The Neighborhood Program of the University of Chicago," Office of Public Information, University of Chicago, August 1961, quoted in Fish, *Black Power/White Control*, p. 14.

48. In life, SB was, finally, on Levi's side. See SB to Mayor Richard M. Daley, 15 November 1996: "Dear Mr. Mayor: This note concerns our friend Jonathan Kleinbard: Jonathan, as I am sure you know, has held the title of vice president of the University of Chicago in four administrations. He served under Edward Levi, under John Wilson and Hanna Gray and is at present on Mr. [Hugo] Sonnenschein's staff. All of Mr. Sonnenschein's predecessors were pleased with him and valued his assistance. . . . Mr. Sonnenschein, however, seems to have come under the influence of Jonathan's opponents and enemies, the PC contingent who were critical of Julian Levi and have apparently never understood that without the Levi plan Hyde Park/Kenwood would have gone the way of other blighted areas. Mr. Sonnenschein has been reducing Jonathan's functions to the vanishing point. . . . He seems to have convinced himself that Jonathan represents all that was wrong with the policies of the University—fifty years of errors."

49. "Mat [*sic*] Wright," in the "Chicago Book."

50. These are terms SB uses to distinguish facts plain and simple from facts charged with imagination: "The fact is a wire through which one sends a current. The voltage of the current is determined by the writer's own belief as to what matters, by his own caring or not-caring, by passionate choice. It is not *in news* that it matters whether a man lives or dies. The mattering is not a product of facts, but of judgment, of caring" (quoted in the introduction to *To Fame and Fortune*, p. 11). SB might have mentioned the presence of a third black man in the novel, the American ambassador to Romania. The ambassador is an attractive figure: calm, concerned, handsome, "with something about him—breeding, delicacy." He listens sympathetically to Corde's difficulties and offers practical advice. Bellow describes him as "quite black, very slender, had style, class, cultivation. He wore a light gray well-cut suit, and an Hermes necktie (Corde recognized the stirrup motif), and narrow black shoes" (p. 64). Corde has met black men like the ambassador before. "They had summer homes in Edgartown [on Martha's Vineyard]" (p. 66).

51. Atlas, *Biography*, p. 512.

52. Ibid., p. 495. David Mikics, *Bellow's People: How Saul Bellow Made Life into Art* (New York: W. W. Norton, 2016), p. 201, inaccurately follows Atlas's lead about Grew threatening a witness.

53. A cricketing term which in this context means something like avoiding answering a question, or deflecting a question, though the term can also mean behaving honestly or decently. Here both meanings fit, since by keeping his views to himself SB might have been seeking to avoid upset, thus behaving decently.

54. See SB to Alan Lelchuk, 22 March 1976: "Where does one live, in Cambridge, in Brookline, in Newton? I was rather attracted to the Jewish ambience of Brookline. It felt something like the Montreal I knew when I was a kid. But is that enough?"

55. Artur Sammler condemns Marcuse, whom he groups with Norman O. Brown. Lelchuk thinks Marcuse and SB may have had lunch together during SB's time at Brandeis, "or maybe they just shook hands."

56. The only other member of the Brandeis English Department whom Alexandra remembers she and Bellow socialized with was Milton Hindus, a scholar of wide and eccentric interests, perhaps best known for having visited Céline in 1948, from which he came away convinced that Céline was not an anti-Semite. This view he argues in *Céline: The Crippled Giant* (1950), perhaps his best-known book. Lelchuk, who befriended Hindus, describes him as "a strange kind of fellow and right-wing." "We learned things of such an arcane nature from him," Alexandra remembers.

57. Email to the author, 11 October 2015.

58. There were also money worries at this time. As Bellow complained to Julian Behrstock in a letter of May 24, 1978, "The IRS presented its bill and cleaned me out so I had to dig out some old sermons and fly to Texas and to Indianapolis and to Montreal. . . . Anyway I had a sudden and unhappy need for dollars and so I went on the road, and every time I gave a talk Washington took away 50% of the fee."

59. The recollection comes from Bettyann Kevles, "The Dean Remembered," *Engineering and Science*, no. 3 (2005) (*Engineering and Science* was the name of the Caltech magazine).

60. SB, foreword to *Clean Hands, Dirty Hands: Clair Patterson's Crusade Against Environmental Lead Contamination*, ed. Cliff L. Davidson (Commack, N.Y.: Nova Science Publishers, 1999).

61. Also in the *Engineering and Science* article, Bettyann Kevles remembers SB's telling another questioner that he reread all of Shakespeare "every year or two."

62. This quotation is from a three-page single-spaced letter to the Norsk Nobel-Komité, 20 January 1981, in which SB makes the case for awarding Patterson the 1981 Nobel Peace Prize. The letter was accompanied by materials documenting Patterson's "persistent efforts to make the world aware of the danger it faces."

7. NADIR

1. See Lionel Adey, *C. S. Lewis' "Great War" with Owen Barfield* (2000). When SB and Alexandra were in Victoria, Patrick Grant was finishing a book entitled *Literature of Mysticism in Western Tradition* (1983).

2. SB, foreword to Rudolf Steiner, *The Boundaries of Natural Science* (1920), trans. Frederick Amrine and Konrad Oberhuber (Spring Valley, N.Y.: The Anthroposophic Press, 1983), the translation of the fourth edition of the German text *Grenzsen der Naturerkenntnis*, consisting of shorthand notes of eight lectures given by Steiner in Dornach, Switzerland, from 27 September to 3 October 1920. It is available online at wn.rsarchive.org/Lectures/GA322/English/AP1983/BndSci_index.html.

3. This advice Walter Pozen strenuously opposed. Shawmut, in "Him with His Foot in His Mouth," comes to see similar advice as "fatal" (p. 378).

4. In the same letter, Roth also says, "You'll find out now what it's like to write for Harper's," by which he means Harper & Row the publisher, not *Harper's* the magazine. Harper & Row published a book-club edition of *The Dean's December* in 1981, before full trade publication in February 1982. SB was unhappy not only with the sales and marketing of *The Dean's December* but with the firm's handling of the collection *Him with His Foot in His Mouth and Other Stories* (1984).

5. The first of SB's public lectures at the University of Victoria was in January, to an audience of six or seven hundred respectful listeners. After his experiences at San Francisco State and elsewhere, he had requested police protection at the event, but, as Alexandra puts it, "Things went well, and we were both pleased and relieved."

6. According to an email to the author, 3 December 2015, from Charles Doyle, a poet and member of the English Department. Basil Bunting, a previous Lansdowne Visiting Professor, had made a similar complaint.

7. In an email to the author, 3 February 2016, Alexandra writes: "We were amused to discover that the study was filled with 'rapid guides' to all the cultures of the world, books containing resumés, plots of all the classics. 'I told Michael Best,' Saul said, 'that the house is full of kitsch.' I must have looked shocked, for he immediately reassured me: 'Look, I have never been afraid to tell these characters what I really think. If that ever happens, it means I am finished.'" SB described the house as "dinky" to Barnett Singer, according to his memoir, "Looking for Mr. Bellow," *Jewish Dialog*, Hannukah 1982, p. 15.

8. Singer, "Looking for Mr. Bellow," p. 15.

9. Alexandra Bellow, "Victoria B.C.—Winter of 82: Comments and Answers by Alexandra Bellow (January 2016) to Zachary Leader's Earlier Questions," p. 1 of an email attachment sent on 3 February 2016.

10. Charles Doyle, email to the author, 3 December 2015.

11. This is Doyle's description of P. K. Page, in ibid. "We saw quite a bit of her," Alexandra writes. She was "the 'grande dame' of poetry in Victoria" (email to the author, 3 February 2016).

12. Singer, "Looking for Mr. Bellow," p. 23. It is on this page also that SB describes P. K. Page as taking "issue" with him.

13. Barnett Singer, "More Proustian Memories of Bellow," p. 11, addendum to "Looking for Mr. Bellow," attachment to email to the author, 5 August 2015. It is not clear how Singer knows that this was the first time SB had used the line or that he put it in "Him with His Foot in His Mouth" that very night or the next morning.

14. Alexandra Bellow, "Victoria B.C.—Winter of 82," p. 2.

15. Ibid., p. 4.

16. Singer, "Looking for Mr. Bellow," pp. 18, 26, 36, 27.

17. Ibid., p. 16.

18. At the suggestion of Ed Burlingame, his editor at Harper & Row, SB had written to Senator Patrick Moynihan, Burlingame's friend and an admirer of SB's books. Had Moynihan not interceded with the Romanian ambassador in Washington, SB wrote to him in a note of 14 July 1981, "I think Aunt Ana would still be in Romania."

19. Alexandra Bellow, "Victoria B.C.—Winter of 82," pp. 4–5.

20. Singer, "Looking for Mr. Bellow," pp. 2, 3.

21. Ibid., p. 4.

22. See SB to Barnett Singer, 9 November 1972: "Dear Barney Singer—I'm awfully slow, but I do eventually acknowledge good letters, and yours was very

good." See also SB to Barnett Singer, 18 May 1976: "Throw your letters away? Never! I read them carefully and Esther [Corbin, SB's secretary] saves them for me. I attach great value to them."

23. Singer, "Looking for Mr. Bellow," p. 4.

24. Ibid. When his girlfriend meets SB, walking with Singer, her reaction, Singer reports, is that they were "roughly the same height, and with roughly the same look in our eyes. Julia said later we could easily be father and son" (p. 14).

25. Ibid., p. 4.

26. Ibid., pp. 5, 8.

27. Ibid., p. 8. Singer seems to be alone in thinking SB spoke with a slight lisp.

28. Ibid., pp. 6, 7, 11, 7, 14, 15.

29. Ibid., p. 14.

30. Ibid.

31. Ibid., pp. 16, 18.

32. See SB to Barnett Singer, 25 August 1975: "In reading your mss my interest was greatly stirred. And I assure you that I'm a pitiless reader. I make allowances neither for myself nor anyone else. Not much less relentless than Jehovah was when he watched the children of Israel behaving inartistically with the golden calf. To be brief with you, you may be a natural writer, for you have the energy and you have a certain hectic charm. You are a buttonholing writer by whom the reader is quite willing to be detained." See also SB to Barnett Singer, 8 November 1978: "I don't know if the story is publishable, which means I rather doubt it, but there certainly are valuable glints in the ore you sent me. I wouldn't give up yet. . . . Look out for yourself and make sure that you are not overcome by your own charm. You emit so much of it that it returns to you in the form of radiation, and you think it's the other party."

33. Singer, "Looking for Mr. Bellow," pp. 19, 20.

34. It recalls Mason Zaehner's "hey-presto" insolence in *The Dean's December*, though Mason is neither passive nor a complainer.

35. Singer, "Looking for Mr. Bellow," pp. 26, 22.

36. Ibid., pp. 23, 31.

37. Ibid., pp. 27, 30, 31.

38. Ibid., p. 34.

39. This undated note is written in pencil on a manila envelope dated July 1982. The poet in question was Alan Bell, whom SB had met in Victoria. The note continues: "A Xerox [of the poems] might be advisable. This seems to be the only copy (or is alleged to be, for purposes of menace). No more of this." For Dean Borok, see *To Fame and Fortune*, chapter 10.

40. The letter from Raymond Kuby is dated January 1981. I have decided against identifying these unhappy correspondents, all of whose letters are among the SB Papers.

41. Louis Gallo to SB, 12 February 1961.

42. Louis Gallo to SB, 7 April 1961.

43. SB to Louis Gallo, 15 June 1961.

44. Louis Gallo to SB, 19 February 1966.

45. Louis Gallo to SB, 29 January 1966.

46. The publisher of the 1966 edition was Dimensions Press. The ninety-eight-page book has been digitized.

47. See "Him with His Foot in His Mouth," pp. 387–88.

48. SB to Daniel Bellow, 31 January 1980.

49. According to Adam, Bellow was planning a second book about the Middle East, though no mention of such a book exists among the SB Papers in the Regenstein.

50. Adam also decided to leave the Committee because "I didn't feel that I'd become part of Bloom's inner circle. I felt I'd been held at arm's length, and I was very sensitive to that." "Allan didn't want me in that circle, and he didn't want anything to get in the way of the relation with Saul."

51. Greg Bellow, *Saul Bellow's Heart: A Son's Memoir* (London and New York: Bloomsbury, 2013), p. 135.

52. SB's increasing doubts about psychotherapy may have owed something to the views of his colleagues at the Committee on Social Thought, principally Edward Shils, who thought Freud undervalued human solidarity, seeing it primarily as a product of fear rather than "respect, obligation, humane impulse" (as David Mikics puts it in *Bellow's People: How Saul Bellow Made Life into Art* [New York: W. W. Norton, 2016], p. 155), and Allan Bloom, for whom the Freudian account was overly pessimistic, "as is apparent from his crude observations about art and philosophy" (*The Closing of the American Mind: How Higher Education Has Failed Democracy and Impoverished the Souls of Today's Students* [New York: Simon & Schuster, 1987], p. 137). That Freudian theory calls agency, human will and freedom, into question, is another likely source of SB's resistance, even hostility, to psychotherapy.

53. Greg Bellow, *Saul Bellow's Heart*, pp. 183–84, 185.

54. Ibid., p. 185.

55. Ibid., pp. 149, 150.

56. Ibid., pp. 155, 156.

57. Ibid., pp. 169, 170.

58. Ibid., pp. 135, 136.

59. Juliet admits that Bellow could be playfully affectionate. In 1982, when she was nine, Bellow sent her a gift of stamps. "I don't know whether you're still collecting, but I assume you're not one of those changeable girls who change their hobbies with their hair-ribbons. Much love from your sillybilly grandfather." In 1986, on her thirteenth birthday, he wrote, "Dear Granddaughter, you are now—congratulations—a teenager, ready to be an adult or a dolt or an adult colt."

60. From an interview with Martin Amis. This was also the year in which Amis discovered Vladimir Nabokov, his other great literary idol.

61. Martin Amis, "Saul Bellow's December," *Observer*, 11 December 1983, reprinted as "Saul Bellow in Chicago," in Amis, *The Moronic Inferno and Other Visits to America* (London: Jonathan Cape, 1986), p. 201.

62. Ibid., pp. 202, 201, 200.

63. Ibid., p. 200.

64. Ibid., p. 202.

65. Ibid., pp. 203, 204.

66. Ibid., p. 206.

67. John Updike, "Toppling Towers Seen by a Whirling Soul," *The New Yorker*, 22 February 1982. The novel made it to number six on the *New York Times* Best Seller list, though only briefly, and Harper & Row, which had paid SB a $600,000 advance, made back only $360,000 on sales and subsidiary rights. According to Atlas, *Biography*, p. 501, "Bellow, to his credit, was concerned about what he described as his 'debt' to Harper and Row and raised the possibility of extending the unrecovered advance to his next book, possibly a collection of short stories and novellas."

68. Updike's criticisms of SB's novels did not prevent him from praising later work. On 16 December 1983, in a letter to Rust Hills in praise of the fiftieth-anniversary issue of *Esquire* (December 1983), he added, "Of the things I read I especially liked the Bellow on Roosevelt ["In the Days of Mr. Roosevelt"]—beautiful, the way that image of the people sitting in their cars along

the Midway smoking, especially for those of us who were alive in the Thirties and can remember the texture of the life then." Hills sent SB a Xerox of Updike's note in a letter of 20 December.

69. Other comparably eminent figures are similarly ignored: Nabokov is referred to only once, Mailer four times.

70. SB, *Recent American Fiction: A Lecture Presented Under the Auspices of the Gertrude Clarke Whittall Poetry and Literature Fund* (Washington, D.C.: Library of Congress, 1963), p. 6; see also SB, "Some Notes on Recent American Fiction," *Encounter*, November 1963. William H. Pritchard, in *Updike: America's Man of Letters* (South Royalton, Vt.: Steerforth Press, 2000), p. 73, connects SB's reservations about the story to "the fact that he was about to publish *Herzog*. His most ambitious attempt to connect public and private realms."

71. By "reviews" in the phrase "outside of reviews" I mean not only Updike's reviews of SB's fiction but of other novelists' works, in which SB is a number of times mentioned in passing, always favorably, usually accompanied by a memorable quotation. SB's name appears in Adam Begley, *Updike* (New York: HarperCollins, 2014), four times, in each case in a list of authors, without comment. In his review of *To Fame and Fortune* in the *TLS* ("Saul Bellow Squares Up," 20 May 2015), Begley complains that Wordsworth is mentioned more frequently than Updike, Salinger, and Cheever combined. *To Fame and Fortune* ends in 1964, before Updike was much of a presence in SB's mind (which was true also of Cheever). Begley has nothing to say of the relations between Updike and SB after 1964. Salinger is not mentioned once in Benjamin Taylor's edition of SB's *Letters*, and the single pre-1964 reference to him in the interviews and profiles collected by Cronin and Siegel in *Conversations with SB* appears in David D. Galoway, "An Interview with Saul Bellow," *Audit-Poetry*, vol. 3 (1963), where he is unfavorably compared to William Golding. In the reference, SB calls Salinger "an excellent craftsman" but has little time for his "Rousseauian critique of society . . . as though civilization were something from which youth had the privilege of withdrawing" (p. 23). Updike is not mentioned at all. Wordsworth is mentioned in *To Fame and Fortune* more frequently than Updike, Cheever, and Salinger combined because he was more important to SB than Updike, Cheever, and Salinger combined, certainly pre-1964.

72. Quoted in *The Letters of John Cheever*, ed. Benjamin Cheever (London: Jonathan Cape, 1989), p. 245.

73. In later years, Cheever "was always courteous to me and increasingly friendly and kind" (John Updike, *Odd Jobs: Essays and Criticism* [New York: Alfred A. Knopf, 1991], pp. 117, 118).

74. To Adam Begley, in *Updike*, it was Cheever who was rivalrous: "Complicating matters was the fact that the pair of them were close friends with Bill Maxwell [of *The New Yorker*], who edited their stories and acted on occasion as mentor to both—there was in Cheever's attitude toward Updike a hint of sibling rivalry" (p. 267). Cheever's irritation with Updike on the Russia trip was sometimes recorded in his journals, as when he complains that Updike "hogged the lecture platform" at one of their events at the University of Leningrad. Begley thinks Cheever, a high-school dropout, "may have been intimidated by Updike's intellect." He also thinks that some of Cheever's complaints about Updike in the Exley letter were fantasies, "obviously concocted for Exley's amusement" (p. 268).

75. Begley, *Updike*, p. 267; when *Bech: A Book* was published, Updike was startled by its good notices, joking, "As everybody treats Bech so courteously, I'm beginning to wonder if there isn't indeed a Jewish Mafia" (quoted in ibid., p. 322).

76. Ibid., p. 267.

77. Ibid., p. 265.

78. Philip Larkin, "Posterity," in *High Windows* (London: Faber and Faber, 1974), p. 21. The poem was meant to provoke (as was Updike's Henry Bech): "It gets in Yanks, yids, wives, kids, Coca Cola, Protest and the Theatre—pretty good list of hates, eh?" (Philip Larkin to Monica Jones, 30 June 1968, in *Philip Larkin: Letters to Monica*, ed. Anthony Thwaite [London: Faber and Faber, 2000], p. 387). But to the Irish poet Richard Murphy, Larkin wrote: "I'm sorry if Jake Balokowsky seemed an unfair portrait. As you see, the idea of the poem was imagining the ironical situation in which one's posthumous reputation was entrusted to somebody as utterly unlike oneself as could be. It was only after the poem had been published that I saw that Jake, wanting to do one thing but having to do something else, was really not so unlike me, and indeed had probably unconsciously been drawn to my work for this reason, which explains his bitter resentment of it" (quoted in John Osborne, *Larkin, Ideology, and Critical Violence: A Case of Wrongful Conviction* [London: Palgrave, 2008], p. 211).

79. For Pritchard, in *Updike: America's Man of Letters*, p. 155, what Bech himself calls the Jewish writer's "domination of the literary world" only in part inspired his creation as a character. Updike may well have said to himself, "Let me, a Protestant, churchgoing exception to the literary rule, get into the act," but he had other motives: "to bring off something new and unexpected"; to indulge Nabokovian "formal highjinks" (the mock foreword, the appendices); to indulge "the metafictional playfulness of John Barth"; to give expression to strong opinions "under the protective guise of a fictional character superficially unlike John Updike." Finally, "Bech was as useful an alter ego to his creator as Rabbit had been and would be; both characters exist at greater distance from the writer than do the protagonists of *Marry Me* and *Couples*."

80. Quoted in Blake Bailey, *Cheever: A Life* (New York: Alfred A. Knopf, 2009), p. 227. On 9 October 1957, Cheever wrote to Felicia Geffen, executive secretary of the National Institute of Arts and Letters, describing SB as "the most original writer in America. No one has done so much to display, creatively, the versatility of life and speech in this country" (quoted in *Letters of John Cheever*, ed. Benjamin Cheever, p. 209).

81. Bailey, *Cheever: A Life*, pp. 227, 228.

82. Quoted in Atlas, *Biography*, p. 246.

83. Quoted in Bailey, *Cheever: A Life*, pp. 228–29, 375, 661.

84. Ibid., p. 455. Nine months earlier, Cheever had also presented Bellow with the Gold Medal for Fiction from the Academy of Arts and Letters.

85. Dana Gioia, "Meeting Mr. Cheever," *Hudson Review*, vol. 39, no. 3 (Autumn 1986), p. 431. See also Charlie Hall and Dana Gioia, "Bellow: A Nervous Hermit," *Stanford Daily*, 29 January 1976, which begins as follows: "'The problem with Saul Bellow,' a former attorney of his once said, is that he is 'a great artist but a lousy friend.' Bellow, who appeared at Stanford last week in an unpublicized visit, consistently confirmed this view, giving the impression of a man able to write warm, compassionate prose, and yet unable to relax among a public that has admired his work for more than 20 years." The authors recount two moments that may help to explain SB's mood, or at least to explain why it never lifted. After a talk on his first night, "he bristled visibly when he had to answer such uninformed questions as 'Who are you?' and 'I've heard your name; why should I know it?'" The second moment occurred the next morning. SB had requested that his visit—which was primarily for Alexandra—not be publicized. When the student newspaper reported the campus location of an informal talk he was to give that afternoon, SB "angrily cancelled the talk."

86. Bailey, *Cheever: A Life*, p. 530. As Gioia, "Meeting Mr. Cheever," p. 421, puts it: "January 1976 marked the nadir of Cheever's literary reputation. His last

novel, *Bullet Park* (1969) had received poor reviews. . . . His work had stopped appearing in *The New Yorker* and now appeared at the rate of about one story per year only in magazines like *The Saturday Evening Post* and *Playboy*. . . . He was not so much discussed as dismissed as a dated suburban satirist, and he had become a sort of ceremonial scapegoat for all the real and imagined sins of *The New Yorker*." As for SB, "he had accompanied [his wife] to tease the University with the prospect of a package deal. The Administration exhibited no hesitation in swallowing the bait" (p. 429). SB's testiness also may have owed something to his schedule: "The Administration had eagerly crammed Bellow's short stay with meetings, parties, speeches, and public appearances" (p. 429).

87. John Cheever to SB, 25 April 1982, *Letters of John Cheever*, ed. Benjamin Cheever, p. 378.

88. See John Cheever to SB, 3 April 1982, in ibid., p. 377: "I was told last week—one could have guessed it—that the miracle worker who can cure my cancer is in Bucharest. I can see him watering his dying cyclamens between administering huge doses of horse urine."

89. SB, "John Cheever" (1972), in *IAAU*, p. 273. This seems to have been mostly true, though Bailey, *Cheever: A Life*, p. 576, records that, "on the bleak autumn day when Bellow was named the winner [of the Nobel Prize], Cheever took a dejected walk with Gurganus [Alan Gurganus, the novelist] . . . starting a little when they came to the statue of the nineteenth-century explorer Alexander von Humboldt: 'Oh my God!' he said. 'They're already putting up statues!' But once his dismay had passed, he gladly conceded the 'exemplary and tireless grace' Bellow had shown as laureate."

90. SB, "John Cheever," pp. 273–74.

91. SB to Jessica Burstein, July 16, 1966, a student at the time, later an English professor at the University of Washington.

92. According to a letter of 13 November 1983 by Andreas Brown, who purchased the Gotham Book Mart from Steloff in 1967, a purchase engineered by Goldberg.

93. Interview with Curt Suplee, "Getting It Right," *Washington Post*, 20 May 1984.

94. These and other details come from Joshua Hammer, "Saul Bellow Returns to Canada, Searching for the Phantoms That Shaped His Life and Art," *People*, 25 June 1984; "Bellow Returns to Lachine," *Gazette*, 7 June 1984; and Harriet Wasserman, *Handsome Is: Adventures with Saul Bellow* (New York: Fromm International, 1977), pp. 103–10.

95. Wasserman, *Handsome Is*, pp. 109, 110.

96. Marvin Gameroff was among the speakers, each of whom was supposed to speak for three minutes maximum. Poems were recited and songs sung between the speeches, and the brunch did not conclude until 3:00 p.m., when everyone sang "Happy Birthday."

97. According to Ruth Wisse, "Bellow's Gift—A Memoir," *Commentary* (1 December 2001), "The one thing you could not raise with him was anything about his books, he did not take offense at political matters."

98. Wisse, ibid., adds: "The Talmud says, 'Who is a hero? He who resists his evil urge'—meaning, according to some, his sexual urge. Yiddish speakers add, 'he who resists his urge to pun,' thereby identifying a besetting sin of *their* civilization." In Bellow's present case, both fit. At this party, Wisse also discovered a bond between herself and Alexandra, who knew the Romanian city of Czernowitz (now part of Ukraine), where Wisse was born in 1936. Alexandra not only knew the city but knew the obstetrician who, Wisse later discovered, had saved her mother's life and given Ruth her name. "Tamara" was her mother's choice, but the obstetrician

advised her that "now is not the time for a Jewish name." So her mother chose "Ruth," or "Rut," "a good Romanian name."

99. See, in particular, laudatory reviews by Cynthia Ozick, "Farcical Combat in a Busy World," *New York Times Book Review*, 20 May 1984; Peter S. Prescott, "Him at His Most Impressive," *Newsweek*, 14 May 1984; Robert M. Adams, "Winter's Tale," *New York Review of Books*, 19 July 1984; D. J. Enright, "Exuberance-Hoarding," *Times Literary Supplement*, 22 June 1984; Eugene Goodheart, "Parables of the Artist," *Partisan Review*, vol. 52, no. 2 (1985).

100. Anatole Broyard, review of SB, *Him with His Foot in His Mouth and Other Stories*, *New York Times*, 11 May 1984.

101. According to an email to the author, 1 July 2011, from Rosemarie Sanchez-Fraser, who worked with Anita at Kaiser for nearly forty years, she was a tough but fair boss, who "respected you as long as you were honest with her." Sanchez-Fraser worked under Anita for her first sixteen years at Kaiser, and Anita "became like a mother to me and taught me to appreciate horticulture, art, opera and politics (she was the most liberal woman I'd ever met)."

102. Greg Bellow, *Saul Bellow's Heart*, pp. 158–59.

103. Georgia death records say Maury died on 1 May 1985. Atlas, *Biography*, p. 516, says he died a week or so later. Atlas also says he died of liver cancer. Rachel Schultz, a physician, and her mother, Lesha Greengus, are certain Maury died of colon cancer, though the cancer may also have spread to the liver.

104. Ruth Miller, *Saul Bellow: A Biography of the Imagination* (New York: St. Martin's Press, 1991), p. 303.

105. Ibid.

106. Ibid. According to Maury's son, Joel, who received a similar call, it was Joyce, not Maury, who told Bellow to "come now."

107. Miller, *Saul Bellow: A Biography of the Imagination*, p. 302.

108. Joel Bellows, email to the author, 1 April 2016.

109. Ibid.

110. Ibid.

111. Ibid., the source also of Joel's respectful inquiry about Maury's health, quoted in previous paragraph.

112. Leonard reacted to Maury's reneging on his promises by quitting work for Maury and starting a rival company, taking with him "every single person" from the old firm. According to Mark Rotblatt, when Maury told Lynn what he intended to do, "my mother said, You can't do that, and my grandfather just said, I'll do what I want." Then he told Lynn she should leave her husband, move to Florida, and live with her mother (Marge, his first wife). "I'll get you a nursemaid to look after the kids. You'll be fine." Lynn, pregnant with Maureen, Mark's sister, refused.

113. Miller, *Saul Bellow: A Biography of the Imagination*, p. 304. For Greg Bellow's earlier reference to Sam's being "no fool," see *Saul Bellow's Heart*, p. 160.

114. Quoted in Ruth Miller, *Saul Bellow: A Biography of the Imagination*, p. 304. Sam Bellows's obituary in the *Chicago Tribune*, "Samuel Bellows, 74, Jewish Leader," appeared on 4 June 1985.

115. When news of the seriousness of Sam's illness reached Daniel in Paris, he wrote to his father, on 25 April: "I had a wonderful time with Dave Peltz when he came here, we went walking around St. Germain and Chatelet, getting drunk in cafés. His goodness is so self-evident, he melted the ice in the hearts of Parisian café waitresses—he can walk as fast as I can in the street. He's the greatest, I like him even more now than I did when I was little. I hope things are better with Uncle Sam. I can only imagine how difficult that is for you. Tell him I send love. Also tell Lesha. I'm sorry, Pop. I wish there was something I could do or say for

you to make it any better, but there ain't. Just know that I am fine and healthy, and that I love you."

116. For the Asher quotation, see Atlas, *Biography*, p. 517; for SB's upset over the marketing of *Him with His Foot in His Mouth and Other Stories*, see chapter 12 of *To Fame and Fortune*, p. 505.

117. Atlas, *Biography*, pp. 492–93, describes the workings of the MacArthur "genius" program, naming other members of the board during SB's tenure as Kenneth Keniston, Jonas Salk, Jerome Wiesner, Edward Levi, Leon Botstein, and Murray Gell-Mann (to which number could be added Marian Wright Edelman and John Hope Franklin). Botstein, the president of Bard College, remembers: "I got the composers, the musicians, and Saul got the writers." Botstein got on well with SB, sharing his amused view not only of "this genius award thing" but of their fellow evaluators, in particular the Nobel Prize–winning physicist Murray Gell-Mann, "a man who knows everything better, what in Yiddish is called a *besserwisser*." Gell-Mann not only "knows everything better," but "what he doesn't know isn't worth knowing." As Botstein puts it: "Saul was not modest, but Gell-Mann drove people nuts." On one occasion, SB and Gell-Mann joined forces to tease their fellow evaluator Jonas Salk, who had a chip on his shoulder about never having won the Nobel Prize. When a Nobel Prize–winning economist was under consideration for an award, the two laureates made snide comments about how the economics prize was not a real Nobel Prize, not being one of the original prizes, like theirs, created in Alfred Nobel's will (a view taken by some of Nobel's descendants). Despite making jokes and cynical remarks, SB took his duties as evaluator seriously, according to Botstein. He made every effort not only to help his friends, arguing successfully on behalf of Robert Penn Warren, William Kennedy, and Bette Howland, but to veto those whose views and talents he disapproved of or questioned (Amiri Baraka, Edward Said, Susan Sontag). Freund's successor, Kenneth Hope, in a letter of 14 December 1984, praised SB as the "longest-standing" of the program's evaluators: "You, in fact, helped us get this program going, and your wisdom and charm have made us both more confident and, more simply, more able to make this Program work."

118. Alfred Kazin, review of *Mr. Sammler's Planet*, "Though He Slay Me . . . ," *New York Review of Books*, 3 December 1970. After the Freund dinner, in a journal entry of 1 June 1985, Kazin describes his and SB's cronies as "a lost generation—poor boys, 'intellectuals.' To their fingertips, brought up to be adversaries of power types and the 'established order'—who now turn out to be the voices of 'privilege,' messengers, auxiliaries, 'conservatives.' . . . O my! How our social opinions reflect our top lofty incomes, and what excuses we do find (we who once had no trouble execrating everyone in power . . .)."

119. Alfred Kazin, entry of 8 May 1979, in *Alfred Kazin's Journals*, ed. Richard M. Cook (New Haven, Conn.: Yale University Press, 2011), p. 470. According to Judith Dunford, there was a second meeting in Chicago, not recorded in *Alfred Kazin's Journals* (Dunford thinks it might have been in 1984). The Kazins came to tea at the Sheridan Road apartment, where Dunford met Bellow for the first time. She recalls finding him "so intensely intelligent it was hard to resist." Alexandra, who had known Dunford's brother, a mathematician, she recalls as "very gracious, very nice." She remembers that Bellow did a lot of "smiling at [Alexandra] and hovering." Although Kazin was apprehensive before this visit, "which always made him combative," the Bellows "were very polite." There was no talk of politics.

120. Richard M. Cook, *Alfred Kazin: A Biography* (New Haven, Conn.: Yale University Press, 2007), pp. 369, 368 (for Kazin's hatred of Likud).

121. Leon Wieseltier's two-part essay, "Hannah Arendt and the Jews," was

published in consecutive issues of *The New Republic*, 7 and 14 October 1981. Part I was titled "Understanding Anti-Semitism," Part II "Pariahs and Politics."

122. Cook, *Alfred Kazin: A Biography*, p. 368. In a letter of 13 April 1999, Kazin's friend Morris Dickstein wrote to SB to thank him for shedding light on "that ill-fated dinner." SB's account "sounds all too much like Alfred at his most uncensored. But it was equally in character for him to feel hurt and bewildered afterward." Dickstein tries to explain the upset caused by SB's remark about Franco: "As he was a child of the 30s, hatred of Franco and grief over the Spanish Civil War were matters of faith to him. Coincidentally, last week on cable we saw a low-budget documentary on 'Franco's Jews.' It seems Franco *had* no policy toward the Jews, except to protect those who had any claim to Spanish nationality. This led to contradictory actions and inaction. But the lack of a policy enabled a few individual diplomats in occupied cities like Paris, Salonika, and Budapest to dispense Spanish papers to Jews, which sometimes provided a temporary shield against deportation."

123. Alfred Kazin, entries of 29 May 1985 and 1 June 1985, in *Alfred Kazin's Journals*, ed. Cook, pp. 522, 523.

124. SB was later to soften toward Kazin. See his letter of 26 October 1988 to Margaret Mills of the American Academy and Institute of Arts and Letters, who had asked him to serve with Eudora Welty and Kazin on a panel to recommend candidates for the Gold Medal in Fiction: "I don't mind chatting with Eudora Welty on the phone. Alfred Kazin and I, who have known each other from the beginning of time, always found it difficult to agree. I like to think, though, that while he has grown more rigid I have grown more flexible. I shouldn't be surprised if he were to accuse *me* of rigidity and claim flexibility for himself. Still, I see no reason why we shouldn't produce a good list."

125. Alexandra Bellow, email to Benjamin Taylor, 20 June 2010.

126. Alexandra Bellow, "A Mathematical Life (Una Vida Matematica)," p. 8, an 11-page typescript dated 29 September 2001, published as "Un vida matematica," *La Gaceta de la Real Sociedad Matematica Española*, vol. 5, no. 1 (January–April 2002), pp. 62–71.

127. Alexandra Bellow, email to the author, 18 April 2016.

128. Greg Bellow, *Saul Bellow's Heart*, pp. 162, 161. See SB to Mark Smith, 17 October 1982: "I have no clear picture of the coming spring. My wife and I will have an empty house in Vermont and it appears that I will be in charge of furnishing it because she always goes into a mathematical trance towards April in preparation for June math conferences in Germany and France."

129. Greg Bellow, *Saul Bellow's Heart*, p. 161.

130. Alexandra Bellow, email to the author, 10 April 2016.

131. These anecdotes are from Wasserman, *Handsome Is*, pp. 117–21.

132. Quotations in Atlas, *Biography*, p. 519.

133. The date of SB's speech, "The Mind of the Reader and the Expectation of the Writer in America," is given in the 6 September letter to Barley Alison, in which he asks if he can stay with her when he arrives in London on the fifteenth. On 6 October, he writes to William Kennedy that he is departing for Dublin on the ninth. However, in a letter of 15 October to Robert Hivnor, SB says, "I can't sign this because my secretary is taking this from dictation and I am going to Dublin day after tomorrow." Kennedy writes to SB on 25 October, "By the time you get this you will have returned from Ireland." So it appears that the dates of the talk and trip were rescheduled.

134. A typescript of SB's talk, entitled "Transcript of Remarks of Mr. Saul Bellow Made on October 31, 1985 at the Whiting Foundation Writers' Program Ceremony," in SB Papers.

135. For "pressed into attending," see SB to John Auerbach, 18 November 1985. Who did the pressing is not identified.

136. Maggie Simmons, email to Benjamin Taylor, 21 January 2011, remembers Alexandra's asking SB for a divorce much earlier: "What I vividly remember is Saul's calling me on the evening before or on his 70th birthday to tell me that Alexandra was asking him for a divorce right on the heels of his brothers' deaths. He was desolate. I remember thinking that he must have done something remarkable (that he wasn't telling me) to anger/upset Alexandra enough to end the marriage on that day. I was living on Central Park West at the time. It sticks in my mind. I thought he was in Chicago when he called but I'm not sure about that part." This can't be right, given SB's correspondence in the autumn, in which he reports on his and Alexandra's movements and plans, in letters addressed from the Sheridan Road apartment. SB's friend Eugene Kennedy recalls the final split as coming after his return from California, remembered by Greg Bellow as "around the New Year," recollections which fit with Alexandra's insistence that she asked for a divorce and for SB to move out of the Sheridan Road apartment in December. It is possible that Maggie is conflating an unhappy phone call on 9 June 1985 from Vermont, perhaps one in which SB told her of a threat of divorce, with one in December, after his return from California.

137. Quoted in Atlas, *Biography*, p. 521.

138. Greg Bellow, *Saul Bellow's Heart*, p. 162.

139. Quoted in Atlas, *Biography*, p. 521.

140. Quoted in David Mikics, *Bellow's People*, pp. 215–16. According to Eugene Kennedy, SB complained about Alexandra's absenting herself in the evenings as well as the mornings: "She had her own life and left him. She would go into her room in the evening and talk on the phone. I might as well have been living here alone." To Kennedy, "there was something crushing in the loneliness he was feeling." That SB would complain about Alexandra's working in the morning is odd, given that he also reserved mornings for work.

8. JANIS FREEDMAN/ALLAN BLOOM/POLITICS

1. See SB to Harvey Stein, assistant director, International Student Services, University of Chicago, in an undated draft.

2. SB to Fellowships Division, Social Science and Humanities Research Council of Canada, 4 November 1981.

3. Allan Bloom, *The Closing of the American Mind: How Higher Education Has Failed Democracy and Impoverished the Souls of Today's Students* (New York: Simon & Schuster, 1987), p. 243. Henceforth cited in the text by page number.

4. Quoted in James Atlas, "Chicago's Grumpy Guru: Best-Selling Professor Allan Bloom and the Chicago Intellectuals," *New York Times Magazine*, 3 January 1988; an abridged version of this article is reprinted in *Essays on the Closing of the American Mind*, ed. Robert L. Stone (Chicago: Chicago Review Press, 1989). Henceforth abbreviated as *Essays on the Closing*, ed. Stone.

5. See Caleb Rossiter, "Cornell's Student Revolt of 1969: A Rare Case of Democracy on Campus," *Progressive*, 5 May 1999. Rossiter writes sympathetically of the protesters, but throws doubt on one of the chief causes of the 1969 revolt. "The takeover was spurred by a faculty-student judicial board's decision to punish black students for a disruptive protest the previous December, and by a cross-burning at a black women's dorm that most black students believed was the work of whites (although it may have been a closely-held provocation by a small cell of blacks)."

6. Clifford Orwin, in "Remembering Allan Bloom," *American Scholar*, vol. 62, no. 3 (Summer 1993), describes Bloom's reaction to an attempt in 1974 on the part of "some New Leftists" at the University of Toronto physically to prevent a distinguished visitor from speaking. "In fielding a question about the dramatic character of the *Republic*, he spoke more movingly than ever about the rarity of the kind of discussion reported therein. He talked of how in times of darkness and crisis for Athens, a few people had gathered to consider the timeless issues of politics, of how the trial of Socrates cast its long shadow over the conversation, and how we must cherish and defend the opportunities for such discussions that the university afforded us today."

7. This account of the Cornell student revolt derives from Rossiter, and also from George Lowery, "A Campus Takeover That Symbolized an Era of Change," *Cornell Chronicle*, 22 May 2016; and Donald Alexander Downs, *Cornell '69: Liberalism and the Crisis of the American University* (1999; Ithaca and London: Cornell University Press, 2012). For Sowell's remark about the protesters, see Thomas Sowell, "The Day Cornell Died," *Hoover Digest*, 30 November 1999.

8. Nathan Tarcov, "The Last Four Years at Cornell," *Public Interest*, vol. 13 (1968).

9. According to Nicholas Lemann, "The Republicans: A Government Waits in the Wings," *Washington Post*, 27 May 1980, most of the so-called neoconservatives who worked for Ronald Reagan, including Jeane Kirkpatrick, Eugene Rostow, Paul Wolfowitz, Elliott Abrams, and Douglas Feith, "have one problem: most of them are registered Democrats."

10. Allan Bloom, "Western Civ," in *Giants and Dwarfs: Essays 1960–1990* (New York: Simon & Schuster, 1990), p. 17; Bloom blames the misattribution on "the fact that I am also not in any current sense a liberal, although the preservation of liberal society is of central concern to me."

11. Orwin, "Remembering Allan Bloom."

12. Ibid.

13. Bloom, "Western Civ," p. 14.

14. Leo Strauss, *Persecution and the Art of Writing* (1952; Chicago: University of Chicago Press, 1988), p. 25.

15. Mark Lilla, "Leo Strauss: The European," *New York Review of Books*, 21 October 2004, part 1 of a two-part omnibus review of books about Strauss and his influence.

16. See Bloom, *The Closing of the American Mind*, p. 73: "Rock music has one appeal only, a barbaric appeal, to sexual desire—not love, not *eros*, but sexual desire undeveloped and untutored. . . . Young people know that rock has the beat of sexual intercourse. That is why Ravel's *Bolero* is the one piece of classical music that is commonly known and liked by them."

17. Harriet Wasserman, *Handsome Is: Adventures with Saul Bellow* (New York: Fromm International, 1997), p. 137.

18. Ibid, p. 142.

19. See Mark Lilla, "The Closing of the Straussian Mind," *New York Review of Books*, 4 November 2004, part 2 of the omnibus review mentioned in note 15, above. The Mark Blitz quotation is from *Leo Strauss, the Straussians, and the American Regime*, ed. Kenneth L. Deutsch and John A. Murley (Lanham, Md.: Rowman & Littlefield, 1999).

20. Lilla, "Closing of the Straussian Mind."

21. Ibid. See also, Leo Strauss, *Natural Right and History* (1953; Chicago: University of Chicago Press, 1965), p. 6, where Strauss asserts that the historicist "voice of reason . . . tells us that our principles are in themselves as good or as bad as any

other principles. The more we cultivate reason, the more we cultivate nihilism" (p. 6). In defense of historicism in "Straussianism, Democracy, and Allan Bloom I: That Old Time Philosophy," *New Republic*, 4 April 1988, reprinted in *Essays on the Closing*, ed. Stone, Richard Rorty quotes John Rawls, an eloquent defender of historicism: "What justifies a conception of justice is not its being true to an order antecedent to and given to us, but its congruence with our deeper understanding of ourselves and our aspirations, and our realization that, given our history and the traditions embedded in our public lives, it is the most reasonable doctrine for us." For Rorty, a fellow historicist, "we shall never have anything firmer to fall back on than our accumulated experience of the advantages and disadvantages of various concrete alternatives (judged by nothing more immutable than our common sense, the judgment of the latest, best-informed, and freest of the children of time)."

22. Critics of John M. Olin see his conservatism as a product in part of opposition to government interference, in particular the prosecution of industrial malfeasance. See Bill McKibben, "The Koch Brothers' New Brand," *New York Review of Books*, 10 March 2016, a review of Jane Mayer, *Dark Money: The Hidden History of the Billionaires Behind the Rise of the Radical Right:* "John M. Olin, for instance, who would fund an unprecedented effort to push his libertarian philosophy on campuses across America, was constantly embroiled in defending egregious pollution at his chemical plants across America. The company was pouring mercury into the Niagara River, and turning a Virginia town so toxic that it became one of the first names on the EPA's 'Superfund' list of especially dirty sites."

23. For the John M. Olin Center Web site, see http://olincenter.uchicago.edu/. According to Nathan Tarcov, in Jeff Wolf and Jeff Taylor, "Profs See Olin Foundation as Asset Here," *Chicago Maroon*, 14 October 1983, the center "is not meant to be just another policy-oriented think tank, but a home for inquiry into the practical problems and policy dilemmas of contemporary democracy on the basis of theoretical reflection," principally on classic texts of political theory. "The Olin Foundation is a conservative one," Tarcov admitted, "but their interest in this case is to support a completely independent center which will examine the problems of free institutions." The Olin Center at the University of Chicago closed in 2001, after twenty-one years' existence.

24. Here is SB to Rudi Lissau, in a letter of 23 July 1990: "I can't blame you for saying that my interest in anthroposophy is waning. All doctrines have to be squared with my own outlook—I nearly said my innate outlook. It was in fact that same outlook that led me to find Steiner so compelling."

25. The Committee on the Present Danger shared this view, declaring in an early position paper, "The Soviet military buildup of all its armed forces over the past quarter century is, in part, reminiscent of Nazi Germany's rearmament in the 1930s." It was fruitless to negotiate arms reduction with Hitler, and it would be no less fruitless to try to do so with Soviet Russia: "The Salt 1 arms limitation agreements have had no visible effect on the Soviet buildup. Indeed, their principal effect so far has been to restrain the United States in the development of those weapons in which it enjoys an advantage" (quoted in *Alerting America: The Papers of the Committee on the Present Danger*, ed. Charles Tyroler II, intro. Max Kampelman [New York: Pergamon-Brassey, 1984]).

26. The press releases of the Committee on the Present Danger issued on 11 November 1976 were entitled "How the Committee Will Operate—What It Will Do, and What It Will *Not* Do" and "Common Sense and the Common Danger."

27. Quoted in David Mikics, *Bellow's People: How Saul Bellow Made Life into Art* (New York: W. W. Norton, 2016), p. 146. In an interview, Epstein says the phrase Shils used in describing what he didn't want the Committee to become

was a "farm team" (for non–North American readers, a baseball term, denoting a second-division team), not a "rest home" for SB's "*nafkas*." Quotations from Epstein come from interviews with the author, plus emails of 7, 8, 14, and 17 June 2016.

28. Mikics, *Bellow's People*, pp. 147, 148.

29. The *Sammler* manuscript containing Shils's annotations is located in the Berg Collection in the New York Public Library. The passages quoted are from pp. 272, 273.

30. Mikics, *Bellow's People*, p. 148.

31. In fact, according to SB to François Furet, 2 February 1992, the "unlanced boil" description came from David Grene. In reply to Furet's description of an awkward Committee on Social Thought meeting, SB regrets missing it: "I should have liked at least to have been there in spirit, haunting the walls. Nasty Shils the ultimate Dickensian funny monster giving his wickedest performance. Bloom is mad with delight, beside himself when he describes the scene. David Grene once said that Edward was an unlanced boil (*un furuncle*, to you)."

32. This is not how Epstein remembers the encounter, according to an email to the author, 24 January 2018: "I recall getting into the very small elevator at Jack Cella's (and Edward Shils's) apartment building, and seeing Saul and Janis B. I greeted Saul (I did not know his wife), and then turned around, if only because the elevator was too small for five people (I believe my wife was with us) for easy conversation. Later, at Jack C's, Saul came up to talk with me. In any case, I did not snub the Bellows."

33. Peter Ahrensdorf, email to the author, 22 June 2016; Janis Freedman Bellow, email to the author, 19 June 2016.

34. Janis Freedman Bellow, "Passionate Longing: Women in the Novel from Rousseau to Flaubert" (1992), a dissertation submitted to the Committee on Social Thought, pp. 3–4. Henceforth cited within the text by page number.

35. The opening pages of the dissertation offer an example of the extremity of female longing. Janis focuses on the real-life model for Sophie in *Émile*, a character who falls passionately in love with the hero of Fénelon's novel *The Adventures of Telemachus* (1699). Fénelon's Telemachus is much more hot-blooded than Homer's Telemachus, and the real-life Sophie, Rousseau tells us, sees him, in Janis's paraphrase, as "emotionally identical with herself. Both share a taste for the beautiful, the noble and virtuous, a longing for self-mastery" (p. 10). As it turns out, Telemachus's longings, as depicted in Fénelon's novel, "may be fierce, but they are in no way a match for hers [that is, the real-life Sophie's]. She is an uncompromising extremist" (p. 17). Nor are Sophie's longings sublimated, as Rousseau says they are in most women. After her account of Sophie in *Émile* and of Julie in *La Nouvelle Héloïse*, Janis turns to Flaubert's *Novembre*, in chapter 2 of the dissertation, before devoting a final three chapters to *Madame Bovary*.

36. The books she considers are Margaret Diehl's *Men* (1988) and Elizabeth McNeill's *Nine and a Half Weeks* (1978). (Elizabeth McNeill is a pseudonym; the author's real name is Ingeborg Day.)

37. Atlas, *Biography*, pp. 520–21, offers an account of the breakup that mixes together SB's January return from California with the earlier ultimatum—either the December one, the date of which SB may have misremembered, or one sometime earlier: "The final parting from Alexandra was acrimonious. As Bellow told it, he had arrived back from Vermont and was standing in the living room with his suitcase when she announced that she wanted a divorce. She had put red tags on his possessions. To Stuart Brent, he described in lurid detail how she had stormed about the apartment, slamming doors. The four bathrooms were employed to dramatic effect: 'She used the first bathroom to get dressed, the second to put on her lipstick; the third to put on her stockings, shoes and gloves; then she came out of

the fourth and said, "You used me for your fucking novels and you drained me dry; go ahead and sue me. I want you out of the house in 24 hours." '"

38. Remarks like these played a part in a temporary cooling of the friendship between SB and Stern, as did Bellow's tendency "to simplify me as a liberal," testing him by making illiberal remarks.

39. Kennedy claimed in an interview that once, when he was visiting SB at the apartment at Sheridan Road, Alexandra said goodbye, then returned unexpectedly, trying, Kennedy was certain, to catch them *in flagrante*. The closeness between the two men is affirmed in "Saul Bellow's Tribute to Gene Kennedy in Celebration of His 70th Birthday," an undated document from 1998 (Kennedy was born on 28 August 1928) among the SB Papers in the Regenstein: "I can tell him openly what I am thinking, feeling, dreading, down to the most shameful, corrosive details. We speak very directly and plainly to each other and this is possible not because I am good (I am too cockeyed to be good) but because *he* is. He is a big man and his size frequently suggests full occupancy of the physical plant by the superabundant goodness of the man."

40. Quoted in Atlas, *Biography*, p. 521.

41. Greg Bellow, *Saul Bellow's Heart: A Son's Memoir* (London and New York: Bloomsbury, 2013), p. 163.

42. Richard Stern, "Penned In," *Critical Inquiry*, vol. 13, no. 1 (Autumn 1986), p. 24.

43. Rhoda Koenig, "At Play in the Fields of the Word: Alienation, Imagination, Feminism, and the Foolishness of PEN," *New York*, 3 February 1986.

44. PEN was founded at the end of the First World War by H. G. Wells, John Galsworthy, and others, with the aim of "rescuing the world's writers from the political consequences of their work," a phrase from Stern, "Penned Up," p. 3n.

45. David Lehman, "When Pen Pals Collide," *Partisan Review*, vol. 53, no. 2 (1986), p. 190.

46. Daniel Fuchs, "Literature and Politics: The Bellow/Grass Confrontation," in *Writers and Thinkers: Selected Literary Criticism* (Piscataway, N.J.: Transaction Publishers, 2015), pp. 144–45.

47. Ibid., p. 144.

48. SB, "Writers, Intellectuals, Politics: Mainly Reminiscence," in *IAAU*, pp. 111–12. Henceforth cited within the text by page number.

49. Grass's exact words, as quoted in Lehman, "When Pen Pals Collide," p. 197, were: "I'm wondering when you're explaining that democracy gave people not only freedom but also shelter and food. I would like to see the echo of your words in the South Bronx, where people don't have shelter, don't have food and no possibility to have the freedom you have, or some have in this country."

50. Koenig, "At Play in the Fields of the Word."

51. R. Z. Sheppard, "Independent States of Mind," *Time*, 27 January 1986.

52. Koenig, "At Play in the Fields of the Word."

53. For the quotations from Rushdie and Gordimer, see Fuchs, "Literature and Politics," p. 150, which also quotes the Peruvian writer Mario Vargas Llosa, another delegate to the congress, who had rejected political office two years earlier on the grounds that once a writer "becomes an instrument of power he is not a writer anymore." In a later session, as reported by Richard Stern in "Some Members of the Congress," *Critical Inquiry*, vol. 14, no. 4 (Summer 1988), p. 885, the second of Stern's articles on the congress, Vargas Llosa said: "The writer in totalitarian states was reduced to being either a courtesan or a dissident. In other societies his problem was how *not* to become an ambassador or minister of state. In countries which pay serious attention to writers, they're frequently arrested. In countries like the United States, writers feel they're simply entertainers."

54. David Lehman, "When Pen Pals Collide," p. 197.
55. Ibid., p. 198.
56. Stern, "Some Members of the Congress," p. 863.
57. Lehman, "When Pen Pals Collide," pp. 198–99.
58. Fuchs, "Literature and Politics," p. 149.
59. Adam Bellow, in "Our Father's Politics: Gregory, Adam, and Daniel Bellow," in *A Political Companion to Saul Bellow*, ed. Gloria L. Cronin and Lee Trepanier (Lexington: University Press of Kentucky, 2013), p. 205. Adam's summary of his father's congress speech, also on p. 205, is that "he basically got up in front of a room full of writers from all over the world and insulted them. I mean really insulted them, calling them (in effect) political ninnies who should be minding their own business. He was like a bullfighter who was constantly concealing his sword behind his cape." SB's memory of the confrontation with Grass, in James Wood, "Einstein of the Common Life," *Guardian*, 21 April 1990, was still bitter, four years later:

> I was supposed to talk about alienation and the state, and I said that certain things had been promised by the American constitution, which were more or less provided—life, liberty, the pursuit of happiness, goods, laws—but that the higher things had never been promised by the constitution; in other words, it was for the middle range of life that everything was arranged in this country.
>
> And Grass said, "Yes, but what about the people in the South Bronx?" Well, I know more about the people in the South Bronx than he does. What had *he* done? He'd got someone to take him on a tour. I live in the midst of it. What the hell does he know about it?

60. Stern, "Penned In," p. 13.
61. This SB phrase comes from *The Adventures of Augie March* (1953), reprinted in *Saul Bellow: Novels 1944–1953* (New York: Library of America, 2003), p. 414.
62. From a draft of Martin Amis's autobiographical novel *Inside Story*, pages of which he sent to the author on 25 September 2009. For Ijah's "basso profundo" see "Cousins," SB, *CS*, p. 205.
63. Amis, *Inside Story*.
64. Quoted in Atlas, *Biography*, p. 522.
65. This last quote, about SB's silence, comes from ibid., p. 522.
66. Timothy Garton Ash, from an email to the author, 15 April 2010.
67. Atlas, *Biography*, p. 522.
68. Wasserman, *Handsome Is*, p. 129.
69. The article caused a stir at the University of Chicago in particular, where on 7 January 1983, an undergraduate *Maroon* staffer, David Brooks, later a columnist in *The New York Times* and a PBS commentator, wrote a riposte entitled "To Allan Bloom: We're Not Empty, Just Self-Centered." Brooks calls Bloom's article "courageous and important" but takes issue with its claim that today's students are "aimless," or that "our relativism, our tolerance," destroys "moral rules or the notions of good and evil, or even God." As for Bloom's views on rock music, they are "nonsense."
70. Wasserman, *Handsome Is*, p. 133. Lehmann-Haupt's "Books of the Times" review of 23 March was followed by Roger Kimball's review of 5 April, "The Groves of Ignorance," in *The New York Times Book Review*. Kimball called the book "genuinely profound," "essential reading for anyone concerned with the state of liberal education in this society."
71. Wasserman, *Handsome Is*, pp. 133–34.
72. Ibid., pp. 140–41.
73. Sales details from ibid., pp. 133–43.

74. Ibid., p. 135.

75. SB, foreword to Bloom, *Closing of the American Mind*, p. 13. Henceforth cited within the text by page number.

76. Werner J. Dannhauser, "Allan Bloom and His Critics," *American Spectator*, October 1988. According to Nathan Tarcov in an interview, it took a while for the book to be adopted by the right. The early rave reviews, by Christopher Lehmann-Haupt in the daily *Times* and Frederick Starr, the president of Oberlin College, in *The Washington Post*, were written by liberals: "It was only later, six months, nine months later, that conservatives started saying, 'this is our book,' and some people on the left saying, 'well, then it isn't ours.' "

77. Robert Pattison, "On the Finn Syndrome and the Shakespeare Paradox," *Nation*, 30 May 1987, in a review of *The Closing of the American Mind* and E. D. Hirsch's *Cultural Literacy*.

78. Dannhauser, "Allan Bloom and His Critics." Bloom was also accused of being un-American as well as undemocratic, in David Rieff, "The Colonel and the Professor," *Times Literary Supplement*, pp. 153–54, reprinted in *Essays on the Closing*, ed. Stone: "He hates American mores, decries American families, despises American teenagers, and takes no notice of the beauty of the American landscape. . . . The real glories of American culture, which, whether Bloom likes it or not, are Hollywood movies and pop music, come in for the professor's special scorn." Rieff, at the time an editor at Farrar, Straus and Giroux, compared Bloom in the review to Colonel Oliver North and described *The Closing of the American Mind* as a book "decent people would be ashamed to have written."

79. Martha Nussbaum, "Undemocratic Vistas," *New York Review of Books*, 5 November 1987, reprinted in *Essays on the Closing*, ed. Stone. Richard Rorty, in "Straussianism, Democracy and Allan Bloom I," makes a similar objection to Straussians in general, who "typically do not countenance alternative, debatable interpretations . . . but rather distinguish between their own 'authentic understandings' and other 'misunderstandings.' In this respect they resemble the Marxists and the Catholics. The tone in which Bloom writes about Plato is the same as that in which Althusser and Fredric Jameson write about Marx."

80. Atlas, *Biography*, p. x.

81. Ibid., p. xi. The title of Atlas's 1986 novel was *The Great Pretender*. In his memoir, *The Shadow in the Garden: A Biographer's Tale* (New York: Pantheon, 2017), p. 175, when he describes the novel as having "annoyed the critics," Atlas elaborates: "The protagonist, Ben Janis, turned out to be a pretentious jerk."

82. Atlas, *Biography*, pp. xii–xiii.

83. James Atlas, "The Shadow in the Garden," *The New Yorker*, 3 July 1995, the source of all unattributed quotations in this paragraph.

84. SB was unbothered by a throwaway line Atlas had attributed to him in the Bloom profile, taken from a telephone conversation: "Who is the Tolstoy of the Zulus? The Proust of the Papuans?" Bellow had asked. This flip question was to lead, as we shall see, to accusations of racism, a charge SB vigorously denied.

85. The corrected title is given in Atlas, *Biography*, p. 556; the misremembering from notes is described in Atlas's book-length memoir, *The Shadow in the Garden*, p. 293, where the "shadow of the tombstone" is said to be "in" the garden, not "falling across" it.

86. *More Die of Heartbreak* was published by William Morrow and Company, the publishers SB moved to after his disappointment with Harper & Row over their promotion of *Him with His Foot in His Mouth and Other Stories*. According to Atlas, *Biography*, p. 527, SB had had little rapport with his editor at Harper & Row, Ed Burlingame, who he thought was insufficiently attentive: "One day Harriet Wasserman called him up and said, 'Saul will never speak to you again.' What

infraction had Burlingame committed now? He had failed to call Bellow to commiserate about a negative review 'in the *Hartford Courant* (or it may have been the *Sacramento Bee*).'" Atlas also quotes a letter Burlingame wrote to Barley Alison on 12 February 1986, which attributes SB's unhappiness to Wasserman: "Our problems with Harriet worsen every week. She is utterly impossible to do business with and she seizes every opportunity to create worry on his part, so that her role as watchdog and defender is magnified" (p. 528).

87. SB explained the novel's genesis in a letter of 7 January 1987 to Martin Amis: "First my elder brothers died, both of them, and then Alexandra after twelve years of marriage decided to divorce me, releasing me at the age of seventy to begin a new life. These events left me reeling for six months. To stave off sordid depression—if not insanity—I went back to work last June and wrote a book—a short one called *More Die of Heartbreak*, in which, naturally, I make fun of heartbreak: with a familiar mixture of obstinacy and high-voltage absurdity."

88. For Bentchka, see chapter 2 of *To Fame and Fortune*, p. 58. Ellen Pifer, *Saul Bellow Against the Grain* (Philadelphia: University of Pennsylvania Press, 1990), pp. 153, 200–201n1, compares Benn's way of seeing to Rudolf Steiner's account of "inward" vision. Kenneth is interesting on eyes: "One of my Russian philosophers says that human eyes fall into one of two categories, the receptive and the will-emanating. . . . The first was Uncle's category, of course" (*More Die of Heartbreak*, p. 47). For similarities between Bentchka's and Benn's and SB's way of seeing and Wordsworth's creative perception, see chapter 2 of *To Fame and Fortune*, pp. 53–57.

89. Although Benn, like Bellow, "couldn't leave the women alone" (p. 190), it is hard to apply Kenneth's account of Benn as "fried" by the women he took up with to SB, just as it is hard to see SB as "a sex-abused man, a mere victim of so many Dellas and Carolines, not to mention the Rajashwaris and other ladies of the Third World" (pp. 112–13).

90. As Kenneth puts it, about Benn's love needs: "The demand then was for a sharer, a charming woman, such a woman as Swedenborg describes—made by God to instruct a man, to lead him to the exchange of souls. Maybe to teach him, as Diotima taught Socrates about love" (p. 46).

91. Pifer, *Saul Bellow Against the Grain*, p. 156.

92. As for Benn's rivals, "According to Doctor, she passed up a national network anchorman, then a fellow who was now on the federal appeals bench, plus a tax genius consulted by Richard Nixon" (p. 126).

93. On 19 May 1983, in response to an unnamed article in which SB admitted that he liked to do dishes, Clarence Brown, professor of comparative literature at Princeton, wrote with advice: "Dear Mr. Bellow, I thought you might like to know about a product called Soft-Scrub, put out by the Clorox people (with whom I have no affiliation). It is a sort of white gunk that cuts grease out of a sink like nobody's business. Same for pots. I sent Nadia Mandelstam, God rest her soul, a bottle and she had people in to watch it work. It does linoleum too. Yours truly, Clarence Brown."

94. The title of the interview is "Saul Bellow Teaches an 'Object' Lesson." That SB knew of the corruption of love from the inside is suggested in a letter to Bloom of 28 February 1983. After an exhausting trip to the market, SB recounts in the letter, "I took off all my clothing and got into bed for an hour of angelic purity and meditation, browsing in Pieper's book on the *Phaedrus*. I saw how bad the sophists were, and it comforted me to be on the right side, faithful to Eros and repudiating spurious sexuality. I am old enough at last to see things in a true light."

95. As SB puts it in "Saul Bellow Teaches an 'Object' Lesson," his *Chicago Tribune* interview with Kennedy, the cause of this damaging literalism is loss of faith in "the ageless truths of human nature. . . . In the nature-nurture controversy,

nurture has been regarded as *everything.* I never believed that. The Bible, Shakespeare, Homer and the Greek playwrights believed there was some stable character to human nature. Now, some people are trying to get rid of the very concept of a durable human nature. That is why the affective lives of people have changed, and why the bonds between persons have grown weaker."

96. See also Pifer, *Saul Bellow Against the Grain*, p. 156: "By insisting that his fascination with Matilda's alluring beauty *is* love, Benn undergoes his version of the West's current 'ordeal of desire.'" Matilda, too, sees only parts, not wholes, like Angela in *Mr. Sammler's Planet*, seeking an impossible ideal made of them: "a little Muhammad Ali for straight sex, some of Kissinger for savvy, Cary Grant for looks, Jack Nicholson for entertainment, plus André Malraux or some Jew for brains. Commonest fantasy there is" (p. 176).

97. Roger Kaplan, email to the author, 17 September 2008.

98. As Dr. Layamon explains to Benn, Vilitzer "was on the zoning commission and he did have advance information" (p. 158). He also has the judge who ruled against Benn and his sister in his pocket, in addition to giving him a kickback after the ruling. This judge is now being threatened with a federal indictment, and it would be a bad time for news of his crooked dealings with Vilitzer to be revealed. The prosecutor would like nothing better than to go after Vilitzer. "You send Vilitzer to jail and you have a clear path to the U.S. Senate. Or you become governor and you're even mentioned for the presidency, maybe. That's how our present governor did it" (p. 160).

99. Martin Amis, introduction, Penguin Classics edition (the edition used here) of *More Die of Heartbreak*, p. vii.

100. See Atlas, *Biography*, p. 530: "Women came and went from the apartment on Dorchester with unabated frequency. . . . Both new and old flames were recruited to fill the gap left by Alexandra's departure. Monique Gonthier [a journalist whom SB had met in James Jones's apartment in Paris] arrived . . . to interview him for a French magazine. Zita Cogan, who had been in love with Bellow since their Tuley days and who kept prominently displayed on her bookshelves copies of his books inscribed 'the second-story man' and 'second-story Bellow from Humboldt Park' . . . came to him with a proposition: 'If you're not married by the time you're 78, I'll take care of you if you'll take care of me.'"

101. Pifer, *Saul Bellow Against the Grain*, p. 160 (the page numbers for Pifer's quotations from the novel have been changed to those from the Penguin Classics edition, the edition used here; hence the square brackets). Kenneth's child is a little girl, not an adolescent boy, but she functions, less crudely, in the role of Allan Bloom's caricature in *The Closing of the American Mind* of a typical adolescent American: "Picture a thirteen-year-old boy sitting in the living room of his family home doing his math assignment while wearing his Walkman headphones or watching MTV. He enjoys the liberties hard won over centuries by the alliance of philosophic genius and political heroism, consecrated by the blood of martyrs; he is provided with comfort and leisure by the most productive economy ever known to mankind; science has penetrated the secrets of nature in order to provide him with the marvelous, lifelike electronic sound and image reproduction he is enjoying. And in what does progress culminate? A pubescent child whose body throbs with orgasmic rhythms; whose feelings are made articulate in hymns to the joys of onanism or the killing of parents; whose ambition is to win fame and wealth in imitating the drag-queen who makes the music" (pp. 74–75), presumably Mick Jagger.

102. According to Atlas, *Biography*, p. 537, though *More Die of Heartbreak* was on the best-seller list for thirteen weeks, it sold less than half its six hundred thousand copies.

103. In an interview, Wieseltier claims that his initial motive in writing the review was "to defend Benn Crader . . . And then I wrote one fateful paragraph near the end. . . . What I said was something like . . . he's just afraid of women, uncomfortable with women." What he said was this:

> There is still another impediment to the American Contemplative in Bellow's account. . . . Specifically, it is women. *More Die of Heartbreak* is unrelenting in its disgust for women, who are portrayed as if their reason for being is the frustration of the better selves of men. Matilda, Treckie, Caroline, Della: they are all curses in makeup, utterly ridiculous figures, plotting predators, exploiters of desire. (There is also one Dita, with whom Trachtenberg finds respite, who is exempt from the great excoriation; but she is also exempt from sexual interest.) At one point Bellow's horror of women is promoted into a theory of history: "The East has the ordeal of privation, the West has the ordeal of desire"—sort of a cross between Strindberg and Solzhenitsyn.

Wieseltier as champion of women has its ironies, given accusations made against him by female staff at *The New Republic*, a personal "ordeal of desire" that cost him dearly. Also costly was the belief that his defense of the metaphysical aspects of the novel would please SB. "I sent him the fucking galleys, like an idiot." The result was disastrous. SB was "very angry and very hurt." In a letter of 11 March 1990 to Wieseltier's boss at *The New Republic*, Martin Peretz, labeled "*CONFIDENTIAL*," SB complained: "Leon said that I was a misogynist, a racist, a sexist, a colonialist, a reactionary, and he charged me with disliking our country and just about everything else he could think of short of downright treason. . . . But even this is not the whole story. Together with a copy of this ignoble review there came a syrupy letter from Leon filled with protestations of friendship and deep loyalty (despite my shortcomings and sins)." Later, Wieseltier recalls, SB appeared on television "and attacked the review as a trendy left-wing rant." Wieseltier protested that all he "meant to say" was that the treatment of women in the novel "seemed like a lapse." He was both "very wounded" and disappointed in SB's reaction: "He was too smart for this reaction. . . . Saul really didn't need people to tell him he was a genius." Here are the other passages of Wieseltier's review (aside from the ones about women) SB took exception to in his letter to Peretz: "Though Bellow's novel is brimming with American energies and American excesses, it is, in a sense, spiritually anti-American. America is presented as a disperser of the spirit, a commotion of deceits and distractions, a shallow, crowded, broken-down, tawdry shrine to money and power"; "His book is sprinkled, for example, with an unworthy scorn for what he calls 'the Third World.' It is saddening to see Bellow become a party to the fashionable neo-colonialist rant."

104. These words from the *New York Times* article are also found on pp. 16–17 of SB's foreword to *The Closing of the American Mind*.

105. "They all worked so hard to turn me around [into a schemer, that is] that I did turn around. At last I entered into it also. . . . This once I've done it, and never again" (pp. 325, 326).

9. TO SEVENTY-FIVE

1. Philip Roth to SB and Janis Bellow, 22 October 1995. The quoted sentence is what the letter read in its entirety. Janis's review of *Sabbath's Theater* and Martin Amis's *The Information*, under the title "Necropolis of the Heart," appeared in the Fall 1995 issue of *Partisan Review*. She had defended Roth the year before, in an article in *Bostonia* taking issue with criticisms of *Operation Shylock* (1993).

2. SB, "Vermont: The Good Place," *Travel Holiday*, July 1990, reprinted in SB, *IAAU*, pp. 250–51.

3. Joseph Epstein, "Another Rare Visit with Noah Danzig," *Commentary*, October 1990. The story is narrated by "a biographer and literary man" interested in "the manifold connections between life and work—and especially the almost inevitable clash between decent behavior and the production of stellar art." Noah Danzig is clearly to be identified with SB and Epstein with the narrator. They meet because the narrator has been commissioned to write a piece about Danzig for *The New York Times*, as Epstein had been commissioned by the *Times* to write a piece about SB. Their place of meeting is the Whitehall Club, where SB and Epstein frequently dined. Danzig has SB's appearance, described as "like some prehistorical version of a Jewish eagle." His clothes are SB's clothes, as in the "checked suit, with sharply cut lapels and small, high pockets cut into the trousers." The heroes in Danzig's novels (Epstein takes the Updike line, or perhaps it's the other way around) "were plainly himself, got up in various wigs, false noses and glasses, taped-on mustaches, and other easily penetrated disguises." One of Danzig's persistent themes in conversation is the irrelevance of the artist in modern society. And so forth. He is shown in a consistently bad light, and though the story concludes that he is of a type, he's the worst of the type. "I took him for a man, when he was that quite different thing, an artist—less than a great one, to be sure, but psychologically a perfect type. . . . But the larger point, I began to see, was that the more complete the artist the less complete the man. Men didn't come much more incomplete than Noah."

The source of the narrator's animus is an unflattering portrait of him in one of Danzig's novels, "a portrait of me as something of an updated Sammy Glick." Epstein had never suffered such a fate, but he believed his friend the art critic Hilton Kramer had, when portrayed in *Humboldt's Gift* as "just a careerist." Epstein had introduced Kramer to SB at "a perfectly agreeable dinner" at the Whitehall Club. According to Epstein, the thinly disguised portrait of Kramer as a cowardly careerist character named Magnasco is both inaccurate (among other things, in its implied account of Kramer's relations with Delmore Schwartz, Humboldt's acknowledged model) and gratuitous. In a letter of February 12, 1991, to Ruth Wisse, Bellow characterized Epstein's story as "gross, moronic and clumsily written."

4. Shawmut's and SB's propensity to make wounding remarks is discussed in chapter 3 of *To Fame and Fortune*, pp. 103–4. It was a quality remarked on admiringly by his son Daniel: "He was truly Pop when he was saying something particularly wicked. You grow up with it and you think it's normal, but I've never met anybody like him" ("Our Father's Politics," in *A Political Companion to Saul Bellow*, ed. Gloria L. Cronin and Lee Trepanier [Lexington: University Press of Kentucky, 2013], p. 221). Kingsley Amis, no admirer of SB, tells a story in his *Memoirs* (Harmondsworth, U.K.: Penguin, 1991) about the novelist Anthony Powell that sheds light upon the "German-Jewish bullshit" story. When Amis and Powell were recording a radio interview at the BBC in 1955, it became clear to them that the interview had been set up as a sort of confrontation: Amis, the angry young man, versus the older, upper-class novelist Powell. What the producer did not know is that the two novelists were friends and admired each other's work. They also took an instant dislike to what Amis calls the producer's "autocratic" manner. Soon after the interview began, as Amis was reading out his introduction, a light flashed and the producer's voice sounded from a loudspeaker; then he bustled in, "clearly dissatisfied."

> "You're sticking to the actual novels, the text" [said the producer].
>
> "I thought that was what we were supposed to be discussing," I said.

"No no, that's not what I want. I want something about the status of the novel in general, its place in society and so on."

Tony said, "We don't care what you want. We're going to do what we want. And if you don't like it we're walking out of this studio. Now."

What impressed me about this utterance, even more than its style and content, was its placid, conversational delivery. That's the upper classes for you, I thought to myself; I might have been able to summon the guts to say something along those lines, but I should have had to lose my temper to do it. Anyway, that short speech of Tony's knocked all the fight out of the producer.

"There's no need to take that tone," he said.

"Oh, good," said Tony appreciatively. [p. 152].

The equivalent of this last exchange ("'Oh, good,' said Tony appreciatively") in the SB story is the way he calmly resumes eating, though in this case sangfroid or self-possession is no product of social class. SB met Anthony Powell once, in London in 1949, according to Thomas Barnard, his insurance agent, in an unpublished memoir he gave me entitled "Saul Bellow, a Gift for Friendship" (2015). "Bellow had pronounced his name Powell," Barnard writes, "but Powell, nose to the sky, said it was pronounced Pole. 'I thought the hell with you.'"

5. Christopher Hitchens, *Hitch-22: A Memoir* (London: Atlantic Books, 2010), p. 398.

6. Ibid., p. 399.

7. Martin Amis, *Experience* (2000; London: Vintage, 2001), p. 261.

8. Ibid., pp. 261, 267.

9. Edward Said, "An Exchange on Edward Said and Difference III: Response," *Critical Inquiry*, vol. 15, no. 3 (Spring 1989).

10. In the unedited typescript of "A Talk with Saul Bellow," *Israel Scene*, April 1988, an interview conducted in Haifa between SB and Leila H. Goldman and Ada Aharoni, SB comments on Gore Vidal: "I've known Gore Vidal a long time. I know he is a bit meshuggah [crazy]. He is a good writer in his way which is not as good a way as he thinks. He has certain gifts which are not as imposing as he would like them to be . . . and he is one of these people who feels that he belongs to patrician America, to the old America, and he takes the view of immigrants and the melting pot [that] old America . . . very often preferred to take, namely that we are an intrusion, a barbarian and hybrid population, we're dragging the country down and lowering its ancient and holy standards and all the rest of that. Well he's full of it." This passage is cut from the published interview, where its themes are woven into other questions. The interviewers liken Vidal to Allbee, the anti-Semite in *The Victim*, and SB concurs: "Allbee does remind one in many ways of Vidal."

11. Hitchens, *Hitch-22*, p. 400.

12. Janis Bellow's account of the European trip comes from entries in the journal she kept from 1987 to 2002.

13. For these and other quotations from the interview, see Leila H. Goldman and Ada Aharoni, "A Talk with Saul Bellow."

14. Atlas, *Biography*, p. 534, where Atlas claims that SB "read every word of the *Saul Bellow Journal*," though in a letter of 5 August 1987 to A. B. Yehoshua, SB says of the editors of the *Journal*, "I shrank from reading their publications."

15. Andrew Gordon, "The Ancient Mariner, and Other Encounters with Saul Bellow," *Saul Bellow Journal*, vol. 10, no. 1 (1991), pp. 64, 65.

16. Ann Cheroff Weinstein, *Me and My (Tor)mentor, Saul Bellow: A Memoir of My Literary Love Affair* (New York: iUniverse, 2007), p. 25.

17. Amis, *Experience*, p. 201. SB, "A Matter of the Soul," *Opera News*, 11 January 1975, reprinted in SB, *IAAU*, p. 76.

18. Ellen Pifer, email to the author, 25 August 2016.

19. For Amis's account of the Haifa conference and the subsequent stay in Jerusalem see *Experience*, pp. 221–26.

20. Atlas, *Biography*, p. 539, misdates SB and Janis's European holiday as after, not before the Haifa conference. He also claims that, upon returning to Vermont, SB immediately set off for Montreal, where he gave a speech at the Montreal Council of Foreign Relations, was interviewed at the Jewish Public Library, and visited Lachine with Ruth Wisse on his way to the airport. Janis Bellow, however, has no record in her journals of a visit to Montreal at this time, nor has the Jewish Public Library a record of such an interview, nor is there any record of SB's giving a talk at the Montreal Council of Foreign Relations (their records don't go back that far). In an email to the author of 17 August 2016, Shannon Hodge, of the Jewish Public Library in Montreal, attributes the misdating to a file in the library that "was horribly misdated." The talk Atlas refers to was given in 1990. Ann Weinstein says its title was "What Does It Mean to Be a Jewish Writer?" But Atlas quotes a passage from this talk, a copy of which was given to him by Weinstein, that clearly refers to the April 1987 trip to Europe, and seems to suggest that SB really did deliver it in 1987:

> I became very tired and went to take a holiday in Europe. I ended up by flying from place to place and tried to catch up with the train from Avignon to Lyon which was determined to leave me behind and then I got on to the railroad station in Lyon and asked where the hotel where I had a reservation was located. . . . I shot up in an elevator to the 48th floor and there I found myself sealed in one of these modern hotel rooms where you couldn't even open a window, where you could scarcely breathe and I thought, "This is Lyon: Is this the holiday where I regrow my depleted tissues?" The answer was No and flying around from place to place was all a big mistake and then I came back to the U.S. I land in Boston. I go to Vermont. I drive up to Lachine because it is impossible for me to refuse an invitation from M. Descary [the mayor of Lachine] and so here I am still on the run, on the lam, so to speak [p. 539].

21. According to Adam Bellow, Sonya Freedman's brother, a musician, was also initially opposed to the relationship, telling Adam at one point, "We're all very upset. I'm very upset."

22. SB, "All Marbles Still Accounted For," p. 21, in SB Papers, Regenstein. In some ways, Hilbert Faucil is like SB: He grew up on the West Side of Chicago and had an education like SB's. That his paper concerns itself with highbrow literary and philosophical matters as well as lowbrow tabloid fare suggests a range like that of SB's fiction.

23. The idea of writing down notes about her life with Bellow came to Janis at the suggestion of Sophie Wilkins, an editor at Knopf, a translator, and the wife of the poet Karl Shapiro.

24. George Walden, *Lucky George: Memoirs of an Anti-Politician* (1999; London: Penguin, 2000), p. 328.

25. The quotations from "Marbles" about ninety-three-year old Hilbert Faucil, the hero, being cheated by his accountant come from p. 23 of the "Marbles" manuscript. The cheating accountant, "the man who took full charge of my financial affairs," is called Rupert Tarquino (p. 21), a boyish-looking man in his mid-thirties. "Looking for signs of honesty in his face you could never be really certain; if you looked for the other thing all you could fix upon was his mouth and

especially the swell of the lower lip when he stared at you during the intervals of fluency. Lip and stare were connected, asserting honesty but unable to eliminate certain traces of guile" (p. 22). Here is how Rupert Tarquino talks:

> At this point in time we should go into condominium sharing on the gulf coast. The group down there is over-extended, with a second-mortgage problem. To invest smartly at this point in time would yield special advantages, taxwise and futurewise, and with your retirement capital setup this one would be a sweetheart. Because we could do it extended, willing to reinvest capital gains. By conceding on distributions you can get special terms from the Firefly Group which is into this up to its kazoo [p. 21].

Among the SB Papers in the Regenstein are letters from his lawyers to Jeffrey W. Krol, his accountant and financial adviser, along with a "Verified Complaint in Chancery for Accounting and Other Relief" filed with the Circuit Court of Cook County, Illinois, Chancery Division. Krol had first served as SB's accountant while at Peat, Marwick and Mitchell in the 1970s. From 1981, having left the firm, he continued to act as SB's accountant and adviser. From 1981 to 1989, the Chancery Complaint reads, SB, "as a result of Defendant's suggestions, recommendations and urgings, invested substantial sums of money in various real estate and other investment vehicles and securities including several partnerships and limited partnerships." Unhappy with his returns, or lack of returns, from these investments, SB made repeated demands to see Krol's books and records. When Krol failed to produce these, SB filed his complaint. According to Janis Bellow, SB lost a very large sum of money and had great difficulty extricating himself from various bad investment deals. "'Very truly yours,' he would sign off," Janis remembers.

26. For SB on the Egypt-Israel Treaty ceremonies see SB, "Saul Bellow's Account of the Mideast Peace Ceremony," *Newsday*, March 31, 1979.

27. Paul Glastris, "The Powers That Shouldn't Be: Five Washington Insiders the Next Democratic President Shouldn't Hire," *Washington Monthly*, October 1987.

28. See SB, "All Marbles Still Accounted For," pp. 113–14 (of the 279-page manuscript), for a fictionalized version of the incident with Schlesinger. Former Secretary of Defense Brushmore is introduced to Hilbert Faucil at a White House dinner:

> He didn't stumble, it was no accident, for he picked up my necktie and spilled red wine on it. The cause, I never actually determined. . . . One thing that may have displeased the Secretary was that the tie, I admit, was a very loud one covered with sprigs of cherry blossom. This is not the kind of thing you can easily get over. He picked it up from the bottom as if he had studied the doing of this for years and tipped his wineglass over it all the way to the knot. Who can know why? The custodian of atomic bombs and missiles took against me. . . . "Why did you do that?" I said. And as he was already turning away I let fly at him with my fist. But I never touched him because I was caught from behind, under the arms. This incident was witnessed by the President's mother, Miz Lillian, who said "See here! None of this!" She wasn't scolding, she gave me her protection. "What did you do to that fella to make him do a thing like that?"
>
> "I only asked him how he was."
>
> "Maybe he's drunk."
>
> "He's one-hundred percent sober. They shouldn't have stopped me."
>
> "Well, for a senior citizen you are a gutsy fellow, you don't take any whatchamacallit."

"I should have smashed him one."

"It would have been in all the papers so I'm glad you didn't."

29. SB, in Manea, "Conversation," p. 32.

30. Adam Bellow, in Gloria L. Cronin, "Our Father's Politics: Gregory, Adam, and Daniel Bellow," in *Political Companion to SB*, ed. Cronin and Trepanier, p. 201.

31. Ibid., p. 216.

32. Walden, *Lucky George*, p. 272.

33. The television program Bloom appeared on was *The Late Show with Clive James*, BBC, 17 February 1979. The other guests were Anthony Burgess and Carmen Callil.

34. Walden, *Lucky George*, pp. 274, 275.

35. Ibid., pp. 275, 276.

36. In addition to the Kennedy op-ed piece, I have drawn on articles in *The New York Times* by Dirk Johnson, "Black-Jewish Hostility Rouses Leaders in Chicago to Action," 29 July 1988, and "Racial Politics: Chicago's Raw Nerve," 19 February 1989; and Anthony Lewis, "A Dangerous Poison," 31 July 1988.

37. Cokely not only believed that Jewish doctors had injected black children with AIDS, he claimed to have uncovered a number of corporate conspiracies, including by the Trilateral Commission, the Bilderberg Group, the Rothschilds, and the Rockefellers. He also said that Jesse Jackson and the CIA had conspired together to assassinate Martin Luther King, Jr.

38. These quotations are reported in excerpts from the speech published on 25 April 1989 in the *Chicago Tribune* under the title "Bellow Sees Good Signs for Future." According to Kennedy, one reason Daley asked Bellow to speak at the inaugural was that his wife, Maggie Daley, was a fan of Bellow's novels.

39. Robert D, McFadden, "John Silber Dies at 86; Led Boston University," *New York Times*, 27 September 2012, the main source also of accounts of Silber's tenure as president of Boston University. For this tenure, see also Roger Kimball, "John Silber, 1926–2012," *New Criterion*, vol. 31, no. 3 (November 2012), and three letters, 18 June, 23 October, and 6 November 1980, to *New York Review of Books* from prominent BU faculty denouncing, defending, then again denouncing Silber.

40. Botsford's and SB's friend John Hunt had something to do with the appointment at Texas. Hunt, who worked undercover for the CIA, and was later to head the Institute for Advanced Studies at Princeton and the Aspen Institute, had known Botsford when they were both at the University of Iowa. In 1962, Hunt invited Botsford to join the Congress for Cultural Freedom and become its "permanent roving representative" in Latin America. After three years based in Rio de Janeiro and Mexico City, Hunt sent Botsford to London, to work as deputy secretary of International PEN. There Botsford helped to organize PEN's first Bled Congress in Yugoslavia, to which Soviet writers were invited. In 1965, less than a year after arriving in London, Botsford got the Texas appointment. See Frances Stonor Saunders, *Who Paid the Piper: The CIA and the Cold War* (1999; Granta Books, 2000), pp. 241–43, 348.

41. According to Atlas, *The Shadow in the Garden: A Biographer's Tale* (New York: Pantheon, 2017), p. 186, when question-and-answer periods followed SB's readings the procedure "was always the same: members of the audience would write down their questions on file cards that had been included with their programs and hand them to the ushers going through the aisles. . . . When the stack of cards arrived, Bellow leafed through it and picked out the ones that interested him, muttering aloud, to great laughter from the audience, the best of the rejects ('What are you doing tonight after the reading?')."

42. See Harriet Wasserman, *Handsome Is: Adventures with Saul Bellow* (New York: Fromm International, 1997), p. 164, where she names only *Esquire* and the *Atlantic Monthly* as having declined to publish *A Theft*. "What to do? I certainly didn't want to risk another turndown," she adds on the next page, before discussing the decision to publish as a paperback original. Atlas, *Biography*, p. 542, mentions *Vanity Fair* and *The New Yorker* as also having turned the novella down. In an interview, Janis recalls waiting for the *New Yorker* decision. Also, Alan Cheuse, in his review of *A Theft* in the *Chicago Tribune* ("Saul Bellow's Ring of Truth," 5 March 1989), mentions *The New Yorker*'s decision.

43. Edwin McDowell, "Trade Paperbacks Gaining in Role of a Happy Medium," *New York Times*, 17 October 1988.

44. Wasserman, *Handsome Is*, p. 165.

45. Atlas, *Biography*, p. 543. John Updike reviewed *A Theft* in *The New Yorker* with Anita Brookner's *Latecomers*, under the ironic title "Nice Tries" (1 May 1989); Robert Towers reviewed it in *The New York Review of Books*, 27 April 1989, with Margaret Atwood's *Cat's Eye* and Susanna Moore's *The Whiteness of Bones*, under the title "Mystery Women." Joyce Carol Oates's review, "Clara's Gift," appeared in *The New York Times Book Review* on 5 March 1989.

46. Henry James, *Collected Novels and Tales*, 24 vols. (1907–9; New York: Charles Scribner and Sons, 1935), vol. 20, p. viii.

47. SB, *A Theft*, in *CS*, p. 124. Henceforth cited within the text by page number.

48. John Banville, "International Tale," *London Review of Books*, 30 March 1989.

49. Maggie Staats Simmons, email to the author, 14 September 2016, the source also of the earlier description of the novella as "an act of expiation."

50. Maggie Staats Simmons, email to the author, 5 September 2016.

51. Maggie Staats Simmons, email to the author, 6 September 2016.

52. Ibid. Fanny Assingham, referred to as a sort of Clara, is a character in James's *The Golden Bowl*. Also Jamesian is a strand of the novella concerning Clara's young daughter, Lucy, who proves another exceptional character. Like a child in a Henry James story, Lucy is involved in adult machinations, being the one Gina chooses to get the ring back to Clara. "I see how you brought it all together through my own child," Clara tells Gina. "You gave her something significant to do, and she was equal to it. Most amazing to me is the fact that she didn't talk, she only watched. That level of control and observation in a girl of ten . . . how do you suppose it feels to discover that?" (p. 171).

53. Ithiel "was committed to high civility, structure, order; nevertheless he took chances with women, he was a gambler, something of an anarchist" (p. 138).

54. For David Denby, in a review of *A Theft* and *The Bellarosa Connection* in *The New Republic* ("Memory in America," 1 January 1990), "Bellow's eager new sophistication [about the world of East Side privilege] fits badly with the highfalutin, morally strenuous tone of the exchanges between Clara and Gina. . . . The irony of a noble character triumphing in such worldly and gilded circumstances doesn't come through with any force."

55. I am drawing from a typed copy of the speech, "A Jewish Writer in America," April 1988, in the SB Papers in the Regenstein. Appended to it is an alternative ending of several sentences and a handwritten note dated 18 May: "Dear Cynthia [Ozick]—This is the added paragraph for the end of the Philadelphia paper. I sent a typed copy." Henceforth, this copy will be cited within the text by page numbers. Versions of the speech were reprinted in *The New York Review of Books* (27 October and 10 November 2011) and in SB, *There Is Simply Too Much to Think About: Collected Nonfiction*, ed. Benjamin Taylor (New York: Viking Penguin, 2015), pp. 356–73.

56. For the theory of the *egregore*, see Valentin Tomberg, *Meditations on the Tarot: A Journey into Christian Hermeticism*, trans. Robert Powell (Amity, N.Y.: Amity House, 1985).

57. P. 30 of the typed copy is the one with the added paragraph sent to Cynthia Ozick.

58. SB to Cynthia Ozick, 18 May 1988: "Among the other speakers I make exception for Potok, who gave a very good talk, and gave it in his own words." Chaim Potok, the novelist and rabbi, had been editor-in-chief of the JPS.

59. Janis Bellow's account of this dinner party is mentioned in the introduction to *To Fame and Fortune*, in a discussion of SB's use of sources.

60. SB to Evelyn Nef, 15 November 1998: "I'm glad you liked the novellas. I can't say that I ever had any real contact with Billy Rose, but I was staying in the King David Hotel in Jerusalem when Billy turned up with Noguchi [Isamu Noguchi, the Japanese American artist and landscape gardener]. They had come to lay out Billy's great gift to the city, a sculpture garden. Noguchi was in charge of this project. This is where I saw and heard Billy screaming with rage in the lobby because his luggage had been lost by El Al. The performance was terribly enjoyable. I had no other contact whatever with this pair but I kept them in my sights for a couple of weeks and enjoyed every minute of my vigil."

61. SB, *The Bellarosa Connection* (1989), reprinted in SB, *CS*, p. 35. Henceforth cited within the text by page numbers.

62. For "distraction" as a key theme in *The Bellarosa Connection*, see Ezra Cappell, "Sorting the Vital from the Useless: Holocaust Memory in Saul Bellow's *The Bellarosa Connection*," *Saul Bellow Journal*, vol. 23, nos. 1–2 (Fall 2007 / Winter 2008).

63. David Denby, in his review of *A Theft* and *The Bellarosa Connection* ("Memory in America," *New Republic*, 1 January 1990), thinks the admiring depiction of Sorella extraordinary because SB's descriptions of her body are "grounded so firmly in sexual disgust." The passage he quotes in support of this view, however, shows nothing of the kind: "She was very heavy and she wore makeup. Her cheeks were downy. Her hair was done up in a beehive. A pince-nez, highly unusual, a deliberate disguise, gave her a theatrical air" (p. 37).

64. SB to Michael Alison (Barley's brother), 12 June 1989.

65. SB, "In Memory of Robert Penn Warren," September 1989, written for Warren's memorial service, SB Papers in the Regenstein.

66. Atlas, *Biography*, p. 550.

67. SB to Sanford Pinsker, 25 July 1988.

68. Andrew Patner, "Dr. Demopoulos Sells a 'Fountain of Youth' to Rich and Famous," *Wall Street Journal*, 8 November 1989. See also SB to Harry B. Demopoulos, 9 August 1994: "Joking aside I have been taking your vitamins and antioxidants for about ten years and in that time I have had no serious diseases. An early benefit of the Health Performance Packs was that I was able to give up beta-blockers or whatever it is cardiologists give for the control of high blood pressure. I have registered 130/70 for a decade now. The only disorder I have to cope with is an arrhythmia for which I take Quinine tablets. At the age of 79 I am therefore virtually drug free and know how well I have been protected by your vitamins. I am willing to say as much at a banquet, before a professional meeting or in print."

69. The "Zetland" manuscripts and SB's relations with Reichian therapy are discussed in chapter 10 of *To Fame and Fortune*.

70. Atlas, *Biography*, p. 554.

71. Philip Roth to SB, 11 June 1990. SB replied on 24 June: "I am very fond of Cousin Volya, who was something of a hero in the Old Country, serving in the

Russian cavalry from Leningrad to Berlin. It's easy to mistake him for somebody else. When he explained the difference between Latvia and Lithuania to Steinberg, Steinberg said it was like a piece of dialogue out of a Marx Brothers' movie."

10. PAPUANS AND ZULUS

1. Details of the party come from Jerry Nemanic, "Politicians Sing of Bellow's Gift to Fiction, City," *Chicago Tribune*, 9 October 1990; Mary A. Johnson, "Bellow Marks His 75th," *Chicago Sun-Times*, 8 October 1990; and John Blades, "Birthday Salute," *Chicago Tribune*, 4 October 1990.

2. Furet was president of the École des Hautes Études en Sciences Sociales. The school was in some ways like the Committee on Social Thought: it prided itself on standing apart from the formal university world, the world of the Sorbonne, and encouraged interdisciplinary study. Furet's own research on the French Revolution brought him into bitter conflict with the Marxist historians of the Sorbonne. He had been a communist in his youth but left the party in 1956, later becoming a significant anti-communist commentator on contemporary French politics.

3. Clifford Orwin, "Remembering Allan Bloom," p. 8 of a 23-page typescript of an essay published under the same title in *The American Scholar*, vol. 62, no. 3 (Summer 1993), pp. 423–30; I quote from the typescript, which is labeled "The Final Version."

4. Spiekerman's recollections, here and elsewhere, come from emails to the author, 5 and 17 August 2016.

5. In an interview with the Canadian psychiatrist Norman Doidge, later used in a profile Doidge wrote for *Saturday Night* magazine in 2000, SB is asked if Bloom "changed" him. I quote from a fax Doidge sent SB on 26 April 2000, which contains his answer to this question (it had been answered over the telephone): "Bellow: He lightened me up, and cleaned up my mental life very considerably. . . . He made me take myself much less seriously. So that I stopped being so serious beyond my own depth. He made me see I didn't have as many options as I thought I did, and that I couldn't expect to render verdicts on all the questions we faced, and that it was comical to be straining for answers I didn't have. There were things he allowed me to get away with because I was a dear friend and because I was a writer. I became interested in Rudolf Steiner, a thinker, and he thought this was just baloney, and he'd say, 'This is inappropriate; I give you license to do it at the back of your mind, for working up some literary themes, but don't expect me to take it seriously.' I thought he was unfair. But according to him I was not a hundred percent serious person."

6. Allan Bloom, *Love & Friendship* (New York: Simon & Schuster, 1993), pp. 208, 209.

7. According to Atlas, *Biography*, p. 564, Bloom's return to normal activities was "sustained by the cartons of Marlboros that he had dispatched Janis to bring him."

8. As recalled by Richard Stern, quoted in ibid., p. 653.

9. Orwin, "Remembering Allan Bloom," typescript, p. 22.

10. SB to Rosanna Warren, 21 October 1992.

11. Andrew Gordon, "Choosing the Necessary: Remarks by Saul Bellow to Padget Powell's Graduate Class in Fiction Writing at the University of Florida, Gainesville, February 21, 1992," http://users.clas.ufl.edu/agordon/beluf.htm. My account of SB's visit to Florida also draws on a fuller draft of the article in the SB Papers in Regenstein, one sent to SB by Powell.

12. Gordon himself calls SB's remarks Wordsworthian; they recall the sonnet "The World Is Too Much With Us" (1807), with its complaint that, "getting and spending, we lay waste our powers."

13. SB, "Mozart: An Overture," *Bostonia*, Spring 1992, delivered at the Mozart Bicentennial, 5 December 1991, in Florence, Italy, reprinted in SB, *IAAU*, p. 3. Henceforth cited in the text by page numbers.

14. See Teddy Kollek to SB, 26 January 1992; the description of Kollek as "schemer," etc., is from SB to Ruth Wisse, 20 February 1992.

15. See Janis Freedman Bellow, "Double Trouble in the Promised Land," a review of Philip Roth, *Operation Shylock*, in *Bostonia*, Winter 1993. *Bostonia* was funded by BU and edited by Keith Botsford, who was transforming it from an alumni magazine to a publication of broader cultural appeal. Janis also discusses Roth's fiction in "Necropolis of the Heart," a review of Martin Amis's *The Information* and Philip Roth's *Sabbath's Theater*, in *Partisan Review*, vol. 4 (1995), pp. 699–718. The quotation about the "manhandling" comes from SB, in John Blades, "Bellow's Latest Chapter," *Chicago Tribune*, 19 June 1994.

16. Roger Kaplan, email to the author, 12 September 2008. Attached to this email was a draft of a memoir of SB and Janis's stay in Paris, "Bellow and Furet." It is thirty-nine single-spaced pages long.

17. Roger Kaplan, email to the author, 20 July 2008; subsequent quotations from Roger come from this and other emails, and from "Bellow and Furet."

18. Roger Kaplan, email to the author, 18 July 2008.

19. For the University Professors, a creation of John Silber, see chapter 9. The University Professors program granted both undergraduate and graduate degrees in fields that combined or fell between traditional disciplines. Students for both graduate and undergraduate degrees were interviewed by faculty and consulted closely with them in designing their course of study. The program was phased out in 2011. When SB joined the program in 1993, other University Professors in literature included Geoffrey Hill, William Arrowsmith, D. S. Carne-Ross, Roger Shattuck, and the poet Rosanna Warren, daughter of Robert Penn Warren and Eleanor Clark. Christopher Ricks refused to join the program, but was more in sympathy with members of its arts-and-literature group than he was with many English Department colleagues.

20. The unnamed friends are quoted in Atlas, *Biography*, p. 566.

21. See Jennifer Rossa, "Nobel Laureate Leaves for BU," *Chicago Maroon*, 26 May 1993. In John Blades, "Bellow Leaving Chicago in Body But Not in Spirit," *Chicago Tribune*, 25 May 1993, SB explains: "I thought I was due for a change. Lots of people leave Chicago in my time of life, and nobody thinks anything of it." The article also quotes Mayor Daley, who called himself SB's "good friend" and hoped he would keep a voting address in Chicago.

22. Manea, "Conversation," pp. 20–21.

23. Atlas, *Biography*, p. 566.

24. For this SB quotation and details of the unveiling ceremony, see Charles Storch, "Bellow's Defection No Match for Affection from Hometown," *Chicago Tribune*, 9 November 1993.

25. Blades, "Bellow Leaving Chicago in Body."

26. For these details of the "Idiosyncratic Survey," see Blades, "Bellow's Latest Chapter." In addition to teaching his one course in the spring, SB was also listed as teaching "Directed Study" for most spring semesters, part of the University Professors program's offerings. According to Chris Walsh, email to the author, 22 November 2016, "Typically the enrollment for those classes was zero, a couple of times he had one student. (The same is true for other University Professor Profs.)"

27. On Botsford and SB's Jewishness, see *To Fame and Fortune*, chapter 13, pp. 551–52.

28. That Botsford was a "terrible, terrible parent," Nathalie claims, all of his children "would agree, though they all love him." She adds: "He's the ideal parent to call at three o'clock in the morning if you've just been arrested, but he's the worst possible parent to bring to the school play in which you've got the leading role, because he'll say afterwards that everyone was dreadful including you, and what a waste of money it was to send you to the school."

29. Keith Botsford, email to the author, 11 January 2017. The Botsford quote about reading eleven languages comes from Fred A. Bernstein, "In Costa Rica, Built for Books and Breezes," *New York Times Magazine*, 1 October 2007, a profile not only of Botsford but of his house in Costa Rica.

30. Botsford's tolerant response is quoted in Atlas, *Biography*, p. 431. I first met Botsford in 2008 in Cahuita, Costa Rica, where he was living with his latest wife, an ex-student from BU, fifty-two years his junior. He seemed very much like Thaxter. When my wife and I arrived at his house, he was napping (there had been a "mix-up" about arrival times, and no one met us at the deserted airport, little more than a field with a single tiny "terminal"; we had no address, only a post-office box number). Botsford emerged from his house bare-chested, in red silk pajama bottoms, drank Pepsi (or was it Coke?) continuously, scattered cigarette ash everywhere, never slept, and took an unsettling interest in my wife. The house he lived in was spectacular. It had been designed by his architect son, Gianni, had won prizes, and was featured in a lavish spread in *The New York Times Magazine* (see note 29 above, www.nytimes.com/2007/10/04/garden/04costarica.html). Everyone in Cahuita knew Botsford as "Kikay," spelled, disconcertingly, "Kike" on the large mailbox at the beginning of his drive. At the local restaurant, the proprietor-chef greeted him with great affection. He always ordered off-menu. Generous with his time, he had much to say about SB, as well as about himself, and over the course of several days he must have mentioned the names of perhaps a hundred places, writers, and books I'd never heard of, let alone been to or read. He was generous in other ways, supplying me with photographs and with not-yet-published drafts of *Fragments*, his multivolume memoir. He was charming—endearing, even—as well as peremptory and condescending.

31. On 14 October 1997, in the course of asking James Wood if he'd received his copy of *News from the Republic of Letters*, SB explained its origins and aims. He and Botsford "have done this sort of thing in the past. In the Fifties we brought out a journal called *The Noble Savage*. The idea has always been to show how the needs of writers might be met. . . . Botsford and I have no publishing house behind us [as they had with *The Noble Savage*]—no corporation, no philanthropical foundations, no patron. We pay for *TROL* ourselves. We do it on the cheap—printing no more than 1,500 copies. We tried to get Barnes and Noble to take it but B and N does not deal with magazines directly. Only with official distributors. We thought we'd run it for a year in the hope of attracting five or six hundred subscribers. Six or seven hundred good men and true would make it possible for *TROL* to survive. Nothing like a boyish enterprise to give old guys the shocks they badly need or crave. I feel I owe you this explanation, since you were good enough to let us publish your Ibsen-Chekhov piece. We couldn't afford to pay you properly for it. So you are entitled to a description of what it is we are doing." In the same letter, SB explains that Chris Walsh, who would become the magazine's managing editor, would be helping out Botsford, described as "a very gifted man but he isn't dependably efficient." Botsford was in the south of France for the summer (where he at this time had a house), and also recovering from a car accident. See SB to Christopher Ricks, 7 July 1997: "Who but Keith could launch a magazine and immediately disappear for two months! Chris Walsh and I have to try to run the shop. I can't even

begin to guess when the next number (including your exchanges with Empson) will appear." See also SB's letters to Sophie Wilkins (17 June 1998), Philip Roth, and Cynthia Ozick (both 18 June 1998), soliciting pieces for the magazine and explaining its aims and character.

32. Christopher Ricks, *T. S. Eliot and Prejudice* (London: Faber & Faber, 1988).

33. In fact, these may not have been exactly the words SB spoke. In his memoir, *The Shadow in the Garden: A Biographer's Tale* (New York: Pantheon, 2017), p. 178n., Atlas writes: "Alas, I have come across the notebook in which I scrawled this now-famous (or infamous) line, and it turns out that the word Bellow used was 'Polynesians,' unless I mistranscribed it—which is quite possible. . . . If it turns out that 'Papuans' is a later embellishment (we'll never know), apologies to untold numbers of journalists who may have misquoted Bellow's comic and wildly offensive remark over the years." In what follows, Papuans stay Papuans, as in public controversy.

34. The extract in *The New York Times Magazine*, from which all my quotations are taken, was titled "Into the White Ivory Tower."

35. In *The Shadow in the Garden*, p. 268, Atlas describes Staples as "a big guy . . . and it was a point of honor for him to dress in scruffy clothes, as if to say *this is who I am*."

36. In "When the Artist Is a Cannibal," an entry in an online exchange with A. O. Scott about Atlas's *Biography* (2000), Staples writes, "I never meant to harm him, just to give him a dose of those menacing black characters he produced in *Mr. Sammler's Planet*, *Dean's December*, and *Humboldt's Gift* and so on." The exchange appeared in the online magazine *Slate*, 16 October 2000.

37. See Harriet Wasserman, *Handsome Is: Adventures with Saul Bellow* (New York: Fromm International, 1997), pp. 170–71. There were, of course, earlier accusations. When *Esquire* published "Something to Remember Me By," the story SB thought had "everything in it," the issue it appeared in (July 1990) also contained an article on American fiction by Edward Hoagland which rehearsed charges of racism against him. On 15 June, having seen an advance copy of the issue, Harriet Wasserman wrote to the magazine's editor, Lee Eisenberg, to complain: "What a betrayal, what trickery, to buy the rights to publish a story and then put the story in a hostile and pejorative setting." At the time of the Papuans-and-Zulus controversy, "Something to Remember Me By" was SB's most recent publication.

38. James Atlas, email to the author, 30 November 2016. In *The Shadow in the Garden: A Biographer's Tale*, p. 262, Atlas describes SB's failure to "remember the name of the journalist who went on to become your biographer . . . [as] what Annie [his wife, a psychoanalyst] would call a narcissistic injury. And I resented being called the 'interviewer.' I was the biographer." At the same time, "I was pleased to see Bellow fighting back against the bullying strictures of political correctness. And maybe he really *didn't* remember that I'd interviewed him."

39. In an email of 28 November 2017 the journalist and writer Rhoda Koenig comments: "He made the remark nearly ten years earlier at the PEN conference that I covered for New York magazine in 1986. I quoted it in my piece. I remember, clear as a bell, that I was very surprised that, when he said it, there were no noises of protest or even indignation. There were no gasps, much less anyone calling out an angry remark, even among all those liberals."

40. Sarah Lyall, "Saul Bellow's Words," *New York Times Book Review*, 16 March 1994.

41. "Political corrector" comes from an unsigned Wieseltier editorial in *The New Republic*, 28 March 1994 (which Lyall presumably saw before publication). It is titled "Mr. Staples's Planet" and begins with a quote: "'I don't think Bellow's work is sufficiently tainted with anti-black attitudes that it poisons his whole work.' Tainted,

we are to infer, but not sufficiently tainted. This, according to *The Boston Globe* a few weeks ago, was how Cambridge novelist Paul Buttenweiser explained his decision not to withdraw an invitation to Saul Bellow to appear as a guest at a Boston Library dinner. In his own eyes, no doubt, Buttenweiser is a hero of political incorrectness; but with friends like this, a writer needs no enemies. The political corrector, in this case, was Brent Staples, whose recent memoir, *Parallel Time*, recounts his years as a graduate student at the University of Chicago, where, among other distinctions, he stalked Saul Bellow." Later in the *New Republic* piece, which appears as one of several items under the heading "Notes," the anonymous editor refers to Rinaldo Cantabile, who utters the "crazy buffaloes" and "pork chops" epithets, as "a tawdry little hood." Of Staples's objection to Bellow's depictions of black sexuality and violence, the editor observes that the objection occurs in a chapter "riddled with black pimps and black prostitutes, compared to whom Bellow's little menaces are quaint."

42. Hilton Kramer, "Saul Bellow, Our Contemporary," *Commentary*, June 1994.

43. For a clearer and more straightforward, if hardly problem-free, account of multiculturalism, see SB's answers to Robert Fulford in "A Thousand Years to Be Born: Robert Fulford Speaks with Saul Bellow," *Books in Canada: The Canadian Review of Books*, September 1996: "We always had multiculturalism in America. The melting pot was multicultural. People seem to forget that. Only those who hated the immigrants, or had some impossible idea about WASP purity, like Henry Adams, were shocked by this. Everybody else took it as a matter of course. . . . I think it's natural to this civilization to be multicultural, but I don't think that this means that all cultures are clearly equal. It's a crazy distortion of the idea of equality. I always tell students when they ask me about multiculturalism that they don't know their own culture yet."

44. See Manea, "Conversation," p. 18; SB, "The French as Dostoyevsky Saw Them," in *IAAU*, pp. 45–46 (for full bibliographical details of the Dostoevsky piece, plus further discussion of SB's sense of the claims of the novel, see the introduction to *To Fame and Fortune*, pp. 8–10).

45. See chapter 8 and note 85 for the titles of Atlas's *New Yorker* and book-length memoirs. In Atlas's reading, the tombstone in "The Shadow of the Tombstone falling across [or "in"] the Garden," is a biography and the shadow a biographer, later "the gravedigger."

46. Atlas, *Shadow in the Garden*, p. 256.

47. See James Atlas, "The Biographer and the Murderer," *New York Times Magazine*, 12 December 1993: "That Saul Bellow, two weeks after his 21st birthday, officially changed his name from Solomon provides a clue to the name changes of his characters."

48. Atlas, *Shadow in the Garden*, p. 268.

49. Rebecca Sinkler's offense was to ask SB to cut three pages from an article he had offered her for the *Book Review*. Among the unpleasing observations in Peter S. Prescott, "Mr. Bellow's Planetoid," *New York Times Book Review*, 10 April 1994, is the following: "Mr. Bellow has recently been bombarded for remarking that the Zulus and Papuans seem disinclined to write three-decker novels in the best 19th-century European tradition. Something sounds phony about both the attack and Mr. Bellow's defense of himself, simply because no one who has read his novels could possibly be surprised that he would say such a thing." Atlas's remark about SB's anger and about his saying that *The New York Times* was "out to get me" come from *Shadow in the Garden*, p. 269.

50. Atlas, *Shadow in the Garden*, p. 271.

51. Ibid., p. 293.

52. See James Atlas, "Starting Out in Chicago," in *Granta 41: Biography* (5 November 1992), an issue that also contains an extract from "Memoirs from a

Bootlegger's Son." *Granta* was at the time edited by Bill Buford, and it was while preparing the excerpt from Atlas's biography that Buford learned of the existence of the journals (according to Atlas's letter to SB of 24 May 1995).

53. Atlas, *Shadow in the Garden*, pp. 294, 293. That Atlas was right to fear the consequences of publishing the journal entries is clear from SB's interview with Robert Fulford, "A Thousand Years to Be Born." Fulford asks SB what he feels about Atlas's impending biography: "I don't like it one bit. I have nothing to do with this biography. Atlas has given people to understand (so they've told me) that his book is being written with my consent. That's not true. I *did* talk to him a few times, but I stopped because he had begun to publish notes about his work-in-progress and I could see that he had misunderstood many of the things I'd said to him. He is inclined to doubt everything he hears and behaves as if his informants were trying to put something over on him. The whole thing is very uncomfortable."

54. Atlas, *Shadow in the Garden*, p. 295.

55. See, for example, SB to the political sociologist Paul Hollander, 7 September 1995: "He [Atlas] has given the impression that he was writing this book of his with my blessing—that it was 'authorized.' Nothing of the sort. He simply informed me that he had signed a contract to write a book about me. For years now he has done nothing but depress me—nosing out facts about sexual activities and startling me with his incredible 'analyses' of my motives." According to Atlas, however, in an email of 5 February 2018 relayed by his agent to the author, "to others he [Bellow] described the biography as 'neither authorized nor unauthorized,' and continued to meet with Atlas up until the summer before publication."

56. James Atlas, "The Quest for Bellow," *New York Times Book Review*, 16 November 1980.

57. See Atlas, *Biography*, pp. 486–87.

58. See Edward Klagsbrun, of Deutsch Klagsbrun & Blasband, SB's lawyers, to Michael Denneny of St. Martin's Press, 1 February 1990 (the letter is copied to the St. Martin's lawyer, David N. Kaye). SB's objections are keyed to manuscript pages and instruct Miller to remove quotes or assertions or attributions variously deemed "untrue," "misunderstood," "inaccurate," "misrepresented," "utterly absurd," "totally false," "preposterous," "riddled with untruths," "extremely disagreeable," and "highly irresponsible" (phrases gathered from the first two pages of SB's objections alone). Michael Denneny had been a student at the Committee on Social Thought. He was the editor to whom SB recommended Roger Kaplan's novel. SB's threat to refuse Miller permission to quote from unpublished works may have owed something to two recently publicized cases: Peter Ackroyd's attempt to write T. S. Eliot's biography, which was radically altered and diminished when he was forbidden by the Eliot estate to quote not only from all unpublished work and correspondence but from published work (the resulting book, *T. S. Eliot*, was published in 1984); and Ian Hamilton's attempt to publish "J. D. Salinger: A Writing Life," which had to be scrapped when Salinger sued (Hamilton then published *In Search of J. D. Salinger* [New York: Random House, 1988], about his difficulties attempting to write the biography).

59. Ruth Miller, *Saul Bellow: A Biography of the Imagination* (New York: St. Martin's Press, 1991), p. xxiii. According to John Blades, "Stop the Presses: Bellow's Clout Delays Biography," *Chicago Tribune*, 18 April 1990, SB "had initially cooperated, assuming it would be a purely academic exploration of his work." After SB objected, St. Martin's agreed to postpone the book, and Miller, now at the Hebrew University of Jerusalem—previously, for twenty-two years, a professor of English at the State University of New York at Stony Brook (where she was a colleague of Jack Ludwig)—agreed to make changes. According to Blades, she described the

changes as "minor revisions," clearing up "problems with footnotes, chapter titles, quotations," but she also talked of "depersonalizing the book, changing the point of view from the first to the third person, which would suggest that the alterations would be more substantial than she indicated." She told Blades that it was SB who had urged her to write the book, having been "impressed with her similarly constructed biography of Emily Dickinson." She described the biographical passages in the book as "based on lengthy conversations with Bellow [over] four decades, many of which [she] recorded in her journal."

60. Atlas, *Biography*, p. 557, quoting from Miller's journal.

61. She was not the first person to have such an idea. SB signed a contract with Harper & Row for just such a collection, to be titled "Occasional Pieces"—on condition that it be edited by Ruth Miller (a signed copy of the contract exists in the Regenstein, dated November 1982, as does a revised draft of Ruth Miller's proposed preface to the volume). On 8 February 1983, Aaron Asher of Harper & Row wrote to SB in praise of his travel piece "My Paris," *New York Times Magazine, Part 2, The Sophisticated Traveler*, calling it "good enough to be an Occasional Piece." It is unclear not only whether the essays for the volume were ever selected and compiled by Miller, but also why Harper & Row dropped the book. Though the Regenstein contains galleys of a volume to be entitled "Occasional Pieces," these galleys were created in the early 1990s by Viking, not Harper & Row, for a volume that started off with the title "Occasional Pieces" but eventually became *It All Adds Up: From the Dim Past to the Uncertain Future—A Nonfiction Collection*. According to Beena Kamlani of Viking Penguin, who worked on the book with Bellow, "We got many individual essays from Harriet Wasserman that were then collated to form the volume It All Adds Up. I sent Saul a suggested structure for the essays, based on part heading that he approved, and most of the pieces naturally fitted into one or other of the sections. Those that didn't were discarded. I am sure there was a lot of overlap between [the Harper & Row "Occasional Pieces"] and It All Adds Up, but I never saw the earlier volume" (email to the author, 15 March 2017).

62. Wasserman, *Handsome Is*, p. 166.

63. For Wasserman's quotes on the genesis of *IAAU*, see *Handsome Is*, pp. 167–69.

64. Wasserman, *Handsome Is*, p. 176.

65. These and other details of the stay at St. Martin come from Janis Bellow, email to the author, 14 December 2016.

11. INTENSIVE CARE

1. See SB to Joe Cuomo, a lecturer in English at CUNY Queens College and a friend of Norman Manea, 1 March 1995: "The doctors tell me that 40% of people in intensive care never make it, that an additional 20% who do make it are forever basket cases. Coming out intact I belong to a lucky minority."

2. When Rachel says she "insisted that they make the switch" and "really pushed" for it, she means with both doctors and family: "I don't think the family was all that concerned about the extra cost. They just wanted to do everything to get Saul better. The hospital gave us a bit of a push back, because valium is a much cheaper drug than versed. And also Saul would need more doses of the versed than the valium because the valium has a longer half-life. But valium also has metabolically active metabolites that hang around and especially in older people, they can accumulate, making extubation from a ventilator more difficult" (Rachel Greengus Schultz, email to the author, 24 March 2017, the source also of her quotes from the main text).

3. See Harriet Wasserman, *Handsome Is: Adventures with Saul Bellow* (New York: Fromm International, 1997), pp. 178–79.

4. Greg Bellow, *Saul Bellow's Heart: A Son's Memoir* (London and New York: Bloomsbury, 2013), p. 193. SB's lawyer at the time was Ed Klagsbrun. Among the friends and colleagues in this last ring, who called for updates, were Philip Roth, Saul Steinberg, John Auerbach, Bette Howland, Nathalie Botsford, Mary Ann McGrail (a fellow University Professor at BU), and the Hillmans from Vermont. To this list Janis adds: "my entire family" (those who came to help were "my mother, my sister Wendy, my brother Robert, my uncle Michael"), "Delba and Harvey Mansfield [both of Harvard], the Wisses [Ruth and Len], my friend Gayle McKeen . . . Walter Pozen, Cliff Orwin, the Kleinbards, Martin Amis" (email to the author, 17 January 2017).

5. Greg Bellow, *Saul Bellow's Heart*, pp. 193–94.

6. Janis Bellow, email to the author, 17 January 2017.

7. Ibid.

8. It was Eugene Kennedy's wife, Sara C. Charles, a professor of psychiatry and an M.D., who arranged for SB to address the conference, which was sponsored by the Council of Medical Specialty Societies. I quote from p. 4 of the transcript of the talk, a copy of which is among the SB Papers in the Regenstein (henceforth cited within the text by page number). "View from Intensive Care" was published in the first issue of *News from the Republic of Letters*, later excerpted in the September 1997 issue of *Harper's*, and reprinted in full in SB and Keith Botsford, *Editors: The Best from Five Decades* (London and Connecticut: Toby Press, 2001), pp. 73–82 (henceforth cited within the text by page number).

9. In a letter of 1 August 2000, to Jay D. Hoffman, chair of the Promotions Committee at the BU Department of Medicine, SB wrote of Dr. Barnardo: "To say that he saved my life would not be an overstatement, but my reasons for recommending him go well beyond personal gratitude. As an attending physician he is undoubtedly brilliant, energetic, devoted, but perhaps his qualities as a human being are even more rare and worthy of recognition. In the days following my extubation when I began to take note of my surroundings Dr. Barnardo emerged as something of a guardian angel. . . . He was there as I took my first tentative steps towards recovery. He made time for me. He cheered me with his shy, dry and wry conversation. . . . I knew that he was giving up personal time to tend me. . . . Such things mean a great deal to a needy patient. For my wife, the fact that Dr. Barnardo was willing to wait extra hours to get the results of a catscan, or to calm us when the world seemed to be spinning out of control quite literally kept her from despair. Furthermore, we knew that we weren't being singled out for special attention. Dr. Barnardo is exceptionally devoted to all of his patients."

10. Rachel Greengus Schultz, email to the author, 3 September 2010. "I knew Uncle Saul would never get off the vent if he was given Valium, so I spoke with the doctor in the ICU . . . about using a different more short acting sedative with no active metabolites, specifically midazolam (Versed). (A bit of background: Both Valium and Versed are benzodiazepines, anxiolytics that cause retrograde amnesia.). . . . [SB's] memory would still have been challenged by the Valium, although he probably wouldn't have remembered it because of all the active metabolites working in concert with the Valium. That bit of information stopped his complaining."

11. Greg Bellow, *Saul Bellow's Heart*, p. 194.

12. Ibid., p. 196.

13. Daniel Bellow, email to the author, 24 March 2017.

14. In *Saul Bellow's Heart*, Greg offers a theory about why Janis might have sought to discredit the sons (a claim she denies): "I have come to believe that after caring for a husband in a weakened condition for six months and the prospect of

having to do so perhaps for years, Allan Bloom's notions about making sacrifices purely for love no longer proved a sufficient rationale," and that "she came to feel a need to go beyond ensuring her primacy in Saul's affection to exert a level of control that expanded well past his daily life to include financial, legal, and literary decision making" (pp. 195, 196).

15. Ibid., p. 195.

16. While Bellow was in the ICU, Walter Pozen received a call from Ed Klagsbrun, Harriet Wasserman's lawyer, also SB's, on occasion, who said, "We're going to take over" (by which he meant take over financial matters). As Pozen remembered it: "I said, Look here, he has a wife, she's the legal representative. You have no authority whatsoever and if you try to take any action we will immediately bring an action in the supreme court of the state of New York. I never heard from him again." In an email of 29 June 2017, Lesha Greengus writes about the matter of financial advice: "Although Saul and I, on various occasions, discussed financial matters and concerns, I did not in fact act as his financial advisor. In 1986, Saul was planning to come to Cincinnati in December to attend my daughter Judith's wedding. I arranged for him to meet with William Friedlander, who was at that time chairman of the investment firm of Bartlett & Co., which was founded in Cincinnati in 1898 (and still continues today). Mr. Friedlander agreed to act as investment manager for Saul's account. . . . Saul asked me to monitor his account and asked that Bartlett send me copies of his monthly statements, along with the personal statements that we were receiving for our own account at Bartlett."

17. Greg Bellow, *Saul Bellow's Heart*, p. 194. That SB had matters of money, inheritance, and filial piety in mind is clear from an interview with Robert Fulford, "A Thousand Years to Be Born: Robert Fulford Speaks with Saul Bellow," *Books in Canada: The Canadian Review of Books* (September 1996):

> Let me give you an example from a course I'm giving now on the ambitious young man in European literature. . . . When we were doing *Père Goriot*, I asked the students what they thought of the behavior of Goriot's daughters, who wouldn't come to the deathbed of the father who had given them everything, ruined himself for them. I said it was true that he had an *idée fixe*, and like so many of the characters in Balzac, he went to the extreme with this; but he had done them a lot of good, and he had been a loving father. They didn't come to his deathbed and they didn't go to his funeral—and they sent their empty carriages to the funeral procession. And one of the students said, "Well, he had no self-respect and he didn't esteem himself, and the daughters felt this, and they became estranged from him." They didn't become estranged from his money, but they did become estranged from him. I could see that this young woman spoke with the support of a great many of her classmates.

18. Greg Bellow, *Saul Bellow's Heart*, p. 197. The word "coup," used by Greg to characterize Janis's behavior, has been used of Greg himself, together with Lesha. I was told by friends of SB that during the period when he was in the hospital, Greg and Lesha briefly considered moving him from Boston to Cincinnati (where Lesha and her family lived, as well as Bellow's sister, Jane). Neither Dan nor Adam knew anything of this story, says Greg, which he labels "ridiculous" in his memoir, a sign of "what extreme concern there must have been about the influence of Saul's family." In an interview of 23 February 2017, however, Adam told me he had heard Lesha and Greg raise the idea, though it was quickly rejected. "I remember it being mentioned, but it did not have an energy about it. Everybody was behaving a little crazily. . . . That the possibility of such a move was considered was warranted by the circumstances." Daniel can't remember if he heard the idea raised at the time,

but he heard of it after Bellow's release from the hospital. The friends of SB who repeated the Cincinnati story were Jonathan Kleinbard, from the University of Chicago, Walter Pozen, and Will Lautzenheiser, who would take over from Chris Walsh in 2000 as SB's assistant at BU.

19. Greg Bellow, *Saul Bellow's Heart*, p. 196.

20. Atlas, *Biography*, p. 579.

21. In *The Shadow in the Garden: A Biographer's Tale* (New York: Pantheon, 2017), p. 235, Atlas describes Shils in the following terms: "Shils was not kind. He brutally disparaged his colleagues, both friends and enemies, as 'idiots' and 'worthless fellows.' He had a sour view of life, thought human beings were corrupt, showed contempt for the living and the dead. All the same, I enjoyed his company. He had one of the most penetrating minds I'd ever encountered, and there were times when I suspected his negativity was a pose. Intellectual challenges stimulated him; he was a natural pedagogue. As it turned out, I, too, would become a disciple of Shils."

22. This is one of a series of answers to questions posed by *Figaro Littéraire*, from a fax of 23 December 1997. In another answer, about writing short stories rather than novels, SB claimed, "It was not at all a challenge to write short. As one grows older, one eliminates superfluities of all kinds." The fax is among the SB Papers in the Regenstein.

23. Quoted in Atlas, *Biography*, p. 577.

24. SB, "By the St. Lawrence," reprinted in SB, *CS*, p. 1 (henceforth cited within the text by page number).

25. On the Gameroff cousins, see *To Fame and Fortune*, chapter 3.

26. Wasserman, *Handsome Is*, pp. 180–94.

27. As SB was in Chicago on 5 December, giving a speech, his call to Wasserman must have been after he returned to Vermont. See SB to Julian Behrstock, 19 January 1996: "Just as I was about to emerge from the woods and to feel approximately normal, the doctors caught up with me and back to the hospital I went for gall-bladder surgery. This imposed a second convalescence on the first, which wasn't quite over. I found myself in the same hospital corridor, only two doorways away from the room I occupied last January. . . . The surgery is about three weeks behind me now."

28. Adam Bellow describes Wasserman as "always difficult, very proprietary with Saul, and it was clear that she was very uncomfortable with the marriage to Janis. . . . She would call and not even say hello to Janis." He adds, "She was very nice to me."

29. Wylie tells a good story about how Atlas became his author: "Round the time of Salman Rushdie's visit to the United States [while in hiding from the *fatwa*] . . . we made arrangements for a couple of conversations, one in print, one televised. *The New York Times* had a position, and *60 Minutes* had a position. Everything was confidential, but there was a cocktail party, and of course everybody from the *Times* and everybody from *60 Minutes* all went to it. And they all felt that they had somehow been given less than the full picture [Wylie had promised each an "exclusive" interview, by which he meant one exclusive for print and one exclusive for television]. I was brought into the *Times* and faced a semicircle of employees; in the semicircle was Gerry Marzorati, whom we represented; Jim Atlas, whom we did not represent. And I was told that the *Times* would no longer do business with the Wylie Agency. . . . And then I said, 'Well, thank you very much,' and I left and went back to the office. And after a little while the phone rang, and it was Philip Roth, and he said, 'What's the matter with you?' And I told him, and he said, 'Huh!' Two weeks went by, and I had another phone call from Philip. He said, 'Andrew, Jim Atlas from *The New York Times* says call me; they want to do a profile for the *Times Magazine*, so I want you to get back to me.' I said, Philip, understandably, you've forgotten the conversation we had. He said, 'No, I didn't forget—why don't you tell them we want the cover and

the amount of money we should be paid.' I said okay. So I called Atlas and I said [all this] and Atlas said . . . 'I can't do business with you.' I said, 'Well, I guess you can't do business with Philip.' And he said, 'Well, I'll get back to you.' So he came back to me and he said, 'Price is okay, but we can't guarantee the cover.' I said, 'Well, then, there's no deal.' So then he called back and said, 'We can guarantee the cover.' And then, a week later, he called and said he'd like to fire Georges Borchardt [his agent] and would like to have me be his agent, and could I renegotiate the advance for the Bellow?" In an email of 27 July 2018, Atlas disputes this account: "I asked Judith Thurman if she would inquire of Andrew whether he was interested in representing me. He called . . . and said he had heard I was thinking of 'changing representation.' That's the whole story."

30. SB, "Literature in a Democracy: From Tocqueville to the Present," typed manuscript, in the Regenstein, p. 1 (henceforth cited within the text by page numbers). The lecture was revised and published under the title "Problems in American Literature," in *Literary Imagination, Ancient and Modern: Essays in Honor of David Grene*, ed. Todd Breyfogle (Chicago: University of Chicago Press, 1999).

31. SB, "Problems in American Literature," in *Literary Imagination, Ancient and Modern*, ed. Todd Breyfogle, pp. 387, 386, 388.

32. Atlas, *Biography*, p. 582.

33. See Sabrina L. Miller, "Bellow's Return: It All Adds Up," *Chicago Tribune*, 7 December 1995.

34. "Final Paper Assignment: UNI ID 202 Professor Bellow," in SB papers in the Regenstein.

35. For these and other details of the wedding, see Margo Howard, "Hell's Bells," *Boston* magazine, September 1996. Howard was a friend of Susan Glassman, mother of the groom. For Daniel, the glitz of the wedding began with the limo driver hired for his stag party, who had been Madonna's driver when she came to Miami. "He knew some places, but that's another story" (email to the author, 5 February 2017).

36. See SB to Martin Amis, 13 March 1996, on his Russian Jewish father: "I understand your saying that you are your dad. With a fair degree of accuracy I can see this in my own father. He and I never *seemed* to be in rapport: Our basic assumptions were *very* different. But that now looks superficial. I treat my sons much as he treated me: out of breath with impatience—and then a long inhalation of affection." See also Daniel's contribution to "Our Father's Politics," in *A Political Companion to Saul Bellow*, ed. Gloria L. Cronin and Lee Trepanier (Lexington: University of Kentucky Press, 2013), p. 217: "He took a very keen interest in my literary education and was handing me things like *David Copperfield* to read when I was ten. He just said, 'Oh, you can read that.' I said, 'Pop, it's a huge book and it's got all these tiny letters in it.' And he would say, 'You can read it.' There was nothing better than hearing Pop read out loud. He read me Jack London's *The Call of the Wild* when I was six years old. When Adam was a teenager, he read us both the Dudley Fitts translation of *The Odyssey*. I've never had to reread it because I remember it all so well—the Cyclops, Polyphemus, smashing the guys' heads together. Adam and I after dinner would say, 'Pop. What are we reading tonight? Pop, will you read to us.'"

37. Daniel Bellow, in "Our Father's Politics," p. 217.

38. Ibid., p. 220.

39. Ibid. Daniel also used this image to describe his father's behavior during the confrontation in Vermont, when he accused Daniel and his brothers of "sitting around in the hospital waiting for him to die" (Daniel's email to the author, 24 March 2017).

40. Daniel Bellow, in "Our Father's Politics," p. 215.

41. On Arthur Lidov, see *To Fame and Fortune*, chapter 7, pp. 286–88.

42. SB, "All Marbles Still Accounted For," typescript in Regenstein, p. 204. The face that exactly resembles Nellie Bassix's belongs to an American Airlines stewardess named Muriel, who knows nothing of Nellie and is no relation to her.

43. SB, *The Actual* (New York: Viking Penguin, 1997), pp. 26–27 (henceforth cited within the text by page numbers). Two other characters in the novella, Bodo and Madge Heisinger, are moneyed versions of Duane and Marlene Swimley, whose notorious divorce case Bellow wrote up in the "Chicago Book" and later fictionalized in *The Dean's December* (where it is recounted in Albert Corde's *Harper's* articles). Like Marlene Swimley, Madge Heisinger tries to have her husband murdered; unlike Duane Swimley, Bodo Heisinger forgives his wife, welcoming her back to his home after her prison term. The Heisingers figure in the story because the Adletskys are trying to buy their apartment, which Amy is to decorate. Madge, however, is a dangerous woman and drives a hard bargain.

44. When questioned, Harry describes the antiquities deal as "sufficiently legal" (ibid., p. 9).

45. For Eleanor Fox, see chapter 4 of *To Fame and Fortune*, pp. 158–60. The persistence of Harry's love for Amy relates to SB's persistent fascination with Eleanor Fox, in life as in his fiction. "Even after I was married," she told me in an interview, "he was always calling me. He never stopped calling me in all these years. Both my husbands said, Get rid of anything related to Saul Bellow and tell him to quit calling here. . . . They weren't concerned that I was going to go off and leave them, obviously, but what's he bothering you for?"

46. In an interview of 31 December 1999 with Thomas Petzinger, Jr., in *The Wall Street Journal Millennium* (http://interactive.wsj.com/millennium/articles/flash-SB944523384413082346.htm), SB declares: "Lately, sex has done a lot of damage to love. By which I mean, sex is now so available that it has become a substitute for love. But on the other hand, I think of it as a mark of sanity that people should be capable of falling in love nevertheless, because in love we discover an unlimited generosity. You don't often think of love as a generosity, but it is. . . . It collides with self-interest, which is one of the springs of market theory. I used to have long conversations with [economist] Milton Friedman, who was a neighbor of mine back in Chicago in the old days. He used to say 'Get real! This is a market problem.'"

47. Almost exactly the same words are used in "Marbles" (p. 205) to describe Muriel the stewardess, the spitting image of Hilbert Faucil's high-school love Nellie Bassix:

> There was a sexual message also in the imperfect application of her lipstick. That was the whole power of it. Just as mortal for me was the shape of her bottom as she carried trays back to the galley. She didn't walk like a stewardess. The faulty management of her pumps, dropping on the minor beat—this syncopation was the telling idiosyncrasy which bound all the other traits together. Her swaying was not the movement of somebody in the service sector. Front or rear she brought back grippingly an earlier style of vision. But threescore ten and then some, with two world wars and about twenty presidential campaigns between, plus all the transformations of the present age had no power to change these looks—the size of her eyes or the brevity of her teeth. There's the persistence of Eros for you: it runs its own show and it holds its own for all your dimming, graying, tooth loss, decay and the rest of it.

The Muriel/Nellie episode takes up eight pages of the "Marbles" typescript (pp. 204–11) and is not referred to again.

48. James Wood, "Essences Rising," *New Republic*, 16 June 1997.

12. *RAVELSTEIN*

1. SB's unfinished novel, "All Marbles Still Accounted For," exists in its fullest form in a 279-page typescript dated June–October 1994; henceforth cited within the text by page number.

2. Janis Bellow, email to the author, 11 April 2017.

3. Rachel Cooke, "His Gift Was to Love and to Be Loved," *Observer*, 10 October 2010.

4. Malcolm Jones, "Odd Outing: A Conservative Critic Makes a Gay Appearance," *Newsweek*, 7 February 2000.

5. These words were quoted on p. 7 of the introduction to *To Fame and Fortune*, which contains an extended discussion of SB's use of real-life models in his fiction. The words come from *Ravelstein* (New York: Viking Penguin, 2000), p. 13 (henceforth cited within the text by page numbers).

6. Ravelstein shares some of this conservative uneasiness: "He despised campy homosexuality and took a very low view of 'gay pride'" (*Ravelstein*, p. 160). Bloom also had professional reasons to be uneasy, as does Ravelstein, according to his friend Chick: "Teaching, as Ravelstein understood teaching, was tricky work. You couldn't afford to let the facts be generally known. But unless the facts *were* known, no real life was possible" (p. 59).

7. Dinitia Smith, "A Bellow Novel Eulogizes a Friendship," *New York Times*, 27 January 2000. What SB means here about Bloom's not having anything to hide is unclear. Perhaps he meant to hide from Bloom himself. The quotation from *Ravelstein* in the preceding endnote, in which making "the facts" (his homosexuality) "generally known" is something one can't afford to do, suggests otherwise.

8. In Julia Keller, "Between the Covers, Bellow Sparks Firestorm," *Chicago Tribune*, 30 April 2000, Frank Palella, "a physician who specializes in infectious diseases and an associate professor at the Northwestern University School of Medicine," is quoted: "The presence or absence of AIDS on a death certificate is not a reliable indicator of whether or not AIDS was a contributing factor. . . . A peptic ulcer is not HIV-associated. And liver failure can be associated with anything. It's completely non-specific. . . . Distressingly in our society . . . AIDS carries not just a clinical diagnosis, but a moral stigma. It implies a behavior."

9. Nikki, the Michael Wu figure, is described by Chick as having "the instincts of a prince, he dressed like one—in Nikki, Ravelstein saw a brilliant young man who had every right to assert himself. This was not a matter of style or self-presentation. We are speaking here of a young man's nature and not his strategies" (p. 22). When he learns of Ravelstein's illness, Nikki, "an accredited maître d'" (p. 19), is "at his hotel school in Geneva" (Wu was training to be a chef); he immediately returns to Chicago. "Nobody questioned the strength of Nikki's attachment to Abe. Nikki was perfectly direct—direct, by nature, a handsome, smooth-skinned, black-haired, Oriental, graceful, boyish man. He had an exotic conception of himself. I don't mean that he put on airs. He was never anything but natural." Chick at first thought Nikki "somewhat spoiled. I was wrong, there, too. . . . He was more intelligent and discerning than many better-educated people. He had, what is more, the courage to assert his right to be exactly what he seemed to be" (p. 68). Nikki was physically brave. As Ravelstein tells Chick, "he's always ready for a fight. And his sense of himself is such that . . . [Bellow's ellipses] I've often had to hold him back" (p. 69). Chick describes Nikki as having "his own kind of princely Asiatic mildness, but if you were to offend him Nikki would tear your head off" (p. 145). For Nikki, Chick and Rosamund "were the people Abe talked to about matters he . . . was not interested in" (p. 77). He wasn't supposed to look after Ravelstein's finances, but when, from time to time, he did, "his only

aim was to protect Abe. It was thanks to Nikki that a major swindler in Singapore was discovered" (p. 29). When it is clear that Ravelstein is mortally ill, Nikki drops the hotel training course. Chick describes him swabbing Ravelstein's face in the hospital, leaving his side only for the medical staff. Back in the apartment, it is Nikki who turns away guests, politely but firmly, when Ravelstein isn't strong enough to see them.

In contrast, there is Nikki's initial appearance in the novel, which comes early. When Chick and Rosamund are breakfasting in Ravelstein's suite in the Hotel Crillon, "we kept our voices low because Nikki, Abe's companion, was still sleeping. It was Nikki's habit, back in the U.S., to watch kung fu films from his native Singapore until four o'clock in the morning. Here too he was up most of the night. The waiter had rolled shut the sliding doors so that Nikki's silken sleep should not be disturbed. I glanced through the window from time to time at his round arms and the long shifting layers of black hair reaching his glossy shoulders. In his early thirties, handsome Nickki was boyish still" (p. 5). This initial impression, of Nikki as lounging catamite, deeply upset Nathan Tarcov. As Ravelstein is dying, Chick would come by his apartment after breakfast and, again, Nikki "would be fast asleep until 10, whereas Ravelstein dozed because he had no company and lay with his large knees asprawl" (p. 173).

Michael Wu told me he had "no problem" with SB's "caricature of me," adding, "it's true I stay up late, I'm a night person, I have insomnia . . . and he was hallucinating, I had to stay up with him. . . . It's true I come out as rather superficial. . . . I really don't care what he did to my character." In Tarcov's view, the novel depicts Nikki "as a useless, lazy parasite, sycophant, which is nothing like Michael, who took care of Allan, nursed him, helped him, worked hard as a student, as a chef; it just seemed gratuitous, and partly also the structure of the book is such that it leads the reader to compare Rosamund/Chick to Nikki/Ravelstein with the implication—maybe I'm being too harsh—that Rosamund is much better than Nikki; you almost get the sense that Ravelstein dies because he doesn't have someone like Rosamund to look after him the way Chick does, and this is the thing I found really offensive. . . . What bothered me was the portrayal of their relationship in a way that hurt Michael, hurt his feelings; in the way *Sammler's Planet* hurt my mother."

10. Ravelstein objects to Chick's depiction of Vela in the same way that SB says Bloom objected to his depiction of Alexandra in *The Dean's December:* "He said about Vela, 'You gave in—you tried to sell me a colored cutout of the woman like the cardboard personalities they used to hang in movie lobbies in the old days. You know, Chick, you sometimes say there's nothing you can't tell me. But you falsified the image of your ex-wife. You'll say that it was done for the sake of marriage but what kind of morality is *that*?' " (P. 176.)

11. On the matter of secrecy, see SB, *Ravelstein*, p. 160: "He was doomed to die because of his irregular sexual ways. About these he was entirely frank with me, with all his close friends"; p. 59: "There were two people in Paris who knew him intimately and three on this side of the Atlantic. I was one of them"; and, finally, p. 142: "Abe was taking the common drug prescribed for his condition but he didn't want it to be known. I remember how much it shocked him when the nurse walked in—the room was full of friends. She said, 'It's time for your AZT.' He said to me the next day, 'I could have killed the woman.' "

12. After reading this chapter in draft, Nathan Tarcov, email to the author, 4 July 2017, offered the following response: "I don't recall my exact words to either Max or you, but I believe that I tried to stick to the facts rather than beliefs. And as you properly report . . . the doctors never said that Allan died of AIDS and there is probably no way of knowing whether the internal bleeding and liver failure that killed Allan were related to HIV as they can be caused by all sorts of

things. I recall one doctor earlier worrying that the steroids Allan was prescribed for Guillain-Barré may have damaged his liver. Bellow himself is quoted by Max as admitting 'I don't know if he died of AIDS, really,' in which case I think it was irresponsible to say he did by saying so of Ravelstein and then through interviews in Janis's words 'demolishing the wall separating novel from memoir.' The issue is clouded somewhat . . . by conflating the questions of whether Allan had HIV/AIDS and whether he died of it. . . . Actually I don't think it should matter (though it did and perhaps still does to some people) what Allan died of. I just didn't and still don't think something should be reported as fact that isn't supported by the facts."

13. Harry V. Jaffa, "Humanizing Certitudes and Impoverishing Doubts: A Critique of *The Closing of the American Mind* by Allan Bloom," *Interpretation: A Journal of Political Philosophy*, vol. 16, no. 1 (Fall 1988), p. 112.

14. Ibid., pp. 113–14.

15. See Jeffrey Rosen, "Sodom and Demurrer," *New Republic*, 29 November 1993.

16. Nowhere in *The Closing of the American Mind: How Higher Education Has Failed Democracy and Impoverished the Souls of Today's Students* (New York: Simon & Schuster, 1987) does Bloom discuss homosexuality or gay liberation. The closest he comes to doing so is in a passage about Thomas Mann's *Death in Venice:* "There is no place in Freud for the satisfaction of the kinds of desires to which Mann gives voice in *Death in Venice*. They are explained and cured by Freud but not accepted on their own terms. In Mann they are somehow premonitory and like cries of the damned plunging into nothingness. . . . These desires are certainly not satisfied with the transfer of their cases from the tribunal of the judge and the priest to that of the doctor. Or with being explained away . . . Neither bourgeois society nor natural science has a place for the nonreproductive aspect of sex. With the slackening of bourgeois austerity and the concomitant emancipation of the harmless pleasures, a certain tolerance of harmless sex came into fashion. But this was not enough, because nobody really wants his dearest desires to be put in the same category as itching and scratching" (p. 234). The "dearest desires" in Mann's Aschenbach's case are for a young boy, and though doom hangs over them, they are more elevated than "itching and scratching," a phrase from Plato's *Gorgias*. David Mikics, *Bellow's People: How Saul Bellow Made Life into Art* (New York: W. W. Norton, 2016), p. 213, draws attention to the way this passage is written: "Bloom's paragraph on Mann, like his description of Nietzsche, has a taut personal intensity lacking from his mentions of Plato. . . . Mann hymns eros: its glory, its piercing independence from all social use and responsibility." As Mikics sees it, Bloom, too, "championed erotic and spiritual torment" (though Mikics doesn't say where, whether in *The Closing of the American Mind* or elsewhere), and he believes that in *Ravelstein* Bellow omitted that dimension of his character, transforming Bloom "into a *shadchen* or matchmaker, an apostle of love and friendship. Gone was the severe Nietzschean Bloom of his bestselling book. In his place was Ravelstein with his intense sociability" (p. 213). Bloom talks more directly about homosexuality (though impersonally, without "taut personal intensity") in part III of the posthumously published *Love & Friendship* (New York: Simon & Schuster, 1993), in discussion of Plato, pp. 436–37 and 468–69.

17. Janis Freedman Bellow, "Rosamund and *Ravelstein:* The Discandying of a Creator's Confection," in *On Life-Writing*, ed. Zachary Leader (Oxford: Oxford University Press, 2015), p. 113; henceforth cited within the text by page number.

18. Christopher Hitchens, "Bloom's Way," *The Nation*, 15 May 2005, unearthed a more substantive excision, from the same page as the last example Max cites:

> Even towards the end Ravelstein was still cruising. It turned out that he went to gay bars.

One day he said to me, "Chick, I need a check drawn. It's not a lot. Five hundred bucks."

"Why can't you write it yourself?"

"I want to avoid trouble with Nikki. He'd see it on the check-stub."

"All right. How do you want it drawn?"

"Make it out to Eulace Harms."

"Eulace?"

"That's how the kid spells it. Pronounced Ulysee."

There was no need to ask Ravelstein to explain. Harms was a boy he had brought home one night. . . . Eulace was the handsome little boy who had wandered about his apartment in the nude . . . physically so elegant. "No older than sixteen. Very well built . . ."

I wanted to ask, what did the kid do or offer that was worth five hundred dollars. . . .

19. Helen Small, *The Long Life* (Oxford: Oxford University Press, 2007), p. 106. Among the most notable of the novel's repetitions is that of Ravelstein's baldness. In "Throwing Away the Clef," *New Republic*, 22 May 2000, Cynthia Ozick gathers the instances: "'On his bald head you felt that what you were looking at were the finger marks of its shaper.' 'This tall pin- or chalk-striped dude with his bald head (you always felt there was something dangerous about its whiteness, its white force, its dents).' 'He liked to raise his long arms over the light gathered on his bald head and give a comic cry.' 'There are bald heads that concentrated in that bald, cranial watchtower of his.' 'You couldn't imagine an odder container for his odd intellect. Somehow his singular, total, almost geological baldness implied that there was nothing hidden about him.' 'The famous light of Paris was concentrated on his bald head.' And so on, image upon image. Ravelstein's is not so much a man's head as it is a lit dome: the dome of some high-ceilinged cathedral or broad-corridored library. Ravelstein's ideas—also his gossip, his extravagant wants—are solidly housed."

20. Cynthia Ozick, in "Throwing Away the Clef," shared Janis's view. For her, the whole poisoned-fish-and-Rosamund episode "seems out of kilter with the rich thick Ravelstein stew that precedes it. Chick's preoccupations veer off the Ravelsteinian tracks into the demands of his own circumstances, much as Bellow, in his foreword to Bloom's blockbuster, ran off the Bloomian rails to grapple with his own spirit."

21. In the end, Janis admits in her essay, she had undervalued Rosamund's strengths. She singles out a passage she had "completely overlooked" (p. 120): "Rosamund, normally flexible, ladylike, deferential, and genteel now revealed (no question about it) an underlying hardness and the will that showed how prepared she was" (*Ravelstein*, p. 199). In the ICU, as Janis puts it, Rosamund is determined to keep Chick alive. The weeks he spent unconscious and near death "had also to be endured by Rosamund, who was fully awake" (p. 121).

22. Samuel Taylor Coleridge, "The Eolian Harp" (composed 1795, published 1796). The lines quoted below (lines 26–33) were added in a revised version of 1817:

O! The one Life within us and abroad.
Which meets all motion and becomes its soul,
A light in sound, a sound-like power in light,
Rhythm in all thought, and joyance everywhere—
Methinks, it should have been impossible
Not to love all things in a world so filled;

Where the breeze warbles, and the mute still air
Is music slumbering on her instrument.

23. For Daniel Carleton Gajdusek (1923–2008), the American physician, medical researcher, and SB's fellow Nobel Prize winner, see chapter 11, which also discusses his journals.

24. SB may have been thinking of Ioan Couliano (1950–91), a Romanian historian of religion who taught at the University of Chicago from 1980 until his death in 1991, and who was murdered in a men's room at the university's divinity school. The murder was thought to be politically motivated, a consequence of Couliano's attacks on the Romanian government.

25. T. S. Eliot, "Ben Jonson," in *The Sacred Wood* (1920; London: Methuen, 1928), p. 115: "If we look at the works of Jonson's great contemporaries, Shakespeare, and also Donne and Webster and Tourneur (and sometimes Middleton) have a depth, a third dimension, as Mr. Gregory Smith rightly calls it, which Jonson's work has not. Their words often have a network of tentacular roots reaching down to the deepest terrors and desires."

26. Leah Garrett, "The Late Bellow: *Ravelstein* and the Novel of Ideas," in *The Cambridge Companion to Saul Bellow*, ed. Victoria Aarons (Cambridge, U.K.: Cambridge University Press, 2017), p. 175.

27. This description was uttered affectionately as well as with impatience. Daniel liked Bloom, "spent hours and hours talking with him. He was just endlessly patient. He was fascinating." He admits that initially he'd had no sense that Bloom was gay, which amazed his brother Adam ("You've led a very sheltered life," Adam told him). Norman Podhoretz, who also remembers Bloom affectionately, described him in an interview in 2008 as a "flamer," a word he told me he'd only just learned.

28. This phrase from SB (quoted in chapter 2 of *To Fame and Fortune*, p. 69) comes from a speech he gave to the Anti-Defamation League on 14 November 1976, published as "I Said I Was an American, a Jew, a Writer by Trade," *New York Times*, 14 December 1976.

29. See SB, *Dangling Man* (1944), in *Saul Bellow Novels: 1944–1953* (New York: Library of America, 2003), pp. 86–87, where Joseph describes a "bare and ominous" dream he has had "in which the dead of a massacre were lying." He thinks the dream might have been set in Bucharest, where "those slain by the Iron Guard were slung from hooks in a slaughterhouse."

30. SB, *Humboldt's Gift* (1975; Harmondsworth, U.K.: Penguin, 1977), pp. 62, 109.

31. It is clear that Ravelstein's book is a fictional equivalent of *The Closing of the American Mind*, its argument being "that while you could get an excellent technical training in the U.S., liberal education had shrunk to the vanishing point" (p. 47).

32. Ravelstein is comparably clear-eyed about French thought and manners: "Very few French intellectuals got high marks from Abe Ravelstein. He did not care for foolish anti-Americanism. He had no need to be loved or pampered by Parisians. On the whole, he liked their wickedness more than their civility" (p. 103).

33. On p. 138 of *Ravelstein*, SB talks of the deterioration of his nonagenarian mother and stepfather: "I'll beat them both, though. At this rate, I'll reach the finish line before my mom. Maybe I'll be waiting for her." "That's aimed at me, isn't it?" "Well, Chick, you've often talked about the life to come." "And you're a self-described atheist, since no philosopher can believe in God. But this is no belief with me."

34. "I didn't like Grielescu but I did find him a funny man, and to Ravelstein this was a cop-out, and it was also characteristic of me. To say he was amusing was to give him a pass" (*Ravelstein*, p. 202).

35. Small, *Long Life*, pp. 108, 116.

36. When I taught *Ravelstein* to students at the Committee on Social Thought, not all my students approved either of its author or of the friend the novel memorialized. One pointed out the deleterious impact of such parrots on the Illinois farming industry. But in Eric Brodie, "Hyde Park Parrots Continue to Thrive," *Chicago Maroon*, 26 September 1990, when the U.S. Department of Agriculture threatened to eradicate the Hyde Park nests, the local community rose up in protest, demanding evidence that the parrots posed a danger to grain fields or orchard fruits or that there had been local complaint. No action was taken by the USDA.

13. LOVE AND STRIFE

1. James Atlas, *Bellow: A Biography* (New York: Random House, 2000), p. 596.

2. James Atlas, *The Shadow in the Garden: A Biographer's Tale* (New York: Pantheon, 2017), p. 315.

3. Ibid., p. 307.

4. Ibid., pp. 314–15.

5. Ibid., pp. 301, 302.

6. Ibid., p. 212.

7. Ibid., p. 333.

8. Richard Stern, "On Atlas on Bellow," reprinted in Richard Stern, *What Is What Was: Essays, Stories, Poems* (Chicago: University of Chicago Press, 2002), p. 132.

9. Atlas, *Shadow in the Garden*, p. 313.

10. Philip Roth, "'I Got a Scheme!': The Words of Saul Bellow," *The New Yorker*, 25 April 2005.

11. Claudia Roth Pierpont, "The Book of Laughter: Philip Roth and His Friends," *The New Yorker*, 30 September 2013, the source also of subsequent quotes from Pierpont or recounted by her. The *New Yorker* article was excerpted from Pierpont's *Roth Unbound: A Writer and His Books* (London: Jonathan Cape, 2014).

12. There is an oddity in the 20 March 1997 letter to Glotzer. Bellow writes to report that "Daniel's mother (aged 62) died suddenly of an aneuryism a few weeks ago." In fact, she died twenty-one weeks earlier, a discrepancy that recalls the unfairness of having Vela kick Chick out in *Ravelstein* within a week of his brother's death (rather than six months, as was the case when Alexandra kicked SB out after Maury's and Sam's deaths).

13. Quoted in Atlas, *Biography*, p. 587.

14. SB to Michael Millgate, 31 August 1998. Millgate taught English at the University of Toronto.

15. Walsh's thesis title was "Craven Images: Cowardice in American Literature from the Revolutionary War to the Nuclear Era." A revised version of the thesis, *Cowardice: A Brief History*, was published in 2014 by Princeton University Press.

16. Martin Amis, email to the author, 26 April 2017. Quotes from Thomas Barber come from an interview with the author and emails of 30 and 31 May 2017.

17. Will Lautzenheiser, email to the author, 31 May 2017.

18. Janis Bellow, email to the author, 8 June 2017.

19. Papers for the course were marked in detail by Wood and then briefly by SB. Among SB's typical handwritten comments: "Obviously Joyce wants more than a 'story.' He aims to create a work of art"; "'interpersonal' is a term used by psychologists or sociologists, not by writers"; "I agree" [with Wood's comments or

marks]; "I too approve of your paper and esp. of your analytic skill"; "Joyce's prose in *The Dead* is markedly poetic. His language is poetic and musical. The language of the [Victorians?] advances the narrative, and little else"; "You are close to Hamsun's aim here"; "Absolutely—the core of the story."

20. Juliet thinks that there were problems with Rosie, who was two and a half, and that Janis was reluctant to leave her: "My personal feeling is that . . . it was right at the time that they were leaving that [Rosie] had a severe problem, and I think it was just too much for Janis. That seems to me to be the timing, but I may not be right on that."

21. Greg Bellow, *Saul Bellow's Heart: A Son's Memoir* (London and New York: Bloomsbury, 2013), p. 204.

22. In an email to the author of 30 May 2017, after reviewing his notes for the meeting of 4 September 2002, Dr. Barber wrote that the meeting was "a routine follow-up . . . not for any urgent issue. Janis was present with Saul. We reviewed his level of functioning in detail. The focus was mainly on his memory and insight, which were both declining. He was having episodes of agitation and anger, especially when Janis was not present. I made note that he was always warm and kind and interested in his two-year-old daughter, but that he was not sustaining interest in much else at that time. He was not writing. . . . I have no notes about a specific conversation about the wedding, but it is clear to me that we were concerned about his progressively limited function in settings in which he was not very familiar and without structure and support. I would have supported any plan to modify social arrangements 'for medical reasons' if Saul were not up to it. And his functional status did vary from day to day during this time, with very good days, and others when he functioned poorly. This is a common pattern in people with vascular dementia. . . . I remember no instance in which Saul or Janis expressed any negative statements about going to the wedding or not going."

23. Greg Bellow, *Saul Bellow's Heart*, p. 205.

24. Thomas Barber, email to the author, 31 May 2017.

25. Greg Bellow, *Saul Bellow's Heart*, p. 205.

26. SB to Martin Amis, 7 February 2000.

27. Greg Bellow, *Saul Bellow's Heart*, pp. 206, 207.

28. Ibid., pp. 206–9.

29. Ibid., p. 211.

30. Ibid., p. 212.

31. Before Martin Amis's session, on Conrad's *The Shadow-Line*, Janis took him aside and whispered about Bellow, "Can't read anymore."

32. Walter Pozen also emphasized SB's hearing problems: "He couldn't hear. 'I hear everything,' he told Janis. . . . I could get his attention, but he didn't really care."

33. Rosie Bellow, emails to the author, 18 May 2014.

34. Daniel Bellow, email to the author, 4 June 2017.

35. Janis had moved from undergraduate teaching at BU to a teaching job at Tufts University, in Medford, Massachusetts, where she still teaches.

36. Janis later described SB's dying to Adam "as something he *did* rather than something that happened to him. . . . It wasn't a passive process. She felt that he had decided to die and that his body was still holding on. That he'd decided, just like in 'A Silver Dish,' to go out on his own terms at a moment of his choosing."

37. Janis Bellow, email to the author, 8 July 2017, describes David Grene's companion, Stephanie Nelson, as "a huge help, support and source of continuous kindness to Saul in the last couple of years—more than anyone except Will."

In the summer of 2011, at age thirty-seven, Will moved from Boston to Montana to take up a job in the film department at Montana State University. Two weeks after his arrival, he was stricken by a bacterial infection so aggressive that it nearly killed him. All four of his limbs were amputated, and he spent ten months in hospitals before resettling in Brookline with his partner, Angel Gonzalez. In 2014, at Boston's Brigham and Women's Hospital, he underwent a double arm transplant, a nine-hour operation involving thirteen surgeons. He is making gains in independence and now speaks regularly to hospital groups, therapists, and others about disability, patient experiences, and organ donation and transplantation. An award-winning film about his ordeal, *Stumped*, was released in 2017.

38. Greg Bellow, *Saul Bellow's Heart*, p. 213.

39. Although Greg was on tenterhooks all through 5 April 2005, he was not easy to reach. "My noble daughter tried to spare me from the coldness she had already suffered, frantically calling every place I might be, without success" (ibid., p. 213).

40. This was Nathalie Botsford's observation, also Ruth Wisse's. I visited the gravesite in 2008, and the approach to the Jewish section of the cemetery was still as they had described it.

41. Greg Bellow, *Saul Bellow's Heart*, p. 211. Lesha Greengus, email to the author, 29 June 2017, says the following about where and whether Bellow wished to be buried in Chicago: "Over the years, Saul had repeatedly spoken about being buried next to his mother and father. . . . He eventually asked me to contact Waldheim Cemetery to see if there were actually plots available . . . located adjacent to the burial plots where his mother and father were buried. He said that he very much wanted to be buried next to them. I looked into purchasing six plots for him and for his family's future use. . . . Saul was disappointed when he learned that the six plots next to his parents were already either occupied or held by other families. (Four of six original Abraham Bellow plots were used for Robert, Larry, and Charlie Kauffman and the last remaining plot was left for Jane.) So he reluctantly abandoned the idea of buying burial plots at Waldheim."

42. Ruth Wisse, email to the author, 6 June 2017, quoted from notes she'd made after the funeral, explaining why she thought she was asked to speak: "Janis might have worried that Saul's Jewish soul would otherwise never have been brought to rest."

43. Greg Bellow, *Saul Bellow's Heart*, p. 213.

44. Ruth Wisse, email to the author, 6 June 2017.

45. Greg Bellow, *Saul Bellow's Heart*, p. 214.

46. Ibid.

47. Every time they met, or so it seemed to Kaplan, Greg said to him: "You know, my father wasn't a good man, and your father wasn't a good man. You're denying it."

48. Joel Bellows remembers remarking that, though Jonathan Kleinbard "looked like shit," Roth looked worse, not only "sad, remorseful," but "like he just fucked the family dinner." Roth overheard this remark, and turned round to ask Joel, "Do I look that bad?"

49. Philip Roth, *Everyman* (2006; New York: Vintage, 2007), pp. 14–15.

50. Ibid., p. 94.

51. Ibid., pp. 59–60, 61.

52. SB, "A Silver Dish," in *CS*, p. 33.

Index

Works by Saul Bellow (SB) appear directly under title; works by others under author's name. Page numbers in *italic* refer to illustrations in text

PERMISSIONS

Grateful acknowledgment is made to the following for permission to reprint the following previously published and unpublished material:

Rosie Alison: Excerpts of letters from Barley Alison to Saul Bellow, December 12, 1960, and February 5, 1967. Reprinted by permission of Rosie Alison.

Linda Asher: Excerpt of letter from Aaron Asher to Saul Bellow, December 23, 1964. Reprinted by permission of Linda Asher.

Owen A. Barfield, Trustee for Owen Barfield Literary Estate: Excerpt of letters from Owen Barfield to Saul Bellow, dated: March 17, 1976; September 18, 1976; and August 23, 1979. Copyright © Owen Barfield Literary Estate. Reprinted by permission of Owen A. Barfield, Trustee for Owen Barfield Literary Estate.

Adam Bellow: Excerpts of letters from Saul Bellow. Reprinted by permission of Adam Bellow.

Daniel Bellow: Excerpts of letters from Saul Bellow. Reprinted by permission of Daniel Bellow.

Joseph Epstein: Excerpts of letters from Edward Shils to Saul Bellow. Reprinted by permission of Joseph Epstein.

Frances Gendlin: Excerpts from "Away for the Summer Again" by Frances Gendlin and other quotes. Reprinted by permission of Frances Gendlin.

Georges Borchardt, Inc. on behalf of Harriet Wasserman: Excerpt of *Handsome Is* by Harriet Wasserman. Copyright © 1997 by Harriet Wasserman. Reprinted by permission of Georges Borchardt, Inc., on behalf of Harriet Wasserman.

Tom Gidwitz: Excerpt of letter from Tom Gidwitz to Saul Bellow, December 23, 1983. Reprinted by permission of Tom Gidwitz.

Philip Grew: Excerpts of emails from Philip Grew to Zachary Leader. Reprinted by permission of Philip Grew.

Gertrude Himmelfarb: Excerpt of an unpublished letter from Irving Kristol to Saul Bellow. Reprinted by permission of Gertrude Himmelfarb.

Lynn Hoffman: Excerpt of letter from Ted Hoffman to Saul Bellow, January 5, 1950. Reprinted by permission of Lynn Hoffman.

Jacob Howland: Excerpts of letters from Bette Howland to Saul Bellow, September 24, 1968, and January 21, 1970. Reprinted by permission of Jacob Howland.

Arlette Jassel: Excerpts of letters and interview answers from Arlette Jassel. Reprinted by permission of Arlette Jassel.

Russell & Volkening, Inc.: Excerpts of correspondence from Henry Volkening to Saul Bellow. Reprinted by permission of Russell & Volkening, Inc.

Pantheon Books, an imprint of the Knopf Doubleday Publishing Group, a division of Penguin Random House LLC: Excerpts from *The Shadow in the Garden: A Biographer's Tale* by James Atlas, copyright © 2017 by James Atlas. Reprinted by permission of Pantheon Books, an imprint of the Knopf Doubleday Publishing Group, a division of Penguin Random House LLC. All rights reserved.

Random House, an imprint and division of Penguin Random House LLC: Excerpts from *Bellow: A Biography* by James Atlas, copyright © 2000 by James Atlas. Reprinted by permission of Random House, an imprint and division of Penguin Random House LLC. All rights reserved.

Katherine Peltz Rivera: Excerpt of letter from David Peltz to Saul Bellow. Reprinted by permission of Katherine Peltz Rivera.

Philip Roth: Excerpt of letter from Philip Roth to Saul Bellow, December 5, 1981. Reprinted by permission of Philip Roth.

The Wylie Agency LLC: Excerpts of unpublished letters by Lionel Trilling. Reprinted by permission of The Wylie Agency LLC.

A NOTE ABOUT THE AUTHOR

ZACHARY LEADER is professor of English literature at the University of Roehampton in London. Although born and raised in the United States, he has lived in Britain for more than forty years and has dual British and American citizenship. In addition to teaching at Roehampton, he has held visiting professorships at Caltech and the University of Chicago. He was educated at Northwestern University; Trinity College, Cambridge; and Harvard University; and is the author of *Reading Blake's Songs*, *Writer's Block*, *Revision and Romantic Authorship*, *The Life of Kingsley Amis*, a finalist for the 2008 Pulitzer Prize in Biography, and *The Life of Saul Bellow: To Fame and Fortune 1915–1964*. He has edited *Romantic Period Writings, 1798–1832: An Anthology* (with Ian Haywood); *The Letters of Kingsley Amis; On Modern British Fiction; Percy Bysshe Shelley: The Major Works* (with Michael O'Neill); *The Movement Reconsidered: Essays on Larkin, Amis, Gunn, Davie, and Their Contemporaries;* and *On Life-Writing*. He is a Fellow of the Royal Society of Literature and General Editor of *The Oxford History of Life-Writing*, a seven-volume series.

A NOTE ON THE TYPE

This book was set in Janson, a typeface long thought to have been made by the Dutchman Anton Janson, who was a practicing typefounder in Leipzig during the years 1668–1687. However, it has been conclusively demonstrated that these types are actually the work of Nicholas Kis (1650–1702), a Hungarian, who most probably learned his trade from the master Dutch typefounder Dirk Voskens. The type is an excellent example of the influential and sturdy Dutch types that prevailed in England up to the time William Caslon (1692–1766) developed his own incomparable designs from them.

Composed by North Market Street Graphics,
Lancaster, Pennsylvania

Printed and bound by LSC,
Crawfordsville, Indiana

Designed by Cassandra J. Pappas